SHORT STORY INDEX

2005–2009

PERMANENT CUMULATIONS

SHORT STORY INDEX

2005-2009

AN INDEX TO STORIES IN
COLLECTIONS AND PERIODICALS

Edited by

JOHN GREENFIELDT

NEW YORK • DUBLIN
THE H. W. WILSON COMPANY
2009

ISSN 0360-9774

Library of Congress Control Number 75-649762

Printed in the United States of America

Visit H.W. Wilson's Web site at: www.hwwilson.com

CONTENTS

PREFACE

This cumulative volume of *Short Story Index* covers short stories written in or translated into English that have appeared in collections and selected periodicals between 2005 and 2009. The periodicals are those indexed in two other Wilson publications: *Readers' Guide to Periodical Literature* and *Humanities Index*.

Short Story Index is issued annually with a cumulation every five years. This cumulation indexes 20,280 stories. Of these, 16,393 stories appeared in collections and 3,887 in periodicals. There are 1,006 collections and 166 periodicals indexed.

As in previous volumes, the arrangement is by author, title, and subject in one alphabet. Stories in periodicals are indexed only by author and title. The author entry, which indicates the collection or periodical where the story can be found, is the fullest entry. A List of Collections Indexed and a Directory of Periodicals complete the volume. Further information about the content of entries is provided in the Directions for Use.

DIRECTIONS FOR USE

Part I of *Short Story Index*, the Author, Title, and Subject Index, is arranged in dictionary form with all entries in one alphabet. Part II is a List of Collections indexed. Part III is a Directory of Periodicals. The following directions apply to Part I.

Author entry

The author entry gives the name of the author and title of the story. For stories found in collections it also gives the title and editor of the collection. For stories found in periodicals it provides the periodical title, volume number, page numbers, and date.

Sample entry from a collection:

> **Niles, Chris**
> Ladies' man
> Brooklyn noir; edited by Tim McLoughlin

The above example shows that the story by Chris Niles entitled "Ladies' man" appeared in *Brooklyn noir*, edited by Tim McLoughlin. Further information about the book is given in the List of Collections Indexed.

Sample entry from a periodical:

> **Friedman, Bruce Jay**
> The savior
> *The Antioch Review* v67 no3 p234-41 Spr 2009

The above example indicates that the story by Bruce Jay Friedman entitled "The savior" appeared in *The Antioch Review*, volume 67, number 3, pages 234-41, in the Spring 2009 issue. For fuller information about the periodical consult the Directory of Periodicals.

Title entry

Title entries are used to identify the author under whose name the source of the story will be found. The first word (not an article) of each title is in boldface type.

Sample entries:

> **Ladies'** man. Niles. C.
> The **savior**. Friedman, B. J.

Subject entry

Stories found in collections are listed under subjects with which they deal in whole or in part. Subject entries are printed in capital letters, in boldface type. Consult the author entry for the title of the story collection.

Sample entry:

> **FRIENDSHIP**
> McGuane, T. Old friends

SHORT STORY INDEX, 2005-2009

PART I

Author, Title, and Subject Index

1-900. Bausch, R.
1%. Young, H.
2hot. Charters, D.
2+2=5. Rucker, R. v. B. and Bisson, T.
3 kills for 1. Woolrich, C.
4H. Martone, M.
7C. Roberts, J.
8. Solomon, S.
13 O'clock. O'Driscoll, M.
The **13th** Egg. Snyder, S.
14 days. D'Allesandro, S.
18 1/2. Butler, R. O.
18 Small Apocalypses. Corin, L.
19 amenities. Barkley, B.
20 tanks from Kasseldown. Bukowski, C.
20th century ghost. Hill, J.
The **"23"**. Edwinson, W.
23 December. Thormahlen, A.
26 monkeys, also the abyss. Johnson, K.
31/10. Volk, S.
32.05864991%. Yu, C.
50 WPM. Card, O. S.
53rd American dream. Sallis, J.
56 Water Street. Searls, D.
57% Irish. Doyle, R.
59th parallel. Novakovich, J.
68° 07' 15N, 31° 36' 44W. Williams, C.
70 is the new 30!. Rushkoff, D.
75 Grand [variant title: 75,000] Chekhov, A. P.
80 centimeters of bad temper. Biller, M.
'80s lilies. Svoboda, T.
The **'84** regress. Lain, D.
86 things that happened between 2:35 and 2:38 while I was lying on my bed trying to take a nap. Tognazzini, A.
304, Adolph Hitler Strasse. Tidhar, L.
401(k). Yu, C.
1688: Osaka: Ihara Saikaku Tells a Cautionary Tale [From The ten virtues of tea that all disappeared at once] Saikaku, I.
1858: East Indies: Alfred Russel Wallace Advances a Theory [Reprint] Mason, D.
1887: Russia: Anton Chekhov Runs the Numbers [Excerpt from The lottery ticket] Chekhov, A. P.
1905: New York: War Prayer [Reprint] Twain, M.
1914: Penal Colony: Franz Kafka Translates a Text [Excerpt from In the Penal Colony] Kafka, F.
1926: New York City: Tell Me about It [Excerpt from Travelogue] Parker, D.
1938: Los Angeles: Waldo's Last Move [Excerpt from Red Wind] Chandler, R.
1941: Fifth Avenue: Window Shopping [From The standard of living] Parker, D.

1948: Smalltown, U.S.A.: Shirley Jackson Casts the First Stone [Excerpt from The Lottery] Jackson, S.
1955: Georgia: Flannery O'Connor Stages a Moral [Excerpt from Good Country People] O'Connor, F.
1956: Shady Hill: Carl Warburton's Wallet [Excerpt from The Housebreaker of Shady Hill] Cheever, J.
1963: Wyoming: After Midnight [Excerpt from Brokeback Mountain] Proulx, A.
1964. Soueif, A.
1966. Johnson, D.
1981: New York City: Donald Barthelme Teaches Philosophy [Excerpt from The School] Barthelme, D.
1987, the races. Pizzolatto, N.
2007: New York City: This Is How You Lose Her. Diaz, J.
2015. Wang Xiaobo
75,000. See Chekhov, A. P. 75 Grand [variant title: 75,000]
93990. Saunders, G.

A

A.K.A.. Yori, T.
a.k.a., Moises Rockafella. Holmes, E.
A! tangled web. Haldeman, J. W.
AAA Plus. Doyle, B.
Aaron, personal. Clayton, J. J.
Abalone, Ebony and Tusk. Murphy, Y.
An **Abalone** Opportunity. Rosenbaum, S. A.
Abandon. Coake, C.
Abandoned belongings. Tognazzini, A.
ABANDONED CHILDREN
    See also Orphans
  Angel, J. Rounding third
  Broches, R. Little Abrahams
  Das, K. The hijra
  Erdrich, L. The blue velvet box
  Green, C. Lakeside
  Hoffman, A. Insulting the angels
  Leonard, E. The kid [variant title: The gift of Regalo]
  Thon, M. R. Heavenly creatures: for wandering children and their delinquent mother
  Turner, M. W. The baby in the night deposit box
Abandoned children of this planet. Ōe, K.
ABANDONED TOWNS *See* Extinct cities
ABANDONMENT OF FAMILY *See* Desertion and nonsupport

Abani, Chris
Albino Crow
  Callaloo v30 no3 p721-9 Summ 2007
Three Letters, One Song & A Refrain
  Daedalus v137 no1 p87-91 Wint 2008
Abbenyi, Juliana Makuchi Nfah- *See* Nfah-
  Abbenyi, Juliana Makuchi, 1958-
ABBESSES *See* Nuns
Abbey, Linda J.
The Root of the Problem
  Journal of the American Geriatrics Society
  v53 no6 p1071 Je 2005
Abbey, Lynn
Good neighbors
  Thieves' world; enemies of fortune; edited by
  Lynn Abbey
ABBEYS
    See also Cathedrals; Churches; Convent
  life
Abbott, Jeff
Bet on red
  The Best American mystery stories, 2004; ed-
  ited and with an introduction by Nelson
  DeMille; Otto Penzler, series editor
  The World's finest mystery and crime stories,
  fifth annual collection; edited by Ed
  Gorman and Martin H. Greenberg
Do unto others [excerpt]
  Lone Star sleuths; an anthology of Texas
  crime fiction; edited and with an introduc-
  tion by Bill Cunningham, Steven L. Davis,
  and Rollo K. Newsom.
A few small repairs
  Mystery Writers of America presents death do
  us part; new stories about love, lust, and
  murder; edited by Harlan Coben
Karma hits dogma
  Greatest hits; original stories of assassins,
  hitmen, and hired guns; edited by Robert J.
  Randisi
Abbott, Jillian
Jihad sucks; or, The conversion of the Jews
  Queens noir; edited by Robert Knightly
Abbott, Lee K.
As fate would have it
  Abbott, L. K. All things, all at once; new and
  selected stories
Category Z
  Abbott, L. K. All things, all at once; new and
  selected stories
Dreams of distant lives
  Abbott, L. K. All things, all at once; new and
  selected stories
The eldest of things
  Abbott, L. K. All things, all at once; new and
  selected stories
The end of grief
  Abbott, L. K. All things, all at once; new and
  selected stories
The final proof of fate and circumstance
  Abbott, L. K. All things, all at once; new and
  selected stories
Gravity
  Abbott, L. K. All things, all at once; new and
  selected stories
  The Georgia Review v59 no3 p614-33 Fall
  2005

A Great Piece of Elephant
  The Georgia Review v61 no1 p56-68 Spr
  2007
How love is lived in paradise
  Abbott, L. K. All things, all at once; new and
  selected stories
The human use of inhuman beings
  Abbott, L. K. All things, all at once; new and
  selected stories
Love is the crooked thing
  Abbott, L. K. All things, all at once; new and
  selected stories
Martians
  Abbott, L. K. All things, all at once; new and
  selected stories
Men of rough persuasion
  Abbott, L. K. All things, all at once; new and
  selected stories
Ninety nights on Mercury
  Abbott, L. K. All things, all at once; new and
  selected stories
One of star wars, one of doom
  Abbott, L. K. All things, all at once; new and
  selected stories
Revolutionaries
  Abbott, L. K. All things, all at once; new and
  selected stories
Sweet cheeks
  Abbott, L. K. All things, all at once; new and
  selected stories
The talk talked between worms
  Abbott, L. K. All things, all at once; new and
  selected stories
The valley of sin
  Abbott, L. K. All things, all at once; new and
  selected stories
The view of me from Mars
  Abbott, L. K. All things, all at once; new and
  selected stories
The way sin is said in wonderland
  Abbott, L. K. All things, all at once; new and
  selected stories
What Y was
  Abbott, L. K. All things, all at once; new and
  selected stories
When our dream world finds us, and these hard
  times are gone
  Abbott, L. K. All things, all at once; new and
  selected stories
The who, the what, and the why
  Abbott, L. K. All things, all at once; new and
  selected stories
X
  Abbott, L. K. All things, all at once; new and
  selected stories
Abbott, Megan
Hollywood lanes
  Queens noir; edited by Robert Knightly
Our eyes couldn't stop opening
  Detroit noir; edited by E. J. Olsen & John C.
  Hocking
Abbott, Patricia
A saving grace
  A Prisoner of memory and 24 of the year's
  finest crime and mystery stories; edited by
  Ed Gorman & Martin H. Greenberg
Abbreviation. Winton, T.

Abdoh, Salar
Scotland
Bomb no97 p108-10 Fall 2006
Water
Callaloo v31 no2 p402-13 Spr 2008
Abducted souls. Reed, R.
Abductio ad absurdum. Friesner, E. M.
ABDUCTION *See* Kidnapping
Abduction. Nelson, R. F.
The **abduction**. Wendroff, Z.
Abegunde, Maria Eliza Hamilton
The Ariran's Last Life
The Kenyon Review v30 no1 p145-62 Wint
2008
ABEL (BIBLICAL FIGURE)
About
Scholes, K. East of Eden and just a little bit
south
Abel, Robert H.
Golden Birds
The Massachusetts Review v50 no1-2 p199-
210 Spr/Summ 2009
The Vulgari Connection
The North American Review v291 no3/4
p58-9 My/Ag 2006
The **Abelard** sanction. Morrell, D.
Abella, Alex
Shanghai
Havana noir; edited by Achy Obejas
Abel's Eden. García Márquez, G.
Abenshushan, Vivian
La cama de Lukin/Lukin's bed
Best of contemporary Mexican fiction; Alvaro
Uribe, editor; Olivia Sears, translation edi-
tor
Abidi, Azhar
The Secret History of the Flying Carpet
Southwest Review v91 no1 p28-35 2006
Abikú. Depestre, Y.
Abinusawa, Adetayo
Charbel Maklouf, the Hermit of Lebanon: His
Afterlife and the Words We Say to Each
Other While Speaking to Those Who Are
No Longer Alive
Hanging Loose no94 p81-5 2009
Abio or love at first sight. Bluestein, E.
Abish, Walter
Even Vienna could not forever endure this
struggle
The Review of Contemporary Fiction v24 no3
p117-21 Fall 2004
The **Abjection**. Mejia, M.
ABNORMALITIES AND DEFORMITIES *See*
Deformities; Dwarfs; Eye—Abnormalities
and deformities; Face—Abnormalities and
deformities; Monsters
ABOLITIONISTS
See also Slavery
Abolitionists of Mars. Douglass, F. R.
The **abominable** ice man. Powell, M.
ABOMINABLE SNOWMAN *See* Yeti
Abominations. Raphael, L.
The **abominations** of Yondo. Smith, C. A.
ABORIGINES, AUSTRALIAN *See* Australian
aborigines
The **aborigines** of Oakland. Bierce, A.
ABORTION
Bacigalupi, P. Small offerings
Boudinot, R. On sex and relationships

Bradford, A. Orderly: how I spent that year af-
ter high school
Crone, M. It
Curtis, R. The near-son
Dooling, R. Roe #5
Hawes, L. All the pale women
Hempel, A. Beg, sl tog, inc, cont, rep
Holland, N. What begins with bird
Johnson, D. Dirty wedding
King, O. We're all in this together
King, O. Wonders
LaBrie, A. The last dead boyfriend
Lefer, D. Angle and grip
Li Yiyun. The princess of Nebraska
Macy, C. The secret vote
Margulis, L. Conceits
McInerney, J. I love you, honey
Monk, B. Flying lesson
Preddy, M. The coffee break
Rivera-Valdes, S. Blue like bluing
Shroff, M. F. Haraami
Sterling, B. Are you for 86?
Aboulela, Leila
The museum
The Anchor book of modern African stories;
edited by Nadežda Obradovic; with a fore-
word by Chinua Achebe
About a burning girl. Mueenuddin, D.
About face. Snyder, S.
About Kamyshinskiy. Litman, E.
About kid Deth. Whitfield, R.
Above Asmara. Guirado, T.
Above the houses. Engberg, S.
Above the law, below the box springs. Allen, W.
Above the line. Sayles, J.
Abraham, Daniel
The cambist and Lord Iron: a fairy tale of eco-
nomics
The Best science fiction and fantasy of the
year: volume two; edited by Jonathan
Strahan
The Year's best fantasy and horror: twenty-
first annual collection; edited by Ellen
Datlow and Kelly Link & Gavin J. Grant
Leviathan wept
The Year's best science fiction: twenty-
second annual collection; edited by Gardner
Dozois
Abraham, Pearl
Hasidic noir
Brooklyn noir; edited by Tim McLoughlin
The seven fat brides
Scribblers on the roof; contemporary Ameri-
can Jewish fiction; edited by Melvin Jules
Bukiet and David G. Roskies
Abraham, Ruth
The Circle
Journal of the American Geriatrics Society
v55 no12 p2088-9 D 2007
Collecting Stones
Journal of the American Geriatrics Society
v53 no11 p2032 N 2005
Abraham Lincoln has been shot. Alarcón, D.
Abraham's boys. Hill, J.
Abrams, Linsey
Taj Mahal
Pushcart prize XXXI: best of the small press-
es 2007; edited by Bill Henderson; with the
Pushcart Prize editors

Abreu, Caio Fernando
Dragons . . .
Oxford anthology of the Brazilian short story; edited by K. David Jackson
ABREU MEJÍA, RAFAEL, 1939-
About
Báez, A. The loss
The **Abridged** Versions. Cameron, P.
Absalom. Anaya, R. A.
Absalom's mother. Marley, L.
Absence. Alarcón, D.
Absence. Shields, C.
An **absence** of cousins. Segal, L. G.
Absence of Oxygen in Town Creek. Goedjen, T.
Absent. Khedairi, B.
Absolut Boudinot. Boudinot, R.
Absolute Numbers. Ackland, K.
Absolute Zero. Schwartz, S.
Absolutely charming. Stackpole, M. A.
Absolutely inflexible. Silverberg, R.
Abu-Jaber, Diana
Clean Room
The Southern Review (Baton Rouge, La.) v41 no4 p683-96 Aut 2005
ABUSE OF CHILDREN *See* Child abuse
ABUSED WIVES *See* Wife abuse
ABYSSINIA *See* Ethiopia
The **Academy** of Chaos and Self-Command. Shepard, J.
ACADIANS
Louisiana
See Cajuns
Acampora, Lauren
How Deep Is the Ocean?
New England Review v27 no3 p22-31 2006
Waterfast
The Antioch Review v63 no1 p163-72 Wint 2005
The **accelerating** expansion of the universe. Updike, J.
Acceptence. Toer, P. A.
Access fantasy. Lethem, J.
Accident. Lý Lan
The **Accident**. McGarry, J.
The **accident** at John Stam's. See Leonard, E. The nagual [variant title: The accident at John Stam's]
Accident Brief. Russell, K.
Accident brief, occurrence # 00/422. Russell, K.
Accident by escalator. Tognazzini, A.
Accident report. McBain, E.
ACCIDENTAL DEATH *See* Accidents
The **accidental** detective. Lippman, L.
The **Accidental** Homeowner. Greenside, M.
Accidental invasion. Bergstrom, E.
The **accidental** murderess. Jeffers, H. P.
Accidentally, like a Martyr. Coleman, R. F.
ACCIDENTS
See also Airplane accidents; Drowning; Fires; Hunting accidents; Railroad accidents; Shipwrecks and castaways; Traffic accidents
Aira, C. An episode in the life of a landscape painter [excerpt]
Amdahl, G. The barber-chair
Archer, J. A Greek tragedy
Ardai, C. The home front
'Arimi, S. a.- . Ghomran's oil field
Barthelme, D. Tales of the Swedish army

Bishop, T. The contest
Boyd, B. Scarecrow
Bradbury, R. The great collision of Monday last
Brennan, K. Saw
Buckler, E. The bars and the bridge
Buckler, E. Just like everyone else
Campbell, B. J. Storm warning
Coleman, W. Backcity transit by day
Curtis, R. The witches
Dalton, Q. Lennie remembers the angels
Davidson, C. Rust and bone
Davis, C. Balance
Donoghue, E. Oops
Donovan, G. By Irish nights
Fulton, J. Real grief
Gardam, J. Snap
Gilchrist, E. The brown cape
Golden, M. After [excerpt]
Granados, C. The latchkey chronicles: Goldfinger
Granville-Barker, H. The fire that burned in the corner
Greene, G. The basement room
Grimes, C. We stand here, swinging cats
Groff, L. Watershed
Hautman, P. The guy
Hawes, L. The knack
Hawes, L. Our lady of sorrows
Herren, G. Annunciation shotgun
Johnson, G. Evening at home
Kennedy, C. What thou and I did, till we loved
L'Amour, L. The admiral
Lennon, J. R. Eight pieces for the left hand
Lott, B. An evening on the cusp of the apocalypse
Luvaas, W. How I died
Malla, P. Timber on the wheel of everyone
Matheson, R. Girl of my dreams
Meacham, R. Worship for shut-ins
Michaels, L. Isaac
Mina, D. An invisible minus sign
Monis, V. O. Woes of the middle class
Mordecai, P. Alvin's ilk
Muñoz, M. The faith healer of Olive Avenue
Murphy, Y. Lester
Oates, J. C. Special
Ockert, J. Jakob Loomis
Ohlin, A. The tennis partner
Ohlin, A. Wonders never cease
Oz, A. The way of the wind
Panayotopoulos, N. The strength of materials
Patterson, S. Aground and aloft
Pollock, D. R. Blessed
Porter, A. Hole
Powers, T. The better boy
Proulx, A. Testimony of the donkey
Quiroga, H. The son
Rash, R. Blackberries in June
Reinhorn, H. Charlotte
Robinson, S. Too hot to hoot
Sakey, M. Gravity and need
Scholes, K. So sang the girl who had no name
Scott, J. Heaven and Hell
Shields, C. The harp
Shomer, E. Rapture
Shukman, H. The garden of God: 1988
Sillitoe, A. The second chance
Simpson, H. Every third thought
Snyder, S. Happy Fish, Plus Coin

ACTORS—*Continued*
Woronov, M. The rise and fall
Yellin, T. Strangers on a train
Yu, C. My last days as me
Zoshchenko, M. The actor
Actors. Ozick, C.
The **actor's** face. LaSalle, P.
ACTRESSES
See also Motion picture actors and actresses; Theater life
Barrett, L. Blue vandas
Bender, A. Motherfucker
Benioff, D. Garden of no
Boyd, W. Notebook no. 9
Brodsky, M. Crisis in the life of an actress
Buckler, E. Nettles into orchids
Carlson, P. M. Frighted out of fear; or, the bombs bursting in air
Dean, D. The queen mother
Dean, D. Romance manual
Diaconú, A. The evil eye
Domecq, B. The eternal theater
Egan, J. Selling the general
Fitch, J. The method
Gordimer, N. A beneficiary
Kelly, R. Scream queen
LaBute, N. Los feliz
Leung, B. Who knew her best
Levinson, R. S. Chapter 82: Myrna Lloyd is missing
Macy, C. Eden's gate
Magee, K. Knock them down
Malone, M. Red clay
Monk, B. Now you don't
Monk, B. Now you see it
Monk, B. Small fry
Nolan, W. F. In real life
Nolan, W. F. Mama's boy
Oates, J. C. Fat man my love
Orr, M. The wisdom of Eve
Phillips, S. The girl who kissed Barnaby Jones
Pratt, T. Terrible ones
Read, C. Hungry enough
Singer, I. B. The manuscript
Vidal, G. Erlinda and Mr. Coffin
Wolfe, G. Seven American nights
Acts of faith (Chicago, 1963). Mohanraj, M. A.
Acts of God. Bova, B.
Actual seasons. Moceri, M.
The **actual** thing. Maxwell, W.
Actually, I've had some phenomenal hard-ons lately. Keret, E.
Ad Vesperas. Menceboni, M.
Adair's. Kun, M.
ADAM (BIBLICAL FIGURE)
About
Bierce, A. Hades in trouble
Webb, J. Paradise design'd
Adam Robinson. Jones, E. P.
Adam Robinson acquires grandparents and a little sister. Jones, E. P.
Adameşteanu, Gabriela
Provisional [excerpt]
Words without borders; the world through the eyes of writers; an anthology; edited by Samantha Schnee, Alane Salierno Mason, and Dedi Felman

ADAMS, ANSEL, 1902-1984
About
Cheuse, A. Moonrise, Hernandez, New Mexico, 1941
Adams, Colin
Journey to the Center of Mathematics
The Mathematical Intelligencer v28 no4 p13-16 Fall 2006
A Killer Theorem
The Mathematical Intelligencer v29 no3 p26-9 Summ 2007
Riot at the Calc Exam
The Mathematical Intelligencer v31 no1 p2-3 Wint 2009
Adams, Linda P.
The Year I Went Insane
Calyx v22 no3 p22-32 Summ 2005
Adams. Saunders, G.
Adam's curse. Downs, G.
Adam's house. Watkins, S.
ADAPTATION (BIOLOGY)
Zelazny, R. The keys to December
Adcock, Justin
(jt. auth) See Kuskin, William and Adcock, Justin
Adcock, Siobhan
Nice Guys
The Massachusetts Review v47 no3 p571-90 Fall 2006
This Is What We're Doing
TriQuarterly no129 p138-59 2007
Adcock, Thomas
Lawyers' tongues
New Orleans noir; edited by Julie Smith
You want I should whack monkey boy?
Bronx noir; edited by S. J. Rozan
Add infinite item. Zelazny, R.
Addiction to nicotine. Valtinos, T.
Addison, Marianne
My Cousin Coyote, as Told by Dog
Tribal College Journal of American Indian Higher Education v19 no1 p49-50 Fall 2007
Shimá Sani' (excerpt)
Tribal College Journal of American Indian Higher Education v19 no1 p50-1 Fall 2007
Addleman, Katie
Sami Works at Night
Dalhousie Review v87 no1 p71-80 Spr 2007
Addonizio, Kim
Egg
Southwest Review v89 no2/3 p320-34 2004
Adelaide's body. Domecq, B.
Adelia. Klassen, S.
Adichie, Chimamanda
The Thing Around Your Neck
Ms. v16 no3 p64-70 Summ 2006
Adichie, Chimamanda Ngozi
The American Embassy
Adichie, C. N. The thing around your neck
The arrangers of marriage
Adichie, C. N. The thing around your neck
Cell one
Adichie, C. N. The thing around your neck
The New Yorker v82 no47 p72-7 Ja 29 2007
Ghosts
Adichie, C. N. The thing around your neck
The Grief of Strangers
Granta no88 p65-81 Wint 2004

ADOLESCENCE—*Continued*

Puchner, E. Essay #3: Leda and the swan
Radojcic, N. Shades of mango
Rash, R. The projectionist's wife
Raymond, J. Young bodies
Reidy, D. Thingless
Reinhorn, H. Fuck you
Richter, S. Duet
Richter, S. Habits and habitat of the southwestern bad boy
Richter, S. The long hall
Rickert, M. Angel face
Rivas, M. Saxophone in the mist
Romano, T. New neighborhood
Rucker, R. v. B. The men in the back room at the country club
Russell, K. The City of Shells
Russell, K. Lady Yeti and the palace of artificial snows
Russell, K. Z.Z.'s sleep-away camp for disordered dreamers
Rylands, J. T. Youth
Scott, J. Or else, part I: In the automat
Selgin, P. Sawdust
Sellers, H. Fla. boys
Sheehy, H. The invisibles
Shepard, J. Courtesy for beginners
Shepard, J. Glut your soul on my accursed ugliness
Shepard, J. Trample the dead, hurdle the weak
Shepard, L. The ease with which we freed the beast
Sherman, R. The first hurt
Sherman, R. Proof
Sherman, R. The reaper
Shimamoto, R. Inside
Shirley, J. Nineteen seconds
Shomer, E. Sweethearts
Silverberg, R. Push no more
Simpson, H. Up at a villa
Smith, N. Green fluorescent protein
Sokoloff, A. The edge of seventeen
Somerville, P. Black earth, early winter morning
Somerville, P. Crow moon
Somerville, P. English cousin
Somerville, P. Puberty
Somerville, P. So long, anyway
Somerville, P. The whales
Soueif, A. 1964
Steinberg, S. Hydroplane
Swann, M. Secret
Taraqqi, G. My little friend
Thompson, J. The brat
Thompson, J. The five senses
Thompson, J. Hunger
Threatt, A. Bela Lugosi's dead
Tobar, H. Once more, Lazarus
Tognazzini, A. Gainesville, Oregon—1962
Tognazzini, A. Westminster march
Tomlinson, J. Singing second part
Tower, W. Wild America
Trevor, D. Haircuts
Trevor, W. An afternoon
Trevor, W. Rose wept
Trezise, R. The Joneses
Turzillo, M. A. Pride
Updike, D. In the age of convertibles
Updike, D. The woman from out of town
Varallo, A. Be true to your school

Varallo, A. In the age of automobiles
Varallo, A. Sunday wash
Verghese, A. If brains was gas
Vidal, G. Clouds and eclipses
Vollmer, M. The digging
Vukcevich, R. Jumping
Waldrop, H. Thin, on the ground
Watkins, S. Critterworld
Watkins, S. Driver's ed
Welch, N. The cheating kind
Welch, N. The Good Humor man
Welch, N. The road from prosperity
Welch, N. Running to Ethiopia
Welch, N. Sweet Maddy
Welch, N. Thanatology
West, D. The birthday party
Westcott, G. Adolescence
Wilkins, K. The forest
Wilson, K. Go, fight, win
Wilson, K. Mortal kombat
Windley, C. Home schooling
Winton, T. Abbreviation
Winton, T. Boner McPharlin's moll
Winton, T. Cockleshell
Winton, T. Damaged goods
Winton, T. Long, clear view
Winton, T. Small mercies
Wolfe, G. Golden city far
Wolff, T. Deep kiss
Wolff, T. Smorgasbord
Wolff, T. Two boys and a girl
Wood, D. The deflowering of Rosie Little
Wood, D. Rosie Little in the Mother Country
Yanique, T. Gita Pinky Manachandi
Zebrowski, G. First love, first fear
Zumas, L. How he was a wicked son

Adolescence. Westcott, G.

ADOLESCENTS *See* Adolescence

Adonis, Isabel

Drawing apart
Urban Welsh; new short fiction; edited by Lewis Davies

ADOPTED CHILDREN *See* Adoption; Foster children

ADOPTION

See also Foster children

Akins, E. Her book
Crane, E. Promise
Erdrich, L. Future home of the living God
Gaitskill, M. Don't cry
Gerrold, D. The Martian child
Gerrold, D. Pickled mongoose
Hawes, L. All the pale women
Hempel, A. The center
Irvine, A. C. The uterus garden
Jones, E. P. Adam Robinson acquires grandparents and a little sister
Jones, N. Carrying
Li Yiyun. The arrangement
MacLeod, I. The bonny boy
Monk, B. Now you don't
Mordecai, P. The burning tree and the balloon man
Munro, A. Trespasses
Nelson, A. We and they
Phan, A. Motherland
Redmann, J. M. The intersection of camp and St. Mary
Richard, N. What you do next

ADOPTION—*Continued*

Sayles, J. Casa de los Babys
Sundaresan, I. Shelter of rain
Tabor, M. L. Riptide
Theroux, P. Warm dogs
Wald, A. H. The virgin's heart

Adoshem. Shabtai, Y.

Adrian, Chris

A better angel
  Best American fantasy; guest editors Ann &
    Jeff VanderMeer; series editor Matthew
    Cheney
  Adrian, C. A better angel; stories
  The New Yorker v82 no7 p68-75 Ap 3 2006

The changeling
  Adrian, C. A better angel; stories

A child's book of sickness and death
  Adrian, C. A better angel; stories

A hero of Chickamauga
  Adrian, C. A better angel; stories

High speeds
  Adrian, C. A better angel; stories

Promise Breaker
  Esquire v148 no6 p141-2, 144, 146, 150, 152,
    154 D 2007

Stab
  The Best American mystery stories 2007; ed-
    ited and with and introduction by Carl
    Hiaasen; Otto Penzler, series editor
  Adrian, C. A better angel; stories

The sum of our parts
  Adrian, C. A better angel; stories

A Tiny Feast
  The New Yorker v85 no10 p90-9 Ap 20 2009

The vision of Peter Damien
  Adrian, C. A better angel; stories

Why antichrist?
  Adrian, C. A better angel; stories

Adriana. Coetzee, J. M.

Adrift and distant. Ockert, J.

Adult Education. Wyatt, J.

Adult fiction. Clayton, J. J.

Adult video. Boyd, W.

The **Adulterous** Wife. Camus, A.

ADULTERY *See* Marriage problems

Adultery. Davis, C.

Adultery. McCauley, W.

Advance notice. Matheson, R.

Advanced Latin. Bingham, S.

The **Advancer**. Stern, D.

Advancing Luna—and Ida B. Wells. Walker, A.

ADVENTURE

    See also Buried treasure; Escapes; Inter-
    national intrigue; Manhunts; Pirates; Sci-
    ence fiction; Sea stories; Soldiers of for-
    tune; Spies; Underwater exploration; Voy-
    ages and travels; Western stories

Andersen, H. C. The Snow Queen
Anderson, B. The man with the plug in his nose
Asher, N. Shell game
Austin, M. H. The girls at Overtown
Baumbach, J. Bright is innocent: scenes from an
  imaginary movie
Brockmeier, K. The human soul as a Rube
  Goldberg device: a choose-your-own-
  adventure story
Chandler, A. B. Grimes and the Gaijin Daimyo
Clark, S. The extraordinary limits of darkness
Di Filippo, P. Eel pie stall

Dominik, H. A free flight in 2222
Goodis, D. Caravan to Tarim
Gorriti, J. M. The quena
Gorriti, J. M. The treasure of the Incas
Gorriti, J. M. A year in California
Hammett, D. The road home
Hodgson, W. H. Captain Dang
Hodgson, W. H. How Sir Jerrold Treyn dealt
  with the Dutch in Caunston Cove
Hughes, M. Help wanted
Hughes, M. Inner huff
Hughes, M. A little learning
Kessel, J. Events preceding the Helvetican re-
  naissance
Lake, J. and Nestvold, R. The big ice
Lamb, H. Alamut
Lamb, H. Ameer of the sea
Lamb, H. The baiting of the warriors
Lamb, H. Bogatyr
Lamb, H. The bride of Jagannath
Lamb, H. Chang Nor
Lamb, H. City under the sea
Lamb, H. Cossack wolf
Lamb, H. The curved sword
Lamb, H. The devil's song
Lamb, H. An edge to a sword
Lamb, H. Khlit
Lamb, H. The king dies
Lamb, H. Koum
Lamb, H. Law of fire
Lamb, H. The lion cub
Lamb, H. Mark of Astrakhan
Lamb, H. The masterpiece of death
Lamb, H. Men from below
Lamb, H. The mighty manslayer
Lamb, H. The moon of Shawwul
Lamb, H. The outrider
Lamb, H. Over the river
Lamb, H. The phantom caravan
Lamb, H. The post in the steppe
Lamb, H. Prophecy of the blind
Lamb, H. Red hands
Lamb, H. The rider of the gray horse
Lamb, H. Roof of the world
Lamb, H. Rose face
Lamb, H. Said Afzel's elephant
Lamb, H. Sangar
Lamb, H. Singing girl
Lamb, H. The skull of Shirzad Mir
Lamb, H. The star of evil omen
Lamb, H. The stone woman
Lamb, H. Tal Taulai Khan
Lamb, H. The bride of Jagannath
Lamb, H. The two swords of Genghis Khan
Lamb, H. The vampire of Khor
Lamb, H. White falcon
Lamb, H. The white Khan
Lamb, H. The winged rider
Lamb, H. The witch of Aleppo
Lamb, H. Witch woman
Lamb, H. Wolf-hounds of the steppe
Lamb, H. The wolf master
Lamb, H. Wolf's war
L'Amour, L. Coast patrol
L'Amour, L. The diamond of Jeru
L'Amour, L. East of Gorontalo
L'Amour, L. From here to Banggai
L'Amour, L. The house of Qasavara
L'Amour, L. May there be a road

ADVENTURE—*Continued*

L'Amour, L. Mission to Siberut
L'Amour, L. On the road to Amurang
L'Amour, L. Pirates of the sky
L'Amour, L. Pirates with wings
L'Amour, L. South of Suez
L'Amour, L. Tailwind to Tibet
L'Amour, L. Well of the unholy light
L'Amour, L. Wings over Brazil
L'Amour, L. Wings over Khabarovsk
Levine, D. D. Titanium Mike saves the day
Martin, G. R. R. The hedge knight: a tale of the seven kingdoms
Moorcock, M. The roaming forest
Neggers, C. On the run
Nix, G. Holly and iron
Nix, G. Sir Hereward and Mister Fitz go to war again
Reed, R. Five thrillers
Reynolds, A. Nightingale
Sanders, W. Amba
Swanwick, M. The skysailor's tale
Weber, D. A beautiful friendship
The **adventure**. Fleischman, C.
An **adventure** at Brownville. Bierce, A.
An **adventure** in futurity. Smith, C. A.
The **Adventure** of a Photographer. Calvino, I.
The **adventure** of Maltree Abbey. Jeffers, H. P.
The **adventure** of the Abbey Grange. Doyle, Sir A. C.
The **adventure** of the agitated actress. Stashower, D.
The **adventure** of the blarney stone. Jeffers, H. P.
The **adventure** of the Boston Dromio. Pearl, M.
The **adventure** of the coughing dentist. Estleman, L. D.
An **adventure** of the deep waters. Hodgson, W. H.
The **adventure** of the dog in the nighttime. Cohen, P.
The **adventure** of the grand old man. Jeffers, H. P.
The **adventure** of the late orang outang. Linscott, G.
The **adventure** of the librarian's ghost. Breen, J. L.
The **adventure** of the missing detective. Lovisi, G.
The **adventure** of the missing three quarters. Breen, J. L.
The **adventure** of the mooning sentry. Breen, J. L.
The **adventure** of the needle's eye. Queen, E.
The **adventure** of the **Sally Martin**. Jeffers, H. P.
The **adventure** of the southsea trunk. McDevitt, J.
The **Adventure** of the Speckled Band. Doyle, Sir A. C.
The **adventure** of the St. Marylebone ghoul. Crider, B.
The **adventure** of the stuttering ghost. Jeffers, H. P.
The **adventure** of the three students. Doyle, Sir A. C.
The **adventure** of the Voorish Sign. Lupoff, R. A.
The **adventure** of the White City. Crider, B.
The **adventure** of voodoo moon. Thomas, E.
Adventures in dementia. Apple, M.
The **adventures** of Captain Black Heart Wentworth: a nautical tail. Swirsky, R.
The **adventures** of King Dong. Baumbach, J.
The **adventures** of the peerless peer. Farmer, P. J.

ADVERTISING

See also Publicity

Arjouni, J. Idiots
Gospodinov, G. On the taste of names
Kim, H. From powder to powder
Rich, M. The beauty monster
Saunders, G. In persuasion nation
Saunders, G. My flamboyant grandson
Winsor, C. The Hilton epiphany
Advice for New Faculty Members: An Open Letter to J.A. Fleisher, K.
Advocates. Charnas, S. M.
Aeken, Hieronymus van *See* Bosch, Hieronymus, d. 1516
Aelita. Tolstoy, A. N., graf
Aerial Bombardment. Tilghman, C.
Aerialist. Burgin, R.

AERONAUTICS

See also Air pilots; Airships; Flight

Bradbury, R. Icarus Montgolfier Wright
Greenman, B. In the air room

Accidents

Silverberg, R. One way journey

Flights

See Air travel

AERONAUTICS, MILITARY *See* Military aeronautics

Aëronauts. Klimasewiski, M. N.

AESCHYLUS

About

Shepard, J. My Aeschylus

AESOP

About

Coover, R. Aesop's forest
Aesop's forest. Coover, R.

AESTHETICS

Henry, O. Art and the bronco
Zelazny, R. A thing of terrible beauty

Affabee, Eric, 1943-

For works written by this author under other names see Stine, R. L., 1943-

The **affair**. Gilchrist, E.
The **affair** at Coulter's Notch. Bierce, A.
An **affair** of outposts. Bierce, A.
The **affair** of the wooden boy. Odom, M.
The **Affinities**. Wilson, R. C.
An **Affliction** of Starlings. Bernier, C.

AFGHANISTAN

Bissell, T. Death defier
Brockmeier, K. The air is full of little holes

Kabul

Howard, C. Blues in the Kabul night

AFGHANS

United States

Hosseini, K. The kite runner [excerpt]

Afolabi, Segun

Gifted
Granta no92 p77-90 Wint 2005

Afraid. Deaver, J.
Afraid to Say. Partin, B.

AFRICA

See also Central Africa; East Africa; North Africa; South Africa; West Africa

Beagle, P. S. The fable of the ostrich
Bhêly-Quénum, O. A child in the bush of ghosts
Clark, S. The extraordinary limits of darkness
Deb, A. The three-piece suit
Eberhardt, I. One night in Africa
Eberhardt, I. The tears of the almond tree

AFRICA—*Continued*

Enekwe, O. O. The last battle
Gifford, B. African adventure story
Green, D. Clockwork atom bomb
Honwana, L. B. Papa, snake & I
Howard, R. E. The hills of the dead
Inyama, N. Hot days, long nights
Lopes, H. The advance
McDonald, I. Tendeléo's story
Okorafor, N. When scarabs multiply
Ousmane, Sembène. Her three days
Resnick, M. The pale, thin god
Resnick, M. Safari 2103 A.D.
Rickards, J. Twenty dollar future
Saro-Wiwa, K. Africa kills her sun
Shepard, L. The arcevoalo
Shepard, L. Crocodile rock
Updike, D. Love songs from America
Waldrop, H. The lions are asleep this night

Native peoples

See also Kikuyu (African people)
D'Souza, T. Djamilla
Johnson, C. R. The gift of the Osuo
Mungoshi, C. The brother
Smith, C. A. The venus of Azombeii
Timm, U. Morenga [excerpt]

Politics

See Politics—Africa

AFRICA, CENTRAL *See* Central Africa
AFRICA, EAST *See* East Africa
AFRICA, GERMAN EAST *See* East Africa
AFRICA, NORTH *See* North Africa
AFRICA, SOUTH *See* South Africa
AFRICA, WEST *See* West Africa
Africa. Reinhorn, H.
Africa under Her Skin. Drayer, J.
African adventure story. Gifford, B.

AFRICAN AMERICAN CHILDREN

West, D. The five dollar bill
West, D. A tale of Christmas and love

AFRICAN AMERICAN SERVANTS

Crone, M. Mr. Sender
Crone, M. Pipe smoke
Dunbar, P. L. Aunt Tempe's triumph
Dunbar, P. L. A blessed deceit
Dunbar, P. L. A lady slipper
Dunbar, P. L. Mammy Peggy's pride
Dunbar, P. L. The Stanton coachman
Dunbar, P. L. The trouble about Sophiny
Dunbar, P. L. Who stand for the gods
Jeffers, H. F. A plate of mojo
West, D. Mammy (a short story)

AFRICAN AMERICAN SOLDIERS

Irsfeld, J. H. Ambivalence Hardy Fire
Leonard, E. "Hurrah for Captain Early"

AFRICAN AMERICAN WOMEN

Anthony, H. B. Two worlds
Barnes, Z. L. Requiem
Boehm, L. Two-bit piece
Bonner, M. O. Corner store
Bonner, M. O. Of Jimmie Harris
Bonner, M. O. There were three
Bright, N. R. Black
Brown, R. Means and ends
Challeno, E. D. A day's pay: a short story
Day, C. B. The pink hat
Dungyc, D. Sally
Fowler, M. Hall of liberty
Hurston, Z. N. Muttsy

Jones, E. P. Blindsided
Jones, E. P. The Devil swims across the Anacostia River
Layer, F. E. Mrs. Millennium
Lowe, R. The woman in the window
Minus, M. The fine line: a story of the color line
Mull, H. F. Excess baggage
Mull, H. F. White only: a story of the color line
Rumford, J. Elise
Selgin, P. The sinking ship man
Walker, A. Advancing Luna—and Ida B. Wells
Walker, A. To my young husband
West, D. Cook
West, D. Hannah Byde

AFRICAN AMERICANS

See also African American children; African American servants; African American soldiers; African American women; Blacks; Mulattoes; Slavery
Adcock, T. Lawyers' tongues
Allen, J. R. Bread and the land
Allen, J. R. Dog tags
Allen, J. R. The green apocalypse
Allen, J. R. Holding pattern
Allen, J. R. Mississippi story
Allen, J. R. Same
Allen, J. R. Shimmy
Allen, J. R. Toilet training
Allen, P. L. Crip
Apple, M. Indian giver
Baldwin, J. Going to meet the man
Baraka, I. A. Dig this! Out?
Baraka, I. A. From war stories
Baraka, I. A. Heathen technology at the end of the twentieth century
Baraka, I. A. My man came by the crib the other day . . .
Baraka, I. A. Neo-American
Baraka, I. A. The rejected buppie
Barnes, H. L. Minimal damage
Barnes, Z. L. Portrait of a citizen
Bear, E. Shoggoths in bloom
Berniker, S. J. Aqua Velva Smitty
Boehm, L. Condemned house: a short story
Bohanon, M. L. Nothing changes
Bonner, M. O. Black fronts
Bonner, M. O. The makin's
Bonner, M. O. Tin can
Boof, Kola. The one you meet everywhere
Boyers, R. Samantha
Burgin, R. My black Rachmaninoff
Campbell, H. V. Part of the pack: another view of night life in Harlem
Capote, T. Preacher's legend
Capotosto, M. The souls of white children
Carl, L. S. Way down in Egypt's land
Carrow, E. Too much pigment
Clayton, J. J. Voices
Clement, T. T. Faith: a story
Coleman, A. S. The eternal quest
Coleman, W. Backcity transit by day
Coleman, W. Jazz at twelve
Coleman, W. My brain's too tired to think
Coleman, W. Pepper
Coleman, W. Shark liver oil
Coleman, W. Winona's choice
Cook, C. F. A slave for life: a story of the long ago

AFRICAN AMERICANS—*Continued*

Cooper, J. C. As time goes by
Cooper, J. C. Catch a falling heart
Cooper, J. C. The eye of the beholder
Cooper, J. C. Just-life politics
Cooper, J. C. Rushing nowhere
Cooper, J. C. Success
Cooper, J. C. Wait a minute, world!
Davis, J. S. Ava Bean
Doran, M. M. A time too soon
Doyle, R. Home to Harlem
Dunbar, P. L. Aunt Mandy's investment
Dunbar, P. L. The boy and the bayonet
Dunbar, P. L. The colonel's awakening
Dunbar, P. L. A council of state
Dunbar, P. L. The defection of Maria Ann Gibbs
Dunbar, P. L. A defender of the faith
Dunbar, P. L. The emancipation of Evalina Jones
Dunbar, P. L. The finish of Patsy Barnes
Dunbar, P. L. The fruitful sleeping of the Rev. Elisha Edwards
Dunbar, P. L. The home-coming of 'Rastus Smith
Dunbar, P. L. How Brother Parker fell from grace
Dunbar, P. L. The ingrate
Dunbar, P. L. The interference of Patsy Ann
Dunbar, P. L. The intervention of Peter
Dunbar, P. L. Jimmy Weedon's contretemps
Dunbar, P. L. Jim's probation
Dunbar, P. L. Johnsonham, Junior
Dunbar, P. L. A judgment of Paris
Dunbar, P. L. The last fiddling of Mordaunt's Jim
Dunbar, P. L. The lynching of Jube Benson
Dunbar, P. L. A matter of doctrine
Dunbar, P. L. A mess of pottage
Dunbar, P. L. The mission of Mr. Scatters
Dunbar, P. L. Mt. Pisgah's Christmas 'possum
Dunbar, P. L. Old Abe's conversion
Dunbar, P. L. Ole Conju'in Joe
Dunbar, P. L. One man's fortunes
Dunbar, P. L. The ordeal at Mt. Hope
Dunbar, P. L. The promoter
Dunbar, P. L. The scapegoat
Dunbar, P. L. Schwalliger's philanthropy
Dunbar, P. L. Silas Jackson
Dunbar, P. L. Silent Sam'el
Dunbar, P. L. Sister Jackson's superstitions
Dunbar, P. L. The strength of Gideon
Dunbar, P. L. The tragedy at Three Forks
Dunbar, P. L. The trial sermons on Bull-Skin
Dunbar, P. L. The triumph of ol' Mis' Pease
Dunbar, P. L. The trousers
Dunbar, P. L. Viney's free papers
Dunbar, P. L. The walls of Jericho
Dunbar, P. L. The way of a woman
Dunbar, P. L. The wisdom of silence
Dunbar-Nelson, A. M. Summer session
Effinger, G. A. Everything but honor
Eisenberg, F. A street car ride
Ferrell, C. Documents of passion love
Fisher, P. High falutin'
Fowler, M. Southern circumstance
France, L. R. School girl
Fusilli, J. The next best thing
Gaines, E. J. A long day in November

Gautier, A. The ease of living
Gifford, B. The lost tribe
Graves, P. The bishop and the landlady
Hambly, B. There shall your heart be also
Haywood, G. A. The first rule is
Hellmann, L. F. High yellow
Holmes, E. Dangerous days
Howard, R. E. Kelly the conjure-man
Hughes, L. Trouble with the angels
Hunter, S. Stephen Longacre's greatest match
Johnson, C. R. Executive decision
Johnson, D. Melvin in the sixth grade
Johnson, T. G. Winter never quits
Jones, E. P. Old boys, old girls
Jones, E. P. Resurrecting Methuselah
Jones, E. P. Tapestry
Kalamu ya Salaam. All I could do was cry
Kamp, S. Big Joe: a short short story
Keene, J. Annotations [excerpt]
Kelley, N. The messenger of soulsville
Knight, M. Gerald's monkey
Lawson, J. E. The ankle–biter's guide to slithering
Lewis, W. H. Crusade
Lewis, W. H. For the brothers who ain't here
Lewis, W. H. I got somebody in Staunton
Lewis, W. H. In the swamp
Lewis, W. H. Kudzu
Lewis, W. H. Potcake
Lewis, W. H. Rossonian days
Lewis, W. H. Shades
Lewis, W. H. Urban renewal
Lewis, W. H. Why we jump
Lovell, G. Hit and run
Mayfield, J. The last days of Duncan Street
Mazor, J. Washington
Menger-Anderson, K. Happy effects, 1741
Miller, A. L. Hawaii
Miller, M. One blue star
Minus, M. Half-bright: a short story
Mosley, W. Archibald Lawless, anarchist at large: walking the line
Mull, H. F. Uncle Ben
Murray, A. I. The simple one
Neal, L. Our bright tomorrows
Nelson, R. F. Refiner's fire
Nichols, L. D. Prodigal
O'Connor, F. The artificial nigger
Packer, Z. The ant of the self
Packer, Z. Doris is coming
Parker, M. Off island
Parry, E. A. The little that is everything
Pelecanos, G. P. The confidential informant
Pelecanos, G. P. String music
Peters, D. "Faith"
Pezzullo, R. Step up
Phillips, G. Roger Crumbler considered his shave
Porter, K. A. The journey
Porter, K. A. The witness
Rash, R. Overtime
Reeves, E. W. Not in the record
Riley, E. Dark Laughter
Rohrlich, R. Citizen in the south
Row, J. The ferry
Rozan, S. J. Building
Ruffin, P. The day J. P. saved the South
Shell, L. Recompense
Shuman, S. N. Concerto

AFRICAN AMERICANS—*Continued*

Simms, E. Tell it to us easy
Smith, C. T. Black brother
Smith, J. Loot
Solomon, A. Lotto
Spencer, M. E. Beyond the years
Stiefel, B. Dark quarry
Stoddard, F. J. Street of the mortar and pestle: a story of color in the capital
Tervalon, J. The battling priests of Corpus Christi
Thomas, A. Gold is where you find it
Thompson, E. B. Mademoiselle 'Tasie-a story
Thompson, I. M. Ebony-a story
Tompkins, G. W. Across the line
Tompkins, G. W. The fugitive
Tompkins, G. W. The red dress: a short story
Toomer, J. Avey
Vega Yunqué, E. Eight morenos
West, D. Jack in the pot
West, D. Prologue to a life
West, D. The typewriter
Westcott, G. In a thicket
Wideman, J. E. Are dreams faster than the speed of light
Wideman, J. E. Fanon
Wideman, J. E. Hunters
Wideman, J. E. Sharing
Wideman, J. E. Sightings
Wideman, J. E. Weight
Wideman, J. E. Who invented the jump shot
Wideman, J. E. Who weeps when one of us goes down blues
Williams, J. Spring is now
Wilson, R. C. The peaceable land; or, The unbearable vision of Harriet Beecher Stowe
Wisdom, R. The light and the dark
Wright, R. The man who killed a shadow
Wynbush, O. B. The noose

Civil rights

Bennett, L. The convert
Billingslea-Brown, A. J. Moonshot
Brown, R. Means and ends
Cassill, R. V. The first day of school
Coleman, V. Paying my dues
Dumas, H. The marchers
Edwards, J. Liars don't qualify
Grooms, A. Flora Devine
Grooms, A. Food that pleases, food to take home
Grooms, A. Negro progress
Leedom-Ackerman, J. The beginning of violence
Martin, L. The welcome table
Oliver, D. Neighbors
Petesch, N. L. M. Selma
Thelwell, M. Direct action
Thompson, J. W. See what tomorrow brings
Updike, J. Marching through Boston
Welty, E. Where is the voice coming from?

Relations with Jews

Lynn, D. H. Chrysalis
Moise, L. Cuck(h)olding a stranger

California

Beatty, P. The white boy shuffle [excerpt]
Mosley, W. After the wedding
Mosley, W. The apology
Mosley, W. The big nickcl
Mosley, W. Black dog
Mosley, W. Breeding ground

Mosley, W. Details
Mosley, W. Maxie
Mosley, W. Red caddy
Mosley, W. The right mistake
Mosley, W. The trail
Mosley, W. Traitor
Mosley, W. Trifecta
Mosley, W. Two women
Phillips, G. House of tears

Chicago (Ill.)

Ojikutu, B. The gospel of moral ends

Detroit (Mich.)

Cooper, D. Night coming

Florida

Hurston, Z. N. Drenched in light
Hurston, Z. N. John Redding goes to sea

France

Reid, G. Lollipop

Illinois

Maxwell, W. Billie Dyer
Maxwell, W. The front and back parts of the house

Italy

Reid, G. The champion

Kentucky

Dunbar, P. L. The deliberation of Mr. Dunkin

Massachusetts

West, D. My baby . . .

Michigan

Allyn, D. Wolf Woman Bay

Mississippi

Waldrop, H. A dozen tough jobs

New York (N.Y.)

Campbell, H. V. The parasites
Dunbar, P. L. Buss Jenkins up nawth
Dunbar, P. L. How George Johnson "won out"
Dunbar, P. L. Jimsella
Dunbar, P. L. An old-time Christmas
Dunbar, P. L. One Christmas at Shiloh
Dunbar, P. L. Yellowjack's game of craps
Hurston, Z. N. Muttsy
Petry, A. L. On Saturday the siren sounds at noon

North Carolina

Lee, A. Anthropology

Ohio

Dunbar, P. L. The independence of Silas Bollender
Dunbar, P. L. The minority committee
Dunbar, P. L. The mortification of the flesh
Dunbar, P. L. The visiting of Mother Danbury
Dunbar, P. L. The white counterpane
Miller, A. L. Getting to know the world

Southern States

Chesnutt, C. W. The sheriff's children
Dalton, Q. The music you never hear
Howard, R. E. Black Canaan
Hurston, Z. N. Spunk
Kalamu ya Salaam. Alabama

Washington (D.C.)

Dunbar, P. L. Mr. Cornelius Johnson, office-seeker
Jones, E. P. Adam Robinson acquires grandparents and a little sister
Jones, E. P. All Aunt Hagar's children
Jones, E. P. Bad neighbors
Jones, E. P. Common law
Jones, E. P. In the blink of God's eye
Jones, E. P. Marie

The **agreement**. Barthelme, D.

Agresta, Michael
　Mugger and Mouse Get Married
　　Boston Review v33 no1 p29-31 Ja/F 2008

AGRICULTURAL LABORERS *See* Farm workers

Aground and aloft. Patterson, S.

Aguilar, Alejandro
　The Colonel's Allegro
　　The Review of Contemporary Fiction v26 no3
　　p73-5 Fall 2006
　Waters
　　The Review of Contemporary Fiction v26 no3
　　p69-72 Fall 2006

Aguilar, Lou
　The mirror cracked
　　Kolchak: the night stalker chronicles; 26 original tales of the surreal, the bizarre, the macabre; edited by Joe Gentile, Garrett Anderson, Lori Gentile; Kolchak created by Jeff Rice

Aguilera, Carolina Garcia- *See* Garcia-Aguilera, Carolina

Aguirre, Forrest
　Andretto walks the king's way
　　Sedia, E. Paper cities; an anthology of urban fantasy

Agustin. Meloy, M.

Ah, sweet mystery of life. Dahl, R.

Ah, Xiao Xie. Zhu Wen

AHAB, CAPTAIN (FICTITIOUS CHARACTER)
　Finger, A. Moby Dick; or, The leg

Ahdal, Wajdi al-
　To return by foot
　　Oranges in the sun; short stories from the Arabian Gulf; edited and translated by Deborah S. Akers, Abubaker A. Bagader

Ahmed, Fatima
　"Return"
　　Multicultural literature in contemporary Italy; edited by Marie Orton and Graziella Parati

Ahmed, Naylah
　Aqua Blue
　　Her Majesty; 21 stories by women; edited by Jackie Gay and Emma Hargrave

Ahmed, Sharbari
　The Ocean of Mrs. Nagai
　　Gettysburg Review v18 no4 p613-27 Wint 2005

Ahrens, Lynn
　Babka
　　The Kenyon Review v29 no4 p125-34 Fall 2007
　Byobu
　　Calyx v25 no1 p103-10 Wint 2009

AIDS (DISEASE)
　Baingana, D. A thank-you note
　Benioff, D. When the nines roll over and other stories
　Burke, T. On the front
　Currans-Sheehan, T. The men with the leopard wallpaper
　Eldridge, C. Young professionals
　Faber, M. Bye-bye Natalia
　Finger, A. Gloucester
　Jay, K. Speeding cars
　Kercheval, J. L. Damage

　Leung, B. Fire walk: an old-fashioned AIDS story
　Martel, Y. The facts behind the Helsinki Roccamatios
　McCann, R. The universe, concealed
　McFarland, D. Nothing to ask for
　Miner, V. Vital signs
　Montgomery, L. These hours
　Moss, B. K. Little Edens
　Newman, L. Something shiny
　Nfah-Abbenyi, J. M. Slow poison
　Nolan, W. F. Behind the curtain
　Pollack, E. Beached in Boca
　Qi, S. The girl in blue jeans
　Shabtai, Y. Twilight
　Shannon, J. The legend of Bayboy and the Mexican surfer
　Shroff, M. F. Love in the time of AIDS
　Smith, M. Imagine this!
　Stevens, J. D. Great myths of our time
　Twelve, O. Fluff

Aidt, Naja Marie
　Blackberries
　　The Literary Review (Madison, N.J.) v51 no3 p55-8 Spr 2008

Aiken, Joan
　Goblin music
　　The Best science fiction and fantasy of the year: volume three; edited by Jonathan Strahan

Ailoura. Di Filippo, P.

Ain't I a king, too? Downs, G.

AIR
　Chiang, T. Exhalation

Air, a romance. Krysl, M.

Air and Water. Khadivi, L.

Air conditioning and heat. Brazaitis, M.

AIR CRASHES *See* Airplane accidents

The **air** is full of little holes. Brockmeier, K.

AIR PILOTS
　　　　See also Women air pilots
　Anderson, P. Kings who die
　Blish, J. Tomb tapper
　Bradbury, R. Icarus Montgolfier Wright
　Connell, E. S. Yellow raft
　Dahl, R. An African story
　Dahl, R. Beware of the dog
　Dahl, R. Death of an old man
　Dahl, R. Katina
　Dahl, R. Madame Rosette
　Dahl, R. Only this
　Dahl, R. A piece of cake
　Dahl, R. Someone like you
　Dahl, R. They shall not grow old
　Dahl, R. Yesterday was beautiful
　Gallagher, S. The box
　Holder, B. and Holder, N. Another exciting adventure of Lightning Merriemouse-Jones: a touching ghost story
　Koretsky, J. L. Deliberate men
　L'Amour, L. Coast patrol
　L'Amour, L. Down Paagumene way
　L'Amour, L. Flight to Enbetu
　L'Amour, L. Flight to the north
　L'Amour, L. The Goose flies South
　L'Amour, L. Mission to Siberut
　L'Amour, L. Pirates of the sky
　L'Amour, L. Pirates with wings
　L'Amour, L. Tailwind to Tibet

AIR PILOTS—*Continued*
  L'Amour, L. Wings over Brazil
  L'Amour, L. Wings over Khabarovsk
  LaSalle, P. A guide to some small border airports
  Shepard, J. Climb aboard the mighty flea
  Smith, C. A. The dimension of change
  Snyder, S. The star attraction of 1919
  Watkins, S. A jelly of light
Air raid. Varley, J.
AIR RAID SHELTERS
  Benioff, D. De composition
  Budnitz, J. Preparedness
  Matheson, R. Descent
  McCann, R. Dream house
AIR SHIPS *See* Airships
AIR TRAVEL
  Barthelme, D. Up, aloft in the air
  Homes, A. M. Cindy Stubenstock
  July, M. Roy Spivey
  Keret, E. A visit to the cockpit
  O'Shaughnessy, P. Tiny angels
  Taraqqı, G. The unfinished game
AIR WARFARE *See* Military aeronautics; World War, 1939-1945—Aerial operations
Aira, César
  An episode in the life of a landscape painter [excerpt]
    Terrestrial intelligence; international fiction now from New Directions; edited by Barbara Epler
Airborne all the way!. Drake, D.
Aird, Catherine
  A change of heart
    Aird, C. Chapter and hearse
  Chapter and hearse
    Aird, C. Chapter and hearse
  Child's play
    Aird, C. Chapter and hearse
  Cold comfort
    Aird, C. Chapter and hearse
  Coup de grâce
    Aird, C. Chapter and hearse
  Dead letters
    Aird, C. Chapter and hearse
  A different cast of mind
    Aird, C. Chapter and hearse
  Due dilligence
    Aird, C. Chapter and hearse
  Dummy run
    Aird, C. Chapter and hearse
  Examination results
    Aird, C. Chapter and hearse
  Exit strategy
    Aird, C. Chapter and hearse
  Gold, frankincense and murder
    Aird, C. Chapter and hearse
  Handsel Monday
    Aird, C. Chapter and hearse
  The holly and the poison ivy
    A New omnibus of crime; edited by Tony Hillerman and Rosemary Herbert; contributing editors Sue Grafton and Jeffery Deaver
  Like to die
    Aird, C. Chapter and hearse
  Losing the plot
    Aird, C. Chapter and hearse

Preyed in aid
  Aird, C. Chapter and hearse
A soldier of the queen
  Aird, C. Chapter and hearse
Time, gentlemen, please
  Aird, C. Chapter and hearse
Touch not the cat
  Aird, C. Chapter and hearse
The trouble and strife
  Aird, C. Chapter and hearse
The widow's might
  Aird, C. Chapter and hearse
The wild card
  Aird, C. Chapter and hearse
AIRLINES
  See also Airports
    Flight attendants
    See Flight attendants
Airman Basic Training. Rosario, N.
AIRMEN *See* Air pilots
Airplane. Corin, L.
AIRPLANE ACCIDENTS
  Bennett, T. Antioxidants
  Connell, E. S. Yellow raft
  Gee, M. Good people
  Irsfeld, J. H. Finderkeepers
  L'Amour, L. Crash landing
  McBain, E. Death flight [variant title: Ticket to death]
  Murphy, Y. Pan, pan, pan
  Russell, K. Accident brief, occurrence # 00/422
Airplane; or, How he talked to himself as if reciting poetry. Murakami, H.
AIRPLANES
  DeMarinis, R. Desperado
  Gaitskill, M. The girl on the plane
  Gordimer, N. Safety procedures
  Irsfeld, J. H. The man who watched airplanes
  Kalotay, D. Calamity
  Lam, V. Night flight
  Matheson, R. Nightmare at 20,000 feet
  Tsutsui, Y. Farmer airlines
    Accidents
    See Airplane accidents
    Pilots
    See Air pilots
AIRPORTS
  Carcaterra, L. A thousand miles from nowhere
  Gospodinov, G. Peonies and forget-me-nots
  Greenman, B. How little we know about cast polymers, and about life
  Hempel, A. To those of you who missed your connecting flights out of O'Hare
  Irsfeld, J. H. The man who watched airplanes
  Kasischke, L. If a stranger approaches you about carrying a foreign object with you onto the plane . . .
  Kesey, R. Wait
  King, P. Baggage claim
  LaBute, N. Layover
  Lippman, L. Dear Penthouse Forum (a first draft)
  Moceri, M. Einstein made easy
  Monteleone, T. F. It's in the bag
  Otis, M. Triage
  Shepard, J. Runway
  Van Booy, S. The shepherd on the rock
  Zar'uni, A. a.- . Surprise at the airport
Airports of light. Meno, J.

AIRSHIPS
Baxter, S. The pacific mystery
Moorcock, M. Benediction: excerpt from The warlord of the air
Rosenbaum, B. Biographical notes to "A discourse on the nature of causality, with airplanes," by Benjamin Rosenbaum
Snyder, S. Blue yodel
Swanwick, M. The skysailor's tale
VanderMeer, J. Fixing Hanover
Waldrop, H. You could go home again

Aisemberg, Isaac
Ramón Acuña's time
Passport to crime; the finest mystery stories from International Crime Writers; edited by Janet Hutchings

Aiyejina, Funso
The one-handed hero
The Anchor book of modern African stories; edited by Nadežda Obradovic; with a foreword by Chinua Achebe

AJAX AMSTERDAM (SOCCER TEAM)
Shepard, J. Ajax is all about attack

Aji, Aron
(tr.) See Karasu, Bilge

Ajidarma, Seno Gumira
Children of the sky
Words without borders; the world through the eyes of writers; an anthology; edited by Samantha Schnee, Alane Salierno Mason, and Dedi Felman

Aka St. Mark's place. Bowes, R.

Akerman, Beverly
The Mysteries
Dalhousie Review v89 no1 p63-72 Spr 2009

Akiko, Sugimoto
Three Chinese stories
The East v42 no3 p40-2 S/O 2006

Akins, Ellen
Her book
So the story goes; twenty-five years of the Johns Hopkins short fiction series; edited by John T. Irwin and Jean McGarry; with a foreword by John Barth

Akins, Morgan
Que-Linda takes the rite aid
Playboy's college fiction; a collection of 21 years of contest winners; edited by Alice K. Turner; foreword by Thom Jones

Akmakjian, Hiag
Sunday
Noise; fiction inspired by Sonic Youth; edited bt Peter Wild; introduction by Lee Ranaldo

Akpan, Uwem
Communion
The New Yorker v84 no17 p62 Je 9-16 2008
An Ex-Mas Feast
The New Yorker v81 no17 p94, 96, 101-6, 108, 110-12, 114, 117 Je 13-20 2005
My Parents' Bedroom
The New Yorker v82 no17 p130-4, 136, 138, 140-2, 144-5 Je 12 2006

Akpan, Uwem Celestine
An Ex-mas feast
Akpan, U. C. Say you're one of them; [by] Uwem Akpan
Fattening for Gabon
Akpan, U. C. Say you're one of them; [by] Uwem Akpan

Luxurious hearses
Akpan, U. C. Say you're one of them; [by] Uwem Akpan
My parent's bedroom
Akpan, U. C. Say you're one of them; [by] Uwem Akpan
What language is that?
Akpan, U. C. Say you're one of them; [by] Uwem Akpan

Akunin, Boris
Table talk, 1882
Passport to crime; the finest mystery stories from International Crime Writers; edited by Janet Hutchings

Akutagawa, Ryunosuke
In a grove
Adaptations: from short story to big screen; 35 great stories that have inspired great films; edited by Stephanie Harrison

Al. Emshwiller, C.
Al-Assadiah. Mahrus, H. 'I. a.- .
Al-Atrash, Laila
The letter
Qissat; short stories by Palestinian women; edited by Jo Glanville

Al Nasiri, Buthaina
The Return of the Prisoner
Southwest Review v94 no1 p66-72 2009

Al Roosten. Saunders, G.

Al-Shaykh, Samah
At the hospital
Qissat; short stories by Palestinian women; edited by Jo Glanville

Al-Tahawy, Miral
Blue Aubergine
Southwest Review v94 no1 p80-105 2009

ALABAMA
Bierce, A. An occurrence at Owl Creek Bridge
Bisson, T. The edge of the universe
Bohanon, M. L. Nothing changes
Capote, T. A Christmas memory
Capote, T. My side of the matter
Capote, T. One Christmas
Capote, T. The Thanksgiving visitor
Davis, J. S. Detritus
Davis, J. S. Giving up the ghost
Franklin, T. Grit
Kiernan, C. R. In the water works (Birmingham, Alabama 1888)
Knight, M. Birdland
Magee, K. Not people, not this
Pendarvis, J. Lumber land
Petesch, N. L. M. Selma
Ruffin, P. Time of the panther
Ruffin, P. The well
Selgin, P. Boy b
Shirley, P. The consequence of summer heat
Welty, E. Where is the voice coming from?
Wyss, G. Kids make their own houses

Birmingham
Grooms, A. Negro progress
Singleton, G. Director's cut

Mobile
Benford, G. Dark heaven

Alabama. Kalamu ya Salaam
Alam, Rumaan
The Healing Power of Pets
Gettysburg Review v18 no2 p307-17 Summ 2005

Alamut. Lamb, H.
Alarcón, Daniel
  Abraham Lincoln has been shot
    Best American fantasy; guest editors Ann &
      Jeff VanderMeer; series editor Matthew
      Cheney
  Absence
    Alarcón, D. War by candlelight; stories
  The Bridge
    Granta no103 p180-212 Fall 2008
  A Circus at the Center of the World
    The Virginia Quarterly Review v83 no1 p78-
    88 Wint 2007
  City of clowns
    Alarcón, D. War by candlelight; stories
  Flood
    Alarcón, D. War by candlelight; stories
  The Idiot President
    The New Yorker v84 no31 p74-80 O 6 2008
  Lima, Peru; July 28, 1979
    Alarcón, D. War by candlelight; stories
    [Reprint]
    Harper's v309 p24, 26-30 N 2004
  República and Grau
    The New Yorker v82 no35 p82-6, 87 O 30
    2006
  A science for being alone
    Alarcón, D. War by candlelight; stories
  A strong dead man
    Alarcón, D. War by candlelight; stories
  Third Avenue suicide
    Alarcón, D. War by candlelight; stories
  The visitor
    Alarcón, D. War by candlelight; stories
  War by candlelight
    Alarcón, D. War by candlelight; stories
Alaree. Silverberg, R.
Alas! Alas! this woeful fate. Zelazny, R.
Alas, Falada!. Lefer, D.
Alas–I recovered. Wendroff, Z.
ALASKA
  Armstrong, M. The boy who chased seagulls
  Barnes, S. The boat
  Cass, R. Come back
  DeNiro, A. Taiga, taiga, burning bright
  L'Amour, L. With these hands
  Mueller, D. The night my brother worked the
    header
  Reynolds, B. The twin
  Sanders, W. Sitka
  Shepard, J. Pleasure boating in Lituya Bay
  Thompson, J. The inside passage
  Tulathimutte, T. Scenes from the life of the only
    girl in Water Shield, Alaska
  Vann, D. The higher blue
  Vann, D. Ichthyology
  Vann, D. Ketchikan
  Vann, D. A legend of good men
  Vann, D. Rhoda
  Vann, D. Sukkwam Island
        Anchorage
  Doogan, M. War can be murder
Alaska. Sallis, J.
ALBANIA
  Hamilton, D. At the drop of a hat
  Kadare, I. Agamemnon's daughter
  Mehadheb, I. "Undertow"
The **Albanian** Writers' Union as Mirrored By a
  Woman. Kadare, I.

ALBANIANS
        Italy
  Kubati, R. "Leaving with no return"
        Spain
  Swan, G. Exiles
The **albatross**. Hodgson, W. H.
Albemarle. Smith, C.
Albert, Elisa
  Etta or Bessie or Dora or Rose
    Albert, E. How this night is different; stories
  Everything but
    Albert, E. How this night is different; stories
  Hotline
    Albert, E. How this night is different; stories
  How this night is different
    Albert, E. How this night is different; stories
  The living
    Albert, E. How this night is different; stories
  The mother is always upset
    Albert, E. How this night is different; stories
  So long
    Albert, E. How this night is different; stories
  Spooked
    Albert, E. How this night is different; stories
  We have trespassed
    Albert, E. How this night is different; stories
  When you say you're a Jew
    Albert, E. How this night is different; stories
Albert, Susan Wittig
  Bloom where you're planted
    Albert, S. W. An unthymely death and other
    garden mysteries
  A deadly chocolate valentine
    Albert, S. W. An unthymely death and other
    garden mysteries
  Death of a Rose Rustler
    Albert, S. W. An unthymely death and other
    garden mysteries
  Ivy's wild, wonderful weeds
    Albert, S. W. An unthymely death and other
    garden mysteries
  The knat who became a hero
    Albert, S. W. An unthymely death and other
    garden mysteries
  Mustard madness
    Albert, S. W. An unthymely death and other
    garden mysteries
  The pennyroyal plot
    Albert, S. W. An unthymely death and other
    garden mysteries
  The Rosemary caper
    Albert, S. W. An unthymely death and other
    garden mysteries
  Rosemary remembered [excerpt]
    Lone Star sleuths; an anthology of Texas
    crime fiction; edited and with an introduc-
    tion by Bill Cunningham, Steven L. Davis,
    and Rollo K. Newsom.
  An unthymely death
    Albert, S. W. An unthymely death and other
    garden mysteries
  A violet death
    Albert, S. W. An unthymely death and other
    garden mysteries
ALBERTA *See* Canada—Alberta
The **Albertine** notes. Moody, R.
Alberto and Diego Giacometti. Levy, J.
The **Albian** message. Morton, O.
The **albino**. Uchida, H.

Aldiss, Brian Wilson
Multi-value motorway
  New worlds; an anthology; edited by Michael
    Moorcock
Supertoys last all summer long
  Adaptations: from short story to big screen;
    35 great stories that have inspired great
    films; edited by Stephanie Harrison
Tiger in the night
  Elemental; the Tsunami relief anthology; sto-
    ries of science fiction and fantasy; [edited
    by] Steven Savile and Alethea Kontis; in-
    troduction by Arthur C. Clarke
Aleas, Richard *See* Ardai, Charles, 1969-
Aleichem, Shalom *See* Sholem Aleichem, 1859-
  1916
Aleichem, Sholem *See* Sholem Aleichem, 1859-
  1916
Alem, Kangni
The spider's fart
  From Africa; new francophone stories; edited
    by Adele King
Alessio, Carolyn
Mijo
  TriQuarterly no125 p151-8 2006
Alessio, Carolyn
Casualidades
  Pushcart prize XXVII; best of the small
    presses; edited by Bill Henderson with the
    Pushcart prize editors
Alewives. McNett, M.
Alex and the toyceivers. Meloy, P.
Alex Pinto hears the bell. Sullivan, C. J.
Alex, the Barista. Turner, J. E.
Alexa and the German. Ottey, J.
Alexander, Donnell
Beneficient diversions from the crackdkins diet
  The cocaine chronicles; edited by Gary Phil-
    lips and Jervey Tervalon
Alexander, Skye
Life, death, love, and baseball
  Fenway fiction; short stories from Red Sox
    nation; edited by Adam Emerson Pachter
ALEXANDRIA (EGYPT) *See* Egypt—Alexandria
Alexie, Sherman
Ghost dance
  McSweeney's mammoth treasury of thrilling
    tales; edited by Michael Chabon
  The living dead; edited by John Joseph Ad-
    ams
Green World [Part of a forum: My Great De-
  pression]
  Harper's v318 p42-4 Je 2009
This is what it means to say Phoenix, Arizona
  Adaptations: from short story to big screen;
    35 great stories that have inspired great
    films; edited by Stephanie Harrison
The toughest Indian in the world
  The New Granta book of the American short
    story; edited and introduced by Richard
    Ford
The toughnest Indian in the world
  Beha, C. R. The Ecco anthology of contem-
    porary American short fiction; selected by
    Joyce Carol Oates and Christopher R.
    Beha.
War Dances
  The New Yorker v85 no24 p64-73 Ag 10-17
    2009

What ever happened to Frank Snake Church?
  Best stories of the American West, v1; edited
    by Marc Jaffe
What you pawn I will redeem
  The O. Henry Prize stories, 2005; edited and
    with an introduction by Laura Furman
What you pawn I will return
  The Best American short stories, 2004; edited
    by Lorrie Moore; Katrina Kenison series
    editor
Alfar, Dean Francis
L'Aquilone du estrellas (The kite of stars)
  The Year's best fantasy and horror: seven-
    teenth annual collection; edited by Ellen
    Datlow, Kelly Link and Gavin J. Grant
Alfaro, Luis
Border Crossings
  Bomb no98 p84-6 Wint 2007
ALGERIA
Shukman, H. The garden of God: 1976
Shukman, H. The garden of God: 1988
ALGERIANS
               Italy
Dekhis, A. "Salvation"
Algiers. Fulmer, D.
Ali, Mohammed Naseehu
Faith
  Ali, M. N. The prophet of Zongo Street; sto-
    ries
Live-in
  Ali, M. N. The prophet of Zongo Street; sto-
    ries
Mallam Sile
  Ali, M. N. The prophet of Zongo Street; sto-
    ries
  The New Yorker v81 no8 p66-71 Ap 11 2005
Man pass man
  Ali, M. N. The prophet of Zongo Street; sto-
    ries
The manhood test
  Ali, M. N. The prophet of Zongo Street; sto-
    ries
Mysteries of Flight
  The New Yorker v84 no17 p85 Je 9-16 2008
The prophet of Zongo Street
  Ali, M. N. The prophet of Zongo Street; sto-
    ries
Rachmaninov
  Ali, M. N. The prophet of Zongo Street; sto-
    ries
The story of day and night
  Ali, M. N. The prophet of Zongo Street; sto-
    ries
The true Aryan
  Ali, M. N. The prophet of Zongo Street; sto-
    ries
Ward G-4
  Ali, M. N. The prophet of Zongo Street; sto-
    ries
Ali, Monica
Sundowners
  The New Yorker v81 no45 p72-85 Ja 23-30
    2006
ALI, MUHAMMAD, 1942-
               About
Bear, E. Sonny Liston takes the fall
The **alibi.** Archer, J.
The **Alibi.** DeGross, J. M.

ALIBIS

Holmes, R. The monks of the Abbey Victoria

Alice. Capps, T.

Alice and the Old Lady. Tezza, C.

Alice fantastic. Estep, M.

Alice in Dairyland. Kercheval, J. L.

Alice in the time of the Jabberwock. Coover, R.

The **alien**. Nolan, W. F.

Alien archeology. Asher, N.

The **alien** enemy. Anderson, P.

Alien fantasies. Melko, P.

Alien Life. Umminger, A.

Alien radio. DiChario, N.

ALIENATION (SOCIAL PSYCHOLOGY)

See also Social isolation

Davis, J. S. Lovely Lily

Dobozy, T. The inert landscapes of György Ferenc

Dobozy, T. The man who came out of the corner of my eye

July, M. The man on the stairs

July, M. Something that needs nothing

Lefer, D. California transit

Mindt, A. An artist at work

Murakami, H. Blind willow, sleeping woman

Tawada, Y. The shadow man

ALIENS, ILLEGAL *See* Undocumented aliens

ALIENS, UNDOCUMENTED *See* Undocumented aliens

Aliens. Cohen, R.

Aliens. McGuane, T.

Aliens ate my pickup. Lackey, M.

The **aliens** who knew, I mean, everything. Effinger, G. A.

Alighieri, Dante *See* Dante Alighieri, 1265-1321

Alison, Jane

Bilbao

TriQuarterly no132 p64-75 2008

All about balls. Skinner, J.

All Aunt Hagar's children. Jones, E. P.

All because of a needle. Libin, Z.

All black. Faber, M.

All bleeding stops . . . eventually. Sheard, T.

All day breakfast. Stewart, P.

All happy families. Ervin, A.

All I could do was cry. Kalamu ya Salaam

All in the execution. Waggoner, T.

All life's grandeur. Kalotay, D.

All my bloody things. Niles, S.

All my darling daughters. Willis, C.

All my roe. Ruefle, M.

The **all-night** bodega of souls. Whitehead, C.

The **all-night** dentist. Kovar, V.

All of a Sudden. Panciera, C.

All of me. Rybicki, E.

All of us can almost . . . Emshwiller, C.

All over, Rover. Morison, N.

All quiet. Lutz, J.

All riptides roar with sand from opposing shores. Vaz, K.

All roads lead to flesh and bone. Rahman, I.

All Roads to Lhasa. Wang Ping

All Saints Day. Pneuman, A.

All that Glass. Hendry, K.

All That I Am and Ever Will Be. Hoffman, A.

All that is gone. Toer, P. A.

All that matters. Binchy, M.

All that's missing. Stamm, P.

All the America you want. Magee, K.

All the bad stuff. Graham, B.

All the Color in the World. Haythe, J.

All the days and nights. Maxwell, W.

All the last wars at once. Effinger, G. A.

All the Necessary Things. Dason, S. B.

All the pale women. Hawes, L.

All the same. Bennett, T.

All the wrecks I've crawled out of. Boyle, T. C.

All These Questions. Raimo, C.

All through the house. Coake, C.

All-U-Can-Eat. Panning, A.

All washed up while looking for a better world. Emshwiller, C.

All We Have. Stansel, I.

All Who Die Share One Breath. Kwong, W. T.-Y.

Allaback, Steven

Big Guy, Bug Guy

The North American Review v290 no1 p40-6 Ja/F 2005

Allam and son. Naiyer Masud

Allan, John B.

For works written by this author under other names see Westlake, Donald E.

Allan, Stephen

If there's a hell below, we're all gonna go

Hardcore hardboiled; edited by Todd Robinson; introduction by Otto Penzler

Allardice, James

The Dancer

Iowa Review v38 no3 p134-6 Wint 2008/2009

Allegiance. Kyle, A.

Allegiance. Silber, J.

Allegorical story with literal window. Tognazzini, A.

ALLEGORIES

See also Fables; Fantasies; Good and evil; Parables; Symbolism

Andersen, H. C. The Snow Queen

Blish, J. The box

Bradbury, R. Death and the maiden

Bradford, K. T. Black feather

Brau, E. The blessing

Brau, E. The prisoner

Bulgakov, M. A. The master and Margarita [excerpt]

Đoàn, L. Achieving flyhood

Englander, N. The tumblers

Garrett, G. P. Epilogue: my life as a home movie

Gordimer, N. Tape measure

Horn, D. Readers Digest

Kadare, I. The blinding order

Kleinheincz, C. A drop of raspberry

Lebbon, T. In the valley where belladonna grows

Maḥfūẓ, N. The haunted wood

Martin, G. R. R. In the lost lands

Okri, B. What the tapster saw

Palwick, S. Elephant

Resnick, M. Bwana

Richards, S. S. Gawain and the horsewoman

Rucker, R. v. B. and Shirley, J. Pockets

Silverberg, R. Sundance

Stone, E. J. Taint of treason

Tolstaia, T. Serafim

Ts'an-hsüeh. Top floor

Yamada, E. Fiesta

Zebrowski, G. General Jaruzelski at the zoo

Zucker, G. Punishment

Allen, Dwight
  The Baby and the Moth
    New England Review v29 no4 p152-65 2008
Allen, Dwight, Jr.
  The green suit
    Barnstorm; contemporary Wisconsin fiction;
      edited by Raphael Kadushin
Allen, Ed
  Chesting, or: The Little League Bounce Can Be
    Stopped
    The Antioch Review v66 no3 p421-33 Summ
      2008
Allen, Henry W., 1912-1991
    *For works by this author under other
      names see* Henry, Will, 1912-1991
Allen, Jeffery Renard
  Barbershop Quartet
    Callaloo v28 no2 p280-8 Spr 2005
  Bread and the land
    Allen, J. R. Holding pattern; stories
  Dog tags
    Allen, J. R. Holding pattern; stories
  The green apocalypse
    Allen, J. R. Holding pattern; stories
  Holding pattern
    Allen, J. R. Holding pattern; stories
  It shall be again
    Allen, J. R. Holding pattern; stories
  Mississippi story
    Allen, J. R. Holding pattern; stories
  The near remote
    Chicago noir; edited by Neal Pollack
    Allen, J. R. Holding pattern; stories
  Same
    Allen, J. R. Holding pattern; stories
  Shimmy
    Allen, J. R. Holding pattern; stories
  Toilet training
    Allen, J. R. Holding pattern; stories
Allen, Karen Jordan
  Alternate anxieties
    Interfictions; an anthology of interstitial writ-
      ing; edited by Delia Sherman and Theodora
      Goss
Allen, M. S.
  Wish You Were Here
    The Georgia Review v58 no3 p537-68 Fall
      2004
Allen, Nancy J.
  Calculation
    Southwest Review v93 no2 p240-51 2008
Allen, Paula Gunn
  Burned alive in the blues
    Reckonings; contemporary short fiction by
      Native American women; edited by Hertha
      D. Sweet Wong, Lauren Stuart Muller, Jana
      Sequoya Magdaleno
  Deer woman
    Reckonings; contemporary short fiction by
      Native American women; edited by Hertha
      D. Sweet Wong, Lauren Stuart Muller, Jana
      Sequoya Magdaleno
Allen, Preston L.
  Crip
    Las Vegas noir; edited by Jarrett Keene &
      Todd James Pierce.
Allen, Woody
  Above the law, below the box springs
    Allen, W. Mere anarchy

Attention geniuses: cash only
  Allen, W. Mere anarchy
Calisthenics, poison ivy, final cut
  Allen, W. Mere anarchy
Caution, falling moguls
  Allen, W. Mere anarchy
Glory hallelujah, sold!
  Allen, W. Mere anarchy
How deadly your taste buds, my sweet
  Allen, W. Mere anarchy
Nanny dearest
  Allen, W. Mere anarchy
No kaddish for Weinstein
  Inside the hornet's head; an anthology of
    Jewish American writing; edited by Jerome
    Charyn
On a bad day you can see forever
  Allen, W. Mere anarchy
Pinchuck's law
  Allen, W. Mere anarchy
The rejection
  Telling tales; edited by Nadine Gordimer
  Allen, W. Mere anarchy
Sam, you made the pants too fragrant
  Allen, W. Mere anarchy
Sing, you sacher tortes
  Allen, W. Mere anarchy
Strung out
  Allen, W. Mere anarchy
Surprise rocks Disney trial
  Allen, W. Mere anarchy
Tandoori ransom
  Allen, W. Mere anarchy
This nib for hire
  Allen, W. Mere anarchy
Thus ate Zarathustra
  Allen, W. Mere anarchy
To err is human—to float, divine
  Allen, W. Mere anarchy
Allen-Agostini, Lisa
  Pot luck
    Trinidad noir; edited by Lisa Allen-Agostini
      & Jeanne Mason.
Allen met the Devil. Roberts, A.
Allende, Isabel
  The Guggenheim lovers
    The Year's best fantasy and horror: nineteenth
      annual collection; edited by Ellen Datlow
      and Kelly Link & Gavin J. Grant
    The Virginia Quarterly Review v81 no3 p102-
      11 Summ 2005
Allergies. McCauley, W.
ALLERGY
  Boudinot, R. Bee beard
  Luvaas, W. The woman who was allergic to
    herself
  McCauley, W. Allergies
Allerleirauh. Yolen, J.
Allesverloren. Gordimer, N.
The **alley.** Hallabi, N. a.- .
Alliances of youth. Johnson, G.
The **alligator** man. Woronov, M.
Alligator story. Koretsky, J. L.
ALLIGATORS
  Poissant, D. J. Lizard man
  Russell, K. Ava wrestles the alligator
  Shirley, P. The story of William B. Greene

Allio, Kirstin

Clothed, Female Figure

Iowa Review v38 no2 p1-26 Fall 2008

Allison, Hughes

Corollary

Black noir; mystery, crime and suspense stories by African-American writers; edited by Otto Penzler

Allman, John

Waiting for Z

Michigan Quarterly Review v47 no3 p493-508 Summ 2008

Allowing the lion. Sallis, J.

Allred, Lee

East of Appomattox

Alternate generals III; edited by Harry Turtledove and Roland J. Green

The **Allure** of All This. Slomski, H. A.

Allyn, Douglas

Dead as a dog

A Prisoner of memory and 24 of the year's finest crime and mystery stories; edited by Ed Gorman & Martin H. Greenberg

The murder ballads

The World's finest mystery and crime stories, fourth annual collection; edited by Ed Gorman and Martin H. Greenberg

Palace in the pines

The World's finest mystery and crime stories, fifth annual collection; edited by Ed Gorman and Martin H. Greenberg

Wolf Woman Bay

Wolf Woman Bay; and nine more of the finest crime and mystery novellas of the year; edited by Ed Gorman and Martin H. Greenberg

Alma. Díaz, J.

Almond, Steve

The American Male in Serious Decline

The Georgia Review v59 no4 p768-74 Wint 2005

Announcement

StoryQuarterly v41 p193-4 2005

Appropriate sex

Almond, S. The evil B. B. Chow and other stories

At Age 91, Anna Smolz of the Gmersh Unit Speaks

StoryQuarterly v40 p126-7 2004

Behold the Don

The Southern Review (Baton Rouge, La.) v43 no2 p417 Spr 2007

Blue messiah

2033; the future of misbehavior: interplanetary dating, Madame President, socialized plastic surgery, and other good news from the future; from the editors of Nerve.com; instigated by Svedka

The breakup vows

Best of Tin House; stories; foreword by Dorothy Allison

Come and Take Me

The Southern Review (Baton Rouge, La.) v43 no2 p419 Spr 2007

Companions

New England Review v28 no1 p108-10 2007

Controversial Author and Cultural Icon Found Dead

The Virginia Quarterly Review p133-9 2006 supp

The darkness together

The Pushcart Prize XXX: best of the small presses 2006; edited by Bill Henderson with the Pushcart Prize editors

Don't Listen to This

StoryQuarterly v41 p91-2 2005

The evil B. B. Chow

Almond, S. The evil B. B. Chow and other stories

First Date Back

New England Review v29 no1 p159-68 2008

A happy dream

Almond, S. The evil B. B. Chow and other stories

Hating Monet

New England Review v27 no1 p76-84 2006

I am as I am

Almond, S. The evil B. B. Chow and other stories

The idea of Michael Jackson's dick

Almond, S. The evil B. B. Chow and other stories

In Love Blood Shall Follow

Bomb no91 p84-6 Spr 2005

Larsen's novel

Almond, S. The evil B. B. Chow and other stories

Liberation Theology

Western Humanities Review v61 no1 p22 Wint 2007

Lincoln, arisen

Almond, S. The evil B. B. Chow and other stories

Miller

Western Humanities Review v61 no1 p23 Wint 2007

Old Waitresses

StoryQuarterly v42 p61-2 2006

Open Up and Say Ow

New England Review v26 no1 p36-44 2005

The pass

Pushcart prize XXVII; best of the small presses; edited by Bill Henderson with the Pushcart prize editors

The problem of human consumption

Almond, S. The evil B. B. Chow and other stories

Shotgun wedding

Before; short stories about pregnancy from our top writers; edited by Emily Franklin and Heather Swain

Skull

Almond, S. The evil B. B. Chow and other stories

The soul molecule

Almond, S. The evil B. B. Chow and other stories

Summer, as in love

Almond, S. The evil B. B. Chow and other stories

Tamalpais

The Virginia Quarterly Review v82 no1 p160-73 Wint 2006

Almond, Steve—*Continued*
  The true republic
    Sex for America; politically inspired erotica;
      edited by Stephen Elliott
  What the Bird Says
    The Southern Review (Baton Rouge, La.) v40
      no4 p703-15 Aut 2004
  When the Toasts Stopped Being Funny
    StoryQuarterly v41 p74 2005
  Wired for life
    Almond, S. The evil B. B. Chow and other
      stories
  Young Body Dream
    The Southern Review (Baton Rouge, La.) v43
      no2 p418 Spr 2007
  Young Waitresses
    StoryQuarterly v42 p60 2006
Almonds. Stern, R. G.
An **almost-blue** arm. Galanaki, R.
Almost home. Bisson, T.
Almost not beautiful. Boswell, R.
Almost Oriental. Gifford, B.
Almost soup. Erdrich, L.
Almost the last story by almost the last man.
  Edelman, S.
Almost two thousand years. Arnow, H. L. S.
Alms. Khan, R.
ALMSHOUSES
  Singer, I. B. A night in the poorhouse
  Stafford, J. Life is no abyss
Alo-Cabalquinto, Carla
  Summer of 2003: New Girl in Idaho
    Idaho Magazine v3 no11 p30-1 Ag 2004
Alone. James, H.
Alone. Lansdale, J. R. and Hall, M. M.
Along the Highways. Arvin, N.
Along the Lake. Brown, R.
Along the Pecos. See Leonard, E. The rustlers
  [variant title: Along the Pecos]
ALPHABET
  Irvine, A. C. Reformation
Alphabet soup. Sankaran, L.
Alphonsus, João
  Sardanapalo
    Oxford anthology of the Brazilian short story;
      edited by K. David Jackson
The **alpine** slide. Curtis, R.
Alsup, Benjamin
  Happy?
    Esquire v142 no6 p143-4, 146, 148, 150, 232
      D 2004
Altenberg, Peter
  Telegrams of the Soul: A Selection
    New England Review v26 no2 p167-74 2005
Alter Ego. Leach, A.
Alter Iteleh's and his daughters. Molodowsky, K.
The **alternate**. Krasikov, S.
The **alternate**. Zebrowski, G.
Alternate anxieties. Allen, K. J.
Alternative. Keret, E.
Alternative endings: the first sense. Gordimer, N.
Alternative endings: the second sense. Gordimer,
  N.
Alternative endings: the third sense. Gordimer, N.
The **Altman** sonata. Stern, D.
Altomonte, Elizabeth
  Being Chandra
    The Kenyon Review v28 no2 p148-54 Spr
      2006

Altschul, Andrew Foster
  Leaving Idyllwild
    StoryQuarterly v42 p63-87 2006
  A new kind of gravity
    The O. Henry Prize stories 2007; edited and
      with an introduction by Laura Furman; with
      essays on the story they admire most by ju-
      rors Charles D'Ambrosio, Ursula K. Le
      Guin, Lily Tuck
    StoryQuarterly v41 p133-59 2005
  Requiem for Sammy the magic cat
    Stumbling and raging; more politically in-
      spired fiction; edited by Stephen Elliott;
      with associate editors Greg Larson [et al.]
  y = mx+b
    Ploughshares v34 no4 p25-8 Wint 2008/2009
ALUMNI, COLLEGE *See* College alumni
The **alumni** interview. Levithan, D.
Alvarado, Beth
  Bastille Day
    Alvarado, B. Not a matter of love
  Can you hear me?
    Alvarado, B. Not a matter of love
  Comadres in the kitchen
    Alvarado, B. Not a matter of love
  Emily's exit
    Alvarado, B. Not a matter of love
  In box canyon
    Alvarado, B. Not a matter of love
  Just family
    Alvarado, B. Not a matter of love
    Ploughshares v31 no2/3 p8-30 Fall 2005
  Limbo
    Alvarado, B. Not a matter of love
  Not a matter of love
    Alvarado, B. Not a matter of love
  Phoenix
    Alvarado, B. Not a matter of love
  What Lydia thinks of roses
    Alvarado, B. Not a matter of love
Alvarez, Julia
  The blood of the Conquistadores
    Colchie, T. A whistler in the nightworld;
      short fiction from the Latin Americas; ed-
      ited by Thomas Colchie
  A Cafecito [Excerpt from A Cafecito Story/El
    Cuento del Cafecito]
    Américas v59 no2 p64 Mr/Ap 2007
Álvaro Rousselot's Journey. Bolaño, R.
Alvin's ilk. Mordecai, P.
Always. Fowler, K. J.
Alyósha Gorshok: Alyósha-the-Pot. Tolstoy, L.
ALZHEIMER'S DISEASE
  Apple, M. Adventures in dementia
  Apple, M. Strawberry shortcake
  Barnes, J. Appetite
  Buentello, J. A certain recollection
  Burke, T. Pomo basuto
  Dufresne, J. Close by me forever
  Gay, W. Those Deep Elm Brown's Ferry Blues
  Guista, M. A walk outside
  Hauser, E. The charm of the highway median
  MacLaverty, B. The assessment
  McHugh, M. F. Oversite
  McHugh, M. F. Presence
  Munro, A. The bear came over the mountain
  Pierce, T. J. Arise and walk, Christopher Reeve
  Pollock, D. R. Honolulu
  Rickert, M. Anyway

Amado, Jorge
  How Porciúncula the mulatto got the corpse off
    his back
    Oxford anthology of the Brazilian short story;
      edited by K. David Jackson
Amakusa, Jeronimo *See* Amakusa, Shiro, 1621 or
    2-1638
AMAKUSA, SHIRO, 1621 OR 2-1638
                    About
  Fowler, K. J. Shimabara
Amanda and the alien. Silverberg, R.
Amanuensis. Chapman, J. D.
Amaryllis. Jen, G.
An **Amateur's** Story. Bly, C.
The **amazing** planet. See Smith, C. A. A captivity
    in Serpens [variant title: The amazing plan-
    et]
The **Amazon.** Woronov, M.
AMAZON RIVER VALLEY
  Woronov, M. The Amazon
Amba. Sanders, W.
AMBASSADORS *See* Diplomatic life
The **ambassador's** son. Bissell, T.
Amberstone, Celu
  Refugees
    So long been dreaming; postcolonial science
      fiction & fantasy; Nalo Hopkinson &
      Uppinder Mehan, eds
AMBITION
  Amdahl, G. The free fall
  Auchincloss, L. The conversion of Fred Coates
  Cooper, J. C. As time goes by
  Dunbar, P. L. One man's fortunes
  Dunbar, P. L. Silas Jackson
  Gordon, M. Eileen
  Hayashi, M. One year later
  Judah, S. Dreams
  Koumandareas, M. Seraphim
  Lobato, J. B. M. The funnyman who repented
  Molodowsky, K. The son-in-law
  Monk, B. Flying lesson
  Orr, M. The wisdom of Eve
  Rachel, D. The last man I killed
  Rucker, R. v. B. and Sterling, B. Junk DNA
  Sandford, J. Lucy had a list
  Sterling, B. and Rucker, R. v. B. Junk DNA
  Ulitskaya, L. Zurich
  Wang Ping. Forage
Ambition. Charters, D.
Ambition. Martinez, M.
Ambivalence. Julavits, H.
An **ambulance.** Chekhov, A. P.
AMBULANCES
  Chekhov, A. P. An ambulance
  Foxwell, E. No man's land
  Wingate, S. Three a.m. ambulance driver
The **ambush.** Tartt, D.
Amdahl, Gary
  Across My Big Brass Bed
    Agni no69 p58-113 2009
  The barber-chair
    Amdahl, G. Visigoth; stories
  The bouncers
    Amdahl, G. Visigoth; stories
  The flight from California
    Amdahl, G. Visigoth; stories
  The flyweight
    Amdahl, G. Visigoth; stories

  The free fall
    Amdahl, G. Visigoth; stories
  The Lesser Evil
    Agni no68 p167-72 2008
  Narrow road to the deep north
    Amdahl, G. Visigoth; stories
  Visigoth
    Amdahl, G. Visigoth; stories
  The volunteer
    Amdahl, G. Visigoth; stories
Ameer of the sea. Lamb, H.
Amend, Allison
  Dominion Over Every Erring Thing
    Prairie Schooner v82 no2 p75-90 Summ 2008
AMERICA
            See also Central America
America. Bonnefoy, Y.
America. Liebrecht, S.
America. Romano, T.
America 1911. Messina, M.
America 1918. Messina, M.
America, you S.O.B. Kobrin, L.
An **American** affair. Brazaitis, M.
The **American** Boyfriend. Hwawon, L.
American Breakfast—Mexican Dinner. Daugharty,
    J.
American Child. Menon, M.
AMERICAN CIVIL WAR, 1861-1865 *See* Unit-
    ed States—Civil War, 1861-1865
American commando. Hemon, A.
American Curls. Springer, N.
American Dhansak and the Holy Man of Oaxaca.
    Rustomji, R.
The **American** dream. Halaby, L.
American dreaming. Iarovici, D.
The **American** Embassy. Adichie, C. N.
American food. Chilson, P.
The **American** girl. Row, J.
American Idyll. Spencer, R.
The **American** Male in Serious Decline. Almond,
    S.
American morons. Hirshberg, G.
An **American** proverb. Glancy, D.
American Purgatorio. Haskell, J.
AMERICAN REVOLUTION, 1775-1783 *See*
    United States—Revolution, 1775-1783
American Silk. Scott, J.
American Ska. Pope, D.
AMERICAN SOLDIERS *See* Soldiers—United
    States
American son [excerpt] Roley, B. A.
An **American** Story. Kiš, D.
An **American** Story; or, What Unfortunately Hap-
    pened. Wheelwright, T.
The **American** Sun & Wind Moving Picture Com-
    pany. Neugeboren, J.
American waitress. Fowler, C.
The **American** Woman's Cookbook. O'Brien, S.
    L.
AMERICANIZATION
  Sankaran, L. Apple pie, one by two
  Sankaran, L. Birdie num-num
AMERICANS
                Afghanistan
  Bissell, T. Death defies
                  Africa
  Burke, T. Basutoland Christmas
  Burke, T. Pomo basuto
  Chilson, P. Toumani Ogun

AMERICANS—Africa—*Continued*
D'Souza, T. Djamilla
Koënings, N. S. Theft
Nelson, R. F. Breaker

Argentina
Groff, L. Sir fleeting
LaSalle, P. Tell Borges if you see him
Unger, D. The perfect wife

Bahamas
Bishop, T. Bonefish in Wyoming

Belize
Massie, E. The landlock
Winn, T. Gumbo limbo

Bolivia
Brazaitis, M. The race

Canada
DuBois, B. An empire's reach
Hirshberg, G. Millwell

Caribbean region
Williams, J. Charity

Central Asia
Berry, S. The devils' due
Bissell, T. Aral
Bissell, T. Expensive trips nowhere
McInerney, J. In the north-west frontier province

China
L'Amour, L. Beyond the great snow mountains

Colombia
Fountain, B. Near-extinct birds of the central cordillera
Tudish, C. Where the devil lost his blanket

Costa Rica
Burgin, R. Bodysurfing
Eggers, D. The only meaning of the oil-wet water

Cuba
Gifford, B. Dancing with Fidel
Obejas, A. Zenzizenzic
Shepard, J. Batting against Castro

Eastern Europe
Bissell, T. The ambassador's son

Egypt
Smith, D. L. The charnel house

El Salvador
Shepard, L. Salvador

England
Gordon, M. Sick in London
Hornung, E. W. A trap to catch a cracksman
Mason, B. A. The prelude
Mason, B. A. Proper gypsies
McClanahan, E. A foreign correspondence
Pearlman, E. If love were all
Schutt, C. Young
Smith, M. M. Being right

Ethiopia
Gaitskill, M. Don't cry

Europe
Barthelme, D. Edward and Pia
McKenzie, E. Stop that girl
Scott, J. Or else, part II: What will happen
Stafford, J. The children's game
Stern, R. G. Gaps
Stern, R. G. Zhoof

France
Baumbach, J. French history
Baumbach, J. Reverie
Bingham, S. Pleyben
Bingham, S. Sagesse
Bingham, S. Sweet peas
Boyd, W. Visions fugitives
Boyers, R. The French lesson
Dymond, J. Cherubs
Fitzgerald, F. S. Babylon revisited
Gardiner, J. R. Fugitive color
Gifford, B. The sculptor's son
Gifford, B. What happened in Japan
Gildner, G. Somewhere geese are flying
Groff, L. Delicate edible birds
Holder, N. Little Dedo
Holthe, T. U. The five-forty-five to Cannes
Holthe, T. U. Homecoming
L'Amour, L. The cross and the candle
LaSalle, P. The cities he would never be sure of
LaSalle, P. French sleeping pills
LaSalle, P. Nocturne
Maxwell, W. The gardens of Mount-Saint-Michel
Maxwell, W. The pilgrimage
Neville, K. The Tuesday club
Raphael, L. Free man in Paris
Reid, G. Lollipop
Robinson, R. Assez
Robinson, R. Choosing sides
Robinson, R. Pilgrimage
Shields, C. Hinterland
Stafford, J. Maggie Meriwether's rich experience
Stern, R. G. My ex, the moral philosopher
Vidal, G. Pages from an abandoned journal
Westcott, G. The sailor

Germany
Gifford, B. One leg
Helms, B. American wives
Kercheval, J. L. A story set in Germany
Michaels, L. A girl with a monkey
Miller, A. The performance
Porter, K. A. The leaning tower
Stafford, J. The echo and the nemesis
Stafford, J. The maiden
Tomlinson, J. Berliner

Ghana
Brown, E. Mules

Greece
Blackwell, K. The minaret
Gildner, G. The roots of Western civilization
Segal, L. G. Leslie's shoes
Thor, B. The Athens solution

Guatemala
Brady, C. The dazzling world
Brazaitis, M. An American affair
Brazaitis, M. Before the wedding
Brazaitis, M. The day and the night of the day
Brazaitis, M. The ferry
Brazaitis, M. Iris, thirty years later
Brazaitis, M. The life he left behind
Williams, J. Fortune

Haiti
Fountain, B. Rêve Haitien
Miller, A. The turpentine still

Honduras
Sayles, J. To the light

Hong Kong
Row, J. The American girl
Row, J. The ferry
Row, J. For you
Row, J. Revolutions
Row, J. The secrets of bats

AMERICANS—*Continued*
Iceland
Anderson, P. The man who came early
India
Connell, E. S. Lost in Uttar Pradesh
Freudenberger, N. Lucky girls
Freudenberger, N. The tutor
LaSalle, P. The cities he would never be sure of
Lynn, D. H. Children of God
Lynn, D. H. Mistaken identity
Theroux, P. The elephant god
Theroux, P. The gateway of India
Theroux, P. Monkey Hill
Updike, J. The apparition
Watkins, S. Kafka's sister
Iran
Le, N. Tehran calling
Ireland
Boyle, T. C. The miracle at Ballinspittle
Bradbury, R. Getting through Sunday somehow
Bradbury, R. The great collision of Monday last
Bradbury, R. A wild night in Galway
Bruen, K. Fade to . . . Brooklyn
Coleman, R. F. Portrait of the killer as a young man
Enright, A. Switzerland
Gordon, M. The baby
Gordon, M. Bishop's house
Keane, J. B. Guaranteed pure
Kiely, B. The dogs in the great Glen
Kiely, B. Rich and rare were the gems she wore
Phillips, G. The man for the job
Starr, J. Lost in Dublin
Swierczynski, D. Lonely and gone
Israel
Hasak-Lowy, T. On the grounds of the complex commemorating the Nazis' treatment of the Jews
Singer, M. Deir Yassin
Singer, M. Helicopter days
Italy
Baumbach, J. The Villa Mondare
Beattie, A. Lavande
Beattie, A. Mostre
Bunin, I. A. The gentleman from San Francisco
Clayton, J. J. Night talk
Dormen, L. General strike
Eisenberg, D. Like it or not
Genna, G. Caput Mundi
Gordon, M. Death in Naples
Helms, B. Men in Italy
Herrmann, M. Cooking lessons
Herrmann, M. Signaling for rescue
Herrmann, M. You only want to scare her
Hirshberg, G. American morons
Holthe, T. U. The five-forty-five to Cannes
Holthe, T. U. Weightless
Kalotay, D. Difficult thoughts
Lannes, R. The anguish of departure
Macy, C. Bait and switch
Ozick, C. At Fumicaro
Parks, T. Changing address
Reid, G. The champion
Stern, R. G. Orvieto dominos, bolsena eels
Stern, R. G. A recital for the Pope
Wolff, T. The benefit of the doubt
Woolson, C. F. Dorothy
Woolson, C. F. A Florentine experiment
Woolson, C. F. "Miss Grief"

Woolson, C. F. A transplanted boy
Japan
Stern, R. G. In return
Woolrich, C. Death in the Yoshiwara
Kenya
Stern, R. G. Oscar and Hypatia
Watkins, S. Family of man
Mali
Haschemeyer, O. The fantome of Fatma
Mexico
Bensko, J. Out from Guadalajara
Crumley, J. Whores
Duncklee, J. The mines of Magdalena
Etchison, D. The dark country
Gifford, B. The stars above Veracruz
Julavits, H. Ambivalence
LaSalle, P. The Christmas bus
Lefer, D. California transit
McBain, E. Carrera's woman
Panning, A. Chiclets
Porter, K. A. Flowering Judas
Puchner, E. Legends
Sayles, J. Casa de los Babys
Selgin, P. The sea cure
Stern, R. G. Gifts
Waldrop, H. Thin, on the ground
White, E. Cinnamon skin
Morocco
Burke, T. Quite normal
Burke, T. Where is home?
Macy, C. Taroudant
McCann, R. Some threads through the Medina
Updike, J. Morocco
Myanmar
Fountain, B. Asian tiger
Netherlands
Speegle, D. Peace rituals
Niger
Chilson, P. Tea with soldiers
Pakistan
Hillhouse, R. Diplomatic constraints
Palestine
Stumacher, A. The Neon desert
Panama
Henriquez, C. Chasing birds
Philippines
Battles, B. Perfect gentleman
Carron, H. B. A favor for the mayor
Poland
Albert, E. The living
Michaels, L. Nachman
Oates, J. C. My Warszawa: 1980
Portugal
Albert, E. When you say you're a Jew
Schappell, E. That sort of woman
Romania
Gifford, B. Almost Oriental
Rome
Harleman, A. Will build to suit
Russia
Bissell, T. God lives in St. Petersburg
Harleman, A. Street of swans
Novakovich, J. Tchaikovsky's bust
Parker, J. False cognate
Saudi Arabia
Ward, A. E. Motherhood and terrorism
Scotland
Nadelson, S. Return
Rankin, I. Graduation day

And proudly die. L'Amour, L.

And seven times never kill man. Martin, G. R. R.

And So. Vernon, O.

And such small deer. Roberson, C.

And the darkness is harsh. Zelazny, R.

And the deep blue sea. Bear, E.

And the dish ran away with the spoon. Di Filippo, P.

And the sea shall give up its dead. Mueller, R.

And the winner is . . . Levinson, R. S.

And then. Barthelme, D.

And then I wrote . . . McClanahan, E.

And Then, One Day, the Rains. Markus, P.

And then she was gone. Matthews, C.

And then you stand up. Feitell, M.

And tomorrow and. Roberts, A.

And we will be here. Yoon, P.

And weel no wot to do. Featherstone, G.

And what shall we call you? Phillips, G.

And when they appear. Wolfe, G.

And Where She Stops . . . A Story. Friedman, B. J.

And you read your Emily Dickinson. Mazelis, J.

Andahazi, Federico

The sleep of the just

   Colchie, T. A whistler in the nightworld; short fiction from the Latin Americas; edited by Thomas Colchie

Anda's game. Doctorow, C.

Anderle, Helga

The rival

   The World's finest mystery and crime stories, fifth annual collection; edited by Ed Gorman and Martin H. Greenberg

Anders, Charlie

Transfixed, helpless, and out of control; election night 2004

   Sex for America; politically inspired erotica; edited by Stephen Elliott

Andersen, Hans Christian

The Snow Queen; a tale in seven stories

   Tales before Narnia; the roots of modern fantasy and science fiction; edited by Douglas A. Anderson

The Ugly Duckling

   Configurations v15 no1 p9-16 Wint 2007

Anderson, Barbara

Balance

   Anderson, B. Collected stories

Commitment

   Anderson, B. Collected stories

The daggy end

   Anderson, B. Collected stories

Day out

   Anderson, B. Collected stories

Discontinuous lives

   Anderson, B. Collected stories

Egypt is a timeless land

   Anderson, B. Collected stories

Fast post

   Anderson, B. Collected stories

Feeding the sparrows

   Anderson, B. Collected stories

The girls

   Anderson, B. Collected stories

Glorious things

   Anderson, B. Collected stories

The grateful dead

   Anderson, B. Collected stories

I thought there'd be a couch

   Anderson, B. Collected stories

I want to get out, I said

   Anderson, B. Collected stories

It is necessary I have a balloon

   Anderson, B. Collected stories

Living on the beach

   Anderson, B. Collected stories

The man with the plug in his nose

   Anderson, B. Collected stories

One potato two potato

   Anderson, B. Collected stories

The peacocks

   Anderson, B. Collected stories

Peppermint frogs

   Anderson, B. Collected stories

Poojah

   Anderson, B. Collected stories

Real beach weather

   Anderson, B. Collected stories

The right sort of ears

   Anderson, B. Collected stories

Rollo's dairy (Jake and Deedee)

   Anderson, B. Collected stories

School story

   Anderson, B. Collected stories

Shanties

   Anderson, B. Collected stories

So lovely of them

   Anderson, B. Collected stories

Subalpine meadow

   Anderson, B. Collected stories

Tuataras

   Anderson, B. Collected stories

Up the river with Mrs Gallant

   Anderson, B. Collected stories

We could celebrate

   Anderson, B. Collected stories

The westerly

   Anderson, B. Collected stories

Anderson, Barth

Clockmaker's requiem

   Realms

The last escape

   Sedia, E. Paper cities; an anthology of urban fantasy

Anderson, Dale Gregory

The Hole

   The North American Review v289 no5 p16-22 S/O 2004

Anderson, Forrest

Coupons

   South Carolina Review v40 no2 p19-27 Spr 2008

Anderson, Frederick Irving

Blind man's buff

   The Penguin book of Gaslight crime; con artists, burglars, rogues, and scoundrels from the time of Sherlock Holmes; edited with an introduction and notes by Michael Sims.

Anderson, Kevin J.

Frog kiss

   This is my funniest 2; leading science fiction writers present their funniest stories ever; edited by Mike Resnick

(jt. auth) See Herbert, Brian and Anderson, Kevin J.

Anderson, Kevin J. and Moesta, Rebecca
　Loincloth
　　Pandora's closet; edited by Jean Rabe and
　　Martin H. Greenberg.
Anderson, Kirsten
　The Service of God
　　Confrontation no102/103 p96-110 Wint
　　2008/Spr 2009
Anderson, Lars
　Black Legion
　　The Black Lizard big book of pulps; edited
　　by Otto Penzler
Anderson, M. T.
　The gray boy's work
　　The Year's best fantasy and horror: twenty-
　　first annual collection; edited by Ellen
　　Datlow and Kelly Link & Gavin J. Grant
　Watch and wake
　　The Year's best fantasy and horror: eighteenth
　　annual collection; edited by Ellen Datlow,
　　Kelly Link & Gavin J. Grant
ANDERSON, MARIAN, 1897-1993
　　　　　About
　Marley, L. Deep river
Anderson, Poul
　The alien enemy
　　Anderson, P. Call me Joe; edited by Rick
　　Katze and Lis Carey
　Backwardness
　　Anderson, P. Call me Joe; edited by Rick
　　Katze and Lis Carey
　Barnacle bull
　　Anderson, P. Call me Joe; edited by Rick
　　Katze and Lis Carey
　Call me Joe
　　Anderson, P. Call me Joe; edited by Rick
　　Katze and Lis Carey
　The doubled-dyed villains
　　Anderson, P. Call me Joe; edited by Rick
　　Katze and Lis Carey
　Enough rope
　　Anderson, P. Call me Joe; edited by Rick
　　Katze and Lis Carey
　Flight to forever
　　Anderson, P. Call me Joe; edited by Rick
　　Katze and Lis Carey
　Genius
　　Anderson, P. Call me Joe; edited by Rick
　　Katze and Lis Carey
　The helping hand
　　Anderson, P. Call me Joe; edited by Rick
　　Katze and Lis Carey
　The immortal game
　　Anderson, P. Call me Joe; edited by Rick
　　Katze and Lis Carey
　Journey's end
　　Anderson, P. Call me Joe; edited by Rick
　　Katze and Lis Carey
　Kings who die
　　Anderson, P. Call me Joe; edited by Rick
　　Katze and Lis Carey
　The live coward
　　Anderson, P. Call me Joe; edited by Rick
　　Katze and Lis Carey
　Logic
　　Anderson, P. Call me Joe; edited by Rick
　　Katze and Lis Carey

The man who came early
　Anderson, P. Call me Joe; edited by Rick
　Katze and Lis Carey
The Martian crown jewels
　Anderson, P. Call me Joe; edited by Rick
　Katze and Lis Carey
Prophecy
　Anderson, P. Call me Joe; edited by Rick
　Katze and Lis Carey
The sharing of flesh
　Anderson, P. Call me Joe; edited by Rick
　Katze and Lis Carey
Starfog
　Anderson, P. Call me Joe; edited by Rick
　Katze and Lis Carey
Time heals
　Anderson, P. Call me Joe; edited by Rick
　Katze and Lis Carey
Time lag
　Anderson, P. Call me Joe; edited by Rick
　Katze and Lis Carey
Time patrol
　Anderson, P. Call me Joe; edited by Rick
　Katze and Lis Carey
Tomorrow's children
　Anderson, P. Call me Joe; edited by Rick
　Katze and Lis Carey
Turning point
　Anderson, P. Call me Joe; edited by Rick
　Katze and Lis Carey
Welcome
　Anderson, P. Call me Joe; edited by Rick
　Katze and Lis Carey
Wildcat
　Anderson, P. Call me Joe; edited by Rick
　Katze and Lis Carey
Anderson, Robert Mailer
　Briley boy
　　San Francisco noir; edited by Peter Maravelis
Anderson, Timothy J.
　Newbie wrangler
　　Year's best fantasy 6; edited by David G.
　　Hartwell & Kathryn Cramer
Andrade, Carlos Drummond de
　Miguel's theft
　　Oxford anthology of the Brazilian short story;
　　edited by K. David Jackson
Andrade, Lourdes
　Grito en la Oscuridad
　　Artes de Mexico no73 p supp12-supp13 2005
Andrade, Mário de
　The Christmas turkey
　　Oxford anthology of the Brazilian short story;
　　edited by K. David Jackson
　It can hurt plenty
　　Oxford anthology of the Brazilian short story;
　　edited by K. David Jackson
Andrea is changing her name. Brockmeier, K.
Andreas-Salomé, Lou
　At one, again, with nature
　　Andreas-Salomé, L. The human family; sto-
　　ries; translated and with an introduction by
　　Raleigh Whitinger
　Before the awakening
　　Andreas-Salomé, L. The human family; sto-
　　ries; translated and with an introduction by
　　Raleigh Whitinger

Andreas-Salomé, Lou—*Continued*

A death

Andreas-Salomé, L. The human family; stories; translated and with an introduction by Raleigh Whitinger

Incognito

Andreas-Salomé, L. The human family; stories; translated and with an introduction by Raleigh Whitinger

Maidens' roundelay

Andreas-Salomé, L. The human family; stories; translated and with an introduction by Raleigh Whitinger

On their way

Andreas-Salomé, L. The human family; stories; translated and with an introduction by Raleigh Whitinger

One night

Andreas-Salomé, L. The human family; stories; translated and with an introduction by Raleigh Whitinger

Paradise

Andreas-Salomé, L. The human family; stories; translated and with an introduction by Raleigh Whitinger

A reunion

Andreas-Salomé, L. The human family; stories; translated and with an introduction by Raleigh Whitinger

Unit for "Men, internal"

Andreas-Salomé, L. The human family; stories; translated and with an introduction by Raleigh Whitinger

ANDRÉE, SALOMON AUGUST, 1854-1897

About

Klimasewiski, M. N. Aëronauts

Andretto walks the king's way. Aguirre, F.

Andrew Chang. Levithan, D.

Andrews, Chris

(tr.) *See* Bolaño, Roberto

Andrews, Colin *See* Wilson, F. Paul (Francis Paul)

Andrews, Donna

Cold spell

Powers of detection; stories of mystery & fantasy; edited by Dana Stabenow

Spellbound

Unusual suspects; stories of mystery & fantasy; edited by Dana Stabenow.

Andrews, Jancis M.

A Fool for Truth

Dalhousie Review v88 no2 p241-8 Summ 2008

Andrews, Robert

Solomon's alley

D. C. noir; edited by George Pelecanos

The Best American mystery stories 2007; edited and with and introduction by Carl Hiaasen; Otto Penzler, series editor

Androcles and the lion. James, C. L. R.

The **Andromeda** Nebula [abridged] Efremov, I. A.

Andy comes back. Faber, M.

Anesthesia. Roley, B. A.

ANEURYSMS

Messinger, J. Bicycle kick

Angel, Jodi

Donny

Angel, J. The history of Vegas; stories

The history of Vegas

Angel, J. The history of Vegas; stories

Portions

Angel, J. The history of Vegas; stories

Push

Angel, J. The history of Vegas; stories

Rolling over

Angel, J. The history of Vegas; stories

Rounding third

Angel, J. The history of Vegas; stories

Seconds

Angel, J. The history of Vegas; stories

The skin from the muscle

Angel, J. The history of Vegas; stories

Supplement

Angel, J. The history of Vegas; stories

Whistle pig

Angel, J. The history of Vegas; stories

Angel. Kennedy, C.

Angel. Ulitskaya, L.

Angel, dark angel. Zelazny, R.

Angel face. Rickert, M.

Angel face [variant title: Murder in wax] Woolrich, C.

Angel, his rabbit, and Kyle McKell. Tomlinson, J.

The **angel** in the darkness. Baker, K.

The **angel** of Entropy. Harleman, A.

Angel of light. Haldeman, J. W.

The **angel** of loneliness. LaValle, V.

Angel of Mercy. Oates, J. C.

Angel of wrath. Oates, J. C.

Angel Talkies. Adiga, A.

Angelique's. Beswetherick, S.

ANGELS

Abbott, L. K. The human use of inhuman beings

Adrian, C. A better angel

Anderson, M. T. The gray boy's work

Beagle, P. S. Uncle Chaim and Aunt Rifke and the angel

Beagle, P. S. We never talk about my brother

Bear, E. Inelastic collisions

Bowes, R. If angels fight

Carey, J. In the matter of fallen angels

Coville, B. The box

Friesner, E. M. Abductio ad absurdum

Martin, J. I'm not quite finished yet

Maxey, J. To know all things that are in the earth

Messinger, J. Christmas spirit

Ruffin, P. Harvey Watson and the angel

Smith, M. M. Being right

Stevenson, J. Walking with angels

Swann, S. A. Fealty

Webb, J. Paradise design'd

Winsor, C. The end of the world

Angels. McAllister, B.

Angels and Martyrs. Grimmett, N.

Angel's house of ice. With, C.

Angels of the marquees. Fonseca, R.

ANGER

Alvarado, B. What Lydia thinks of roses

Amdahl, G. The volunteer

Appel, R. Bloody hot

Bierce, A. The Scolliver pig

Blackshaw, G. Girlfriend

Block, L. Terrible Tommy Terhune

Clarke, B. The apology

Dalton, Q. Graceland

Dalton, Q. How to clean your apartment

Another exciting adventure of Lightning Merriemouse-Jones: a touching ghost story. Holder, B. and Holder, N.

Another First. Schrader, E. K.

Another fish story. Newman, K.

Another great moment in sports. McClanahan, E.

Another life. Donovan, G.

Another life. Raphael, L.

Another little piece. Dean, D.

Another Manhattan. Antrim, D.

Another perfect catastrophe. Barkley, B.

Another Sad, Bizarre Chapter in Human History. Markovits, B.

Another Simple Encounter. Downs, E.

Another story; or, A fisherman of the inland sea. Le Guin, U. K.

Another Warning. Park, S.

Another way to make Cleopatra cry. Winn, T.

Another Word for Dead. Williams, K.

Another word for map is faith. Rowe, C.

Anselmo Merino. Di Filippo, P.

Ansky, S.
Mendel the Turk
No star too beautiful; Yiddish stories from 1382 to the present; compiled and translated by Joachim Neugroschel
The starveling
No star too beautiful; Yiddish stories from 1382 to the present; compiled and translated by Joachim Neugroschel

Answering machine. Tognazzini, A.

The **ant** king: a California fairy tale. Rosenbaum, B.

The **ant** of the self. Packer, Z.

ANTARCTIC REGIONS
See also Arctic regions
Green, Dominic. Send me a mentagram
Rand, K. The find
Rand, K. The swimmer

Anteaters don't dream. Hawes, L.

The **antelope** wife. Erdrich, L.

ANTELOPES
Lefer, D. Alas, Falada!

Anthony, Helen Bayne
Two worlds
"Tell it to us easy" and other stories; a complete short fiction anthology of African American women writers in Opportunity magazine, (1923-1948); edited by Judith Musser.

ANTHROPOLOGISTS
Fowler, K. J. What I didn't see
Murphy, P. Inappropriate behavior
Row, J. The American girl
Skinner, J. All about balls

Anthropology. Lee, A.

The **anthropology** of sex. McPhee, M.

The **anti-Santa.** Bradfield, S.

Antibodies. Stross, C.

ANTICHRIST
Moorcock, M. Lunching with the Antichrist
Traviss, K. The man who did nothing

Antickes and frets. Clarke, S.

Antigone. Bunin, I. A.

Antin, Charles
The Iraq Show
The Virginia Quarterly Review v84 no4 p100-15 Fall 2008

Antioxidants. Bennett, T.

ANTIQUE DEALERS
See also Art dealers
Dahl, R. Parson's pleasure
Morgan, J. M. Scratch that one

ANTIQUES
Gash, J. Death by golf
Robinson, R. Pilgrimage
Rylands, J. T. Finish
Silverberg, R. The artifact business

ANTIQUITIES
See also Archeology

ANTISEMITISM
See also Holocaust, Jewish (1933-1945); Jews—Persecutions
Ames, J. Looking for the answers
Apple, M. Indian giver
Busch, F. Frost line
Englander, N. How we avenged the Blums
Fountain, B. Fantasy for eleven fingers
Newman, L. Flashback
Perlman, E. Spitalnic's last year
Perlman, E. A tale in two cities
Raphael, L. The Cossacks
Spinosa, T. Killing O'Malley
Wilson, F. P. Aryans and Absinthe
Yates, R. Oh, Joseph, I'm so tired

Antoni, Robert
How to make photocopies in the Trinidad & Tobago national archives
Trinidad noir; edited by Lisa Allen-Agostini & Jeanne Mason.

Antoni Kosmatka resists the goddess of love. Bukoski, A.

Antonio de Juvita. Monteiro, L.

Antonio sings his song. Duncklee, J.

Antosia, Mike
The Last King of China
The Massachusetts Review v49 no3 p341-50 Aut 2008

Antrim, Donald
Another Manhattan
The New Yorker v84 no42 p52-61 D 22-29 2008
Solace
The New Yorker v81 no7 p78-87 Ap 4 2005

Antrim, Kathleen
Through a veil darkly
Thriller 2; stories you just can't put down; edited by Clive Cussler; [stories by] Kathleen Antrim . . . [et al.]

ANTS
Burke, K. The excursion
Ford, J. A few things about ants
Pohl, F. Let the ants try
Sampsell, K. Homewreckers

ANXIETY *See* Fear

An **anxious** man. Lasdun, J.

Any Landlord's Dream. Spatz, G.

Any ordinary uncle. Flanagan, E.

"**Anyone** could have done it. But only James had a crisp £5 note, a stepladder, a key to the chemistry cupboard marked 'Flammable' and a misdirected sense of curiosity...". Phinn, G.

Anything that floats. Johnston, B. A.

Anyway. Rickert, M.

Apache agent. See Leonard, E. Trail of the Apache [variant title: Apache agent]

APACHE INDIANS

Haycox, E. Stage to Lordsburg

Leonard, E. Apache medicine [variant title: Medicine]

Leonard, E. The boy who smiled

Leonard, E. The colonel's lady [variant title: Road to Inspiration]

Leonard, E. Under the friar's ledge

Leonard, E. You never see Apaches . . . [variant title: Eight days from Willcox]

Silko, L. Mistaken identity

Silko, L. Old pancakes

Wars, 1883-1886

Leonard, E. Cavalry boots

Leonard, E. Red hell hits Canyon Diablo [variant title: Tizwin]

Leonard, E. Trail of the Apache [variant title: Apache agent]

Apache medicine [variant title: Medicine] Leonard, E.

APARTHEID See South Africa—Race relations

The **Apartment**. Chang, D.

The **apartment**. Schor, L.

Apartment 1-A. Mehringer, A.

APARTMENT HOUSES

Alarcón, D. Third Avenue suicide

Angel, J. Whistle pig

Asís, M. Murder at 503 La Rosa

Cheever, J. Christmas is a sad season for the poor

Cony, C. H. Order of the day

Dalton, Q. How to clean your apartment

Dobson, J. Hey, girlie

Ducornet, R. The doorman's swellage

Eisenberg, D. Twilight of the superheroes

Glatt, L. What Milton heard

Hospital, J. T. Credit repair

Lamsley, T. So long Gerry

Larsen, T. Lids

Martin, G. R. R. The pear-shaped man

Maxwell, W. The thistles in Sweden

McGruder, K. Clan of marsupials

Meacham, R. Worship for shut-ins

Mustecaplioglu, B. An extra body

Parks, T. Annette and Frank

Parks, T. Mary knew about Marilyn

Pintado, M. F. The scene

Sallis, J. Under construction

Santangelo, E. Eaten alive

Schor, L. The apartment

Scott, J. Across from the Shannonso

Scott, J. The most beautiful apartment in New York

Simmons, P. Night vision

Sundaresan, I. Hunger

Wolff, T. Firelight

Zoshchenko, M. Crisis

Zoshchenko, M. Does a man need much?

Zoshchenko, M. Electrification

Zoshchenko, M. Firewood

Zoshchenko, M. Nervous people

Zoshchenko, M. Pushkin

Zoshchenko, M. A summer break

APARTMENTS See Apartment houses

The **ape** in the face. Richards, S. S.

The **ape** man. MacBride, A.

Apecon. Delaplace, B.

APES

See also Gorillas

Baumbach, J. The adventures of King Dong

Delaplace, B. Apecon

Howard, R. E. Golnor the Ape

Kiernan, C. R. The ape's wife

MacBride, A. The ape man

Oakley, R. Jack Jaw and the Arab's ape

Schaller, E. Monkey shines

Vaswani, N. The pelvis series

The **ape's** wife. Kiernan, C. R.

The **aphid**. Lee, S.

An **apiary** of white bees. Thomas, L.

Apikuni See Schultz, James Willard, 1859-1947

Apocalypse then. DeMarinis, R.

Apoikis. Lasswitz, K.

APOLLO (GREEK DEITY)

Cadnum, M. Daphne

James, C. L. R. The Nobbie stories for children and adults

Apólogo del Juglar y de la Domadora / Apologue of the Juggler and the Lion Tamer. Torres Bodet, J.

The **apology**. Barthelme, D.

The **apology**. Clarke, B.

The **apology**. Mosley, W.

Apology for a journey not taken: how to write a story. Beattie, A.

Apostol, Gina

Tita Beth

Gettysburg Review v19 no2 p273-81 Summ 2006

APOTHECARIES See Pharmacists

The **Apotheosis** of Hard Knock Johnson. Curtin, J. M.

APPALACHIAN REGION

Cady, J. The souls of Drowning Mountain

Rash, R. Blackberries in June

Rash, R. Cold Harbor

Rash, R. Deep Gap

Rash, R. Pemberton's bride

Rash, R. The projectionist's wife

The **apparition**. Updike, J.

Apparitions. Walters, A. L.

Appearances. Cross, E.

Appearences. Parry, O.

Appel, Jacob M.

The Apprenticeship

The North American Review v291 no3/4 p3-9 My/Ag 2006

The Atatürk of the Outer Boroughs

Raritan v24 no3 p78-93 Wint 2005

Bury Me Someplace Warm and Lovely

South Carolina Review v37 no2 p207-16 Spr 2005

Choose Your Own Genetics

Michigan Quarterly Review v47 no4 p571-92 Fall 2008

Gadney's Immunity

Southwest Review v89 no4 p580-92 2004

Hearth and Home

Confrontation no90/91 p87-99 Spr/Summ 2005

Helen of Sparta

Iowa Review v38 no3 p36-48 Wint 2008/2009

Long Term

Prairie Schooner v83 no2 p135-49 Summ 2009

Appel, Jacob M.—*Continued*

Measures of Sorrow
StoryQuarterly v41 p25-45 2005

Phoebe with Impending Frost
Southwest Review v94 no3 p386-405 2009

Rods and Cones
Southwest Review v92 no3 p354-72 2007

The Savior
River Styx no69/70 p43-56 2005

Scouting for the Reaper
The Virginia Quarterly Review v85 no3 p169-80 Summ 2009

Winter Honeymoon
River Styx no79 p45-59 2009

Appel, René

Bloody hot
Passport to crime; the finest mystery stories from International Crime Writers; edited by Janet Hutchings

Appelfeld, Aharon and Green, Jeffrey M.

Giant
Southwest Review v90 no4 p620-9 2005

The **appendix** and the spectacles. Breuer, M. J.

Appetite for murder. Green, S. R.

Applause, applause. Thompson, J.

Apple, Jessica

One Act
The Southern Review (Baton Rouge, La.) v43 no4 p852-8 Aut 2007

Apple, Max

Adventures in dementia
Apple, M. The Jew of Home Depot and other stories

"The eighth day"
Scribblers on the roof; contemporary American Jewish fiction; edited by Melvin Jules Bukiet and David G. Roskies

House of the lowered
Apple, M. The Jew of Home Depot and other stories

Indian giver
Apple, M. The Jew of Home Depot and other stories

The Jew of Home Depot
Apple, M. The Jew of Home Depot and other stories

Peace
Apple, M. The Jew of Home Depot and other stories

Proton decay
Apple, M. The Jew of Home Depot and other stories

Sized up
Apple, M. The Jew of Home Depot and other stories

Stabbing an elephant
Apple, M. The Jew of Home Depot and other stories

Stepdaughters
Apple, M. The Jew of Home Depot and other stories

Strawberry shortcake
Apple, M. The Jew of Home Depot and other stories

Talker
Apple, M. The Jew of Home Depot and other stories

Threads
Apple, M. The Jew of Home Depot and other stories

Yao's chick
Apple, M. The Jew of Home Depot and other stories

Apple-core Baltimore. Bradbury, R.

An **apple** could make you laugh. Meno, J.

The **apple** of her eye. Lee, M.

The **apple** orchard. Anaya, R. A.

Apple pie, one by two. Sankaran, L.

APPLE TREES

Samphire, P. Crab apple

Van Booy, S. Apples

Apples. Van Booy, S.

Apples and Angels. Collins, E.

The **apples** of Venus. Rich, M.

The **applicant.** Bierce, A.

Applied mathematical theology. Benford, G.

Appointment. Dobrovodsky, M.

Appraisal. Lott, B.

APPRENTICES

Uchida, H. Jintoshi

Uchida, H. Santo Kyoden

The **apprentice's** guide to modern magic. Davidson, C.

The **Apprenticeship.** Appel, J. M.

Appropriate sex. Almond, S.

Approval. Gerber, M. J.

Approximate Past. Searcy, D.

April. Olafsson, O.

April 20, 2008. Percy, B.

An **April** story. Nisbet, R.

Aprille. Wahl, B.

Apropos Opa. Butschkow, J.

Aqua Blue. Ahmed, N.

Aqua Velva Smitty. Berniker, S. J.

Aquarium. Josephsen, M.

AQUEDUCT RACE TRACK (NEW YORK, N.Y.)

Estep, M. Alice fantastic

Aquifer. Winton, T.

Aquinas, Saint Thomas *See* Thomas, Aquinas, Saint, 1225?-1274

Aquinas, Thomas *See* Thomas, Aquinas, Saint, 1225?-1274

ARAB AMERICANS

Halaby, L. The American dream

ARAB-JEWISH RELATIONS *See* Jewish-Arab relations

ARABIA *See* Arabian Peninsula

ARABIAN NIGHTS

Parodies, imitations, etc.

Bierce, A. The history of windbag the sailor

ARABIAN PENINSULA

Howard, R. E. The fire of Asshurbanipal

ARABIC LANGUAGE

Drosso, A.-M. Egyptians who cannot fill in a form in Arabic

ARABS

See also Jewish-Arab relations; Palestinian Arabs

Gurnah, A. Bossy

Joyce, G. An ordinary soldier of the Queen

Keret, E. Vladimir Hussein

LaSalle, P. Tunis and time

Lynds, D. Success of a mission

Papernick, J. An unwelcome guest

Sterling, B. We see things differently

ARABS—*Continued*

Italy

Genna, G. Caput Mundi

Lamri, T. "The pilgrimage"

Aral. Bissell, T.

Araminta, or, The wreck of the Amphidrake. Novik, N.

Arango, Arturo

Murder, according to my mother-in-law

Havana noir; edited by Achy Obejas

Aranitsis, Evyenios

Jesus aged twelve in the temple

Angelic & black; contemporary Greek short stories; edited and translated by David Connolly; with an introduction by Vangelis Hatzivassileiou

Arbor. McLeod, C.

ARBUCKLE, FATTY, 1887-1933

About

Matthews, C. For benefit of Mr. Means

Arbuckle, Roscoe *See* Arbuckle, Fatty, 1887-1933

The **Arbus** Factor. Segal, L.

The **arbutus** tree. With, C.

Arcadia. Dills, T.

Arcady and After. MacInnes, M.

Arcana, Judith

A Matter of Fact

Feminist Studies v34 no3 p425-30 Fall 2008

The **arcevoalo**. Shepard, L.

The **Arch**. Mozina, A.

The **archaeologist's** daughter. Ingalls, R.

ARCHEOLOGISTS

See also Women archeologists

De Camp, L. S. Lest darkness fall

Donovan, G. Archeologists

Drosso, A.-M. He has aged

Faber, M. The hundred and ninety-nine steps

Fowler, K. J. Private grave 9

Gerrold, D. Digging in Gehenna

Howard, R. E. The noseless horror

Kemnitzer, L. The boulder

Langan, J. On Skua Isalnd

Silverberg, R. The artifact business

Smith, C. A. The invisible city

Smith, C. A. An offering to the moon

Archeologists. Donovan, G.

ARCHEOLOGY

See also Prehistoric man

Lovecraft, H. P. At the mountains of madness

SInger, M. Hazor

Archer, Jeffrey

The alibi

Archer, J. Cat o'nine tales and other stories; drawings by Ronald Searle

Charity begins at home

Archer, J. Cat o'nine tales and other stories; drawings by Ronald Searle

The commissioner

Archer, J. Cat o'nine tales and other stories; drawings by Ronald Searle

Don't drink the water

Archer, J. Cat o'nine tales and other stories; drawings by Ronald Searle

A Greek tragedy

Archer, J. Cat o'nine tales and other stories; drawings by Ronald Searle

In the eye of the beholder

Archer, J. Cat o'nine tales and other stories; drawings by Ronald Searle

It can't be October already

Archer, J. Cat o'nine tales and other stories; drawings by Ronald Searle

Know what I mean?

Archer, J. Cat o'nine tales and other stories; drawings by Ronald Searle

Maestro

Archer, J. Cat o'nine tales and other stories; drawings by Ronald Searle

The man who robbed his own post office

Archer, J. Cat o'nine tales and other stories; drawings by Ronald Searle

The red king

Archer, J. Cat o'nine tales and other stories; drawings by Ronald Searle

The wisdom of Solomon

Archer, J. Cat o'nine tales and other stories; drawings by Ronald Searle

Archibald Lawless, anarchist at large: walking the line. Mosley, W.

The **architect**. Biller, M.

ARCHITECTS

See also Building

Biller, M. The architect

Boyd, W. A haunting

Clayton, J. J. The builder

Clayton, J. J. Soap opera

Flewelling, L. Perfection

Hawes, L. Anteaters don't dream

James, C. L. R. The Liverpool cathedral

Lefer, D. At the site where vision is most perfect

Liebrecht, S. Hiroshima

McIntyre, V. Dunford

Stevenson, J. Light my fire

The **architecture** of the moon. Meno, J.

The **Archivist** Says Goodbye to His Daily Routine. Presser, A. L.

ARCHIVISTS

Antoni, R. How to make photocopies in the Trinidad & Tobago national archives

Krasznahorkai, L. War and war [excerpt]

The **Archivist's** Story. Holland, T.

Archon LLC. Ball, D.

ARCTIC REGIONS

See also Alaska; Antarctic regions

DeAndrea, W. L. A friend of mine

Faber, M. The Fahrenheit twins

King, O. Frozen animals

Silko, L. Storyteller

Arcturus. Connell, E. S.

Ardai, Charles

The good samaritan

Manhattan noir; edited by Lawrence Block

The home front

Mystery Writers of America presents death do us part; new stories about love, lust, and murder; edited by Harlan Coben

Arden, William, 1924-

For works written by this author under other names see Collins, Michael, 1924-2005; Lynds, Dennis, 1924-2005

ARDENNES (BELGIUM AND FRANCE)

McNally, T. M. Bastogne

The **ardent** admirer. McCauley, W.

Ardent clouds. Sussex, L.

Are dreams faster than the speed of light. Wideman, J. E.

Are we dwelling deep yet? Krysl, M.

Are we not men? Gee, H.
Are you for 86? Sterling, B.
Are You Passing? Gee, A.
Are You There. Taylor, L.
Arends, Marthe *See* MacAlister, Katie
ARGENTINA
    See also Patagonia (Argentina and Chile)
Aisemberg, I. Ramón Acuña's time
Brau, E. Bárcena's dog
Brau, E. The blessing
Brau, E. Casablanca
Coloane, F. Forgotten land [variant title: Land of oblivion]
Coloane, F. How the Chilote Otey died
Cozarinsky, E. The bride from Odessa
Forn, J. Swimming at night
Gorriti, J. M. The black glove
Gorriti, J. M. The dead man's fiancée
Gorriti, J. M. Gubi Amaya
Gorriti, J. M. The mazorquero's daughter
Heker, L. Far away
Hernández, J. J. For Christmas
Kozameh, A. Impression of heights
Lojo, Maria Rosa. Compound eyes
Roffé, R. Transforming the desert
Solá, M. Kind's silence [excerpt]
          Politics
    See Politics—Argentina
          Rural life
Saer, J. J. Baked mud
          Buenos Aires
Grimes, C. Examination of an afflicted man
ARGENTINE REPUBLIC *See* Argentina
ARGENTINES
          France
Shua, A. M. The white Guanaco in the middle of France
ARGENTINIANS *See* Argentines
ARGUS blinked. Di Filippo, P.
Ariadne's mother. Ford, J.
Arif's Refusal to Bargain. Czyz, V.
The **Arimaspian** legacy. Wolfe, G.
'Arimi, Su'ad al-
Ghomran's oil field
    Oranges in the sun; short stories from the Arabian Gulf; edited and translated by Deborah S. Akers, Abubaker A. Bagader
The **Ariran's** Last Life. Abegunde, M. E. H.
Arise and walk, Christopher Reeve. Pierce, T. J.
ARISTOCRACY
          England
Arnott, J. Ten lords a-leaping
          France
Barnes, J. Bark
Harris, J. Eau de toilette
          Ireland
McCabe, E. The master
          Italy
Palazzeschi, A. Bistino and the Marquis
          Russia
Bunin, I. A. The scent of apples
Bunin, I. A. Sukhodol
Zoshchenko, M. A victim of the revolution
          Scotland
Brown, G. M. The fires of Christmas
ARISTOTLE, 384-322 B.C.
          About
De Camp, L. S. Aristotle and the gun
Aristotle and the gun. De Camp, L. S.

Aristotle OS. Ballantyne, T.
ARIZONA
Alvarado, B. Emily's exit
Alvarado, B. Limbo
Alvarado, B. Phoenix
Bierce, A. A mirage in Arizona
Bierce, A. The stranger
Dee, E. The tailman
Duncklee, J. The developers
Duncklee, J. The last breakfast
Duncklee, J. The miner
Duncklee, J. The mines of Magdalena
Green, A. Food stamp
Howard, C. Arizona heat
Nolan, W. F. Ripper!
Richter, S. Christ, their Lord
Rodriguez, A. Imagining Bisbee
Romm, R. Lost and found
Welsh, I. Miss Arizona
Wheeler, R. S. Hearts
          Flagstaff
Wingate, S. In flagstaff
          Phoenix
McNally, T. M. Network
          Scottsdale
Deaver, J. A dish served cold
          Tucson
Alvarado, B. Bastille Day
Arizona heat. Howard, C.
Arjouni, Jakob
At peace
    Arjouni, J. Idiots; five fairy tales and other stories; translated from the German by Anthea Bell
Defeated
    Arjouni, J. Idiots; five fairy tales and other stories; translated from the German by Anthea Bell
A friend
    Arjouni, J. Idiots; five fairy tales and other stories; translated from the German by Anthea Bell
Happy ending
    Arjouni, J. Idiots; five fairy tales and other stories; translated from the German by Anthea Bell
Idiots
    Arjouni, J. Idiots; five fairy tales and other stories; translated from the German by Anthea Bell
In the valley of death
    Arjouni, J. Idiots; five fairy tales and other stories; translated from the German by Anthea Bell
The inner man
    Arjouni, J. Idiots; five fairy tales and other stories; translated from the German by Anthea Bell
The Rudolf family does good works
    Arjouni, J. Idiots; five fairy tales and other stories; translated from the German by Anthea Bell
Self-defense
    Arjouni, J. Idiots; five fairy tales and other stories; translated from the German by Anthea Bell
The **ark**. McAllister, B.
ARKANSAS
Barthelme, D. The reference

Arnow, Harriette Louisa Simpson—*Continued*

The goat who was a cow
  Arnow, H. L. S. The collected short stories of Harriette Simpson Arnow; Sandra L. Ballard & Haeja K. Chung, editors
Home coming
  Arnow, H. L. S. The collected short stories of Harriette Simpson Arnow; Sandra L. Ballard & Haeja K. Chung, editors
The hunter
  Arnow, H. L. S. The collected short stories of Harriette Simpson Arnow; Sandra L. Ballard & Haeja K. Chung, editors
Interruptions to school at home
  Arnow, H. L. S. The collected short stories of Harriette Simpson Arnow; Sandra L. Ballard & Haeja K. Chung, editors
Ketchup-making Saturday
  Arnow, H. L. S. The collected short stories of Harriette Simpson Arnow; Sandra L. Ballard & Haeja K. Chung, editors
King Devil's bargain
  Arnow, H. L. S. The collected short stories of Harriette Simpson Arnow; Sandra L. Ballard & Haeja K. Chung, editors
Love?
  Arnow, H. L. S. The collected short stories of Harriette Simpson Arnow; Sandra L. Ballard & Haeja K. Chung, editors
Marigolds and mules
  Arnow, H. L. S. The collected short stories of Harriette Simpson Arnow; Sandra L. Ballard & Haeja K. Chung, editors
A mess of pork
  Arnow, H. L. S. The collected short stories of Harriette Simpson Arnow; Sandra L. Ballard & Haeja K. Chung, editors
No lady
  Arnow, H. L. S. The collected short stories of Harriette Simpson Arnow; Sandra L. Ballard & Haeja K. Chung, editors
Sugar Tree Holler
  Arnow, H. L. S. The collected short stories of Harriette Simpson Arnow; Sandra L. Ballard & Haeja K. Chung, editors
Tin cup
  Arnow, H. L. S. The collected short stories of Harriette Simpson Arnow; Sandra L. Ballard & Haeja K. Chung, editors
The two hunters
  Arnow, H. L. S. The collected short stories of Harriette Simpson Arnow; Sandra L. Ballard & Haeja K. Chung, editors
The un-American activities of Miss Prink
  Arnow, H. L. S. The collected short stories of Harriette Simpson Arnow; Sandra L. Ballard & Haeja K. Chung, editors
The washerwoman's day
  Arnow, H. L. S. The collected short stories of Harriette Simpson Arnow; Sandra L. Ballard & Haeja K. Chung, editors
White collar woman
  Arnow, H. L. S. The collected short stories of Harriette Simpson Arnow; Sandra L. Ballard & Haeja K. Chung, editors
Winky Creek's new song
  Arnow, H. L. S. The collected short stories of Harriette Simpson Arnow; Sandra L. Ballard & Haeja K. Chung, editors

Zekie, the hill-billy mouse
  Arnow, H. L. S. The collected short stories of Harriette Simpson Arnow; Sandra L. Ballard & Haeja K. Chung, editors
Arnzen, Michael A.
The dead lantern
  Poe's lighthouse; all new collaborations with Edgar Allan Poe; edited by Christopher Conlon
The **aroma** of death. Fiorillo, H.
Around here, somewhere. Sezginturedi, A.
Around the great Samovar. Wendroff, Z.
The **arrangement**. Li Yiyun
Arrangements at the Gulf. Stern, R. G.
The **arrangers** of marriage. Adichie, C. N.
ARRESTS
Barry, R. Newspaper clipping
Chilson, P. American food
Jablonski, N. Wanting out
Lucarelli, C. Beret
McCauley, W. Tradition
Qi, S. The evidence
Arria Marcella. Gautier, T.
Arrival. Cadnum, M.
The **arrival**. Romm, R.
Arrival and departure. Bradbury, R.
Arrivederci, Aldo. Sykes, K.
Arrogance. Panselinos, A.
Arsenault, Michael
A Halloween like any other
  Witpunk; edited by Claude Lalumière and Marty Halpern
Arsenieva, Elena
A birch tree, a white fox
  The SFWA European hall of fame; sixteen contemporary masterpieces of science fiction from the continent; edited by James Morrow and Kathryn Morrow
ARSON
Akins, M. Que-Linda takes the rite aid
Block, L. A fire at night
Chazin, S. Burnout
Hammett, D. Faith
Hoch, E. D. The retired arsonist
Jones, H. G. Proof of God
Lansdale, J. R. Veil's visit
Magee, K. All the America you want
Manotti, D. Ethnic cleansing
Meaker, M. Round heels
Menger-Anderson, K. Happy effects, 1741
Parker, M. The right to remain
Rusch, K. K. Patriotic gestures
Shomer, E. Sweethearts
Sillitoe, A. The firebug
Smith, R. T. Blaze
Vanbeck, M. Given her history
Westcott, G. The runaways
Wharton, E. Mrs. Manstey's view
Wolven, S. Controlled burn
Arsonists. Pancake, A.
ART
Dedman, S. Lost arts
Disch, T. M. Canned goods
Kiernan, C. R. Ode to Katan Amano
Klassen, S. Still life
Lasdun, J. Annals of honorary secretary
Millhauser, S. A precursor of the cinema
Moss, B. K. The consolations of art
Weil, G. Guernica

ARTISTS—*Continued*

Burke, T. Landscape portrait
Busch, F. The rescue mission
Carroll, J. The sadness of detail
Cooper, D. Graduate seminar
Copper, B. Voices in the water
Cozarinsky, E. Budapest
DeMarinis, R. Hell's cartoonist
DeMarinis, R. Palochky
Disch, T. M. Painting eggplants
Disch, T. M. The Wall of America
Ducornet, R. She thinks dots
Ducornet, R. Thumbtacks
Erdrich, L. Revival Road
Farland, D. The mooncalfe
Ford, J. Coffins on the river
Gabrielyan, N. The house in Metekhi Lane
Gardiner, J. R. Fugitive color
Gee, M. The artist
Gifford, B. The sculptor's son
Hawes, L. Mr. Mix-Up
Helms, B. Once
Helms, B. Oysters
Hempel, A. What were the white things?
Hernandez, L. Pinky Sandoval
Homenidis, C. Not all fingers are equal
Jhabvala, R. P. Refuge in London
Koretsky, J. L. The disintegrating man
Lake, J. Chewing up the innocent
Langan, J. Laocöon, or the singularity
Le, N. Meeting Elise
Lermontov, M. I. Shtoss
Lumley, B. The house of the temple
Martin, V. Beethoven
Martin, V. The change
Martin, V. His blue period
Matheson, R. The children of Noah
Michalopoulou, A. I'd like
Michalopoulou, A. I'd like (orchestral version)
Ohlin, A. You are here
Pierce, T. J. Newsworld
Pizzolatto, N. Nepal
Porter, K. A. The martyr
Reidy, D. Look and feel
Reynolds, A. Zima blue
Row, J. Revolutions
Rowe, C. The voluntary state
Rylands, J. T. Art
Selgin, P. Boy b
Shepard, L. The man who painted the dragon
    griaule
Sillitoe, A. Guzman, go home
Smith, C. A. The light from beyond
Smith, C. A. The secret of the cairn [variant ti-
    tle: The light from beyond]
Smith, N. The butterfly box
Sojka, C. Art can be murder
Stern, R. G. Milius and Melanie
Templeton, E. Irresistibly
Thomas, E. The artist
Thomas, E. The ship of swallows
Tomlinson, J. So exotic
Totton, S. Bluecoat Jack
Ulitskaya, L. Sonechka
Updike, J. The guardians
Wilson, G. The outermost borough
Wilson, R. C. YFL–500
Wood, D. Eden
Zelazny, R. A museum piece

The **artist's** model. Auchincloss, L.
ARTISTS' MODELS

Auchincloss, L. The artist's model
Boyers, R. Torso
Crone, M. It
Đoàn, L. The venus of Chua village
Farris, J. The Ransome women
Finger, A. The artist and the dwarf
Shabtai, Y. Model
Stafford, J. The philosophy lesson

The **artist's** story. Bluestein, E.
Arts and crafts of American WASPs. Montgom-
ery, L.
Arvin, Nick

Along the Highways
    The New Yorker v81 no12 p72-9 My 9 2005

Aryans and Absinthe. Wilson, F. P.
As fate would have it. Abbott, L. K.
As human as you are standing here. Magee, K.
As I was saying . . . Barth, J.
As if there were trees. McCann, C.
As it is in heaven. Cherry, K.
As much below as up above. Van Booy, S.
As time goes by. Cooper, J. C.
Asal. Krasikov, S.
The **ascension**. Uchida, H.
Ascent. Brown, D.
Ascent of man. Brown, E.
An **ascent** of the moon. Sallis, J.
Asch, Sholem

Children
    Shining and shadow; an anthology of early
        Yiddish stories from the Lower East Side;
        edited and translated by Albert Waldinger
Leybel is dead—Leybel lives
    Shining and shadow; an anthology of early
        Yiddish stories from the Lower East Side;
        edited and translated by Albert Waldinger
The magnetic boarder
    Shining and shadow; an anthology of early
        Yiddish stories from the Lower East Side;
        edited and translated by Albert Waldinger
A mannequin
    Shining and shadow; an anthology of early
        Yiddish stories from the Lower East Side;
        edited and translated by Albert Waldinger
On the bank of an alien stream
    Shining and shadow; an anthology of early
        Yiddish stories from the Lower East Side;
        edited and translated by Albert Waldinger
The story of beautiful Marie
    No star too beautiful; Yiddish stories from
        1382 to the present; compiled and translat-
        ed by Joachim Neugroschel
A surrendered home
    Shining and shadow; an anthology of early
        Yiddish stories from the Lower East Side;
        edited and translated by Albert Waldinger

Aschkenas, Lea

La Coca-Cola del olvido
    Havana noir; edited by Achy Obejas

Ascribed this day to the affidavit. Ruefle, M.
ASEXUAL REPRODUCTION

See also Fertilization in vitro
Bisson, T. Macs
Chiang, T. Seventy-two letters
Johnston, A. Fat farm
McHugh, M. F. Frankenstein's daughter
Reed, R. The cuckoo's boys

The **assassination** weapon. Ballard, J. G.
Assassins. Reich, C.
Assassins Project: Storyboards to Date. Domini, J.
ASSAULT AND BATTERY
    Kiely, B. Through the fields in gloves
    Manotti, D. Zero tolerance
    Michaels, L. The deal
    Michaels, L. Going places
    O'Connor, F. Revelation
    O'Mahony, M. Every ounce of soul
    Reid, G. Soon we will be blind
    Stern, R. G. Ins and outs
ASSES AND MULES
    Barlow, J. The donkey wedding at Gomersal, recounted by an inhabitant of that place
    Lansdale, J. R. The mule rustlers
    Lansdale, J. R. White mule, spotted pig
    Peelle, L. Mule killers
    Taha, M. A. The freak
The **assessment**. MacLaverty, B.
Assessment of an amateur. Stern, R. G.
Assez. Robinson, R.
Assignment. Chekhov, A. P.
The **assignment**. Meacham, R.
The **assistants**. Sotiropoulou, E.
Assisted living. Barth, J.
Association test. McBain, E.
Associations in blue. Wolf, C.
Assumption. Giles, M.
Assurance. Singleton, G.
Asteroid Ceres. Bova, B.
ASTEROIDS
    Bova, B. Two years before the mast
    Finlay, C. C. The seal hunter
    Gerrold, D. Riding Janis
    Haldeman, J. W. Giza
    Rich, M. The asking place
    Scheerbart, P. Malvu the helmsman: a story of vesta
ASTHMA
    Leavitt, C. Breathe
Asthma attack. Keret, E.
The **astrologer** who predicted his own murder. Tremayne, P.
ASTROLOGERS
    Smith, C. A. The last hieroglyph
ASTROLOGY
    Bennett, T. Checkout #5
Astronaut of the year. Meno, J.
ASTRONAUTS
    See also Women astronauts
    Arsenieva, E. A birch tree, a white fox
    Blish, J. Common time
    Bova, B. The supervisor's tale
    Bradbury, R. June 2001: And the moon be still as bright
    Brown, E. Ulla, ulla
    Dalton, Q. Back on earth
    DeAndrea, W. L. Sabotage
    DuBois, B. Falling star
    Eschbach, A. Wonders of the universe
    Ford, J. The dismantled invention of fate
    Irvine, A. C. Pictures from an expedition
    Jacobs, H. Gravity
    Kress, N. First flight
    Meno, J. Astronaut of the year
    Pohl, F. The gold at the starbow's end
    Pohl, F. Speed trap
    Rich, M. Forever down the ringing groves

    Shepard, J. Eros 7
    Silverberg, R. The feast of St. Dionysus
    Sterling, B. Join the navy and see the worlds
    Swanwick, M. Slow life
The **Astronauts**. Pinches, B.
ASTRONOMERS
    Bear, E. Stella nova
    Roberts, J. 7C
ASTRONOMY
    See also Outer space; Stars names of individual planets
    Benford, G. Bow shock
    Pohl, F. Shaffery among the immortals
Astrosapiens. Marrak, M.
Astute fiery luxurious. Smith, A.
Asunder. Lopez, R.
At 8:15 on Tuesday Morning. Blackman, S.
At Age 91, Anna Smolz of the Gmersh Unit Speaks. Almond, S.
At five in the afternoon. Steiner, G.
At Fumicaro. Ozick, C.
At Home on This Movable Earth. Kloefkorn, W.
At Olivehill. Trevor, W.
At one. Lovegrove, J.
At one, again, with nature. Andreas-Salomé, L.
At peace. Arjouni, J.
At reparata. Ford, J.
At Schindler's. Malouf, D.
At sea. See Chekhov, A. P. On the sea: a sailor's story [variant title: At sea]
At Shaft 11. Dunbar, P. L.
At the attorney's. Pinski, D.
At the beach. Robinson, R.
At the bran foundry. Effinger, G. A.
At the Café Lovely. Lapcharoensap, R.
At the cemetery. Chekhov, A. P.
At the Concert of Alternative Music. Spilman, R.
At the drop of a hat. Hamilton, D.
At the gates of the animal kingdom. Hempel, A.
At the hospital. Al-Shaykh, S.
At the huts of Ajala. Shawl, N.
At the mountains of madness. Lovecraft, H. P.
At the mouth of the river of bees. Johnson, K.
At the Powwow Hotel. Jensen, T.
At the Rialto. Willis, C.
At the seminary. Oates, J. C.
At the site where vision is most perfect. Lefer, D.
At the sound of the last post. Gappah, P.
At the top of his game. Rhodes, S.
At the Top of the Hill on Water. Miller, S. G.
At the Zoo. Horrocks, C.
At Vega's taqueria. Lupoff, R. A.
At whom the dog barks. Segal, L. G.
The **Atatürk** of the Outer Boroughs. Appel, J. M.
ATHEISM
    Shabtai, Y. The voyage to Mauritius
Atheling, William, Jr. *See* Blish, James, 1921-1975
ATHENA (GREEK DEITY)
    Cadnum, M. Medusa
ATHENS (GREECE) *See* Greece—Athens
The **Athens** solution. Thor, B.
ATHLETES
    See also Olympic Games
    Archer, J. In the eye of the beholder
    Bass, R. Field events
    Clarke, B. Geronimo
    DuBois, B. The taste of silver
    Fisher, C. Tin man square

Atwood, Margaret—*Continued*
White horse
Atwood, M. Moral disorder; stories
Atxaga, Bernardo
Pirpo and Chanberlán, Murderers
The Paris Review v47 p225-30 Spr 2005
Et **au** diable les frontières . . . Mercier, M.
Au Pair. Gordon, M.
AU PAIRS
Doyle, R. The pram
Komla-Ebri, K. "Home . . . sickness"
Krasikov, S. Asal
Sherman, R. Homestay
Simpson, H. The year's midnight
Wright, P. Looking for Aimee
Aubrey's Boyfriend. Czepiel, K. L.
Auchincloss, Louis
The artist's model
Auchincloss, L. The young Apollo and other
stories
The attributions
Auchincloss, L. The young Apollo and other
stories
The call of the wild
Auchincloss, L. The friend of women and
other stories
A case history
Auchincloss, L. The young Apollo and other
stories
The conversion of Fred Coates
Auchincloss, L. The friend of women and
other stories
The devil and Rufus Lockwood
Auchincloss, L. The friend of women and
other stories
Due process
Auchincloss, L. The young Apollo and other
stories
The grandeur that was Byzantium
Auchincloss, L. The young Apollo and other
stories
Her better half
Auchincloss, L. The young Apollo and other
stories
An hour and a lifetime
Auchincloss, L. The young Apollo and other
stories
Lady Kate
Auchincloss, L. The young Apollo and other
stories
L'ami des femmes
Auchincloss, L. The friend of women and
other stories
The omelette and the egg
Auchincloss, L. The friend of women and
other stories
Other times, other ways
Auchincloss, L. The young Apollo and other
stories
Pandora's box
Auchincloss, L. The young Apollo and other
stories
Pa's darling
Auchincloss, L. The young Apollo and other
stories
The Best American short stories, 2007; select-
ed from U. S. and Canadian magazines by
Stephen King with Heidi Pitlor; with an in-
troduction by Stephen King

The Yale Review v94 no1 p123 35 Ja 2006
The young Apollo
Auchincloss, L. The young Apollo and other
stories
AUCTIONS
Buckler, E. Humble pie
Swan, G. Cochise
Weaver, W. Dispersal
Yellin, T. Dan
Audience. Franck, T.
The **audition.** Bova, B.
AUDUBON, JOHN JAMES, 1785-1851
About
Turtledove, H. Audubon in Atlantis
Audubon in Atlantis. Turtledove, H.
Auggie Wren's Christmas story. Auster, P.
An **augury.** Brown, R.
August. Olafsson, O.
August. Slouka, M.
The **Aunt** and Amabel. Nesbit, E.
Aunt Germaine. Murphy, Y.
Aunt Juliana's Indian. Gappah, P.
Aunt Mandy's investment. Dunbar, P. L.
Aunt 'Phroney's boy. Baum, L. F.
Aunt Severina. Neera
Aunt Telephone. Pearlman, E.
Aunt Tempe's revenge. Dunbar, P. L.
Aunt Tempe's triumph. Dunbar, P. L.
Aunt Zézé's tears. Dolores, C.
Auntie Kadrajan. Siba'i, A. a.- .
Auntie Maim. Lalui, A.
AUNTS
See also Nieces
Arnow, H. L. S. No lady
Averill, T. F. Matty
Bashar, B. a.- . The jewelry box
Bergua, A. G. Los conservadores/The preservers
Bierce, A. Curried cow
Binchy, M. All that matters
Crone, M. Salvage
Dolores, C. Aunt Zézé's tears
Drosso, A.-M. They took everything
Erdrich, L. Morphine
Fincke, G. Rip his head off
Flanagan, E. Laws of relativity
Fulton, A. The glorious mysteries
Gordon, M. The healing
Gordon, M. The thorn
Granados, C. Enough
Granados, C. Pecado
Hinton, S. E. Sentenced
Hwang, F. Giving a clock
Johnson, G. Escalators
Johnson, G. Schadenfreude
Kiely, B. Elm Valley Valerie
Ludwig, S. Holding my breath underwater
Lunstrum, K. S. Baby love
Luvaas, W. Original sin
Malik, M. 'A. a.- . That winter
Mastretta, A. Aunt Concha Esparza
Maxwell, W. The woman who had no eye for
small details
Meno, J. How to say good night
Miller, A. L. My summer of love
Munro, A. The ticket
Murphy, Y. Aunt Germaine
Naipaul, V. S. My aunt Gold Teeth
Naiyer Masud. Obscure domains of fear and de-
sire

AUTUMN
  Luvaas, W. Season of limb fall
Autumn. Erdrich, L.
Autumn. Ryunosuke, A.
Autumn, 1911. Harleman, A.
Autumn Alchemy. Braverman, K.
Autumn's Girl. Giraldi, W.
Ava Bean. Davis, J. S.
Ava wrestles the alligator. Russell, K.
Avalanche! (a fairy tale). Montgomery, L.
AVALANCHES
  Montgomery, L. Avalanche! (a fairy tale)
AVANT GARDE STORIES See Experimental
   stories
AVARICE
    See also Misers
  Boyle, T. C. The devil and Irv Cherniske
  Cadnum, M. The flounder's kiss
  Dawson, P. Hell for homesteaders
  Douka, M. Carré fix
  Fowler, C. The threads
  Gorriti, J. M. The quena
  Gorriti, J. M. The treasure of the Incas
  Gorriti, J. M. A year in California
  Irsfeld, J. H. Finderkeepers
  L'Amour, L. Off the mangrove coast
  Light, L. The lamented
  Ma Jian. The golden crown
  Matheson, R. Button, button
  Matheson, R. Girl of my dreams
  McInerney, J. Summary judgment
  Molodowsky, K. Off the track
  Stevenson, R. L. The Waif woman: a cue–from
    a saga
  Strasser, D. Conquest
  Valdés, J. People like us
  Wilson, F. P. RAPED
  Zahn, T. The ring
Avast, abaft!. Waldrop, H.
Avatar. Chambers, C.
The **avatar** of background noise. Finley, T. K.
Ave Maria. Morrissette, M.
The **avenging** chance. Berkeley, A.
Averill, Thomas Fox
  The Bocce brothers
    Averill, T. F. Ordinary genius
  Bus
    Averill, T. F. Ordinary genius
  During the twelfth summer of Elmer D.
    Peterson
    Averill, T. F. Ordinary genius
  Garden Plots: A Collection of Short-Shorts
    The North American Review v293 no3/4
    p30-1 My/Ag 2008
  The man who ran with deer
    Averill, T. F. Ordinary genius
  Matty
    Averill, T. F. Ordinary genius
  Memphis, 1825: The Nerve and the Blood
    The North American Review v292 no1 p17-24
    Ja/F 2007
  Midlin, Kansas, jump shot
    Averill, T. F. Ordinary genius
  The musical genius of Moscow, Kansas
    Averill, T. F. Ordinary genius
  The onion and I
    Averill, T. F. Ordinary genius
  Red River Valley
    New Letters v74 no1 p89-105 2007/2008

  Shopping
    Averill, T. F. Ordinary genius
  The summer grandma was supposed to die
    Averill, T. F. Ordinary genius
  Topeka underground
    Averill, T. F. Ordinary genius
AVERROËS, 1126-1198
       About
  Hussin, J. Y. The day in Buenos Aires
Avery, Andrea
  Maps
    Ploughshares v32 no2/3 p8-9 Fall 2006
"**Avery,** If It's a Girl". Mitchard, J.
Avey. Toomer, J.
AVIATION See Aeronautics
AVIATORS See Air pilots
Aviva's back. Biller, M.
Avoid agony. Agnihotri, S.
Avoiding penance. Stewart, P.
Aw, Tash
  To the City
    Granta v100 p247-57 Wint 2007
Awaiting orders. Wolff, T.
Awake. Wolff, T.
The **awakening**. Báez, A.
Awakening the genius within. Gregory, D.
Away ground. Petsetidis, D.
AWK. Wunsch, K.
Ax Handle. Chin, M.
Ax of the apostles. McGraw, E.
Ayana. King, S.
Aydinoglu, Yasemin
  One among us
    Istanbul noir; edited by Mustafa Ziyalan &
    Amy Spangler; translated by Amy Spangler
    & Mustafa Ziyalan.
AYERS ROCK (AUSTRALIA)
  Malouf, D. Mrs. Porter and the rock
Aylett, Steve
  The man whose head expanded
    Perverted by language; fiction inspired by The
    Fall; edited and introduced by Peter Wild.
  Voyage of the Iguana
    Fast ships, black sails; edited by Ann & Jeff
    VanderMeer
Ayres, N. J.
  Black Zak and the heart attack
    Creature cozies; edited by Jill M. Morgan
  Rust
    At the scene of the crime; forensic mysteries
    from today's best writers; edited by Dana
    Stabenow
    The Best American mystery stories, 2009; ed-
    ited and with an introduction by Jeffery
    Deaver
AZERBAIJAN
  Sterling, B. Hollywood kremlin
Azevedo, Kathleen de
  Behold My Son Issac
    Gettysburg Review v19 no3 p341-50 Aut
    2006
  Together we are lost
    New stories from the Southwest; edited by D.
    Seth Horton; foreword by Ray Gonzalez.
Aziz Mishri, 'Abd al-
  Reaching you through the letter carrier
    Oranges in the sun; short stories from the
    Arabian Gulf; edited and translated by Deb-
    orah S. Akers, Abubaker A. Bagader

Azorno [excerpt] Christensen, I.
AZTECS
  Buckell, T. S. The people's machine
  Rosenblum, M. H. Sacrifice
Azul. Porter, A.
Azzam, Samira
  Her tale
    Qissat; short stories by Palestinian women; edited by Jo Glanville

B

The **B** & W. Rheinheimer, K.
"The **B-line**". de Caldas Brito, C.
B. Traven is alive and well in Cuernavaca. Anaya, R. A.
The **B9ers**. Smith, N.
Baantjer
  DeKok and the hammer blow
    Passport to crime; the finest mystery stories from International Crime Writers; edited by Janet Hutchings
Baba Yaga and the sorcerer's son. McKillip, P. A.
Babe. West, D.
Babel, Isaac
  First love
    My mistress's sparrow is dead; great love stories, from Chekhov to Munro; edited by Jeffrey Eugenides
  The sin of Jesus
    A cross of centuries; twenty-five imaginative tales about the Christ; edited by Michael Bishop
Babel interface. Finch, S.
Babette. Gardam, J.
Babic, Mary Jean
  What Coal Tastes Like
    Iowa Review v34 no3 p41-64 Wint 2004/2005
Babilla, Assurbanipal
  (tr.) See Ravanipour, Moniro
Babka. Ahrens, L.
BABOONS
  Rollins, J. Kowalski's in love
  Smith, M. Baboons
  Smith, T. A troop [sic] of baboons
Baboons. Kohler, S.
Baboons. Smith, M.
Babs. Phillips, S.
Babu Barrah Takka. Shroff, M. F.
The **baby**. Gordon, M.
The **Baby** and the Moth. Allen, D.
The **Baby** Cooper Dollar Bill. Gerrold, D.
Baby doll. Sinisalo, J.
Baby Fat. Margolis, D.
Baby girl. Leebron, F. G.
The **baby** in rose tarlatan. Barreto, P.
The **baby** in the night deposit box. Turner, M. W.
A **Baby** Is a Baby Is a Baby. Stuart, M.
Baby Jane. Lanagan, M.
Baby love. Lunstrum, K. S.
Baby Pictures. Pratt, B.
Baby R. Poverman, C. E.
BABY SITTERS
  Goldfaden, J. The Veronese circle
  James, C. L. R. The babysitter
  Jones, C. The babysitter
  LaBrie, A. Ducklings
  Lippman, L. The babysitter's code

Litman, E. Charity
Lott, B. Nostaglia
Macy, C. Bad ghost
Ohlin, A. Edgewater
Sherman, R. Set man
Stafford, J. The darkening moon
Sutton, B. Rabbit punch
The **Baby** Store. Gorman, E.
A **baby** tramp. Bierce, A.
The **baby** who saved Hanukkah. Hope, T. G.
Babylon. Ohlin, A.
Babylon revisited. Fitzgerald, F. S.
The **babysitter**. James, C. L. R.
The **babysitter**. Jones, C.
The **babysitter's** code. Lippman, L.
Bach, Mischa
  Full moon
    Passport to crime; the finest mystery stories from International Crime Writers; edited by Janet Hutchings
Bachelder, Chris
  Blue Knights bounced from CVD Tourney
    New stories from the South: the year's best, 2006; selected from U.S. magazines by Allan Gurganus with Kathy Pories; with an introduction by Allan Gurganus
BACHELORS *See* Single men
Bachman, Richard *See* King, Stephen, 1947-
Bacigalupi, Paolo
  Calorie man
    The Year's best science fiction: twenty-third annual collection; edited by Gardner Dozois
    Rewired; the post-cyberpunk anthology; James Patrick Kelly & John Kessel, editors
    Bacigalupi, P. Pump six and other stories
  The fluted girl
    The Year's best science fiction: twenty-first annual collection; edited by Gardner Dozois
    The Year's best fantasy and horror: seventeenth annual collection; edited by Ellen Datlow, Kelly Link and Gavin J. Grant
    Bacigalupi, P. Pump six and other stories
  The gambler
    The Best science fiction and fantasy of the year: volume three; edited by Jonathan Strahan
  The pasho
    Bacigalupi, P. Pump six and other stories
  The people of sand and slag
    The Year's best science fiction: twenty-second annual collection; edited by Gardner Dozois
    Bacigalupi, P. Pump six and other stories
  Pocketful of dharma
    Bacigalupi, P. Pump six and other stories
  Pop squad
    Bacigalupi, P. Pump six and other stories
  Pump six
    Bacigalupi, P. Pump six and other stories
  Small offerings
    Fast forward 1; future fiction from the cutting edge; edited by Lou Anders
  Softer
    Bacigalupi, P. Pump six and other stories
  The tamarisk hunter
    Bacigalupi, P. Pump six and other stories
  Yellow card man
    The Year's best science fiction: twenty-fourth annual collection; edited by Gardner Dozois

Bacigalupi, Paolo—*Continued*
Bacigalupi, P. Pump six and other stories
Back. Marcus, J. S.
Back across the Light Years. Pastan, R.
"**Back** alleys". Quijada, C.
Back Home at the Driftwood Lodge. Miner, V.
Back in the Day. Lee, H. E.
The **Back** Nine. Haverty, C.
Back of beyond. Rash, R.
The **back** of his hand. Gallagher, S.
Back on earth. Dalton, Q.
The **back** page. Kellerman, F.
Back to School. Parvulescu, C.
Back-trail betrayal. Dawson, P.
Backcity transit by day. Coleman, W.
BACKGAMMON
Papernick, J. An unwelcome guest
The **backgammon** monster. Keret, E.
Backsliders. DeMarinis, R.
Backwardness. Anderson, P.
BACTERIOLOGISTS
Rose, A. Micrographia esoterica
Bactine. McNett, M.
Bactine. Pollock, D. R.
Bad blood. Malouf, D.
Bad blood. Weaver, W.
Bad Boo-boo-loo and the shark fight. James, C. L. R.
Bad Boo-boo-loo messes up the time. James, C. L. R.
Bad Boo-boo-loo rides in a horse race. James, C. L. R.
Bad business. Chekhov, A. P.
Bad characters. Stafford, J.
Bad Dreams. Hospital, J. T.
Bad for the heart. Tsutsui, Y.
Bad ghost. Macy, C.
Bad girl on the curb. Glatt, L.
A **bad** habit. Zoshchenko, M.
Bad habits. Oates, J. C.
Bad karma girl wins a t bingo. Braffet, K.
Bad luck, trouble, death, and vampire sex. Nix, G.
The **bad** magician. Raines, P. and Welles, H.
Bad neighbors. Jones, E. P.
The **bad** news. Atwood, M.
Bad News. Holt, T. E.
The **bad** night. Block, L.
The **bad** sex weekend. Enright, A.
A **Bad** Spell. Lowe, B.
The **bad** thing. Gates, D.
"A **bad** woman". Bierce, A.
The **badger** game. Block, L.
BADGERS
Proulx, A. The old badger game
Badib, 'Ali 'Awad
Trilling cries of joy
Oranges in the sun; short stories from the Arabian Gulf; edited and translated by Deborah S. Akers, Abubaker A. Bagader
Badlands Billy, the wolf that won. Seton, E. T.
Badr, Liyānah
Other cities
Qissat; short stories by Palestinian women; edited by Jo Glanville
Baer, Will Christopher
Deception of the thrush
San Francisco noir; edited by Peter Maravelis

Báez, Annecy
Amor es. . . Love is
Báez, A. My daughter's eyes, and other stories
Amor sucks
Báez, A. My daughter's eyes, and other stories
Aura
Báez, A. My daughter's eyes, and other stories
The awakening
Báez, A. My daughter's eyes, and other stories
Casa-Arte
Báez, A. My daughter's eyes, and other stories
Como se dice success in Spanish?
Báez, A. My daughter's eyes, and other stories
The loss
Báez, A. My daughter's eyes, and other stories
My daughter's eyes
Báez, A. My daughter's eyes, and other stories
The Pinocchio
Báez, A. My daughter's eyes, and other stories
The red shoes
Báez, A. My daughter's eyes, and other stories
The silence of angels
Báez, A. My daughter's eyes, and other stories
The storyteller
Báez, A. My daughter's eyes, and other stories
The time keeper
Báez, A. My daughter's eyes, and other stories
To tell the truth
Báez, A. My daughter's eyes, and other stories
Wildflow
Báez, A. My daughter's eyes, and other stories
A wrinkle in the eye
Báez, A. My daughter's eyes, and other stories
Zulieka
Báez, A. My daughter's eyes, and other stories
BAG LADIES *See* Homeless persons
"**bag** of mice". Flynn, N. and Neufeld, J.
Bagdasarian, Adam
Clay
The Antioch Review v63 no3 p511-22 Summ 2005
Baggage. Charters, D.
Baggage. Donoghue, E.
Baggott, Julianna
Girl-child X: a story of birthing told through three eras
Before; short stories about pregnancy from our top writers; edited by Emily Franklin and Heather Swain
Baghdad at seven-thirty. Biller, M.

Bagi, Yassir 'Abd al-
Bus #99
  Oranges in the sun; short stories from the
  Arabian Gulf; edited and translated by Deb-
  orah S. Akers, Abubaker A. Bagader
Bahah, Muhammad O.
A parting shot
  Oranges in the sun; short stories from the
  Arabian Gulf; edited and translated by Deb-
  orah S. Akers, Abubaker A. Bagader
BAHAMAS
Bishop, T. Bonefish in Wyoming
McBain, E. Every morning
Shukman, H. Castaway
BAHIA (BRAZIL) *See* Brazil—Bahia
Bahr, Aida
Black and White
  The Review of Contemporary Fiction v26 no3
  p114-27 Fall 2006
Baikal. Lum, E.
Bailey, Dale
Death and suffrage
  The living dead; edited by John Joseph Ad-
  ams
The end of the world as we know it
  Nebula Awards showcase 2007; the year's
  best SF and fantasy; selected by the Sci-
  ence Fiction and Fantasy Writers of Ameri-
  ca; edited by Mike Resnick
Hunger: a confession
  The Year's best fantasy and horror: seven-
  teenth annual collection; edited by Ellen
  Datlow, Kelly Link and Gavin J. Grant
Bailey, Hilary
Dr. Gelabius
  New worlds; an anthology; edited by Michael
  Moorcock
Bailey, Mary
Gingerbread
  Confrontation no101 p173-91 Spr/Summ 2008
Bailey, Robin Wayne
Protection
  Thieves' world; enemies of fortune; edited by
  Lynn Abbey
Baingana, Doreen
First kiss
  Baingana, D. Tropical fish; tales from Enteb-
  be
Green stones
  Baingana, D. Tropical fish; tales from Enteb-
  be
Hunger
  Baingana, D. Tropical fish; tales from Enteb-
  be
Kadongo Kamu—One Beat
  StoryQuarterly v41 p120-32 2005
Lost in Los Angeles
  Baingana, D. Tropical fish; tales from Enteb-
  be
Passion
  Baingana, D. Tropical fish; tales from Enteb-
  be
Questions of home
  Baingana, D. Tropical fish; tales from Enteb-
  be
A thank-you note
  Baingana, D. Tropical fish; tales from Enteb-
  be

Tropical fish
  Baingana, D. Tropical fish; tales from Enteb-
  be
Baird, Robert P.
(tr.) See Wu Ming
Bait. Dybek, S.
Bait and switch. Macy, C.
The **baiting** of the warriors. Lamb, H.
Bajpe. Adiga, A.
Baked Beans in Redwoods. Carney, R.
Baked mud. Saer, J. J.
Baker, Kage
The angel in the darkness
  Baker, K. Gods and pawns
The Briscian saint
  Baker, K. Mother Aegypt and other stories
Calamari Curls
  Baker, K. Dark Mondays; stories
The catch
  Baker, K. Gods and pawns
Desolation Rose
  Baker, K. Mother Aegypt and other stories
Hellfire at twilight
  Baker, K. Gods and pawns
  The Year's best science fiction: twenty-fifth
  annual collection; edited by Gardner Dozois
Her father's eyes
  Baker, K. Mother Aegypt and other stories
How they tried to talk Indian Tony down
  Baker, K. Mother Aegypt and other stories
I begyn as I mean to go on
  Fast ships, black sails; edited by Ann & Jeff
  VanderMeer
Katherine's story
  Baker, K. Dark Mondays; stories
Leaving his cares behind
  Baker, K. Mother Aegypt and other stories
Maelstrom
  The new space opera; edited by Gardner
  Dozois and Jonathan Strahan
The maid on the shore
  Baker, K. Dark Mondays; stories
Merry Christmas from Navarro Lodge, 1928
  Baker, K. Mother Aegypt and other stories
Miss Yahoo has her say
  Baker, K. Mother Aegypt and other stories
Monkey day
  Baker, K. Dark Mondays; stories
Mother Aegypt
  Baker, K. Mother Aegypt and other stories
  The Year's best science fiction: twenty-
  second annual collection; edited by Gardner
  Dozois
A night on the Barbary Coast
  Baker, K. Gods and pawns
Nightmare Mountain
  Baker, K. Mother Aegypt and other stories
Oh, false young man!
  Baker, K. Dark Mondays; stories
Plotters and shooters
  Fast forward 1; future fiction from the cutting
  edge; edited by Lou Anders
Portrait, with flames
  Baker, K. Dark Mondays; stories
Pueblo, Colorado has the answers
  Baker, K. Mother Aegypt and other stories
The ruby incomparable
  Wizards; edited by Jack Dann and Gardner
  Dozois

Baker, Kage—*Continued*
Year's best fantasy 8; edited by David G. Hartwell, Kathryn Cramer
Running the snake
Sideways in crime; an alternate mystery anthology; edited by Lou Anders
Silent Leonardo
Baker, K. Dark Mondays; stories
So this guy walks into a lighthouse—
Poe's lighthouse; all new collaborations with Edgar Allan Poe; edited by Christopher Conlon
Baker, K. Dark Mondays; stories
Standing in his light
Baker, K. Gods and pawns
The summer people
Baker, K. Mother Aegypt and other stories
To the land beyond the sunset
Baker, K. Gods and pawns
Two old men
Baker, K. Mother Aegypt and other stories
The two old women
Baker, K. Dark Mondays; stories
Welcome to Olympus, Mr. Hearst
The Year's best science fiction: twenty-first annual collection; edited by Gardner Dozois
Baker, K. Gods and pawns
What the tyger told her
Baker, K. Mother Aegypt and other stories
Where the golden apples grow
The Year's best science fiction: twenty-fourth annual collection; edited by Gardner Dozois

Baker, Kevin
The cheers like waves
Bronx noir; edited by S. J. Rozan

Baker, Linda P.
The opposite of solid
Pandora's closet; edited by Jean Rabe and Martin H. Greenberg.

Baker, Olaf
Where the buffaloes begin
Adventures in the West; stories for young readers; edited by Susanne George Bloomfield and Eric Melvin Reed

BAKERIES AND BAKERS
Dalton, Q. Dough
Duval, P. Bakery
Luongo, M. Cake
McKinstray, S. No one here says what they mean
Pifer, D. Fruitcakes and fiction
The **baker's** dog. Kun, M.
Bakery. Duval, P.

Bakhsawayn, 'Abd Allah
The silver polisher
Oranges in the sun; short stories from the Arabian Gulf; edited and translated by Deborah S. Akers, Abubaker A. Bagader

Bakken, Kerry Neville
The body/love problem
Bakken, K. N. Necessary lies
The effects of light
Bakken, K. N. Necessary lies
Eggs
Bakken, K. N. Necessary lies
Indignity
Gettysburg Review v21 no1 p124-51 Spr 2008
Necessary lies
Bakken, K. N. Necessary lies

Remains
Bakken, K. N. Necessary lies
Renter's guide to the Hamptons
Bakken, K. N. Necessary lies
Vigil
Bakken, K. N. Necessary lies

Bakopoulos, Dean
Cougar & Zeke
The Virginia Quarterly Review v82 no4 p150-64 Fall 2006
Happy
Barnstorm; contemporary Wisconsin fiction; edited by Raphael Kadushin

Bakr, Salwá
Thirty-one beautiful green trees
The Anchor book of modern African stories; edited by Nadežda Obradovic; with a foreword by Chinua Achebe

Balance. Anderson, B.
Balance. Davis, C.
Balboa. Murray, S.
Bald island. Dourado, A.

Baldeosingh, Kevin
The rape
Trinidad noir; edited by Lisa Allen-Agostini & Jeanne Mason.

Balding, Nate
Twenty2. The city without secrets
Nature v443 p480 S 28 2006

BALDNESS
Holmes, A. The league of bald-headed men

Baldwin, D. N.
The Rat Hunt
The Sewanee Review v117 no1 p38-54 Wint 2009
Razing Temples
The Sewanee Review v113 no2 p207-27 Spr 2005

Baldwin, James
Going to meet the man
Short stories of the civil rights movement; an anthology; edited by Margaret Earley Whitt
A **Bale** of Salt. Koo, H.-S. and Anthony
The **balers**. Currans-Sheehan, T.

Balint, Anna
Goulash
Calyx v24 no1 p6-12 Summ 2007
The **Balkan** House. Wingate, S.
Balked eclogue. Lynn, D. H.

Ball, Jesse
Archon LLC
The Paris Review v50 p142-51 Fall 2008
The Early Deaths of Lubeck, Brennan, Harp, and Carr
The Paris Review v49 p155-85 Wint 2007
Plainface
The Paris Review v51 p102-31 Spr 2009

Ball, Peter M.
The last great house of Isla Tortuga
Dreaming again; thirty-five new stories celebrating the wild side of Australian fiction; edited by Jack Dann

BALL GAMES
See also Baseball; Basketball; Football; Soccer; Softball; Tennis
Ball lighting. Gifford, B.
Ball lightning reported. Wolven, S.
A **ball** of malt and Madame Butterfly. Kiely, B.

The **ball** room. Miéville, C. and others
Ballad. Bunin, I. A.
A **Ballad** for Ginny Brothers. Kalpakian, L.
The **ballad** of Moosecock Lip. Thomas, J.
The **Ballad** of Poor Lucy Miller. Holdstock, N.
The **ballad** of the flexible bullet. King, S.
Ballantyne, Tony
  Aristotle OS
    Fast forward 1; future fiction from the cutting
      edge; edited by Lou Anders
  Takeaway
    Nature v458 p376 Mr 19 2009
Ballard, J. G.
  The assassination weapon
    New worlds; an anthology; edited by Michael
      Moorcock
  The Autobiography of J.G.B.
    The New Yorker v85 no13 p96-7 My 11 2009
  The index
    The Paris review book for planes, trains, ele-
      vators, and waiting rooms; by the editors of
      the Paris review; with an introduction by
      Richard Powers
BALLET
    See also Dancers
  Gilman, G. I. Down the wall
  Ward, A. E. On Messalonskee Lake
Ballingrud, Nathan
  The monsters of heaven
    The Year's best fantasy and horror: twenty-
      first annual collection; edited by Ellen
      Datlow and Kelly Link & Gavin J. Grant
    Inferno; new tales of terror and the supernatu-
      ral; edited by Ellen Datlow.
  North American lake monsters
    The Del Rey book of science fiction and fan-
      tasy; sixteen original works by speculative
      fiction's finest voices; edited by Ellen
      Datlow
  You go where it takes you
    The Year's best fantasy and horror: seven-
      teenth annual collection; edited by Ellen
      Datlow, Kelly Link and Gavin J. Grant
BALLOON ASCENSIONS
  Bishop, E. A flight of fancy
BALLOONS
  Drake, D. Airborne all the way!
  Wolfe, G. Straw
BALLS (PARTIES) *See* Parties
Balsamo's mirror. De Camp, L. S.
BALTIMORE (MD.) *See* Maryland—Baltimore
Baltimore. Rheinheimer, K.
Balto. Boyle, T. C.
Balzac, Honoré de
  The last Napoleon
    Paris tales; stories; translated by Helen Con-
      stantine
Balzac. Domecq, B.
Bamber, Linda
  In the Forest
    The Kenyon Review v29 no1 p106-45 Wint
      2007
  In the Yucatan
    Harvard Review (1992) no32 p102-14 2007
Bambino road, chapter one. Tan, C.
Bamer, Linda
  Casting Call
    Southwest Review v90 no2 p214-45 2005

Bamia, Aida
  (tr.) See Khalifeh, Sahar
Banana love. Crane, E.
BANANAS
  Crane, E. Banana love
Bandit Jim Crow. Baum, L. F.
The **bandit** of sanity. Lannes, R.
BANDITS *See* Brigands and robbers
BANDS (MUSIC)
  Barthelme, D. The police band
  Chattin, J. So far from the stage
  Doyle, R. The deportees
  Randolph, L. It's cheaper to live in the dark
  Tognazzini, A. Westminster march
Bang. Zeman, A.
Bang crunch. Smith, N.
Banger Finds Out: A Story. Cherry, K.
Bangkok, Jeffrey
  Counterfeit love
    Hardcore hardboiled; edited by Todd Robin-
      son; introduction by Otto Penzler
BANGKOK (THAILAND) *See* Thailand—Bang-
    kok
Bangkok. Salter, J.
BANGLADESH
    See also Bengal (India and Bangladesh)
  Khan, R. Alms
Bank, Melissa
  Run Run Run Run Run Run Run Away
    Ploughshares v31 no1 p56-66 Spr 2005
BANK CLERKS *See* Clerks
Bank of America. Lange, R.
BANK ROBBERS
  Arjouni, J. The inner man
  Breuer, M. J. Millions for defense
  Crumley, J. Hostages
  Ervin, A. All happy families
  Fusilli, J. The next best thing
  Garrett, G. P. The misery and the glory of Tex-
    as Pete
  Humphrey, W. A voice from the woods
  Lange, R. Bank of America
  Lansdale, J. R. Dirt devils
  Leonard, E. Blood money [variant title: Rich
    Miller's hand]
  Lochte, D. Low tide
  Lupoff, R. A. Streamliner
  McBain, E. The big day
  Meno, J. Stockholm 1973
  Rivas, M. What do you want with me, love?
  Symons, J. Flowers that bloom in the spring
  Wolff, T. Bullet in the brain
Bank shots. DeNymme, S.
The **bank** teller's game. Brodsky, M.
BANKERS
  Bierce, A. Banking at Mexican Hill
  Charters, D. 2hot
  Charters, D. After dark
  Charters, D. Ambition
  Charters, D. Baggage
  Charters, D. Big break
  Charters, D. Bonus round
  Charters, D. Diary
  Charters, D. Dinner party
  Charters, D. Expenses
  Charters, D. If you can't take a joke . . .
  Charters, D. Infatuation
  Charters, D. Inside track
  Charters, D. Lawsuit

BASTARDY *See* Illegitimacy
Bastille Day. Alvarado, B.
Bastogne. McNally, T. M.
Basutoland Christmas. Burke, T.
Bat. Varble, V.
BAT MITZVAH
  Albert, E. Everything but
BATES, DAISY
         About
  Rickert, M. Map of dreams
Bates, James W.
  The ungrateful dead
    Kolchak: the night stalker chronicles; 26 original tales of the surreal, the bizarre, the macabre; edited by Joe Gentile, Garrett Anderson, Lori Gentile; Kolchak created by Jeff Rice
Bates, Joseph
  Butterfinger
    South Carolina Review v37 no1 p209-13 Fall 2004
BATH (ENGLAND) *See* England—Bath
The **bath**. Lunstrum, K. S.
A **bathhouse**. Zoshchenko, M.
Bathroom. Mozetič, B.
Baths. Mounts, M.
Batistatou, Anna and Charalabopoulos, Konstantinos
  The picture of Oscar X
    Nature v455 p834 O 9 2008
Batki, John
  (tr.) *See* Krudy, Gyula
Batley, Nicholas J.
  Mister Doctor Batley [Medical Humanities, 32 no1 June 2006]
    Journal of Medical Ethics v32 no6 p44-5 Je 2006 supp
Batteiger, Paul
  A cold day in hell
    Fast ships, black sails; edited by Ann & Jeff VanderMeer
BATTERED WIVES *See* Wife abuse
Battersby, Lee
  Father muerte & the flesh
    The Year's best fantasy and horror: twentieth annual collection; edited by Ellen Datlow and Kelly Link & Gavin J. Grant
  In from the sow
    Dreaming again; thirty-five new stories celebrating the wild side of Australian fiction; edited by Jack Dann
Batting cleanup. Greenman, B.
Battle of wizards. Hubbard, L. R.
Battles, Brett
  Perfect gentleman
    Killer year; stories to die for . . . from the hottest new crime writers; edited by Lee Child
BATTLES
    See also names of individual battles
  Bierce, A. An affair of outposts
  Bierce, A. The coup de grâce
  Carl, L. S. Over the sea from Skye
  Davies, C. P. The defenders
  Saumont, A. Léna
  Tarr, J. Measureless to man
  Weber, D. Sword brother
BATTLESHIPS *See* Warships
The **battling** priests of Corpus Christi. Tervalon, J.

Bauer, Christian
  The Breakfast Burrito
    Southwest Review v90 no3 p402-11 2005
Baum, L. Frank
  Aunt 'Phroney's boy
    Adventures in the West; stories for young readers; edited by Susanne George Bloomfield and Eric Melvin Reed
  Bandit Jim Crow
    Baum, L. F. The Twinkle tales; illustrations by Maginel Wright Enright; introduction by Katharine M. Rogers
  Mr. Woodchuck
    Baum, L. F. The Twinkle tales; illustrations by Maginel Wright Enright; introduction by Katharine M. Rogers
  Policeman Bluejay
    Baum, L. F. The Twinkle tales; illustrations by Maginel Wright Enright; introduction by Katharine M. Rogers
  Prairie-Dog Town
    Baum, L. F. The Twinkle tales; illustrations by Maginel Wright Enright; introduction by Katharine M. Rogers
  Prince Mud-Turtle
    Baum, L. F. The Twinkle tales; illustrations by Maginel Wright Enright; introduction by Katharine M. Rogers
  Sugar-Loaf Mountain
    Baum, L. F. The Twinkle tales; illustrations by Maginel Wright Enright; introduction by Katharine M. Rogers
  Twinkle's enchantment
    Baum, L. F. The Twinkle tales; illustrations by Maginel Wright Enright; introduction by Katharine M. Rogers
BAUM, L. FRANK, 1856-1919
    Parodies, imitations, etc.
  De Camp, L. S. and Pratt, F. Sir Harold and the gnome king
  Marley, L. Technicolor
Baum, Lyman Frank *See* Baum, L. Frank, 1856-1919
The **Baum** plan for financial independence. Kessel, J.
Baumbach, Jonathan
  The adventures of King Dong
    Baumbach, J. On the way to my father's funeral; new and selected stories
  Bright is innocent: scenes from an imaginary movie
    Baumbach, J. On the way to my father's funeral; new and selected stories
  Courtship
    Baumbach, J. On the way to my father's funeral; new and selected stories
  The dinner party
    Baumbach, J. On the way to my father's funeral; new and selected stories
  Drool
    Baumbach, J. On the way to my father's funeral; new and selected stories
  Familiar games
    Baumbach, J. On the way to my father's funeral; new and selected stories
  The fell of love
    Baumbach, J. On the way to my father's funeral; new and selected stories

Baumbach, Jonathan—*Continued*

The fields of obscurity
   Baumbach, J. On the way to my father's funeral; new and selected stories

French history
   Baumbach, J. On the way to my father's funeral; new and selected stories

The life and times of Major Fiction
   Baumbach, J. On the way to my father's funeral; new and selected stories

Lost in translation
   Baumbach, J. On the way to my father's funeral; new and selected stories

Men at lunch
   Baumbach, J. On the way to my father's funeral; new and selected stories

Oh, hum
   Baumbach, J. On the way to my father's funeral; new and selected stories

On the way to my father's funeral, he tells me his story
   Baumbach, J. On the way to my father's funeral; new and selected stories

Passion?
   Baumbach, J. On the way to my father's funeral; new and selected stories

Past perfect
   Baumbach, J. On the way to my father's funeral; new and selected stories

The psychopathology of everyday life
   Baumbach, J. On the way to my father's funeral; new and selected stories

The relationship
   Baumbach, J. On the way to my father's funeral; new and selected stories

The return of service
   Baumbach, J. On the way to my father's funeral; new and selected stories

Reverie
   Baumbach, J. On the way to my father's funeral; new and selected stories

Spooky in Florida
   Baumbach, J. On the way to my father's funeral; new and selected stories

The traditional story returns
   Baumbach, J. On the way to my father's funeral; new and selected stories

The Villa Mondare
   Baumbach, J. On the way to my father's funeral; new and selected stories

Who shall escape whipping
   Baumbach, J. On the way to my father's funeral; new and selected stories

Window in the woods
   Baumbach, J. On the way to my father's funeral; new and selected stories

Baumgartner, Mark

Landing on Water
   The Southern Review (Baton Rouge, La.) v44 no3 p513-18 Summ 2008

Bausch, Richard

1-900
   Beha, C. R. The Ecco anthology of contemporary American short fiction; selected by Joyce Carol Oates and Christopher R. Beha.

Ancient history
   The New Granta book of the American short story; edited and introduced by Richard Ford

Byron the Lyron
   StoryQuarterly v41 p278-302 2005

The weight
   Pushcart prize XXVII; best of the small presses; edited by Bill Henderson with the Pushcart prize editors

Baxter, Charles

The Clothes of the Master
   TriQuarterly no130 p18-26 2008

Ghosts
   Pushcart prize XXXIII: best of the small presses 2009; edited by Bill Henderson with the Pushcart Prize editors
   Ploughshares v33 no1 p9-30 Spr 2007

Gina's death
   The Pushcart Prize XXIX: best of the small presses 2005; edited by Bill Henderson with the Pushcart Prize editors

Gryphon
   Children playing before a statue of Hercules; edited and introduced by David Sedaris

Innocent
   Politically inspired; edited by Stephen Elliott; assistant editor, Gabriel Kram; associate editors, Elizabeth Brooks [et al.]

Poor devil
   Beha, C. R. The Ecco anthology of contemporary American short fiction; selected by Joyce Carol Oates and Christopher R. Beha.

Royal Blue
   The American Scholar v77 no2 p91-102 Spr 2008

Saul and Patsy are in labor
   Before; short stories about pregnancy from our top writers; edited by Emily Franklin and Heather Swain

Baxter, Greg

Fighting Continues in Najaf
   Southwest Review v91 no4 p594-603 2006

Baxter, Stephen

Children of time
   The Year's best science fiction: twenty-third annual collection; edited by Gardner Dozois
   Asimov's science fiction: 30th anniversary anthology; edited by Sheila Williams

Fate and the fire-lance
   Sideways in crime; an alternate mystery anthology; edited by Lou Anders

Last contact
   The Best science fiction and fantasy of the year: volume two; edited by Jonathan Strahan
   The Year's best science fiction: twenty-fifth annual collection; edited by Gardner Dozois

Mayflower II
   The Year's best science fiction: twenty-second annual collection; edited by Gardner Dozois

No more stories
   Fast forward 1; future fiction from the cutting edge; edited by Lou Anders

The pacific mystery
   The Year's best science fiction: twenty-fourth annual collection; edited by Gardner Dozois

Bear, Elizabeth
And the deep blue sea
  Bear, E. The chains that you refuse
Annie Webber: The customer is always right
  Nature v451 p604 Ja 31 2008
Botticelli
  Bear, E. The chains that you refuse
The chains that you refuse
  Bear, E. The chains that you refuse
The company of four
  Bear, E. The chains that you refuse
The devil you don't
  Bear, E. The chains that you refuse
The dying of the light
  Bear, E. The chains that you refuse
Follow me light
  Bear, E. The chains that you refuse
  The Year's best fantasy and horror: nineteenth
    annual collection; edited by Ellen Datlow
    and Kelly Link & Gavin J. Grant
Gone to flowers
  Bear, E. The chains that you refuse
High iron
  Bear, E. The chains that you refuse
Ice
  Bear, E. The chains that you refuse
Inelastic collisions
  Inferno; new tales of terror and the supernatu-
    ral; edited by Ellen Datlow.
L'esprit d'escalier
  Bear, E. The chains that you refuse
Old leatherwings
  Bear, E. The chains that you refuse
One-Eyed Jack and the Suicide King
  Bear, E. The chains that you refuse
Orm the beautiful
  The Best science fiction and fantasy of the
    year: volume two; edited by Jonathan
    Strahan
  Realms
Schrödinger's cat chases the super string
  Bear, E. The chains that you refuse
Seven Dragons Mountains
  Bear, E. The chains that you refuse
Shoggoths in bloom
  The Best science fiction and fantasy of the
    year: volume three; edited by Jonathan
    Strahan
Sleeping dogs lie
  Bear, E. The chains that you refuse
The something-dreaming game
  Fast forward 1; future fiction from the cutting
    edge; edited by Lou Anders
Sonny Liston takes the fall
  The Del Rey book of science fiction and fan-
    tasy; sixteen original works by speculative
    fiction's finest voices; edited by Ellen
    Datlow
Stella nova
  Bear, E. The chains that you refuse
This tragic glass
  Bear, E. The chains that you refuse
Tideline
  The Year's best science fiction: twenty-fifth
    annual collection; edited by Gardner Dozois
Tiger! Tiger!
  Bear, E. The chains that you refuse
Two dreams on trains
  Bear, E. The chains that you refuse

The Year's best science fiction: twenty-third
    annual collection; edited by Gardner Dozois
  Rewired; the post-cyberpunk anthology;
    James Patrick Kelly & John Kessel, editors
When you visit the Magoebaskloof Hotel, be
    certain not to miss the samango monkeys
  Bear, E. The chains that you refuse
Bear, Elizabeth and Monette, Sarah
Boojum
  Fast ships, black sails; edited by Ann & Jeff
    VanderMeer
The ile of dogges
  The Year's best science fiction: twenty-fourth
    annual collection; edited by Gardner Dozois
Bear, Greg
Darwin's radio [excerpt]
  Nebula awards showcase 2002; edited by Kim
    Stanley Robinson
Ram shift phase 2
  This is my funniest 2; leading science fiction
    writers present their funniest stories ever;
    edited by Mike Resnick
  Nature v438 p1050 D 15 2005
The **bear** came over the mountain. Munro, A.
The **Bear** cub. Remizov, A.
Bear it away. Cadnum, M.
The **bear** itself. DeMarinis, R.
Bear meat. Levi, P.
Bear story. Marsters, S.
Bear trap. Stross, C.
Beard, Alan
Huddersfield versus Crewe
  Going the distance; edited by Alan Beard
The **bearded** lady of Rutgers Street. Gifford, B.
The **Bearded** Man. Hlehel, A.
BEARDS
  Proulx, A. The contest
Bearing up. Hughes, M.
BEARS
  Bierce, A. Boarding a bear
  Bierce, A. The following bear
  Bierce, A. The grateful bear
  Bierce, A. How to saw bears
  Bierce, A. Juniper
  Bierce, A. Stringing a bear
  Bradfield, S. Goldilocks tells all
  Cadnum, M. Bear it away
  DeNiro, A. Taiga, taiga, burning bright
  Hughes, M. Bearing up
  Lansdale, J. R. Mr. Bear
  Misha. Memekwesiw
  Moffett, J. The bear's baby
  Murphy, Y. In a bear's eye
  Murphy, Y. Real enough
  Percy, B. When the bear came
  Seton, E. T. Johnny Bear
  Seton, E. T. Monarch, the big bear of Tallac
  Stelmok, J. Not your average bear
Bear's Wood Main Line. Tsutsui, Y.
The **beast**. McHugh, M. F.
The **beast**. Ulitskaya, L.
A **beast** for Norn. Martin, G. R. R.
The **Beast** of Averoigne. Smith, C. A.
Beast of Burden. Chin, M.
Beast of the heartland. Shepard, L.
Beasts. Kercheval, J. L.
BEAT GENERATION See Bohemianism
Beat me to death. Valdés, J.
Beating around the burning bush. Roth, M.

BEATLES
Fulton, A. The real Eleanor Rigby
Lain, D. I read the news today
BEATNIKS *See* Bohemianism
Beatrice Trueblood's story. Stafford, J.
Beats of seven. Orullian, P.
Beattie, Ann
Apology for a journey not taken: how to write a story
   Beattie, A. Follies; new stories
The Confidence Decoy
   The New Yorker v82 no39 p134, 136-8, 140, 142-50 N 27 2006
Coping Stones
   The New Yorker v81 no27 p78-89 S 12 2005
Duchais
   Beattie, A. Follies; new stories
Find and replace
   Beattie, A. Follies; new stories
Fléchette follies
   Beattie, A. Follies; new stories
The garden game
   Beattie, A. Follies; new stories
Horatio's trick
   The Ecco book of Christmas stories; edited by Alberto Manguel
Just going out
   Beattie, A. Follies; new stories
The last odd day in L. A.
   Beattie, A. Follies; new stories
Lavande
   Beha, C. R. The Ecco anthology of contemporary American short fiction; selected by Joyce Carol Oates and Christopher R. Beha.
   Granta no94 p189-203 Summ 2006
Mostre
   Beattie, A. Follies; new stories
The rabbit hole as likely explanation
   The New Granta book of the American short story; edited and introduced by Richard Ford
The rabbitt hole as likely explanantion
   Beattie, A. Follies; new stories
Solid wood
   The Best American short stories, 2007; selected from U. S. and Canadian magazines by Stephen King with Heidi Pitlor; with an introduction by Stephen King
Talk
   Ploughshares v31 no4 p8-31 Wint 2005/2006
Tending something
   Beattie, A. Follies; new stories
   TriQuarterly no121 p180-93 2005
Wheeling
   The American Scholar v76 no1 p108-13 Wint 2007
Beattie, Ann and Mathews, Harry
Mr. Nobody at all
   The Best American short stories, 2006; selected from U.S. and Canadian magazines by Ann Patchett with Katrina Kenison; with an introduction by Ann Patchett
Beatty, Paul
The white boy shuffle [excerpt]
   California uncovered; stories for the 21st century; edited by Chitra Banerjee Divakaruni, William E. Justice, and James Quay
A **beau** for Aunt Sheree. Stolz, K.

Beau Séjour. Riva, P. L.
Beaulieu, Bradley P.
Chasing humanity
   Man vs. machine; edited by John Helfers and Martin H. Greenberg.
In the eyes of the empress's cat
   Orson Scott Card's Intergalctic medicine show; [edited by] Edmund R. Schubert and Orson Scott Card
Beaumont, Matt
Contraflow
   Perverted by language; fiction inspired by The Fall; edited and introduced by Peter Wild.
Beautiful. Henriquez, C.
Beautiful Consuela. Rhodes, D.
Beautiful day. Ruefle, M.
Beautiful for a Day. Welsch, G.
A **beautiful** friendship. Weber, D.
The **beautiful** Gelreesh. Ford, J.
The **beautiful** king. Palazzeschi, A.
Beautiful stuff. Palwick, S.
Beautiful things. Gee, M.
The **Beautiful** Uncut Hair of Graves. Matthews, C.
Beautiful Wreck. Semeiks, J.
BEAUTY *See* Aesthetics
BEAUTY, PERSONAL *See* Personal beauty
The **Beauty.** Ha Jin
Beauty and the opéra; or, The phantom beast. Charnas, S. M.
Beauty and virtue. Maes, A.
The **beauty** contest. Alcântara Machado, A. d.
BEAUTY CONTESTS
Alcântara Machado, A. d. The beauty contest
Bluestein, E. Skin deep
Matheson, R. Miss Stardust
Randolph, L. Miss Kielbasa
Troy, M. The most beautiful girl in the world
Ward, A. E. Miss Montana's wedding day
The **beauty** in bulls. Murphy, Y.
Beauty in the night. Silverberg, R.
Beauty Is a Fate Better than Death. Jelloun, T. B.
The **beauty** monster. Rich, M.
BEAUTY SHOPS
Gardam, J. The hair of the dog
Halpern, F. Goodbye, honey
Michaels, L. Nachman burning
Qi, S. The evidence
         Employees
Jablonski, N. Pam calls her mother on five-cent Sundays
Shayla, H. Himmelen
Beauty Sleeping [Includes a commentary] Kushner, E.
Beauty stolen from another world. Erdrich, L.
BEAVERS
Miller, A. Beavers
Moceri, M. Proper fires
Beavers. Miller, A.
Because his youth or the parrot's Spanish. Ducornet, R.
Bech noir. Updike, J.
Becker, Geoffrey
Black Days
   New England Review v30 no2 p78-87 2009
Cowboy Honeymoon
   Ploughshares v31 no2/3 p31-45 Fall 2005
The Naked Man
   Gettysburg Review v22 no2 p257-66 Summ 2009

Becker, Gina Young
Blood Loss
Southern Humanities Review v40 no3 p266-79
Summ 2006
Beckett, Chris
Piccadilly circus
The Year's best science fiction: twenty-third
annual collection; edited by Gardner Dozois
BECKWOURTH, JAMES PIERSON, 1798-1866
About
Bierce, A. Jim Beckwourth's pond
Bierce, A. Mr. Jim Beckwourth's adventure
Becky Ship: A letter to my patients [Medical Humanities, 31 no1 June 2005] Ship, B.
Become a warrior. Yolen, J.
Becoming number 1. Smith, F.
Becoming revolutionary. Bercovitch, B.
The **bed**. Barthelme, D.
Bed and breakfast. Wolfe, G.
Bed Times. Bonavoglia, A.
Bedard, Brian
Curse of the Corn Borer
The North American Review v291 no3/4 p36-
41 My/Ag 2006
Bedbug. McBain, E.
Bedfordshire. Crowther, P.
Bedforshire. Crowther, P.
The **bedroom** light. Ford, J.
BEDS
Collins, W. A terribly strange bed
Harrison, W. Eleven beds
Reed, K. Escape from shark island
Waters, D. Sheets
Bedtime for Mr. Li. Montgomery, D. J.
A **Bedtime** Story. Clayton, J. J.
Bee beard. Boudinot, R.
Beebe, Lauren
Young Invention
Hanging Loose no86 p103 2005
Beech Hill. Wolfe, G.
Beehive. Erdrich, L.
Been so good to me. McIlvoy, K.
Beep. Blish, J.
BEES
Boudinot, R. Bee beard
Dahl, R. Royal jelly
Hemon, A. The bees, part 1
Johnson, K. At the mouth of the river of bees
Thomas, L. An apiary of white bees
The **bees**. Chaon, D.
The **bees**, part 1. Hemon, A.
BEETHOVEN, LUDWIG VAN, 1770-1827
Smith, A. Fidelio and Bess
Beethoven. Martin, V.
Beethoven was one-sixteenth black. Gordimer, N.
Beethoven's Nephew. Friedman, S.
La **Befana**. Wolfe, G.
Before high desert. Malae, P. N.
Before Lawrence Became Known as Ty McKeesport, PA August 1911. Pilkington, M.
Before light. Lam, V.
Before long. Laken, V.
Before snow comes. Sillitoe, A.
Before the awakening. Andreas-Salomé, L.
Before the wedding. Brazaitis, M.
Beg, sl tog, inc, cont, rep. Hempel, A.

Begamudré, Ven
Out of sync
So long been dreaming; postcolonial science
fiction & fantasy; Nalo Hopkinson &
Uppinder Mehan, eds
"The **beggar**". de Caldas Brito, C.
BEGGARS
Adiga, A. The Cool Water Well Junction
Ajidarma, S. G. Children of the sky
Bacigalupi, P. Pocketful of dharma
Bierce, A. Feodora
Bradbury, R. The beggar on O'Connell Bridge
Daeninckx, D. The man with the collecting-box
de Caldas Brito, C. "The beggar"
Dokey, R. The beggar of Union Square
Fonseca, R. The other
Khan, R. Alms
Modisane, B. The dignity of begging
Walpole, Sir H. The silver mask
Watkins, S. Kafka's sister
Beggars in Spain. Kress, N.
Beginners. Carver, R.
Beginning. Engberg, S.
The **beginning** of grief. Montemarano, N.
The **beginning** of violence. Leedom-Ackerman, J.
Begley, Louis
Cowboys and Indians
The American Scholar v76 no1 p114-20 Wint
2007
BEHAVIOR MODIFICATION
See also Brainwashing
Behind the brick wall. Déry, T.
Behind the curtain. Nolan, W. F.
Behind the veil. Bierce, A.
Behling, Elizabeth Harris
(tr.) See Mozzi, Giulio
Behold My Son Issac. Azevedo, K. de
Behold the Don. Almond, S.
Behold the man. Moorcock, M.
Behrens, Peter
Feel This
The Walrus v5 no9 p60-63 D 2008
The Smell of Smoke
The Walrus v3 no8 p76-80 O 2006
Beigbeder, Frederic
Manuscript found at Saint-Germain-des-Prés
Paris tales; stories; translated by Helen Constantine
BEIJING (CHINA) *See* China—Beijing
Being. Matheson, R.
Being and nothingness. Hecht, J.
Being Chandra. Altomonte, E.
Being here. Lalumière, C.
Being like bulls. Malla, P.
Being right. Smith, M. M.
BEIRUT (LEBANON) *See* Lebanon—Beirut
Bela Lugosi's dead. Threatt, A.
Bela's plot. Kiernan, C. R.
BELFAST (NORTHERN IRELAND) *See* Northern Ireland—Belfast
A **Belfast** memory. MacLaverty, B.
BELGIUM
Koënings, N. S. Pearls to swine
Bruges
Gardam, J. The virgins of Bruges
Belief. Barthelme, D.
Believers. Keane, M. B.
Belinda. Gaige, A.
Belisario. Piñera, V.

BELIZE
  Daughtry, P. Jungle roads
  Daughtry, P. Trickle Creek
  Massie, E. The landlock
  Meno, J. Ghost plane
Bell, Anthea
  (tr.) See Biller, Maxim
Bell, Julia
  Help the aged
    Going the distance; edited by Alan Beard
Bell, Katherine
  The casual car pool
    The Best American short stories, 2006; select-
    ed from U.S. and Canadian magazines by
    Ann Patchett with Katrina Kenison; with an
    introduction by Ann Patchett
    Ploughshares v31 no2/3 p46-64 Fall 2005
Bell, M. Shayne
  Anomalous structures of my dreams
    The Year's best science fiction: twenty-first
    annual collection; edited by Gardner Dozois
Bell, Steinur
  Someone Had to Tell Them
    South Carolina Review v37 no1 p159-68 Fall
    2004
Bell, Ted
  The powder monkey
    Thriller; edited by James Patterson
The **bell-curve** drug. Kling, J.
The **bell** . . . from HELL!!!. Strand, J.
The **bell** ringer. Burnside, J.
BELL-RINGERS *See* Bells and bell ringers
Bellatin, Mario
  The Sheika's condition
    Words without borders; the world through the
    eyes of writers; an anthology; edited by
    Samantha Schnee, Alane Salierno Mason,
    and Dedi Felman
La **Belle** Dame. Ronk, M. C.
Belle Haven. Pietrzyk, L.
BELLINI, VINCENZO, 1801-1835
                  About
  Green, G. "Such dear ecstasy"
Bellos, David
  (tr.) See Kadare, Ismail
Bellow, Saul
  Grandma Lausch
    Inside the hornet's head; an anthology of
    Jewish American writing; edited by Jerome
    Charyn
Bellows, Nathaniel
  First four measures
    The Best American short stories, 2005; select-
    ed from U.S. and Canadian magazines by
    Michael Chabon with Katrina Kenison;
    with an introduction by Michael Chabon
BELLS AND BELL RINGERS
  Burnside, J. The bell ringer
The **bells** of Shoredan (Dilvish 3 of 11). Zelazny,
  R.
Bell's station. Cook, W.
Belly. Krysl, M.
Belmar. Martin, J.
Belonging impossible, longing all there is. Breslin,
  S.
Beloved of the Sky. Conkie, J. L.
Below the Gospels. Gildner, G.

Belrose, J. L.
  House built of sticks
    Women of mystery; an anthology; Katherine
    V. Forrest, editor
Beltrame, Sara
  Sara Beltrame
    The Literary Review (Madison, N.J.) v49 no1
    p148-54 Fall 2005
Beltran, Rosa
  Shere-Sade/Sheri-Sade
    Best of contemporary Mexican fiction; Alvaro
    Uribe, editor; Olivia Sears, translation edi-
    tor
Bely, Andrey
  Petersburg [excerpt]
    Worlds apart; an anthology of Russian fantasy
    and science fiction; edited and with com-
    mentary by Alexander Levitsky; translated
    by Alexander Levitsky and Martha T.
    Kitchen
Belyĭ, Andreĭ *See* Bely, Andrey, 1880-1934
Benaron, Naomi
  The Chemical Nature of Things
    Calyx v23 no3 p12-18 Wint 2007
  Directions
    New Letters v73 no4 p105-14 2007
Benbow, Margaret
  Egyptian
    Barnstorm; contemporary Wisconsin fiction;
    edited by Raphael Kadushin
The **bench**. Ruefle, M.
Benchley, Robert
  The mystery of the poisoned kipper
    The vicious circle; mystery and crime stories
    by members of the Algonquin Round Ta-
    ble; edited by Otto Penzler
Bender, Aimee
  The case of the salt and pepper shakers
    McSweeney's mammoth treasury of thrilling
    tales; edited by Michael Chabon
    Bender, A. Willful creatures; stories
  Dearth
    Bender, A. Willful creatures; stories
    The James Tiptree Award Anthology 3; edited
    by Karen Joy Fowler [et al.]
  Death wish
    Bender, A. Willful creatures; stories
  Debbieland
    Bender, A. Willful creatures; stories
  End of the line
    Bender, A. Willful creatures; stories
    The Pushcart Prize XXX: best of the small
    presses 2006; edited by Bill Henderson
    with the Pushcart Prize editors
    Best of Tin House; stories; foreword by Dor-
    othy Allison
  Even Steven
    Stumbling and raging; more politically in-
    spired fiction; edited by Stephen Elliott;
    with associate editors Greg Larson [et al.]
  Fruit and words
    Bender, A. Willful creatures; stories
  The girl in the flammable skirt
    The Anchor book of new American short sto-
    ries; edited by Ben Marcus
  The healer
    Feeling very strange; the Slipstream antholo-
    gy; James Patrick Kelly & John Kessel, ed-
    itors

Bender, Aimee—*Continued*

Hymn
  Bender, A. Willful creatures; stories
I will pick out your ribs (from my teeth)
  Bender, A. Willful creatures; stories
Ironhead
  Bender, A. Willful creatures; stories
Jinx
  Pushcart prize XXVII; best of the small
    presses; edited by Bill Henderson with the
    Pushcart prize editors
  Bender, A. Willful creatures; stories
Job's jobs
  Bender, A. Willful creatures; stories
The leading man
  Bender, A. Willful creatures; stories
Marzipan
  Before; short stories about pregnancy from
    our top writers; edited by Emily Franklin
    and Heather Swain
The meeting
  Bender, A. Willful creatures; stories
Motherfucker
  Bender, A. Willful creatures; stories
Off
  Bender, A. Willful creatures; stories
  Beha, C. R. The Ecco anthology of contem-
    porary American short fiction; selected by
    Joyce Carol Oates and Christopher R.
    Beha.
Two days
  This is not chick lit; original stories by Amer-
    ica's best women writers; edited by Eliza-
    beth Merrick

Bender, Karen E.

Candidate
  New stories from the South; the year's best,
    2008; selected from U.S. magazines by ZZ
    Packer with Kathy Pories; with an introduc-
    tion by ZZ Packer
Refund
  Pushcart prize XXXI: best of the small press-
    es 2007; edited by Bill Henderson; with the
    Pushcart Prize editors
  Ploughshares v31 no1 p71-87 Spr 2005
Reunion
  Ploughshares v33 no2/3 p7-32 Fall 2007
Theft
  The Best American Mystery Stories, 2006;
    edited and with an introduction by Scott
    Turow; Otto Penzler, series editor
  Harvard Review (1992) no29 p37-50 2005
The Visiting Child
  Granta no91 p77-93 Fall 2005
What the Cat Said
  Harvard Review (1992) no34 p56-60 2008
The **Bends**. Mott, J.
Beneath. Gollatz, G.
Beneath Black Bayou. Kelly, R.
Beneath the deep, slow motion. Barkley, B.
Benedict, Elizabeth
FAQ
  The dictionary of failed relationships; 26 tales
    of love gone wrong; edited by Meredith
    Broussard

Benedict, Pinckney

Bridge of sighs
  New stories from the South; the year's best,
    2008; selected from U.S. magazines by ZZ
    Packer with Kathy Pories; with an introduc-
    tion by ZZ Packer
Irish mountain
  Pushcart Prize XXVIII: best of the small
    presses 2004; edited by Bill Henderson and
    the Pushcart prize editors
Mercy
  Pushcart prize XXXII: best of the small
    presses 2008; edited by Bill Henderson
    with the Pushcart Prize editors
  Beha, C. R. The Ecco anthology of contem-
    porary American short fiction; selected by
    Joyce Carol Oates and Christopher R.
    Beha.
Mudman
  Best of Tin House; stories; foreword by Dor-
    othy Allison
Pig Helmet & The Wall of Life
  StoryQuarterly v42 p25-40 2006
Benediction. McGahan, J.
Benediction: excerpt from The warlord of the air.
  Moorcock, M.
A **beneficiary**. Gordimer, N.
Beneficient diversions from the crackdkins diet.
  Alexander, D.
The **benefit** of the doubt. Wolff, T.
The **benefits** of culture. Zoshchenko, M.
A **Benevolence** of Ladybugs. Slater, J.
Benford, Gregory
Applied mathematical theology
  Nature v440 p126 Mr 2 2006
Bow shock
  The Year's best science fiction: twenty-fourth
    annual collection; edited by Gardner Dozois
Dark heaven
  The Year's best science fiction: twenty-fifth
    annual collection; edited by Gardner Dozois
How to write a scientific paper
  This is my funniest 2; leading science fiction
    writers present their funniest stories ever;
    edited by Mike Resnick
SETI for profit
  Nature v452 p1032 Ap 24 2008
The worm turns
  The new space opera; edited by Gardner
    Dozois and Jonathan Strahan
(jt. auth) See Eklund, Gordon and Benford,
  Gregory
Bengal, Rebecca
Mash Turning
  Southwest Review v90 no2 p290-308 2005
BENGAL (INDIA AND BANGLADESH)
  Dahl, R. Poison
Benioff, David
The barefoot girl in clover
  Benioff, D. When the nines roll over and oth-
    er stories
De composition
  Benioff, D. When the nines roll over and oth-
    er stories
The devil comes to Orekhovo
  Benioff, D. When the nines roll over and oth-
    er stories

Benioff, David—*Continued*
Garden of no
　Benioff, D. When the nines roll over and other stories
Neversink
　Benioff, D. When the nines roll over and other stories
When the nines roll over
　Benioff, D. When the nines roll over and other stories
When the nines roll over and other stories
　Benioff, D. When the nines roll over and other stories
Zoanthropy
　Benioff, D. When the nines roll over and other stories
　Best of Tin House; stories; foreword by Dorothy Allison
Benjamin, Carol Lea
The last supper
　Manhattan noir; edited by Lawrence Block
Benjamin, Paul *See* Auster, Paul, 1947-
Benji's pencil. McAllister, B.
Benmalek, Anouar
Eve
　World Literature Today v82 no1 p50-2 Ja/F 2008
Bennett, Arnold
A comedy on the gold coast
　The Penguin book of Gaslight crime; con artists, burglars, rogues, and scoundrels from the time of Sherlock Holmes; edited with an introduction and notes by Michael Sims.
Murder!
　The Mammoth book of vintage whodunnits; edited by Maxim Jakubowski
Bennett, Enoch Arnold *See* Bennett, Arnold, 1867-1931
Bennett, Gertrude Barrows *See* Stevens, Francis, b. 1884
Bennett, Lerone
The convert
　Short stories of the civil rights movement; an anthology; edited by Margaret Earley Whitt
Bennett, Penelope
Just a Speck
　Confrontation no101 p144-61 Spr/Summ 2008
Bennett, Terry
All the same
　Bennett, T. Antioxidants and other stories
Antioxidants
　Bennett, T. Antioxidants and other stories
Blind faith
　Bennett, T. Antioxidants and other stories
Checkout #5
　Bennett, T. Antioxidants and other stories
Filigree
　Bennett, T. Antioxidants and other stories
Lesson plan
　Bennett, T. Antioxidants and other stories
Matinee
　Bennett, T. Antioxidants and other stories
Saving Grace
　Bennett, T. Antioxidants and other stories
Trading corners
　Bennett, T. Antioxidants and other stories
Wishbone
　Bennett, T. Antioxidants and other stories

Bennett, Terrence James *See* Bennett, Terry, 1948-
Bennie Rojas and the rough riders. Medina, P.
BENNY, JACK, 1894-1974
About
　Betancourt, J. G. Invasion of the Jack Benny snatchers
Benny. Raymond, J.
Benny gets the blame. Boylan, C.
Benny's space. Muller, M.
Bensko, John
A cabin in the woods
　Bensko, J. Sea dogs
Creeping things
　Bensko, J. Sea dogs
Flying St. Croix
　Bensko, J. Sea dogs
The ocean
　Bensko, J. Sea dogs
Out from Guadalajara
　Bensko, J. Sea dogs
Painted animals
　Bensko, J. Sea dogs
The Painted Snake
　The Georgia Review v60 no1 p36-50 Spr 2006
The palm and the cat
　Bensko, J. Sea dogs
The robber
　Bensko, J. Sea dogs
Sea dogs
　Bensko, J. Sea dogs
Sirens
　Bensko, J. Sea dogs
A spell
　Bensko, J. Sea dogs
Summer girls
　Bensko, J. Sea dogs
Tequila worms
　Bensko, J. Sea dogs
Bent twig. West, D.
Bentham, Rachel
When should we live?
　Her Majesty; 21 stories by women; edited by Jackie Gay and Emma Hargrave
Bentil, Thomas
Lost and found
　Bronx noir; edited by S. J. Rozan
Benvenuto, Christine
Sextet
　Gettysburg Review v19 no3 p425-45 Aut 2006
Ber-Lulu. Hammett, D.
Bercovitch, Bryna
Becoming revolutionary
　Arguing with the storm; stories by Yiddish women writers; edited and with a preface by Rhea Tregebov; introduction by Kathryn Hellerstein.
Berdeshevsky, Margo
Donkeys
　Confrontation no102/103 p66-73 Wint 2008/Spr 2009
Pas de Deux, à Trois
　Agni no66 p10-17 2007
Troika for Lovers
　Agni no69 p146-51 2009
BEREAVEMENT
　Abbott, L. K. The end of grief

Berg, Elizabeth—*Continued*

The only one of millions just like him
  Berg, E. The day I ate whatever I wanted;
    and other small acts of liberation
Over the hill and into the woods
  Berg, E. The day I ate whatever I wanted;
    and other small acts of liberation
The party
  Berg, E. The day I ate whatever I wanted;
    and other small acts of liberation
Rain
  Berg, E. The day I ate whatever I wanted;
    and other small acts of liberation
Returns & Exchanges
  Good Housekeeping v246 no5 p203, 205,
    207-8, 210-14 My 2008
Returns and exchanges
  Berg, E. The day I ate whatever I wanted;
    and other small acts of liberation
Sin city
  Berg, E. The day I ate whatever I wanted;
    and other small acts of liberation
Truth or dare
  Berg, E. The day I ate whatever I wanted;
    and other small acts of liberation

Berg, Mary A.
  (tr.) See García González, Francisco
  (tr.) See García Somodevilla, Alexis Sebas-
    tián
  (tr.) See Vega Serova, Anna Lidia

Berg, Mary G.
  (tr.) See Fernández de Jaun, Adelaida

Bergelson, David
The deal man
  No star too beautiful; Yiddish stories from
    1382 to the present; compiled and translat-
    ed by Joachim Neugroschel
Two roads
  No star too beautiful; Yiddish stories from
    1382 to the present; compiled and translat-
    ed by Joachim Neugroschel
Without a trace
  No star too beautiful; Yiddish stories from
    1382 to the present; compiled and translat-
    ed by Joachim Neugroschel

Bergen, David
Just the Thing
  The Walrus v5 no1 p75-6 Ja/F 2008
Saved
  The Walrus v6 no2 p51-5 Mr 2009

Berger, Barbara Helen
Brother Simple
  Parabola v32 no3 p24-7 Fall 2007
Mistakes [With commentary]
  Parabola v32 no1 p90-1 Spr 2007

Berger, Sande Boritz
A Split-Level Life
  TriQuarterly no126 p131-42 2006

Bergman, Lucy
Damned if you don't
  Nature v435 p1002 Je 16 2005

Bergstrom, Elaine
Accidental invasion
  Kolchak: the night stalker chronicles; 26 orig-
    inal tales of the surreal, the bizarre, the ma-
    cabre; edited by Joe Gentile, Garrett Ander-
    son, Lori Gentile; Kolchak created by Jeff
    Rice

Bergua, Ana Garcia
Los conservadores/The preservers
  Best of contemporary Mexican fiction; Alvaro
    Uribe, editor; Olivia Sears, translation edi-
    tor

Berkeley, Anthony
The avenging chance
  Murder short & sweet; edited by Paul D.
    Staudohar
Dark journey
  Murder short & sweet; edited by Paul D.
    Staudohar

BERKELEY (CALIF.) *See* California—Berkeley
BERLIN (GERMANY) *See* Germany—Berlin
A **Berlin** Story. Stern, R.
BERLIN WALL
  Oates, J. C. Our wall

Berliner, Janet
High kicks and misdemeanors
  The Horror Writers Association presents
    Blood lite; an anthology of humorous hor-
    ror stories; edited by Kevin J. Anderson
The road to Rachel
  Las Vegas noir; edited by Jarrett Keene &
    Todd James Pierce.

Berliner. Tomlinson, J.
Berlinski, Mischa
In the Dark
  New England Review v28 no1 p99-104 2007

Berman, Steve
Tearjerker
  Sedia, E. Paper cities; an anthology of urban
    fantasy

BERMUDA
  Maxwell, W. Grape Bay (1941)
Bern. Daugherty, T.
Bernard, Kenneth
Flâneur
  Salmagundi no144/145 p88-91 Fall 2004/Wint
    2005
Out of Time, Out of Place
  Salmagundi no155/156 p241-50 Summ/Fall
    2007

Bernardo's house. Kelly, J. P.
Berner, Jennie
The Dance
  Boston Review v31 no4 p25 Jl/Ag 2006

Bernhardt-House, Phillip A.
Epicycle: King Niall and the Child without a
    Father
  Parabola v32 no2 p18-20 Summ 2007

Bernheimer, Kate
A Cuckoo Tale
  Western Humanities Review v62 no1 p68-78
    Wint 2008

Berniced. Minot, E.
Bernier, Craig
An Affliction of Starlings
  Western Humanities Review v61 no1 p56-66
    Wint 2007
Migration
  Detroit noir; edited by E. J. Olsen & John C.
    Hocking

Berniker, Sara Joan
Aqua Velva Smitty
  Playboy's college fiction; a collection of 21
    years of contest winners; edited by Alice
    K. Turner; foreword by Thom Jones

Bernstein, Leonard S.
Dating Deborah Kerr
   Prairie Schooner v80 no1 p181-5 Spr 2006
Searching for Seventh Avenue
   Prairie Schooner v81 no2 p44-9 Summ 2007
Bernstein, Susan David
Transparent
   Women's Studies Quarterly v36 no3/4 p271-8
   Fall/Wint 2008
Berrada, Mohammed
A life in detail
   The Anchor book of modern African stories;
   edited by Nadežda Obradovic; with a fore-
   word by Chinua Achebe
Berreby, David
The punishment fits the crime
   Nature v440 p254 Mr 9 2006
Berrington, Lucy
Love Good Hate Evil
   New England Review v30 no2 p28-60 2009
Berry, Jedediah
Inheritance
   Best new American voices 2008; guest editor
   Richard Bausch; series editors John Kulka
   and Natalie Danford
To measure the earth
   Salon fantastique; edited and with an intro-
   duction by Ellen Datlow and Terri
   Windling
Berry, P.
Guesswork and guilt—the mind of a suicide
   [Medical Humanities, v30 no2 December
   2004]
   Journal of Medical Ethics v30 no2 p82-4 D
   2004 supp
Berry, Steve
The devils' due
   Thriller; edited by James Patterson
Berry, Wendell
Burley Coulter's Fortunate Fall
   The Sewanee Review v116 no2 p264-73 Spr
   2008
The Dark Country
   The Sewanee Review v117 no2 p163-80 Spr
   2009
A Desirable Woman
   The Hudson Review v61 no2 p295-314 Summ
   2008
The hurt man
   The O. Henry Prize stories, 2005; edited and
   with an introduction by Laura Furman
   The Pushcart Prize XXIX: best of the small
   presses 2005; edited by Bill Henderson
   with the Pushcart Prize editors
Mike
   New stories from the South: the year's best,
   2006; selected from U.S. magazines by Al-
   lan Gurganus with Kathy Pories; with an
   introduction by Allan Gurganus
   The Sewanee Review v113 no1 p1-15 Wint
   2005
A Place in Time: Some Chapters of a Telling
   Story
   The Hudson Review v62 no2 p217-38 Summ
   2009
The Requirement
   Harper's v314 p77-80 Mr 2007

Return to Port William
   The Christian Century v124 no1 p20-5 Ja 9
   2007
Whitefoot
   Orion v26 no1 p44-52 Ja/F 2007
Berry, Betsy
Family and flood
   Lone Star literature; from the Red River to
   the Rio Grande; edited by Don Graham
Bertino, Maria-Helene
Free Ham
   The North American Review v292 no3/4 p16-
   20 My/Ag 2007
Bertino, Marie
North of
   Pushcart prize XXXIII: best of the small
   presses 2009; edited by Bill Henderson
   with the Pushcart Prize editors
Bertino, Marie-Helene
Free Ham
   The North American Review v293 no5 p30-4
   S/O 2008
Berwin, Margot
Perfection
   2033; the future of misbehavior: interplane-
   tary dating, Madame President, socialized
   plastic surgery, and other good news from
   the future; from the editors of Nerve.com;
   instigated by Svedka
Beside dreams. Sundaresan, I.
Besserman, Perle
The Sackman Street Boys
   Agni no67 p24-31 2008
Bessie. West, D.
Bessora
The milka cow
   From Africa; new francophone stories; edited
   by Adele King
Best, Laura
The Bread Poultice
   Dalhousie Review v87 no2 p225-32 Summ
   2007
Windows
   Dalhousie Review v86 no2 p283-9 Summ
   2006
The **best**. Rippen, C.
The **best** Christmas ever. Kelly, J. P.
Best eaten cold. Wilson, L.
The **best** friend-murder. Westlake, D. E.
The **best** jeweler. Martin, C.
The **best** laid plans. Maloney, D.
The **best** man. Dean, D.
Best man wins. Waterman, F.
Best new horror. Hill, J.
The **best** of Betty. Willett, J.
The **best** part. Spiegelman, P.
The **best** place to be. Dormen, L.
The **best** revenge. Newman, L.
The **best** time for planting. Coelen, I.
Best western. Erdrich, L.
The **Best** Year of My Life. Theroux, P.
BESTIALITY
   Sinha, U. Parvati
Bestiary. O'Connor, S.
The **Bestseller** of Beau Diamond. Ewing, B.

Bestwick, Simon
  Hazy shade of winter
    The Year's best fantasy and horror: eighteenth
      annual collection; edited by Ellen Datlow,
      Kelly Link & Gavin J. Grant
  Hushabye
    Inferno; new tales of terror and the supernatu-
      ral; edited by Ellen Datlow.
Beswetherick, Sandra
  Angelique's
    Cat tales: fantastic feline fiction; edited by
      George H. Scithers
A **Bet**. Keret, E.
Bet on red. Abbott, J.
Betancourt, John Gregory
  Invasion of the Jack Benny snatchers
    This is my funniest 2; leading science fiction
      writers present their funniest stories ever;
      edited by Mike Resnick
Betancourt, Luis Adrián
  Guilty
    Passport to crime; the finest mystery stories
      from International Crime Writers; edited by
      Janet Hutchings
Bête noire. DeMarinis, R.
Bethany's wood. Finch, P.
Beth's law. Lane, J.
Betrayal. Chen, W.
Betrayals. Hassan, I.
Betrayed by David Bowie. Raphael, L.
BETROTHALS
  Albert, E. So long
  Collins, M. A. and Clemens, M. V. East Side,
    West Side
  Dunbar, P. L. His bride of the tomb
  Dunbar, P. L. Jimmy Weedon's contretemps
  Iarovici, D. Facts
  Jones, N. Home for a short time
  Judah, S. The courtship of Naomi Samuel
  Judah, S. Dropped from heaven
  Judah, S. A girl from my hometown
  Judah, S. My friend Joseph
  Kun, M. The handwriting patient
  Mohanraj, M. A. The emigrant (Colombo, 1979)
  Mohanraj, M. A. A gentle man (Massachusettes,
    1979)
  Munro, A. The ticket
  Opatoshu, J. A house on Gorek Street
  Opatoshu, J. Saloon—night
  Rheinheimer, K. Debut
  Romano, T. Silences
  Ward, A. E. Butte as in beautiful
  Westcott, G. The dove came down
  Williams, C. The night before
  Wingate, S. Meeting Grace
  Wood, D. The depthlessness of soup
BETS See Wagers
Betsy. Fonseca, R.
A **better** angel. Adrian, C.
The **better** boy. Powers, T.
Better guns. Rabe, J.
Better half. Krasikov, S.
Better luck next time. Zellar, B.
Better lucky than good. Stein, J. C.
A **better** mousetrap. Resnick, M.
Better than counting sheep. Johnson, C. R.
Better Than Court TV: Sensational Cases from the
  NYC Courts. Novack, C.
Better than home. Hill, J.

A **better** view of paradise [Adaptation] Coburn, R.
  S.
A **better** view of paradise [Adapted from the nov-
  el] Coburn, R. S.
A **better** view of paradise [Excerpt] Coburn, R. S.
A **better** world's in birth!. Waldrop, H.
BETTING See Gambling
Betting on Men. Frank, J.
Betts, Kristie
  Breeding Season
    Southern Humanities Review v40 no3 p252-61
      Summ 2006
Betty Brown Calling. Byers, M.
Betty the zombie. Crane, E.
Between. Long, N. A.
Between Camelots. Ebenbach, D. H.
Between eight and nine o'clock. Garton, R.
Between here and the yellow sea. Pizzolatto, N.
Between Here and the Yellow Sea. Pizzolatto, N.
Between here and there. Messinger, J.
Between states. Downs, G.
Between the Devil and the Deep Sea. Dayan, C.
. . . **Between** the gargoyle trees. Kiernan, C. R.
Between the lines. Cotrina, J. A.
Between the lines. Dexter, C.
Between the porch and the altar. Stafford, J.
Between the sheets. Corso, P.
Between Wrecks. Singleton, G.
Beulah Berlin, an A-Z. Boyd, W.
Beulah land. McGruder, K.
BEVERLY HILLS (CALIF.) See California—
  Beverly Hills
Beverly Home. Johnson, D.
Bevete del vino. Reid, G.
Beware of the dog. Dahl, R.
Beware the pale horse comes riding. Wieland, M.
Beyond All Blessing and Song, Praise and Conso-
  lation. Raffel, D.
Beyond Mao. Di Filippo, P.
Beyond pain. Faber, M.
Beyond Rapture. Miller, T.
Beyond the Aquila rift. Reynolds, A.
Beyond the border. Klassen, S.
Beyond the clouds. Maḥfūẓ, N.
Beyond the great snow mountains. L'Amour, L.
Beyond the Overpass. Winter, M.
Beyond the Pale: A Story. Epstein, J.
Beyond the river. Lane, J.
Beyond the sea gate of the scholar-pirates of
  Sarsköe. Nix, G.
Beyond the singing flame. Smith, C. A.
Beyond the wall. Bierce, A.
Beyond the wall. Stanchfield, J.
Beyond the years. Spencer, M. E.
Bezmozgis, David
  Natasha
    The Best American short stories, 2005; select-
      ed from U.S. and Canadian magazines by
      Michael Chabon with Katrina Kenison;
      with an introduction by Michael Chabon
    My mistress's sparrow is dead; great love sto-
      ries, from Chekhov to Munro; edited by
      Jeffrey Eugenides
  A new gravestone for an old grave
    The Best American short stories, 2006; select-
      ed from U.S. and Canadian magazines by
      Ann Patchett with Katrina Kenison; with an
      introduction by Ann Patchett

Bezmozgis, David—*Continued*

The Proposition
Harper's v315 p80-4 S 2007

The Russian Riviera
The New Yorker v81 no15 p74-85 My 30 2005

Bhêly-Quénum, Olympe

A child in the bush of ghosts
The Anchor book of modern African stories; edited by Nadežda Obradovic; with a foreword by Chinua Achebe

Biaz, Brooke

The Disappearing Father
Dalhousie Review v84 no3 p463-9 Summ 2004

BIBLE

SInger, M. Hazor

BIBLE. N.T. CORINTHIANS

Mordecai, P. Corinthians thirteen thirteen

The **Bible**. Duras, M.

BIBLICAL STORIES

Barnard, R. The Cairo Road

Borges, J. L. The Gospel according to Mark

Brett, S. Cain was innocent

Cutler, J. Judith

Disch, T. M. Torah! Torah! Torah!: three Bible tales for the third millennium

Douglas, C. N. Strangers in a strange land

James, C. L. R. David and Goliath

Pollack, R. Burning Beard: the dreams and visions of Joseph Ben Jacob, Lord Viceroy of Egypt

Rosenbaum, B. The book of Jashar

Singer, I. B. The death of Methuselah

Winsor, C. The last Israelite in the Red Sea

Bicycle kick. Messinger, J.

The **Bicycle** Lesson. Campbell, E. P.

BICYCLE RACING

Roberts, A. Tour de Lune

Bicycle repairman. Sterling, B.

BICYCLES AND BICYCLING

Boyd, W. Varengeville

Capps, T. Alice

Estep, M. Boneshaker

Feitell, M. Bike New York!

Kadetsky, E. Men more than mortal

Malla, P. Timber on the wheel of everyone

Peck, D. Dues

Pinski, D. At the attorney's

Sillitoe, A. The bike

Sterling, B. Bicycle repairman

Zhu Wen. Wheels

Bid Don's dream of soccerdemia. Walker, G.

Bid farewell to her many horses. Urrea, L. A.

The **Bidden**. Gray, V.

Biely, Andrei *See* Bely, Andrey, 1880-1934

Bierce, Ambrose

The aborigines of Oakland
Bierce, A. The short fiction of Ambrose Bierce, volume 1; edited by S. T. Joshi, Lawrence I. Berkove, and David E. Schultz

Across the continent
Bierce, A. The short fiction of Ambrose Bierce, volume 1; edited by S. T. Joshi, Lawrence I. Berkove, and David E. Schultz

An adventure at Brownville
Bierce, A. The short fiction of Ambrose Bierce, volume 2; edited by S. T. Joshi, Lawrence I. Berkove, and David E. Schultz

The affair at Coulter's Notch
Bierce, A. The short fiction of Ambrose Bierce, volume 2; edited by S. T. Joshi, Lawrence I. Berkove, and David E. Schultz

An affair of outposts
Bierce, A. The short fiction of Ambrose Bierce, volume 3; edited by S. T. Joshi, Lawrence I. Berkove, and David E. Schultz

An ancient hunter
Bierce, A. The short fiction of Ambrose Bierce, volume 3; edited by S. T. Joshi, Lawrence I. Berkove, and David E. Schultz

The applicant
Bierce, A. The short fiction of Ambrose Bierce, volume 2; edited by S. T. Joshi, Lawrence I. Berkove, and David E. Schultz

Ashes of the beacon
Bierce, A. The short fiction of Ambrose Bierce, volume 3; edited by S. T. Joshi, Lawrence I. Berkove, and David E. Schultz

Authenticating a ghost
Bierce, A. The short fiction of Ambrose Bierce, volume 1; edited by S. T. Joshi, Lawrence I. Berkove, and David E. Schultz

A baby tramp
Bierce, A. The short fiction of Ambrose Bierce, volume 2; edited by S. T. Joshi, Lawrence I. Berkove, and David E. Schultz

"A bad woman"
Bierce, A. The short fiction of Ambrose Bierce, volume 1; edited by S. T. Joshi, Lawrence I. Berkove, and David E. Schultz

Banking at Mexican Hill
Bierce, A. The short fiction of Ambrose Bierce, volume 1; edited by S. T. Joshi, Lawrence I. Berkove, and David E. Schultz

The baptism of Dobsho
Bierce, A. The short fiction of Ambrose Bierce, volume 1; edited by S. T. Joshi, Lawrence I. Berkove, and David E. Schultz

Behind the veil
Bierce, A. The short fiction of Ambrose Bierce, volume 2; edited by S. T. Joshi, Lawrence I. Berkove, and David E. Schultz

Beyond the wall
Bierce, A. The short fiction of Ambrose Bierce, volume 3; edited by S. T. Joshi, Lawrence I. Berkove, and David E. Schultz

A bit of chivalry
Bierce, A. The short fiction of Ambrose Bierce, volume 1; edited by S. T. Joshi, Lawrence I. Berkove, and David E. Schultz

The boarded window
Bierce, A. The short fiction of Ambrose Bierce, volume 2; edited by S. T. Joshi, Lawrence I. Berkove, and David E. Schultz

Boarding a bear
Bierce, A. The short fiction of Ambrose Bierce, volume 1; edited by S. T. Joshi, Lawrence I. Berkove, and David E. Schultz

Bodies of the dead [I]
Bierce, A. The short fiction of Ambrose Bierce, volume 2; edited by S. T. Joshi, Lawrence I. Berkove, and David E. Schultz

Bodies of the dead [II]
Bierce, A. The short fiction of Ambrose Bierce, volume 2; edited by S. T. Joshi, Lawrence I. Berkove, and David E. Schultz

Bierce, Ambrose—*Continued*

Killed at Resaca
  Bierce, A. The short fiction of Ambrose
    Bierce, volume 2; edited by S. T. Joshi,
    Lawrence I. Berkove, and David E. Schultz

The kingdom of Tortirra
  Bierce, A. The short fiction of Ambrose
    Bierce, volume 2; edited by S. T. Joshi,
    Lawrence I. Berkove, and David E. Schultz

L. S.
  Bierce, A. The short fiction of Ambrose
    Bierce, volume 1; edited by S. T. Joshi,
    Lawrence I. Berkove, and David E. Schultz

A lady from Redhorse
  Bierce, A. The short fiction of Ambrose
    Bierce, volume 2; edited by S. T. Joshi,
    Lawrence I. Berkove, and David E. Schultz

The land beyond the blow
  Bierce, A. The short fiction of Ambrose
    Bierce, volume 3; edited by S. T. Joshi,
    Lawrence I. Berkove, and David E. Schultz

Largo al Gapperino
  Bierce, A. The short fiction of Ambrose
    Bierce, volume 1; edited by S. T. Joshi,
    Lawrence I. Berkove, and David E. Schultz

The late Dowling, senior
  Bierce, A. The short fiction of Ambrose
    Bierce, volume 1; edited by S. T. Joshi,
    Lawrence I. Berkove, and David E. Schultz

The late John Sweetbosh, Esq.
  Bierce, A. The short fiction of Ambrose
    Bierce, volume 1; edited by S. T. Joshi,
    Lawrence I. Berkove, and David E. Schultz

A leaf blown in from days to be
  Bierce, A. The short fiction of Ambrose
    Bierce, volume 3; edited by S. T. Joshi,
    Lawrence I. Berkove, and David E. Schultz

Letters from a Hdkhoite
  Bierce, A. The short fiction of Ambrose
    Bierce, volume 1; edited by S. T. Joshi,
    Lawrence I. Berkove, and David E. Schultz

The lion at bay
  Bierce, A. The short fiction of Ambrose
    Bierce, volume 1; edited by S. T. Joshi,
    Lawrence I. Berkove, and David E. Schultz

A literary riot
  Bierce, A. The short fiction of Ambrose
    Bierce, volume 1; edited by S. T. Joshi,
    Lawrence I. Berkove, and David E. Schultz

Little Larry
  Bierce, A. The short fiction of Ambrose
    Bierce, volume 1; edited by S. T. Joshi,
    Lawrence I. Berkove, and David E. Schultz

The little story
  Bierce, A. The short fiction of Ambrose
    Bierce, volume 1; edited by S. T. Joshi,
    Lawrence I. Berkove, and David E. Schultz

"Love's labor lost"
  Bierce, A. The short fiction of Ambrose
    Bierce, volume 1; edited by S. T. Joshi,
    Lawrence I. Berkove, and David E. Schultz

The magician's little joke
  Bierce, A. The short fiction of Ambrose
    Bierce, volume 1; edited by S. T. Joshi,
    Lawrence I. Berkove, and David E. Schultz

The maid of Podunk
  Bierce, A. The short fiction of Ambrose
    Bierce, volume 3; edited by S. T. Joshi,
    Lawrence I. Berkove, and David E. Schultz

The major's tale
  Bierce, A. The short fiction of Ambrose
    Bierce, volume 2; edited by S. T. Joshi,
    Lawrence I. Berkove, and David E. Schultz

The man and the snake
  Bierce, A. The short fiction of Ambrose
    Bierce, volume 2; edited by S. T. Joshi,
    Lawrence I. Berkove, and David E. Schultz

The man out of the nose
  Bierce, A. The short fiction of Ambrose
    Bierce, volume 2; edited by S. T. Joshi,
    Lawrence I. Berkove, and David E. Schultz

The man overboard
  Bierce, A. The short fiction of Ambrose
    Bierce, volume 1; edited by S. T. Joshi,
    Lawrence I. Berkove, and David E. Schultz

A man with two lives
  Bierce, A. The short fiction of Ambrose
    Bierce, volume 3; edited by S. T. Joshi,
    Lawrence I. Berkove, and David E. Schultz

Marooned on Ug
  Bierce, A. The short fiction of Ambrose
    Bierce, volume 3; edited by S. T. Joshi,
    Lawrence I. Berkove, and David E. Schultz

Maud's papa
  Bierce, A. The short fiction of Ambrose
    Bierce, volume 1; edited by S. T. Joshi,
    Lawrence I. Berkove, and David E. Schultz

Maumee's mission
  Bierce, A. The short fiction of Ambrose
    Bierce, volume 1; edited by S. T. Joshi,
    Lawrence I. Berkove, and David E. Schultz

The middle toe of the right foot
  Bierce, A. The short fiction of Ambrose
    Bierce, volume 2; edited by S. T. Joshi,
    Lawrence I. Berkove, and David E. Schultz

A midsummer day's dream
  Bierce, A. The short fiction of Ambrose
    Bierce, volume 1; edited by S. T. Joshi,
    Lawrence I. Berkove, and David E. Schultz

The miraculous guest
  Bierce, A. The short fiction of Ambrose
    Bierce, volume 1; edited by S. T. Joshi,
    Lawrence I. Berkove, and David E. Schultz

A mirage in Arizona
  Bierce, A. The short fiction of Ambrose
    Bierce, volume 1; edited by S. T. Joshi,
    Lawrence I. Berkove, and David E. Schultz

The mocking-bird
  Bierce, A. The short fiction of Ambrose
    Bierce, volume 2; edited by S. T. Joshi,
    Lawrence I. Berkove, and David E. Schultz

The moonlit road
  Bierce, A. The short fiction of Ambrose
    Bierce, volume 3; edited by S. T. Joshi,
    Lawrence I. Berkove, and David E. Schultz

A mournful property
  Bierce, A. The short fiction of Ambrose
    Bierce, volume 1; edited by S. T. Joshi,
    Lawrence I. Berkove, and David E. Schultz

Moxon's master
  Bierce, A. The short fiction of Ambrose
    Bierce, volume 3; edited by S. T. Joshi,
    Lawrence I. Berkove, and David E. Schultz

Mr. Barcle's mill
  Bierce, A. The short fiction of Ambrose
    Bierce, volume 1; edited by S. T. Joshi,
    Lawrence I. Berkove, and David E. Schultz

Bierce, Ambrose—*Continued*

Seafaring

Bierce, A. The short fiction of Ambrose Bierce, volume 1; edited by S. T. Joshi, Lawrence I. Berkove, and David E. Schultz

The secret of Macarger's Gulch

Bierce, A. The short fiction of Ambrose Bierce, volume 2; edited by S. T. Joshi, Lawrence I. Berkove, and David E. Schultz

A shipwreckollection

Bierce, A. The short fiction of Ambrose Bierce, volume 1; edited by S. T. Joshi, Lawrence I. Berkove, and David E. Schultz

Snaking

Bierce, A. The short fiction of Ambrose Bierce, volume 1; edited by S. T. Joshi, Lawrence I. Berkove, and David E. Schultz

A son of the gods

Bierce, A. The short fiction of Ambrose Bierce, volume 2; edited by S. T. Joshi, Lawrence I. Berkove, and David E. Schultz

Sons of the fair star

Bierce, A. The short fiction of Ambrose Bierce, volume 2; edited by S. T. Joshi, Lawrence I. Berkove, and David E. Schultz

Storm and sunshine

Bierce, A. The short fiction of Ambrose Bierce, volume 1; edited by S. T. Joshi, Lawrence I. Berkove, and David E. Schultz

A story at the club

Bierce, A. The short fiction of Ambrose Bierce, volume 1; edited by S. T. Joshi, Lawrence I. Berkove, and David E. Schultz

The story of a conscience

Bierce, A. The short fiction of Ambrose Bierce, volume 2; edited by S. T. Joshi, Lawrence I. Berkove, and David E. Schultz

The stranger

Bierce, A. The short fiction of Ambrose Bierce, volume 3; edited by S. T. Joshi, Lawrence I. Berkove, and David E. Schultz

Stringing a bear

Bierce, A. The short fiction of Ambrose Bierce, volume 1; edited by S. T. Joshi, Lawrence I. Berkove, and David E. Schultz

The suitable surroundings

Bierce, A. The short fiction of Ambrose Bierce, volume 2; edited by S. T. Joshi, Lawrence I. Berkove, and David E. Schultz

Sundered hearts

Bierce, A. The short fiction of Ambrose Bierce, volume 1; edited by S. T. Joshi, Lawrence I. Berkove, and David E. Schultz

A tale of Spanish vengeance

Bierce, A. The short fiction of Ambrose Bierce, volume 1; edited by S. T. Joshi, Lawrence I. Berkove, and David E. Schultz

A tale of the bosphorus

Bierce, A. The short fiction of Ambrose Bierce, volume 1; edited by S. T. Joshi, Lawrence I. Berkove, and David E. Schultz

The Tamtonians

Bierce, A. The short fiction of Ambrose Bierce, volume 2; edited by S. T. Joshi, Lawrence I. Berkove, and David E. Schultz

That dog

Bierce, A. The short fiction of Ambrose Bierce, volume 1; edited by S. T. Joshi, Lawrence I. Berkove, and David E. Schultz

The thing at Nolan

Bierce, A. The short fiction of Ambrose Bierce, volume 2; edited by S. T. Joshi, Lawrence I. Berkove, and David E. Schultz

Three and one are one

Bierce, A. The short fiction of Ambrose Bierce, volume 3; edited by S. T. Joshi, Lawrence I. Berkove, and David E. Schultz

To Fiji and return

Bierce, A. The short fiction of Ambrose Bierce, volume 1; edited by S. T. Joshi, Lawrence I. Berkove, and David E. Schultz

Tony Rollo's conclusion

Bierce, A. The short fiction of Ambrose Bierce, volume 1; edited by S. T. Joshi, Lawrence I. Berkove, and David E. Schultz

A tough tussle

Bierce, A. The short fiction of Ambrose Bierce, volume 2; edited by S. T. Joshi, Lawrence I. Berkove, and David E. Schultz

Trustland: a tale of a traveler

Bierce, A. The short fiction of Ambrose Bierce, volume 3; edited by S. T. Joshi, Lawrence I. Berkove, and David E. Schultz

Two haunted houses

Bierce, A. The short fiction of Ambrose Bierce, volume 2; edited by S. T. Joshi, Lawrence I. Berkove, and David E. Schultz

Two military executions

Bierce, A. The short fiction of Ambrose Bierce, volume 3; edited by S. T. Joshi, Lawrence I. Berkove, and David E. Schultz

Two stories about Johnson

Bierce, A. The short fiction of Ambrose Bierce, volume 1; edited by S. T. Joshi, Lawrence I. Berkove, and David E. Schultz

An upper class misdemeanant

Bierce, A. The short fiction of Ambrose Bierce, volume 1; edited by S. T. Joshi, Lawrence I. Berkove, and David E. Schultz

A vine on a house

Bierce, A. The short fiction of Ambrose Bierce, volume 3; edited by S. T. Joshi, Lawrence I. Berkove, and David E. Schultz

The war with Wug

Bierce, A. The short fiction of Ambrose Bierce, volume 3; edited by S. T. Joshi, Lawrence I. Berkove, and David E. Schultz

A watcher by the dead

Bierce, A. The short fiction of Ambrose Bierce, volume 2; edited by S. T. Joshi, Lawrence I. Berkove, and David E. Schultz

San Francisco noir 2; the classics; edited by Peter Maravelis.

Whither?

Bierce, A. The short fiction of Ambrose Bierce, volume 2; edited by S. T. Joshi, Lawrence I. Berkove, and David E. Schultz

Why I am not editing "The stinger"

Bierce, A. The short fiction of Ambrose Bierce, volume 1; edited by S. T. Joshi, Lawrence I. Berkove, and David E. Schultz

The widower Turmore

Bierce, A. The short fiction of Ambrose Bierce, volume 2; edited by S. T. Joshi, Lawrence I. Berkove, and David E. Schultz

Bierce, Ambrose—_Continued_

The wizard of Bumbassa

    Bierce, A. The short fiction of Ambrose Bierce, volume 2; edited by S. T. Joshi, Lawrence I. Berkove, and David E. Schultz

The wreck of the Orion

    Bierce, A. The short fiction of Ambrose Bierce, volume 1; edited by S. T. Joshi, Lawrence I. Berkove, and David E. Schultz

Big 32. Monson, A.

The **big** and the little. Asimov, I.

Big Bear, California. Curtis, R.

Big-bellied cow. Piñon, N.

Big bird. Rand, K.

Big blonde. Parker, D.

The **big** blow. Lansdale, J. R.

Big Blue. Parsons, R.

Big Bob. Manley, C.

Big break. Charters, D.

The **big** broadcast of 1938. Barthelme, D.

Big brother iron. Stross, C.

Big bucks. Trevor, W.

Big "C". Lumley, B.

Big cats. Reinhorn, H.

Big city girls. Malla, P.

The **big** day. McBain, E.

Big Doug rides torch. Messinger, J.

Big Fast Thing. Tower, W.

The **big** five. Wallace, J.

Big Fork Campground. Howard, B.

The **big** garbage dump. Naiyer Masud

Big girls don't cry. Raphael, L.

Big guy. Jablonski, N.

Big Guy, Bug Guy. Allaback, S.

The **big** hunt [variant title: Matt Gordon's boy] Leonard, E.

The **big** ice. Lake, J. and Nestvold, R.

Big Joe: a short short story. Kamp, S.

Big Mama. Qi, S.

Big medicine. Bower, B. M.

Big midnight special. Burke, J. L.

The **big** nickel. Mosley, W.

The **big** no. Bingham, S.

The **big** O. Hendricks, V.

The **Big** Picture. Stowe, R.

Big River. Rolnick, J.

The **big** scream. See McBain, E. Dummy [variant title: The big scream]

Big surprise. Matheson, R.

Big world. Winton, T.

The **bigamist**. Granville-Barker, H.

BIGAMY

    Alarcón, D. City of clowns

    Collins, W. A marriage tragedy

    Granville-Barker, H. The bigamist

    Mandelbaum, P. Changeling

    Mandelman, A. Mish-mash

Bigamy. Smith, C.

The **biggest** and the best. Holladay, C. C.

BIGOTRY _See_ Prejudices

Biguenet, John

An Encounter at Nightfall

    The Southern Review (Baton Rouge, La.) v43 no1 p38-41 Wint 2007

The work of art

    Wide awake in the Pelican State; stories by contemporary Louisiana writers; edited by Ann Brewster Dobie; with a foreword by Ernest J. Gaines

The **bike**. Sillitoe, A.

Bike New York!. Feitell, M.

Bikwan, Wong

She is a Woman; I am Also a Woman

    The Literary Review (Madison, N.J.) v48 no1 p7-22 Fall 2004

Bilal, Ahmad

A voice from the earth

    Oranges in the sun; short stories from the Arabian Gulf; edited and translated by Deborah S. Akers, Abubaker A. Bagader

Bilal, Mehmet

The stepson

    Istanbul noir; edited by Mustafa Ziyalan & Amy Spangler; translated by Amy Spangler & Mustafa Ziyalan.

Bilbao. Alison, J.

Bile. Jones, S. G.

Bill. Wingate, S.

Bill, the little steam shovel. Lansdale, J. R.

Bill, Wyoming. Marquiss, T.

Biller, Maxim

80 centimeters of bad temper

    Biller, M. Love today; translated from the German by Anthea Bell

The architect

    Biller, M. Love today; translated from the German by Anthea Bell

Aviva's back

    Biller, M. Love today; translated from the German by Anthea Bell

Baghdad at seven-thirty

    Biller, M. Love today; translated from the German by Anthea Bell

Butterflies

    Biller, M. Love today; translated from the German by Anthea Bell

Dear Arthur

    Biller, M. Love today; translated from the German by Anthea Bell

Fearing for Ilana

    Biller, M. Love today; translated from the German by Anthea Bell

Happy ending with sticky tape

    Biller, M. Love today; translated from the German by Anthea Bell

In bed with Sheikh Yassin

    Biller, M. Love today; translated from the German by Anthea Bell

It's a sad story

    Biller, M. Love today; translated from the German by Anthea Bell

The mahogany elephant

    Biller, M. Love today; translated from the German by Anthea Bell

    The New Yorker v83 no18 p62-4 Jl 2 2007

The maserati years

    Biller, M. Love today; translated from the German by Anthea Bell

    The New Yorker v83 no28 p148, 150 S 24 2007

Melody

    Biller, M. Love today; translated from the German by Anthea Bell

My name was Singer

    Biller, M. Love today; translated from the German by Anthea Bell

Biller, Maxim—*Continued*
On a cold, dark night
  Biller, M. Love today; translated from the German by Anthea Bell
The right of young men
  Biller, M. Love today; translated from the German by Anthea Bell
The right time of the month
  Biller, M. Love today; translated from the German by Anthea Bell
Seven attempts at loving
  Biller, M. Love today; translated from the German by Anthea Bell
Song number 7
  Biller, M. Love today; translated from the German by Anthea Bell
The statement of Amos Oz
  Biller, M. Love today; translated from the German by Anthea Bell
The suicide
  Biller, M. Love today; translated from the German by Anthea Bell
The sweet whore
  Biller, M. Love today; translated from the German by Anthea Bell
Two Israelis in Prague
  Biller, M. Love today; translated from the German by Anthea Bell
We were sitting in Cibo Matto
  Biller, M. Love today; translated from the German by Anthea Bell
Yellow sandals
  Biller, M. Love today; translated from the German by Anthea Bell
You're Greta
  Biller, M. Love today; translated from the German by Anthea Bell
Ziggy stardust
  Biller, M. Love today; translated from the German by Anthea Bell
BILLIARDS
Bear, E. Inelastic collisions
Holden, C. Red quarters
Keret, E. Angle
Billie Dyer. Maxwell, W.
Billing, Robert
Harnessing the brane-deer
  Nature v456 p1008 D 18-25 2008
Billingham, Mark
Dancing towards the blade
  The Best British mysteries, 2005; edited by Maxim Jakubowski
Stroke of luck
  The Best British mysteries, 2006; edited by Maxim Jakubowski
Billingslea-Brown, Alma Jean
Moonshot
  Short stories of the civil rights movement; an anthology; edited by Margaret Earley Whitt
A billion eves. Reed, R.
Billman, Jon
Inkneck
  Ploughshares v31 no2/3 p65-91 Fall 2005
Billon, Lydia
(tr.) See Rheda, Regina
BILLY, THE KID
            About
Duncklee, J. The last breakfast
Henry, W. A bullet for Billy the Kid

Billy. Gordon, M.
Billy. Randolph, L.
Billy and the wizard. Bisson, T.
Billy Bird. Wilson, L.
Billy Budd. Di Filippo, P.
Billy Jazz. Savage, R.
Bilwakesh, Champa
The "Boston Globe" Personal Line
  The Kenyon Review v27 no4 p10-26 Fall 2005
Bimko, Felix
The encounter
  No star too beautiful; Yiddish stories from 1382 to the present; compiled and translated by Joachim Neugroschel
Bin Laden, Osama *See* Osama bin Laden
Bin Laden's hiding in my liver. Fourgs, T.
Binchy, Maeve
All that matters
  New Dubliners; edited by Oona Frawley
Binder, L. Annette
Dead Languages
  The Southern Review (Baton Rouge, La.) v45 no1 p50-5 Wint 2009
Binge. McIntyre, V.
Bingham, Sallie
Advanced Latin
  Bingham, S. Red car; stories
The big no
  Bingham, S. Red car; stories
Doing good
  Bingham, S. Red car; stories
A gift for burning
  Bingham, S. Red car; stories
His sons
  Bingham, S. Red car; stories
Pleyben
  Bingham, S. Red car; stories
Porn
  Bingham, S. Red car; stories
Red car
  Bingham, S. Red car; stories
Sagesse
  Bingham, S. Red car; stories
The shot tower
  Bingham, S. Red car; stories
Sweet peas
  Bingham, S. Red car; stories
That winter
  Bingham, S. Red car; stories
Bingle, Donald J.
Attached to the land
  Future Americas; edited by Martin H. Greenberg and John Helferd
Cursory review
  Pandora's closet; edited by Jean Rabe and Martin H. Greenberg.
BINGO
Viets, E. Sex and bingo
With, C. Grangran Warmfeather's sitting on a hot bingo
Bingo master's break out. Griffiths, N.
The bingo van. Erdrich, L.
Biodegradable. Nelson, A.
BIOENGINEERING
Rand, K. The swimmer
Rich, M. Impossible alone
Stableford, B. The immortals of Atlantis
Swanwick, M. Wild minds

Biofeedback. Milofsky, D.
BIOGRAPHERS *See* Authors
Biographical notes to "A discourse on the nature of causality, with air-planes,". Rosenbaum, B.
Biographical notes to "A discourse on the nature of causality, with air-planes," by Benjamin Rosenbaum. Rosenbaum, B.
Biography of a House. Lee, J. C.
BIOLOGICAL WARFARE
   Pohl, F. The kindly isle
   Rollins, J. Kowalski's in love
BIOLOGISTS
   Bissell, T. Aral
   Boyle, T. C. Dogology
Biology. Spivack, K.
BIONICS
   Bacigalupi, P. The people of sand and slag
   Cadigan, P. The final remake of *The return of Little Latin Larry,* with a completely remastered soundtrack and the original audience
   McHugh, M. F. Nekropolis
   McHugh, M. F. Special economics
   Sterling, B. Twenty evocations
A **birch** tree, a white fox. Arsenieva, E.
Birchiam pier. Richards, T.
Bird, Carmel
   Her Voice Was Full of Money and They Were Careless People
   The Review of Contemporary Fiction v27 no3 p13-19 Fall 2007
The **bird**. Taha, M. A.
The **bird** and the cage. Taha, M. A.
Bird day. Shawl, N.
The **bird** of time. Yolen, J.
The **Bird** Sisters. Rasmussen, R.
BIRD WATCHERS
   Boyle, T. C. Swept away
   Hornsby, W. Dust up
   McLean, S. Burd
   Singleton, G. Migration over Gruel
BIRDCAGES
   Ducornet, R. The one marvelous thing
Birdie num-num. Sankaran, L.
Birdland. Knight, M.
BIRDS
     See also Hawks; Ostriches; Owls; Parrots; Pigeons
   Anderson, B. Feeding the sparrows
   Barry, R. How to save a wounded bird
   Baum, L. F. Bandit Jim Crow
   Baum, L. F. Policeman Bluejay
   Bradbury, R. Once more, Legato
   Carl, L. S. A mimicry of mockingbirds
   Colfer, E. A fowl tale
   Corso, P. Nose dive
   Daughtry, P. A grace of shadows
   Daughtry, P. Season of broken wings
   Emshwiller, C. All of us can almost . . .
   Gerber, M. J. The Cleopatra birds
   Gifford, B. The god of birds
   Gilman, G. I. Down the wall
   Harjo, J. The crow and the snake
   Lanagan, M. A feather in the breast of god
   Lange, R. Telephone bird
   Maxwell, W. The blue finch of Arabia
   Morrissette, M. Ave Maria
   Ochsner, G. Last words of the mynah bird

   Purdy, J. Entre dos luces
   Rosa, J. G. Treetops
   Ruefle, M. My search among the birds
   Scoville, S. Pu'u Pu'iwa
   Shawl, N. Bird day
   Smith, C. A. The voyage of King Euvoran
   Taha, M. A. The bird
   Taha, M. A. The bird and the cage
   Thomas, E. Birds of a feather flock together
   Thomas, E. One swallow doesn't make a summer
   Uchida, H. The water bird
   Varon, P. The feast
   Vidal, G. The robin
   Williams, L. The hide
   Wolfe, G. Castaway
   Yolen, J. The bird of time
   Yolen, J. The hundredth dove
Birds. Kwa'mboka
The **birds** below. Messinger, J.
Birds in the house. Wilson, K.
Birds of a feather flock together. Thomas, E.
Birds of Providence. Tomlinson, J.
Birds of the mountain west. DeMarinis, R.
Birmingham, John
   Heere be monsters
     Dreaming again; thirty-five new stories celebrating the wild side of Australian fiction; edited by Jack Dann
BIRMINGHAM (ALA.) *See* Alabama—Birmingham
Birnkrandt and Kamenski. Lynn, D. H.
The **birth**. Taha, M. A.
BIRTH CONTROL
     See also Abortion
   Feeny, P. Like rabbits
   Morrow, J. Auspicious eggs
Birth Data. Corcoran, M.
Birthday dance. Robinson, P.
The **birthday** girl. Canty, K.
Birthday girl. Murakami, H.
BIRTHDAY PARTIES *See* Birthdays
The **birthday** party. McLean, S.
The **birthday** party. West, D.
Birthday surprises. Cule, E.
BIRTHDAYS
   Anderson, B. It is necessary I have a balloon
   Anderson, B. Peppermint frogs
   Angel, J. Rounding third
   Beattie, A. Tending something
   Butcher, J. It's my birthday, too
   Caine, R. The first day of the rest of your life
   Crider, B. I was a teenage vampire
   Espinosa, G. Family birthday wishes
   Feitell, M. The Dumpling King
   Golden, C. The mournful cry of owls
   Hallaway, T. Fire and ice and linguini for two
   Harris, C. Dracula night
   Hawes, L. Mr. Mix-Up
   Hempel, A. The children's party
   Hinton, S. E. Full moon birthday
   Jung, H.-Y. Han Gahp
   Kelner, T. L. P. How Stella got her grave back
   Keret, E. Goody bags
   Keret, E. Happy birthday to you
   Keret, E. A no-magician birthday
   Kim, M. Scarlet fingernails
   Malouf, D. Great Day
   Matthews, C. For benefit of Mr. Means

Bishop, Tom—*Continued*

Cardinals and Tanagers flying by
 Bishop, T. The great Mormon cricket fly-fishing festival and other western stories
The contest
 Bishop, T. The great Mormon cricket fly-fishing festival and other western stories
Courting Miss Ellen
 Bishop, T. The great Mormon cricket fly-fishing festival and other western stories
The fragile commandment
 Bishop, T. The great Mormon cricket fly-fishing festival and other western stories
The great Mormon cricket fly-fishing festival
 Bishop, T. The great Mormon cricket fly-fishing festival and other western stories
A Hoover steak
 Bishop, T. The great Mormon cricket fly-fishing festival and other western stories
I cain't go
 Bishop, T. The great Mormon cricket fly-fishing festival and other western stories
Someone's dog
 Bishop, T. The great Mormon cricket fly-fishing festival and other western stories
The vision of Hehaka 'To
 Bishop, T. The great Mormon cricket fly-fishing festival and other western stories
The **bishop** and the landlady. Graves, P.
BISHOPS, CATHOLIC *See* Catholic bishops
Bishop's house. Gordon, M.
BISMARCK, OTTO, FÜRST VON, 1815-1898
 About
Moorcock, M. The pleasure garden of Felipe Sagittarius
BISON
Baker, O. Where the buffaloes begin
Erdrich, L. History of the Puyats
Leonard, E. The big hunt [variant title: Matt Gordon's boy]
Proulx, A. Deep-blood-greasy-bowl
Schultz, J. W. The buffalo hunt
Bissell, Tom
The ambassador's son
 Bissell, T. God lives in St. Petersburg; and other stories
Animals in our lives
 Bissell, T. God lives in St. Petersburg; and other stories
Aral
 Bissell, T. God lives in St. Petersburg; and other stories
Death defier
 The Best American short stories, 2005; selected from U.S. and Canadian magazines by Michael Chabon with Katrina Kenison; with an introduction by Michael Chabon
Death defies
 Bissell, T. God lives in St. Petersburg; and other stories
Expensive trips nowhere
 Bissell, T. God lives in St. Petersburg; and other stories
God lives in St. Petersburg
 Bissell, T. God lives in St. Petersburg; and other stories
 The Pushcart Prize XXIX: best of the small presses 2005; edited by Bill Henderson with the Pushcart Prize editors

My interview with the Avenger
 Burnham, C. Who can save us now?; brand-new superheroes and their amazing [short] stories; edited by Owen King and John McNally; [illustrations by Chris Burnham]
 The Best American mystery stories, 2009; edited and with an introduction by Jeffery Deaver
 The Virginia Quarterly Review v84 no2 p28-41 Spr 2008
Bisson, Terry
Almost home
 The Year's best fantasy and horror: seventeenth annual collection; edited by Ellen Datlow, Kelly Link and Gavin J. Grant
 Bisson, T. Greetings
Billy and the wizard
 Wizards; edited by Jack Dann and Gardner Dozois
BYOB FAQ
 Nature v449 p754 O 11 2007
Come dance with me
 Bisson, T. Greetings
Dear Abbey
 The Year's best science fiction: twenty-first annual collection; edited by Gardner Dozois
 Bisson, T. Greetings
Death's door
 Bisson, T. Greetings
The edge of the universe
 Bisson, T. Numbers don't lie
Get me to the church on time
 Bisson, T. Numbers don't lie
Greetings
 Bisson, T. Greetings
He loved Lucy
 This is my funniest 2; leading science fiction writers present their funniest stories ever; edited by Mike Resnick
The hole in the hole
 Bisson, T. Numbers don't lie
I saw the light
 Bisson, T. Greetings
Macs
 Nebula awards showcase 2002; edited by Kim Stanley Robinson
The old rugged cross
 Bisson, T. Greetings
Openclose
 Bisson, T. Greetings
Scout's honor
 The Year's best science fiction: twenty-second annual collection; edited by Gardner Dozois
 Bisson, T. Greetings
Super 8
 Bisson, T. Greetings
 (jt. auth) See Rucker, Rudy von Bitter and Bisson, Terry
Bistino and the Marquis. Palazzeschi, A.
Bit forgive. Chapman, M.
A **bit** of chivalry. Bierce, A.
A **bit** on the side. Trevor, W.
Bitch. Dahl, R.
Bitch Curve. Blanchard, E.
Bitches of the night. Kilpatrick, N.
Bite the hand. Cadnum, M.
The **biter** bit. Collins, W.
Bits and pieces. McKellar, C.

Bitter almonds and absinthe. Murphy, J.
Bitter grounds. Gaiman, N.
Bitter sorrows. Gomez, D. R.
Bitterblooms. Martin, G. R. R.
BITTERROOT RANGE (IDAHO AND MONT.)
 Burke, J. L. A season of regret
The **Bittersweet** Salvation . . . of Tim Mason. Perrotta, T.
Bitterwolf. Smith, R. T.
The **bizarre** wooden building. Ts'an-hsüeh
Black, Alethea
 Good in a Crisis
  The North American Review v292 no6 p20-7 N/D 2007
 That of Which We Cannot Speak
  The Antioch Review v65 no3 p469-81 Summ 2007
Black, Cara
 Mosquito incense
  Meeting across the river; stories inspired by the haunting Bruce Springsteen song; edited by Jessica Kaye and Richard J. Brewer
 The redhead
  Paris noir; capital crime fiction; edited by Maxim Jakubowski
Black, Holly
 The coat of stars
  The Best science fiction and fantasy of the year: volume two; edited by Jonathan Strahan
 Paper cuts scissors
  Year's best fantasy 8; edited by David G. Hartwell, Kathryn Cramer
 A reversal of fortune
  The Year's best fantasy and horror: twenty-first annual collection; edited by Ellen Datlow and Kelly Link & Gavin J. Grant
 Virgin
  The Best science fiction and fantasy of the year: volume three; edited by Jonathan Strahan
Black, Michael A.
 Articulation of murder
  At the scene of the crime; forensic mysteries from today's best writers; edited by Dana Stabenow
 Chasing the blues
  Chicago blues; edited by Libby Fischer Hellmann
Black, Robin
 . . . Divorced, beheaded, survived
  The Best of the Bellevue Literary Review; edited by Dannielle Ofri and the staff of the Bellevue Literary Review
 A Fence Between Our Homes
  The Southern Review (Baton Rouge, La.) v42 no4 p689-99 Aut 2006
Black, William
 Midnight Thoughts on the Law of Probability
  Prairie Schooner v79 no3 p57-72 Fall 2005
Black. Bright, N. R.
Black. Mandelman, A.
Black. Stewart, P.
Black and White. Bahr, A.
Black brother. Smith, C. T.
Black Canaan. Howard, R. E.
The **Black** Carpet. Crone, M.
The **black** cat. Poe, E. A.

BLACK CHILDREN *See* African American children
Black Days. Becker, G.
Black dog. Mosley, W.
Black dogs. Fry, G.
The **black** dress: a short short story. West, D.
Black dust. Joyce, G.
Black earth, early winter morning. Somerville, P.
The **black** eyed blonde. Schutz, B. M.
Black-eyed Susan. Lippman, L.
Black feather. Bradford, K. T.
Black Fields, Black Horses. Van Winckel, N.
Black fronts. Bonner, M. O.
Black, gray, green, red, blue: a letter from a famous painter on the moon. Greenman, B.
Black harvest. Kelly, R.
Black heart and cabin girl. Costa, S.
The **black** hero of the ranges. Mills, E. J.
The **black** hole of San Francisco. Twain, M.
BLACK HOLES (ASTRONOMY)
 Benford, G. The worm turns
 Bova, B. Einstein
 Bova, B. Surprise, surprise
 Kress, N. Shiva in shadow
 Swanwick, M. Ginungagap
Black hoodie. Doyle, R.
BLACK HUMOR *See* Humor; Satire
Black Ice. Kennedy, C.
Black ice. Stamm, P.
Black is the color of my true love's hair. Hoffman, A.
BLACK-JEWISH RELATIONS *See* African Americans—Relations with Jews
Black Legion. Anderson, L.
BLACK MAGIC *See* Witchcraft
The **black** mark. Palazzeschi, A.
BLACK MARKETS
 Kalfus, K. Pu-239
 L'Amour, L. A friend of the general
 Mehadheb, I. "Undertow"
 Sterling, B. Hollywood kremlin
The **black** Mercedes. Yates, D.
Black Mill Cove. Morton, L.
The **black** mirror. Simo, E.
Black palace. Ziyalan, M.
The **black** phone. Hill, J.
Black pockets. Zebrowski, G.
Black pork. Downs, G.
Black pudding. Goodis, D.
Black pumps & a skanky tom. Esden, P.
Black Rabbit. Hoffman, A.
BLACK SERVANTS *See* African American servants
Black shoes. Wolfe, G.
BLACK SOLDIERS *See* African American soldiers
Black Step. Woodrell, D.
The **black** stone. Howard, R. E.
Black stuff. Bruen, K.
Black Tie. Corriveau, A.
BLACK WOMEN *See* African American women
Black Zak and the heart attack. Ayres, N. J.
Blackberries. Aidt, N. M.
Blackberries in June. Rash, R.
Blackbird on a bramble bough. Kiely, B.

Blackford, Jenny
Trolls' night out
  Dreaming again; thirty-five new stories cele-
    brating the wild side of Australian fiction;
    edited by Jack Dann
Blackford, Russell
Manannan's children
  Dreaming again; thirty-five new stories cele-
    brating the wild side of Australian fiction;
    edited by Jack Dann
BLACKMAIL
  See also Extortion
Block, L. Man with a passion
Block, L. Sweet little racket
Bova, B. Diamond Sam
Collins, W. The fourth poor traveller
Franceschini, E. Roman holidays
Friesner, E. M. The fraud
Fusilli, J. The dupe
Haldeman, J. W. To Howard Hughes: a modest
    proposal
Hamilton, S. Room for a fourth
Hammett, D. The scorched face
Harvey, J. Promise
Holding, J. The inquisitive butcher of Nice
Hughes, M. Thwarting Jabbi Gloond
Khan, R. Alms
Lange, R. Culver City
Lescroart, J. T. The cover story is always a lie
Lippman, L. One true love
Matheson, R. The distributor
McDermid, V. Four calling birds
McInerney, J. The business
Moore, D. Bumping uglies
Parker, M. Everything was paid for
Saylor, S. A twist at the end [excerpt]
Trevor, W. The dressmaker's child
Trevor, W. Men of Ireland
Trezise, R. But not really
Vidal, G. Clouds and eclipses
Blackman, Nicole
Dumped
  Brooklyn noir; edited by Tim McLoughlin
Blackman, Sarah
At 8:15 on Tuesday Morning
  Gettysburg Review v19 no4 p571-8 Wint
    2006
Blackout. Richter, S.
BLACKS
  See also African Americans
Billingham, M. Dancing towards the blade
Bradbury, R. June 2003: Way in the middle of
    the air
De Mazia, V. The legend of Ngurangurante (the
    son of the crocodile)
Gardam, J. Waiting for a stranger
Gordimer, N. Beethoven was one-sixteenth
    black
Miller, M. One blue star
Packer, Z. Gideon
Shawl, N. Deep end
Shawl, N. Good boy
Thomas, S. R. The grassdreaming tree
        Europe
Tawada, Y. The shadow man
        Ireland
Bruen, K. Black stuff
Doyle, R. Black hoodie
Doyle, R. Guess who's coming for the dinner

        Wales
Adonis, I. Drawing apart
Brito, L. The last jumpshot
Blackshaw, Gemma
Girlfriend
  Her Majesty; 21 stories by women; edited by
    Jackie Gay and Emma Hargrave
Going the distance
  Going the distance; edited by Alan Beard
Blacksmith street. Wendroff, Z.
BLACKSMITHS
Wendroff, Z. Blacksmith street
Wingate, S. Beaching it
Blacksoil country. Malouf, D.
Blackwell, Kate
Carpe diem
  Blackwell, K. You won't remember this; sto-
    ries
Duckie's okay
  Blackwell, K. You won't remember this; sto-
    ries
George, Nadia, Blaise
  Blackwell, K. You won't remember this; sto-
    ries
Heartbeatland
  Blackwell, K. You won't remember this; sto-
    ries
The minaret
  Blackwell, K. You won't remember this; sto-
    ries
My first wedding
  Blackwell, K. You won't remember this; sto-
    ries
The obi tree
  Blackwell, K. You won't remember this; sto-
    ries
Pepper hunt
  Blackwell, K. You won't remember this; sto-
    ries
Queen of the May
  Blackwell, K. You won't remember this; sto-
    ries
The secret life of peonies
  Blackwell, K. You won't remember this; sto-
    ries
What we do for love
  Blackwell, K. You won't remember this; sto-
    ries
You won't remember this
  Blackwell, K. You won't remember this; sto-
    ries
Blackwood, Grant
Sacrificial lion
  Thriller; edited by James Patterson
Blackwood, Scott
Orson Welles' Blue Brocade Vest
  Western Humanities Review v61 no1 p98-112
    Wint 2007
The **Blackwood** Oak. Gallagher, S.
The **Blade**. Means, D.
Blade. Poch, J.
Blade and bone. Lamsley, T.
Blades, Leon
The glumbo glisae
  Going the distance; edited by Alan Beard

Blaeser, Kimberly M.
Growing things
    Reckonings; contemporary short fiction by Native American women; edited by Hertha D. Sweet Wong, Lauren Stuart Muller, Jana Sequoya Magdaleno
Like some old story
    Reckonings; contemporary short fiction by Native American women; edited by Hertha D. Sweet Wong, Lauren Stuart Muller, Jana Sequoya Magdaleno
Blair, David
Gravitational astronomy 101
    Nature v457 p122 Ja 1 2009
Blair, John
Low Tide Turning
    The Sewanee Review v113 no2 p174-92 Spr 2005
Motorhead
    The Antioch Review v63 no3 p479-96 Summ 2005
Blake, Glenn
Marsh
    So the story goes; twenty-five years of the Johns Hopkins short fiction series; edited by John T. Irwin and Jean McGarry; with a foreword by John Barth
BLAKE, WILLIAM, 1757-1827
About
Aldiss, B. W. Tiger in the night
Blakinger, Kate
Inside This New Skin
    Iowa Review v38 no3 p155-9 Wint 2008/2009
Blanchard, Elizabeth
Bitch Curve
    Dalhousie Review v87 no2 p241-8 Summ 2007
Bland, Eleanor Taylor
The canasta club
    Black noir; mystery, crime and suspense stories by African-American writers; edited by Otto Penzler
Blank. Baraka, I. A.
The **blanks**. Bluestein, E.
Blanqué, Andrea
Immensely Eunice
    Violations; stories of love by Latin American women; edited and with an introduction by Psiche Hughes; foreword by Brian Matthews
Blarney. Hockensmith, S.
Blaschke, Jayme Lynn
The whale below
    Fast ships, black sails; edited by Ann & Jeff VanderMeer
Blasted. Logue, M.
Blauner, Peter
Going, going, gone
    Hard boiled Brooklyn; edited by Reed Farrel Coleman
    The Best American mystery stories 2007; edited and with and introduction by Carl Hiaasen; Otto Penzler, series editor
BLAVATSKY, H. P. (HELENA PETROVNA), 1831-1891
About
Linaweaver, B. A good bag
Blavatsky, Helene Petrovna *See* Blavatsky, H. P. (Helena Petrovna), 1831-1891

Blaylock, James P.
Lord Kelvin's machine
    Steampunk; edited by Ann & Jeff VanderMeer
The **blaze**. Remizov, A.
Blaze. Smith, R. T.
Blaze of glory. Silverberg, R.
Blaze of glory. Weaver, W.
Bleak Bay. Sallis, J.
Bleeck, Oliver *See* Thomas, Ross, 1926-1995
Bleed into me. Jones, S. G.
The **bleeding** heart. Stafford, J.
The **blemish**. Tremayne, P.
The **Blemmye's** stratagem. Sterling, B.
Bless Everybody. Schwartz, S.
Blessed. Pollock, D. R.
Blessed—blessed. Arnow, H. L. S.
Blessed by an angel. Hamilton, P. F.
A **blessed** deceit. Dunbar, P. L.
Blessed hands. Halpern, F.
Blessed Virgin Mary, Saint *See* Mary, Blessed Virgin, Saint
The **blessing**. Brau, E.
Blessing. D'Ambrosio, C., Jr.
A **blessing**. Ochsner, G.
A **blessing** of frogs. Linscott, G.
Bletter, Diana
Waiting to Be Reborn
    The North American Review v290 no1 p34-9 Ja/F 2005
Blickle, Peter
(tr.) *See* Hoben, Josef
Bligh, Tom
Inventions
    The Southern Review (Baton Rouge, La.) v41 no4 p813-25 Aut 2005
BLIMPS *See* Airships
Blincoe, Nicholas
Lucifer over Lancashire
    Perverted by language; fiction inspired by The Fall; edited and introduced by Peter Wild.
BLIND
Auster, P. Auggie Wren's Christmas story
Bennett, T. Blind faith
Bensko, J. Tequila worms
Bissell, T. Aral
Brau, E. The Buddha's eyes
Dahl, R. The bookseller
Elkins, K. What is visible
Erdrich, L. The leap
Finger, A. The blind marksman
Gordon, M. The magician's wife
Gorman, E. Yesterday's dreams
Gospodinov, G. Blind Vaysha
Hart, E. Blind sided
Hempel, A. The dog of the marriage
Jones, E. P. Blindsided
Judah, S. Shame under the chuppah
King, L. R. Weaving the dark
Laken, V. Before long
Lange, R. Blind-made products
Lansdale, J. R. Mister weed-eater
McGlynn, D. The eyes to see
Means, D. It counts as seeing
Morrow, B. Amazing Grace
Reid, G. Pavilion 24
Roberts, A. Blindness and invisibility
Rock, P. Blooms
Row, J. The American girl

Block, Lawrence—*Continued*
  Keller's double dribble
    Murder at the foul line; edited by Otto
      Penzler
    The Best American mystery stories 2007; ed-
      ited and with and introduction by Carl
      Hiaasen; Otto Penzler, series editor
  Keller's karma
    Greatest hits; original stories of assassins,
      hitmen, and hired guns; edited by Robert J.
      Randisi
  Lie back and enjoy it
    Block, L. One night stands and lost weekends
  Look death in the eye
    Block, L. One night stands and lost weekends
  Man with a passion
    Block, L. One night stands and lost weekends
  A moment of wrong thinking
    The World's finest mystery and crime stories,
      fourth annual collection; edited by Ed
      Gorman and Martin H. Greenberg
  Murder is my business
    Block, L. One night stands and lost weekends
  The naked and the deadly
    Block, L. One night stands and lost weekends
  Nor iron bars a cage
    Block, L. One night stands and lost weekends
  One night of death
    Block, L. One night stands and lost weekends
  Package deal
    Block, L. One night stands and lost weekends
  Professional killer
    Block, L. One night stands and lost weekends
  Pseudo identity
    Block, L. One night stands and lost weekends
  Ride a white horse
    Block, L. One night stands and lost weekends
  Rude awakening
    Bronx noir; edited by S. J. Rozan
  A shroud for the damned
    Block, L. One night stands and lost weekends
  Stag party girl
    Block, L. One night stands and lost weekends
  Sweet little racket
    Block, L. One night stands and lost weekends
  Terrible Tommy Terhune
    Murder is my racquet; edited by Otto Penzler
  Twin call girls
    Block, L. One night stands and lost weekends
  A vision in white
    A Prisoner of memory and 24 of the year's
      finest crime and mystery stories; edited by
      Ed Gorman & Martin H. Greenberg
  The way to power
    Block, L. One night stands and lost weekends
  Welcome to the real world
    Murder in the rough; edited by Otto Penzler
  You can't lose
    Block, L. One night stands and lost weekends
BLOCK ISLAND (R.I.)
  Stamm, P. Flotsam
Block Island. Lynch, T.
Block out. Shields, C.
Blog. Kane, A. D.
BLOOD
  Francisco, B. and Lynch, C. This is my blood
Blood. Mordecai, P.
Blood and Wine. Parotti, P.

BLOOD DONORS
  Sutton, B. The rest of Esther
Blood duty. Stackpole, M. A.
The **blood** jet. Schutt, C.
Blood Loss. Becker, G. Y.
Blood management. Waters, D.
Blood money [variant title: Rich Miller's hand]
  Leonard, E.
Blood moon. Le May, A.
Blood of Jose Rizal. Roley, B. A.
The **blood** of Peter Francisco. Park, P.
Blood of sorcery. Roberson, J.
Blood relatives I: My mother was a monster.
  Boudinot, R.
Blood relatives II: Profession. Boudinot, R.
Blood sky. Cook, W.
Blood sky. Nolan, W. F.
Blood son. Matheson, R.
Blood suede shoes. Kelly, R.
Blood wrapped. Huff, T.
Bloodless Byrne of a Monday. Kiely, B.
Bloodlines. Hines, J. C.
Bloodstains on the wall. Bogary, A.
The **bloody** horn. Cetin, I.
Bloody hot. Appel, R.
Bloody Mary morning. Farris, J.
Bloom, Amy
  I love to see you coming, I hate to see you go
    Best of Tin House; stories; foreword by Dor-
      othy Allison
  The Old Impossible
    Ploughshares v32 no2/3 p10-23 Fall 2006
Bloom, Steven
  I Never Know What I Want to Say Until I See
    What I've Written
    Confrontation no98/99 p120-30 Spr/Summ
      2007
  Two Tickets for "Turandot"
    Confrontation no90/91 p11-27 Spr/Summ
      2005
Blooming. Weinman, S.
Blooms. Rock, P.
Bloomsbury Nights: Being, Food, and Love. Tay-
  lor, S.
Blossom. Schow, D. J.
Blotilla takes the cake. Zumas, L.
The **Blow**. Coetzee, J. M.
The **blow**. Rosenbaum, B.
Blow-up. Cortázar, J.
Blowing up on the spot. Wilson, K.
Blown from the bridge. Means, D.
Blown upon: or, The sagacious reporter Bendel-
  Simso, M. M., ed. Early American detec-
  tive stories; an anthology; edited by LeRoy
  Lad Panek and Mary M. Bendel-Simso.
Blows with Sticks Raining Hard. Gifford, B.
Blue, Eleanor
  The cut the crap machine
    Bluestein, E. Tea & other Ayama Na tales
Blue/Green. Ronk, M. C.
The **blue**. Gee, M.
Blue. Johnson, S. M.
Blue abstraction. MacEnulty, P.
A **blue** and cloudless sky. Ribbeck, B.
Blue As Blue Can Be. Oates, N.
Blue Aubergine. Al-Tahawy, M.
The **blue** book of dogs. Graham, T.
Blue boy. Canty, K.
Blue country. Mason, B. A.

The **blue** engines. Kun, M.
The **blue** finch of Arabia. Maxwell, W.
The **blue** flame. Ward, A. E.
Blue funk. Ducornet, R.
Blue girl. Crane, E.
Blue gloves. Pflug, U.
Blue grass, green sky. Chattin, J.
The **blue** handkerchief. James, H.
Blue hour. Hwang, F.
The **blue** hour. Templeton, E.
Blue house. Clayton, J. J.
The **blue** house. Gilchrist, E.
Blue is for bravery. Woolrich, C.
Blue Kiss.
Blue Knights bounced from CVD Tourney. Bachelder, C.
Blue light. Updike, J.
Blue light in the sky. Ts'an-hsüeh
Blue like bluing. Rivera-Valdes, S.
The **blue** line. Levitsky, R.
Blue messiah. Almond, S.
The **blue** monkey. Holladay, C. C.
Blue moon. Davis, J. S.
Blue note. Kaminsky, S. M.
The **blue** road: a fairy tale. Compton, W.
The **blue** room. Randolph, L.
The **Blue** Room. Schrader, E. K.
The **blue** sweetheart. Goodis, D.
Blue tango. Winn, T.
A **Blue** to the Shadow's Black. Yardumian, R.
Blue vandas. Barrett, L.
The **blue** velvet box. Erdrich, L.
Blue yodel. Snyder, S.
BLUEBEARD (LEGENDARY CHARACTER)
  Coover, R. The last one
Bluebell Meadow. Kiely, B.
Blueberry Pie. Harshbarger, K.
Bluecoat Jack. Totton, S.
Blued moon. Willis, C.
BLUES (MUSIC)
  Allen, P. G. Burned alive in the blues
  Fredrickson, J. Good evenin', blues
  Guilfoile, K. O death where is thy sting?
  Hellmann, L. F. Your sweet man
  Shepard, B. Sweet Benny and the Sanchez penitentiary band
Blues and the abstract truth. Dann, J. and Malzberg, B. N.
Blues in the Kabul night. Howard, C.
Bluestein, Eleanor
  Abio or love at first sight
    Bluestein, E. Tea & other Ayama Na tales
  The artist's story
    Bluestein, E. Tea & other Ayama Na tales
  The blanks
    Bluestein, E. Tea & other Ayama Na tales
  Hamburger School
    Bluestein, E. Tea & other Ayama Na tales
  North of the Faro
    Bluestein, E. Tea & other Ayama Na tales
  Pineapple wars
    Bluestein, E. Tea & other Ayama Na tales
  A ruined world
    Bluestein, E. Tea & other Ayama Na tales
  Skin deep
    Bluestein, E. Tea & other Ayama Na tales
  Tea
    Bluestein, E. Tea & other Ayama Na tales
Bluffs. Singleton, G.

Blum, Jonathan
  The kind of luxuries we felt we deserved
    Playboy's college fiction; a collection of 21 years of contest winners; edited by Alice K. Turner; foreword by Thom Jones
Blumenthal, Michael
  The Death of Fekete
    Legal Studies Forum v31 no1 p127-38 2007
Bly, Carol
  An Amateur's Story
    Prairie Schooner v80 no2 p54-65 Summ 2006
Blythe. Groff, L.
Boar Lake. Van Name, M. L.
Boar Taint. Campbell, B. J.
The **boarded** window. Bierce, A.
The **boarder**. Johnson, G.
The **Boarder**. Szilágyi, A.
BOARDERS *See* Boarding houses
Boarders. Pendleton, J.
Boarding a bear. Bierce, A.
BOARDING HOUSES
  Bensko, J. A spell
  Bierce, A. The new bedder
  Gordon, C. The presence
  Henry, O. The furnished room
  Jhabvala, R. P. Refuge in London
  Johnson, G. The boarder
  Kiely, B. The house in Jail Square
  MacLaverty, B. The wedding ring
  Porter, K. A. The leaning tower
  Qi, S. The tenants
  Singer, I. B. Escape from civilization
  Stafford, J. The tea time of stouthearted ladies
  Vidal, G. Erlinda and Mr. Coffin
  Wendroff, Z. A secure lodging
  Wharton, E. Mrs. Manstey's view
BOARDING SCHOOLS *See* School life
Boast, Will
  In the Leaves
    The Southern Review (Baton Rouge, La.) v42 no4 p729-42 Aut 2006
  Weather enough
    Best new American voices 2009; guest editor Mary Gaitskill; series editors John Kulka and Natalie Danford
The **boat**. Barnes, S.
The **boat**. Le, N.
A **boat** crossing. Zhu Wen
Boat taint. Campbell, B. J.
Boatman's holiday. Ford, J.
BOATMEN
  Bensko, J. Tequila worms
BOATS AND BOATING
       See also Rafting (Sports); Sailing vessels
  Anderson, B. Up the river with Mrs Gallant
  Barnes, S. The boat
  Bierce, A. The wreck of the Orion
  Chercover, S. A calculated risk
  Connell, N. Ozark Lake
  Curtis, R. The witches
  Gardiner, J. R. Leaving Port McHair
  González, K. A. Wake
  Helprin, M. Sail shining in white
  Hodgson, W. H. The sea horses
  Maupassant, G. d. Mouche
  McCauley, W. The mix
  Olafsson, O. On the lake
  Palazzeschi, A. Summer noontide
  Parks, T. In defiance of club rules

BOATS AND BOATING—*Continued*

Rodgers, S. J. The two husbands

Ruffin, P. The queen

Sayles, J. Cruisers

Vermeulen, J. The corpse that lost its head

Boats of Mine a-Boating. Lobsenz, R.

Boats of Mount Desert Island. Magnussen, L.

Bob Dylan Goes Tubing. Jackson, M.

Bobby Conroy comes back from the dead. Hill, J.

Bobby Kagan knows everything. Langer, A.

Bobby the prop buys in. Corbett, D.

Bobes, Marilyn

In Florence ten years later

Violations; stories of love by Latin American women; edited and with an introduction by Psiche Hughes; foreword by Brian Matthews

Bobis, Merlinda

The Sweetest Potato

World Literature Today v83 no1 p32-5 Ja/F 2009

Bobo the self-hating chimp. Auslander, S.

Bobok. Dostoyevsky, F.

Bobrinsky, Count

Peacock from Heaven

Parabola v30 no4 p81-7 Wint 2005

The **Bocce** Ball King of Farragut Road. Randisi, R. J.

The **Bocce** brothers. Averill, T. F.

Bocky-Bocky. Watkins, S.

The **Bodhisattva**. Dean, D.

Bodies. Vollmer, M.

Bodies at Rest. Haines, H. A.

Bodies in motion (Chicago, 1999). Mohanraj, M. A.

Bodies like mouths. Clayton, J. J.

Bodies of knowledge. Feldman, S.

Bodies of the dead [I]. Bierce, A.

Bodies of the dead [II]. Bierce, A.

Bodies of the rich. Clayton, J. J.

Bodrov, Sergei

Cross-Eyed Sasha

Studies in Russian & Soviet Cinema v1 no1 p69-109 2007

The **body/love** problem. Bakken, K. N.

Body. Evenson, B.

The **body**. Houliaras, N.

The **body**. Lispector, C.

Body and blood. Marley, L.

Body and Soul. Tihanyi, E.

Body count. Singer, M.

The **body** in the dovecote. Emerson, K. L.

Body language. Magee, K.

The **body** shop. Glatt, L.

BODYBUILDERS

Houliaras, N. The body

Kelts, R. N. Equilibrium

BODYBUILDING *See* Weight lifting

BODYGUARDS

Gischler, V. Kill posse

Hasak-Lowy, T. Will Power, Inc.

Lupica, M. Mrs. Cash

Reynolds, A. Fury

Bodysurfing. Burgin, R.

Boehm, Lucille

Condemned house: a short story

"Tell it to us easy" and other stories; a complete short fiction anthology of African American women writers in Opportunity magazine, (1923-1948); edited by Judith Musser.

Two-bit piece

"Tell it to us easy" and other stories; a complete short fiction anthology of African American women writers in Opportunity magazine, (1923-1948); edited by Judith Musser.

Bogary, Ahmad

Bloodstains on the wall

Oranges in the sun; short stories from the Arabian Gulf; edited and translated by Deborah S. Akers, Abubaker A. Bagader

Bogatyr. Lamb, H.

Bogdanov, Alexey Alexeevich

Red star

Worlds apart; an anthology of Russian fantasy and science fiction; edited and with commentary by Alexander Levitsky; translated by Alexander Levitsky and Martha T. Kitchen

Boggs, Johnny D.

Red River Crossing

Best stories of the American West, v1; edited by Marc Jaffe

Bogieman. Douglas, C. N.

The **Bogo-Indian** defense. Lange, R.

Bohanon, Mary Louise

Nothing changes

"Tell it to us easy" and other stories; a complete short fiction anthology of African American women writers in Opportunity magazine, (1923-1948); edited by Judith Musser.

The **Bohemian** of the Arbat. Pinborough, S.

BOHEMIANISM

Nolan, J. Open mike

Reid, G. After the rain

BOHEMIANS

United States

See Czechs—United States

Bohemians. Saunders, G.

BOHR, NIELS HENRIK DAVID, 1885-1962

About

Bear, E. Schrödinger's cat chases the super string

Sullivan, J. Niels Bohr and the sleeping dane

Boilard, Jon

The Train

Dalhousie Review v88 no3 p373-8 Aut 2008

Bojaxhiu, Agnes Gonxha *See* Teresa, Mother, 1910-1997

Bola de la fortuna. Tel, J.

Boland, Joe

The night watchman is asleep

Detroit noir; edited by E. J. Olsen & John C. Hocking

Bolaño, Roberto

Álvaro Rousselot's Journey

The New Yorker v83 no37 p116, 118-28 N 26 2007

Anne Moore's life

Bolaño, R. Last evenings on Earth; translated from the Spanish by Chris Andrews

Bonham, Frank—*Continued*

The phantom bandit

Bonham, F. The phantom bandit: western stories; edited by Bill Pronzini

A river man goes to war

Bonham, F. The phantom bandit: western stories; edited by Bill Pronzini

Wanted!

Bonham, F. The phantom bandit: western stories; edited by Bill Pronzini

Bonnefoy, Yves

America

Southern Humanities Review v42 no4 p334-9 Fall 2008

Bonner, Marita

The hands: a sroty

"Tell it to us easy" and other stories; a complete short fiction anthology of African American women writers in Opportunity magazine, (1923-1948); edited by Judith Musser.

Bonner, Marita O.

Black fronts

"Tell it to us easy" and other stories; a complete short fiction anthology of African American women writers in Opportunity magazine, (1923-1948); edited by Judith Musser.

Corner store

"Tell it to us easy" and other stories; a complete short fiction anthology of African American women writers in Opportunity magazine, (1923-1948); edited by Judith Musser.

The makin's

"Tell it to us easy" and other stories; a complete short fiction anthology of African American women writers in Opportunity magazine, (1923-1948); edited by Judith Musser.

Of Jimmie Harris

"Tell it to us easy" and other stories; a complete short fiction anthology of African American women writers in Opportunity magazine, (1923-1948); edited by Judith Musser.

A sealed pod

"Tell it to us easy" and other stories; a complete short fiction anthology of African American women writers in Opportunity magazine, (1923-1948); edited by Judith Musser.

There were three

"Tell it to us easy" and other stories; a complete short fiction anthology of African American women writers in Opportunity magazine, (1923-1948); edited by Judith Musser.

Tin can

"Tell it to us easy" and other stories; a complete short fiction anthology of African American women writers in Opportunity magazine, (1923-1948); edited by Judith Musser.

Bonney, William H. *See* Billy, the Kid

Bonnie. Purdy, J.

The **bonny** boy. MacLeod, I.

Bonobo Momma. Oates, J. C.

Bonsai. Zambra, A.

Bontly, Thomas

Immortal Remains

The Sewanee Review v113 no4 p518-25 Fall 2005

Listening for the Silences

The Sewanee Review v116 no4 p542-59 Fall 2008

Bonus round. Charters, D.

Boo-boo. LaBute, N.

Boobs. Charnas, S. M.

Boof, Kola

The one you meet everywhere

Politically inspired; edited by Stephen Elliott; assistant editor, Gabriel Kram; associate editors, Elizabeth Brooks [et al.]

Boojum. Bear, E. and Monette, S.

A **book** for Michael Sama. McCauley, W.

BOOK OF A THOUSAND AND ONE NIGHTS

See Arabian nights

The **Book** of Angels. McMillan, D.

The **book** of Jashar. Rosenbaum, B.

The **book** of names. Langer, A.

The **book** of panegyrics. Fonseca, R.

A **Book** of Swoons. Santos, J. P.

The **Book** of Tobit. Jeffers, H. P.

The **book** of Yul. Burke, K.

Book owner. Fincke, G.

BOOK RARITIES *See* Rare books

BOOK SHOPS *See* Booksellers and bookselling

The **book** signing. Hamill, P.

Booker, Brian

Sequelæ

The Antioch Review v63 no1 p122-3 Wint 2005

Train Delayed Due to Horrible, Horrible Accident

TriQuarterly no125 p44-71 2006

Bookman, Marc

The Get

Confrontation no90/91 p107-24 Spr/Summ 2005

Oath

The Antioch Review v64 no2 p267-82 Spr 2006

Bookmarks. Kelly, R.

BOOKS

See also Books and reading; Manuscripts; Rare books

Black, H. Paper cuts scissors

Campisi, S. The title of this story

Dunbar, P. L. The vindication of Jared Hargot

Effinger, G. A. Target: Berlin! The role of the Air Force four-door hardtop

Horn, D. Readers Digest

Kiely, B. Bon ami, Emile

Michaelopoulou, A. Lermontov

Pendarvis, J. Our spring catalog

Schow, D. J. The pyre and others

Tabor, M. L. The woman who never cooked

BOOKS, RARE *See* Rare books

BOOKS AND READING

Adiga, A. Lighthouse Hill

Baumbach, J. The life and times of Major Fiction

Bicrce, A. The captain of the Camel

Bolaño, R. Vagabond in France and Belgium

Bradbury, R. A literary encounter

Brockmeier, K. The view from the seventh layer

Chadbourn, M. Farewell to the 21st century girl

BOOKS AND READING—*Continued*
Cooper, J. C. The eye of the beholder
Cotrina, J. A. Between the lines
Davidson, J. The other amazon
Disch, T. M. The man who read a book
Gordon, M. The Epiphany Branch
Gunn, E. Coming to terms
Haldeman, J. W. Angel of light
Hammett, D. Itchy
Hand, E. The least Trumps
James, C. L. R. Delphi and Herodotus discussion
Julavits, H. Judge Gladys Parks-Schultz
Kelly, J. P. The edge of nowhere
Klages, E. Travel agency
Kun, M. The last chance Texaco
L'Amour, L. The man who stole Shakespeare
Levi, P. The girl in the book
Levi, P. In the park
Link, K. Pretty monsters
Monteleone, T. F. Present perfect
Painter, P. Reading in his wake
Resnick, M. Travels with my cats
Rock, P. Blooms
Ronk, M. C. Page 42
Ruefle, M. Woman with a yellow scarf
Samuels, M. A gentleman from Mexico
Shirley, P. The story of William B. Greene
Soueif, A. 1964
Ulitskaya, L. Sonechka
Westerfeld, S. Ass-hat magic spider
Wolfe, G. The Arimaspian legacy
Wolfe, G. The island of Doctor Death and other stories
Yates, D. Reading Erica Jong
Yu, C. Realism
Zelazny, R. The Malatesta collection
The **bookseller**. Dahl, R.

BOOKSELLERS AND BOOKSELLING
Clayton, J. J. Adult fiction
Cowdrey, A. E. Twilight states
Dahl, R. The bookseller
Gardiner, J. R. The Ricus Adams
Harper, J. After hours
King, L. Five Tuesdays in winter
LaSalle, P. The spaces inside sleep
Lupoff, R. A. Fourth Avenue interlude
Pickman, R. Dark delicacies of the dead
Salter, J. Bangkok
Tea, M. 9/11 L.A. bookstore
Vazquez, Maria Esther. Returning by train with Borges
Wolfe, G. From the cradle
Boomerang. Keret, E.
Boon, J.-P. and others
A concrete example
Nature v444 p122 N 2 2006
Boosta
Silence is golden
Rome noir; edited by Chiara Stangalino & Maxim Jakubowski; translated by Anne Milano Appel, Ann Goldstein, and Kathrine Jason
Booth, Charles G.
Stag party
The Black Lizard big book of pulps; edited by Otto Penzler

BOOTH, JOHN WILKES, 1838-1865
About
Smith, R. T. Shooting Booth
Booth, Marilyn
(tr.) See Ramadan, Somaya
Boothby, Guy
The Duchess of Wiltshire's diamonds
The Penguin book of Gaslight crime; con artists, burglars, rogues, and scoundrels from the time of Sherlock Holmes; edited with an introduction and notes by Michael Sims.
The **bootleg** heart. Lane, J.
Bootleggers. Bishop, T.
The **Boots**. Kealey, T.

BOOTS AND SHOES
Báez, A. The red shoes
Baraka, I. A. Mchawi
Bradbury, R. The sound of summer running
Marley, L. Technicolor
Stevens, J. D. JFK's shoes
Tambour, A. The shoe in SHOES window
Thawabteh, N. My shoe size and other people's views on the matter!
Wolfe, G. Black shoes
Zettel, S. The red shoes
Zoshchenko, M. The galosh
Zoshchenko, M. The Tsar's boots
Booze Bag. Devereaux, K. C.
The **boozer**. Choe, I.
The **bordello** in faerie. Swanwick, M.
Border. Hagy, A.
Border Crossings. Alfaro, L.
Border crossings. Pflug, U.
Borderland. Singer, M.
Bordersnakes [excerpt] Crumley, J.
Bordiuk, Amy
Infestation
The Massachusetts Review v48 no4 p604-8 Wint 2007
Pure Love
The Massachusetts Review v50 no1-2 p223-30 Spr/Summ 2009
The **boreal** forest. Canty, K.

BOREDOM
Barrett, M. Suspects wanted
Barthelme, D. Edwards, Amelia
Bradford, R. Carolina live
Colombi, M. Winter evenings
Davis, C. Electric
Elkin, S. The guest
Keret, E. Gur's theory of boredom
Kun, M. A place like here, only different
Rheinheimer, K. FLA
Rock, P. Disentangling
Boredom, Or, The Yellow Trousers. Stacey, T.

BORES (PERSONS)
Molodowsky, K. Herschel Eisengold
Borges, Jorge Luis
The Gospel according to Mark
A cross of centuries; twenty-five imaginative tales about the Christ; edited by Michael Bishop

BORGES, JORGE LUIS, 1899-1986
About
Grimes, C. Examination of an afflicted man
Vazquez, Maria Esther. Returning by train with Borges
Parodies, imitations, etc.
Hussin, J. Y. The day in Buenos Aires

Borges's Dagger. Hinojosa-Smith, R.
The **Borgia** hand. Zelazny, R.
Boring Baby. Paul, J.
Born, James O.
The drought
Mystery Writers of America presents the blue religion; new stories about cops, criminals, and the chase; edited by Michael Connelly
Tourist trade
Dublin noir; the Celtic tiger vs. the ugly American; edited by Ken Bruen
Born bad. Deaver, J.
Born of man and woman. Matheson, R.
Born of the winds. Lumley, B.
Born with the dead. Silverberg, R.
BORNEO
L'Amour, L. The diamond of Jeru
L'Amour, L. Off the mangrove coast
Borough of cemeteries. Shaw, I.
El **Borrachito**. Vaca, N. C.
Borscht. Vapnyar, L.
Borthwick, J. S.
The case of the hooked-billed kites [excerpt]
Lone Star sleuths; an anthology of Texas crime fiction; edited and with an introduction by Bill Cunningham, Steven L. Davis, and Rollo K. Newsom.
BOSCH, HIERONYMUS, D. 1516
About
Rucker, R. v. B. Guadalupe and Hieronymus Bosch
Bosco, Monique
Sara Sage [excerpt]
Contemporary Jewish writing in Canada; an anthology; edited by Michael Greenstein
BOSNIA AND HERCEGOVINA
Fais, M. Halima, Desdemona, Bubu
Hemon, A. Everything
Reid, G. Pavilion 24
Sarajevo
Hemon, A. American commando
Hemon, A. The conductor
Hemon, A. The noble truths of suffering
Novakovich, J. Hail
Novakovich, J. The stamp
BOSNIANS
Canada
Hemon, A. The bees, part 1
United States
Hemon, A. American commando
Hemon, A. The conductor
Hemon, A. Good living
Hemon, A. Szmura's room
Novakovich, J. Spleen
Wieland, M. Swan in retreat
Zaire
Hemon, A. Stairway to heaven
BOSTON (MASS.) See Massachusetts—Boston
The **"Boston** Globe" Personal Line. Bilwakesh, C.
BOSTON RED SOX (BASEBALL TEAM)
Evich, M. Fischer at Fenway
Pachter, A. E. Green monster
Parenti, J. The opposite field
Pariseau, E. Heirloom
Polyak, S. and Polyak, C. The prophecy: a Red Sox alternate history
Saks, A. My night at Fenway
Snee, T. First start

Boswell, Marshall
The Remotes
New England Review v27 no3 p214-23 2006
Boswell, Robert
Almost not beautiful
Boswell, R. The heyday of the insensitive bastards; stories
City bus
Boswell, R. The heyday of the insensitive bastards; stories
Guests
Boswell, R. The heyday of the insensitive bastards; stories
The heyday of the insensitive bastards
Boswell, R. The heyday of the insensitive bastards; stories
In a foreign land
Boswell, R. The heyday of the insensitive bastards; stories
Lacunae
Boswell, R. The heyday of the insensitive bastards; stories
Miss Famous
Boswell, R. The heyday of the insensitive bastards; stories
No river wide
Boswell, R. The heyday of the insensitive bastards; stories
The Southern Review (Baton Rouge, La.) v43 no2 p371-400 Spr 2007
A sketch of highway on the nap of a mountain
Boswell, R. The heyday of the insensitive bastards; stories
Skin deep
Boswell, R. The heyday of the insensitive bastards; stories
Smoke
Boswell, R. The heyday of the insensitive bastards; stories
Story Ideas
Callaloo v32 no2 p345-9 Spr 2009
Supreme beings
Boswell, R. The heyday of the insensitive bastards; stories
A walk in winter
Boswell, R. The heyday of the insensitive bastards; stories
Bosworth, Beth
Tell Me Again
Hanging Loose no90 p10-12 2007
With Thee Conversing
Hanging Loose no92 p14-21 2008
BOTANISTS
Chilson, P. Disturbance-loving species
The **Botch**. Means, D.
Botch Town. Ford, J.
Botero, Juan Carlos
The execution
The Flight of the condor; stories of violence and war from Colombia; translated and compiled by Jennifer Gabrielle Edwards; foreword by Hugo Chaparro Valderrama.
Botticelli. Bear, E.
Bottle. Keret, E.
A **bottle** of brown sherry. Kiely, B.
Bottle of cana. See Coloane, F. The empty bottle [variant title: Bottle of cana]
Bottom deal. Browne, R. G.
Bottom feeding. Pratt, T.

Bowen, Rhys

Doppelganger

    The World's finest mystery and crime stories, fifth annual collection; edited by Ed Gorman and Martin H. Greenberg

Bowen. Connell, E. S.

Bower, B. M.

Big medicine

    Bower, B. M. Law on the Flying U: western stories; edited by Kate Baird Anderson

By gollies, yes!

    Bower, B. M. Law on the Flying U: western stories; edited by Kate Baird Anderson

Happy Jack, wild man

    Bower, B. M. Law on the Flying U: western stories; edited by Kate Baird Anderson

The intervention of almighty voice

    Bower, B. M. Law on the Flying U: western stories; edited by Kate Baird Anderson

The land shark

    Bower, B. M. Law on the Flying U: western stories; edited by Kate Baird Anderson

Law on the Flying U

    Bower, B. M. Law on the Flying U: western stories; edited by Kate Baird Anderson

On the middle guard

    Bower, B. M. Law on the Flying U: western stories; edited by Kate Baird Anderson

The outlaw

    Bower, B. M. Law on the Flying U: western stories; edited by Kate Baird Anderson

The tale of a native son

    Bower, B. M. Law on the Flying U: western stories; edited by Kate Baird Anderson

The **bower.** Martin, V.

Bowerbird. Schor, L.

Bowes, Richard

Aka St. Mark's place

    The Del Rey book of science fiction and fantasy; sixteen original works by speculative fiction's finest voices; edited by Ellen Datlow

Dust devil on a quiet street

    Salon fantastique; edited and with an introduction by Ellen Datlow and Terri Windling

If angels fight

    The Best science fiction and fantasy of the year: volume three; edited by Jonathan Strahan

The mask of the Rex

    Nebula Awards showcase 2005; the year's best SF and fantasy; selected by the Science Fiction and Fantasy Writers of America; edited by Jack Dann

BOWIE, DAVID

About

Raphael, L. Betrayed by David Bowie

Bowie, James *See* Bowie, Jim, 1796-1836

BOWIE, JIM, 1796-1836

About

Card, O. S. The Yazoo Queen

Bowker, David

Johnny Seven

    Expletive deleted; edited by Jen Jordan

The **bowler** hat. Uchida, H.

Bowman, Jeffrey Robert

Stonewalls

    The Best American mystery stories, 2004; edited and with an introduction by Nelson DeMille; Otto Penzler, series editor

Box, C. J.

Pirates of Yellowstone

    Meeting across the river; stories inspired by the haunting Bruce Springsteen song; edited by Jessica Kaye and Richard J. Brewer

    The Best American Mystery Stories, 2006; edited and with an introduction by Scott Turow; Otto Penzler, series editor

The **box.** Blish, J.

The **box.** Coville, B.

The **box.** Gallagher, S.

Box. Stevens, J. D.

Box. White, S.

The **box** house and the snow. Henriquez, C.

The **box** of beautiful things. Dolton, B.

The **Box** of Water [Tlingit story retold by John E. Smelcer]

The **boxcar.** Kelly, R.

BOXERS

Davidson, C. Rust and bone

Muller, E. Kid's last fight

Shepard, L. Beast of the heartland

Sullivan, C. J. Alex Pinto hears the bell

Sullivan, C. J. The last round

BOXING

Bear, E. Sonny Liston takes the fall

Bennett, T. Trading corners

Davidson, C. Life in the flesh

Dobozy, T. Into the ring

Edwards, S. The long count

Faust, C. Cutman

Gifford, B. This coulda happened anywhere

Hodgson, W. H. How the honourable Billy Darrell raised the wind

Hornung, E. W. A trap to catch a cracksman

Howard, R. E. The spirit of Tom Molyneaux

Kiely, B. Eton Crop

Lansdale, J. R. The big blow

Matheson, R. Steel

Mazor, J. Washington

Oates, J. C. Golden gloves

Oates, J. C. The man who fought Roland LaStarza

Resnick, R. Muay Thai

Tognazzini, A. Macho outing

Villoro, J. Lightweight champ

Wolven, S. El Rey

Boy. Mozetič, B.

The **boy** and the bayonet. Dunbar, P. L.

Boy b. Selgin, P.

The **Boy** Friend Test. Huntington, C. R.

The **boy** from Dos Cabezas. See Leonard, E. Jugged [variant title: The boy from Dos Cabezas]

The **boy** from Lam Kien. July, M.

A **boy** in Cathyland. Marusek, D.

The **boy** in the band uniform. Randolph, L.

A **boy** in the house. West, D.

The **boy** in the tree. Spencer, E.

The **boy** in Zaquitos. McAllister, B.

The **boy** on the far left. Cooper, D.

BOY SCOUTS

Maxwell, W. With reference to an incident at a bridge

The **Boy** Scouts of Westhampton. Goodman, P.

The **boy** who drew unicorns. Yolen, J.

The **Boy** Who Had Never Seen the Sea. Le Clézio, J. M. G.

The **boy** who hooked the sun. Wolfe, G.

A **boy** who picked the sun. Taha, M. A.

The **boy** who sang for death. Yolen, J.

The **boy** who smiled. Leonard, E.

The **boy** who was a chirping oriole. Meno, J.

Boyagoda, Randy

Water Spider

The Walrus v3 no2 p68-71 Mr 2006

Boyd, Betsy

Scarecrow

Pushcart prize XXXIII: best of the small presses 2009; edited by Bill Henderson with the Pushcart Prize editors

Boyd, John P.

The icosahedral anaster

Nature v453 p256 My 8 2008

Boyd, Paula

Hot enough to kill [excerpt]

Lone Star sleuths; an anthology of Texas crime fiction; edited and with an introduction by Bill Cunningham, Steven L. Davis, and Rollo K. Newsom.

Boyd, William

Adult video

Boyd, W. Fascination; stories

Beulah Berlin, an A-Z

Boyd, W. Fascination; stories

Fantasia on a favorite waltz

Boyd, W. Fascination; stories

Fascination

Boyd, W. Fascination; stories

The ghost of a bird

Boyd, W. Fascination; stories

A haunting

Boyd, W. Fascination; stories

Incandescence

Boyd, W. Fascination; stories

The mind/body problem

Boyd, W. Fascination; stories

Notebook no. 9

Boyd, W. Fascination; stories

The pigeon

Boyd, W. Fascination; stories

The Kenyon Review v27 no1 p1-11 Wint 2005

Varengeville

Boyd, W. Fascination; stories

The view from Yves Hill

Boyd, W. Fascination; stories

Visions fugitives

Boyd, W. Fascination; stories

The woman on the beach with a dog

Boyd, W. Fascination; stories

Boyden, Amanda

The eleventh

2033; the future of misbehavior: interplanetary dating, Madame President, socialized plastic surgery, and other good news from the future; from the editors of Nerve.com; instigated by Svedka

Boyer, J.

The Night Mechanic

Ploughshares v32 no4 p41-8 Wint 2006/2007

Boyers, Robert

An excitable woman

Boyers, R. Excitable women, damaged men

The French lesson

Boyers, R. Excitable women, damaged men

A Friend of Dr. Reis

Michigan Quarterly Review v44 no4 p758-81 Fall 2005

In hiding

Boyers, R. Excitable women, damaged men

A perfect stranger

Boyers, R. Excitable women, damaged men

Samantha

Boyers, R. Excitable women, damaged men

The Pushcart Prize XXX: best of the small presses 2006; edited by Bill Henderson with the Pushcart Prize editors

Secrets and sons

Boyers, R. Excitable women, damaged men

The Yale Review v93 no3 p119-38 Jl 2005

The Sister

The Antioch Review v64 no3 p474-92 Summ 2006

Torso

Boyers, R. Excitable women, damaged men

Tribunal

Boyers, R. Excitable women, damaged men

The visit

Boyers, R. Excitable women, damaged men

BOYES, JOHN, B. 1874

About

Resnick, M. Bully!

Boyfriend of the World. Murphy, R.

Boyfriends. Luongo, M.

Boyfriends. Weiner, C.

Boyko, Craig

The Intruder

The Walrus v6 no4 p49, 51, 53 My 2009

Boylan, Clare

Benny gets the blame

New Dubliners; edited by Oona Frawley

Boylan, James *See* Boylan, Jennifer Finney, 1958-

Boylan, Jennifer Finney

Thirty-six miracles of Lyndon Johnson

So the story goes; twenty-five years of the Johns Hopkins short fiction series; edited by John T. Irwin and Jean McGarry; with a foreword by John Barth

Boyle, Nicholas

The churring

The Year's best fantasy and horror: twentieth annual collection; edited by Ellen Datlow and Kelly Link & Gavin J. Grant

Boyle, T. C.

Balto

The Best American short stories, 2007; selected from U. S. and Canadian magazines by Stephen King with Heidi Pitlor; with an introduction by Stephen King

The Paris Review v48 p51-69 Wint 2006

Bulletproof

Best Life v5 no7 p130-5, 158-160 S 2008

The devil and Irv Cherniske

The best American Catholic short stories; a Sheed & Ward collection; edited by Daniel McVeigh and Patricia Schnapp

Hands On

The Kenyon Review v29 no3 p29-37 Summ 2007

Bradbury, Ray—*Continued*
When the bough breaks
    Bradbury, R. We'll always have Paris; stories
The whole town's sleeping
    Bradbury, R. Bradbury stories; 100 of his
    most celebrated tales
A wild night in Galway
    Bradbury, R. Bradbury stories; 100 of his
    most celebrated tales
The wilderness
    Fourth planet from the sun; tales of Mars
    from The Magazine of Fantasy & Science
    Fiction; edited by Gordon Van Gelder
The wind
    Bradbury, R. Bradbury stories; 100 of his
    most celebrated tales
The wish
    Bradbury, R. Bradbury stories; 100 of his
    most celebrated tales
The witch doctor
    Bradbury, R. Bradbury stories; 100 of his
    most celebrated tales
The woman on the lawn
    Bradbury, R. Bradbury stories; 100 of his
    most celebrated tales
The wonderful death of Dudley Stone
    Bradbury, R. Bradbury stories; 100 of his
    most celebrated tales
Zero hour
    Bradbury, R. Bradbury stories; 100 of his
    most celebrated tales
BRADBURY, RAY, 1920-
        Parodies, imitations, etc.
Card, O. S. Feed the baby of love
Konrath, J. A. and Wilson, F. P. The sound of
    blunder
Wilson, F. P. The November game
Bradbury, Walter I.
(tr.) See Monterroso, Augusto
Bradbury weather. Kiernan, C. R.
Bradfield, Scott
Angry duck
    Bradfield, S. Hot animal love; tales of mod-
    ern romance
The anti-Santa
    Bradfield, S. Hot animal love; tales of mod-
    ern romance
Dazzle redux
    Bradfield, S. Hot animal love; tales of mod-
    ern romance
Dazzle's inferno
    Bradfield, S. Hot animal love; tales of mod-
    ern romance
The devil disinvests
    Bradfield, S. Hot animal love; tales of mod-
    ern romance
Doggy love
    Bradfield, S. Hot animal love; tales of mod-
    ern romance
Goldilocks tells all
    Bradfield, S. Hot animal love; tales of mod-
    ern romance
Heaven sent
    Bradfield, S. Hot animal love; tales of mod-
    ern romance
Men and women in love
    Bradfield, S. Hot animal love; tales of mod-
    ern romance

Penguins for lunch
    Bradfield, S. Hot animal love; tales of mod-
    ern romance
Pig paradise
    Bradfield, S. Hot animal love; tales of mod-
    ern romance
Queen of the Apocalypse
    Bradfield, S. Hot animal love; tales of mod-
    ern romance
The reflection once removed
    Bradfield, S. Hot animal love; tales of mod-
    ern romance
Bradford, Arthur
Build It Up, Knock It Down
    StoryQuarterly v42 p321-33 2006
Orderly: how I spent that year after high school
    Before; short stories about pregnancy from
    our top writers; edited by Emily Franklin
    and Heather Swain
Bradford, Becky
More than skin deep
    Getting even; revenge stories; edited by Mitzi
    Szereto
Bradford, K. Tempest
Black feather
    Interfictions; an anthology of interstitial writ-
    ing; edited by Delia Sherman and Theodora
    Goss
Bradford, Rachel
Carolina live
    Her Majesty; 21 stories by women; edited by
    Jackie Gay and Emma Hargrave
Bradley, Darin C.
They would only be roads
    Sedia, E. Paper cities; an anthology of urban
    fantasy
Bradley, George
An East Egg Update
    The Yale Review v96 no4 p126-37 O 2008
Bradshaw, Heather
Sanctity: All life is here
    Nature v453 p426 My 15 2008
Bradway, Becky
Provenance
    The Antioch Review v65 no1 p135-48 Wint
    2007
Sara in the Apartments of the Countess
    Southern Humanities Review v40 no2 p151-63
    Spr 2006
Brady, Catherine
The dazzling world
    Brady, C. The mechanics of falling and other
    stories
Last of the true believers
    Brady, C. The mechanics of falling and other
    stories
Looking for a female tenet
    Brady, C. The mechanics of falling and other
    stories
The mechanics of falling
    Brady, C. The mechanics of falling and other
    stories
Much have I traveled
    Brady, C. The mechanics of falling and other
    stories
Scissors, paper, rock
    Brady, C. The mechanics of falling and other
    stories

Brady, Catherine—*Continued*

Seven remedies

Brady, C. The mechanics of falling and other stories

The Kenyon Review v26 no4 p69-84 Fall 2004

Slender little thing

Brady, C. The mechanics of falling and other stories

Those who walk during the day

Brady, C. The mechanics of falling and other stories

Wait for instructions

Brady, C. The mechanics of falling and other stories

Wicked stepmother

Brady, C. The mechanics of falling and other stories

Written in stone

The Best American short stories, 2004; edited by Lorrie Moore; Katrina Kenison series editor

Brady, William S., 1938-

For works written by this author under other names see Harvey, John, 1938-

Braffet, Kelly

Bad karma girl wins a t bingo

Burnham, C. Who can save us now?; brand-new superheroes and their amazing [short] stories; edited by Owen King and John McNally; [illustrations by Chris Burnham]

BRAHE, SOPHIA, 1556-1643

About

Bear, E. Stella nova

BRAHE, TYCHO, 1546-1601

About

Bear, E. Stella nova

BRAHMS, JOHANNES, 1833-1897

About

Marley, L. P dolce

Brahms Second, in Color. Rabin, A.

BRAIN

Dahl, R. William and Mary

Gregory, D. Dead horse point

Rose, A. Enchanted looms

Silverberg, R. In the House of Double Minds

Zelazny, R. No award

Experiments

Menger-Anderson, K. Doctor Olaf van Schuler's brain, 1664

Surgery

Menger-Anderson, K. My name is Lubbert Das, 1765

Menger-Anderson, K. The siblings, 1910

Shannon, H. A host of shadows

BRAIN DAMAGE

Fulton, J. The sleeping woman

The **brainiacs**. Cooper, D.

The **braining** of Mother Lamprey. Ings, S. D.

BRAINWASHING

Gorman, E. Moral imperative

Robson, J. The girl hero's mirror says he's not the one

The **brake** fluid at Gina's. Trezise, R.

Bramah, Ernest

The disappearance of Marie Severe

The Mammoth book of vintage whodunnits; edited by Maxim Jakubowski

Brammer, Billy Lee

The Gay Place [excerpt]

Lone Star literature; from the Red River to the Rio Grande; edited by Don Graham

Brammer, Sidney

When Leslie Got the Call

Southwest Review v94 no2 p189-211 2009

Brammer, William *See* Brammer, Billy Lee, 1929-1978

Brand, Rebecca *See* Charnas, Suzy McKee

A **brand** new you. Kalotay, D.

Brandner, Gary

Words, words, words!

Dark delicacies 2; fear: more original tales of terror and the macabre by the world's greatest horror writers; edited by Del Howison and Jeff Gelb

Brandon, Jay

Pushed or was fell

Mystery Writers of America presents death do us part; new stories about love, lust, and murder; edited by Harlan Coben

Brandon, Paul and Dann, Jack

The transformation of Targ

Eclipse one; new science fiction and fantasy; edited by Jonathan Strahan

Brant, Beth E.

Swimming upstream

Reckonings; contemporary short fiction by Native American women; edited by Hertha D. Sweet Wong, Lauren Stuart Muller, Jana Sequoya Magdaleno

Turtle gal

Reckonings; contemporary short fiction by Native American women; edited by Hertha D. Sweet Wong, Lauren Stuart Muller, Jana Sequoya Magdaleno

Brant bites back. Bruen, K.

The **Brasher** girl. Gorman, E.

The **Brass** Ring. Popowich, N.

The **brat**. Thompson, J.

Brau, Edgar

Bárcena's dog

Brau, E. Casablanca and other stories; translated from the Spanish by Andrea G. Labinger, Joanne M. Yates, and Donald A. Yates; introduction by Donald A. Yates

The blessing

Brau, E. Casablanca and other stories; translated from the Spanish by Andrea G. Labinger, Joanne M. Yates, and Donald A. Yates; introduction by Donald A. Yates

The Buddha's eyes

Brau, E. Casablanca and other stories; translated from the Spanish by Andrea G. Labinger, Joanne M. Yates, and Donald A. Yates; introduction by Donald A. Yates

The calendar

Brau, E. Casablanca and other stories; translated from the Spanish by Andrea G. Labinger, Joanne M. Yates, and Donald A. Yates; introduction by Donald A. Yates

Casablanca

Brau, E. Casablanca and other stories; translated from the Spanish by Andrea G. Labinger, Joanne M. Yates, and Donald A. Yates; introduction by Donald A. Yates

BRAZIL—Amazon River Valley—*Continued*
 Verissimo, J. Returning from rubber gathering
Bahia
 Amado, J. How Porciúncula the mulatto got the
  corpse off his back
Manaus
 Hatoum, M. The truth is a seven-headed animal
Rio de Janeiro
 Barreto, P. The baby in rose tarlatan
 D'Allesandro, S. 14 days
 Daughtry, P. The mescaline runes
 Machado, A. The death of the standard-bearer
 Machado de Assis. The fortune-teller
 Machado de Assis. The nurse
 Machado de Assis. The secret heart
 Rebelo, M. Down our street
São Paulo
 Andrade, M. d. It can hurt plenty
 Lobato, J. B. M. The funnyman who repented
Brazil. Kercheval, J. L.
BRAZILIANS
New York (N.Y.)
 Lessa, O. Marta
Breach of promise of marriage. James, H.
Bread and bombs. Rickert, M.
Bread and the land. Allen, J. R.
The **bread** of the departed. Percoto, C.
The **Bread** Poultice. Best, L.
The **break**. Lamsley, T.
Break In. Williams, I.
Break it down. Davis, L.
Breakdown. Grey, E.
Breaker. Nelson, R. F.
The **Breakfast** Burrito. Bauer, C.
Breakfast in the house of the rising sun. Kiernan,
  C. R.
Breakfast on the West Side. Gangemi, K.
Breakfast serial. Kelly, R.
BREAKFASTS
 Harris, J. Breakfast at Tescos
Breaking and Crumbling from the 17th Floor.
  Braver, A.
Breaking and entering. Levithan, D.
The **breaking** of the bread. Lispector, C.
Breakout. Vollmann, W. T.
The **breakup**. Castillon, C.
Breakup Stories. Franzen, J.
The **breakup** vows. Almond, S.
BREAST
 Charnas, S. M. Boobs
 Goto, H. Tales from the breast
 Harris, A. L. Still life with boobs
 Hoffman, N. K. Savage breasts
 Menger-Anderson, K. The story of her breasts,
  1971
 Rodgers, S. J. Bust
 Romm, R. Where nothing is
 Sampsell, K. Swimsuit issue
 Schor, L. The history of my breasts
Breasts. Dybek, S.
A **Breath** of Air. Frame, R.
Breathe. Leavitt, C.
Breathe deep. Westlake, D. E.
BREATHING *See* Respiration
Breathing. Davis, C.
Breathing in public. Daughtry, P.
Breathing Jesus. Hempel, A.
Breathless in Bombay. Shroff, M. F.
Breathmoss. MacLeod, I.

Breathnach, Clare
 (jt. auth) See Breathnach, Michéal and
  Breathnach, Clare
Breathnach, Michéal and Breathnach, Clare
 The Coole Park problem
  Ghosts in Baker Street; edited by Martin H.
   Greenberg, Jon Lellenberg, Daniel
   Stashower
Brecious. Keret, E.
Breckenridge and the continuum. Silverberg, R.
A **breed** apart. Rand, K.
Breeding ground. Mosley, W.
Breeding maze. Niven, L.
Breeding Season. Betts, K.
Breen, Jon L.
 The adventure of the librarian's ghost
  Ghosts in Baker Street; edited by Martin H.
   Greenberg, Jon Lellenberg, Daniel
   Stashower
 The adventure of the missing three quarters
  Sherlock Holmes in America; edited by Mar-
   tin H. Greenberg, Jon L. Lellenberg, and
   Daniel Stashower.
 The adventure of the mooning sentry
  The World's finest mystery and crime stories,
   fourth annual collection; edited by Ed
   Gorman and Martin H. Greenberg
 All-star team
  Breen, J. L. Kill the umpire; the calls of Ed
   Gorgon
 The Babe Ruth murder case
  Breen, J. L. Kill the umpire; the calls of Ed
   Gorgon
 The body in the bullpen
  Breen, J. L. Kill the umpire; the calls of Ed
   Gorgon
 Designated murderer
  Breen, J. L. Kill the umpire; the calls of Ed
   Gorgon
 Diamond Dick
  Breen, J. L. Kill the umpire; the calls of Ed
   Gorgon
 Fall of a hero
  Breen, J. L. Kill the umpire; the calls of Ed
   Gorgon
 Horsehide sleuth
  Breen, J. L. Kill the umpire; the calls of Ed
   Gorgon
 Insider trading
  Breen, J. L. Kill the umpire; the calls of Ed
   Gorgon
 Instant replay
  Breen, J. L. Kill the umpire; the calls of Ed
   Gorgon
 Kill the umpire
  Breen, J. L. Kill the umpire; the calls of Ed
   Gorgon
 Malice at the mike
  Breen, J. L. Kill the umpire; the calls of Ed
   Gorgon
 The Mother's-Day doubleheader
  Breen, J. L. Kill the umpire; the calls of Ed
   Gorgon
 The number 12 jinx
  Breen, J. L. Kill the umpire; the calls of Ed
   Gorgon
 Old-timers' game
  Breen, J. L. Kill the umpire; the calls of Ed
   Gorgon

Breuer, Miles J.—*Continued*

Mechanocracy

    Breuer, M. J. The man with the strange head and other early science fiction stories; [by] Miles J. Breuer; edited and with an introduction by Michael R. Page.

Millions for defense

    Breuer, M. J. The man with the strange head and other early science fiction stories; [by] Miles J. Breuer; edited and with an introduction by Michael R. Page.

On board the martian liner

    Breuer, M. J. The man with the strange head and other early science fiction stories; [by] Miles J. Breuer; edited and with an introduction by Michael R. Page.

The oversight

    Breuer, M. J. The man with the strange head and other early science fiction stories; [by] Miles J. Breuer; edited and with an introduction by Michael R. Page.

A problem in communication

    Breuer, M. J. The man with the strange head and other early science fiction stories; [by] Miles J. Breuer; edited and with an introduction by Michael R. Page.

Brewer, Richard J.

Keeping it good

    Meeting across the river; stories inspired by the haunting Bruce Springsteen song; edited by Jessica Kaye and Richard J. Brewer

The **brewer's** son. Millett, L.

BREWSTER, SIR DAVID, 1781-1868

About

    Enright, A. Men and angels

Brian aka "Bear". Cooper, D.

BRIBERY

    Bierce, A. Corrupting the press

    Hodgson, W. H. The red herring

    McCauley, W. Palaver

    Zoshchenko, M. Loose packaging

Bricks. Bushnell, J. T.

The **bride.** Granados, C.

Bride 91. Silverberg, R.

The **bride** of Jagannath. Lamb, H.

Bride of violence. Block, L.

Brides by night. Diago, E. R.

Bridesmaid. Ebenbach, D. H.

BRIDGE (GAME)

    Dahl, R. My lady love, my dove

The **Bridge.** Alarcón, D.

The **Bridge.** Blish, J.

The **bridge.** Yanique, T.

Bridge O' doom. Rand, K.

Bridge of sighs. Benedict, P.

Bridge ship Golden Gate. Bova, B.

Bridge ship Golden Gate [continued] Bova, B.

The **bridge** under the Danube. Novakovich, J.

BRIDGES

    Bell, K. The casual car pool

    Clarke, S. Tom Brightwind; or, How the fairy bridge was built at Thoresby

    Treat, J. Covered bridge

    Yanique, T. The bridge

    Zelazny, R. Threshold of the prophet

The **brief** cure of Aunt Fanny. Dunbar, P. L.

Brief encounters with Che Guevara. Fountain, B.

A **brief** exercise in the absurd. Domecq, B.

Brief flower. Piñón, N.

The **Brief** Gravity of the Earth and Eighteen. Cinadr, B. D.

A **brief** history of death switches. Eagleman, D.

The **brief** history of the dead. Brockmeier, K.

A **brief** history of us. Dean, D.

Brief interviews with hideous men. Wallace, D. F.

The **Briefcase.** Makkai, R.

Brierley, Shirley

    Shirley Brierley: Screaming and Shouting [Medical Humanities, 31 no1 June 2005]

    Journal of Medical Ethics v31 no6 p48 Je 2005 supp

BRIGANDS AND ROBBERS

    See also Outlaws; Robbery

    Allen, W. Tandoori ransom

    Barnard, R. The Cairo Road

    Liss, D. The double dealer

    Saro-Wiwa, K. Africa kills her sun

    Smith, M. Pajamas

Bright, Nellie R.

Black

    "Tell it to us easy" and other stories; a complete short fiction anthology of African American women writers in Opportunity magazine, (1923-1948); edited by Judith Musser.

The **bright** graves. Kiely, B.

Bright is innocent: scenes from an imaginary movie. Baumbach, J.

Bright morning. Ford, J.

Bright waters. Brown, J.

Brighten up. Vonnegut, K.

Brightly shine the stars tonight. Guo, S.

Briley boy. Anderson, R. M.

Brilliant Billy dubbs on the ocean floor. LaSalle, P.

A **brilliant** idea and his own. Helprin, M.

Brimacombe, M.

    Gunman aimed to please [Medical Humanities, v30 no2 December 2004]

    Journal of Medical Ethics v30 no2 p93-4 D 2004 supp

Brin, David

Ickies in mirrorshades

    This is my funniest; leading science fiction writers present their funniest stories ever; edited by Mike Resnick

Bring brang brung. Muñoz, M.

Bring everybody. Yates, D.

Bringing Belle home. Campbell, B. J.

Bringing up baby. Wilde, H.

The **bris.** Pollack, E.

The **Briscian** saint. Baker, K.

Brite, Poppy Z.

Calcutta, lord of nerves

    The living dead; edited by John Joseph Adams

Crown of thorns

    Brite, P. Z. Antediluvian tales

The devil of Delery street

    McSweeney's enchanted chamber of astonishing stories; edited by Michael Chabon; illustrations by Mike Mignola

    Brite, P. Z. Antediluvian tales

The feast of St. Rosalie

    Brite, P. Z. Antediluvian tales

Four flies and a swatter

    Brite, P. Z. Antediluvian tales

Brite, Poppy Z.—*Continued*
  Henry goes shopping
    Brite, P. Z. Antediluvian tales
  The working slob's prayer; (being a night in the
      history of the Peychaud grill)
    Brite, P. Z. Antediluvian tales
  Wound Man and horned melon go to Hell
    Brite, P. Z. Antediluvian tales
BRITISH
                    Africa
  James, C. L. R. Ghana independence
  Resnick, M. The lord of the jungle
  Smith, M. Game drive
                    Asia
  Lamb, H. Ameer of the sea
  Lamb, H. Prophecy of the blind
  Lamb, H. Rose face
  Lamb, H. Said Afzel's elephant
                  Bahamas
  Shukman, H. Castaway
                  Belgium
  Faber, M. The courage consort
                  Ecuador
  Kuprin, A. I. Liquid sunshine
                    Egypt
  Dahl, R. Madame Rosette
  Soueif, A. Sandpiper
              Foreign countries
  Aird, C. The widow's might
                    France
  Lowry, M. June the 30th, 1934
  Perry, A. A tale of one city
  Williams, C. The owl
                    Greece
  Dahl, R. Katina
  Dahl, R. Yesterday was beautiful
                    India
  Hoch, E. D. The face of Ali Baba
  Parashuram. The scripture read backward
                  Indonesia
  Toer, P. A. Revenge
                  Ireland
  Kiely, B. The weavers at the mill
                    Italy
  Barnard, R. The path to the shroud
  Donoghue, E. The dormition of the virgin
  Palazzeschi, A. Dagobert
  Templeton, E. The blue hour
  Templeton, E. Nymph & faun
  Wright, P. 'Tutto bene?'
                  Malaysia
  Sillitoe, A. The gate of a great mansion
                    Mexico
  Glantz, M. English love
  Lowry, M. Under the volcano
  Samuels, M. A gentleman from Mexico
                North Africa
  Fowler, C. The threads
                    Russia
  Archer, J. Don't drink the water
  Pinborough, S. The Bohemian of the Arbat
                South Africa
  Gordimer, N. Beethoven was one-sixteenth
      black
                    Spain
  Sillitoe, A. Guzman, go home
                Switzerland
  James, C. L. R. Ghana independence

                Trinidad and Tobago
  Jardim, K. The jaguar
                    Uganda
  Baingana, D. Tropical fish
                United States
  Dunbar, P. L. The case of Cadwallader
  Johnson, R. K. Hey love
  Kyle, A. Allegiance
  Park, P. The blood of Peter Francisco
  Robinson, R. A perfect stranger
  Scott, J. Freeze-out
BRITISH ARISTOCRACY *See* Aristocracy—En-
      gland
BRITISH COLUMBIA *See* Canada—British Co-
      lumbia
BRITISH GUIANA *See* Guyana
British horror weekend British invasion; edited by
      Christopher Golden, Tim Lebbon & James
      A. Moore
BRITISH SOLDIERS *See* Soldiers—Great Brit-
      ain
BRITISH VIRGIN ISLANDS
  González, K. A. Wake
BRITISH WEST INDIES *See* West Indies
Brito, Leonora
  The last jumpshot
    Urban Welsh; new short fiction; edited by
      Lewis Davies
BRITTANY (FRANCE) *See* France—Brittany
Brittany? Oh: she's in translucent blue. Shirley, J.
Briussov, Valeri *See* Bryusov, Valery
      Yakovlevich, 1873-1924
Brkic, Courtney Angela
  Departure
    The Kenyon Review v28 no2 p4-10 Spr 2006
  the offering
    The North American Review v290 no6 p30-3
      N/D 2005
  The translator
    Stumbling and raging; more politically in-
      spired fiction; edited by Stephen Elliott;
      with associate editors Greg Larson [et al.]
The **broad** estates of death. Fox, P.
Broches, Rochel
  Little Abrahams
    Arguing with the storm; stories by Yiddish
      women writers; edited and with a preface
      by Rhea Tregebov; introduction by Kathryn
      Hellerstein.
Brochure. Haldeman, J. W.
Brock, Geoffrey
  (tr.) *See* Eco, Umberto
Brockmeier, Kevin
  The air is full of little holes
    Brockmeier, K. The view from the seventh
      layer
  Andrea is changing her name
    Brockmeier, K. The view from the seventh
      layer
    New stories from the South; the year's best,
      2008; selected from U.S. magazines by ZZ
      Packer with Kathy Pories; with an introduc-
      tion by ZZ Packer
  The brief history of the dead
    The Year's best fantasy and horror: seven-
      teenth annual collection; edited by Ellen
      Datlow, Kelly Link and Gavin J. Grant
    The O. Henry Prize stories, 2005; edited and
      with an introduction by Laura Furman

BROTHERS—*Continued*

Stevens, J. D. Clara's PC and the second coming

Stevens, J. D. Flying

Stewart, P. Red means stop

Tenorio, L. The brothers

Tomlinson, J. Lake Charles

Tower, W. Retreat

Trevor, D. Haircuts

Uchida, H. The companion

Unger, D. Looking for war

Unger, D. Matisse

Upadhyay, S. The royal ghosts

Valdés, J. Cornelia

Varallo, A. Pool season

Watkins, S. Adam's house

Westcott, G. The sailor

Westermann, J. The secret

Wilson, K. Blowing up on the spot

Wingate, S. Faster

Winton, T. Family

Winton, T. Sand

Wolff, T. The rich brother

Wolven, S. Atomic supernova

Wolven, S. St. Gabriel

Woolson, C. F. The South Devil

Brothers. Chase, M.

Brothers. Molodowsky, K.

Brothers. Sillitoe, A.

The **brothers**. Tenorio, L.

BROTHERS AND SISTERS

See also Twins

Adichie, C. N. Cell one

Adichie, C. N. Tomorrow is too far

Adiga, A. The Cathedral of Our Lady of Valencia

Ahmed, N. Aqua Blue

Akpan, U. C. Fattening for Gabon

Allen, J. R. The green apocalypse

Alvarado, B. Can you hear me?

Alvarado, B. What Lydia thinks of roses

Anderson, B. Tuataras

Angel, J. Supplement

Arnow, H. L. S. The goat who was a cow

Azzam, S. Her tale

Bakken, K. N. The effects of light

Bass, R. Field events

Bass, R. Her first elk

Beagle, P. S. El regalo

Beattie, A. Mostre

Beattie, A. The rabbit hole as likely explanation

Beattie, A. The rabbitt hole as likely explanantion

Black, H. The coat of stars

Black, R. . . . Divorced, beheaded, survived

Bluestein, E. Tea

Boyd, W. The pigeon

Boylan, C. Benny gets the blame

Bukoski, A. A guide to American trees

Bukoski, A. Hello from Ture

Burgin, R. Miles

Burgin, R. My sister's house

Burke, T. On the front

Burke, T. Pomo basuto

Cassill, R. V. The first day of school

Chattin, J. The nearest thing in the world

Chekhov, A. P. The brother: a slice of life

Chilson, P. Disturbance-loving species

Cody, L. Turning it round

Cox, F. B. Madeline's version

Crider, B. I was a teenage vampire

Crouse, D. The observable universe

Daley-Clarke, D. Saturday soup

D'Ambrosio, C., Jr. Blessing

Davidson, C. The apprentice's guide to modern magic

Desaulniers, J. After Rosa Parks

Donoghue, E. Baggage

Donoghue, E. Necessary noise

Doran, M. M. A well-arranged life

Dormen, L. General strike

Dormen, L. Gladiators

Dybek, S. The Palatski Man

Effgen, R. The inappropriate behavior of our alleged loved ones

Eisenberg, D. Some other, better Otto

Encinosa Fú, M. What for, this burden

Engberg, S. River hills

Erdrich, L. The blue velvet box

Espinosa, G. Family birthday wishes

Faber, M. The Fahrenheit twins

Feitell, M. Here beneath low-flying planes

Fincke, G. Rip his head off

Frost, G. Divertimento

Fuentes, M. Looking for eight

Gaitskill, M. College town, 1980

Gifford, B. Ball lighting

Gilman, G. I. Down the wall

Goonan, K. A. Sundiver day

Gordon, M. Storytelling

Granados, C. The latchkey chronicles: Goldfinger

Granados, C. The latchkey chronicles: Manguera wars

Granados, C. The latchkey chronicles: Séance

Halam, A. Cheats

Harleman, A. Romantic fever

Haslett, A. Devotion

Hawes, L. Summerlands

Hempel, A. Cotton Flat Road

Hempel, A. The lady will have the Slug Louie

Hempel, A. Today will be a quiet day

Hernandez, L. Count the raindrops

Hernandez, L. The red curtain

Hoffman, A. The summer kitchen

Holladay, C. C. The quick-change artist

Hospital, J. T. North of nowhere

Hyde, M. Everything valuable and portable

Jablonski, N. Succor

James, H. My lost darling

Judah, S. Rats and cobras

Kent, L. T. In common

Kercheval, J. L. Damage

Kercheval, J. L. Honors

Komla-Ebri, K. "Home . . . sickness"

LaBrie, A. Snowball

Lahiri, J. Only goodness

Lamsley, T. Running in the family

Lanagan, M. Singing my sister down

Lange, R. Fuzzyland

Lasdun, J. The incalculable life gesture

Lin, T. Sincerity

Lordon, R. Like a sore thumb

Luongo, M. Every year the baby dies

Luvaas, W. The sexual revolution

Magee, K. The business of souls

Malla, P. The past composed

Mandelbaum, P. Lynn, raving

Brumfiel, Geoff
The crime of the century
Nature v438 p256 N 10 2005
Brun, Lisbeth
Excerpts from a novel
The Literary Review (Madison, N.J.) v51 no3 p128-38 Spr 2008
BRUNEI
Sterling, B. Green days in Brunei
Bruno and Leo have a fight. James, C. L. R.
Bruno the bulldog has heart pain. James, C. L. R.
Bruno the bulldog has heart pain--Continued. James, C. L. R.
Brust, Steven
The man from Shemhaza
Thieves' world; enemies of fortune; edited by Lynn Abbey
BRUTALITY *See* Cruelty; Violence
BRYAN, WILLIAM JENNINGS, 1860-1925
About
Landis, G. A. The eyes of America
Bryan Dead. Justice, J. R.
Bryant, Cullene
The Exhibition
Dalhousie Review v88 no2 p249-54 Summ 2008
Bryant, Deyonne
Tough Love
Callaloo v29 no1 p45-54 Wint 2006
Bryusov, Valery Yakovlevich
The Republic of Southern Cross
Worlds apart; an anthology of Russian fantasy and science fiction; edited and with commentary by Alexander Levitsky; translated by Alexander Levitsky and Martha T. Kitchen
Bub, Barry
Going to the DOCS [Medical Humanities, 32 no1 June 2006]
Journal of Medical Ethics v32 no6 p45-6 Je 2006 supp
Bubba. Solomita, S.
Bubba Ho-Tep. Lansdale, J. R.
"The **bubble** reputation". Bierce, A.
Bubbles. Sallis, J.
Buber, Martin
Epicycle: Here Where One Stands
Parabola v31 no4 p45 Wint 2006
BUBONIC PLAGUE *See* Plague
Buchan, Elizabeth
Precious pearls
Good Housekeeping v241 no4 p269-71 O 2005
Buchanan, Carolyn
The Road
The Kenyon Review v30 no2 p115-22 Spr 2008
Buchanan, W. W.
In the cellar
Bendel-Simso, M. M., ed. Early American detective stories; an anthology; edited by LeRoy Lad Panek and Mary M. Bendel-Simso.
The **Buchovskys** on Their Own. Raeff, A.
Buck fever [excerpt] Rehder, B.
Buckbee, Brian
My Trip to the Aquarium
The Georgia Review v61 no2 p386-96 Summ 2007

Buckell, Tobias S.
Necahual
So long been dreaming; postcolonial science fiction & fantasy; Nalo Hopkinson & Uppinder Mehan, eds
Nord's gambit
This is my funniest 2; leading science fiction writers present their funniest stories ever; edited by Mike Resnick
The people's machine
Sideways in crime; an alternate mystery anthology; edited by Lou Anders
Toy planes
Nature v437 p1064 O 13 2005
Buckets of blood. Hadley, T.
Buckeye the elder. Udall, B.
Buckingham, Polly
My Doppelganger's Arms
The North American Review v292 no3/4 p28-32 My/Ag 2007
Buckler, Ernest
Another Christmas
Buckler, E. Thanks for listening; stories and short fictions by Ernest Buckler; selected and edited by Marta Dvořak
The bars and the bridge
Buckler, E. Thanks for listening; stories and short fictions by Ernest Buckler; selected and edited by Marta Dvořak
Children
Buckler, E. Thanks for listening; stories and short fictions by Ernest Buckler; selected and edited by Marta Dvořak
The choice
Buckler, E. Thanks for listening; stories and short fictions by Ernest Buckler; selected and edited by Marta Dvořak
The Christmas order
Buckler, E. Thanks for listening; stories and short fictions by Ernest Buckler; selected and edited by Marta Dvořak
Cleft rock, with spring
Buckler, E. Thanks for listening; stories and short fictions by Ernest Buckler; selected and edited by Marta Dvořak
The clumsy one
Buckler, E. Thanks for listening; stories and short fictions by Ernest Buckler; selected and edited by Marta Dvořak
The doctor and the patient
Buckler, E. Thanks for listening; stories and short fictions by Ernest Buckler; selected and edited by Marta Dvořak
The dream and the triumph
Buckler, E. Thanks for listening; stories and short fictions by Ernest Buckler; selected and edited by Marta Dvořak
Education at Mimi's
Buckler, E. Thanks for listening; stories and short fictions by Ernest Buckler; selected and edited by Marta Dvořak
The finest tree
Buckler, E. Thanks for listening; stories and short fictions by Ernest Buckler; selected and edited by Marta Dvořak
The first born son
Buckler, E. Thanks for listening; stories and short fictions by Ernest Buckler; selected and edited by Marta Dvořak

Bukoski, Anthony—*Continued*

The sons of the desert [variant title: Stan and Ollie]
> Bukoski, A. Twelve below zero: new and expanded edition; stories

Twelve below zero
> Bukoski, A. Twelve below zero: new and expanded edition; stories

A walk down lonely street
> Bukoski, A. North of the port; stories

The Wally na Zdrowie show
> Bukoski, A. North of the port; stories

The wand of youth
> Bukoski, A. North of the port; stories

Wesolewski, Hedwig room 301 [variant title: Harry and the dancer]
> Bukoski, A. Twelve below zero: new and expanded edition; stories

The woman who ate cat food
> Bukoski, A. Twelve below zero: new and expanded edition; stories

The wood-bat league
> Bukoski, A. Twelve below zero: new and expanded edition; stories

Your hit parade
> Bukoski, A. Twelve below zero: new and expanded edition; stories

Bukowski, Charles

20 tanks from Kasseldown
> Bukowski, C. Portions from a wine-stained notebook; uncollected stories and essays, 1944-1990; edited and with an introduction by David Stephen Calonne

Aftermath of a lengthy rejection slip
> Bukowski, C. Portions from a wine-stained notebook; uncollected stories and essays, 1944-1990; edited and with an introduction by David Stephen Calonne

Distraction in the literary life
> Bukowski, C. Portions from a wine-stained notebook; uncollected stories and essays, 1944-1990; edited and with an introduction by David Stephen Calonne

Hard without music
> Bukowski, C. Portions from a wine-stained notebook; uncollected stories and essays, 1944-1990; edited and with an introduction by David Stephen Calonne

Just passing time
> Bukowski, C. Portions from a wine-stained notebook; uncollected stories and essays, 1944-1990; edited and with an introduction by David Stephen Calonne

The night nobody believed I was Allen Ginsberg
> Bukowski, C. Portions from a wine-stained notebook; uncollected stories and essays, 1944-1990; edited and with an introduction by David Stephen Calonne

The way it happened
> Bukowski, C. Portions from a wine-stained notebook; uncollected stories and essays, 1944-1990; edited and with an introduction by David Stephen Calonne

Workout
> Bukowski, C. Portions from a wine-stained notebook; uncollected stories and essays, 1944-1990; edited and with an introduction by David Stephen Calonne

Bulgakov, Mikhail Afanas´evich

The fatal eggs
> Worlds apart; an anthology of Russian fantasy and science fiction; edited and with commentary by Alexander Levitsky; translated by Alexander Levitsky and Martha T. Kitchen

The master and Margarita [excerpt]
> Worlds apart; an anthology of Russian fantasy and science fiction; edited and with commentary by Alexander Levitsky; translated by Alexander Levitsky and Martha T. Kitchen

BULGARIA

Gospodinov, G. First steps

Gospodinov, G. Forging the Bulgarian earring

Bulgarin, Faddeĭ Venedikovitch

[Im-] Plausible fantasies, or A journey in the 29th century [abridged]
> Worlds apart; an anthology of Russian fantasy and science fiction; edited and with commentary by Alexander Levitsky; translated by Alexander Levitsky and Martha T. Kitchen

BULIMIA

Meacham, R. Weights and measures

Bull, Jesse Short

Dot Com Indian
> *Tribal College Journal of American Indian Higher Education* v18 no1 p32-3 Fall 2006

Bull, Scott Emerson

Mr. Sly stops for a cup of joe
> The Year's best fantasy and horror: seventeenth annual collection; edited by Ellen Datlow, Kelly Link and Gavin J. Grant

Bull, Warren

Heidegger's cat
> Medium of murder; edited by Susan Budavari and Suzanne Flaig

Bull in the heather. Mebus, S.

The **Bull** Moose at bay. Resnick, M.

Bulldog. Miller, A.

Bulldozer. Barron, L.

BULLDOZERS

Sturgeon, T. Killdozer!

A **bullet** for Billy the Kid. Henry, W.

Bullet in the brain. Wolff, T.

Bulletproof. Boyle, T. C.

Bulletproof girl. Dalton, Q.

BULLFIGHTERS AND BULLFIGHTING

Zelazny, R. Corrida

BULLFIGHTING *See* Bullfighters and bullfighting

Bullfighting. Doyle, R.

Bullheads. Lorrie, M.

Bullion. Hodgson, W. H.

Bullock, John

Taller
> *The Antioch Review* v66 no4 p764-76 Fall 2008

The **bullock** run. McDonald, R.

The **Bulls** at San Luis. Waters, D.

Bull's-eye. Kellerman, F.

The **Bull's** Eye. Schram, P.

Bully!. Resnick, M.

BULLYING

Anderson, B. Discontinuous lives

Baker, K. Plotters and shooters

Crone, M. The odd fellow

BULLYING—*Continued*
  Doyle, R. New boy
  Englander, N. How we avenged the Blums
  Fujino, C. Her room
  Granados, C. My girlfriend Bobbi
  Le, N. Halflead Bay
  Rickert, M. More beautiful than you
  Somerville, P. English cousin
  Starr, J. The last pick
  Wallace, J. Dead man
Bulushi, Saud
  Sounds of the sea
    Oranges in the sun; short stories from the
      Arabian Gulf; edited and translated by Deb-
      orah S. Akers, Abubaker A. Bagader
The **bumblety's** marble. Rambo, C.
Bump. Deaver, J.
Bump. Pourciau, G.
Bumping uglies. Moore, D.
Bums. Krueger, W. K.
Bunch, Chris
  Murdering Uncle Ho
    Alternate generals III; edited by Harry Turtle-
      dove and Roland J. Green
Bunch, Rose
  Season
    River Styx no79 p80-1 2009
A **bunch** of broccoli and the third shelf. Vapnyar,
  L.
The **Bunder**. Adiga, A.
Bunin, Ivan Alekseevich
  Antigone
    Bunin, I. A. The collected stories of Ivan Bu-
      nin; translated from the Russian, and with
      an introduction by Graham Hettlinger
  Ballad
    Bunin, I. A. The collected stories of Ivan Bu-
      nin; translated from the Russian, and with
      an introduction by Graham Hettlinger
  Calf's head
    Bunin, I. A. The collected stories of Ivan Bu-
      nin; translated from the Russian, and with
      an introduction by Graham Hettlinger
  Calling cards
    Bunin, I. A. The collected stories of Ivan Bu-
      nin; translated from the Russian, and with
      an introduction by Graham Hettlinger
  Caucasus
    Bunin, I. A. The collected stories of Ivan Bu-
      nin; translated from the Russian, and with
      an introduction by Graham Hettlinger
  Chang's dreams
    Bunin, I. A. The collected stories of Ivan Bu-
      nin; translated from the Russian, and with
      an introduction by Graham Hettlinger
  Cleansing Monday
    Bunin, I. A. The Elagin affair and other sto-
      ries; translated from the Russian, with an
      introduction, by Graham Hettlinger
    Bunin, I. A. The collected stories of Ivan Bu-
      nin; translated from the Russian, and with
      an introduction by Graham Hettlinger
  Cold fall [Same as: Cold autumn]
    Bunin, I. A. The collected stories of Ivan Bu-
      nin; translated from the Russian, and with
      an introduction by Graham Hettlinger

Cranes
  Bunin, I. A. The collected stories of Ivan Bu-
    nin; translated from the Russian, and with
    an introduction by Graham Hettlinger
The Elagin affair
  Bunin, I. A. The Elagin affair and other sto-
    ries; translated from the Russian, with an
    introduction, by Graham Hettlinger
  Bunin, I. A. The collected stories of Ivan Bu-
    nin; translated from the Russian, and with
    an introduction by Graham Hettlinger
The eve
  Bunin, I. A. The collected stories of Ivan Bu-
    nin; translated from the Russian, and with
    an introduction by Graham Hettlinger
First class
  Bunin, I. A. The collected stories of Ivan Bu-
    nin; translated from the Russian, and with
    an introduction by Graham Hettlinger
The gentleman from San Francisco
  Bunin, I. A. The collected stories of Ivan Bu-
    nin; translated from the Russian, and with
    an introduction by Graham Hettlinger
The hunchback's affair [Same as: Hunchback's
  romance]
  Bunin, I. A. The collected stories of Ivan Bu-
    nin; translated from the Russian, and with
    an introduction by Graham Hettlinger
Ida
  Bunin, I. A. The collected stories of Ivan Bu-
    nin; translated from the Russian, and with
    an introduction by Graham Hettlinger
In Paris
  Bunin, I. A. The collected stories of Ivan Bu-
    nin; translated from the Russian, and with
    an introduction by Graham Hettlinger
Late hour
  Bunin, I. A. The collected stories of Ivan Bu-
    nin; translated from the Russian, and with
    an introduction by Graham Hettlinger
Light breathing [Same as: Gentle breathing]
  Bunin, I. A. The collected stories of Ivan Bu-
    nin; translated from the Russian, and with
    an introduction by Graham Hettlinger
Little fool
  Bunin, I. A. The collected stories of Ivan Bu-
    nin; translated from the Russian, and with
    an introduction by Graham Hettlinger
Mitya's love
  Bunin, I. A. The Elagin affair and other sto-
    ries; translated from the Russian, with an
    introduction, by Graham Hettlinger
  Bunin, I. A. The collected stories of Ivan Bu-
    nin; translated from the Russian, and with
    an introduction by Graham Hettlinger
Muza
  Bunin, I. A. The collected stories of Ivan Bu-
    nin; translated from the Russian, and with
    an introduction by Graham Hettlinger
Old and young
  Bunin, I. A. The collected stories of Ivan Bu-
    nin; translated from the Russian, and with
    an introduction by Graham Hettlinger
On onc familiar street
  Bunin, I. A. The collected stories of Ivan Bu-
    nin; translated from the Russian, and with
    an introduction by Graham Hettlinger

Bunin, Ivan Alekseevich—*Continued*
Raven
  Bunin, I. A. The collected stories of Ivan Bu-
    nin; translated from the Russian, and with
    an introduction by Graham Hettlinger
Rusya
  Bunin, I. A. The collected stories of Ivan Bu-
    nin; translated from the Russian, and with
    an introduction by Graham Hettlinger
The scent of apples
  Bunin, I. A. The Elagin affair and other sto-
    ries; translated from the Russian, with an
    introduction, by Graham Hettlinger
  Bunin, I. A. The collected stories of Ivan Bu-
    nin; translated from the Russian, and with
    an introduction by Graham Hettlinger
Sky above a wall
  Bunin, I. A. The collected stories of Ivan Bu-
    nin; translated from the Russian, and with
    an introduction by Graham Hettlinger
Styopa
  Bunin, I. A. The collected stories of Ivan Bu-
    nin; translated from the Russian, and with
    an introduction by Graham Hettlinger
Sukhodol
  Bunin, I. A. The Elagin affair and other sto-
    ries; translated from the Russian, with an
    introduction, by Graham Hettlinger
  Bunin, I. A. The collected stories of Ivan Bu-
    nin; translated from the Russian, and with
    an introduction by Graham Hettlinger
Summer day
  Bunin, I. A. The collected stories of Ivan Bu-
    nin; translated from the Russian, and with
    an introduction by Graham Hettlinger
Sunstroke
  Bunin, I. A. The collected stories of Ivan Bu-
    nin; translated from the Russian, and with
    an introduction by Graham Hettlinger
Tanya
  Bunin, I. A. The Elagin affair and other sto-
    ries; translated from the Russian, with an
    introduction, by Graham Hettlinger
  Bunin, I. A. The collected stories of Ivan Bu-
    nin; translated from the Russian, and with
    an introduction by Graham Hettlinger
Wolves
  Bunin, I. A. The collected stories of Ivan Bu-
    nin; translated from the Russian, and with
    an introduction by Graham Hettlinger
Zoyka and Valeriya
  Bunin, I. A. The collected stories of Ivan Bu-
    nin; translated from the Russian, and with
    an introduction by Graham Hettlinger
Bunn, Austin
The ledge
  Best American fantasy; guest editors Ann &
    Jeff VanderMeer; series editor Matthew
    Cheney
Buonarotti, Michelangelo *See* Michelangelo Buo-
    narroti, 1475-1564
Buonarroti, Michel Angelo *See* Michelangelo
    Buonarroti, 1475-1564
Buoyant. Luongo, M.
Burbank's crime. Bierce, A.
Burch, Beverly
The Second Life
  New England Review v30 no1 p104-14 2009
Burd. McLean, S.

The **Burden**. Foy, D.
Bureau of vital statistics. Levi, P.
BUREAUCRACY
    See also Civil service
  Barthelme, D. The new member
  Barthelme, D. Subpoena
  Finger, A. Vincent
  Grimes, C. Customs in a developing country: a
    prefatory story
  Grimes, C. The inspection
  Jones, E. P. Marie
  Levi, P. Bureau of vital statistics
  Lewis, A. R. Request for proposal
  Li Yiyun. Persimmons
  Lima Barreto, A. H. d. The man who knew
    Javanese
  May, S. The wizard of Khao-I-Dang
  Nelson, R. F. Mechanical men
  Parks, T. Changing address
  Powers, J. F. Dawn
  Quiroga, H. The incense tree roof
  Rylands, J. T. Service
  Sayles, J. Casa de los Babys
  Scholes, K. The doom of love in small places
  Scholes, K. The doom of love is small spaces
  Sherman, J. The usurper memos
  Tambour, A. The shoe in SHOES window
  Tomlinson, J. First husband, first wife
  Zhu Wen. Ah, Xiao Xie
  Zoshchenko, M. A bathhouse
  Zoshchenko, M. A crime report
  Zoshchenko, M. The galosh
  Zoshchenko, M. The photograph
  Zoshchenko, M. Red tape
Burgess, Marie
Remember the Time
  Women's Studies Quarterly v36 no1/2 p236-
    48 Spr/Summ 2008
Burgess. Minoff, A.
Burgin, Richard
Aerialist
  Burgin, R. The identity club; new and select-
    ed stories
Bodysurfing
  So the story goes; twenty-five years of the
    Johns Hopkins short fiction series; edited
    by John T. Irwin and Jean McGarry; with
    a foreword by John Barth
  Burgin, R. The identity club; new and select-
    ed stories
Carbo's
  Burgin, R. The identity club; new and select-
    ed stories
The Dinner
  River Styx no69/70 p92-106 2005
Ghost parks
  Burgin, R. The identity club; new and select-
    ed stories
The horror conference
  Burgin, R. The identity club; new and select-
    ed stories
The identity club
  The Best American mystery stories, 2005; ed-
    ited and with an introduction by Joyce Car-
    ol Oates; Otto Penzler, series editor
  Burgin, R. The identity club; new and select-
    ed stories

Burgin, Richard—*Continued*

Beha, C. R. The Ecco anthology of contemporary American short fiction; selected by Joyce Carol Oates and Christopher R. Beha.

Jonathan and Lillian
TriQuarterly no123 p203-23 2005

A Letter in Las Vegas
TriQuarterly no129 p45-65 2007

The liar
Burgin, R. The identity club; new and selected stories

Memo and Oblivion
Confrontation no104 p37-60 Summ 2009

Mercury
Burgin, R. The identity club; new and selected stories

Miles
Burgin, R. The identity club; new and selected stories

My black Rachmaninoff
Burgin, R. The identity club; new and selected stories

My sister's house
Burgin, R. The identity club; new and selected stories

Notes on Mrs. Slaughter
Burgin, R. The identity club; new and selected stories

The park
Burgin, R. The identity club; new and selected stories

Simone
Burgin, R. The identity club; new and selected stories

Song of the earth
Burgin, R. The identity club; new and selected stories

The spirit of New York
Burgin, R. The identity club; new and selected stories

The urn
Burgin, R. The identity club; new and selected stories
The Antioch Review v63 no3 p497-510 Summ 2005

Vacation
Burgin, R. The identity club; new and selected stories
Pushcart prize XXXI: best of the small presses 2007; edited by Bill Henderson; with the Pushcart Prize editors

The victims
Burgin, R. The identity club; new and selected stories

With all my heart
Burgin, R. The identity club; new and selected stories

The **burglar**. Tabor, M. L.

BURGLARS *See* Thieves

BURIAL *See* Funeral rites and ceremonies

BURIAL, PREMATURE *See* Premature burial

The **burial**. Carew, J.

Burial. Gildner, G.

Burial. Ts'an-hsüeh

BURIED ALIVE *See* Premature burial

Buried in the sky. Shirley, J.

Buried talents. Matheson, R.

BURIED TREASURE

Hambly, B. There shall your heart be also
Hodgson, W. H. In the Wailing Gully
L'Amour, L. Off the mangrove coast
Lupoff, R. A. Treasure of the red robe men
Peelle, L. Shadow on a weary land
Pohl, F. The merchants of Venus
Queen, E. The adventure of the needle's eye
Sayles, J. Treasure
Silverberg, R. The sixth palace
Valdés, J. People like us

Burke, Alafair

Winning
Mystery Writers of America presents the blue religion; new stories about cops, criminals, and the chase; edited by Michael Connelly
The Best American mystery stories, 2009; edited and with an introduction by Jeffery Deaver

Burke, Bridgit M.

My Quinn Lee Story
Thomas M. Cooley Journal of Practical & Clinical Law v8 no1 p43-54 2006

Burke, James Lee

Big midnight special
The Best American mystery stories, 2009; edited and with an introduction by Jeffery Deaver

The burning of the flag
New stories from the South: the year's best, 2005; edited by Shannon Ravenel; with a preface by Jill McCorkle
Burke, J. L. Jesus out to sea; stories

The convict
Wide awake in the Pelican State; stories by contemporary Louisiana writers; edited by Ann Brewster Dobie; with a foreword by Ernest J. Gaines

Jesus out to sea
Burke, J. L. Jesus out to sea; stories
Esquire v145 no4 p158-61, 184 Ap 2006

Mist
Burke, J. L. Jesus out to sea; stories
The Best American mystery stories, 2008; edited and with an introduction by George Pelecanos; Otto Penzler, series editor
The Southern Review (Baton Rouge, La.) v43 no1 p133-45 Wint 2007

The molester
Burke, J. L. Jesus out to sea; stories

The night Johnny Ace died
Burke, J. L. Jesus out to sea; stories
Esquire v147 no3 p134, 136, 138, 140, 142, 144, 146 Mr 2007

A season of regret
Burke, J. L. Jesus out to sea; stories
New stories from the South: the year's best, 2007; selected from U.S. magazines by Edward P. Jones with Kathy Pories; with an introduction by Edward P. Jones
The Best American mystery stories 2007; edited and with and introduction by Carl Hiaasen; Otto Penzler, series editor

Texas City, 1947
Burke, J. L. Jesus out to sea; stories

The village
Burke, J. L. Jesus out to sea; stories

Water people
Burke, J. L. Jesus out to sea; stories

By hook or by crook. Drees, C.
By Irish nights. Donovan, G.
By moonlight. Beagle, P. S.
By Now It Should Sound Like Music. Sheets, N.
By the Pool. McDonald, F.
By the ruins of "El Walarieh". L'Amour, L.
By the scruff of the soul. Davis, D. S.
By the time I get to Phoenix. Roberson, J.
By the time you get this. Reinhorn, H.
By the waters of San Tadeo. L'Amour, L.
By the Wolf. Trethewey, E.
Byatt, A. S.
 The Narrow Jet
  The Paris Review v47 p81-104 Spr 2005
Byblis. Kanner, R.
Bychkov, Andrey
 The Hunter
  Iowa Review v35 no1 p70-5 Spr 2005
Bye Bye Brewster. Barthelme, S.
Bye-bye Larry. Karlin, K.
Bye-bye Natalia. Faber, M.
Byers, Michael
 Bartholomew's Island
  Chicago Review v54 no3 p115-27 Wint 2009
 Betty Brown Calling
  Michigan Quarterly Review v48 no2 p175-84
   Spr 2009
 Mister Jerry Is a Big One
  Western Humanities Review v59 no1 p88-97
   Spr 2005
Bynum, Sarah Shun-Lien
 Accomplice
  The Best American short stories, 2004; edited
   by Lorrie Moore; Katrina Kenison series
   editor
 Creep
  TriQuarterly no121 p18-35 2005
 The Voyage Over
  The Literary Review (Madison, N.J.) v48 no3
   p8-24 Spr 2005
 Yurt
  The New Yorker v84 no21 p74-81 Jl 21 2008
BYOB FAQ. Bisson, T.
Byobu. Ahrens, L.
Byrne, Joe
 Coral
  Hanging Loose no94 p98-101 2009
 Ice Water
  Hanging Loose no93 p97-8 2008
 Waking Up
  Hanging Loose no93 p94-6 2008
Byrne, Mary
 Only the strong survive
  Queens noir; edited by Robert Knightly
Byrne, Eugene
 Bagged 'n' tagged
  Witpunk; edited by Claude Lalumière and
   Marty Halpern
**BYRON, GEORGE GORDON BYRON, 6TH
 BARON, 1788-1824**
       About
 Crowley, J. Missolonghi 1824
 Michaels, L. Annabella's hat
 Zelazny, R. There shall be no moon!
Byron the Lyron. Bausch, R.
BYZANTINE EMPIRE
 DeNiro, A. Our Byzantium

C

c. 1600: China Sea: True Blue [Excerpt from The
  Young Man with the Carnation] Dinesen, I.
c. 1970: Vietnam: First Blood [From The things
  they carried] O'Brien, T.
"C.S.A.". Arnold, G.
CAB DRIVERS
 Chekhov, A. P. Ivan the cabman
 Coleman, W. My son, my son
 Davies, L. The fare
 Maloney, D. The best laid plans
 Schwarzschild, E. What to expect
 Shaw, I. Borough of cemeteries
 Villard, M. The lookout
CABALA
 Auslander, S. One death to go
Cabbages and kale or: How we downsized North
  America. Marusek, D.
A **cabin** on the coast. Wolfe, G.
CABINETMAKERS
 Brockmeier, K. A fable with a photograph of a
  glass mobile on the wall
 Vonnegut, K. The commandant's desk
CABLE NEWS NETWORK
 Dalton, Q. Back on earth
ČABRINOVIC, NEDELJKO, 1895-1916
       About
 Novakovich, J. The stamp
Cacek, P. D. (Patricia D.)
 The keeper
  Inferno; new tales of terror and the supernatu-
   ral; edited by Ellen Datlow.
Cacek, Patricia D. *See* Cacek, P. D. (Patricia D.)
Cadaver dog. Quertermous, B.
Cadbury, Alison
 Dimitra's Path
  The Georgia Review v60 no3/4 p553-61
   Fall/Wint 2006
CADETS
 Harrison, H. Space rats of the CCC
Cadigan, Pat
 The day the Martels got the cable
  This is my funniest 2; leading science fiction
   writers present their funniest stories ever;
   edited by Mike Resnick
 The final remake of *The return of Little Latin
  Larry,* with a completely remastered
   soundtrack and the original audience
  Rewired; the post-cyberpunk anthology;
   James Patrick Kelly & John Kessel, editors
 Jimmy
  The Del Rey book of science fiction and fan-
   tasy; sixteen original works by speculative
   fiction's finest voices; edited by Ellen
   Datlow
 Mother's milt
  Witpunk; edited by Claude Lalumière and
   Marty Halpern
 Nothing personal
  The Year's best science fiction: twenty-fifth
   annual collection; edited by Gardner Dozois
 Stilled life
  Inferno; new tales of terror and the supernatu-
   ral; edited by Ellen Datlow.
  Year's best fantasy 8; edited by David G.
   Hartwell, Kathryn Cramer

Cadigan, Pat—*Continued*

Worlds of possibilities

Sideways in crime; an alternate mystery anthology; edited by Lou Anders

Cadillac. Barrett, M.

Cadillac Hearse. Conley, C.

CADILLAC MOTOR CAR DIVISION

Hernandez, L. The last car

Hernandez, L. This is our song for today

Hernandez, L. Tuesday morning

Hernandez, L. We have a job for you

Hernandez, L. Yes I am a virgin

Cadnum, Michael

Arrival

Cadnum, M. Can't catch me and other twice-told tales

Bear it away

Cadnum, M. Can't catch me and other twice-told tales

Bite the hand

Cadnum, M. Can't catch me and other twice-told tales

Can't catch me

Cadnum, M. Can't catch me and other twice-told tales

Daphne

Cadnum, M. Can't catch me and other twice-told tales

Elf trap

Cadnum, M. Can't catch me and other twice-told tales

Ella and the canary prince

Cadnum, M. Can't catch me and other twice-told tales

The flounder's kiss

Cadnum, M. Can't catch me and other twice-told tales

Give him the eye

Cadnum, M. Can't catch me and other twice-told tales

Gravity

Cadnum, M. Can't catch me and other twice-told tales

Hungry

Cadnum, M. Can't catch me and other twice-told tales

Medusa

Cadnum, M. Can't catch me and other twice-told tales

Mrs. Big

Cadnum, M. Can't catch me and other twice-told tales

Naked little men

Cadnum, M. Can't catch me and other twice-told tales

Or be to not

Cadnum, M. Can't catch me and other twice-told tales

P-bird

Cadnum, M. Can't catch me and other twice-told tales

Toad-rich

Cadnum, M. Can't catch me and other twice-told tales

Together again

Cadnum, M. Can't catch me and other twice-told tales

Cady, Jack

The souls of Drowning Mountain

The Year's best fantasy and horror: nineteenth annual collection; edited by Ellen Datlow and Kelly Link & Gavin J. Grant

Caesar and Nero. Wendroff, Z.

Caesar in Paris. Carew, J.

A **Cafecito** [Excerpt from A Cafecito Story/El Cuento del Cafecito] Alvarez, J.

CAFÉS *See* Restaurants, lunchrooms, etc.

Caffè Doppio. Frame, R.

Cagnone, Nanni

Dying Away

FMR (Black Edition) no20 p157-64 Jl/Ag 2007

Cahoots. Dunbar, P. L.

CAIN (BIBLICAL FIGURE)

About

Brett, S. Cain was innocent

Irvine, A. C. The fall at Shanghai

Scholes, K. East of Eden and just a little bit south

Cain, James M. (James Mallahan)

Pastorale

The Black Lizard big book of pulps; edited by Otto Penzler

Cain, Paul

One, two, three

The Black Lizard big book of pulps; edited by Otto Penzler

Pigeon blood

The Black Lizard big book of pulps; edited by Otto Penzler

Cain, Shannon

Cultivation

Pushcart prize XXXIII: best of the small presses 2009; edited by Bill Henderson with the Pushcart Prize editors

The necessity of certain behaviors

The O. Henry Prize stories 2008; edited and with an introduction by Laura Furman; with essays on the stories they admire most by jurors Chimamanda Ngozi Adiche, David Leavitt, David Means

New England Review v27 no2 p156-65 2006

The Queer Zoo

The Massachusetts Review v48 no1 p9-23 Spr 2007

Cain was innocent. Brett, S.

Caine, Rachel

The first day of the rest of your life

Many bloody returns; edited by Charlaine Harris and Toni L. P. Kelner

Roman holidays; or, SPQ-arrrrr

My big fat supernatural honeymoon; edited by P.N. Elrod.

Cairene dawn. Caselberg, J.

The **Cairene** Purse. Moorcock, M.

The **cairn** on the headland. Howard, R. E.

CAIRO (EGYPT) *See* Egypt—Cairo

The **Cairo** Road. Barnard, R.

The **cajun** knot. Fazi, M.

CAJUNS

Davis, A. B. The significance of importance

DeGravelles, C. The last man on Earth to play the bones

Donoghue, E. Enchantment

Soileau, S. The boucherie

Cake. Luongo, M.

CALIFORNIA—*Continued*

Yates, D. Oceanside, 1985
Yates, D. The sleep machine

19th century
Muller, M. The Indian witch

1846-1900
Gorriti, J. M. A year in California
Muller, M. The cyaniders

Gold discoveries
See California—1846-1900

Berkeley
Brady, C. Last of the true believers

Beverly Hills
Morrison, P. Morocco Junction 90210

Fresno
Muñoz, M. Bring brang brung
Muñoz, M. The faith healer of Olive Avenue
Muñoz, M. The good brother
Muñoz, M. The heart finds its own conclusion
Muñoz, M. Ida y vuelta
Muñoz, M. Lindo y querido
Muñoz, M. Señor X
Muñoz, M. Tell him about Brother John
Muñoz, M. When you come into your kingdom

Hollywood
Abbott, L. K. As fate would have it
Barrett, L. Blue vandas
Ellison, H. The resurgence of Miss Ankle-strap Wedgie
Fowler, C. The univited
Fuchs, D. Florida
Fuchs, D. The golden West
Fuchs, D. A Hollywood diary
Fuchs, D. Triplicate
Goldberg, L. Jack Webb's star
Hallberg, G. R. Early humans
Hart, C. G. Murder for lunch
Kiernan, C. R. Bela's plot
Levinson, R. S.
Matthews, C. And then she was gone
Pierce, T. J. Studio sense
Read, C. Hungry enough
Sayles, J. Dillinger in Hollywood
Shepard, L. Larissa Miusov
Willis, C. At the Rialto
Willis, C. Inside job

Los Angeles
Bacigalupi, P. The gambler
Baingana, D. Lost in Los Angeles
Bradbury, R. Another fine mess
Brown, F. The wench is dead
Coleman, W. Backcity transit by day
Coleman, W. Shark liver oil
Connelly, M. Mulholland dive
Deaver, J. The voyeur
Donoghue, E. Baggage
Due, T. Amusement
Fitch, J. The method
Flynn, T. T. Brother murder
Gerrold, D. Report from the near future: crystallization
Green, G. "Your sister and some wine!"
Hamilton, D. Midnight in Silicon Valley
Haywood, G. A. Heatseeker
Haywood, G. A. Moving pictures
Hirahara, N. Number 19
Holmes, E. Dangerous days
Kiernan, C. R. San Andreas (1998)
Lange, R. Bank of America

Lange, R. Blind-made products
Lange, R. The Bogo-Indian defense
Lange, R. Culver City
Lange, R. Dead boys
Lange, R. Everything beautiful is far away
Lange, R. Fuzzyland
Lange, R. The hero shot
Lange, R. Long lost
Lange, R. Loss prevention
Lange, R. Love lifted me
Lange, R. Telephone bird
Leung, B. Drawings by Andy Warhol
Levinson, R. S. And the winner is . . .
Marks, N. Down and out in Brentwood
McGlynn, D. Moonland on fire
Meloy, M. Liliana
Meyers, A. It's too late, baby
Michaels, L. Nachman from Los Angeles
Michaels, L. Of mystery there is no end
Mohan, S. Our flag was still there
Monk, B. Small fry
Montgomery, L. Avalanche! (a fairy tale)
Mosley, W. After the wedding
Mosley, W. The apology
Mosley, W. The big nickel
Mosley, W. Black dog
Mosley, W. Breeding ground
Mosley, W. Details
Mosley, W. Maxie
Mosley, W. Red caddy
Mosley, W. The right mistake
Mosley, W. The trail
Mosley, W. Traitor
Mosley, W. Trifecta
Mosley, W. Two women
Nelson, A. Dick
Neri, K. Hocus-pocus on Friday the 13th
Nolan, W. F. The small world of Lewis Stillman
Pascoe, J. The kidnapper bell
Phillips, G. Roger Crumbler considered his shave
Phillips, G. Swift boats for Jesus
Phillips, G. Where all our dreams come true
Phillips, S. The girl who kissed Barnaby Jones
Pollack, N. City of commerce
Pratt, T. and Van Eekhout, G. Robots and falling hearts
Pronzini, B. I wasn't there
prostitutes. See stories by Trezise, R.
Reinhorn, H. By the time you get this
Rice, C. Over thirty
Roley, B. A. American son [excerpt]
Roley, B. A. Kinship
Shirley, J. Brittany? Oh: she's in translucent blue
Shirley, J. Buried in the sky
Shirley, J. One stick: both ends sharpened
Siegel, J. Empathy
Silver, L. Fish
Straight, S. The Golden Gopher
Straub, P. Lapland; or, Film noir
Tea, M. 9/11 L.A. bookstore
Tobar, H. Once more, Lazarus
Tomlinson, J. Paragon tea
Trezise, R. On the strip
Van Booy, S. The world laughs in flowers
Wagman, D. What you see
Weil, G. The house in the desert
Williams, N. J. Rickshaw runner

Calypso in Berlin. Hand, E.
Cam, Nguyen Nguyet
  (tr.) See Nguyen Viet Ha
La **cama** de Lukin/Lukin's bed. Abenshushan, V.
Camaro blue. Moody, B.
Camas Man. Mannan, H.
Cambias, James L.
  The oceans of the blind
    The Year's best science fiction: twenty-
    second annual collection; edited by Gardner
    Dozois
  See my king all dressed in red
    Crossroads; tales of the southern literary fan-
    tastic; edited by F. Brett Cox and Andy
    Duncan
The **cambist** and Lord Iron: a fairy tale of eco-
  nomics. Abraham, D.
CAMBODIA
  Ahmed, F. "Return"
  May, S. The monkey king
  Moorcock, M. Crossing into Cambodia
  Ryman, G. The last ten years in the life of Hero
    Kai
  Ryman, G. Pol Pot's beautiful daughter (fantasy)
CAMBODIAN REFUGEES
  Lapcharoensap, R. Priscilla the Cambodian
  May, S. The wizard of Khao-I-Dang
CAMBODIANS
            Thailand
  Lapcharoensap, R. Priscilla the Cambodian
CAMBRIDGE (MASS.) *See* Massachusetts—
  Cambridge
Cambridge is sinking!. Clayton, J. J.
CAMELS
  Fischer, J. Undead camels ate their flesh
Camenietzki, Shalom
  A Dry Depression
    Dalhousie Review v85 no1 p81-93 Spr 2005
The **camera** and the cobra. Nash, R.
Camera obscura. Monteleone, T. F.
CAMERAS
  Milionis, C. The find
  Nash, R. The camera and the cobra
Cameron, Bill
  Slice of pie
    Killer year; stories to die for . . . from the
    hottest new crime writers; edited by Lee
    Child
Cameron, Peter
  The Abridged Versions
    The Yale Review v94 no3 p150-4 Jl 2006
CAMEROON
  Mokoso, N. God of meme
El **Camino** del Rio [excerpt] Sanderson, J.
Caminsky, Jeffrey
  Crapshoot
    The Michigan Bar Journal v86 no8 p30-4 Ag
    2007
  Crucible of Justice
    The Michigan Bar Journal v88 no8 p28-31
    Ag 2009
Camoin, Francois
  A Difficult Man
    Western Humanities Review v62 no1 p109-16
    Wint 2008
Camouflage. Reed, R.
Camouflage. Watkins, S.
Camouflage [excerpt] Haldeman, J. W.

Camp, John, 1944-
    See also Sandford, John, 1944-
CAMP COUNSELORS
  Delfosse, O. G. Men and Boys
  Sherman, R. Keeping time
Camp whitehorse. Erian, A.
Camp William. Ruefle, M.
Campagnoli, Michael
  The Company of Strangers
    Southern Humanities Review v39 no1 p48-67
    Wint 2005
Campaign Pictures. Schrader, S.
CAMPAIGNS, PRESIDENTIAL
          United States
    See Presidents—United States—Election
Campbell, Bonnie Jo
  Boar Taint
    The Kenyon Review v30 no3 p60-73 Summ
    2008
  Boat taint
    Campbell, B. J. American salvage; stories
  Bringing Belle home
    Campbell, B. J. American salvage; stories
  The burn
    Campbell, B. J. American salvage; stories
  Falling
    Campbell, B. J. American salvage; stories
  Family reunion
    Campbell, B. J. American salvage; stories
  Fuel for the millennium
    Campbell, B. J. American salvage; stories
  The inventor, 1972
    Campbell, B. J. American salvage; stories
    The Southern Review (Baton Rouge, La.) v44
    no1 p15-24 Wint 2008
  King Cole's American Salvage
    Campbell, B. J. American salvage; stories
  September News from Susanna's Farm
    TriQuarterly no133 p176-85 2009
  The solutions to Brian's problem
    Campbell, B. J. American salvage; stories
  Storm warning
    Campbell, B. J. American salvage; stories
  The trespasser
    Campbell, B. J. American salvage; stories
  Winter life
    Campbell, B. J. American salvage; stories
  World of gas
    Campbell, B. J. American salvage; stories
  The yard man
    Campbell, B. J. American salvage; stories
    The Southern Review (Baton Rouge, La.) v44
    no3 p397-418 Summ 2008
Campbell, Bruce
  (tr.) See Majfud, Jorge
Campbell, Ellen Prentiss
  The Bicycle Lesson
    The Massachusetts Review v49 no3 p353-62
    Aut 2008
Campbell, Ewing
  Floaters
    The Georgia Review v59 no3 p535-45 Fall
    2005
  The Levanto
    The Georgia Review v58 no4 p887-97 Wint
    2004

Campbell, Felicia
Murder is academic
Las Vegas noir; edited by Jarrett Keene & Todd James Pierce.
Campbell, Hazel V.
The parasites
"Tell it to us easy" and other stories; a complete short fiction anthology of African American women writers in Opportunity magazine, (1923-1948); edited by Judith Musser.
Part of the pack: another view of night life in Harlem
"Tell it to us easy" and other stories; a complete short fiction anthology of African American women writers in Opportunity magazine, (1923-1948); edited by Judith Musser.
Campbell, J. R.
The entwined
Gaslight grimoire; fantastic tales of Sherlock Holmes; edited by J. R. Campbell and Charles Prepolec
Campbell, Ramsey
The announcement
Dark delicacies; original tales of terror and the macabre by the world's greatest horror writers; edited by Del Howison and Jeff Gelb
Raised by the moon
Weird shadows over Innsmouth; edited by Stephen Jones; illustrated by Randy Broecker [et al.]
Respects
British invasion; edited by Christopher Golden, Tim Lebbon & James A. Moore
Seeing the world
Summer chills; strangers in stranger lands; edited by Stephen Jones
The voice of the beach
Poe's children; the new horror: an anthology; [edited by] Peter Straub.
CAMPING
See also Wilderness survival
Alvarado, B. In box canyon
Anaya, R. A. The place of the swallows
Bishop, T. I cain't go
D'Ambrosio, C., Jr. The high divide
Link, K. Monster
Morton, L. Black Mill Cove
Preston, D. and Child, L. Gone fishing
Raymond, J. Old joy
Rock, P. Stranger
Shiina, M. The yellow tent on the roof
Stamm, P. Everyone's right
Steck, U. Phantoms
Trezise, R. The magician
Wallace, R. Logjam
Wilcox, J. Camping out
Camping in. Moss, B. K.
Camping out. Wilcox, J.
Campisi, Stephanie
The title of this story
Sedia, E. Paper cities; an anthology of urban fantasy

Campo, Ángel del
Papando moscas / Catching Flies [Part of a special issue: Elogio de la mosca en el arte / In Praise of Flies in Art]
Artes de Mexico no93 p48-9, 86-7 Mr 2009
Campra, Rosalba
Dream tiger
English translations of short stories by contemporary Argentine women writers; edited by Eliana Cazaubon Hermann; translated by Sally Webb Thornton
CAMPS, SUMMER *See* Summer camps
CAMPUS LIFE *See* College life
Camus, Albert
The Adulterous Wife
The Kenyon Review v28 no2 p42-57 Spr 2006
CAMUS, ALBERT, 1913-1960
About
Di Filippo, P. Sisyphus and the stranger
About
Di Filippo, P. Sisyphus and the stranger
A **can** of worms. Bova, B.
Can we talk. Barthelme, D.
Can Xue *See* Ts'an-hsüeh, 1953-
Can you hear me? Alvarado, B.
Can you help me out here? Ferrigno, R.
CANADA
de Chambrey, M. Hurting Hugh
Martel, Y. The facts behind the Helsinki Roccamatios
Robinson, E. Terminal Avenue
Willis, C. Daisy, in the sun
Windley, C. Home schooling
Zentner, A. Touch
Rural life
Buckler, E. Another Christmas
Buckler, E. Cleft rock, with spring
Buckler, E. The clumsy one
Buckler, E. The dream and the triumph
Buckler, E. The first born son
Buckler, E. Goodbye, prince
Buckler, E. Just like everyone else
Buckler, E. Return trip to Christmas
Buckler, E. You could go anywhere now
Munro, A. Half a grapefruit
Munro, A. Working for a living
Alberta
Hirshberg, G. Millwell
British Columbia
Lowry, M. The forest path to the spring
Munro, A. Silence
Roden, B. Northwest passage
Calgary
Lam, D. The seventy-two-ounce steak challenge
Rees, R. Hand of a thief
Rees, R. If a mote
Rees, R. Solange
Rees, R. Tunnels
Rees, R. Upstairs
Manitoba
Leiren-Young, M. Frost-bitten
Lumley, B. Born of the winds
Shields, C. Reportage
Montreal
Cohen, L. The favourite game [excerpt]
Ebenbach, D. H. Rue Rachel
Ohlin, A. Edgewater
Nova Scotia
Buckler, E. The bars and the bridge

Canfield, Henry Spofford
The common sense of John Thomas
Adventures in the West; stories for young readers; edited by Susanne George Bloomfield and Eric Melvin Reed
Canin, Ethan
The palace thief
The Paris review book for planes, trains, elevators, and waiting rooms; by the editors of the Paris review; with an introduction by Richard Powers
The **caning**. Percoto, C.
Cann, Dana
Caterpillar
Gettysburg Review v22 no2 p229-32 Summ 2009
Canned goods. Disch, T. M.
CANNERIES
Mueller, D. The night my brother worked the header
CANNES (FRANCE) *See* France—Cannes
CANNIBALISM
Alexie, S. Ghost dance
Anderson, P. The sharing of flesh
Anderson, P. Welcome
Battersby, L. In from the sow
Bierce, A. To Fiji and return
Boudinot, R. Blood relatives I: My mother was a monster
Dunsany, E. J. M. D. P., Baron. The two bottles of relish
Ellin, S. The specialty of the house
Evenson, B. An accounting
Holder, N. I know who you ate last summer
Holder, N. Out twelve-steppin, summer of AA
Klages, E. Be prepared
Lanagan, M. The goosle
Matheson, R. The children of Noah
Niles, S. All my bloody things
Rahman, I. Eating, Ohio
Silverberg, R. Road to nightfall
Stafford, J. A modest proposal
Stokes, C. The man who ate Michael Rockefeller
Wolfe, G. The hero as werwolf
Canning, Rick
Take It from Me
New England Review v27 no3 p6-19 2006
The **cannon**. Link, K.
Canoeists. Bass, R.
CANOES AND CANOEING
Bass, R. Canoeists
Gebert, A. Two in the same boat
Mattison, A. The odds it would be you
Rosa, J. G. The third bank of the river
Can't catch me. Cadnum, M.
Can't catch me. Morrissey, T.
Cantogallo. Winn, T.
Cantor, Rachel
Tibet, New York
New England Review v29 no4 p140-8 2008
The **Cantoria** delle Messe by Luca Della Robbia. Mencoboni, M.
The **cantor's** daughter. Nadelson, S.
Canty, Kevin
The birthday girl
Canty, K. Where the money went; stories

Blue boy
The New Granta book of the American short story; edited and introduced by Richard Ford
The boreal forest
Canty, K. Where the money went; stories
Burning bridges, breaking glass
Canty, K. Where the money went; stories
The emperor of ice cream
Canty, K. Where the money went; stories
In the burn
Canty, K. Where the money went; stories
No place in this world for you
Canty, K. Where the money went; stories
Sleeping beauty
Canty, K. Where the money went; stories
They were expendable
Canty, K. Where the money went; stories
Where the money went
Canty, K. Where the money went; stories
Canyon Ghosts [Excerpt from There's This River] Sadler, C.
Canyons. Varble, V.
Capacity to kill. Montierth, D. A.
The **cape**. Hill, J.
CAPE COD (MASS.) *See* Massachusetts—Cape Cod
Cape tribulation. Hospital, J. T.
Capel, Theo
The red Mercedes
Passport to crime; the finest mystery stories from International Crime Writers; edited by Janet Hutchings
Capildeo, Vahni
Peacock blue
Trinidad noir; edited by Lisa Allen-Agostini & Jeanne Mason.
Capital of the world. Patton, J.
CAPITAL PUNISHMENT
Barnes, H. L. Punishment
Bierce, A. An execution in Batrugia
Hillerman, T. First lead gasser
Hogan, C. Two thousand volts
Lanagan, M. Singing my sister down
Martel, Y. Manners of dying
Capital punishment. Henry, L.
CAPITALISM
Bierce, A. The fall of the Republic
Bierce, A. Trustland: a tale of a traveler
CAPITALISTS AND FINANCIERS
See also Bankers; Millionaires; Wealth
Auchincloss, L. Other times, other ways
Charters, D. 2hot
Charters, D. After dark
Charters, D. Ambition
Charters, D. Baggage
Charters, D. Big break
Charters, D. Bonus round
Charters, D. Diary
Charters, D. Dinner party
Charters, D. Expenses
Charters, D. If you can't take a joke . . .
Charters, D. Infatuation
Charters, D. Inside track
Charters, D. Lawsuit
Charters, D. May Day
Charters, D. Merger
Charters, D. Misdial
Charters, D. Off-site

Carey, Jacqueline
In the matter of fallen angels
Elemental; the Tsunami relief anthology; stories of science fiction and fantasy; [edited by] Steven Savile and Alethea Kontis; introduction by Arthur C. Clarke
Carey, Kevin
Woods Hole Film Festival
The Literary Review (Madison, N.J.) v50 no2 p132-6 Wint 2007
Carey, Peter
The fat man in history
What are you looking at?; the first fat fiction anthology; edited by Donna Jarrell and Ira Sukrungruang
Carey, Robert *See* Monmouth, Robert Carey, 1st Earl of, 1560?-1639
Cargo. Fincke, G.
A **cargo** of cat. Bierce, A.
CARIBBEAN ISLANDS *See* West Indies
Caribbean provedor. Connell, E. S.
CARIBBEAN REGION
Adisa, O. P. The living roots
Chercover, S. A calculated risk
Hopkinson, N. The glass bottle trick
McGuane, T. The refugee
Rabe, J. Hang ten
Shomer, E. Rapture
Shukman, H. Darien dogs
Shukman, H. Old Providence
Updike, D. The last of the Caribs
Yanique, T. The bridge
El **Caribe** Hilton. Schrader, E. K.
Carker. Gershow, M.
Carl, Lillian Stewart
A mimicry of mockingbirds
The World's finest mystery and crime stories, fourth annual collection; edited by Ed Gorman and Martin H. Greenberg
The necromancer's apprentice
The Adventure of the missing detective and 19 of the year's finest crime and mystery stories!; edited by Ed Gorman and Martin H. Greenberg
Over the sea from Skye
Alternate generals III; edited by Harry Turtledove and Roland J. Green
Way down in Egypt's land
Thou shalt not kill; biblical mystery stories; edited by Anne Perry
Carleton, Lindsay
Everything I Have Made or Bought or Become
The Massachusetts Review v48 no1 p73-9 Spr 2007
Carlin, Paul
Fuel
Critical Quarterly v48 no3 p81-8 Aut 2006
Carlos I, King of Spain *See* Charles V, Holy Roman Emperor, 1500-1558
Carlson, P. M.
Frighted out of fear; or, the bombs bursting in air
Sisters on the case; celebrating twenty years of Sisters in Crime; edited by Sara Paretsky
Carlson, Ron
Beanball
The Best American mystery stories, 2009; edited and with an introduction by Jeffery Deaver

The Exploits of the Adventure Boys
Best Life v5 no10 p134-9, 153 D 2008/Ja 2009
In the Old Firehouse
Ploughshares v31 no4 p32-3 Wint 2005/2006
Introduction to Speech
Harper's v309 p80-5 D 2004
The Slump Buster
The Southern Review (Baton Rouge, La.) v41 no4 p858-64 Aut 2005
Victory at Sea
Iowa Review v38 no3 p96-109 Wint 2008/2009
Carmel. Lunstrum, K. S.
Carmell, Pamela
(tr.) *See* Curbelo, Jesús David
(tr.) *See* Mejides, Miguel
(tr.) *See* Portela, Ena Lucía
(tr.) *See* Yáñez, Mirta
Carmiña. Rivas, M.
Carmody, Isobelle
Perchance to dream
Dreaming again; thirty-five new stories celebrating the wild side of Australian fiction; edited by Jack Dann
Carnacki, the ghost finder. Hodgson, W. H.
Carney, Megan
Flighty Youth
Raritan v25 no4 p75-9 Spr 2006
Carney, Rob
Baked Beans in Redwoods
River Styx no76/77 p119 2008
Carnie. Means, D.
CARNIVAL
Barreto, P. The baby in rose tarlatan
Machado, A. The death of the standard-bearer
Carnival, Las Tablas. Henríquez, C.
CARNIVALS (CIRCUS) *See* Amusement parks
Carny. With, C.
Carofiglio, Gianrico
Christmas Eves
Rome noir; edited by Chiara Stangalino & Maxim Jakubowski; translated by Anne Milano Appel, Ann Goldstein, and Kathrine Jason
Carol head Lina heart. Steen, E. v.
Carolina live. Bradford, R.
Carolina Reel. Frame, R.
The **Carolingian** Period. Rhodes, D.
Carousel. White, B.
The **carp**. Uchida, H.
CARPACCIO, VITTORE, CA. 1465-1525 OR 6
  About
Denevi, M. Victor Scarpazo; or, The end of the pursuit
CARPATHIAN MOUNTAINS
Klassen, S. The Carpathians
The **Carpathians**. Klassen, S.
Carpe diem. Blackwell, K.
Carpenter, Megan M.
The Lexical Heart: A Dictionary
Legal Studies Forum v32 no1 p137-52 2008
The **carpenter**. Maxwell, W.
CARPENTERS
D'Ambrosio, C., Jr. The dead fish museum
Simpson, H. The door
Carpentry. Luvaas, W.
CARPETS
Saadat, R. Uncle Mehdi's carpet deal

CASABLANCA (MOTION PICTURE)
Brau, E. Casablanca
Casablanca. Brau, E.
CASANOVA, GIACOMO, 1725-1798
About
Schnitzler, A. Casanova's homecoming
Casanova's homecoming. Schnitzler, A.
Cascade Lake. McIlvoy, K.
Cascom Mountain Road. Williams, A. J.
Case closed. Manfredo, L.
The **case** for bread and sausage. Bukoski, A.
A **case** history. Auchincloss, L.
The **case** of Cadwallader. Dunbar, P. L.
The **case** of Charles Dexter Ward. Lovecraft, H. P.
The **case** of Colonel Crockett's violin. Linscott, G.
The **case** of Colonel Warburton's madness. Faye, L.
A **case** of conscience. Blish, J.
A **case** of consilience. MacLeod, K.
The **case** of Mr and Mrs Stetson. Oppenheim, E. P.
The **case** of Peter the painter. Thomas, D. S.
The **case** of the Greek key. Thomas, D. S.
The **case** of the hooked-billed kites [excerpt] Borthwick, J. S.
The **case** of the killer-diller. Woolrich, C.
The **case** of the king's evil. Thomas, D. S.
The **case** of the laughing queen. Goodis, D.
The **case** of the Peasenhall murder. Thomas, D. S.
The **case** of the phantom chambermaid. Thomas, D. S.
The **case** of the Portuguese sonnets. Thomas, D. S.
The **case** of the rival queens. Wheat, C.
The **case** of the salt and pepper shakers. Bender, A.
The **Case** of the Severed Hand. Coover, R.
The **case** of the tell-tale hands. Thomas, D. S.
The **case** of the Zimmermann telegram. Thomas, D. S.
A **case** study of emergency room procedure and risk management by hospital staff members in the urban facility. Richter, S.
Caselberg, Jay
Cairene dawn
Powers of detection; stories of mystery & fantasy; edited by Dana Stabenow
Casey, John
Rapunzel
Ploughshares v32 no4 p49-65 Wint 2006/2007
Casey, Pamela
(tr.) See Guo, Xiaolu
Casey, Sean
The Contents of This Shoe Box Are of Greater Worth Than Your Life
The Massachusetts Review v49 no3 p303-11 Aut 2008
Casey Smithers Jones. Johnston, P. E.
Cash crop. Willis, C.
Casimir Antoine's Jazzy Cancun Vacation. Chassagne, L.
CASINOS
Erdrich, L. Fuck with Kayla and you die
Steele, A. M. High roller
The **casket**. Romano, T.
Cason, Pat
Mermaid Fire
Calyx v24 no2 p81-92 Wint 2008
Casonetto's last song. Howard, R. E.

Cass, Meagan
Pas de Chat
South Carolina Review v40 no1 p39-53 Fall 2007
Cass, Richard
Come back
Best stories of the American West, v1; edited by Marc Jaffe
CASSIDY, BUTCH, B. 1866
About
Duncklee, J. The last breakfast
Cassill, R. V.
The first day of school
Short stories of the civil rights movement; an anthology; edited by Margaret Earley Whitt
Cassill, Ronald Verlin *See* Cassill, R. V., 1919-2002
Cassirer, Nadine Gordimer *See* Gordimer, Nadine, 1923-
Cassutt, Michael
The last Mars trip
Fourth planet from the sun; tales of Mars from The Magazine of Fantasy & Science Fiction; edited by Gordon Van Gelder
Cast a yellow shadow [excerpt] Thomas, R.
Castaneda, Ruben
Coyote hunt
D. C. noir; edited by George Pelecanos
Castaway. Shukman, H.
Castaway. Wolfe, G.
CASTE
Upadhyay, S. Father, daughter
India
Adiga, A. St. Alfonso's Boys' High School and Junior College
Das, K. The hijra
Lynn, D. H. Children of God
Mahāsvetā Debī. Bayen
Castelli, Carole
(tr.) See Glockner, Julio
Castillo, Ana
Remembering Las Cartoneras
Feminist Studies v34 no1/2 p263-75 Spr/Summ 2008
Castillo, Rafael
The battle of the Alamo
Lone Star literature; from the Red River to the Rio Grande; edited by Don Graham
Castillon, Claire
The breakup
Castillon, C. My mother never dies; stories; translated from the French by Alison Anderson.
I said one
Castillon, C. My mother never dies; stories; translated from the French by Alison Anderson.
The insect
Castillon, C. My mother never dies; stories; translated from the French by Alison Anderson.
Knots and nuts
Castillon, C. My mother never dies; stories; translated from the French by Alison Anderson.
Letter time
Castillon, C. My mother never dies; stories; translated from the French by Alison Anderson.

Castillon, Claire—*Continued*

Liar
    Castillon, C. My mother never dies; stories; translated from the French by Alison Anderson.

Munchhausen syndrome by proxy
    Castillon, C. My mother never dies; stories; translated from the French by Alison Anderson.

My best friend
    Castillon, C. My mother never dies; stories; translated from the French by Alison Anderson.

My dad's not a monster, mom
    Castillon, C. My mother never dies; stories; translated from the French by Alison Anderson.

My mother never dies
    Castillon, C. My mother never dies; stories; translated from the French by Alison Anderson.

A parka and some fur-lined boots
    Castillon, C. My mother never dies; stories; translated from the French by Alison Anderson.

A pink baby
    Castillon, C. My mother never dies; stories; translated from the French by Alison Anderson.

Punching bag
    Castillon, C. My mother never dies; stories; translated from the French by Alison Anderson.

Shame
    Castillon, C. My mother never dies; stories; translated from the French by Alison Anderson.

Ten operations in ten years
    Castillon, C. My mother never dies; stories; translated from the French by Alison Anderson.

There's a pill for that
    Castillon, C. My mother never dies; stories; translated from the French by Alison Anderson.

They drank champagne at the restaurant
    Castillon, C. My mother never dies; stories; translated from the French by Alison Anderson.

With affectionate kisses
    Castillon, C. My mother never dies; stories; translated from the French by Alison Anderson.

You'll be a woman, my girl
    Castillon, C. My mother never dies; stories; translated from the French by Alison Anderson.

Casting Call. Bamer, L.

Castle, Mort

The watcher at the window
    Poe's lighthouse; all new collaborations with Edgar Allan Poe; edited by Christopher Conlon

Castle, Sarah K.

Life, abundant and with simple joy
    Nature v450 p920 D 6 2007

The **castle** of iron. De Camp, L. S. and Pratt, F.

Castle of tears. Cook, G.

The **castle** on the hill. Crouse, D.

CASTLES

Lovecraft, H. P. The outsider
Resnick, L. Lady Roxanne La Belle
Templeton, E. Equality cake

Castor on troubled waters. Hughes, R.

CASTRATI *See* Eunuchs

CASTRATION

Baraka, I. A. Norman's date
Groff, L. L. DeBard and Aliette
Groff, L. L. DeBard and Aliette: a love story

Castro, Adam-Troy

Dead like me
    The living dead; edited by John Joseph Adams
Of a sweet slow dance in the wake of temporary dogs
    Nebula Awards showcase 2005; the year's best SF and fantasy; selected by the Science Fiction and Fantasy Writers of America; edited by Jack Dann

CASTRO, FIDEL, 1926-
About

McAllister, B. Southpaw
Unger, D. Cuban nights
Zebrowski, G. I walked with Fidel

The **casual** car pool. Bell, K.

Casual Labor. Miller, K. T.

Casual work. Zoshchenko, M.

CASUALTIES (WORLD WAR, 1914-1918) *See* World War, 1914-1918—Casualties

The **cat**. Uchida, H.

The **cat** bride. Yolen, J.

Cat call. Wentworth, K. D.

The **cat** from hell. King, S.

Cat got your tongue? MacAlister, K.

Cat 'n' mouse. Millhauser, S.

The **cat-woman**. Gardner, E. S.

CATACOMBS

Lane, J. The city of love

Catalog sales. McNett, M.

Catalogue. Reents, S.

Catalogue Sales. McNett, M.

Catastrophe Baker and a canticle for Leibowitz. Resnick, M.

Catastrophe baker and the cold equations. Resnick, M.

CATASTROPHES *See* Disasters

Catcalling: A Desire Story in Nine Parts. Rosenwaike, P.

The **catch**. Baker, K.

The **catch**. Hall, J. W.

Catch a falling heart. Cooper, J. C.

Category Z. Abbott, L. K.

CATERERS AND CATERING

Moody, R. The Mansion on the Hill

Caterina's loom. Messina, M.

Caterpillar. Cann, D.

Caterpillars. Lasdun, J.

Catfish. Manley, C.

CATFISHES

Ruffin, P. Teaching her about catfish

The **Cathedral** of Our Lady of Valencia. Adiga, A.

CATHEDRALS

Daniel, T. Ex cathedra
Thormahlen, A. A talk with Thomas

CATHER, WILLA, 1873-1947
About

Johnson, G. Women I've known

CELEBRITIES—*Continued*

Kaminsky, S. M. The shooting of John Roy Worth

Montgomery, L. Avalanche! (a fairy tale)

Pierce, T. J. Studio sense

Prior, A. Like he was just anyone else

Richter, S. My mother the rock star

Van Eekhout, G. Ghost market

Wellman, A. M. The Madison Heights syndrome

Celia. Gordon, P.

Celia is back. Hempel, A.

Celia's fish. Romm, R.

CELIBACY

See also Virginity

Celik, Behcet

So very familiar

Istanbul noir; edited by Mustafa Ziyalan & Amy Spangler; translated by Amy Spangler & Mustafa Ziyalan.

Cell call. Laidlaw, M.

Cell one. Adichie, C. N.

Cell phone. Schulze, I.

The **cellar**. Roth, H.

CELLISTS

Rhodes, D. The violoncello

Richter, S. Duet

CELTS

De Camp, L. S. and Pratt, F. The green magician

CEMETERIES

See also Tombstones

Bear, E. The dying of the light

Bierce, A. The City of the Gone Away

Bradbury, R. The handler

Capote, T. Among the paths to Eden

Chédid, A. The joyful death of Fassola

Chekhov, A. P. At the cemetery

Chekhov, A. P. A night at the cemetery [variant title: In the cemetery; In the graveyard]

Chercover, S. A sleep not unlike death

Ðoàn, L. The cemetery of Chua village

Dunbar, P. L. His bride of the tomb

Finch, P. The crazy helmets

Fonseca, R. The flesh and the bones

Gaiman, N. The witch's headstone

Gospodinov, G. One last tale of the nineties

Hamilton, L. K. Those who seek forgiveness

Hempel, A. The annex

Hempel, A. Church cancels cow

Howard, R. E. The cairn on the headland

Howard, R. E. The horror from the mound

Hyde, M. Miracle-Gro

Kiernan, C. R. Lafayette

Lovecraft, H. P. The statement of Randolph Carter

Machado, A. The first corpse

Maḥfūẓ, N. The rose garden

Munro, A. What do you want to know for?

Porter, K. A. The grave

Rivas, M. Havana's vast cemetery

Sillitoe, A. Spitfire

Symons, J. Flowers that bloom in the spring

Ts'an-hsüeh. Snake Island

Woolson, C. F. Rodman the keeper

Zebrowski, G. Earth around his bones

Zelazny, R. The man who loved the Faioli

Zelazny, R. The stainless steel leech

Zelazny, R. Walpurgisnacht

The **cemetery** of Chua village. Ðoàn, L.

CENSORSHIP

Levi, P. Censorship in Bitinia

Censorship in Bitinia. Levi, P.

The **centaur**. DeNiro, A.

The **centaur**. Saramago, J.

CENTAURS

Saramago, J. The centaur

Waldrop, H. Wild, wild horses

The **centaur's** son. Daughtry, P.

The **center**. Hempel, A.

The **center** of the world. Clark, G. M.

Centner, C. Martin

The Target

The Humanist v67 no5 p40-1 S/O 2007

CENTRAL AFRICA

Resnick, M. Bully!

CENTRAL AMERICA

Howard, R. E. The thing on the roof

Shepard, L. The Drive-In Puerto Rico

Shepard, L. The lepidopterist

CENTRAL ASIA

Berry, S. The devils' due

Lamb, H. The baiting of the warriors

Lamb, H. Bogatyr

Lamb, H. City under the sea

Lamb, H. Cossack wolf

Lamb, H. The devil's song

Lamb, H. An edge to a sword

Lamb, H. The king dies

Lamb, H. Koum

Lamb, H. Mark of Astrakhan

Lamb, H. Men from below

Lamb, H. The moon of Shawwul

Lamb, H. The outrider

Lamb, H. Over the river

Lamb, H. The phantom caravan

Lamb, H. The post in the steppe

Lamb, H. Red hands

Lamb, H. Sangar

Lamb, H. Singing girl

Lamb, H. The stone woman

Lamb, H. The two swords of Genghis Khan

Lamb, H. The vampire of Khor

Lamb, H. White falcon

Lamb, H. The winged rider

Lamb, H. The witch of Aleppo

Lamb, H. Witch woman

Lamb, H. Wolf-hounds of the steppe

Lamb, H. The wolf master

Livings, J. The heir

McInerney, J. In the north-west frontier province

Central Square. Trevor, D.

Centrally isolated. Fulton, A.

Cepeda Samudio, Alvaro

The soldiers

The Flight of the condor; stories of violence and war from Colombia; translated and compiled by Jennifer Gabrielle Edwards; foreword by Hugo Chaparro Valderrama.

CERAMICS *See* Pottery

Cercas, Javier

Agamemnon's Truth

Granta v98 p183-204 Summ 2007

CEREBRAL PALSY

Cooney, E. See the girl

McNett, M. Helping

The **cerebral** passion. Kelly, R.

CEREBROVASCULAR DISEASE
Clayton, J. J. Old friends
Eisenberg, D. Revenge of the dinosaurs
Hernandez, L. Over the Belle Isle boundary
Milofsky, D. Biofeedback
Minor, K. A day meant to do less
Ockert, J. Scarecrowed
Percy, B. Whisper
Sutton, B. The brotherhood of healing
Thompson, J. Escape
Tóibín, C. A journey
CEREMONIES *See* Rites and ceremonies
A **certain** recollection. Buentello, J.
A **certain** samaritan. Yates, D.
A **certain** swirl. Ruefle, M.
A **certain** talent. Weber, D.
A **Certain** Time. Bujinowski, A.
**CERVANTES SAAVEDRA, MIGUEL DE,
1547-1616**
Parodies, imitations, etc.
Pierson, C. What Quig found
CESTODA
Gordimer, N. Tape measure
Cetin, Inan
The bloody horn
Istanbul noir; edited by Mustafa Ziyalan &
Amy Spangler; translated by Amy Spangler
& Mustafa Ziyalan.
CEYLON *See* Sri Lanka
Chabon, Michael
The god of dark laughter
Feeling very strange; the Slipstream antholo-
gy; James Patrick Kelly & John Kessel, ed-
itors
The Martian agent, a planetary romance
McSweeney's mammoth treasury of thrilling
tales; edited by Michael Chabon
Steampunk; edited by Ann & Jeff
VanderMeer
Son of the wolfman
Beha, C. R. The Ecco anthology of contem-
porary American short fiction; selected by
Joyce Carol Oates and Christopher R.
Beha.
Chacón, Daniel
What Manner of Light?
Callaloo v32 no2 p354-60 Spr 2009
Chadbourn, Mark
Farewell to the 21st century girl
British invasion; edited by Christopher Gol-
den, Tim Lebbon & James A. Moore
Who slays the gyant, wounds the beast
Year's best fantasy 8; edited by David G.
Hartwell, Kathryn Cramer
Ch'ae, Manshik
The wife and children
Land of exile: contemporary Korean fiction;
translated and edited by Marshall Pihl,
Bruce Fulton, and Ju-Chan Fulton
Chagall's Wife. Ulman, A.
Chain. McIlvoy, K.
The **chain.** Wolff, T.
The **chain** of Aforgomon. Smith, C. A.
The **chains** that you refuse. Bear, E.
Chainsaw Putt-Putt. Gardner, P.
The **chair** of philanthromathematics. Henry, O.
CHAIRS
Crowther, P. Sitting pretty

Chalar, Julio C.
Taking a Statement
Legal Studies Forum v32 no1 p35-7 2008
Chalar, Laura
The Custodian
Legal Studies Forum v32 no1 p23-6 2008
A Great Day for Surubí
Legal Studies Forum v32 no1 p27-34 2008
Mortis Causa
Legal Studies Forum v32 no1 p15-22 2008
Chalele. Vermeulen, J.
Chalk [variant title: I killed Jennie] McBain, E.
Chalk it up. Mordecai, P.
Challah (Philadelphia, 1998). Mohanraj, M. A.
CHALLENGER (SPACE SHUTTLE)
DeAndrea, W. L. Sabotage
Challeno, Elise D.
A day's pay: a short story
"Tell it to us easy" and other stories; a com-
plete short fiction anthology of African
American women writers in Opportunity
magazine, (1923-1948); edited by Judith
Musser.
The **chambered** fruit. Rickert, M.
Chamberlin, Jeremiah
Missionaries
Michigan Quarterly Review v46 no1 p38-56
Wint 2007
Chamberlin, Joseph Edgar
(jt. auth) See Freeman, Mary Eleanor Wilkins
and Chamberlin, Joseph Edgar
Chambers, Christopher
Avatar
The darker mask; edited by Gary Phillips and
Christopher Chambers.
Chambers, Whitman
The duchess pulls a fast one
The Black Lizard big book of pulps; edited
by Otto Penzler
Chameleons. Moon, E.
Champion, Laurie
Where Has Your Lover Gone?
Callaloo v32 no2 p361-5 Spr 2009
The **champion.** Reid, G.
A **champion** of the sex. Bierce, A.
The **champion** of the world. Dahl, R.
CHANCE
Gallo, L. The king of slack
Garrett, G. P. Epilogue: my life as a home mov-
ie
Munro, A. Chance
Murakami, H. Chance traveler
Papadimitrakopoulos, I. H. Rosamund
Yates, D. Buster
Yates, D. Cartography
Chance. Harvey, J.
Chance. Munro, A.
Chance. Willis, C.
Chance traveler. Murakami, H.
Chandail. Beagle, P. S.
Chandler, A. Bertram
Giant killer
The Mammoth book of golden age science
fiction; edited by Isaac Asimov, Charles G.
Waugh and Martin H. Greenberg
Grimes and the Gaijin Daimyo
Dreaming again; thirty-five new stories cele-
brating the wild side of Australian fiction;
edited by Jack Dann

Chandler, Elizabeth
(tr.) See Platonov, Andrei
Chandler, Raymond
1938: Los Angeles: Waldo's Last Move [Excerpt from Red Wind]
Lapham's Quarterly v2 no2 p50-1 Spr 2009
Finger man
The Black Lizard big book of pulps; edited by Otto Penzler
Killer in the rain
The Black Lizard big book of pulps; edited by Otto Penzler
Red wind
A New omnibus of crime; edited by Tony Hillerman and Rosemary Herbert; contributing editors Sue Grafton and Jeffery Deaver
The Black Lizard big book of pulps; edited by Otto Penzler
Chandler, Robert
(tr.) See Platonov, Andrei
Chandler, Laurel *See* Holder, Nancy, 1953-
Chandra, Viola
"Light beer and peanuts"
Multicultural literature in contemporary Italy; edited by Marie Orton and Graziella Parati
Chang, Ai-ling *See* Chang, Eileen, 1920-1995
Chang, Diane
The Apartment
Prairie Schooner v79 no1 p98-109 Spr 2005
Chang, Eileen
Red rose, white rose
My mistress's sparrow is dead; great love stories, from Chekhov to Munro; edited by Jeffrey Eugenides
Chang, Lan Samantha
The Other Country
TriQuarterly no131 p39-44 2008
Chang, Leonard
Wood Chips
Prairie Schooner v79 no2 p114-21 Summ 2005
Chang Nor. Lamb, H.
The **change**. Keane, J. B.
The **change**. Martin, V.
A **change** in fashion. Millhauser, S.
A **change** in his heart. Fredrickson, J.
A **change** in the weather. Dann, J. and Dozois, G. R.
Change of Address. Tilghman, C.
A **change** of heart. Aird, C.
CHANGE OF LIFE *See* Menopause
A **change** of scene. Malouf, D.
A **change** of scenery. Lieberman, R.
Change the world. Mazza, C.
The **changeling**. Adrian, C.
Changeling. Hoffman, A.
Changeling. Mandelbaum, P.
The **changeling's** tale. Swanwick, M.
Changes. Lawrence, H.
Changing address. Parks, T.
Changing of the guard. Monteleone, T. F.
Chang's dreams. Bunin, I. A.
CHANNEL ISLANDS
Bell, T. The powder monkey
Chantal. Carew, J.
Chanting the violet dog down: a tale of Noreela. Lebbon, T.

Chaon, Dan
The bees
McSweeney's mammoth treasury of thrilling tales; edited by Michael Chabon
The Year's best fantasy and horror: seventeenth annual collection; edited by Ellen Datlow, Kelly Link and Gavin J. Grant
Poe's children; the new horror: an anthology; [edited by] Peter Straub.
I demand to know where you're taking me
Pushcart prize XXVII; best of the small presses; edited by Bill Henderson with the Pushcart prize editors
Shepherdess
Pushcart prize XXXII: best of the small presses 2008; edited by Bill Henderson with the Pushcart Prize editors
The Virginia Quarterly Review v82 no4 p174-87 Fall 2006
CHAPLIN, CHARLIE, 1889-1977
About
Williams, N. J. Rickshaw runner
Chapman, J. D.
Amanuensis
New stories from the South: the year's best, 2006; selected from U.S. magazines by Allan Gurganus with Kathy Pories; with an introduction by Allan Gurganus
King of the World
South Carolina Review v39 no2 p129-36 Spr 2007
The Museum of Wooden Architecture
Southern Humanities Review v41 no1 p62-71 Wint 2007
Sugar
River Styx no76/77 p79-90 2008
Chapman, Maile
Bit forgive
Best American fantasy; guest editors Ann & Jeff VanderMeer; series editor Matthew Cheney
Compulsion Vigil
The Literary Review (Madison, N.J.) v48 no3 p106-12 Spr 2005
Chapman, Stepan
Minutes of the last meeting
Steampunk; edited by Ann & Jeff VanderMeer
The revenge of the callico cat
The Year's best fantasy and horror: eighteenth annual collection; edited by Ellen Datlow, Kelly Link & Gavin J. Grant
Chaponda, Daliso
Heroic proportions
Passport to crime; the finest mystery stories from International Crime Writers; edited by Janet Hutchings
Chappell, Crissa-Jean
Practical Gifts
Southwest Review v90 no2 p195-202 2005
Chappell, Fred
Creeper shadows
Cat tales: fantastic feline fiction; edited by George H. Scithers
Dance of shadows
Year's best fantasy 8; edited by David G. Hartwell, Kathryn Cramer

Charters, David—*Continued*
Misdial
Charters, D. The insiders; a portfolio of stories from high finance
Off-site
Charters, D. The insiders; a portfolio of stories from high finance
Playing the game
Charters, D. The insiders; a portfolio of stories from high finance
Regrets
Charters, D. The insiders; a portfolio of stories from high finance
Riff-raff
Charters, D. The insiders; a portfolio of stories from high finance
Signing ceremony
Charters, D. The insiders; a portfolio of stories from high finance
Smart people
Charters, D. The insiders; a portfolio of stories from high finance
Takeover
Charters, D. The insiders; a portfolio of stories from high finance
Team move
Charters, D. The insiders; a portfolio of stories from high finance
Words
Charters, D. The insiders; a portfolio of stories from high finance
CHARWOMEN
See also Cleaning women
Charyn, Jerome
Letter from Mogilev
Inside the hornet's head; an anthology of Jewish American writing; edited by Jerome Charyn
La shampouineuse
Paris noir; capital crime fiction; edited by Maxim Jakubowski
White trash
Bronx noir; edited by S. J. Rozan
Young Isaac
Manhattan noir 2; the classics; edited by Lawrence Block
Chase, Anthony
One Hundred Four
UMKC Law Review v76 no3 p803-9 Spr 2008
Chase, Katie
Man and wife
Pushcart prize XXXIII: best of the small presses 2009; edited by Bill Henderson with the Pushcart Prize editors
Chase, Melvyn
Brothers
Chase, M. The terminal project and other voyages of discovery; stories
The busker
Chase, M. The terminal project and other voyages of discovery; stories
Dawn
Chase, M. The terminal project and other voyages of discovery; stories
False start
Chase, M. The terminal project and other voyages of discovery; stories

Leapers
Chase, M. The terminal project and other voyages of discovery; stories
The perimeter
Chase, M. The terminal project and other voyages of discovery; stories
The terminal project
Chase, M. The terminal project and other voyages of discovery; stories
Weekend
Chase, M. The terminal project and other voyages of discovery; stories
Wet
Chase, M. The terminal project and other voyages of discovery; stories
Wheeler-dealer
Chase, M. The terminal project and other voyages of discovery; stories
The word
Chase, M. The terminal project and other voyages of discovery; stories
CHASIDISM *See* Hasidism
Chasin, Alexandra
The Clawed Claims of Bear Love
Agni no63 p114-34 2006
Chasing birds. Henriquez, C.
Chasing humanity. Beaulieu, B. P.
Chasing the blues. Black, M. A.
The **chasm**. Keeble, J.
Chassagne, Leslie
Casimir Antoine's Jazzy Cancun Vacation
Callaloo v31 no3 p852-70 Summ 2008
CHATEAUX *See* Castles
Chattin, John
Blue grass, green sky
Chattin, J. Cars go fast; stories
The deer
Chattin, J. Cars go fast; stories
My brother, mine
Chattin, J. Cars go fast; stories
The nearest thing in the world
Chattin, J. Cars go fast; stories
Nowheresville
Chattin, J. Cars go fast; stories
Outer banks
Chattin, J. Cars go fast; stories
People like that
Chattin, J. Cars go fast; stories
So far from the stage
Chattin, J. Cars go fast; stories
So much rain, so much thirst
Chattin, J. Cars go fast; stories
The split
Chattin, J. Cars go fast; stories
Things you have to ask
Chattin, J. Cars go fast; stories
The wand
Chattin, J. Cars go fast; stories
CHAUFFEURS
Coleman, R. F. Portrait of the killer as a young man
Hajiri, M. a.- . The checkpoint
Le Queux, W. The story of a secret
Meno, J. Astronaut of the year
Rifai, T. a.- . Bashrawi
Rodriguez, L. J. My ride, my revolution
Sankaran, L. The red carpet
Waters, D. Blood management
Williams, N. J. Rickshaw runner

Chekhov, Anton Pavlovich—*Continued*
Fire in the steppe: an evil night
  Chekhov, A. P. A night in the cemetery and other stories of crime & suspense; translated by Peter Sekirin
Ignoramus
  Chekhov, A. P. A night in the cemetery and other stories of crime & suspense; translated by Peter Sekirin
In the darkness of the night [variant title: Darkness]
  Chekhov, A. P. A night in the cemetery and other stories of crime & suspense; translated by Peter Sekirin
The intentional deception
  Chekhov, A. P. A night in the cemetery and other stories of crime & suspense; translated by Peter Sekirin
Ivan the cabman
  Chekhov, A. P. A night in the cemetery and other stories of crime & suspense; translated by Peter Sekirin
The lady with the little dog
  My mistress's sparrow is dead; great love stories, from Chekhov to Munro; edited by Jeffrey Eugenides
The lady with the pet dog
  Adaptations: from short story to big screen; 35 great stories that have inspired great films; edited by Stephanie Harrison
The man who wanted revenge
  Chekhov, A. P. A night in the cemetery and other stories of crime & suspense; translated by Peter Sekirin
Misfortune
  Chekhov, A. P. A night in the cemetery and other stories of crime & suspense; translated by Peter Sekirin
Murder (abridged)
  Chekhov, A. P. A night in the cemetery and other stories of crime & suspense; translated by Peter Sekirin
A night at the cemetery [variant title: In the cemetery; In the graveyard]
  Chekhov, A. P. A night in the cemetery and other stories of crime & suspense; translated by Peter Sekirin
A night of horror [variant title: Dreadful night]
  Chekhov, A. P. A night in the cemetery and other stories of crime & suspense; translated by Peter Sekirin
On the sea: a sailor's story [variant title: At sea]
  Chekhov, A. P. A night in the cemetery and other stories of crime & suspense; translated by Peter Sekirin
The only way out
  Chekhov, A. P. A night in the cemetery and other stories of crime & suspense; translated by Peter Sekirin
Perpetual mobile [variant title: Perpetuum mobile]
  Chekhov, A. P. A night in the cemetery and other stories of crime & suspense; translated by Peter Sekirin
Psychopaths
  Chekhov, A. P. A night in the cemetery and other stories of crime & suspense; translated by Peter Sekirin

The Swedish match
  Chekhov, A. P. A night in the cemetery and other stories of crime & suspense; translated by Peter Sekirin
Task
  Chekhov, A. P. A night in the cemetery and other stories of crime & suspense; translated by Peter Sekirin
A thief
  Chekhov, A. P. A night in the cemetery and other stories of crime & suspense; translated by Peter Sekirin
Thieves
  Chekhov, A. P. A night in the cemetery and other stories of crime & suspense; translated by Peter Sekirin
Too much talking! (abridged)
  Chekhov, A. P. A night in the cemetery and other stories of crime & suspense; translated by Peter Sekirin
The wallet
  Chekhov, A. P. A night in the cemetery and other stories of crime & suspense; translated by Peter Sekirin
What you usually find in novels [variant title: Elements most often found in novels, short stories, etc.]
  Chekhov, A. P. A night in the cemetery and other stories of crime & suspense; translated by Peter Sekirin
Willow
  Chekhov, A. P. A night in the cemetery and other stories of crime & suspense; translated by Peter Sekirin

CHEKHOV, ANTON PAVLOVICH, 1860-1904
About
Carver, R. Errand
MacLaverty, B. The clinic
Parodies, imitations, etc.
Boyd, W. The woman on the beach with a dog
Brockmeier, K. The lady with the pet tribble
Rock, P. Lights
Chellini's solution. Fusilli, J.
The **chemical** brothers. Rees, C.
The **Chemical** Nature of Things. Benaron, N.
CHEMICALS
Bacigalupi, P. Small offerings
Kelly, R. Tyrophex-fourteen
Moore, D. W. Wide awake in Baton Rouge
Chemistry. Rash, R.
Chemistry. Shields, C.
Chemistry. Ward, R.
The **chemistry** between us. Nelson, L.
CHEMISTS
Dahl, R. Bitch
Margulis, L. Gases
Molodowsky, K. Elaine
Rucker, R. v. B. Six thought experiments concerning the nature of computation: Experiment 3: Aint paint
Chen, Willi
Betrayal
  Trinidad noir; edited by Lisa Allen-Agostini & Jeanne Mason.
Cheney, Dick *See* Cheney, Richard B.

Chiang, Ted
Exhalation
    Strahan, J. Eclipse two; new science fiction
        and fantasy; edited by Jonathan Strahan
    The Best science fiction and fantasy of the
        year: volume three; edited by Jonathan
        Strahan
Hell is the absence of God
    Feeling very strange; the Slipstream antholo-
        gy; James Patrick Kelly & John Kessel, ed-
        itors
Liking what you see: a documentary
    The James Tiptree Award Anthology 3; edited
        by Karen Joy Fowler [et al.]
The merchant and the alchemist's gate
    The Best science fiction and fantasy of the
        year: volume two; edited by Jonathan
        Strahan
    The Year's best science fiction: twenty-fifth
        annual collection; edited by Gardner Dozois
    The Year's best fantasy and horror: twenty-
        first annual collection; edited by Ellen
        Datlow and Kelly Link & Gavin J. Grant
    Nebula Awards showcase 2009; the year's
        best SF and fantasy; selected by the Sci-
        ence Fiction and Fantasy Writers of Ameri-
        ca; edited by Ellen Datlow
Seventy-two letters
    Steampunk; edited by Ann & Jeff
        VanderMeer
What's expected of us
    Nature v436 p150 Jl 7 2005
CHICAGO (ILL.) *See* Illinois—Chicago
Chicago. Grimwood, J. C.
Chicago confetti. Rollins, W.
Chicago cryptogram. Coover, R.
CHICAGO CUBS (BASEBALL TEAM)
    Brod, D. C. My heroes have always been short-
        stops
Chicago, in the depths of feeling. Stern, R. G.
CHICANOS *See* Mexican Americans
CHICKAMAUGA, BATTLE OF, 1863
    Bierce, A. Chickamauga
Chickamauga. Bierce, A.
The **chicken**. Lispector, C.
Chicken. Pomfret, S.
Chicken. Sillitoe, A.
Chicken with Plums [Graphic novel] Satrapi, M.
Chicken with Plums: Part 2 [Graphic novel]
    Satrapi, M.
CHICKENS
    Auslander, S. God is a big happy chicken
    Duncan, A. Unique chicken goes in reverse
    Kelly, R. The hatchling
    Lispector, C. The chicken
    Pratchett, T. Hollywood chickens
    Schmuck, R. The results of a dog going blind
    Trezise, R. Chickens
    Wang Ping. Crush
Chickens. Carter, R.
Chickens. Fisher, C.
Chickens. Keeble, J.
Chickens. Trezise, R.
Chicks Love Scars. Taylor, S.
Chiclets. Panning, A.
Chicory. Zimmer, P.
Chicxulub. Boyle, T. C.
CHIEF JUSTICE OF THE SUPREME COURT
    See United States. Supreme Court

Ch'ien, Evelyn Nien-Ming
    (tr.) See Bikwan, Wong
The **chiker**. Sillitoe, A.
Chikwava, Brian
    A Rigor Mortis of the Tongue & Other Earthly
        Things
        The Literary Review (Madison, N.J.) v52 no2
        p182-6 Wint 2009
Child, Lee
    The greatest trick of all
        Greatest hits; original stories of assassins,
            hitmen, and hired guns; edited by Robert J.
            Randisi
    James Penney's new identity
        Thriller; edited by James Patterson
    Safe enough
        Mystery Writers of America presents death do
            us part; new stories about love, lust, and
            murder; edited by Harlan Coben
    Ten keys
        The cocaine chronicles; edited by Gary Phil-
            lips and Jervey Tervalon
Child, Lincoln
    (jt. auth) See Preston, Douglas and Child, Lin-
        coln
The **child**. Doyle, R.
The **child**. Smith, A.
CHILD ABUSE
    Bach, M. Full moon
    Bishop, T. The fragile commandment
    Boudinot, R. Newholly
    Bowker, D. Johnny Seven
    Burke, J. L. Texas City, 1947
    Desaulniers, J. Who knows more than you
    Faber, M. The smallness of the action
    Garrett, G. P. Pornographers
    Green, C. Lakeside
    Hawes, L. Small hands
    Henry, S. Sister death
    Holthe, T. U. The ferry driver of Portofino
    Montemarano, N. Note to future self
    Montemarano, N. To fall apart
    Montemarano, N. The worst degree of unforgiv-
        able
    Murphy, Y. Story of the spirit
    Nolan, W. F. Mommy, Daddy, & Mollie
    Opatoshu, J. On the other side of the bridge
    Otis, M. Picture head
    Palwick, S. Elephant
    Rickert, M. The Christmas witch
    Riley, P. Damping down the road
    Schutz, B. M. Expert opinion
    Trezise, R. A little boy
    Tuttle, L.
    Wilson, F. P. Please don't hurt me
    Wolff, T. The night in question
CHILD AND PARENT *See* Parent and child
The **child** and the giant. Barfield, O.
Child assassin. DeNiro, A.
Child, dead, in the rose garden. Doctorow, E. L.
CHILD LABOR
    Doctorow, C. Anda's game
    Child Locked in Car. Hood, D.
CHILD MOLESTING *See* Child sexual abuse
Child of God. Moses, J.
CHILD SEXUAL ABUSE
    Adcock, T. Lawyers' tongues
    Anderson, B. One potato two potato
    Báez, A. The Pinocchio

Chin, Marilyn—_Continued_
Singing Worm
    Michigan Quarterly Review v47 no2 p309-12
        Spr 2008
The Wolf and the Chinese Pug
    Prairie Schooner v82 no2 p7-9 Summ 2008
Chin, Mei
A Chinese Folktale
    Bomb no91 p100-2, 104-6 Spr 2005
CHINA
Bacigalupi, P. Pocketful of dharma
Bear, E. Seven Dragons Mountains
Card, O. S. Cheater
Chang, E. Red rose, white rose
Lam, V. Contact tracing
L'Amour, L. A friend of the general
Li Yiyun. Immortality
Livings, J. The heir
McHugh, M. F. Special economics
Qi, S. Buddha's feet
Roberson, C. Gold mountain
Roberson, C. The sky is large and the earth is
    small
Smith, C. A. The willow landscape
Tarr, J. Measureless to man
Ts'an-hsüeh. Meteorite mountain
Ts'an-hsüeh. The spring
To 1643
Bradbury, R. The flying machine
Kadare, I. The Great Wall
1900-1949
L'Amour, L. Beyond the great snow mountains
1949-
Li Yiyun. After a life
Li Yiyun. The arrangement
Li Yiyun. Love in the marketplace
Li Yiyun. Persimmons
Ma Jian. Where are you running to?
Ts'an-hsüeh. Snake Island
Wang Ping. Crush
Wang Ping. Maverick
Wang Ping. Where the poppies blow
Zhu Wen. Ah, Xiao Xie
Zhu Wen. A boat crossing
Zhu Wen. A hospital night
Zhu Wen. I love dollars
Zhu Wen. Pounds, ounces, meat
Zhu Wen. Wheels
Peasant life
See Peasant life—China
Politics
See Politics—China
Prisoners and prisons
See Prisoners and prisons—China
Rural life
Doerr, A. Village 113
Ts'an-hsüeh. Blue light in the sky
Ts'an-hsüeh. Burial
Ts'an-hsüeh. Helin
Ts'an-hsüeh. The lure of the sea
Ts'an-hsüeh. Mosquitoes and mountain ballads
Ts'an-hsüeh. My brother
Ts'an-hsüeh. Night in the mountain village
Ts'an-hsüeh. Snake island
Beijing
Li Yiyun. Death is not a bad joke if told the
    right way
Li Yiyun. Extra
Li Yiyun. Son

Livings, J. The dog
Slate, E. V. Purple Bamboo Park
Wang Ping. The homecoming of an old Beijing
    man
Hong Kong
See Hong Kong
Peking
See China—Beijing
Shanghai
Irvine, A. C. The fall at Shanghai
L'Amour, L. The admiral
L'Amour, L. The man who stole Shakespeare
L'Amour, L. Shanghai, not without gestures
Tibet
L'Amour, L. May there be a road
L'Amour, L. Tailwind to Tibet
Linaweaver, B. A good bag
Ma Jian. The eight-fanged roach
Ma Jian. The final initiation
Ma Jian. The golden crown
Ma Jian. The smile of Lake Drolmula
Ma Jian. The woman and the blue sky
Shepard, J. Ancestral legacies
Shomer, E. Chosen
China. Lowry, M.
CHINESE
Australia
Lam, V. A long migration
California
Bierce, A. The haunted valley
Wilson, F. P. Part of the game
Wilson, F. P. Sex slaves of the dragon tong
Cuba
Ortiz, O. F. Settling of scores
Italy
Gangbo, J. M. "Rometta and Giulieo"
Pincio, T. The melting pot
Jamaica
Mordecai, P. Alvin's ilk
Latin America
Rosenblum, M. H. Sacrifice
United States
Cheng, T. Gold mountain
Ha Jin. The house behind a weeping cherry
Hwang, F. The old gentleman
Li Yiyun. The princess of Nebraska
Li Yiyun. Prison
Li Yiyun. A thousand years of good prayers
Norris, F. The third circle
Rozan, S. J. Undocumented
Schor, L. Collateral damage
Wang Ping. Forage
Wang Ping. House of anything you wish
Wang Ping. The last communist virgin
CHINESE AMERICANS
Apple, M. Yao's chick
Hwang, F. The modern age
Leung, B. Dog sleep
Leung, B. Six ways to jump off a bridge
Leung, B. White hand
Leung, B. Who knew her best
Li Yiyun. Son
Lu, A. Le rouge et le noir
Michaels, L. Tell me everything
Richter, J. The gambling master of Shanghai
Row, J. Heaven Lake
Rozan, S. J. Sunset
The **Chinese** boy. Stapleton, A.
A **Chinese** Folktale. Chin, M.

Chinese puzzle. McBain, E.
Chintamani's women. Upadhyay, S.
Chipmunks. McKinley, J.
CHIPPEWA INDIANS
Erdrich, L. The antelope wife
Erdrich, L. Fleur
Erdrich, L. History of the Puyats
Erdrich, L. The painted drum
Erdrich, L. The plunge of the brave
Erdrich, L. Pounding the dog
Erdrich, L. The world's greatest fishermen
The **chirashi** covenant. Hirahara, N.
Chiu, Lily
(tr.) See Lý Lan
CHIVALRY
See also Knights and knighthood; Middle Ages
Bierce, A. A bit of chivalry
Bierce, A. A champion of the sex
Ferrigno, R. The hour when the ship comes in
L'Amour, L. Shanghai, not without gestures
Chkhartishvili, Grigory See Akunin, Boris, 1956-
Cho, Chŏngnae
Land of exile
Land of exile: contemporary Korean fiction; translated and edited by Marshall Pihl, Bruce Fulton, and Ju-Chan Fulton
Cho, Grace M.
Homecoming
Feminist Studies v32 no2 p365-79 Summ 2006
Chocolate milkshake. O'Shaughnessy, P.
Chocolates from Paris. Moser, E.
Choe, Inho
The boozer
Land of exile: contemporary Korean fiction; translated and edited by Marshall Pihl, Bruce Fulton, and Ju-Chan Fulton
Ch'oe, Such'ol
Conviction
Land of exile: contemporary Korean fiction; translated and edited by Marshall Pihl, Bruce Fulton, and Ju-Chan Fulton
Ch'oe, Yun
The last of Hanak'o
Land of exile: contemporary Korean fiction; translated and edited by Marshall Pihl, Bruce Fulton, and Ju-Chan Fulton
There a petal silently falls
Ch'oe, Y. There a petal silently falls; three stories; by Ch'oe Yun; translated by Bruce and Ju-Chan Fulton
The thirteen-scent flower
Ch'oe, Y. There a petal silently falls; three stories; by Ch'oe Yun; translated by Bruce and Ju-Chan Fulton.
Whisper yet
Ch'oe, Y. There a petal silently falls; three stories; by Ch'oe Yun; translated by Bruce and Ju-Chan Fulton.
The **choice**. Buckler, E.
A **choice** of accommodations. Lahiri, J.
The **choir** director affair (The baby's teeth). Wilson, K.
CHOIRS (MUSIC)
Tomlinson, J. Singing second part
CHOLERA
McGrath, P. The year of the gibbet

Chon, Kwangyong
Kapitan Ri
Land of exile: contemporary Korean fiction; translated and edited by Marshall Pihl, Bruce Fulton, and Ju-Chan Fulton
Choose Your Own Genetics. Appel, J. M.
Choosing sides. Robinson, R.
Chop-Chop Block. Esser, S.
The **chop** girl. MacLeod, I.
CHOREOGRAPHERS
Dunyach, J.-C. Separations
Chosen. Shomer, E.
The **Chosen** One. Sundaresan, I.
Chosen to die. White, L. T.
Chou d'amour. Kohler, S.
Choudhry, Roohi
Flame Lilies
Callaloo v31 no2 p436-42 Spr 2008
Chrenkoff, Arthur
The aching of Dion Harper
Nature v441 p254 My 11 2006
Christ See Jesus Christ
The **Christ** of San Buenaventura. Parra, E. A.
Christ, their Lord. Richter, S.
Christ walked down Market Street. Gaines, E. J.
Christ Walked down Market Street [With an introduction by the author] Gaines, E. J.
CHRISTENINGS
Hardy, T. The three strangers
Christensen, Inger
Azorno [excerpt]
Terrestrial intelligence; international fiction now from New Directions; edited by Barbara Epler
CHRISTIAN LIFE
Burke, K. First pastoral
Gardiner, J. R. North of ordinary
Granville-Barker, H. Souls on fifth
Klassen, S. The seven steps
Lewis, Mark Ray. Scordatura
Manley, C. Church booty
Manley, C. Everything is going to be alright
Manley, C. How I got saved
Manley, C. Louella and the Holy Ghost
Manley, C. Raising Cane
Manley, C. Resurrection Sunday
Manley, C. Saturday night at the Fluff and Fold
McGlynn, D. Seventeen one-hundredths of a second
Monteiro, L. The whirling dove
Rogers, B. H. Cross carriers
Thompson, J. The woman at the well
Westcott, G. The dove came down
CHRISTIAN MARTYRS See Martyrs
CHRISTIANITY
See also Catholic faith names of Christian churches or sects
Akpan, U. C. What language is that?
Baingana, D. Hunger
Frost, G. Touring Jesusworld
Judson, T. The sultan's emissary
Mead, D. A thing forbidden
Thormahlen, A. The churchgoer
CHRISTIANS
Beaumont, M. Contraflow
Christie, Agatha
Philomel cottage
Murder short & sweet; edited by Paul D. Staudohar

Christie. Macy, C.
CHRISTINA, QUEEN OF SWEDEN, 1626-1689
About
Johnson, C. R. The queen and the philosopher
Christine waving from the train. Gospodinov, G.
CHRISTMAS
McInerney, J. Simple gifts
Christmas. Nabokov, V. V.
Christmas. Saunders, G.
Christmas 1910. Butler, R. O.
Christmas at Helaman's house. Card, O. S.
The **Christmas** bus. LaSalle, P.
A **Christmas** carol. Williamson, J.
A **Christmas** Carol [Reprint] Heath, A. B.
The **Christmas** club. Kalpakian, L.
Christmas Eve. Farmer, L.
Christmas Eves. Carofiglio, G.
A **Christmas** in 1945 [With an introduction by the translator] Stern, M. R.
Christmas in Dodge City. Schutz, B. M.
Christmas in Gruel. Singleton, G.
Christmas is a sad season for the poor. Cheever, J.
The **Christmas** Joe. Parry, O.
A **Christmas** memory. Capote, T.
The **Christmas** order. Buckler, E.
The **Christmas** soul of a pig. Gospodinov, G.
Christmas spirit. Messinger, J.
CHRISTMAS STORIES
Akpan, U. C. An Ex-mas feast
Anderson, B. Poojah
Andrade, M. d. The Christmas turkey
Auster, P. Auggie Wren's Christmas story
Báez, A. The time keeper
Beattie, A. Horatio's trick
Bestwick, S. Hazy shade of winter
Bradbury, R. Bless me, Father, for I have sinned
Buckler, E. Another Christmas
Buckler, E. The Christmas order
Buckler, E. The finest tree
Buckler, E. Goodbye, prince
Buckler, E. Just like everyone else
Buckler, E. A present for Miss Merriam
Buckler, E. Return trip to Christmas
Capote, T. A Christmas memory
Capote, T. One Christmas
Card, O. S. Christmas at Helaman's house
Card, O. S. Dust
Card, O. S. Homeless in hell
Carofiglio, G. Christmas Eves
Cheever, J. Christmas is a sad season for the poor
Clayton, J. J. An old 3 a.m. story
Daugherty, T. Lamplighter
DeAndrea, W. L. The adventure of the Christmas tree
Dickens, C. The story of the goblins who stole a sexton
Donoghue, E. Do they know it's Christmas?
Doran, M. M. They shall have music
Dufresne, J. Close by me forever
Dunbar, P. L. Ash-Cake Hannah and her Ben
Dunbar, P. L. A defender of the faith
Dunbar, P. L. An old-time Christmas
Dunbar, P. L. One Christmas at Shiloh
Ebenbach, D. H. I'll be home
Ford, R. Crèche
Gardam, J. The zoo at Christmas
Gerrold, D. . . . And eight rabid pigs

Goldsworthy, P. Run silent, run deep
Gospodinov, G. The Christmas soul of a pig
Hinojosa-Smith, Rolando. The Gulf Oil -Can Santa Claus
Holladay, C. C. Hollyhocks
Hunton, E. R. Who gives himself
Iagnemma, K. A little advance
Keane, J. B. The curriculum vitae
Keane, J. B. The woman who hated Christmas
Kelly, J. P. The best Christmas ever
Lange, R. Long lost
Lenz, S. A risk for Father Christmas
MacLeod, A. Winter dog
McLean, S. Dave cooks the turkey
Mendoza Zambrano, M. A Christmas story
Messinger, J. Christmas spirit
Nabokov, V. V. Christmas
Nelson, A. Obo
Odrach, T. The night before Christmas
Paley, G. The loudest voice
Parry, O. Appearences
Parry, O. The Christmas Joe
Parry, O. Coal and iron
Parry, O. How Jimmy Mulvaney astonished the world for Christmas
Parry, O. The lie of the land
Powers, T. We traverse afar
Pratchett, T. Twenty pence with envelope and seasonal greeting
Reynolds, C. A train to catch
Richter, S. Christ, their Lord
Roberson, J. A compromised Christmas
Robinson, R. Family Christmas
Saunders, G. Christmas
Shepherd, J. Red Ryder nails the Hammond kid
Simpson, H. The green room
Simpson, H. The year's midnight
Singleton, G. Christmas in Gruel
Singleton, G. The opposite of zero
Smith, A. Present
Spark, M. The leaf-sweeper
Stamm, P. In the outer suburbs
Stern, R. G. La pourriture noble
Temple, S. A roomful of Christmas
Tournier, M. Mother Christmas
Trevor, W. Another Christmas
Waldrop, H. Household words; or, The powers-that-be
Williamson, J. A Christmas carol
Willis, C. Inn
Willis, C. Just like the ones we used to know
Willis, C. Newsletter
Winterson, J. O'Brien's first Christmas
Winton, T. Reunion
Wolfe, G. And when they appear
Yasuoka, S. Jingle bells
Christmas Stories. Luce, K.
A **Christmas** story. Mendoza Zambrano, M.
CHRISTMAS TREES
Dostoyevsky, F. The little boy at the Savior's Christmas tree
Meloy, M. O Tannenbaum
Mun, N. Shelter
Thormahlen, A. 23 December
The **Christmas** turkey. Andrade, M. d.
The **Christmas** witch. Rickert, M.
Christus destitutus. Webster, B.
Chrysalis. Lynn, D. H.
Chrysanthemum. Uchida, H.

Chuang Tzu
    The Swimmer [Taoist story retold by Yitzhak
      Buxbaum]
        Parabola v34 no2 p74-7 Summ 2009
Chuck the Terrible, Chuck of the Deep. Broudy,
    O.
Chuculate, Eddie
    Galveston Bay, 1826
        The O. Henry Prize stories 2007; edited and
          with an introduction by Laura Furman; with
          essays on the story they admire most by ju-
          rors Charles D'Ambrosio, Ursula K. Le
          Guin, Lily Tuck
    Winter, 1979
        Ploughshares   v30   no4   p23-31   Wint
          2004/2005
Chupa mi pena, baby. Robson, L. L.
CHURCH ATTENDANCE
    Dunbar, P. L. The defection of Maria Ann
      Gibbs
    Dunbar, P. L. Lafe Halloway's two fights
    Dunbar, P. L. One Christmas at Shiloh
    Manley, C. Everything is going to be alright
    Manley, C. How I got saved
    Manley, C. Raising Cane
    Westcott, G. The dove came down
Church booty. Manley, C.
Church cancels cow. Hempel, A.
The **Church** of the Fellowship of Something. Nis-
    sen, T.
Church Owl. Norman, H.
CHURCH SCHOOLS
        See also School life
    Kiely, B. The shortest way home
    Ochsner, G. A darkness held
    Scoville, S. The pin collectors
    Shepard, J. Eustace
CHURCHES
        See also Cathedrals
    Dunbar, P. L. A judgment of Paris
    Dunbar, P. L. The minority committee
    Dunbar, P. L. One Christmas at Shiloh
    Farley, B. The investigation
    Hughes, R. J. A visit to St. Nick's
    Klassen, S. Wednesday is adoration
    Lain, D. The suburbs of the citadel of thought
    Lovecraft, H. P. The haunter of the dark
    Martin, S. H. How the parsonage was papered
    Nichols, L. D. Prodigal
    Thormahlen, A. The churchgoer
    Williams, J. M. Passion
    Willis, C. Inn
The **churchgoer**. Thormahlen, A.
CHURCHILL, SIR WINSTON, 1874-1965
                About
    Hughes, M. The devil you don't
    Wolfe, G. Donovan sent us
The **churching** of Grandma Pleasant. Dunbar, P.
    L.
The **churring**. Boyle, N.
Chute, Carolyn
    "Ollie, oh . . ."
        Contemporary Maine fiction; an anthology of
          short stories; edited by Wesley McNair
Ciaccia, Jillian
    Manufacture of Non-bleeding Maraschino Cher-
      ries
        Women's Studies Quarterly v37 no1/2 p261-6
          Spr/Summ 2009

Peaches
        Women's Studies Quarterly v37 no1/2 p256-
          60 Spr/Summ 2009
    StockingS
        Women's Studies Quarterly v37 no1/2 p251-5
          Spr/Summ 2009
Ciancianedda. Messina, M.
Cibola. Willis, C.
Cicada Queen. Sterling, B.
Cicero Waiting. Gautier, A.
Cielo Azul. Connelly, M.
Cigar box. Kun, M.
Cigarette. Woolrich, C.
Cigarettes. Lewin, M. Z.
Cinadr, Brian David
    The Brief Gravity of the Earth and Eighteen
        South Carolina Review v37 no2 p192-6 Spr
          2005
CINCINNATI (OHIO) *See* Ohio—Cincinnati
CINDERELLA (LEGENDARY CHARACTER)
    Bierce, A. A tale of the bosphorus
    Cadnum, M. Ella and the canary prince
    Harris, J. The Ugly Sister
Cinderella School. Vapnyar, L.
Cindy Stubenstock. Homes, A. M.
Cinema. Mozetič, B.
Cinnamon skin. White, E.
The **cinquefoil**. Brown, G. M.
Cioffari, Philip
    Turns
        Southern Humanities Review v41 no2 p169-81
          Spr 2007
CIRCE (LEGENDARY CHARACTER)
    Zelazny, R. Circe has her problems
Circe has her problems. Zelazny, R.
The **Circle**. Abraham, R.
The **circle**. Hewson, D.
The **circle**. Tolstaia, T.
Circle of prayer. Munro, A.
CIRCUMCISION
    Albert, E. The mother is always upset
    Apple, M. "The eighth day"
    Kwa'mboka. Birds
    Pollack, E. The bris
    Raphael, L. Roy's Jewish problem
    Toer, P. A. Circumcision
Circumcision. Toer, P. A.
CIRCUS
    Bradbury, R. Pietà summer
    DeNiro, A. Fuming woman
    Erdrich, L. The leap
    James, H. In a circus
    Porter, K. A. The circus
    Rich, M. The suckers
    Riley, E. Dark Laughter
    Robbins, T. Spurs
    Ruffin, P. In search of the tightrope walker
    Smith, C. A. The root of Ampoi
    Stamm, P. The wall of fire
    Uchida, H. The lizard
The **circus**. Déry, T.
The **circus**. Porter, K. A.
Λ **Circus** at the Center of the World. Alarcón, D.
Circus bezerk. Flanagan, E.
The **circus** house. Judah, S.

Cisneros, Sandra
  Machu Picchu
    Stumbling and raging; more politically inspired fiction; edited by Stephen Elliott; with associate editors Greg Larson [et al.]
The **cistern**. Kelly, R.
Citchens, Addie
  Indelible Ink
    Callaloo v29 no1 p93-5 Wint 2006
CITIES AND TOWNS
        See also Extinct cities; Imaginary cities
  Barthelme, D. I bought a little city
  Boyle, T. C. Jubilation
  Brockmeier, K. The year of silence
  Chapman, S. The revenge of the callico cat
  Crane, E. Clearview
  Ducornet, R. Blue funk
  Ford, J. Daltharee
  Millhauser, S. The other town
  Rose, A. Picture this
  Samperio, G. La mujer de la gabardina roja/The woman in the red coat
  Valdés, J. Beat me to death
  Zelazny, R. The hounds of sorrow
CITIES AND TOWNS, RUINED, EXTINCT, ETC. *See* Extinct cities
Cities Beneath Them. Lanoie, C.
The **cities** he would never be sure of. LaSalle, P.
Citizen in the south. Rohrlich, R.
The **City** and the Moon. Schwartz, D.
City boy. Michaels, L.
City bus. Boswell, R.
City codes. Daugherty, T.
City Demolition Industry, Inc. Isozaki, A.
A **city** divided. Zelazny, R.
City Hall. Romano, T.
City hobgoblins. Mellick, C.
City in aspic. Williams, C.
City life. Gordon, M.
The **city** never sleeps. Walsh, H.
City of clowns. Alarcón, D.
City of commerce. Pollack, N.
The **city** of hell!. White, L. T.
The **city** of love. Lane, J.
The **City** of Shells. Russell, K.
The **City** of the Gone Away. Bierce, A.
The **city** of the singing flame. Smith, C. A.
City under the sea. Lamb, H.
City visit. Haslett, A.
Civil disobedience. Haldeman, J. W.
CIVIL RIGHTS DEMONSTRATIONS *See* African Americans—Civil rights
CIVIL SERVICE
  Barthelme, D. The reference
  Bierce, A. The civil service in Florida
  Chekhov, A. P. Death of an office worker [variant titles: Death of a government clerk; Death of an official]
  Gogol´, N. V. Diary of a madman
  Quiroga, H. The incense tree roof
The **civil** service in Florida. Bierce, A.
CIVIL WAR
        England
        See England—17th century
        United States
        See United States—Civil War, 1861-1865
CIVILIZATION *See* Social problems
Civilization. Boudinot, R.

CIVILIZATION AND TECHNOLOGY *See* Technology and civilization
CivilWarLand in bad decline. Saunders, G.
Claim. Pourciau, G.
Claire, Alexandra
  Playing the odds
    Urban Welsh; new short fiction; edited by Lewis Davies
Claire. Barthelme, S.
Claire. Hale, J. C.
CLAIRVOYANCE
  Bradbury, R. The illustrated man
  D'Ambrosio, C., Jr. The scheme of things
  DeNiro, A. If I leap
  Hughes, M. The devil you don't
  Long, A. Clairvoyant
  Scurati, A. Eternal Rome
Clairvoyant. Long, A.
Clan of marsupials. McGruder, K.
CLANS
        See also Tribes
CLANTON, IKE, D. 1887
            About
  Duncklee, J. The last breakfast
The **clapping** hands of God. Flynn, M.
Clara. Bolaño, R.
Clara's PC and the second coming. Stevens, J. D.
Clare, Jai
  The Hand of Fatima
    Agni no60 p68-76 2004
CLARE (IRELAND) *See* Ireland—Clare
Clare Connolly: WIND in Bradford playground, 17 January 2003 [Medical Humanities, 31 no1 June 2005] Connolly, C.
Clarence 13X *See* Smith, Clarence, 1928-1969
Clarence Cummins and the semi-permanent loan. Richards, S. S.
Clarfield, A. Mark
  Fathers and Sons
    Journal of the American Geriatrics Society v54 no2 p365-6 F 2006
Clark, Curt
    For works written by this author under other names see Westlake, Donald E.
Clark, George Makana
  The center of the world
    The O. Henry Prize stories, 2006; edited and with an introduction by Laura Furman; jurors: Kevin Brockmeier, Francine Prose, Colm Toibin
Clark, Mathilde Walter
  The Fish Shop Owner's Wife
    Iowa Review v37 no2 p119-24 Fall 2007
Clark, Matt
  The Crowned Heads of Pecos
    Southwest Review v91 no3 p359-65 2006
  The secret heart of Christ
    New stories from the Southwest; edited by D. Seth Horton; foreword by Ray Gonzalez.
Clark, May Roberts
  Her neighbor's claim
    Adventures in the West; stories for young readers; edited by Susanne George Bloomfield and Eric Melvin Reed
Clark, Shane
  Kidroid
    Nature v456 p674 D 4 2008

Clark, Simon
The extraordinary limits of darkness
The Year's best fantasy and horror: twentieth annual collection; edited by Ellen Datlow and Kelly Link & Gavin J. Grant
Langthwaite Road
Fourbodings; [by] Simon Clark . . . [et al.]; edited by Peter Crowther

Clarke, Arthur C.
Crime on Mars
Fourth planet from the sun; tales of Mars from The Magazine of Fantasy & Science Fiction; edited by Gordon Van Gelder
The sentinel
Adaptations: from short story to big screen; 35 great stories that have inspired great films; edited by Stephanie Harrison

Clarke, Austin
Don't Shoot, Don't Shoot!
Callaloo v29 no2 p254-63 Spr 2006

Clarke, Brock
The apology
Clarke, B. Carrying the torch; stories
The Pushcart Prize XXIX: best of the small presses 2005; edited by Bill Henderson with the Pushcart Prize editors
Carrying the torch
Clarke, B. Carrying the torch; stories
For those of us who need such things
Clarke, B. Carrying the torch; stories
The fund-raiser's dance card
Clarke, B. Carrying the torch; stories
Geronimo
Clarke, B. Carrying the torch; stories
The ghosts we love
Clarke, B. Carrying the torch; stories
The Virginia Quarterly Review v81 no3 p160-77 Summ 2005
The Hotel Utica
Clarke, B. Carrying the torch; stories
The Pity Palace
The Virginia Quarterly Review p43-65 2006 supp
The Price of the Haircut
Agni no61 p50-60 2005
The reason was us
Clarke, B. Carrying the torch; stories
The son's point of view
Clarke, B. Carrying the torch; stories
That Which We Will Not Give
New England Review v27 no1 p8-21 2006

Clarke, Susanna
Antickes and frets
Clarke, S. The ladies of Grace Adieu and other stories; illustrated by Charles Vess
The Duke of Wellington misplaces his horse
Clarke, S. The ladies of Grace Adieu and other stories; illustrated by Charles Vess
John Uskglass and the Cumbrian charcoal burner
Clarke, S. The ladies of Grace Adieu and other stories; illustrated by Charles Vess
The ladies of Grace Adieu
Clarke, S. The ladies of Grace Adieu and other stories; illustrated by Charles Vess
Lickerish Hill
Clarke, S. The ladies of Grace Adieu and other stories; illustrated by Charles Vess

Mr Simonelli; or, The fairy widower
Clarke, S. The ladies of Grace Adieu and other stories; illustrated by Charles Vess
Mrs Mabb
Clarke, S. The ladies of Grace Adieu and other stories; illustrated by Charles Vess
Tom Brightwind; or, How the fairy bridge was built at Thoresby
Clarke, S. The ladies of Grace Adieu and other stories; illustrated by Charles Vess

Clarke, Will
The pentecostal home for flying children
Burnham, C. Who can save us now?; brand-new superheroes and their amazing [short] stories; edited by Owen King and John McNally; [illustrations by Chris Burnham]

Claro. Williams, J.

Clary, Ryan
Leave It on the Counter
New Letters v75 no1 p121-2 2008/2009
Wedding Reception
New Letters v75 no1 p123-5 2008/2009

Class Day. Foster, P.

CLASS DISTINCTION
See also Middle classes; Social classes
Clayton, J. J. Bodies of the rich
Crouse, D. The ugliest boy
Dunbar, P. L. The lion tamer
Gardiner, J. R. The Magellan House
Lehane, D. Gone down to Corpus
McInerney, J. The waiter
Munro, A. Passion
Petry, A. L. The bones of Louella Brown
Raymond, J. The suckling pig
Rust, E. M. The prisoner pear
Sayers, V. Walker Evans is a spy on the Lexington Avenue local
Sillitoe, A. The devil's almanack
Taraqqi, G. The maid
Trevor, D. Girls I know
Trevor, D. Haircuts
Wendroff, Z. Blacksmith street
Westermann, J. The secret
Williams, J. Charity

Classic Combo [Graphic fiction] Heatley, D.

Classy lady. Zoshchenko, M.

Claudine, Sidonie Gabrielle *See* Colette, 1873-1954

Claud's dog: Mr Feasey. Dahl, R.

Claud's dog: Mr Hoddy. Dahl, R.

Claud's dog: Rummins. Dahl, R.

Claud's dog: The ratcatcher. Dahl, R.

CLAUSTROPHOBIA
Fujino, C. The housewife and the police box

Claustrophobia. Reed, P.

The **Clawed** Claims of Bear Love. Chasin, A.

Clay, Cassius *See* Ali, Muhammad, 1942-

Clay. Bagdasarian, D.

The **clay** is vile. Hyde, M.

Clayton, John J.
A Bedtime Story
TriQuarterly no130 p180-92 2008
Getting Out in One Piece
The Sewanee Review v117 no3 p359-77 Summ 2009
Many Seconds Into the Future—A Story
Commentary v124 no5 p32-41 D 2007
Vertigo: A Story
Commentary v118 no5 p50-6 D 2004

Clayton, John Jacob

Aaron, personal
  Clayton, J. J. Wrestling with angels; new and collected stories; [by] John J. Clayton

Adult fiction
  Clayton, J. J. Wrestling with angels; new and collected stories; [by] John J. Clayton

Blue house
  Clayton, J. J. Wrestling with angels; new and collected stories; [by] John J. Clayton

Bodies like mouths
  Clayton, J. J. Wrestling with angels; new and collected stories; [by] John J. Clayton

Bodies of the rich
  Clayton, J. J. Wrestling with angels; new and collected stories; [by] John J. Clayton

The builder
  Clayton, J. J. Wrestling with angels; new and collected stories; [by] John J. Clayton

Cambridge is sinking!
  Clayton, J. J. Wrestling with angels; new and collected stories; [by] John J. Clayton

The company you keep
  Clayton, J. J. Wrestling with angels; new and collected stories; [by] John J. Clayton

The contract
  Clayton, J. J. Wrestling with angels; new and collected stories; [by] John J. Clayton

Dance to the old words
  Clayton, J. J. Wrestling with angels; new and collected stories; [by] John J. Clayton

Fables of the erotic other
  Clayton, J. J. Wrestling with angels; new and collected stories; [by] John J. Clayton

Fantasy for a Friday afternoon
  Clayton, J. J. Wrestling with angels; new and collected stories; [by] John J. Clayton

Friends
  Clayton, J. J. Wrestling with angels; new and collected stories; [by] John J. Clayton

Glory
  Clayton, J. J. Wrestling with angels; new and collected stories; [by] John J. Clayton

History lessons
  Clayton, J. J. Wrestling with angels; new and collected stories; [by] John J. Clayton

I'm here, you're there
  Clayton, J. J. Wrestling with angels; new and collected stories; [by] John J. Clayton

Light at the end of the tunnel
  Clayton, J. J. Wrestling with angels; new and collected stories; [by] John J. Clayton

Losers in paradise
  Clayton, J. J. Wrestling with angels; new and collected stories; [by] John J. Clayton

The man who could see radiance
  Clayton, J. J. Wrestling with angels; new and collected stories; [by] John J. Clayton

Muscles
  Clayton, J. J. Wrestling with angels; new and collected stories; [by] John J. Clayton

Night talk
  Clayton, J. J. Wrestling with angels; new and collected stories; [by] John J. Clayton

An old 3 a.m. story
  Clayton, J. J. Wrestling with angels; new and collected stories; [by] John J. Clayton

Old friends
  Clayton, J. J. Wrestling with angels; new and collected stories; [by] John J. Clayton

Open-heart surgery
  Clayton, J. J. Wrestling with angels; new and collected stories; [by] John J. Clayton

Part-time father
  Clayton, J. J. Wrestling with angels; new and collected stories; [by] John J. Clayton

Prewar quality
  Clayton, J. J. Wrestling with angels; new and collected stories; [by] John J. Clayton

The promised land
  Clayton, J. J. Wrestling with angels; new and collected stories; [by] John J. Clayton

Soap opera
  Clayton, J. J. Wrestling with angels; new and collected stories; [by] John J. Clayton

Talking to Charlie
  Clayton, J. J. Wrestling with angels; new and collected stories; [by] John J. Clayton

Time exposure
  Clayton, J. J. Wrestling with angels; new and collected stories; [by] John J. Clayton

Vertigo
  Clayton, J. J. Wrestling with angels; new and collected stories; [by] John J. Clayton

Voices
  Clayton, J. J. Wrestling with angels; new and collected stories; [by] John J. Clayton

Waiting for Polly Adler
  Clayton, J. J. Wrestling with angels; new and collected stories; [by] John J. Clayton

Clean as a whistle. Coville, B.

A **clean** getaway. DeCandido, K. R. A.

Clean Room. Abu-Jaber, D.

A **clean** sheet. Tolstaia, T.

Cleaning house. Miller, A. L.

Cleaning up. Gordon, M.

CLEANING WOMEN
  See also Maids (Servants)
  Boswell, R. Miss Famous
  Brady, C. Seven remedies
  Cooper, J. C. Just-life politics
  Dormen, L. Gladiators
  Hecht, J. Get money
  Iarovici, D. American dreaming
  Klages, E. Basement magic
  Macy, C. The red coat
  Mayer, L. N. Love for Miss Dottie
  Moss, B. K. Camping in
  West, D. Mrs. Creel
  Winton, T. On her knees

Cleanness. Lasdun, J.

Cleansing Monday. Bunin, I. A.

Clearview. Crane, E.

Clearwater. Stone, R.

Cleft rock, with spring. Buckler, E.

Clegg, Douglas

The skin of the world
  The Year's best fantasy and horror: eighteenth annual collection; edited by Ellen Datlow, Kelly Link & Gavin J. Grant

Clegg, Sally Anne

You Are Your Own Very Unique Snowflake
  Bomb no107 p supp10-supp11 Spr 2009

Clemens, Matthew V.

(jt. auth) See Collins, Max Allan and Clemens, Matthew V.

Clemens, Samuel Langhorne *See* Twain, Mark, 1835-1910
Clement, Thelma T.
  Faith: a story
    "Tell it to us easy" and other stories; a complete short fiction anthology of African American women writers in Opportunity magazine, (1923-1948); edited by Judith Musser.
CLEOPATRA, QUEEN OF EGYPT, D. 30 B.C.
  About
  Fiscus, J. The road to endless sleep
The **Cleopatra** birds. Gerber, M. J.
Cleopatra Brimstone. Hand, E.
CLERGY
    See also Evangelists; Rabbis; Women clergy
  Aniebo, I. N. C. Four dimensions
  Bierce, A. "A bad woman"
  Bierce, A. The new church that was not built
  Bierce, A. A providential intimation
  Bradbury, R. The Messiah
  Clarke, S. Mr Simonelli; or, The fairy widower
  Coake, C. His mission
  Dahl, R. Georgy Porgy
  Deaver, J. Chapter and verse
  Dunbar, P. L. The finding of Martha
  Dunbar, P. L. The fruitful sleeping of the Rev. Elisha Edwards
  Dunbar, P. L. The last fiddling of Mordaunt's Jim
  Dunbar, P. L. A matter of doctrine
  Dunbar, P. L. Mt. Pisgah's Christmas 'possum
  Dunbar, P. L. The ordeal at Mt. Hope
  Dunbar, P. L. The trial sermons on Bull-Skin
  Dunbar, P. L. The trousers
  Dunbar, P. L. Uncle Simon's Sundays out
  Dunbar, P. L. The walls of Jericho
  Gardam, J. Waiting for a stranger
  Graves, P. The bishop and the landlady
  Lansdale, J. R. Deadman's road
  Lansdale, J. R. The fat man and the elephant
  Lansdale, J. R. The gentleman's hotel
  Lowry, M. June the 30th, 1934
  Manley, C. Kitty litter
  Manley, C. Louella and the Holy Ghost
  Manley, C. Repo
  Manley, C. Resurrection Sunday
  Martin, G. R. R. The way of cross and dragon
  Martin, S. H. How the parsonage was papered
  McCafferty, J. The pastor's brother
  McCauley, W. Wedding party
  McGlynn, D. Landslide
  McNett, M. One dog happy
  Minor, K. A day meant to do less
  Powers, T. Through and through
  Shirley, P. Charisma
  Smith, M. Motorcycles
  Stern, R. G. Lesson for the day
  Sutton, B. Tra il devoto et profano
  Thomas, E. The friend of the blackbird
  Troy, J. The order of things
  Vidal, G. Clouds and eclipses
  Willis, C. Epiphany
  Willis, C. Samaritan
  Woolson, C. F. Jeannette
  Zettel, S. The red shoes
CLERGY, ANGLICAN AND EPISCOPAL *See* Anglican and Episcopal clergy

CLERGY, CATHOLIC *See* Catholic priests
The **clergyman's** confession. Collins, W.
CLERKS
    See also Civil service
  Machado de Assis. A woman's arms
  Naiyer Masud. The big garbage dump
  Tomlinson, J. So exotic
A **clerk's** life. Parker, B.
CLEVELAND (OHIO) *See* Ohio—Cleveland
Clevenger, Craig
  The numbers game
    San Francisco noir 2; the classics; edited by Peter Maravelis.
Cleverly, Barbara
  Love-lies-bleeding
    The Best British mysteries, 2006; edited by Maxim Jakubowski
Clevidence, Carin
  The Cult of the Bed
    Michigan Quarterly Review v45 no1 p184-95 Wint 2006
Click. Crouse, D.
The **Click**. Frame, R.
Click Click. Stark, C.
The **Cliffs**. Norman, D.
Clift, G. W.
  Pink-haired.alt/pix_girls
    The North American Review v292 no3/4 p59-60 My/Ag 2007
Clifton, Ashley
  Martin Hellinger
    The Massachusetts Review v48 no3 p422-31 Fall 2007
CLIMATE CHANGE
  Chase, M. Wet
Climate change. Hanlon, M.
The **climb**. Mukhopadhyay, T.
Climb the wind. Sargent, P.
Climbing redemption mountain. Trimm, M.
Climbing to the window, pretending to dance. Eggers, D.
The **clinic**. MacLaverty, B.
CLINICS
  Kulpa, K. Maintaining
Clip art. Klages, E.
CLIPPER SHIPS *See* Sailing vessels
The **Clipping**. Perkins-Valdez, D.
CLOAKS
  Stackpole, M. A. Seamless
The **Clock**. Koulack, D.
The **Clockmaker**. Stevenson, R. L.
Clockmaker's requiem. Anderson, B.
CLOCKS AND WATCHES
  Anderson, B. Clockmaker's requiem
  Báez, A. The time keeper
  Bierce, A. John Bartine's watch
  Frost, G. From hell again
  Kiely, B. The jeweller's boy
  Maxwell, W. The marble watch
  Singer, M. Borderland
  Williams, C. Perhaps the last
Clockwork atom bomb. Green, D.
The **clone**. Đoàn, L.
CLONES *See* Asexual reproduction
CLONING
  Bova, B. Takes two to tangle
  Rich, M. The asking place
  Rich, M. The real thing

Cody, Liza—*Continued*
Turning it round
The Best British mysteries, 2005; edited by Maxim Jakubowski
The uniform
Cody, L. Lucky dip and other stories
Walking blues
Cody, L. Lucky dip and other stories
Where's Stacey?
Cody, L. Lucky dip and other stories
Woke up this morning
Cody, L. Lucky dip and other stories
The World's finest mystery and crime stories, fifth annual collection; edited by Ed Gorman and Martin H. Greenberg

Coe, Tucker
For works written by this author under other names see Westlake, Donald E.

Coelacanths. Reed, R.

Coelen, Ina
The best time for planting
The World's finest mystery and crime stories, fourth annual collection; edited by Ed Gorman and Martin H. Greenberg

Coen, Ethan
The Russian
Pushcart prize XXXIII: best of the small presses 2009; edited by Bill Henderson with the Pushcart Prize editors

Coetzee, J. M.
Adriana
Harper's v319 p77-82 S 2009
The Blow
The New Yorker v81 no18 p76-89 Je 27 2005

Cofer, Judith Ortiz
Give Us This Day
The North American Review v293 no3/4 p59 My/Ag 2008

COFFEE
Ford, J. The empire of ice cream
Gospodinov, G. Gaustine
The **coffee** break. Preddy, M.
Coffee Pot Tree. Lovelace, S.
Coffee Time. Shami, J. B.
A **coffeehouse** acquaintance. Templeton, E.

COFFINS
Chekhov, A. P. A night of horror [variant title: Dreadful night]
Gappah, P. The Mupandawana dancing champion
Coffins on the river. Ford, J.

Coffman, Lucinda Harrison
The dream lover
New stories from the South: the year's best, 2005; edited by Shannon Ravenel; with a preface by Jill McCorkle

Cognetti, Paolo
Use the Stars to Get Your Bearings
The Literary Review (Madison, N.J.) v49 no1 p51-65 Fall 2005

Cohen, Gabriel
Right is right
Hard boiled Brooklyn; edited by Reed Farrel Coleman

Cohen, Jack
Omphalosphere: New York 2057
Nature v435 p1136 Je 23 2005
Schrödinger's mousetrap. Part 8: The outcast
Nature v434 p143 Mr 10 2005

Cohen, Joshua
Last transmission; or, Man with a robotic ermine
Text: Ur; the new book of masks; [edited by Forrest Aguirre]

Cohen, Leonard
The favourite game [excerpt]
Contemporary Jewish writing in Canada; an anthology; edited by Michael Greenstein
The history of them all
Inside the hornet's head; an anthology of Jewish American writing; edited by Jerome Charyn

Cohen, Matt
The sins of Tomas Benares
Contemporary Jewish writing in Canada; an anthology; edited by Michael Greenstein

Cohen, Meyer H. *See* Cohen, Mickey, 1914-1976
COHEN, MICKEY, 1914-1976
About
Levinson, R. S. And the winner is . . .

Cohen, Paula
The adventure of the dog in the nighttime
Ghosts in Baker Street; edited by Martin H. Greenberg, Jon Lellenberg, Daniel Stashower
Recalled to life
Sherlock Holmes in America; edited by Martin H. Greenberg, Jon L. Lellenberg, and Daniel Stashower.

Cohen, Phyllis
Designer justice
Mystery Writers of America presents the prosecution rests; new stories about courtrooms, criminals, and the law; edited by Linda Fairstein.

Cohen, Robert
Aliens
The Virginia Quarterly Review v81 no1 p64-79 Wint 2005

Cohen, Stanley
A girl named Charlie
The World's finest mystery and crime stories, fourth annual collection; edited by Ed Gorman and Martin H. Greenberg
Why'd you bring me here?
The Deadly Bride; and 21 of the year's finest crime and mystery stories; including complete coverage of the year in mystery and crime fiction; edited by Ed Gorman and Martin H. Greenberg

COINS
Kenyon, S. Where angels fear to tread

Cokal, Susann
Shooting Snakes
Prairie Schooner v79 no4 p135-52 Wint 2005

Colbert, Jaimee Wriston
The Manager's Son
Prairie Schooner v79 no3 p35-44 Fall 2005
Cold as ice. Peterson, Q.
Cold autumn. See Bunin, I. A. Cold fall
Cold-blooded. Rykena, S.
Cold comfort. Aird, C.
Λ **cold** day in hell. Batteiger, P.
Cold dead fingers. Coleman, L. L.
Cold fall. Bunin, I. A.
Cold-Fire. Williams, A. J.
Cold fires. Rickert, M.
Cold Harbor. Rash, R.

The **cold,** hard truth. McMahan, R.
The **Cold** Outside. Burnside, J.
Cold snap. Kennedy, C.
Cold spell. Andrews, D.
The **Cold** War. Somerville, P.
A **Cold** War Story. Wang, J.
A **colder** war. Stross, C.
Cole, Adrian
Indian Night
  The North American Review v291 no2 p22-5
    Mr/Ap 2006
Cole, Andrea Nacina
Leaving Women
  Ploughshares v35 no1 p43-63 Spr 2009
Coleman, Anita Scott
Cross crossings cautiously
  "Tell it to us easy" and other stories; a com-
    plete short fiction anthology of African
    American women writers in Opportunity
    magazine, (1923-1948); edited by Judith
    Musser.
The eternal quest
  "Tell it to us easy" and other stories; a com-
    plete short fiction anthology of African
    American women writers in Opportunity
    magazine, (1923-1948); edited by Judith
    Musser.
Coleman, Layne
Oasis of Hope
  The Walrus v4 no5 p66-74 Je 2007
Coleman, Loren L.
Cold dead fingers
  Man vs. machine; edited by John Helfers and
    Martin H. Greenberg.
Coleman, Reed Farrel
Accidentally, like a Martyr
  The darker mask; edited by Gary Phillips and
    Christopher Chambers.
Pearls
  Expletive deleted; edited by Jen Jordan
Portrait of the killer as a young man
  Dublin noir; the Celtic tiger vs. the ugly
    American; edited by Ken Bruen
Coleman, Val
Paying my dues
  Short stories of the civil rights movement; an
    anthology; edited by Margaret Earley Whitt
Coleman, Wanda
Backcity transit by day
  Coleman, W. Jazz & twelve o'clock tales;
    new stories
Butterfly meat
  Coleman, W. Jazz & twelve o'clock tales;
    new stories
Darkness
  Coleman, W. Jazz & twelve o'clock tales;
    new stories
Dunny
  Coleman, W. Jazz & twelve o'clock tales;
    new stories
Hibernation
  Coleman, W. Jazz & twelve o'clock tales;
    new stories
Jazz at twelve
  Coleman, W. Jazz & twelve o'clock tales;
    new stories
Joy ride
  Coleman, W. Jazz & twelve o'clock tales;
    new stories

My brain's too tired to think
  Coleman, W. Jazz & twelve o'clock tales;
    new stories
My son, my son
  Coleman, W. Jazz & twelve o'clock tales;
    new stories
Pepper
  Coleman, W. Jazz & twelve o'clock tales;
    new stories
Purgatory
  Coleman, W. Jazz & twelve o'clock tales;
    new stories
Shark liver oil
  Coleman, W. Jazz & twelve o'clock tales;
    new stories
Winona's choice
  Coleman, W. Jazz & twelve o'clock tales;
    new stories
COLERIDGE, SAMUEL TAYLOR, 1772-1834
About
Mason, B. A. The prelude
Colette
Montmartre cemetery and flora and fauna in Pa-
  ris
  Paris tales; stories; translated by Helen Con-
    stantine
Colfer, Eoin
A fowl tale
  Wizards; edited by Jack Dann and Gardner
    Dozois
Taking on PJ
  Dublin noir; the Celtic tiger vs. the ugly
    American; edited by Ken Bruen
Colin Kelly's Kids. Elkin, S.
COLLABORATIONISTS *See* World War, 1939-
  1945—Collaborationists
Collateral damage. Greer, R. O.
Collateral damage. Schor, L.
Collateral Damage. Van Dyke, H.
The **Collected** Short Stories of Summer Style.
  Wray, J.
Collecting dust. Frost, G.
Collecting Stones. Abraham, R.
Collecting team. Silverberg, R.
The **collection** treatment. Schonfeld, Y.
COLLECTIVE SETTLEMENTS
Donoghue, E. The welcome
Israel
Liebrecht, S. Kibbutz
Mandelman, A. Talking to the enemy
Oz, A. The way of the wind
Shabtai, Y. Uncle Shmuel
United States
Lefer, D. The prosperity of cities and desert
  places
The **collector** comes after payday. Flora, F.
COLLECTORS AND COLLECTING
Chappell, F. Dance of shadows
Erdrich, L. The painted drum
Goldfaden, J. Disorder destroyers
Guilfoile, K. O death where is thy sting?
Higgins, G. V. The last wash of the teapot
Klages, E. Clip art
Morrow, B. The hoarder
Ozick, C. Stone
Rucker, R. v. B. Guadalupe and Hieronymus
  Bosch
Scholes, K. Fearsome Jones' discarded love col-
  lection

COLLECTORS AND COLLECTING—*Continued*

Straub, P. Little Red's tango
Zelazny, R. Collector's fever
Collector's fever. Zelazny, R.
COLLEGE ALUMNI
Ebenbach, D. H. Getting back onto solid foods
Wilson, K. Tunneling to the center of the earth
COLLEGE AND SCHOOL DRAMA
Paley, G. The loudest voice
COLLEGE LIFE
See also College students; School life; Students; Teachers
Ducornet, R. Koi
Rich, M. Smoking gun
Sutton, B. The rest of Esther
Yellin, T. Naphtali

Japan
Murakami, H. Firefly
Uchida, H. Chrysanthemum

United States
Amdahl, G. Visigoth
Barth, J. Tell me
Brown, D. The dangers of salmonella
Burke, K. Mrs. Maecenas
Crane, E. What our week was like
Fowler, M. Hall of liberty
Henry, O. The chair of philanthromathematics
Kessel, J. The snake girl
LaSalle, P. Where we last saw time
Lynn, D. H. Life sentences
Martin, V. The open door
Matheson, R. Old haunts
McCauley, C. S. Two left shoes
McKenzie, E. Caveat emptor
Oates, J. C. Landfill
Parker, J. and Parker, R. B. Galahad, Inc.
Rachel, D. The last man I killed
Raphael, L. Roy's Jewish problem
Raphael, L. Welcome to Beth Homo
Russo, R. Horseman
Singleton, G. The novels of Raymond Carver
Smith, N. Scrapbook
Tallent, E. Eros 101
Willis, C. Ado
Willis, C. In the late Cretaceous
COLLEGE STUDENTS
See also College life
Adichie, C. N. The shivering
Albert, E. Hotline
Albert, E. We have trespassed
Almond, S. Appropriate sex
Ames, J. Womb shelter
Barry, R. How to save a wounded bird
Beattie, A. Duchais
Boyers, R. Samantha
Clarke, B. Geronimo
Clayton, J. J. Bodies like mouths
Crone, M. It
Curtis, R. Big Bear, California
Curtis, R. Summer, with twins
Dormen, L. The secret of drawing
Fincke, G. The serial plagiarist
Gaitskill, M. College town, 1980
Gardiner, J. R. North of ordinary
Gerber, M. J. Tell me your secret
Gilchrist, E. Lunch at the best restaurant in the world
Griffiths, N. Freshers' week

Guista, M. The year of release
Hand, E. Wonderwall
Hernandez, L. Count the raindrops
Iagnemma, K. On the nature of human romantic interaction
Johnson, T. G. Winter never quits
Jones, H. G. Proof of God
Kercheval, J. L. Brazil
Klassen, S. Adelia
Kulpa, K. Cristina in another country
LaBute, N. Spring break
Lahiri, J. Nobody's business
Lain, D. The Sea Monkey conspiracy
Lawrence, H. Changes
Leedom-Ackerman, J. The beginning of violence
Ligon, S. Dirty boots
Lunstrum, K. S. Dangerous women
Lynn, D. H. Dean of women
Margulis, L. Sunday morning with J. Robert Oppenheimer
McInerney, J. The waiter
McKenzie, E. Look out, kids
McKenzie, E. S.O.S.
Michaels, L. Nachman from Los Angeles
Moffett, K. Space
Molodowsky, K. Elaine
Neal, L. Our bright tomorrows
Nelson, A. Stitches
Oates, J. C. Three girls
Ohlin, A. You are here
Parker, M. Hidden meanings: treatment of time, supreme irony, and life experiences in the song "Ain't gonna bump no more no big fat woman"
Perlman, E. Spitalnic's last year
Pierce, T. J. Sirens
Qi, S. The girl in blue jeans
Qi, S. The tenants
Randolph, L. The girls
Raphael, L. Betrayed by David Bowie
Raphael, L. The Cossacks
Reed, R. Abducted souls
Richter, S. Blackout
Roberts, A. Blindness and invisibility
Schutt, C. Weather is here, wish you were beautiful
Scott, J. Or else, part III: Rain on concrete
Shomer, E. The summer of questions
Stafford, J. The echo and the nemesis
Stafford, J. The tea time of stouthearted ladies
Stern, R. G. A counterfactual proposition
Stern, R. G. Wissler remembers
Thelwell, M. Direct action
Thompson, J. Lost
Trevor, D. Girls I know
Trevor, D. The river
Vollmer, M. Stewards of the earth
Ward, A. E. Miss Montana's wedding day
Windley, C. Sand and frost
Yates, D. Bring everybody
Yellin, T. Issachar
COLLEGE TEACHERS *See* Teachers
College town, 1980. Gaitskill, M.
A **collegiate** casting-out of devilish devices. Pratchett, T.
Collings, P. d'A.
The Mynah Bird
The Advocate (Vancouver, B.C.) v66 pt2 p298-304 Mr 2008

Collins, Barbara
Trailer trashed
   Deadly housewives; edited by Christine Matthews
Collins, Cat
Breia's diamond
   Places to be, people to kill; edited by Martin H. Greenberg and Brittianey A. Koren
Collins, Elizabeth
Apples and Angels
   The Massachusetts Review v50 no1-2 p233-42 Spr/Summ 2009
Collins, Max Allan
Open house
   Kolchak: the night stalker chronicles; 26 original tales of the surreal, the bizarre, the macabre; edited by Joe Gentile, Garrett Anderson, Lori Gentile; Kolchak created by Jeff Rice
Quarry's luck
   Greatest hits; original stories of assassins, hitmen, and hired guns; edited by Robert J. Randisi
Scrap
   Chicago blues; edited by Libby Fischer Hellmann
That kind of nag
   Murder at the racetrack; edited by Otto Penzler
Collins, Max Allan and Clemens, Matthew V.
East Side, West Side
   The Adventure of the missing detective and 19 of the year's finest crime and mystery stories!; edited by Ed Gorman and Martin H. Greenberg
The high life: a heartland homicide story
   At the scene of the crime; forensic mysteries from today's best writers; edited by Dana Stabenow
Murderlized
   Hollywood and crime; original crime stories set during the history of Hollywood; edited by Robert J. Randisi
Collins, Merle
The Wealth of the Dreams
   TriQuarterly no120 p49-56 2005
Collins, Michael
The kidnapping of Xiang Fei
   The International Association of Crime Writers presents Murder in Vegas; new crime tales of gambling and desperation; edited by Michael Connelly
Collins, Michael, 1924-
   For works written by this author under other names see Lynds, Dennis, 1924-2005
Collins, Myfanwy
'Have You Seen Us?'
   The Kenyon Review v29 no3 p101-15 Summ 2007
Collins, Paul
Lure
   Dreaming again; thirty-five new stories celebrating the wild side of Australian fiction; edited by Jack Dann
Collins, Ron
Picasso's cat
   Nature v443 p722 O 12 2006

Collins, Stephen
Water hazard
   Murder in the rough; edited by Otto Penzler
Collins, Wilkie
The biter bit
   The Mammoth book of vintage whodunnits; edited by Maxim Jakubowski
The clergyman's confession
   Collins, W. Sensation stories; tales of mystery and suspense; edited and introduced by Peter Haining
The diary of Ann Rodway
   Collins, W. Sensation stories; tales of mystery and suspense; edited and introduced by Peter Haining
The dream woman
   Collins, W. Sensation stories; tales of mystery and suspense; edited and introduced by Peter Haining
The fourth poor traveller
   Collins, W. Sensation stories; tales of mystery and suspense; edited and introduced by Peter Haining
The last stage coachman
   Collins, W. Sensation stories; tales of mystery and suspense; edited and introduced by Peter Haining
Love's random shot
   Collins, W. Sensation stories; tales of mystery and suspense; edited and introduced by Peter Haining
A marriage tragedy
   Collins, W. Sensation stories; tales of mystery and suspense; edited and introduced by Peter Haining
Nine o'clock
   Collins, W. Sensation stories; tales of mystery and suspense; edited and introduced by Peter Haining
A terribly strange bed
   Collins, W. Sensation stories; tales of mystery and suspense; edited and introduced by Peter Haining
Volpurno—or the Student
   The Times Literary Supplement no5518 p14-15 Ja 2 2009
Who is the thief?
   Collins, W. Sensation stories; tales of mystery and suspense; edited and introduced by Peter Haining
COLLINS, WILKIE, 1824-1889
About
Edwards, M. The house of the red candle
Collision. Shields, C.
Coloane, Francisco
The empty bottle [variant title: Bottle of cana]
   Coloane, F. Tierra del Fuego; translated from the Spanish by Howard Curtis
Five sailors and a green coffin [variant title: Five mariners and a green coffin]
   Coloane, F. Tierra del Fuego; translated from the Spanish by Howard Curtis
Forgotten land [variant title: Land of oblivion]
   Coloane, F. Tierra del Fuego; translated from the Spanish by Howard Curtis
The hidden part of the iceberg [variant title: Submerged iceberg]
   Coloane, F. Tierra del Fuego; translated from the Spanish by Howard Curtis

Coloane, Francisco—_Continued_
How the Chilote Otey died
    Coloane, F. Tierra del Fuego; translated from
    the Spanish by Howard Curtis
The lighthouse builder
    Coloane, F. Tierra del Fuego; translated from
    the Spanish by Howard Curtis
On the horse of dawn
    Coloane, F. Tierra del Fuego; translated from
    the Spanish by Howard Curtis
Passage to Puerto Edén
    Coloane, F. Tierra del Fuego; translated from
    the Spanish by Howard Curtis
Tierra del Fuego
    Coloane, F. Tierra del Fuego; translated from
    the Spanish by Howard Curtis
Colombi, Marchesa
Dear hope
    Writing to delight; Italian short stories by
    nineteenth-century women writers; edited
    by Antonia Arslan and Gabriella Romani
Learn a trade for a rainy day
    Writing to delight; Italian short stories by
    nineteenth-century women writers; edited
    by Antonia Arslan and Gabriella Romani
Winter evenings
    Writing to delight; Italian short stories by
    nineteenth-century women writers; edited
    by Antonia Arslan and Gabriella Romani
COLOMBIA
Fountain, B. Near-extinct birds of the central
    cordillera
Le, N. Cartagena
Mendoza, P. The day we buried our weapons
Rendall, P. Flowers for Doña Alicia
Suescun, N. My father was blue
COLOMBIANS
United States
Leonard, E. When the women come out to
    dance
The **Colonel's** Allegro. Aguilar, A.
The **colonel's** awakening. Dunbar, P. L.
The **colonel's** lady [variant title: Road to Inspira-
    tion] Leonard, E.
COLONIALISM _See_ Imperialism
COLONIES, ARTIST _See_ Artist colonies
Colony of New York, 1712. Johnson, M.
COLOR
Silverberg, R. World of a thousand colors
Zelazny, R. The House of the Hanged Man
The **Color** of Darkness. Mas, A.
The **Color** of Shadows. Tóibín, C.
Color of the sea. Selgin, P.
The **Color** of Wheat in Winter. Ellison, J.
Color Struck. Perry, P.
Color vision. Rosenblum, M. H.
COLORADO
Bingham, S. That winter
Bingle, D. J. Attached to the land
Hinton, S. E. Full moon birthday
Krysl, M. Dinner with Osama
Olafsson, O. March
Stafford, J. Bad characters
Stafford, J. A reading problem
Frontier and pioneer life
    See Frontier and pioneer life—Colorado
Denver
Lewis, W. H. Rossonian days
Willis, C. Cibola

Il **colore** ritrovato. Helprin, M.
COLOSSEUM (ROME, ITALY)
Scurati, A. Eternal Rome
The **colossus** of Ylourgne. Smith, C. A.
Colour. Moorcock, M.
The **colour** out of space. Lovecraft, H. P.
The **coloured** lands. Chesterton, G. K.
Columbia Revolt. Obenzinger, H.
**COLUMBIA RIVER GORGE (OR. AND
    WASH.)**
Keeble, J. The cross
Columbine: the musical. Pierce, T. J.
COLUMNISTS _See_ Journalists
Colvin, Clare
Love and death in renaissance Italy
    Getting even; revenge stories; edited by Mitzi
    Szereto
Comadres in the kitchen. Alvarado, B.
COMANCHE INDIANS
Graves, J. The last running
Comba, Gretchen
The Close and Faraway
    South Carolina Review v39 no1 p181-7 Fall
    2006
Combatant love. Mercado, T.
Comber. Wolfe, G.
COMBUSTION, SPONTANEOUS
Menger-Anderson, K. The burning, 1725
Wilson, K. Blowing up on the spot
Come and Take Me. Almond, S.
Come away with me. Bradbury, R.
Come back. Cass, R.
Come dance with me. Bisson, T.
Come Day, Go Day. Jeffers, H. F.
Come sta? come va? Gildner, G.
Come to me dying!. Goodis, D.
Come to me not in winter's white. Zelazny, R.
Come together, fall apart. Henriquez, C.
COMEDIANS
Dann, J. Fairy tale
Dean, D. What the left hand is saying
Hempel, A. Three popes walk into a bar
Lobato, J. B. M. The funnyman who repented
Nelson, R. F. In the picking room
Pearlman, E. How to fall
Reidy, D. Captive audience
Schulberg, B. Your Arkansas traveler
A **comedy** on the gold coast. Bennett, A.
Comes now the power. Zelazny, R.
Comet. Salter, J.
COMETS
Hempel, A. Under no moon
Pohl, F. Some joys under the star
The **comeuppance** of Lupe Rivera. Muñoz, M.
Comfort. Granados, C.
COMIC BOOKS, STRIPS, ETC.
Clowes, D. Justin M. Damiano
Ducornet, R. The butcher's comics
Lupoff, R. A. The Crimson Wizard
Pendarvis, J. Sex devil
Romano, T. Comic books
Ware, C. Jordan Wellington Lint
Comic books. Romano, T.
The **coming.** Cave, H. B.
Coming home. Brazaitis, M.
Coming of age. Lane, J.
Coming of age. Schor, L.
Coming of Age in Faheete. Leong, S.

COMPOSERS—*Continued*

Green, G. Voices in a mask

Greenman, B. The duck knows how to make the most of things

Ha Jin. A composer and his parakeets

Lain, D. Music lessons

MacLeod, I. The noonday pool

Malouf, D. The domestic cantata

Moon, E. New world symphony

Shields, C. New music

Stern, D. Fabrikant's way

Stern, R. G. Double Charley

Stern, R. G. Veni, vidi . . . wendt

Westcott, G. The whistling swan

Wingate, S. Knuckles

The **compound**. Smith, M. M.

A **compromised** Christmas. Roberson, J.

Compton, Wayde

The blue road: a fairy tale

So long been dreaming; postcolonial science fiction & fantasy; Nalo Hopkinson & Uppinder Mehan, eds

Compulsion Vigil. Chapman, M.

COMPULSIVE BEHAVIOR

Cook, T. H. The odds

Corso, P. Roman arches

Guilfoile, K. Zero zero day

Parks, T. Annette and Frank

COMPULSORY MILITARY SERVICE *See* Draft

COMPUTER CRIMES

Modesitt, L. E., Jr. The great American economy

Computer friendly. Gunn, E.

COMPUTER GAMES

Crouse, D. The forgotten kingdom

Faber, M. Mouse

COMPUTER PROGRAMMING *See* Programming (Computers)

COMPUTER SIMULATION *See* Virtual reality

Computer virus. Kress, N.

COMPUTERS

See also Programming (Computers)

Almond, S. Wired for life

Averill, T. F. The onion and I

Ballantyne, T. Aristotle OS

Bradley, D. C. They would only be roads

Chase, M. Wet

Doctorow, C. OwnzOreo

Egan, G. Crystal nights

Egan, G. Luminous

Finlay, C. C. The factwhore proposition

Gaiman, N. Goliath

Gerrold, D. The Baby Cooper Dollar Bill

Grimes, C. Subdivisions of space

Gunn, E. Computer friendly

Irvine, A. C. Reformation

Kress, N. Computer virus

Kuper, T. Project 38; or, The game of small causes

Lupoff, R. A. The turret

Modesitt, L. E., Jr. Rule of law

Pratchett, T. FTB

Pratchett, T. # ifdefDEBUG + "world/enough" + "time"

Roberts, A. New model computer

Roberts, A. Swiftly

Rucker, R. v. B. MS found in a minidrive

Scalzi, J. The tale of the wicked

Shawl, N. Good boy

Silverberg, R. The Macauley circuit

Stackpole, M. A. Kid binary and the two-bit gang

Sterling, B. Code

Sterling, B. The lustration

Sterling, B. Maneki Neko

Stevens, J. D. Clara's PC and the second coming

Stross, C. Antibodies

Stross, C. Down on the farm

Stross, C. Toast: a con report

Swanwick, M. Trojan horse

Updike, J. Bech noir

Zelazny, R. Angel, dark angel

Zelazny, R. For a breath I tarry

Zelazny, R. Heritage

Zelazny, R. My lady of the diodes

The **computiful** game. Miller, P. S.

Comrade Luxemburg and Comrade Gramsci pass each other at a Congress of the Second International in Switzerland on the 10th of March, 1912. Finger, A.

Con doctor. McInerney, J.

CON MEN *See* Swindlers and swindling

Conard, Robert C.

(tr.) See Timm, Uwe

Concealed weapon. Torrey, R.

Concealment shoes. Youmans, M.

Conceits. Margulis, L.

Conceived. Morse, D. L.

CONCENTRATION CAMPS

See also Auschwitz (Poland: Concentration camp); Political prisoners; World War, 1939-1945—Prisoners and prisons

Dann, J. and Dozois, G. R. Down among the dead men

Conception. Van Booy, S.

Concerning balloons. Bierce, A.

Concerning the case of Bobby T. Oates, J. C.

Concerning the Correct Way to Make Cabbage. Sulaitis, D. S.

Concerning the So-Called One and Only God, as Told by Anu the All-Seeing Lord of the World-Covering Sky Vault. Mathews, B.

Concerto. Shuman, S. N.

CONCERTS

Barnes, J. Vigilance

Charnas, S. M. Listening to Brahms

La **Conchita**. Boyle, T. C.

A **concrete** example. Boon, J.-P. and others

The **Concrete** Village. Le Minh Khue

Condé, Maryse

Family portrait

Paris tales; stories; translated by Helen Constantine

Condemned house: a short story. Boehm, L.

The **condom** and the clarinet. Stern, D.

CONDOMS

Daughtry, P. French letters

CONDUCT OF LIFE *See* Ethics

The **conductor**. Hemon, A.

CONDUCTORS (MUSIC)

Beagle, P. S. Mr. Sigerson

Cones. Ronk, M. C.

Conescu, William

Brought To You By

New Letters v73 no2 p57-62 2007

CONEY ISLAND (NEW YORK, N.Y.) *See* New
    York (N.Y.)—Coney Island
Coney Island. Trezise, R.
CONFEDERACY *See* Confederate States of
    America
CONFEDERATE AGENTS *See* Spies
CONFEDERATE STATES OF AMERICA
    Allred, L. East of Appomattox
CONFEDERATE STATES OF AMERICA.
    ARMY
    Bierce, A. One of the missing
    Bierce, A. Parker Adderson, philosopher
    Smith, R. T. Wretch like me
The **conference**. Singer, I. B.
CONFESSION
    Anderson, B. Feeding the sparrows
    Bierce, A. A bottomless grave
    Bierce, A. Burbank's crime
    Bierce, A. The City of the Gone Away
    Bierce, A. His Waterloo
    Bierce, A. The hypnotist
    Bierce, A. My favorite murder
    Bierce, A. Oil of dog
    Bierce, A. The widower Turmore
    Depestre, Y. Abikú
    Fonseca, R. Winning the game
    Manotti, D. Zero tolerance
    Rickert, M. Art is not a violent subject
    Sakey, M. No one
    Trevor, W. Solitude
    Tuma, H. The Waldiba story
    Weinman, S. Hen night
CONFESSION (CATHOLIC)
    Bradbury, R. Bless me, Father, for I have sinned
    Duval, P. Pious objects
    Trevor, W. Justina's priest
A **confession**. Chekhov, A. P.
Confession for Raymond Good Bird. Thon, M. R.
Confessions. Mantel, T.
Confessions of a dial-up gigolo. Pollack, N.
Confessions of a falling woman. Dean, D.
Confessions of a sad dog. Bierce, A.
Confessions of a sex maniac. Sterry, D. H.
The **Confidence** Decoy. Beattie, A.
Confidences. Romano, T.
The **confidential** informant. Pelecanos, G. P.
The **conflagration** in Ghargaroo. Bierce, A.
CONFLICT OF GENERATIONS
    Deaver, J. The poker lesson
    Dunbar, P. L. The minority committee
    Dunbar, P. L. Old Abe's conversion
    Judah, S. A girl from my hometown
    Judah, S. Old man Moses
    Kobrin, L. Door number one
    Petsetidis, D. Away ground
    Pilcer, S. "Paskudnyak"
    Pinski, D. At the attorney's
    Reisen, A. Mother goes to the library
Conford, M. G.
    Bombing (1)
        Dalhousie Review v89 no1 p87-94 Spr 2009
CONFORMITY
    Baraka, I. A. The rejected buppie
    Douka, M. Carré fix
    Gordin, J. What will people say?
    Gorman, E. Moral imperative
    Kadare, I. The blinding order
    Keret, E. A thought in the shape of a story
    Palazzeschi, A. The black mark

Russell, K. St. Lucy's home for girls raised by
    wolves
    Silverberg, R. Caliban
Confrontation. Sillitoe, A.
Confusions most monstrous. Emerson, K. L.
Conga, conga. Rivas, M.
Congenital agenesis of gender ideation by K. N.
    Sirsi and Sandra Botkin. Carter, R.
Congratulations Goldie Katowitz. Monk, B.
Congress. Williams, J.
CONGRESSES AND CONFERENCES
        See also Meetings
    Margulis, L. Meeting
    Pohl, F. Speed trap
    Singer, I. B. The conference
Conjugal ties (1). Fuentes, C.
Conjugal ties (2). Fuentes, C.
Conjugation [short story by Lee Henderson] Hen-
    derson, L.
The **conjurer's** handbook. Hoffman, A.
The **conjuring** contest. Dunbar, P. L.
Conkie, Jennifer Law
    Beloved of the Sky
        The Advocate (Vancouver, B.C.) v66 pt4
        p515-19 Jl 2008
Conley, Charles
    Cadillac Hearse
        The Southern Review (Baton Rouge, La.) v43
        no3 p707-16 Summ 2007
    The Final Cold
        Harvard Review (1992) no35 p8-29 2008
Conlon, Christopher
    Darkness, and she was alone
        Poe's lighthouse; all new collaborations with
        Edgar Allan Poe; edited by Christopher
        Conlon
Connected. Mennuti, N. D.
Connected. Mueller, D.
CONNECTICUT
    Chase, M. The busker
    Pope, D. Karaoke Night
    Porter, A. Connecticut
    Selgin, P. The girl in the story
Connecticut. Porter, A.
Connection completed. Merril, J.
Connections. Zoshchenko, M.
Connell, Brendan
    We sleep on a thousand waves beneath the stars
        Fast ships, black sails; edited by Ann & Jeff
        VanderMeer
Connell, Evan S.
    Ancient musick
        Connell, E. S. Lost in Uttar Pradesh; new and
        selected stories
    Arcturus
        Connell, E. S. Lost in Uttar Pradesh; new and
        selected stories
    Assassin
        Connell, E. S. Lost in Uttar Pradesh; new and
        selected stories
    Bowen
        Connell, E. S. Lost in Uttar Pradesh; new and
        selected stories
    Caribbean provedor
        Connell, E. S. Lost in Uttar Pradesh; new and
        selected stories
    The Cuban Missle Crisis
        Connell, E. S. Lost in Uttar Pradesh; new and
        selected stories

Connell, Evan S.—*Continued*

Election eve

Pushcart Prize XXVIII: best of the small presses 2004; edited by Bill Henderson and the Pushcart prize editors

Connell, E. S. Lost in Uttar Pradesh; new and selected stories

Guadalcanal [variant title: The Marine]

Connell, E. S. Lost in Uttar Pradesh; new and selected stories

Hooker

Connell, E. S. Lost in Uttar Pradesh; new and selected stories

The land where lemon trees bloom

Connell, E. S. Lost in Uttar Pradesh; new and selected stories

Lion

Connell, E. S. Lost in Uttar Pradesh; new and selected stories

Lost in Uttar Pradesh

Connell, E. S. Lost in Uttar Pradesh; new and selected stories

Harper's v311 p76-84 D 2005

Mrs. Proctor Bemis

Connell, E. S. Lost in Uttar Pradesh; new and selected stories

Nan Madol

Connell, E. S. Lost in Uttar Pradesh; new and selected stories

Noah's Ark

Connell, E. S. Lost in Uttar Pradesh; new and selected stories

Octopus, the Sausalito quarterly of new writing, art & ideas

Connell, E. S. Lost in Uttar Pradesh; new and selected stories

The palace of the moorish kings

Connell, E. S. Lost in Uttar Pradesh; new and selected stories

Proctor Bemis

Connell, E. S. Lost in Uttar Pradesh; new and selected stories

Puig's wife

Connell, E. S. Lost in Uttar Pradesh; new and selected stories

St. Augustine's pigeon

Connell, E. S. Lost in Uttar Pradesh; new and selected stories

The walls of Avila

Connell, E. S. Lost in Uttar Pradesh; new and selected stories

Yellow raft

Connell, E. S. Lost in Uttar Pradesh; new and selected stories

Connell, Myra

The shirt

Her Majesty; 21 stories by women; edited by Jackie Gay and Emma Hargrave

Connell, Nick

Ozark Lake

Playboy's college fiction; a collection of 21 years of contest winners; edited by Alice K. Turner; foreword by Thom Jones

Connell, Richard Edward

A reputation

Adaptations: from short story to big screen; 35 great stories that have inspired great films; edited by Stephanie Harrison

Connelly, Mark

Coroner's inquest

The vicious circle; mystery and crime stories by members of the Algonquin Round Table; edited by Otto Penzler

Connelly, Michael

Cielo Azul

Dangerous women; edited by Otto Penzler

Father's day

Mystery Writers of America presents the blue religion; new stories about cops, criminals, and the chase; edited by Michael Connelly

The Best American mystery stories, 2009; edited and with an introduction by Jeffery Deaver

Mulholland dive

Los Angeles noir; edited by Denise Hamilton

A Prisoner of memory and 24 of the year's finest crime and mystery stories; edited by Ed Gorman & Martin H. Greenberg

The Best American mystery stories, 2008; edited and with an introduction by George Pelecanos; Otto Penzler, series editor

One–dollar jackpot

Dead man's hand; crime fiction at the poker table; edited by Otto Penzler.

Suicide run

Hollywood and crime; original crime stories set during the history of Hollywood; edited by Robert J. Randisi

Connolly, Clare

Clare Connolly: WIND in Bradford playground, 17 January 2003 [Medical Humanities, 31 no1 June 2005]

Journal of Medical Ethics v31 no6 p45-6 Je 2005 supp

Connolly, John

The inkpot monkey

The Best British mysteries, 2006; edited by Maxim Jakubowski

Mr. Gray's folly

Dangerous women; edited by Otto Penzler

Connor, Joan

The Folly of Being Comforted

TriQuarterly no123 p169-77 2005

The Landmark Hotel

The Antioch Review v64 no1 p164-75 Wint 2006

Palimpsest

Gettysburg Review v18 no2 p173-85 Summ 2005

What it is

Pushcart Prize XXVIII: best of the small presses 2004; edited by Bill Henderson and the Pushcart prize editors

The **conqueror**. Matheson, R.

The **conquest** [excerpt] Murray, Y. M.

The **conquest** of Gola. Stone, L. F.

Conquist. Strasser, D.

CONRAD, JOSEPH, 1857-1924
About
Ozick, C. Dictation
Parodies, imitations, etc.
Clark, S. The extraordinary limits of darkness

Conrad Loomis & the Clothes Ray. Baraka, I. A.

Conroy-Goldman, Melanie

The Mistress of Leche Island

StoryQuarterly v41 p502-26 2005

Conroy-Goldman, Melanie—*Continued*
Rock Star
The Southern Review (Baton Rouge, La.) v43
no3 p583-95 Summ 2007
CONSCIENCE
See also Ethics; Guilt
Oates, J. C. Concerning the case of Bobby T.
Stevenson, R. L. Markheim
The **consequence** of summer heat. Shirley, P.
Consequences. Nye, J. L.
Consequences of knowledge. McGlynn, D.
Los **conservadores/The** preservers. Bergua, A. G.
Conservation. Spark, D.
CONSERVATIONISTS
Bass, R. Titan
Consideration of the force required to break an
arm. Monson, A.
Consolation. Brown, R.
The **consolation** blonde. McDermid, V.
The **consolations** of art. Moss, B. K.
CONSPIRACIES
Baraka, I. A. My man came by the crib the oth-
er day . . .
Baraka, I. A. Post–and pre–mortem dialogue
Baraka, I. A. The used saver
Barthelme, D. Hiding man
Barthelme, D. Pages from the annual report
Chase, M. The perimeter
De Camp, L. S. The isolinguals
Gregory, D. Damascus
Lain, D. The Sea Monkey conspiracy
L'Amour, L. South of Suez
L'Amour, L. Voyage to Tobolai
L'Amour, L. Wings over Brazil
MacLaverty, B. A trusted neighbour
Matheson, R. Legion of plotters
McAuley, P. J. and Newman, K. Prisoners of
the action
Mejides, M. Nowhere man
Moody, R. The Omega Force
Silverberg, R. The littlest Jackal
Waldrop, H. The horse of a different color (That
you rode in on)
Conspiracies: a very condensed 937-page novel.
Resnick, M. and Flint, E.
The **constable** of Abal. Link, K.
A **Constant** History. Wheat, C.
The **constant** past. McMullen, S.
CONSTANTINOPLE *See* Turkey—Istanbul
Constellations. Monson, A.
Constitutional. Simpson, H.
CONSTRUCTION INDUSTRY
Allyn, D. Palace in the pines
Erdrich, L. Scales
Thormahlen, A. The construction worker
The **construction** worker. Thormahlen, A.
CONSULS *See* Diplomatic life
Consuming the View. Malerba, L.
Consumption. Kelly, R.
Contact. Gunn, E.
Contact. Schossler, J.
Contact and cover. Rucka, G.
Contact tracing. Lam, V.
Contaminant. Boudinot, R.
Contemplating a thing about a person. Greenman,
B.
CONTENTMENT
See also Happiness

The **Contents** of This Shoe Box Are of Greater
Worth Than Your Life. Casey, S.
Contessa Lara *See* Lara, Contessa, 1849-1896
The **contest**. Bishop, T.
The **contest**. Cook, W.
The **contest**. Proulx, A.
CONTESTS
Baker, K. Plotters and shooters
Bierce, A. A literary riot
Bishop, T. The contest
Bishop, T. The great Mormon cricket fly-fishing
festival
Dunbar, P. L. A judgment of Paris
Hubbard, L. R. Battle of wizards
James, C. L. R. Serial not cereal
Lam, D. The seventy-two-ounce steak challenge
Parker, M. Results for novice males
Proulx, A. The contest
Rucker, R. v. B. and Bisson, T. 2+2=5
Sterling, B. Sunken gardens
Wilson, K. Birds in the house
Conti, Gregory
(tr.) *See* Stern, Mario Rigoni
Continental. Pagès, V.
Continental grip. Morrell, D.
Continuity. Kelton, E.
CONTRACEPTION *See* Birth control
The **contract**. Clayton, J. J.
Contract bridge. Lane, J.
CONTRACTORS
Allen, W. On a bad day you can see forever
Helprin, M. Monday
Contraflow. Beaumont, M.
Contrails. Maliszewski, P.
Controlled burn. Wolven, S.
Controversial Author and Cultural Icon Found
Dead. Almond, S.
Conundrums to guess. Crowther, P.
CONVENT LIFE
See also Nuns
Phan, A. The Delta
Phan, A. Miss Lien
Ruiz Rosas, T. Santa Catalina, Arequipa
Stern, R. G. A recital for the Pope
CONVENTS *See* Convent life
CONVENTS AND NUNNERIES *See* Convent
life
CONVERSATION
Baraka, I. A. Dream comics
Baraka, I. A. A Monk story
Baraka, I. A. My man came by the crib the oth-
er day . . .
Barthelme, D. The apology
Barthelme, D. Basil from her garden
Barthelme, D. Belief
Barthelme, D. The discovery
Barthelme, D. The Viennese Opera Ball
Barthelme, D. Wrack
Barthelme, D. You are cordially invited
Carver, R. What we talk about when we talk
about love
Maxwell, W. The woman with a talent for talk-
ing
Pickard, N. I killed
Porter, J. A. West Baltimore
Tognazzini, A. What comes of conversation
Wolfe, T. Only the dead know Brooklyn
Conversation. Walbert, K.

Conversation of a drunken man with a sober devil. Chekhov, A. P.

The **conversation** of a man with a dog. Chekhov, A. P.

Conversations at ma maia metron. Meadley, R.

Conversations in prosperity. Gordon, M.

Conversations with Godard. Whalen, T.

Converse, Karna
  Grandpa's Letters
    Nebraska Life v12 no3 p28-9 My/Je 2008

CONVERSION
  Bierce, A. The baptism of Dobsho
  Donoghue, E. Enchantment
  Donoghue, E. The man who wrote on beaches
  Ebenbach, D. H. I'll be home
  Gordon, M. Temporary shelter
  Mandelbaum, P. The omelet king
  Riley, P. Wisteria
  Wendroff, Z. The abduction

The **conversion**. Cherne, B.

The **conversion** of Fred Coates. Auchincloss, L.

The **convert**. Bennett, L.

Converting a prodigal. Bierce, A.

The **convict**. Burke, J. L.

Conviction. Ch'oe, S.

CONVICTS *See* Crime and criminals; Ex-convicts; Prisoners and prisons

CONVICTS, ESCAPED *See* Escaped convicts

Cony, Carlos Heitor
  Order of the day
    Oxford anthology of the Brazilian short story; edited by K. David Jackson

Coo people. Emshwiller, C.

Cook, Coralie Franklin
  A slave for life: a story of the long ago
    "Tell it to us easy" and other stories; a complete short fiction anthology of African American women writers in Opportunity magazine, (1923-1948); edited by Judith Musser

Cook, Glen
  Call for the dead
    Cook, G. An empire unacquainted with defeat; stories of the Dread Empire
  Castle of tears
    Cook, G. An empire unacquainted with defeat; stories of the Dread Empire
  Filed teeth
    Cook, G. An empire unacquainted with defeat; stories of the Dread Empire
  Finding Svale's daughter
    Cook, G. An empire unacquainted with defeat; stories of the Dread Empire
  Ghost stalk
    Cook, G. An empire unacquainted with defeat; stories of the Dread Empire
  Hell's forge
    Cook, G. An empire unacquainted with defeat; stories of the Dread Empire
  The nights of dreadful silence
    Cook, G. An empire unacquainted with defeat; stories of the Dread Empire
  Severed heads
    Cook, G. An empire unacquainted with defeat; stories of the Dread Empire
  Silverheels
    Cook, G. An empire unacquainted with defeat; stories of the Dread Empire

Soldier of an empire unacquainted with defeat
    Cook, G. An empire unacquainted with defeat; stories of the Dread Empire

Cook, Rebecca
  You Girls Have the Loveliest Legs
    New England Review v29 no2 p120-7 2008

Cook, Thomas H.
  The odds
    Murder at the racetrack; edited by Otto Penzler
  Rain
    Manhattan noir; edited by Lawrence Block
  What she offered
    Dangerous women; edited by Otto Penzler

Cook, Will
  Bell's station
    Cook, W. Blood sky; western stories; edited by Bill Pronzini
  Blood sky
    Cook, W. Blood sky; western stories; edited by Bill Pronzini
  The contest
    Cook, W. Blood sky; western stories; edited by Bill Pronzini
  The far-travelin' man
    Cook, W. Blood sky; western stories; edited by Bill Pronzini
  The fight at Renegade Basin
    Cook, W. Blood sky; western stories; edited by Bill Pronzini
  Let's all go kill the scared old man
    Cook, W. Blood sky; western stories; edited by Bill Pronzini
  Wildcat on the prod
    Cook, W. Blood sky; western stories; edited by Bill Pronzini

Cook. West, D.

COOKERY
  Allen, W. Thus ate Zarathustra
  Barnes, J. Appetite
  Corso, P. Freezer burn
  Cross, E. The recipe
  Dahl, R. Pig
  Harris, J. Gastronomicon
  Hogan, L. Bush's mourning feast
  Klages, E. Be prepared
  Paschal, D. Sauteing the playtgast
  Ruffin, P. The hands of John Merchant
  Scego, I. "Faduma & Barni (April, 2003)"
  Vapnyar, L. Borscht
  Vapnyar, L. Luda and Milena

Cookie Lily. Troy, M.

The **cookie** monster. Vinge, V.

Cooking lessons. Herrmann, M.

COOKS
  Adiga, A. Valencia (to the first crossroads)
  Barrett, M. Skyliner
  Barry, R. Snow fever
  Burke, T. Quite normal
  Cavin, R. Even gamblers have to eat
  Coloane, F. Passage to Puerto Edén
  Ducornet, R. Panna cotta
  Dunbar, P. L. The brief cure of Aunt Fanny
  Gerencer, T. Primordial chili
  Goldfaden, J. Nautical intervention
  Hempel, A. Du jour
  Herrmann, M. Cooking lessons
  Holthe, T. U. Weightless
  Kamlani, B. Zanzibar

CORONERS—*Continued*

Brite, P. Z. Wound Man and horned melon go to Hell

Levi, J. The scrimshaw violin

Coroner's inquest. Connelly, M.

CORPORATIONS *See* Business

The **corpse** in the crystal. McCandless, D. B.

The **corpse** in the parlor. Trevisan, D.

Corpse on a holy day. Tremayne, P.

The **corpse** that lost its head. Vermeulen, J.

CORPULENCE *See* Obesity

Corpus Christi. Marston, E.

Correa, Arnaldo

Olúo

Havana noir; edited by Achy Obejas

Correa Baez, Arnaldo, 1938- *See* Correa, Arnaldo, 1938-

A **correct** life. Nguyen, V. T.

The **correct** names of things. Kennedy, C.

Corrections to my memoirs. Kun, M.

Correspondence with a breeder. Ian, J.

Correspondent. Ingalls, R.

Corrida. Zelazny, R.

Corrigall, Melodie

Without the China

Dalhousie Review v87 no2 p281-5 Summ 2007

Corriveau, Art

Black Tie

Southwest Review v91 no2 p229-37 2006

Corrupting the press. Bierce, A.

CORRUPTION (IN POLITICS)

See also Bribery

Artemis, B. Slingin'

Baraka, I. A. Neo-American

Baraka, I. A. New & old

Bierce, A. Burbank's crime

Bierce, A. The fall of the Republic

Bierce, A. His Waterloo

Bierce, A. The Tamtonians

Davis, M. Negative Nixons

Dunbar, P. L. The scapegoat

Fountain, B. Asian tiger

Fusilli, J. The dupe

Grady, J. The bottom line

Greer, R. O. Collateral damage

Hautman, P. Pork

Hinojosa, R. Partners in crime [excerpt]

James, D. The art of avarice

Lamar, J. Madame secretary's lover man

Light, L. The lamented

Martinez, M. Ambition

McCauley, W. The turning over

Nganang, P. Our neighborhood fool

Phelan, T. Strange bedfellows

Phillips, G. Swift boats for Jesus

Rakotoson, M. The ballad of a shipwreck

Rusch, K. K. G-Men

Rylands, J. T. Service

White, L. T. The city of hell!

Wishnia, K. J. A. Dissed

CORSAIRS *See* Pirates

Corso, Paola

Between the sheets

Corso, P. Giovanna's 86 circles

The drying corner

Corso, P. Giovanna's 86 circles

Freezer burn

Corso, P. Giovanna's 86 circles

Giovanna's 86 circles

Corso, P. Giovanna's 86 circles

Nose dive

Corso, P. Giovanna's 86 circles

Raw egg in beer

Corso, P. Giovanna's 86 circles

Roman arches

Corso, P. Giovanna's 86 circles

Shelf life

Corso, P. Giovanna's 86 circles

Unraveled

Corso, P. Giovanna's 86 circles

Yesterday's news

Corso, P. Giovanna's 86 circles

Cortázar, Julio

Blow-up

Adaptations: from short story to big screen; 35 great stories that have inspired great films; edited by Stephanie Harrison

COSA NOSTRA *See* Mafia

Cosas. Carrillo, H. G.

Cosman, Carol

(tr.) See Camus, Albert

Cosmic Joke. Stone, L. F.

Cosmonauts. Frazier, K.

Cosmopolitan. Sharma, A.

Cosper, Darcy

Love, American style, 2033

2033; the future of misbehavior: interplanetary dating, Madame President, socialized plastic surgery, and other good news from the future; from the editors of Nerve.com; instigated by Svedka

Cossack wolf. Lamb, H.

COSSACKS

Lamb, H. Alamut

Lamb, H. Ameer of the sea

Lamb, H. The baiting of the warriors

Lamb, H. Bogatyr

Lamb, H. The bride of Jagannath

Lamb, H. Chang Nor

Lamb, H. City under the sea

Lamb, H. Cossack wolf

Lamb, H. The curved sword

Lamb, H. The devil's song

Lamb, H. An edge to a sword

Lamb, H. Khlit

Lamb, H. The king dies

Lamb, H. Koum

Lamb, H. Law of fire

Lamb, H. The lion cub

Lamb, H. Mark of Astrakhan

Lamb, H. The masterpiece of death

Lamb, H. Men from below

Lamb, H. The mighty manslayer

Lamb, H. The moon of Shawwul

Lamb, H. The outrider

Lamb, H. Over the river

Lamb, H. The phantom caravan

Lamb, H. The post in the steppe

Lamb, H. Prophecy of the blind

Lamb, H. Red hands

Lamb, H. The rider of the gray horse

Lamb, H. Roof of the world

Lamb, H. Rose face

Lamb, H. Sangar

Lamb, H. Singing girl

Lamb, H. The star of evil omen

Lamb, H. The stone woman

COSSACKS—*Continued*
 Lamb, H. Tal Taulai Khan
 Lamb, H. The bride of Jagannath
 Lamb, H. The two swords of Genghis Khan
 Lamb, H. The vampire of Khor
 Lamb, H. White falcon
 Lamb, H. The white Khan
 Lamb, H. The winged rider
 Lamb, H. The witch of Aleppo
 Lamb, H. Witch woman
 Lamb, H. Wolf-hounds of the steppe
 Lamb, H. The wolf master
 Lamb, H. Wolf's war
The **Cossacks**. Raphael, L.
The **cost** of things. Donoghue, E.
The **cost** to be wise. McHugh, M. F.
Costa, Margaret Jull
 (tr.) See Atxaga, Bernardo
Costa, Shelley
 Black heart and cabin girl
  The World's finest mystery and crime stories,
  fifth annual collection; edited by Ed
  Gorman and Martin H. Greenberg
 From the Personal Record Collection of
  Beniamino Gigli
  The Georgia Review v58 no3 p616-33 Fall
  2004
COSTA RICA
 Link, K. The surfer
The **costly** kiss: a New York detective experience
 Bendel-Simso, M. M., ed. Early American
 detective stories; an anthology; edited by
 LeRoy Lad Panek and Mary M. Bendel-
 Simso.
COSTUME PARTIES *See* Parties
Côté, Estelle
 Un goût de terre
  Canadian Woman Studies v26 no1 p35-6
  Wint/Spr 2007
Cotrina, José Antonio
 Between the lines
  The SFWA European hall of fame; sixteen
  contemporary masterpieces of science fic-
  tion from the continent; edited by James
  Morrow and Kathryn Morrow
Cotsirilos, Teresa
 My Fourth
  Hanging Loose no88 p83-7 2006
 Obituary in Three Drafts
  Hanging Loose no88 p88-90 2006
The **cottagers** and Mrs. Carmody. West, D.
Cotton Flat Road. Hempel, A.
Coudriet, Daniel
 Geese
  Best American fantasy; guest editors Ann &
  Jeff VanderMeer; series editor Matthew
  Cheney
Cougar & Zeke. Bakopoulos, D.
A **council** of state. Dunbar, P. L.
Counihan, Elizabeth
 Acting up
  Nature v452 p502 Mr 27 2008
COUNSELING
 Luongo, M. What Nina wants
Count the raindrops. Hernandez, L.
COUNTER CULTURE
 Wild, P. Radical adults lick godhead style
COUNTERESPIONAGE *See* International in-
 trigue; Spies

A **counterfactual** proposition. Stern, R. G.
Counterfactuals. Davies, T.
Counterfeit love. Bangkok, J.
The **Counterfeit** Sock. Frazer, R.
COUNTERFEITERS
 Higgins, G. V. The devil is real
The **Counterpart**. Kalman, N.
Counterpart. Silverberg, R.
Counterparts. Means, D.
Counterparts. Shishin, A.
The **countess**. Cherne, B.
Counting coup. McGruder, K.
Counting Pages. Goodman, A.
COUNTRY CLUBS
 Coyne, T. A gentleman's game [excerpt]
 Hunter, S. Stephen Longacre's greatest match
 Liddell, R. Whatever happened to Sébastien
  Grosjean?
 Morrell, D. Continental grip
 Rucker, R. v. B. The men in the back room at
  the country club
 Stashower, D. A peach of a shot
The **country** girl. Levin, Z.
The **Country** House. Stewart, D.
COUNTRY LIFE
  See also Farm life; Plantation life; Ranch
  life; Small town life
 Berry, W. Mike
 Bierce, A. Sundered hearts
 Christie, A. Philomel cottage
 Chute, C. "Ollie, oh . . ."
 Franklin, T. Those good days
 Grimes, C. Farmer, pointing the way with a rad-
  ish
 Keeble, J. The chasm
 Keeble, J. The cross
 Keeble, J. The fishers
 Keeble, J. Freezing the apes
 Keeble, J. I could love you (if I wanted)
 Keeble, J. The transmission
 Keeble, J. Zeta's house
 Kincaid, N. The currency of love
 Lasdun, J. Oh, death
 McMahan, R. The cold, hard truth
 Meacham, R. Good fences
 Moceri, M. Proper fires
 Munro, A. Home
 Smith, R. T. Razorhead the axeman
 Smith, R. T. Tastes like chicken
 Smith, R. T. Tube Rose
 Somerville, P. Black earth, early winter morning
 Strom, D. Grass roof, tin roof [excerpt]
 Swann, M. Secret
 Thomas, E. The artist
 Thomas, E. Milking
 Tomlinson, J. Lake Charles
 Tomlinson, J. Stainless
 Wood, D. Eden
A **country** love story. Stafford, J.
Country manners. DuBois, B.
COUNTRY MUSIC
 Ferris, J. Ghost town choir
 Snyder, S. Dumpster Tuesday
The **country** of glass. Lane, J.
Country of the grand. Donovan, G.
The **country** where nobody ever grew old and
 died. Maxwell, W.
Coup de grâce. Aird, C.
The **coup** de grâce. Bierce, A.

The **couple** behind the curtain. O'Shaughnessy, P.

The **couple** next door. Millar, M.

"A **couple** of words". Reisen, A.

Couple strike it rich on second honeymoon. Parker, M.

Coupons. Anderson, F.

COUPS D'ÉTAT
> Brazaitis, M. The foreign correspondent

COURAGE
> *See also* Heroism
> Bierce, A. George Thurston
> Bierce, A. Killed at Resaca
> Bierce, A. A son of the gods
> Hughes, M. Bearing up
> Khalifah, 'A. A. The dogs
> Levi, P. Bear meat
> Levi, P. The death of Marinese
> Smith, M. Pajamas
> Thompson, J. W. See what tomorrow brings

The **courage** consort. Faber, M.

Courageous blast: the legacy of America's most radical gum. Pendarvis, J.

Court. Steinberg, S.

A **court** case [variant title: In the court] Chekhov, A. P.

The **court** investigator. See Chekhov, A. P. Criminal investigator [variant title: The court investigator]

COURTESANS
> *See also* Prostitutes
> Ducornet, R. La Goulue in retirement

Courtesy for beginners. Shepard, J.

The **Courthouse**. Anam, T.

Courting Miss Ellen. Bishop, T.

Courting the Lady Scythe. Parks, R.

COURTROOM SCENES *See* Trials

COURTSHIP
> Anderson, B. Glorious things
> Anderson, B. The man with the plug in his nose
> Andreas-Salomé, L. Maidens' roundelay
> Buckler, E. Squares
> Colombi, M. Learn a trade for a rainy day
> Dahl, R. Claud's dog: Mr Hoddy
> Dann, J. and Dozois, G. R. Time bride
> Dunbar, P. L. Aunt Tempe's triumph
> Dunbar, P. L. The conjuring contest
> Dunbar, P. L. The deliberation of Mr. Dunkin
> Dunbar, P. L. Dizzy-headed Dick
> Dunbar, P. L. The finding of Martha
> Dunbar, P. L. A lady slipper
> Dunbar, P. L. Mammy Peggy's pride
> Dunbar, P. L. The mortification of the flesh
> Dunbar, P. L. Silent Sam'el
> Dunbar, P. L. Uncle Simon's Sundays out
> Dunbar, P. L. The way of a woman
> Dunbar, P. L. The way of love
> Dunbar, P. L. The white counterpane
> Dunbar, P. L. Who stand for the gods
> Endrezze, A. Grandfather sun falls in love with a moon-faced woman
> Freed, L. The widow's daughter
> James, H. Breach of promise of marriage
> James, H. A hasty marriage
> James, H. One evening's work
> James, H. The rainy day
> James, H. The sprite tranformed
> James, H. A summer adventure
> James, H. Unto the least of these
> James, H. The village belle

> James, H. Woman's influence; or, Incidents of a courtship
> Koënings, N. S. Setting up shop
> Lara, Contessa. The coral necklace
> Miura, T. A portrait of Shino
> Molodowsky, K. A long journey
> Molodowsky, K. The shared sukkah
> Nolan, W. F. The mating of Thirdburt
> Ploetz, S. In love with Rachel
> Reisen, A. Brother and beau
> Rhodes, D. Landfill
> Rhodes, D. Mademoiselle Arc-en-ciel
> Row, J. The train to Lo Wu
> Schwartz, D. In dreams begin responsibilities [excerpt]
> Zoshchenko, M. Classy lady
> Zoshchenko, M. Love

Courtship. Baumbach, J.

The **courtship** of Naomi Samuel. Judah, S.

The **Cousin** that Wasn't. Johnston, P. D.

A **cousin** without charm. Fuentes, C.

Cousins, Eleri
> In the Jura
> *The Writer* v119 no9 p24-5 S 2006

COUSINS
> Andreas-Salomé, L. At one, again, with nature
> Beattie, A. Just going out
> Bezmozgis, D. Natasha
> Blackwell, K. My first wedding
> Capote, T. A Christmas memory
> Capote, T. One Christmas
> Capote, T. The Thanksgiving visitor
> Chekhov, A. P. Murder (abridged)
> Coleman, W. Shark liver oil
> Crow, L. Cowboys and Indians
> Currans-Sheehan, T. And now he's gone and you're back
> Erdrich, L. Hairy buffalo
> Erdrich, L. The little book
> Fuentes, C. A cousin without charm
> Galaviz-Budziszewski, A. Maximillian
> Harrison, W. Looking for Greywolf
> Hinton, S. E. Full moon birthday
> Hinton, S. E. Homecoming
> Hinton, S. E. Sentenced
> Hwang, F. A visit to the suns
> Johnson, G. Leavings
> Kress, N. The most famous little girl in the world
> Lee, A. Anthropology
> Lunstrum, K. S. Baby love
> Malouf, D. Dream stuff
> Mandelman, A. Black
> McGruder, K. Like dancing on both feet
> McHugh, M. F. Laika comes back safe
> McIntyre, V. Foray
> Meno, J. How to say good night
> Mohanraj, M. A. Sins of the father (Jaffna, 1977)
> Mohanraj, M. A. Wood and flesh (Berkeley, 1999)
> Muñoz, M. The heart finds its own conclusion
> Murakami, H. Blind willow, sleeping woman
> Oates, J. C. Honor code
> Roley, B. A. Kinship
> Sarris, G. The magic pony
> Selgin, P. My search for red and gray wide-striped pajamas
> Shomer, E. The summer of questions

COUSINS—*Continued*

Sillitoe, A. A time to keep

Somerville, P. English cousin

Stafford, J. Life is no abyss

Swan, G. Uncle Lazarus

Tabor, M. L. Guarding the pie

Tower, W. Wild America

West, D. A tale of Christmas and love

Wood, D. Elephantiasis

Woronov, M. We were Jewish for a little while

The **cousins**. Oates, J. C.

COUSTEAU, JACQUES YVES, 1910-1997
About
Malla, P. When Jacques Cousteau gave Pablo Picasso a piece of black coral

Couture, Kevin A.

The Cartographer

Dalhousie Review v89 no1 p75-83 Spr 2009

Covenant. Laken, V.

Covenant. Rycraft, R. A.

The **cover** story is always a lie. Lescroart, J. T.

Coverdale, Linda

(tr.) See Duras, Marguerite

Covered bridge. Treat, J.

Coverson, Michael

Dance with me

Going the distance; edited by Alan Beard

Coville, Bruce

The box

Coville, B. The One right thing; edited by Deb Geisler

Clean as a whistle

Coville, B. The One right thing; edited by Deb Geisler

The giant's tooth

Coville, B. The One right thing; edited by Deb Geisler

Guardian of memory

Coville, B. The One right thing; edited by Deb Geisler

I, earthling

Coville, B. The One right thing; edited by Deb Geisler

A life in miniature

Coville, B. The One right thing; edited by Deb Geisler

The metamorphosis of Justin Jones

Coville, B. The One right thing; edited by Deb Geisler

My little brother is a monster

Coville, B. The One right thing; edited by Deb Geisler

Old glory

Coville, B. The One right thing; edited by Deb Geisler

Saying no to Nick

Coville, B. The One right thing; edited by Deb Geisler

The stinky princess

Coville, B. The One right thing; edited by Deb Geisler

The troddler

Coville, B. The One right thing; edited by Deb Geisler

With his head tucked underneath his arm

Coville, B. The One right thing; edited by Deb Geisler

Wizard's boy

Coville, B. The One right thing; edited by Deb Geisler

The world's worst fairy godmother

Coville, B. The One right thing; edited by Deb Geisler

The **cow**. Scliar, M.

A **cow** in the house. Kiely, B.

The **Cow** of the Ocean. Moody, R.

Coward, Mat

Offenders

The World's finest mystery and crime stories, fifth annual collection; edited by Ed Gorman and Martin H. Greenberg

Room to move

The Best British mysteries, 2005; edited by Maxim Jakubowski

Cowboy. McGuane, T.

Cowboy Grace. Rusch, K. K.

Cowboy Honeymoon. Becker, G.

COWBOYS

Boggs, J. D. Red River Crossing

Daughtry, P. Trickle Creek

Evans, M. Once a cowboy

Hadley, D. The teachings of Bronc Buster Billy Brown

Hickey, D. I'm bound to follow the longhorn cows

James, C. L. R. Mighty Mouse and the conceited cowboy

Julavits, H. Little little big man

L'Amour, L. Lit a shuck for Texas

Leonard, E. "Hurrah for Captain Early"

Leonard, E. Long night

Leonard, E. The longest day of his life

Leonard, E. Man with the iron arm [variant title: The one arm man]

Leonard, E. The rustlers [variant title: Along the Pecos]

Marley, L. Small in the saddle

McElrath, F. A native teacher

McGuane, T. Cowboy

Meloy, M. Travis, B.

Osborn, C. My brother is a cowboy

Seton, E. T. The pacing mustang

Vaile, C. M. Sister Anne and the cowboy

Veríssimo, É. Fandango

Cowboys. Stuck, C.

Cowboys and East Indians. McConigley, N.

Cowboys and Indians. Begley, L.

Cowboys and Indians. Crow, L.

Cowdrey, Albert E.

The tribes of Bela

The Year's best science fiction: twenty-second annual collection; edited by Gardner Dozois

Twilight states

The Year's best fantasy and horror: nineteenth annual collection; edited by Ellen Datlow and Kelly Link & Gavin J. Grant

Cowgirls. Fairless, J.

COWHANDS *See* Cowboys

COWS *See* Cattle

Cox, Ana Marie
Tabloids bring back family values!
2033; the future of misbehavior: interplanetary dating, Madame President, socialized plastic surgery, and other good news from the future; from the editors of Nerve.com; instigated by Svedka
Cox, Anthony Berkeley *See* Berkeley, Anthony, 1893-1971
Cox, F. Brett
Madeline's version
Crossroads; tales of the southern literary fantastic; edited by F. Brett Cox and Andy Duncan
Cox, John K.
(tr.) See Kiš, Danilo
Coxe, George Harmon
Murder picture
The Black Lizard big book of pulps; edited by Otto Penzler
Coyne, Stephen
Hunting country
Best of the South: from the second decade of New stories from the South; selected and introduced by Anne Tyler
The Mercy of the World
New England Review v28 no2 p60-7 2007
Still Life
South Carolina Review v40 no1 p181-7 Fall 2007
Coyne, Stephen and Wiese, Jill
Jill's Story
The North American Review v292 no2 p26-8 Mr/Ap 2007
Coyne, Tom
A gentleman's game [excerpt]
On the Mason-Dixon line; an anthology of contemporary Delaware writers; edited by Billie Travalini and Fleda Brown.
The **Coyote**. Lintelmann, J.
Coyote hunt. Castaneda, R.
COYOTES
Seton, E. T. Tito, the story of the coyote that learned how
Slouka, M. Dominion
Spears, J. R. Smiley Hewitt and the prairie-wolf
Wieland, M. The prodigal son
Coyotes. McQueen, L.
Coyotes. Porter, A.
Cozarinsky, Edgardo
The bride from Odessa
Cozarinsky, E. The bride from Odessa; translated from the Spanish by Nick Caistor
Budapest
Cozarinsky, E. The bride from Odessa; translated from the Spanish by Nick Caistor
Days of 1937
Cozarinsky, E. The bride from Odessa; translated from the Spanish by Nick Caistor
Emigré hotel
Cozarinsky, E. The bride from Odessa; translated from the Spanish by Nick Caistor
Literature
Cozarinsky, E. The bride from Odessa; translated from the Spanish by Nick Caistor
Obscure loves
Cozarinsky, E. The bride from Odessa; translated from the Spanish by Nick Caistor

Real estate
Cozarinsky, E. The bride from Odessa; translated from the Spanish by Nick Caistor
View of dawn over the lake
Cozarinsky, E. The bride from Odessa; translated from the Spanish by Nick Caistor
Crab apple. Samphire, P.
CRABS
Hodgson, W. H. From the tideless sea (first part)
Hodgson, W. H. From the tideless sea (second part)
Crabs. Danticat, E.
Crabs. Murakami, H.
Crabwise. Rust, E. M.
Crace, Jim
Too Young for Funerals
Harvard Review (1992) no28 p6-7 2005
CRACK (DRUG)
Alexander, D. Beneficient diversions from the crackdkins diet
Angel, J. Push
Lippman, L. The crack cocaine diet
Lippman, L. The crack cocaine diet (Or: how to lose a lot of weight and change your life in just one weekend)
Straight, S. Poinciana
The **crack** cocaine diet. Lippman, L.
The **crack** cocaine diet (Or: how to lose a lot of weight and change your life in just one weekend). Lippman, L.
The **cracked** looking-glass. Porter, K. A.
The **cracked**, pink lips of Rosie's bridegroom. Gappah, P.
Crackers. Haverty, C.
Cracklegrackle. Robson, J.
The **cracks** in the sidewalk. Muller, M.
Cragun, Jenni
Flour Baby
Western Humanities Review v63 no2 p86-93 Summ 2009
Craig, Alisa *See* MacLeod, Charlotte
Craig, Kit, 1932-
See also Reed, Kit, 1932-
Cramer, Kathryn
Sandcastles: a dystopia
Nature v437 p926 O 6 2005
Cramp bark. Hecht, J.
Cramps. Keret, E.
Crane, Elizabeth
Banana love
Crane, E. You must be this happy to enter; stories
Betty the zombie
Crane, E. You must be this happy to enter; stories
Blue girl
Crane, E. You must be this happy to enter; stories
Clearview
Crane, E. You must be this happy to enter; stories
Donovan's closet
Crane, E. You must be this happy to enter; stories
Emmanuel
Crane, E. You must be this happy to enter; stories

Crane, Elizabeth—*Continued*

The glistening head of Ricky Ricardo begs further experimentation
  Crane, E. You must be this happy to enter; stories
The most everything in the world
  Crane, E. You must be this happy to enter; stories
My life is awesome! and great!
  Crane, E. You must be this happy to enter; stories
Nate Pinckney-Alderson, superhero
  Burnham, C. Who can save us now?; brand-new superheroes and their amazing [short] stories; edited by Owen King and John McNally; [illustrations by Chris Burnham]
Notes for a story about people with weird phobias
  Crane, E. You must be this happy to enter; stories
Promise
  Crane, E. You must be this happy to enter; stories
Sally (featuring: Lollipop the rainbow unicorn)
  Crane, E. You must be this happy to enter; stories
Varieties of loudness in Chicago
  Crane, E. You must be this happy to enter; stories
What happens when the mipods leave their milieu
  Crane, E. You must be this happy to enter; stories
What our week was like
  Crane, E. You must be this happy to enter; stories
You must be this happy to enter
  Crane, E. You must be this happy to enter; stories

CRANE, HART, 1899-1932
About
Zelazny, R. Threshold of the prophet
Crane, Stephen
A poker game
  Manhattan noir 2; the classics; edited by Lawrence Block
CRANES (BIRDS)
Mindt, A. Karrooo
Cranes. Bunin, I. A.
Crank. Wolven, S.
Cranley Meadows. Lasdun, J.
Crapshoot. Caminsky, J.
Crash. Percy, B.
Crash course. Shomer, E.
Crash landing. L'Amour, L.
Craters. Rusch, K. K.
Cravings. Panning, A.
Crawl. Hershon, J.
Crazy. Latiolais, M.
Crazy glue. Keret, E.
The **crazy** helmets. Finch, P.
CRAZY HORSE, SIOUX CHIEF, CA. 1842-1877
About
Rand, K. Medicine
Crazy Jill saves the slinky. Solomita, S.
Crazy ladies. Johnson, G.
Crazy Red Head Devil. Thornton, M. B.
Create a real available beach. With, C.

Created he them. Jones, A. E.
CREATION
Domecq, B. Lillith
Domecq, B. Sammaël
Domecq, B. Sammaël and Lillith
Gerencer, T. Primordial chili
Pratt, T. and Van Eekhout, G. Robots and falling hearts
Wolfe, G. The god and his nman
CREATION (LITERARY, ARTISTIC, ETC.)
See also Authorship
Chase, M. Wet
Greenman, B. In the air room
Irvine, A. C. Gus dreams of biting the mailman
Creation myths of the recently extinct. Pohl, F.
The **creation** of Bennie Good. Sallis, J.
Creature features. McNally, J.
A **creature** of accident. Monteleone, T. F.
Creatures of the mind. Green, G.
Crèche. Ford, R.
CREDIBILITY *See* Truthfulness and falsehood
Credit repair. Hospital, J. T.
Creep. Bynum, S. S.-L.
Creeper shadows. Chappell, F.
Creeping. Swann, M.
The **creeping** Siamese. Hammett, D.
The **creeping** terror. Matheson, R.
Creepy World. Taylor, M.
Crees, Stuart
What friction? What factions?
  Going the distance; edited by Alan Beard
CREMATION
Clark, G. M. The center of the world
Gerber, M. J. I don't believe this
Goswami, M. R. The empty chest
Kim, H. From powder to powder
Lange, R. The Bogo-Indian defense
Ruffin, P. When momma came home for Christmas and Talmidge quoted Frost
Stern, R. G. Packages
Waters, D. What to do with the dead
The **cremation** ground. Mahajan, K.
Crenshaw, Paul
Diving
  Confrontation no96/97 p128-40 Fall 2006/Wint 2007
CREOLES
Thompson, E. B. Mademoiselle 'Tasie-a story
Crêpe de chine. McCann, R.
Crepuscule with Mickey [Reprint] Sorrentino, C.
The **crest.** Erdrich, L.
CRETE
Blackwell, K. The minaret
Selgin, P. Color of the sea
Crew cut. Umansky, E.
The **crew** of the Lancing. Hodgson, W. H.
Crichton, Michael
Blood doesn't come out
  McSweeney's mammoth treasury of thrilling tales; edited by Michael Chabon
CRICKET
Hernandez, L. Over the Belle Isle boundary
CRICKETS
Butler, R. O. Crickets
Matheson, R. Crickets
Rand, K. Crickets everywhere
Crickets. Butler, R. O.
Crickets. Matheson, R.
Crickets everywhere. Rand, K.

Crider, Bill

The adventure of the St. Marylebone ghoul
   Ghosts in Baker Street; edited by Martin H. Greenberg, Jon Lellenberg, Daniel Stashower

The adventure of the White City
   Sherlock Holmes in America; edited by Martin H. Greenberg, Jon L. Lellenberg, and Daniel Stashower.

I was a teenage vampire
   Many bloody returns; edited by Charlaine Harris and Toni L. P. Kelner

The man on the cross
   Thou shalt not kill; biblical mystery stories; edited by Anne Perry

Top of the world
   The World's finest mystery and crime stories, fourth annual collection; edited by Ed Gorman and Martin H. Greenberg

Winning can be murder [excerpt]
   Lone Star sleuths; an anthology of Texas crime fiction; edited and with an introduction by Bill Cunningham, Steven L. Davis, and Rollo K. Newsom.

Cridland, Cassandra

The Last Hunt
   Idaho Magazine v5 no1 p28-31 O 2005

A **crime:** a double murder case. Chekhov, A. P.

CRIME AND CRIMINALS

   See also Arson; Atrocities; Bank robbers; Brigands and robbers; Child abuse; Counterfeiters; Escaped convicts; Extortion; Gangs; Gangsters; Hostages; Juvenile delinquency; Kidnapping; Mafia; Murder stories; Rape; Smuggling; Swindlers and swindling; Thieves; Underworld; Vandalism; War criminals; Wife abuse

Abbott, J. Bet on red
Abbott, L. K. Men of rough persuasion
Adcock, T. You want I should whack monkey boy?
Agnihotri, S. Avoid agony
Allen, P. L. Crip
Allen, W. Above the law, below the box springs
Archer, J. It can't be October already
Auchincloss, L. Other times, other ways
Bangkok, J. Counterfeit love
Banks, R. Wrong 'em, boyo
Beane, J. Jeanette
Bentil, T. Lost and found
Bierce, A. A bottomless grave
Bierce, A. Oil of dog
Bierce, A. An upper class misdemeanant
Bissell, T. My interview with the Avenger
Black, C. Mosquito incense
Block, L. The bad night
Block, L. The badger game
Block, L. The dope
Block, L. You can't lose
Boland, J. The night watchman is asleep
Box, C. J. Pirates of Yellowstone
Brewer, R. J. Keeping it good
Brodsky, M. Limit point
Brown, S. Water babies
Bruen, K. Black stuff
Bruen, K. Spittin iron
Bruen, K. Stones
Bruen, K. Time of the green
Burke, J. L. Mist

Burke, J. L. The night Johnny Ace died
Burke, J. L. Why Bugsy Siegel was a friend of mine
Byrne, M. Only the strong survive
Campbell, B. J. King Cole's American Salvage
Capel, T. The red Mercedes
Carlson, R. Beanball
Charles, P. In the midnight hour
Charyn, J. La shampouineuse
Charyn, J. White trash
Charyn, J. Young Isaac
Chekhov, A. P. Psychopaths
Cody, L. Lucky dip
Colfer, E. Taking on PJ
Cook, T. H. Rain
Corbett, D. Bobby the prop buys in
Coxe, G. H. Murder picture
Crider, B. Top of the world
David, P. Killing time by the River Styx
Davis, J. M. Iggy's stuff
Dawson, J. Invisible time
De Silva, D. Don't talk to the passenger
Deaver, J. Born bad
Disch, T. M. Ringtime
Doctorow, C. Printcrime
Dokey, R. Monkey
Encinosa Fú, M. What for, this burden
Estep, M. Boneshaker
Estep, M. Luck be a lady
Everheart, C. Chili dog
Ferrigno, R. Can you help me out here?
Fonseca, R. Angels of the marquees
Fuentes, C. The mariachi's mother
Garcia, E. Meeting across the river
Gardner, E. S. Honest money
George, N. New Lots Avenue
Gerlach, G. Wedding in Voerde
Gifford, B. Wanted man
Goldberg, L. Jack Webb's star
Goodis, D. Black pudding
Goodis, D. The blue sweetheart
Goodis, D. The dead laugh last
Goodis, D. The time of your kill
Gordon, A. Bottom of the sixth
Gorman, E. Yesterday's dreams
Gospodinov, G. L.
Guerriero, L. Eating Italian
Haldeman, J. W. Four short novels
Hamilton, S. One fast Packard
Hammett, D. The green elephant
Hammett, D. Itchy
Hammett, D. The sardonic star of Tom Doody
Hartlaub, J. Crossed double
Harvey, J. Sack o' woe
Hayter, S. Deus ex machina
Healy, J. F. Grieving Las Vegas
Helfers, J. Deadhand
Hellmann, L. F. The jade elephant
Hogan, C. One good one
Holmes, E. a.k.a., Moises Rockafella
Hornsby, W. Dust up
Houston, P. Cherry looks back
Howard, C. The leper colony
Howard, C. To live and die in Midland, Texas
Hurwitz, G. The real thing
Huston, C. Interrogation B
Irby, L. God don't like ugly
Jardim, K. The jaguar
Jasper, K. First

CRIME PASSIONEL *See* Crimes of passion
A **crime** report. Zoshchenko, M.
CRIMEA (UKRAINE) *See* Ukraine—Crimea
CRIMES OF PASSION
    See also Murder stories
  Bunin, I. A. The Elagin affair
  Woolrich, C. New York blues
CRIMINAL INVESTIGATION
  Cody, L. Reconstruction
Criminal investigator [variant title: The court investigator] Chekhov, A. P.
CRIMINALLY INSANE *See* Insane, Criminal and dangerous
CRIMINALS *See* Crime and criminals
The **crimson** curtain. Barbey d'Aurevilly, J.
The **Crimson** Wizard. Lupoff, R. A.
The **Crimson** Wizard and the jewels of Lemuria. Lupoff, R. A.
Crip. Allen, P. L.
Crisis. Zoshchenko, M.
A **crisis** at sea. Rashid, 'A. M.
Crisis in the life of an actress. Brodsky, M.
Cristina in another country. Kulpa, K.
Critical Paranoia. Frame, R.
Criticality. Pohl, F.
Critterworld. Watkins, S.
CRO-MAGNON MAN *See* Prehistoric man
CROATIA
  Novakovich, J. Ribs
The **crocodile**. Hernández, F.
The **Crocodile** Lover. Habila, H.
Crocodile rock. Shepard, L.
CROCODILES
  Palazzeschi, A. Dagobert
CROMWELL, OLIVER, 1599-1658
         About
  Judson, T. The sultan's emissary
Crone, Moira
  The Black Carpet
    Callaloo v29 no4 p1118-26 Fall 2006
  Fever
    Wide awake in the Pelican State; stories by contemporary Louisiana writers; edited by Ann Brewster Dobie; with a foreword by Ernest J. Gaines
  The ice garden
    Crone, M. What gets into us; stories
    New stories from the South: the year's best, 2007; selected from U.S. magazines by Edward P. Jones with Kathy Pories; with an introduction by Edward P. Jones
    TriQuarterly no125 p96-132 2006
  It
    Crone, M. What gets into us; stories
  Mr. Sender
    New stories from the South: the year's best, 2005; edited by Shannon Ravenel; with a preface by Jill McCorkle
    Crone, M. What gets into us; stories
  The odd fellow
    Crone, M. What gets into us; stories
  Paradise
    Crone, M. What gets into us; stories
  Pipe smoke
    Crone, M. What gets into us; stories
  Salvage
    Crone, M. What gets into us; stories
  Where what gets into people comes from
    Crone, M. What gets into us; stories

White sky in May
    Crone, M. What gets into us; stories
Crone's Revenge. McCauley, C. S.
Cronin, Justin
  Oysters
    StoryQuarterly v42 p375-84 2006
Crook, Jeff
  Ever: Picture perfect
    Nature v451 p1028 F 21 2008
  Hotdogs at the end of the world
    Nature v444 p1104 D 21-28 2006
Crooked mirror (a Christmas story). See Chekhov, A. P. Curved mirror [variant title: Crooked mirror (a Christmas story)]
Cross, Brian P.
  The Talibé
    Confrontation no94/95 p83-98 Spr/Summ 2006
Cross, Esther
  Appearances
    Díaz, G. J. Women and power in Argentine literature; stories, interviews, and critical essays; [by] Gwendolyn Díaz
  The recipe
    Díaz, G. J. Women and power in Argentine literature; stories, interviews, and critical essays; [by] Gwendolyn Díaz
Cross, Eugene
  Eyes Closed
    Callaloo v29 no2 p336-43 Spr 2006
Cross, Helen
  The uniform
    Her Majesty; 21 stories by women; edited by Jackie Gay and Emma Hargrave
The **cross**. Hernandez, L.
The **cross**. Keeble, J.
The **Cross**. Zoshchenko, M.
The **cross** and the candle. L'Amour, L.
Cross carriers. Rogers, B. H.
Cross country. Coake, C.
Cross crossings cautiously. Coleman, A. S.
Cross-Eyed Sasha. Bodrov, S.
A **Cross** for Sister Mary Joseph. Williford, L.
A **cross** of centirues. Kuttner, H.
Crossbones. Michaels, L.
Crossed double. Hartlaub, J.
The **Crossing**. Varga, M.
Crossing into Cambodia. Moorcock, M.
Crossing over. Signor, R. M.
Crossing the River 1932. Ford, K.
"**Crossroads** identity". Komla-Ebri, K.
Crosstown traffic. Bishop, S.
CROSSWORD PUZZLES
  Paz Soldán, E. Dochera
Crouch, Blake
  Remaking
    Thriller 2; stories you just can't put down; edited by Clive Cussler; [stories by] Kathleen Antrim . . . [et al.]
Crouse, David
  The castle on the hill
    Crouse, D. The man back there and other stories
  Click
    Crouse, D. Copy cats; stories
  Code
    Crouse, D. Copy cats; stories
  Copy Kats
    Crouse, D. Copy cats; stories

CRUELTY—*Continued*

Ockert, J. Adrift and distant

Pratt, T. The tyrant in love

Puchner, E. Child's play

Rash, R. Honesty

Rickert, M. Moorina of the seals

Seton, E. T. Tito, the story of the coyote that learned how

Shepard, L. The Drive-In Puerto Rico

Shirley, J. In the road

Solá, M. Kind's silence [excerpt]

Stamm, P. What we can do

Swanwick, M. Radiant doors

Trevor, W. Folie à deux

Vidal, G. The robin

Zelazny, R. But not the Herald

CRUELTY TO CHILDREN *See* Child abuse

The **cruise**. Enright, A.

Cruisers. Sayles, J.

Cruiser's Creek. Wild, P.

Cruising. Gurba, M.

Crumey, Andrew

Calculation Quest

Nature v437 p1206 O 20 2005

Crumley, James

Bordersnakes [excerpt]

Lone Star sleuths; an anthology of Texas crime fiction; edited and with an introduction by Bill Cunningham, Steven L. Davis, and Rollo K. Newsom.

Hostages

A New omnibus of crime; edited by Tony Hillerman and Rosemary Herbert; contributing editors Sue Grafton and Jeffery Deaver

Whores

Lone Star literature; from the Red River to the Rio Grande; edited by Don Graham

Crusade. Lewis, W. H.

CRUSADES

See also Knights and knighthood

Sterling, B. The Blemmye's stratagem

Crush. Wang Ping

Cry Baby. Weiss, D.

A **Cry** of Ice. Madden, D.

Cry "wolf!". Tremayne, P.

Crybaby. Crouse, D.

CRYING Women I have made cry

Crying and Smoking. Taylor, K.

The **Crying** Bride. Youngblood, S.

Crying with Audrey Hepburn. Xu Xi

CRYOGENICS *See* Low temperatures

CRYONICS

Zelazny, R. Go starless in the night

Cryptograph. Pizzolatto, N.

CRYPTOGRAPHY

Aird, C. Child's play

Cryptology. Michaels, L.

The **Cryptozoologist**. Earley, T.

Crystal nights. Egan, G.

Crystal's big night. Gorman, E.

Csilla's story. Goss, T.

CUBA

Meno, J. In the arms of someone you love

Michaels, L. Viva la Tropicana

Radojcic, N. Shades of mango

Rivera-Valdes, S. Ana at four times: Ana and the magic wand

Rivera-Valdes, S. Ana at four times: Ana and the moon

Unger, D. Cuban nights

Prisoners and prisons

See Prisoners and prisons—Cuba

Havana

Abella, A. Shanghai

Arango, A. Murder, according to my mother-in-law

Aschkenas, L. La Coca-Cola del olvido

Asís, M. Murder at 503 La Rosa

Correa, A. Olúo

Cuesta, M. Virgins of Regla

Depestre, Y. Abikú

Encinosa Fú, M. What for, this burden

Garcia-Aguilera, C. The dinner

Gifford, B. Dancing with Fidel

Gutiérrez, P. J. Nothing to do

Malla, P. The love life of the automation Turk

Mejides, M. Nowhere man

Obejas, A. Zenzizenzic

Ortiz, O. F. Settling of scores

Padura Fuentes, L. Staring at the sun

Pintado, M. F. The scene

Portela, E. L. The last passenger

Rivas, M. Havana's vast cemetery

Rivera-Valdes, S. Blue like bluing

Rivera-Valdes, S. The deepest seed of the lemon

Rivera-Valdes, S. Life leads

Roque, M. V. The orchid

Yoss. The red bridge

CUBAN AMERICANS

Mestre-Reed, E. After Elián

CUBAN MISSILE CRISIS, OCT. 1962

Connell, E. S. The Cuban Missle Crisis

Waldrop, H. The other real world

The **Cuban** Missle Crisis. Connell, E. S.

CUBAN REFUGEES

Asís, M. Murder at 503 La Rosa

Medina, P. Johnny Ventura's seventh try

Padura Fuentes, L. Staring at the sun

Rivera-Valdes, S. Ana at four times: Ana and the lemon balm

Rivera-Valdes, S. Ana at four times: Ana and the snow

Rivera-Valdes, S. Sunday at the same time

CUBANS

Italy

Bobes, M. In Florence ten years later

United States

Medina, P. Bennie Rojas and the rough riders

Michaels, L. Viva la Tropicana

Obejas, A. Destiny returns

Obejas, A. Zenzizenzic

Cubby Grumbles makes a change. Friesner, E. M.

The **cubicles**. Searls, D.

CUBS (BASEBALL TEAM) *See* Chicago Cubs (Baseball team)

Cuck(h)olding a stranger. Moise, L.

A **Cuckoo** Tale. Bernheimer, K.

The **cuckoo's** boys. Reed, R.

Un **Cuento** de Alta Montaña / An Alpine Tale. Soler Frost, P.

Cuentos Volcánicos: Recopilados por Julio Glockner / Volcanic Tales: Compiled by Julio Glockner. Glockner, J.

CUERNAVACA (MEXICO) *See* Mexico—Cuernavaca

Cuerpo presente/Requiem. Parra, E. A.

Cuesta, Mabel
Virgins of Regla
Havana noir; edited by Achy Obejas
Cul-De-Sac. Pearlman, E.
Cule, Erika
Birthday surprises
Nature v456 p420 N 20 2008
Cull the steel heart, melt the ice one, love the weak thing; say nothing of consolation, but irrelevance, disaster, and nonexistence; have no hope or hate—nothing; ruin yourself exclusively, completely, and whenever possible. Lin, T.
Cully, Seth
Roadkill
Bandersnatch; edited by Paul Tremblay and Sean Wallace
The **Cult** of the Bed. Clevidence, C.
Cultivation. Cain, S.
CULTS
Allen, W. To err is human—to float, divine
Barron, L. The imago sequence
Breuer, M. J. A problem in communication
Chabon, M. The god of dark laughter
Crane, E. What happens when the mipods leave their milieu
DeNiro, A. The caliber
DeNiro, A. Quiver
Evenson, B. An accounting
Farley, B. The investigation
Fowler, K. J. Always
Gregory, D. Damascus
Howard, R. E. The black stone
Howard, R. E. The children of the night
Howard, R. E. Untitled fragment
Kelley, N. The messenger of soulsville
Kelly, R. Devil's Creek
Kiernan, C. R. The pearl diver
Lovecraft, H. P. The call of Cthulhu
Mokoso, N. God of meme
Munro, A. Silence
Palazzeschi, A. Servite domino in laetitia
Pierce, T. J. The Yoshi Compound: a story of post-Waco Texas
Scott, J. The Queen of Sheba is afraid of snow
Shirley, J. Sweet armageddon
Shunn, W. Inclination
Smith, C. A. An offering to the moon
Stackpole, M. A. Seamless
Cultural relativity. Johnson, C. R.
CULTURE CONFLICT
Adichie, C. N. The thing around your neck
Anderson, P. The helping hand
Bacigalupi, P. The pasho
Baingana, D. Lost in Los Angeles
Butler, R. O. Crickets
Chilson, P. American food
Divakaruni, C. B. Mrs. Dutta writes a letter
D'Souza, T. Djamilla
Ghermandi, G. "The village telephone"
Grimes, C. Customs in a developing country: a prefatory story
Hawes, L. My last Indian
Hosseini, K. The kite runner [excerpt]
Kobrin, L. Door number one
L'Amour, L. By the ruins of "El Walarieh"
Libin, Z. Two shrines
Libin, Z. A Yiddish-speaking socialist
Monk, B. Epilogue: Excellent sperm

Monk, B. The great wall
Naipaul, V. S. My aunt Gold Teeth
Perlman, E. A tale in two cities
Rodriguez, L. J. My ride, my revolution
Ryman, G. Have not have
Serna, E. Tesoro viviente/Living treasure
Theroux, P. Monkey Hill
Wadia, L.-A. L. "Ravi's wedding"
Yellin, T. Manasseh
Culver, Timothy J.
For works written by this author under other names see Westlake, Donald E.
Culver City. Lange, R.
The **Culvert**. Morris, K. L.
Cumberland, William Augustus, Duke of See William Augustus, Duke of Cumberland, 1721-1765
Cummings, John Michael
Marshmallow People
The Kenyon Review v30 no1 p89-99 Wint 2008
The Scratchboard Project
Iowa Review v36 no1 p108-35 Spr 2006
Cummins, Ann
Where I work
The Anchor book of new American short stories; edited by Ben Marcus
Cunningham, M. Allen
Twelve Monthly Devotions
The Kenyon Review v28 no3 p96-122 Summ 2006
Cunt crazy. Roth, P.
Cup and table. Pratt, T.
A **Cup** of Coffee in the Café on Ostozhenka. Shklovsky, Y.
Curado. Monteiro, L.
The **Curandeiro**. Monteleone, T. F.
Curbelo, Jesús David
How Much I Love You
The Review of Contemporary Fiction v26 no3 p141-5 Fall 2006
The Lady with the Pooch
The Review of Contemporary Fiction v26 no3 p128-40 Fall 2006
The **Cure** for Cancer. Milward, A. M.
A **cure** for coquettes. James, H.
Curie, Maria Sklodowska See Curie, Marie, 1867-1934
CURIE, MARIE, 1867-1934
                    About
Bear, E. Schrödinger's cat chases the super string
CURIE, PIERRE, 1859-1906
                    About
Bear, E. Schrödinger's cat chases the super string
A **Curious** Assignment. Olson, R. J.
The **curious** child. Matheson, R.
The **curious** inventions of Mr. H. Di Filippo, P.
A **Curious** Race. Magee, R. M.
Curly Hamson and the Lucky Couple. Schiffman, C.
Curran, Colleen
LDR
The dictionary of failed relationships; 26 tales of love gone wrong; edited by Meredith Broussard

Currans-Sheehan, Tricia

And now he's gone and you're back
 Currans-Sheehan, T. The egg lady and other neighbors
The balers
 Currans-Sheehan, T. The egg lady and other neighbors
Called for action
 Currans-Sheehan, T. The egg lady and other neighbors
The egg lady
 Currans-Sheehan, T. The egg lady and other neighbors
The last trapshoot
 Currans-Sheehan, T. The egg lady and other neighbors
The many stages of their making
 Currans-Sheehan, T. The egg lady and other neighbors
Margaret
 Currans-Sheehan, T. The egg lady and other neighbors
The men with the leopard wallpaper
 Currans-Sheehan, T. The egg lady and other neighbors
The raffle
 Currans-Sheehan, T. The egg lady and other neighbors
The secrets that men have
 Currans-Sheehan, T. The egg lady and other neighbors
The wild club
 Currans-Sheehan, T. The egg lady and other neighbors
The **currency** of love. Kincaid, N.

Currey, Richard

The names of the lost
 D. C. noir; edited by George Pelecanos
The **curriculum** vitae. Keane, J. B.
Curried cow. Bierce, A.

Currier, Jameson

Manhattan Transfer
 Confrontation no101 p84-105 Spr/Summ 2008
Curse. Mandelman, A.
The **curse** of kings. Willis, C.
Curse of the Corn Borer. Bedard, B.

CURSES

Erdrich, L. Snares
Ford, J. A night in the Tropics
Fowler, C. The threads
Hurd, D. L. Guadalupe and the taxman
Jones, E. P. A poor Guatemalan dreams of a Downtown in Peru
Lumley, B. The house of the temple
Mandelman, A. Curse
Opatoshu, J. Saloon—night
Schuster, F. African Christmas
Shepard, L. Crocodile rock
Willis, C. The curse of kings
Zahn, T. The ring
CURSES, FAMILY *See* Family curses
Cursory review. Bingle, D. J.
Curtains. Grimes, C.

Curtin, John M.

The Apotheosis of Hard Knock Johnson
 Arizona Attorney v43 no8 p26-8, 30, 32-4 Ap 2007

The Legacy of Bernie the Loser
 Arizona Attorney v44 no9 p20-2, 24, 26, 28 My 2008

Curtis, Rebecca

The alpine slide
 Curtis, R. Twenty grand and other tales of love and money
Big Bear, California
 Curtis, R. Twenty grand and other tales of love and money
Hungry self
 What are you looking at?; the first fat fiction anthology; edited by Donna Jarrell and Ira Sukrungruang
 Curtis, R. Twenty grand and other tales of love and money
Monsters
 Curtis, R. Twenty grand and other tales of love and money
The near-son
 Curtis, R. Twenty grand and other tales of love and money
The Sno-Kone Cart
 Curtis, R. Twenty grand and other tales of love and money
Solicitation
 Curtis, R. Twenty grand and other tales of love and money
Summer, with twins
 Curtis, R. Twenty grand and other tales of love and money
 The O. Henry Prize stories 2007; edited and with an introduction by Laura Furman; with essays on the story they admire most by jurors Charles D'Ambrosio, Ursula K. Le Guin, Lily Tuck
 Harper's v310 p75-80 Je 2005
To the Interstate
 Curtis, R. Twenty grand and other tales of love and money
Twenty grand
 Curtis, R. Twenty grand and other tales of love and money
 The New Yorker v81 no41 p78-85 D 19 2005
The witches
 Curtis, R. Twenty grand and other tales of love and money
The wolf at the door
 Curtis, R. Twenty grand and other tales of love and money
 StoryQuarterly v40 p88-94 2004
Curved mirror [variant title: Crooked mirror (a Christmas story)] Chekhov, A. P.
The **curved** sword. Lamb, H.
Curvy. Dormen, L.

Cusset, Catherine

Spoiled Brat
 Women's Studies Quarterly v34 no3/4 p183-98 Fall/Wint 2006
The **Custodian**. Chalar, L.
The **custodian**. Eisenberg, D.
Custody. Naiyer Masud

CUSTODY OF CHILDREN

Davis, C. Balance
Desaulniers, J. Mothers without children
Harleman, A. Street of swans
Naiyer Masud. Custody
Palwick, S. The fate of mice
Siegel, J. Empathy

Dahl, Roald—*Continued*
  William and Mary
    Dahl, R. Collected stories; edited and intro-
      duced by Jeremy Treglown
  The wish
    Dahl, R. Collected stories; edited and intro-
      duced by Jeremy Treglown
  Yesterday was beautiful
    Dahl, R. Collected stories; edited and intro-
      duced by Jeremy Treglown
Dahlia season. Gurba, M.
Daidō, Tamaki
  Milk
    Inside and other short fiction; Japanese wom-
      en by Japanese women; with a foreword by
      Ruth Ozeki; compiled by Cathy Layne
Dain, Catherine
  Dreams of Jeannie
    The World's finest mystery and crime stories,
      fifth annual collection; edited by Ed
      Gorman and Martin H. Greenberg
Dainty shoes. Messina, M.
Daisy, in the sun. Willis, C.
Dakai, Rebecca
  Deadly Alaska
    *Tribal College Journal of American Indian
      Higher Education* v19 no1 p46-7 Fall 2007
DAKOTA INDIANS
  Bierce, A. A remarkable adventure
  Proulx, A. The Indian wars refought
DALAI LAMAS
  Bacigalupi, P. Pocketful of dharma
Dalby, Andrew
  The "Satyrica" Concluded
    Gastronomica (Berkeley, Calif.) v5 no4 p60-
      72 Fall 2005
Daldorph, Brian
  Death and Children
    The North American Review v293 no3/4 p13-
      15 My/Ag 2008
  Methadone
    The North American Review v290 no3/4
      p63-4 My/Ag 2005
Daley-Clarke, Donna
  Saturday soup
    Her Majesty; 21 stories by women; edited by
      Jackie Gay and Emma Hargrave
DALLAS (TEX.) *See* Texas—Dallas
D'Allesandro, Sam
  14 days
    D'Allesandro, S. The wild creatures; collected
      stories of Sam D'Allesandro; edited by
      Kevin Killian
  Electrical type of thing
    D'Allesandro, S. The wild creatures; collected
      stories of Sam D'Allesandro; edited by
      Kevin Killian
  A fine feat hered friend
    D'Allesandro, S. The wild creatures; collected
      stories of Sam D'Allesandro; edited by
      Kevin Killian
  Giovanni's apartment
    D'Allesandro, S. The wild creatures; collected
      stories of Sam D'Allesandro; edited by
      Kevin Killian
  How I came to dinosaur pond
    D'Allesandro, S. The wild creatures; collected
      stories of Sam D'Allesandro; edited by
      Kevin Killian

Jane and Sam
  D'Allesandro, S. The wild creatures; collected
    stories of Sam D'Allesandro; edited by
    Kevin Killian
My day with Judy
  D'Allesandro, S. The wild creatures; collected
    stories of Sam D'Allesandro; edited by
    Kevin Killian
Nothing ever just disappears
  D'Allesandro, S. The wild creatures; collected
    stories of Sam D'Allesandro; edited by
    Kevin Killian
Travels with my mother
  D'Allesandro, S. The wild creatures; collected
    stories of Sam D'Allesandro; edited by
    Kevin Killian
The wild creatures
  D'Allesandro, S. The wild creatures; collected
    stories of Sam D'Allesandro; edited by
    Kevin Killian
The zombie pit
  D'Allesandro, S. The wild creatures; collected
    stories of Sam D'Allesandro; edited by
    Kevin Killian
Daltharee. Ford, J.
Dalton, John
  The Grand Ballroom
    Western Humanities Review v59 no2 p104-17
      Fall 2005
Dalton, Quinn
  Back on earth
    Dalton, Q. Bulletproof girl; stories
  Bulletproof girl
    Dalton, Q. Bulletproof girl; stories
  Dinner at Josette's
    Dalton, Q. Bulletproof girl; stories
  Dough
    Dalton, Q. Bulletproof girl; stories
  Endurance tests
    Dalton, Q. Bulletproof girl; stories
  Graceland
    Dalton, Q. Bulletproof girl; stories
  How to clean your apartment
    Dalton, Q. Bulletproof girl; stories
  Lennie remembers the angels
    Dalton, Q. Bulletproof girl; stories
  Midnight bowling
    Dalton, Q. Bulletproof girl; stories
  The music you never hear
    New stories from the South: the year's best,
      2006; selected from U.S. magazines by Al-
      lan Gurganus with Kathy Pories; with an
      introduction by Allan Gurganus
  Package
    Dalton, Q. Bulletproof girl; stories
  Shed this life
    Dalton, Q. Bulletproof girl; stories
Dalton, Trinie
  Lou in the Moonlight
    Bomb no91 p82-3 Spr 2005
Damage. Kercheval, J. L.
Damage. Nelson, K.
Damaged goods. Winton, T.
Damascus. Gregory, D.
D'Amato, Barbara
  The lower wacker Hilton
    Chicago blues; edited by Libby Fischer
      Hellmann

DANES—*Continued*
Switzerland
Stamm, P. The kiss
United States
Sherman, R. Homestay
D'Angelo, Jill Sand
(tr.) See Oz, Amos
Danger Dog and I Are Going In. Schille, C. B. K.
Danger in the dark. Hubbard, L. R.
Dangerous days. Holmes, E.
The **dangerous** dimension. Hubbard, L. R.
Dangerous laughter. Millhauser, S.
The **Dangerous** Lay of the Land. Driscoll, J.
Dangerous love. Rash, R.
Dangerous women. Lunstrum, K. S.
Dangers. Gardam, J.
The **dangers** of salmonella. Brown, D.
Daniel, Tony
Ex cathedra
Strahan, J. Eclipse two; new science fiction
and fantasy; edited by Jonathan Strahan
The Valley of the Gardens
The new space opera; edited by Gardner
Dozois and Jonathan Strahan
The Best science fiction and fantasy of the
year: volume two; edited by Jonathan
Strahan
Daniells, Rowena Cory
Purgatory
Dreaming again; thirty-five new stories cele-
brating the wild side of Australian fiction;
edited by Jack Dann
Dann, Jack
Fairy tale
This is my funniest 2; leading science fiction
writers present their funniest stories ever;
edited by Mike Resnick
(jt. auth) See Brandon, Paul and Dann, Jack
(jt. auth) See Dozois, Gardner R. and Dann,
Jack
Dann, Jack and Dozois, Gardner R.
A change in the weather
Dann, J. The fiction factory; by Jack Dann
with Susan Casper . . . [et al.]
Down among the dead men
Dann, J. The fiction factory; by Jack Dann
with Susan Casper . . . [et al.]
Playing the game
Dann, J. The fiction factory; by Jack Dann
with Susan Casper . . . [et al.]
Slow dancing with Jesus
Dann, J. The fiction factory; by Jack Dann
with Susan Casper . . . [et al.]
Time bride
Dann, J. The fiction factory; by Jack Dann
with Susan Casper . . . [et al.]
Dann, Jack and Frost, Gregory
The incompleat Ripper
Dann, J. The fiction factory; by Jack Dann
with Susan Casper . . . [et al.]
Dann, Jack and Haldeman, Jack C.
High steel
Dann, J. The fiction factory; by Jack Dann
with Susan Casper . . . [et al.]
Dann, Jack and Malzberg, Barry N.
Art appreciation
Dann, J. The fiction factory; by Jack Dann
with Susan Casper . . . [et al.]

Blues and the abstract truth
Dann, J. The fiction factory; by Jack Dann
with Susan Casper . . . [et al.]
Life in the air
Dann, J. The fiction factory; by Jack Dann
with Susan Casper . . . [et al.]
Dann, Jack and Swanwick, Michael
Ships
Dann, J. The fiction factory; by Jack Dann
with Susan Casper . . . [et al.]
Dann, Jack and Webb, Janeen
Niagara falling
Dann, J. The fiction factory; by Jack Dann
with Susan Casper . . . [et al.]
Dann, Jack and Zebrowski, George
Yellowhead
Dann, J. The fiction factory; by Jack Dann
with Susan Casper . . . [et al.]
Dann, Jack and others
Afternoon at Schrafft's
Dann, J. The fiction factory; by Jack Dann
with Susan Casper . . . [et al.]
The clowns
Dann, J. The fiction factory; by Jack Dann
with Susan Casper . . . [et al.]
The gods of Mars
Dann, J. The fiction factory; by Jack Dann
with Susan Casper . . . [et al.]
Golden apples of the sun
Dann, J. The fiction factory; by Jack Dann
with Susan Casper . . . [et al.]
Touring
Dann, J. The fiction factory; by Jack Dann
with Susan Casper . . . [et al.]
Dannay, Frederic, 1905-1982
For works written by this author in collab-
oration with Manfred Lee see Queen,
Ellery
Danny's very long trip. Moscoe, M.
Dans le Vent [With photograph by Eduardo
Momeñe] Mingarelli, H.
Dansky, Richard E.
Killer App
Man vs. machine; edited by John Helfers and
Martin H. Greenberg.
DANTE ALIGHIERI, 1265-1321
About
Farmer, P. J. A hole in Hell
Parodies, imitations, etc.
Roberts, A. Dantesque
Dantesque. Roberts, A.
Danticat, Edwidge
Crabs
The New Yorker v84 no17 p78 Je 9-16 2008
Elsie
Callaloo v29 no1 p22-9 Wint 2006
Ghosts
The New Yorker v84 no38 p108-13 N 24
2008
The Indigo Girl
Sojourners v33 no12 p28-30 D 2004
Lélé
The book of other people; edited by Zadie
Smith
Night women
Beha, C. R. The Ecco anthology of contem-
porary American short fiction; selected by
Joyce Carol Oates and Christopher R.
Beha.

Danticat, Edwidge—*Continued*
  Reading Lessons
    The New Yorker v80 no42 p66-73 Ja 10 2005
Daphne. Cadnum, M.
Darien dogs. Shukman, H.
DARK AGES *See* Middle Ages
The **Dark** Between Them. Ray, S.
The **Dark** Country. Berry, W.
The **dark** country. Etchison, D.
Dark delicacies of the dead. Pickman, R.
The **dark** eidolon. Smith, C. A.
The **Dark** Forces. Justice, J. R.
Dark heaven. Benford, G.
Dark integers. Egan, G.
Dark journey. Berkeley, A.
Dark Laughter. Riley, E.
Dark Matter. Williams, J. A.
Dark moon rising. Tremayne, P.
Dark nights. Theodore, J.
Dark of the Moon. Masters, A.
Dark of the moon. Offutt, A.
The **Dark** Part of the Road. Siegal, L.
Dark quarry. Stiefel, B.
Dark return. Nolan, W. F.
Dark Room. Brown, J.
Dark roots. Kennedy, C.
The **dark** side of town. Kelly, J. P.
The **dark** snow. DuBois, B.
Dark times. Crowther, P.
The **dark** tribe. Kelly, R.
A **Dark** Turn. Strickley, S. A.
Dark urgings of the blood. Nayman, S.
The **darkening** moon. Stafford, J.
The **darkest** night. Parra, E. A.
Darkest of all. Schutt, C.
The **Darkest** Skies in North America. Root, M.
Darkness. Coleman, W.
Darkness. Greer, A. S.
Darkness. See Chekhov, A. P. In the darkness of
    the night [variant title: Darkness]
Darkness, and she was alone. Conlon, C.
A **darkness** held. Ochsner, G.
The **darkness** together. Almond, S.
Darlington, Tenaya
  Great North American Trees
    The North American Review v292 no1 p35-40
    Ja/F 2007
  A patch of skin
    Barnstorm; contemporary Wisconsin fiction;
    edited by Raphael Kadushin
The **Darlington** substitution. Jeffers, H. P.
The **dart** and the drill. Ruefle, M.
Dart-Thornton, Cecilia
  The lanes of Camberwell
    Dreaming again; thirty-five new stories cele-
    brating the wild side of Australian fiction;
    edited by Jack Dann
The **darts** of Cupid. Templeton, E.
Das, Kamala
  The hijra
    Gibson, M. E. Separate journeys; short stories
    by contemporary Indian women; edited by
    Geeta Dharmarajan; introduction by Mary
    Ellis Gibson

Das, Varsha
  I am complete
    Gibson, M. E. Separate journeys; short stories
    by contemporary Indian women; edited by
    Geeta Dharmarajan; introduction by Mary
    Ellis Gibson
Dason, Shymala B.
  All the Necessary Things
    The Massachusetts Review v45 no3 p229-40
    Aut 2004
The **date**. Lazellari, E.
Date 1965: modern warfare. Hodgson, W. H.
Date with a bird. Tolstaia, T.
Dates and bitter coffee. Ismaeel, D. E.
DATING (SOCIAL CUSTOMS)
  Almond, S. The evil B. B. Chow
  Almond, S. A happy dream
  Alvarado, B. What Lydia thinks of roses
  Báez, A. Amor es. . . Love is
  Báez, A. The time keeper
  Baingana, D. First kiss
  Barrett, M. Skyliner
  Bender, A. Two days
  Benedict, E. FAQ
  Boudinot, R. Bee beard
  Boyers, R. Tribunal
  Burgin, R. Carbo's
  Burgin, R. The liar
  Curran, C. LDR
  Curtis, R. Big Bear, California
  de Chambrey, M. Hurting Hugh
  Dormen, L. Figure of a woman
  Duffy, S. Un bon repas doit commencer par la
    faim. . .
  Edgerton, C. Debra's flap and snap
  Eng, V. The flower of flushing
  Freed, L. The curse of the appropriate man
  Gospodinov, G. Peonies and forget-me-nots
  Hawes, L. A fine mess
  Hayes, D. Twenty-six hours, twenty-five min-
    utes
  Houston, P. Nightmare
  Kalotay, D. Prom season
  Keret, E. An exclusive
  Keret, E. The girl on the fridge
  Keret, E. One hundred percent
  Keret, E. Through walls
  Kirkman, J. The single girl's guide to compro-
    mising homeland security
  Krause, E. Zero
  Krysl, M. Air, a romance
  LaBrie, A. Encore
  LaBrie, A. The last dead boyfriend
  LaBrie, A. Wanted
  LaBrie, A. What she should do
  LaBrie, A. Wonderful girl
  LaBrie, A. Words to live by
  Lam, V. How to get into medical school, part I
  Lam, V. How to get into medical school, part II
  Levithan, D. The alumni interview
  Levithan, D. Andrew Chang
  Levithan, D. The escalator, a love story
  Levithan, D. The number of people who meet
    on airplanes
  Levithan, D. Starbucks boy

DATING (SOCIAL CUSTOMS)—*Continued*

Lin, T. Cull the steel heart, melt the ice one, love the weak thing; say nothing of consolation, but irrelevance, disaster, and nonexistence; have no hope or hate—nothing; ruin yourself exclusively, completely, and whenever possible

Lin, T. Insomnia for a better tomorrow

Lin, T. Love is a thing on sale for more money than there exists

Lin, T. Sincerity

Litman, E. The trajectory of frying pans

McHugh, M. F. In the air

McLean, S. Valentine's Day

Meno, J. Mr. Song

Merino, J. F. The sixth commandment

Messinger, J. Between here and there

Messinger, J. The birds below

Messinger, J. One valve opens

Moceri, M. The mystery spot

Moise, L. Cuck(h)olding a stranger

Molodowsky, K. Eternal summer

Monson, A. Forecast

Nissen, T. Etiquette

Parker, M. Smoke from Chester leading me down to see Dogman

Penn, V. Trim

Piatote, B. H. Life-size Indian

Porter, A. Departure

Pruett, L. Shouting Nazarene

Rash, R. Honesty

Rich, M. The real thing

Riley, G. Au pont du font

Rosen, J. First date

Shaw, H. Single white farmhouse

Shroff, M. F. Babu Barrah Takka

Sohn, A. Call-hell

Tower, W. On the show

Trevor, W. An evening out

Tsutsui, Y. Rumours about me

Unferth, D. O. Juan the cell phone salesman

Upadhyay, S. Chintamani's women

Valdés, J. Orquidea

Ward, A. E. The way the sky changed

Welch, N. Sweet Maddy

Yasuoka, S. The wandering minstrel

Dating Deborah Kerr. Bernstein, L. S.

Dating for the wired generation. Gaskell, S.

Daugharty, Janice

American Breakfast—Mexican Dinner

The Georgia Review v58 no3 p585-97 Fall 2004

Dumdum

New stories from the South: the year's best, 2005; edited by Shannon Ravenel; with a preface by Jill McCorkle

Daugherty, Tracy

Anna Lia

Daugherty, T. Late in the standoff; stories and a novella

Bern

The Georgia Review v62 no1 p100-29 Spr 2008

City codes

Daugherty, T. Late in the standoff; stories and a novella

Lamplighter

Daugherty, T. Late in the standoff; stories and a novella

Magnitude

The Georgia Review v60 no3/4 p577-95 Fall/Wint 2006

Power lines

Daugherty, T. Late in the standoff; stories and a novella

Purgatory, Nevada

Southwest Review v93 no3 p379-84 2008

The Saint

Prairie Schooner v81 no4 p83-102 Wint 2007

The standoff

Daugherty, T. Late in the standoff; stories and a novella

The **daughter-in-law**. Molodowsky, K.

A **daughter** in time. Caponegro, M.

A **daughter** of my own. Gerber, M. J.

The **Daughter** of the Bearded Lady. Precht, V.

Daughter of the clay. Lanagan, M.

DAUGHTERS *See* Fathers and daughters; Mothers and daughters; Stepdaughters

Barthelme, D. The agreement

Barthelme, D. You are as brave as Vincent Van Gogh

Gordon, M. Eleanor's music

Rickert, M. Night blossoms

Daughters. Karmazin, M.

DAUGHTERS-IN-LAW

Cody, L. Indian throw

Cohen, M. The sins of Tomas Benares

Feitell, M. Such a big Mr. England

Gordon, M. Death in Naples

McCauley, W. Edna's mission

Rash, R. Last rite

Roggie, D. The mushroom Duchess

Schwarzschild, E. What to expect

Stevenson, J. Garden guerrillas

Daughters of earth. Merril, J.

The **Daughters** of the Moon. Calvino, I.

Daughtry, Philip

Another country

Daughtry, P. The centaur's son

Breathing in public

Daughtry, P. The centaur's son

The centaur's son

Daughtry, P. The centaur's son

French letters

Daughtry, P. The centaur's son

A grace of shadows

Daughtry, P. The centaur's son

Haunted sailors

Daughtry, P. The centaur's son

Jungle roads

Daughtry, P. The centaur's son

The mescaline runes

Daughtry, P. The centaur's son

The mouse's aura

Daughtry, P. The centaur's son

Season of broken wings

Daughtry, P. The centaur's son

Street of wounded Mercedes

Daughtry, P. The centaur's son

Tinker's turn

Daughtry, P. The centaur's son

Trickle Creek

Daughtry, P. The centaur's son

Dauntless women of the Russian steppe. Ulitskaya, L.

D'Aurevilly, J. Barbey *See* Barbey d'Aurevilly, J., 1808-1889

Dave cooks the turkey. McLean, S.
Davenport, Guy
A field of snow on a slope of the Rosenberg
So the story goes; twenty-five years of the Johns Hopkins short fiction series; edited by John T. Irwin and Jean McGarry; with a foreword by John Barth
Davenport, Steve
Oh My Darling
The Literary Review (Madison, N.J.) v51 no4 p C18-C20 Summ 2008
Rivers to Gilead
The Southern Review (Baton Rouge, La.) v45 no1 p20-7 Wint 2009
Where the Water Runs Uphill
The Literary Review (Madison, N.J.) v51 no4 p C21-C26 Summ 2008
You Be Wing
The Literary Review (Madison, N.J.) v51 no4 p C14-C17 Summ 2008
Davenport, T. F.
Penance
Nature v457 p1046 F 19 2009
DAVID, KING OF ISRAEL
About
James, C. L. R. Michelangelo and the statue of David
Rosenbaum, B. The book of Jashar
David, Jonathan
The Sub
TriQuarterly no126 p143-9 2006
David, Peter
Killing time by the River Styx
Meeting across the river; stories inspired by the haunting Bruce Springsteen song; edited by Jessica Kaye and Richard J. Brewer
What monsters do
Kolchak: the night stalker chronicles; 26 original tales of the surreal, the bizarre, the macabre; edited by Joe Gentile, Garrett Anderson, Lori Gentile; Kolchak created by Jeff Rice
David and Goliath. James, C. L. R.
David Wassermann. Burke, K.
Davidson, Chad
(tr.) See Pariani, Laura
Davidson, Craig
The apprentice's guide to modern magic
Davidson, C. Rust and bone; stories
Friction
Davidson, C. Rust and bone; stories
Life in the flesh
Davidson, C. Rust and bone; stories
A mean utility
Davidson, C. Rust and bone; stories
On sleepless roads
Davidson, C. Rust and bone; stories
The rifleman
Davidson, C. Rust and bone; stories
Rocket ride
Davidson, C. Rust and bone; stories
Rust and bone
Davidson, C. Rust and bone; stories
Davidson, Hilary
Anniversary
A Prisoner of memory and 24 of the year's finest crime and mystery stories; edited by Ed Gorman & Martin H. Greenberg

Davidson, Jenny
The other amazon
Realms
Davidson, Rjurik
Twilight in Caeli-Amur
Dreaming again; thirty-five new stories celebrating the wild side of Australian fiction; edited by Jack Dann
Davies, Colin P.
The defenders
The Year's best science fiction: twenty-second annual collection; edited by Gardner Dozois
Davies, Lewis
The fare
Urban Welsh; new short fiction; edited by Lewis Davies
Davies, Tristan
Counterfactuals
So the story goes; twenty-five years of the Johns Hopkins short fiction series; edited by John T. Irwin and Jean McGarry; with a foreword by John Barth
Davis, Albert Belisle
The significance of importance
Wide awake in the Pelican State; stories by contemporary Louisiana writers; edited by Ann Brewster Dobie; with a foreword by Ernest J. Gaines
Davis, Bob
Death of a deer
On the Mason-Dixon line; an anthology of contemporary Delaware writers; edited by Billie Travalini and Fleda Brown.
Davis, Carol Anne
Starting over
The World's finest mystery and crime stories, fifth annual collection; edited by Ed Gorman and Martin H. Greenberg
Davis, Claire
Adultery
Davis, C. Labors of the heart; stories
Balance
Davis, C. Labors of the heart; stories
Electric
Davis, C. Labors of the heart; stories
Grounded
Davis, C. Labors of the heart; stories
Labors of the heart
Davis, C. Labors of the heart; stories
Mouse rampant
Davis, C. Labors of the heart; stories
The same sky
Davis, C. Labors of the heart; stories
Stiff soup
Davis, C. Labors of the heart; stories
Tap
Davis, C. Labors of the heart; stories
Trash
Davis, C. Labors of the heart; stories
Davis, Cortney
Breathing
The Best of the Bellevue Literary Review; edited by Dannielle Ofri and the staff of the Bellevue Literary Review

Davis, Dorothy Salisbury
By the scruff of the soul
  A New omnibus of crime; edited by Tony
    Hillerman and Rosemary Herbert; contrib-
    uting editors Sue Grafton and Jeffery
    Deaver
Dies Irae
  Sisters on the case; celebrating twenty years
    of Sisters in Crime; edited by Sara Paretsky
  A Prisoner of memory and 24 of the year's
    finest crime and mystery stories; edited by
    Ed Gorman & Martin H. Greenberg
Davis, Frederick C.
The sinister sphere
  The Black Lizard big book of pulps; edited
    by Otto Penzler
Davis, J. Madison
Iggy's stuff
  The International Association of Crime Writ-
    ers presents Murder in Vegas; new crime
    tales of gambling and desperation; edited
    by Michael Connelly
DAVIS, JEFFERSON, 1808-1889
                About
Smith, R. T. Trousseau
Davis, Jennifer S.
Ava Bean
  This is not chick lit; original stories by Amer-
    ica's best women writers; edited by Eliza-
    beth Merrick
  Davis, J. S. Our former lives in art; (stories)
Bliss
  The Georgia Review v59 no2 p258-74 Summ
    2005
Blue moon
  Davis, J. S. Our former lives in art; (stories)
Detritus
  Davis, J. S. Our former lives in art; (stories)
Giving up the ghost
  Davis, J. S. Our former lives in art; (stories)
  The Paris Review v46 p143-60 Wint 2004
Lovely Lily
  Davis, J. S. Our former lives in art; (stories)
Our former lives in art
  Davis, J. S. Our former lives in art; (stories)
Pilgrimage in Georgia
  Davis, J. S. Our former lives in art; (stories)
Rapture
  Davis, J. S. Our former lives in art; (stories)
Witnessing
  Davis, J. S. Our former lives in art; (stories)
Davis, Lindsey
'Going anywhere nice?'
  The Detection collection; edited by Simon
    Brett
Something spooky on Geophys
  The Best British mysteries, 2005; edited by
    Maxim Jakubowski
Davis, Lisa Selin
Relationship Resume
  The Literary Review (Madison, N.J.) v48 no1
    p97-8 Fall 2004
  The Literary Review (Madison, N.J.) v48 no1
    p99-100 Fall 2004

Davis, Lydia
Break it down
  The Paris review book for planes, trains, ele-
    vators, and waiting rooms; by the editors of
    the Paris review; with an introduction by
    Richard Powers
The old dictionary
  The Anchor book of new American short sto-
    ries; edited by Ben Marcus
Television
  Beha, C. R. The Ecco anthology of contem-
    porary American short fiction; selected by
    Joyce Carol Oates and Christopher R.
    Beha.
Three Letters of Complaint
  The Literary Review (Madison, N.J.) v48 no4
    p9-15 Summ 2005
Davis, Michael
The Problem of Evil in Hauberk, Missouri
  The Georgia Review v59 no4 p828-47 Wint
    2005
Davis, Mike
Negative Nixons
  Politics noir; dark tales from the corridors of
    power; edited by Gary Phillips.
Davis, Norbert
The price of a dime
  The Black Lizard big book of pulps; edited
    by Otto Penzler
You'll die laughing
  The Black Lizard big book of pulps; edited
    by Otto Penzler
Davis, Ree
I Kneel Before You
  Daedalus v135 no1 p116-19 Wint 2006
Davis, Robert Hambling See Davis, Bob
Davis, Russell
Engines of desire & despair
  Man vs. machine; edited by John Helfers and
    Martin H. Greenberg.
Davis, Susanne
Our Lady of Sorrows
  Feminist Studies v32 no2 p422-33 Summ
    2006
Davis, Wendi See Holder, Nancy, 1953-
Dawidziak, Mark
Interview with a vampire?
  Kolchak: the night stalker chronicles; 26 orig-
    inal tales of the surreal, the bizarre, the ma-
    cabre; edited by Joe Gentile, Garrett Ander-
    son, Lori Gentile; Kolchak created by Jeff
    Rice
Dawn. Chase, M.
Dawn. Powers, J. F.
Dawn-strider. Yolen, J.
Dawson, Janet
Invisible time
  San Francisco noir 2; the classics; edited by
    Peter Maravelis.
Dawson, Peter
Back-trail betrayal
  Dawson, P. Showdown at Anchor; a western
    quintet
Hell for homesteaders
  Dawson, P. Showdown at Anchor; a western
    quintet
Showdown at Anchor
  Dawson, P. Showdown at Anchor; a western
    quintet

Dawson, Peter—_Continued_
  A tinhorn takes a tank town
    Dawson, P. Showdown at Anchor; a western
    quintet
  Unwanted gold
    Dawson, P. Showdown at Anchor; a western
    quintet
Dawson, Robert
  Good Hands
    StoryQuarterly v41 p350-60 2005
Dawson's folly. Hawes, L.
Day, Andrew
  Our Agreement
    New England Review v26 no2 p49-52 2005
Day, Angie
  In the darkness
    Before; short stories about pregnancy from
    our top writers; edited by Emily Franklin
    and Heather Swain
Day, Caroline Bond
  The pink hat
    "Tell it to us easy" and other stories; a com-
    plete short fiction anthology of African
    American women writers in Opportunity
    magazine, (1923-1948); edited by Judith
    Musser.
Day, Robert
  Free Writing
    New Letters v73 no2 p141-55 2007
  My Uncle's Poor French
    New Letters v71 no3 p119-52 2005
  The Skull Hunter
    New Letters v71 no1 p135-53 2004/2005
  Some Notes on the Cold War in Kansas
    New Letters v73 no2 p157-71 2007
  The Story I'm Pitching
    New Letters v71 no1 p155-83 2004/2005
The **day** and the night of the day. Brazaitis, M.
The **day** I ate nothing I even remotely wanted.
  Berg, E.
The **day** I ate whatever I wanted. Berg, E.
The **day** I had everything. Hempel, A.
The **day** in Buenos Aires. Hussin, J. Y.
A **day** in the life of Justin Argento Morrel. Frost,
  G.
A **Day** in the Park. Leslie, N.
The **day** J. P. saved the South. Ruffin, P.
A **day** meant to do less. Minor, K.
Day million. Pohl, F.
The **day** of glory. Drake, D.
Day of reckoning [variant titles: The faces; Grave-
  yard shift] Matheson, R.
The **day** of settlement. Romano, T.
The **day** of the bullett. Ellin, S.
Day of the dead. Pierce, T. J.
The **day** of two cars. Linscott, G.
Day off. Butcher, J.
A **day** off. McLean, S.
Day out. Anderson, B.
The **day** the Gorf took over. Nolan, W. F.
The **Day** the Governor Came to Lunch. Hartman,
  R. A.
The **day** the icicle works closed. Pohl, F.
The **day** the invaders came. Effinger, G. A.
The **day** the Martels got the cable. Cadigan, P.
The **day** the Martians came. Pohl, F.
The **day** we buried our weapons. Mendoza, P.
The **Day** We Exist Again. Maisto, M.

The **day** we went through the transition. De la
  Casa, R. and Romero, P. J.
The **day** we were set free. Tognazzini, A.
A **day** with Charulata. Niranjana, A.
Dayan, Colin
  Between the Devil and the Deep Sea
    Boston Review v34 no4 p43-5 Jl/Ag 2009
Daylight come. Hempel, A.
Daymare. Brown, F.
The **Days** Down Here. White, J.
Days of 1978. Bolaño, R.
The **days** of other light. Di Filippo, P.
The **Days** of the Peppers. Holladay, C.
Days of the wheel. Crowther, P.
A **day's** pay: a short story. Challeno, E. D.
A **day's** work. Porter, K. A.
A **day's** worth of beauty. Gifford, B.
Daytrip. Probst, M.
Dazzle redux. Bradfield, S.
Dazzled. Singer, I. B.
Dazzle's inferno. Bradfield, S.
The **dazzling** world. Brady, C.
De Andrade, Mário _See_ Andrade, Mário de,
  1893-1945
De Azevedo, Kathleen
  Together We Are Lost
    TriQuarterly no125 p72-81 2006 _See_
    Azevedo, Kathleen de, 1955-
De Balzac, Honoré _See_ Balzac, Honoré de, 1799-
  1850
de Caldas Brito, Christiana
  "The B-line"
    Multicultural literature in contemporary Italy;
    edited by Marie Orton and Graziella Parati
  "The beggar"
    Multicultural literature in contemporary Italy;
    edited by Marie Orton and Graziella Parati
De Camp, L. Sprague
  Aristotle and the gun
    De Camp, L. S. Years in the making; the
    time-travel stories of L. Sprague de Camp;
    edited by Mark L. Olson
  Balsamo's mirror
    De Camp, L. S. Years in the making; the
    time-travel stories of L. Sprague de Camp;
    edited by Mark L. Olson
  The gnarly man
    De Camp, L. S. Years in the making; the
    time-travel stories of L. Sprague de Camp;
    edited by Mark L. Olson
  A gun for dinosaur
    De Camp, L. S. Years in the making; the
    time-travel stories of L. Sprague de Camp;
    edited by Mark L. Olson
  The isolinguals
    De Camp, L. S. Years in the making; the
    time-travel stories of L. Sprague de Camp;
    edited by Mark L. Olson
  Language for time travelers
    De Camp, L. S. Years in the making; the
    time-travel stories of L. Sprague de Camp;
    edited by Mark L. Olson
  Lest darkness fall
    De Camp, L. S. Years in the making; the
    time-travel stories of L. Sprague de Camp;
    edited by Mark L. Olson

Dean, Debra

The afterlife of Lyle Stone
    Dean, D. Confessions of a falling woman;
    and other stories

Another little piece
    Dean, D. Confessions of a falling woman;
    and other stories

The best man
    Dean, D. Confessions of a falling woman;
    and other stories

The Bodhisattva
    Dean, D. Confessions of a falling woman;
    and other stories

A brief history of us
    Dean, D. Confessions of a falling woman;
    and other stories

Confessions of a falling woman
    Dean, D. Confessions of a falling woman;
    and other stories

Dan in the gray flannel rat suit
    Dean, D. Confessions of a falling woman;
    and other stories

The queen mother
    Dean, D. Confessions of a falling woman;
    and other stories

Romance manual
    Dean, D. Confessions of a falling woman;
    and other stories

What the left hand is saying
    Dean, D. Confessions of a falling woman;
    and other stories

Dean of women. Lynn, D. H.

DeAndrea, William L.

The adventure of the Christmas tree
    DeAndrea, W. L. Murder-all kinds; introduc-
    tion by Jane Haddam

The adventure of the cripple parade
    DeAndrea, W. L. Murder-all kinds; introduc-
    tion by Jane Haddam

A friend of mine
    DeAndrea, W. L. Murder-all kinds; introduc-
    tion by Jane Haddam

Hero's welcome
    DeAndrea, W. L. Murder-all kinds; introduc-
    tion by Jane Haddam

Killed in good company
    DeAndrea, W. L. Murder-all kinds; introduc-
    tion by Jane Haddam

Killed in midstream
    DeAndrea, W. L. Murder-all kinds; introduc-
    tion by Jane Haddam

Killed top to bottom
    DeAndrea, W. L. Murder-all kinds; introduc-
    tion by Jane Haddam

Murder at the end of the world
    DeAndrea, W. L. Murder-all kinds; introduc-
    tion by Jane Haddam

Prince Charming
    DeAndrea, W. L. Murder-all kinds; introduc-
    tion by Jane Haddam

Sabotage
    DeAndrea, W. L. Murder-all kinds; introduc-
    tion by Jane Haddam

Snowy reception
    DeAndrea, W. L. Murder-all kinds; introduc-
    tion by Jane Haddam

DEANS (CATHEDRAL AND COLLEGIATE)
    See Anglican and Episcopal clergy

Dear. Crouse, D.

Dear Abbey. Bisson, T.

Dear Arthur. Biller, M.

Dear Daniel Davis or How I Came to Know Jesus
    Christ as My Personal Lord and Savior.
    Haynes, D.

Dear diary. Matheson, R.

Dear Dr. Haskell. Treat, J.

Dear hope. Colombi, M.

Dear husband,. Oates, J. C.

Dear Joyce Carol,. Oates, J. C.

Dear leader. Working, R.

Dear Mr. Klezcka. Orner, P.

Dear Penthouse Forum (a first draft). Lippman, L.

Dear People Magazine, keep up the great cyclops
    coverage. Pendarvis, J.

Dear Prudence. Savile, S.

Dear X. Greenman, B.

Dearborn and LaSalle. Manley, C.

Dearth. Bender, A.

DEATH

    See also Bereavement; Dead; Deathbed
    scenes

Abbott, J. A few small repairs

Abbott, L. K. The human use of inhuman beings

Abbott, M. Our eyes couldn't stop opening

Aird, C. A different cast of mind

Alarcón, D. A strong dead man

Alarcón, D. The visitor

Alexie, S. This is what it means to say Phoenix,
    Arizona

Ali, M. N. Ward G-4

Almond, S. The problem of human consumption

Anaya, R. A. Jerónimo's journey

Anderson, B. Fast post

Anderson, R. M. Briley boy

Andreas-Salomé, L. A death

Arnold, G. Heart trouble

Atwood, M. The age of lead

Auslander, S. Somebody up there likes you

Báez, A. The loss

Barron, L. The lagerstatte

Barry, R. Lucy's last hurrah

Beagle, P. S. We never talk about my brother

Bender, A. Death wish

Bender, A. Marzipan

Bierce, A. A diagnosis of death

Bierce, A. The Golampians

Bierce, A. A watcher by the dead

Bingham, S. Pleyben

Bishop, E. Gwendolyn

Bissell, T. Death defier

Bisson, T. Come dance with me

Bisson, T. Death's door

Black, R. . . . Divorced, beheaded, survived

Bluestein, E. North of the Faro

Boast, W. Weather enough

Bogary, A. Bloodstains on the wall

Boyd, B. Scarecrow

Bradbury, R. Death and the maiden

Bradbury, R. The Kilimanjaro device

Bradbury, R. The miracles of Jamie

Bradbury, R. No news; or, What killed the dog?

Brandner, G. Words, words, words!

Brant, B. E. Turtle gal

Brau, E. The calendar

Brau, E. The siesta

Brown, E. Hunting the Slarque

Brown, G. M. The interrogator

Buckler, E. Long, long after school

DEATH—*Continued*

Buckler, E. The orchard
Bulushi, S. Sounds of the sea
Bunin, I. A. The gentleman from San Francisco
Campbell, R. Respects
Card, O. S. Missed
Card, O. S. Vessel
Chekhov, A. P. Criminal investigator [variant title: The court investigator]
Chilson, P. Disturbance-loving species
Clarke, B. The ghosts we love
Clayton, J. J. Glory
Clayton, J. J. I'm here, you're there
Clayton, J. J. Vertigo
Collins, W. Nine o'clock
Colombi, M. Dear hope
Corso, P. Raw egg in beer
Crone, M. Salvage
Crouch, B. Remaking
Crowther, P. Even beggars would ride
Crowther, P. Stand-by
Dalton, Q. Endurance tests
Dalton, Q. Midnight bowling
Daniells, R. C. Purgatory
Dann, J. and Dozois, G. R. Down among the dead men
Danticat, E. Lélé
Daugherty, T. Anna Lia
Daughtry, P. Another country
Davis, C. Breathing
Dills, T. Arcadia
Đoàn, L. Guot's love
Đoàn, L. A question mark for God
Dobozy, T. Radio Blik
Donoghue, E. The dormition of the virgin
Donovan, G. Glass
Dostoyevsky, F. The little boy at the Savior's Christmas tree
Dowling, T. The fooly
Downs, G. Between states
Dufresne, J. The dead of night
Dufresne, J. Died and gone to heaven
Dufresne, J. I will eat a piece of the roof and you can eat the window
Dunbar, P. L. A prophesy of fate
Eisenberg, D. The girl who left her sock on the floor
Enright, A. The cruise
Enright, A. Until the girl died
Erdrich, L. Le Mooz
Erdrich, L. The plunge of the brave
Fawcett, B. You'll catch your death of colds
Ferrigno, R. The hour when the ship comes in
Fiorillo, H. The aroma of death
Fonseca, R. Betsy
Fonseca, R. The flesh and the bones
Fonseca, R. Pride
Ford, J. Present from the past
Formetta, C. D. Last summer together
Francisco, B. and Lynch, C. This is my blood
Frankel-Zaltzman, P. A natural death
Freudenberger, N. Lucky girls
Fromm, P. Snow cave
Fulton, J. Real grief
Gappah, P. Something nice from London
García Márquez, G. Death constant beyond love
Gardiner, J. R. The voyage out
Gee, M. Starting at last
Gerber, M. J. Tell me your secret

Gerber, M. J. We know that your hearts are heavy
Gifford, B. Johnny Across
Gilchrist, E. The blue house
Gildner, G. Burial
Gildner, G. The rock
Gold, H. Death in Miami Beach
Goonan, K. A. Sundiver day
Gordin, J. Missus, your soup is cold
Gorman, E. Different kinds of dead
Gospodinov, G. A living soul
Graham, T. Heaven's gate
Granville-Barker, H. The fire that burned in the corner
Green, G. "This very vivd morn"
Guista, M. Kiltee
Gunn, E. Coming to terms
Haines, C. The wish
Hammett, D. The dimple
Hand, E. Pavane for a prince of the air
Harland, R. A guided tour in the kingdom of the dead
Harper, B. Yellowstone
Hasak-Lowy, T. How Keith's dad died
Hawes, L. Summerlands
Hempel, A. At the gates of the animal kingdom
Hempel, A. In the cemetery where Al Jolson is buried
Hempel, A. When it's human instead of when it's dog
Henriquez, C. Ashes
Henry, S. Sister death
Herlihy, J. The core
Hernandez, L. Death in the sidesaddle
Higgins, G. V. Slowly now the dancer
Hill, S. The sin-eater
Hirshberg, G. The two Sams
Hodgson, W. H. The goddess of death
Hodgson, W. H. The heaving of the log
Horgan, P. The peach stone
Houston, P. Waltzing the cat
Hyde, M. Second-hand
Irsfeld, J. H. Death of a soldier
Irsfeld, J. H. My neighbor Mr. Young
Isaka, K. The precision of the agent of death
Ison, T. Wig
Jablonski, N. The good life
Jamieson, T. The new deal
Johnson, G. Escalators
Johnston, T. Irish girl
Jones, S. G. Bleed into me
Julavits, H. Judge Gladys Parks-Schultz
Karlin, K. Bye-bye Larry
Keeble, J. The chasm
Keeble, J. Freezing the apes
Kellerman, F. Malibu dog
Kelly, R. Forever angels
Kenney, S. The death of the dog and other rescues
Kercheval, J. L. Honors
Keret, E. Himme
Keret, E. Sidewalks
Keret, E. Without her
Kim, H. From powder to powder
Kim, S. Findings & impressions
Klimasewiski, M. N. Tanner and Jun Hee
Koretsky, J. l. Snapshot
Kress, N. Elevator
Kress, N. Fountain of age

Desaulniers, Janet—*Continued*

Everyone is wearing a hat

Desaulniers, J. What you've been missing; by Janet Desaulniers

The good fight

Desaulniers, J. What you've been missing; by Janet Desaulniers

Mothers without children

Desaulniers, J. What you've been missing; by Janet Desaulniers

Never, ever, always

Desaulniers, J. What you've been missing; by Janet Desaulniers

The next day

Desaulniers, J. What you've been missing; by Janet Desaulniers

Real love

Desaulniers, J. What you've been missing; by Janet Desaulniers

Roll

Desaulniers, J. What you've been missing; by Janet Desaulniers

Where we all should have been

Desaulniers, J. What you've been missing; by Janet Desaulniers

Who knows more than you

Desaulniers, J. What you've been missing; by Janet Desaulniers

DESCARTES, RENÉ, 1596-1650

About

Johnson, C. R. The queen and the philosopher

Descent. Brown, D.

Descent. Hogan, L.

Descent. Matheson, R.

The **Descent** of the River Ganges [Hindu story retold by D. K. M. Kartha]

Description. Gaitskill, M.

Desert breakdown, 1968. Wolff, T.

The **desert** here and the desert far away. Sakey, M.

Desert shield. Millet, L.

DESERTED HOUSES

Bierce, A. A vine on a house

Hyde, M. The clay is vile

DESERTION, MILITARY *See* Military desertion

DESERTION AND NONSUPPORT

Brazaitis, M. The life he left behind

Drosso, A.-M. Penance

Hodgen, C. A jeweler's eye for flaw

Mordecai, P. Corinthians thirteen thirteen

Reed, K. No two alike

Resnick, L. Lady Roxanne La Belle

Singer, I. B. Disguised

Ward, A. E. Nan and Claude

DESERTS

See also Sahara

Dahl, R. The visitor

DeMarinis, R. Bête noire

Eberhardt, I. One night in Africa

Goodis, D. Caravan to Tarim

Hirshberg, G. Dancing men

Klages, E. The green glass sea

Koretsky, J. L. The tormenting eye of God

L'Amour, L. Valley of the sun

Lum, E. What I never said

Nash, R. The camera and the cobra

Padilla, I. The antipodes and the century

Paine, R. D. "Old Glory" in the desert

Rand, K. Buzzards of Oz

Rand, K. Ice folly

Rock, P. Gold Firebird

Sada, D. El fenomeno ominoso/The ominous phenomenon

Sakey, M. The desert here and the desert far away

Schow, D. J. Plot twist

Shepard, J. The First South Central Australian Expedition

Smith, C. A. The abominations of Yondo

Tobin, P. passage

Ts'an-hsüeh. My brother

Welsh, I. Rattlesnakes

Westerfeld, S. Ass-hat magic spider

Wieland, M. God's dogs

Wieland, M. The mistress of the horse god

Wieland, M. Solstice

Wieland, M. Swan's song

Wilce, Y. S. Quartermaster returns

Deserts and dowries. Lynn, D. H.

Desgraciado. Watkins, S.

Design. Rylands, J. T.

The **designator**. Mathieu, R. M.

Designer justice. Cohen, P.

A **Desirable** Woman. Berry, W.

Desolation. Jones, G.

Desolation Rose. Baker, K.

DESPAIR

Bakr, S. Thirty-one beautiful green trees

Ford, J. The drowned life

Harleman, A. Thoreau's laundry

Schonfeld, Y. The collection treatment

Thon, M. R. Confession for Raymond Good Bird

Desperado. DeMarinis, R.

Desperate times. Rand, K.

Desprat, Jean-Paul

I'm No Ingres Odalisque

FMR (Black Edition) no18 p157-64 Ap/My 2007

DESTINY *See* Fate and fatalism

Destiny. Erdrich, L.

Destiny, Inc. Lukyanenko, S.

Destiny returns. Obejas, A.

DESTRUCTION OF EARTH *See* Earth, Destruction of

DESTRUCTION OF THE JEWS *See* Holocaust, Jewish (1933-1945)

Details. Mosley, W.

The **detective** Bendel-Simso, M. M., ed. Early American detective stories; an anthology; edited by LeRoy Lad Panek and Mary M. Bendel-Simso.

DETECTIVE AND MYSTERY STORIES *See* Mystery and detective stories

The **detective** from Baltimore Bendel-Simso, M. M., ed. Early American detective stories; an anthology; edited by LeRoy Lad Panek and Mary M. Bendel-Simso.

The **detective** of dreams. Wolfe, G.

The **detective** story Bendel-Simso, M. M., ed. Early American detective stories; an anthology; edited by LeRoy Lad Panek and Mary M. Bendel-Simso.

Detective William Brown. Woolrich, C.

DETECTIVES

Amlingmeyer, Big Red. See stories by Hockensmith, S.

DETECTIVES—*Continued*

Lupin, Arsène. See stories by Leblanc, M.
MacAlister, Marti. See stories by Bland, E. T.
Malone, Dizzy. See stories by Paul, P.
Marlin, John. See stories by Rehder, B.
Marlowe, Philip. See stories by Chandler, R.
Martinez, Dolph. See stories by Sanderson, J.
Matthews, Charles Timothy. See stories by Meredith, D. R.
McCone, Sharon. See stories by Muller, M.
McDonald, Cal. See stories by Niles, S.
McDonough, Martin. See stories by Rubenstein, B.
McFee. See stories by Booth, C. G.
Meyer, Detective Meyer. See stories by McBain, E.
Millhone, Kinsey. See stories by Grafton, S.
Milodragovitch, Milo. See stories by Crumley, J.
Monaghan, Tess. See stories by Lippman, L.
Morgan, Mariana. See stories by Dain, C.
Moss, Margaret. See stories by Scheen, K.
Navarre, Tres. See stories by Riordan, R.
Nudger, Aldo. See stories by Lutz, J.
Pascoe, Inspector. See stories by Hill, R.
Pigeon, Anna. See stories by Barr, N.
Pine, Leonard. See stories by Lansdale, J. R.
Poole, Tom. See stories by Dold, G.
Popeau, Hercules. See stories by Lowndes, B.
Poteet, Jordan. See stories by Abbott, J.
Quincannon, John. See stories by Pronzini, B.
Rafferty, Shadwell. See stories by Millett, L.
Raffles, A. S. See stories by Hornung, E. W.
Rawlins, Easy. See stories by Mosley, W.
Rebus, Inspector. See stories by Rankin, I.
Repairman Jack. See stories by Wilson, F. P.
Rhodes, Dan. See stories by Crider, B.
Rhyme, Lincoln. See stories by Deaver, J.
Rodrigue, John. See stories by Grissom, K.
Saint, The. See stories by Charteris, L.
Scudder, Matthew. See stories by Block, L.
Shaley, Ben. See stories by Davis, N.
Sheringham, Roger. See stories by Berkeley, A.
Sloan, Inspector. See stories by Aird, C.
Space, Sam. See stories by Nolan, W. F.
Stashower, D. The seven walnuts
Street, Delilah. See stories by Douglas, C. N.
Sughrue, C. W. See stories by Crumley, J.
Taylor, Mitch. See stories by Treat, L.
Thinnes, John. See stories by Dymmoch, M. A.
Thorn, Vince. See stories by Parker, P. S.
Tsung, Ruby. See stories by Cadigan, P.
Twist, Alan. See stories by Halter, P.
Valentino. See stories by Estleman, L. D.
Valmont, Eugene. See stories by Barr, R.
Walker, Amos. See stories by Estleman, L. D.
Warshawski, V. I. See stories by Paretsky, S.
Watson, Sarah. See stories by McCandless, D. B.

DETECTIVES, PRIVATE

Abbott, P. A saving grace
Abella, A. Shanghai
Brodsky, M. Midtown Pythagoras
Cain, P. One, two, three
Cain, P. Pigeon blood
Carrington, T. Last stop, Ditmars
Chandler, R. Killer in the rain
Coen, E. The Russian
Collins, M. A. and Clemens, M. V. East Side, West Side

Collins, M. The kidnapping of Xiang Fei
Crichton, M. Blood doesn't come out
Di Filippo, P. Murder in Geektopia
DuBois, B. Country manners
Gildner, G. Something special
Goodis, D. It's a wise cadaver
Green, S. R. Appetite for murder
Green, S. R. The difference a day makes
Hall, P. Fear of failure
Hammett, D. The scorched face
Harvey, J. Promise
Healy, J. F. A debt to the devil
Herron, D. Knives in the dark
Kaminsky, S. M. Evangeline
Kantner, R. Down home blues
Kinman, G. T. Catnapping
Koretsky, J. L. The cherry on the cake
Levitsky, R. The blue line
Love, R. Riding on the q-ball
MacLean, M. Little sins
Martin, G. R. R. The skin trade
McBain, E. Death flight [variant title: Ticket to death]
McBain, E. Kiss me, Dudley
McNab, C. Animal act
Meaney, J. Via Vortex
Moamrath, M. M. A study in scarlet herrings
Moceri, M. Actual seasons
Moorcock, M. The case of the Nazi canary
Moorcock, M. The flaneur of les arcades de l'opera
Morson, I. The moving-picture mystery
Mosley, W. Karma
Muller, M. Pickpocket
Niles, S. The Y incision
Nolan, W. F. Silk and fire
Parker, J. and Parker, R. B. Galahad, Inc.
Pendarvis, J. Lumber land
Perelman, S. J. Farewell, my lovely appetizer
Petrin, J. R. Car trouble
Pickard, N. There is no crime on Easter Island
Pronzini, B. Souls burning
Pronzini, B. The winning ticket
Redman, B. R. The perfect crime
Richardson, K. The third death of the little clay dog
Robbins, A. B. The magic touch: a Peter Pansy detective yarn
Robinson, P. The cherub affair
Rollins, W. Chicago confetti
Rosenbaum, B. The blow
Rosenblum, M. H. Search engine
Schulz, G. The Panama hen
Smith, A. N. Find me
Sniegoski, T. E. Noah's ophans
Stackpole, M. A. It's the thought that counts
Stewart, P. Mother's day
Swanwick, M. A small room in Koboldtown
Swierczynski, D. The last case of Hilly Palmer
Torrey, R. Concealed weapon
Torrey, R. Mansion of death
Walsh, T. Double check
Wilson, F. P. Part of the game
Wishnia, K. J. A. Viernes loco
Wohlforth, T. The masseuse
Wolfe, G. The detective of dreams
Yorke, C. B. Snowbound

Diaconú, Alina
Blue lagoon
English translations of short stories by contemporary Argentine women writers; edited by Eliana Cazaubon Hermann; translated by Sally Webb Thornton
The evil eye
Díaz, G. J. Women and power in Argentine literature; stories, interviews, and critical essays; [by] Gwendolyn Díaz
The **Diagnosis**. McEwan, I.
A **diagnosis** of death. Bierce, A.
Diago, Evelio Rosero
Brides by night
The Flight of the condor; stories of violence and war from Colombia; translated and compiled by Jennifer Gabrielle Edwards; foreword by Hugo Chaparro Valderrama.
DIALOGUE See Conversation
Dialogue between the two chief world systems. Searls, D.
Diamond, Suzanne
Story: Discovering Ruth
Women's Studies v37 no1 p57-61 Ja/F 2008
Diamond cut diamond with a vengence. Hodgson, W. H.
Diamond dog. Lochte, D.
Diamond girls. Marley, L.
The **diamond** of Jeru. L'Amour, L.
Diamond Sam. Bova, B.
The **diamond** sky. Gerrold, D.
The **diamond** spy. Hodgson, W. H.
Diamond versus Jiminez. Koretsky, J. L.
DIAMONDS
Boothby, G. The Duchess of Wiltshire's diamonds
Dahl, R. The surgeon
Falk, B. There are no pockets in our grave-clothes
Fountain, B. The lion's mouth
Grant, A. The episode of the diamond links
Hodgson, W. H. Diamond cut diamond with a vengence
Irvine, A. C. Shepherded by Galatea
L'Amour, L. The diamond of Jeru
Lecard, M. Teardown
Myers, A. Murder by ghost
Woolrich, C. The heavy sugar
DIANA, PRINCESS OF WALES, 1961-1997
About
Feitell, M. Such a big Mr. England
DIARIES (STORIES ABOUT)
Bingham, S. The big no
Budnitz, J. The kindest cut
Đoàn, L. A question mark for God
Fonseca, R. The notebook
Jackson, S. Vitriol
Levinson, R. S. Chapter 82: Myrna Lloyd is missing
Maxwell, W. What he was like
McCann, R. The diarist
Moceri, M. Actual seasons
Murakami, H. Nausea 1979
Rosenfarb, C. A Friday in the life of Sarah Zonabend
Ruefle, M. The diary
SInger, M. Hazor

DIARIES (STORIES IN DIARY FORM)
See also Letters (Stories in letter form)
Aylett, S. Voyage of the Iguana
Barthelme, D. Me and Miss Mandible
Baumbach, J. Courtship
Bishop, E. Seven-days monologue
Bishop, M. The Yukio Mishima Cultural Association of Kudzu Valley, Georgia
Boyle, T. C. The doubtfulness of water: Madam Knight's journey to New York, 1702
Carl, L. S. Over the sea from Skye
Charnas, S. M. Listening to Brahms
Collins, W. The diary of Ann Rodway
Crowther, P. Bedfordshire
Crowther, P. Bedforshire
Dahl, R. Bitch
Dahl, R. The visitor
Dobozy, T. Radio Blik
France, L. R. School girl
Fuchs, D. A Hollywood diary
Gaiman, N. Pages from a journal found in a shoebox left in a Greyhound bus somewhere between Tulsa, Oklahoma, and Louisville, Kentucky
Guista, M. A walk outside
Hodgson, W. H. The inn of the black crow
Hodgson, W. H. R.M.S. "Empress of Australia"
Martin, G. R. R. From the journal of Xavier Desmond
Martin, G. R. R. The second kind of loneliness
Matheson, R. Dear diary
Michaels, L. Journal
Mohanraj, M. A. Lakshmi's diary (Chicago, 1969)
Munro, A. Powers
Oates, J. C. The fabled light-house at Viña Del Mar
Oates, J. C. Poe posthumous; or, The lighthouse
Roberson, C. And such small deer
Ruefle, M. My search among the birds
Shepard, J. The First South Central Australian Expedition
Shirley, J. Blind eye
Smith, C. A. Beyond the singing flame
Smith, C. A. The city of the singing flame
Smith, C. A. The god of the asteroid [variant title: Master of the asteroid]
Stross, C. Extracts from the club diary
Tham, H. The seventh day
Vidal, G. Pages from an abandoned journal
The **diarist**. McCann, R.
Diary. Charters, D.
The **diary**. Ruefle, M.
Diary of a madman. Gogol', N. V.
The **diary** of Ann Rodway. Collins, W.
Diaz, Junot
2007: New York City: This Is How You Lose Her
Lapham's Quarterly v2 no1 p132-3 Wint 2009
Alma
The New Yorker v83 no41 p52-3 D 24-31 2007
Aurora
The New Granta book of the American short story; edited and introduced by Richard Ford

Diaz, Junot—*Continued*

Beha, C. R. The Ecco anthology of contemporary American short fiction; selected by Joyce Carol Oates and Christopher R. Beha.

The brief wondrous life of Oscar Wao

What are you looking at?; the first fat fiction anthology; edited by Donna Jarrell and Ira Sukrungruang

Edison, New Jersey

Colchie, T. A whistler in the nightworld; short fiction from the Latin Americas; edited by Thomas Colchie

The Paris review book for planes, trains, elevators, and waiting rooms; by the editors of the Paris review; with an introduction by Richard Powers

Wildwood

The PEN/O.Henry Prize stories 2009; chosen and with an introduction by Laura Furman; with essays on the stories They admire most by jurors A. S. Byatt; Anthony Doerr; Tim O'Brien

DiChario, Nick

Alien radio

This is my funniest; leading science fiction writers present their funniest stories ever; edited by Mike Resnick

Dragonhead

The Year's best science fiction: twenty-first annual collection; edited by Gardner Dozois

Dick, Philip K.

The minority report

Adaptations: from short story to big screen; 35 great stories that have inspired great films; edited by Stephanie Harrison

We can remember it for you wholesale

Fourth planet from the sun; tales of Mars from The Magazine of Fantasy & Science Fiction; edited by Gordon Van Gelder

Dick. Nelson, A.

Dick W. and his Pussy, or Tess and her Adequate Dick. Yolen, J.

Dickens, Charles

Hunted down

The Mammoth book of vintage whodunnits; edited by Maxim Jakubowski

The story of the goblins who stole a sexton

Tales before Narnia; the roots of modern fantasy and science fiction; edited by Douglas A. Anderson

DICKENS, CHARLES, 1812-1870

About

Bradbury, R. Any friend of Nicholas Nickleby's is a friend of mine

Edwards, M. The house of the red candle

Waldrop, H. Household words; or, The powers-that-be

Parodies, imitations, etc.

Perry, A. A tale of one city

Dickerson, D. Ellis

Postcretaceous era

The Year's best fantasy and horror: eighteenth annual collection; edited by Ellen Datlow, Kelly Link & Gavin J. Grant

StoryQuarterly no40 p474-82 2004

Dickey, Colin

Keeping Times

TriQuarterly no123 p157-68 2005

Dicking the Buddha. Shivnan, S.

DICKINSON, EMILY, 1830-1886

About

Johnson, G. First surmise

Oates, J. C. EDickinsonRepliLuxe

Willis, C. The soul selects her own society: invasion and repulsion

Willis, C. The soul selects her own society: invasion and repulsion: a chronological reinterpretation of two of Emily Dickinson's poems: a Wellsian perspective

Dickinson, Marc

Something They Hadn't Counted On

The North American Review v292 no3/4 p21-7 My/Ag 2007

Dickinson, Mary Lou

Is

Canadian Woman Studies v26 no1 p14-17 Wint/Spr 2007

Dickinson, Stephanie

Grasshopper Woman

Femspec v7 no1 p91-6 2006

Lucky seven & Dalloway

New stories from the South; the year's best, 2008; selected from U.S. magazines by ZZ Packer with Kathy Pories; with an introduction by ZZ Packer

Man of War

Feminist Studies v31 no2 p310-31 Summ 2005

Slave Quarters

StoryQuarterly v41 p93-117 2005

Unity Cloud

Calyx v24 no3 p26-38 Summ 2008

The **Dickmare**. Ducornet, R.

Dictation. Ozick, C.

DICTATORS

See also Totalitarianism

Bova, B. Sam's war

Budnitz, J. Saving face

Chaponda, D. Heroic proportions

Egan, J. Selling the general

Faber, M. Finesse

Helprin, M. Mar Nueva

James, C. L. R. Emperor Jones and the African drums

Kadare, I. Agamemnon's daughter

Li Yiyun. Immortality

Pratt, T. The tyrant in love

Rivas, M. The girl with the pirate trousers

Shepard, L. Crocodile rock

Zebrowski, G. I walked with Fidel

DICTATORSHIP *See* Dictators

A **dictionary** of saints. Varallo, A.

Did she jump or was she pushed. Kun, M.

Died and gone to heaven. Dufresne, J.

Died and gone to Vegas. Gautreaux, T.

Diehl, Barbara Westwood

Flimflam

Confrontation no90/91 p58-67 Spr/Summ 2005

Diehn, Andi

Walking Circles

The Massachusetts Review v45 no4 p732-41 Wint 2004/2005

Dies Irae. Davis, D. S.

DIETING *See* Reducing

Dietz, William C.
 The run to Hardscrabble Station
  Elemental; the Tsunami relief anthology; sto-
  ries of science fiction and fantasy; [edited
  by] Steven Savile and Alethea Kontis; in-
  troduction by Arthur C. Clarke
Difalco, Salvatore
 The Skunk
  Dalhousie Review v86 no1 p79-87 Spr 2006
The **difference**. Modesitt, L. E., Jr.
The **difference**. Tognazzini, A.
The **difference** a day makes. Green, S. R.
The **difference** between women and men. Lott, B.
A **different** bhel. Shroff, M. F.
A **different** cast of mind. Aird, C.
Different Distances. Kirkpatrick, M.
Different kinds of dead. Gorman, E.
A **different** road. Strout, E.
Different shorelines. Hinton, S. E.
A **Difficult** Man. Camoin, F.
Difficult thoughts. Kalotay, D.
DiFilippo, Paul
 Science fiction
  Witpunk; edited by Claude Lalumière and
  Marty Halpern
Dig for dollars. Wingate, S.
Dig me no grave. Howard, R. E.
Dig this! Out? Baraka, I. A.
The **digging**. Vollmer, M.
Digging his grave. Libin, Z.
Digging in Gehenna. Gerrold, D.
Digression. Hunton, E. R.
Dik, Aizik-Meyer
 The panic; or, The town of Hérres
  No star too beautiful; Yiddish stories from
  1382 to the present; compiled and translat-
  ed by Joachim Neugroschel
The **dilemma** of the dead lady. Woolrich, C.
Dill. Randolph, L.
DILLINGER, JOHN, 1903-1934
             About
  Sayles, J. Dillinger in Hollywood
Dillinger in Hollywood. Sayles, J.
Dills, Todd
 Arcadia
  Chicago noir; edited by Neal Pollack
Dilly. Gordon, M.
Dimension. Munro, A.
The **dimension** of change. Smith, C. A.
The **Dimensions** of Silence. Melnyczuk, A.
Diminished chord. Haldeman, J. W.
Dimitra's Path. Cadbury, A.
Dimitriou, Sotiris
 The plunderer
  Angelic & black; contemporary Greek short
  stories; edited and translated by David
  Connolly; with an introduction by Vangelis
  Hatzivassileiou
Dimitry Gurov's Dowdy wife. Miller, A. L.
Dimmick, Barbara
 Honeymoon
  Ploughshares v34 no1 p46-53 Spr 2008
The **dimple**. Hammett, D.
Dinaburg's Cake. Dorst, D.
Dinesen, Isak
 c. 1600: China Sea: True Blue [Excerpt from
  The Young Man with the Carnation]
  Lapham's Quarterly v2 no3 p181-2 Summ
  2009

Dinezon, Yankev
 The crisis [excerpt]
  No star too beautiful; Yiddish stories from
  1382 to the present; compiled and translat-
  ed by Joachim Neugroschel
Ding-dong-bell. Russell, J.
Dinh, Viet
 Rabbit-in-the-Moon
  Michigan Quarterly Review v44 no1 p79-105
  Wint 2005
 Substitutes
  The PEN/O.Henry Prize stories 2009; chosen
  and with an introduction by Laura Furman;
  with essays on the stories They admire
  most by jurors A. S. Byatt; Anthony Doerr;
  Tim O'Brien
The **Dinner**. Burgin, R.
The **dinner**. Garcia-Aguilera, C.
Dinner at Josette's. Dalton, Q.
Dinner in Audoghast. Sterling, B.
DINNER PARTIES *See* Dinners
The **dinner** party. Baumbach, J.
Dinner party. Charters, D.
The **Dinner** Party. Ferris, J.
Dinner with Osama. Krysl, M.
DINNERS
 Barth, J. Progressive dinner
 Baumbach, J. The dinner party
 Dalton, Q. Dinner at Josette's
 Ducornet, R. Panna cotta
 Dunbar, P. L. A supper by proxy
 Ellin, S. The specialty of the house
 Geary, T. M. Opening day
 Hogan, L. Bush's mourning feast
 Kaftan, V. Scar stories
 Kennedy, C. Wheelbarrow thief
 McLean, S. Dave cooks the turkey
 Myers, A. Murder, the missing heir and the
  boiled egg
 Raymond, J. The suckling pig
 Ronk, M. C. La Belle Dame
 Shields, C. Salt
 Smith, A. End of story
 Steinberg, S. The last guest
 Williams, J. Hammer
Dinners at Six. Leavitt, D.
The **dinosaur**. Taha, M. A.
DINOSAURS
 Beagle, P. S. The fable of the tyrannosaurus rex
 Dann, J. and Dozois, G. R. A change in the
  weather
 De Camp, L. S. A gun for dinosaur
 Dickerson, D. E. Postcretaceous era
 Perlman, E. In the time of the dinosaur
 Powell, M. Sherlock Holmes in the lost world
 Silverberg, R. Hunters in the forest
 Swanwick, M. A great day for brontosaurs
 Swanwick, M. Scherzo with Tyrannosaur
 Swanwick, M. Triceratops summer
 Webb, J. Paradise design'd
 Wolfe, G. Petting zoo
Dintino, Theresa
 Total Lunar Eclipse
  Calyx v25 no1 p13-23 Wint 2009
DIONYSUS
 Silverberg, R. The feast of St. Dionysus
Diorama. Vallese, J.
A **diorama** of the infernal regions; or, The Devil's
 ninth question. Duncan, A.

Dip in the pool. Dahl, R.
DIPENDRA, KING OF NEPAL, 1971-2001
About
Upadhyay, S. The royal ghosts
Diplomatic constraints. Hillhouse, R.
DIPLOMATIC LIFE
Aird, C. The widow's might
Bissell, T. The ambassador's son
Gappah, P. Our man in Geneva wins a million euros
Hemon, A. Stairway to heaven
Hillhouse, R. Diplomatic constraints
Uchida, H. Envoy to Tang China
Ward, A. E. Motherhood and terrorism
DIPLOMATS *See* Diplomatic life
Direct action. Kennedy, C.
Direct action. Thelwell, M.
Directed energy. Hecht, J.
Directions. Benaron, N.
Directions. Wilson, C.
DIRECTORS, MOTION PICTURE *See* Motion picture producers and directors
Director's Cut. Pendleton, J.
Director's cut. Singleton, G.
A **dirge** for Prester John. Valente, C. M.
DIRIGIBLES *See* Airships
Dirt devils. Lansdale, J. R.
Dirt Men. Johnston, T.
Dirty blood. Starr, C.
Dirty boots. Ligon, S.
Dirty Hannah gets hit by a car. Glatt, L.
Dirty heaven. Norton, V.
Dirty laundry. McGruder, K.
Dirty little war. Swanwick, M.
Dirty rice. Erdrich, L.
The **dirty** snowball and white raincoat. James, C. L. R.
Dirty weather. Hurwitz, G.
Dirty wedding. Johnson, D.
Dirty White Dogs. Hoffman, A.
Disability. McIntyre, V.
Disappear. Greenspon, J.
The **disappearance**. Stavans, I.
The **disappearance** of Elaine Coleman. Millhauser, S.
The **disappearance** of Marie Severe. Bramah, E.
DISAPPEARANCES *See* Missing persons
Disappeared girls. Rock, P.
Disappearer. Thorne, M.
Disappearing act. Bova, B.
Disappearing act. Matheson, R.
The **Disappearing** Father. Biaz, B.
The **disaster**. Ibn Sayf Rahabi, M.
Disaster stamps of Pluto. Erdrich, L.
The **disaster** story. Platt, C.
DISASTERS
See also Avalanches; Earthquakes; Epidemics; Famines; Floods; Shipwrecks and castaways
Alarcón, D. The visitor
Brazaitis, M. The ferry
Burke, J. L. Texas City, 1947
DeAndrea, W. L. Sabotage
Finlay, C. C. Footnotes
Lain, D. Shopping at the end of the world
Mukhopadhyay, T. The showers
Pukallus, H. The age of the burning mountains
Shepard, J. Pleasure boating in Lituya Bay
Disasters of War. Smith, R. M.

DISC JOCKEYS
Kelts, R. N. Equilibrium
Pendarvis, J. The pipe
Discarded draft of The shadow over Innsmouth. Lovecraft, H. P.
Discards. Kellerman, F.
Disch, Thomas M.
The abduction of Bunny Steiner; or, A shameless lie
Disch, T. M. The wall of America
Angouleme
New worlds; an anthology; edited by Michael Moorcock
Canned goods
Disch, T. M. The wall of America
A family of the post-apocalypse
Disch, T. M. The wall of America
The first annual performance art festival at the Slaughter Rock Battlefield
Disch, T. M. The wall of America
In praise of older women
Disch, T. M. The wall of America
In Xanadu
Disch, T. M. The wall of America
Jour de fête
Disch, T. M. The wall of America
A knight at the opera
Disch, T. M. The wall of America
The Hudson Review v58 no3 p417-26 Aut 2005
The man who read a book
Disch, T. M. The wall of America
Nights in the garden of the Kerhonkson prison for the aged and infirm
Disch, T. M. The wall of America
One night; or, Scheherazade's bare minimum
Disch, T. M. The wall of America
The owl and the pussycat
Disch, T. M. The wall of America
Painting eggplants
Disch, T. M. The wall of America
Ringtime
Disch, T. M. The wall of America
Three chronicles of Xglotl and Rwang
Disch, T. M. The wall of America
Torah! Torah! Torah!: three Bible tales for the third millennium
Disch, T. M. The wall of America
Voices of the kill
Disch, T. M. The wall of America
The Wall of America
Disch, T. M. The wall of America
The white man
Disch, T. M. The wall of America
Discipline. Pollock, D. R.
Disco. Mozetič, B.
Disco zombies. Phillips, G.
The **discomfited** demon. Bierce, A.
The **discomfiting** brother. Fuentes, C.
Discontinuous lives. Anderson, B.
DISCOTHEQUES
Wilson, F. P. When he was fab
Discourse on the sublime and the beautiful. Grimes, C.
Discovering America. Jones, S. G.
The **discovery**. Barthelme, D.
Diseasemaker's group. Gaiman, N.

DISEASES

See also AIDS (Disease); Alzheimer's disease; Sexually transmitted diseases; Tuberculosis; Vaccines

Accioly, B. João Urso
Anderson, P. Time heals
Atwood, M. Lusus naturae
Bear, G. Darwin's radio [excerpt]
Benedict, P. Bridge of sighs
Butler, O. E. The evening and the morning and the night
Card, O. S. Heal thyself
Cooper, D. Ugly man
Green, Dominic. Send me a mentagram
Jablonski, N. Succor
Lam, V. Contact tracing
Meno, J. Airports of light
Nelson, R. F. River story
Shawl, N. Momi watu
Smith, A. I know something you don't know
Williams, C. Nearly people
Zelazny, R. Come to me not in winter's white

Disentangling. Rock, P.
Disfigured. Palmer, M. and Palmer, D.
The **disgrace** of Jim Scarfedale. Sillitoe, A.

DISGUISES *See* Impersonations

A **dish** served cold. Deaver, J.
The **disinheritors**. Matheson, R.
The **disintegrating** man. Koretsky, J. L.
The **disinterment** of Venus. Smith, C. A.
Dismal light. Zelazny, R.
The **dismantled** invention of fate. Ford, J.

DISMISSAL OF EMPLOYEES

Faiz, J. The prize
Martin, J. Why I got fired
Murr, M. a- . An idyllic world

DISNEY (WALT) COMPANY *See* Walt Disney Company

The **disobedient** son. Fuentes, C.
Disorder destroyers. Goldfaden, J.

DISORDERS OF PERSONALITY *See* Personality disorders

Dispersal. Weaver, W.
The **displaced** person. O'Connor, F.
Displacement. Faust, R.
Disquisition on tears. Reents, S.
Dissecting the soul. Thomas, J.
Dissed. Wishnia, K. J. A.

DISSENTERS

Walbert, K. Do something

DISSIDENTS *See* Dissenters

Distance man. Schwarzschild, E.
Distances. Di Filippo, P.
Distant ships. Van Booy, S.
The **Distant** Sound of Engines [Reprint] Budrys, A.

DISTILLING, ILLICIT *See* Moonshiners

Distraction in the literary life. Bukowski, C.
The **distributor**. Matheson, R.

DISTRICT OF COLUMBIA *See* Washington (D.C.)

Disturbance-loving species. Chilson, P.
The **Disturbing** Occurrences. Mahfouz, N.
The **disturbing** occurrences. Maḥfūẓ, N.

Divakaruni, Chitra Banerjee

The lives of strangers
Pushcart prize XXVII; best of the small presses; edited by Bill Henderson with the Pushcart prize editors

Mrs. Dutta writes a letter
California uncovered; stories for the 21st century; edited by Chitra Banerjee Divakaruni, William E. Justice, and James Quay

Divertimento. Frost, G.
Dives. Parks, T.
Dividing the sustain. Kelly, J. P.
Divination. McGruder, K.
Divine Afflatus. Gilette, J.
Divine droplets. Woods, P. L.
Divine madness. Zelazny, R.

DIVING

Shomer, E. Rapture

Diving. Crenshaw, P.
The **diving** girl. Laymon, R.

DIVORCE

See also Desertion and nonsupport; Divorced persons; Marriage problems

Abbott, L. K. Martians
Apple, M. Talker
Archer, J. The wisdom of Solomon
Auchincloss, L. The call of the wild
Bahah, M. O. A parting shot
Bakken, K. N. The effects of light
Bakken, K. N. Renter's guide to the Hamptons
Bakken, K. N. Vigil
Barnes, S. Earthquake
Barry, R. Men shoot things to kill them
Barthelme, D. The agreement
Barthelme, D. The big broadcast of 1938
Bass, R. Yazoo
Baxter, C. Gina's death
Beattie, A. The garden game
Benjamin, C. L. The last supper
Blum, J. The kind of luxuries we felt we deserved
Castillon, C. Punching bag
Clayton, J. J. An old 3 a.m. story
D'Ambrosio, C., Jr. The high divide
D'Ambrosio, C., Jr. Open house
Desaulniers, J. The good fight
Ducornet, R. Divorce
Gabriele, L. Don't let the 100 percent divorce rate spoil your wedding!
Ghadir, M. A. a- . I was betrayed with a single golden pound
Gonzalez, K. A. Statehood
Gordimer, N. Alternative endings: the first sense
Harleman, A. Sharks
Henriquez, C. Mercury
Higgins, G. V. The easiest thing in the world
Holladay, C. C. The biggest and the best
Keret, E. Himme
Kovar, V. The all-night dentist
Link, K. The great divorce
Lunstrum, K. S. Baby love
Luvaas, W. Carpentry
McCafferty, J. Embraced
McCorkle, J. Crash diet
McGlynn, D. Moonland on fire
McNett, M. Catalog sales
Molodowsky, K. The divorce
Molodowsky, K. A fur coat
Nelson, A. Nothing right
Nelson, A. Some fun
Reah, D. Glazed
Rodgers, S. J. Fits and starts
Shimamoto, R. Inside
Shomer, E. The other mother

DIVORCED PERSONS—*Continued*

Schwarzschild, E. Spring Garden

Selgin, P. Our cups are bottomless

Shinn, S. The house of seven spirits

Shomer, E. Rapture

Sillitoe, A. The meeting

Singer, I. B. Exes

Singleton, G. What attracts us to Gruel

Skabardonis, Y. Mussels in the flower vase

Stamm, P. In strange gardens

Stern, R. G. My ex, the moral philosopher

Swan, G. A garden amid fires

Tait, J. Reasons for concern regarding my girlfriend of five days, Monica Garza

Tallent, E. Tabriz

Thompson, J. Her untold story

Tomlinson, J. First husband, first wife

Tomlinson, J. Squirrels

Tower, W. Down through the valley

Tower, W. On the show

Treat, J. Make a nest

Trevor, W. On the streets

Ulitskaya, L. The queen of spades

Upadhyay, S. The weight of a gun

Updike, J. The journey to the dead

Varallo, A. Pool season

Vogrin, V. The hotel-motel bar & grill

Vollmer, M. Straightedge

Watkins, S. A jelly of light

Weiner, J. Regret

Welch, N. Tender foot

Welsh, I. If you liked school, you'll love work . . .

West, D. The lettters

Wieland, M. The bones of hagerman

Wieland, M. God's dogs

Wieland, M. The king of infinite space

Wieland, M. The mistress of the horse god

Wieland, M. The prodigal son

Wieland, M. Solstice

Wieland, M. Swan in retreat

Wieland, M. Swan's home

Wieland, M. Swan's song

Windley, C. Children's games

DIVORCÉES *See* Divorced persons

DIVORCÉS *See* Divorced persons

Dix, Shane

(jt. auth) See Williams, Sean and Dix, Shane

Dixon, Chuck

Barrens

Kolchak: the night stalker chronicles; 26 original tales of the surreal, the bizarre, the macabre; edited by Joe Gentile, Garrett Anderson, Lori Gentile; Kolchak created by Jeff Rice

Dixon, Kent H.

Wake

The Antioch Review v67 no3 p460-1 Summ 2009

Dixon, Stephen

Down the road

The Anchor book of new American short stories; edited by Ben Marcus

The Fool

New England Review v28 no1 p37-43 2007

Pain

The Best of the Bellevue Literary Review; edited by Dannielle Ofri and the staff of the Bellevue Literary Review

Phone Ring Two

TriQuarterly no123 p238-48 2005

The Shade

StoryQuarterly v40 p413-30 2004

Time to go

So the story goes; twenty-five years of the Johns Hopkins short fiction series; edited by John T. Irwin and Jean McGarry; with a foreword by John Barth

Winter

New England Review v27 no1 p161-3 2006

Dizzy-headed Dick. Dunbar, P. L.

Dizzy when you look down in. Malla, P.

Djamilla. D'Souza, T.

Djebar, Assia

The Attack

The Literary Review (Madison, N.J.) v50 no1 p63-75 Fall 2006

The **Djinn's** wife. McDonald, I.

Do not deny me. Thompson, J.

Do not disturb. Homes, A. M.

Do not revive. Monk, B.

Do something. Walbert, K.

Do that everywhere. Luongo, M.

Do the blind dream? Gifford, B.

Do they know it's Christmas? Donoghue, E.

Do unto others [excerpt] Abbott, J.

Do ya, do ya, wanna dance? Waldrop, H.

Do you think I am who I will be? Schutt, C.

Doak, Emily

Spring across from West Point

Gettysburg Review v21 no4 p553-69 Wint 2008

Đoàn, Lê

Achieving flyhood

Đoàn, L. The cemetery of Chua village and other stories; by Doan Le; chief translator, Rosemary Nguyen, with additional translations by Duong Tuong and Wayne Karlin

The cemetery of Chua village

Đoàn, L. The cemetery of Chua village and other stories; by Doan Le; chief translator, Rosemary Nguyen, with additional translations by Duong Tuong and Wayne Karlin

The clone

Đoàn, L. The cemetery of Chua village and other stories; by Doan Le; chief translator, Rosemary Nguyen, with additional translations by Duong Tuong and Wayne Karlin

The double bed of Chua village

Đoàn, L. The cemetery of Chua village and other stories; by Doan Le; chief translator, Rosemary Nguyen, with additional translations by Duong Tuong and Wayne Karlin

Guot's love

Đoàn, L. The cemetery of Chua village and other stories; by Doan Le; chief translator, Rosemary Nguyen, with additional translations by Duong Tuong and Wayne Karlin

A question mark for God

Đoàn, L. The cemetery of Chua village and other stories; by Doan Le; chief translator, Rosemary Nguyen, with additional translations by Duong Tuong and Wayne Karlin

The real estate of Chua village

Đoàn, L. The cemetery of Chua village and other stories; by Doan Le; chief translator, Rosemary Nguyen, with additional translations by Duong Tuong and Wayne Karlin

Đoàn, Lê—*Continued*

Sesame seed

Đoàn, L. The cemetery of Chua village and other stories; by Doan Le; chief translator, Rosemary Nguyen, with additional translations by Duong Tuong and Wayne Karlin

The venus of Chua village

Đoàn, L. The cemetery of Chua village and other stories; by Doan Le; chief translator, Rosemary Nguyen, with additional translations by Duong Tuong and Wayne Karlin

The wooden cottage

Đoàn, L. The cemetery of Chua village and other stories; by Doan Le; chief translator, Rosemary Nguyen, with additional translations by Duong Tuong and Wayne Karlin

Dobozy, Tamas

Dead letters

Dobozy, T. Last notes and other stories

Four uncles

Dobozy, T. Last notes and other stories

The inert landscapes of György Ferenc

Dobozy, T. Last notes and other stories

Into the ring

Dobozy, T. Last notes and other stories

Last notes

Dobozy, T. Last notes and other stories

The Laughing Cat

Dobozy, T. Last notes and other stories

The man who came out of the corner of my eye

Dobozy, T. Last notes and other stories

Philip's killer hat

Dobozy, T. Last notes and other stories

Radio Blik

Dobozy, T. Last notes and other stories

Stories of Forgery

Confrontation no98/99 p100-19 Spr/Summ 2007

Tales of Hungarian resistance

Dobozy, T. Last notes and other stories

Dobrovodsky, Martin

Appointment

Dalhousie Review v87 no3 p373-81 Aut 2007

Dobson, Clara L.

When Jennie saved the windmill

Adventures in the West; stories for young readers; edited by Susanne George Bloomfield and Eric Melvin Reed

Dobson, Joanne

Hey, girlie

Bronx noir; edited by S. J. Rozan

Docent. Smith, R. T.

The **doctor**. Emshwiller, C.

The **doctor** and the patient. Buckler, E.

Doctor Benn's Astrolabe. Šteger, A.

Doctor Graesler. Schnitzler, A.

Doctor Hood. Gallagher, S.

Doctor Olaf van Schuler's brain, 1664. Menger-Anderson, K.

DOCTOR WHO (TELEVISION PROGRAM: 1963-1989)

Boudinot, R. So little time

Doctorow, Cory

After the siege

Doctorow, C. Overclocked; stories of the future present

Anda's game

The Best American short stories, 2005; selected from U.S. and Canadian magazines by Michael Chabon with Katrina Kenison; with an introduction by Michael Chabon

Doctorow, C. Overclocked; stories of the future present

The Starry rift; tales of new tomorrows: an original science fiction anthology; edited by Jonathan Strahan

I, robot

Doctorow, C. Overclocked; stories of the future present

I, row-boat

Doctorow, C. Overclocked; stories of the future present

The Year's best science fiction: twenty-fourth annual collection; edited by Gardner Dozois

OwnzOreo

Nebula Awards showcase 2005; the year's best SF and fantasy; selected by the Science Fiction and Fantasy Writers of America; edited by Jack Dann

Printcrime

Doctorow, C. Overclocked; stories of the future present

Nature v439 p242 Ja 12 2006

To go boldly

The new space opera 2; edited by Gardner Dozois and Jonathan Strahan

When sysadmins ruled the earth

Doctorow, C. Overclocked; stories of the future present

Rewired; the post-cyberpunk anthology; James Patrick Kelly & John Kessel, editors

Doctorow, E. L.

Child, dead, in the rose garden

The Pushcart Prize XXX: best of the small presses 2006; edited by Bill Henderson with the Pushcart Prize editors

A house on the plains

Beha, C. R. The Ecco anthology of contemporary American short fiction; selected by Joyce Carol Oates and Christopher R. Beha.

Wakefield

The New Yorker v83 no43 p60-6, 68-74 Ja 14 2008

DOCTORS *See* Physicians; Surgeons; Women physicians

The **doctors,** 2006. Menger-Anderson, K.

Doctor's Boys. Watson, L.

Doctor's orders. Cutler, J.

The **doctor's** visit. Garland, H.

Documentary. Goldfaden, J.

Documenting my abduction. Kluge, C. B.

DOCUMENTS *See* Manuscripts

Documents in the case of Elizabeth Akeley. Lupoff, R. A.

Documents of passion love. Ferrell, C.

Dodge, Mary Mapes

The Silver Skates

The Saturday Evening Post v278 no1 p82, 84-5 Ja/F 2006

Dodgson, Charles Lutwidge *See* Carroll, Lewis, 1832-1898

DODOS

Waldrop, H. The ugly chickens

Doench, Meredith
On the Importance of the Lesbian Continuum at Daytona Beach, 2004: A Scale of One Young Woman's Sexuality
Women's Studies Quarterly v34 no3/4 p225-31 Fall/Wint 2006

Doerr, Anthony
The caretaker
The Anchor book of new American short stories; edited by Ben Marcus
Village 113
The O. Henry Prize stories 2008; edited and with an introduction by Laura Furman; with essays on the stories they admire most by jurors Chimamanda Ngozi Adiche, David Leavitt, David Means

Does a man need much? Zoshchenko, M.

Does God obey his own law?: A Sister Fidelma story. Tremayne, P.

Does your job application put your company at risk? Kun, M.

The **Dog**. Doyle, R.

Dog. Lansdale, J. R.

The **dog**. Livings, J.

Dog. Welch, N.

The **Dog** Ate My . . . Siegel, G. L.

Dog-eared paperback of my life. Shepard, L.

The **dog** in Ganegwag. Bierce, A.

Dog loves Ellie. McClanahan, E.

The **dog** of the drops. Wolfe, G.

The **dog** of the marriage. Hempel, A.

Dog person. Nicholson, S.

DOG RACING
Dahl, R. Claud's dog: Mr Feasey
Keane, J. B. A tale of two furs
Livings, J. The dog
The **dog** said bow-wow. Swanwick, M.

DOG SLED RACING *See* Sled dog racing

Dog song. Pancake, A.

Dog stories. Tudish, C.

Dog tags. Allen, J. R.

DOGFIGHTING
Davidson, C. A mean utility
Wolven, S. Barracuda

Dogged. O'Keitinn, R.

A **dogged** sense of smell. Zoshchenko, M.

Doggy love. Bradfield, S.

Dogology. Boyle, T. C.

DOGS
Alarcón, D. Lima, Peru; July 28, 1979
Allyn, D. Dead as a dog
Amdahl, G. The flight from California
Angel, J. Donny
Arnow, H. L. S. The hunter
Arnow, H. L. S. King Devil's bargain
Auslander, S. Heimish knows all
Bach, M. Full moon
Bacigalupi, P. The people of sand and slag
Bear, E. Sleeping dogs lie
Bensko, J. The ocean
Berg, E. The only one of millions just like him
Berry, W. Mike
Bierce, A. The dog in Ganegwag
Bierce, A. "The following dorg"
Bierce, A. How I came to like dogs
Bierce, A. That dog
Bishop, T. Someone's dog
Boggs, J. D. Red River Crossing
Boyle, T. C. Dogology

Bradbury, R. No news; or, What killed the dog?
Bradbury, R. Pater caninus
Bradfield, S. Dazzle redux
Bradfield, S. Dazzle's inferno
Bradfield, S. Doggy love
Bunin, I. A. Chang's dreams
Busch, F. Patrols
Capps, T. Alice
Carver, R. Jerry and Molly and Sam
Chekhov, A. P. 75 Grand [variant title: 75,000]
Chekhov, A. P. The conversation of a man with a dog
Chekhov, A. P. An expensive dog
Cody, L. Listen
Corso, P. Shelf life
Coyne, S. Hunting country
Dahl, R. Claud's dog: Mr Feasey
Desaulniers, J. The next day
Domecq, B. Balzac
Donoghue, E. Do they know it's Christmas?
Doran, M. M. Showdown
Dufresne, J. Electric limits of our widest senses
Dufresne, J. Johnny too bad
Dufresne, J. Squeeze the feeling
Duval, P. Cellular
Eggers, D. After I was thrown in the river and before I drowned
Elyshevitz, A. Hermano
Erdrich, L. Almost soup
Erdrich, L. Father's milk
Erdrich, L. Lazy stitch: almost soup
Faber, M. The hundred and ninety-nine steps
Fisher, C. Chickens
Fox, P. Grace
Gerber, M. J. Dogs bark
Gerrold, D. Chester
Gerrold, D. A shaggy dog story
Gordimer, N. Alternative endings: the third sense
Graham, T. The blue book of dogs
Grimes, C. Vivisection
Hawes, L. Spring cleaning
Hempel, A. Breathing Jesus
Hempel, A. The center
Hempel, A. The children's party
Hempel, A. Church cancels cow
Hempel, A. The dog of the marriage
Hempel, A. Nashville gone to ashes
Henderson, J. Wet dog of Galveston
Heuler, K. Down on the farm
Holappa, P. Boman
Jance, J. A. Highest, best use
Johnson, K. The evolution of trickster stories among the dogs of North Park after the change
Kellerman, F. Malibu dog
Kelly, J. P. The edge of nowhere
Kennedy, C. Kill or cure
Kennedy, C. A pitch too high for the human ear
Kenney, S. The death of the dog and other rescues
Kercheval, J. L. Damage
Keret, E. Actually, I've had some phenomenal hard-ons lately
Keret, E. Shooting Tuvia
Khalifah, 'A. A. The dogs
Kress, N. Laws of survival
Kulpa, K. How the light walks
Kun, M. The baker's dog

DOGS—*Continued*

Langan, J. Episode seven: last stand against the Pack in the kingdom of the purple flowers
Lansdale, J. R. Dog
Lansdale, J. R. The pit
Leung, B. Dog sleep
Lewis, W. H. Potcake
Link, K. The hortlak
Livings, J. The dog
Lochte, D. Diamond dog
Lyons, D. The Greyhound
MacEnulty, P. The bargain
MacLeod, A. Winter dog
Ma'mami, S. a.- . The white dog
Marion, S. Dogs with human faces
Marusek, D. The earth is on the mend
Mason, B. A. Lying doggo
McBain, E. Barking at butterflies
McCafferty, J. The dog who saved her
McHugh, M. F. In the air
McHugh, M. F. Laika comes back safe
McNab, C. Animal act
McNett, M. One dog happy
McRae, D. Never drop by
Meacham, R. Worship for shut-ins
Miller, A. Bulldog
Mindt, A. Ruby
Monk, B. Little yellow dogs
Montemarano, N. Man throws dog out window
Mosley, W. Black dog
Mundis, J. The luger is a 9MM automatic handgun with a parabellum action
Murphy, Y. Into the arms of the man on the moon
Murphy, Y. Is this a land, a continent, can it be conquered?
Murphy, Y. The lost breed
Murphy, Y. Whitely on the tips
Nelson, D. E. Bay
Nicholson, S. Dog person
O'Callaghan, M. Going to the dogs
Ochsner, G. A blessing
Ohlin, A. In trouble with the Dutchman
O'Keitinn, R. Dogged
Pancake, A. Dog song
Pflug, U. Border crossings
Pflug, U. A dog's life
Phillips, G. The accomplice
Qi, S. Love me, love my dog
Quertermous, B. Cadaver dog
Quiroga, H. Sunstroke
Rahman, I. Here come the dog people
Rajaniemi, H. His master's voice
Ramos, G. Whale
Rand, K. Buzzards of Oz
Rand, K. Good dog
Randolph, L. The girls
Raymond, J. Train choir
Reed, R. Roxie
Reese, J. Taser
Reinhorn, H. The white dog
Resnick, M. and Faw, B. A muse with burning eyes
Richter, S. Velvet
Rivas, M. Carmiña
Rivas, M. The coming of wisdom with time
Roberson, J. Sleeping dogs
Rock, P. The silent men
Romm, R. Where nothing is

Rust, E. M. Stealing Yakima
Salter, J. My Lord you
Saunders, G. Puppy
Saunders, G. The red bow
Schmuck, R. The results of a dog going blind
Schuman, D. Stay
Shepard, J. Piano stops here
Shepard, J. Reach for the sky
Shepard, J. Runway
Shiina, M. The yellow tent on the roof
Shrayer-Petrov, D. Rusty
Sillitoe, A. No name in the street
Singleton, G. Lickers
Singleton, G. Runt
Stafford, J. In the zoo
Steele, A. M. The war of dogs and boids
Stefaniak, M. H. You love that dog
Stelmok, J. Maggie
Stine, R. L. Wifey
Strom, D. Grass roof, tin roof [excerpt]
Swanwick, M. The dog said bow-wow
Toganov, B. The children
Treat, J. Listing
Treat, J. Trail
Vollmer, M. Freebleeders
Welch, N. Dog
Welsh, I. The DOGS of Lincoln Park
Wendroff, Z. Caesar and Nero
West, D. Interlude
West, D. Skippy
West, D. Summer setting
Williams, J. Substance
Willis, C. The last of the Winnebagos
Windley, C. The reading Elvis
Wolfe, G. Calamity warps
Wolfe, G. The dog of the drops
Wolfe, G. Golden city far
Wolff, T. The chain
Wolff, T. Her dog
Woolson, C. F. A transplanted boy
Yarbrough, S. Two dogs
Zelazny, R. The last Inn on the road with Dannie Plachta
Zoshchenko, M. A dogged sense of smell

Training

Bass, R. The hermit's story
Burke, J. Lost and found
Roley, B. A. American son [excerpt]

The **dogs**. Khalifah, 'A. A.
Dogs. Marshall, J.
Dogs. Rheinheimer, K.
Dogs bark. Gerber, M. J.
The **dogs** in the great Glen. Kiely, B.
A **dog's** life. Pflug, U.
The **DOGS** of Lincoln Park. Welsh, I.
Dogs with human faces. Marion, S.
Doing good. Bingham, S.

Dokey, Richard

Ace
    Dokey, R. Pale morning dun; stories
The Barber's Tale
    Southern Humanities Review v40 no4 p348-58 Fall 2006
The beggar of Union Square
    Dokey, R. Pale morning dun; stories
Electric dog
    Dokey, R. Pale morning dun; stories

Dokey, Richard—*Continued*
  Flight from Cytherea
    Southern Humanities Review v43 no1 p30-40
      Wint 2009
  The Gambler
    Confrontation no98/99 p51-60 Spr/Summ
      2007
  Hampstead's folly
    Dokey, R. Pale morning dun; stories
  A house in order
    Dokey, R. Pale morning dun; stories
  Monkey
    Dokey, R. Pale morning dun; stories
  The monster
    Dokey, R. Pale morning dun; stories
  The mouse
    Dokey, R. Pale morning dun; stories
  Never trust the weatherman
    Dokey, R. Pale morning dun; stories
  Pale morning dun
    Dokey, R. Pale morning dun; stories
  The shopper
    Dokey, R. Pale morning dun; stories
  The suicide
    Dokey, R. Pale morning dun; stories
  Vital statistics
    Dokey, R. Pale morning dun; stories
Dold, Gaylord
  Bay of sorrows [excerpt]
    Lone Star sleuths; an anthology of Texas
      crime fiction; edited and with an introduc-
      tion by Bill Cunningham, Steven L. Davis,
      and Rollo K. Newsom.
Dolinin, V.
  The Pit: A Novella of Camp Life
    World Literature Today v81 no5 p53-4 S/O
      2007
The **doll**. Tsiaboussis, V.
Doll: a romance of the Mississippi. Oates, J. C.
The **doll** house. Gardiner, J. R.
The **doll** that does everything. Matheson, R.
Dolleman, Rusty
  September, 1981
    Iowa Review v37 no1 p31-42 Spr 2007
Dollface. Arnott, M.
DOLLS
        See also Barbie dolls
  Dalton, Q. Package
  Hawes, L. Spring cleaning
  Jablonski, N. Big guy
  Lefer, D. Angle and grip
  Matheson, R. The doll that does everything
  Matheson, R. Prey
  Nisbet, R. Reconnaissance
  Nye, J. L. The revenge of Chatty Cathy
  Rusch, K. K. Losing Dolly
  Shields, C. Dolls, dolls, dolls, dolls
  Sussex, L. Frozen Charlottes
Dolls, dolls, dolls, dolls. Shields, C.
Dolls, revenge, dolls again. Dunning, C.
Dollywood. Martin, M.
Dolores, Carmen
  Aunt Zézé's tears
    Oxford anthology of the Brazilian short story;
      edited by K. David Jackson
DOLPHINS
  Silverberg, R. Ishmael in love
  Zelazny, R. 'Kjwalll'kje'k'koothaïlll'kje'k

Dolphins Dancing Somewhere off the Coast of
    Cuba. Haken, N.
Dolton, Brian
  The box of beautiful things
    Orson Scott Card's Intergalctic medicine
      show; [edited by] Edmund R. Schubert and
      Orson Scott Card
Dome. Lennon, B.
The **dome**. Millhauser, S.
Domecq, Brianda
  Adelaide's body
    Domecq, B. When I was a horse; translated
      by Kay (Kayla) S. Garcia
  Balzac
    Domecq, B. When I was a horse; translated
      by Kay (Kayla) S. Garcia
  A brief exercise in the absurd
    Domecq, B. When I was a horse; translated
      by Kay (Kayla) S. Garcia
  Earl
    Domecq, B. When I was a horse; translated
      by Kay (Kayla) S. Garcia
  The eternal theater
    Domecq, B. When I was a horse; translated
      by Kay (Kayla) S. Garcia
  Galatea
    Domecq, B. When I was a horse; translated
      by Kay (Kayla) S. Garcia
  Gift of the jaguar
    Domecq, B. When I was a horse; translated
      by Kay (Kayla) S. Garcia
  In memoriam
    Domecq, B. When I was a horse; translated
      by Kay (Kayla) S. Garcia
  The Judas-tail
    Domecq, B. When I was a horse; translated
      by Kay (Kayla) S. Garcia
  Lillith
    Domecq, B. When I was a horse; translated
      by Kay (Kayla) S. Garcia
  Mozart day
    Domecq, B. When I was a horse; translated
      by Kay (Kayla) S. Garcia
  Mr. Clunk!
    Domecq, B. When I was a horse; translated
      by Kay (Kayla) S. Garcia
  Of cheese and Christ
    Domecq, B. When I was a horse; translated
      by Kay (Kayla) S. Garcia
  Sammaël
    Domecq, B. When I was a horse; translated
      by Kay (Kayla) S. Garcia
  Sammaël and Lillith
    Domecq, B. When I was a horse; translated
      by Kay (Kayla) S. Garcia
  The turtle
    Domecq, B. When I was a horse; translated
      by Kay (Kayla) S. Garcia
  When I was a horse
    Domecq, B. When I was a horse; translated
      by Kay (Kayla) S. Garcia
Domestic architecture. Downs, G.
Domestic bliss. Zoshchenko, M.
The **domestic** cantata. Malouf, D.
DOMESTIC RELATIONS *See* Family life
Domestic Relations. Schall, J.
Domingue, Ronlyn
  Broken Silence
    New England Review v26 no1 p46-55 2005

Doogan, Mike

The death of Clickclickwhistle

Powers of detection; stories of mystery & fantasy; edited by Dana Stabenow

Glamour

Unusual suspects; stories of mystery & fantasy; edited by Dana Stabenow.

War can be murder

The World's finest mystery and crime stories, fourth annual collection; edited by Ed Gorman and Martin H. Greenberg

Dooling, Richard

Roe #5

Burnham, C. Who can save us now?; brand-new superheroes and their amazing [short] stories; edited by Owen King and John McNally; [illustrations by Chris Burnham]

DOOLITTLE, JAMES HAROLD, 1896-1993

About

Mina, J. I shall return

Doolittle, Sean

Mr. big deal

Burnham, C. Who can save us now?; brand-new superheroes and their amazing [short] stories; edited by Owen King and John McNally; [illustrations by Chris Burnham]

The **doom** of love in small places. Scholes, K.

The **doom** of love is small spaces. Scholes, K.

The **doom** that came to Dunwich. Lupoff, R. A.

Door. Erdrich, L.

The **door**. Simpson, H.

The **Door** in the Woods. Gossy, D.

Door in your eye. Tower, W.

The **Door** Man. Vogel, L.

Door number 279. Gordin, J.

Door number one. Kobrin, L.

Door of Deception. Wood, S. J. H.

The **door** to Saturn. Smith, C. A.

The **doorman's** swellage. Ducornet, R.

The **doors** of his face, the lamps of his mouth. Zelazny, R.

The **dope**. Block, L.

The **dope** show. Wishnia, K. J. A.

Doppelganger. Bowen, R.

Doran, Maggie Morgan

Billy and Benjamin too

Doran, M. M. Gentle hearts, guilty sins

End October

Doran, M. M. Gentle hearts, guilty sins

The estate of Joseph P. Bosley

Doran, M. M. Gentle hearts, guilty sins

A family in winter

Doran, M. M. Gentle hearts, guilty sins

The giver

Doran, M. M. Gentle hearts, guilty sins

Golden anniversary

Doran, M. M. Gentle hearts, guilty sins

Showdown

Doran, M. M. Gentle hearts, guilty sins

They shall have music

Doran, M. M. Gentle hearts, guilty sins

A time too soon

Doran, M. M. Gentle hearts, guilty sins

Wedding at the Gormay Cafe

Doran, M. M. Gentle hearts, guilty sins

A well-arranged life

Doran, M. M. Gentle hearts, guilty sins

Zachary's miracle cure

Doran, M. M. Gentle hearts, guilty sins

Dorchie. Park, E.

DORDOGNE (FRANCE) *See* France—Dordogne

Dorfman, Ariel

Gringos

The O. Henry Prize stories 2007; edited and with an introduction by Laura Furman; with essays on the story they admire most by jurors Charles D'Ambrosio, Ursula K. Le Guin, Lily Tuck

Stew

Daedalus v135 no4 p105-7 Fall 2006

Dori Bangs. Sterling, B.

Doris is coming. Packer, Z.

Dormen, Lesley

The best place to be

Dormen, L. The best place to be

Curvy

Dormen, L. The best place to be

Ploughshares v31 no2/3 p109-24 Fall 2005

Figure of a woman

Dormen, L. The best place to be

General strike

Dormen, L. The best place to be

Gladiators

Dormen, L. The best place to be

I asked my mother

Dormen, L. The best place to be

The old economy husband

Dormen, L. The best place to be

The secret of drawing

Dormen, L. The best place to be

Dormez Vous? Troy, M.

The **dormition** of the virgin. Donoghue, E.

DORMITORIES

Raphael, L. Roy's Jewish problem

Dorothy. Woolson, C. F.

Dorothy Loves maleman. Fulton, A.

Dörrie, Doris

The Father of the Bride

The Massachusetts Review v48 no2 p225-31 Summ 2007

Dors, mon petit, dors. Nisbet, R.

DORSET (ENGLAND) *See* England—Dorset

Dorsey, Candas Jane

Mom and Mother Teresa

Year's best fantasy 6; edited by David G. Hartwell & Kathryn Cramer

Dorst, Doug

Dinaburg's Cake

StoryQuarterly v42 p176-208 2006

Dosie, of Killakeet Island. Hickam, H.

Dostoevskiĭ, Fedor Mikhaĭlovich *See* Dostoyevsky, Fyodor, 1821-1881

Dostoyevsky, Fyodor

Bobok

Worlds apart; an anthology of Russian fantasy and science fiction; edited and with commentary by Alexander Levitsky; translated by Alexander Levitsky and Martha T. Kitchen

The dream of a ridiculous man

Worlds apart; an anthology of Russian fantasy and science fiction; edited and with commentary by Alexander Levitsky; translated by Alexander Levitsky and Martha T. Kitchen

Dostoyevsky, Fyodor—*Continued*
  The inquisitor general
    A cross of centuries; twenty-five imaginative
      tales about the Christ; edited by Michael
      Bishop
  The little boy at the Savior's Christmas tree
    Worlds apart; an anthology of Russian fantasy
      and science fiction; edited and with com-
      mentary by Alexander Levitsky; translated
      by Alexander Levitsky and Martha T.
      Kitchen
DOSTOYEVSKY, FYODOR, 1821-1881
                    About
  ŤSypkin, L. Summer in Baden-Baden [excerpt]
          Parodies, imitations, etc.
  O'Shaughnessy, P. His master's hand
Dot Com Indian. Bull, J. S.
The **double** bed of Chua village. Đoàn, L.
Double Charley. Stern, R. G.
Double check. Walsh, T.
The **double** crossing. Dexter, C.
The **double** dealer. Liss, D.
Double diet. Berg, E.
The **double-edged** sword. Shinn, S.
Double espresso. Soracco, S.
Double exposure. Johnson, G.
Double feature. Woolrich, C.
The **Double** Happiness Bun. Gilchrist, E.
Double jeopardy. Deaver, J.
The **Double** Knot. Toews, M.
The **double** shadow. Smith, C. A.
Double trouble. Tognazzini, A.
The **doubled-dyed** villains. Anderson, P.
Doubles. Bradbury, R.
The **doubtfulness** of water: Madam Knight's jour-
      ney to New York, 1702. Boyle, T. C.
Doucement, s'il vous plaît. Sallis, J.
Dough. Dalton, Q.
Doughtie, Edward
  Headache
    South Carolina Review v39 no2 p137-43 Spr
      2007
Dougla. Manickchand, R. A.
Douglas, Carole Nelson
  Bogieman
    Unusual suspects; stories of mystery & fanta-
      sy; edited by Dana Stabenow.
  Junior partner in crime
    Creature cozies; edited by Jill M. Morgan
    Wolf Woman Bay; and nine more of the
      finest crime and mystery novellas of the
      year; edited by Ed Gorman and Martin H.
      Greenberg
  Lawn and order
    Deadly housewives; edited by Christine Mat-
      thews
  The riches there that lie
    Poe's lighthouse; all new collaborations with
      Edgar Allan Poe; edited by Christopher
      Conlon
  Strangers in a strange land
    Thou shalt not kill; biblical mystery stories;
      edited by Anne Perry
  Those are pearls that were his eyes
    The World's finest mystery and crime stories,
      fourth annual collection; edited by Ed
      Gorman and Martin H. Greenberg

Douglas, Conda V.
  The Moebius Strip
    Idaho Magazine v3 no12 p56-60 S 2004
Douglas, Marcia
  Marie-Ma
    Femspec v6 no1 p113-21 2005
Douglas, Michael *See* Crichton, Michael, 1942-
      2008
DOUGLASS, FREDERICK, 1817?-1895
                    About
  Almond, S. Lincoln, arisen
Douglass, Frederick Rice
  Abolitionists of Mars
    Raritan v26 no3 p71-81 Wint 2007
Douglass, Sara
  This way to the exit
    Dreaming again; thirty-five new stories cele-
      brating the wild side of Australian fiction;
      edited by Jack Dann
Douka, Marō
  Carré fix
    Angelic & black; contemporary Greek short
      stories; edited and translated by David
      Connolly; with an introduction by Vangelis
      Hatzivassileiou
Dourado, Autran
  Bald island
    Oxford anthology of the Brazilian short story;
      edited by K. David Jackson
Dousie O'Dea. Keane, J. B.
The **dove** came down. Westcott, G.
Dove season. Harrison, W.
Doves in the circle. Moorcock, M.
Dowling, Terry
  Clownette
    The Year's best fantasy and horror: eighteenth
      annual collection; edited by Ellen Datlow,
      Kelly Link & Gavin J. Grant
  Flashmen
    The Year's best science fiction: twenty-first
      annual collection; edited by Gardner Dozois
  The fooly
    Dreaming again; thirty-five new stories cele-
      brating the wild side of Australian fiction;
      edited by Jack Dann
  The magikkers
    Wizards; edited by Jack Dann and Gardner
      Dozois
  La profonde
    The Year's best fantasy and horror: twentieth
      annual collection; edited by Ellen Datlow
      and Kelly Link & Gavin J. Grant
  The suits at Auderlene
    Inferno; new tales of terror and the supernatu-
      ral; edited by Ellen Datlow.
  Toother
    Eclipse one; new science fiction and fantasy;
      edited by Jonathan Strahan
    The Year's best fantasy and horror: twenty-
      first annual collection; edited by Ellen
      Datlow and Kelly Link & Gavin J. Grant
  Truth window: a tale of the bedlam rose
    Strahan, J. Eclipse two; new science fiction
      and fantasy; edited by Jonathan Strahan
Down among the dead men. Dann, J. and Dozois,
      G. R.
Down and out in Brentwood. Marks, N.
Down and out in the Magic Kingdom. Moles, D.
Down dirty. Hernandez, L.

DOYLE, SIR ARTHUR CONAN, 1859-1930—

Parodies, imitations, etc.—*Continued*

Jeffers, H. P. In Flanders fields

Jeffers, H. P. The paradol chamber

Jeffers, H. P. Sherlock Holmes and the mummy's curse

Jeffers, H. P. The singular affair of the dying schoolboys

Kidd, C. and Kennett, R. The Grantchester grimoire

Linscott, G. The adventure of the late orang outang

Linscott, G. The case of Colonel Crockett's violin

Lovisi, G. The adventure of the missing detective

Lupoff, R. A. The adventure of the Voorish Sign

Lupoff, R. A. The incident of the impecunious chevalier

Madison, B. Red sunset

McCrumb, S. The vale of the white horse

McDevitt, J. The adventure of the southsea trunk

Newman, K. The red planet league

Newman, K. A shambles in Belgravia

Pearl, M. The adventure of the Boston Dromio

Pohle, R. W. The flowers of Utah

Powell, M. Sherlock Holmes in the lost world

Roberson, C. Merridew of abominable memory

Roden, B. The things that shall come upon them

Rose, L. Ghosts and the machine

Sequeira, C. His last arrow

Stashower, D. The adventure of the agitated actress

Stashower, D. The seven walnuts

Thomas, D. S. The case of Peter the painter

Thomas, D. S. The case of the Greek key

Thomas, D. S. The case of the king's evil

Thomas, D. S. The case of the Peasenhall murder

Thomas, D. S. The case of the phantom chambermaid

Thomas, D. S. The case of the Portuguese sonnets

Thomas, D. S. The case of the tell-tale hands

Thomas, D. S. The case of the Zimmermann telegram

Thomas, D. S. The execution of Sherlock Holmes

Thomas, D. S. The queen of the night

Thompson, V. The minister's missing daughter

Walsh, M. The song at twilight

Wheat, C. The case of the rival queens

Wheat, C. A scandal in Drury Lane; or, The vampire trap

Doyle, Brian

AAA Plus

Harper's v311 p27-9 S 2005

Denouement

New Letters v72 no2 p137-41 2006

Hürtgen

U.S. Catholic v71 no4 p36-7 Ap 2006

Waking the bishop

U.S. Catholic v72 no3 p34-7 Mr 2007

Doyle, Conan *See* Doyle, Sir Arthur Conan, 1859-1930

Doyle, Roddy

57% Irish

Doyle, R. The deportees and other stories

Black hoodie

Doyle, R. The deportees and other stories

Bullfighting

The New Yorker v84 no11 p64-71 Ap 28 2008

The child

McSweeney's enchanted chamber of astonishing stories; edited by Michael Chabon; illustrations by Mike Mignola

The deportees

Doyle, R. The deportees and other stories

The Dog

The New Yorker v83 no34 p78-83 N 5 2007

Guess who's coming for the dinner

Doyle, R. The deportees and other stories

Home to Harlem

Doyle, R. The deportees and other stories

I understand

Doyle, R. The deportees and other stories

The Joke

The New Yorker v80 no37 p118, 120-2 N 29 2004

New boy

Doyle, R. The deportees and other stories

The Photograph

The New Yorker v82 no33 p162-7 O 16 2006

The pram

Doyle, R. The deportees and other stories

Recuperation

New Dubliners; edited by Oona Frawley

Sleep

The New Yorker v84 no33 p76-9 O 20 2008

Teaching

The New Yorker v83 no6 p68-72 Ap 2 2007

A **dozen** tough jobs. Waldrop, H.

Dozing on doomsday. Libin, Z.

Dozois, Gardner R.

The hanging curve

This is my funniest; leading science fiction writers present their funniest stories ever; edited by Mike Resnick

A knight of ghosts and shadows

Nebula awards showcase 2002; edited by Kim Stanley Robinson

(jt. auth) See Dann, Jack and Dozois, Gardner R.

Dozois, Gardner R. and Dann, Jack

Slow dancing with Jesus

A cross of centuries; twenty-five imaginative tales about the Christ; edited by Michael Bishop

Dr. Cahn's visit. Stern, R. G.

Dr. Deadwood, I presume. Bierce, A.

Dr. Deneau's Punishment. Ostlund, L.

Dr. Gelabius. Bailey, H.

Dr. King's refrigerator. Johnson, C. R.

Dr. Leopold Needs a Little Help. Kobin, J.

Dr. Sullivan's library. Matthews, C.

DR. WHO (TELEVISION PROGRAM: 1962-1989) *See* Doctor Who (Television program: 1963-1989)

Draco campestris. Monctte, S.

DRACULA, COUNT (FICTITIOUS CHARACTER)

Harris, C. Dracula night

Resnick, M. Two hunters in Manhattan

Dracula night. Harris, C.
Draculess. Nelson, V.
DRAFT
  Abbott, L. K. Category Z
  Lapcharoensap, R. Draft day
  McIlvoy, K. Ice
  O'Brien, T. On the rainy river
DRAFT, MILITARY *See* Draft
Draft day. Lapcharoensap, R.
DRAFT RESISTERS *See* Draft
Drafting the field report. Grimes, C.
Dragomán, György
  End of the World
    The Paris Review v49 p141-8 Wint 2007
  Jump
    The Paris Review v48 p169-75 Fall 2006
The **dragon**. Zamíàtin, E. I.
Dragon dreams. Vedam, S.
DRAGONS
  Abreu, C. F. Dragons . . .
  Bear, E. Orm the beautiful
  Bear, E. Seven Dragons Mountains
  Card, O. S. In the dragon's house
  Cook, G. Filed teeth
  Coover, R. Sir John Paper returns to Honah-Lee
  Goss, T. Singing of Mount Abora
  Lynn, E. A. The silver dragon
  Martin, G. R. R. The ice dragon
  McKillip, P. A. The fellowship of the dragon
  McKillip, P. A. The harrowing of the dragon of Hoarsbreath
  Monette, S. Draco campestris
  Moon, E. Judgment
  Purdy, J. A little variety, please
  Reed, R. The dragons of Summer Gulch
  Shawl, N. The pragmatical princess
  Shepard, L. The man who painted the dragon griaule
  Swanwick, M. King dragon
  Weber, D. Sir George and the dragon
  Zelazny, R. The George business
  Zelazny, R. The monster and the maiden
Dragons . . . Abreu, C. F.
Dragons may be the way forward. Zumas, L.
The **dragons** of Summer Gulch. Reed, R.
Drain, Kim
  My Thoughts on Pâté
    Agni no60 p32-9 2004
Drake, David
  Airborne all the way!
    This is my funniest 2; leading science fiction writers present their funniest stories ever; edited by Mike Resnick
  The day of glory
    Elemental; the Tsunami relief anthology; stories of science fiction and fantasy; [edited by] Steven Savile and Alethea Kontis; introduction by Arthur C. Clarke
Drama. Chekhov, A. P.
The **drama** at the hunt. Chekhov, A. P.
DRAMA CRITICS
  Zelazny, R. A thing of terrible beauty
DRAMATISTS
  Blue, E. The cut the crap machine
  Libin, Z. A refurbished play
  McInerney, J. The madonna of turkey season
The **drawing**. Zelazny, R.
Drawing apart. Adonis, I.

Drayer, Jeffrey
  Africa under Her Skin
    The Massachusetts Review v49 no3 p395-402 Aut 2008
Dreadful night. See Chekhov, A. P. A night of horror [variant title: Dreadful night]
Dreadnought. Robson, J.
The **dream**. Kharms, D.
The **Dream**. Ndongo-Bidyogo, D.
The **dream** and the triumph. Buckler, E.
Dream baby. McAllister, B.
Dream city; or, The drugged lake. Fuchs, D.
Dream comics. Baraka, I. A.
The **dream** dust factory. Gresham, W. L.
Dream engine. Pratt, T.
Dream house. McCann, R.
Dream knights. Banks, L. E.
The **dream** lover. Coffman, L. H.
Dream obits for Liz. Monson, A.
The **dream** of a ridiculous man. Dostoyevsky, F.
A **dream** of good fortune. Hwang, S.
Dream of the Revolution. Holland, T.
"The **dream** of x". Hodgson, W. H.
Dream on. Porter, J. A.
The **dream** snake. Howard, R. E.
Dream stuff. Malouf, D.
Dreaming of the dead. Gordimer, N.
The **dreaming** wind. Ford, J.
Dreamland. Raphael, L.
DREAMS
  Abbott, L. K. Dreams of distant lives
  Alcântara Machado, A. d. Gaetaninho
  Asimov, I. Robot dreams
  Banks, L. E. Dream knights
  Baraka, I. A. Dream comics
  Baumbach, J. The dinner party
  Baumbach, J. The return of service
  Bierce, A. Authenticating a ghost
  Bierce, A. The death of Halpin Frayser
  Bisson, T. Super 8
  Brennan, K. Three seaside tales
  Card, O. S. Keeper of lost dreams
  Carmody, I. Perchance to dream
  Catt, D. Evil comes
  Chappell, F. Mankind journeys through forests of symbols
  Chernyshevsky, N. G. Vera Pavlovna's fourth dream
  Collins, W. The dream woman
  Cooney, L. Pink
  Crowther, P. Even beggars would ride
  Curtis, R. The wolf at the door
  Dammaj, H. The nightmare
  Dean, D. The afterlife of Lyle Stone
  Dostoyevsky, F. The dream of a ridiculous man
  Ducornet, R. Who's there?
  Dunbar, P. L. A prophesy of fate
  Galanaki, R. An almost-blue arm
  Gerrold, D. Chester
  Gifford, B. Coda: the ropedancers recurring dream
  Gogol', N. V. Nevsky Prospekt
  Gordimer, N. Dreaming of the dead
  Gordin, J. Yankele's dream
  Gospodinov, G. Forging the Bulgarian earring
  Gospodinov, G. The nightmare of a lady
  Gresham, W. L. The dream dust factory
  Harrison, M. J. The luck in the head
  Hawes, L. Anteaters don't dream

DREAMS—*Continued*

Hogan, L. Bush's mourning feast
Hospital, J. T. Cape tribulation
Hospital, J. T. Night train
Hospital, J. T. Unperformed experiments have no results
Howard, R. E. The dream snake
Hubbard, L. R. He didn't like cats
Hughes, M. Bearing up
Hughes, M. Help wonted
Hussin, J. Y. The day in Buenos Aires
Irvine, A. C. Clownfish
Johnson, C. R. Sweet dreams
July, M. The shared patio
Keret, E. Cramps
Keret, E. Horsie
Keret, E. On the nutritional value of dreams
Kharms, D. The dream
King, S. Harvey's dream
Kulpa, K. The night Copernicus died
Lawrence, J. Kissing frogs
Lin, T. Love is the indifferent god of the religion in which universe is church
Lovecraft, H. P. The dreams in the Witch House
Lovecraft, H. P. The shadow out of time
Lumley, B. Deja viewer
Lumley, B. The horror at Oakdeene
Luongo, M. Buoyant
Luongo, M. Embankment
Machado de Assis. A woman's arms
Maḥfūẓ, N. Beyond the clouds
Maḥfūẓ, N. Forgetfulness
Maḥfūẓ, N. A man of awesome power
McAllister, B. Dream baby
McAllister, B. Little boy blue
Messinger, J. Between here and there
Messinger, J. Scream in the dark
Misha. Memekwesiw
Mukhopadhyay, T. Grey, apple green, and white
O'Driscoll, M. 13 O'clock
Pratt, T. Dream engine
Rand, K. To dream to be
Randolph, L. The picture in her dream
Rickert, M. Night blossoms
Rivera-Garza, C. Nostalgia/Nostalgia
Rock, P. Disappeared girls
Scholes, K. So sang the girl who had no name
Schwartz, D. In dreams begin responsibilities [excerpt]
Sheehy, H. The invisibles
Shirley, J. Miss singularity
Silverberg, R. Something wild is loose
Steinberg, S. Court
Swanwick, M. Slow life
Tabor, M. L. To swim?
Thomas, E. The ship of swallows
Ts'an-hsüeh. Blue light in the sky
Tsutsui, Y. The Dabba Dabba Tree
Uchida, H. The reflection
Van Booy, S. Some bloom in darkness
Webb, D. The great white bed
Welch, N. Welcome to the neighborhood
Wilson, F. P. Dreams
Wilson, R. C. YFL–500
Wolfe, G. The detective of dreams
Wolfe, G. Golden city far
Wolfe, G. Houston, 1943
Yellin, T. Manasseh
Yolen, J. Man of rock, man of stone

Zebrowski, G. Passing nights
Dreams. Chekhov, A. P.
Dreams. Judah, S.
Dreams. Wilson, F. P.
Dreams come true. Arnow, H. L. S.
The **dreams** in the Witch House. Lovecraft, H. P.
Dreams of distant lives. Abbott, L. K.
Dreams of Flying. del Llano, E.
Dreams of Jeannie. Dain, C.
Dreams Where I Can Fly. Barnes, E.
Dred. Rodriguez, J. A.
Drees, Charlie
By hook or by crook
Mystery Writers of America presents the prosecution rests; new stories about courtrooms, criminals, and the law; edited by Linda Fairstein.
Dreifus, Erika
Matrilineal Descent
TriQuarterly no130 p193-205 2008
Drenched in light. Hurston, Z. N.
Dresden. Salisbury, L.
The **dress**. Erdrich, L.
Dress of white silk. Matheson, R.
The **dress** rehearsal. Templeton, E.
Dressing down. Shields, C.
Dressing up. Swann, M.
Dressing up for the carnival. Shields, C.
DRESSMAKERS
James, H. Alone
James, H. The rose-colored silk
The **dressmaker's** child. Trevor, W.
Drew, Flora
(tr.) See Ma Jian
Dreyer, Eileen
Vanquishing the infidel
Deadly housewives; edited by Christine Matthews
DREYFUS, ALFRED, 1859-1935
About
Waldrop, H. Fin de Cyclé
The **Driest** Season. Kenny, M.
Drift. Schwarzschild, E.
Drifting. Quiroga, H.
Driftwood. Uchida, H.
Drill and Song Day. Kozlov, V.
A **drink** of water. Matheson, R.
Drink to long life. Kaye, J.
Driscoll, Jack
The Dangerous Lay of the Land
The Georgia Review v62 no4 p650-65 Wint 2008
Prowlers
Pushcart prize XXXIII: best of the small presses 2009; edited by Bill Henderson with the Pushcart Prize editors
The Georgia Review v61 no3 p462-75 Fall 2007
Wonder
The Southern Review (Baton Rouge, La.) v43 no4 p933-50 Aut 2007
Drive. Henriquez, C.
Drive. Treat, J.
The **Drive-In** Puerto Rico. Shepard, L.
DRIVE-IN THEATERS
Pollock, D. R. Real life
Drive Uncle Randy. With, C.
Driven to distraction. Talley, M.
Driver's ed. Watkins, S.

DRUGS—*Continued*

Nolan, W. F. Toe to tip, tip to toe, pip-pop as you go

Ohlin, A. Edgewater

Pelecanos, G. P. String music

Phillips, G. The man for the job

Phillips, G. Where all our dreams come true

Phillips, S. Babs

Pollock, D. R. Bactine

Pollock, D. R. Pills

Rand, K. Through these eyes

Rash, R. Back of beyond

Richter, S. Blackout

Schanoes, V. Rats

Shepard, L. The ease with which we freed the beast

Shirley, J. Brittany? Oh: she's in translucent blue

Shirley, J. One stick: both ends sharpened

Shirley, J. Sleepwalkers

Shomer, E. Fill in the blank

Shomer, E. Rapture

Silverberg, R. Schwartz between the galaxies

Smith, C. A. The Plutonian drug

Speegle, D. Peace rituals

Spinrad, N. No direction home

Sterling, B. Are you for 86?

Tomlinson, J. First husband, first wife

Wilson, K. Tunneling to the center of the earth

Wolfe, G. Seven American nights

Woronov, M. The white plains of Western Avenue

Drugs and toys. Boudinot, R.

DRUGSTORES *See* Pharmacists

DRUIDS

Howard, R. E. The little people

Drummer unknown. Harvey, J.

DRUMMERS

Bradbury, R. The drummer boy of Shiloh

Sayles, J. Keeping time

Drummond, Robert

The unnecessary man

New stories from the South; the year's best, 2008; selected from U.S. magazines by ZZ Packer with Kathy Pories; with an introduction by ZZ Packer

Drummond & son. D'Ambrosio, C., Jr.

Drummond de Andrade, Carlos *See* Andrade, Carlos Drummond de

Drunk with love. Gilchrist, E.

DRUNKARDS

See also Alcoholism; Temperance

Arjouni, J. At peace

Arjouni, J. Happy ending

Bierce, A. Confessions of a sad dog

Bierce, A. D. T.

Bierce, A. Two stories about Johnson

Choe, I. The boozer

Dahl, R. The umbrella man

Lamsley, T. Running in the family

Lethem, J. The vision

Shroff, M. F. Jamal Haddi's revenge

Westcott, G. Prohibition

Zoshchenko, M. Lemonade

DRUNKENNESS

Anderson, B. We could celebrate

Ayres, N. J. Rust

Barry, R. Love him, Petaluma

Bishop, T. A Hoover steak

Block, L. The burning fury

Bova, B. The supervisor's tale

Boyle, T. C. Balto

Boyle, T. C. When I woke up this morning, everything I had was gone

Busch, F. Something along those lines

Chekhov, A. P. Conversation of a drunken man with a sober devil

Crane, E. What our week was like

Daughtry, P. The mouse's aura

DeMarinis, R. The bear itself

Duval, P. Rear view

Goldfaden, J. Top of the list

Harjo, J. The reckoning

Hemon, A. Everything

Higgins, G. V. A principle of dominant transience

Hinton, S. E. After the party

Holladay, C. C. Hollyhocks

Hunt, H. Sovietski!

Keane, J. B. 'Your're on next Sunday'

LaSalle, P. Preseason: The Texas Football Dead

Nelson, R. F. Pulp life

Oates, J. C. Landfill

Porter, A. River dog

Reid, G. Lollipop

Richter, S. Blackout

Rylands, J. T. Fortune

Scott, J. Everybody loves somebody

Shirley, J. The word "random", deliberately repeated

Singleton, G. John Cheever, rest in peace

Skabardonis, Y. Mussels in the flower vase

Stafford, J. In the zoo

Steinberg, S. The last guest

Swan, G. Traveling light

Drury, David

Things we knew when the house caught fire

The best Christian short stories; edited and with an introduction by Bret Lott

Drury, Joan M.

The "sound" of music

Women of mystery; an anthology; Katherine V. Forrest, editor

Drury, Tom

Path Lights

The New Yorker v81 no32 p156-61 O 17 2005

Drusilla. Gorman, E.

Dry bones. Sanders, W.

DRY CLEANING

Cooper, J. C. The eye of the beholder

Kalotay, D. Sunshine Cleaners

A **Dry** Depression. Camenietzki, S.

A **dry** season. Johnson, G.

DRYADS

Samphire, P. Crab apple

Dryden, Rachel Ann

Respite

Orson Scott Card's Intergalctic medicine show; [edited by] Edmund R. Schubert and Orson Scott Card

The **drying** corner. Corso, P.

D'Souza, Tony

Club Des Amis

The New Yorker v81 no26 p134-41 S 5 2005

Ducornet, Rikki—*Continued*
Divorce
  Ducornet, R. The one marvelous thing; decorated by T. Motley
The doorman's swellage
  Ducornet, R. The one marvelous thing; decorated by T. Motley
Giulia on her knees
  Ducornet, R. The one marvelous thing; decorated by T. Motley
La Goulue in retirement
  Ducornet, R. The one marvelous thing; decorated by T. Motley
Green air
  Ducornet, R. The one marvelous thing; decorated by T. Motley
Koi
  Ducornet, R. The one marvelous thing; decorated by T. Motley
Koi [2]
  Ducornet, R. The one marvelous thing; decorated by T. Motley
Lettuce
  Ducornet, R. The one marvelous thing; decorated by T. Motley
Mimi Ungerer and Janet
  Ducornet, R. The one marvelous thing; decorated by T. Motley
The ominous philologist
  Ducornet, R. The one marvelous thing; decorated by T. Motley
The one marvelous thing
  Ducornet, R. The one marvelous thing; decorated by T. Motley
  Bomb no93 p98-9 Fall 2005
Oops!
  Ducornet, R. The one marvelous thing; decorated by T. Motley
Painter
  Ducornet, R. The one marvelous thing; decorated by T. Motley
Panna cotta
  Ducornet, R. The one marvelous thing; decorated by T. Motley
Poet
  Ducornet, R. The one marvelous thing; decorated by T. Motley
The scouring
  Text: Ur; the new book of masks; [edited by Forrest Aguirre]
  Ducornet, R. The one marvelous thing; decorated by T. Motley
A secret life
  Ducornet, R. The one marvelous thing; decorated by T. Motley
She thinks dots
  Ducornet, R. The one marvelous thing; decorated by T. Motley
A suicide
  Ducornet, R. The one marvelous thing; decorated by T. Motley
Thumbtacks
  Ducornet, R. The one marvelous thing; decorated by T. Motley
Who's there?
  Ducornet, R. The one marvelous thing; decorated by T. Motley

The wild child
  Ducornet, R. The one marvelous thing; decorated by T. Motley
  Agni no62 p92-5 2005
Ziti Motlog
  Ducornet, R. The one marvelous thing; decorated by T. Motley
Dudman, Clare
There's a ghost in my house
  Perverted by language; fiction inspired by The Fall; edited and introduced by Peter Wild.
Due, Tananarive
Amusement
  Dark delicacies 2; fear: more original tales of terror and the macabre by the world's greatest horror writers; edited by Del Howison and Jeff Gelb
  (jt. auth) See Barnes, Steven and Due, Tananarive
Due dilligence. Aird, C.
Due process. Auchincloss, L.
Due West. Othmer, J. P.
Duel. Matheson, R.
DUELING
  Schnitzler, A. Lieutenant Gustl
  Wolfe, G. The hour of the sheep
DUELS *See* Dueling
Dues. Peck, D.
Duet. Richter, S.
Duff, Gerald
The Way a Blind Man Tracks Light
  The Kenyon Review v29 no3 p82-100 Summ 2007
Duffy, Stella
Un bon repas doit commencer par la faim. . .
  Paris noir; capital crime fiction; edited by Maxim Jakubowski
Payment in kind
  Getting even; revenge stories; edited by Mitzi Szereto
Dufresne, John
Arlis & Ivy
  Dufresne, J. Johnny too bad; stories
Based on a true story
  Dufresne, J. Johnny too bad; stories
Close by me forever
  Dufresne, J. Johnny too bad; stories
The dead of night
  Dufresne, J. Johnny too bad; stories
  TriQuarterly no121 p43-52 2005
Died and gone to heaven
  Dufresne, J. Johnny too bad; stories
Electric limits of our widest senses
  Dufresne, J. Johnny too bad; stories
Epithalamion
  Dufresne, J. Johnny too bad; stories
The freezer Jesus
  Wide awake in the Pelican State; stories by contemporary Louisiana writers; edited by Ann Brewster Dobie; with a foreword by Ernest J. Gaines
I will eat a piece of the roof and you can eat the window
  Dufresne, J. Johnny too bad; stories
Johnny too bad
  Dufresne, J. Johnny too bad; stories
Lefty
  Dufresne, J. Johnny too bad; stories

Dunbar, Paul Laurence—*Continued*

A defender of the faith
Dunbar, P. L. The complete stories of Paul
Laurence Dunbar; edited by Gene Andrew
Jarrett and Thomas Lewis Morgan; fore-
word by Shelley Fisher Fishkin

The deliberation of Mr. Dunkin
Dunbar, P. L. The complete stories of Paul
Laurence Dunbar; edited by Gene Andrew
Jarrett and Thomas Lewis Morgan; fore-
word by Shelley Fisher Fishkin

Dizzy-headed Dick
Dunbar, P. L. The complete stories of Paul
Laurence Dunbar; edited by Gene Andrew
Jarrett and Thomas Lewis Morgan; fore-
word by Shelley Fisher Fishkin

The Easter wedding
Dunbar, P. L. The complete stories of Paul
Laurence Dunbar; edited by Gene Andrew
Jarrett and Thomas Lewis Morgan; fore-
word by Shelley Fisher Fishkin

The emancipation of Evalina Jones
Dunbar, P. L. The complete stories of Paul
Laurence Dunbar; edited by Gene Andrew
Jarrett and Thomas Lewis Morgan; fore-
word by Shelley Fisher Fishkin

The faith cure man
Dunbar, P. L. The complete stories of Paul
Laurence Dunbar; edited by Gene Andrew
Jarrett and Thomas Lewis Morgan; fore-
word by Shelley Fisher Fishkin

A family feud
Dunbar, P. L. The complete stories of Paul
Laurence Dunbar; edited by Gene Andrew
Jarrett and Thomas Lewis Morgan; fore-
word by Shelley Fisher Fishkin

The finding of Martha
Dunbar, P. L. The complete stories of Paul
Laurence Dunbar; edited by Gene Andrew
Jarrett and Thomas Lewis Morgan; fore-
word by Shelley Fisher Fishkin

The finding of Zach
Dunbar, P. L. The complete stories of Paul
Laurence Dunbar; edited by Gene Andrew
Jarrett and Thomas Lewis Morgan; fore-
word by Shelley Fisher Fishkin

The finish of Patsy Barnes
Dunbar, P. L. The complete stories of Paul
Laurence Dunbar; edited by Gene Andrew
Jarrett and Thomas Lewis Morgan; fore-
word by Shelley Fisher Fishkin

From impulse
Dunbar, P. L. The complete stories of Paul
Laurence Dunbar; edited by Gene Andrew
Jarrett and Thomas Lewis Morgan; fore-
word by Shelley Fisher Fishkin

The fruitful sleeping of the Rev. Elisha Edwards
Dunbar, P. L. The complete stories of Paul
Laurence Dunbar; edited by Gene Andrew
Jarrett and Thomas Lewis Morgan; fore-
word by Shelley Fisher Fishkin

His bride of the tomb
Dunbar, P. L. The complete stories of Paul
Laurence Dunbar; edited by Gene Andrew
Jarrett and Thomas Lewis Morgan; fore-
word by Shelley Fisher Fishkin

The home-coming of 'Rastus Smith
Dunbar, P. L. The complete stories of Paul
Laurence Dunbar; edited by Gene Andrew
Jarrett and Thomas Lewis Morgan; fore-
word by Shelley Fisher Fishkin

The hoodooing of Mr. Bill Simms
Dunbar, P. L. The complete stories of Paul
Laurence Dunbar; edited by Gene Andrew
Jarrett and Thomas Lewis Morgan; fore-
word by Shelley Fisher Fishkin

How Brother Parker fell from grace
Dunbar, P. L. The complete stories of Paul
Laurence Dunbar; edited by Gene Andrew
Jarrett and Thomas Lewis Morgan; fore-
word by Shelley Fisher Fishkin

How George Johnson "won out"
Dunbar, P. L. The complete stories of Paul
Laurence Dunbar; edited by Gene Andrew
Jarrett and Thomas Lewis Morgan; fore-
word by Shelley Fisher Fishkin

The independence of Silas Bollender
Dunbar, P. L. The complete stories of Paul
Laurence Dunbar; edited by Gene Andrew
Jarrett and Thomas Lewis Morgan; fore-
word by Shelley Fisher Fishkin

The ingrate
Dunbar, P. L. The complete stories of Paul
Laurence Dunbar; edited by Gene Andrew
Jarrett and Thomas Lewis Morgan; fore-
word by Shelley Fisher Fishkin

The interference of Patsy Ann
Dunbar, P. L. The complete stories of Paul
Laurence Dunbar; edited by Gene Andrew
Jarrett and Thomas Lewis Morgan; fore-
word by Shelley Fisher Fishkin

The intervention of Peter
Dunbar, P. L. The complete stories of Paul
Laurence Dunbar; edited by Gene Andrew
Jarrett and Thomas Lewis Morgan; fore-
word by Shelley Fisher Fishkin

Jethro's garden
Dunbar, P. L. The complete stories of Paul
Laurence Dunbar; edited by Gene Andrew
Jarrett and Thomas Lewis Morgan; fore-
word by Shelley Fisher Fishkin

Jimmy Weedon's contretemps
Dunbar, P. L. The complete stories of Paul
Laurence Dunbar; edited by Gene Andrew
Jarrett and Thomas Lewis Morgan; fore-
word by Shelley Fisher Fishkin

Jim's probation
Dunbar, P. L. The complete stories of Paul
Laurence Dunbar; edited by Gene Andrew
Jarrett and Thomas Lewis Morgan; fore-
word by Shelley Fisher Fishkin

Jimsella
Dunbar, P. L. The complete stories of Paul
Laurence Dunbar; edited by Gene Andrew
Jarrett and Thomas Lewis Morgan; fore-
word by Shelley Fisher Fishkin

Johnsonham, Junior
Dunbar, P. L. The complete stories of Paul
Laurence Dunbar; edited by Gene Andrew
Jarrett and Thomas Lewis Morgan; fore-
word by Shelley Fisher Fishkin

Dunbar, Paul Laurence—*Continued*

The scapegoat

Dunbar, P. L. The complete stories of Paul Laurence Dunbar; edited by Gene Andrew Jarrett and Thomas Lewis Morgan; foreword by Shelley Fisher Fishkin

Schwalliger's philanthropy

Dunbar, P. L. The complete stories of Paul Laurence Dunbar; edited by Gene Andrew Jarrett and Thomas Lewis Morgan; foreword by Shelley Fisher Fishkin

Silas Jackson

Dunbar, P. L. The complete stories of Paul Laurence Dunbar; edited by Gene Andrew Jarrett and Thomas Lewis Morgan; foreword by Shelley Fisher Fishkin

Silent Sam'el

Dunbar, P. L. The complete stories of Paul Laurence Dunbar; edited by Gene Andrew Jarrett and Thomas Lewis Morgan; foreword by Shelley Fisher Fishkin

Sister Jackson's superstitions

Dunbar, P. L. The complete stories of Paul Laurence Dunbar; edited by Gene Andrew Jarrett and Thomas Lewis Morgan; foreword by Shelley Fisher Fishkin

The Stanton coachman

Dunbar, P. L. The complete stories of Paul Laurence Dunbar; edited by Gene Andrew Jarrett and Thomas Lewis Morgan; foreword by Shelley Fisher Fishkin

The strength of Gideon

Dunbar, P. L. The complete stories of Paul Laurence Dunbar; edited by Gene Andrew Jarrett and Thomas Lewis Morgan; foreword by Shelley Fisher Fishkin

A supper by proxy

Dunbar, P. L. The complete stories of Paul Laurence Dunbar; edited by Gene Andrew Jarrett and Thomas Lewis Morgan; foreword by Shelley Fisher Fishkin

The tenderfoot

Dunbar, P. L. The complete stories of Paul Laurence Dunbar; edited by Gene Andrew Jarrett and Thomas Lewis Morgan; foreword by Shelley Fisher Fishkin

The tragedy at Three Forks

Dunbar, P. L. The complete stories of Paul Laurence Dunbar; edited by Gene Andrew Jarrett and Thomas Lewis Morgan; foreword by Shelley Fisher Fishkin

The trial sermons on Bull-Skin

Dunbar, P. L. The complete stories of Paul Laurence Dunbar; edited by Gene Andrew Jarrett and Thomas Lewis Morgan; foreword by Shelley Fisher Fishkin

The triumph of ol' Mis' Pease

Dunbar, P. L. The complete stories of Paul Laurence Dunbar; edited by Gene Andrew Jarrett and Thomas Lewis Morgan; foreword by Shelley Fisher Fishkin

The trouble about Sophiny

Dunbar, P. L. The complete stories of Paul Laurence Dunbar; edited by Gene Andrew Jarrett and Thomas Lewis Morgan; foreword by Shelley Fisher Fishkin

The trousers

Dunbar, P. L. The complete stories of Paul Laurence Dunbar; edited by Gene Andrew Jarrett and Thomas Lewis Morgan; foreword by Shelley Fisher Fishkin

The trustfulness of Polly

Dunbar, P. L. The complete stories of Paul Laurence Dunbar; edited by Gene Andrew Jarrett and Thomas Lewis Morgan; foreword by Shelley Fisher Fishkin

Uncle Simon's Sundays out

Dunbar, P. L. The complete stories of Paul Laurence Dunbar; edited by Gene Andrew Jarrett and Thomas Lewis Morgan; foreword by Shelley Fisher Fishkin

The vindication of Jared Hargot

Dunbar, P. L. The complete stories of Paul Laurence Dunbar; edited by Gene Andrew Jarrett and Thomas Lewis Morgan; foreword by Shelley Fisher Fishkin

Viney's free papers

Dunbar, P. L. The complete stories of Paul Laurence Dunbar; edited by Gene Andrew Jarrett and Thomas Lewis Morgan; foreword by Shelley Fisher Fishkin

The visiting of Mother Danbury

Dunbar, P. L. The complete stories of Paul Laurence Dunbar; edited by Gene Andrew Jarrett and Thomas Lewis Morgan; foreword by Shelley Fisher Fishkin

The walls of Jericho

Dunbar, P. L. The complete stories of Paul Laurence Dunbar; edited by Gene Andrew Jarrett and Thomas Lewis Morgan; foreword by Shelley Fisher Fishkin

The way of a woman

Dunbar, P. L. The complete stories of Paul Laurence Dunbar; edited by Gene Andrew Jarrett and Thomas Lewis Morgan; foreword by Shelley Fisher Fishkin

The way of love

Dunbar, P. L. The complete stories of Paul Laurence Dunbar; edited by Gene Andrew Jarrett and Thomas Lewis Morgan; foreword by Shelley Fisher Fishkin

The white counterpane

Dunbar, P. L. The complete stories of Paul Laurence Dunbar; edited by Gene Andrew Jarrett and Thomas Lewis Morgan; foreword by Shelley Fisher Fishkin

Who stand for the gods

Dunbar, P. L. The complete stories of Paul Laurence Dunbar; edited by Gene Andrew Jarrett and Thomas Lewis Morgan; foreword by Shelley Fisher Fishkin

The wisdom of silence

Dunbar, P. L. The complete stories of Paul Laurence Dunbar; edited by Gene Andrew Jarrett and Thomas Lewis Morgan; foreword by Shelley Fisher Fishkin

Yellowjack's game of craps

Dunbar, P. L. The complete stories of Paul Laurence Dunbar; edited by Gene Andrew Jarrett and Thomas Lewis Morgan; foreword by Shelley Fisher Fishkin

Durham, Frank
Supplying Audubon
South Carolina Review v39 no1 p74-9 Fall 2006
Durham, Gregory
Waiting
Southern Humanities Review v43 no1 p43-53 Wint 2009
During the twelfth summer of Elmer D. Peterson. Averill, T. F.
Durrow, Heidi W.
He Runs
The Literary Review (Madison, N.J.) v50 no2 p7-14 Wint 2007
Durtschi, Maxwell
The legend of Andrea Cerameline
Idaho Magazine v5 no9 p19-23 Je 2006
A **dusk** of Idols. Blish, J.
DÜSSELDORF (GERMANY) *See* Germany—Düsseldorf
Dust. Card, O. S.
Dust. Shibli, A.
The **dust** assassin. McDonald, I.
Dust devil on a quiet street. Bowes, R.
Dust devils. Kelly, R.
Dust to dust. Muller, M.
Dust up. Hornsby, W.
Dustman appearances to date. Means, D.
DUTCH

Indonesia
Toer, P. A. In twilight born
Dutch Boy 32-V. Martone, M.
DUTCH EAST INDIES *See* Indonesia
DUTCH GUIANA *See* Suriname
Duval, Pete
Bakery
Duval, P. Rear view
Cellular
Duval, P. Rear view
Fun with mammals
Duval, P. Rear view
Impala
Duval, P. Rear view
Midnight mass
Duval, P. Rear view
Pious objects
Duval, P. Rear view
Rear view
Duval, P. Rear view
Scissors
Duval, P. Rear view
Spectator sport
Duval, P. Rear view
Welcome wagon
Duval, P. Rear view
Wheatback
Duval, P. Rear view
The **dwarf**. Fonseca, R.
DWARFS
Bierce, A. Juniper
Bradbury, R. The dwarf
Connelly, M. Coroner's inquest
Finger, A. The artist and the dwarf
Fonseca, R. The dwarf
Long, A. Clairvoyant
Mejides, M. Nowhere man
Robbins, T. Spurs
Smith, C. A. A captivity in Serpens [variant title: The amazing planet]

Smith, R. T. Uke Rivers delivers
Vidal, G. Erlinda and Mr. Coffin
Dwelle, Jessica
The Engraving
The Georgia Review v59 no2 p368-94 Summ 2005
The **dweller** in the gulf. Smith, C. A.
The **dwellers** under the tomb. Howard, R. E.
DWI. Nelson, A.
DX. Haldeman, J. W.
The **dybbuk** of Mazel Tov IV. Silverberg, R.
Dybek, Stuart
Bait
TriQuarterly no131 p45-7 2008
Breasts
The Best American short stories, 2004; edited by Lorrie Moore; Katrina Kenison series editor
Death of the right fielder
Beha, C. R. The Ecco anthology of contemporary American short fiction; selected by Joyce Carol Oates and Christopher R. Beha.
If I Vanished
The New Yorker v83 no19 p80-7 Jl 9-16 2007
The Palatski Man
The New Granta book of the American short story; edited and introduced by Richard Ford
Pink Ocean
Poetry (Modern Poetry Association) v191 no4 p327-31 Ja 2008
Transaction
New Letters v73 no3 p66-71 2007
We didn't
My mistress's sparrow is dead; great love stories, from Chekhov to Munro; edited by Jeffrey Eugenides
Dyer, Geoff
White Sands
Granta no91 p167-79 Fall 2005
Dying. Stern, R. G.
Dying Away. Cagnone, N.
The **Dying** Country. Espriu, S.
Dying for love. Shields, C.
The **dying** of the light. Bear, E.
Dying room only. Matheson, R.
Dyke Crest Lane no. 1. Thormahlen, A.
DYLAN, BOB, 1941-
About
Bertino, M. North of
Dymmoch, Michael Allen
A shade of blue
Chicago blues; edited by Libby Fischer Hellmann
Dymond, Justine
Cherubs
The O. Henry Prize stories 2007; edited and with an introduction by Laura Furman; with essays on the story they admire most by jurors Charles D'Ambrosio, Ursula K. Le Guin, Lily Tuck
The Massachusetts Review v46 no3 p513-25 Fall 2005
Dynamite hole. Pollock, D. R.
The **dynasters**. Waldrop, H.
Dysfunctional family cat. Melko, P.
The **dystopianist,** thinking of his rival, is interrupted by a knock on the door. Lethem, J.

Dzhugashvili, Iosif Vissarionovich *See* Stalin, Joseph, 1879-1953

E

E for effort. Sherred, T. L.
The **Eagle** Has Landed. Kearns, J. M.
Eagleman, David
  A brief history of death switches
    Nature v443 p882 O 19 2006
EAGLES
  James, C. L. R. Moby Dick fights a strange eagle
Earl. Domecq, B.
Earley, Tony
  The Cryptozoologist
    The New Yorker v81 no43 p74-81 Ja 9 2006
  Mr. Tall
    The Southern Review (Baton Rouge, La.) v45 no2 p345-67 Spr 2009
  Yard art
    New stories from the South: the year's best, 2006; selected from U.S. magazines by Allan Gurganus with Kathy Pories; with an introduction by Allan Gurganus
The **Early** Deaths of Lubeck, Brennan, Harp, and Carr. Ball, J.
Early fall. Torres, S.
The **early** history of Bath. Bierce, A.
Early humans. Hallberg, G. R.
Early marvels. Linney, R.
Early Music. Eugenides, J.
Early one morning. Simpson, H.
Earning Money All Her Own. Fioravanti, V.
EARP, MORGAN, 1851-1882
  About
  Duncklee, J. The last breakfast
EARP, WYATT, 1848-1929
  About
  Duncklee, J. The last breakfast
  Wheeler, R. S. Hearts
EARRINGS
  Piatote, B. H. Beading lesson
  Swails, K. Cake and candy
The **Ears** of the Eyes in the Heart. Simms, L.
EARTH
  Crowther, P. Switching off the lights
  Friedell, E. Is the earth inhabited?
  Silverberg, R. The wind and the rain
  Zelazny, R. The game of blood and dust
  Zelazny, R. The night has 999 eyes
EARTH, DESTRUCTION OF
  Gordon, M. The imagination of disaster
  Pohl, F. The gold at the starbow's end
  Silverberg, R. When we went to see the end of the world
  Smith, C. A. Seedling of Mars
  Tsutsui, Y. The world is tilting
Earth around his bones. Zebrowski, G.
The **earth** is on the mend. Marusek, D.
Earthly Delights. Leong, S.
Earthman, come here. Blish, J.
Earthquake. Barnes, S.
EARTHQUAKES
  See also Disasters
  Harper, B. Yellowstone
  Hodgson, W. H. The crew of the Lancing
  Hodgson, W. H. R.M.S. "Empress of Australia"

  Kercheval, J. L. Damage
  Reinhorn, H. Get away from me, David
  Tsutsui, Y. The world is tilting
The **ease** of living. Gautier, A.
The **ease** with which we freed the beast. Shepard, L.
The **easiest** thing in the world. Higgins, G. V.
EAST AFRICA
  Koënings, N. S. Sisters for Shama
An **East** Egg Update. Bradley, G.
EAST INDIAN AMERICANS
  Lahiri, J. A choice of accommodations
  Lahiri, J. Hell-heaven
  Lahiri, J. Nobody's business
  Lahiri, J. Once in a lifetime
  Lahiri, J. Only goodness
  Lahiri, J. Unaccustomed earth
  Lahiri, J. Year's end
EAST INDIAN SOLDIERS *See* Soldiers—India
EAST INDIANS
      Canada
  Mukherjee, B. The management of grief
      England
  Cutler, J. Doctor's orders
  Gee, M. Ring-barking
      Israel
  Judah, S. A girl from my hometown
      Italy
  Chandra, V. "Light beer and peanuts"
      Trinidad and Tobago
  Antoni, R. How to make photocopies in the Trinidad & Tobago national archives
      United States
  Divakaruni, C. B. Mrs. Dutta writes a letter
  Jones, N. Half the story
  Lahiri, J. Once in a lifetime
  Lahiri, J. When Mr. Pirzada came to dine
  Sankaran, L. Alphabet soup
  Sankaran, L. Apple pie, one by two
  Sharma, A. Cosmopolitan
  Singh, V. The wife
  Sundaresan, I. Shelter of rain
      Zimbabwe
  Gappah, P. Aunt Juliana's Indian
East of Appomattox. Allred, L.
East of Eden and just a little bit south. Scholes, K.
East of Gorontalo. L'Amour, L.
East of the sun. Howard, J.
EAST SIDE, LOWER (NEW YORK, N.Y.) *See* New York (N.Y.)—Lower East Side
East Side, West Side. Collins, M. A. and Clemens, M. V.
East, West . . . Midwest. Stern, R. G.
East Wind. Barnes, J.
EASTER
  Standing, S. Fast Sunday
Easter Flowers. Kantor, M.
EASTER ISLAND
  Pickard, N. There is no crime on Easter Island
Easter Sunday. Lins, O.
The **Easter** wedding. Dunbar, P. L.
EASTERN EUROPE
  Sterling, B. Kiosk
The **Eastvale** Ladies' Poker Circle. Robinson, P.
Easy as a-b-c. Lippman, L.
An **Easy** Day at Easy Red. Poe, D. R.
Eaten alive. Santangelo, E.
Eating Cake. Weatherwax, A.

EATING DISORDERS

Fulton, A. A shadow table
Harris, J. Fish
Otis, M. The straight and narrow
Prose, F. An open letter to Doctor X
Zumas, L. Blotilla takes the cake
Eating Earth. White, M.
Eating hearts. Lee, Y. H.
Eating Italian. Guerriero, L.
Eating, Ohio. Rahman, I.
Eating out. Michaels, L.
Eating the Dream. Laity, K. A.

EAVESDROPPING

Donovan, G. Morning swimmers
Prose, F. An open letter to Doctor X
Singer, I. B. Not for the Sabbath
Eavesdropping at the Van Gogh museum.
Tognazzini, A.

Ebenbach, David Harris

Between Camelots
Ebenbach, D. H. Between Camelots
Bridesmaid
Ebenbach, D. H. Between Camelots
Fighting
Ebenbach, D. H. Between Camelots
Getting back onto solid foods
Ebenbach, D. H. Between Camelots
I'll be home
Ebenbach, D. H. Between Camelots
Jewish Day
The Antioch Review v67 no3 p441-52 Summ
2009
The movements of the body
Ebenbach, D. H. Between Camelots
Nothing ever happens in white America
Ebenbach, D. H. Between Camelots
Out in the open
Ebenbach, D. H. Between Camelots
Rebbetzin
Ebenbach, D. H. Between Camelots
Rue Rachel
Ebenbach, D. H. Between Camelots
Searching the reef in the off-season
Ebenbach, D. H. Between Camelots
Social games
Ebenbach, D. H. Between Camelots

Eberhardt, Isabelle

One night in Africa
"Tell it to us easy" and other stories; a com-
plete short fiction anthology of African
American women writers in Opportunity
magazine, (1923-1948); edited by Judith
Musser.
The tears of the almond tree
"Tell it to us easy" and other stories; a com-
plete short fiction anthology of African
American women writers in Opportunity
magazine, (1923-1948); edited by Judith
Musser.

Eberlein, Xujun

Goldbach's Conjecture
StoryQuarterly v40 p128-63 2004
Pivot Point
Agni no62 p54-72 2005
Ebony-a story. Thompson, I. M.
Ebri, Kossi Komla- *See* Komla-Ebri, Kossi, 1954-
Ecce Homo. Gottreich, L.

ECCENTRICS AND ECCENTRICITIES

See also Recluses
Averill, T. F. Topeka underground
Barlow, J. The donkey wedding at Gomersal, re-
counted by an inhabitant of that place
Barthelme, D. The big broadcast of 1938
Barzak, C. What we know about the lost fami-
lies of — house
Baxter, C. Gryphon
Beattie, A. Duchais
Brau, E. Casablanca
Bukoski, A. The woman who ate cat food
Busch, F. Now that it's spring
Carver, R. Why don't you dance?
Corso, P. Shelf life
Crouse, D. Copy Kats
DeMarinis, R. Structure
D'Souza, T. The man who married a tree
Dybek, S. Breasts
Fulton, A. The glorious mysteries
Gifford, B. The bearded lady of Rutgers Street
Gildner, G. Come sta? come va?
Grimes, C. The public sentence
Groff, L. Blythe
Harrison, M. J. Running down
Hempel, A. At the gates of the animal kingdom
Holladay, C. C. The peacock
Johnson, G. Crazy ladies
Lennon, J. R. Eight pieces for the left hand
Levin, Z. Grammar
Lynn, D. H. Paschal lamb
Massie, E. The next-door collector
Matthews, J. Haunted by name our ignorant lips
Mayer, L. N. Love for Miss Dottie
Moceri, M. The mystery spot
Molodowsky, K. Elaine
Moss, B. K. Camping in
Ohlin, A. Ghostwriting
Palazzeschi, A. Silence
Palazzeschi, A. A solitary gentleman
Pancake, A. Dog song
Reisen, A. He laughed
Rock, P. The sharpest knife
Scoville, S. Pu'u Pu'iwa
Singleton, G. Assurance
Singleton, G. The novels of Raymond Carver
Singleton, G. Soldiers in Gruel
Stamm, P. Deep furrows
Steinberg, S. How it starts
Stern, R. G. La pourriture noble
Thomas, E. Hawthornden
Thomas, E. Morgan
Trevor, D. Saint Francis in Flint
Ts'an-hsüeh. The bizarre wooden building
Vogrin, V. The hotel-motel bar & grill
Wilson, K. The museum of whatnot
Wilson, K. The shooting man

Echenoz, Jean

Plan of occupancy
Paris tales; stories; translated by Helen Constantine

ECHO (LEGENDARY CHARACTER)

Hand, E. Echo
Echo. Hand, E.
Echo. Jackson, R.
The **echo** and the nemesis. Stafford, J.

Eck, Matthew

What I Won't Tell You
New Letters v73 no4 p35-48 2007

Eclipse. Delury, J.
Eclipse tonight. Moceri, M.
ECLIPSES
  Moceri, M. Eclipse tonight
  Stafford, J. The darkening moon
Eco, Umberto
  The Gorge
    The New Yorker v81 no3 p62-73 Mr 7 2005
ECOLOGY
  Kress, N. Wetlands preserve
  Martin, G. R. R. A beast for Norn
  Martin, G. R. R. Guardians
  Silverberg, R. The wind and the rain
ECONOMISTS
  Abraham, D. The cambist and Lord Iron: a fairy
    tale of economics
  Unger, D. The perfect wife
Economy measures. Zoshchenko, M.
Ecstasy.
Ecstasy and Poetry in Chicago. Komie, L. B.
The **Ecstasy** of Alfred Russel Wallace. Mason, D.
ECUADOR
    See also Galapagos Islands
  Bova, B. Sam's war
Edelglass, Elizabeth
  Small Rotations of the Earth
    Michigan Quarterly Review v45 no2 p266-83
    Spr 2006
Edelman, Scott
  Almost the last story by almost the last man
    The living dead; edited by John Joseph Ad-
    ams
  My life is good
    Crossroads; tales of the southern literary fan-
    tastic; edited by F. Brett Cox and Andy
    Duncan
  Survival of the fittest
    Summer chills; strangers in stranger lands; ed-
    ited by Stephen Jones
Edelweiss. Haddam, J.
EDEN
  Domecq, B. Lillith
  Domecq, B. Sammaël
  Domecq, B. Sammaël and Lillith
  Friesner, E. M. Abductio ad absurdum
  Kelly, J. P. Serpent
Eden. Wood, D.
Eden's bodyguard. Bareford, D.
Eden's gate. Macy, C.
The **edge**. Matheson, R.
Edge. Williams, C.
The **edge** of nowhere. Kelly, J. P.
The **edge** of seventeen. Sokoloff, A.
The **edge** of the universe. Bisson, T.
The **edge** of the world. Hoffman, A.
The **edge** of the world. Swanwick, M.
An **edge** to a sword. Lamb, H.
Edgerton, Clyde
  Debra's flap and snap
    Best of the South: from the second decade of
    New stories from the South; selected and
    introduced by Anne Tyler
  The great speckled bird
    New stories from the South; the year's best,
    2008; selected from U.S. magazines by ZZ
    Packer with Kathy Pories; with an introduc-
    tion by ZZ Packer
    The Southern Review (Baton Rouge, La.) v43
    no1 p182-96 Wint 2007

Edgewater. Ohlin, A.
EDickinsonRepliLuxe. Oates, J. C.
Edie's nod. Burke, T.
EDINBURGH (SCOTLAND) *See* Scotland—Ed-
  inburgh
Edinburgh. Kennedy, A. L.
Edinburgh man. MacNeil, K.
**EDISON, THOMAS A. (THOMAS ALVA),
1847-1931**
       About
  Landis, G. A. The eyes of America
Edison, New Jersey. Díaz, J.
Edith-Esther. Shields, C.
Edith Swan-Neck. Leblanc, M.
EDITORS
    See also Journalists
  Bierce, A. "The bubble reputation"
  Bierce, A. Corrupting the press
  Bierce, A. Mr. Masthead, journalist
  Bierce, A. Why I am not editing "The stinger"
  Chase, M. Weekend
  Cooper, D. The anal-retentive line editor
  Effinger, G. A. The thing from the slush
  Hill, J. Best new horror
  King, S. The ballad of the flexible bullet
  Luongo, M. Pretty
  Maleeny, T. Suspension of disbelief
  Malzberg, B. N. A delightful comedic premise
  Marusek, D. Yurek Rutz, Yurek Rutz, Yurek
    Rutz
  Monteleone, T. F. Present perfect
Edmison, Erin
  (tr.) *See* Pletzinger, Thomas
Edmonds, Chris
  Elsa
    Dalhousie Review v88 no3 p397-404 Aut
    2008
Edna's mission. McCauley, W.
Eduardo's hair. McCann, R.
EDUCATION
    See also Books and reading; Literacy;
    Teachers
  Luongo, M. Pedagogy
  Williams, S. and Dix, S. Night of the dolls
Education at Mimi's. Buckler, E.
Education of a Coat-Check Girl. O'Brien, P.
The **Education** of Henry Adams. Freeman, C.
The **education** of Her Majesty the Queen. Max-
  well, W.
EDUCATORS *See* Teachers
Edugyan, Esi
  The Mosque at Larabanga
    The Literary Review (Madison, N.J.) v52 no2
    p117-31 Wint 2009
Edward and Pia. Barthelme, D.
Edward Bear. Scholes, K.
Edward the Conqueror. Dahl, R.
Edwards, Junius
  Liars don't qualify
    Short stories of the civil rights movement; an
    anthology; edited by Margaret Earley Whitt
Edwards, Martin
  The house of the red candle
    The Best British mysteries, 2006; edited by
    Maxim Jakubowski
  The people outside
    Thou shalt not kill; biblical mystery stories;
    edited by Anne Perry

Edwards, Melodie
Fragile: This Side up
  Michigan Quarterly Review v44 no4 p612-34
  Fall 2005
Edwards, Philip K.
Why Wagon Wheels Go Backwards
  South Carolina Review v39 no1 p94-103 Fall
  2006
Edwards, Sam
The long count
  Hardcore hardboiled; edited by Todd Robin-
  son; introduction by Otto Penzler
Edwinson, Will
The "23"
  Idaho Magazine v3 no7 p28-31 Ap 2004
The Blizzard
  Idaho Magazine v3 no8 p44-9 My 2004
Frankie
  Idaho Magazine v3 no6 p8-11 Mr 2004
The Lesson
  Idaho Magazine v3 no4 p5-9 Ja 2004
The Tin Lizzie
  Idaho Magazine v3 no5 p4-8 F 2004
The trees
  Idaho Magazine v5 no10 p41-3 Jl 2006
World War II Holiday Memories
  Idaho Magazine v5 no3 p56-8 D 2005
Edwrads, Amelia. Barthelme, D.
Eel pie stall. Di Filippo, P.
The **Effect**. Whalen, T.
The **effects** of light. Bakken, K. N.
Effgen, Ryan
The inappropriate behavior of our alleged loved
  ones
  Best New American voices 2007; [edited by
  Sue Miller; series editors, John Kulka and
  Natalie Danford]
Effinger, George Alec
Afternoon under glass
  Effinger, G. A. George Alec Effinger live!
  from planet Earth; featuring contributions
  by Neal Barrett Jr. ... {et al.}
The aliens who knew, I mean, everything
  Effinger, G. A. George Alec Effinger live!
  from planet Earth; featuring contributions
  by Neal Barrett Jr. ... {et al.}
All the last wars at once
  Effinger, G. A. George Alec Effinger live!
  from planet Earth; featuring contributions
  by Neal Barrett Jr. ... {et al.}
At the bran foundry
  Effinger, G. A. George Alec Effinger live!
  from planet Earth; featuring contributions
  by Neal Barrett Jr. ... {et al.}
The day the invaders came
  Effinger, G. A. George Alec Effinger live!
  from planet Earth; featuring contributions
  by Neal Barrett Jr. ... {et al.}
Everything but honor
  Effinger, G. A. George Alec Effinger live!
  from planet Earth; featuring contributions
  by Neal Barrett Jr. ... {et al.}
Fatal disk error
  Effinger, G. A. A thousand deaths; with an
  introduction by Mike Resnick and an
  afterword by Andrew Fox

From downtown at the buzzer
  Effinger, G. A. George Alec Effinger live!
  from planet Earth; featuring contributions
  by Neal Barrett Jr. ... {et al.}
From the desk of
  Effinger, G. A. A thousand deaths; with an
  introduction by Mike Resnick and an
  afterword by Andrew Fox
Glimmer, glimmer
  Effinger, G. A. George Alec Effinger live!
  from planet Earth; featuring contributions
  by Neal Barrett Jr. ... {et al.}
Housebound
  Effinger, G. A. George Alec Effinger live!
  from planet Earth; featuring contributions
  by Neal Barrett Jr. ... {et al.}
In the wings
  Effinger, G. A. A thousand deaths; with an
  introduction by Mike Resnick and an
  afterword by Andrew Fox
The man outside
  Effinger, G. A. George Alec Effinger live!
  from planet Earth; featuring contributions
  by Neal Barrett Jr. ... {et al.}
Mango Red goes to war
  Effinger, G. A. A thousand deaths; with an
  introduction by Mike Resnick and an
  afterword by Andrew Fox
My old man
  Effinger, G. A. George Alec Effinger live!
  from planet Earth; featuring contributions
  by Neal Barrett Jr. ... {et al.}
One
  Effinger, G. A. George Alec Effinger live!
  from planet Earth; featuring contributions
  by Neal Barrett Jr. ... {et al.}
Posterity
  Effinger, G. A. A thousand deaths; with an
  introduction by Mike Resnick and an
  afterword by Andrew Fox
Put your hands together
  Effinger, G. A. George Alec Effinger live!
  from planet Earth; featuring contributions
  by Neal Barrett Jr. ... {et al.}
Seven nights in Slumberland
  Effinger, G. A. George Alec Effinger live!
  from planet Earth; featuring contributions
  by Neal Barrett Jr. ... {et al.}
Solo in the spotlight
  Effinger, G. A. George Alec Effinger live!
  from planet Earth; featuring contributions
  by Neal Barrett Jr. ... {et al.}
Target: Berlin! The role of the Air Force four-
  door hardtop
  Effinger, G. A. George Alec Effinger live!
  from planet Earth; featuring contributions
  by Neal Barrett Jr. ... {et al.}
The thing from the slush
  Effinger, G. A. A thousand deaths; with an
  introduction by Mike Resnick and an
  afterword by Andrew Fox
Two bits
  Effinger, G. A. George Alec Effinger live!
  from planet Earth; featuring contributions
  by Neal Barrett Jr. ... {et al.}
Two sadnesses
  Effinger, G. A. George Alec Effinger live!
  from planet Earth; featuring contributions
  by Neal Barrett Jr. ... {et al.}

Effinger, George Alec—*Continued*
The wicked old witch
  Effinger, G. A. A thousand deaths; with an introduction by Mike Resnick and an afterword by Andrew Fox
The wisdom of having money
  Effinger, G. A. George Alec Effinger live! from planet Earth; featuring contributions by Neal Barrett Jr. ... {et al.}
The wooing of Slowboat Sadie
  Effinger, G. A. George Alec Effinger live! from planet Earth; featuring contributions by Neal Barrett Jr. ... {et al.}
Efoui, Kossi
A hunting scene as observed by a sentimental photographer
  From Africa; new francophone stories; edited by Adele King
Efremov, Ivan Antonovich
The Andromeda Nebula [abridged]
  Worlds apart; an anthology of Russian fantasy and science fiction; edited and with commentary by Alexander Levitsky; translated by Alexander Levitsky and Martha T. Kitchen
"**Eft**" or "Epic". Micklem, S.
Egan, Greg
Crystal nights
  The Best science fiction and fantasy of the year: volume three; edited by Jonathan Strahan
Dark integers
  Egan, G. Dark integers and other stories
Glory
  The new space opera; edited by Gardner Dozois and Jonathan Strahan
  Egan, G. Dark integers and other stories
  The Best science fiction and fantasy of the year: volume two; edited by Jonathan Strahan
  The Year's best science fiction: twenty-fifth annual collection; edited by Gardner Dozois
Lost continent
  The Starry rift; tales of new tomorrows: an original science fiction anthology; edited by Jonathan Strahan
Luminous
  Egan, G. Dark integers and other stories
Oceanic
  The Best of the best, volume 2; 20 years of the best short science fiction novels; edited by Gardner Dozois
  Egan, G. Dark integers and other stories
Riding the crocodile
  The Year's best science fiction: twenty-fourth annual collection; edited by Gardner Dozois
  Egan, G. Dark integers and other stories
Steve fever
  The Year's best science fiction: twenty-fifth annual collection; edited by Gardner Dozois
  Technology Review (Cambridge, Mass.: 1998) v110 no6 p60-8 N/D 2007
Yeyuka
  Rewired; the post-cyberpunk anthology; James Patrick Kelly & John Kessel, editors
Egan, Jennifer
Found Objects
  The New Yorker v83 no39 p96-101 D 10 2007

Selling the general
  This is not chick lit; original stories by America's best women writers; edited by Elizabeth Merrick
Egan, Patrick
Horsepower
  South Carolina Review v38 no1 p148-57 Fall 2005
Egg. Addonizio, K.
Egg. Jackson, S.
The **egg** game. Romm, R.
The **egg** lady. Currans-Sheehan, T.
The **Egg** Trick. Svoboda, T.
Eggers, Dave
After I was thrown in the river and before I drowned
  Eggers, D. How we are hungry
Climbing to the window, pretending to dance
  Eggers, D. How we are hungry
Max at Sea
  The New Yorker v85 no25 p60-9 Ag 24 2009
Notes for a story of a man who will not die alone
  Eggers, D. How we are hungry
The only meaning of the oil-wet water
  Eggers, D. How we are hungry
Quiet
  Eggers, D. How we are hungry
Theo
  The book of other people; edited by Zadie Smith
There are some things he should keep to himself
  Eggers, D. How we are hungry
Up the mountain coming down slowly
  Eggers, D. How we are hungry
  McSweeney's mammoth treasury of thrilling tales; edited by Michael Chabon
When they learned to yelp
  Eggers, D. How we are hungry
Your mother and I
  Eggers, D. How we are hungry
  Stumbling and raging; more politically inspired fiction; edited by Stephen Elliott; with associate editors Greg Larson [et al.]
Eggers, Paul
Monsieur le Genius
  Agni no63 p11-40 2006
What's Yours, What's Mine
  New England Review v29 no3 p143-85 2008
Won't You Stay, Please?
  Prairie Schooner v82 no4 p50-82 Wint 2008
Egghead. Mozetič, B.
EGGS
  Currans-Sheehan, T. The egg lady
  Jackson, S. Egg
  Romm, R. The egg game
  Tem, S. R. Eggs
Eggs. Bakken, K. N.
Eggs. Glatt, L.
Eggs. Tem, S. R.
The **eggy** stone. Hadley, T.
EGOISM
  Fuentes, C. The secret marriage
  Hammett, D. Itchy
  James, C. L. R. Bad Boo-boo-loo messes up the time
  James, C. L. R. Mighty Mouse and the conceited cowboy
  Kun, M. The handwriting patient

EGYPT

Drosso, A.-M. Egyptians who cannot fill in a form in Arabic
Drosso, A.-M. Flight to Marsa Matruh
Drosso, A.-M. Meant for each other
Drosso, A.-M. Penance
Drosso, A.-M. Turbulence
Howard, R. E. The noseless horror
L'Amour, L. South of Suez
Maḥfūẓ, N. The seventh heaven
Mamatas, N. Summon bind banish
Moorcock, M. The Cairene Purse
Nash, R. The camera and the cobra
Posadas, Carmen. The Nubian lover
Smith, D. L. The charnel house
Soueif, A. Returning
Sterling, B. The necropolis of Thebes

To 640

Linscott, G. A blessing of frogs

Rural life

Rifaat, A. At the time of the Jasmine

Alexandria

Drosso, A.-M. From Alexandria to Roseville

Cairo

Dahl, R. Madame Rosette
Drosso, A.-M. Fracture
Drosso, A.-M. Heat
Drosso, A.-M. Pasha, be careful
Drosso, A.-M. Twist
Ghitany, G. A drowsy haze
Harland, R. A guided tour in the kingdom of the dead
Ingalls, R. The archaeologist's daughter
Soueif, A. Chez Milou
Soueif, A. I think of you
Soueif, A. Knowing
Wakkas, Y. "The Egyptian lover"

Luxor

Drosso, A.-M. He has aged
Egypt is a timeless land. Anderson, B.
Egyptian. Benbow, M.
"The **Egyptian** lover". Wakkas, Y.

EGYPTIAN MYTHOLOGY

Farmer, P. J. Osiris on crutches
Smith, D. L. The charnel house

EGYPTIANS

England

Aboulela, L. The museum
Soueif, A. 1964

Saudi Arabia

Megid, Ibrahim Abdel. The other city
Egyptians who cannot fill in a form in Arabic. Drosso, A.-M.

Ehikhamenor, Victor
The General's Bulldozers
The Literary Review (Madison, N.J.) v52 no2 p40-56 Wint 2009

Ehle, Rob
Not the Ocean
New England Review v28 no3 p129-41 2007

Ehrenreich, Ben
From "Everything You See Is Real" [Book excerpt]
Bomb no107 p supp17-supp18, supp20-supp23 Spr 2009
Love (ii)
Bomb no99 p106 Spr 2007

Eidus, Janice
Elvis, Axl, and me
Scribblers on the roof; contemporary American Jewish fiction; edited by Melvin Jules Bukiet and David G. Roskies
Eight days from Willcox. See Leonard, E. You never see Apaches . . . [variant title: Eight days from Willcox]
The **Eight** Eating Disorders of Eve. Munch, B.
Eight episodes. Reed, R.
The **eight-fanged** roach. Ma Jian
Eight guns over a dead girl. Templeton, P.
Eight-legged story. McHugh, M. F.
Eight percent of nothing. Keret, E.
Eight pieces for the left hand. Lennon, J. R.
Eight-tenths a man. Kitahara, A.
Eighteenth summer. Mitsuhara, Y.
"The **eighth** day". Apple, M.
The **eighth** fold. Rivera-Valdés, S.
The **eighth** night. Gospodinov, G.
Eileen. Gordon, M.

EINSTEIN, ALBERT, 1879-1955

About

Bear, E. Schrödinger's cat chases the super string
Fowler, K. J. Lieserl
Silverberg, R. The millenium express
Einstein. Bova, B.
Einstein made easy. Moceri, M.

Eisenberg, Deborah
The custodian
The New Granta book of the American short story; edited and introduced by Richard Ford
The flaw in the design
Eisenberg, D. Twilight of the superheroes
The Virginia Quarterly Review v82 no1 p228-45 Wint 2006
The girl who left her sock on the floor
Beha, C. R. The Ecco anthology of contemporary American short fiction; selected by Joyce Carol Oates and Christopher R. Beha.
Like it or not
Eisenberg, D. Twilight of the superheroes
Revenge of the dinosaurs
Eisenberg, D. Twilight of the superheroes
Best of Tin House; stories; foreword by Dorothy Allison
Some other, better Otto
The Best American short stories, 2004; edited by Lorrie Moore; Katrina Kenison series editor
Eisenberg, D. Twilight of the superheroes
My mistress's sparrow is dead; great love stories, from Chekhov to Munro; edited by Jeffrey Eugenides
Someone to talk to
The Anchor book of new American short stories; edited by Ben Marcus
Twilight of the superheroes
Eisenberg, D. Twilight of the superheroes
Window
Eisenberg, D. Twilight of the superheroes
The O. Henry Prize stories, 2006; edited and with an introduction by Laura Furman; jurors: Kevin Brockmeier, Francine Prose, Colm Toibin

Elephantiasis. Wood, D.
ELEPHANTS
  Bausch, R. The weight
  Budnitz, J. Elephant and boy
  Card, O. S. The elephant of Poznan
  Jo Kyung Ran. Looking for the elephant
  Lansdale, J. R. The fat man and the elephant
  Meno, J. Miniature elephants are popular
  Murphy, Y. Abalone, Ebony and Tusk
  Rosenbaum, B. Orphans
  Smith, C. A. The justice of the elephant
  Stoddard, J. The elephant ironclads
  Theroux, P. The elephant god
  Twain, M. The stolen white elephant
  Watkins, S. Critterworld
  Wood, D. Elephantiasis
Elethea, Abba *See* Thompson, James W., 1935-
Elevator. Kress, N.
ELEVATORS
  Enright, A. Shaft
  Kress, N. Elevator
Eleven. Rees, R.
Eleven beds. Harrison, W.
The **eleventh.** Boyden, A.
The **eleventh** juror. Starrett, V.
The **eleventh** of May. Fonseca, R.
"Elevenzerothreetwothousandfour". Lamri, T.
Elf trap. Cadnum, M.
Elgon. Mabura, L.
Eli. Lam, V.
Eliahu Zalkind's bookkeeping. Molodowsky, K.
Elias *See* Elijah (Biblical figure)
Elias, Tony
  The Animal Doctor
    New England Review v28 no3 p95-126 2007
ELIJAH (BIBLICAL FIGURE)
      About
  Yolen, J. Slipping sideways through eternity
ELIOT, T. S. (THOMAS STEARNS), 1888-1965
      About
  Bear, E. L'esprit d'escalier
Eliot, Thomas Stearns *See* Eliot, T. S. (Thomas
  Stearns), 1888-1965
Elise. Rumford, J.
**ELIZABETH I, QUEEN OF ENGLAND, 1533-
  1603**
      About
  Clarke, S. Antickes and frets
Elkassabany, Amani
  The Barber's Son
    Callaloo v31 no3 p808-17 Summ 2008
Elkin, Stanley
  Baseball Story
    New England Review v27 no4 p48-52 2006
  Colin Kelly's Kids
    New England Review v27 no4 p53-6 2006
  The guest
    Inside the hornet's head; an anthology of
    Jewish American writing; edited by Jerome
    Charyn
Elkins, Kimberly
  What is visible
    Best new American voices 2004; guest editor
    John Casey; series editors John Kulka and
    Natalie Danford
Ella and the canary prince. Cadnum, M.
Elle et moi: le sacrifice. Lamar, J.
Ellen at the End of Summer. Downs, M.
Ellie and Eric and Master Ah. Metcalfe, W.

Ellin, Stanley
  The day of the bullett
    Brooklyn noir 2; the classics; edited by Tim
    McLoughlin
  The specialty of the house
    Murder short & sweet; edited by Paul D.
    Staudohar
Elliot, Jessie *See* Grodstein, Lauren
Elliot, Julia
  The Whipping
    The Georgia Review v60 no2 p394-406
    Summ 2006
Elliot, M. J.
  The finishing stroke
    Gaslight grimoire; fantastic tales of Sherlock
    Holmes; edited by J. R. Campbell and
    Charles Prepolec
Elliott, Julia
  The whipping
    Best American fantasy; guest editors Ann &
    Jeff VanderMeer; series editor Matthew
    Cheney
Elliott, Scott
  The Wheelbarrow Man
    The Antioch Review v64 no3 p461-73 Summ
    2006
Elliott, Stephen
  My Friend Petey
    StoryQuarterly v42 p257-61 2006
  The other man
    Homewrecker: an adultery reader; edited by
    Daphne Gottlieb
  The patriot actor
    Politically inspired; edited by Stephen Elliott;
    assistant editor, Gabriel Kram; associate ed-
    itors, Elizabeth Brooks [et al.]
  Social contract
    Sex for America; politically inspired erotica;
    edited by Stephen Elliott
ELLIS, BRET EASTON, 1964-
      Parodies, imitations, etc.
  Winter, D. E. Less than zombies
Ellis, Katherine Malmo
  New Patient Questionnaire
    Gastronomica (Berkeley, Calif.) v8 no3 p70-3
    Summ 2008
Ellis, Seth
  The sidewinders
    Bandersnatch; edited by Paul Tremblay and
    Sean Wallace
Ellison, Harlan
  Goodbye to all that
    McSweeney's mammoth treasury of thrilling
    tales; edited by Michael Chabon
    Nebula Awards showcase 2005; the year's
    best SF and fantasy; selected by the Sci-
    ence Fiction and Fantasy Writers of Ameri-
    ca; edited by Jack Dann
  Incognita, Inc.
    Summer chills; strangers in stranger lands; ed-
    ited by Stephen Jones
  The resurgence of Miss Ankle-strap Wedgie
    Nebula Awards showcase 2007; the year's
    best SF and fantasy; selected by the Sci-
    ence Fiction and Fantasy Writers of Ameri-
    ca; edited by Mike Resnick

Emshwiller, Carol—*Continued*
Josephine
  Emshwiller, C. I live with you
The library
  Emshwiller, C. I live with you
My general
  Emshwiller, C. I live with you
The prince of mules
  Emshwiller, C. I live with you
See no evil, feel no joy
  Emshwiller, C. I live with you
Enchanted looms. Rose, A.
The **enchanted** palace. Kiely, B.
Enchantment. Donoghue, E.
Encho, Sanyutei
Kazikazawa [Redaction of the Meiji-Era story]
  The East v43 no2 p46 Jl/Ag 2007
Encinosa, Michel *See* Encinosa Fú, Michel
Encinosa Fú, Michel
What for, this burden
  Havana noir; edited by Achy Obejas
Enclave. Sallis, J.
Encore. LaBrie, A.
Encore for a neck verse. Emerson, K. L.
An **encounter**. Husayn, 'A. A.
An **Encounter** at Nightfall. Biguenet, J.
An **Encounter** with an Interviewer. Twain, M.
Encounters with the Kodambakkam Hyena.
  Narayanan, V.
The **end**. Barth, J.
The **end**. MacEnulty, P.
The **End** is Nothing, the Road is All. McNally, J.
The **end** of a career. Stafford, J.
The **End** of an Old Song. Fraser, R.
The **end** of Enoch? Sillitoe, A.
The **end** of everything. Jablonski, N.
The **end** of grief. Abbott, L. K.
The **end** of Indian summer. Fitch, S.
The **end** of Larry's wallet. Hasak-Lowy, T.
End of messages. Nevai, L.
The **end** of narrative (1–29; or 29–1). LaSalle, P.
The **End** of Pinky. O'Neill, H.
End of story. Smith, A.
The **End** of Summer. Jones, K.
The **end** of the demon who thought he was God.
  Kartha, D. K. M.
End of the line. Bender, A.
End of the Lot. Horodyski, M.
The **end** of the story. Smith, C. A.
The **end** of the straight and narrow. McGlynn, D.
END OF THE WORLD
  See also Earth, Destruction of
Bailey, D. The end of the world as we know it
Baxter, S. Last contact
Baxter, S. No more stories
Bear, E. And the deep blue sea
Bierce, A. For the Ahkoond
Bishop, M. The angst I kid you not, of god
Bradfield, S. Queen of the Apocalypse
DeAndrea, W. L. Murder at the end of the
  world
DiChario, N. Alien radio
Hautala, R. The hum
King, S. Graduation afternoon
Lane, J. Against my ruins
Lebbon, T. Chanting the violet dog down: a tale
  of Noreela
Lumley, B. The strange years
Magee, K. Heat rises

Matheson, R. The last day
Roberts, J. 7C
Rucker, R. v. B. Guadalupe and Hieronymus
  Bosch
Rucker, R. v. B. The men in the back room at
  the country club
Rucker, R. v. B. Six thought experiments con-
  cerning the nature of computation: Experi-
  ment 1: Lucky number
Skillingstead, J. Life on the preservation
Smith, C. A. The shadows
Svoboda, T. '80s lilies
Willis, C. Daisy, in the sun
Wilson, R. C. Utriusque cosmi
Winsor, C. The end of the world
Zelazny, R. Exeunt omnes
Zelazny, R. Fire and/or ice
End of the World. Dragomán, G.
The **end** of the world. Winsor, C.
The **end** of the world as we know it. Bailey, D.
The **end** of the world (as we know it).
  McClendon, L.
The **end-of-the-world** disco. Hospital, J. T.
End piece: old man with a blade. Lumley, B.
End State. Schultz, J.
An **end** to revels. Higgins, G. V.
Endangered Species. Svoboda, T.
Endicott's girl. Woolrich, C.
Ending, and beginning. Roberson, J.
Ending with poetry. Klassen, S.
Endless Buffets. Jones, S. G.
ENDOWMENTS
Bierce, A. The applicant
Parker, D. Song of the shirt, 1941
Pearlman, E. Rules
Endrezze, Anita
Grandfather sun falls in love with a moon-faced
  woman
  Reckonings; contemporary short fiction by
  Native American women; edited by Hertha
  D. Sweet Wong, Lauren Stuart Muller, Jana
  Sequoya Magdaleno
The humming of stars and bees and waves
  Reckonings; contemporary short fiction by
  Native American women; edited by Hertha
  D. Sweet Wong, Lauren Stuart Muller, Jana
  Sequoya Magdaleno
Endurance tests. Dalton, Q.
Enekwe, Ossie Onuora
The last battle
  The Anchor book of modern African stories;
  edited by Nadežda Obradovic; with a fore-
  word by Chinua Achebe
The **enemy**. Fonseca, R.
The **enemy**. Hadley, T.
Enemy. Schuman, D.
Enemy in the Sand. Layugan, M. M.
Eng, Victoria
The flower of flushing
  Queens noir; edited by Robert Knightly
ENGAGEMENTS *See* Betrothals
Engberg, Susan
Above the houses
  Engberg, S. Above the houses
  Iowa Review v35 no2 p58-88 Fall 2005
Beginning
  Engberg, S. Above the houses
Fortune
  Engberg, S. Above the houses

Engberg, Susan—*Continued*

Moon
Engberg, S. Above the houses
Mother of chartres
Engberg, S. Above the houses
Rain
Engberg, S. Above the houses
Reunion
Engberg, S. Above the houses
River hills
Engberg, S. Above the houses
Time's body
Engberg, S. Above the houses
The Sewanee Review v116 no2 p171-95 Spr 2008

Engel, Patricia

Desaliento
Boston Review v33 no3 p39-41 My/Je 2008
Lucho
Boston Review v32 no4 p23-6 Jl/Ag 2007

ENGELS, FRIEDRICH, 1820-1895
About
Waldrop, H. A better world's in birth!
The **engine** at Heartspring's Center. Zelazny, R.

ENGINEERS
Anderson, P. Barnacle bull
Panayotopoulos, N. The strength of materials
Silber, J. War buddies
Engines of desire & despair. Davis, R.

ENGLAND
See also Thames River (England)
Baker, K. Running the snake
Baxter, S. Fate and the fire-lance
Bradbury, R. Henry the Ninth
Chadbourn, M. Who slays the gyant, wounds the beast
Daughtry, P. Tinker's turn
Judson, T. The sultan's emissary
Lumley, B. The taint
MacLeod, I. The summer isles
Morwood, P. The longest ladder
Shepard, J. Hadrian's wall
Sillitoe, A. Enoch's two letters
Sillitoe, A. The road
Soueif, A. Knowing
Spark, M. The Portobello Road
Stirling, S. M. A murder in Eddsford
Trevor, W. Lovers of their time
Trevor, W. A perfect relationship
11th century
Vonnegut, K. The Unicorn trap
15th century
Marston, E. Corpus Christi
16th century
Garrett, G. P. Ghost me what's holy now
17th century
Baker, K. Hellfire at twilight
Carl, L. S. The necromancer's apprentice
Garrett, G. P. Ghost me what's holy now
Williams, L. Winterborn
18th century
Bishop, E. Mr. Pope's garden
Friesner, E. M. The fraud
Liss, D. The double dealer
19th century
Blaylock, J. P. Lord Kelvin's machine
Collins, W. The diary of Ann Rodway
MacLeod, I. The bonny boy
Swanwick, M. The skysailor's tale

Aristocracy
See Aristocracy—England
Civil War
See England—17th century
Coal mines and mining
See Coal mines and mining—England
Farm life
See Farm life—England
Prisoners and prisons
See Prisoners and prisons—England
Rural life
Barlow, J. The possession of Thomas-Bessie: a Victorian melodrama
Dahl, R. Ah, sweet mystery of life
Dahl, R. The champion of the world
Dahl, R. Claud's dog: Mr Feasey
Dahl, R. Claud's dog: Mr Hoddy
Dahl, R. Claud's dog: Rummins
Dahl, R. Claud's dog: The ratcatcher
Dahl, R. Neck
Dahl, R. Parson's pleasure
Gardam, J. Waiting for a stranger
Keating, H. R. F. The great, the good and the not-so-good
Lumley, B. No way home
Scott, Sir W. The Tapestried Chamber; or, The lady in the sacque
Sillitoe, A. The fiddle
Sillitoe, A. The second chance
Woollcott, A. Moonlight sonata
World War, 1939-1945
See World War, 1939-1945—England
Bath
Bierce, A. The early history of Bath
Channel Islands
See Channel Islands
Cornwall
Trezise, R. The magician
Van Booy, S. Everything is a beautiful trick
Dorset
Gardam, J. The people of Privilege Hill
Hardy, T. The three strangers
Kent
Gardam, J. Pangbourne
Lancashire
Blincoe, N. Lucifer over Lancashire
Harris, J. Never give a sucker . . .
London
Aldiss, B. W. Tiger in the night
Beattie, A. Fléchette follies
Beckett, C. Piccadilly circus
Brenner, Y. H. Out of the depths
Brown, S. Empire
Clayton, J. J. Old friends
Dahl, R. The bookseller
Douglass, S. This way to the exit
Fowler, C. Seven feet
Gardam, J. The flight path
Gardam, J. The hair of the dog
Gardam, J. The latter days of Mr. Jones
Gordon, M. Sick in London
Green, S. R. The difference a day makes
Harvey, J. Chance
Hewson, D. The circle
Holmes, A. The league of bald-headed men
Jackson, R. Echo
Jecks, M. No one can hear you scream
Jhabvala, R. P. Refuge in London
Johnstone, N. Lie dream of a casino soul

Epstein, Jennifer C.

Family Gathering

Confrontation no92/93 p182-203 Fall 2005/Wint 2006

Epstein, Joseph

Bartlestein's First Fling

Commentary v122 no4 p47-54 N 2006

Beyond the Pale: A Story

Commentary v125 no3 p43-51 Mr 2008

Gladrags & Kicks

Commentary v123 no6 p44-8 Je 2007

Life of a Salesman: A Story

Commentary v126 no2 p44-50 S 2008

The Life of Art: A Story

Commentary v119 no6 p54-61 Je 2005

The Love Song of A. Jerome Minkoff: A Story

Commentary v127 no2 p37-42 F 2009

My brother Eli

The Best American short stories, 2007; selected from U. S. and Canadian magazines by Stephen King with Heidi Pitlor; with an introduction by Stephen King

The Hudson Review v59 no3 p385-412 Aut 2006

No Good Deed

Commentary v121 no6 p38-43 Je 2006

The Philosopher and the Checkout Girl: A Story

Commentary v118 no4 p54-60 N 2004

What Are Friends For?

Commentary v128 no2 p53-9 S 2009

Epstein. Roth, P.

Equality cake. Templeton, E.

Equilibrium. Kelts, R. N.

Erdeni's tiger. Sargent, P.

Erdrich, Lise

Attention

Erdrich, L. Night train; stories; [by] Liselotte Erdrich

Autumn

Erdrich, L. Night train; stories; [by] Liselotte Erdrich

Beehive

Erdrich, L. Night train; stories; [by] Liselotte Erdrich

Corn is number one

Erdrich, L. Night train; stories; [by] Liselotte Erdrich

Dirty rice

Erdrich, L. Night train; stories; [by] Liselotte Erdrich

Door

Erdrich, L. Night train; stories; [by] Liselotte Erdrich

Errr

Erdrich, L. Night train; stories; [by] Liselotte Erdrich

F-M

Erdrich, L. Night train; stories; [by] Liselotte Erdrich

Fennel toothpaste

Erdrich, L. Night train; stories; [by] Liselotte Erdrich

Great love poems of the state hospital

Erdrich, L. Night train; stories; [by] Liselotte Erdrich

Hairy buffalo

Erdrich, L. Night train; stories; [by] Liselotte Erdrich

Indian ice cream

Erdrich, L. Night train; stories; [by] Liselotte Erdrich

Jolly Beef, Metis legend

Erdrich, L. Night train; stories; [by] Liselotte Erdrich

Kibble

Erdrich, L. Night train; stories; [by] Liselotte Erdrich

LSD

Erdrich, L. Night train; stories; [by] Liselotte Erdrich

Monday

Erdrich, L. Night train; stories; [by] Liselotte Erdrich

Morphine

Erdrich, L. Night train; stories; [by] Liselotte Erdrich

Night train

Erdrich, L. Night train; stories; [by] Liselotte Erdrich

Other (explain)

Erdrich, L. Night train; stories; [by] Liselotte Erdrich

Psychopharmacology

Erdrich, L. Night train; stories; [by] Liselotte Erdrich

Quotidian

Erdrich, L. Night train; stories; [by] Liselotte Erdrich

Red-eyed helldriver

Erdrich, L. Night train; stories; [by] Liselotte Erdrich

Rerst stop

Erdrich, L. Night train; stories; [by] Liselotte Erdrich

Still life with "marigold" & the blue mumbled earth

Erdrich, L. Night train; stories; [by] Liselotte Erdrich

Tribe unknown (fleur-de-lis)

Erdrich, L. Night train; stories; [by] Liselotte Erdrich

Vroom

Erdrich, L. Night train; stories; [by] Liselotte Erdrich

Well-adjusted individual

Erdrich, L. Night train; stories; [by] Liselotte Erdrich

Wi-Jun-Jon

Erdrich, L. Night train; stories; [by] Liselotte Erdrich

XXXL

Erdrich, L. Night train; stories; [by] Liselotte Erdrich

Y

Erdrich, L. Night train; stories; [by] Liselotte Erdrich

Zanimoo

Erdrich, L. Night train; stories; [by] Liselotte Erdrich

Erdrich, Louise

Almost soup

Reckonings; contemporary short fiction by Native American women; edited by Hertha D. Sweet Wong, Lauren Stuart Muller, Jana Sequoya Magdaleno

Eugenides, Jeffrey—*Continued*
Great Experiment
 The New Yorker v84 no7 p100-9 Mr 31 2008
Eulogy for a Warrior. Lindeman, M.
EUNUCHS
Duchamp, L. T. The gift
Due, T. Amusement
Li Yiyun. Immortality
Europa. Scutt, C.
EUROPE
 See also Eastern Europe
Gospodinov, G. Christine waving from the train
   18th century
Tawada, Y. The shadow man
EUROPE, EASTERN *See* Eastern Europe
European experience. Sallis, J.
EUROPEANS
   United States
Saunders, G. Bohemians
Eustace. Malouf, D.
EUTHANASIA
Bierce, A. The coup de grâce
Bisson, T. Greetings
Cozarinsky, E. View of dawn over the lake
Lundin, L. Quality of mercy
Marion, S. Dogs with human faces
Matheson, R. The test
McAllister, B. Benji's pencil
Miller, M. Elsie Riley
Olsen, E. J. Snow angel
Pintado, M. F. The scene
Pohl, F. Spending a day at the lottery fair
Silverberg, R. Neighbor
Wideman, J. E. Are dreams faster than the speed of light
Zelazny, R. The engine at Heartspring's Center
Evan, Raima
Gittel and the Golden Carp
 Calyx v23 no3 p87-95 Wint 2007
Evangeline. Kaminsky, S. M.
Evangelisti, Valerio
Sepultura
 The SFWA European hall of fame; sixteen contemporary masterpieces of science fiction from the continent; edited by James Morrow and Kathryn Morrow
EVANGELISTS
Barnes, H. L. Snake boy
Evenson, B. Two brothers
Kenagy, M. Loud lake
McGlynn, D. Landslide
Singleton, G. Man oh man — it's Manna Man
Stafford, J. A reading problem
Stelmok, J. The samaritan
Evans, Danielle
Virgins
 The Paris Review v49 p82-94 Fall 2007
EVANS, DWIGHT
   About
Evich, M. Fischer at Fenway
Evans, G. S.
(tr.) See Lustig, Arnošt
Evans, Max
Once a cowboy
 Best stories of the American West, v1; edited by Marc Jaffe

Evans, Miranda
I learned when I was older
 Urban Welsh; new short fiction; edited by Lewis Davies
Evans, Richard.
Touch sensitive
 Perverted by language; fiction inspired by The Fall; edited and introduced by Peter Wild.
EVANS, WALKER, 1903-1975
   About
Sayers, V. Walker Evans is a spy on the Lexington Avenue local
EVE (BIBLICAL FIGURE)
   About
Bierce, A. Hades in trouble
Resnick, L. The capo of darkness
Webb, J. Paradise design'd
Eve. Benmalek, A.
The **eve**. Bunin, I. A.
The **eve** of RUMOKO. Zelazny, R.
Evelyn. Wilbur, E.
Even beggars would ride. Crowther, P.
Even gamblers have to eat. Cavin, R.
"**Even** if he never comes back . . . ". Scott-Fleming, S.
Even Macau Girls Get the Blues. Mukherjee, B.
Even Steven. Bender, A.
Even the queen. Willis, C.
Even Vienna could not forever endure this struggle. Abish, W.
The **evening** and the morning and the night. Butler, O. E.
Evening at home. Johnson, G.
An **Evening** Conversation. Ryunosuke, A.
Evening Game. O, C.-H.
An **evening** on the cusp of the apocalypse. Lott, B.
An **evening** out. Trevor, W.
An **evening** with Al Gore. Harris, C.
Evenson, Brian
An accounting
 Best American fantasy; guest editors Ann & Jeff VanderMeer; series editor Matthew Cheney
Body
 Poe's children; the new horror: an anthology; [edited by] Peter Straub.
Fugue–state
 Text: Ur; the new book of masks; [edited by Forrest Aguirre]
Mudder tongue
 The O. Henry Prize stories 2007; edited and with an introduction by Laura Furman; with essays on the story they admire most by jurors Charles D'Ambrosio, Ursula K. Le Guin, Lily Tuck
Prairie
 The living dead; edited by John Joseph Adams
Two brothers
 The Anchor book of new American short stories; edited by Ben Marcus
Watson's boy
 The new weird; Ann & Jeff VanderMeer, editors
"**Event**". Nilsen, A.
An **Event** in Summer. Gibbons, R.
The **events** concerning a nude fold-out found in a Harlequin romance. Lansdale, J. R.

Ez Eldin, Mansoura
  Maryam's Maze
    Southwest Review v94 no1 p73-9 2009

F

F—. Matheson, R.
F-M. Erdrich, L.
Faber, Michel
  All black
    Faber, M. Vanilla bright like Eminem; stories
  Andy comes back
    Faber, M. Vanilla bright like Eminem; stories
  Beyond pain
    Faber, M. Vanilla bright like Eminem; stories
  Bye-bye Natalia
    The O. Henry Prize stories 2008; edited and
      with an introduction by Laura Furman; with
      essays on the stories they admire most by
      jurors Chimamanda Ngozi Adiche, David
      Leavitt, David Means
    Granta no94 p45-71 Summ 2006
  The courage consort
  Explaining coconuts
    Faber, M. Vanilla bright like Eminem; stories
  The eyes of the soul
    Faber, M. Vanilla bright like Eminem; stories
  The Fahrenheit twins
  Finesse
    Faber, M. Vanilla bright like Eminem; stories
  Flesh remains flesh
    Faber, M. Vanilla bright like Eminem; stories
  Fortress/Deer Park
    Perverted by language; fiction inspired by The
      Fall; edited and introduced by Peter Wild.
  A hole with two ends
    Faber, M. Vanilla bright like Eminem; stories
  The hundred and ninety-nine steps
  Less than perfect
    Faber, M. Vanilla bright like Eminem; stories
  Mouse
    Faber, M. Vanilla bright like Eminem; stories
  The safehouse
    Faber, M. Vanilla bright like Eminem; stories
  Serious swimmers
    Faber, M. Vanilla bright like Eminem; stories
  The smallness of the action
    Faber, M. Vanilla bright like Eminem; stories
  Someone to kiss it better
    Faber, M. Vanilla bright like Eminem; stories
  Tabitha Warren
    Faber, M. Vanilla bright like Eminem; stories
  Vanilla bright like Eminem
    Faber, M. Vanilla bright like Eminem; stories
The **fable** begotten of an echo of a line of verse
    by W. B. Yeats. Maxwell, W.
A **fable** containing a reflection the size of a match
    head in its pupil. Brockmeier, K.
A **fable** ending in the sound of a thousand para-
    keets. Brockmeier, K.
The **fable** of the moth. Beagle, P. S.
The **fable** of the octopus. Beagle, P. S.
The **fable** of the ostrich. Beagle, P. S.
The **fable** of the tyrannosaurus rex. Beagle, P. S.
A **fable** with a photograph of a glass mobile on
    the wall. Brockmeier, K.
A **fable** with slips of white paper spilling from the
    pockets. Brockmeier, K.

The **fabled** light-house at Viña Del Mar. Oates, J.
    C.
FABLES
  See also Allegories
  Barlow, J. The possession of Thomas-Bessie: a
    Victorian melodrama
  Beagle, P. S. The fable of the moth
  Beagle, P. S. The fable of the octopus
  Beagle, P. S. The fable of the ostrich
  Beagle, P. S. The fable of the tyrannosaurus rex
  Bierce, A. The grateful bear
  Bierce, A. Haita the shepherd
  Bierce, A. "Love's labor lost"
  Browne, A. Neverland blues
  Coover, R. Aesop's forest
  Eggers, D. Theo
  Franck, T. Audience
  Hill, J. Pop art
  Johnson, C. R. The gift of the Osuo
  Kang, M. S. A fearful symmetry
  Lethem, J. The dystopianist, thinking of his ri-
    val, is interrupted by a knock on the door
  Martel, Y. The Vita Æterna Mirror Company:
    mirrors to last till kingdom come
  Maxwell, W. All the days and nights
  Maxwell, W. The blue finch of Arabia
  Maxwell, W. The carpenter
  Maxwell, W. The country where nobody ever
    grew old and died
  Maxwell, W. The dancing
  Maxwell, W. The education of Her Majesty the
    Queen
  Maxwell, W. The epistolarian
  Maxwell, W. The fable begotten of an echo of
    a line of verse by W. B. Yeats
  Maxwell, W. The girl with a willing heart and
    a cold mind
  Maxwell, W. The half-crazy woman
  Maxwell, W. The industrious tailor
  Maxwell, W. The kingdom where straightfor-
    ward, logical thinking was admired over
    every other kind
  Maxwell, W. The lamplighter
  Maxwell, W. A love story
  Maxwell, W. The man who had never been sick
    a day in his life
  Maxwell, W. The man who had no friends and
    didn't want any
  Maxwell, W. The man who lost his father
  Maxwell, W. The man who loved to eat
  Maxwell, W. The marble watch
  Maxwell, W. The masks
  Maxwell, W. A mean and spiteful toad
  Maxwell, W. Mushrooms
  Maxwell, W. Newton's law
  Maxwell, W. The old man at the railroad cross-
    ing
  Maxwell, W. The old man who was afraid of
    falling
  Maxwell, W. The old woman whose house was
    beside a running stream
  Maxwell, W. Perfection
  Maxwell, W. The pessimistic fortune-teller
  Maxwell, W. The printing office
  Maxwell, W. The sound of waves
  Maxwell, W. The two women friends
  Maxwell, W. What you can't hang on to
  Maxwell, W. The woman who didn't want any-
    thing more

Falconer, Delia
The Intimacy of the Table
The Review of Contemporary Fiction v27 no3 p55-64 Fall 2007
Falk, Bertil
There are no pockets in our graveclothes
Passport to crime; the finest mystery stories from International Crime Writers; edited by Janet Hutchings
FALL (MUSICAL GROUP)
Williams, J. An older lover etc.
The **fall**. Smith, D. L.
The **fall**. Somers, A.
The **fall** at Shanghai. Irvine, A. C.
The **fall** of a coin. Rendell, R.
The **Fall** of the House of Pirnat. Novak, M.
The **fall** of the Republic. Bierce, A.
Fallenberg, Evan
(jt. auth) See Evron, Gilad and Fallenberg, Evan
The **fallguy's** faith. Coover, R.
Falling. Campbell, B. J.
Falling. Lehman, E. G.
Falling. Mooney, C.
Falling. Rosenbaum, B.
Falling Backward. Greenberg, J.
Falling in love. Troy, M.
Falling star. DuBois, B.
Fallon, Melanie
One, Whispering Pines
The Yale Review v94 no2 p159-75 Ap 2006
Fallout. Kent, T.
Fallow earth. Melko, P.
FALSE ACCUSATION
Busch, F. Metal fatigue
Gardiner, J. R. The head of Farnham Hall
Koretsky, J. L. Diamond versus Jiminez
McCabe, E. Victorian fields
Oates, J. C. Concerning the case of Bobby T.
Schutz, B. M. Not enough monkeys
Shinn, S. The double-edged sword
Smith, J. Loot
False alarm. Smith, J.
False cognate. Parker, J.
False light. Murphy, M.
False start. Chase, M.
Falsetto. Nelson, A.
FAME
Bierce, A. Largo al Gapperino
Garrett, G. P. Spilling the beans: a letter to Linda Evangelista
Greenman, B. Oh Lord! Why not?
Johnson, G. The metamorphosis
Lain, D. The dead celebrity
Pierce, T. J. The real world
Pohl, F. Shaffery among the immortals
Rubin, J. Little stones, little pistols, little clash
Samuels, M. Shallaballah
Singleton, G. Runt
Stein, J. The man who killed (and saved) Wall Street
Familial kindness. Lunstrum, K. S.
Familiar games. Baumbach, J.
FAMILY
Bukoski, A. Great sea battles
Busch, F. The bottom of the glass
Drosso, A.-M. They took everything
Effgen, R. The inappropriate behavior of our alleged loved ones
Lin, T. Three-day cruise

MacLaverty, B. A Belfast memory
Monk, B. Flying lesson
Monk, B. Writing lesson
Phillips, S. The Emerson, 1950
Pizzolatto, N. Amy's watch
Singer, M. Deir Yassin
Singer, M. Expatriate
Walsh, M. O. The Freddies
Family. Lott, B.
Family. Winton, T.
The **family** Barcus. Thompson, J.
Family birthday wishes. Espinosa, G.
Family Christmas. Robinson, R.
FAMILY CHRONICLES
See also Family life
Alvarez, J. The blood of the Conquistadores
Lovecraft, H. P. The shunned house
Maxwell, W. The man in the moon
Trevor, D. Labor Day hurricane, 1935
FAMILY CURSES
Arnott, J. Ten lords a-leaping
Farris, J. Bloody Mary morning
Family Custom Tailor. Marcus, W.
Family epic. Romm, R.
A **family** feud. Dunbar, P. L.
Family Gathering. Epstein, J. C.
A **family** history. Park, P.
Family honor. Taha, M. A.
Family in black. Windley, C.
FAMILY LIFE
See also Aunts; Brothers; Brothers and sisters; Family chronicles; Fathers; Fathers and sons; Fathers-in-law; Grandchildren; Granddaughters; Grandfathers; Grandmothers; Grandparents; Grandsons; Halfbrothers; Half-sisters; Marriage; Marriage problems; Mothers and daughters; Mothers and sons; Mothers-in-law; Nephews; Nieces; Parent and child; Sisters; Stepbrothers; Stepchildren; Stepdaughters; Stepfathers; Stepmothers; Stepsisters; Stepsons; Twins; Uncles
Adrian, C. A hero of Chickamauga
Akpan, U. C. An Ex-mas feast
Akpan, U. C. My parent's bedroom
Albert, E. How this night is different
Albert, E. We have trespassed
Anaya, R. A. Dead end
Anaya, R. A. A story
Andrade, M. d. The Christmas turkey
Angel, J. The history of Vegas
Apple, M. Threads
Arnold, G. Heart trouble
Arnow, H. L. S. Blessed—blessed
Arnow, H. L. S. Dreams come true
Arnow, H. L. S. Ketchup-making Saturday
Arnow, H. L. S. King Devil's bargain
Arnow, H. L. S. Marigolds and mules
Averill, T. F. Matty
Badib, 'A. 'A. Trilling cries of joy
Báez, A. To tell the truth
Bannister, I. Mrs Hyde frolics in the eel pit
Barnes, S. The boat
Barrett, M. The last time I saw my father
Battersby, L. In from the sow
Beagan, G. Messages
Beattie, A. The garden game
Bellow, S. Grandma Lausch
Bender, A. Marzipan

FAMILY LIFE—*Continued*

Berg, E. Over the hill and into the woods
Berry, Betsy. Family and flood
Bertino, M. North of
Bierce, A. A bottomless grave
Bradford, R. Carolina live
Brady, C. Last of the true believers
Brkic, C. A. The translator
Brodkey, H. First love and other sorrows
Brown, D. Hands across America
Brown, G. M. Sealskin
Brown, G. M. The tarn and the rosary
Buckler, E. Goodbye, prince
Buckler, E. The orchard
Buckler, E. The quarrel
Buckler, E. Return trip to Christmas
Bunin, I. A. Sukhodol
Burke, J. L. Texas City, 1947
Byrne, M. Only the strong survive
Capote, T. My side of the matter
Card, O. S. Worthy to be one of us
Chute, C. "Ollie, oh . . ."
Clayton, J. J. Muscles
Clayton, J. J. Time exposure
Colombi, M. Winter evenings
Condé, M. Family portrait
Connell, E. S. Arcturus
Corso, P. Unraveled
Currans-Sheehan, T. The balers
Currans-Sheehan, T. Margaret
Curtis, R. Monsters
Curtis, R. Twenty grand
D'Allesandro, S. The wild creatures
Danticat, E. Lélé
De Varennes, Monique. Cabeza
Dean, D. A brief history of us
Déry, T. Love
Divakaruni, C. B. Mrs. Dutta writes a letter
Domecq, B. Of cheese and Christ
Donoghue, E. Do they know it's Christmas?
Doyle, R. Recuperation
Drosso, A.-M. Next on the list?
Drosso, A.-M. Twist
Dunbar, P. L. A family feud
Dunbar, P. L. The interference of Patsy Ann
Eisenberg, D. The custodian
Elliott, J. The whipping
Emshwiller, C. The general
Engberg, S. Mother of chartres
Enright, A. Caravan
Faber, M. Vanilla bright like Eminem
Fisher, C. Chickens
Foer, J. S. Rhoda
Fonseca, R. Night drive
Ford, J. Present from the past
Ford, R. Crèche
Freed, L. Foreign student
Frost, G. Collecting dust
Fuentes, C. A family like any other
Gaines, E. J. A long day in November
Gee, M. Mornington Place
Gee, M. What was important
Gerber, M. J. A daughter of my own
Gifford, B. Do the blind dream?
Gildner, G. Genealogy
Goldfaden, J. King of the ferns
Granados, C. Inner view
Hamer-Jacklyn, S. No more rabbi!
Harjo, J. The reckoning

Haschemeyer, O. The soldier as a boy
Hemon, A. Stairway to heaven
Hempel, A. Weekend
Henriquez, C. Come together, fall apart
Herman, M. El fin del mundo
Hernández, J. J. For Christmas
Herrmann, M. Everthing and nothing
Hill, J. My father's mask
Hodgen, C. A jeweler's eye for flaw
Hoffman, A. India
Holladay, C. C. The lost pony
Holladay, C. C. Snow day
Honwana, L. B. Papa, snake & I
Horgan, P. The peach stone
Hwang, F. Transparency
Hwang, S. A dream of good fortune
Hyde, M. Everything valuable and portable
Ingalls, R. No love lost
Isaacs, S. My cousin Rachel's uncle Murray
Jablonski, N. The good life
Jablonski, N. Succor
Jiménez, F. Moving still
Jo Kyung Ran. Looking for the elephant
Johnson, G. Crazy ladies
Jones, E. P. Common law
Jones, E. P. A poor Guatemalan dreams of a
    Downtown in Peru
Jones, E. P. Spanish in the morning
Jones, S. G. Bleed into me
Jones, S. G. Filius nervosus
Kalman, J. Personal effects
Keane, J. B. 'The teapots are out'
Keane, J. B. Thrift
Keeble, J. The chasm
Kenney, S. The death of the dog and other res-
    cues
Kercheval, J. L. Family portrait
Kercheval, J. L. Mary
Kercheval, J. L. Night dogs
Kercheval, J. L. Scarce
Kiely, B. Down then by Derry
Kiely, B. Your left foot is crazy
Kim, J. Yangban
Kim, M. Scarlet fingernails
Kim, T. The post horse curse
Klassen, S. Eye of the moon
Klimasewiski, M. N. The third house
Kulpa, K. How the light walks
Lain, D. Music lessons
Lapcharoensap, R. Don't let me die in a place
    like this
Le, T. D. T. The gangster we are all looking for
    [excerpt]
Lefer, D. At the site where vision is most per-
    fect
Leung, B. White hand
Levithan, D. How they met
Li Yiyun. After a life
Liebrecht, S. A good place for the night
Lott, B. An evening on the cusp of the apoca-
    lypse
Lupoff, R. A. The Crimson Wizard
Luvaas, W. Yesterday after the storm . . .
Luxenberg, H. The photograph
Lynn, D. H. Mt. Pleasant
MacLaverty, B. On the roundabout
MacLeod, A. Winter dog
Malouf, D. The domestic cantata
Malouf, D. Great Day

FAMILY LIFE—*Continued*

Taraqqi, G. The maid
Thompson, J. The family Barcus
Toer, P. A. Independence Day
Tóibín, C. A long winter
Trevor, D. Fellowship of the bereaved
Troy, J. Ramone
Troy, M. The most beautiful girl in the world
Troy, M. Talk story
Ts'an-hsüeh. Blue light in the sky
Tsutsui, Y. The very edge of happiness
Udall, B. Buckeye the elder
Upadhyay, S. A refugee
Upadhyay, S. The third stage
Updike, J. The brown chest
Updike, J. The guardians
Updike, J. Kinderszenen
Updike, J. Morocco
Varallo, A. The pines
Varallo, A. Sometimes I'm Becky Macomber
Wallace, D. Justice
Wallace, R. Logjam
Wang Ping. Where the poppies blow
Ward, L. Snowbound
Welch, N. Dog
Welch, N. The Good Humor man
Welch, N. Lifeguarding
Welch, N. Texas sounds like an easy place to leave
Wendroff, Z. Around the great Samovar
Wendroff, Z. I am important
Wendroff, Z. A man of principle
Wendroff, Z. On the way to Wonderland
Wendroff, Z. When it comes to living
West, D. My baby . . .
Winsor, C. Four of the times my sister cried
Wolfe, G. La Befana
Wolff, T. The liar
Yates, R. Oh, Joseph, I'm so tired
Yellin, T. Reuben
Zulkey, C. The great Billik
Family life. Molodowsky, K.
Family Life. Monzó, Q.
A family like any other. Fuentes, C.
Family man. Proulx, A.
Family Matters. Howard, Z.
Family Museum of the Ancient Postcards. Watts, S. P.
Family of man. Watkins, S.
Family of shadows. Freed, L.
A family of the post-apocalypse. Disch, T. M.
Family photos. Swann, S. A.
Family portrait. Condé, M.
Family portrait. Kercheval, J. L.
Family reunion. Campbell, B. J.

FAMILY REUNIONS

Chenoweth, A. Powerman
D'Ambrosio, C., Jr. Blessing
Eisenberg, D. Revenge of the dinosaurs
Gildner, G. Something special
Harrison, W. Looking for Greywolf
Hasak-Lowy, T. The task of this translator
Jensen, B. Wake
McIntyre, V. Nightwalking

FAMILY SAGAS *See* Family chronicles
Family scandal. Tognazzini, A.
Family secrets. Shields, C.
A family Sunday in the park: V. I. Warshawski's first case. Paretsky, S.

Famine. Xu Xi

FAMINES

McCabe, E. The landlord
McCabe, E. The master
McCabe, E. The mother
McCabe, E. The orphan
Famished. Brennan, K.
Famous blue raincoat. Tóibín, C.
The famous Gilson bequest. Bierce, A.
The famous poll at Jody's Bar. Gilchrist, E.

Fan Wu

The Taste of Life
    Ploughshares v34 no4 p161-72 Wint 2008/2009

FANATICISM

Kelly, R. Bookmarks
Lansdale, J. R. The pit
Nevill, A. L. G. Yellow teeth
Williams, L. Mortegarde
FANATICS *See* Fanaticism

Fancher, Jane

(jt. auth) See Cherryh, C. J. and Fancher, Jane

Fancher, Jane and Cherryh, C. J.

Legacies
    Thieves' world; enemies of fortune; edited by Lynn Abbey
Fandango. Veríssimo, É.
The fangs of the trees. Silverberg, R.

Fanning, Erin

Sagebrush Schoolhouse
    Idaho Magazine v7 no4 p41-4 Ja 2008

FANON, FRANTZ, 1925-1961

About

Wideman, J. E. Fanon
Fanon. Wideman, J. E.
Fantasia on a favorite waltz. Boyd, W.

FANTASIES

See also Allegories; End of the world; Experimental stories; Future; Improbable stories; Science fiction; Utopias

Abbey, L. Good neighbors
Abraham, D. The cambist and Lord Iron: a fairy tale of economics
Ackert, D. and Rosenbaum, B. The king of the djinn
Adisa, O. P. The living roots
Adrian, C. A better angel
Aguirre, F. Andretto walks the king's way
Aiken, J. Goblin music
Alarcón, D. Abraham Lincoln has been shot
Alfar, D. F. L'Aquilone du estrellas (The kite of stars)
Ali, M. N. Faith
Allende, I. The Guggenheim lovers
Allred, L. East of Appomattox
Andersen, H. C. The Snow Queen
Anderson, B. Clockmaker's requiem
Anderson, B. The last escape
Anderson, K. J. Frog kiss
Anderson, K. J. and Moesta, R. Loincloth
Anderson, M. T. The gray boy's work
Anderson, P. The immortal game
Anderson, T. J. Newbie wrangler
Andrade, C. D. d. Miguel's theft
Andrews, D. Cold spell
Andrews, D. Spellbound
Aranitsis, E. Jesus aged twelve in the temple
Armstrong, M. The Duh Vice
Arnason, E. Knapsack poems

FANTASIES—*Continued*

FANTASIES—*Continued*

Modesitt, L. E., Jr. Ghost mission
Modesitt, L. E., Jr. The pilots
Modesitt, L. E., Jr. Sisters of Sarronnyn, sisters of Westwind
Modesitt, L. E., Jr. Understanding
Moen, D. S. A sword called Rhonda
Monette, S. Draco campestris
Monette, S. A light in Troy
Monette, S. Three letters from the Queen of Elfland
Monteleone, T. F. Changing of the guard
Monteleone, T. F. Off to see the wizard
Monteleone, T. F. Please stand by
Monteleone, T. F. Taking the night train
Moon, E. And ladies of the club
Moon, E. Fool's gold
Moon, E. Gifts
Moon, E. Gravesite revisited
Moon, E. Judgment
Moon, E. No pain, no gain
Moon, E. Sweet charity
Moorcock, M. Benediction: excerpt from The warlord of the air
Moorcock, M. The flaneur of les arcades de l'opera
Moorcock, M. The pleasure garden of Felipe Sagittarius
Moorcock, M. A portrait in ivory
Moorcock, M. The roaming forest
Moorcock, M. A slow Saturday night at the Surrealist Sporting Club
Moore, R. R. The machine of a religious man
Morris, W. A king's lesson
Morse, D. L. Conceived
Morwood, P. The longest ladder
Moscoe, M. Danny's very long trip
Mueller, R. And the sea shall give up its dead
Murphy, J. Bitter almonds and absinthe
Murphy, Y. Abalone, Ebony and Tusk
Murphy, Y. Into the arms of the man on the moon
Murphy, Y. Legacies
Murphy, Y. Our underwater mother
Murr, M. a.- . An idyllic world
Nesbit, E. The Aunt and Amabel
Newman, K. The gypsies in the wood
Nickels, T. England and nowhere
Nix, G. Bad luck, trouble, death, and vampire sex
Nix, G. Beyond the sea gate of the scholar-pirates of Sarsköe
Nix, G. Holly and iron
Nix, G. Punctuality
Nix, G. Sir Hereward and Mister Fitz go to war again
Nolan, W. F. The clown's daughter
Nolan, W. F. Dark return
Nolan, W. F. Once upon a time
Novik, N. Araminta, or, The wreck of the Amphidrake
Nye, J. L. Consequences
Nye, J. L. The growling
Nye, J. L. The revenge of Chatty Cathy
Nylund, E. S. Butterflies like jewels
Ochsner, G. From the fourth row
Ochsner, G. Song of the selkie
Odom, M. The affair of the wooden boy
Offutt, A. Dark of the moon

Okorafor, N. When scarabs multiply
Olesha, I. K. Love
Orullian, P. Beats of seven
Palazzeschi, A. Little Maria
Palazzeschi, A. The portrait of the queen
Palwick, S. Ever after
Palwick, S. The fate of mice
Palwick, S. Stormdusk
Park, P. A family history
Park, P. Fragrant goddess
Parks, R. Courting the Lady Scythe
Parks, R. Skin deep
Paxson, D. L. and Grey, I. The ghost in the phoenix
Peake, M. L. The party at lady cusp-canine's
Peek, B. The funeral, ruined
Perry, A. The judgement
Pflug, U. Border crossings
Pflug, U. The eyes of Horus
Phillips, G. And what shall we call you?
Phillips, H. The oracle spoke
Phillips, H. The small door
Pierson, C. What Quig found
Pil'níàk, B. The naked year [excerpt]
Platonov, A. The sun, the moon, and the ether channel
Pohl, F. Day million
Poirier, M. J. I, Maggot
Powers, T. Itinerary
Powers, T. Night moves
Powers, T. The way down the hill
Powers, T. Where they are hid
Prabhaker, S. A hard truth about waste management
Pratchett, T. Final reward
Pratchett, T. FTB
Pratchett, T. The Hades business
Pratchett, T. Once and future
Pratchett, T. Theatre of cruelty
Pratchett, T. Troll bridge
Pratchett, T. Turntables of the night
Pratt, T. Bottom feeding
Pratt, T. Cup and table
Pratt, T. Dream engine
Pratt, T. Grander than the sea
Pratt, T. In a glass casket
Pratt, T. Komodo
Pratt, T. Lachrymose and the golden egg
Pratt, T. Life in stone
Pratt, T. Romanticore
Pratt, T. Terrible ones
Pratt, T. and Van Eekhout, G. Robots and falling hearts
Purdy, J. Kitty place
Qi, S. Red Guard fantasies
Rabe, J. Roadshow
Raines, P. and Welles, H. The bad magician
Raines, P. and Welles, H. The fishie
Rambo, C. The bumblety's marble
Rambo, C. I'll gnaw your bones, the manticore said
Rand, K. Crickets everywhere
Rand, K. The eye
Rand, K. The glass army
Rand, K. Hear my plea
Rand, K. Kisses sweeter than wine
Rand, K. Medicine
Rand, K. No wine before its time
Rand, K. "Penny" Joe Crane died for my sins

FANTASIES—*Continued*

Rand, K. Refuge
Rand, K. Sawk
Rand, K. Soul taster
Rand, K. The stranger at Gunnison's camp
Rand, K. Through these eyes
Rand, K. Where angels fear
Reed, K. Incursions
Reed, R. Show me yours
Reese, J. Taser
Reichert, M. Z. Deadly ritual
Remizov, A. The Bear cub
Remizov, A. The blaze
Resnick, L. The capo of darkness
Resnick, L. Lady Roxanne La Belle
Resnick, M. The burning spear at twilight
Resnick, M. The lord of the jungle
Resnick, M. Revolt of the Sugar Plum Fairies
Resnick, M. Stalking the unicorn with guns and camera
Resnick, M. Stalking the vampire
Richards, T. Non-existent cats
Richter, S. A case study of emergency room procedure and risk management by hospital staff members in the urban facility
Richter, S. The cavemen in the hedges
Richter, S. The land of pain
Rickert, M. Bread and bombs
Rickert, M. Don't ask
Rickert, M. Journey into the kingdom
Rickert, M. Leda
Rickert, M. You have never been here
Roberson, C. And such small deer
Roberson, J. Blood of sorcery
Roberson, J. Ending, and beginning
Roberson, J. Fair play
Roberson, J. Garden of glories
Roberson, J. Guinevere's truth
Roberson, J. In his name
Roberson, J. The lady and the Tiger
Roberson, J. A lesser working
Roberson, J. Mad Jack
Roberson, J. Of honor and the lion
Roberson, J. Rite of passage
Roberson, J. Shadows in the wood
Roberson, J. Sleeping dogs
Roberson, J. Spoils of war
Roberson, J. Valley of the shadow
Roberts, A. Allen met the Devil
Roberts, A. Dantesque
Roberts, A. Eleanor
Roberts, A. Swiftly
Roberts, S. M. Eviction notice
Robinson, E. Terminal Avenue
Rodriguez, J. A. Dred
Roe, E. The stolen father
Roggie, D. The mushroom Duchess
Rohrig, J. Revolution: number 9
Rosen, S. Gathering strength
Rosenbaum, B. Biographical notes to "A discourse on the nature of causality, with airplanes,"
Rosenbaum, B. Biographical notes to "A discourse on the nature of causality, with airplanes," by Benjamin Rosenbaum
Rosenbaum, B. The book of Jashar
Rosenbaum, B. Embracing-the-new
Rosenbaum, B. Fig
Rosenbaum, B. The house beyond your sky

Rosenbaum, B. Other cities
Rosenbaum, B. Sense and sensibility
Rosenbaum, B. A siege of cranes
Rosenbaum, B. The valley of giants
Rosenblum, M. H. Color vision
Rosenblum, M. H. Sacrifice
Rowe, C. Another word for map is faith
Rowe, C. Gather
Rubião, M. Zacarias, the pyrotechnist
Rucker, R. v. B. Guadalupe and Hieronymus Bosch
Rucker, R. v. B. The use of the ellipse, the catalog, the meter & the vibrating plane
Rushdie, S. The firebird's nest
Russell, K. Accident brief, occurrence # 00/422
Russell, K. Children's reminiscences of the westward migration
Russell, K. Help wanted
Russell, K. St. Lucy's home for girls raised by wolves
Russell, K. Z.Z.'s sleep-away camp for disordered dreamers
Ryman, G. The last ten years in the life of Hero Kai
Ryman, G. Pol Pot's beautiful daughter (fantasy)
Sallis, J. Two stories: The museum of last week
Sallis, J. Under construction
Samphire, P. Crab apple
Sanders, W. Not fade away
Sargent, P. Amphibians
Sargent, P. Climb the wind
Sargent, P. Erdeni's tiger
Sargent, P. Out of place
Sargent, P. A smaller government
Sargent, P. Spirit brother
Saunders, G. The red bow
Savory, B. A. Messages
Schanoes, V. Serpents
Schoffstall, J. Fourteen experiments in postal delivery
Scholes, K. Action team-ups number thirty-seven
Scholes, K. The doom of love in small places
Scholes, K. The doom of love is small spaces
Scholes, K. Edward Bear
Scholes, K. Hibakusha dreaming in the shadowy land of death
Scholes, K. Into the blank where life is hurled
Scholes, K. Last flight of the Goddess
Scholes, K. The man with great despair behind his eyes
Scholes, K. Of metal men and scarlet thread and dancing with the sunrise
Scholes, K. The Santaman cycle
Scholes, K. So sang the girl who had no name
Scholes, K. Soon we shall all be Saunders
Schwartz, D. J. The ichthyomancer writes his friend with an account of the Yeti's birthday party
Schwartz, D. J. The somnambulist
Schwarzschild, E. Irreversible
Schweighofer, P. Seebohm's cap
Schwitters, K. Fairy tale
Schwitters, K. The fairy tale about happiness
Schwitters, K. Fish and man
Schwitters, K. The fish and the ship's propeller
Schwitters, K. The flat and the round painter
Schwitters, K. The flying fish

FANTASIES—*Continued*

Stevens, F. The nightmare
Stevens, F. Sunfire
Stevens, J. D. Burn
Stone, E. J. Taint of treason
Straley, J. Lovely
Stross, C. Pimpf
Strout, A. M. Lady in red
Sullivan, J. Niels Bohr and the sleeping dane
Sussex, L. Frozen Charlottes
Sussex, L. Robots & Zombies, Inc.
Svoboda, T. The Lindberg baby
Swails, K. Cake and candy
Swainston, S. The ride of the Gabbleratchet
Swann, S. A. Fealty
Swanson, F. For the love of Paul Bunyan
Swanwick, M. The bordello in faerie
Swanwick, M. The changeling's tale
Swanwick, M. Dirty little war
Swanwick, M. The dog said bow-wow
Swanwick, M. The edge of the world
Swanwick, M. An episode of stardust
Swanwick, M. Girls and boys, come out to play
Swanwick, M. King dragon
Swanwick, M. The little cat laughed to see such sport
Swanwick, M. The raggle taggle gypsy-o
Swanwick, M. The skysailor's tale
Swanwick, M. A small room in Koboldtown
Swanwick, M. Urdumheim
Swirsky, R. Marry the sun
Taha, M. A. The freak
Tarr, J. Measureless to man
Teppo, M. The one that got away
Thomas, J. The flaying season
Thomas, S. R. The grassdreaming tree
Tidhar, L. 304, Adolph Hitler Strasse
Tidhar, L. My travels with Al-Qaeda
Tolstaia, T. Date with a bird
Traviss, K. The man who did nothing
Tremblay, P. G. There's no light between floors
Tsutsui, Y. Rumours about me
Turgenev, I. S. The Phantoms [abridged]
Turner, M. W. The baby in the night deposit box
Turtledove, H. Joe Steele
Turtledove, H. Shock and awe
Turzillo, M. A. Pride
Tuttle, L. Wives
Tyent, N. Miriam
Uchida, H. The banquet
Uchida, H. The carp
Uchida, H. The cat
Uchida, H. Chrysanthemum
Uchida, H. Envoy to Tang China
Uchida, H. Fireworks
Uchida, H. Jintoshi
Uchida, H. Kudan
Uchida, H. The leopard
Uchida, H. Magnolia
Uchida, H. The narrow straw mat
Uchida, H. The pier
Uchida, H. The reflection
Uchida, H. Santo Kyoden
Uchida, H. The short night
Uchida, H. The tiny double
Uchida, H. Triumphant march into Port Arthur
Uchida, H. The water bird
Valente, C. M. A gray and soundless tide

Valente, C. M. Palimpsest
Valente, C. M. Urchins, while swimming
Van Eekhout, G. The Holy City and Em's reptile farm
Van Eekhout, G. The osteomancer's son
Van Name, M. L. Boar Lake
VanderMeer, J. Exhibit H: torn pages discovered in the vest pocket of an unidentified tourist
VanderMeer, J. The farmer's cat
VanderMeer, J. The goat variations
VanderMeer, J. The Third Bear
Varley, J. Air raid
Vaughan, E. A. Off the rack
Vaughn, C. The nymph's child
Vedam, S. Dragon dreams
Waggoner, T. All in the execution
Wagman, D. What you see
Waldrop, H. Flatfeet!
Waldrop, H. Heart of whitenesse
Waldrop, H. The lions are asleep this night
Waldrop, H. The Sawing Boys
Waldrop, H. Thin, on the ground
Waldrop, H. Us
Waldrop, H. Wild, wild horses
Waldrop, H. You could go home again
Warren, K. Dead sea fruit
Watson, I. The Moby Clitoris of his beloved
Webb, D. The great white bed
Webb, D. Ool Athag
Weber, D. Sword brother
Weiner, J. League of Justice (Philadelphia Division)
Weller, S. The quick stop 5®
Wells, M. The potter's daughter
Wilce, Y. S. The lineaments of gratified desire
Wilde, O. The selfish giant
Wilkins, K. The forest
Williams, C. MacCreadle's bike
Williams, C. The machine
Williams, C. Nearly people
Williams, C. Other skins
Williams, L. Debatable lands
Williams, L. The hide
Williams, L. Mortegarde
Williams, L. Winterborn
Wilson, F. P. RAPED
Wolfe, G. And when they appear
Wolfe, G. The Arimaspian legacy
Wolfe, G. Bea and her bird brother
Wolfe, G. Bed and breakfast
Wolfe, G. The boy who hooked the sun
Wolfe, G. Build-a-bear
Wolfe, G. Death of the island doctor
Wolfe, G. The detective of dreams
Wolfe, G. The dog of the drops
Wolfe, G. Empires of foliage and flower
Wolfe, G. Game in the pope's head
Wolfe, G. Golden city far
Wolfe, G. The hour of the sheep
Wolfe, G. Hunter Lake
Wolfe, G. The island of Doctor Death and other stories
Wolfe, G. The magic animal
Wolfe, G. Of soil and climate
Wolfe, G. On the train
Wolfe, G. Straw
Wolfe, G. Westwind
Wolfe, G. and Hopkins, B. Rattler
Wood, D. The wardrobe

FANTASIES—*Continued*

Wright, J. C. Awake in the night
Yolen, J. The barbarian and the queen: thirteen views
Yolen, J. Become a warrior
Yolen, J. The bird of time
Yolen, J. The boy who sang for death
Yolen, J. Brother Hart
Yolen, J. The cat bride
Yolen, J. Dawn-strider
Yolen, J. Dick W. and his Pussy, or Tess and her Adequate Dick
Yolen, J. The face in the cloth
Yolen, J. The faery flag
Yolen, J. The fisherman's wife
Yolen, J. Flight
Yolen, J. The foxwife
Yolen, J. The girl who cried flowers
Yolen, J. The golden balls
Yolen, J. Green plague
Yolen, J. The gwynhfar
Yolen, J. Happy dens; or, A day in the old wolves' home
Yolen, J. The honey-stick boy
Yolen, J. The hundredth dove
Yolen, J. Inscription
Yolen, J. The lad who stared everyone down
Yolen, J. The lady and the merman
Yolen, J. The maiden made of fire
Yolen, J. Man of rock, man of stone
Yolen, J. The moon child
Yolen, J. The pot child
Yolen, J. Princess Heart O'Stone
Yolen, J. The promise
Yolen, J. Ride me like a wave
Yolen, J. The river maid
Yolen, J. Sans Soleil
Yolen, J. The seventh mandarin
Yolen, J. Silent Bianca
Yolen, J. Slipping sideways through eternity
Yolen, J. Snow in summer
Yolen, J. The tale of the seventeenth eunuch
Yolen, J. The tree's wife
Yolen, J. The white seal maid
Yolen, J. The wind cap
Yolen, J. Winter's king
Yolen, J. The woman who loved a bear
Yolen, J. Words of power
Yoo, D. The somewhat super
Youmans, M. Concealment shoes
Youmans, M. An incident at Agate Beach
Yu, C. Third class superhero
Zamíàtin, E. I. The cave
Zamíàtin, E. I. The dragon
Zavala, H. L. A golpe de martillo/Hammering away
Zebrowski, G. First love, first fear
Zeidler, C. Pregnant
Zelazny, R. Alas! Alas! this woeful fate
Zelazny, R. The bells of Shoredan (Dilvish 3 of 11)
Zelazny, R. The Borgia hand
Zelazny, R. A city divided
Zelazny, R. Comes now the power
Zelazny, R. Death and the executioner
Zelazny, R. The game of blood and dust
Zelazny, R. Here there be dragons
Zelazny, R. Horseman!
Zelazny, R. The horses of Lir

Zelazny, R. The House of the Hanged Man
Zelazny, R. The insider
Zelazny, R. The Juan's thousandth
Zelazny, R. A knight for Merytha (Dilvish 4 of 11)
Zelazny, R. The last defender of Camelot
Zelazny, R. Love is an imaginary number
Zelazny, R. The man who loved the Faioli
Zelazny, R. The new pleasure
Zelazny, R. The places of Aache
Zelazny, R. Shadowjack
Zelazny, R. The steel general
Zelazny, R. Thelinde's song (Dilvish 2 of 11)
Zelazny, R. Time of night in the 7th room
Zelazny, R. Tower of ice
Zelazny, R. Unicorn variation
Zelazny, R. Way up high
Zelazny, R. The white beast
Zettel, S. The red shoes
Zumas, L. Leopard arms

FANTASTIC FICTION *See* Fantasies; Science fiction

Fantasy. Troy, M.
Fantasy for a Friday afternoon. Clayton, J. J.
Fantasy for eleven fingers. Fountain, B.
Fantasy for six electrodes and one adrenaline drip. Haldeman, J. W.
The **fantome** of Fatma. Haschemeyer, O.
FAQ. Benedict, E.

Faqih, Zayd Salih al-
The veiled one
Oranges in the sun; short stories from the Arabian Gulf; edited and translated by Deborah S. Akers, Abubaker A. Bagader

Far as you can go. Van Eekhout, G.
Far away. Heker, L.
The **far** end of history. Wright, J. C.
The **far** side of the bell-shaped curve. Silverberg, R.
The **far** side of the river. Krueger, W. K.
The **far-travelin'** man. Cook, W.
Farangs. Lapcharoensap, R.
The **fare**. Davies, L.
Farewell, my lovely appetizer. Perelman, S. J.
Farewell My Lovely Drawing Table. Meyerowitz, R.
Farewell navigator. Zumas, L.
Farewell to Douala. Tran Dieu Hang
Farewell to the 21st century girl. Chadbourn, M.

FAREWELLS
Martin, J. Galletas
Smith, M. Katzengela

Fargue, Léon-Paul
The twentieth arrondissement
Paris tales; stories; translated by Helen Constantine

Farland, David
The mooncalfe
Orson Scott Card's Intergalctic medicine show; [edited by] Edmund R. Schubert and Orson Scott Card

Farley, Belinda
The investigation
Queens noir; edited by Robert Knightly

The **farm**. Williams, J.

FARM HANDS *See* Farm workers

FARM LIFE
See also Peasant life
Anderson, B. The girls

FARMWORKERS *See* Farm workers
Farnsworth, Vanessa
  The Plaid Shoes
    Dalhousie Review v87 no3 p357-64 Aut 2007
Faro and the bogus inspector. Knight, A.
Farquhar, Polly
  A Hundred Fires
    Prairie Schooner v80 no3 p93-107 Fall 2006
Farrelly, Michael Garrett
  The liquidators
    Nature v444 p518 N 23 2006
Farrier's Daughter. Wilson, L. J. K.
Farrington, Anthony
  Interrupting Jenny
    The Georgia Review v59 no3 p474-90 Fall
    2005
Farrington, Mandy M.
  The Other Side of the Line
    Calyx v23 no1 p12-25 Wint 2006
Farris, Holly
  Lockjaw
    Frontiers v25 no3 p100-3 2004
Farris, John
  Bloody Mary morning
    Dark delicacies; original tales of terror and
    the macabre by the world's greatest horror
    writers; edited by Del Howison and Jeff
    Gelb
  First born
    Dark delicacies 2; fear: more original tales of
    terror and the macabre by the world's
    greatest horror writers; edited by Del
    Howison and Jeff Gelb
  Hunting meth zombies in the great Nebraskan
    wasteland
    The Year's best fantasy and horror: eighteenth
    annual collection; edited by Ellen Datlow,
    Kelly Link & Gavin J. Grant
  The Ransome women
    Transgressions; edited by Ed McBain
The **farthest** schorr. Di Filippo, P.
Fascination. Boyd, W.
FASCISM
    See also Communism; Dictators; National-
  al socialism; Totalitarianism
FASHION INDUSTRY AND TRADE
  Cross, E. Appearances
  Harris, J. Any girl can be a CandyKiss girl!
  Mendes, B. Fleeting fashion
FASHION MODELS
  Garrett, G. P. Spilling the beans: a letter to Lin-
    da Evangelista
  Hawes, L. The knack
  McInerney, J. Philomena
  Pierce, T. J. Sirens
Fast, Molly Jong- *See* Jong-Fast, Molly
Fast like That. Vandiver, E. B.
Fast post. Anderson, B.
Fast Sunday. Standing, S.
Faster. Wingate, S.
The **Fasterfaster** affair. Nolan, W. F.
FASTING
  Watkins, S. Kafka's sister
Fastosous and avaro. MacGowan, J.
Fat farm. Johnston, A.
The **fat** magician. Wolfe, G.
The **fat** man and the elephant. Lansdale, J. R.
Fat man my love. Oates, J. C.
The **fat** man's race. Erdrich, L.

The **fat** one. Ford, J.
Fatal disk error. Effinger, G. A.
The **fatal** eggs. Bulgakov, M. A.
The **fatal** footlights. Woolrich, C.
Fatal wish. Segal, L. G.
FATE AND FATALISM
  Khan, R. Alms
  Lukyanenko, S. Destiny, Inc.
  Robson, J. The girl hero's mirror says he's not
    the one
  Singer, I. B. There are no coincidences
  Sterling, B. Dori Bangs
Fate and the fire-lance. Baxter, S.
The **fate** of mice. Palwick, S.
The **fate** of the Poseidonia. Harris, C. W.
The **Father**. Gunn, K.
The **father**. Martin, J.
The **Father**. Osborn, C.
Father, daughter. Upadhyay, S.
Father Diodorus. Stella, C.
Father John Melby and the ghost of Amy Eliza-
  beth. Brockmeier, K.
Father muerte & the flesh. Battersby, L.
The **Father** of the Bride. Dörrie, D.
Fatherhood. Qi, S.
FATHERS
    See also Fathers and daughters; Fathers
    and sons; Fathers-in-law; Stepfathers
  Alarcón, D. The visitor
  Berry, W. Mike
  Boswell, R. Lacunae
  Boudinot, R. Blood relatives II: Profession
  Busch, F. Metal fatigue
  Engberg, S. Fortune
  Engberg, S. Rain
  Hempel, A. Celia is back
  Hempel, A. Today will be a quiet day
  Hirshberg, G. The two Sams
  Irvine, A. C. The golems of Detroit
  Jensen, B. Wake
  Kercheval, J. L. Honors
  Keret, E. Bwoken
  Malla, P. The film we made about dads
  Martin, J. The father
  McCafferty, J. Light of Lucy
  McLean, S. Driving lessons
  Mordecai, P. Corinthians thirteen thirteen
  Mordecai, P. Crucial concern
  Nisbet, R. Our father
  Rees, R. Lucky strike
  Reinhorn, H. Good to hear you
  Reisen, A. Over the child
  Roe, E. The stolen father
  Ruefle, M. Hazeline
  Saunders, G. Adams
  Shepard, J. Pleasure boating in Lituya Bay
  Smith, R. T. Jesus wept
  Steinberg, S. The garage
  Stern, R. G. The illegibility of this world
  Swann, M. I may look dumb
  Taraqqi, G. Father
  Thompson, J. The family Barcus
  Thompson, J. Treehouse
  Toer, P. A. In twilight born
  Tran, V. The gift of years
  Van Booy, S. Little birds
  Wolff, T. The night in question
  Yellin, T. Dan
  Zentner, A. Touch

FATHERS AND SONS—*Continued*

Majzels, R. Hellman's scrapbook [excerpt]
Malae, P. N. Reliable vet dad, reliable con son
Malae, P. N. The story
Malla, P. Pushing oceans in and pulling oceans outs
Malla, P. Timber on the wheel of everyone
Malouf, D. Blacksoil country
Mandelbaum, P. Several answers
Mandelman, A. Talking to the enemy
Martin, L. The welcome table
Masello, R. Where there's a will . . .
Matheson, R. The test
Matheson, R. A visit to Santa Claus
Maxwell, W. The man who lost his father
Maxwell, W. My father's friends
Maxwell, W. The value of money
McAllister, B. Assassin
McAllister, B. The man inside
McCann, R. The diarist
McCann, R. Snapshots of the visible man
McClure, M. My son
McGlynn, D. Moonland on fire
McGlynn, D. Testimony
McGrath, P. Julius
McGruder, K. The bereavement of Eugene Wheeler
McGuane, T. The zombie
McGuinness, F. The Sunday father
McIlvoy, K. Last will
McInerney, J. The madonna of turkey season
McLean, S. Polly Anderson's Christmas party
McLoughlin, T. When all this was Bay Ridge
McNally, T. M. Bastogne
McNally, T. M. The gateway
Meno, J. The architecture of the moon
Meno, J. The sound before the end of the world
Messinger, J. Christmas spirit
Messinger, J. Winged attack
Meyer, P. One day this will all be yours
Mindt, A. An artist at work
Mindt, A. Free spirits
Mindt, A. Immigration
Mindt, A. King of America
Mindt, A. Reception
Mindt, A. Ruby
Mindt, A. Stories of the hunt
Miura, T. Face of death
Monson, A. Constellations
Monson, A. Other electricities
Montemarano, N. The other man
Morris, M. Homing instinct
Muller, M. Cave of ice
Muñoz, M. Bring brang brung
Muñoz, M. The faith healer of Olive Avenue
Muñoz, M. Ida y vuelta
Muñoz, M. Tell him about Brother John
Muñoz, M. When you come into your kingdom
Murakami, H. The kidney-shaped stone that moves every day
Murphy, Y. Ready in the night
Murphy, Y. Real enough
Nadelson, S. Model rockets
Naiyer Masud. Weather vane
Nelson, A. Strike anywhere
Nelson, R. F. Breaker
Nimrod. My father's lamp
Oates, J. C. The Glazers
Oates, J. C. Suicide watch

Oates, J. C. The twins: a mystery
Ockert, J. Horseshoes
O'Driscoll, M. 13 O'clock
Olafsson, O. April
Orner, P. Pampkin's lament
Otis, M. Picture head
Oz, A. The way of the wind
Pachter, A. E. Green monster
Packer, Z. The ant of the self
Palwick, S. The old world
Panning, A. Super America
Parker, M. What happens next
Parks, T. Dives
Parra, E. A. The showcase of dreams
Parrish, T. It pours
Peelle, L. Mule killers
Pelecanos, G. P. The confidential informant
Percy, B. Refresh, refresh
Percy, B. Unearthed
Percy, B. When the bear came
Percy, B. The woods
Pizzolatto, N. 1987, the races
Pizzolatto, N. Haunted earth
Poissant, D. J. Lizard man
Pollack, E. The bris
Pollock, D. R. Lard
Pollock, D. R. Real life
Pope, D. Karaoke Night
Porter, A. Coyotes
Puchner, E. Neon tetra
Qadir 'Aqil, 'A. a.- . The siege
Qi, S. Fatherhood
Quiroga, H. The son
Rash, R. Chemistry
Rash, R. Deep Gap
Reed, R. Winemaster
Rheinheimer, K. Moon Beach
Richard, M. Gentleman's agreement
Rifaat, A. At the time of the Jasmine
Rivas, M. The gaffer and iron maiden
Rivas, M. Here and there
Rivas, M. Yoko's light
Roberts, S. M. Eviction notice
Roffé, R. Transforming the desert
Romano, T. Bllod lines
Romano, T. One up
Rosa, J. G. The third bank of the river
Rosenfarb, C. Letters to God
Ruffin, P. J. P. and the water tower
Ruffin, P. The queen
Ruffin, P. The well
Russell, K. Children's reminiscences of the westward migration
Russell, K. Lady Yeti and the palace of artificial snows
Rust, E. M. God and birds
Saer, J. J. Baked mud
Sallis, J. Free time
Sallis, J. Hazards of autobiography
Samphire, P. Crab apple
Santangelo, E. Eaten alive
Schmuck, R. The results of a dog going blind
Schwarzschild, E. No rest for the middleman
Schwarzschild, E. What to expect
Selgin, P. My search for red and gray wide-striped pajamas
Selinger, G. Jack Tar
Seth, R. Just a simple bridge
Shaw, S. Reconstruction

The **favourite** game [excerpt] Cohen, L.
Faw, Bob
  (jt. auth) See Resnick, Mike and Faw, Bob
Fawcett, Bill
  Last of the fourth
    Man vs. machine; edited by John Helfers and
     Martin H. Greenberg.
  You'll catch your death of colds
    This is my funniest; leading science fiction
     writers present their funniest stories ever;
     edited by Mike Resnick
Faye, Lyndsay
  The case of Colonel Warburton's madness
    Sherlock Holmes in America; edited by Mar-
     tin H. Greenberg, Jon L. Lellenberg, and
     Daniel Stashower.
Fayer, Steve
  Sea Dogs
    The North American Review v292 no2 p30-5
    Mr/Ap 2007
Fazi, Melanie
  The cajun knot
    The Year's best fantasy and horror: eighteenth
     annual collection; edited by Ellen Datlow,
     Kelly Link & Gavin J. Grant
FBI *See* United States. Federal Bureau of Investi-
  gation
Fealty. Swann, S. A.
FEAR
  Ahmed, N. Aqua Blue
  Allen, K. J. Alternate anxieties
  Anaya, R. A. The road to Platero
  Arjouni, J. Defeated
  Bierce, A. The man and the snake
  Bierce, A. One officer, one man
  Bierce, A. The suitable surroundings
  Bierce, A. A tough tussle
  Bierce, A. A watcher by the dead
  Bierce, A. The wreck of the Orion
  Birmingham, J. Heere be monsters
  Bradbury, R. The whole town's sleeping
  Bradbury, R. The wind
  Brazaitis, M. The day and the night of the day
  Burgin, R. The identity club
  Burgin, R. The spirit of New York
  Campbell, B. J. Fuel for the millennium
  Copper, B. The cave
  Crane, E. Notes for a story about people with
    weird phobias
  Crouse, D. Code
  Dahl, R. Poison
  Dahl, R. The wish
  D'Allesandro, S. My day with Judy
  Deaver, J. Afraid
  Deaver, J. A dish served cold
  Effinger, G. A. Housebound
  Eldridge, C. Sharks
  Gaiman, N. The Flints of memory lane
  Gordimer, N. Safety procedures
  Gordin, J. Spirited away
  Grooms, A. Negro progress
  Guista, M. Step four
  Hand, E. The Saffron gatherers
  Harleman, A. Romantic fever
  Hempel, A. In a tub
  Hempel, A. To those of you who missed your
    connecting flights out of O'Hare
  Hinton, S. E. No white light no tunnel
  Hodgson, W. H. The haunted *Pampero*

  Hodgson, W. H. The rooms of fear
  Hughes, M. Bearing up
  Irsfeld, J. H. The man who watched airplanes
  James, C. L. R. The teacher who feared rats
  Jones, S. G. The fear of jumping
  July, M. The man on the stairs
  Kadare, I. The blinding order
  Kalotay, D. Calamity
  King, L. R. Cat's paw
  Klages, E. The feed bag
  Klam, M. Adina, Astrid, Chipewee, Jasmine
  L'Amour, L. And proudly die
  Lasdun, J. An anxious man
  MacLaverty, B. The assessment
  Maxwell, W. The French scarecrow
  McLean, S. "Be-bop-a-lula"
  McLean, S. On the roof
  Meacham, R. Simple as that
  Michaels, L. Going places
  Milionis, C. The find
  Moceri, M. Einstein made easy
  Moore, D. W. Wide awake in Baton Rouge
  Murphy, M. False light
  Murray, A. The tonsil machine
  Naiyer Masud. Epistle
  Naiyer Masud. Snake catcher
  Newman, L. Flashback
  Pinborough, S. The nowhere man
  Pizzolatto, N. Ghost birds
  Puchner, E. A fear of invisible tribes
  Quiroga, H. The pursued
  Reed, K. Escape from shark island
  Reed, K. Playmate
  Reed, K. Precautions
  Reed, K. The shop of little horrors
  Rivera-Valdes, S. Ana at four times: Ana and
    the moon
  Shabtai, Y. Adoshem
  Shepard, L. Beast of the heartland
  Shirley, J. Nineteen seconds
  Simpson, H. Every third thought
  Simpson, H. If I'm spared
  Smith, C. A. The second interment
  Smith, D. L. The fall
  Tabor, M. L. Trouble with kitchens
  Taha, M. A. The fear
  Tem, S. R. and Tem, M. The man on the ceiling
  Templeton, E. The blue hour
  Trouillot, E. The Chareron inheritance
  Uchida, H. Driftwood
  Waites, M. Just pretend
  Ward, A. E. Motherhood and terrorism
  Watkins, S. Camouflage
  Weber, D. The traitor
  Wendroff, Z. Homeless
  Wingate, S. Inside the hole
  Zebrowski, G. The wish in the fear
  Zoshchenko, M. A hasty business
  Zoshchenko, M. An unpleasant story
Fear. Mejía Vallejo, M.
The **fear**. Taha, M. A.
Fear and loathing in Chelsea. Orner, E.
Fear and trembling: a Father Dowling story.
  McInerny, R. M.
Fear of failure. Hall, P.
A **fear** of invisible tribes. Puchner, E.
The **fear** of jumping. Jones, S. G.
A **fearful** symmetry. Kang, M. S.
Fearing for Ilana. Biller, M.

Ferrell, Carolyn
Documents of passion love
This is not chick lit; original stories by America's best women writers; edited by Elizabeth Merrick
Ferrer, Hugh
(tr.) See Lauterbach, Benjamin
Ferrero, Adrian
When it rains, you'd better get out of Ulga
Interfictions; an anthology of interstitial writing; edited by Delia Sherman and Theodora Goss
Ferrey, Ashok
Vitamin V
Dalhousie Review v89 no1 p51-7 Spr 2009
Ferrigno, Robert
Can you help me out here?
Thriller 2; stories you just can't put down; edited by Clive Cussler; [stories by] Kathleen Antrim . . . [et al.]
The hour when the ship comes in
Los Angeles noir; edited by Denise Hamilton
The Best American mystery stories, 2008; edited and with an introduction by George Pelecanos; Otto Penzler, series editor
Ferris, Joshua
The Dinner Party
The New Yorker v84 no24 p80-5 Ag 11-18 2008
Ghost town choir
New stories from the South: the year's best, 2007; selected from U.S. magazines by Edward P. Jones with Kathy Pories; with an introduction by Edward P. Jones
Prairie Schooner v80 no3 p35-47 Fall 2006
More Afraid of You
Granta no101 p216-35 Spr 2008
The Valetudinarian
The New Yorker v85 no23 p58-66 Ag 3 2009
The **ferry**. Brazaitis, M.
The **ferry**. Row, J.
The **ferry** driver of Portofino. Holthe, T. U.
Fertility. Ingalls, R.
FERTILIZATION IN VITRO
Bakken, K. N. Eggs
Mandelbaum, P. Several answers
FESTIVALS
Brite, P. Z. The feast of St. Rosalie
Kalokyris, D. Militsa or mid-August reverie
Karystiani, I. Mrs. Cataki
Lanagan, M. Night of the firstlings
Moon, E. Welcome to wheel days
FETISHISM (SEXUAL BEHAVIOR)
Martin, J. Rubber days
FETUS
See also Pregnancy
Wilson, F. P. Foet
Fetzer, Bret
Rosebud
The Literary Review (Madison, N.J.) v48 no1 p79-89 Fall 2004
FEUDALISM
Stackpole, M. A. Blood duty
FEUDS
Howard, R. E. The man on the ground
Montemarano, N. If the sky falls, hold up your hands
Silverberg, R. The outbreeders

FEVER
Parra, E. A. Traveler Hotel
Sillitoe, A. The gate of a great mansion
Fever. Crone, M.
Fever. Johnson, G.
A **Few** Moral Problems You Might Like to Ponder, of a Winter's Evening, in Front of the Fire, with a Cat on Your Lap. Smith, G. B.
A **few** small repairs. Abbott, J.
A **few** things about ants. Ford, J.
Fewell, Richard
Knocking on Doors
African American Review v42 no2 p347-9 Summ 2008
Ffitch, Madeline
The Fisher Cat
Chicago Review v54 no4 p36-46 Spr 2009
Fiber. Bass, R.
Ficowski, Jerzy
Intermission
Chicago Review v51 no3 p53-7 Aut 2005
They Don't Ring at the Bernardines'
Chicago Review v51 no3 p58-60 Aut 2005
Waiting for the Dog to Sleep
Chicago Review v51 no3 p61-2 Aut 2005
Window to the World
Chicago Review v51 no3 p63-4 Aut 2005
Fiction. Munro, A.
Fictional History. Goodman, J.
FICTITIOUS ANIMALS *See* Mythical animals
The **fiddle**. Sillitoe, A.
A **fiddle**. Viderman, A.
The **fiddler** of Bayou Teche. Sherman, D.
FIDDLERS *See* Violinists
Fidelio and Bess. Smith, A.
The **field**. Lovesey, P.
The **field**. Mukhopadhyay, T.
Field events. Bass, R.
A **field** guide to the North American Bigfoot. Greenman, B.
FIELD HOCKEY
Schumacher, J. Resurrection hockey
Field Notes: Day 18. Keith, É. C.
A **Field** of Gray Houses. Zuelke, K.
A **field** of snow on a slope of the Rosenberg. Davenport, G.
Field trip. Downs, G.
The **fields** of obscurity. Baumbach, J.
Fiesta. Yamada, E.
Fiesta. Zabala, M.
Fifteen painted cards from a vampire tarot. Gaiman, N.
The **fifteen** worst Russian gay porn web sites. Cooper, D.
FIFTH COLUMN *See* World War, 1939-1945—Collaborationists
The **fifth** daughter. Kemnitz, C.
The **fifth** head of Cerberus. Wolfe, G.
The **fifth** star in the southern cross. Lanagan, M.
The **fifth** story. Lispector, C.
The **fifth** tale: When the devil met Baldrick Beckenbauer. Miller, T.
The **Fifth** Wall. McCollum, M.
The **fifth** world. Sierra, J.
Fifty cents. Powers, T.
Fig. Rosenbaum, B.
The **fig** tree. Porter, K. A.
Figgy pudding. Kalpakian, L.
Fight. Czyzniejewski, M.

The **find**. Hodgson, W. H.
The **find**. Milionis, C.
The **find**. Rand, K.
Find and replace. Beattie, A.
Find Freddy. Hannaham, J.
Find me. Smith, A. N.
Find Natasha. Murphy, Y.
Find Your High School Classmates!!!. Sellers, H.
Finding my shadow. Haldeman, J. W.
The **finding** of Martha. Dunbar, P. L.
The **finding** of the **Graiken**. Hodgson, W. H.
The **finding** of Zach. Dunbar, P. L.
Finding Sajessarian. Hughes, M.
Finding Svale's daughter. Cook, G.
Findings & impressions. Kim, S.
Findurman's News. Ducker, B.
A **fine** dark line [excerpt] Lansdale, J. R.
A **fine** feat hered friend. D'Allesandro, S.
A **Fine** Hen. Kleinman, S.
The **fine** line: a story of the color line. Minus, M.
A **Fine** Looking Man. Watson, P.
A **fine** mess. Hawes, L.
Finesse. Faber, M.
The **finest** tree. Buckler, E.
Finger, Anne
  The artist and the dwarf
    Finger, A. Call me Ahab; a short story collection
  The blind marksman
    Finger, A. Call me Ahab; a short story collection
  Comrade Luxemburg and Comrade Gramsci pass each other at a Congress of the Second International in Switzerland on the 10th of March, 1912
    Finger, A. Call me Ahab; a short story collection
  Gloucester
    Finger, A. Call me Ahab; a short story collection
  Goliath
    Finger, A. Call me Ahab; a short story collection
  Helen and Frida
    Finger, A. Call me Ahab; a short story collection
  Moby Dick; or, The leg
    Finger, A. Call me Ahab; a short story collection
  Our Ned
    Finger, A. Call me Ahab; a short story collection
  Vincent
    Finger, A. Call me Ahab; a short story collection
Finger man. Chandler, R.
Finger prints. Matheson, R.
FINGERS
  Dahl, R. Man from the South
Fingers and toes. Michaels, L.
The **fingers** of the past. Breuer, M. J.
Finigan, Linda Hanley
  Rain, Heavy at Times
    Confrontation no90/91 p143-57 Spr/Summ 2005
Finish. Rylands, J. T.
The **Finish** Line. Robinson, R.
The **finish** of Patsy Barnes. Dunbar, P. L.
Finish what you started. Weil, G.

The **finishing** stroke. Elliot, M. J.
Finishing touches. Matheson, R.
Finisterra. Moles, D.
FINLAND
  Silverberg, R. The littlest Jackal
Helsinki
Daughtry, P. The mouse's aura
Finlay, Charles Coleman
  After the gaud chrysalis
    Finlay, C. C. Wild things
  The factwhore proposition
    Finlay, C. C. Wild things
  Fading Quayle, dancing Quayle
    Finlay, C. C. Wild things
  Footnotes
    Finlay, C. C. Wild things
  A game of chicken
    Finlay, C. C. Wild things
  Lucy, in her splendor
    Finlay, C. C. Wild things
  Pervert
    Finlay, C. C. Wild things
  The political officer
    Finlay, C. C. Wild things
  The seal hunter
    Finlay, C. C. Wild things
  The smackdown outside Dedham
    Finlay, C. C. Wild things
  Still life with action figure
    Finlay, C. C. Wild things
  We come not to praise Washington
    Finlay, C. C. Wild things
  Wild thing
    Finlay, C. C. Wild things
Finley, Toiya Kristen
  The avatar of background noise
    Text: Ur; the new book of masks; [edited by Forrest Aguirre]
  Zed's fanverse
    Nature v451 p222 Ja 10 2008
Finn, Patrick Michael
  In What She Has Done, and in What She Has Failed to Do
    TriQuarterly no129 p125-37 2007
  Where beautiful ladies dance for you
    The Best American mystery stories, 2004; edited and with an introduction by Nelson DeMille; Otto Penzler, series editor
Finn. Michaels, L.
Finnamore, Suzanne
  X
    The dictionary of failed relationships; 26 tales of love gone wrong; edited by Meredith Broussard
Finney, Ernest J.
  After Eden
    The Sewanee Review v113 no2 p269-91 Spr 2005
  Sequoia Gardens
    The Sewanee Review v116 no1 p1-28 Wint 2008
FINNS
United States
Stamm, P. Flotsam
Fioravanti, Valerie
  Earning Money All Her Own
    The North American Review v291 no1 p16-22 Ja/F 2006

Fiorillo, Heriberto

The aroma of death

The Flight of the condor; stories of violence and war from Colombia; translated and compiled by Jennifer Gabrielle Edwards; foreword by Hugo Chaparro Valderrama.

A **Fire**. Puntí, J.

Fire. Sundaresan, I.

Fire and/or ice. Zelazny, R.

Fire and dust. Tolstaia, T.

Fire and ice and linguini for two. Hallaway, T.

Fire and light. MacEnulty, P.

A **fire** at night. Block, L.

Fire in the steppe: an evil night. Chekhov, A. P.

The **fire** of Asshurbanipal. Howard, R. E.

Fire of spring. Zebrowski, G.

The **Fire** Pit. Leslie, N.

The **fire** that burned in the corner. Granville-Barker, H.

Fire watch. Willis, C.

FIREARMS

Amsden, D. Pull!

Anaya, R. A. The man who found a pistol

Archer, J. A Greek tragedy

Boyd, B. Scarecrow

DeMarinis, R. Bête noire

Esposito, B. Guns don't kill people

Gee, M. Righteousness

Haschemeyer, O. The soldier as a boy

Hodgson, W. H. How Sir Jerrold Treyn dealt with the Dutch in Caunston Cove

Lakin, R. The woman who hated the Bronx

Lethem, J. Light and the sufferer

Liparulo, R. Kill zone

Lippman, L. The babysitter's code

Logue, M. Blasted

Mordecai, P. Crucial concern

Mundis, J. The luger is a 9MM automatic handgun with a parabellum action

Oates, J. C. Panic

Rabe, J. Better guns

Shepard, J. The gun lobby

Sillitoe, A. To be collected

Tobar, H. Once more, Lazarus

Treat, J. Little bitches

Van Vogt, A. E. The weapons shop

Watkins, S. Camouflage

The **firebird's** nest. Rushdie, S.

Firebrace, William

Nantes Notes

AA Files no54 p36-47 Summ 2006

The **firebug**. Sillitoe, A.

FIREFIGHTERS

Barthelme, D. A man

Canty, K. In the burn

Chazin, S. Burnout

Hoch, E. D. The retired arsonist

Firefly. Murakami, H.

The **firefly** hunt. Michalopoulou, A.

Firelight. Wolff, T.

FIRES

See also Arson; Disasters

'Arimi, S. a.- . Ghomran's oil field

Brown, G. M. The burning harp

Chandler, A. B. Grimes and the Gaijin Daimyo

Chekhov, A. P. Fire in the steppe: an evil night

Crowther, P. Days of the wheel

Drury, D. Things we knew when the house caught fire

Erdrich, L. The leap

Flanagan, E. Burn

Gardam, J. Learning to fly

Gifford, B. The Peterson fire

Goss, T. A statement in the case

Güzelsoy, I. The tongues of the flames

Hammett, D. The dimple

Hempel, A. Pool night

McGlynn, D. Moonland on fire

McIlvoy, K. Smoke

Monteiro, L. Antonio de Juvita

Murguía, A. The other Barrio

Murphy, Y. Our underwater mother

Pitts, L. Tchoupitoulas bus stop

Richards, S. S. Grass fires

Scott, J. Across from the Shannonso

Silverberg, R. The time of the burning

Smith, C. A. The phantoms of the fire

Smith, R. T. Blaze

Fires. Lee, J.

Fires. Pflug, U.

The **fires** of Christmas. Brown, G. M.

Firewood. Zoshchenko, M.

FIREWORKS

Meno, J. The boy who was a chirping oriole

Romano, T. Sulfur memories

Fireworks. Ford, R.

Fireworks. Uchida, H.

Firing the cathedral. Moorcock, M.

First. Jasper, K.

First. Schrader, E. K.

First anniversary. Matheson, R.

The **first** annual performance art festival at the Slaughter Rock Battlefield. Disch, T. M.

First born. Farris, J.

The **first** born son. Buckler, E.

First calvary. Knightly, N.

The **first** case Bendel-Simso, M. M., ed. Early American detective stories; an anthology; edited by LeRoy Lad Panek and Mary M. Bendel-Simso.

First, catch your elephant. Friesner, E. M.

First class. Bunin, I. A.

The **first** corpse. Machado, A.

First date. Rosen, J.

First Date Back. Almond, S.

The **first** day of school. Cassill, R. V.

The **first** day of the rest of your life. Caine, R.

First Defeat (1939). Méndez, A.

First Family. Winn, S.

The **first** female president. De Kler, M.

The **first** few kinds of truth. Sallis, J.

First flight. Kress, N.

First four measures. Bellows, N.

The **first** hunger. Barnes, H. L.

The **first** hurt. Sherman, R.

First husband, first wife. Tomlinson, J.

First kiss. Baingana, D.

First kisses from beyond the grave. Houser, N.

First lead gasser. Hillerman, T.

The **first** letter of Rosalind to the four churches of the village Bellevue. Rees, R.

First love. Babel, I.

First love and other sorrows. Brodkey, H.

First love, first fear. Zebrowski, G.

First marriage. Moffett, K.

The **first** Mars mission. Young, R. F.

The **first** of spring. Thomas, E.

The **first** of the year. Higgins, G. V.

First offense. McBain, E.

First pastoral. Burke, K.

The **first** person. Smith, A.

The **first** ride. Arnow, H. L. S.

The **first** rule is. Haywood, G. A.

The **First** Sense. Gordimer, N.

First Sight. Mullins, D. P.

The **First** South Central Australian Expedition. Shepard, J.

The **First** Stage of Life. Stewart, M. W.

First start. Snee, T.

First steps. Gospodinov, G.

First surmise. Johnson, G.

The **First** Time I Met H. McKnight, M.

The **First** Time You Are Punched. Lombardo, B.

The **First** to Look Away. Singleton, G.

First Tuesday. Reed, R.

First was the word. Finch, S.

First whisper of the wind in the willows. Grahame, K.

Firstborn. Woiwode, L.

Fischer, Barbara A.
 Evolution
  Confrontation no96/97 p79-93 Fall 2006/Wint 2007
 Late September
  Calyx v25 no2 p73-82 Summ 2009

Fischer, Jason
 Undead camels ate their flesh
  Dreaming again; thirty-five new stories celebrating the wild side of Australian fiction; edited by Jack Dann

Fischer at Fenway. Evich, M.

Fiscus, Jim
 The road to endless sleep
  Alternate generals III; edited by Harry Turtledove and Roland J. Green

Fish. Lakhan, A.

Fish. Silver, L.

Fish and man. Schwitters, K.

The **fish** and the ship's propeller. Schwitters, K.

The **fish** factory. Oates, J. C.

Fish Heads. Markus, P.

The **fish** keeper. Murphy, Y.

The **fish** of Berlin [excerpt] Hummel, E.

The **Fish** Shop Owner's Wife. Clark, M. W.

Fish sticks. Pollock, D. R.

Fish story. Stevens, J. D.

Fishboy. McIntosh, M.

Fisher, Chris
 Chickens
  Fisher, C. Third and long
 Ground rules
  Fisher, C. Third and long
 Hurdles
  Fisher, C. Third and long
 Lilacs
  Fisher, C. Third and long
 The road es traveled
  Fisher, C. Third and long
 Roll your owns
  Fisher, C. Third and long
 Third and long
  Fisher, C. Third and long
 Tin man square
  Fisher, C. Third and long

Fisher, Clay, 1912-1991
  For works by this author under other names see Henry, Will, 1912-1991

Fisher, Pearl
 High falutin'
  "Tell it to us easy" and other stories; a complete short fiction anthology of African American women writers in Opportunity magazine, (1923-1948); edited by Judith Musser.

Fisher, Rudolph
 John Archer's nose
  Black noir; mystery, crime and suspense stories by African-American writers; edited by Otto Penzler

Fisher, Steve
 You'll always remember me
  The Black Lizard big book of pulps; edited by Otto Penzler

The **Fisher** Cat. Ffitch, M.

FISHERIES
 McCauley, W. The turning over
 Ruffin, P. Teaching her about catfish

The **fisherman** and the jinn. Coover, R.

The **fisherman** who had nobody to go out in his boat with him. Maxwell, W.

Fisherman's delight. Braunbeck, G. A.

Fisherman's friend. Noll, I.

The **fisherman's** wife. Yolen, J.

FISHERMEN
  See also Fishing
 Aird, C. A different cast of mind
 Barnes, H. L. The first hunger
 Bensko, J. The palm and the cat
 Brown, G. M. The girl
 Cadnum, M. The flounder's kiss
 Cadnum, M. Give him the eye
 Cass, R. Come back
 Davis, A. B. The significance of importance
 Donoghue, E. Enchantment
 Duncklee, J. Two gold coins
 Fountain, B. Bouki and the cocaine
 Gifford, B. Murder at the Swordfish Club
 Hoffman, A. The edge of the world
 Hukumenoglu, H. The smell of fish
 Kiely, B. Bluebell Meadow
 Marusek, D. The earth is on the mend
 Maxwell, W. The fisherman who had nobody to go out in his boat with him
 Parker, M. Off island
 Skabardonis, Y. Mussels in the flower vase
 Yolen, J. The fisherman's wife
 Yolen, J. The white seal maid
 Yoon, P. Once the shore

The **fishers**. Keeble, J.

FISHES
 Bear, E. Follow me light
 DeNiro, A. A keeper
 Flanagan, E. Goldfish
 Irvine, A. C. Clownfish
 Keret, E. Halibut
 Means, D. The secret goldfish
 Monteiro, L. Little Star of Bela Lua
 Palazzeschi, A. The portrait of the queen
 Pratt, T. Bottom feeding
 Puchner, E. Neon tetra
 Romm, R. Celia's fish
 Vann, D. Ichthyology

The **fishie**. Raines, P. and Welles, H.

FISHING
  See also Fishermen
 Bensko, J. Sirens

FISHING—*Continued*

Bensko, J. Tequila worms

Bierce, A. Sam Baxter's eel

Bishop, T. Bonefish in Wyoming

Bishop, T. The great Mormon cricket fly-fishing festival

Bishop, T. Someone's dog

Dokey, R. Pale morning dun

Dokey, R. The suicide

German, N. Sportfishing with Cameron

Gordon, C. Old Red

Guthridge, M. The host

Hummel, E. The fish of Berlin [excerpt]

Judah, S. Hunting and fishing

Lin, T. Nine, ten

McGruder, K. A view from Eagle Rock Mountain

Ochsner, G. The fractious south

Rash, R. Speckle trout

Rash, R. Speckled trout

Rash, R. Their ancient, glittering eyes

Rheinheimer, K. Hooks

Ribeiro, E. T. The turn in the river

Rock, P. Shaken

Shepard, J. Astounding stories

Welty, E. Ladies in spring

Zelazny, R. The doors of his face, the lamps of his mouth

Fishing. Kaufman, M.

The **fishing-boat** picture. Sillitoe, A.

The **Fishman** of Point Cripp. McMillan, J.

Fitch, Brian

The Luck of the Hopeless

The North American Review v293 no1 p11-18 Ja/F 2008

When I Fall in Love

The North American Review v290 no6 p22-7 N/D 2005

Fitch, Janet

The method

Los Angeles noir; edited by Denise Hamilton

Fitch, Stona

The end of Indian summer

A hell of a woman; an anthology of female noir; edited by Megan Abbott; foreword by Val McDermid

Fitten, Marc

The Paprika Ewer

Prairie Schooner v82 no1 p158-66 Spr 2008

Fitts, James Franklin

The guest-chamber of the Inn at St. Ives

Bendel-Simso, M. M., ed. Early American detective stories; an anthology; edited by Le-Roy Lad Panek and Mary M. Bendel-Simso.

Fitz, Ezra

(tr.) See Fadanelli, Guillermo

Fitzgerald, Desmond

The Soldier in My Throat

The Hudson Review v61 no1 p66-70 Spr 2008

Fitzgerald, F. Scott (Francis Scott)

Babylon revisited

Adaptations: from short story to big screen; 35 great stories that have inspired great films; edited by Stephanie Harrison

FITZGERALD, F. SCOTT (FRANCIS SCOTT), 1896-1940

Parodies, imitations, etc.

Irsfeld, J. H. Interview with Jordan Baker

Fitzgerald, Francis Scott *See* Fitzgerald, F. Scott (Francis Scott), 1896-1940

FitzGerald, Michael A.

Toxoplasmosis or the Beginning of Things You Can't Take Back

The Massachusetts Review v46 no4 p649-67 Wint 2005/2006

Fitzgerald, Penelope

The Mooi

The Hudson Review v61 no1 p71-7 Spr 2008

Worlds Apart

The Hudson Review v61 no1 p78-86 Spr 2008

Fitzgerald, Samar Farah

A Perfect Rotation of the Earth

The Southern Review (Baton Rouge, La.) v43 no4 p886-99 Aut 2007

Fitzhugh, Bill

The neighbors

Hardcore hardboiled; edited by Todd Robinson; introduction by Otto Penzler

FIVE BLIND BOYS OF ALABAMA (MUSICAL GROUP) *See* Blind Boys of Alabama (Musical group)

The **five** dollar bill. West, D.

The **Five** Eggs. Sweet, R. B.

The **five-forty-five** to Cannes. Holthe, T. U.

Five fucks. Lethem, J.

Five marines and a green coffin. See Coloane, F. Five sailors and a green coffin [variant title: Five mariners and a green coffin]

Five-minute hearts. Otis, M.

Five reasons I miss the laundromat. Panning, A.

Five sailors and a green coffin [variant title: Five mariners and a green coffin] Coloane, F.

The **five** senses. Thompson, J.

Five sorrowful mysteries. Hyzy, J.

Five Things. White, L. M.

Five thousand dollars reward. Standish, H. L.

Five thrillers. Reed, R.

Five Tuesdays in winter. King, L.

The **Five** Wounds. Valdez Quade, K.

The **fix**. Duane, D.

Fixed. Longhi, J.

Fixing a hole. Romano, T.

Fixing Hanover. VanderMeer, J.

FLA. Rheinheimer, K.

Fla. boys. Sellers, H.

FLAGS

Grooms, A. Flora Devine

Flaherty, Kate

The Property of Water

Prairie Schooner v79 no1 p146-58 Spr 2005

Flaig, Suzanne

Texas toast

Medium of murder; edited by Susan Budavari and Suzanne Flaig

The **flame**. Holthe, T. U.

Flame Lilies. Choudhry, R.

FLAMENCO DANCERS *See* Dancers

The **flames** beneath the light. Lebbon, T.

Flanagan, Erin

Any ordinary uncle

Flanagan, E. The usual mistakes

Burn

Flanagan, E. The usual mistakes

Circus bezerk

Flanagan, E. The usual mistakes

Every sad detail

Flanagan, E. The usual mistakes

Flanagan, Erin—*Continued*
  Goldfish
    Flanagan, E. The usual mistakes
  Honda people
    Flanagan, E. The usual mistakes
  In this weather
    Flanagan, E. The usual mistakes
  Intervention
    Flanagan, E. The usual mistakes
  The last girlfriend
    Flanagan, E. The usual mistakes
  Laws of relativity
    Flanagan, E. The usual mistakes
  The story of Gladys
    Flanagan, E. The usual mistakes
  The usual mistakes
    Flanagan, E. The usual mistakes
Flâneur. Bernard, K.
The **flaneur** of les arcades de l'opera. Moorcock, M.
Flash Fictions [8 short short stories, by A. N. Holmes et al.]
Flashback. Newman, L.
The **flashlight** game. Hansen-Young, D.
The **flat** and the round painter. Schwitters, K.
Flatfeet!. Waldrop, H.
Flatties: their various forms and uses. Shields, C.
The **flautist**. Boudinot, R.
The **flaw** in the design. Eisenberg, D.
Flax. Weaver, W.
The **flaying** season. Thomas, J.
The **flea** market. Ronk, M. C.
FLEA MARKETS
  Wingate, S. Bill
Fléchette follies. Beattie, A.
The **fledgling**. Gardam, J.
Fleeting fashion. Mendes, B.
Fleischman, Cyrille
  The adventure
    Paris tales; stories; translated by Helen Constantine
Fleisher, Kass
  Advice for New Faculty Members: An Open Letter to J.A.
    Iowa Review v35 no1 p125-30 Spr 2005
FLEMING, IAN, 1908-1964
          Parodies, imitations, etc.
  Nolan, W. F. The Fasterfaster affair
The **flesh** and the bones. Fonseca, R.
Flesh remains flesh. Faber, M.
Flesh tone. Nelson, A.
The **fleshly** school of poetry. Winsor, C.
Fletcher, George U. *See* Pratt, Fletcher, 1897-1956
Fletcher, Matthew L. M.
  The Legal Fiction of the Lake Matchimanitou Indian School
    American University Journal of Gender, Social Policy & the Law v13 no3 p597-634 2005
  Truck Stop
    UMKC Law Review v76 no3 p843-9 Spr 2008
Fletcher and I. De Camp, L. S. and Pratt, F.
Fleur. Erdrich, L.

Flewelling, Lynn
  Perfection
    Elemental; the Tsunami relief anthology; stories of science fiction and fantasy; [edited by] Steven Savile and Alethea Kontis; introduction by Arthur C. Clarke
Flexion. Kennedy, C.
Flidia. Valdés, J.
FLIERS *See* Air pilots
FLIES
  Dahl, R. Claud's dog: Mr Hoddy
  Đoàn, L. Achieving flyhood
  Gospodinov, G. A fly in the urinal
  Langelaan, G. The fly
Flies. Silverberg, R.
FLIGHT
  Bradbury, R. The flying machine
  Brennan, K. Paradise
  Clarke, W. The pentecostal home for flying children
  Kharms, D. The young man who surprised the watchman
  McCarron, M. The flying woman
Flight. Goldberg, M.
Flight. Hospital, J. T.
Flight. Serizawa, A.
Flight. Yolen, J.
FLIGHT ATTENDANTS
  Fuentes, C. A family like any other
  LaBute, N. Whitecap
The **flight** from California. Amdahl, G.
Flight from Cytherea. Dokey, R.
A **flight** of fancy. Bishop, E.
A **flight** of words. Finch, S.
The **flight** path. Gardam, J.
Flight to Enbetu. L'Amour, L.
Flight to forever. Anderson, P.
Flight to Marsa Matruh. Drosso, A.-M.
Flight to the north. L'Amour, L.
Flights. Tomlinson, J.
Flighty Youth. Carney, M.
The **flim-flam** alien. Roberts, R.
Flimflam. Diehl, B. W.
Flint, Eric
  A soldier's complaint
    This is my funniest 2; leading science fiction writers present their funniest stories ever; edited by Mike Resnick
  (jt. auth) See Freer, David and Flint, Eric
  (jt. auth) See Resnick, Mike and Flint, Eric
The **Flints** of memory lane. Gaiman, N.
Flirting with waiters. Levithan, D.
The **Flirty** Dozen. Buckley, C.
Flitting behavior. Shields, C.
Float. Hernandez, L.
Floaters. Campbell, E.
Floating. Heeger, S.
A **Floating** Life. Livings, J.
Floating on the darkness. MacEnulty, P.
Flochne. Levin, Z.
Flood. Alarcón, D.
The **Flood**. Brown, J.
The **flood**. Harjo, J.
The **Flood**. Wood, A.-E.
A **flood** of memories. Green, G.
FLOODS
          See also Disasters
  Berry, Betsy. Family and flood
  Bierce, A. The new bedder

FLOODS—*Continued*

Cambias, J. L. See my king all dressed in red
Card, O. S. Atlantis
Gurganus, A. Fourteen feet of water in my house
Hempel, A. Pool night
Holladay, C. C. The broken lake
Hospital, J. T. The end-of-the-world disco
Judah, S. Monsoon
Kiernan, C. R. To this water (Johnstown, Pennsylvania 1889)
Oates, J. C. Upon the sweeping flood
Parrish, T. It pours
Peattie, E. W. The McCulloughs of the Bluff
Quiroga, H. In the middle of the night
Rheinheimer, K. The stop
Sterling, B. The denial
Straight, S. El ojo de agua
Ts'an-hsüeh. Night in the mountain village

Flora, Fletcher

The collector comes after payday
San Francisco noir 2; the classics; edited by Peter Maravelis.

Flora, Kate

Ninjettes
Sisters on the case; celebrating twenty years of Sisters in Crime; edited by Sara Paretsky

Flora Devine. Grooms, A.

FLORENCE (ITALY) *See* Italy—Florence

Florence. Yu, C.

Florence Green is 81. Barthelme, D.

A **Florentine** experiment. Woolson, C. F.

Flori. Woolford, L.

FLORIDA

Bensko, J. Painted animals
Bensko, J. The palm and the cat
Bensko, J. The robber
Bierce, A. The civil service in Florida
Bingham, S. Doing good
Bingham, S. Red car
Boswell, R. No river wide
Boyle, T. C. Jubilation
Davis, J. S. Ava Bean
Dean, D. Romance manual
Dufresne, J. Electric limits of our widest senses
Dufresne, J. Johnny too bad
Dufresne, J. Squeeze the feeling
Ferris, J. Ghost town choir
Gautier, A. The ease of living
Gifford, B. Wanted man
Goonan, K. A. Sundiver day
Gordon, C. The presence
Gordon, M. Storytelling
Graham, H. The face in the window
Gurganus, A. My heart is a snake farm
Hendricks, V. The big O
Hurston, Z. N. Drenched in light
Hurston, Z. N. John Redding goes to sea
Kelby, N. Jubilation, Florida
King, J. Snake eyes
King, S. The gingerbread girl
Magee, K. Body language
Magee, K. The business of souls
Magee, K. Heat rises
Martin, J. Hope
McBain, E. Downpour [variant title: Murder on the Keys]
Moffett, K. The gardener of Eden
Moffett, K. The medicine man

Moffett, K. Space
Moffett, K. A statement of purpose
Nichols, J. Slow monkeys
Ockert, J. Adrift and distant
Ockert, J. Deviated septum
Parker, B. A clerk's life
Pierce, T. J. Day of the dead
Pollack, E. Beached in Boca
Powell, P. Scarliotti and the sinkhole
Rheinheimer, K. FLA
Rheinheimer, K. Grand Strand
Russell, K. Ava wrestles the alligator
Sayles, J. Cruisers
Sayles, J. Treasure
Sellers, H. Fla. boys
Shepard, L. Hands up! Who wants to die?
Shomer, E. Chosen
Shomer, E. Sweethearts
Shomer, E. Tourist season
Snyder, S. Voodoo heart
Tea, M. Music from earth
Thompson, J. The five senses
Tower, W. The brown coast
Watkins, S. Adam's house
Watkins, S. A jelly of light
Woolson, C. F. The South Devil
Worley, E. B. Grove
Woronov, M. The alligator man

Jacksonville

Stefaniak, M. H. You love that dog
Watkins, S. Critterworld

Key West

Beattie, A. Solid wood
Johnson, G. Hemingway's cats
McGuane, T. The refugee
Trevor, D. Labor Day hurricane, 1935
Vidal, G. Erlinda and Mr. Coffin
Vidal, G. Three stratagems

Miami

Bond, J. T-Bird
DuBois, B. The temptation of King David
Greenman, B. Clutching and glancing
Hall, J. W. The catch
MacEnulty, P. Singing in the free world
Mestre-Reed, E. After Elián
Rivera-Valdes, S. Sunday at the same time
Sterling, B. We see things differently
Wingate, S. The Balkan House

Miami Beach

Gold, H. Death in Miami Beach

Orlando

Magee, K. Knock them down
Snyder, S. Happy Fish, Plus Coin

Palm Beach

Leonard, E. When the women come out to dance

Tampa

Magee, K. All the America you want
Magee, K. As human as you are standing here

Florida. Fuchs, D.

Florida rental. Proulx, A.

FLORISTS

Nelson, R. F. The guardian

Flotsam. Hoffman, N. K.

Flotsam. Kennedy, C.

Flotsam. Stamm, P.

Flounder. Sanders, T.

The **flounder's** kiss. Cadnum, M.

Flour Baby. Cragun, J.

A **flourish** of strumpets. Matheson, R.
Flower. Sherrill, S.
Flower children. Swann, M.
The **flower-gatherer**. Thomas, E.
The **flower** of flushing. Eng, V.
The **flower-women**. Smith, C. A.
Flowering Judas. Porter, K. A.
FLOWERS
  Arnow, H. L. S. Winky Creek's new song
  Ch'oe, Y. The thirteen-scent flower
  Llah, 'A. a.- . and Qadir, 'A. a.- . A bouquet of
    jasmine
  Uchida, H. Chrysanthemum
  Wang Ping. Where the poppies blow
Flowers. McCarthy, S. P.
Flowers for Benny Black. Lieberman, A.
Flowers for Doña Alicia. Rendall, P.
Flowers of Edo. Sterling, B.
The **flowers** of Utah. Pohle, R. W.
Flowers that bloom in the spring. Symons, J.
Floyd, Charles Arthur *See* Floyd, Pretty Boy,
  1904-1934
FLOYD, PRETTY BOY, 1904-1934
          About
  Leonard, E. Louly and Pretty Boy
Fluff. Twelve, O.
Flush. Budnitz, J.
The **fluted** girl. Bacigalupi, P.
FLUTISTS
  Boudinot, R. The flautist
The **fly**. Langelaan, G.
Fly away home. Bradbury, R.
Fly away home. Rees, R.
A **fly** in the urinal. Gospodinov, G.
Flyboys. Wolff, T.
FLYING *See* Flight
Flying. Stevens, J. D.
FLYING DUTCHMAN
  Zelazny, R. And I only am escaped to tell thee
The **flying** Dutchman. Bova, B.
Flying fast. Teigeler, P.
The **flying** fish. Schwitters, K.
Flying lesson. Monk, B.
Flying lessons. Link, K.
Flying over water. Klages, E.
Flying saucer rock and roll. Waldrop, H.
FLYING SAUCERS
  Abbott, L. K. The talk talked between worms
Flying to America. Barthelme, D.
The **flying** woman. McCarron, M.
Flynn, Michael
  The clapping hands of God
    The Year's best science fiction: twenty-
    second annual collection; edited by Gardner
    Dozois
  On the high frontier
    This is my funniest 2; leading science fiction
    writers present their funniest stories ever;
    edited by Mike Resnick
Flynn, Nick
  A crystal formed entirely of holes
    Sex for America; politically inspired erotica;
    edited by Stephen Elliott
Flynn, Nick and Neufeld, Josh
  "bag of mice"
    World Literature Today v81 no2 p46-7 Mr/Ap
    2007

Flynn, T. T.
  Brother murder
    The Black Lizard big book of pulps; edited
    by Otto Penzler
The **flyweight**. Amdahl, G.
Focus group. Reed, K.
Focus on the Fundamentals. Hamid, M.
Foday. McCauley, W.
Foer, Jonathan Safran
  Rhoda
    The book of other people; edited by Zadie
    Smith
Foet. Wilson, F. P.
FOETUS *See* Fetus
Fog. Ruddock, N.
Fog. Winton, T.
Foggery. Rich, M.
Folie à deux. Trevor, W.
FOLK MEDICINE
  Hwang, F. Remedies
  Tagatac, G. G. Stretched toward him like a dark
    wake
Folk song. Gaitskill, M.
A **folklore** for my generation: a pre-history of
  late-stage capitalism. Murakami, H.
Follow me light. Bear, E.
Follow the Money. Kesey, R.
Followed. McIntosh, W.
The **Follower**. Galgut, D.
The **following** bear. Bierce, A.
"The **following** dorg". Bierce, A.
Following the sea. Bierce, A.
The **Folly** of Being Comforted. Connor, J.
Foltz, Craig
  Miasma
    Chicago Review v53 no4/54 no1/2 p208-9
    Summ 2008
  The Return of the BBQ Killers
    Chicago Review v53 no4/54 no1/2 p210-18
    Summ 2008
Fonalleras, Josep M.
  The Brothers Kóvacks
    The Review of Contemporary Fiction v28 no1
    p62-5 Spr 2008
Fondelle or The whore with a heart of gold.
  McClanahan, E.
Fonseca, Rubem
  Account of the incident
    Fonseca, R. The taker and other stories; trans-
    lated from the Portuguese by Clifford E.
    Landers
  Angels of the marquees
    Fonseca, R. The taker and other stories; trans-
    lated from the Portuguese by Clifford E.
    Landers
  Betsy
    Fonseca, R. The taker and other stories; trans-
    lated from the Portuguese by Clifford E.
    Landers
  The book of panegyrics
    Fonseca, R. The taker and other stories; trans-
    lated from the Portuguese by Clifford E.
    Landers
    The Literary Review (Madison, N.J.) v50 no4
    p154-82 Summ 2007
  The dwarf
    Fonseca, R. The taker and other stories; trans-
    lated from the Portuguese by Clifford E.
    Landers

Fonseca, Rubem—*Continued*

The eleventh of May

Fonseca, R. The taker and other stories; translated from the Portuguese by Clifford E. Landers

The enemy

Fonseca, R. The taker and other stories; translated from the Portuguese by Clifford E. Landers

The flesh and the bones

Fonseca, R. The taker and other stories; translated from the Portuguese by Clifford E. Landers

Guardian Angel

World Literature Today v83 no4 p40-3 Jl/Ag 2009

Happy New Year

Fonseca, R. The taker and other stories; translated from the Portuguese by Clifford E. Landers

Large intestine

Oxford anthology of the Brazilian short story; edited by K. David Jackson

Night drive

Fonseca, R. The taker and other stories; translated from the Portuguese by Clifford E. Landers

The notebook

Fonseca, R. The taker and other stories; translated from the Portuguese by Clifford E. Landers

Olivia and Xania

Bomb no102 p94-7 Wint 2008

The other

Fonseca, R. The taker and other stories; translated from the Portuguese by Clifford E. Landers

Pride

Fonseca, R. The taker and other stories; translated from the Portuguese by Clifford E. Landers

The taker

Fonseca, R. The taker and other stories; translated from the Portuguese by Clifford E. Landers

The Literary Review (Madison, N.J.) v52 no1 p166-81 Fall 2008

Trials of a young writer

Fonseca, R. The taker and other stories; translated from the Portuguese by Clifford E. Landers

Winning the game

Passport to crime; the finest mystery stories from International Crime Writers; edited by Janet Hutchings

FOOD

Bacigalupi, P. Calorie man

Berg, E. The day I ate whatever I wanted

Disch, T. M. Canned goods

Frost, G. The girlfriends of Dorian Gray

Gaiman, N. Sunbird

Holladay, C. C. The blue monkey

Lam, D. The seventy-two-ounce steak challenge

Lispector, C. The breaking of the bread

Maxwell, W. The man who loved to eat

McGraw, E. Ax of the apostles

Mohanraj, M. A. Monsoon day (Colombo, 2002)

Peri Rossi, C. To love or to ingest

Romano, T. Hungers

Romano, T. If you eat, you never die

Sargent, P. Originals

Singleton, G. Slow drink

Tabor, M. L. The woman who never cooked

Xu Xi. Famine

Food is fuel. Nelson, R. F.

Food stamp. Green, A.

Food that pleases, food to take home. Grooms, A.

Food Wars. Foster, P.

The **Fool**. Dixon, S.

The **fool**. King, L. R.

A **Fool** for Truth. Andrews, J. M.

Fool of myself. Hill, R.

FOOLS AND JESTERS

Keret, E. For only 9.99 (inc. tax and postage)

Fool's gold. Moon, E.

The **fooly**. Dowling, T.

FOOTBALL

Abbott, L. K. How love is lived in paradise

Abbott, L. K. Love is the crooked thing

Arndorfer, J. The oldest rivalry

Clarke, B. Geronimo

Fisher, C. Third and long

Hasak-Lowy, T. Raider nation

Mandelbaum, P. Virtue

Nisbet, R. Miss Grey of Market Street

Ockert, J. Des

Robinson, R. The football game

Shepard, J. Messiah

Shepard, J. Trample the dead, hurdle the weak

Sillitoe, A. The match

The **football** game. Robinson, R.

Footnotes. Finlay, C. C.

Footprints in the Snow. Frame, R.

Footvote. Hamilton, P. F.

For a breath I tarry. Zelazny, R.

For benefit of Mr. Means. Matthews, C.

For Christmas. Hernández, J. J.

For he on honeydew hath fed. . . Smaglik, P.

For love. Meek, J.

For Mr. Voss or occupant. Hospital, J. T.

For now it's eight o'clock. Irvine, A. C.

For only 9.99 (inc. tax and postage). Keret, E.

For Sale By Owner. Ma, K.

For sale by owner. Siler, J.

For the Ahkoond. Bierce, A.

For the brothers who ain't here. Lewis, W. H.

For the common good. Sprinkle, P.

For the dead travel slowly. Lumley, B.

For the love of mechanical minds. Cooper, B.

For the love of Paul Bunyan. Swanson, F.

For those of us who need such things. Clarke, B.

For What They Shared. Hua, V.

For White Hill. Haldeman, J. W.

For you. Row, J.

Forage. Wang Ping

Foray. McIntyre, V.

Forbidden brides of the faceless slaves in the secret house of the night of dread desire. Gaiman, N.

Forbidden things. Muller, M.

The **force** that through the circuit drives the current. Zelazny, R.

Forced Return. DuBois, M.

Ford, Elaine

Elwood's last job

Contemporary Maine fiction; an anthology of short stories; edited by Wesley McNair

Ford, Kathleen
Crossing the River 1932
The North American Review v293 no6 p12-17
N/D 2008
Typhoid Mary's Proposal
The Antioch Review v67 no3 p425-40 Summ
2009
Ford, Richard
Calling
Wide awake in the Pelican State; stories by
contemporary Louisiana writers; edited by
Ann Brewster Dobie; with a foreword by
Ernest J. Gaines
Charity
Contemporary Maine fiction; an anthology of
short stories; edited by Wesley McNair
Crèche
The Ecco book of Christmas stories; edited
by Alberto Manguel
Fireworks
My mistress's sparrow is dead; great love sto-
ries, from Chekhov to Munro; edited by
Jeffrey Eugenides
How Was It To Be Dead?
The New Yorker v82 no26 p58-69 Ag 28
2006
Leaving for Kenosha
The New Yorker v84 no3 p68-75 Mr 3 2008
Reunion
Beha, C. R. The Ecco anthology of contem-
porary American short fiction; selected by
Joyce Carol Oates and Christopher R.
Beha.
Forecast. Monson, A.
Foreclosure. Haldeman, J. W.
A **foreign** correspondence. McClanahan, E.
The **foreign** correspondent. Brazaitis, M.
FOREIGN SERVICE *See* Diplomatic life
FOREIGN VISITORS
Ohlin, A. Land of the midnight sun
Foreigners. O'Hagan, A.
FORENSIC SCIENTISTS
Black, M. A. Articulation of murder
Collins, M. A. and Clemens, M. V. The high
life: a heartland homicide story
Lutz, J. Mitt's murder
Rusch, K. K. Patriotic gestures
Stein, J. C. Better lucky than good
The **forerunner**. Uchida, H.
The **forest**. Barron, L.
The **forest**. Wilkins, K.
The **Forest** of Existence. Jeon, S. T.
The **forest** path to the spring. Lowry, M.
Forester, C. S. (Cecil Scott)
The turn of the tide
Murder short & sweet; edited by Paul D.
Staudohar
Forester, Cecil Scott *See* Forester, C. S. (Cecil
Scott), 1899-1966
FORESTS AND FORESTRY
See also Wilderness areas
Green, R. L. The wood that time forgot
Schanoes, V. Serpents
Thormahlen, A. 23 December
Wilkins, K. The forest
Forever. Deaver, J.
Forever after. Gifford, B.
Forever angels. Kelly, R.
Forever down the ringing groves. Rich, M.

The **forever** kitten. Hamilton, P. F.
Forever upward. Lanagan, M.
FORGERY OF WORKS OF ART
Irvine, A. C. The Lorelei
Silverberg, R. The artifact business
Forget-me-not. Kitahara, A.
Forgetfulness. Maḥfūẓ, N.
Forging the Bulgarian earring. Gospodinov, G.
FORGIVENESS
Drury, D. Things we knew when the house
caught fire
Dunbar, P. L. Lafe Halloway's two fights
Dunbar, P. L. Nelse Hatton's vengeance
Forgiveness day. Le Guin, U. K.
Forgotten coast. Porter, J. A.
The **forgotten** god. Brau, E.
The **forgotten** kingdom. Crouse, D.
Forgotten land [variant title: Land of oblivion]
Coloane, F.
The **forgotten** ones. Lowachee, K.
A **forgotten** slogan. Zoshchenko, M.
Fork your own broncs. L'Amour, L.
Forlesen. Wolfe, G.
The **Forlorn** Father's Lone Misguided Son.
Ingraham, C.
Forman, Jacob
Lake Hollywood
Bomb no91 p92-5 Spr 2005
Formetta, Cristina Danila
Last summer together
Rome noir; edited by Chiara Stangalino &
Maxim Jakubowski; translated by Anne Mi-
lano Appel, Ann Goldstein, and Kathrine
Jason
Forn, Juan
Swimming at night
Words without borders; the world through the
eyes of writers; an anthology; edited by
Samantha Schnee, Alane Salierno Mason,
and Dedi Felman
Forrest, Katherine V.
A leopard's spots
Women of mystery; an anthology; Katherine
V. Forrest, editor
**FORSTER, E. M. (EDWARD MORGAN),
1879-1970**
About
Brown, R. Aspects of the novel
Forster, Edward Morgan *See* Forster, E. M. (Ed-
ward Morgan), 1879-1970
The **Fort** Field. Keane, J. B.
Fort Macon. Gullette, D.
FORT WORTH (TEX.) *See* Texas—Fort Worth
Forton, Jean
Nestor
The Southern Review (Baton Rouge, La.) v45
no2 p293-4 Spr 2009
Fortress/Deer Park. Faber, M.
The **fortress**. Martin, G. R. R.
Fortunate Buddhas. Ribeiro, J. U.
Fortune. Engberg, S.
Fortune. Graham, T.
Fortune. Magee, K.
Fortune. Rylands, J. T.
Fortune. Williams, J.
The **fortune-teller**. Machado de Assis
The **fortune** teller. Moffett, K.
FORTUNE TELLING
Bishop, E. Was it in his hand?

Frankenstein, Harriet
(tr.) See Cagnone, Nanni
FRANKENSTEIN (FICTITIOUS CHARAC-TER)
DeAndrea, W. L. A friend of mine
Kessel, J. Pride and Prometheus
Frankenstein's daughter. McHugh, M. F.
FRANKFURT AM MAIN (GERMANY) *See*
Germany—Frankfurt am Main
Frankie. Edwinson, W.
Frankie Floats. Winn, T.
FRANKLIN, BENJAMIN, 1706-1790
About
Neville, K. The Tuesday club
Franklin, Emily
In the herd of elephants
Before; short stories about pregnancy from
our top writers; edited by Emily Franklin
and Heather Swain
Franklin, Tom
Grit
The New Granta book of the American short
story; edited and introduced by Richard
Ford
Nap time
New stories from the South: the year's best,
2005; edited by Shannon Ravenel; with a
preface by Jill McCorkle
Those good days
Murder in the rough; edited by Otto Penzler
Franz, Carlos
Circle
Colchie, T. A whistler in the nightworld;
short fiction from the Latin Americas; ed-
ited by Thomas Colchie
FRANZ FERDINAND, ARCHDUKE OF AUS-TRIA, 1863-1914
About
Novakovich, J. The stamp
Franz Kafka—Serious About Your Safety. Singer,
S.
Franz Kafka, superhero!. Gerrold, D.
Franzen, Cola
(tr.) See Ponte, Antonio José
Franzen, Jonathan
Breakup Stories
The New Yorker v80 no34 p104-8 N 8 2004
Good Neighbors
The New Yorker v85 no17 p78-82, 84-9 Je
8-15 2009
Two's Company
The New Yorker v81 no14 p78-81 My 23
2005
Fraser, Russell
The End of an Old Song
The Sewanee Review v115 no4 p524-39 Fall
2007
Phoebe and the Character of Happiness
The Sewanee Review v113 no2 p228-50 Spr
2005
FRATRICIDE
McBain, E. Kid kill
Smith, C. A. The return of the sorcerer
FRAUD
Cain, P. Pigeon blood
Cohen, G. Right is right
Deaver, J. The poker lesson
Dokey, R. The beggar of Union Square

Gappah, P. Our man in Geneva wins a million
euros
Granados, C. Small time
Mason, B. A. The heirs
McGuane, T. Old friends
Meyers, A. Not just the facts
Pierce, T. J. The Yoshi Compound: a story of
post-Waco Texas
Smith, M. Calculators
The **fraud**. Friesner, E. M.
The **Fräulein**. Harshbarger, K.
Frazer, Ron
The Counterfeit Sock
African American Review v40 no2 p313-18
Summ 2006
Frazier, Kevin
Cosmonauts
South Carolina Review v37 no1 p83-91 Fall
2004
The Great Hate
Dalhousie Review v86 no2 p249-60 Summ
2006
Freak. Nolan, W. F.
The **freak**. Taha, M. A.
FREAK SHOWS
With, C. Carny
Freaks. DeMarinis, R.
Fred Rimble. Keane, J. B.
Freda thinks spring. Monson, A.
Fredd, D. E.
Satan's on Euclid Just off Juniper
Southern Humanities Review v39 no3 p264-74
Summ 2005
Freddie Prinze is my guardian angel. Martinez, L.
The **Freddies**. Walsh, M. O.
Fredrickson, Jack
A change in his heart
Mystery Writers of America presents the blue
religion; new stories about cops, criminals,
and the chase; edited by Michael Connelly
Good evenin', blues
Chicago blues; edited by Libby Fischer
Hellmann
Free. Updike, J.
The **free** fall. Amdahl, G.
A **free** flight in 2222. Dominik, H.
Free Ham. Bertino, M.-H.
Free Ham. Bertino, M.-H.
Free Kick. Kuo, A.
Free man in Paris. Raphael, L.
Free parking. Kellerman, F.
Free radicals. Munro, A.
Free spirits. Mindt, A.
Free time. Sallis, J.
Free Writing. Day, R.
Freebleeders. Vollmer, M.
Freed, Lynn
The curse of the appropriate man
Freed, L. The curse of the appropriate man
An error of desire
Freed, L. The curse of the appropriate man
Family of shadows
Freed, L. The curse of the appropriate man
The first rule of happiness
Freed, L. The curse of the appropriate man
Foreign student
Freed, L. The curse of the appropriate man
Liars, cheats, and cowards
Freed, L. The curse of the appropriate man

Friedell, Egon
Is the earth inhabited?
The black mirror and other stories; an anthology of science fiction from Germany & Austria; edited & with an introduction & notes by Franz Rottensteiner; translated by Mike Mitchell.
Friedland, Bob
Call Me Happy
The Advocate (Vancouver, B.C.) v67 pt4 p503-7 Jl 2009
Friedman, Bruce Jay
And Where She Stops . . . A Story
Commentary v127 no3 p35-8 Mr 2009
Neck and Neck
The Antioch Review v63 no4 p666-73 Fall 2005
The Reversal
The Antioch Review v64 no3 p432-7 Summ 2006
The Savior
The Antioch Review v67 no3 p234-41 Spr 2009
The Secret Man
TriQuarterly no125 p38-43 2006
Friedman, Kinky
Armadillos and old lace [excerpt]
Lone Star sleuths; an anthology of Texas crime fiction; edited and with an introduction by Bill Cunningham, Steven L. Davis, and Rollo K. Newsom.
Tennis, anyone?
Murder is my racquet; edited by Otto Penzler
Friedman, Mack
Setting the lawn on fire
Barnstorm; contemporary Wisconsin fiction; edited by Raphael Kadushin
Friedman, Sanford
Beethoven's Nephew
Confrontation no100 p106-11 Fall 2007/Wint 2008
Friedmann, Patty
Two-story brick houses
New Orleans noir; edited by Julie Smith
A **friend**. Arjouni, J.
A **Friend** of Dr. Reis. Boyers, R.
The **friend** of the blackbird. Thomas, E.
A **friend** of the general. L'Amour, L.
Friendly Fire. Hadley, T.
The **friendly** giants. DeNiro, A.
A **friendly** little game. Lescroart, J. T.
FRIENDS *See* Friendship
Friends. Clayton, J. J.
Friends. Paley, G.
Friends: an elegy. Miller, A. L.
Friends in high places. McDevitt, J.
Friends of Your Enemies. Grunebaum, J.
FRIENDSHIP
See also Love
Abbott, L. K. Martians
Abbott, L. K. Revolutionaries
Aboulela, L. The museum
Adichie, C. N. Ghosts
Akpan, U. C. What language is that?
Almond, S. Larsen's novel
Almond, S. The soul molecule
Anderson, B. Commitment
Anderson, B Day out
Andreas-Salomé, L. Unit for "Men, internal"

Angel, J. Rolling over
Angel, J. Whistle pig
Arjouni, J. At peace
Arjouni, J. A friend
Báez, A. Casa-Arte
Baraka, I. A. Mondongo
Barkley, B. Another perfect catastrophe
Barkley, B. Beneath the deep, slow motion
Barry, R. Love him, Petaluma
Barry, R. Not much is new here
Bass, R. Pagans
Baumbach, J. Men at lunch
Beagle, P. S. A dance for Emilia
Beattie, A. Solid wood
Beattie, A. Tending something
Bellows, N. First four measures
Berg, E. Mrs. Ethel Menafee and Mr. Bridie Stoltz
Bierce, A. The coup de grâce
Blackshaw, G. Girlfriend
Blackwell, K. George, Nadia, Blaise
Blincoe, N. Lucifer over Lancashire
Boswell, R. No river wide
Boudinot, R. On sex and relationships
Boudinot, R. So little time
Bradbury, R. Apple-core Baltimore
Bradbury, R. Last laughs
Bradbury, R. The pumpernickel
Brennan, K. Three seaside tales
Brown, D. Hands across America
Brown, D. Running
Brown, D. Thanksgiving
Budnitz, J. Nadia
Bukoski, A. Mission work
Burgin, R. The victims
Busch, F. The barrens
Busch, F. Manhattans
Carey, P. The fat man in history
Carver, R. What we talk about when we talk about love
Chattin, J. Blue grass, green sky
Chattin, J. So far from the stage
Clayton, J. J. Friends
Clayton, J. J. Glory
Clayton, J. J. Old friends
Clayton, J. J. Prewar quality
Connell, E. S. Puig's wife
Coyne, T. A gentleman's game [excerpt]
Crane, E. Varieties of loudness in Chicago
Crone, M. White sky in May
Crouse, D. Crybaby
Currans-Sheehan, T. The wild club
DeMarinis, R. The bear itself
DeMarinis, R. Birds of the mountain west
Desaulniers, J. The good fight
Dills, T. Arcadia
Dobozy, T. The man who came out of the corner of my eye
Dobozy, T. Radio Blik
Dokey, R. Ace
Dokey, R. The mouse
Donoghue, E. Enchantment
Donoghue, E. Team men
Donoghue, E. Touchy subjects
Donovan, G. Morning swimmers
Dormen, L. Curvy
Dormen, L. Figure of a woman
Dormen, L. The secret of drawing

FRIENDSHIP—*Continued*

Paley, G. Friends
Palwick, S. GI Jesus
Pearlman, E. Shenanigans
Pinkerton, B. Lower wacker blues
Pohl, F. I remember a winter
Pollack, E. Milt and Moose
Pollock, D. R. Schott's Bridge
Pratt, T. Komodo
Purdy, J. No stranger to Luke
Randolph, L. This is not the tropics
Raymond, J. Benny
Raymond, J. The coast
Raymond, J. Old joy
Reddi, R. P. Justice Shiva Ram Murthy
Reidy, D. Captive audience
Reidy, D. The regular
Rheinheimer, K. The B & W
Rheinheimer, K. Hooks
Rich, M. Across the sky
Richter, S. Duet
Richter, S. Habits and habitat of the southwestern bad boy
Richter, S. Young people today
Roberts, N. This is not skin
Rock, P. Halo effect
Romano, T. Comic books
Ronk, M. C. The sofa
Russell, K. Z.Z.'s sleep-away camp for disordered dreamers
Salter, J. Give
Saunders, G. Bohemians
Scego, I. "Faduma & Barni (April, 2003)"
Schutt, C. Winterreise
Selgin, P. The girl in the story
Selgin, P. The wolf house
Shepard, J. Spending the night with the poor
Shirley, P. The story of William B. Greene
Silber, J. War buddies
Silver, L. Fish
Smith, A. End of story
Snyder, S. Happy Fish, Plus Coin
Soueif, A. I think of you
Spark, M. The Portobello Road
Stark, C. Getting out more
Steinberg, S. The last guest
Stella, C. Waiting for Gallo
Stern, R. G. Arrangements at the Gulf
Stern, R. G. Double Charley
Stern, R. G. The girl who loves Schubert
Sutton, B. Risk merchants
Taraqqi, G. My little friend
Thayer, S. Hi, I'm God
Thompson, J. Applause, applause
Thompson, J. The brat
Thompson, J. Throw like a girl
Thompson, J. Wilderness
Thorne, M. My ex-classmates' Kids
Threatt, A. Bela Lugosi's dead
Tomlinson, J. Prologue (two lives in letters)
Tomlinson, J. Shadow flag
Treat, J. More than winter or spring
Tremain, R. A game of cards
Trevor, D. Fellowship of the bereaved
Trevor, D. Girls I know
Trevor, W. Folie à deux
Trezise, R. Jigsaws
Trezise, R. Merry go-rounds
Trezise, R. Valley lines

Troy, M. Happy birthday Gerald Meatloaf
Vapnyar, L. There are Jews in my house
Varallo, A. A dictionary of saints
Varallo, A. The eyes of Dr. T. J. Eckleburg
Varallo, A. Sometimes I'm Becky Macomber
Vida, V. Soleil
Vollmer, M. Oh land of national paradise, how glorious are thy bounties
Welch, N. The cheating kind
Welch, N. Sweet Maddy
Welch, N. Tender foot
Wendroff, Z. Pavlik's mysterious disappearance
Westcott, G. A guilty woman
Wideman, J. E. What we cannot speak about we must pass over in silence
Wieland, M. Swan in retreat
Williams, J. ACK
Williams, J. The visiting privilege
Winn, T. Mrs. Somebody Somebody
Winton, T. Big world
Wolff, T. Flyboys
Wolff, T. Hunters in the snow
Wolff, T. Two boys and a girl
Yanique, T. Gita Pinky Manachandi
Yasuoka, S. The king's ears
Yoss. The red bridge
Zimmer, P. The mechanics

Friendship. Molodowsky, K.
A **Friendship:** How It Ended. Gornick, V.
The **friendship** of Monsieur Jeynois. Hodgson, W. H.

Friesner, Esther M.

Abductio ad absurdum
  Elemental; the Tsunami relief anthology; stories of science fiction and fantasy; [edited by] Steven Savile and Alethea Kontis; introduction by Arthur C. Clarke
Cubby Grumbles makes a change
  The Magic toybox; edited by Denise Little
First, catch your elephant
  Alternate generals III; edited by Harry Turtledove and Roland J. Green
The fraud
  Year's best fantasy 6; edited by David G. Hartwell & Kathryn Cramer
Sweet, savage sorcerer
  This is my funniest; leading science fiction writers present their funniest stories ever; edited by Mike Resnick

Frighted out of fear; or, the bombs bursting in air. Carlson, P. M.
A **frivolous** woman. Gordimer, N.

Frizell, John

Making memories
  Nature v457 p346 Ja 15 2009

Frog kiss. Anderson, K. J.
The **frog** prince. Dunn, L. J.

FROGS

Anderson, K. J. Frog kiss
Danticat, E. Lélé
Davis, C. Stiff soup
Dunn, L. J. The frog prince
Linscott, G. A blessing of frogs
Nolan, W. F. The day the Gorf took over
Yolen, J. The golden balls
Yolen, J. Green plague

Frolic and Banter. Targan, B.
From A Song of Ilan (a novel). Paul, J.
From A to M. Brenner, Y. H.

From Alexandria to Roseville. Drosso, A.-M.

From Alice to everywhere, with love. Brenchley, C.

From Almost Egypt. Moore, A.

From Babel's fall'n glory we fled. Swanwick, M.

From "Barley Patch". Murnane, G.

from Bridge of Sand. Burroway, J.

From cabinet 34, drawer 6. Kiernan, C. R.

From downtown at the buzzer. Effinger, G. A.

From "Everything You See Is Real" [Book excerpt] Ehrenreich, B.

From Farrow to Fork. Bourke, R. W.

From hell again. Frost, G.

From here to Banggai. L'Amour, L.

From How Much of Us There Was. Kimball, M.

From impulse. Dunbar, P. L.

From Kilgore to Kurtz, at the Steak 'n' Stage. Rahman, I.

From Leyb the shoemaker. Molodowsky, K.

From Loneliness to Ubiquitousness. Norrby, E.

From Mars with love. Tang, J.

From Now On, You're Back. Weems, R. K.

from On This Island. Todd, P.

From powder to powder. Kim, H.

From Ray of the Star (a novel). Hunt, L.

From shadowed places. Matheson, R.

From the Archives of Drs. Placek and Arriola . . . Schleef, D.

From the cradle. Wolfe, G.

From the crypts of memory. Smith, C. A.

From the desk of. Effinger, G. A.

From the Desk of Daniel Varsky. Krauss, N.

From the desk of Gilmer C. Merton. Wolfe, G.

From the desk of Jarrod Foster. Shah, B.

From the fourth row. Ochsner, G.

From the heart. Meaney, J.

From the journal of Xavier Desmond. Martin, G. R. R.

From the Personal Record Collection of Beniamino Gigli. Costa, S.

From the tideless sea (first part). Hodgson, W. H.

From the tideless sea (second part). Hodgson, W. H.

From the Window. Kelman, J.

From this Side of the Cloister. Ibarz, M.

From war stories. Baraka, I. A.

Fromm, Pete

Snow cave

Best stories of the American West, v1; edited by Marc Jaffe

The **front** and back parts of the house. Maxwell, W.

The **front** yard. Guista, M.

FRONTIER AND PIONEER LIFE

Bear, E. The devil you don't

Bierce, A. Maumee's mission

Bierce, A. Pernicketty's fright

James, H. A cure for coquettes

Munro, A. The wilds of Morris Township

Russell, K. Children's reminiscences of the westward migration

Scholes, K. A good hairy day in Anarchy

Colorado

Inglis, T. M. Fairy "Spuds"

Kansas

Muller, M. Time of the wolves

Ohio

Bierce, A. The boarded window

South Dakota

Canfield, H. S. The common sense of John Thomas

United States

Mirrielees, E. R. A matter of nationality

Western States

Clark, M. R. Her neighbor's claim

Dobson, C. L. When Jennie saved the windmill

Johnson, D. M. A man called Horse

Lambert, C. The scent of cinnamon

Peattie, E. W. The McCulloughs of the Bluff

Smith, L. K. The successes of Jimmy Sylvester

Wyoming

Proulx, A. Them old cowboy songs

Frood, Arran

Only in your dreams

Nature v449 p376 S 20 2007

Frost, Gregory

Attack of the jazz giants

Frost, G. Attack of the jazz giants and other stories; with a foreword by Karen Joy Fowler and an afterword by John Kessel

The bus

Frost, G. Attack of the jazz giants and other stories; with a foreword by Karen Joy Fowler and an afterword by John Kessel

Collecting dust

Frost, G. Attack of the jazz giants and other stories; with a foreword by Karen Joy Fowler and an afterword by John Kessel

A day in the life of Justin Argento Morrel

Frost, G. Attack of the jazz giants and other stories; with a foreword by Karen Joy Fowler and an afterword by John Kessel

Divertimento

Frost, G. Attack of the jazz giants and other stories; with a foreword by Karen Joy Fowler and an afterword by John Kessel

From hell again

Frost, G. Attack of the jazz giants and other stories; with a foreword by Karen Joy Fowler and an afterword by John Kessel

The girlfriends of Dorian Gray

Frost, G. Attack of the jazz giants and other stories; with a foreword by Karen Joy Fowler and an afterword by John Kessel

How Meersh the bedeviler lost his toes

Frost, G. Attack of the jazz giants and other stories; with a foreword by Karen Joy Fowler and an afterword by John Kessel

In the sunken museum

Frost, G. Attack of the jazz giants and other stories; with a foreword by Karen Joy Fowler and an afterword by John Kessel

Lizaveta

Frost, G. Attack of the jazz giants and other stories; with a foreword by Karen Joy Fowler and an afterword by John Kessel

Madonna of the maquiladora

Frost, G. Attack of the jazz giants and other stories; with a foreword by Karen Joy Fowler and an afterword by John Kessel

The road to recovery

Frost, G. Attack of the jazz giants and other stories; with a foreword by Karen Joy Fowler and an afterword by John Kessel

Frost, Gregory—*Continued*
  Some things are better left
    Frost, G. Attack of the jazz giants and other stories; with a foreword by Karen Joy Fowler and an afterword by John Kessel
  Touring Jesus World
    A cross of centuries; twenty-five imaginative tales about the Christ; edited by Michael Bishop
  Touring Jesusworld
    Frost, G. Attack of the jazz giants and other stories; with a foreword by Karen Joy Fowler and an afterword by John Kessel
  (jt. auth) *See* Dann, Jack and Frost, Gregory
FROST, ROBERT, 1874-1963
About
  Di Filippo, P. A monument to after-thought unveiled
Frost-bitten. Leiren-Young, M.
Frost line. Busch, F.
Frost rides alone. McCoy, H.
Frozen animals. King, O.
Frozen Charlottes. Sussex, L.
Frozen stiff. Block, L.
FRUIT
  Bender, A. Fruit and words
Fruit. Middleton, N.
Fruit and words. Bender, A.
FRUIT PICKERS *See* Migrant labor
The **Fruit** Stand. Gangemi, K.
Fruitcakes and fiction. Pifer, D.
The **fruitful** sleeping of the Rev. Elisha Edwards. Dunbar, P. L.
Fruits of Shinjuku. Morita, R.
Fruits of the dead. Treat, J.
Fry, Gary
  Black dogs
    British invasion; edited by Christopher Golden, Tim Lebbon & James A. Moore
Frym, Gloria
  Message to Legatee
    Women's Studies Quarterly v34 no1/2 p293-4 Spr/Summ 2006
FTB. Pratchett, T.
Fú, Michel Encinosa *See* Encinosa Fú, Michel
Fuchs, Daniel
  Dream city; or, The drugged lake
    Fuchs, D. The golden West; Hollywood stories; selected by Christopher Carduff; introduction by John Updike
  Florida
    Fuchs, D. The golden West; Hollywood stories; selected by Christopher Carduff; introduction by John Updike
  The golden West
    Fuchs, D. The golden West; Hollywood stories; selected by Christopher Carduff; introduction by John Updike
  A Hollywood diary
    Fuchs, D. The golden West; Hollywood stories; selected by Christopher Carduff; introduction by John Updike
  Triplicate
    Fuchs, D. The golden West; Hollywood stories; selected by Christopher Carduff; introduction by John Updike

  West of the Rockies
    Fuchs, D. The golden West; Hollywood stories; selected by Christopher Carduff; introduction by John Updike
Fuck with Kayla and you die. Erdrich, L.
Fuck you. Reinhorn, H.
Fuel. Carlin, P.
Fuel for the fire. Shields, C.
Fuel for the millennium. Campbell, B. J.
Fuentes, Adrián
  The Second Death
    The North American Review v292 no5 p16-23 S/O 2007
Fuentes, Carlos
  The armed family
    Fuentes, C. Happy families; stories; translated by Edith Grossman
  Conjugal ties (1)
    Fuentes, C. Happy families; stories; translated by Edith Grossman
  Conjugal ties (2)
    Fuentes, C. Happy families; stories; translated by Edith Grossman
  A cousin without charm
    Fuentes, C. Happy families; stories; translated by Edith Grossman
  The discomfiting brother
    Fuentes, C. Happy families; stories; translated by Edith Grossman
  The disobedient son
    Fuentes, C. Happy families; stories; translated by Edith Grossman
  Eternal father
    Fuentes, C. Happy families; stories; translated by Edith Grossman
  A family like any other
    Fuentes, C. Happy families; stories; translated by Edith Grossman
  The father's servant
    Fuentes, C. Happy families; stories; translated by Edith Grossman
  The gay divorcee
    Fuentes, C. Happy families; stories; translated by Edith Grossman
  The mariachi's mother
    Fuentes, C. Happy families; stories; translated by Edith Grossman
  Mater Dolorosa
    Fuentes, C. Happy families; stories; translated by Edith Grossman
  The official family
    Fuentes, C. Happy families; stories; translated by Edith Grossman
  The secret marriage
    Fuentes, C. Happy families; stories; translated by Edith Grossman
  The star's son
    Fuentes, C. Happy families; stories; translated by Edith Grossman
  Sweethearts
    Fuentes, C. Happy families; stories; translated by Edith Grossman
Fuentes, Karina
  Twinspeak
    Calyx v24 no1 p92-100 Summ 2007
Fuentes, Marcela
  Looking for eight
    New stories from the Southwest; edited by D. Seth Horton; foreword by Ray Gonzalez.

The **fugitive**. Levi, P.
The **fugitive**. Tompkins, G. W.
Fugitive color. Gardiner, J. R.
Fugitive light, old photos. McCann, R.
Fugitive pieces [excerpt] Michaels, A.
FUGITIVE SLAVES
Cook, C. F. A slave for life: a story of the long ago
Ransom, A. Incident
FUGITIVES
See also Escaped convicts; Fugitive slaves; Manhunts; Outlaws
Coloane, F. Tierra del Fuego
Gardiner, J. R. Leaving Port McHair
Im, C. A shared journey
McBain, E. See him die
Neggers, C. On the run
Parra, E. A. The hunter
Pizzolatto, N. Wanted man
Rosenblum, M. H. Search engine
Shaw, S. Reconstruction
Tompkins, G. W. The fugitive
Fugue. Groff, L.
Fugue–state. Evenson, B.
Fujino, Chiya
Her room
Inside and other short fiction; Japanese women by Japanese women; with a foreword by Ruth Ozeki; compiled by Cathy Layne
The housewife and the police box
Morita, R. Tokyo fragments; Ryuji Morita [et al.]; translated by Giles Murray
Fulcrum. Jones, G. A.
Fulgoni, Dennis
Dead man's nail
New stories from the Southwest; edited by D. Seth Horton; foreword by Ray Gonzalez.
Full circle. Matheson, R.
Full count. Berg, E.
The **Full** Glass. Updike, J.
Full moon. Bach, M.
Full moon birthday. Hinton, S. E.
Full service. LaBute, N.
Fulmer, David
Algiers
New Orleans noir; edited by Julie Smith
Fulton, Alice
Centrally isolated; (Edna Garrahan Kelly O'Keefe)
Fulton, A. The nightingales of Troy; stories of one family's century
Dorothy Loves maleman; (Edna Garrahan Kelly, Dorothy Garrahan)
Fulton, A. The nightingales of Troy; stories of one family's century
The glorious mysteries; (Charlotte Garrahan Willoughby)
Fulton, A. The nightingales of Troy; stories of one family's century
Happy dust; (Mamie Flynn Garrahan)
Fulton, A. The nightingales of Troy; stories of one family's century
If it's not too much to ask; (Ruth Livington)
Fulton, A. The nightingales of Troy; stories of one family's century
L'Air du Temps; (Ruth Livington, Annie Garrahan Livington)
Fulton, A. The nightingales of Troy; stories of one family's century

The nightingales of Troy; (Annie Garrahan)
Fulton, A. The nightingales of Troy; stories of one family's century
Queen Wintergreen; (Peg Flynn)
Fulton, A. The nightingales of Troy; stories of one family's century
The real Eleanor Rigby
The Pushcart Prize XXIX: best of the small presses 2005; edited by Bill Henderson with the Pushcart Prize editors; (Ruth Livington)
Fulton, A. The nightingales of Troy; stories of one family's century
A shadow table; (Charlotte Garrahan)
Fulton, A. The nightingales of Troy; stories of one family's century
Fulton, John
The animal girl
Fulton, J. The animal girl; two novellas and three stories
Hunters
The Pushcart Prize XXX: best of the small presses 2006; edited by Bill Henderson with the Pushcart Prize editors
Fulton, J. The animal girl; two novellas and three stories
The Southern Review (Baton Rouge, La.) v40 no4 p752-78 Aut 2004
Real grief
Fulton, J. The animal girl; two novellas and three stories
The sleeping woman
Fulton, J. The animal girl; two novellas and three stories
A small matter
Fulton, J. The animal girl; two novellas and three stories
Fuming woman. DeNiro, A.
Fumiyo, Saienji
Higurashi
The East v42 no6 p42-4 Mr/Ap 2007
Maeda Keijiro
The East v42 no6 p35-41 Mr/Ap 2007
Rain Shower
The East v43 no1 p44-6 My/Je 2007
Shima Sakon
The East v42 no5 p34-41 Ja/F 2007
Takenaka Hanbei
The East v43 no1 p36-43 My/Je 2007
The **fund-raiser's** dance card. Clarke, B.
FUND RAISING
Clarke, B. The fund-raiser's dance card
Dunbar, P. L. The defection of Maria Ann Gibbs
Pearlman, E. The large lady
Stern, R. G. Idylls of Dugan and Strunk
FUNDAMENTALISM See Fundamentalists
FUNDAMENTALISTS
Bass, R. The lives of rocks
The **funeral**. Judah, S.
The **funeral**. Matheson, R.
FUNERAL DIRECTORS See Undertakers and undertaking
The **funeral** party. Mootoo, S.
FUNERAL RITES AND CEREMONIES
Albert, E. Spooked
Alcântara Machado, A. d. Gaetaninho
Arnow, H. L. S. The washerwoman's day
Banks, R. Wrong 'em, boyo

GANGSTERS

See also Mafia

Alvarado, B. Limbo
Barr, R. The girl who knew too much
Bennett, T. Lesson plan
Bush, G. If you harm us
Byrne, M. Only the strong survive
Carcaterra, L. The strega's last dance
Cavin, R. Even gamblers have to eat
Davis, D. S. Dies Irae
Ellin, S. The day of the bullett
Haringa, J. M. A perfect and unmappable grace
Haywood, G. A. Heatseeker
Hemingway, E. The killers
Konrath, J. A. and Wilson, F. P. The sound of blunder
Leonard, E. Louly and Pretty Boy
Levinson, R. S. And the winner is . . .
Livings, J. The heir
Luman, P. T. Gangster's brand
Martinez, C. The devil's bookkeeper
Nebel, F. Wise guy
Resnick, M. A very special girl
Robinson, P. Birthday dance
Rosen, R. D. Mamzer
Schutz, B. M. Expert opinion
Scott, J. In the zone
Shepard, L. Eternity and afterward
Steiber, R. Mexican gatsby
Turow, S. Loyalty
Welsh, I. Kingdom of Fife
Wignall, K. The preacher
Woolrich, C. Cigarette
Woronov, M. Mobster
The **Gangsters**. Whitehead, C.
Gangster's brand. Luman, P. T.
Ganjefa. Naiyer Masud
Gannon, Frank
I know what I'm doing about all the attention I've been getting
Children playing before a statue of Hercules; edited and introduced by David Sedaris
Gansworth, Eric
True Crime
The Kenyon Review v28 no4 p80-91 Fall 2006
Gappah, Petina
The annex shuffle
Gappah, P. An elegy for easterly; stories
At the sound of the last post
Gappah, P. An elegy for easterly; stories
Aunt Juliana's Indian
Gappah, P. An elegy for easterly; stories
The cracked, pink lips of Rosie's bridegroom
Gappah, P. An elegy for easterly; stories
An elegy for Easterly
Gappah, P. An elegy for easterly; stories
In the heart of the golden triangle
Gappah, P. An elegy for easterly; stories
The maid from Lalapanzi
Gappah, P. An elegy for easterly; stories
Midnight at the Hotel California
Gappah, P. An elegy for easterly; stories
The Mupandawana dancing champion
Gappah, P. An elegy for easterly; stories
My cousin-sister Rambanai
Gappah, P. An elegy for easterly; stories
The negotiated settlement
Gappah, P. An elegy for easterly; stories

Our man in Geneva wins a million euros
Gappah, P. An elegy for easterly; stories
Something nice from London
Gappah, P. An elegy for easterly; stories
Gaps. Long, A.
Gaps. Stern, R. G.
The **garage**. Steinberg, S.
Garbage thief. Segal, L. G.
Garcia, Eric
Meeting across the river
Meeting across the river; stories inspired by the haunting Bruce Springsteen song; edited by Jessica Kaye and Richard J. Brewer
Garcia-Aguilera, Carolina
The dinner
Havana noir; edited by Achy Obejas
García González, Francisco
Women of the Federation
The Review of Contemporary Fiction v26 no3 p85-96 Fall 2006
García Márquez, Gabriel
Abel's Eden
Americas v57 no1 p64, Inside Back Cover Ja/F 2005
Death constant beyond love
Telling tales; edited by Nadine Gordimer
García Somodevilla, Alexis Sebastián
Mirages of Daily Life
The Review of Contemporary Fiction v26 no3 p97-9 Fall 2006
Gardam, Jane
Babette
Gardam, J. The people on Privilege Hill and other stories
Dangers
Gardam, J. The people on Privilege Hill and other stories
The fledgling
Gardam, J. The people on Privilege Hill and other stories
The flight path
Gardam, J. The people on Privilege Hill and other stories
The hair of the dog
Gardam, J. The people on Privilege Hill and other stories
The last reunion
Gardam, J. The people on Privilege Hill and other stories
The latter days of Mr. Jones
Gardam, J. The people on Privilege Hill and other stories
Learning to fly
Gardam, J. The people on Privilege Hill and other stories
The Milly Ming
Gardam, J. The people on Privilege Hill and other stories
Pangbourne
Gardam, J. The people on Privilege Hill and other stories
The people of Privilege Hill
Gardam, J. The people on Privilege Hill and other stories
Snap
Gardam, J. The people on Privilege Hill and other stories

Garrett, George P.—*Continued*
  Heroes
    Garrett, G. P. Empty bed blues
  The misery and the glory of Texas Pete
    Garrett, G. P. Empty bed blues
  A perfect stranger
    Garrett, G. P. Empty bed blues
  Pornographers
    Garrett, G. P. Empty bed blues
  A short history of the Civil War
    Garrett, G. P. Empty bed blues
  Spilling the beans: a letter to Linda Evangelista
    Garrett, G. P. Empty bed blues
  A story goes with it
    Garrett, G. P. Empty bed blues
  Tanks
    Garrett, G. P. Empty bed blues
  With my body, I thee worship
    Garrett, G. P. Empty bed blues
Garrett, Percy
  The knotted handkerchief
    Bendel-Simso, M. M., ed. Early American detective stories; an anthology; edited by LeRoy Lad Panek and Mary M. Bendel-Simso.
Garrett in the wild. Mandelbaum, P.
Garrett in wedlock. Mandelbaum, P.
Garro, Elena
  The Little Shoemaker from Guanajuato
    StoryQuarterly v41 p249, 251, 253, 255, 257, 259, 261, 263, 265, 267, 269, 271, 273, 275 2005
  El zapaterito de Guanajuato
    StoryQuarterly v41 p248, 250, 252, 254, 256, 258, 260, 262, 264, 266, 268, 270, 272, 274 2005
Gartner, Zsuzsi
  Summer of the Flesh Eater
    The Walrus v6 no7 p54-7, 59-63 S 2009
Garton, Ray
  Between eight and nine o'clock
    Dark delicacies 2; fear: more original tales of terror and the macabre by the world's greatest horror writers; edited by Del Howison and Jeff Gelb
Garwin, Laura
  Schrödinger's mousetrap. Part 4: A very public humiliation
    Nature v433 p579 F 10 2005
Garza, Cristina Rivera- *See* Rivera-Garza, Cristina, 1964-
Garza, Oscar
  Land of a thousand dances: an R&B fable
    Popular Music v24 no3 p429-37 O 2005
Gas Bar. Vigna, J.
Gases. Margulis, L.
Gash, Jonathan
  Death by golf
    Murder in the rough; edited by Otto Penzler
Gaskell, Stephen
  Dating for the wired generation
    Nature v450 p584 N 22 2007
Gaskell, Whitney
  Trying again
    Before; short stories about pregnancy from our top writers; edited by Emily Franklin and Heather Swain
GASOLINE STATIONS *See* Automobiles—Service stations

Gass, William H.
  A little history of modern music
    The O. Henry Prize stories 2008; edited and with an introduction by Laura Furman; with essays on the stories they admire most by jurors Chimamanda Ngozi Adiche, David Leavitt, David Means
The **gate** of a great mansion. Sillitoe, A.
A **gated** community. Segal, L. G.
Gates, David
  Aces & eights
    The World's finest mystery and crime stories, fifth annual collection; edited by Ed Gorman and Martin H. Greenberg
  The bad thing
    My mistress's sparrow is dead; great love stories, from Chekhov to Munro; edited by Jeffrey Eugenides
  The Man Who Knew Beckett
    Agni no65 p43-8 2007
  A Secret Station
    The New Yorker v81 no6 p56-65 Mr 28 2005
Gates of Saigon. Phan, A.
The **gates** of Sodom. McCauley, W.
The **gateway**. McNally, T. M.
The **gateway** of India. Theroux, P.
The **gateway** of the monster. Hodgson, W. H.
Gather. Rowe, C.
Gather blue roses. Sargent, P.
Gathering genius. Marley, L.
Gathering of the clans. Lopes, R. J.
The **gathering** squall. Oates, J. C.
Gathering strength. Rosen, S.
Gator bait. Garrett, G. P.
Los Gatos bus. Kulpa, K.
Gatsby, tender, paradise. Fincke, G.
Gauger, Soren
  (tr.) See Ficowski, Jerzy
GAULS *See* Celts
Gault, Michael Bay
  O Liberated Eyes
    Agni no68 p48-62 2008
Gauss, Marianne
  A life like Maggy's
    Adventures in the West; stories for young readers; edited by Susanne George Bloomfield and Eric Melvin Reed
Gaustine. Gospodinov, G.
Gautier, Amina
  Cicero Waiting
    The North American Review v290 no5 p36-40 S/O 2005
  Dance for Me
    Southwest Review v91 no2 p177-87 2006
  The ease of living
    New stories from the South; the year's best, 2008; selected from U.S. magazines by ZZ Packer with Kathy Pories; with an introduction by ZZ Packer
  Girl of Wisdom
    The Kenyon Review v29 no3 p116-22 Summ 2007
  Housegirl
    StoryQuarterly v40 p388-91 2004
  Minnow
    River Styx no79 p79 2009
  Some Other Kind of Happiness
    The North American Review v293 no5 p24-7 S/O 2008

Geezers. Thompson, B.
Gefen, Nan Fink
  The Gift
    Tikkun v19 no6 p28-30 N/D 2004
Geiger, Scott
  The Frank Orison
    Pushcart prize XXXI: best of the small press-
    es 2007; edited by Bill Henderson; with the
    Pushcart Prize editors
Gelatin. Kremer, H.
Gelernter, David
  The Passion of Emma: A Story
    Commentary v126 no5 p40-55 D 2008
GEMS *See* Diamonds; Emeralds; Rubies
The **Gendarme**. Lustig, A.
GENEALOGY
  Shawl, N. The Raineses´
  Westlake, D. E. Never shake a family tree
Genealogy. Gildner, G.
General Jaruzelski at the zoo. Zebrowski, G.
**GENERAL MOTORS CORP. CADILLAC
  MOTOR CAR DIVISION** *See* Cadillac
  Motor Car Division
**GENERAL MOTORS CORP. CHEVROLET
  MOTOR DIVISION** *See* Chevrolet Motor
  Division
General strike. Dormen, L.
GENERALS
  Bradbury, R. The drummer boy of Shiloh
  Brazaitis, M. The poet and the general
  Ford, J. The seventh expression of the robot
    general
  Fuentes, C. The armed family
  Guo, S. Brightly shine the stars tonight
  Sallis, J. Jeremiad
  Scott, Sir W. The Tapestried Chamber; or, The
    lady in the sacque
The **General's** Bulldozers. Ehikhamenor, V.
GENERATION GAP *See* Conflict of generations
Geneseo. Deaver, P. F.
Genesis and catastrophe. Dahl, R.
Genesis to revelation. Plate, P.
GENETIC ENGINEERING
  Bacigalupi, P. Calorie man
  Chase, M. False start
  Haldeman, J. W. Giza
  Kiernan, C. R. Faces in revolving souls
  Kress, N. Fountain of age
  Lindskold, J. Unlimited
  Marusek, D. We were out of our minds with joy
  McAllister, B. Angels
  Rajaniemi, H. His master's voice
  Rand, K. One person
  Reed, R. Five thrillers
GENETIC EXPERIMENTATION *See* Genetics
GENETIC RESEARCH *See* Genetics
GENETICS
  Baxter, S. No more stories
  Heuler, K. Down on the farm
  Kress, N. Beggars in Spain
  Steele, A. M. Moreau
  Sterling, B. Our neural Chernobyl
  Wolfe, G. The fat magician
GENGHIS KHAN, 1162-1227
        About
  Sargent, P. Spirit brother
Geni, Abby
  Landscaping
    Confrontation no104 p127-31 Summ 2009

GENIUS
    See also Gifted children
  Anderson, P. Logic
  Di Filippo, P. Up!
  Lawson, J. E. A serenade to beauty everlasting
  Marley, L. Gathering genius
  Nelson, A. People people
  Pohl, F. To see another mountain
  Silverberg, R. The man who never forgot
Genius. Anderson, P.
Genius Loci. Smith, C. A.
Genius Loci. Weinberg, R.
Genna, Giuseppe
  Caput Mundi
    Rome noir; edited by Chiara Stangalino &
    Maxim Jakubowski; translated by Anne Mi-
    lano Appel, Ann Goldstein, and Kathrine
    Jason
GENOA (ITALY) *See* Italy—Genoa
GENOCIDE
  Mueller, R. And the sea shall give up its dead
Gentile, Joe
  The shrug of Atlas
    Kolchak: the night stalker chronicles; 26 orig-
    inal tales of the surreal, the bizarre, the ma-
    cabre; edited by Joe Gentile, Garrett Ander-
    son, Lori Gentile; Kolchak created by Jeff
    Rice
Gentle, Mary
  A sun in the attic
    Steampunk; edited by Ann & Jeff
    VanderMeer
Gentle breathing. See Bunin, I. A. Light breathing
A **gentle** man (Massachusettes, 1979). Mohanraj,
  M. A.
A **gentleman** from Mexico. Samuels, M.
The **gentleman** from San Francisco. Bunin, I. A.
A **gentleman** of the old school. Yarbro, C. Q.
Gentleman's agreement. Richard, M.
A **gentleman's** game [excerpt] Coyne, T.
The **gentleman's** hotel. Lansdale, J. R.
Gentry, Elizabeth
  In Exchange
    Confrontation no100 p73-83 Fall 2007/Wint
    2008
Geoffrey says. Whiteley, A.
GEOGRAPHERS
  Rowe, C. Another word for map is faith
Geography. Kadetsky, E.
GEOLOGISTS
  Bass, R. The lives of rocks
  Farmer, P. J. The volcano
  Lovecraft, H. P. At the mountains of madness
George, Diana
  Filzbad
    Chicago Review v51 no3 p73-84 Aut 2005
George, Nelson
  New Lots Avenue
    Brooklyn noir; edited by Tim McLoughlin
George, Sherri
  Nine-Tenths of the Law
    Idaho Magazine v4 no12 p46-9 S 2005
George. Jose, N.
The **George** business. Zelazny, R.
George, Nadia, Blaise. Blackwell, K.
George Thurston. Bierce, A.
George Washington. Zimmer, P.
Georgeoliani, Dinara
  (tr.) See P´yetsukh, V. A.

GEORGIA

Bishop, M. The Yukio Mishima Cultural Association of Kudzu Valley, Georgia
Davis, J. S. Pilgrimage in Georgia
Johnson, G. Leavings
Kantner, R. Down home blues
Kessel, J. Every angel is terrifying
Kincaid, N. The currency of love
Pierce, T. J. Newsworld
Pierce, T. J. Newsworld II
Pratt, T. Bottom feeding
Stiefel, B. Dark quarry
Watkins, S. Ice age

Atlanta

Clarke, B. Carrying the torch
Grimsley, J. Jesus is sending you this message
Grooms, A. Flora Devine
Johnson, G. The boarder
Kiernan, C. R. Mercury
Kiernan, C. R. A story of Edward Gorey
O'Connor, F. The artificial nigger

Savannah

Clarke, B. For those of us who need such things

Georgiana. Granville-Barker, H.
Georgy Porgy. Dahl, R.
Geraldine. Purdy, J.
Gerald's monkey. Knight, M.
Geranium. Updike, D.
Gérard de Nerval *See* Nerval, Gérard de, 1808-1855

Gerber, Merrill Joan

Approval
    Gerber, M. J. This is a voice from your past; new and selected stories
The Cleopatra birds
    Gerber, M. J. This is a voice from your past; new and selected stories
A daughter of my own
    Gerber, M. J. This is a voice from your past; new and selected stories
Dogs bark
    Gerber, M. J. This is a voice from your past; new and selected stories
Honeymoon
    Gerber, M. J. This is a voice from your past; new and selected stories
I don't believe this
    Gerber, M. J. This is a voice from your past; new and selected stories
Latitude
    Gerber, M. J. This is a voice from your past; new and selected stories
My suicides
    Gerber, M. J. This is a voice from your past; new and selected stories
Night stalker
    Gerber, M. J. This is a voice from your past; new and selected stories
See Bonnie & Clyde death car
    Gerber, M. J. This is a voice from your past; new and selected stories
Tell me your secret
    Gerber, M. J. This is a voice from your past; new and selected stories
This is a voice from your past
    Gerber, M. J. This is a voice from your past; new and selected stories

We know that your hearts are heavy
    Gerber, M. J. This is a voice from your past; new and selected stories

Gerencer, Tom

Primordial chili
    This is my funniest; leading science fiction writers present their funniest stories ever; edited by Mike Resnick

Geriatric ward. Card, O. S.

Gerlach, Gunter

Wedding in Voerde
    Passport to crime; the finest mystery stories from International Crime Writers; edited by Janet Hutchings

German, Norman

Sportfishing with Cameron
    Wide awake in the Pelican State; stories by contemporary Louisiana writers; edited by Ann Brewster Dobie; with a foreword by Ernest J. Gaines

GERMAN AMERICANS

Erdrich, L. The butcher's wife
Nayman, S. The house on Kronenstrasse
Nayman, S. The lamp
Nayman, S. The porcelain monkey

GERMAN EAST AFRICA *See* East Africa
German lessons. Updike, J.

GERMAN REFUGEES

Jhabvala, R. P. Refuge in London

GERMAN SOLDIERS *See* Soldiers—Germany
German summer. Schuster, F.
GERMAN WEST AFRICA *See* Cameroon

Germanacos, Anne

The Marriage
    Southern Humanities Review v40 no2 p166-75 Spr 2006

GERMANS

Argentina

Aira, C. An episode in the life of a landscape painter [excerpt]

England

Wolfe, G. Donovan sent us

France

Weil, G. Little Sonja Rosenkranz

Mexico

Weil, G. Finish what you started

Russia

Hummel, E. The fish of Berlin [excerpt]

South Africa

Gordimer, N. Mother tongue

Spain

Sillitoe, A. Guzman, go home

Tibet

Shepard, J. Ancestral legacies

United States

Keeble, J. Chickens
Lowry, M. Kristbjorg's story: in the Black Hills
Porter, K. A. Holiday
Scott, J. X number of possibilities
Updike, J. German lessons
Weil, G. Guernica
Weil, G. The house in the desert
Wingate, S. Dig for dollars

GERMANY

Kramlovsky, B. Silk road
Lenz, S. A risk for Father Christmas
Noll, I. Fisherman's friend
Parks, T. Keeping distance
Schulze, I. Cell phone

GERMANY—*Continued*

Weil, G. Don't touch me

17th century

Weber, D. In the Navy

1918-1945

Wilson, F. P. Aryans and Absinthe

1945-

Stafford, J. The maiden

Vollmann, W. T. Lost victories

American occupation, 1945-1955

See Germany—1945-

Communism

See Communism—Germany

World War, 1939-1945

See World War, 1939-1945—Germany

Berlin

Arjouni, J. Idiots

Biller, M. My name was Singer

Kiesbye, S. Islanders

Miller, A. The performance

Oates, J. C. Our wall

Düsseldorf

Sterling, B. Deep Eddy

Frankfurt am Main

Biller, M. The right of young men

Heidelberg

Nayman, S. The house on Kronenstrasse

Munich

Liebrecht, S. Munich

GERMS *See* Microorganisms

GERONIMO, APACHE CHIEF, 1829-1909

About

Silko, L. Mistaken identity

Silko, L. Old pancakes

Geronimo. Clarke, B.

GERONTOLOGISTS *See* Physicians

Gerrold, David

. . . And eight rabid pigs

Gerrold, D. The involuntary human

The Baby Cooper Dollar Bill

Gerrold, D. The involuntary human

Chess with a dragon

Gerrold, D. The involuntary human

Chester

Gerrold, D. The involuntary human

Dancer in the dark

Gerrold, D. The involuntary human

The diamond sky

Gerrold, D. The involuntary human

Digging in Gehenna

Gerrold, D. The involuntary human

Franz Kafka, superhero!

This is my funniest; leading science fiction writers present their funniest stories ever; edited by Mike Resnick

The green man

Gerrold, D. The involuntary human

In the quake zone

The Year's best science fiction: twenty-third annual collection; edited by Gardner Dozois

It needs salt

Gerrold, D. The involuntary human

The Kennedy enterprise

Gerrold, D. The involuntary human

King Kong: behind the scenes

Gerrold, D. The involuntary human

The Martian child

Gerrold, D. The involuntary human

Pickled mongoose

Gerrold, D. The involuntary human

Report from the near future: crystallization

Elemental; the Tsunami relief anthology; stories of science fiction and fantasy; [edited by] Steven Savile and Alethea Kontis; introduction by Arthur C. Clarke

Riding Janis

Gerrold, D. The involuntary human

A shaggy dog story

Gerrold, D. The involuntary human

The strange death of Orson Welles

Gerrold, D. The involuntary human

Thirteen o'clock

Gerrold, D. The involuntary human

Gershow, Miriam

Carker

The Georgia Review v61 no2 p283-301 Summ 2007

GERSHWIN, GEORGE, 1898-1937

Smith, A. Fidelio and Bess

Gertrude Stein solves a mystery. O'Shaughnessy, P.

GESTAPO *See* National socialism

Gestella. Palwick, S.

Gesture. Lott, B.

The **Get**. Bookman, M.

Get away from me, David. Reinhorn, H.

Get Drunk and Screw. Gardner, P.

Get it out. Monteleone, T. F.

Get me to the church on time. Bisson, T.

Get money. Hecht, J.

Get-Rich-Quick Wallingford. Chester, G. R.

Get some young. Hannah, B.

Get started. Monson, A.

Get well, Seymour!. Meno, J.

The **Getaway**. Redhill, M.

Getting across. Silverberg, R.

Getting back onto solid foods. Ebenbach, D. H.

Getting By. Nelson, R. J.

The **getting** even of "Parson" Guyles. Hodgson, W. H.

The **getting** even of Tommy Dodd. Hodgson, W. H.

Getting in touch with Lonnie. McInerney, J.

Getting it back. Reed, K.

Getting It Right. O'Sullivan, V.

Getting lucky. Michaels, L.

Getting older. Tognazzini, A.

Getting Out in One Piece. Clayton, J. J.

Getting out more. Stark, C.

Getting Shot from a Tree. Donaldson, J. W.

Getting to know the world. Miller, A. L.

Getting to know you. Marusek, D.

Getting to Yes. Walsh, K. M.

GETTY CENTER (LOS ANGELES, CALIF.)

Murray, Y. M. The conquest [excerpt]

GEYSERS

Bierce, A. Jim Beckwourth's pond

Ghadir, Munirah A. al-

I was betrayed with a single golden pound

Oranges in the sun; short stories from the Arabian Gulf; edited and translated by Deborah S. Akers, Abubaker A. Bagader

GHANA

Ali, M. N. Mallam Sile

Ali, M. N. Man pass man

Ali, M. N. The manhood test

Ali, M. N. The prophet of Zongo Street

GHOST STORIES—*Continued*

Grimes, C. Seven stories to live by
Harman, C. The last to be found
Henderson, J. Wet dog of Galveston
Hill, J. 20th century ghost
Hill, J. Dead-wood
Hill, J. My father's mask
Hirshberg, G. Dancing men
Hirshberg, G. The muldoon
Hirshberg, G. The two Sams
Hodgson, W. H. Carnacki, the ghost finder
Hodgson, W. H. The find
Hodgson, W. H. The gateway of the monster
Hodgson, W. H. The ghost pirates
Hodgson, W. H. The haunting of the Lady Shannon
Hodgson, W. H. The hog
Hodgson, W. H. The horse of the invisible
Hodgson, W. H. The house among the laurels
Hodgson, W. H. The searcher of the end house
Hodgson, W. H. The thing invisible
Hodgson, W. H. The Valley of Lost Children
Hodgson, W. H. The whistling room
Holder, B. and Holder, N. Another exciting adventure of Lightning Merriemouse-Jones: a touching ghost story
Howard, R. E. The cairn on the headland
Howard, R. E. Delenda est
Howard, R. E. Dermod's bane
Howard, R. E. The shadow of the beast
Howard, R. E. Spectres in the dark
Howard, R. E. The spirit of Tom Molyneaux
Irvine, A. C. Green River chantey
Jackson, S. Here is the church
James, C. L. R. The ghost at the window
Jones, N. What you call winter
Joyce, G. Black dust
Kang, M. S. A fearful symmetry
Keane, J. B. 'Your're on next Sunday'
Kelly, R. The cistern
Kihn, G. Queen of the groupies
King, L. R. The house
King, S. The reach
King, S. Willa
Lamsley, T. Inheritance
Lamsley, T. Running in the family
Lennon, J. R. Death to our friends
Ligotti, T. Purity
Link, K. The constable of Abal
Link, K. Louise's ghost
Link, K. Stone animals
Liu, M. M. Where the heart lives
Lovecraft, H. P. The lurking fear
Luvaas, W. Trespass
Lytton, B. The house and the brain
MacAlister, K. Cat got your tongue?
Mandelbaum, P. Several answers
Marías, J. When I was mortal
Martin, G. R. R. The exit to San Breta
Martin, G. R. R. Nightflyers
Matheson, R. Old haunts
Matheson, R. Slaughter house
Matheson, R. Wet straw
McCrumb, S. The gallows necklace
McMahan, G. Hum drum
Messinger, J. Scream in the dark
Miéville, C. and others. The ball room
Modesitt, L. E., Jr. The dock to heaven
Modesitt, L. E., Jr. Ghost mission

Monette, S. Drowning Palmer
Monteleone, T. F. The prisoner's tale
Muller, M. Dust to dust
Murakami, H. Hanalei Bay
Murphy, Y. Is this a land, a continent, can it be conquered?
Nelson, A. Flesh tone
Nelson, D. E. Bay
Nevill, A. L. G. Where angels come in
Nolan, W. F. Mommy, Daddy, & Mollie
Ochsner, G. Articles of faith
Ochsner, G. How one carries another
Ochsner, G. When the dark is light enough
O'Driscoll, M. The silence of the falling stars
Oliver, F. Dancing on air
Oliver, R. Among the tombs
Powers, T. Fifty cents
Qadir 'Aqil, 'A. a.- . The siege
Reed, K. Yard sale
Resnick, M. Travels with my cats
Richards, S. S. The ape in the face
Richards, S. S. Man walking
Rickards, J. Twenty dollar future
Rickert, M. The chambered fruit
Rickert, M. Holiday
Rickert, M. Journey into the kingdom
Rickert, M. More beautiful than you
Roberts, S. M. Eviction notice
Rock, P. Gold firebird
Rock, P. Shaken
Rock, P. Signal mirror
Rubião, M. Zacarias, the pyrotechnist
Russell, K. Haunting Olivia
Scott, Sir W. The Tapestried Chamber; or, The lady in the sacque
Sezginturedi, A. Around here, somewhere
Shawl, N. The Raineses´
Shepard, L. Delta Sly Honey
Shepard, L. The lepidopterist
Shepard, L. Only partly here
Shinn, S. The house of seven spirits
Sillitoe, A. The caller
Silver, M. The visitor
Silverberg, R. Push no more
Smith, C. A. Thirteen phantasms
Smith, R. T. Little Sorrel
Snell, D. L. Love seat solitaire
Spark, M. The leaf-sweeper
Spark, M. The Portobello Road
Stackpole, M. A. When you're dead
Stelmok, J. Maxfield Ridge
Sterling, B. The denial
Sterns, A. The rest is silence
Swan, G. Cochise
Tham, H. The seventh day
Thormahlen, A. 23 December
Ts'an-hsüeh. Snake Island
Vidal, G. A moment of green laurel
Volk, S. 31/10
Vukcevich, R. Pretending
Wagner, K. E. In the pines
Waldrop, H. A better world's in birth!
Weinberg, R. Genius Loci
Wilhelm, K. Rules of the game
Williams, C. The night before
Williams, C. The suicide pit
Williams, W. J. Ligdan and the young pretender
Willis, C. Service for the burial of the dead
Wilson, F. P. Aftershock

GHOST STORIES—*Continued*

Yeaman, R. N. A world more real

Ghost town choir. Ferris, J.

GHOST TOWNS *See* Extinct cities

Ghost writer. Braver, G.

Ghost writer. Law, J.

GHOSTS *See* Ghost stories

Ghosts. Adichie, C. N.

Ghosts. Baxter, C.

Ghosts. Danticat, E.

Ghosts. Manley, C.

Ghosts and the machine. Rose, L.

The **ghosts** of the 'Glen Doon'. Hodgson, W. H.

The **ghosts** we love. Clarke, B.

The **Ghostwriter**. Lychack, W.

Ghostwriting. Ohlin, A.

The **ghoul**. Smith, C. A.

GHOULS AND OGRES

Griffith, C. and Griffith, S. The source

Smith, C. A. The ghoul

GI Jesus. Palwick, S.

Giant. Appelfeld, A. and Green, J. M.

Giant killer. Chandler, A. B.

Giant Land. Ford, J.

Giant Things. Martin, S. H.

GIANTS

Barfield, O. The child and the giant

Bierce, A. No charge for attendance

Cadnum, M. Mrs. Big

Chandler, A. B. Giant killer

Coville, B. The giant's tooth

DeNiro, A. The friendly giants

Eggers, D. Theo

Ford, J. Giant Land

Rosenbaum, B. The valley of giants

Smith, C. A. The root of Ampoi

Thomas, E. The making of the worlds, of gods, and of giants

Wilde, O. The selfish giant

Yolen, J. Dawn-strider

The **giant's** tooth. Coville, B.

Gibb, Camilla

The Principles of Exile

The Walrus v4 no6 p70-5 Jl/Ag 2007

When She Was Small

Harvard Review (1992) no25 p191-6 Fall 2003

Gibbons, Reginald

An Event in Summer

StoryQuarterly v41 p276-7 2005

Island

TriQuarterly no131 p49-56 2008

Some of the Art of Fiction

StoryQuarterly v41 p243-7 2005

Giberga, Jane Sughrue

Runaway

Good Housekeeping v241 no3 p225-6, 228, 230-2, 234 S 2005

Gibson, Stephen

The Story behind the Photograph

Michigan Quarterly Review v45 no1 p182-3 Wint 2006

Gibson, William

Thirteen views of a cardboard city

Rewired; the post-cyberpunk anthology; James Patrick Kelly & John Kessel, editors

Gideon. Packer, Z.

Gifford, Barry

African adventure story

Gifford, B. Do the blind dream?; new novellas and stories

After hours at La Chinita

San Francisco noir; edited by Peter Maravelis

Gifford, B. The stars above Veracruz

Almost Oriental

Gifford, B. The stars above Veracruz

Ball lighting

Gifford, B. Do the blind dream?; new novellas and stories

The bearded lady of Rutgers Street

Gifford, B. The stars above Veracruz

Blows with Sticks Raining Hard

Southwest Review v92 no1 p93-5 2007

The ciné

Gifford, B. Do the blind dream?; new novellas and stories

Coda: the ropedancers recurring dream

Gifford, B. The stars above Veracruz

Dancing with Fidel

Gifford, B. The stars above Veracruz

A day's worth of beauty

Gifford, B. Do the blind dream?; new novellas and stories

Détente at the Flying Horse

Southwest Review v92 no1 p89-92 2007

Do the blind dream?

Gifford, B. Do the blind dream?; new novellas and stories

Forever after

Gifford, B. Do the blind dream?; new novellas and stories

The god of birds

Gifford, B. The stars above Veracruz

Havana Moon

Gifford, B. Do the blind dream?; new novellas and stories

Holiday from women

Gifford, B. Do the blind dream?; new novellas and stories

Johnny Across

Gifford, B. Do the blind dream?; new novellas and stories

The law of affection

Gifford, B. The stars above Veracruz

Life is like this sometimes

Gifford, B. Do the blind dream?; new novellas and stories

The lost tribe

Gifford, B. Do the blind dream?; new novellas and stories

Murder at the Swordfish Club

Gifford, B. The stars above Veracruz

My catechism

Gifford, B. The stars above Veracruz

New mysteries of Paris

Paris noir; capital crime fiction; edited by Maxim Jakubowski

One leg

Gifford, B. The stars above Veracruz

Ploughshares v32 no1 p15-18 Spr 2006

The Peterson fire

Gifford, B. Do the blind dream?; new novellas and stories

The ropedancer: an introduction

Gifford, B. The stars above Veracruz

Giraldi, William—*Continued*
  Two Backyards
     Confrontation no92/93 p141-7 Fall 2005/Wint
        2006
The **girl**. Brown, G. M.
The **Girl** at the Station. Varallo, A.
Girl-child X: a story of birthing told through three
    eras. Baggott, J.
The **girl** detective Bendel-Simso, M. M., ed. Early
    American detective stories; an anthology;
    edited by LeRoy Lad Panek and Mary M.
    Bendel-Simso.
The **girl** from beyond. Rosa, J. G.
A **girl** from my hometown. Judah, S.
The **girl** hero's mirror says he's not the one. Rob-
    son, J.
The **girl** in blue jeans. Qi, S.
The **girl** in the book. Levi, P.
The **girl** in the flammable skirt. Bender, A.
The **girl** in the story. Selgin, P.
A **girl** is like a colt. Le May, A.
A **girl** like you. Gorman, E.
A **girl** named Charlie. Cohen, S.
Girl of my dreams. Matheson, R.
Girl of Wisdom. Gautier, A.
The **girl** on the fridge. Keret, E.
Girl reporter. Harrell, S.
Girl Talk. Van den Berg, L.
Girl . . . There Was a Time. Harlow, E.
The **girl** who ate butterflies. Rickert, M.
The **girl** who cried flowers. Yolen, J.
The **girl** who kissed Barnaby Jones. Phillips, S.
The **girl** who knew too much. Barr, R.
The **girl** who left her sock on the floor. Eisenberg,
    D.
The **girl** who loved animals. McAllister, B.
The **girl** who loved movies. Hinton, S. E.
The **girl** who loves Schubert. Stern, R. G.
The **Girl** Who Proposed. Smither, E.
The **girl** who was plugged in. Tiptree, J.
A **girl** with a monkey. Michaels, L.
The **girl** with a willing heart and a cold mind.
    Maxwell, W.
The **girl** with the blackened eye. Oates, J. C.
The **girl** with the grey eyes. Hodgson, W. H.
The **Girl** with the Metal Hair. Morris, A.
The **girl** with the pirate trousers. Rivas, M.
The **girl** with the silver eyes. Hammett, D.
Girlfriend. Blackshaw, G.
The **girlfriend**. Meloy, M.
The **girlfriend** from another planet. Lombardi, T.
The **girlfriends** of Dorian Gray. Frost, G.
Girlieman. Hauser, P.
GIRLS
        See also Adolescence; Children; Youth
  Abbott, L. K. Gravity
  Abbott, M. Our eyes couldn't stop opening
  Adrian, C. A child's book of sickness and death
  Akpan, U. C. My parent's bedroom
  Allen, P. L. Crip
  Alvarado, B. What Lydia thinks of roses
  Anderson, B. Discontinuous lives
  Anderson, B. One potato two potato
  Askins, C. Kit
  Atwell, M. S. Blue night, Clover Lake
  Atwood, M. The art of cooking and serving
  Atwood, M. Lusus naturae
  Atwood, M. My last Duchess

  Averill, T. F. The musical genius of Moscow,
    Kansas
  Baer, W. C. Deception of the thrush
  Báez, A. The awakening
  Báez, A. To tell the truth
  Báez, A. Wildflow
  Baingana, D. First kiss
  Baingana, D. Green stones
  Baker, K. Her father's eyes
  Barnes, S. The boat
  Barnes, S. Calling home
  Barnes, S. Earthquake
  Barzak, C. The guardian of the egg
  Baum, L. F. Bandit Jim Crow
  Baum, L. F. Mr. Woodchuck
  Baum, L. F. Prince Mud-Turtle
  Baum, L. F. Twinkle's enchantment
  Baxter, C. Gina's death
  Bear, E. The something-dreaming game
  Beattie, A. The garden game
  Belrose, J. L. House built of sticks
  Bender, A. Debbieland
  Bender, A. Jinx
  Bender, A. Marzipan
  Berg, E. Full count
  Bishop, E. Gwendolyn
  Bishop, T. The fragile commandment
  Black, H. Virgin
  Blackshaw, G. Going the distance
  Boyd, B. Scarecrow
  Braffet, K. Bad karma girl wins a t bingo
  Brockmeier, K. Andrea is changing her name
  Brown, D. Descent
  Brown, D. Hands across America
  Brown, D. Running
  Brown, K. Isabel's daughter
  Brown, R. The trenches
  Brown, R. Means and ends
  Budnitz, J. Immersion
  Bunin, I. A. Light breathing
  Cacek, P. D. The keeper
  Card, O. S. Inventing lovers on the phone
  Castillon, C. Knots and nuts
  Castillon, C. Letter time
  Castillon, C. Liar
  Castillon, C. Punching bag
  Castillon, C. Shame
  Castillon, C. There's a pill for that
  Castillon, C. You'll be a woman, my girl
  Chase, K. Man and wife
  Chattin, J. The wand
  Cherne, B. The countess
  Cherry, K. Where she was
  Cooney, E. See the girl
  Cooney, L. Pink
  Cooper, J. C. Rushing nowhere
  Corso, P. Giovanna's 86 circles
  Coville, B. Clean as a whistle
  Crone, M. Mr. Sender
  Crone, M. Where what gets into people comes
    from
  Crone, M. White sky in May
  Crowther, P. Conundrums to guess
  Crowther, P. Even beggars would ride
  Currans-Sheehan, T. The balers
  Currans-Sheehan, T. Margaret
  Daidō, T. Milk
  Dammaj, Z. M. The corn seller
  Daugherty, T. Lamplighter

Glasby, John S.
The quest for Y'ha-nthlei
Weird shadows over Innsmouth; edited by
Stephen Jones; illustrated by Randy
Broecker [et al.]
GLASGOW (SCOTLAND) *See* Scotland—Glasgow
Glass, Leslie
The Herald
Mystery Writers of America presents the blue
religion; new stories about cops, criminals,
and the chase; edited by Michael Connelly
GLASS
Pizzolatto, N. Nepal
Glass. Donovan, G.
Glass. Gregory, D.
A **glass.** Zoshchenko, M.
The **glass** army. Rand, K.
The **glass** bottle trick. Hopkinson, N.
Glass box. Winn, T.
Glass coffin. Kiernan, C. R.
Glass eyes. Rhodes, D.
The **glass** flower. Martin, G. R. R.
Glass grapes. Ronk, M. C.
A **glass** of water. Ruefle, M.
A **Glass** Shard and Memory. Steinfeld, J. J.
The **glass** slipper. Yasuoka, S.
Glasser, Perry
Satan Takes 12 Steps
Hanging Loose no87 p46-53 2005
The **glasses.** Lethem, J.
Glatt, Lisa
Animals
Glatt, L. The apple's bruise; stories
Bad girl on the curb
Glatt, L. The apple's bruise; stories
The body shop
Glatt, L. The apple's bruise; stories
Dirty Hannah gets hit by a car
Glatt, L. The apple's bruise; stories
Eggs
Glatt, L. The apple's bruise; stories
Grip
Glatt, L. The apple's bruise; stories
Ludlow
Glatt, L. The apple's bruise; stories
Soup
Glatt, L. The apple's bruise; stories
The study of lightning injury
Glatt, L. The apple's bruise; stories
Tag
Glatt, L. The apple's bruise; stories
Waste
Glatt, L. The apple's bruise; stories
What Milton heard
Glatt, L. The apple's bruise; stories
Glave, Thomas
He Who Would Have Become "Joshua," 1791
Callaloo v30 no2 p420-38 Spr 2007
Invasion: Evening: Two
The Massachusetts Review v49 no3 p281-301
Aut 2008
The Torturer's Wife
The Kenyon Review v30 no4 p144-76 Fall
2008
Glavin, Anthony
Patio nights
New Dubliners; edited by Oona Frawley
Glazed. Reah, D.

The **Glazers.** Oates, J. C.
The **gleaners.** Weaver, W.
Gleason, Katherine A.
Sweet Treat
River Styx no74 p62 2007
Gleason. Erdrich, L.
Glen echo. Luongo, M.
Gliders though they be. Emshwiller, C.
Glimmer, glimmer. Effinger, G. A.
A **glimmer** of youth. Molodowsky, K.
The **glistening** head of Ricky Ricardo begs further
experimentation. Crane, E.
Glittery eyes. Keret, E.
Globetrotters. Parks, T.
Glockner, Julio
Cuentos Volcánicos: Recopilados por Julio
Glockner / Volcanic Tales: Compiled by
Julio Glockner
Artes de Mexico no73 p26-7, 71-2 2005
Soñando al maíz / Dreaming of Corn
Artes de Mexico no79 p32-3, 71 2006
Glorious! Glorious!. L'Amour, L.
The **glorious** mysteries. Fulton, A.
Glorious things. Anderson, B.
Glory. Clayton, J. J.
Glory. Egan, G.
Glory hallelujah, sold!. Allen, W.
Gloss, Molly
Lambing season
Nebula Awards showcase 2005; the year's
best SF and fantasy; selected by the Science Fiction and Fantasy Writers of America; edited by Jack Dann
Gloucester. Finger, A.
GLOVES
Lumley, B. Gaddy's gloves
Smith, N. Extremities
Glue trap. Grimes, C.
The **glumbo** glisae. Blades, L.
The **gnarly** man. De Camp, L. S.
GNOMES *See* Fairies
Go, fight, win. Wilson, K.
Go on, sleep!. Zoshchenko, M.
Go Ride the Train. Holden, M.
Go Sell it on the Mountain. Shivani, A.
Go starless in the night. Zelazny, R.
Go tell the Phoenicians. Hughes, M.
Go ugly early. Parker, M.
Goanna. Madrid, G.
Goat. Kamlani, B.
The **goat** variations. VanderMeer, J.
The **goat** who was a cow. Arnow, H. L. S.
GOATS
L'Amour, L. By the ruins of "El Walarieh"
Malzberg, B. N. The passion of Azazel
Goats. Bass, R.
Goblin music. Aiken, J.
GOD
Auslander, S. God is a big happy chicken
Auslander, S. Prophet's dilemma
Auslander, S. Somebody up there likes you
Auslander, S. They're all the same
Bender, A. Job's jobs
Bradbury, R. The man
Brockmeier, K. A fable with slips of white paper spilling from the pockets
Clayton, J. J. The builder
DeLuca, M. J. The utter proximity of God
Klages, E. Intelligent design

Goldstein, Ann
  (tr.) See Baricco, Alessandro
  (tr.) See Levi, Primo
Goldstein, Imre
  (tr.) See Nádas, Péter
Goldstein, Yael
  Tastes Like Regular
    The Literary Review (Madison, N.J.) v50 no4
      p184-201 Summ 2007
Goldsworthy, Peter
  Run silent, run deep
    The Ecco book of Christmas stories; edited
      by Alberto Manguel
GOLEM
  Auslander, S. It ain't easy bein' supremey
  Foster, A. D. We three kings
  Irvine, A. C. The golems of Detroit
  Lake, J. The god-clown is near
  Malzberg, B. N. The passion of Azazel
  Sullivan, J. Niels Bohr and the sleeping dane
The **golems** of Detroit. Irvine, A. C.
GOLF
  Abbott, L. K. The valley of sin
  Block, L. Welcome to the real world
  Brett, S. The man who didn't play golf
  Bruen, K. Spittin iron
  Coake, C. His mission
  Collins, S. Water hazard
  Coyne, T. A gentleman's game [excerpt]
  Fountain, B. Asian tiger
  Franklin, T. Those good days
  Gash, J. Death by golf
  Hamilton, S. Room for a fourth
  Higgins, G. V. The heroic cat in the bag
  Keating, H. R. F. Miss Unwin plays by the rules
  Lippman, L. A good fuck spoiled [variant title:
    A good **** spoiled]
  Lippman, L. A good **** spoiled [variant title:
    A good fuck spoiled]
  Morrow, B. The hoarder
  Rankin, I. Graduation day
  Sandford, J. Lucy had a list
  Tapply, W. G. Unplayable lies
  Westermann, J. The secret
GOLIATH (BIBLICAL FIGURE)
                  About
  Finger, A. Goliath
Goliath. Finger, A.
Goliath. Gaiman, N.
Goliger, Gabriella
  Maladies of the inner ear
    Contemporary Jewish writing in Canada; an
      anthology; edited by Michael Greenstein
Gollatz, Garner
  Beneath
    Confrontation no102/103 p111-24 Wint
      2008/Spr 2009
Golllub, Dan
  The chess players
    Nature v455 p430 S 18 2008
Golnick's Fortune. Langer, A.
Golnor the Ape. Howard, R. E.
A **golpe** de martillo/Hammering away. Zavala, H.
  L.
Gombrowicz, Witold
  The Memoirs of Stefan Czarniecki
    The Georgia Review v58 no3 p670-81 Fall
      2004

Gomez, Dario Ruiz
  Bitter sorrows
    The Flight of the condor; stories of violence
      and war from Colombia; translated and
      compiled by Jennifer Gabrielle Edwards;
      foreword by Hugo Chaparro Valderrama.
Gomez, Reid
  Electric gods
    Reckonings; contemporary short fiction by
      Native American women; edited by Hertha
      D. Sweet Wong, Lauren Stuart Muller, Jana
      Sequoya Magdaleno
Gómez Palacio. Bolaño, R.
Gonatas, E. H.
  The preparation
    Angelic & black; contemporary Greek short
      stories; edited and translated by David
      Connolly; with an introduction by Vangelis
      Hatzivassileiou
Gone. Jensen, B.
Gone. Lazarin, D.
Gone. Molodowsky, K.
Gone down to Corpus. Lehane, D.
Gone fishin'. Rand, K.
Gone fishin' [excerpt] Mosley, W.
Gone fishing. Preston, D. and Child, L.
Gone girl. Macdonald, R.
Gone to flowers. Bear, E.
Gonzales, Michael A.
  The whores of Onyx City
    The darker mask; edited by Gary Phillips and
      Christopher Chambers.
Gonzalez, Kevin A.
  Statehood
    Playboy's college fiction; a collection of 21
      years of contest winners; edited by Alice
      K. Turner; foreword by Thom Jones
    Best new American voices 2009; guest editor
      Mary Gaitskill; series editors John Kulka
      and Natalie Danford
  Wake
    Best New American voices 2007; [edited by
      Sue Miller; series editors, John Kulka and
      Natalie Danford]
    The Virginia Quarterly Review v82 no2 p160-
      79 Spr 2006
Good and dead. McBain, E.
GOOD AND EVIL
              See also Sin; Suffering
  Baker, K. The ruby incomparable
  Beagle, P. S. Barrens dance
  Bonner, M. O. Tin can
  Fowler, C. The univited
  Levi, P. The magic paint
  Maḥfūẓ, N. The seventh heaven
  Matheson, R. The distributor
  Monteiro, L. Little Star of Bela Lua
  Moorcock, M. Lunching with the Antichrist
  Rickert, M. The harrowing
  Singer, I. B. The Jew from Babylon
  Stevenson, R. L. Markheim
  Valdés, J. Neighbors
  Vonnegut, K. Armageddon in retrospect
  Wilson, R. C. The Cartesian theater
  Zelazny, R. Tower of icc
A **good** bag. Linaweaver, B.
Good boy. Shawl, N.
Good boys deserve favors. Gaiman, N.
The **good** brother. Muñoz, M.

Gordon, Mary—*Continued*
City life
  Gordon, M. The stories of Mary Gordon
Cleaning up
  Gordon, M. The stories of Mary Gordon
Conversations in prosperity
  Gordon, M. The stories of Mary Gordon
The dancing party
  Gordon, M. The stories of Mary Gordon
The deacon
  Gordon, M. The stories of Mary Gordon
Death in Naples
  The Pushcart Prize XXIX: best of the small
    presses 2005; edited by Bill Henderson
    with the Pushcart Prize editors
  Gordon, M. The stories of Mary Gordon
Delia
  Gordon, M. The stories of Mary Gordon
Dilly
  Daedalus v136 no4 p89-100 Fall 2007
Eileen
  Gordon, M. The stories of Mary Gordon
Eleanor's music
  Gordon, M. The stories of Mary Gordon
  The Best American short stories, 2007; select-
    ed from U. S. and Canadian magazines by
    Stephen King with Heidi Pitlor; with an in-
    troduction by Stephen King
  Ploughshares v32 no1 p26-41 Spr 2006
The Epiphany Branch
  Gordon, M. The stories of Mary Gordon
  This is not chick lit; original stories by Amer-
    ica's best women writers; edited by Eliza-
    beth Merrick
The healing
  Gordon, M. The stories of Mary Gordon
I need to tell three stories and to speak of love
    and death
  Gordon, M. The stories of Mary Gordon
  Salmagundi no148/149 p108-16 Fall
    2005/Wint 2006
The imagination of disaster
  Gordon, M. The stories of Mary Gordon
Intertextuality
  Gordon, M. The stories of Mary Gordon
The magician's wife
  Gordon, M. The stories of Mary Gordon
Mrs. Cassidy's last year
  Gordon, M. The stories of Mary Gordon
  The best American Catholic short stories; a
    Sheed & Ward collection; edited by Daniel
    McVeigh and Patricia Schnapp
My podiatrist tells me a story about a boy and
    a dog
  Gordon, M. The stories of Mary Gordon
The neighborhood
  Gordon, M. The stories of Mary Gordon
Now I am married
  Gordon, M. The stories of Mary Gordon
The only son of the doctor
  Gordon, M. The stories of Mary Gordon
The other woman
  Gordon, M. The stories of Mary Gordon
Out of the fray
  Gordon, M. The stories of Mary Gordon
Rosecliff
  Gordon, M. The stories of Mary Gordon
Safe
  Gordon, M. The stories of Mary Gordon

Separation
  Gordon, M. The stories of Mary Gordon
Sick in London
  Gordon, M. The stories of Mary Gordon
  New Letters v73 no1 p31-59 2006/2007
Storytelling
  Gordon, M. The stories of Mary Gordon
Temporary shelter
  Gordon, M. The stories of Mary Gordon
The thorn
  Gordon, M. The stories of Mary Gordon
Three men tell me stories about their boyhoods
  Gordon, M. The stories of Mary Gordon
The translator's husband
  Gordon, M. The stories of Mary Gordon
Violation
  Gordon, M. The stories of Mary Gordon
Vision
  Gordon, M. The stories of Mary Gordon
Walt
  Gordon, M. The stories of Mary Gordon
Watching the tango
  Gordon, M. The stories of Mary Gordon
A writing lesson
  Gordon, M. The stories of Mary Gordon
Gordon, Peter
Celia
  Ploughshares v31 no2/3 p125-37 Fall 2005
Man Receives Letter
  The Southern Review (Baton Rouge, La.) v42
    no3 p625-38 Summ 2006
Gordon, Susan J.
Molly's menorah
  Good Housekeeping v241 no6 p225-7, 229-31
    D 2005
Gordon. O'Hagan, A.
Gordon, the self-made cat. Beagle, P. S.
Gordy gave me your name. Giles, J.
GORE, AL, 1948-
About
  Pierce, T. J. Wrestling Al Gore
Gore, Albert, Jr. *See* Gore, Al, 1948-
Gores, Joe
The second coming
  San Francisco noir 2; the classics; edited by
    Peter Maravelis.
Gores, Joseph N. *See* Gores, Joe
The **Gorge**. Eco, U.
The **Gorgon**. Smith, C. A.
The **Gorgon** [Variant title: Symposium of the Gor-
    gon] Smith, C. A.
Gorgon planet. Silverberg, R.
GORILLAS
  Fowler, K. J. What I didn't see
  Gardam, J. Pangbourne
  Howard, R. E. The shadow of the beast
  Resnick, M. The lord of the jungle
Gorman, Edward
The Baby Store
  Future Americas; edited by Martin H.
    Greenberg and John Helferd
The Brasher girl
  Gorman, E. Different kinds of dead and other
    tales
The broker
  Gorman, E. Different kinds of dead and other
    tales
Crystal's big night
  Creature cozies; edited by Jill M. Morgan

Gorman, Edward—*Continued*

Deathman
  Gorman, E. Different kinds of dead and other tales

Different kinds of dead
  Gorman, E. Different kinds of dead and other tales

Drusilla
  Places to be, people to kill; edited by Martin H. Greenberg and Brittianey A. Koren

Emma Baxter's boy
  Gorman, E. Different kinds of dead and other tales

A girl like you
  Gorman, E. Different kinds of dead and other tales

Junior
  Gorman, E. Different kinds of dead and other tales

The long sunset
  Gorman, E. Different kinds of dead and other tales

Lover boy
  Gorman, E. Different kinds of dead and other tales

Masque
  Gorman, E. Different kinds of dead and other tales

Moral imperative
  Man vs. machine; edited by John Helfers and Martin H. Greenberg.

Muse
  Gorman, E. Different kinds of dead and other tales

Riff
  Gorman, E. Different kinds of dead and other tales

Second most popular
  Gorman, E. Different kinds of dead and other tales

Survival
  Gorman, E. Different kinds of dead and other tales

A trip home
  Greatest hits; original stories of assassins, hitmen, and hired guns; edited by Robert J. Randisi

Yesterday's dreams
  Gorman, E. Different kinds of dead and other tales

Gorman, Edward and Starr, Richard Dean

The shadow that shapes the light
  Kolchak: the night stalker chronicles; 26 original tales of the surreal, the bizarre, the macabre; edited by Joe Gentile, Garrett Anderson, Lori Gentile; Kolchak created by Jeff Rice

Gornick, Vivian

A Friendship: How It Ended
  O: the Oprah Magazine v6 no4 p169-70, 172-3 Ap 2005

Gorodischer, Angélica

How to succeed in life
  Díaz, G. J. Women and power in Argentine literature; stories, interviews, and critical essays; [by] Gwendolyn Díaz

Gorriti, Juana Manuela

The black glove
  Gorriti, J. M. Dreams and realities; selected fiction of Juana Manuela Gorriti; translated from the Spanish by Sergio Waisman; edited, with an introduction and notes by Francine Masiello

The dead man's fiancée
  Gorriti, J. M. Dreams and realities; selected fiction of Juana Manuela Gorriti; translated from the Spanish by Sergio Waisman; edited, with an introduction and notes by Francine Masiello

Gubi Amaya
  Gorriti, J. M. Dreams and realities; selected fiction of Juana Manuela Gorriti; translated from the Spanish by Sergio Waisman; edited, with an introduction and notes by Francine Masiello

If you do wrong, expect no good
  Gorriti, J. M. Dreams and realities; selected fiction of Juana Manuela Gorriti; translated from the Spanish by Sergio Waisman; edited, with an introduction and notes by Francine Masiello

The mazorquero's daughter
  Gorriti, J. M. Dreams and realities; selected fiction of Juana Manuela Gorriti; translated from the Spanish by Sergio Waisman; edited, with an introduction and notes by Francine Masiello

The quena
  Gorriti, J. M. Dreams and realities; selected fiction of Juana Manuela Gorriti; translated from the Spanish by Sergio Waisman; edited, with an introduction and notes by Francine Masiello

The treasure of the Incas
  Gorriti, J. M. Dreams and realities; selected fiction of Juana Manuela Gorriti; translated from the Spanish by Sergio Waisman; edited, with an introduction and notes by Francine Masiello

A year in California
  Gorriti, J. M. Dreams and realities; selected fiction of Juana Manuela Gorriti; translated from the Spanish by Sergio Waisman; edited, with an introduction and notes by Francine Masiello

Gorse Is Not People. Frame, J.

The **Gospel** according to Mark. Borges, J. L.

The **gospel** of Mark Schneider. Vollmer, M.

The **gospel** of moral ends. Ojikutu, B.

Gospodinov, Georgi

Blind Vaysha
  Gospodinov, G. And other stories; translated from the Bulgarian by Alexis Levitin and Magdalena Levy

Blind Vaysha (an unfinished story)
  The Literary Review (Madison, N.J.) v49 no4 p9-11 Summ 2006

Christine waving from the train
  Gospodinov, G. And other stories; translated from the Bulgarian by Alexis Levitin and Magdalena Levy

The Christmas soul of a pig
  Gospodinov, G. And other stories; translated from the Bulgarian by Alexis Levitin and Magdalena Levy

Goswami, Mamoni Raisom
The empty chest
Gibson, M. E. Separate journeys; short stories by contemporary Indian women; edited by Geeta Dharmarajan; introduction by Mary Ellis Gibson
Got it one last time. Malae, P. N.
GOTHIC ROMANCES
See also Horror stories
Goto, Hiromi
Nostalgia
Nature v437 p168 S 1 2005
Tales from the breast
Witpunk; edited by Claude Lalumière and Marty Halpern
Götterdämmerung, in which Nora Jane and Freddy Harwood confront evil in a world they never made. Gilchrist, E.
Gottlieb, Daphne
Undone
Sex for America; politically inspired erotica; edited by Stephen Elliott
Gottlieb, Roger S.
The Occupation: One Fable, Three Commentaries
Tikkun v22 no4 p64-7 Jl/Ag 2007
Gottreich, Lisa
Ecce Homo
The Georgia Review v61 no1 p105-18 Spr 2007
Goudelis, Tassos
Afternoon with alcoholic view
Angelic & black; contemporary Greek short stories; edited and translated by David Connolly; with an introduction by Vangelis Hatzivassileiou
Gough, John
Julia
Going the distance; edited by Alan Beard
Gough, Thomas
Talk with Men
New England Review v29 no4 p41-52 2008
Goulart, Ron
The robot who came to dinner
This is my funniest 2; leading science fiction writers present their funniest stories ever; edited by Mike Resnick
Goulash. Balint, A.
Goulet, John
The Accompanist
The Literary Review (Madison, N.J.) v50 no2 p84-97 Wint 2007
La **Goulue** in retirement. Ducornet, R.
Gourevitch, Philip
Enough
The Paris Review v51 p154-8 Spr 2009
Gouroyannis, Vassilis
The cock's crowing
Angelic & black; contemporary Greek short stories; edited and translated by David Connolly; with an introduction by Vangelis Hatzivassileiou
Un **goût** de terre. Côté, E.
Govan, Babak
Fighting Fish
The North American Review v291 no1 p12-13 Ja/F 2006

GOVERNESSES
See also Housekeepers
Allen, W. Nanny dearest
Flanagan, E. Burn
Keating, H. R. F. Miss Unwin plays by the rules
Macy, C. Annabel's mother
Sankaran, L. Two four six eight
Tolstaia, T. Loves me, loves me not
GOVERNMENT, RESISTANCE TO *See* Resistance to government
Government Cows. Miller, K.
GOVERNMENTAL INVESTIGATIONS
DeNiro, A. The fourth
Lehane, D. ICU
Gower, Jon
TV land
Urban Welsh; new short fiction; edited by Lewis Davies
Goyette, Marie E.
One Pink, One Black
Feminist Studies v34 no3 p476-96 Fall 2008
Something Dreaming
The North American Review v292 no5 p25-32 S/O 2007
Grace, Patricia
Headlights
World Literature Today v83 no3 p31-4 My/Je 2009
Pa Wars
Harvard Review (1992) no35 p136-54 2008
Grace. Barry, R.
Grace. Fox, P.
Grace. Messina, M.
A **grace** of shadows. Daughtry, P.
Graceland. Dalton, Q.
Gracious silence. Linscott, G.
The **Grackel** question. Nolan, W. F.
Grada, Hector Luis
(tr.) *See* Esquinca, Bernardo
Graduate seminar. Cooper, D.
GRADUATION *See* Commencements
Graduation afternoon. King, S.
Graduation day. Rankin, I.
Grady, James
The bottom line
D. C. noir; edited by George Pelecanos
Kiss the sky
D.C. noir 2; the classics; edited by George Pelecanos.
Grady, Janett L.
Faux-pas, Doc
Nature v455 p1278 O 30 2008
Grady, Wayne
The Man on the Island
The Walrus v4 no3 p60-8 Apr 2007
GRAFFITI
Dann, J. and Zebrowski, G. Yellowhead
Magee, K. Vertical mile
Pizzolatto, N. Cryptograph
Schwartz, L. S. Mrs. Saunders writes to the world
Williams, C. Known
Graffiti. McCoy, L.
Graft vs. Host. Smith, R.

Grafton, Sue
A poison that leaves no trace
A New omnibus of crime; edited by Tony Hillerman and Rosemary Herbert; contributing editors Sue Grafton and Jeffery Deaver

Graham, Barry
All the bad stuff
Homewrecker: an adultery reader; edited by Daphne Gottlieb

Graham, Heather
The face in the window
Thriller; edited by James Patterson

Graham, Ottie B.
Slackened caprice
"Tell it to us easy" and other stories; a complete short fiction anthology of African American women writers in Opportunity magazine, (1923-1948); edited by Judith Musser.

Graham, Seana
The pirate's true love
The Best of Lady Churchill's rosebud wristlet; edited by Kelly Link & Gavin J. Grant; introduction by Dan Chaon

Graham, Tom *See* Lewis, Sinclair, 1885-1951

Graham, Toni
The blue book of dogs
Graham, T. Waiting for Elvis; stories
Eyes of glass
Graham, T. Waiting for Elvis; stories
Fortune
Graham, T. Waiting for Elvis; stories
God's Playground
Confrontation no98/99 p227-42 Spr/Summ 2007
Guest
Graham, T. Waiting for Elvis; stories
Heaven's gate
Graham, T. Waiting for Elvis; stories
Here and now
Graham, T. Waiting for Elvis; stories
In the realm of the senses
Graham, T. Waiting for Elvis; stories
Kilter
Graham, T. Waiting for Elvis; stories
Twins
Graham, T. Waiting for Elvis; stories
Ultrasaurus
Graham, T. Waiting for Elvis; stories
Waiting for Elvis
Graham, T. Waiting for Elvis; stories

Grahame, Kenneth
First whisper of the wind in the willows
Tales before Narnia; the roots of modern fantasy and science fiction; edited by Douglas A. Anderson

GRAIL
Pratt, T. Cup and table

Graillis's legacy. Trevor, W.

Grainger, Paul
To look too closely
Nature v450 p1276 D 20-27 2007

The **Gramercy** Park mystery Bendel-Simso, M. M., ed. Early American detective stories; an anthology; edited by LeRoy Lad Panek and Mary M. Bendel-Simso.

Grammar. Levin, Z.

GRAMSCI, ANTONIO, 1891-1937
About
Finger, A. Comrade Luxemburg and Comrade Gramsci pass each other at a Congress of the Second International in Switzerland on the 10th of March, 1912

Gran, Sara
The token booth clerk
A hell of a woman; an anthology of female noir; edited by Megan Abbott; foreword by Val McDermid

El **Gran** Enano / The Great Dwarf. Olmos, G.

Granados, Christine
The bride
Granados, C. Brides and sinners in El Chuco; short stories
Comfort
Granados, C. Brides and sinners in El Chuco; short stories
Enough
Granados, C. Brides and sinners in El Chuco; short stories
Haunts
Callaloo v32 no2 p378-84 Spr 2009
Inner view
Granados, C. Brides and sinners in El Chuco; short stories
The latchkey chronicles: Goldfinger
Granados, C. Brides and sinners in El Chuco; short stories
The latchkey chronicles: Manguera wars
Granados, C. Brides and sinners in El Chuco; short stories
The latchkey chronicles: Séance
Granados, C. Brides and sinners in El Chuco; short stories
Love web
Granados, C. Brides and sinners in El Chuco; short stories
Man of the house
Granados, C. Brides and sinners in El Chuco; short stories
My girlfriend Bobbi
Granados, C. Brides and sinners in El Chuco; short stories
Pecado
Granados, C. Brides and sinners in El Chuco; short stories
A scenic night
Granados, C. Brides and sinners in El Chuco; short stories
Small time
Granados, C. Brides and sinners in El Chuco; short stories
Vieja chueca
Granados, C. Brides and sinners in El Chuco; short stories

The **Grand** Ballroom. Dalton, J.

GRAND CANYON (ARIZ.)
Magee, K. Vertical mile
McKenzie, E. We know where we are, but not why

The **grand** inquisitor. Muller, E.

Grand opening. Reed, K.

Grand slam. LaBute, N.

Grand stand-in. Wilson, K.

Grand Strand. Rheinheimer, K.

Grand Tour. Seay, M.

Great Men and Famous Deeds. Peery, J.

Great moments in sports. McClanahan, E.

The **great** Mormon cricket fly-fishing festival. Bishop, T.

Great myths of our time. Stevens, J. D.

Great North American Trees. Darlington, T.

A **Great** Piece of Elephant. Abbott, L. K.

Great sea battles. Bukoski, A.

The **great** slow kings. Zelazny, R.

The **great** speckled bird. Edgerton, C.

The **great** strike of 1895. Bierce, A.

The **great** switcheroo. Dahl, R.

The **Great** Talent [Story originally published in German in 1915] Walser, R.

The **great,** the good and the not-so-good. Keating, H. R. F.

Great unreported discoveries no. 163. Resnick, M.

The **Great** Wall. Kadare, I.

The **great** wall. Monk, B.

Great wall: a story from the zombie war. Brooks, M.

The **great** white bed. Webb, D.

The **Greatest** Loss. Reuben, D. B.

The **greatest** trick of all. Child, L.

Grebec. Hardwell, J.

Greco, Ralph

The protocol: Your children deserve the best
Nature v452 p252 Mr 13 2008

Greco, El *See* El Greco, 1541-1614

GREECE

Archer, J. A Greek tragedy

Bakken, K. N. The effects of light

Crowley, J. Missolonghi 1824

De Camp, L. S. Aristotle and the gun

Douka, M. Carré fix

Lasdun, J. The natural order

Michalopoulou, A. Dad and childhood

Michalopoulou, A. I'd like

Michalopoulou, A. I'd like (orchestral version)

Michalopoulou, A. What will you do next?

Persian Wars, 500-449 B.C.

James, C. L. R. The Nobbie stories for children and adults

Politics

See Politics—Greece

Rural life

Kaisaridis, Y. The old man and the tree

Motz, J. With a little help from your friends

Valtinos, T. Addiction to nicotine

Zateli, Z. The ivory buttons

Athens

Koumandareas, M. Seraphim

Koustas, P. Athos Emfovos in the temple of sound

Panselinos, A. Arrogance

Thor, B. The Athens solution

Delphi

James, C. L. R. The Nobbie stories for children and adults

GREED *See* Avarice

GREEK AMERICANS

Ingalls, R. The icon

Pelecanos, G. P. The dead their eyes implore us

Selgin, P. My search for red and gray wide-striped pajamas

GREEK MYTHOLOGY

Link, K. Flying lessons

Sterling, B. The sword of Damocles

Swanwick, M. Girls and boys, come out to play

A **Greek** tragedy. Archer, J.

GREEKS

Egypt

Drosso, A.-M. Fracture

Soueif, A. Chez Milou

England

Milionis, C. The find

Turkey

Cetin, I. The bloody horn

Yemni, S. Burn and go

Green, Angel

Cornetta's Roominghouse
African American Review v42 no2 p339-41 Summ 2008

Green, Angel Y.

Wild Grape
African American Review v39 no4 p581-95 Wint 2005

Green, Anna

Food stamp
New stories from the Southwest; edited by D. Seth Horton; foreword by Ray Gonzalez.

Green, Arthur

(tr.) See Nahman

Green, Charles

Snowball
New England Review v25 no3 p174-87 2004

Green, Christopher

Lakeside
Dreaming again; thirty-five new stories celebrating the wild side of Australian fiction; edited by Jack Dann

Green, Dominic

Clockwork atom bomb
The Year's best science fiction: twenty-third annual collection; edited by Gardner Dozois

Green, Geoffrey

Creatures of the mind
Green, G. Voices in a mask; stories

A flood of memories
Green, G. Voices in a mask; stories

The keeper of the list
Green, G. Voices in a mask; stories

Overture
Green, G. Voices in a mask; stories

"Such dear ecstasy"
Green, G. Voices in a mask; stories

"This very vivd morn"
Green, G. Voices in a mask; stories

Voices in a mask
Green, G. Voices in a mask; stories

"Your sister and some wine!"
Green, G. Voices in a mask; stories

Green, Jeffrey M.

(jt. auth) See Appelfeld, Aharon and Green, Jeffrey M.

Green, Julien

In Notre-Dame
Paris tales; stories; translated by Helen Constantine

Green, Roger Lancelyn

The wood that time forgot; The Enchanted Wood

Tales before Narnia; the roots of modern fantasy and science fiction; edited by Douglas A. Anderson

Green, Roland J.
"It isn't every day of the week . . ."
    Alternate generals III; edited by Harry Turtle-dove and Roland J. Green

Green, Simon R.
Appetite for murder
    Unusual suspects; stories of mystery & fantasy; edited by Dana Stabenow.
The difference a day makes
    Butcher, J. Mean streets; [by] Jim Butcher ... [et al]
The nightside, needless to say
    Powers of detection; stories of mystery & fantasy; edited by Dana Stabenow

Green. Enright, A.

Green. Minot, S.

Green air. Ducornet, R.

The **green** apocalypse. Allen, J. R.

Green days in Brunei. Sterling, B.

Green, Dominic
Send me a mentagram
    The Year's best science fiction: twenty-first annual collection; edited by Gardner Dozois

The **green** elephant. Hammett, D.

Green fire. Gunn, E.

Green fluorescent protein. Smith, N.

The **green** glass sea. Klages, E.

Green heat. Zeman, A.

Green is the Most Difficult Colour. Tihanyi, E.

The **green** lanes. Kiely, B.

The **green** leopard plague. Williams, W. J.

The **green** magician. De Camp, L. S. and Pratt, F.

The **green** man. Gerrold, D.

The **green** monster. Nerval, G. d.

Green monster. Pachter, A. E.

Green plague. Yolen, J.

Green River chantey. Irvine, A. C.

The **green** room. Simpson, H.

Green stones. Baingana, D.

The **green** suit. Allen, D., Jr.

Green Tea. Hoffman, A.

A **green** thought. Michaels, L.

The **Green** Violinist, After Chagall. Vega Serova, A. L.

The **green** word. Ford, J.

Green World [Part of a forum: My Great Depression] Alexie, S.

Greenberg, Joanne
Falling Backward
    Commentary v127 no6 p51-5 Je 2009

Greene, A. C.
The girl at Cabe ranch
    Lone Star literature; from the Red River to the Rio Grande; edited by Don Graham

Greene, Graham
The basement room
    Adaptations: from short story to big screen; 35 great stories that have inspired great films; edited by Stephanie Harrison
A visit to Morin
    The Ecco book of Christmas stories; edited by Alberto Manguel

Greene, Maggie
The sixteen parts
    Homewrecker: an adultery reader; edited by Daphne Gottlieb

Greenfeld, Karl Taro
Noisemaker
    The Paris Review v50 p170-82 Summ 2008

Silver
    The Paris Review v49 p142-54 Spr 2007

The **greening** of Bed-Stuy. Pohl, F.

Greenland, Colin
Timothy
    Interfictions; an anthology of interstitial writing; edited by Delia Sherman and Theodora Goss

Greenleaf, Fitzroy
Our first well in Nebraska
    Adventures in the West; stories for young readers; edited by Susanne George Bloomfield and Eric Melvin Reed

Greenman, Ben
Batting cleanup
    Greenman, B. A circle is a balloon and compass both; stories about human love
Black, gray, green, red, blue: a letter from a famous painter on the moon
    Greenman, B. A circle is a balloon and compass both; stories about human love
Clutching and glancing
    Greenman, B. A circle is a balloon and compass both; stories about human love
Contemplating a thing about a person
    Greenman, B. A circle is a balloon and compass both; stories about human love
Dear X
    Greenman, B. A circle is a balloon and compass both; stories about human love
The duck knows how to make the most of things
    Greenman, B. A circle is a balloon and compass both; stories about human love
A field guide to the North American Bigfoot
    Greenman, B. A circle is a balloon and compass both; stories about human love
How little we know about cast polymers, and about life
    Stumbling and raging; more politically inspired fiction; edited by Stephen Elliott; with associate editors Greg Larson [et al.]
    Greenman, B. A circle is a balloon and compass both; stories about human love
In the air room
    Greenman, B. A circle is a balloon and compass both; stories about human love
Keep your eye on the bishop
    Greenman, B. A circle is a balloon and compass both; stories about human love
Mr. Mxyzptlk's opus
    Politically inspired; edited by Stephen Elliott; assistant editor, Gabriel Kram; associate editors, Elizabeth Brooks [et al.]
My decorous pornography
    Greenman, B. A circle is a balloon and compass both; stories about human love
Oh Lord! Why not?
    Greenman, B. A circle is a balloon and compass both; stories about human love
The re-education of M. Grooms
    Greenman, B. A circle is a balloon and compass both; stories about human love
Signs
    Greenman, B. A circle is a balloon and compass both; stories about human love

Greenside, Mark
The Accidental Homeowner
Good Housekeeping v248 no6 p167-70, 172
Je 2009
Greensleeves. Simpson, H.
Greenspon, Jaq
Disappear
Las Vegas noir; edited by Jarrett Keene &
Todd James Pierce.
GREENWICH VILLAGE (NEW YORK, N.Y.)
See New York (N.Y.)—Greenwich Village
Greer, Andrew Sean
Darkness
The PEN/O.Henry Prize stories 2009; chosen
and with an introduction by Laura Furman;
with essays on the stories They admire
most by jurors A. S. Byatt; Anthony Doerr;
Tim O'Brien
Newton Wicks
The book of other people; edited by Zadie
Smith
Greer, Robert O.
Collateral damage
Politics noir; dark tales from the corridors of
power; edited by Gary Phillips.
Oprah's song
Black noir; mystery, crime and suspense sto-
ries by African-American writers; edited by
Otto Penzler
Greetings. Bisson, T.
Greetings from Hollywood, 1979. Selgin, P.
Gregor, Nadia
Faure, envenomed, dictates
Text: Ur; the new book of masks; [edited by
Forrest Aguirre]
Gregor. Gordimer, N.
Gregory, Daniel
Awakening the genius within
Nature v444 p788 D 7 2006
Gregory, Daryl
Damascus
The Year's best science fiction: twenty-fourth
annual collection; edited by Gardner Dozois
Dead horse point
The Best science fiction and fantasy of the
year: volume two; edited by Jonathan
Strahan
Glass
Technology Review (Cambridge, Mass.: 1998)
v111 no6 p74-6 N/D 2008
The illustrated biography of Lord Grimm
Strahan, J. Eclipse two; new science fiction
and fantasy; edited by Jonathan Strahan
Second person, present tense
The Year's best science fiction: twenty-third
annual collection; edited by Gardner Dozois
Unpossible
Year's best fantasy 8; edited by David G.
Hartwell, Kathryn Cramer
Gregory, Rebecca Brown
Staying
River Styx no74 p65 2007
Gregovich, Andrea
(tr.) See Kozlov, Vladimir
Grendel. Taylor, E.
Grenier, Roger
The house in the Place des Fêtes
Paris tales; stories; translated by Helen Con-
stantine

Grenville, Kate
Bushfire
Harvard Review (1992) no30 p60-3 2006
Gresham, William Lindsay
The dream dust factory
Tales before Narnia; the roots of modern fan-
tasy and science fiction; edited by Douglas
A. Anderson
Gretchen of Cemetary Lane. Wendroff, Z.
Grey, Elisabeth
Breakdown
Southern Humanities Review v43 no2 p157-69
Spr 2009
Grey, Ian
(jt. auth) See Paxson, Diana L. and Grey, Ian
Grey, apple green, and white. Mukhopadhyay, T.
The **Greyhound**. Lyons, D.
Gribnis. Cheuse, A.
GRIEF *See* Bereavement
The **Grief** of Strangers. Adichie, C. N.
Grieving Las Vegas. Healy, J. F.
Griffin, Daniel
The Last Great Works of Alvin Cale
Dalhousie Review v88 no2 p283-96 Summ
2008
Saturday Night
Dalhousie Review v86 no3 p405-12 Aut 2006
GRIFFINS
Beagle, P. S. Two hearts
Griffin's egg. Swanwick, M.
Griffith, Clay and Griffith, Susan
The source
Kolchak: the night stalker chronicles; 26 orig-
inal tales of the surreal, the bizarre, the ma-
cabre; edited by Joe Gentile, Garrett Ander-
son, Lori Gentile; Kolchak created by Jeff
Rice
Griffith, Susan
(jt. auth) See Griffith, Clay and Griffith, Susan
Griffiths, Niall
Bingo master's break out
Perverted by language; fiction inspired by The
Fall; edited and introduced by Peter Wild.
Freshers' week
Urban Welsh; new short fiction; edited by
Lewis Davies
Never die
Getting even; revenge stories; edited by Mitzi
Szereto
Griffiths, Paul
Postcards from the Flood
StoryQuarterly v41 p496-501 2005
Grilley, Kate
Maubi and Jumbies
Sisters on the case; celebrating twenty years
of Sisters in Crime; edited by Sara Paretsky
Grillo, Christine
Hot Coffee, Summer
The Southern Review (Baton Rouge, La.) v41
no2 p263-70 Spr 2005
Grimes, Christopher
Curtains
Grimes, C. Public works
Customs in a developing country: a prefatory
story
Grimes, C. Public works
Discourse on the sublime and the beautiful
Grimes, C. Public works

GUILT—*Continued*

Trevor, W. The dressmaker's child

Updike, D. Kinds of love

Van Booy, S. As much below as up above

Van Booy, S. Distant ships

Villoro, J. Lightweight champ

Vollmer, M. Oh land of national paradise, how glorious are thy bounties

Weil, G. The most beautiful spot in the world

Williams, J. The girls

Windley, C. What Saffi knows

Zoshchenko, M. A dogged sense of smell

Guilty. Betancourt, L. A.

A **guilty** woman. Westcott, G.

Guimarães Rosa, João *See* Rosa, João Guimarães, 1908-1967

GUINEA PIGS

Davidson, C. On sleepless roads

McLean, S. The pig

GUINEVERE, QUEEN (LEGENDARY CHARACTER) *See* Guenevere, Queen (Legendary character)

Guinevere's truth. Roberson, J.

Guirado, Tamara

Above Asmara

StoryQuarterly v42 p480-508 2006

Guista, Michael

California

Guista, M. Brain work; stories

Down to the roots

Guista, M. Brain work; stories

Filling the spaces between us

Guista, M. Brain work; stories

The front yard

Guista, M. Brain work; stories

Godcrazy

Guista, M. Brain work; stories

The interviewer

Guista, M. Brain work; stories

Kiltee

Guista, M. Brain work; stories

Let me introduce to you

Guista, M. Brain work; stories

The old country

Guista, M. Brain work; stories

Secrets

Guista, M. Brain work; stories

Step four

Guista, M. Brain work; stories

A walk outside

Guista, M. Brain work; stories

The whole world's guilt

Guista, M. Brain work; stories

The year of release

Guista, M. Brain work; stories

GUITARISTS

Coake, C. Pitch black

Di Filippo, P. Slowhand and Little Sister

Magris, C. To have been

Reidy, D. Thingless

Guixà, Pere

You Can't Not Feel It

The Review of Contemporary Fiction v28 no1 p133-6 Spr 2008

The **Gulch**. Means, D.

GULF OF MEXICO

Guthridge, M. The host

GULF WAR, 1991 *See* Persian Gulf War, 1991

Gullard, Pamela

A Place for Fine Hats

TriQuarterly no129 p223-37 2007

Trapper Lake

The North American Review v293 no3/4 p6-12 My/Ag 2008

Gullette, David

Fort Macon

Ploughshares v34 no2/3 p62-74 Fall 2008

Gulliver in Icelandic. Keret, E.

Gumbo limbo. Winn, T.

A **gun** for dinosaur. De Camp, L. S.

A **gun** for Kilkenny. L'Amour, L.

GUNBOATS *See* Warships

Gunman aimed to please [Medical Humanities, v30 no2 December 2004] Brimacombe, M.

Gunn, Eileen

Coming to terms

Gunn, E. Stable strategies and others

Nebula Awards showcase 2006; the year's best SF and fantasy; selected by the Science Fiction and Fantasy Writers of America; edited by Gardner Dozois

Computer friendly

Gunn, E. Stable strategies and others

Contact

Gunn, E. Stable strategies and others

Fellow Americans

Gunn, E. Stable strategies and others

Green fire

Gunn, E. Stable strategies and others

Ideological labile fruit crisp

Gunn, E. Stable strategies and others

Lichen and rock

Gunn, E. Stable strategies and others

Nirvana High

Gunn, E. Stable strategies and others

The sock story

Gunn, E. Stable strategies and others

Speak, geek

Nature v442 p956 Ag 24 2006

Spring conditions

Gunn, E. Stable strategies and others

Stable strategies for middle management

Gunn, E. Stable strategies and others

Up the fire road

Eclipse one; new science fiction and fantasy; edited by Jonathan Strahan

The Year's best fantasy and horror: twenty-first annual collection; edited by Ellen Datlow and Kelly Link & Gavin J. Grant

What are friends for?

Gunn, E. Stable strategies and others

Gunn, Eileen and What, Leslie

Nirvana High

The James Tiptree Award Anthology 2; edited by Karen Joy Fowler [et al.]

Gunn, James E.

The listeners

Nebula Awards showcase 2008; the year's best SF and fantasy; selected by the Science Fiction and Fantasy Writers of America; edited by Ben Bova

Gunn, Kirsty

The Father

Granta no104 p213-17 Wint 2008

GUNS *See* Firearms

Guns and jasmine. Salih, L. M.

Guns before butter. Vonnegut, K.

Guns don't kill people. Esposito, B.

The **guns** talk loud. L'Amour, L.

The **gunshot**. Shirley, J.

Guo, Songfen

Brightly shine the stars tonight
  Guo, S. Running mother and other stories; edited and with an introduction by John Balcom.

Clover
  Guo, S. Running mother and other stories; edited and with an introduction by John Balcom.

Moon seal
  Guo, S. Running mother and other stories; edited and with an introduction by John Balcom.

Running mother
  Guo, S. Running mother and other stories; edited and with an introduction by John Balcom.

Snow blind
  Guo, S. Running mother and other stories; edited and with an introduction by John Balcom.

Wailing moon
  Guo, S. Running mother and other stories; edited and with an introduction by John Balcom.

Guo, Xiaolu

Winter Worm, Summer Weed
  Ploughshares v33 no1 p80-3 Spr 2007

Guot's love. Đoàn, L.

Gurba, Myriam

Cruising
  Gurba, M. Dahlia season; stories & a novella

Dahlia season
  Gurba, M. Dahlia season; stories & a novella

Just drift
  Gurba, M. Dahlia season; stories & a novella

Primera comunión
  Gurba, M. Dahlia season; stories & a novella

White girl
  Gurba, M. Dahlia season; stories & a novella

Gurganus, Allan

Fourteen feet of water in my house
  New stories from the South: the year's best, 2007; selected from U.S. magazines by Edward P. Jones with Kathy Pories; with an introduction by Edward P. Jones
  Harper's v312 p74-9 Ja 2006

My heart is a snake farm
  New stories from the South: the year's best, 2005; edited by Shannon Ravenel; with a preface by Jill McCorkle
  The New Yorker v80 no36 p72-83 N 22 2004

Gurnah, Abdulrazak

Bossy
  The Anchor book of modern African stories; edited by Nadežda Obradovic; with a foreword by Chinua Achebe

The **guro** artists. Cooper, D.

Gur's theory of boredom. Keret, E.

Gurski, Edward T.

(tr.) See Mayoral, Marina

Gus dreams of biting the mailman. Irvine, A. C.

Gusev, Mariya

(tr.) See Klyuchareva, Natalya

Gustafson, Katherine

Parijaat
  Iowa Review v36 no3 p67-79 Wint 2006/2007

Gustav Amlingmeyer, Holmes of the range. Hockensmith, S.

Gustine, Amy

Nectarine Love
  The North American Review v290 no3/4 p52-61 My/Ag 2005

Guthridge, Marcia

The host
  Best of the South: from the second decade of New stories from the South; selected and introduced by Anne Tyler

Guthrie, Allan

Call me, I'm dying
  A hell of a woman; an anthology of female noir; edited by Megan Abbott; foreword by Val McDermid

Gutiérrez, Pedro Juan

Nothing to do
  Colchie, T. A whistler in the nightworld; short fiction from the Latin Americas; edited by Thomas Colchie

Guts. Palahniuk, C.

Guts and viscera in the chicken farm. Malae, P. N.

The **Gutter** sees the light that never shines. Rennie, A.

The **guy**. Hautman, P.

Guy Georges' final crime. Slocombe, R.

The **guy** not taken. Weiner, J.

The **guy** you said Joyce is fucking. McCauley, W.

GUYANA

Carew, J. Bra Anancy and Tiger

Carew, J. The burial

Carew, J. Chantal

Carew, J. Hunters and hunted

Carew, J. The initiation of Belfon

Carew, J. Tilson Ezekiel alias Ti - Zek

Carew, J. The visit

Guyot, Paul

Barry of Hollywood
  Hollywood and crime; original crime stories set during the history of Hollywood; edited by Robert J. Randisi

The closers
  Greatest hits; original stories of assassins, hitmen, and hired guns; edited by Robert J. Randisi

What a wonderful world
  Mystery Writers of America presents the blue religion; new stories about cops, criminals, and the chase; edited by Michael Connelly

Guys day out. Klages, E.

Güzelsoy, Ismail

The tongues of the flames
  Istanbul noir; edited by Mustafa Ziyalan & Amy Spangler; translated by Amy Spangler & Mustafa Ziyalan.

Guzman, go home. Sillitoe, A.

Gwartney, Larry

The Great fourth grade Powered Glider Caper of 1928
  Idaho Magazine v6 no1 p41-6 O 2006

Gwendolyn. Bishop, E.

The **gwynhfar**. Yolen, J.

Gym. Mozetič, B.

GYPSIES
    Daughtry, P. Street of wounded Mercedes
    Gospodinov, G. On the stealing of stories
    Scholes, K. Of metal men and scarlet thread and
        dancing with the sunrise
    Toganov, B. The children
    Weaver, W. Bad blood
Gypsies. Mozetič, B.
Gypsies Came to Call. Goeden, J.
The **gypsies** in the wood. Newman, K.
The **gypsy**. Mindt, A.

H

H as in homicide. Treat, L.
Ha Jin
    The Beauty
        Michigan Quarterly Review v47 no2 p182-
        200 Spr 2008
    A composer and his parakeets
        The O. Henry Prize stories 2008; edited and
        with an introduction by Laura Furman; with
        essays on the stories they admire most by
        jurors Chimamanda Ngozi Adiche, David
        Leavitt, David Means
    The house behind a weeping cherry
        The PEN/O.Henry Prize stories 2009; chosen
        and with an introduction by Laura Furman;
        with essays on the stories They admire
        most by jurors A. S. Byatt; Anthony Doerr;
        Tim O'Brien
    The Perp [Excerpt from The Bridegroom]
        Lapham's Quarterly v2 no2 p20-4 Spr 2009
Habayeb, Huzama
    A thread snaps
        Qissat; short stories by Palestinian women;
        edited by Jo Glanville
Habemus papam. Mommers, H. W.
Habila, Helon
    The Crocodile Lover
        Granta v99 p225-38 Fall 2007
    The Hotel Malogo
        The Virginia Quarterly Review v83 no2 p190-
        203 Spr 2007
    The Witch's Dog
        Granta no92 p183-90 Wint 2005
Habit. Kennedy, C.
The **habitants** of Middle Islet. Hodgson, W. H.
Habitat new Chicago. Bova, B.
Habits and habitat of the southwestern bad boy.
    Richter, S.
The **habits** of the animals: the progress of the sea-
    sons. Higgins, G. V.
Hacienda. Porter, K. A.
Had he but known. Millhiser, M.
Haddam, Jane
    Edelweiss
        Creature cozies; edited by Jill M. Morgan
        The Best American Mystery Stories, 2006;
        edited and with an introduction by Scott
        Turow; Otto Penzler, series editor
The **Hades** business. Pratchett, T.
Hades in trouble. Bierce, A.
Hadley, Drum
    The teachings of Bronc Buster Billy Brown
        Best stories of the American West, v1; edited
        by Marc Jaffe

Hadley, Tessa
    Buckets of blood
        Hadley, T. Sunstroke and other stories
        Granta no89 p167-86 Spr 2005
    The card trick
        The O. Henry Prize stories, 2005; edited and
        with an introduction by Laura Furman
        Hadley, T. Sunstroke and other stories
    The eggy stone
        Hadley, T. Sunstroke and other stories
    The enemy
        Hadley, T. Sunstroke and other stories
    Exchanges
        Hadley, T. Sunstroke and other stories
    Friendly Fire
        The New Yorker v83 no46 p62-6 F 4 2008
    In the Country
        Granta v99 p149-68 Fall 2007
    Married Love
        The New Yorker v83 no30 p80-7 O 8 2007
    Matrilineal
        Hadley, T. Sunstroke and other stories
        Granta no94 p235-50 Summ 2006
    Mother's son
        Hadley, T. Sunstroke and other stories
    A Mouthful of Cut Glass
        The New Yorker v81 no16 p84-5, 88-93 Je 6
        2005
    Phosphorescence
        Hadley, T. Sunstroke and other stories
    She's the One
        The New Yorker v85 no6 p62-9 Mr 23 2009
    Sunstroke
        Hadley, T. Sunstroke and other stories
    The surrogate
        Hadley, T. Sunstroke and other stories
Hadrian's wall. Shepard, J.
**HAECKEL, ERNST HEINRICH PHILIPP AU-
    GUST, 1834-1919**
        About
    Rose, A. Micrographia esoterica
Haeckel's tale. Barker, C.
Hag. Riley, A.
Hagar & Ishmael. Heller, J.
Hagelstein, Chris
    Rossberger
        Confrontation no101 p231-5 Spr/Summ 2008
Hagelstein, Robert
    L.I.U. My World in the Early 60s
        Confrontation no101 p23-5 Spr/Summ 2008
Hagenston, Becky
    In Case Someone Comes Looking for Me
        Gettysburg Review v20 no3 p357-63 Aut
        2007
HAGER, JENNA
        About
    Rucker, R. v. B. Jenna and me
Hagiography. Tuttle, S.
Hagkull, Jeff
    Who Goes Up the Mountain
        The Literary Review (Madison, N.J.) v48 no2
        p134-45 Wint 2005
Hagy, Alyson
    Border
        Ploughshares v31 no1 p148-61 Spr 2005
    The Long Lost Soul of Mabry McKee
        Western Humanities Review v59 no2 p5-10
        Fall 2005

Haldeman, Joe W.—*Continued*
Finding my shadow
  Haldeman, J. W. A separate war and other
    stories
For White Hill
  Haldeman, J. W. A separate war and other
    stories
Foreclosure
  Haldeman, J. W. A separate war and other
    stories
Four short novels
  Haldeman, J. W. A separate war and other
    stories
Giza
  Haldeman, J. W. War stories
  Haldeman, J. W. A separate war and other
    stories
Graves
  Haldeman, J. W. War stories
Heartwired
  Haldeman, J. W. A separate war and other
    stories
The Hemingway hoax
  The Best of the best, volume 2; 20 years of
    the best short science fiction novels; edited
    by Gardner Dozois
Memento mori
  Haldeman, J. W. A separate war and other
    stories
The monster
  Haldeman, J. W. War stories
Out of phase
  Haldeman, J. W. A separate war and other
    stories
Power complex
  Haldeman, J. W. A separate war and other
    stories
The private war of Private Jacob
  Haldeman, J. W. War stories
A separate war
  Haldeman, J. W. War stories
  Haldeman, J. W. A separate war and other
    stories
Time piece
  Haldeman, J. W. War stories
To Howard Hughes: a modest proposal
  Haldeman, J. W. War stories
War year
  Haldeman, J. W. War stories
Hale, Daniel J.
My brother's keeper
  Mystery Writers of America presents the
    prosecution rests; new stories about court-
    rooms, criminals, and the law; edited by
    Linda Fairstein.
Hale, Janet Campbell
Claire
  Reckonings; contemporary short fiction by
    Native American women; edited by Hertha
    D. Sweet Wong, Lauren Stuart Muller, Jana
    Sequoya Magdaleno
Hale and hallowed. Erpenbeck, J.
Half a day in Halifax. Nadelson, S.
Half a grapefruit. Munro, A.
Half-bright: a short story. Minus, M.
HALF-BROTHERS
Barnes, H. L. The first hunger
Lange, R. Long lost
Roley, B. A. American son [excerpt]

Shepard, J. Trample the dead, hurdle the weak
HALF-CASTES *See* Mixed bloods
The **half-crazy** woman. Maxwell, W.
Half of being married. Saintcrow, L.
The **half** sister. Lasdun, J.
HALF-SISTERS
Erdrich, L. Future home of the living God
A **half-sketched** head. Ruefle, M.
The **half-skinned** steer. Proulx, A.
Half the story. Jones, N.
Halfie. Lara, A.-M.
Halfjack. Zelazny, R.
Halflead Bay. Le, N.
Halfpastdoom. Mitsora, M.
The **Halfway** Diner. Sayles, J.
Halfway house. Hardinge, F.
Halfway house. Silverberg, R.
The **halfway** house at the heart of darkness. Spen-
  cer, W. B.
Halibut. Keret, E.
Halima, Desdemona, Bubu. Fais, M.
Hall, Charles F.
The man who lived backwards
  Tales before Narnia; the roots of modern fan-
    tasy and science fiction; edited by Douglas
    A. Anderson
Hall, Emily
(tr.) *See* Cognetti, Paolo
Hall, H. Palmer
Strung Out in Suburbia
  The North American Review v291 no5 p18-23
    S/O 2006
Hall, James W.
The catch
  Greatest hits; original stories of assassins,
    hitmen, and hired guns; edited by Robert J.
    Randisi
  The Deadly Bride; and 21 of the year's finest
    crime and mystery stories; including com-
    plete coverage of the year in mystery and
    crime fiction; edited by Ed Gorman and
    Martin H. Greenberg
Six love
  Murder is my racquet; edited by Otto Penzler
Hall, Melissa Mia
(jt. auth) *See* Lansdale, Joe R. and Hall, Melissa
  Mia
Hall, Nancy Abraham
(tr.) *See* Poniatowska, Elena
Hall, Parnell
Deal me in
  Dead man's hand; crime fiction at the poker
    table; edited by Otto Penzler.
Fear of failure
  Murder at the foul line; edited by Otto
    Penzler
Hall, Sands
Hide & Go Seek
  Iowa Review v38 no3 p121-33 Wint
    2008/2009
Hall, W. David
Prince Valiant Works the Black Seam
  Callaloo v31 no2 p454-60 Spr 2008
Sandlot
  The Kenyon Review v30 no4 p45-63 Fall
    2008
Hall of liberty. Fowler, M.
The **hall** of the meteorites. Morris, M.

Hallabi, Nasir al-
The alley
  Oranges in the sun; short stories from the
    Arabian Gulf; edited and translated by Deb-
    orah S. Akers, Abubaker A. Bagader
Hallaway, Tate
Fire and ice and linguini for two
  Many bloody returns; edited by Charlaine
    Harris and Toni L. P. Kelner
Hallberg, Garth Risk
Early humans
  Best new American voices 2008; guest editor
    Richard Bausch; series editors John Kulka
    and Natalie Danford
Haller's second home. Maxwell, W.
Halliday, Lisa
Stump Louie
  The Paris Review v47 p155-64 Summ 2005
HALLOWEEN
Abbott, L. K. As fate would have it
Arsenault, Michael. A Halloween like any other
Atwood, M. The headless horseman
Boudinot, R. Absolut Boudinot
Boudinot, R. The littlest Hitler
Brite, P. Z. Crown of thorns
Crouse, D. Morte infinita
Gardam, J. Waiting for a stranger
Hempel, A. Rapture of the deep
Nolan, W. F. Year of the witch
Pierce, T. J. Day of the dead
Puchner, E. Child's play
Working, R. Halloween, via dolorosa
Halloween. Jones, S. G.
Halloween, via dolorosa. Working, R.
Hallowell, Janis
Safekeeping
  Ploughshares v32 no4 p96-113 Wint
    2006/2007
Hallucigenia. Barron, L.
HALLUCINATIONS AND ILLUSIONS
  See also Personality disorders
Bierce, A. Confessions of a sad dog
Bierce, A. D. T.
Bierce, A. A mirage in Arizona
Bierce, A. An occurrence at Owl Creek Bridge
Bierce, A. The realm of the unreal
Bierce, A. A remarkable adventure
Bradbury, R. The cistern
Cheever, J. The swimmer
Corso, P. Between the sheets
Guista, M. The interviewer
Jackson, M. Totally wired
Jo Kyung Ran. Looking for the elephant
Judah, S. Her three soldiers
Lovecraft, H. P. The dreams in the Witch House
Lovecraft, H. P. The shunned house
McGuinness, F. The Sunday father
Montgomery, L. Hats
Nelson, R. F. River story
Ozick, C. Levitation
Palazzeschi, A. Silence
Panayotopoulos, N. The strength of materials
Pratt, T. Lachrymose and the golden egg
Reents, S. Disquisition on tears
Reinhorn, H. Get away from me, David
Scurati, A. Eternal Rome
Shepard, L. Salvador
Shirley, J. The gunshot
Silverberg, R. In entropy's jaws

Smith, C. A. Thirteen phantasms
Wolfe, G. Seven American nights
Halmi, Suzanne
Maps of Old Battles
  Southern Humanities Review v42 no4 p367-79
    Fall 2008
Halo. Lott, B.
Halo effect. Rock, P.
Halperin, Mark
(tr.) See P'yetsukh, V. A.
Halpern, Frume
Blessed hands
  Arguing with the storm; stories by Yiddish
    women writers; edited and with a preface
    by Rhea Tregebov; introduction by Kathryn
    Hellerstein.
Goodbye, honey
  Arguing with the storm; stories by Yiddish
    women writers; edited and with a preface
    by Rhea Tregebov; introduction by Kathryn
    Hellerstein.
Three meetings
  Arguing with the storm; stories by Yiddish
    women writers; edited and with a preface
    by Rhea Tregebov; introduction by Kathryn
    Hellerstein.
Halpern, Frume
Dog Blood
  No star too beautiful; Yiddish stories from
    1382 to the present; compiled and translat-
    ed by Joachim Neugroschel
Halter, Paul
The call of the Lorelei
  Passport to crime; the finest mystery stories
    from International Crime Writers; edited by
    Janet Hutchings
Halves of a whole. Ochsner, G.
Halweil, Brian
Think Globally, Eat Locally
  World Watch v18 no5 p3 S/O 2005
Ham. Stewart, P.
Hamadani, Malak Roya
Looking for Shahbazi
  The Massachusetts Review v45 no3 p267-84
    Aut 2004
Hambly, Barbara
The lost boy
  Gaslight grimoire; fantastic tales of Sherlock
    Holmes; edited by J. R. Campbell and
    Charles Prepolec
Sunrise on running water
  Dark delicacies 2; fear: more original tales of
    terror and the macabre by the world's
    greatest horror writers; edited by Del
    Howison and Jeff Gelb
There shall your heart be also
  New Orleans noir; edited by Julie Smith
Hamburger School. Bluestein, E.
Hamby, Barbara
Invasion of the Haoles
  Harvard Review (1992) no36 p116-32 2009
Lester Higata's String Theory Paradise
  TriQuarterly no130 p60-8 2008
Hamel, Ruth
The Providence Trip
  New England Review v25 no3 p198-211 2004

Hamer-Jacklyn, Sarah

A guest

Arguing with the storm; stories by Yiddish women writers; edited and with a preface by Rhea Tregebov; introduction by Kathryn Hellerstein.

A love story

Arguing with the storm; stories by Yiddish women writers; edited and with a preface by Rhea Tregebov; introduction by Kathryn Hellerstein.

No more rabbi!

Arguing with the storm; stories by Yiddish women writers; edited and with a preface by Rhea Tregebov; introduction by Kathryn Hellerstein.

Hamid, Mohsin

Focus on the Fundamentals

The Paris Review v48 p11-40 Fall 2006

Hamid Ahmad, 'Abd al-

The plight

Oranges in the sun; short stories from the Arabian Gulf; edited and translated by Deborah S. Akers, Abubaker A. Bagader

Hamill, Denis

Under the Throg Neck Bridge

Queens noir; edited by Robert Knightly

Hamill, Pete

The book signing

Brooklyn noir; edited by Tim McLoughlin

The men in black raincoats

Brooklyn noir 2; the classics; edited by Tim McLoughlin

Hamilton, Clive *See* Lewis, C. S. (Clive Staples), 1898-1963

Hamilton, Denise

At the drop of a hat

Thriller; edited by James Patterson

Midnight in Silicon Valley

Los Angeles noir; edited by Denise Hamilton

Hamilton, Jane

The short history of a prince [excerpt]

Barnstorm; contemporary Wisconsin fiction; edited by Raphael Kadushin

Hamilton, Laurell K.

Those who seek forgiveness

The living dead; edited by John Joseph Adams

Hamilton, Peter F.

Blessed by an angel

The new space opera; edited by Gardner Dozois and Jonathan Strahan

Footvote

The Year's best science fiction: twenty-second annual collection; edited by Gardner Dozois

The forever kitten

Nature v436 p602 Jl 28 2005

Hamilton, Steve

One fast Packard

Meeting across the river; stories inspired by the haunting Bruce Springsteen song; edited by Jessica Kaye and Richard J. Brewer

Room for a fourth

Murder in the rough; edited by Otto Penzler

Hammad, Hamad al-

The return of a captive

Oranges in the sun; short stories from the Arabian Gulf; edited and translated by Deborah S. Akers, Abubaker A. Bagader

Hammer. Williams, J.

The **Hammer-Bashing** Society: A Parable for our Times [Reprinted from July/August 1978 issue] Goldsmith, E.

Hammett, Dashiell

The barber and his wife

Hammett, D. Lost stories; 21 long-lost stories from the best selling creator of Sam Spade, The Maltese Falcon, and The Thin Man; introduction by 3-time Edgar Award winner Joe Gores; edited by Vince Emery

Ber-Lulu

Hammett, D. Lost stories; 21 long-lost stories from the best selling creator of Sam Spade, The Maltese Falcon, and The Thin Man; introduction by 3-time Edgar Award winner Joe Gores; edited by Vince Emery

The creeping Siamese

The Black Lizard big book of pulps; edited by Otto Penzler

The dimple

Hammett, D. Lost stories; 21 long-lost stories from the best selling creator of Sam Spade, The Maltese Falcon, and The Thin Man; introduction by 3-time Edgar Award winner Joe Gores; edited by Vince Emery

Esther entertains

Hammett, D. Lost stories; 21 long-lost stories from the best selling creator of Sam Spade, The Maltese Falcon, and The Thin Man; introduction by 3-time Edgar Award winner Joe Gores; edited by Vince Emery

Faith

The Black Lizard big book of pulps; edited by Otto Penzler

The girl with the silver eyes

A New omnibus of crime; edited by Tony Hillerman and Rosemary Herbert; contributing editors Sue Grafton and Jeffery Deaver

The Black Lizard big book of pulps; edited by Otto Penzler

The green elephant

Hammett, D. Lost stories; 21 long-lost stories from the best selling creator of Sam Spade, The Maltese Falcon, and The Thin Man; introduction by 3-time Edgar Award winner Joe Gores; edited by Vince Emery

Holiday

Hammett, D. Lost stories; 21 long-lost stories from the best selling creator of Sam Spade, The Maltese Falcon, and The Thin Man; introduction by 3-time Edgar Award winner Joe Gores; edited by Vince Emery

Itchy

Hammett, D. Lost stories; 21 long-lost stories from the best selling creator of Sam Spade, The Maltese Falcon, and The Thin Man; introduction by 3-time Edgar Award winner Joe Gores; edited by Vince Emery

HAND-TO-HAND FIGHTING
  See also Karate; Kung fu; Wrestling
  Boswell, R. Guests
  Brown, G. M. The fight at Greenay
  Crouse, D. The man back there
  Dunbar, P. L. The trouble about Sophiny
  Granados, C. The latchkey chronicles: Manguera
    wars
  Johnson, C. R. Kwoon
  Lansdale, J. R. The pit
  Ockert, J. Mother may I
  Ockert, J. Some storm
  Perry, G. S. Hold autumn in your hand
  Pollock, D. R. Real life
  Pronzini, B. and Malzberg, B. N. Me and Mitch
  Raymond, J. The wind
  Smith, B. Broken arrow
  Starr, J. Bar fight
  Yoss. The red bridge
Handal, Nathalie
  Umm Kulthoum at midnight
    Qissat; short stories by Palestinian women;
      edited by Jo Glanville
Handfasting. Zumas, L.
A **handful** of dates. Ṣāliḥ, a.-
Handler, Daniel
  Delmonico
    The Best American mystery stories, 2005; ed-
      ited and with an introduction by Joyce Car-
      ol Oates; Otto Penzler, series editor
Handler, David
  Delmonico
    McSweeney's enchanted chamber of astonish-
      ing stories; edited by Michael Chabon; il-
      lustrations by Mike Mignola
Hands. Ronk, M. C.
The **hands**: a sroty. Bonner, M.
Hands across America. Brown, D.
The **hands** of John Merchant. Ruffin, P.
The **hands** of Mr. Ottermole. Burke, T.
Hands On. Boyle, T. C.
The **Hands** That Hold the Hammer. Markus, P.
Hands up! Who wants to die? Shepard, L.
Handsel Monday. Aird, C.
The **handwriting** patient. Kun, M.
Handyman. DeMarinis, R.
HANDYMEN *See* Hired men
HANDYWOMEN *See* Hired women
Hanford Reach. Wilson, M.
Hang ten. Rabe, J.
The **hanged** man. Rankin, I.
The **hanging**. Keane, J. B.
The **hanging** curve. Dozois, G. R.
The **hanging** in the foaling barn. Richards, S. S.
The **Hanging** Lanterns of Ido. Yoon, P.
The **hanging** of Bobby Valdez. See Leonard, E.
    Saint with a six-gun [variant title: The
    hanging of Bobby Valdez]
HANGINGS
  Bierce, A. Mr. Swiddler's flip-flap
  Bierce, A. An occurrence at Owl Creek Bridge
  Howard, R. E. Restless waters
The **hangman's** beautiful daughter. Barnard, R.
Hanlon, Matthew
  The long, dark voyage
    Fenway fiction; short stories from Red Sox
      nation; edited by Adam Emerson Pachter

Hanlon, Michael
  Climate change
    Nature v435 p384 My 19 2005
Hannah, Barry
  Get some young
    The New Granta book of the American short
      story; edited and introduced by Richard
      Ford
Hannah, James
  History Lessons
    Dalhousie Review v85 no1 p53-61 Spr 2005
Hannah and Benjamin. Judah, S.
Hannah Byde. West, D.
Hannaham, James
  Find Freddy
    The Literary Review (Madison, N.J.) v48 no2
      p53-64 Wint 2005
  Sneezing Lessons
    The Literary Review (Madison, N.J.) v49 no4
      p17-26 Summ 2006
Hanner's wit. Bierce, A.
HANNIBAL, 247-183 B.C.
                      About
  Friesner, E. M. First, catch your elephant
Hanoosh, Yasmeen
  (tr.) See Shibli, Adania
Hans & his daughter. Treat, J.
Hans and Grete: a fairy tale about children who
    live in the woods. Schwitters, K.
Hansen, Ron
  Hopkins in Wales
    The Virginia Quarterly Review p71-84 2006
      supp
  Playland
    The best American Catholic short stories; a
      Sheed & Ward collection; edited by Daniel
      McVeigh and Patricia Schnapp
  Wilde in Omaha
    Prairie Schooner v79 no2 p5-23 Summ 2005
Hansen-Young, Diana
  The flashlight game
    Mystery Writers of America presents the
      prosecution rests; new stories about court-
      rooms, criminals, and the law; edited by
      Linda Fairstein.
  Oaths, Ohana, and everything
    Mystery Writers of America presents the blue
      religion; new stories about cops, criminals,
      and the chase; edited by Michael Connelly
Hanson, Kate Myers
  Not Quite a Murder Mystery
    The North American Review v290 no5 p9-16
      S/O 2005
  Pilgrims
    South Carolina Review v40 no1 p132-40 Fall
      2007
Hanson, Rachel
  A Place of Serenity
    *Tribal College Journal of American Indian
      Higher Education* v19 no1 p43 Fall 2007
HANUKKAH
  Gordin, J. Yankele's dream
Hanway, Nancy Scott
  Names
    Southern Humanities Review v41 no1 p31-48
      Wint 2007
Hanwell in Hell. Smith, Z.
Hanwell Senior. Smith, Z.
Hanwell Snr. Smith, Z.

Happily ever after. Nolan, W. F.

HAPPINESS
 See also Joy and sorrow
 Bierce, A. Haita the shepherd
 Brennan, K. Happy girl
 Crane, E. You must be this happy to enter
 Disch, T. M. A knight at the opera
 Faber, M. Vanilla bright like Eminem
 July, M. This person
 Mueenuddin, D. A spoiled man
 Thormahlen, A. A happy man
 Tsutsui, Y. The very edge of happiness

Happiness. Schwitters, K.
Happiness will be yours. Meno, J.
Happy?. Alsup, B.
Happy. Bakopoulos, D.
Happy Accidents. McCorkle, J.
Happy birthday, 1951. Vonnegut, K.
Happy birthday Gerald Meatloaf. Troy, M.
Happy birthday to you. Keret, E.
Happy country. Schwitters, K.
A **happy** day in 2381. Silverberg, R.
The **Happy** Death of Alborada Almanza. Padura Fuentes, L.
Happy dens; or, A day in the old wolves' home. Yolen, J.
A **happy** dream. Almond, S.
Happy dust. Fulton, A.
Happy effects, 1741. Menger-Anderson, K.
Happy ending. Arjouni, J.
Happy ending with sticky tape. Biller, M.
Happy Fish, Plus Coin. Snyder, S.
Happy for You. Spatz, G.
Happy girl. Brennan, K.
Happy Jack, wild man. Bower, B. M.
A **Happy** Life. Mozzi, G.
The **happy** man. Lethem, J.
A **happy** man. Thormahlen, A.
The **Happy** Memories Club. Smith, L.
Happy New Year. Fonseca, R.
Happy trails to you. Hecht, J.
Happy with Crocodiles. Shepard, J.
Haraami. Shroff, M. F.

HARASSMENT, SEXUAL *See* Sexual harassment

Harbinger Hall. Roorbach, B.

HARBORS
 Campbell, R. Raised by the moon
 Lumley, B. The taint
California
 Lupoff, R. A. Brackish waters
Massachusetts
 Cave, H. B. The coming
 Glasby, J. S. The quest for Y'ha-nthlei
 Lovecraft, H. P. Discarded draft of The shadow over Innsmouth
 Lovecraft, H. P. The shadow over Innsmouth
 Tem, S. R. Eggs

Harborview. Miller, S. G.
Hard blows. Swingle, M.
Hard Body. Treuer, D.
Hard-boiled detective. Ruefle, M.
Hard Times. Rash, R.
Hard times. Wilson, R., Jr.
A **hard** truth about waste management. Prabhaker, S.
The **hard** way. Leonard, E.
Hard-Wired. Callan, L.
Hard without music. Bukowski, C.

The **Hardest** Thing. Kavaler, R.

Harding, Paul
 Miss Hale
  Harvard Review (1992) no33 p123-34 2007

Harding, S. M.
 The medium is the message
  Medium of murder; edited by Susan Budavari and Suzanne Flaig

Hardinge, Frances
 Halfway house
  The Year's best fantasy and horror: twentieth annual collection; edited by Ellen Datlow and Kelly Link & Gavin J. Grant

Hardly knew her. Lippman, L.

Hardwell, Jesus
 Grebec
  Dalhousie Review v87 no3 p427-35 Aut 2007

Hardy, Edward
 Welding
  New England Review v30 no2 p123-37 2009

Hardy, Myronn
 Vasco Da Gama's Pigeons
  Callaloo v28 no4 p1041-6 Fall 2005

Hardy, Nye Joell
 Chess's game
  Nature v451 p744 F 7 2008

Hardy, Thomas
 The three strangers
  The Mammoth book of vintage whodunnits; edited by Maxim Jakubowski

HARELIP *See* Face—Abnormalities and deformities

HAREM LIFE
 Smith, C. A. The kiss of Zoraida

Hareven, Gail
 The Slows
  The New Yorker v85 no12 p60-4 My 4 2009

Harihan, Githa
 Diablo Baby
  The Kenyon Review v30 no4 p134-7 Fall 2008

Haringa, Jack M.
 A perfect and unmappable grace
  Bandersnatch; edited by Paul Tremblay and Sean Wallace
  The Year's best fantasy and horror: twenty-first annual collection; edited by Ellen Datlow and Kelly Link & Gavin J. Grant

Harjo, Joy
 The crow and the snake
  Reckonings; contemporary short fiction by Native American women; edited by Hertha D. Sweet Wong, Lauren Stuart Muller, Jana Sequoya Magdaleno
 The flood
  Reckonings; contemporary short fiction by Native American women; edited by Hertha D. Sweet Wong, Lauren Stuart Muller, Jana Sequoya Magdaleno
 The reckoning
  Reckonings; contemporary short fiction by Native American women; edited by Hertha D. Sweet Wong, Lauren Stuart Muller, Jana Sequoya Magdaleno
 The woman who fell from the sky
  Reckonings; contemporary short fiction by Native American women; edited by Hertha D. Sweet Wong, Lauren Stuart Muller, Jana Sequoya Magdaleno

Harland, Richard
A guided tour in the kingdom of the dead
Dreaming again; thirty-five new stories celebrating the wild side of Australian fiction; edited by Jack Dann
HARLEM (NEW YORK, N.Y.) *See* New York (N.Y.)—Harlem
HARLEM GLOBETROTTERS
Wideman, J. E. Who invented the jump shot
Harleman, Ann
The angel of Entropy
Harleman, A. Thoreau's laundry; stories
Autumn, 1911
Harleman, A. Thoreau's laundry; stories
Biscuit baby
Harleman, A. Thoreau's laundry; stories
Iggy ugly
Harleman, A. Thoreau's laundry; stories
Meanwhile
Harleman, A. Thoreau's laundry; stories
My Romance
Southwest Review v89 no2/3 p368-89 2004
The ones without visas
Harleman, A. Thoreau's laundry; stories
Princess in Disguise
Good Housekeeping v246 no1 p159, 162-6 Ja 2008
Romantic fever
Harleman, A. Thoreau's laundry; stories
Sharks
Harleman, A. Thoreau's laundry; stories
Stalin dreaming
Harleman, A. Thoreau's laundry; stories
The stand-in
Good Housekeeping v242 no4 p211-12, 214, 216-18 Ap 2006
Street of swans
Harleman, A. Thoreau's laundry; stories
Thoreau's laundry
Harleman, A. Thoreau's laundry; stories
Will build to suit
Harleman, A. Thoreau's laundry; stories
Harlequin Valentine. Gaiman, N.
Harlow, Enid
Girl . . . There Was a Time
TriQuarterly no129 p113-24 2007
Harman, Christopher
The last to be found
The Year's best fantasy and horror: twentieth annual collection; edited by Ellen Datlow and Kelly Link & Gavin J. Grant
Harmon, A. G.
Native Language
The Antioch Review v66 no3 p489-502 Summ 2008
A Thing of Beauty
TriQuarterly no129 p198-222 2007
Harmon, Joshua
The Passion of Asa Fitch
New England Review v28 no4 p54-81 2007
Harness, Charles L.
Quarks at Appomattox
Nebula Awards showcase 2005; the year's best SF and fantasy; selected by the Science Fiction and Fantasy Writers of America; edited by Jack Dann
The **harness**. Buckler, E.
Harnessing the brane-deer. Billing, R.

Harnett, Catherine
Her Gorgeous Grief
The Hudson Review v58 no1 p29-36 Spr 2005
Harold Carlisle. Troy, J.
Harold Plays the Pauper. Sheehy, H.
The **harp**. Shields, C.
Harper, Baird
Yellowstone
Best new American voices 2009; guest editor Mary Gaitskill; series editors John Kulka and Natalie Danford
Harper, Candice L.
Mai Tais and Sticky Rice
Calyx v23 no1 p60-1 Wint 2006
Harper, Jonathan
After hours
Homewrecker: an adultery reader; edited by Daphne Gottlieb
Harper, Jordan
Johnny Cash is dead
Hardcore hardboiled; edited by Todd Robinson; introduction by Otto Penzler
Harper, Larry
No One Told Them
Western Humanities Review v61 no2 p132-3 Spr/Summ 2007
HARPISTS
Bradbury, R. Getting through Sunday somehow
Shields, C. The harp
Harrell, Stephanie
Girl reporter
Burnham, C. Who can save us now?; brand-new superheroes and their amazing [short] stories; edited by Owen King and John McNally; [illustrations by Chris Burnham]
Harrington, Kim
Low drama
The Deadly Bride; and 21 of the year's finest crime and mystery stories; including complete coverage of the year in mystery and crime fiction; edited by Ed Gorman and Martin H. Greenberg
Harris, Anne L.
Still life with boobs
Year's best fantasy 6; edited by David G. Hartwell & Kathryn Cramer
Nebula Awards showcase 2007; the year's best SF and fantasy; selected by the Science Fiction and Fantasy Writers of America; edited by Mike Resnick
Harris, Charlaine
Dracula night
Many bloody returns; edited by Charlaine Harris and Toni L. P. Kelner
An evening with Al Gore
The Horror Writers Association presents Blood lite; an anthology of humorous horror stories; edited by Kevin J. Anderson
Fairy dust
Powers of detection; stories of mystery & fantasy; edited by Dana Stabenow
Lucky
Unusual suspects; stories of mystery & fantasy; edited by Dana Stabenow.
Harris, Clare Winger
The fate of the Poseidonia
Daughters of earth; feminist science fiction in the twentieth century; edited by Justine Larbalestier

Hassler, Jon
  Keepsakes
    The best American Catholic short stories; a
      Sheed & Ward collection; edited by Daniel
      McVeigh and Patricia Schnapp
  Resident priest
    The best American Catholic short stories; a
      Sheed & Ward collection; edited by Daniel
      McVeigh and Patricia Schnapp
Hassouneh, Rima
  (tr.) See Hlehel, Ala
Hasta namaste, baby. Erdrich, L.
A **hasty** business. Zoshchenko, M.
A **hasty** marriage. James, H.
Hat trick. Keret, E.
Hatch. Reed, R.
The **hatchling**. Kelly, R.
HATE
  Higgins, G. V. Slowly now the dancer
  Lispector, C. The buffalo
  Smith, C. A. The maker of gargoyles
  Trevisan, D. The corpse in the parlor
Hate goes courting. Block, L.
Hating Monet. Almond, S.
Hatoum, Milton
  The truth is a seven-headed animal
    Oxford anthology of the Brazilian short story;
      edited by K. David Jackson
HATRED See Hate
HATS
  Day, C. B. The pink hat
  Lubar, D. Hats off
  Schweighofer, P. Seebohm's cap
  Uchida, H. The bowler hat
Hats. Montgomery, L.
Hats off. Lubar, D.
Haunted by name our ignorant lips. Matthews, J.
Haunted earth. Pizzolatto, N.
HAUNTED HOUSES See Ghost stories
The **haunted Jarvee**. Hodgson, W. H.
The **haunted Pampero**. Hodgson, W. H.
Haunted sailors. Daughtry, P.
The **haunted** valley. Bierce, A.
The **haunted** wood. Maḥfūẓ, N.
The **haunter** of the dark. Lovecraft, H. P.
The **haunter** of the ring. Howard, R. E.
A **haunting**. Boyd, W.
The **haunting**. Oates, J. C.
The **haunting** of Sherlock Holmes. Jeffers, H. P.
The **haunting** of the Lady Shannon. Hodgson, W.
  H.
Haunting Olivia. Russell, K.
Haunts. Granados, C.
Hauser, Ethan
  The charm of the highway median
    New stories from the South: the year's best,
      2005; edited by Shannon Ravenel; with a
      preface by Jill McCorkle
  Nashville
    Ploughshares v31 no2/3 p157-75 Fall 2005
Hauser, Pierre
  Girlieman
    Confrontation no104 p103-13 Summ 2009
  How to Date a Dead Guy
    Iowa Review v37 no2 p151-66 Fall 2007
  Teachable Moment
    Bomb no93 p114-16, 118-20 Fall 2005

Hautala, Rick
  The hum
    Man vs. machine; edited by John Helfers and
      Martin H. Greenberg.
Hautman, Pete
  The guy
    Twin cities; edited by Julie Schaper & Steven
      Horwitz
  Pork
    Politics noir; dark tales from the corridors of
      power; edited by Gary Phillips.
HAVANA (CUBA) *See* Cuba—Havana
Havana Moon. Gifford, B.
Havana's vast cemetery. Rivas, M.
Havazelet, Ehud
  Law of Return
    Ploughshares v33 no4 p47-66 Wint
      2007/2008
Have not have. Ryman, G.
Have you seen her? Kulpa, K.
'**Have** You Seen Us?'. Collins, M.
Haverty, Charles
  The Back Nine
    Gettysburg Review v19 no1 p37-52 Spr 2006
  Crackers
    Agni no60 p128-42 2004
  Excommunicados
    Agni no68 p28-44 2008
  Search Party
    Agni no65 p144-59 2007
  Two Virgins
    Confrontation no104 p201-12 Summ 2009
HAWAII
  Downs, G. Domestic architecture
  Mitchell, D. What you do not know you want
  Murakami, H. Hanalei Bay
  Obejas, A. Zenzizenzic
  Panning, A. Tidal wave wedding
  Panning, A. What happened
  Scoville, S. Pu'u Pu'iwa
  Scoville, S. Ulu's dog
  Todd, R. L. Vinegar
  Troy, M. Cookie Lily
  Troy, M. Fantasy
  Troy, M. Group home
  Troy, M. Island entertainment
  Troy, M. The most beautiful girl in the world
  Troy, M. Talk story
Hawaii. Miller, A. L.
HAWAIIAN ISLANDS *See* Hawaii
Hawes, Louise
  All the pale women
    Hawes, L. Anteaters don't dream and other
      stories
  Anteaters don't dream
    Hawes, L. Anteaters don't dream and other
      stories
  Dawson's folly
    Hawes, L. Anteaters don't dream and other
      stories
  A fine mess
    Hawes, L. Anteaters don't dream and other
      stories
  Halcyon House
    Hawes, L. Anteaters don't dream and other
      stories
  The knack
    Hawes, L. Anteaters don't dream and other
      stories

He. Porter, K. A.

He. Schwitters, K.

He ain't Jesus. McCollum, M.

He didn't like cats. Hubbard, L. R.

He got what he asked for. McCandless, D. B.

He has aged. Drosso, A.-M.

He Himself and His Wife Alena. Radzinsky, O.

He laughed. Reisen, A.

He loved Lucy. Bisson, T.

He loved to go for drives with his father. McCall Smith, A.

He Runs. Durrow, H. W.

He said . . . she said. Muller, M.

He Sets Me in the Stream. Duncan, D. J.

He that moves. Zelazny, R.

He who is mentally retarded. Schwitters, K.

He who shapes. Zelazny, R.

He Who Would Have Become "Joshua," 1791. Glave, T.

Head, Bessie

The coming of the Christ-Child

The Ecco book of Christmas stories; edited by Alberto Manguel

Head, Gwen

The Story about Lefty

The Yale Review v93 no3 p139-61 Jl 2005

HEAD-HUNTERS

L'Amour, L. The diamond of Jeru

The **head** of Farnham Hall. Gardiner, J. R.

Headache. Doughtie, E.

The **headhunter.** Nadelson, S.

The **headless** horseman. Atwood, M.

Headlights. Grace, P.

The **headline** trick. Lain, D.

Headlock. Pinkerton, D.

HEADMASTERS *See* School superintendents and principals; Teachers

HEADMISTRESSES *See* School superintendents and principals; Teachers

Heads down, thumbs up. Grant, G. J.

Heads or Tails. Lakoseljac, B.

The **headstrong** historian. Adichie, C. N.

Heal thyself. Card, O. S.

The **healer.** Bender, A.

The **healing.** Gordon, M.

The **Healing** Power of Pets. Alam, R.

HEALTH RESORTS

See also Summer resorts

Stuckey-French, E. Mudlavia

The **healthiest** girl in town. Stafford, J.

Healy, J. F. (Jeremiah F.)

Aftermath

The World's finest mystery and crime stories, fourth annual collection; edited by Ed Gorman and Martin H. Greenberg

A debt to the devil

Murder is my racquet; edited by Otto Penzler

Grieving Las Vegas

The International Association of Crime Writers presents Murder in Vegas; new crime tales of gambling and desperation; edited by Michael Connelly

Wolf Woman Bay; and nine more of the finest crime and mystery novellas of the year; edited by Ed Gorman and Martin H. Greenberg

I/M-print: a Tess Cassidy short story

At the scene of the crime; forensic mysteries from today's best writers; edited by Dana Stabenow

A matter of honor

The Deadly Bride; and 21 of the year's finest crime and mystery stories; including complete coverage of the year in mystery and crime fiction; edited by Ed Gorman and Martin H. Greenberg

Prayers for the dying

A Prisoner of memory and 24 of the year's finest crime and mystery stories; edited by Ed Gorman & Martin H. Greenberg

Proportionate response

The World's finest mystery and crime stories, fifth annual collection; edited by Ed Gorman and Martin H. Greenberg

Healy, Jeremiah F. *See* Healy, J. F. (Jeremiah F.), 1948-

Healy, Mick

Ashes and Spit

The North American Review v293 no3/4 p33-9 My/Ag 2008

Hear my plea. Rand, K.

Hearing her name. Dunlap, S.

Hearn, Lafcadio

(tr.) See Gautier, Théophile

Hearon, Shelby

A prince of a fellow [excerpt]

Lone Star literature; from the Red River to the Rio Grande; edited by Don Graham

Pushers

The Southern Review (Baton Rouge, La.) v42 no3 p605-16 Summ 2006

HEARST, PATRICIA CAMPBELL

About

McCarthy, T. Kool things: or why I want to fuck Patty Hearst

HEARST, WILLIAM RANDOLPH, 1863-1951

About

Baker, K. Welcome to Olympus, Mr. Hearst

HEART

Landis, G. A. Lazy Taekos

Disease

Drosso, A.-M. Hand on heart

Luongo, M. If the heart is lean

Percy, B. The faulty builder

Tsutsui, Y. Bad for the heart

Diseases

Castillon, C. They drank champagne at the restaurant

Clayton, J. J. Open-heart surgery

DeMarinis, R. The life and times of a forty-nine-pound man

Dokey, R. Electric dog

Johnson, G. Fever

Novakovich, J. A purple story

Ohlin, A. Transcription

Perlman, E. Spitalnic's last year

Temple, S. A roomful of Christmas

Heart Farm. Quarry, J.

The **heart** finds its own conclusion. Muñoz, M.

Heart for heart's sake. Thomas, J.

The **heart** is katmandu [excerpt] Hoffmann, Y.

Heart of the fields. Weaver, W.

Heart of whitenesse. Waldrop, H.

Heart shaped rock. Nelson, A.

Heart sockets. Zumas, L.

Heart suit. Coover, R.
The heart sutra. Oates, J. C.
Heart trouble. Arnold, G.
Heart Woods. Sanders, S. R.
Heartbeatland. Blackwell, K.
Hearth and Home. Appel, J. M.
Heartland. Fowler, K. J.
Hearts. Wheeler, R. S.
Heartwired. Haldeman, J. W.
HEAT
Lott, B. The issue of money
Heat. Drosso, A.-M.
Heat. Oates, J. C.
The heat death of the universe. Zoline, P.
Heat from another sun [excerpt] Lindsey, D. L.
Heat lightning. Krueger, W. K.
Heat rises. Magee, K.
Heath, Aloise Buckley
　A Christmas Carol [Reprint]
　　National Review v59 no24 p36-8 D 31 2007
Heathcock, Alan
　Peacekeeper
　　The Best American Mystery Stories, 2006;
　　　edited and with an introduction by Scott
　　　Turow; Otto Penzler, series editor
　　The Virginia Quarterly Review v81 no4 p186-
　　　203 Fall 2005
　Smoke
　　The Kenyon Review v29 no3 p12-27 Summ
　　　2007
　The Staying Freight
　　Harvard Review (1992) no31 p28-52 2006
Heathen technology at the end of the twentieth
　century. Baraka, I. A.
Heathens. Jones, A.
Heathen's revenge. Hodgson, W. H.
Heather. Barthelme, D.
Heatley, David
　Classic Combo [Graphic fiction]
　　Granta no102 p97-107 Summ 2008
Heatseeker. Haywood, G. A.
Heatwave. Sylvain, D.
HEAVEN
Bierce, A. My credentials
Bradfield, S. Heaven sent
Brett, S. Cain was innocent
Hughes, M. A little learning
Maḥfūẓ, N. The seventh heaven
Millhauser, S. The tower
Monk, B. Mrs. Herbinko's birthday party
Reeves, E. W. Not in the record
Roberts, A. Dantesque
Heaven. Holladay, C. C.
Heaven and Hell. Scott, J.
Heaven help me. Kun, M.
Heaven Lake. Row, J.
Heaven lies about us. McCabe, E.
Heaven sent. Bradfield, S.
Heavenly creatures: for wandering children and
　their delinquent mother. Thon, M. R.
Heavenly flame. Tolstaia, T.
Heaven's gate. Graham, T.
The heaving of the log. Hodgson, W. H.
The heavy sugar. Woolrich, C.
Hecht, Jeff
　Directed energy
　　Nature v440 p968 Ap 13 2006
　Operation Tesla
　　Nature v443 p604 O 5 2006

Hecht, Julie
　Being and nothingness
　　Hecht, J. Happy trails to you
　Cramp bark
　　Hecht, J. Happy trails to you
　Get money
　　Hecht, J. Happy trails to you
　Happy trails to you
　　Hecht, J. Happy trails to you
　A little present on this dark November day
　　Hecht, J. Happy trails to you
　Over there
　　Hecht, J. Happy trails to you
　Thank you for the mittens
　　Hecht, J. Happy trails to you
The hedge knight: a tale of the seven kingdoms.
　Martin, G. R. R.
HEDONISM
Welsh, I. Rattlesnakes
Heeger, Susan
　Floating
　　Good Housekeeping v243 no1 p211-12, 214,
　　　216, 218-20 Jl 2006
　Planting Happiness
　　Good Housekeeping v245 no2 p163-4, 166,
　　　168, 170-3 Ag 2007
Heer, Liliana
　Red summer
　　Díaz, G. J. Women and power in Argentine
　　　literature; stories, interviews, and critical
　　　essays; [by] Gwendolyn Díaz
Heere be monsters. Birmingham, J.
Heeren, Fredric
　Making the sale
　　Nature v444 p242 N 9 2006
Heidegger's cat. Bull, W.
Height advantage. Carroll, W. J.
Heighton, Steven
　The Dead Are More Visible
　　The Walrus v4 no10 p92-7 D 2007
The heights. Reinhorn, H.
Heim, Michael
　(tr.) See Bodrov, Sergei
Heimish knows all. Auslander, S.
Heink, Ernestine Schumann- See Schumann-
　Heink, Ernestine, 1861-1936
HEINLEIN, ROBERT A. (ROBERT ANSON),
　1907-1988
About
Gunn, E. Green fire
The heir. Livings, J.
The heir-apparent. Tremayne, P.
The Heiress from Horn Lake. Taylor, K.
HEIRESSES See Inheritance and succession;
　Wealth
Heirloom. Pariseau, E.
Heirloom. Stewart, P.
HEIRLOOMS
Templeton, E. Nymph & faun
HEIRS See Inheritance and succession; Wealth
The heirs. Mason, B. A.
Heirs. Oz, A.
Heirs of the perisphere. Waldrop, H.
HEISENBERG, WERNER, 1901-1976
About
Bear, E. Schrödinger's cat chases the super
　string

Heker, Liliana

Far away

Díaz, G. J. Women and power in Argentine literature; stories, interviews, and critical essays; [by] Gwendolyn Díaz

Spick and span

Violations; stories of love by Latin American women; edited and with an introduction by Psiche Hughes; foreword by Brian Matthews

Helen and Frida. Finger, A.

Helen of Sparta. Appel, J. M.

Helfers, John

Ancestral armor

Pandora's closet; edited by Jean Rabe and Martin H. Greenberg.

Deadhand

Places to be, people to kill; edited by Martin H. Greenberg and Brittianey A. Koren

Helicopter days. Singer, M.

Helin. Ts'an-hsüeh

HELL

Bierce, A. Hades in trouble

Bingle, D. J. Cursory review

Card, O. S. Homeless in hell

Farmer, P. J. A hole in Hell

Gaiman, N. Other people

Hevesi, L. Jules Verne in hell: a letter to the editor from the late writer

Hughes, M. A little learning

Lansdale, J. R. Way down there

Lethem, J. The happy man

Pratchett, T. The Hades business

Proulx, A. The hellhole

Roberts, A. Dantesque

Scholes, K. Into the blank where life is hurled

Singer, I. B. Sabbath in Gehenna

Soulban, L. Hell in a handbasket

Swanwick, M. North of Diddy-Wah-Diddy

Thisted, V. Letters from hell: letter III

Williams, C. Et in Sempiternum pereant

Zelazny, R. Mr. Fuller's revolt

Hell for homesteaders. Dawson, P.

Hell-heaven. Lahiri, J.

Hell in a handbasket. Soulban, L.

Hell in Dakota. Bonham, F.

Hell is the absence of God. Chiang, T.

Hell is where the heart is. Szereto, M.

Hell just over the hill. Zebrowski, G.

Hellas is Florida. Eklund, G. and Benford, G.

Hellem, Aaron

The Ghost of Stephen Foster

The Massachusetts Review v50 no1-2 p151-3 Spr/Summ 2009

Heller, Joseph

Hagar & Ishmael

The Paris Review v48 p96-112 Wint 2006

Hellfire at twilight. Baker, K.

The **hellhole**. Proulx, A.

Hellmann, Libby Fischer

High yellow

A hell of a woman; an anthology of female noir; edited by Megan Abbott; foreword by Val McDermid

House rules

The International Association of Crime Writers presents Murder in Vegas; new crime tales of gambling and desperation; edited by Michael Connelly

The jade elephant

Expletive deleted; edited by Jen Jordan

The whole world is watching

Sisters on the case; celebrating twenty years of Sisters in Crime; edited by Sara Paretsky

Your sweet man

Chicago blues; edited by Libby Fischer Hellmann

Hellman's scrapbook [excerpt] Majzels, R.

Hello, Astrid. Denza, K.

Hello from Ture. Bukoski, A.

Hello, hello, hello!. Tsutsui, Y.

Hello Jack. Michaels, L.

"Hello," said the stick. Swanwick, M.

Hell's cartoonist. DeMarinis, R.

Hell's forge. Cook, G.

Hellweg, Paul

Love/A Story

The North American Review v290 no6 p17 N/D 2005

Helms, Beth

American wives

Helms, B. American wives

Antique map collecting

Helms, B. American wives

Collected stories

Helms, B. American wives

The confines of civilized behavior

Helms, B. American wives

Glazing

Helms, B. American wives

Men in Italy

Helms, B. American wives

Once

Helms, B. American wives

Oysters

Helms, B. American wives

Telling stories

Helms, B. American wives

Help. Working, R.

Help the aged. Bell, J.

Help wanted. Russell, K.

Help wonted. Hughes, M.

A **Helpful** Nurse. O'Hanlon, S.

Helping. McNett, M.

Helping. Rea, A.

Helping. Stone, R.

The **helping** hand. Anderson, P.

Helprin, Mark

A brilliant idea and his own

Helprin, M. The Pacific and other stories

Charlotte of the Utrechtseweg

Helprin, M. The Pacific and other stories

Il colore ritrovato

Helprin, M. The Pacific and other stories

Jacob Bayer and the telephone

Helprin, M. The Pacific and other stories

Last tea with armorers

Helprin, M. The Pacific and other stories

Mar Nueva

Helprin, M. The Pacific and other stories

Monday

Helprin, M. The Pacific and other stories

The Pacific

Helprin, M. The Pacific and other stories

Passchendaele

Helprin, M. The Pacific and other stories

Perfection

Helprin, M. The Pacific and other stories

Helprin, Mark—*Continued*

Perfection: A Story

Commentary v118 no3 p17-47 O 2004

Prelude

Helprin, M. The Pacific and other stories

Rain

Helprin, M. The Pacific and other stories

Reconstruction

Helprin, M. The Pacific and other stories

Sail shining in white

Helprin, M. The Pacific and other stories

Sidney Balbion

Helprin, M. The Pacific and other stories

Vandevere's house

Helprin, M. The Pacific and other stories

HELSINKI (FINLAND) *See* Finland—Helsinki

Hemingway, Ernest

The killers

Adaptations: from short story to big screen; 35 great stories that have inspired great films; edited by Stephanie Harrison

HEMINGWAY, ERNEST, 1899-1961

About

Bradbury, R. The Kilimanjaro device

Haldeman, J. W. The Hemingway hoax

Oates, J. C. Papa at Ketchum, 1961

Scholes, K. Summer on Paris, light from the sky

Silverberg, R. The millenium express

Parodies, imitations, etc.

Effinger, G. A. Afternoon under glass

Hemingway, John

Uncle Gus

The Saturday Evening Post v281 no4 p31-3 Jl/Ag 2009

The **Hemingway** hoax. Haldeman, J. W.

Hemingway's cats. Johnson, G.

Hemley, Robin

Local Time

The Southern Review (Baton Rouge, La.) v41 no3 p507-23 Summ 2005

The warehouse of saints

Best American fantasy; guest editors Ann & Jeff VanderMeer; series editor Matthew Cheney

Hemmingson, Michael

How to have an affair

Homewrecker: an adultery reader; edited by Daphne Gottlieb

Hemon, Aleksandar

American commando

Hemon, A. Love and obstacles; stories

The bees, part 1

Hemon, A. Love and obstacles; stories

The conductor

The Best American short stories, 2006; selected from U.S. and Canadian magazines by Ann Patchett with Katrina Kenison; with an introduction by Ann Patchett

Hemon, A. Love and obstacles; stories

The New Yorker v81 no2 p70-7 F 28 2005

Everything

Hemon, A. Love and obstacles; stories

Good living

Hemon, A. Love and obstacles; stories

The liar

The book of other people; edited by Zadie Smith

The life and work of Alphonse Kauders

The Anchor book of new American short stories; edited by Ben Marcus

Love and Obstacles

The New Yorker v81 no38 p132, 134-6, 138-40, 142-3 N 28 2005

The noble truths of suffering

Hemon, A. Love and obstacles; stories

The New Yorker v84 no29 p76-85 S 22 2008

Stairway to heaven

Hemon, A. Love and obstacles; stories

The New Yorker v82 no34 p72-81 O 23 2006

Szmura's room

Hemon, A. Love and obstacles; stories

Hempel, Amy

The afterlife

Hempel, A. The dog of the marriage; stories

Hempel, A. The collected stories of Amy Hempel; with an introduction by Rick Moody

And lead us not into Penn Station

Hempel, A. The collected stories of Amy Hempel; with an introduction by Rick Moody

The annex

Hempel, A. The collected stories of Amy Hempel; with an introduction by Rick Moody

At the gates of the animal kingdom

Hempel, A. The collected stories of Amy Hempel; with an introduction by Rick Moody

Beach town

Hempel, A. The dog of the marriage; stories

Hempel, A. The collected stories of Amy Hempel; with an introduction by Rick Moody

Beg, sl tog, inc, cont, rep

Hempel, A. The collected stories of Amy Hempel; with an introduction by Rick Moody

Breathing Jesus

Hempel, A. The collected stories of Amy Hempel; with an introduction by Rick Moody

Celia is back

Hempel, A. The collected stories of Amy Hempel; with an introduction by Rick Moody

The center

Hempel, A. The collected stories of Amy Hempel; with an introduction by Rick Moody

The children's party

Hempel, A. The collected stories of Amy Hempel; with an introduction by Rick Moody

Church cancels cow

Hempel, A. The collected stories of Amy Hempel; with an introduction by Rick Moody

Cotton Flat Road

Daugherty, T. Late in the standoff; stories and a novella

The day I had everything

Hempel, A. The collected stories of Amy Hempel; with an introduction by Rick Moody

Hempel, Amy—*Continued*
Weekend
  Hempel, A. The collected stories of Amy
    Hempel; with an introduction by Rick
    Moody
What were the white things?
  Hempel, A. The dog of the marriage; stories
  Hempel, A. The collected stories of Amy
    Hempel; with an introduction by Rick
    Moody
  The Best of the Bellevue Literary Review;
    edited by Dannielle Ofri and the staff of
    the Bellevue Literary Review
When it's human instead of when it's dog
  Hempel, A. The collected stories of Amy
    Hempel; with an introduction by Rick
    Moody
Why I'm here
  Hempel, A. The collected stories of Amy
    Hempel; with an introduction by Rick
    Moody
Henchman. Johnson, M.
Henderson, C. J.
What every coin has
  Kolchak: the night stalker chronicles; 26 orig-
    inal tales of the surreal, the bizarre, the ma-
    cabre; edited by Joe Gentile, Garrett Ander-
    son, Lori Gentile; Kolchak created by Jeff
    Rice
Henderson, Eleanor
The Farms
  Agni no68 p81-93 2008
The Kissing Disease
  The North American Review v292 no3/4 p33-
    41 My/Ag 2007
Henderson, Jason
Wet dog of Galveston
  Kolchak: the night stalker chronicles; 26 orig-
    inal tales of the surreal, the bizarre, the ma-
    cabre; edited by Joe Gentile, Garrett Ander-
    son, Lori Gentile; Kolchak created by Jeff
    Rice
Hendricks, Vicki
Be very afraid
  Getting even; revenge stories; edited by Mitzi
    Szereto
The big O
  A hell of a woman; an anthology of female
    noir; edited by Megan Abbott; foreword by
    Val McDermid
Purrz, baby
  Deadly housewives; edited by Christine Mat-
    thews
HENDRIX, JIMI
About
Moorcock, M. A dead singer
Hendry, Kate
All that Glass
  Harper's v312 p22-5 Mr 2006
Hendry, Rebecca
The Legacy
  Dalhousie Review v87 no1 p59-69 Spr 2007
Henion, Kathryn
A Red Pen
  Confrontation no104 p161-75 Summ 2009

Henkel, Oliver
Hitler on the campaign trail in America
  The black mirror and other stories; an anthol-
    ogy of science fiction from Germany &
    Austria; edited & with an introduction &
    notes by Franz Rottensteiner; translated by
    Mike Mitchell.
Henningsen, Gail R.
Strokes
  Gettysburg Review v20 no1 p41-51 Spr 2007
Henrietta and Alexandra. Barthelme, D.
Henriquez, Cristina
Ashes
  Henriquez, C. Come together, fall apart; a no-
    vella and stories
  The New Yorker v81 no19 p68-73 Jl 4 2005
Beautiful
  Henriquez, C. Come together, fall apart; a no-
    vella and stories
The box house and the snow
  Henriquez, C. Come together, fall apart; a no-
    vella and stories
Carnival, Las Tablas
  The New Yorker v82 no20 p64-71 Jl 3 2006
Chasing birds
  Henriquez, C. Come together, fall apart; a no-
    vella and stories
  Ploughshares v32 no1 p49-62 Spr 2006
Come together, fall apart
  Henriquez, C. Come together, fall apart; a no-
    vella and stories
Drive
  Henriquez, C. Come together, fall apart; a no-
    vella and stories
Gabriella, my heart
  This is not chick lit; original stories by Amer-
    ica's best women writers; edited by Eliza-
    beth Merrick
Mercury
  Henriquez, C. Come together, fall apart; a no-
    vella and stories
The wide, pale ocean
  Henriquez, C. Come together, fall apart; a no-
    vella and stories
Yanina
  Henriquez, C. Come together, fall apart; a no-
    vella and stories
Henry, Brian
(tr.) See Šteger, Aleš
Henry, Liz
Capital punishment
  Sex for America; politically inspired erotica;
    edited by Stephen Elliott
Henry, O
The Gift of the Magi
  The Saturday Evening Post v279 no6 p46-7
    N/D 2007
Henry, O.
Art and the bronco
  Lone Star literature; from the Red River to
    the Rio Grande; edited by Don Graham
The chair of philanthromathematics
  The Penguin book of Gaslight crime; con art-
    ists, burglars, rogues, and scoundrels from
    the time of Sherlock Holmes; edited with
    an introduction and notes by Michael Sims.
The furnished room
  Manhattan noir 2; the classics; edited by
    Lawrence Block

Hernandez, Kathy-Ann

Sometimes
Callaloo v31 no3 p840-3 Summ 2008

Hernandez, Lisa

The Catholic girl
Hernandez, L. Migrations and other stories
Count the raindrops
Hernandez, L. Migrations and other stories
The cross
Hernandez, L. Migrations and other stories
Migrations
Hernandez, L. Migrations and other stories
My little tyrant heart
Hernandez, L. Migrations and other stories
The neighbor
Hernandez, L. Migrations and other stories
Ojitos
Hernandez, L. Migrations and other stories
Pinky Sandoval
Hernandez, L. Migrations and other stories
The red curtain
Hernandez, L. Migrations and other stories
Somewhere between Santa Monica and
incarnacion de Cristo
Hernandez, L. Migrations and other stories
The swap meet
Hernandez, L. Migrations and other stories

Hernandez, Lolita

Autopsy of an engine
Hernandez, L. Autopsy of an engine and oth-
er stories from the Cadillac plant
Death in the sidesaddle
Hernandez, L. Autopsy of an engine and oth-
er stories from the Cadillac plant
Down dirty
Hernandez, L. Autopsy of an engine and oth-
er stories from the Cadillac plant
Float
Hernandez, L. Autopsy of an engine and oth-
er stories from the Cadillac plant
The last car
Hernandez, L. Autopsy of an engine and oth-
er stories from the Cadillac plant
Manuel, Manuel everywhere
Hernandez, L. Autopsy of an engine and oth-
er stories from the Cadillac plant
Over the Belle Isle boundary
Detroit noir; edited by E. J. Olsen & John C.
Hocking
Preparing for a strike
Hernandez, L. Autopsy of an engine and oth-
er stories from the Cadillac plant
Thanks to Abbie Wilson
Hernandez, L. Autopsy of an engine and oth-
er stories from the Cadillac plant
This is our song for today
Hernandez, L. Autopsy of an engine and oth-
er stories from the Cadillac plant
Tuesday morning
Hernandez, L. Autopsy of an engine and oth-
er stories from the Cadillac plant
We have a job for you
Hernandez, L. Autopsy of an engine and oth-
er stories from the Cadillac plant
Yes I am a virgin
Hernandez, L. Autopsy of an engine and oth-
er stories from the Cadillac plant

Herndon, Nancy

Time bombs [excerpt]
Lone Star sleuths; an anthology of Texas
crime fiction; edited and with an introduc-
tion by Bill Cunningham, Steven L. Davis,
and Rollo K. Newsom.
The **hero.** Martin, G. R. R.
The **hero.** Schroeder, K.
The **hero** as werwolf. Wolfe, G.
A **hero** of Chickamauga. Adrian, C.
The **hero** shot. Lange, R.
Hero, the movie. McAllister, B.
Hero Vale. Lanagan, M.

HERODOTUS

About

James, C. L. R. Delphi and Herodotus discussion

HEROES

See also Heroism

Barnes, S. and Due, T. Trickster
Bissell, T. My interview with the Avenger
Blackford, R. Manannan's children
Chambers, C. Avatar
Clarke, W. The pentecostal home for flying
children
Coover, R. The Invisible Man
Crane, E. Nate Pinckney-Alderson, superhero
Czyzniejewski, M. When the heroes came to
town
Doolittle, S. Mr. big deal
Harrell, S. Girl reporter
Haynes, D. The lives of ordinary superheroes
Jablonski, N. The snipper
Johnson, M. Henchman
Joyce, G. The oversoul
King, O. The meerkat
Levine, D. D. Titanium Mike saves the day
Martin, G. R. R. Shell games
McNally, J. Remains of the night
Melko, P. Doctor Mighty & the case of ennui
Nolan, W. F. The clown's daughter
Scholes, K. Edward Bear
Shepard, J. In cretaceous seas
Singleton, G. Man oh man — it's Manna Man
Udall, B. Buckeye the elder
Weller, S. The quick stop 5®
Yoo, D. The somewhat super
Young, D. Housework
Yu, C. Third class superhero
Heroes. Garrett, G. P.
The **heroes** in the dark house. Kiely, B.
Heroes of the Revolution. Matthews, B.
The **heroic** cat in the bag. Higgins, G. V.
Heroic proportions. Chaponda, D.

HEROIN

Block, L. Ride a white horse
MacEnulty, P. Floating on the darkness
Trezise, R. On the strip

HEROISM

See also Courage; Heroes

Austin, M. H. The girls at Overtown
Coake, C. A single awe
Dobozy, T. Tales of Hungarian resistance
Irvine, A. C. Shepherded by Galatea
L'Amour, L. Crash landing
Ryman, G. The last ten years in the life of Hero
Kai
Hero's way. Merril, J.

HERPETOLOGISTS

Peelle, L. Reasons for and advantages of breathing

Herr Schulz destroys my career. Wendroff, Z.

Herren, Greg

Annunciation shotgun

New Orleans noir; edited by Julie Smith

Herrman, Heather

Monsoon

South Carolina Review v38 no2 p129-34 Spr 2006

Herrmann, Marianne

Cooking lessons

Herrmann, M. Signaling for rescue

Ducklings

Herrmann, M. Signaling for rescue

Everthing and nothing

Herrmann, M. Signaling for rescue

Leonardo's baby

Herrmann, M. Signaling for rescue

Signaling for rescue

Herrmann, M. Signaling for rescue

Stones

Herrmann, M. Signaling for rescue

You only want to scare her

Herrmann, M. Signaling for rescue

Herron, Don

Knives in the dark

San Francisco noir 2; the classics; edited by Peter Maravelis.

Herschel Eisengold. Molodowsky, K.

Hershey, Edward

A Brooklyn Exile's Return

Confrontation no101 p25-7 Spr/Summ 2008

Hershon, Joanna

Crawl

The Virginia Quarterly Review v81 no3 p62-77 Summ 2005

Hervey, Evelyn *See* Keating, H. R. F. (Henry Reymond Fitzwalter), 1926-

Herwitz, Daniel

Homecoming

Michigan Quarterly Review v46 no3 p489-504 Summ 2007

Migration

Michigan Quarterly Review v44 no3 p419-33 Summ 2005

Hesperia and glory. Leckie, A.

Hester Street. Yezierska, A.

Heti, Sheila

Ticknor, Beginning

New England Review v26 no4 p162-74 2005

Heuler, Karen

Down on the farm

Bandersnatch; edited by Paul Tremblay and Sean Wallace

Hevesi, Ludwig

Jules Verne in hell: a letter to the editor from the late writer

The black mirror and other stories; an anthology of science fiction from Germany & Austria; edited & with an introduction & notes by Franz Rottensteiner; translated by Mike Mitchell.

Hewson, David

The circle

Thriller 2; stories you just can't put down; edited by Clive Cussler; [stories by] Kathleen Antrim . . . [et al.]

Hey, girlie. Dobson, J.

Hey love. Johnson, R. K.

Hey, mister!. Reid, G.

Hey Shoobie!. McClanahan, E.

The **heyday** of the insensitive bastards. Boswell, R.

HEYDRICH, REINHARD, 1904-1942

About

Shepard, J. The assassination of Reinhard Heydrich

Heydt-Minor, Will

An unfortunate book tour

Nature v444 p400 N 16 2006

The **Heyworth** fragment. Lupoff, R. A.

Hezekiah Number Three. Parsons, R.

Hi! Howya doin!. Oates, J. C.

Hi, I'm God. Thayer, S.

Hibakusha dreaming in the shadowy land of death. Scholes, K.

Hibernation. Coleman, W.

Hickam, Homer

Dosie, of Killakeet Island

The best Christian short stories; edited and with an introduction by Bret Lott

Hickey, Dave

I'm bound to follow the longhorn cows

Lone Star literature; from the Red River to the Rio Grande; edited by Don Graham

Hicks, Jeremy

(tr.) See Zoshchenko, Mikhail

Hicok, Bob

Coming to life

Iowa Review v37 no3 p131 Wint 2007/2008

The Raft

The Southern Review (Baton Rouge, La.) v41 no1 p11-15 Wint 2005

Hidden in the Trees. Oates, N.

Hidden meanings: treatment of time, supreme irony, and life experiences in the song "Ain't gonna bump no more no big fat woman". Parker, M.

The **hidden** part of the iceberg [variant title: Submerged iceberg] Coloane, F.

Hidden Works. Troyan, S.

The **hide**. Williams, L.

Hide & Go Seek. Hall, S.

Hidian. Lopez, Z.

Hiding man. Barthelme, D.

Hiding out. Messinger, J.

Higgins, George V.

The devil is real

Higgins, G. V. The easiest thing in the world; the uncollected fiction of George V. Higgins; edited by Matthew J. Bruccoli

The easiest thing in the world

Higgins, G. V. The easiest thing in the world; the uncollected fiction of George V. Higgins; edited by Matthew J. Bruccoli

An end to revels

Higgins, G. V. The easiest thing in the world; the uncollected fiction of George V. Higgins; edited by Matthew J. Bruccoli

The first of the year

Higgins, G. V. The easiest thing in the world; the uncollected fiction of George V. Higgins; edited by Matthew J. Bruccoli

Hill, Joe—*Continued*

Pop art

Hill, J. 20th century ghosts; introduction by Christopher Golden

Voluntary committal

Hill, J. 20th century ghosts; introduction by Christopher Golden

The widow's breakfast

Hill, J. 20th century ghosts; introduction by Christopher Golden

You will hear the locust sing

Hill, J. 20th century ghosts; introduction by Christopher Golden

Hill, Kathleen

Who Occupies this House

Ploughshares v34 no4 p42-58 Wint 2008/2009

Hill, Nathan

I Have Seen Some Dirty Things

Gettysburg Review v19 no2 p219-26 Summ 2006

The New Year's Child

The Antioch Review v65 no3 p482-95 Summ 2007

Hill, Reginald

Fool of myself

The Detection collection; edited by Simon Brett

The game of dog

The Best British mysteries, 2005; edited by Maxim Jakubowski

Hill, Sam

The sin-eater

Chicago blues; edited by Libby Fischer Hellmann

The stake

Dead man's hand; crime fiction at the poker table; edited by Otto Penzler.

The **hill**. Lee, T.

Hillbillies. Panning, A.

Hillerman, Tony

Chee's witch

A New omnibus of crime; edited by Tony Hillerman and Rosemary Herbert; contributing editors Sue Grafton and Jeffery Deaver

First lead gasser

A New omnibus of crime; edited by Tony Hillerman and Rosemary Herbert; contributing editors Sue Grafton and Jeffery Deaver

Hillhouse, Raelynn

Diplomatic constraints

Thriller; edited by James Patterson

The **hills** of the dead. Howard, R. E.

Hilltop (an American story). Luvaas, W.

Hilst, Hilda

Agda

Oxford anthology of the Brazilian short story; edited by K. David Jackson

The **Hilton** epiphany. Winsor, C.

HIMALAYA MOUNTAINS

Shepard, J. Ancestral legacies

Singer, M. Borderland

Himes, Chester

Strictly business

Black noir; mystery, crime and suspense stories by African-American writers; edited by Otto Penzler

Himme. Keret, E.

Himmelen. Shayla, H.

Hinde the gardener. Molodowsky, K.

HINDENBURG (AIRSHIP)

Shepard, J. Love and hydrogen

HINDUISM

Wadia, L.-A. L. "Ravi's wedding"

HINDUS

Naipaul, V. S. My aunt Gold Teeth

Reddi, R. P. Justice Shiva Ram Murthy

England

See also East Indians—England

India

Judah, S. Rakhi

Hines, Jim C.

Bloodlines

Places to be, people to kill; edited by Martin H. Greenberg and Brittianey A. Koren

The eyes of Ra

Cat tales: fantastic feline fiction; edited by George H. Scithers

Hinojosa, Francisco

La muda boca/The muted mouth

Best of contemporary Mexican fiction; Alvaro Uribe, editor; Olivia Sears, translation editor

Hinojosa, Rolando

Partners in crime [excerpt]

Lone Star sleuths; an anthology of Texas crime fiction; edited and with an introduction by Bill Cunningham, Steven L. Davis, and Rollo K. Newsom.

Hinojosa-Smith, R. Rolando *See* Hinojosa, Rolando, 1929-

Hinojosa-Smith, Rolando

Borges's Dagger

Bomb no98 p98-9 Wint 2007

Notes from a Forgotten War, So-called

Callaloo v32 no2 p404-7 Spr 2009

Hinojosa-Smith, Rolando

The Gulf Oil -Can Santa Claus

Lone Star literature; from the Red River to the Rio Grande; edited by Don Graham

Hinterland. Shields, C.

Hinton, S. E.

After the party

Hinton, S. E. Some of Tim's stories

Different shorelines

Hinton, S. E. Some of Tim's stories

Full moon birthday

Hinton, S. E. Some of Tim's stories

The girl who loved movies

Hinton, S. E. Some of Tim's stories

Homecoming

Hinton, S. E. Some of Tim's stories

Jailed

Hinton, S. E. Some of Tim's stories

The missed trip

Hinton, S. E. Some of Tim's stories

No white light no tunnel

Hinton, S. E. Some of Tim's stories

Sentenced

Hinton, S. E. Some of Tim's stories

The sweetest sound

Hinton, S. E. Some of Tim's stories

Visit

Hinton, S. E. Some of Tim's stories

What's your poison?

Hinton, S. E. Some of Tim's stories

His bride of the tomb. Dunbar, P. L.
His last arrow. Sequeira, C.
His last role. Sourounis, A.
His majesty, almighty death [excerpt] Anissimov, M.
His master's hand. O'Shaughnessy, P.
His master's voice. Rajaniemi, H.
His mission. Coake, C.
His own time. Thompson, J.
His parents, naked. Johnson, G.
His sons. Bingham, S.
His trip to America. Reisen, A.
His Waterloo. Bierce, A.

HISPANIC AMERICANS
Alvarado, B. Just family
Alvarado, B. Limbo
Granados, C. The bride
Granados, C. Inner view
Granados, C. Man of the house
Granados, C. Vieja chueca
Hernandez, L. Tuesday morning
Magee, K. All the America you want
Magee, K. Body language
Murguía, A. The other Barrio
Soracco, S. Double espresso
Sullivan, C. J. Alex Pinto hears the bell
Tait, J. Reasons for concern regarding my girlfriend of five days, Monica Garza

HISTORIANS
MacLeod, I. The summer isles
Pendarvis, J. The mysterious secret of the valuable treasure
Swann, S. A. The historian's apprentice
Willis, C. Fire watch

The **historian's** apprentice. Swann, S. A.
Historical letters. Enright, A.

HISTORICAL REENACTMENTS
Adrian, C. A hero of Chickamauga

Histories of the undead. Braverman, K.
History. Gordimer, N.
History. Lott, B.
History. Sherwood, F.
History. Wisniewski, M.
History lessons. Clayton, J. J.
History Lessons. Hannah, J.
History of a disturbance. Millhauser, S.
The **history** of history. Smith, A.
The **history** of my breasts. Schor, L.
The **history** of staying awake. Fincke, G.
A **History** of the Ghosts of Judy, Tennessee. Poore, M.
History of the Puyats. Erdrich, L.
The **history** of them all. Cohen, L.
The **history** of Vegas. Angel, J.
The **history** of windbag the sailor. Bierce, A.
The **hit**. Levinson, R. S.
Hit and run. Lovell, G.

HIT-AND-RUN DRIVERS
Dubus, A. A father's story
Endrezze, A. Grandfather sun falls in love with a moon-faced woman
Fonseca, R. Night drive
Guista, M. The whole world's guilt
Willis, C. The last of the Winnebagos

HITCHCOCK, ALFRED, 1899-1980
About
Oates, J. C. Fat man my love
The **hitchhiker**. Dahl, R.

HITCHHIKERS
Alexie, S. The toughest Indian in the world
Alexie, S. The toughnest Indian in the world
Arjouni, J. A friend
Block, L. Lie back and enjoy it
Dahl, R. The hitchhiker
Duval, P. Rear view
Ford, J. On the road to new Egypt
Irsfeld, J. H. Have you knocked on Cleopatra?
Kelly, R. Yea, though I drive
King, S. Mute
Magee, K. The Niña, the Pinta, the Santa Maria
Marsters, S. Bear story
Shields, C. Poaching
Shirley, P. Charisma
Smith, C. Albemarle
Tilmac, F. Hitching in the lodos
Williams, J. Charity

The **hitchhiking** game. Kundera, M.
Hitching in the lodos. Tilmac, F.
Hither from Hades. Bierce, A.

HITLER, ADOLF, 1889-1945
About
Anaya, R. A. The captain
Bradbury, R. Darling Adolf
Henkel, O. Hitler on the campaign trail in America
Miller, A. The performance
Moorcock, M. The flaneur of les arcades de l'opera
Moorcock, M. The pleasure garden of Felipe Sagittarius
Scholes, K. Summer on Paris, light from the sky
Zelazny, R. The Borgia hand

Hitler on the campaign trail in America. Henkel, O.

Hlehel, Ala
The Bearded Man
World Literature Today v81 no1 p48-51 Ja/F 2007

HO CHI MINH CITY (VIETNAM) *See* Vietnam—Ho Chi Minh City

Hoagland, Edward
The Devil's Tub
The Yale Review v93 no4 p102-38 O 2005
In Africa
New Letters v74 no4 p43-76 2008

Hoar frost. Rees, R.
The **hoarder**. Morrow, B.

HOAXES
Grant, A. The episode of the diamond links
Keane, J. B. Fred Rimble
Omari, I. Obeah catastrophe

The **hob-nailed** shoes Bendel-Simso, M. M., ed.
Early American detective stories; an anthology; edited by LeRoy Lad Panek and Mary M. Bendel-Simso.

Hoben, Josef
Departure
The Antioch Review v66 no1 p99-110 Wint 2008

HOBOKEN (N.J.) *See* New Jersey—Hoboken

Hoch, Edward D.
The face of Ali Baba
The World's finest mystery and crime stories, fifth annual collection; edited by Ed Gorman and Martin H. Greenberg

Hoch, Edward D.—*Continued*

Friday night luck

Mystery Writers of America presents the blue religion; new stories about cops, criminals, and the chase; edited by Michael Connelly

The retired arsonist

At the scene of the crime; forensic mysteries from today's best writers; edited by Dana Stabenow

The secret session

Mystery Writers of America presents the prosecution rests; new stories about courtrooms, criminals, and the law; edited by Linda Fairstein.

The vampire theme

The World's finest mystery and crime stories, fourth annual collection; edited by Ed Gorman and Martin H. Greenberg

Hochstein, Rolaine

Art in America

Confrontation no96/97 p26-36 Fall 2006/Wint 2007

Bronik Returns to Vienna

Prairie Schooner v82 no2 p140-51 Summ 2008

Hockensmith, Steve

Blarney

Mystery Writers of America presents death do us part; new stories about love, lust, and murder; edited by Harlan Coben

Excerpts from an unpublished memoir found in the basement of the home for retired actors

Sherlock Holmes in America; edited by Martin H. Greenberg, Jon L. Lellenberg, and Daniel Stashower.

Gustav Amlingmeyer, Holmes of the range

Wolf Woman Bay; and nine more of the finest crime and mystery novellas of the year; edited by Ed Gorman and Martin H. Greenberg

HOCKEY

Amdahl, G. Visigoth

Amdahl, G. The volunteer

Angrist, M. So much the better

Fisher, C. The road es traveled

Fisher, C. Tin man square

McLean, S. The jockstrap

Hocus-pocus. Monk, B.

Hocus-pocus on Friday the 13th. Neri, K.

Hodge, Brian

With acknowledgements to Sun Tzu

The Year's best fantasy and horror: seventeenth annual collection; edited by Ellen Datlow, Kelly Link and Gavin J. Grant

Hodgen, Christie

A jeweler's eye for flaw

Pushcart Prize XXVIII: best of the small presses 2004; edited by Bill Henderson and the Pushcart prize editors

Mike Beaudry 1950-1988 An Elegy

The Southern Review (Baton Rouge, La.) v44 no3 p551-74 Summ 2008

Tom & Jerry

Ploughshares v34 no1 p68-91 Spr 2008

Hodgins, Eric

Mr. Blandings builds his castle

Adaptations: from short story to big screen; 35 great stories that have inspired great films; edited by Stephanie Harrison

Hodgson, William Hope

An adventure of the deep waters

Hodgson, W. H. Adrift on the haunted seas; the best short stories of William Hope Hodgson; edited and with an introduction by Douglas A. Anderson

Hodgson, W. H. The dream of X and other fantastic visions; being the fifth volume of The collected fiction of William Hope Hodgson; edited by Douglas A. Anderson

The albatross

Hodgson, W. H. The ghost pirates and other revenants of the sea; being the third volume of The collected fiction of William Hope Hodgson; edited by Jeremy Lassen

Bullion

Hodgson, W. H. The house on the borderland and other mysterious places; being the second volume of The collected fiction of William Hope Hodgson; edited by Jeremy Lassen

Captain Dan Danblasten

Hodgson, W. H. The dream of X and other fantastic visions; being the fifth volume of The collected fiction of William Hope Hodgson; edited by Douglas A. Anderson

Captain Dang

Hodgson, W. H. The dream of X and other fantastic visions; being the fifth volume of The collected fiction of William Hope Hodgson; edited by Douglas A. Anderson

Captain Gunbolt Charity and the painted lady

Hodgson, W. H. The dream of X and other fantastic visions; being the fifth volume of The collected fiction of William Hope Hodgson; edited by Douglas A. Anderson

The captain of the onion boat

Hodgson, W. H. The night land and other perilous romances; being the fourth volume of The collected fiction of William Hope Hodgson; edited by Jeremy Lassen

Carnacki, the ghost finder

Hodgson, W. H. The dream of X and other fantastic visions; being the fifth volume of The collected fiction of William Hope Hodgson; edited by Douglas A. Anderson

The crew of the Lancing

Hodgson, W. H. The dream of X and other fantastic visions; being the fifth volume of The collected fiction of William Hope Hodgson; edited by Douglas A. Anderson

Date 1965: modern warfare

Hodgson, W. H. The dream of X and other fantastic visions; being the fifth volume of The collected fiction of William Hope Hodgson; edited by Douglas A. Anderson

Demons of the sea

Hodgson, W. H. Adrift on the haunted seas; the best short stories of William Hope Hodgson; edited and with an introduction by Douglas A. Anderson

Hodgson, William Hope—*Continued*

The haunting of the Lady Shannon
Hodgson, W. H. The house on the borderland and other mysterious places; being the second volume of The collected fiction of William Hope Hodgson; edited by Jeremy Lassen

Heathen's revenge
Hodgson, W. H. The house on the borderland and other mysterious places; being the second volume of The collected fiction of William Hope Hodgson; edited by Jeremy Lassen

The heaving of the log
Hodgson, W. H. The ghost pirates and other revenants of the sea; being the third volume of The collected fiction of William Hope Hodgson; edited by Jeremy Lassen

The hog
Hodgson, W. H. The house on the borderland and other mysterious places; being the second volume of The collected fiction of William Hope Hodgson; edited by Jeremy Lassen

The homecoming of Captain Dan
Hodgson, W. H. The house on the borderland and other mysterious places; being the second volume of The collected fiction of William Hope Hodgson; edited by Jeremy Lassen

The horse of the invisible
Hodgson, W. H. The house on the borderland and other mysterious places; being the second volume of The collected fiction of William Hope Hodgson; edited by Jeremy Lassen

The house among the laurels
Hodgson, W. H. The house on the borderland and other mysterious places; being the second volume of The collected fiction of William Hope Hodgson; edited by Jeremy Lassen

How Sir Jerrold Treyn dealt with the Dutch in Caunston Cove
Hodgson, W. H. The dream of X and other fantastic visions; being the fifth volume of The collected fiction of William Hope Hodgson; edited by Douglas A. Anderson

How the honourable Billy Darrell raised the wind
Hodgson, W. H. The dream of X and other fantastic visions; being the fifth volume of The collected fiction of William Hope Hodgson; edited by Douglas A. Anderson

In the danger zone
Hodgson, W. H. The ghost pirates and other revenants of the sea; being the third volume of The collected fiction of William Hope Hodgson; edited by Jeremy Lassen

In the Wailing Gully
Hodgson, W. H. The night land and other perilous romances; being the fourth volume of The collected fiction of William Hope Hodgson; edited by Jeremy Lassen

The inn of the black crow
Hodgson, W. H. The dream of X and other fantastic visions; being the fifth volume of The collected fiction of William Hope Hodgson; edited by Douglas A. Anderson

The island of the crossbones
Hodgson, W. H. The ghost pirates and other revenants of the sea; being the third volume of The collected fiction of William Hope Hodgson; edited by Jeremy Lassen

Jack Grey, second mate
Hodgson, W. H. The ghost pirates and other revenants of the sea; being the third volume of The collected fiction of William Hope Hodgson; edited by Jeremy Lassen

Jem Binney and the safe at Lockwood Hall
Hodgson, W. H. The dream of X and other fantastic visions; being the fifth volume of The collected fiction of William Hope Hodgson; edited by Douglas A. Anderson

Judge Barclay's wife
Hodgson, W. H. The dream of X and other fantastic visions; being the fifth volume of The collected fiction of William Hope Hodgson; edited by Douglas A. Anderson

Kind, kind and gentle is she
Hodgson, W. H. The night land and other perilous romances; being the fourth volume of The collected fiction of William Hope Hodgson; edited by Jeremy Lassen

The last word in mysteries
Hodgson, W. H. The dream of X and other fantastic visions; being the fifth volume of The collected fiction of William Hope Hodgson; edited by Douglas A. Anderson

Merciful plunder
Hodgson, W. H. The house on the borderland and other mysterious places; being the second volume of The collected fiction of William Hope Hodgson; edited by Jeremy Lassen

Mr. Jock Danplank
Hodgson, W. H. The house on the borderland and other mysterious places; being the second volume of The collected fiction of William Hope Hodgson; edited by Jeremy Lassen

My house shall be called the house of prayer
Hodgson, W. H. The dream of X and other fantastic visions; being the fifth volume of The collected fiction of William Hope Hodgson; edited by Douglas A. Anderson

The mystery of Captain Chappel
Hodgson, W. H. The house on the borderland and other mysterious places; being the second volume of The collected fiction of William Hope Hodgson; edited by Jeremy Lassen

The mystery of missing ships
Hodgson, W. H. The ghost pirates and other revenants of the sea; being the third volume of The collected fiction of William Hope Hodgson; edited by Jeremy Lassen

The mystery of the derelict
Hodgson, W. H. Adrift on the haunted seas; the best short stories of William Hope Hodgson; edited and with an introduction by Douglas A. Anderson

The mystery of the water-logged ship
Hodgson, W. H. The house on the borderland and other mysterious places; being the second volume of The collected fiction of William Hope Hodgson; edited by Jeremy Lassen

Hodgson, William Hope—*Continued*

Through the vortex of a cyclone
>Hodgson, W. H. Adrift on the haunted seas; the best short stories of William Hope Hodgson; edited and with an introduction by Douglas A. Anderson

A timely escape
>Hodgson, W. H. The night land and other perilous romances; being the fourth volume of The collected fiction of William Hope Hodgson; edited by Jeremy Lassen

A tropical horror
>Hodgson, W. H. Adrift on the haunted seas; the best short stories of William Hope Hodgson; edited and with an introduction by Douglas A. Anderson

>Hodgson, W. H. The ghost pirates and other revenants of the sea; being the third volume of The collected fiction of William Hope Hodgson; edited by Jeremy Lassen

The Valley of Lost Children
>Hodgson, W. H. The dream of X and other fantastic visions; being the fifth volume of The collected fiction of William Hope Hodgson; edited by Douglas A. Anderson

The voice in the dawn
>Hodgson, W. H. Adrift on the haunted seas; the best short stories of William Hope Hodgson; edited and with an introduction by Douglas A. Anderson

The voice in the night
>Hodgson, W. H. Adrift on the haunted seas; the best short stories of William Hope Hodgson; edited and with an introduction by Douglas A. Anderson

>Hodgson, W. H. The ghost pirates and other revenants of the sea; being the third volume of The collected fiction of William Hope Hodgson; edited by Jeremy Lassen

We two and Bully Dunkan
>Hodgson, W. H. The ghost pirates and other revenants of the sea; being the third volume of The collected fiction of William Hope Hodgson; edited by Jeremy Lassen

What happened in the Thunderbolt
>Hodgson, W. H. The dream of X and other fantastic visions; being the fifth volume of The collected fiction of William Hope Hodgson; edited by Douglas A. Anderson

The whistling room
>Hodgson, W. H. The house on the borderland and other mysterious places; being the second volume of The collected fiction of William Hope Hodgson; edited by Jeremy Lassen

The wild man of the sea
>Hodgson, W. H. Adrift on the haunted seas; the best short stories of William Hope Hodgson; edited and with an introduction by Douglas A. Anderson

>Hodgson, W. H. The ghost pirates and other revenants of the sea; being the third volume of The collected fiction of William Hope Hodgson; edited by Jeremy Lassen

HODGSON, WILLIAM HOPE, 1877-1918
Parodies, imitations, etc.

Wright, J. C. Awake in the night

Hoffa, James Riddle *See* Hoffa, Jimmy, b. 1913

HOFFA, JIMMY, B. 1913
About

Resnick, M. and Flint, E. Conspiracies: a very condensed 937-page novel

Hoffman, Alice

All That I Am and Ever Will Be
>*Harvard Review (1992)* no31 p100-8 2006

Black is the color of my true love's hair
>Hoffman, A. Blackbird house

Black Rabbit
>*Southwest Review* v94 no3 p335-48 2009

Changeling
>*The Kenyon Review* v29 no2 p123-30 Spr 2007

The conjurer's handbook
>Hoffman, A. Blackbird house
>*Southwest Review* v89 no2/3 p213-25 2004

Dirty White Dogs
>*Prairie Schooner* v81 no2 p11-19 Summ 2007

The edge of the world
>Hoffman, A. Blackbird house

Green Tea
>*Southwest Review* v91 no4 p467-76 2006

India
>Hoffman, A. Blackbird house

Insulting the angels
>Hoffman, A. Blackbird house

Lionheart
>Hoffman, A. Blackbird house
>*Harvard Review (1992)* no25 p6-12 Fall 2003

The pear tree
>Hoffman, A. Blackbird house

Saint Helene
>*Ploughshares* v31 no4 p84-95 Wint 2005/2006

The summer kitchen
>Hoffman, A. Blackbird house

The token
>Hoffman, A. Blackbird house

The wedding of snow and ice
>Hoffman, A. Blackbird house

Wish you were here
>Hoffman, A. Blackbird house

The witch of Truro
>Hoffman, A. Blackbird house
>The Year's best fantasy and horror: eighteenth annual collection; edited by Ellen Datlow, Kelly Link & Gavin J. Grant

Hoffman, Barry

I've been waiting for you
>Poe's lighthouse; all new collaborations with Edgar Allan Poe; edited by Christopher Conlon

Hoffman, Daniel

Interview
>*Gettysburg Review* v18 no3 p487-91 Aut 2005

Hoffman, Nina Kiriki

Flotsam
>The Year's best fantasy and horror: seventeenth annual collection; edited by Ellen Datlow, Kelly Link and Gavin J. Grant

Savage breasts
>Witpunk; edited by Claude Lalumière and Marty Halpern

Hoffman, Nina Kiriki—*Continued*
Sea air
Elemental; the Tsunami relief anthology; stories of science fiction and fantasy; [edited by] Steven Savile and Alethea Kontis; introduction by Arthur C. Clarke
Year's best fantasy 7; edited by David G. Hartwell & Kathryn Cramer
The third dead body
The living dead; edited by John Joseph Adams

HOFFMANN, E. T. A. (ERNST THEODOR AMADEUS), 1776-1822
About
Green, G. Creatures of the mind

Hoffmann, Ernst Theodor Amadeus *See* Hoffmann, E. T. A. (Ernst Theodor Amadeus), 1776-1822

Hoffmann, Yoel
The heart is katmandu [excerpt]
Terrestrial intelligence; international fiction now from New Directions; edited by Barbara Epler

The **hog**. Hodgson, W. H.

Hogan, Chuck
One good one
The Best American mystery stories, 2008; edited and with an introduction by George Pelecanos; Otto Penzler, series editor
Two thousand volts
The Best American mystery stories, 2009; edited and with an introduction by Jeffery Deaver

Hogan, Desmond
Pictures
New Dubliners; edited by Oona Frawley

Hogan, Ernest
Coyote goes Hollywood
Witpunk; edited by Claude Lalumière and Marty Halpern

Hogan, Linda
Bush's mourning feast
Reckonings; contemporary short fiction by Native American women; edited by Hertha D. Sweet Wong, Lauren Stuart Muller, Jana Sequoya Magdaleno
Descent
Reckonings; contemporary short fiction by Native American women; edited by Hertha D. Sweet Wong, Lauren Stuart Muller, Jana Sequoya Magdaleno

Hoggard, James
The scapegoat
Lone Star literature; from the Red River to the Rio Grande; edited by Don Graham

Holappa, Pentti
Boman
The Year's best fantasy and horror: nineteenth annual collection; edited by Ellen Datlow and Kelly Link & Gavin J. Grant

Holcombe, Alec
(tr.) See Nguyen Viet Ha

Hold fast. Meacham, R.
Hold on to your hat. Meno, J.

Holden, Craig
Red quarters
Detroit noir; edited by E. J. Olsen & John C. Hocking

Holden, Mark
Go Ride the Train
The North American Review v290 no3/4 p3-8 My/Ag 2005
Maybe Someone Should Call the Commodores
The North American Review v292 no3/4 p8-15 My/Ag 2007
The Unnecessary Cat
The Georgia Review v61 no2 p348-56 Summ 2007

Holder, Belle and Holder, Nancy
Another exciting adventure of Lightning Merriemouse-Jones: a touching ghost story
Pandora's closet; edited by Jean Rabe and Martin H. Greenberg.

Holder, Nancy
I know who you ate last summer
The Horror Writers Association presents Blood lite; an anthology of humorous horror stories; edited by Kevin J. Anderson
Little Dedo
Summer chills; strangers in stranger lands; edited by Stephen Jones
Out twelve-steppin, summer of AA
Dark delicacies; original tales of terror and the macabre by the world's greatest horror writers; edited by Del Howison and Jeff Gelb
Passion play
The living dead; edited by John Joseph Adams
(jt. auth) See Holder, Belle and Holder, Nancy

Holding, James
The inquisitive butcher of Nice
Murder short & sweet; edited by Paul D. Staudohar

Holding my breath underwater. Ludwig, S.
Holding pattern. Allen, J. R.

Holdstock, Nick
The Ballad of Poor Lucy Miller
The Southern Review (Baton Rouge, La.) v45 no2 p314-21 Spr 2009

HOLDUPS *See* Robbery
The **Hole**. Anderson, D. G.
Hole. Porter, A.
A **hole** in Hell. Farmer, P. J.
The **hole** in the hole. Bisson, T.
A **hole** with two ends. Faber, M.
The **holes** in the system. Muller, M.
The **holiday**. Francis, C.
Holiday. Hammett, D.
Holiday. Porter, K. A.
Holiday. Rickert, M.
Holiday at the Shamrock. Waters, D.
A **holiday** experience. Bierce, A.
Holiday from women. Gifford, B.
The **holiday** man. Matheson, R.
HOLIDAYS
See also Christmas stories; New Year; Passover; Thanksgiving Day; Vacations; Valentine's Day; Yom Kippur
Anaya, R. A. Jerónimo's journey
Kobrin, L. The freed children of the shtetl
Luongo, M. Cake
Pinski, D. "Our" first of May
Waters, D. Holiday at the Shamrock
The **holiness** of Azédarac. Smith, C. A.

Holinger, Richard

The Huntsman

Iowa Review v36 no3 p172-80 Wint 2006/2007

Holladay, Cary

The Days of the Peppers

The Southern Review (Baton Rouge, La.) v40 no4 p741-51 Aut 2004

Every High Hill

The Hudson Review v61 no3 p473-88 Aut 2008

The Hudson Review v61 no4 p473-88 Wint 2009

Monstrosities

The Georgia Review v59 no4 p860-80 Wint 2005

The Runaway Stagecoach

The Southern Review (Baton Rouge, La.) v44 no3 p429-45 Summ 2008

Holladay, Cary C.

The biggest and the best

Holladay, C. C. The quick-change artist; stories

The blue monkey

Holladay, C. C. The quick-change artist; stories

The broken lake

Holladay, C. C. The quick-change artist; stories

The burning

New stories from the South: the year's best, 2006; selected from U.S. magazines by Allan Gurganus with Kathy Pories; with an introduction by Allan Gurganus

Heaven

Holladay, C. C. The quick-change artist; stories

Hollyhocks

New stories from the South: the year's best, 2007; selected from U.S. magazines by Edward P. Jones with Kathy Pories; with an introduction by Edward P. Jones

The horses are loose

Burnham, C. Who can save us now?; brand-new superheroes and their amazing [short] stories; edited by Owen King and John McNally; [illustrations by Chris Burnham]

The interview

Holladay, C. C. The quick-change artist; stories

The iron road

Holladay, C. C. The quick-change artist; stories

Jane's hat

New stories from the South: the year's best, 2005; edited by Shannon Ravenel; with a preface by Jill McCorkle

Holladay, C. C. The quick-change artist; stories

The lost pony

Holladay, C. C. The quick-change artist; stories

The peacock

Holladay, C. C. The quick-change artist; stories

The quick-change artist

Holladay, C. C. The quick-change artist; stories

Sailor's valentine

Holladay, C. C. The quick-change artist; stories

Snow day

Holladay, C. C. The quick-change artist; stories

Syrup and feather

Holladay, C. C. The quick-change artist; stories

Holland, Barbara

Sinners

Going the distance; edited by Alan Beard

Holland, Noy

Coquina

Holland, N. What begins with bird

Fairway

Holland, N. What begins with bird

Rooster, pollard, cricket, goose

Holland, N. What begins with bird

Someone is always missing

Holland, N. What begins with bird

Time for the flat-headed man

Holland, N. What begins with bird

What begins with bird

Holland, N. What begins with bird

Holland, Travis

The Archivist's Story

Michigan Quarterly Review v46 no1 p57-65 Wint 2007

Dream of the Revolution

Ploughshares v30 no4 p52-66 Wint 2004/2005

HOLLAND *See* Netherlands

Holland. McLean, S.

Hollinghurst, Alan

Highlights

Granta v100 p193-206 Wint 2007

Hollingshead, Greg

Whyte Avenue Blue

The Walrus v5 no1 p74-5 Ja/F 2008

The **Hollow.** Lasdun, J.

HOLLY, BUDDY, 1936-1959

About

Dann, J. and others. Touring

Holly and iron. Nix, G.

The **holly** and the poison ivy. Aird, C.

Hollyhocks. Holladay, C. C.

HOLLYWOOD (CALIF.) *See* California—Hollywood

Hollywood chickens. Pratchett, T.

A **Hollywood** diary. Fuchs, D.

Hollywood kremlin. Sterling, B.

Hollywood lanes. Abbott, M.

Holmes, Andrew

The league of bald-headed men

Perverted by language; fiction inspired by The Fall; edited and introduced by Peter Wild.

Holmes, Charlotte

Taken

New Letters v72 no3/4 p215-38 2006

Holmes, Emory

a.k.a., Moises Rockafella

The Best American Mystery Stories, 2006; edited and with an introduction by Scott Turow; Otto Penzler, series editor

Dangerous days

Los Angeles noir; edited by Denise Hamilton

Holmes, Mary Jane
　　Excerpt from "Adam Floyd" (1892)
　　　Legacy v25 no1 p155-61 2008
Holmes, Rupert
　　The monks of the Abbey Victoria
　　　Dead man's hand; crime fiction at the poker
　　　　table; edited by Otto Penzler.
　　　The Best American mystery stories, 2008; ed-
　　　　ited and with an introduction by George
　　　　Pelecanos; Otto Penzler, series editor
HOLOCAUST, JEWISH (1933-1945)
　　　See also Jews—Persecutions
　　Anissimov, M. His majesty, almighty death [ex-
　　　cerpt]
　　Auslander, S. Holocaust tips for kids
　　Finger, A. The artist and the dwarf
　　Friedmann, P. Two-story brick houses
　　Hasak-Lowy, T. On the grounds of the complex
　　　commemorating the Nazis' treatment of the
　　　Jews
　　Molodowsky, K. Gone
　　Newman, L. Flashback
　　Raphael, L. Big girls don't cry
　　Raphael, L. War stories
　　Segal, L. G. The reverse bug
　　Sherez, S. God-box
　　Sullivan, J. Niels Bohr and the sleeping dane
　　Weil, G. Little Sonja Rosenkranz
A **holocaust** in my breakfast room. Cherne, B.
HOLOCAUST SURVIVORS
　　Cacek, P. D. The keeper
　　Currey, R. The names of the lost
　　Freed, L. Songbird
　　Gordimer, N. A frivolous woman
　　Helprin, M. Perfection
　　Hirshberg, G. Dancing men
　　Hoffman, A. The conjurer's handbook
　　Majzels, R. Hellman's scrapbook [excerpt]
　　Michaels, A. Fugitive pieces [excerpt]
　　Moss, B. K. December birthday
　　Oates, J. C. The cousins
　　Pearlman, E. Madame Guralnik
　　Perlman, E. A tale in two cities
　　Pilcer, S. "Paskudnyak"
　　Rosenfarb, C. A Friday in the life of Sarah
　　　Zonabend
　　Rosenfarb, C. Letters to God
　　Singer, I. B. The bird
　　Updike, D. Old girlfriends
　　Weil, G. And I? witness to pain
　　Weil, G. Don't touch me
　　Weil, G. Finish what you started
　　Weil, G. The most beautiful spot in the world
　　Zelazny, R. Monologue for two
Holocaust tips for kids. Auslander, S.
The **Holographic** Soul. Lazarin, D.
Holt, T. E.
　　Bad News
　　　Boston Review v31 no4 p26-9 Jl/Ag 2006
Holthe, Tess Uriza
　　The bruiser
　　　Holthe, T. U. The five-forty-five to Cannes
　　The ferry driver of Portofino
　　　Holthe, T. U. The five-forty-five to Cannes
　　The five-forty-five to Cannes
　　　Holthe, T. U. The five-forty-five to Cannes
　　The flame
　　　Holthe, T. U. The five-forty-five to Cannes

Homecoming
　　Holthe, T. U. The five-forty-five to Cannes
The last bullfight
　　Holthe, T. U. The five-forty-five to Cannes
The necklace
　　Holthe, T. U. The five-forty-five to Cannes
The pointer
　　Holthe, T. U. The five-forty-five to Cannes
The three widows of Signor Alberto Moretti
　　Holthe, T. U. The five-forty-five to Cannes
Weightless
　　Holthe, T. U. The five-forty-five to Cannes
The **Holy** City and Em's reptile farm. Van
　　Eekhout, G.
HOLY GRAIL *See* Grail
Holy Ground. Quatro, J.
The **holy** pair. Reisen, A.
A **holy** terror. Bierce, A.
The **holy** terror. Maxwell, W.
Holy water. Kellerman, F.
Holy Week. Thompson, J.
Holyoke, Mass.: An Ethnography. Rodriguez, I.
Home. Barrett, M.
Home. Litman, E.
Home. Munro, A.
Home. Shields, C.
Home. Thomas, E.
Home coming. Arnow, H. L. S.
Home coming. Todd, C.
The **home-coming** of 'Rastus Smith. Dunbar, P. L.
Home delivery. King, S.
HOME ECONOMICS
　　Tsutsui, Y. Hello, hello, hello!
　　Zoline, P. The heat death of the universe
Home for a short time. Jones, N.
Home for Passover. Molodowsky, K.
The **home** front. Ardai, C.
HOME HEALTH AIDES
　　Montemarano, N. Shift
　　Montemarano, N. The usual human disabilities
Home in the valley. L'Amour, L.
Home is the hangman. Zelazny, R.
Home movies. Rosenblum, M. H.
Home of the. DeNiro, A.
Home on the rain. Carroll, J.
Home remedies. Kalpakian, L.
Home schooling. Pearlman, E.
Home schooling. Windley, C.
"**Home** . . . sickness". Komla-Ebri, K.
Home sweet home. Kitt, S.
Home to Harlem. Doyle, R.
Home videos. Brockmeier, K.
Homecalling. Merril, J.
Homecoming. Cho, G. M.
Homecoming. Herwitz, D.
Homecoming. Hinton, S. E.
Homecoming. Holthe, T. U.
Homecoming. Maxwell, W.
Homecoming. Miura, T.
Homecoming. West, D.
The **homecoming** of an old Beijing man. Wang
　　Ping
The **homecoming** of Captain Dan. Hodgson, W.
　　H.
HOMECOMINGS
　　Anaya, R. A. Jerónimo's journey
　　Baingana, D. Questions of home
　　Barrett, M. Cadillac
　　Brazaitis, M. Coming home

HOMECOMINGS—*Continued*

Ch'ae, M. The wife and children

Clarke, B. The Hotel Utica

Connell, E. S. The palace of the moorish kings

Currans-Sheehan, T. And now he's gone and you're back

Dunbar, P. L. The home-coming of 'Rastus Smith

Gharbi 'Umran, M. a.- . Sanaa does not know me

Gildner, G. A week in South Dakota

Hamilton, J. The short history of a prince [excerpt]

Hammad, H. a.- . The return of a captive

Hernandez, L. Migrations

Hinton, S. E. Homecoming

Hospital, J. T. The ocean of Brisbane

Jafta, M. The home-coming

Judah, S. The funeral

Kiely, B. Homes on the mountain

Ma Jian. The smile of Lake Drolmula

McGruder, K. Beulah land

McGuinness, F. The Sunday father

Miura, T. Homecoming

Mullan, P. Tribunal

Muller, M. Forbidden things

Naiyer Masud. Epistle

Nisbet, R. Nightingale

Nisbet, R. Time to go home

Pawar, U. Justice

Qi, S. The long march, sort of

Rashid, F. Syra

Reed, K. Visiting the dead

Rheinheimer, K. Telling Brenda

Rifai, T. a.- . Bashrawi

Sankaran, L. Alphabet soup

Sankaran, L. Apple pie, one by two

Sankaran, L. Birdie num-num

Seth, R. Just a simple bridge

Sillitoe, A. Canals

Soueif, A. Returning

Templeton, E. Equality cake

Ts'an-hsüeh. Snake island

Wang Ping. The homecoming of an old Beijing man

Westcott, G. Goodbye, Wisconsin

Westcott, G. The whistling swan

Homeland Hijab. Lewis, T.

The **homeland** is far away, the roads are many. Uthman, L. a.- .

Homeless. Wendroff, Z.

Homeless in hell. Card, O. S.

HOMELESS PERSONS

Alexie, S. What you pawn I will redeem

Alexie, S. What you pawn I will return

Ames, J. Looking for the answers

Archer, J. It can't be October already

Ardai, C. The good samaritan

Barkley, B. St. Jimmy

Boyle, T. C. Here comes

Bradbury, R. The dead man

Brady, C. Those who walk during the day

Carofiglio, G. Christmas Eves

Chekhov, A. P. Dreams

Cody, L. Lucky dip

Curtis, R. To the Interstate

D'Amato, B. The lower wacker Hilton

Donoghue, E. Good deed

Estep, M. Triple Harrison

Faber, M. The safehouse

Fischer, J. Undead camels ate their flesh

Flanagan, E. Every sad detail

Fonseca, R. Angels of the marquees

Frost, G. The bus

Gaines, E. J. Christ walked down Market Street

Gee, M. Mornington Place

Gospodinov, G. The late gift

Halpern, F. Three meetings

Hatoum, M. The truth is a seven-headed animal

Hill, J. The widow's breakfast

Holladay, C. C. Syrup and feather

Kiernan, C. R. The last child of Lir

Krueger, W. K. Bums

L'Amour, L. Death, Westbound

Lane, J. Scratch

McCabe, E. Roma

McInerney, J. The queen and I

McLean, S. Emil

Miles, K. Old bag dad

Muller, M. The cracks in the sidewalk

Mun, N. Shelter

Neera. The lady of the evening

Nelson, A. Eminent domain

Nelson, A. Strike anywhere

Nichols, J. Slow monkeys

Parra, E. A. The well

Peelle, L. The still point

Rice, C. Over thirty

Rivera-Valdes, S. Life leads

Rock, P. Disentangling

Slavin, J. Squatters

Somerville, P. Trouble and the shadowy death-blow

Stewart, P. Walk left stand right

Straight, S. The Golden Gopher

Thon, M. R. Letters in the snow—for kind strangers and unborn children—for the ones lost and most beloved

Van Booy, S. The shepherd on the rock

Webster, B. Christus destitutus

Wendroff, Z. Homeless

Zadoorian, M. The lost Tiki palaces of Detroit

Homenidis, Christos

Not all fingers are equal

Angelic & black; contemporary Greek short stories; edited and translated by David Connolly; with an introduction by Vangelis Hatzivassileiou

HOMER

Parodies, imitations, etc.

Winsor, C. The art of war

Homer, Paul

International Law 101

Legal Studies Forum v33 no2 p273-97 2009

Proof of Heirship

Legal Studies Forum v32 no1 p51-61 2008

The Secret

Legal Studies Forum v32 no1 p63-6 2008

Homer's Childhood Games. Epstein, A.

Homes, A. M.

Brother on Sunday

The New Yorker v85 no3 p60-5 Mr 2 2009

Cindy Stubenstock

The book of other people; edited by Zadie Smith

Do not disturb

The Anchor book of new American short stories; edited by Ben Marcus

HOMOSEXUALITY—*Continued*

Mattison, A. The odds it would be you
McCafferty, J. Elizabeth Tines
McCann, R. Eduardo's hair
McCann, R. My brother in the basement
McCann, R. Some threads through the Medina
McCann, R. The universe, concealed
McFarland, D. Nothing to ask for
McIntyre, V. Disability
McIntyre, V. ONJ.com
Mohanraj, M. A. Challah (Philadelphia, 1998)
Montgomery, L. Hats
Mozetič, B. Bathroom
Mozetič, B. The beach
Mozetič, B. Boy
Mozetič, B. Cinema
Mozetič, B. Dancing
Mozetič, B. Disco
Mozetič, B. Egghead
Mozetič, B. G.
Mozetič, B. Gym
Mozetič, B. Gypsies
Mozetič, B. Hairdresser
Mozetič, B. Interloper
Mozetič, B. Ivan
Mozetič, B. The letter
Mozetič, B. Library
Mozetič, B. Lover boy
Mozetič, B. The mayor
Mozetič, B. Nino
Mozetič, B. No. 6
Mozetič, B. Oblivion
Mozetič, B. The poem
Mozetič, B. The poet
Mozetič, B. Rage
Mozetič, B. The rails
Mozetič, B. Rape
Mozetič, B. Razorblade
Mozetič, B. The reader
Mozetič, B. The soldiers
Mozetič, B. The station
Mozetič, B. The street
Mozetič, B. Telephone
Mozetič, B. The unfortunate
Mozetič, B. Video
Mozetič, B. Woman
Mozetič, B. You
Muñoz, M. The comeuppance of Lupe Rivera
Muñoz, M. The good brother
Muñoz, M. Ida y vuelta
Muñoz, M. Lindo y querido
Muñoz, M. Señor X
Muñoz, M. Tell him about Brother John
Munro, A. The turkey season
Newman, L. A letter to Harvey Milk
Nguyen, V. T. A correct life
Nisbet, J. Facilis descensus averno
Oates, J. C. Life after high school
Orner, E. Fear and loathing in Chelsea
Peck, D. Dues
Pierce, T. J. Newsworld
Poirier, M. J. I, Maggot
Pollock, D. R. Schott's Bridge
Pomfret, S. Chicken
Porter, A. Azul
Porter, J. A. Pending
Porter, J. A. Solstice
Randolph, L. This is not the tropics
Raphael, L. Abominations

Raphael, L. Another life
Raphael, L. Betrayed by David Bowie
Raphael, L. The children
Raphael, L. Dancing on Tisha B'Av
Raphael, L. Gimme shelter
Raphael, L. The pathfinder
Raphael, L. Secret anniversaries of the heart
Raphael, L. Shouts of joy
Raphael, L. Welcome to Beth Homo
Raphael, L. Your papers, please
Raphael, L. You're breaking my heart!
Resnick, R. Muay Thai
Rice, C. Man catch
Rice, C. Over thirty
Richter, S. Habits and habitat of the southwestern bad boy
Rickards, J. Wish
Roberts, A. Blindness and invisibility
Roberts, N. This is not skin
Romano, T. Comic books
Rylands, J. T. Fortune
Ryman, G. Birth days
Salter, J. Give
Sayre-Roberts, A. Death mouth
Selgin, P. Sawdust
Shunn, W. Inclination
Singer, I. B. Two
Smith, N. Green fluorescent protein
Smith, N. Isolettes
Sonnenberg, B. Taiping
Stahl, J. Li'l Dickens
Stamm, P. In the outer suburbs
Starr, C. Dirty blood
Stella, C. Father Diodorus
Stevens, J. D. Great myths of our time
Swofford, A. Escape and evasion
Thomas, L. An apiary of white bees
Tobin, P. passage
Tóibín, C. Three friends
Tomlinson, J. Angel, his rabbit, and Kyle McKell
Trezise, R. Valley lines
Upadhyay, S. The royal ghosts
Vallorani, N. Pasolini's shadow
Vidal, G. Pages from an abandoned journal
Vidal, G. Three stratagems
Vidal, G. The Zenner trophy
Vollmer, M. Second home
Waters, D. Sheets
White, E. Cinnamon skin
With, C. Angel's house of ice
With, C. The arbutus tree
Wolff, T. Awaiting orders
Zumas, L. How he was a wicked son

HOMOSEXUALS *See* Homosexuality; Lesbianism

Honda people. Flanagan, E.

HONDURAS

Gifford, B. The law of affection

Honegger, Gitta

(tr.) *See* Reinerová, Lenka

An **honest** day's work. Lanagan, M.

Honest money. Gardner, E. S.

HONESTY

See also Truthfulness and falsehood

Keret, E. Surprise egg
L'Amour, L. The Dancing Kate
L'Amour, L. Old Doc Yak

Honesty. Rash, R.

Horgan, Paul
 The devil in the desert
   The best American Catholic short stories; a
    Sheed & Ward collection; edited by Daniel
    McVeigh and Patricia Schnapp
 The peach stone
   The best American Catholic short stories; a
    Sheed & Ward collection; edited by Daniel
    McVeigh and Patricia Schnapp
Horizon. Mountford, P.
Horn, Dara
 Readers Digest
   Scribblers on the roof; contemporary Ameri-
    can Jewish fiction; edited by Melvin Jules
    Bukiet and David G. Roskies
Hornby, Nick
 J. Johnson
   The book of other people; edited by Zadie
    Smith
 Otherwise pandemonium
   McSweeney's mammoth treasury of thrilling
    tales; edited by Michael Chabon
Hornsby, Wendy
 Dust up
   The International Association of Crime Writ-
    ers presents Murder in Vegas; new crime
    tales of gambling and desperation; edited
    by Michael Connelly
   The Best American Mystery Stories, 2006;
    edited and with an introduction by Scott
    Turow; Otto Penzler, series editor
   The Deadly Bride; and 21 of the year's finest
    crime and mystery stories; including com-
    plete coverage of the year in mystery and
    crime fiction; edited by Ed Gorman and
    Martin H. Greenberg
Hornung, Ernest William
 Nine points of the law
   The Penguin book of Gaslight crime; con art-
    ists, burglars, rogues, and scoundrels from
    the time of Sherlock Holmes; edited with
    an introduction and notes by Michael Sims.
 A trap to catch a cracksman
   The Mammoth book of vintage whodunnits;
    edited by Maxim Jakubowski
Horodyski, Mary
 End of the Lot
   Dalhousie Review v86 no1 p61-70 Spr 2006
The **horoscope** never lies. Judah, S.
Horowitz, James *See* Salter, James
Horrocks, Caitlin
 At the Zoo
   The Paris Review v51 p70-80 Spr 2009
 Steal Small
   Prairie Schooner v83 no2 p67-81 Summ 2009
 This is not your city
   The PEN/O.Henry Prize stories 2009; chosen
    and with an introduction by Laura Furman;
    with essays on the stories They admire
    most by jurors A. S. Byatt; Anthony Doerr;
    Tim O'Brien
 Zolaria
   The Southern Review (Baton Rouge, La.) v44
    no3 p471-80 Summ 2008
Horrocks, Kaitlin
 In the Gulf of Aden, Past the Cape of Guardafui
   Gettysburg Review v21 no2 p173-85 Summ
    2008
The **horror** at Oakdeene. Lumley, B.

The **horror** at Red Hook. Lovecraft, H. P.
The **horror** conference. Burgin, R.
The **horror** from the mound. Howard, R. E.
The **horror** south of Red Hook. Lupoff, R. A.
HORROR STORIES
      See also Ghost stories; Murder stories;
       Supernatural phenomena; Vampires; Were-
       wolves
 Aguilar, L. The mirror cracked
 Aguirre, F. Andretto walks the king's way
 Anderson, M. T. Watch and wake
 Arnzen, M. A. The dead lantern
 Atkins, P. Stacy and her idiot
 Baker, K. I begyn as I mean to go on
 Ballingrud, N. The monsters of heaven
 Ballingrud, N. You go where it takes you
 Banks, L. E. What the devil won't take . . .
 Barker, C. Haeckel's tale
 Barker, C. In the hills, the cities
 Barker, C. Sex, death and starshine
 Barron, L. Bulldozer
 Barron, L. The forest
 Barron, L. Hallucigenia
 Barron, L. The imago sequence
 Barron, L. Proboscis
 Battersby, L. Father muerte & the flesh
 Bear, E. Inelastic collisions
 Bear, E. Tiger! Tiger!
 Bergstrom, E. Accidental invasion
 Berliner, J. High kicks and misdemeanors
 Bestwick, S. Hazy shade of winter
 Bierce, A. An adventure at Brownville
 Bierce, A. The boarded window
 Bierce, A. The death of Halpin Frayser
 Bierce, A. A diagnosis of death
 Bierce, A. The secret of Macarger's Gulch
 Bierce, A. Two haunted houses
 Bierce, A. A watcher by the dead
 Birmingham, J. Heere be monsters
 Borges, J. L. The Gospel according to Mark
 Boyle, N. The churring
 Bradbury, R. April 2005: Usher II
 Bradbury, R. The Finnegan
 Bradbury, R. Heavy set
 Bradbury, R. Let's play poison
 Bradbury, R. The reincarnate
 Bradbury, R. Trapdoor
 Bradbury, R. The watchers
 Bradbury, R. The whole town's sleeping
 Bradbury, R. Zero hour
 Brandner, G. Words, words, words!
 Brenchley, C. The house of mechanical pain
 Brennan, T. Scarecrow
 British horror weekend
 Brown, S. Water babies
 Bull, S. E. Mr. Sly stops for a cup of joe
 Burgin, R. The horror conference
 Burke, K. P. Mutiny
 Cadigan, P. Stilled life
 Campbell, R. Raised by the moon
 Campbell, R. Respects
 Campbell, R. The voice of the beach
 Card, O. S. Waterbaby
 Cave, H. B. The coming
 Chadbourn, M. Farewell to the 21st century girl
 Charnas, S. M. Evil thoughts
 Chekhov, A. P. Curved mirror [variant title:
    Crooked mirror (a Christmas story)]
 Clark, S. The extraordinary limits of darkness

HORROR STORIES—*Continued*

Kelly, R. The dark tribe
Kelly, R. Dead skin
Kelly, R. Devil's Creek
Kelly, R. Exit
Kelly, R. Forever angels
Kelly, R. Grandma's favorite recipe
Kelly, R. The hatchling
Kelly, R. Impressions in oak
Kelly, R. Midnight grinding
Kelly, R. Miss Abigail's delicate condition
Kelly, R. Oh, sordid shame!
Kelly, R. Old Hacker
Kelly, R. Papa's exile
Kelly, R. Romicide
Kelly, R. Scream queen
Kelly, R. Thinning the herd
Kelly, R. The web of La Sanguinaire
Kelly, R. Whorehouse Hollow
Kelly, R. The winds within
Kelly, R. Yea, though I drive
Kenyon, S. Where angels fear to tread
Kessel, J. Every angel is terrifying
Kiernan, C. R. Estate
Kiernan, C. R. Glass coffin
Kiernan, C. R. In the water works (Birmingham, Alabama 1888)
Kiernan, C. R. The last child of Lir
Kiernan, C. R. The long hall on the top floor
Kiernan, C. R. Mercury

Kiernan, C. R. Paedomorphosis
Kiernan, C. R. Postcards from the King of Tides
Kiernan, C. R. Rats live on no evil star
Kiernan, C. R. Salammbô
Kiernan, C. R. Salammbô redux (2007)
Kiernan, C. R. Salmagundi (New York City, 1981)
Kiernan, C. R. San Andreas (1998)
Kiernan, C. R. A story of Edward Gorey
Kiernan, C. R. Superheroes
Kiernan, C. R. Tears seven times salt
King, S. The cat from hell
King, S. The gingerbread girl
King, S. Home delivery
King, S. N.
King, S. The reach
King, S. Stationary bike
King, S. A very tight place
Kirtley, D. B. The skull-faced boy
Konrath, J. A. and Wilson, F. P. The sound of blunder
Kress, N. To cuddle Amy
Kuhoric, J. A. Man or monster
Lamsley, T. Blade and bone
Lamsley, T. The break
Lamsley, T. The extension
Lamsley, T. The outer darkness
Lamsley, T. Screens
Lamsley, T. So long Gerry
Lamsley, T. Someone to dump on
Lamsley, T. The toddler
Lamsley, T. Walking the dog
Lanagan, M. A pig's whisper
Lane, J. Among the dead
Lane, J. Beyond the river
Lane, J. The city of love
Lane, J. Coming of age

Lane, J. Contract bridge
Lane, J. Like shattered stone
Lane, J. The lost district
Lane, J. The plans they made
Lane, J. The quiet hours
Lane, J. Reservoir
Lane, J. You could have it all
Langan, J. Episode seven: last stand against the Pack in the kingdom of the purple flowers
Langan, J. Laocöon, or the singularity
Langan, J. Mr. Gaunt
Langan, J. On Skua Isalnd
Langan, J. Tutorial
Lannes, R. The anguish of departure
Lansdale, J. R. Dog
Lansdale, J. R. The gentleman's hotel
Lansdale, J. R. Janet finds the razor
Lansdale, J. R. King of shadows
Lansdale, J. R. The long dead day
Lansdale, J. R. Mr. Bear
Lansdale, J. R. Night they missed the horror show
Lansdale, J. R. The shaggy house
Lebbon, T. The flames beneath the light
Lebbon, T. In the valley where belladonna grows
Lee, T. The hill
Leiren-Young, M. Frost-bitten
Ligotti, T. Notes of the writing of horror: a story
Ligotti, T. A soft voice whispers nothing
Link, K. Catskin
Link, K. The hortlak
Link, K. The specialist's hat
Little, B. We find things old
Lockley, S. and Lewis, P. Never go back
Lovecraft, H. P. The call of Cthulhu
Lovecraft, H. P. The cats of Ulthar
Lovecraft, H. P. The colour out of space
Lovecraft, H. P. Cool air
Lovecraft, H. P. Discarded draft of The shadow over Innsmouth
Lovecraft, H. P. The Dunwich horror
Lovecraft, H. P. Herbert West—reanimator
Lovecraft, H. P. Herbert West—reanimator: six shots by moonlight
Lovecraft, H. P. The music of Erich Zann
Lovecraft, H. P. The outsider
Lovecraft, H. P. Pickman's model
Lovecraft, H. P. The rats in the walls
Lovecraft, H. P. The shadow over Innsmouth
Lovecraft, H. P. The statement of Randolph Carter
Lovecraft, H. P. The thing on the doorstep
Lovecraft, H. P. The whisperer in darkness
Lovegrove, J. At one
Ludwigsen, W. A good psycho is hard to find
Lumley, B. Born of the winds
Lumley, B. Deja viewer
Lumley, B. End piece: old man with a blade
Lumley, B. The fairground horror
Lumley, B. Feasibility study
Lumley, B. For the dead travel slowly
Lumley, B. Gaddy's gloves
Lumley, B. Harry and the pirates
Lumley, B. The horror at Oakdeene
Lumley, B. The house of the temple
Lumley, B. Lord of the worms
Lumley, B. The man who felt pain

HORROR STORIES—*Continued*

Lumley, B. The man who saw no spiders
Lumley, B. No way home
Lumley, B. Snarker's son
Lumley, B. The strange years
Lumley, B. The sun, the sea and the silent scream
Lumley, B. The taint
Luongo, M. Embankment
Luongo, M. Pedagogy
Lupoff, R. A. The adventure of the Voorish Sign
Lupoff, R. A. Brackish waters
Lupoff, R. A. The devil's hop yard
Lupoff, R. A. Documents in the case of Elizabeth Akeley
Lupoff, R. A. The doom that came to Dunwich
Lupoff, R. A. The horror south of Red Hook
Lupoff, R. A. The secret of the Sahara
Maḥfūẓ, N. The haunted wood
Maḥfūẓ, N. The only man
Maḥfūẓ, N. Room no. 12
Maḥfūẓ, N. The vapor of darkness
Martin, G. R. R. The pear-shaped man
Martin, G. R. R. Remembering Melody
Masdon, J. Jack's mantle
Masello, R. Where there's a will . . .
Massie, E. The landlock
Matheson, R. Big surprise
Matheson, R. Blood son
Matheson, R. Buried talents
Matheson, R. Button, button
Matheson, R. The children of Noah
Matheson, R. Crickets
Matheson, R. Day of reckoning [variant titles: The faces; Graveyard shift]
Matheson, R. Deadline
Matheson, R. The doll that does everything
Matheson, R. A drink of water
Matheson, R. Duel
Matheson, R. Dying room only
Matheson, R. The edge
Matheson, R. First anniversary
Matheson, R. The holiday man
Matheson, R. Lemmings
Matheson, R. The likeness of Julie
Matheson, R. Little girl lost
Matheson, R. Long distance call
Matheson, R. Nightmare at 20,000 feet
Matheson, R. Prey
Matheson, R. Shockwave
Matheson, R. The wedding
Matheson, R. Witch war
Matthews, B. The pretty dead girl
McAuley, P. J. Take me to the river
McDowell, I. Making faces
Meloy, P. The vague

Mitchell, D. What you do not know you want
Monteleone, T. F. The dancer in the darkness
Monteleone, T. F. A spell for Jonathan
Monteleone, T. F. The white man
Morris, M. Puppies for sale
Morris, M. Stamps
Morton, L. Black Mill Cove
Moser, Elise. The seven-day itch
Newman, K. Richard Riddle, boy detective, in "The case of the French spy"
Nicholson, S. Last writes

Nolan, W. F. Depompa
Nutman, P. The misadventure of Eat Man and Little Boy, or, How I made a monster
Oates, J. C. *BD* 11 1 87
Oates, J. C. Face [2007]
Oates, J. C. Madison at Guignol
Oates, J. C. The museum of Dr. Moses
O'Bryan, J. The unlikely redemption of Jared Pearce
O'Connell, J. The swag from Doc Hawthorne's
O'Driscoll, M. 13 O'clock
Oliver, R. Mr. Poo-Poo
Palahniuk, C. Guts
Palahniuk, C. Hot potting
Pascoe, J. The kidnapper bell
Phillips, G. Searching for Cisa
Pickman, R. Dark delicacies of the dead
Pinborough, S. The Bohemian of the Arbat
Poe, E. A. The black cat
Pohl, F. Let the ants try
Powell, M. The abominable ice man
Powers, T. Pat Moore
Powers, T. Where they are hid
Pratchett, T. Twenty pence with envelope and seasonal greeting
Quiroga, H. Anaconda
Quiroga, H. The dead man
Quiroga, H. The decapitated chicken
Quiroga, H. Drifting
Quiroga, H. The feather pillow
Quiroga, H. In the middle of the night
Raines, P. and Welles, H. The bad magician
Rand, K. Last vision
Rath, T. A trick of the dark
Reed, K. Escape from shark island
Reed, K. No two alike
Reed, K. Precautions
Reed, K. Visiting the dead
Reed, K. The zombie prince
Reed, R. She sees my monsters now
Reed, R. Show me yours
Rhine, R. S. The seer
Rhodes, D. Glass eyes
Richards, T. Birchiam pier
Rickert, M. A very little madness goes a long way
Roberts, J. 7C
Roden, B. Northwest passage
Rosenbaum, B. A siege of cranes
Royle, N. The goldfinch

Rucker, R. v. B. MS found in a minidrive
Samuels, M. A gentleman from Mexico
Samuels, M. Ghorla
Samuels, M. Shallaballah
Saunders, G. Sea Oak
Schlich, S. Inside the Iron Maiden
Schow, D. J. The pyre and others
Shawl, N. Cruel Sistah
Shirley, J. Blind eye
Shirley, J. Buried in the sky
Shirley, J. Isolation Point, California
Shirley, J. Miss singularity
Shirley, J. Skeeter junkie
Shirley, J. Sleepwalkers
Shirley, J. The word "random", deliberately repeated
Silverberg, R. Not our brother
Silverberg, R. Road to nightfall

HORROR STORIES—*Continued*

Smith, C. A. The devotee of evil
Smith, C. A. The dweller in the gulf
Smith, C. A. The epiphany of death
Smith, C. A. The ghoul
Smith, C. A. The Gorgon
Smith, C. A. The hunters from beyond
Smith, C. A. The immeasurable horror
Smith, C. A. The maker of gargoyles
Smith, C. A. The nameless offspring
Smith, C. A. The ninth skeleton
Smith, C. A. The resurrection of the rattlesnake
Smith, C. A. The return of the sorcerer
Smith, C. A. The satyr
Smith, C. A. The second interment
Smith, C. A. The seed from the sepulcher
Smith, C. A. The tale of Satampra Zeiros
Smith, C. A. The treader of the dust
Smith, C. A. Ubbo-Sathla
Smith, C. A. The vaults of Yoh-Vombis
Smith, D. L. The charnel house
Smith, D. L. The fall
Smith, M. M. Fair exchange
Spencer, W. B. The essayist in the wilderness
Spencer, W. B. The ocean and all its devices
Spencer, W. B. The tenth muse
Stevens, F. Behind the curtain
Stevens, F. The labyrinth
Stevens, F. The nightmare
Stevens, F. Serapion
Stevens, F. Unseen—unfeared
Stevenson, R. P. Insect dreams
Stone, E. J. PR problems
Strand, J. The bell . . . from HELL!!!
Straub, P. Little Red's tango
Straub, P. Mr. Aickman's air rifle
Strieber, W. Kaddish
Tantimedh, A. Kali's final cut
Tem, S. R. Eggs
Tem, S. R. and Tem, M. The man on the ceiling
Tessier, T. In praise of folly
Tham, H. The seventh day
Thomas, J. The reflections of ghosts
Thomas, L. An apiary of white bees
Travis, J. King of the maggots
Tumasonis, D. The swing
Tuttle, L.
Uchida, H. The companion
Uchida, H. The forerunner
Uchida, H. The lizard
Uchida, H. The narrow straw mat
Uchida, H. Seaweed
Uchida, H. The war museum
Ulanski, D. It came from Monkey Skull Creek
Van Eekhout, G. Ghost market
Van Lente, F. Don't even blink

Volk, S. 31/10
Walter, P. Splitfoot
Warren, K. Down to the silver spirits
Welch, C. The Eldritch Pastiche from Beyond the Shadow of Horror
Williams, C. 68° 07' 15N, 31° 36' 44W
Williams, C. The burn
Williams, C. City in aspic
Williams, C. Edge
Williams, C. Excuse the unusual approach
Williams, C. The light that passes through you
Williams, C. Nest of salt

Williams, C. The owl
Williams, C. Slitten gorge
Williams, C. Supple bodies
Williams, C. The windmill
Williams, C. Wire
Wilson, C. Directions
Wilson, F. P. Anna
Wilson, F. P. Dreams
Wilson, F. P. Foet
Wilson, F. P. Itsy bitsy spider
Wilson, F. P. Part of the game
Wilson, F. P. Sole custody
Wilson, F. P. When he was fab
Wilson, G. The outermost borough
Wolfe, G. Black shoes
Wolfe, G. The hero as werwolf
Wolfe, G. Houston, 1943
Wolfe, G. Lord of the land
Wolfe, G. Mute
Wolfe, G. Sob in the silence
Wolfe, G. The tree is my hat
Wolfe, G. Try and kill it
Woollcott, A. Moonlight sonata
Zebrowski, G. The alternate
Zebrowski, G. Black pockets
Zebrowski, G. Earth around his bones
Zebrowski, G. Fire of spring
Zebrowski, G. First love, first fear
Zebrowski, G. Hell just over the hill
Zebrowski, G. Jumper
Zebrowski, G. Lords of imagination
Zebrowski, G. My first world
Zebrowski, G. Nappy
Zebrowski, G. Passing nights
Zebrowski, G. A piano full of dead spiders
Zebrowski, G. The soft terrible music
Zebrowski, G. Takes you back
Zebrowski, G. The wish in the fear
Zelazny, R. Corrida
The **horse** dealer's lovers. DeMarinis, R.

HORSE FARMS

Reinhorn, H. Africa
Richards, S. S. Clarence Cummins and the semi-permanent loan
Richards, S. S. The murderer, the pony, and Miss Brown to you
Horse, Girl, Landscape. Sheehan, A.
The **Horse** in Our History. Woodrell, D.
The **horse** of a different color (That you rode in on). Waldrop, H.
The **horse** of the invisible. Hodgson, W. H.

HORSE RACING

See also Jockeys

Bierce, A. The miraculous guest
Bierce, A. The race at Left Bower
Block, L. Keller by a nose
Burke, J. Zuppa Inglese
Carcaterra, L. Yellow Mama's long weekend
Dunbar, P. L. The finish of Patsy Barnes
Dunbar, P. L. Schwalliger's philanthropy
Ford, J. What's sure to come
L'Amour, L. Ride or start shootin'
Malone, M. Raindancer
Martinez, M. The long shot
Michaels, L. Nachman at the races
Oates, J. C. Meadowlands
Oates, J. C. Raven's Wing
Pizzolatto, N. 1987, the races
Richards, S. S. Gawain and the horsewoman

HORSE RACING—*Continued*
Smith, J. Hotwalking
Wolven, S. Pinwheel

HORSE THIEVES
Askins, C. Kit
The **Horse** Thieves of Rockaway Beach. Magill, M.

Horseman. Russo, R.
Horseman!. Zelazny, R.
A **horseman** in the sky. Bierce, A.

HORSEMANSHIP
Arnow, H. L. S. The first ride
Macy, C. Spoiled

Horsepower. Egan, P.

HORSES
Atwood, M. White horse
Benedict, P. Mercy
Blackford, R. Manannan's children
Brady, C. The mechanics of falling
Burke, J. Zuppa Inglese
Carcaterra, L. Yellow Mama's long weekend
Coloane, F. On the horse of dawn
Daughtry, P. The centaur's son
Daughtry, P. The mescaline runes
Davis, C. The same sky
Estep, M. Triple Harrison
Garland, H. The doctor's visit
Holladay, C. C. Heaven
James, C. L. R. Bad Boo-boo-loo rides in a horse race
Koretsky, J. L. Deliberate men
Malone, M. Raindancer
Mills, E. J. The black hero of the ranges
O'Hara, M. My friend Flicka
Peelle, L. Sweethearts of the rodeo
Proulx, A. The great divide
Reinhorn, H. Africa
Richards, S. S. The hanging in the foaling barn
Saramago, J. The centaur
Sarris, G. The magic pony
Seton, E. T. Coaly-bay, the outlaw horse
Seton, E. T. The pacing mustang
Shroff, M. F. The queen guards her own
Smith, R. T. Little Sorrel
Welsh, I. Kingdom of Fife
Wieland, M. The bones of hagerman
Zelazny, R. The horses of Lir

Horses. Dumbleton, M.
Horses. Powell, P.
The **horses** are loose. Holladay, C. C.
The **horses** of Lir. Zelazny, R.
Horseshoes. Ockert, J.
Horsey ride. Stewart, P.
Horsie. Keret, E.
The **hortlak**. Link, K.

HOSPICES (TERMINAL CARE)
Palahniuk, C. Escort

Hospital, Janette, Turner
Bad Dreams
Southern Humanities Review v40 no3 p237-46 Summ 2006
Cape tribulation
Hospital, J. T. North of nowhere, south of loss
Credit repair
Hospital, J. T. North of nowhere, south of loss

The end-of-the-world disco
Hospital, J. T. North of nowhere, south of loss
Flight
Hospital, J. T. North of nowhere, south of loss
For Mr. Voss or occupant
Hospital, J. T. North of nowhere, south of loss
Frames and wonders
Hospital, J. T. North of nowhere, south of loss
Litany for the homeland
Hospital, J. T. North of nowhere, south of loss
Nativity
Hospital, J. T. North of nowhere, south of loss
Night train
Hospital, J. T. North of nowhere, south of loss
North of nowhere
Hospital, J. T. North of nowhere, south of loss
The ocean of Brisbane
Hospital, J. T. North of nowhere, south of loss
Our own little Kakadu
Hospital, J. T. North of nowhere, south of loss
South of loss
Hospital, J. T. North of nowhere, south of loss
Unperformed experiments have no results
Hospital, J. T. North of nowhere, south of loss

The **hospital** and the bar. Bova, B.
A **hospital** night. Zhu Wen
Hospitality. Arnold, G.

HOSPITALS AND SANATORIUMS
Adrian, C. A child's book of sickness and death
Adrian, C. The sum of our parts
Al-Shaykh, S. At the hospital
Ali, M. N. Ward G-4
Anderson, B. Balance
Andreas-Salomé, L. One night
Angrist, M. So much the better
Bell, M. S. Anomalous structures of my dreams
Berg, E. Mrs. Ethel Menafee and Mr. Bridie Stoltz
Bradford, A. Orderly: how I spent that year after high school
Buitrago, F. The sea from the window
Chapman, J. D. Amanuensis
Coleman, A. S. The eternal quest
Cooney, E. See the girl
Davis, C. Breathing
Dunn, G. Only on a Sunday morning
Effinger, G. A. Posterity
Emshwiller, C. The assassin; or, Being the loved one
Erdrich, L. Errr
Finger, A. Gloucester
Flanagan, E. The usual mistakes
Gordon, M. Sick in London
Gorman, E. Survival
Haldeman, J. W. Memento mori
Hallabi, N. a.- . The alley
Harleman, A. Meanwhile

Howard, Clark—*Continued*

Crowded lives
> Manhattan noir 2; the classics; edited by Lawrence Block

The leper colony
> The World's finest mystery and crime stories, fifth annual collection; edited by Ed Gorman and Martin H. Greenberg

Manila burning
> The Best American mystery stories, 2009; edited and with an introduction by Jeffery Deaver

To live and die in Midland, Texas
> The World's finest mystery and crime stories, fourth annual collection; edited by Ed Gorman and Martin H. Greenberg

Under suspicion
> Murder short & sweet; edited by Paul D. Staudohar

Howard, Hannah

Men, Monsters, and Mothers
> *Hanging Loose* no86 p106-9 2005

Howard, Jennifer

East of the sun
> D. C. noir; edited by George Pelecanos

Howard, Robert Ervin

Black Canaan
> Howard, R. E. The horror stories of Robert E. Howard; illustrated by Greg Staples.

The black stone
> Howard, R. E. The horror stories of Robert E. Howard; illustrated by Greg Staples.

The cairn on the headland
> Howard, R. E. The horror stories of Robert E. Howard; illustrated by Greg Staples.

Casonetto's last song
> Howard, R. E. The horror stories of Robert E. Howard; illustrated by Greg Staples.

The children of the night
> Howard, R. E. The horror stories of Robert E. Howard; illustrated by Greg Staples.

The dead remember
> Howard, R. E. The horror stories of Robert E. Howard; illustrated by Greg Staples.

Delenda est
> Howard, R. E. The horror stories of Robert E. Howard; illustrated by Greg Staples.

Dermod's bane
> Howard, R. E. The horror stories of Robert E. Howard; illustrated by Greg Staples.

Dig me no grave
> Howard, R. E. The horror stories of Robert E. Howard; illustrated by Greg Staples.

The dream snake
> Howard, R. E. The horror stories of Robert E. Howard; illustrated by Greg Staples.

The dwellers under the tomb
> Howard, R. E. The horror stories of Robert E. Howard; illustrated by Greg Staples.

The fire of Asshurbanipal
> Howard, R. E. The horror stories of Robert E. Howard; illustrated by Greg Staples.

Golnor the Ape
> Howard, R. E. The horror stories of Robert E. Howard; illustrated by Greg Staples.

The haunter of the ring
> Howard, R. E. The horror stories of Robert E. Howard; illustrated by Greg Staples.

The hills of the dead
> Howard, R. E. The horror stories of Robert E. Howard; illustrated by Greg Staples.

The hoofed thing
> Howard, R. E. The horror stories of Robert E. Howard; illustrated by Greg Staples.

The horror from the mound
> Howard, R. E. The horror stories of Robert E. Howard; illustrated by Greg Staples.

The hosue
> Howard, R. E. The horror stories of Robert E. Howard; illustrated by Greg Staples.

The house of Arabu
> Howard, R. E. The horror stories of Robert E. Howard; illustrated by Greg Staples.

In the forest of Villefère
> Howard, R. E. The horror stories of Robert E. Howard; illustrated by Greg Staples.

Kelly the conjure-man
> Howard, R. E. The horror stories of Robert E. Howard; illustrated by Greg Staples.

The little people
> Howard, R. E. The horror stories of Robert E. Howard; illustrated by Greg Staples.

The man on the ground
> Howard, R. E. The horror stories of Robert E. Howard; illustrated by Greg Staples.

The noseless horror
> Howard, R. E. The horror stories of Robert E. Howard; illustrated by Greg Staples.

Old Garfield's heart
> Howard, R. E. The horror stories of Robert E. Howard; illustrated by Greg Staples.

Out of the deep
> Howard, R. E. The horror stories of Robert E. Howard; illustrated by Greg Staples.

People of the dark
> Howard, R. E. The horror stories of Robert E. Howard; illustrated by Greg Staples.

Pigeons from hell
> Howard, R. E. The horror stories of Robert E. Howard; illustrated by Greg Staples.

Rattles of bones
> Howard, R. E. The horror stories of Robert E. Howard; illustrated by Greg Staples.

Restless waters
> Howard, R. E. The horror stories of Robert E. Howard; illustrated by Greg Staples.

The shadow of the beast
> Howard, R. E. The horror stories of Robert E. Howard; illustrated by Greg Staples.

Spectres in the dark
> Howard, R. E. The horror stories of Robert E. Howard; illustrated by Greg Staples.

The spirit of Tom Molyneaux
> Howard, R. E. The horror stories of Robert E. Howard; illustrated by Greg Staples.

The thing on the roof
> Howard, R. E. The horror stories of Robert E. Howard; illustrated by Greg Staples.

The touch of death
> Howard, R. E. The horror stories of Robert E. Howard; illustrated by Greg Staples.

Untitled fragment
> Howard, R. E. The horror stories of Robert E. Howard; illustrated by Greg Staples.

The valley of the lost
> Howard, R. E. The horror stories of Robert E. Howard; illustrated by Greg Staples.

Howard, Robert Ervin—*Continued*
Wolfshead
Howard, R. E. The horror stories of Robert E. Howard; illustrated by Greg Staples.
Worms of the earth
Howard, R. E. The horror stories of Robert E. Howard; illustrated by Greg Staples.
HOWARD, ROBERT ERVIN, 1906-1936
Parodies, imitations, etc.
Di Filippo, P. Observable things
Howard, Zoë
Family Matters
Dalhousie Review v88 no3 p425-8 Aut 2008
How'd It Go? Moulthrop, R.
HOWE, GORDIE
About
Popkes, S. The ice
Howe, Gordon *See* Howe, Gordie
Howe, Justin
Skillet and saber
Fast ships, black sails; edited by Ann & Jeff VanderMeer
Howell, Carol K.
I am Meyer
Bandersnatch; edited by Paul Tremblay and Sean Wallace
Sourballs
Western Humanities Review v63 no2 p116-28 Summ 2009
Howls. Dabrowski, S. A.
How's death? Sallis, J.
How's that again? McClanahan, E.
Hoyt, Daniel A.
The Immaculate Collection
Confrontation no90/91 p158-65 Spr/Summ 2005
Hoyt, Sarah A.
Elvis died for your sins
This is my funniest 2; leading science fiction writers present their funniest stories ever; edited by Mike Resnick
While horse and hero fell
Places to be, people to kill; edited by Martin H. Greenberg and Brittianey A. Koren
Hua, Vanessa
For What They Shared
River Styx no78 p6-21 2008
Hubbard, Jennifer R.
Lunch with His Mother
The North American Review v293 no3/4 p48 My/Ag 2008
Hubbard, L. Ron (La Fayette Ron)
Battle of wizards
Hubbard, L. R. The professor was a thief
Danger in the dark
Hubbard, L. R. Danger in the dark
The dangerous dimension
Hubbard, L. R. The professor was a thief
He didn't like cats
Hubbard, L. R. Danger in the dark
The professor was a thief
Hubbard, L. R. The professor was a thief
The room
Hubbard, L. R. Danger in the dark
Hubbard, La Fayette Ron *See* Hubbard, L. Ron (La Fayette Ron), 1911-1986

Huberath, Marek S.
"Yoo retoont, sneogg. Ay noo."
The SFWA European hall of fame; sixteen contemporary masterpieces of science fiction from the continent; edited by James Morrow and Kathryn Morrow
Huddersfield versus Crewe. Beard, A.
Huddle, David
Volunteer
The Georgia Review v63 no1 p123-42 Spr 2009
Hudson, Jeffery *See* Crichton, Michael, 1942-2008
Huff, Tanya
Blood wrapped
Many bloody returns; edited by Charlaine Harris and Toni L. P. Kelner
Exactly
Places to be, people to kill; edited by Martin H. Greenberg and Brittianey A. Koren
A huge, old radio. Monson, A.
Hughes, Langston
Spanish blood
Manhattan noir 2; the classics; edited by Lawrence Block
Trouble with the angels
D.C. noir 2; the classics; edited by George Pelecanos.
Hughes, Mary-Beth
Honeymoon
The dictionary of failed relationships; 26 tales of love gone wrong; edited by Meredith Broussard
Hughes, Matthew
Bearing up
Hughes, M. The gist hunter and other stories
The devil you don't
Hughes, M. The gist hunter and other stories
Falberoth's ruin
Hughes, M. The gist hunter and other stories
Finding Sajessarian
Hughes, M. The gist hunter and other stories
The gist hunter
Hughes, M. The gist hunter and other stories
Go tell the Phoenicians
Hughes, M. The gist hunter and other stories
Help wonted
Hughes, M. The gist hunter and other stories
Inner huff
Hughes, M. The gist hunter and other stories
A little learning
Hughes, M. The gist hunter and other stories
Mastermindless
Hughes, M. The gist hunter and other stories
Relics of the Thim
Hughes, M. The gist hunter and other stories
Shadow man
Hughes, M. The gist hunter and other stories
Thwarting Jabbi Gloond
Hughes, M. The gist hunter and other stories
Hughes, Rhys
Castor on troubled waters
Fast ships, black sails; edited by Ann & Jeff VanderMeer
Hughes, Robert J.
A visit to St. Nick's
Bronx noir; edited by S. J. Rozan
Hughes, Ryan *See* Oltion, Jerry

Hughes, Tristan
Twelve beer blues
Urban Welsh; new short fiction; edited by Lewis Davies

Hugo, Ulrike
Undines Herz: Eine Erzählung über die (Un)Möglichkeit, sich im Wasser zu lieben . . .
Wagadu v3 p217-37 2006

Hugus, Frank
(tr.) See Brun, Lisbeth
(tr.) See Butschkow, Julia
(tr.) See Jensen, Kristian Ditlev
(tr.) See Josephsen, Mikael
(tr.) See Munch, Birgit

Hukumenoglu, Hikmet
The smell of fish
Istanbul noir; edited by Mustafa Ziyalan & Amy Spangler; translated by Amy Spangler & Mustafa Ziyalan.

Hulme, Juliet *See* Perry, Anne, 1938-
The **hum**. Hautala, R.
Hum drum. McMahan, G.

HUMAN ANATOMY
See also Eye; Nose; Teeth
The **Human** Atlas of Hackensack. Kuris, G.
The **human** front. MacLeod, K.

HUMAN SACRIFICE
Anaya, R. A. The village that the gods painted yellow
Cave, H. B. The coming
Kelly, R. Black harvest
Lovecraft, H. P. Discarded draft of The shadow over Innsmouth
Lovecraft, H. P. The shadow over Innsmouth
Smith, C. A. An offering to the moon
Wallace, D. Justice
The **human** season. Schutt, C.
The **human** soul as a Rube Goldberg device: a choose-your-own-adventure story. Brockmeier, K.
The **human** use of inhuman beings. Abbott, L. K.

Humaydan, Ibrahim Nassir al-
The shelter
Oranges in the sun; short stories from the Arabian Gulf; edited and translated by Deborah S. Akers, Abubaker A. Bagader

Humble pie. Buckler, E.

Hummel, Eleonora
The fish of Berlin [excerpt]
Words without borders; the world through the eyes of writers; an anthology; edited by Samantha Schnee, Alane Salierno Mason, and Dedi Felman
The **humming** of stars and bees and waves. Endrezze, A.

HUMOR
See also Parodies; Practical jokes; Satire
Allen, W. Above the law, below the box springs
Allen, W. Attention geniuses: cash only
Allen, W. Calisthenics, poison ivy, final cut
Allen, W. Caution, falling moguls
Allen, W. Glory hallelujah, sold!
Allen, W. How deadly your taste buds, my sweet
Allen, W. Nanny dearest
Allen, W. No kaddish for Weinstein
Allen, W. On a bad day you can see forever
Allen, W. Pinchuck's law

Allen, W. The rejection
Allen, W. Sam, you made the pants too fragrant
Allen, W. Sing, you sacher tortes
Allen, W. Strung out
Allen, W. Surprise rocks Disney trial
Allen, W. Tandoori ransom
Allen, W. This nib for hire
Allen, W. Thus ate Zarathustra
Allen, W. To err is human—to float, divine
Andrade, M. d. The Christmas turkey
Aylett, S. Voyage of the Iguana
Barthelme, D. Flying to America
Barthelme, D. Heather
Barthelme, D. Henrietta and Alexandra
Barthelme, D. The reference
Barthelme, D. Tales of the Swedish army
Bierce, A. A bit of chivalry
Bierce, A. Concerning balloons
Bierce, A. The failure of Hope & Wandel
Bierce, A. "The following dorg"
Bierce, A. Following the sea
Bierce, A. A holiday experience
Bierce, A. An imperfect conflagration
Bierce, A. Jeph Benedick's grandmother
Bierce, A. Jupiter Doke, Brigadier-General
Bierce, A. The miraculous guest
Bierce, A. Mrs. Dennison's head
Bierce, A. My credentials
Bierce, A. My favorite murder
Bierce, A. My muse
Bierce, A. Oil of dog
Bierce, A. Perry Chumly's eclipse
Bierce, A. The race at Left Bower
Bierce, A. A revolt of the gods
Bierce, A. Samuel Baxter, M.D.
Bierce, A. A scientific dream
Bierce, A. Sundered hearts
Bierce, A. That dog
Bierce, A. Why I am not editing "The stinger"
Bierce, A. The widower Turmore
Bierce, A. The wreck of the Orion
Bishop, T. The great Mormon cricket fly-fishing festival
Capote, T. Among the paths to Eden
Capote, T. My side of the matter
Cody, L. Where's Stacey?
Dann, J. and others. Afternoon at Schrafft's
De Camp, L. S. The gnarly man
Delaplace, B. Apecon
DiChario, N. Alien radio
Doctorow, C. To go boldly
Domecq, B. Mr. Clunk!
Donoghue, E. Do they know it's Christmas?
Donoghue, E. Touchy subjects
Downs, G. Freedom rides
Doyle, R. 57% Irish
Dozois, G. R. The hanging curve
Drake, D. Airborne all the way!
Fawcett, B. You'll catch your death of colds
Friesner, E. M. Abductio ad absurdum
Gaiman, N. Diseasemaker's group
Gaiman, N. Forbidden brides of the faceless slaves in the secret house of the night of dread desire
Gerencer, T. Primordial chili
Gerlach, G. Wedding in Voerde
Ghermandi, G. "The village telephone"
Greenman, B. A field guide to the North American Bigfoot

HUMOR—*Continued*

Greenman, B. Keep your eye on the bishop

Grimes, C. Farmer, pointing the way with a radish

Gunn, E. Stable strategies for middle management

Harris, A. L. Still life with boobs

Howe, J. Skillet and saber

Irvine, A. C. Gus dreams of biting the mailman

Íṣ.l'olá, A. The uses of English

Keret, E. Fatso

Keret, E. For only 9.99 (inc. tax and postage)

Keret, E. A good-looking couple

Kobrin, L. What he saw at the Yiddish theater

Kun, M. That will be ten cents

Kun, M. Touched, very touched

Lansdale, J. R. White mule, spotted pig

Lazellari, E. The date

Libin, Z. Digging his grave

Libin, Z. The impure street

Luongo, M. Boyfriends

Luongo, M. If the heart is lean

Malzberg, B. N. A delightful comedic premise

Marillier, J. Tough love 3001

Matheson, R. Clothes make the man

Matheson, R. The splendid source

Maxwell, W. A love story

Merril, J. Rain check

Merril, J. Stormy weather

Merril, J. Woman's work is never done!

Miller, T. The fifth tale: When the devil met Baldrick Beckenbauer

Molodowsky, K. The queen

Montemarano, N. The usual human disabilities

Moon, E. Say cheese

Niven, L. Breeding maze

Nolan, W. F. Hopping for Abe

Nolan, W. F. Killing Charlie

Nye, J. L. The growling

Palazzeschi, A. Dagobert

Parker, M. Hidden meanings: treatment of time, supreme irony, and life experiences in the song "Ain't gonna bump no more no big fat woman"

Pendarvis, J. Attention Johnny America! Please read!

Pendarvis, J. Dear People Magazine, keep up the great cyclops coverage

Pendarvis, J. My high, squeaky voice

Pendarvis, J. Our spring catalog

Powers, T. The better boy

Pratchett, T. Final reward

Pratchett, T. The Hades business

Pratchett, T. Hollywood chickens

Pratchett, T. # ifdefDEBUG + "world/enough" + "time"

Pratchett, T. The sea and little fishes

Pratchett, T. Theatre of cruelty

Pratchett, T. Turntables of the night

Rahman, I. All roads lead to flesh and bone

Rahman, I. Call me Manny

Rahman, I. Eating, Ohio

Rahman, I. From Kilgore to Kurtz, at the Steak 'n' Stage

Rahman, I. Here come the dog people

Rahman, I. I, Claudius

Rahman, I. I dream of microwaves

Rahman, I. Real, actual life

Reisen, A. Brother and beau

Reisen, A. "A couple of words"

Reisen, A. His trip to America

Reisen, A. Show-windows

Resnick, L. The capo of darkness

Resnick, M. Catastrophe Baker and a canticle for Leibowitz

Rich, M. Across the sky

Rich, M. Foggery

Rich, M. The real thing

Rickert, M. Angel face

Robinson, F. M. The Santa Claus planet

Robinson, S. Too hot to hoot

Rucker, R. v. B. Six thought experiments concerning the nature of computation: Experiment 1: Lucky number

Sargent, P. A smaller government

Scholes, K. Action team-ups number thirty-seven

Scholes, K. East of Eden and just a little bit south

Silverberg, R. The Science Fiction Hall of Fame

Singleton, G. The novels of Raymond Carver

Singleton, G. Soldiers in Gruel

Singleton, G. Soles in Gruel

Stevens, J. D. The joke

Tatsopoulos, P. A smelly weakness

Turtledove, H. Myth Manners' Guide to Greek Missology #1: Andromeda and Perseus

Veiga, J. J. The misplaced machine

Wadia, L.-A. L. "Ravi's wedding"

Wakkas, Y. "The Egyptian lover"

Waldrop, H. Avast, abaft!

Waldrop, H. The ugly chickens

Westlake, D. E. Love in the lean years

Westlake, D. E. Walking around money

Yates, D. Gophers

Yates, D. Persimmons

Yates, D. Reading Erica Jong

Zelazny, R. Fire and/or ice

Zelazny, R. Late, late show

Zoshchenko, M. The actor

Zoshchenko, M. A bad habit

Zoshchenko, M. Classy lady

Zoshchenko, M. The galosh

Zoshchenko, M. A glass

Zoshchenko, M. A hasty business

Zoshchenko, M. In praise of transport

Zoshchenko, M. Passenger

Zoshchenko, M. Red tape

Zoshchenko, M. The thief

Zoshchenko, M. What generosity

The **humorist**. Levin, Z.

HUMOROUS STORIES *See* Humor

Humphrey, William

A voice from the woods

Lone Star literature; from the Red River to the Rio Grande; edited by Don Graham

Humphreys, Helen

The Whole Story

The Walrus v6 no3 p48-9, 51 Ap 2009

Hunault, Adam

The Royal Flush Saga

Iowa Review v36 no3 p80-96 Wint 2006/2007

The **hunchback**. Palazzeschi, A.

HUNCHBACKS

Palazzeschi, A. The hunchback

Vila-Matas, E. Bartleby & Co. [excerpt]

The **hunchback's** affair. Bunin, I. A.

Hunchback's romance. *See* Bunin, I. A. The hunchback's affair

The **hundred** and ninety-nine steps. Faber, M.

A **Hundred** Fires. Farquhar, P.

The **hundredth** dove. Yolen, J.

The **hundredth** kill. Marco, J.

Hungarian lessons. Steinhauer, O.

HUNGARIANS

Canada

Dobozy, T. Four uncles

Dobozy, T. The inert landscapes of György Ferenc

South Africa

Gordimer, N. Alternative endings: the first sense

United States

Goss, T. A statement in the case

HUNGARY

Dobozy, T. Four uncles

Gospodinov, G. A second story

Krasznahorkai, L. War and war [excerpt]

Communism

See Communism—Hungary

World War, 1939-1945

See World War, 1939-1945—Hungary

Budapest

Cozarinsky, E. Budapest

Déry, T. Behind the brick wall

Déry, T. The circus

Déry, T. Games of the underworld

Déry, T. Love

Déry, T. Reckoning

Déry, T. Two women

James, C. L. R. Children in the resistance

Kalman, J. Personal effects

HUNGER

See also Starvation

Andrade, M. d. It can hurt plenty

Baingana, D. Hunger

Frankel-Zaltzman, P. A natural death

Gordimer, N. The ultimate safari

Rivera-Valdes, S. Life leads

Roman, C. Vendors of peculiar objects

Shafi'i, M. a.- . Hunger

Watkins, S. Family of man

Williams, W. J. The Green Leopard Plague

Xu Xi. Famine

Zoshchenko, M. Casual work

Hunger. Baingana, D.

Hunger. Lam, A.

Hunger. Means, D.

Hunger. Oates, J. C.

Hunger. Shafi'i, M. a.- .

Hunger. Singh, V.

Hunger. Stevens, J. D.

Hunger. Sundaresan, I.

Hunger. Thompson, J.

Hunger: a confession. Bailey, D.

Hungers. Romano, T.

Hungry. Cadnum, M.

Hungry de catch me. McCauley, W.

Hungry enough. Read, C.

Hungry self. Curtis, R.

Hunsicker, Harry

Iced

Thriller 2; stories you just can't put down; edited by Clive Cussler; [stories by] Kathleen Antrim . . . [et al.]

Hunt, Howard

Sovietski!

Best of Tin House; stories; foreword by Dorothy Allison

Hunt, Laird

From Ray of the Star (a novel)

Western Humanities Review v62 no2 p16-22 Spr/Summ 2008

Kissability

Noise; fiction inspired by Sonic Youth; edited bt Peter Wild; introduction by Lee Ranaldo

Hunt, Samantha

Love machine

This is not chick lit; original stories by America's best women writers; edited by Elizabeth Merrick

Three Days

The New Yorker v81 no44 p68-75 Ja 16 2006

The **hunt** for Dmitri. Lynds, G.

Hunted down. Dickens, C.

Hunter, Evan

The last spin

Manhattan noir 2; the classics; edited by Lawrence Block

Hunter, Evan, 1926-2005

For works written by this author under other names see McBain, Ed, 1926-2005

Hunter, Stephen

Stephen Longacre's greatest match

Murder is my racquet; edited by Otto Penzler

Hunter/Trapper. Nersesian, A.

The **hunter**. Arnow, H. L. S.

The **Hunter**. Bychkov, A.

The **hunter**. Oates, J. C.

The **hunter**. Parra, E. A.

Hunter, Killer. Gallagher, S.

Hunter Lake. Wolfe, G.

HUNTERS *See* Hunting

Hunters. Fulton, J.

Hunters. Ruffin, P.

Hunters. Wideman, J. E.

Hunters and Gatherers. Patterson, C.

Hunters and hunted. Carew, J.

The **hunters** from beyond. Smith, C. A.

Hunters in the forest. Silverberg, R.

Hunters in the snow. Wolff, T.

Hunter's Moon. Lynch, T.

The **Hunters,** the Hunted. Opie, J.

HUNTING

See also Duck hunting; Fox hunting; Trappers and trapping

Allyn, D. Dead as a dog

Angel, J. The skin from the muscle

Asher, N. Softly spoke the gabbleduck

Bass, R. Her first elk

Bierce, A. An ancient hunter

Bierce, A. A mirage in Arizona

Bishop, T. The contest

Bishop, T. The vision of Hehaka 'To

Blaeser, K. M. Like some old story

Buckler, E. The wild goose

Campbell, B. J. Family reunion

Coyne, S. Hunting country

Currans-Sheehan, T. The last trapshoot

D'Ambrosio, C., Jr. Up North

De Camp, L. S. A gun for dinosaur

Erdrich, L. History of the Puyats

Fulton, J. Hunters

Harrison, W. Dove season

HUNTING—*Continued*

Haschemeyer, O. The soldier as a boy
Hildebrand, J. Touching bottom
Jones, S. G. Nobody knows this
Judah, S. Hunting and fishing
Kelly, J. P. Luck
Leonard, E. The big hunt [variant title: Matt Gordon's boy]
Malouf, D. The Valley of Lagoons
Mindt, A. Stories of the hunt
Percy, B. When the bear came
Percy, B. The woods
Quiroga, H. The son
Rand, K. Trophy kill
Resnick, M. Bwana
Resnick, M. Hunting the snark
Resnick, M. The soul eater
Resnick, M. Stalking the unicorn with guns and camera
Rickert, M. Moorina of the seals
Rosa, J. G. The jaguar
Ruffin, P. Hunters
Sanders, W. Amba
Seton, E. T. Badlands Billy, the wolf that won
Seton, E. T. Monarch, the big bear of Tallac
Shepard, L. The jaguar hunter
Shirley, P. The turkey hunt
Shroff, M. F. A different bhel
Sillitoe, A. The other John Peel
Silverberg, R. Hunters in the forest
Smith, R. T. Bitterwolf
Steele, A. M. The teb hunter
Swann, M. The outlaws
Tudish, C. Jordan's stand
Wallace, J. The big five
Weaver, W. Heart of the fields
Weaver, W. Marked for death
Westcott, G. The whistling swan
Wolfe, G. Try and kill it
Wolff, T. Hunters in the snow
Yolen, J. Brother Hart

HUNTING ACCIDENTS

Abrams, L. Taj Mahal
Hunting and fishing. Judah, S.
Hunting country. Coyne, S.
Hunting knife. Murakami, H.
Hunting meth zombies in the great Nebraskan wasteland. Farris, J.
Hunting rogues. Russell, W.
Hunting the Slarque. Brown, E.
Hunting the snark. Resnick, M.
Hunting the wooly mammoth. Tolstaia, T.

Huntington, Clara
The Wildflower
Idaho Magazine v3 no10 p4-6 Jl 2004

Huntington, Clara R.
The Boy Friend Test
Idaho Magazine v4 no9 p50-5 Je 2005

Hunton, Eunice Roberta
Digression
"Tell it to us easy" and other stories; a complete short fiction anthology of African American women writers in Opportunity magazine, (1923-1948); edited by Judith Musser.

Replica
"Tell it to us easy" and other stories; a complete short fiction anthology of African American women writers in Opportunity magazine, (1923-1948); edited by Judith Musser.
Who gives himself
"Tell it to us easy" and other stories; a complete short fiction anthology of African American women writers in Opportunity magazine, (1923-1948); edited by Judith Musser.
Huntress moon. York, R.
The **Huntsman**. Holinger, R.

Hurd, Donald Lucio
Guadalupe and the taxman
New stories from the Southwest; edited by D. Seth Horton; foreword by Ray Gonzalez.

Hurdi, Carolyn Ann Marie DeGarza
Noel
Tribal College Journal of American Indian Higher Education v18 no1 p33 Fall 2006
Hurdles. Fisher, C.
The **hurler**. Ochsner, G.
"**Hurrah** for Captain Early". Leonard, E.
The **hurricane** dance. MacEnulty, P.

HURRICANE KATRINA, 2005

Adcock, T. Lawyers' tongues
Allan, S. If there's a hell below, we're all gonna go
Atkins, A. Angola South
Burke, J. L. Jesus out to sea
Burke, J. L. Mist
Rossi, J. C. And hell walked in
Smith, J. Loot
Tan, M. Muddy pond
Wiltz, C. Night taxi
Hurricane Party, 2002. Jahna, R.

HURRICANES

Burke, J. L. Water people
Davis, J. S. Rapture
Dufresne, J. Johnny too bad
Graham, H. The face in the window
Gurganus, A. Fourteen feet of water in my house
Helprin, M. Sail shining in white
Hendricks, V. The big O
Hogan, L. Descent
Kazumi Stahl, A. Natural disasters
McGlynn, D. The end of the straight and narrow
Oates, J. C. Upon the sweeping flood
Trevor, D. Labor Day hurricane, 1935
Hurry call for hangin' Gus. Bonham, F.

Hurston, Zora Neale
Drenched in light
"Tell it to us easy" and other stories; a complete short fiction anthology of African American women writers in Opportunity magazine, (1923-1948); edited by Judith Musser.
John Redding goes to sea
"Tell it to us easy" and other stories; a complete short fiction anthology of African American women writers in Opportunity magazine, (1923-1948); edited by Judith Musser.

Hurston, Zora Neale—*Continued*

Muttsy
  "Tell it to us easy" and other stories; a complete short fiction anthology of African American women writers in Opportunity magazine, (1923-1948); edited by Judith Musser.

Spunk
  "Tell it to us easy" and other stories; a complete short fiction anthology of African American women writers in Opportunity magazine, (1923-1948); edited by Judith Musser.

HURSTON, ZORA NEALE, 1891-1960
About

Duncan, A. Zora and the zombie

The **hurt** man. Berry, W.

Hürtgen. Doyle, B.

Hurting Hugh. de Chambrey, M.

Hurwitz, Gregg

Dirty weather
  Thriller; edited by James Patterson

The real thing
  Meeting across the river; stories inspired by the haunting Bruce Springsteen song; edited by Jessica Kaye and Richard J. Brewer

Husayn, 'Abd Allah

An encounter
  Oranges in the sun; short stories from the Arabian Gulf; edited and translated by Deborah S. Akers, Abubaker A. Bagader

Husband. Jackson, S.

HUSBAND AND WIFE

See also Desertion and nonsupport; Marriage

Abbott, L. K. What Y was

Aird, C. Due dilligence

Ali, M. N. The manhood test

Amdahl, G. The free fall

Anaya, R. A. Iliana of the pleasure dreams

Anderson, B. Commitment

Anderson, B. Real beach weather

Anderson, B. Rollo's dairy (Jake and Deedee)

Anderson, B. Shanties

Anderson, B. So lovely of them

Archer, J. Don't drink the water

Archer, J. The man who robbed his own post office

Arnow, H. L. S. The first ride

Arnow, H. L. S. Love?

Auchincloss, L. The omelette and the egg

Auslander, S. The war of the Bernsteins

Averill, T. F. The man who ran with deer

Baingana, D. Green stones

Barkley, B. The properties of stainless steel

Barkley, B. The small machine

Barnes, J. Appetite

Barnes, J. The fruit cage

Barr, N. GDMFSOB

Barry, R. Men shoot things to kill them

Barth, J. Assisted living

Barthelme, D. Tickets

Bass, R. The windy day

Baumbach, J. The fields of obscurity

Beagle, P. S. The last and only or, Mr. Moscowitz becomes french

Beagle, P. S. The last and only, or Mr. Moskowitz becomes french

Bennett, T. Antioxidants

Bennett, T. Matinee

Bensko, J. A cabin in the woods

Bensko, J. Flying St. Croix

Berg, E. Double diet

Berg, E. The only one of millions just like him

Berg, E. Returns and exchanges

Bierce, A. The affair at Coulter's Notch

Bierce, A. Hanner's wit

Bierce, A. The man out of the nose

Bierce, A. The widower Turmore

Bingham, S. Pleyben

Bingham, S. Porn

Blackwell, K. George, Nadia, Blaise

Blackwell, K. Heartbeatland

Blackwell, K. The minaret

Blackwell, K. The obi tree

Blackwell, K. Queen of the May

Blackwell, K. The secret life of peonies

Boudinot, R. Newholly

Bradbury, R. And the sailor, home from the sea

Bradbury, R. Arrival and departure

Bradbury, R. Doubles

Bradbury, R. A literary encounter

Bradbury, R. Miss Appletree and I

Bradbury, R. Remember Sascha?

Brady, C. Last of the true believers

Brady, C. Much have I traveled

Brady, C. Seven remedies

Brazaitis, M. The race

Brenchley, C. Going the Jerusalem mile

Buckler, E. Cleft rock, with spring

Buckler, E. The finest tree

Buckler, E. Glance in the mirror

Buckman, D. Pure products

Budnitz, J. Underdog

Bukoski, A. I, miss Lillian [variant title: I, Lillian]

Bukoski, A. Shovel work

Busch, F. The barrens

Busch, F. The hay behind the house

Busch, F. Manhattans

Busch, F. Now that it's spring

Cadnum, M. Bite the hand

Cadnum, M. Elf trap

Cadnum, M. The flounder's kiss

Caine, R. Roman holidays; or, SPQ-arrrrrr

Campbell, B. J. The solutions to Brian's problem

Campra, Rosalba. Dream tiger

Caponegro, M. Ashes ashes we all fall down

Capote, T. Mojave

Ch'ae, M. The wife and children

Chekhov, A. P. The intentional deception

Chekhov, A. P. The man who wanted revenge

Christie, A. Philomel cottage

Clarke, B. The Hotel Utica

Clarke, S. Lickerish Hill

Clayton, J. J. The contract

Clayton, J. J. Night talk

Coake, C. Solos

Coben, H. Entrapped

Coleman, W. Pepper

Coloane, F. The lighthouse builder

Connell, E. S. Mrs. Proctor Bemis

Cooper, D. Night coming

Crane, E. The most everything in the world

Crouse, D. Retreat

Crowther, P. The space between the lines

Cutler, J. Judith

HUSBAND AND WIFE—*Continued*

HUSBAND AND WIFE—*Continued*

Spencer, E. The boy in the tree
Spies, O. The love of a strong man
Steinke, D. Orgasm
Sterling, B. The denial
Sterling, B. and Di Filippo, P. The scab's progress
Stern, D. The future
Stern, R. G. Dr. Cahn's visit
Stern, R. G. Gardiner's legacy
Stevens, J. D. Fish story
Stewart, P. Ham
Swan, G. Women who don't tell war stories
Tabor, M. L. The burglar
Tabor, M. L. Guarding the pie
Tabor, M. L. To swim?
Tabor, M. L. Trouble with kitchens
Takagi, N. The shadow of the orchid
Talley, M. Driven to distraction
Tambour, A. Gladiolus ezposed
Tan, C. Bambino road, chapter one
Tem, S. R. Eggs
Templeton, E. The blue hour
Theroux, P. Monkey Hill
Thompson, J. Escape
Thompson, J. Liberty tax
Todd, R. L. Vinegar
Tomlinson, J. Overburden
Tomlinson, J. Rose
Treat, J. Beached
Trevor, D. The surprising weight of the body's organs
Trevor, W. Another Christmas
Trezise, R. A little boy
Ts'an-hsüeh. Burial
Ts'an-hsüeh. The lure of the sea
Tudish, C. Pigeon
Turnbull, P. Max Winner's shadow
Uchida, H. The pier
Unger, D. Tide pool
Updike, J. The apparition
Updike, J. Marching through Boston
Van Booy, S. Conception
Van Booy, S. Everyday things
Van Booy, S. Everything is a beautiful trick
Van Booy, S. Snow falls and then disappears
Viets, E. Red meat
Wallace, D. Slippered feet
Wallace, D. A terrible thing
Ward, A. E. Motherhood and terrorism
Ward, A. E. Shakespeare.com
Ward, A. E. She almost wrote
Ward, A. E. Should I be scared?
Ward, A. E. The stars are bright in Texas
Waters, D. Little sins
Watkins, S. Camouflage
Watkins, S. Painting the baby's room
Weaver, W. Blaze of glory
Weaver, W. The gleaners
Welch, N. Texas sounds like an easy place to leave
Welch, N. Welcome to the neighborhood
Wendroff, Z. Zlatte's misfortune
West, D. Bent twig
West, D. Wives and women
Westlake, D. E. Love in the lean years
Wilhelm, K. No light in the window
Williams, C. The owl

Wilson, K. The choir director affair (The baby's teeth)
Winn, T. Blue tango
Winn, T. Glass box
Winn, T. Gumbo limbo
Winton, T. Damaged goods
Winton, T. Defender
Wolff, T. Desert breakdown, 1968
Wolff, T. Lady's dream
Wolff, T. Next door
Wolff, T. Say yes
Wood, M. Ernie's ark
Working, R. The sky ranch
Woronov, M. The Amazon
Yellin, T. Naphtali
Yellin, T. Strangers on a train
Youmans, M. An incident at Agate Beach
Yu, C. 401(k)
Yu, F. S. Social contract
Zelazny, R. Come to me not in winter's white
Zelazny, R. Final dining
Zoshchenko, M. An anonymous friend

Husband of the Bee. Sonnenmoser, R.
Husband, wife. Strom, D.
A **hush**. Levin, Z.
Hushabye. Bestwick, S.

Hussein, Ameena
  An Ordinary Death
    Iowa Review v36 no2 p63-5 Fall 2006

Hussin, Jabbar Yussin
  The day in Buenos Aires
    Words without borders; the world through the eyes of writers; an anthology; edited by Samantha Schnee, Alane Salierno Mason, and Dedi Felman

The **hustle**. Jordan, P.

Huston, Charlie
  Interrogation B
    A hell of a woman; an anthology of female noir; edited by Megan Abbott; foreword by Val McDermid
  Like a lady
    Expletive deleted; edited by Jen Jordan

Huston, Nancy
  Faces of Dawn
    Salmagundi no144/145 p47-80 Fall 2004/Wint 2005

Hutchins, Feng Feng
  The Tab
    Feminist Studies v33 no3 p510-17 Fall 2007

Hutchins, Scott
  Jack
    StoryQuarterly v42 p443-62 2006

Hutchinson, Dave
  The pavement artist
    The Year's best fantasy and horror: nineteenth annual collection; edited by Ellen Datlow and Kelly Link & Gavin J. Grant

Hwang, Frances
  Blue hour
    Hwang, F. Transparency; stories
  Garden city
    Hwang, F. Transparency; stories
  Giving a clock
    Hwang, F. Transparency; stories
  Intruders
    Hwang, F. Transparency; stories
  The modern age
    Hwang, F. Transparency; stories

Hwang, Frances—*Continued*
The old gentleman
Best of Tin House; stories; foreword by Dorothy Allison
Hwang, F. Transparency; stories
Remedies
Hwang, F. Transparency; stories
Sonata for the left hand
Hwang, F. Transparency; stories
Transparency
Hwang, F. Transparency; stories
A visit to the suns
Hwang, F. Transparency; stories
Hwang, Sogyong
A dream of good fortune
Land of exile: contemporary Korean fiction; translated and edited by Marshall Pihl, Bruce Fulton, and Ju-Chan Fulton
Hwang, Sunwon
Mountains
Land of exile: contemporary Korean fiction; translated and edited by Marshall Pihl, Bruce Fulton, and Ju-Chan Fulton
Hwawon, Lim
The American Boyfriend
Harper's v312 p24-5 Je 2006
Hyacinths. Randolph, L.
Hyde, Catherine Ryan
Dancing with Elinor
Gettysburg Review v19 no2 p189-200 Summ 2006
Hyde, Michael
The clay is vile
Hyde, M. What are you afraid of?
Everything valuable and portable
Hyde, M. What are you afraid of?
Her Hollywood
Hyde, M. What are you afraid of?
Hydra
Hyde, M. What are you afraid of?
Life among the bulrushes
Hyde, M. What are you afraid of?
Miracle-Gro
Hyde, M. What are you afraid of?
People's choice
Hyde, M. What are you afraid of?
Second-hand
Hyde, M. What are you afraid of?
What are you afraid of?
Hyde, M. What are you afraid of?
What is now proved was once only imagined
Hyde, M. What are you afraid of?
Hyder, Qurratulain
The sermons of Haji Gul Baba Bektashi
Gibson, M. E. Separate journeys; short stories by contemporary Indian women; edited by Geeta Dharmarajan; introduction by Mary Ellis Gibson
Hydra. Hyde, M.
HYDROGEN BOMB *See* Atomic bomb
Hydroplane. Steinberg, S.
Hymn. Bender, A.
Hymn to Kalliope. Taylor, E.
HYPNOSIS *See* Hypnotism
HYPNOTISM
Bierce, A. An adventure at Brownville
Bierce, A. The hypnotist
Bierce, A. The realm of the unreal
Menger-Anderson, K. The baquet, 1850

The **hypnotist**. Bierce, A.
HYPOCHONDRIA
Gaiman, N. Diseasemaker's group
Stafford, J. The liberation
HYPOCRISY
Barnard, R. The life-lie
Bierce, A. The conflagration in Ghargaroo
Bierce, A. The famous Gilson bequest
Modesitt, L. E., Jr. Second coming
Molodowsky, K. The meeting
Hypocrites. Saunders, G.
Hysteria, 1820. Menger-Anderson, K.
Hyzy, Julie
Five sorrowful mysteries
At the scene of the crime; forensic mysteries from today's best writers; edited by Dana Stabenow

I

I/M-print: a Tess Cassidy short story. Healy, J. F.
I. Bano, J.
I Am a Novelist. Murakami, R.
I am as I am. Almond, S.
I Am Awake. McDermott, A.
I am coming to live in your mouth. Hirshberg, G.
I am complete. Das, V.
I am dangerous. Johnson, G.
I am important. Wendroff, Z.
I Am Listening. Turner, P.
I am Meyer. Howell, C. K.
I Am Not Your Happiness. Hepler, H.
I am not your mother. Mattison, A.
I Am the Author of My Own Life. McCarthy, R.
I am the news. Busch, F.
I and You. Stevens, J. D.
I asked my mother. Dormen, L.
I begyn as I mean to go on. Baker, K.
I bring the lip balm. Tognazzini, A.
I cain't go. Bishop, T.
I can hear the grass grow. Ray, R.
I can speak!. Saunders, G.
I carry a hammer in my pocket for occasions such as these. Tognazzini, A.
I, Claudius. Rahman, I.
I could love you (if I wanted). Keeble, J.
I don't believe this. Gerber, M. J.
I don't fool around. Block, L.
I dream of microwaves. Rahman, I.
I, earthling. Coville, B.
I got somebody in Staunton. Lewis, W. H.
I Hate the Moon. Yang Xianhui
I have lost my right. Smith, R. T.
I Have Seen Some Dirty Things. Hill, N.
I have work to do. Gildner, G.
I hold my father's paws. Levine, D. D.
I killed. Pickard, N.
I killed Jennie. See McBain, E. Chalk [variant title: I killed Jennie]
I kiss a door. July, M.
I Kneel Before You. Davis, R.
I know something you don't know. Smith, A.
I know what I'm doing about all the attention I've been getting. Gannon, F.
I know who you ate last summer. Holder, N.
I learned when I was older. Evans, M.
I left my heart in Skaftafell. LaValle, V.

The **ile** of dogges. Bear, E. and Monette, S.
Iles, Francis *See* Berkeley, Anthony, 1893-1971
Iliana of the pleasure dreams. Anaya, R. A.
Ilk. Shields, C.
I'll be doggone. Woods, P. L.
I'll be home. Ebenbach, D. H.
I'll be your sailor. Meno, J.
I'll give you my word. Jones, D. W.
I'll gnaw your bones, the manticore said. Rambo, C.
I'll take the high road. Bonham, F.
Ill-timed. Caponegro, M.
ILLEGAL ALIENS *See* Undocumented aliens
The **illegibility** of this world. Stern, R. G.
ILLEGITIMACY
> *See also* Unmarried mothers
> Arnow, H. L. S. No lady
> Babel, I. The sin of Jesus
> Bunin, I. A. Little fool
> Dalton, Q. The music you never hear
> Gallagher, S. The Plot
> Gautreaux, T. Welding with children
> Iarovici, D. Facts
> Ingalls, R. The archaeologist's daughter
> Ingalls, R. Fertility
> Lins, O. Baroque tale; or, Tripartite unity
> Morrison, P. Morocco Junction 90210
> Robinson, R. Choosing sides
> Sundaresan, I. The most unwanted

ILLINOIS
> Maxwell, W. Billie Dyer
> McIlvoy, K. The rhino in the barn
> Orner, P. Pampkin's lament
> **Politics**
> *See* Politics—Illinois
> **Chicago**
> Allen, J. R. Bread and the land
> Allen, J. R. Dog tags
> Black, M. A. Chasing the blues
> Brod, D. C. My heroes have always been short-stops
> Butcher, J. Day off
> Butcher, J. Heorot
> Butcher, J. The warrior
> Carlson, P. M. Frighted out of fear; or, the bombs bursting in air
> Crane, E. Varieties of loudness in Chicago
> Dills, T. Arcadia
> Dybek, S. Breasts
> Dybek, S. The Palatski Man
> Engberg, S. Reunion
> Fredrickson, J. Good evenin', blues
> Galaviz-Budziszewski, A. Maximillian
> Gifford, B. The ciné
> Gifford, B. My catechism
> Gorman, E. Yesterday's dreams
> Greenman, B. Batting cleanup
> Grimwood, J. C. Chicago
> Hellmann, L. F. The whole world is watching
> Hellmann, L. F. Your sweet man
> Hemon, A. Good living
> Hemon, A. Szmura's room
> Kaminsky, S. M. Blue note
> Konrath, J. A. Epitaph
> LaBrie, A. Look at the sky and tell me what you see
> LaBrie, A. Six different ways to die in the windy city!
> LaBrie, A. Tribute to an optometrist

> LaBrie, A. Wanted
> Langer, A. Bobby Kagan knows everything
> Levitsky, R. The blue line
> Li Yiyun. The princess of Nebraska
> Lunstrum, K. S. The bath
> Mandel, S. B. Blind man blue
> Margulis, L. Conceits
> Meno, J. Like a rocket with a beat
> Meyers, M. K. Monkey head
> Obejas, A. Destiny returns
> Ojikutu, B. The gospel of moral ends
> Pinkerton, B. Lower wacker blues
> Reaves, S. The test
> Rollins, W. Chicago confetti
> Sakey, M. No one
> Saunders, G. Christmas
> Stern, R. G. Chicago, in the depths of feeling
> Stern, R. G. East, West . . . Midwest
> Stern, R. G. Idylls of Dugan and Strunk
> Stern, R. G. Ins and outs
> Stern, R. G. La pourriture noble
> Sullivan, C. J. Alex Pinto hears the bell
> Walker, D. J. A weekend in the country
> Welk, M. V. Code blue
> Welsh, I. The DOGS of Lincoln Park
> Working, R. The tin man
> Zulkey, C. The great Billik
Illinois. Munro, A.
ILLITERACY *See* Literacy
ILLNESS
> *See also* Invalids; Mental illness; Terminal illness
> Adrian, C. The sum of our parts
> Andreas-Salomé, L. Unit for "Men, internal"
> Arnold, G. Heart trouble
> Arnow, H. L. S. Tin cup
> Barkley, B. The way it's lasted
> Baumbach, J. The Villa Mondare
> Beattie, A. The rabbit hole as likely explanation
> Beattie, A. The rabbitt hole as likely explanantion
> Bender, A. Death wish
> Caponegro, M. Ill-timed
> Ch'oe, S. Conviction
> Cozarinsky, E. View of dawn over the lake
> Davis, J. S. Lovely Lily
> DeMarinis, R. Freaks
> Desaulniers, J. Never, ever, always
> Dunbar, P. L. The faith cure man
> Dunbar, P. L. The finish of Patsy Barnes
> Fincke, G. The Armstrong view
> Finlay, C. C. Lucy, in her splendor
> Finlay, C. C. Still life with action figure
> Gordon, M. Sick in London
> Goss, T. Lily, with clouds
> Graham, B. All the bad stuff
> Grimes, C. Examination of an afflicted man
> Guista, M. The old country
> Hanlon, M. The long, dark voyage
> Hempel, A. What were the white things?
> Hwang, F. Transparency
> Jablonski, N. The good life
> James, C. L. R. Bruno the bulldog has heart pain
> James, C. L. R. Bruno the bulldog has heart pain--Continued
> Jones, S. G. Carbon
> Kenney, S. The death of the dog and other rescues

ILLNESS—*Continued*

Lanagan, M. Night of the firstlings

Lapcharoensap, R. Don't let me die in a place like this

Lapcharoensap, R. Sightseeing

Lupoff, R. A. The Crimson Wizard

Mandelbaum, P. The explorers

Marusek, D. Listen to me

McCauley, W. Foday

McIntyre, V. Disability

McKenzie, E. We know where we are, but not why

Meno, J. A strange episode of *Aqua Voyage*

Monk, B. Do not revive

Munro, A. Home

Murray, A. The tonsil machine

Naiyer Masud. Weather vane

Nfah-Abbenyi, J. M. Slow poison

Olafsson, O. January

Olafsson, O. July

O'Shaughnessy, P. To still the beating of her heart

Pearlman, E. Signs of life

Qi, S. Fatherhood

Reinhorn, H. The heights

Rheinheimer, K. Hooks

Robinson, R. The treatment

Rust, E. M. Vital organs

Seamon, H. The plagiarist

Shepard, J. Proto-scorpions of the silurian

Shua, A. M. Death as a side effect

Simpson, H. If I'm spared

Stafford, J. A country love story

Stamm, P. The stop

Stewart, P. Shit happens

Stuckey-French, E. Mudlavia

Thomas, E. The friend of the blackbird

Thomas, J. Pink pills

Ts'an-hsüeh. Helin

Uchida, H. The ascension

Unger, D. Tide pool

Wendroff, Z. Alas–I recovered

Wendroff, Z. I am important

Willis, C. Cash crop

Working, R. Inmates

Woronov, M. The Amazon

Wright, P. Looking for Aimee

Illumination. Gilman, L. A.

The **Illusionist**. Sweetman, C.

ILLUSIONS *See* Hallucinations and illusions

The **illustrated** biography of Lord Grimm. Gregory, D.

ILLUSTRATORS

Murakami, H. Nausea 1979

Ochsner, G. From the fourth row

Im, Choru

A shared journey

Land of exile: contemporary Korean fiction; translated and edited by Marshall Pihl, Bruce Fulton, and Ju-Chan Fulton

Im, Mary

To the Lady that Thinks She Knows

Amerasia Journal v35 no1 p192 2009

I'm going on strike. Gordin, J.

I'm here, you're there. Clayton, J. J.

I'm No Ingres Odalisque. Desprat, J.-P.

I'm Not Italian. Fagan, C.

I'm not quite finished yet. Martin, J.

I'm on Fire. O'Loughlin, J.

[Im-] Plausible fantasies, or A journey in the 29th century [abridged] Bulgarin, F. V.

I'm slavering. Lipsyte, S.

IMAGINARY ANIMALS *See* Mythical animals

IMAGINARY CITIES

Goss, T. The rapid advance of sorrow

Pratt, T. Dream engine

Rosenbaum, B. Other cities

Silverberg, R. Getting across

Smith, C. A. Beyond the singing flame

Smith, C. A. The city of the singing flame

Smith, C. A. The seven geases

Sterling, B. Dinner in Audoghast

Swann, S. A. The historian's apprentice

Valente, C. M. Palimpsest

Wolfe, G. Comber

IMAGINARY KINGDOMS

Bierce, A. The City of the Gone Away

Bierce, A. The dog in Ganegwag

Bierce, A. An execution in Batrugia

Bierce, A. The Golampians

Bierce, A. The kingdom of Tortirra

Bierce, A. The land beyond the blow

Bierce, A. Marooned on Ug

Bierce, A. Sons of the fair star

Bierce, A. The Tamtonians

Bierce, A. Trustland: a tale of a traveler

Bierce, A. The wizard of Bumbassa

Chase, M. The terminal project

Flewelling, L. Perfection

Ford, J. At reparata

Johnson, J. Birthright

Meaney, J. Sideways from now

Palazzeschi, A. The beautiful king

Shinn, S. The double-edged sword

Wells, M. The potter's daughter

Williams, L. Mortegarde

Yolen, J. Evian steel

York, R. Huntress moon

IMAGINARY PLAYMATES

Rich, M. The suckers

Whiteley, A. Geoffrey says

IMAGINARY WARS AND BATTLES

Coleman, L. L. Cold dead fingers

Cook, G. Filed teeth

Dellamonica, A. M. Time of the snake

Dietz, W. C. The run to Hardscrabble Station

Drake, D. The day of glory

Fawcett, B. Last of the fourth

Lindskold, J. and Saberhagen, F. Servant of death

McDonald, I. Sanjeev and Robotwallah

Nye, J. L. The growling

Robson, J. The girl hero's mirror says he's not the one

The **imagination** of disaster. Gordon, M.

Imagine this!. Smith, M.

Imagining Bisbee. Rodriguez, A.

The **imago** sequence. Barron, L.

Imitate the sun. Sholer, L.

Imitation. Adichie, C. N.

The **Immaculate** Collection. Hoyt, D. A.

The **immeasurable** horror. Smith, C. A.

Immersion. Budnitz, J.

IMMIGRANTS

Ahmed, F. "Return"

Alarcón, D. Absence

Andrews, R. Solomon's alley

Asch, S. A surrendered home

INSANITY—*Continued*

Spark, M. The leaf-sweeper

Stevens, F. Unseen—unfeared

Van Booy, S. The shepherd on the rock

An **Insanity,** a Madness, a Furor. Rinaldi, N.

Inscription. Yolen, J.

The **insect.** Castillon, C.

Insect dreams. Stevenson, R. P.

Insect men of Boston. Sallis, J.

INSECTS

Bensko, J. Creeping things

Klages, E. Intelligent design

Sterling, B. Luciferase

Stevenson, R. P. Insect dreams

Wilson, F. P. Part of the game

Zelazny, R. Stand pat, Ruby Stone

INSEMINATION, ARTIFICIAL *See* Artificial insemination

Insensates. Kulpa, K.

Inside. Shimamoto, R.

Inside job. Willis, C.

Inside out. MacEnulty, P.

Inside Out. Mo Yan

Inside Outside. Reeve, F. D.

The **inside** passage. Thompson, J.

An **Inside** Story. Strand, M.

Inside the Dog.

Inside the hole. Wingate, S.

Inside the Iron Maiden. Schlich, S.

Inside This New Skin. Blakinger, K.

Inside track. Charters, D.

The **insider.** Zelazny, R.

Insiders. Palahniuk, C.

An **insistent** tide. Lam, V.

INSOMNIA

Chazin, S. Burnout

Fincke, G. The history of staying awake

Ford, J. The bedroom light

Johnson, C. R. Better than counting sheep

Meno, J. A strange episode of *Aqua Voyage*

Sallis, J. I saw Robert Johnson

Insomnia for a better tomorrow. Lin, T.

The **inspection.** Grimes, C.

INSPIRATION *See* Creation (Literary, artistic, etc.)

Instant labor. Lain, D.

Instituto. Kesey, R.

Instructions for a substitute bus driver. Barry, R.

Instructions for surviving the destruction of Star-Probe X-11-57. Brown, E.

INSTRUCTORS *See* Teachers

The **Insufferable** Gaucho. Bolaño, R.

Insulting the angels. Hoffman, A.

INSURANCE

Bierce, A. Insurance in ancient America

Bova, B. Acts of God

Goodis, D. Never too old to burn

INSURANCE, LIFE *See* Life insurance

The **Insurance** Adjuster. Toma, T. L.

INSURANCE BROKERS

Baker, K. The angel in the darkness

Gappah, P. Midnight at the Hotel California

Moody, R. K & K

Insurance in ancient America. Bierce, A.

Integration. Rylands, J. T.

INTELLECTUALS

See also Scholars

Allen, W. No kaddish for Weinstein

Machado de Assis. The Siamese academies

Michaelopoulou, A. Lermontov

INTELLIGENCE AGENTS *See* Secret service

Intelligent design. Klages, E.

Intensive care. Manley, C.

The **intentional** deception. Chekhov, A. P.

INTER-RACIAL MARRIAGE *See* Interracial marriage

The **interceptor.** Malzberg, B. N.

Intercourse. Butler, R. O.

Intercourse: Couples in Six Stories. Butler, R. O.

Interest. Matheson, R.

Interesting Facts about the Austrian Glass Trade. Magnussen, L.

INTERFAITH MARRIAGE

Gordon, M. Delia

Konkle, M. Resolved

Michaels, L. Intimations

Ozick, C. Levitation

Redhill, M. Martin Sloane [excerpt]

Silverberg, R. The mutant season

The **interference** of Patsy Ann. Dunbar, P. L.

The **interior** castle. Stafford, J.

Interloper. Mozetič, B.

Interlude. West, D.

Interlude at Duane's. Wilson, F. P.

Interment. Nevai, L.

Intermission. Ficowski, J.

Internal Affairs. Roncagliolo, S.

INTERNATIONAL INTRIGUE

See also Adventure; Secret service; Spies

Berry, S. The devils' due

Blackwood, G. Sacrificial lion

Deaver, J. The weapon

Hamilton, D. At the drop of a hat

Jakubowski, M. L'Americaine

Lynds, D. Success of a mission

Lynds, G. The hunt for Dmitri

Morrell, D. The Abelard sanction

Reich, C. Assassins

Thomas, R. Cast a yellow shadow [excerpt]

International Law 101. Homer, P.

INTERNATIONAL MARRIAGES

Auchincloss, L. Her better half

Biller, M. Melody

Brazaitis, M. Coming home

Chandra, V. "Light beer and peanuts"

Enright, A. Here's to love

Klimasewiski, M. N. Tanner

Klimasewiski, M. N. Tanner and Jun Hee

Rushdie, S. The firebird's nest

Simpson, P. Playing the joker

Strom, D. Neighbors

Ulitskaya, L. Zurich

Wadia, L.-A. L. "Ravi's wedding"

INTERNATIONAL WILDLIFE CONSERVATION PARK (NEW YORK, N.Y.) *See* Bronx Zoo

INTERNET

Doctorow, C. When sysadmins ruled the earth

Faber, M. Bye-bye Natalia

Rice, C. Man catch

Savage, T. Cyberdate.com

Stross, C. Unwirer

Treat, J. Dear Dr. Haskell

The **Interoperation.** Sterling, B.

INTERPLANETARY COMMUNICATION *See* Interstellar communication

INTERPLANETARY TRAVEL *See* Interplanetary voyages

INTERPLANETARY VISITORS

IRANIANS
France
Taraqqī, G. The bizarre comportment of Mr. Alpha in exile
Taraqqī, G. My little friend
United States
Brady, C. Written in stone
Moss, B. K. Rug weaver
Okasi, M. T. Salvation army
Sterling, B. In paradise
Wolfe, G. Seven American nights
IRAQ
Douglas, C. N. Strangers in a strange land
The **Iraq** Show. Antin, C.
IRAQ WAR, 2003-
Biller, M. Baghdad at seven-thirty
Busch, F. Patrols
Flynn, N. A crystal formed entirely of holes
Hays, D. Ackerman in Eden
Henry, L. Capital punishment
Litzky, T. Purple tulip
Morgana, M. An open letter to the Bush administration
Percy, B. Refresh, refresh
Shepard, L. A walk in the garden
Simpson, H. The phlebotomist's love life
Tea, M. Music from earth
Winn, T. Cantogallo
Irby, Lee
There Is No Place That Does Not See You
The North American Review v292 no2 p20-4
Mr/Ap 2007
Irby, Lester
God don't like ugly
D. C. noir; edited by George Pelecanos
IRELAND
See also Northern Ireland; Ulster (Ireland and Northern Ireland)
Bradbury, R. Banshee
Bradbury, R. One for his lordship, and one for the road
Daughtry, P. French letters
Daughtry, P. Season of broken wings
De Camp, L. S. and Pratt, F. Fletcher and I
Donoghue, E. Speaking in tongues
Donovan, G. Archeologists
Donovan, G. By Irish nights
Donovan, G. Country of the grand
Donovan, G. Glass
Donovan, G. Harry Dietz
Donovan, G. How long until
Donovan, G. New deal
Donovan, G. Shoplifting in the USA
Donovan, G. The summer of birds
Donovan, G. Visit
Doyle, R. 57% Irish
Doyle, R. Guess who's coming for the dinner
Glavin, A. Patio nights
Hogan, D. Pictures
Howard, R. E. The cairn on the headland
Kiely, B. Bon ami, Emile
Kiely, B. A bottle of brown sherry
Kiely, B. The bright graves
Kiely, B. A cow in the house
Kiely, B. Down then by Derry
Kiely, B. The enchanted palace
Kiely, B. The green lanes
Kiely, B. The house in Jail Square
Kiely, B. The shortest way home

Kiely, B. The white wild bronco
O'Shaughnessy, P. A grandmother's tale
Redhill, M. Martin Sloane [excerpt]
Stamm, P. Deep furrows
Thomas, E. The land of youth
Tóibín, C. Donal Webster
Tóibín, C. Famous blue raincoat
Tóibín, C. A journey
Tóibín, C. The name of the game
Tóibín, C. A priest in the family
Tóibín, C. Three friends
Trevor, W. At Olivehill
Trevor, W. Big bucks
Trevor, W. The dressmaker's child
Trevor, W. Justina's priest
Trevor, W. Men of Ireland
Trevor, W. Sacred statues
Aristocracy
See Aristocracy—Ireland
Farm life
See Farm life—Ireland
Race relations
Doyle, R. Black hoodie
Doyle, R. I understand
Lambe, P. J. The new prosperity
Rural life
Bradbury, R. The first night of Lent
Bradbury, R. The great collision of Monday last
Hodgson, W. H. My house shall be called the house of prayer
Keane, J. B. The change
Keane, J. B. The curriculum vitae
Keane, J. B. Death be not proud
Keane, J. B. Dousie O'Dea
Keane, J. B. Faith
Keane, J. B. Fred Rimble
Keane, J. B. The hanging
Keane, J. B. Under the sycamore tree
Keane, J. B. The woman who hated Christmas
Kiely, B. Bloodless Byrne of a Monday
Kiely, B. Bluebell Meadow
Kiely, B. The dogs in the great Glen
Kiely, B. Elm Valley Valerie
Kiely, B. The fairy women of Lisbellaw
Kiely, B. God's own country
Kiely, B. A great god's angel standing
Kiely, B. The heroes in the dark house
Kiely, B. Homes on the mountain
Kiely, B. A journey to the seven streams
Kiely, B. The little wrens and robins
Kiely, B. Maiden's leap
Kiely, B. Mock battle
Kiely, B. Near Banbridge town
Kiely, B. An old friend
Kiely, B. The players and the kings
Kiely, B. A room in Linden
Kiely, B. Secondary top
Kiely, B. Soldier, red soldier
Kiely, B. There are meadows in Lanark
Kiely, B. A walk in the wheat
Kiely, B. The weavers at the mill
Kiely, B. The wild boy
Kiely, B. Wild rover no more
McCabe, E. Cancer
McCabe, E. The landlord
McCabe, E. The master
McCabe, E. The mother
McCabe, E. Music at Annahullion
McCabe, E. The orphan

ISLAM—*Continued*
Sterling, B. The compassionate, the digital
Taha, M. A. The legislation of sheikh mal-allah
Island. Gibbons, R.
Island. Macaire, J.
The **island**. Watts, P.
Island entertainment. Troy, M.
The **island** of Doctor Death and other stories. Wolfe, G.
The **island** of the crossbones. Hodgson, W. H.
Island time. Brennan, K.
Islanders. Kiesbye, S.
Islanders. Kostival, B.
Islanders. Smith, M.
ISLANDS
 See also names of individual islands and groups of islands
 Bowes, R. The mask of the Rex
 Boyle, T. C. Rastrow's island
 Boyle, T. C. Swept away
 Brockmeier, K. The view from the seventh layer
 Budnitz, J. Motherland
 Butner, R. The wounded
 Coloane, F. The hidden part of the iceberg [variant title: Submerged iceberg]
 Coloane, F. Passage to Puerto Edén
 Davies, C. P. The defenders
 Emshwiller, C. All washed up while looking for a better world
 Freed, L. Twilight
 Hodgson, W. H. The habitants of Middle Islet
 Hodgson, W. H. The island of the crossbones
 Hodgson, W. H. The voice in the dawn
 Holland, N. Coquina
 Jacobsen, J. On the island
 King, S. Home delivery
 Lanagan, M. Forever upward
 Langan, J. On Skua Isalnd
 Lasswitz, K. Apoikis
 Lumley, B. Rising with Surtsey
 Lunstrum, K. S. Islands
 Nelson, R. F. Breaker
 Parker, M. Off island
 Rose, A. Ultima thule
 Sandstrom, E. K. The people's wat
 Schutt, C. Unrediscovered, unrenameable
 Smith, C. A. The uncharted isle
 Stevens, F. Friend island
 Stevens, F. Sunfire
 Unger, D. Tide pool
 Windley, C. Home schooling
 Wolfe, G. The death of Dr. Island
 Wolfe, G. Death of the island doctor
 Woolson, C. F. Jeannette
 Woolson, C. F. St. Clair Flats
Islands. Lunstrum, K. S.
ISLANDS OF THE INDIAN OCEAN
 Koënings, N. S. Setting up shop
ISLANDS OF THE PACIFIC
 See also Solomon Islands
 Hubbard, L. R. Danger in the dark
 Murphy, P. Inappropriate behavior
The **isle** of the torturers. Smith, C. A.
Isle Royale. Monson, A.
Ismaeel, Donia Elamal
 Dates and bitter coffee
  Qissat; short stories by Palestinian women; edited by Jo Glanville
Isnis. Richards, T.

Íṣ·l'olá, Akínwùmí
 The uses of English
  Words without borders; the world through the eyes of writers; an anthology; edited by Samantha Schnee, Alane Salierno Mason, and Dedi Felman
Isolation area. Bova, B.
Isolation Point, California. Shirley, J.
Isolettes. Smith, N.
The **isolinguals**. De Camp, L. S.
Ison, Tara
 Wig
  Getting even; revenge stories; edited by Mitzi Szereto
Isozaki, Arata
 City Demolition Industry, Inc.
  The South Atlantic Quarterly v106 no4 p853-8 Fall 2007
 Rumor City
  The South Atlantic Quarterly v106 no4 p859-69 Fall 2007
ISRAEL
 See also Jerusalem; Zionism
 Anaya, R. A. Absalom
 Asch, S. On the bank of an alien stream
 Helprin, M. Last tea with armorers
 Keret, E. Halibut
 Keret, E. Journey
 Keret, E. Knockoff Venus
 Keret, E. Loquat
 Keret, E. Moral something
 Keret, E. The night the buses died
 Keret, E. The Nimrod flipout
 Keret, E. A no-magician birthday
 Keret, E. Not human beings
 Keret, E. Vladimir Hussein
 Liebrecht, S. America
 Mandelman, A. Black
 Mandelman, A. Curse
 Mandelman, A. Mish-mash
 Mandelman, A. Terror
 Molodowsky, K. Godl the shoemaker of Rehovot
 Molodowsky, K. A house with seven windows
 Singer, I. B. The psychic journey
 Singer, M. Helicopter days
 Stollman, A. L. Mr. Mitochondria
   Haifa
 Hoffmann, Y. The heart is katmandu [excerpt]
   Tel Aviv
 Biller, M. In bed with Sheikh Yassin
 Brown, D. Land of ass and honey
 Brown, D. Selling the apartment
 Brown, D. Your own private America
 Liebrecht, S. Tel Aviv
 Shabtai, Y. Adoshem
 Shabtai, Y. Past continuous
 Shabtai, Y. Uncle Peretz takes off
 Shabtai, Y. The visit
 Singer, I. B. Brother Beetle
ISRAEL. MOSSAD
 Mandelman, A. Pity
 Mandelman, A. Talking to the enemy
 Mandelman, A. Test
ISRAELI-ARAB RELATIONS
 Singer, M. Body count
 Singer, M. The pale of settlement
 Stumacher, A. The Neon desert
 Taha, M. A. A boy who picked the sun

Jablonski, Noria—*Continued*
The snipper
  Burnham, C. Who can save us now?; brand-
  new superheroes and their amazing [short]
  stories; edited by Owen King and John
  McNally; [illustrations by Chris Burnham]
Solo in the spotlight
  Jablonski, N. Human oddities; stories
Succor
  Jablonski, N. Human oddities; stories
Wanting out
  Jablonski, N. Human oddities; stories
Jabr, Kulthum
A night of sorrow
  Oranges in the sun; short stories from the
  Arabian Gulf; edited and translated by Deb-
  orah S. Akers, Abubaker A. Bagader
Jabs, Kathleen Toomey
Deep water
  Good Housekeeping v244 no3 p201-4, 206-9
  Mr 2007
The **jacaranda** wife. Slatter, A.
Jack. Hutchins, S.
Jack. Miéville, C.
Jack. Robinson, M.
Jack. Willis, C.
Jack Daw's pack. Gilman, G. I.
Jack Duggan's law. Higgins, G. V.
Jack Grey, second mate. Hodgson, W. H.
Jack in the pot. West, D.
Jack Jaw and the Arab's ape. Oakley, R.
Jack, part one. Woronov, M.
Jack, part two. Woronov, M.
Jack Tar. Selinger, G.
JACK THE RIPPER
                   About
  Dann, J. and Frost, G. The incompleat Ripper
  Frost, G. From hell again
  Masdon, J. Jack's mantle
  Nolan, W. F. Ripper!
  Resnick, M. Redchapel
  Shepard, L. Jack's decline
  Wolfe, G. Game in the pope's head
Jack Webb's star. Goldberg, L.
Jacko's ranch. Malouf, D.
Jack's decline. Shepard, L.
Jack's mantle. Masdon, J.
Jackson, Lawrence
To Danville
  New England Review v28 no1 p150-67 2007
Jackson, Lisa
Vintage death
  Thriller 2; stories you just can't put down;
  edited by Clive Cussler; [stories by] Kath-
  leen Antrim . . . [et al.]
Jackson, Marni
Bob Dylan Goes Tubing
  The Walrus v4 no6 p64-9 Jl/Ag 2007
Jackson, Merilyn Oniszczuk
A Sow of Violence
  The Massachusetts Review v45 no3 p367-76
  Aut 2004
JACKSON, MICHAEL, 1958-2009
                   About
  Almond, S. The idea of Michael Jackson's dick
  Browne, A. Neverland blues

Jackson, Mick
Totally wired
  Perverted by language; fiction inspired by The
  Fall; edited and introduced by Peter Wild.
Jackson, Rosie
Echo
  Getting even; revenge stories; edited by Mitzi
  Szereto
Jackson, Shelley
Egg
  Pushcart Prize XXVIII: best of the small
  presses 2004; edited by Bill Henderson and
  the Pushcart prize editors
Here is the church
  The Year's best fantasy and horror: eighteenth
  annual collection; edited by Ellen Datlow,
  Kelly Link & Gavin J. Grant
Husband
  The Year's best fantasy and horror: seven-
  teenth annual collection; edited by Ellen
  Datlow, Kelly Link and Gavin J. Grant
My friend goo
  Noise; fiction inspired by Sonic Youth; edited
  bt Peter Wild; introduction by Lee Ranaldo
  The Massachusetts Review v49 no1/2 p48-60
  Spr/Summ 2008
Vitriol
  The dictionary of failed relationships; 26 tales
  of love gone wrong; edited by Meredith
  Broussard
Jackson, Shirley
1948: Smalltown, U.S.A.: Shirley Jackson Casts
  the First Stone [Excerpt from The Lottery]
  Lapham's Quarterly v2 no2 p117-23 Spr
  2009
JACKSON, STONEWALL, 1824-1863
                   About
  Bowman, J. R. Stonewalls
  Smith, R. T. I have lost my right
  Smith, R. T. Little Sorrel
Jackson, Thomas Jonathan *See* Jackson, Stone-
  wall, 1824-1863
Jackson, Tina
Smell the cheese
  Her Majesty; 21 stories by women; edited by
  Jackie Gay and Emma Hargrave
Jackson of Horntown. L'Amour, L.
Jacob Bayer and the telephone. Helprin, M.
Jacob the Angel [Includes a commentary]
  Schwartz, H.
Jacobs, Harvey
Gravity
  New worlds; an anthology; edited by Michael
  Moorcock
Jacobs, Mark
Perfect Rush
  Southwest Review v90 no3 p445-62 2005
Jacobsen, Josephine
On the island
  So the story goes; twenty-five years of the
  Johns Hopkins short fiction series; edited
  by John T. Irwin and Jean McGarry; with
  a foreword by John Barth
Jade Buddhas, red bridges, fruits of love.
  Gilchrist, E.
The **jade** elephant. Hellmann, L. F.

James, C. L. R. (Cyril Lionel Robert)—*Continued*

Delphi and Herodotus discussion
    James, C. L. R. The Nobbie stories for children and adults; edited and introduced by Constance Webb; foreword by Anna Grimshaw

The dirty snowball and white raincoat
    James, C. L. R. The Nobbie stories for children and adults; edited and introduced by Constance Webb; foreword by Anna Grimshaw

Emperor Jones and the African drums
    James, C. L. R. The Nobbie stories for children and adults; edited and introduced by Constance Webb; foreword by Anna Grimshaw

The fossil fight
    James, C. L. R. The Nobbie stories for children and adults; edited and introduced by Constance Webb; foreword by Anna Grimshaw

Ghana independence
    James, C. L. R. The Nobbie stories for children and adults; edited and introduced by Constance Webb; foreword by Anna Grimshaw

The ghost at the window
    James, C. L. R. The Nobbie stories for children and adults; edited and introduced by Constance Webb; foreword by Anna Grimshaw

The Liverpool cathedral
    James, C. L. R. The Nobbie stories for children and adults; edited and introduced by Constance Webb; foreword by Anna Grimshaw

Michelangelo and the statue of David
    James, C. L. R. The Nobbie stories for children and adults; edited and introduced by Constance Webb; foreword by Anna Grimshaw

Mighty Mouse and the conceited cowboy
    James, C. L. R. The Nobbie stories for children and adults; edited and introduced by Constance Webb; foreword by Anna Grimshaw

Mighty Mouse and the sinking ship
    James, C. L. R. The Nobbie stories for children and adults; edited and introduced by Constance Webb; foreword by Anna Grimshaw

Mighty Mouse to the rescue—again
    James, C. L. R. The Nobbie stories for children and adults; edited and introduced by Constance Webb; foreword by Anna Grimshaw

Moby Dick fights a strange eagle
    James, C. L. R. The Nobbie stories for children and adults; edited and introduced by Constance Webb; foreword by Anna Grimshaw

The monster in the park
    James, C. L. R. The Nobbie stories for children and adults; edited and introduced by Constance Webb; foreword by Anna Grimshaw

The Nobbie stories for children and adults
    James, C. L. R. The Nobbie stories for children and adults; edited and introduced by Constance Webb; foreword by Anna Grimshaw

Nobbie's birthday
    James, C. L. R. The Nobbie stories for children and adults; edited and introduced by Constance Webb; foreword by Anna Grimshaw

Police proclamation
    James, C. L. R. The Nobbie stories for children and adults; edited and introduced by Constance Webb; foreword by Anna Grimshaw

Roundheads and Cavaliers
    James, C. L. R. The Nobbie stories for children and adults; edited and introduced by Constance Webb; foreword by Anna Grimshaw

Serial not cereal
    James, C. L. R. The Nobbie stories for children and adults; edited and introduced by Constance Webb; foreword by Anna Grimshaw

The shark fight—Second installment
    James, C. L. R. The Nobbie stories for children and adults; edited and introduced by Constance Webb; foreword by Anna Grimshaw

Sir Lancelot and the tack
    James, C. L. R. The Nobbie stories for children and adults; edited and introduced by Constance Webb; foreword by Anna Grimshaw

The teacher who feared rats
    James, C. L. R. The Nobbie stories for children and adults; edited and introduced by Constance Webb; foreword by Anna Grimshaw

Ulysses—a great hero
    James, C. L. R. The Nobbie stories for children and adults; edited and introduced by Constance Webb; foreword by Anna Grimshaw

James, Cyril Lionel Robert *See* James, C. L. R. (Cyril Lionel Robert), 1901-1989

James, Darrell

The art of avarice
    Politics noir; dark tales from the corridors of power; edited by Gary Phillips.

JAMES, FRANK, 1844-1915
About
Peelle, L. Shadow on a weary land

James, Gay

Wordwatching
    Boston Review v33 no5 p33 S/O 2008

James, Henry

Alone
    James, H. The uncollected Henry James; newly discovered stories; edited by Floyd R. Horowitz

The blue handkerchief
    James, H. The uncollected Henry James; newly discovered stories; edited by Floyd R. Horowitz

Jane and Sam. D'Alessandro, S.

Jane crying. Sallis, J.

Jane, Dreaming. Grimm, M.

Jane from Cameroon. Tait, J.

The **Jane** from Hell's Kitchen. Paul, P.

Jane's hat. Holladay, C. C.

Janet finds the razor. Lansdale, J. R.

JANITORS

Davis, C. Labors of the heart

Gifford, B. The lost tribe

Hernandez, L. Float

Hyde, M. Miracle-Gro

Sayles, J. Keeping time

Jansen, Julie

Morpho sanguinalis

Nature v453 p696 My 29 2008

January. Olafsson, O.

The **janus** tree. Hirshberg, G.

JAPAN

Beagle, P. S. The tale of Junko and Sayuri

Black, C. Mosquito incense

Daidō, T. Milk

Fowler, K. J. Shimabara

Fujino, C. Her room

Hasegawa, J. The unfertilized egg

Murakami, H. The seventh man

Murakami, H. Tony Takitani

Shimamoto, R. Inside

Stackpole, M. A. Blood duty

Sterling, B. Flowers of Edo

Sterling, B. Maneki Neko

Takagi, N. The shadow of the orchid

Uchida, S. My son's lips

Watson, I. The Moby Clitoris of his beloved

19th century

Kitahara, A. The budding tree

Kitahara, A. Eight-tenths a man

Kitahara, A. Forget-me-not

Kitahara, A. Innocent in love

Kitahara, A. Love's chill wind

Kitahara, A. No time for tears

1945-

Kōno, T. Bone meat

Miura, T. And all promenade!

Miura, T. Face of death

Miura, T. Homecoming

Miura, T. Magic lantern show

Miura, T. Shame in the blood

Seikoh, I. God is nowhere; God is now here

Yasuoka, S. The glass slipper

Yasuoka, S. Homework

Yasuoka, S. The house guard

Yasuoka, S. Jingle bells

Yasuoka, S. The medal

Yasuoka, S. The sword dance

Yasuoka, S. The wandering minstrel

College life

See College life—Japan

Rural life

Waters, M. Y. Mirror studies

Hiroshima

Le, N. Hiroshima

Liebrecht, S. Hiroshima

Kyoto

Daughtry, P. A grace of shadows

Tokyo

Fujino, C. The housewife and the police box

Hayashi, M. One year later

Miura, T. A portrait of Shino

Morita, R. Fruits of Shinjuku

Murakami, H. Firefly

Murakami, H. A folklore for my generation: a pre-history of late-stage capitalism

Muramatsu, T. Yumeko

Muroi, Y. Piss

Shiina, M. The yellow tent on the roof

Sholer, L. Imitate the sun

Woolrich, C. Death in the Yoshiwara

Yasuoka, S. Homework

Yasuoka, S. The medal

Yasuoka, S. A room in Tsukiji

Yokohama

Hodgson, W. H. R.M.S. "Empress of Australia"

JAPAN. ARMY

Tsutsui, Y. Commuter army

JAPANESE

Canary Islands

Tawada, Y. Saint George and the translator

China

Uchida, H. Envoy to Tang China

Germany

Tawada, Y. In front of Trang Tien Bridge

Tawada, Y. The shadow man

Greece

Murakami, H. Man-eating cats

Hawaii

Troy, M. Luau

United States

Knightly, R. Take the man's pay

Sterling, B. Are you for 86?

Wolven, S. Pinwheel

JAPANESE AMERICANS

Hirahara, N. The chirashi covenant

Rock, P. Shaken

Williams, N. J. Rickshaw runner

JAPANESE SOLDIERS *See* Soldiers—Japan

Jardim, Keith

The jaguar

Trinidad noir; edited by Lisa Allen-Agostini & Jeanne Mason.

Jarrar, Randa

Barefoot bridge

Qissat; short stories by Palestinian women; edited by Jo Glanville

Jarrell, Donna

The displaced overweight homemaker's guide to finding a man

What are you looking at?; the first fat fiction anthology; edited by Donna Jarrell and Ira Sukrungruang

JARRY, ALFRED, 1873-1907

About

Waldrop, H. Fin de Cyclé

JARUZELSKI, WOJCIECH

About

Zebrowski, G. General Jaruzelski at the zoo

Jasper, Kenji

First

D. C. noir; edited by George Pelecanos

Thursday

Brooklyn noir; edited by Tim McLoughlin

Jasper, Michael

Painting Haiti

Sedia, E. Paper cities; an anthology of urban fantasy

Jay, Karla
Speeding cars
Women of mystery; an anthology; Katherine V. Forrest, editor
Jaybird. Smith, N.
JAZZ
Matheson, R. Jazz machine
Jazz at twelve. Coleman, W.
Jazz machine. Matheson, R.
JAZZ MUSIC
Baraka, I. A. Dig this! Out?
Baraka, I. A. Heathen technology at the end of the twentieth century
Baraka, I. A. Retrospection
Coleman, W. Jazz at twelve
Frost, G. Attack of the jazz giants
Gorman, E. Riff
Harvey, J. Minor key
Kaminsky, S. M. Blue note
Lewis, W. H. Rossonian days
Straub, P. Little Red's tango
Thomas, J. Precious metal
Woolrich, C. The case of the killer-diller
JEALOUSY
Barry, R. Men shoot things to kill them
Billingham, M. Stroke of luck
Blackwell, K. The secret life of peonies
Bonner, M. O. A sealed pod
Brodsky, M. Crisis in the life of an actress
Brown, R. The movie
Coake, C. Unmade bed
Collins, B. Trailer trashed
Colvin, C. Love and death in renaissance Italy
Cooper, J. C. Rushing nowhere
Dunbar, P. L. Dizzy-headed Dick
Dunbar, P. L. The triumph of ol' Mis' Pease
Dunbar-Nelson, A. M. Summer session
Eldridge, C. Becky
Forrest, K. V. A leopard's spots
Grant, J. Tails
Greenman, B. Oh Lord! Why not?
Hammett, D. Ber-Lulu
Haywood, G. A. The first rule is
Humphrey, W. A voice from the woods
Irvine, A. C. Shepherded by Galatea
Irvine, A. C. Volunteers
Kellerman, F. The back page
Kundera, M. The hitchhiking game
Lispector, C. Plaza Mauá
Machado, A. The death of the standard-bearer
Machado de Assis. The Siamese academies
Marz, M. Miscast
Maxted, A. Dagenham
McBain, E. The innocent one
Meacham, R. The assignment
Meno, J. A town of night
Molodowsky, K. A glimmer of youth
Murphy, D. R. Sounds of silence
Neera. Paolina
Oates, J. C. Special
O'Shaughnessy, P. Trio
Perry, A. Sneaker wave
Pickard, N. Joy ride
Quertermous, B. Murder boy
Rash, R. Blackberries in June
Rhodes, D. Mademoiselle Arc-en-ciel
Sakey, M. No one
Schuster, F. Two sisters
Selgin, P. The girl in the story

Shua, A. M. Farewell, my love
Singer, I. B. The impresario
Snyder, S. About face
Talley, M. The queen is dead, long live the queen
Tower, W. Wild America
Uchida, H. Afterglow
Winton, T. Sand
Zelazny, R. My lady of the diodes
Jealousy. Shivani, A.
Jealousy and Doubt. Brenna, D.
Jeanette. Beane, J.
Jeanne d'Arc, Saint *See* Joan, of Arc, Saint, 1412-1431
Jeannette. Woolson, C. F.
Jecks, Michael
No one can hear you scream
The Best British mysteries, 2005; edited by Maxim Jakubowski
Jeffers, H. Paul (Harry Paul)
The accidental murderess
Jeffers, H. P. The forgotten adventures of Sherlock Holmes; based on the original radio plays by Anthony Boucher and Denis Green
The adventure of Maltree Abbey
Jeffers, H. P. The forgotten adventures of Sherlock Holmes; based on the original radio plays by Anthony Boucher and Denis Green
The adventure of the blarney stone
Jeffers, H. P. The forgotten adventures of Sherlock Holmes; based on the original radio plays by Anthony Boucher and Denis Green
The adventure of the grand old man
Jeffers, H. P. The forgotten adventures of Sherlock Holmes; based on the original radio plays by Anthony Boucher and Denis Green
The adventure of the *Sally Martin*
Jeffers, H. P. The forgotten adventures of Sherlock Holmes; based on the original radio plays by Anthony Boucher and Denis Green
The adventure of the stuttering ghost
Jeffers, H. P. The forgotten adventures of Sherlock Holmes; based on the original radio plays by Anthony Boucher and Denis Green
The Book of Tobit
Jeffers, H. P. The forgotten adventures of Sherlock Holmes; based on the original radio plays by Anthony Boucher and Denis Green
The clue of the hungry cat
Jeffers, H. P. The forgotten adventures of Sherlock Holmes; based on the original radio plays by Anthony Boucher and Denis Green
The Darlington substitution
Jeffers, H. P. The forgotten adventures of Sherlock Holmes; based on the original radio plays by Anthony Boucher and Denis Green

Jeffers, H. Paul (Harry Paul)—*Continued*

The haunting of Sherlock Holmes

> Jeffers, H. P. The forgotten adventures of Sherlock Holmes; based on the original radio plays by Anthony Boucher and Denis Green

In Flanders fields

> Jeffers, H. P. The forgotten adventures of Sherlock Holmes; based on the original radio plays by Anthony Boucher and Denis Green

The paradol chamber

> Jeffers, H. P. The forgotten adventures of Sherlock Holmes; based on the original radio plays by Anthony Boucher and Denis Green

Sherlock Holmes and the mummy's curse

> Ghosts in Baker Street; edited by Martin H. Greenberg, Jon Lellenberg, Daniel Stashower

The singular affair of the dying schoolboys

> Jeffers, H. P. The forgotten adventures of Sherlock Holmes; based on the original radio plays by Anthony Boucher and Denis Green

Jeffers, Harry Paul *See* Jeffers, H. Paul (Harry Paul), 1934-

Jeffers, Honorée Fanonne

Come Day, Go Day

> *The Kenyon Review* v28 no1 p128-41 Wint 2006

If You Get There Before I Do

> *StoryQuarterly* v41 p199-219 2005

Miss Baby, O Lovely and Dark (as Told to Mr. J. C. Harris)

> *Callaloo* v28 no2 p265-71 Spr 2005

A plate of mojo

> Crossroads; tales of the southern literary fantastic; edited by F. Brett Cox and Andy Duncan

Soon One Morning

> *New England Review* v25 no4 p138-47 2004

JEFFERSON, THOMAS, 1743-1826

About

Carl, L. S. A mimicry of mockingbirds

JEHOVAH'S WITNESSES

Luvaas, W. Hilltop (an American story)

Watts, S. P. Unassigned territory

Jelloun, Tahar Ben

Beauty Is a Fate Better than Death

> *The New Yorker* v81 no42 p108-11 D 26 2005/Ja 2 2006

A **jelly** of light. Watkins, S.

Jem Binney and the safe at Lockwood Hall. Hodgson, W. H.

Jen, Gish

Amaryllis

> *The Paris Review* v48 p160-74 Wint 2006

Gratitude

> *Ploughshares* v32 no2/3 p98-117 Fall 2006

Jenna and me. Rucker, R. v. B.

Jenny among the zeebs. Nolan, W. F.

Jensen, Beverly

Gone

> *New England Review* v28 no2 p151-69 2007

Pan-Fried

> *New England Review* v29 no4 p115-32 2008

Wake

> The Best American short stories, 2007; selected from U. S. and Canadian magazines by Stephen King with Heidi Pitlor; with an introduction by Stephen King
>
> *New England Review* v27 no2 p65-87 2006

Jensen, Kristian Ditlev

And in India

> *The Literary Review (Madison, N.J.)* v51 no3 p82-90 Spr 2008

Jensen, Mrs. Oliver *See* Stafford, Jean, 1915-1979

Jensen, Toni

At the Powwow Hotel

> New stories from the South: the year's best, 2007; selected from U.S. magazines by Edward P. Jones with Kathy Pories; with an introduction by Edward P. Jones
>
> New stories from the Southwest; edited by D. Seth Horton; foreword by Ray Gonzalez.

Rabids

> *Dalhousie Review* v85 no1 p73-4 Spr 2005

Jeph Benedick's grandmother. Bierce, A.

Jeremiad. Sallis, J.

Jerk. Cooper, D.

Jernigan, R. Kirk

What it Takes to Spice Up a Haircut

> *The North American Review* v290 no5 p31-5 S/O 2005

Jerónimo's journey. Anaya, R. A.

Jerreat, Jerri

Featheredge

> *Dalhousie Review* v85 no1 p43-51 Spr 2005

Jerry and Molly and Sam. Carver, R.

JERUSALEM

Hasak-Lowy, T. On the grounds of the complex commemorating the Nazis' treatment of the Jews

Liebrecht, S. Jerusalem

Pearlman, E. The message

Jerusalem. Liebrecht, S.

Jeschke, Wolfgang

Partners for life

> The black mirror and other stories; an anthology of science fiction from Germany & Austria; edited & with an introduction & notes by Franz Rottensteiner; translated by Mike Mitchell.

Jeschonek, Robert T.

Acirema the rellik

> Future Americas; edited by Martin H. Greenberg and John Helferd

JESTERS *See* Fools and jesters

Jesus aged twelve in the temple. Aranitsis, E.

JESUS CHRIST

About

Aranitsis, E. Jesus aged twelve in the temple

Babel, I. The sin of Jesus

Bishop, M. Sequel on Skorpiós

Dann, J. and Dozois, G. R. Slow dancing with Jesus

Di Filippo, P. Lignum Crucis

Dostoyevsky, F. The inquisitor general

Dozois, G. R. and Dann, J. Slow dancing with Jesus

Ford, J. On the road to new Egypt

Frost, G. Touring Jesus World

Gaines, E. J. Christ walked down Market Street

Kuttner, H. A cross of centirues

Johnson, Charles Richard—*Continued*

The gift of the Osuo
  Johnson, C. R. Dr. King's refrigerator and other bedtime stories; [by] Charles Johnson

Kwoon
  Johnson, C. R. Dr. King's refrigerator and other bedtime stories; [by] Charles Johnson

The queen and the philosopher
  Johnson, C. R. Dr. King's refrigerator and other bedtime stories; [by] Charles Johnson

Sweet dreams
  Johnson, C. R. Dr. King's refrigerator and other bedtime stories; [by] Charles Johnson

Johnson, Dana

Melvin in the sixth grade
  California uncovered; stories for the 21st century; edited by Chitra Banerjee Divakaruni, William E. Justice, and James Quay

Threesome
  The dictionary of failed relationships; 26 tales of love gone wrong; edited by Meredith Broussard

Johnson, Denis

1966
  The New Yorker v83 no16 p106-10, 112-15 Je 11-18 2007

Beverly Home
  The Paris review book for planes, trains, elevators, and waiting rooms; by the editors of the Paris review; with an introduction by Richard Powers

Dirty wedding
  My mistress's sparrow is dead; great love stories, from Chekhov to Munro; edited by Jeffrey Eugenides

Emergency
  Adaptations: from short story to big screen; 35 great stories that have inspired great films; edited by Stephanie Harrison
  Beha, C. R. The Ecco anthology of contemporary American short fiction; selected by Joyce Carol Oates and Christopher R. Beha.

Work
  The New Granta book of the American short story; edited and introduced by Richard Ford

Xmas in Las Vegas
  Best of Tin House; stories; foreword by Dorothy Allison

Johnson, Dorothy M.

A man called Horse
  Adaptations: from short story to big screen; 35 great stories that have inspired great films; edited by Stephanie Harrison

Johnson, Drew

The Last Dead
  The Virginia Quarterly Review v84 no1 p106-25 Wint 2008

Johnson, Emily D.

(tr.) See Dolinin, V.

Johnson, George Clayton

A literary forgery
  Poe's lighthouse; all new collaborations with Edgar Allan Poe; edited by Christopher Conlon

Johnson, Greg

Alliances of youth
  Johnson, G. Women I've known; new and selected stories

The boarder
  Johnson, G. Women I've known; new and selected stories

Crazy ladies
  Johnson, G. Women I've known; new and selected stories

Double exposure
  Johnson, G. Women I've known; new and selected stories
  Beha, C. R. The Ecco anthology of contemporary American short fiction; selected by Joyce Carol Oates and Christopher R. Beha.

A dry season
  Johnson, G. Women I've known; new and selected stories

Escalators
  Johnson, G. Women I've known; new and selected stories

Evening at home
  Johnson, G. Women I've known; new and selected stories

Fever
  Johnson, G. Women I've known; new and selected stories

First surmise
  Johnson, G. Women I've known; new and selected stories

Hemingway's cats
  So the story goes; twenty-five years of the Johns Hopkins short fiction series; edited by John T. Irwin and Jean McGarry; with a foreword by John Barth
  Johnson, G. Women I've known; new and selected stories

His parents, naked
  Johnson, G. Women I've known; new and selected stories
  TriQuarterly no129 p187-97 2007

I am dangerous
  Johnson, G. Women I've known; new and selected stories

Last encounter with the enemy
  Johnson, G. Women I've known; new and selected stories

Leavings
  Johnson, G. Women I've known; new and selected stories

The metamorphosis
  Johnson, G. Women I've known; new and selected stories

Scene of the crime
  Johnson, G. Women I've known; new and selected stories

Schadenfreude
  Johnson, G. Women I've known; new and selected stories

Shameless
  Johnson, G. Women I've known; new and selected stories

To the madhouse
  Johnson, G. Women I've known; new and selected stories

Jones, Holly Goddard—*Continued*
Life expectancy
New stories from the South: the year's best, 2007; selected from U.S. magazines by Edward P. Jones with Kathy Pories; with an introduction by Edward P. Jones
The Kenyon Review v29 no1 p154-72 Wint 2007
Parts
The Hudson Review v60 no4 p569-86 Wint 2008
Proof of God
The Best American mystery stories, 2008; edited and with an introduction by George Pelecanos; Otto Penzler, series editor
Retrospective
The Kenyon Review v30 no3 p4-45 Summ 2008
Theory of Realty
Gettysburg Review v20 no4 p635-60 Wint 2007
Theory of relity
New stories from the South; the year's best, 2008; selected from U.S. magazines by ZZ Packer with Kathy Pories; with an introduction by ZZ Packer

JONES, JOHN PAUL, 1747-1792
About
Weber, D. The Captain from Kirkbean

Jones, Kimberly
The End of Summer
Calyx v22 no3 p102-8 Summ 2005

Jones, Langdon
The eye of the lens
New worlds; an anthology; edited by Michael Moorcock

Jones, LeRoi *See* Baraka, Imamu Amiri, 1934-

Jones, Louis B.
The epicurean
Pushcart prize XXXIII: best of the small presses 2009; edited by Bill Henderson with the Pushcart Prize editors

Jones, Nalini
The bold, the beautiful
Jones, N. What you call winter; stories
Carrying
Jones, N. What you call winter; stories
The crow and the monkey
Jones, N. What you call winter; stories
Half the story
Jones, N. What you call winter; stories
Home for a short time
Jones, N. What you call winter; stories
In the garden
Jones, N. What you call winter; stories
This is your home also
Jones, N. What you call winter; stories
We think of you every day
Jones, N. What you call winter; stories
What you call winter
Jones, N. What you call winter; stories

Jones, Stephen Graham
Bile
Jones, S. G. Bleed into me; a book of stories
Bleed into me
Jones, S. G. Bleed into me; a book of stories
Captivity narrative 109
Jones, S. G. Bleed into me; a book of stories

Carbon
Jones, S. G. Bleed into me; a book of stories
Discovering America
Jones, S. G. Bleed into me; a book of stories
Endless Buffets
Western Humanities Review v63 no2 p64-9 Summ 2009
Episode 43: incest
Jones, S. G. Bleed into me; a book of stories
Every night was Halloween
Jones, S. G. Bleed into me; a book of stories
The fear of jumping
Jones, S. G. Bleed into me; a book of stories
Filius nervosus
Jones, S. G. Bleed into me; a book of stories
Halloween
Jones, S. G. Bleed into me; a book of stories
Last success
Jones, S. G. Bleed into me; a book of stories
Nobody knows this
Jones, S. G. Bleed into me; a book of stories
Raphael
The Year's best fantasy and horror: twentieth annual collection; edited by Ellen Datlow and Kelly Link & Gavin J. Grant
These are the names I know
Jones, S. G. Bleed into me; a book of stories
To run without falling
Jones, S. G. Bleed into me; a book of stories
Venison
Jones, S. G. Bleed into me; a book of stories

Jones, Thom
The pugilist at rest
The New Granta book of the American short story; edited and introduced by Richard Ford

The **Joneses**. Trezise, R.

Jong-Fast, Molly
Letters from a young fetus
Before; short stories about pregnancy from our top writers; edited by Emily Franklin and Heather Swain

Jonjo's Present. Foden, G.

JOPLIN, JANIS, 1943-1970
About
Baker, L. P. The opposite of solid
Dann, J. and others. Touring
Swanwick, M. The feast of Saint Janis

Jordan, Pat
The hustle
Murder at the racetrack; edited by Otto Penzler

Jordan, Ruth
Little blue pill
Expletive deleted; edited by Jen Jordan

Jordan Wellington Lint. Ware, C.

Jordan's stand. Tudish, C.

Jo's hair. Palwick, S.

Jose, Nicholas
George
The Review of Contemporary Fiction v27 no3 p205-9 Fall 2007

JOSEPH (BIBLICAL FIGURE)
About
Pollack, R. Burning Beard: the dreams and visions of Joseph Ben Jacob, Lord Viceroy of Egypt

JUDAISM—*Continued*

Molodowsky, K. In a living room

Moss, B. K. The palm tree of Dilys Cathcart

Potash, R. Rumiya and the shofar

The **Judas-tail**. Domecq, B.

Judd, Randy

Nobody's Fool

The Michigan Bar Journal v86 no8 p24-7 Ag 2007

Judge Barclay's wife. Hodgson, W. H.

Judge Gladys Parks-Schultz. Julavits, H.

The **judgement**. Perry, A.

JUDGES

Archer, J. The wisdom of Solomon

Auchincloss, L. Pa's darling

Chekhov, A. P. Evildoer

Hoch, E. D. The secret session

Hodgson, W. H. Judge Barclay's wife

Modesitt, L. E., Jr. Rule of law

Mueenuddin, D. About a burning girl

Rozan, S. J. Night court

Wheat, C. The only good judge

Judgment. Moon, E.

A **judgment** of Paris. Dunbar, P. L.

JUDITH (BIBLICAL FIGURE)

About

Cutler, J. Judith

Judith. Cutler, J.

Judith Castle. Mitchell, D.

Judson, Theodore

The sultan's emissary

Sideways in crime; an alternate mystery anthology; edited by Lou Anders

The thief catcher

Future Americas; edited by Martin H. Greenberg and John Helferd

Jugged [variant title: The boy from Dos Cabezas] Leonard, E.

Juggernaut. Bradbury, R.

Juggernaut. O'Shaughnessy, P.

JUKEBOXES

Crowther, P. Three plays a quarter

Julavits, Heidi

Ambivalence

The dictionary of failed relationships; 26 tales of love gone wrong; edited by Meredith Broussard

Judge Gladys Parks-Schultz

The book of other people; edited by Zadie Smith

Little little big man

Before; short stories about pregnancy from our top writers; edited by Emily Franklin and Heather Swain

The miniaturist

McSweeney's enchanted chamber of astonishing stories; edited by Michael Chabon; illustrations by Mike Mignola

The Santosbrazzi Killer

Harper's v318 p63-8 Ja 2009

Jules Verne in hell: a letter to the editor from the late writer. Hevesi, L.

Julia. Gough, J.

Julia and Byron. Raine, C.

Julian, a Christmas story. Wilson, R. C.

Julius. McGrath, P.

July, Miranda

Birthmark

July, M. No one belongs here more than you; stories

The boy from Lam Kien

July, M. No one belongs here more than you; stories

How to tell stories to children

July, M. No one belongs here more than you; stories

I kiss a door

July, M. No one belongs here more than you; stories

It was romance

July, M. No one belongs here more than you; stories

Majesty

July, M. No one belongs here more than you; stories

Making love in 2003

July, M. No one belongs here more than you; stories

The man on the stairs

July, M. No one belongs here more than you; stories

Mon plaisir

July, M. No one belongs here more than you; stories

The moves

July, M. No one belongs here more than you; stories

Roy Spivey

The book of other people; edited by Zadie Smith

The New Yorker v83 no16 p90-3 Je 11-18 2007

The shared patio

July, M. No one belongs here more than you; stories

The sister

July, M. No one belongs here more than you; stories

Something that needs nothing

July, M. No one belongs here more than you; stories

My mistress's sparrow is dead; great love stories, from Chekhov to Munro; edited by Jeffrey Eugenides

The New Yorker v82 no29 p68-77 S 18 2006

The swim team

July, M. No one belongs here more than you; stories

Harper's v314 p79-80 Ja 2007

Ten true things

July, M. No one belongs here more than you; stories

This person

July, M. No one belongs here more than you; stories

July. Olafsson, O.

Jump. Dragomán, G.

Jumper. Zebrowski, G.

Jumping man. Johnston, T.

Jumping Monkey Hill. Adichie, C. N.

Jun Hee. Klimasewiski, M. N.

June. Olafsson, O.

June the 30th, 1934. Lowry, M.

Jung, Ha-Yun
  Han Gahp
    Best of Tin House; stories; foreword by Dorothy Allison
JÜNGER, ERNST, 1895-1998
About
  Grass, G. Witnesses of an era
Jungle roads. Daughtry, P.
The **Jungle** Rot Kid on the nod. Farmer, P. J.
JUNGLES
  Alarcón, D. War by candlelight
  Daughtry, P. Jungle roads
  Fowler, K. J. What I didn't see
  Rand, K. Here there be humans
  Reed, K. Into the jungle
  Resnick, M. The lord of the jungle
  Shepard, L. The arcevoalo
  Smith, C. A. The maze of Maal Dweb
  Smith, C. A. The maze of the enchanter [variant title: The maze of Maal Dweb]
Jung's Nightmare of Watches. Epstein, A.
Junior. Gorman, E.
Junior achievement. Caponegro, M.
Junior partner in crime. Douglas, C. N.
Juniper. Bierce, A.
The **Juniper** tree. Kessel, J.
The **Juniper** Tree. Moore, L.
Junk [Fictional account of a future with genetically modified humans] Sellar, G.
Junk DNA. Rucker, R. v. B. and Sterling, B.
Junk DNA. Sterling, B. and Rucker, R. v. B.
JUPITER (PLANET)
  Anderson, P. Call me Joe
  Blish, J. The Bridge
  Roberts, A. Jupiter magnified
  Rosenblum, M. H. Splinters of glass
Jupiter Doke, Brigadier-General. Bierce, A.
Jupiter magnified. Roberts, A.
Jupiter's skull. Ford, J.
Jurado, Alicia
  Saying goodbye through twenty-five centuries
    English translations of short stories by contemporary Argentine women writers; edited by Eliana Cazaubon Hermann; translated by Sally Webb Thornton
JURY DUTY See Trials
Jury duty. Rusch, K. K.
The **jury** in ancient America. Bierce, A.
Jus' a Pinch of the Yellow Powder. Shaw, A.
Juska, Elise
  Blind date
    Good Housekeeping v240 no6 p195-6, 198, 200-202, 204, 206 Je 2005
  Driving Aunt Edna
    Good Housekeeping v242 no1 p193-9 Ja 2006
  The Summer Guest
    Good Housekeeping v247 no2 p173-4, 177-8, 182-3 Ag 2008
Just, Ward S.
  Nora
    D.C. noir 2; the classics; edited by George Pelecanos.
Just a saxophone. Telles, L. F.
Just a simple bridge. Seth, R.
Just a smile. Mukhopadhyay, T.
Just a Speck. Bennett, P.
Just Another Abortion Story. Pietrzyk, L.
Just Because I Said So. Stazinski, J.
Just don't take the little I got. Parra, E. A.

Just drift. Gurba, M.
Just family. Alvarado, B.
Just going out. Beattie, A.
Just in the niche of time. Monteleone, T. F.
Just-life politics. Cooper, J. C.
Just like everyone else. Buckler, E.
Just like the ones we used to know. Willis, C.
Just one summer. Amery, C.
Just passing time. Bukowski, C.
Just pretend. Waites, M.
Just surviving another day. Jones, D.
Just the Thing. Bergen, D.
Just window shopping. Block, L.
Just you and me, Sammy. Vonnegut, K.
Justice, Jean Ross
  Bryan Dead
    The Yale Review v95 no1 p129-43 Ja 2007
  The Dark Forces
    The Yale Review v93 no1 p144-56 Ja 2005
  Miami, 1959
    The Antioch Review v65 no2 p346-51 Spr 2007
  The Smell of Ashes
    The Sewanee Review v117 no3 p394-409 Summ 2009
  The Two of Us
    Southwest Review v91 no4 p582-93 2006
JUSTICE
  Berniker, S. J. Aqua Velva Smitty
  Orphée, E. Justice shall be done
  Solá, M. Natural paradises
  Taha, M. A. The legislation of sheikh mal-allah
Justice. Brown, R.
Justice. Lette, K.
Justice. Pawar, U.
Justice. Wallace, D.
Justice—A Beginning. Paley, G.
Justice is a two-edged sword. Stabenow, D.
The **justice** of the elephant. Smith, C. A.
Justice served. Stewart, M.
Justice shall be done. Orphée, E.
Justice Shiva Ram Murthy. Reddi, R. P.
Justin M. Damiano. Clowes, D.
Justina's priest. Trevor, W.
JUVENILE DELINQUENCY
  Chase, M. Dawn
  Harleman, A. The ones without visas
  Hart, E. Blind sided
  Klassen, S. Wednesday is adoration
  McBain, E. First offense
  Nadelson, S. Model rockets
  Nelson, A. Only a thing
  Oates, J. C. How I contemplated the world from the Detroit House of Corrections, and began my life over again
  Russell, K. Out to sea
  Russell, K. The star-gazer's log of summer-time crime
  Sillitoe, A. The decline and fall of Frankie Buller
  Swann, M. Secret
  Varallo, A. The pines

K

K & K. Moody, R.
K-Ush: The Legend of the Last Wero. Salaam, K. I.

KABBALA
Kabbala
See also Cabala
The **Kabbalist** of Madison Avenue. Leonard, A.
Kabbani, Nizar *See* Qabbānī, Nizār, 1923-1998
KACZYNSKI, THEODORE J.
About
Hunt, S. Love machine
Meno, J. The Unabomber and my brother
Kadare, Ismail
Agamemnon's daughter
    Kadare, I. Agamemnon's daughter; a novella and stories; translated from the French of Tedi Papavrami and Jusuf Vrioni by David Bellos
The Albanian Writers' Union as Mirrored By a Woman
    The New Yorker v81 no42 p112-27 D 26 2005/Ja 2 2006
The blinding order
    Kadare, I. Agamemnon's daughter; a novella and stories; translated from the French of Tedi Papavrami and Jusuf Vrioni by David Bellos
    World Literature Today v80 no5 p4-6 S/O 2006
The Great Wall
    Kadare, I. Agamemnon's daughter; a novella and stories; translated from the French of Tedi Papavrami and Jusuf Vrioni by David Bellos
    Granta no91 p147-65 Fall 2005
Kaddish. Strieber, W.
Kadesch, Margot C.
Lacunae
    Calyx v22 no3 p49-64 Summ 2005
Kadetsky, Elizabeth
Geography
    The Antioch Review v67 no3 p462-79 Summ 2009
Men more than mortal
    Best new American voices 2008; guest editor Richard Bausch; series editors John Kulka and Natalie Danford
The poison that purifies you
    The Pushcart Prize XXIX: best of the small presses 2005; edited by Bill Henderson with the Pushcart Prize editors
Kadish, Rachel
Killer
    Gettysburg Review v21 no4 p615-24 Wint 2008
Love Story
    New England Review v28 no3 p183-7 2007
Kadongo Kamu—One Beat. Baingana, D.
Kafka, Franz
1914: Penal Colony: Franz Kafka Translates a Text [Excerpt from In the Penal Colony]
    Lapham's Quarterly v2 no2 p134-6 Spr 2009
KAFKA, FRANZ, 1883-1924
About
Gordimer, N. Gregor
Tognazzini, A. Working out with Kafka
Parodies, imitations, etc.
Gerrold, D. Franz Kafka, superhero!
Kafka the Bagger. Meins, S. R.
Kafka's sister. Watkins, S.

Kaftan, Vylar
Godivy
    Sedia, E. Paper cities; an anthology of urban fantasy
Lydia's body
    Realms
Scar stories
    Bandersnatch; edited by Paul Tremblay and Sean Wallace
Kahanovitch, Pinhas *See* Der Nister, 1884-1950
KAHLO, FRIDA, 1907-1954
About
Finger, A. Helen and Frida
Kaisaridis, Yannis
The old man and the tree
    Angelic & black; contemporary Greek short stories; edited and translated by David Connolly; with an introduction by Vangelis Hatzivassileiou
Kalamu ya Salaam
Alabama
    Crossroads; tales of the southern literary fantastic; edited by F. Brett Cox and Andy Duncan
All I could do was cry
    New Orleans noir; edited by Julie Smith
Kalfus, Ken
Professor Arecibo
    Agni no67 p134-40 2008
Pu-239
    Scribblers on the roof; contemporary American Jewish fiction; edited by Melvin Jules Bukiet and David G. Roskies
Kali's final cut. Tantimedh, A.
Kalman, Judith
Personal effects
    Contemporary Jewish writing in Canada; an anthology; edited by Michael Greenstein
Kalman, Nadia
The Counterpart
    The Walrus v4 no6 p56-62 Jl/Ag 2007
Kalokyris, Dimitris
Militsa or mid-August reverie
    Angelic & black; contemporary Greek short stories; edited and translated by David Connolly; with an introduction by Vangelis Hatzivassileiou
Kalotay, Daphne
All life's grandeur
    Kalotay, D. Calamity and other stories
Anniversary
    Kalotay, D. Calamity and other stories
A brand new you
    Kalotay, D. Calamity and other stories
Calamity
    Kalotay, D. Calamity and other stories
Difficult thoughts
    Kalotay, D. Calamity and other stories
The man from Allston Electric
    Kalotay, D. Calamity and other stories
Prom season
    Kalotay, D. Calamity and other stories
Rehearsal dinner
    Kalotay, D. Calamity and other stories
Serenade
    Kalotay, D. Calamity and other stories
Snapshots
    Kalotay, D. Calamity and other stories

Kalotay, Daphne—*Continued*
Sunshine Cleaners
Kalotay, D. Calamity and other stories
Wedding at Rockport
Kalotay, D. Calamity and other stories
What Madame Lipsky Wanted
Good Housekeeping v240 no1 p183-6, 188, 190 Ja 2005
Kalpakian, Laura
A Ballad for Ginny Brothers
Prairie Schooner v80 no3 p136-42 Fall 2006
The Christmas club
Good Housekeeping v241 no6 p232-4, 236-41 D 2005
Figgy pudding
Good Housekeeping v239 no6 p197-8, 200, 202-4 D 2004
Home remedies
Good Housekeeping v240 no3 p225-32 Mr 2005
The key of love
Good Housekeeping v243 no2 p189-90, 192, 195-8 Ag 2006
Romance in the blue bathroom
Good Housekeeping v241 no2 p175-8, 180-3 Ag 2005
Kamila and the king of kandy. Powell, G. C.
Kaminsky, Stuart M.
Blue note
Chicago blues; edited by Libby Fischer Hellmann
Evangeline
Hollywood and crime; original crime stories set during the history of Hollywood; edited by Robert J. Randisi
The night talker
Kolchak: the night stalker chronicles; 26 original tales of the surreal, the bizarre, the macabre; edited by Joe Gentile, Garrett Anderson, Lori Gentile; Kolchak created by Jeff Rice
The shooting of John Roy Worth
The Best American mystery stories, 2005; edited and with an introduction by Joyce Carol Oates; Otto Penzler, series editor
Kamlani, Beena
Goat
Ploughshares v33 no1 p131-44 Spr 2007
Zanzibar
Pushcart prize XXXIII: best of the small presses 2009; edited by Bill Henderson with the Pushcart Prize editors
The Virginia Quarterly Review v83 no3 p118-32 Summ 2007
Kamp, Stella
Big Joe: a short short story
"Tell it to us easy" and other stories; a complete short fiction anthology of African American women writers in Opportunity magazine, (1923-1948); edited by Judith Musser.
KAMPUCHEA *See* Cambodia
Kanakia, Rahul
The cheap crusade
Nature v455 p1006 O 16 2008
Kane, Alice DeBerry
Blog
Western Humanities Review v62 no2 p78-93 Spr/Summ 2008

Kane, Jessica Francis
The Inquiry
The Virginia Quarterly Review v85 no2 p182-92 Spr 2009
Kang, Min Soo
A fearful symmetry
The Year's best fantasy and horror: twentieth annual collection; edited by Ellen Datlow and Kelly Link & Gavin J. Grant
KANGAROOS
Levi, P. Buffet dinner
Murakami, H. A perfect day for kangaroos
Kanner, Rebecca
Byblis
The Kenyon Review v29 no2 p77-107 Spr 2007
KANSAS
Averill, T. F. The Bocce brothers
Averill, T. F. Bus
Averill, T. F. During the twelfth summer of Elmer D. Peterson
Averill, T. F. The man who ran with deer
Averill, T. F. Matty
Averill, T. F. Midlin, Kansas, jump shot
Averill, T. F. The musical genius of Moscow, Kansas
Averill, T. F. The onion and I
Averill, T. F. Shopping
Averill, T. F. The summer grandma was supposed to die
Averill, T. F. Topeka underground
Bierce, A. Mr. Masthead, journalist
Nelson, A. Obo
Nelson, P. Burying Mr. Henry
Frontier and pioneer life
See Frontier and pioneer life—Kansas
Kansas. Nelson, A.
KANSAS CITY (MO.) *See* Missouri—Kansas City
Kantner, Rob
Down home blues
The Best American mystery stories, 2009; edited and with an introduction by Jeffery Deaver
How Wendy Tudhope was saved from sure and certain death
The Best American mystery stories, 2004; edited and with an introduction by Nelson DeMille; Otto Penzler, series editor
Kantor, MacKinlay
Easter Flowers
The Saturday Evening Post v280 no2 p90-3, 96-7 Mr/Ap 2008
Kapel, Alexander
How long does a pogrom last?
No star too beautiful; Yiddish stories from 1382 to the present; compiled and translated by Joachim Neugroschel
Kapitan Ri. Chon, K.
KARAOKE
Reidy, D. The regular
Karaoke Night. Pope, D.
Karasu, Bilge
Essay on a Dark Yali
World Literature Today v80 no2 p24-8 Mr/Ap 2006
KARATE
Johnson, C. R. Kwoon

Kardos, Michael P.
Maximum Security
The Southern Review (Baton Rouge, La.) v44 no1 p113-27 Wint 2008
Metamorphosis
Prairie Schooner v83 no1 p90-103 Spr 2009

Karel the Walker. Rogers, M.

Karl V, Emperor of Germany *See* Charles V, Holy Roman Emperor, 1500-1558

Karlin, Katherine
Bye-bye Larry
Pushcart prize XXXI: best of the small presses 2007; edited by Bill Henderson; with the Pushcart Prize editors

Karma. Mosley, W.

Karma hits dogma. Abbott, J.

Karmazin, Margaret
Daughters
Confrontation no90/91 p224-33 Spr/Summ 2005

Karmel, Miriam
The caves of Lascaux
The Best of the Bellevue Literary Review; edited by Dannielle Ofri and the staff of the Bellevue Literary Review

Karodia, Farida
The woman in green
The Anchor book of modern African stories; edited by Nadežda Obradovic; with a foreword by Chinua Achebe

Karpinovitsh, Avrom
Zubak
No star too beautiful; Yiddish stories from 1382 to the present; compiled and translated by Joachim Neugroschel

Karrooo. Mindt, A.

Kartha, D. K. M.
The end of the demon who thought he was God
Parabola v33 no2 p78-9 Summ 2008

Karystiani, Ioanna
Mrs. Cataki
Angelic & black; contemporary Greek short stories; edited and translated by David Connolly; with an introduction by Vangelis Hatzivassileiou

KASHMIR VALLEY (INDIA) *See* India—Vale of Kashmir

Kasischke, Laura
If a stranger approaches you about carrying a foreign object with you onto the plane . . .
Pushcart prize XXXI: best of the small presses 2007; edited by Bill Henderson; with the Pushcart Prize editors
Ploughshares v31 no2/3 p176-89 Fall 2005

Kasper, Catherine
The theater spectacular
Text: Ur; the new book of masks; [edited by Forrest Aguirre]

Kassak, Fred
Who's afraid of Ed Garpo?
Passport to crime; the finest mystery stories from International Crime Writers; edited by Janet Hutchings

Kate Nace Day. Day, K. N.

Katherine's story. Baker, K.

Katina. Dahl, R.

Kato and the Indians from here. Murphy, Y.

Kattan, Naim
The dancer
Contemporary Jewish writing in Canada; an anthology; edited by Michael Greenstein

Katz, Michael R.
(tr.) See Tolstoy, Leo

Katzengela. Smith, M.

Kauffman, Janet
Monitoring: 10 Spot Samples
New England Review v26 no3 p76-80 2005

Kaufman, Margaret
Fishing
The Kenyon Review ns27 no3 p95-104 Summ 2005

Kava, Alex
Goodnight, sweet mother
Thriller; edited by James Patterson

Kava, Sharon M. *See* Kava, Alex

Kavaler, Rebecca
The Hardest Thing
The Antioch Review v63 no2 p317-28 Spr 2005

Kavanagh, Paul *See* Block, Lawrence, 1938-

Kavita through glass. Raboteau, E.

Kawakami, Hiromi
Mogera Wogura
The Paris Review v47 p143-59 Spr 2005

Kay, Jackie
The Last of the Smokers
Granta v98 p145-55 Summ 2007
You go when you can no longer stay
The O. Henry Prize stories, 2006; edited and with an introduction by Laura Furman; jurors: Kevin Brockmeier, Francine Prose, Colm Toibin

Kaye, Jessica
Drink to long life
Meeting across the river; stories inspired by the haunting Bruce Springsteen song; edited by Jessica Kaye and Richard J. Brewer

Kazikazawa [Redaction of the Meiji-Era story] Encho, S.

Kazoo. Sallis, J.

Kazumi Stahl, Anna
Natural disasters
Colchie, T. A whistler in the nightworld; short fiction from the Latin Americas; edited by Thomas Colchie

Kealey, Tom
The Boots
StoryQuarterly v42 p134-52 2006

Keane, John B.
The change
Keane, J. B. The teapots are out; and other eccentric tales from Ireland
The curriculum vitae
Keane, J. B. The teapots are out; and other eccentric tales from Ireland
Death be not proud
Keane, J. B. The teapots are out; and other eccentric tales from Ireland
Dousie O'Dea
Keane, J. B. The teapots are out; and other eccentric tales from Ireland
Faith
Keane, J. B. The teapots are out; and other eccentric tales from Ireland

Kelly, James Patrick—*Continued*

Serpent

Kelly, J. P. The wreck of the Godspeed; with a foreword by Bob Eggleton

Shoppers: No purchase necessary

Nature v452 p663 Ap 3 2008

The wreck of the Godspeed

Kelly, J. P. The wreck of the Godspeed; with a foreword by Bob Eggleton

Kelly, Ronald

Beneath Black Bayou

Kelly, R. Midnight grinding and other twilight terrors

Black harvest

Kelly, R. Midnight grinding and other twilight terrors

Blood suede shoes

Kelly, R. Midnight grinding and other twilight terrors

Bookmarks

Kelly, R. Midnight grinding and other twilight terrors

The boxcar

Kelly, R. Midnight grinding and other twilight terrors

Breakfast serial

Kelly, R. Midnight grinding and other twilight terrors

The cerebral passion

Kelly, R. Midnight grinding and other twilight terrors

The cistern

Kelly, R. Midnight grinding and other twilight terrors

Consumption

Kelly, R. Midnight grinding and other twilight terrors

The dark tribe

Kelly, R. Midnight grinding and other twilight terrors

Dead skin

Kelly, R. Midnight grinding and other twilight terrors

Depravity road

Kelly, R. Midnight grinding and other twilight terrors

Devil's Creek

Kelly, R. Midnight grinding and other twilight terrors

Dust devils

Kelly, R. Midnight grinding and other twilight terrors

Exit

Kelly, R. Midnight grinding and other twilight terrors

Forever angels

Kelly, R. Midnight grinding and other twilight terrors

Grandma's favorite recipe

Kelly, R. Midnight grinding and other twilight terrors

The hatchling

Kelly, R. Midnight grinding and other twilight terrors

Impressions in oak

Kelly, R. Midnight grinding and other twilight terrors

Midnight grinding

Kelly, R. Midnight grinding and other twilight terrors

Miss Abigail's delicate condition

Kelly, R. Midnight grinding and other twilight terrors

Oh, sordid shame!

Kelly, R. Midnight grinding and other twilight terrors

Old Hacker

Kelly, R. Midnight grinding and other twilight terrors

Papa's exile

Kelly, R. Midnight grinding and other twilight terrors

Romicide

Kelly, R. Midnight grinding and other twilight terrors

Scream queen

Kelly, R. Midnight grinding and other twilight terrors

Thinning the herd

Kelly, R. Midnight grinding and other twilight terrors

Tyrophex-fourteen

Kelly, R. Midnight grinding and other twilight terrors

The web of La Sanguinaire

Kelly, R. Midnight grinding and other twilight terrors

Whorehouse Hollow

Kelly, R. Midnight grinding and other twilight terrors

The winds within

Kelly, R. Midnight grinding and other twilight terrors

Yea, though I drive

Kelly, R. Midnight grinding and other twilight terrors

Kelly, Frederic Michael. Nolan, W. F.

Kelly the conjure-man. Howard, R. E.

Kelman, James

From the Window

Southwest Review v90 no4 p545-51 2005

Naval History

Southwest Review v90 no4 p533-44 2005

Kelman, Judith

No strings

Murder is my racquet; edited by Otto Penzler

Kelner, Toni L. P.

How Stella got her grave back

Many bloody returns; edited by Charlaine Harris and Toni L. P. Kelner

The **Kelpie** from Rhum. Stacey, T.

Kelton, Elmer

Continuity

Best stories of the American West, v1; edited by Marc Jaffe

North of the big river

Lone Star literature; from the Red River to the Rio Grande; edited by Don Graham

Kelts, Roland N.

Equilibrium

Playboy's college fiction; a collection of 21 years of contest winners; edited by Alice K. Turner; foreword by Thom Jones

Kemnitz, Charles
The fifth daughter
New stories from the Southwest; edited by D.
Seth Horton; foreword by Ray Gonzalez.
Kemnitzer, Lucy
The boulder
The Year's best fantasy and horror: twenty-
first annual collection; edited by Ellen
Datlow and Kelly Link & Gavin J. Grant
Kempadoo, Oonya
Standing on thin skin
Trinidad noir; edited by Lisa Allen-Agostini
& Jeanne Mason.
Kenagy, Mary
Loud lake
The best Christian short stories; edited and
with an introduction by Bret Lott
Kennedy, A. L.
Frank
The book of other people; edited by Zadie
Smith
Story of My Life
Granta no105 p44-55 Spr 2009
Wasps
The New Yorker v83 no21 p72-5 Jl 30 2007
Kennedy, Cate
Angel
Kennedy, C. Dark roots
Black Ice
The New Yorker v82 no28 p70-5 S 11 2006
Cold snap
Kennedy, C. Dark roots
The correct names of things
Kennedy, C. Dark roots
Dark roots
Kennedy, C. Dark roots
Direct action
Kennedy, C. Dark roots
Flexion
Harvard Review (1992) no34 p122-30 2008
Flotsam
Kennedy, C. Dark roots
Habit
Kennedy, C. Dark roots
Kill or cure
Kennedy, C. Dark roots
The light of coincidence [no subjects]
Kennedy, C. Dark roots
A pitch too high for the human ear
Kennedy, C. Dark roots
Resize
Kennedy, C. Dark roots
Sea burial
Kennedy, C. Dark roots
Seizure
Kennedy, C. Dark roots
Soundtrack
Kennedy, C. Dark roots
The testosterone club
Kennedy, C. Dark roots
What thou and I did, till we loved
Kennedy, C. Dark roots
Wheelbarrow thief
Kennedy, C. Dark roots
KENNEDY, JOHN F. (JOHN FITZGERALD),
1917-1963
About
Gerrold, D. The Kennedy enterprise
Lansdale, J. R. Bubba Ho-Tep

Stevens, J. D. JFK's shoes
Assassination
Cadigan, P. Jimmy
Kennedy, Pagan
Queer
The dictionary of failed relationships; 26 tales
of love gone wrong; edited by Meredith
Broussard
KENNEDY, ROBERT F., 1925-1968
About
Rusch, K. K. G-Men
Kennedy, Thomas E.
Let Everyone Forget Everyone
South Carolina Review v40 no2 p28-35 Spr
2008
(tr.) See Aidt, Naja Marie
(tr.) See Brøgger, Suzanne
The **Kennedy** enterprise. Gerrold, D.
Kennett, Rick
(jt. auth) See Kidd, Chico and Kennett, Rick
Kenney, Susan
The death of the dog and other rescues
Contemporary Maine fiction; an anthology of
short stories; edited by Wesley McNair
Kenny, Meghan
The Driest Season
Iowa Review v35 no3 p7-13 Wint 2005/2006
These Things Happen
Gettysburg Review v18 no3 p473-81 Aut
2005
Kent, Arthur
Warlord Reborn
The Literary Review (Madison, N.J.) v48 no4
p66-85 Summ 2005
Kent, Laura Tilden
In common
Adventures in the West; stories for young
readers; edited by Susanne George Bloom-
field and Eric Melvin Reed
Kent, Trilby
Fallout
African American Review v42 no2 p327-30
Summ 2008
KENT (ENGLAND) *See* England—Kent
KENTUCKY
Cady, J. The souls of Drowning Mountain
Downs, G. Between states
Downs, G. Indoor plumbing
Downs, G. Snack cakes
Dungye, D. Sally
Irvine, A. C. Green River chantey
Mason, B. A. The heirs
Mason, B. A. Spence + Lila
McClanahan, E. Hey Shoobie!
Richards, S. S. Magic lantern
Richards, S. S. The murderer, the pony, and
Miss Brown to you
Tomlinson, J. The accomplished son
Tomlinson, J. Berliner
Tomlinson, J. Birds of Providence
Tomlinson, J. Lake Charles
Tomlinson, J. A male influence in the house
Tomlinson, J. Nothing like an ocean
Tomlinson, J. Overburden
Tomlinson, J. The persistence of ice
Tomlinson, J. Prologue (two lives in letters)
Tomlinson, J. Shadow flag
Tomlinson, J. Singing second part
Tomlinson, J. So exotic

KENTUCKY—*Continued*
Tomlinson, J. Things kept
Tomlinson, J. Things left behind
Van Booy, S. Not the same shoes
Farm life
See Farm life—Kentucky
Lexington
McClanahan, E. How's that again?
Tomlinson, J. First husband, first wife
KENYA
Akpan, U. C. An Ex-mas feast
Resnick, M. The burning spear at twilight
Watkins, S. Family of man
Nairobi
Íṣ̣·l'olá, A. The uses of English
Tidhar, L. My travels with Al-Qaeda
KENYATTA, JOMO, CA. 1891-1978
About
Resnick, M. The burning spear at twilight
Kenyon, Kay
The acid test
This is my funniest 2; leading science fiction
writers present their funniest stories ever;
edited by Mike Resnick
Kenyon, Sherrilyn
Where angels fear to tread
The Horror Writers Association presents
Blood lite; an anthology of humorous hor-
ror stories; edited by Kevin J. Anderson
KEPLER, JOHANNES, 1571-1630
About
Bear, E. Stella nova
Keppel, Tim
Paternity
South Carolina Review v39 no1 p188-95 Fall
2006
Keppler, Johannes *See* Kepler, Johannes, 1571-
1630
Kercheval, Jesse Lee
Alice in Dairyland
Kercheval, J. L. The Alice stories
Beasts
Kercheval, J. L. The Alice stories
Brazil
Barnstorm; contemporary Wisconsin fiction;
edited by Raphael Kadushin
Damage
Kercheval, J. L. The Alice stories
Family portrait
Kercheval, J. L. The Alice stories
Prairie Schooner v81 no2 p87-95 Summ 2007
Honors
Kercheval, J. L. The Alice stories
Mary
Kercheval, J. L. The Alice stories
Prairie Schooner v81 no2 p96-106 Summ
2007
New rooms
Kercheval, J. L. The Alice stories
Night dogs
Kercheval, J. L. The Alice stories
Scarce
Kercheval, J. L. The Alice stories
A story set in Germany
Kercheval, J. L. The Alice stories

Keret, Etgar
Actually, I've had some phenomenal hard-ons
lately
Keret, E. The Nimrod flipout; translated from
the Hebrew by Miriam Shlesinger and Son-
dra Silverston
Alternative
Keret, E. The girl on the fridge; stories; trans-
lated from the Hebrew by Miriam
Shlesinger and Sondra Silverston
Angle
Keret, E. The Nimrod flipout; translated from
the Hebrew by Miriam Shlesinger and Son-
dra Silverston
Asthma attack
Keret, E. The girl on the fridge; stories; trans-
lated from the Hebrew by Miriam
Shlesinger and Sondra Silverston
Atonement
Keret, E. The girl on the fridge; stories; trans-
lated from the Hebrew by Miriam
Shlesinger and Sondra Silverston
The backgammon monster
Keret, E. The girl on the fridge; stories; trans-
lated from the Hebrew by Miriam
Shlesinger and Sondra Silverston
A Bet
The Paris Review v47 p145-6 Summ 2005
Boomerang
Keret, E. The girl on the fridge; stories; trans-
lated from the Hebrew by Miriam
Shlesinger and Sondra Silverston
Bottle
Keret, E. The Nimrod flipout; translated from
the Hebrew by Miriam Shlesinger and Son-
dra Silverston
Brecious
The Virginia Quarterly Review v85 no3 p118-
19 Summ 2009
Bwoken
Keret, E. The Nimrod flipout; translated from
the Hebrew by Miriam Shlesinger and Son-
dra Silverston
Cheerful colors
Keret, E. The girl on the fridge; stories; trans-
lated from the Hebrew by Miriam
Shlesinger and Sondra Silverston
Cramps
Keret, E. The girl on the fridge; stories; trans-
lated from the Hebrew by Miriam
Shlesinger and Sondra Silverston
Crazy glue
Keret, E. The girl on the fridge; stories; trans-
lated from the Hebrew by Miriam
Shlesinger and Sondra Silverston
Eight percent of nothing
Keret, E. The Nimrod flipout; translated from
the Hebrew by Miriam Shlesinger and Son-
dra Silverston
An exclusive
Keret, E. The girl on the fridge; stories; trans-
lated from the Hebrew by Miriam
Shlesinger and Sondra Silverston
Fatso
Keret, E. The Nimrod flipout; translated from
the Hebrew by Miriam Shlesinger and Son-
dra Silverston

Keret, Etgar—*Continued*

For only 9.99 (inc. tax and postage)
  Keret, E. The Nimrod flipout; translated from the Hebrew by Miriam Shlesinger and Sondra Silverston

Freeze!
  Keret, E. The girl on the fridge; stories; translated from the Hebrew by Miriam Shlesinger and Sondra Silverston

Gaza blues
  Keret, E. The girl on the fridge; stories; translated from the Hebrew by Miriam Shlesinger and Sondra Silverston

The girl on the fridge
  Keret, E. The girl on the fridge; stories; translated from the Hebrew by Miriam Shlesinger and Sondra Silverston

Glittery eyes
  Keret, E. The Nimrod flipout; translated from the Hebrew by Miriam Shlesinger and Sondra Silverston

A good-looking couple
  Keret, E. The Nimrod flipout; translated from the Hebrew by Miriam Shlesinger and Sondra Silverston

Goody bags
  Keret, E. The girl on the fridge; stories; translated from the Hebrew by Miriam Shlesinger and Sondra Silverston

Gulliver in Icelandic
  Keret, E. The girl on the fridge; stories; translated from the Hebrew by Miriam Shlesinger and Sondra Silverston

Gur's theory of boredom
  Keret, E. The Nimrod flipout; translated from the Hebrew by Miriam Shlesinger and Sondra Silverston

Halibut
  Keret, E. The Nimrod flipout; translated from the Hebrew by Miriam Shlesinger and Sondra Silverston

Happy birthday to you
  Keret, E. The girl on the fridge; stories; translated from the Hebrew by Miriam Shlesinger and Sondra Silverston

Hat trick
  Keret, E. The girl on the fridge; stories; translated from the Hebrew by Miriam Shlesinger and Sondra Silverston

Himme
  Keret, E. The Nimrod flipout; translated from the Hebrew by Miriam Shlesinger and Sondra Silverston

Horsie
  Keret, E. The Nimrod flipout; translated from the Hebrew by Miriam Shlesinger and Sondra Silverston

Ironclad rules
  Keret, E. The Nimrod flipout; translated from the Hebrew by Miriam Shlesinger and Sondra Silverston

Journey
  Keret, E. The girl on the fridge; stories; translated from the Hebrew by Miriam Shlesinger and Sondra Silverston

Knockoff Venus
  Keret, E. The girl on the fridge; stories; translated from the Hebrew by Miriam Shlesinger and Sondra Silverston

Like Bats
  World Literature Today v82 no5 p63 S/O 2008

Loquat
  Keret, E. The girl on the fridge; stories; translated from the Hebrew by Miriam Shlesinger and Sondra Silverston

Monkey say, monkey do
  Keret, E. The girl on the fridge; stories; translated from the Hebrew by Miriam Shlesinger and Sondra Silverston

Moral something
  Keret, E. The girl on the fridge; stories; translated from the Hebrew by Miriam Shlesinger and Sondra Silverston

More life
  Keret, E. The Nimrod flipout; translated from the Hebrew by Miriam Shlesinger and Sondra Silverston

My best friend
  Keret, E. The girl on the fridge; stories; translated from the Hebrew by Miriam Shlesinger and Sondra Silverston

My girlfriend's naked
  Keret, E. The Nimrod flipout; translated from the Hebrew by Miriam Shlesinger and Sondra Silverston

Myth milk
  Keret, E. The girl on the fridge; stories; translated from the Hebrew by Miriam Shlesinger and Sondra Silverston

The night the buses died
  Keret, E. The girl on the fridge; stories; translated from the Hebrew by Miriam Shlesinger and Sondra Silverston
  Bomb no95 p94 Spr 2006

The Nimrod flipout
  Keret, E. The Nimrod flipout; translated from the Hebrew by Miriam Shlesinger and Sondra Silverston

A no-magician birthday
  Keret, E. The girl on the fridge; stories; translated from the Hebrew by Miriam Shlesinger and Sondra Silverston

No politics
  Keret, E. The girl on the fridge; stories; translated from the Hebrew by Miriam Shlesinger and Sondra Silverston

Not human beings
  Keret, E. The girl on the fridge; stories; translated from the Hebrew by Miriam Shlesinger and Sondra Silverston

Nothing
  Keret, E. The girl on the fridge; stories; translated from the Hebrew by Miriam Shlesinger and Sondra Silverston

On the nutritional value of dreams
  Keret, E. The girl on the fridge; stories; translated from the Hebrew by Miriam Shlesinger and Sondra Silverston

One hundred percent
  Keret, E. The girl on the fridge; stories; translated from the Hebrew by Miriam Shlesinger and Sondra Silverston

One kiss on the mouth in Mombasa
  Keret, E. The Nimrod flipout; translated from the Hebrew by Miriam Shlesinger and Sondra Silverston

Kim, Sungok
Seoul: 1964, winter
  Land of exile: contemporary Korean fiction;
    translated and edited by Marshall Pihl,
    Bruce Fulton, and Ju-Chan Fulton
Kim, Tongni
The post horse curse
  Land of exile: contemporary Korean fiction;
    translated and edited by Marshall Pihl,
    Bruce Fulton, and Ju-Chan Fulton
Kimball, L. E.
Space Dwellers
  The Massachusetts Review v46 no2 p295-311
    Summ 2005
Kimball, Michael
From How Much of Us There Was
  Prairie Schooner v79 no3 p5-13 Fall 2005
Kimber, Josie
A cake story
  Getting even; revenge stories; edited by Mitzi
    Szereto
Kin. McAllister, B.
Kincaid, Jamaica
What I have been doing lately
  The Paris review book for planes, trains, ele-
    vators, and waiting rooms; by the editors of
    the Paris review; with an introduction by
    Richard Powers
Kincaid, Nanci
The currency of love
  New stories from the South: the year's best,
    2006; selected from U.S. magazines by Al-
    lan Gurganus with Kathy Pories; with an
    introduction by Allan Gurganus
Kind. Miller, L. E.
The **kind** assassin. Boyle, T. C.
Kind, kind and gentle is she. Hodgson, W. H.
A **kind** of love story. Pande, M.
The **kind** of luxuries we felt we deserved. Blum,
  J.
KINDERGARTEN
Gordon, M. Separation
Kinderscenen. Updike, J.
Kinderszenen. Updike, J.
The **kindest** cut. Budnitz, J.
The **kindly** isle. Pohl, F.
Kindly omit flowers. Winchell, P.
KINDNESS
Bashar, B. a.- . The jewelry box
Donoghue, E. Good deed
Hawes, L. Halcyon House
James, C. L. R. Androcles and the lion
James, H. Alone
James, H. A winter story
Kennedy, C. Seizure
Meno, J. Be a good citizen
Michaels, A. Fugitive pieces [excerpt]
Molodowsky, K. The daughter-in-law
Molodowsky, K. To hear the megillah on Purim
Molodowsky, K. Tulia Shor's stories: King Sol-
  omon's bride
Molodowsky, K. Tulia Shor's stories: The cap-
  tain
Molodowsky, K. Tulia Shor's stories: The fourth
  Mitzvah
Naiyer Masud. Resting place
Nisbet, R. Ladies' man
Percoto, C. The bread of the departed
Rani, T. J. The decision

Rylands, J. T. Integration
Kindness. McLean, K.
Kinds of love. Updike, D.
Kind's silence [excerpt]. Solá, M.
King, C. Daly (Charles Daly)
The episode of *Torment IV*
  The Mammoth book of vintage whodunnits;
    edited by Maxim Jakubowski
King, Charles Daly *See* King, C. Daly (Charles
  Daly), 1895-1963
King, Francis
The sitting tenant
  The Best British mysteries, 2005; edited by
    Maxim Jakubowski
King, John
(tr.) *See* Vargas Llosa, Mario
King, Jonathon
Snake eyes
  The Best American mystery stories, 2004; ed-
    ited and with an introduction by Nelson
    DeMille; Otto Penzler, series editor
King, Joseph Hillstrom *See* Hill, Joe
KING, LARRY, 1933-
About
Zebrowski, G. The coming of Christ the joker
King, Laurie R.
Cat's paw
  Murder at the foul line; edited by Otto
    Penzler
The fool
  Mystery Writers of America presents the blue
    religion; new stories about cops, criminals,
    and the chase; edited by Michael Connelly
The house
  Unusual suspects; stories of mystery & fanta-
    sy; edited by Dana Stabenow.
Weaving the dark
  McSweeney's mammoth treasury of thrilling
    tales; edited by Michael Chabon
King, Lily
Five Tuesdays in winter
  Contemporary Maine fiction; an anthology of
    short stories; edited by Wesley McNair
  Ploughshares v31 no2/3 p190-204 Fall 2005
Reading his heart
  Good Housekeeping v242 no5 p261-4, 266-9
    My 2006
KING, MARTIN LUTHER, JR., 1929-1968
About
Johnson, C. R. Dr. King's refrigerator
King, Owen
Frozen animals
  King, O. We're all in this together; a novella
    and stories
The meerkat
  Burnham, C. Who can save us now?; brand-
    new superheroes and their amazing [short]
    stories; edited by Owen King and John
    McNally; [illustrations by Chris Burnham]
My second wife
  King, O. We're all in this together; a novella
    and stories
Snake
  King, O. We're all in this together; a novella
    and stories
We're all in this together
  King, O. We're all in this together; a novella
    and stories

King, Owen—*Continued*
Wonders
King, O. We're all in this together; a novella and stories
King, Patricia
Baggage claim
Queens noir; edited by Robert Knightly
King, Sharon
Quiescent
Femspec v6 no2 p112-21 2005
King, Stephen
Ayana
King, S. Just after sunset; stories
The Paris Review v49 p160-74 Fall 2007
The ballad of the flexible bullet
Poe's children; the new horror: an anthology; [edited by] Peter Straub.
The cat from hell
King, S. Just after sunset; stories
The gingerbread girl
King, S. Just after sunset; stories
Esquire v148 no1 p87, 89-110 Jl 2007
Graduation afternoon
King, S. Just after sunset; stories
Harvey's dream
The Best American mystery stories, 2004; edited and with an introduction by Nelson DeMille; Otto Penzler, series editor
The Year's best fantasy and horror: seventeenth annual collection; edited by Ellen Datlow, Kelly Link and Gavin J. Grant
King, S. Just after sunset; stories
Home delivery
The living dead; edited by John Joseph Adams
Lisey and the madman
McSweeney's enchanted chamber of astonishing stories; edited by Michael Chabon; illustrations by Mike Mignola
Morality [Cover story; part of a special section: Stories of Our Time]
Esquire v152 no1 p57-67, 110-11 Jl 2009
Mute
King, S. Just after sunset; stories
N.
King, S. Just after sunset; stories
The New York Times at special bargain rates
King, S. Just after sunset; stories
The Best science fiction and fantasy of the year: volume three; edited by Jonathan Strahan
The reach
Contemporary Maine fiction; an anthology of short stories; edited by Wesley McNair
Rest stop
King, S. Just after sunset; stories
Stationary bike
King, S. Just after sunset; stories
The tale of the Gray Dick
McSweeney's mammoth treasury of thrilling tales; edited by Michael Chabon
The things they left behind
Transgressions; edited by Ed McBain
King, S. Just after sunset; stories
A very tight place
King, S. Just after sunset; stories
Willa
King, S. Just after sunset; stories
The **King** and I. Schrader, S.

The **king** butcher of Bristol Bay. Peñaranda, O.
King Cole's American Salvage. Campbell, B. J.
King Devil's bargain. Arnow, H. L. S.
The **king** dies. Lamb, H.
King dragon. Swanwick, M.
KING KONG (FICTITIOUS CHARACTER)
Kiernan, C. R. The ape's wife
KING KONG (MOTION PICTURE: 1933)
Gerrold, D. King Kong: behind the scenes
King Kong: behind the scenes. Gerrold, D.
King Log in Exile. Atwood, M.
King of America. Mindt, A.
King of Bums. Mlalazi, C.
The **king** of infinite space. Wieland, M.
The **King** of Kohlrabi. Ohlin, A.
The **King** of Sentences. Lethem, J.
King of shadows. Lansdale, J. R.
The **king** of slack. Gallo, L.
The **king** of the djinn. Ackert, D. and Rosenbaum, B.
King of the ferns. Goldfaden, J.
King of the Gypsies. Myka, L.
King of the maggots. Travis, J.
King of the World. Chapman, J. D.
The **king** of where-I-go. Waldrop, H.
King Pelles the sure. Beagle, P. S.
King Rat. Fowler, K. J.
King Solomon's ring. Zelazny, R.
A **king** without people. Schwitters, K.
Kingdom of Fife. Welsh, I.
The **kingdom** of the worm. Smith, C. A.
The **kingdom** of Tortirra. Bierce, A.
The **kingdom** where straightforward, logical thinking was admired over every other kind. Maxwell, W.
Kingfish. Stockton, C. R.
KINGS AND RULERS
See also names of kings and rulers
Beagle, P. S. King Pelles the sure
Coville, B. With his head tucked underneath his arm
DeNiro, A. A keeper
Morris, W. A king's lesson
Palazzeschi, A. The beautiful king
Smith, C. A. The death of Malygris
Smith, C. A. The seven geases
Smith, C. A. The voyage of King Euvoran
Smith, M. Protocol
Yolen, J. Allerleirauh
Yolen, J. The seventh mandarin
Zelazny, R. The great slow kings
The **king's** ears. Yasuoka, S.
A **king's** lesson. Morris, W.
Kings who die. Anderson, P.
Kinman, Gay Toltl
Catnapping
The International Association of Crime Writers presents Murder in Vegas; new crime tales of gambling and desperation; edited by Michael Connelly
iRomance
Medium of murder; edited by Susan Budavari and Suzanne Flaig
Kinney, Alison Lee
Term
The Literary Review (Madison, N.J.) v48 no4 p124-45 Summ 2005

Klages, Ellen—*Continued*
  Be prepared
    Klages, E. Portable childhoods; stories
  Clip art
    Klages, E. Portable childhoods; stories
  The feed bag
    Klages, E. Portable childhoods; stories
  Flying over water
    Klages, E. Portable childhoods; stories
  The green glass sea
    Klages, E. Portable childhoods; stories
    Poe's children; the new horror: an anthology;
      [edited by] Peter Straub.
  Guys day out
    Klages, E. Portable childhoods; stories
  In the house of the seven librarians
    Klages, E. Portable childhoods; stories
    The Year's best fantasy and horror: twentieth
      annual collection; edited by Ellen Datlow
      and Kelly Link & Gavin J. Grant
  Intelligent design
    Klages, E. Portable childhoods; stories
  Möbius, stripped of a muse
    Klages, E. Portable childhoods; stories
  Mrs. Zeno's paradox
    Eclipse one; new science fiction and fantasy;
      edited by Jonathan Strahan
  Portable childhoods
    Klages, E. Portable childhoods; stories
  Ringing up baby
    Klages, E. Portable childhoods; stories
    Nature v440 p1244 Ap 27 2006
  A taste of summer
    Klages, E. Portable childhoods; stories
  Time gypsy
    Klages, E. Portable childhoods; stories
  Travel agency
    Klages, E. Portable childhoods; stories
  Triangle
    Klages, E. Portable childhoods; stories
Klam, Matthew
  Adina, Astrid, Chipewee, Jasmine
    Beha, C. R. The Ecco anthology of contem-
      porary American short fiction; selected by
      Joyce Carol Oates and Christopher R.
      Beha.
    The New Yorker v82 no13 p70-9 My 15 2006
  Issues I dealt with in therapy
    The New Granta book of the American short
      story; edited and introduced by Richard
      Ford
Klaskin, Ronnie
  Nickels and dimes
    The International Association of Crime Writ-
      ers presents Murder in Vegas; new crime
      tales of gambling and desperation; edited
      by Michael Connelly
Klass, Philip *See* Tenn, William, 1920-
Klassen, Sarah
  Adelia
    Klassen, S. A feast of longing
  Beyond the border
    Klassen, S. A feast of longing
  The Carpathians
    Klassen, S. A feast of longing
  Ending with poetry
    Klassen, S. A feast of longing
  Eye of the moon
    Klassen, S. A feast of longing

In such circumstances
    Klassen, S. A feast of longing
  A perfect location
    Klassen, S. A feast of longing
  Saved
    Klassen, S. A feast of longing
  The seven steps
    Klassen, S. A feast of longing
  Still life
    Klassen, S. A feast of longing
  Surprised
    Klassen, S. A feast of longing
  Thursday at Agape Table
    Klassen, S. A feast of longing
  Wednesday is adoration
    Klassen, S. A feast of longing
  The wind blows where it chooses
    Klassen, S. A feast of longing
Klavan, Andrew
  Her Lord and Master
    Dangerous women; edited by Otto Penzler
    The Best American Mystery Stories, 2006;
      edited and with an introduction by Scott
      Turow; Otto Penzler, series editor
KLEBOLD, DYLAN, 1981-1999
  About
  Pierce, T. J. Columbine: the musical
Kleinheincz, Csilla
  A drop of raspberry
    Interfictions; an anthology of interstitial writ-
      ing; edited by Delia Sherman and Theodora
      Goss
Kleinman, Sherryl
  A Fine Hen
    Calyx v23 no2 p66-70 Summ 2006
Kletter, Dana
  Night Song
    Michigan Quarterly Review v47 no4 p625-39
      Fall 2008
Klimasewiski, Marshall N.
  Aëronauts
    Klimasewiski, M. N. Tyrants; stories
  Jun Hee
    Klimasewiski, M. N. Tyrants; stories
  The last time I saw Richard
    Klimasewiski, M. N. Tyrants; stories
  Nobile's airship
    Klimasewiski, M. N. Tyrants; stories
  Some thrills
    Klimasewiski, M. N. Tyrants; stories
  Tanner
    Klimasewiski, M. N. Tyrants; stories
  Tanner and Jun Hee
    Klimasewiski, M. N. Tyrants; stories
  The third house
    Best of Tin House; stories; foreword by Dor-
      othy Allison
    Klimasewiski, M. N. Tyrants; stories
  Tyrants
    Klimasewiski, M. N. Tyrants; stories
Kling, Jim
  The bell-curve drug
    Nature v436 p1064 Ag 18 2005
  Semi-autonomous
    Nature v442 p108 Jl 6 2006

Klinkowitz, Jerome
  Basepaths
    So the story goes; twenty-five years of the Johns Hopkins short fiction series; edited by John T. Irwin and Jean McGarry; with a foreword by John Barth
Kloefkorn, William
  At Home on This Movable Earth
    Iowa Review v35 no2 p97-111 Fall 2005
Klonimos, Samuel
  I Santi delle Anitre
    Raritan v26 no4 p68-83 Spr 2007
  The Relation
    Raritan v28 no2 p54-100 Fall 2008
Kluge, Alexander
  Six stories
    Terrestrial intelligence; international fiction now from New Directions; edited by Barbara Epler
Kluge, Christine Boyka
  Documenting my abduction
    Text: Ur; the new book of masks; [edited by Forrest Aguirre]
  No mooing in the moonlight
    Text: Ur; the new book of masks; [edited by Forrest Aguirre]
  Parchment and twigs
    Text: Ur; the new book of masks; [edited by Forrest Aguirre]
Klyuchareva, Natalya
  One Year in Paradise
    The Virginia Quarterly Review v85 no3 p137-47 Summ 2009
The **knack**. Hawes, L.
Knall. Levi, P.
Knall [Excerpt from A Tranquil Star] Levi, P.
Knapsack poems. Arnason, E.
KNICKKNACKS
  Abbott, L. K. Sweet cheeks
Knife/Tape/Rope. Cooper, D.
The **knife**. Oates, J. C.
Knife, Barn, My Harvey. Houtrides, R.
Knife fight. Goldman, J.
KNIFE THROWING
  Rash, R. Dangerous love
Knight, Alanna
  Faro and the bogus inspector
    The Best British mysteries, 2006; edited by Maxim Jakubowski
Knight, Michael
  Birdland
    Best of the South: from the second decade of New stories from the South; selected and introduced by Anne Tyler
  Gerald's monkey
    Playboy's college fiction; a collection of 21 years of contest winners; edited by Alice K. Turner; foreword by Thom Jones
  Smash and grab
    The Best American mystery stories, 2004; edited and with an introduction by Nelson DeMille; Otto Penzler, series editor
  Thanksgiving
    The Southern Review (Baton Rouge, La.) v41 no4 p737-54 Aut 2005
KNIGHT, SARAH KEMBLE, 1666-1727
  About
  Boyle, T. C. The doubtfulness of water: Madam Knight's journey to New York, 1702

A **knight** at the opera. Disch, T. M.
A **knight** for Merytha (Dilvish 4 of 11). Zelazny, R.
KNIGHTHOOD *See* Knights and knighthood
Knightly, Robert
  First calvary
    Queens noir; edited by Robert Knightly
  One more for the road
    Brooklyn noir; edited by Tim McLoughlin
  Take the man's pay
    Manhattan noir; edited by Lawrence Block
    The Best American mystery stories 2007; edited and with and introduction by Carl Hiaasen; Otto Penzler, series editor
KNIGHTS AND KNIGHTHOOD
    See also Chivalry; Middle Ages
  De Camp, L. S. and Pratt, F. The mathematics of magic
  La Motte-Fouqué, F. H. K., Freiherr von. Undine
  Smith, C. A. The kingdom of the worm
  Zelazny, R. The George business
The **knights** of Arthur. Pohl, F.
KNIGHTS OF COLUMBUS
  Currans-Sheehan, T. The secrets that men have
KNITTING
  Atwood, M. The art of cooking and serving
  Hempel, A. Beg, sl tog, inc, cont, rep
Knives. Erdrich, L.
Knives in the dark. Herron, D.
Knock them down. Magee, K.
Knockemstiff. Pollock, D. R.
Knocking on Doors. Fewell, R.
Knockoff Venus. Keret, E.
The **knot**. Varallo, A.
Knots and nuts. Castillon, C.
The **knotted** handkerchief. Garrett, P.
Know what I mean? Archer, J.
Knowing. Soueif, A.
Knowing his secret. Shamlan, S. a.- .
Known. Williams, C.
Knuckle Curve. Mepham, A.
Knuckles. Wingate, S.
Kobayashi, Tamai
  Panopte's eye
    So long been dreaming; postcolonial science fiction & fantasy; Nalo Hopkinson & Uppinder Mehan, eds
Kobin, Joann
  Dr. Leopold Needs a Little Help
    New England Review v28 no1 p24-36 2007
Kobrin, Leon
  America, you S.O.B.
    Shining and shadow; an anthology of early Yiddish stories from the Lower East Side; edited and translated by Albert Waldinger
  Apartment no. four
    No star too beautiful; Yiddish stories from 1382 to the present; compiled and translated by Joachim Neugroschel
  The calamity of Mottel Hannah-Beyle's
    Shining and shadow; an anthology of early Yiddish stories from the Lower East Side; edited and translated by Albert Waldinger
  Door number one
    Shining and shadow; an anthology of early Yiddish stories from the Lower East Side; edited and translated by Albert Waldinger

Kobrin, Leon—*Continued*
The freed children of the shtetl
   Shining and shadow; an anthology of early
      Yiddish stories from the Lower East Side;
      edited and translated by Albert Waldinger
What he saw at the Yiddish theater
   Shining and shadow; an anthology of early
      Yiddish stories from the Lower East Side;
      edited and translated by Albert Waldinger
Kocsis, Andre
The English Tutor
   Dalhousie Review v86 no2 p237-47 Summ
   2006
Kodama, María
Leonor
   Díaz, G. J. Women and power in Argentine
   literature; stories, interviews, and critical
   essays; [by] Gwendolyn Díaz
Koënings, N. S.
Pearls to swine
   Koënings, N. S. Theft; stories
Setting up shop
   Koënings, N. S. Theft; stories
Sisters for Shama
   Koënings, N. S. Theft; stories
Theft
   Koënings, N. S. Theft; stories
Wondrous strange
   Koënings, N. S. Theft; stories
Kohler, Sheila
Baboons
   Beha, C. R. The Ecco anthology of contem-
   porary American short fiction; selected by
   Joyce Carol Oates and Christopher R.
   Beha.
Chou d'amour
   The Yale Review v95 no2 p136-54 Ap 2007
Symbols
   The American Scholar v77 no3 p124-9 Summ
   2008
The transitional object
   The O. Henry Prize stories 2008; edited and
   with an introduction by Laura Furman; with
   essays on the stories they admire most by
   jurors Chimamanda Ngozi Adiche, David
   Leavitt, David Means
Köhlmeier, Paula
The Man with the Black Hair and the Many
   Tattoos
   Southern Humanities Review v40 no4 p360-7
   Fall 2006
Koi. Ducornet, R.
Koi [2]. Ducornet, R.
Koja, Kathe
The neglected garden
   The new weird; Ann & Jeff VanderMeer, edi-
   tors
Kolchak & the cult murders. Barr, M. W.
Koldys, Sayzie
Mona, Yehya, Basma
   New England Review v29 no1 p120-34 2008
Kolendo, Anastasia
Wintering
   Best new American voices 2009; guest editor
   Mary Gaitskill; series editors John Kulka
   and Natalie Danford

Kolosov, Jacqueline
Solstice in the Jardin du Luxembourg
   Western Humanities Review v61 no2 p150-68
   Spr/Summ 2007
Komie, Lowell B.
Ecstasy and Poetry in Chicago
   Legal Studies Forum v32 no1 p45-50 2008
Mombasa
   Legal Studies Forum v33 no2 p267-72 2009
Origami Aeroplane
   Legal Studies Forum v32 no1 p39-44 2008
Komla-Ebri, Kossi
"Crossroads identity"
   Multicultural literature in contemporary Italy;
   edited by Marie Orton and Graziella Parati
"Home . . . sickness"
   Multicultural literature in contemporary Italy;
   edited by Marie Orton and Graziella Parati
Komodo. Pratt, T.
Konkle, Marsena
Resolved
   The best Christian short stories; edited and
   with an introduction by Bret Lott
Kōno, Taeko
Bone meat
   Terrestrial intelligence; international fiction
   now from New Directions; edited by Bar-
   bara Epler
Konrath, J. A.
Epitaph
   Thriller; edited by James Patterson
Overproof
   Chicago blues; edited by Libby Fischer
   Hellmann
Konrath, J. A. and Wilson, F. Paul (Francis Paul)
The sound of blunder
   The Horror Writers Association presents
   Blood lite; an anthology of humorous hor-
   ror stories; edited by Kevin J. Anderson
Konrath, Joe *See* Konrath, J. A., 1970-
Kooker, Jonathan
Measures of Height, Heat and Time
   The Literary Review (Madison, N.J.) v50 no2
   p137-40 Wint 2007
Kool things: or why I want to fuck Patty Hearst.
   McCarthy, T.
KOREA
Ch'ae, M. The wife and children
Cho, C. Land of exile
Choe, I. The boozer
Ch'oe, S. Conviction
Ch'oe, Y. There a petal silently falls
Ch'oe, Y. The thirteen-scent flower
Ch'oe, Y. Whisper yet
Chon, K. Kapitan Ri
Hwang, S. A dream of good fortune
Hwang, S. Mountains
Im, C. A shared journey
Jo Kyung Ran. Looking for the elephant
Jung, H.-Y. Han Gahp
Kim, H. From powder to powder
Kim, M. Scarlet fingernails
Kim, S. Seoul: 1964, winter
Kim, T. The post horse curse
O, C. The bronze mirror
Pak, W. Winter outing
Yoon, P. And we will be here

KOREA—*Continued*
Yun, H. The man who was left as nine pairs of shoes
KOREAN AMERICANS
Apple, M. Peace
Beagle, P. S. El regalo
July, M. The shared patio
Kim, J. Yangban
Klimasewiski, M. N. Jun Hee
Klimasewiski, M. N. Tanner
Klimasewiski, M. N. Tanner and Jun Hee
KOREAN REFUGEES
Working, R. Dear leader
Korean Standards. Park, M.-G. and Anthony
KOREAN WAR, 1950-1953
Daugherty, T. Lamplighter
Garrett, G. P. Heroes
KOREANS
China
Working, R. Dear leader
Italy
Ch'oe, Y. The last of Hanak'o
United States
Hirahara, N. Number 19
Koretsky, J. Lea
Alligator story
Koretsky, J. L. Snapshot; collected stories
The cherry on the cake
Koretsky, J. L. Snapshot; collected stories
Deliberate men
Koretsky, J. L. Snapshot; collected stories
A delicate balance
Koretsky, J. L. Snapshot; collected stories
Diamond versus Jiminez
Koretsky, J. L. Snapshot; collected stories
The disintegrating man
Koretsky, J. L. Snapshot; collected stories
The man of the house
Koretsky, J. L. Snapshot; collected stories
Root
Koretsky, J. L. Snapshot; collected stories
Snapshot
Koretsky, J. L. Snapshot; collected stories
A stranger among them
Koretsky, J. L. Snapshot; collected stories
Timeline
Koretsky, J. L. Snapshot; collected stories
The tormenting eye of God
Koretsky, J. L. Snapshot; collected stories
Korn, Rokhl
The end of the road
No star too beautiful; Yiddish stories from 1382 to the present; compiled and translated by Joachim Neugroschel
Kornbluth, C. M. (Cyril M.)
(jt. auth) See Pohl, Frederik and Kornbluth, C. M. (Cyril M.)
Kornbluth, Cyril M. *See* Kornbluth, C. M. (Cyril M.), 1923-1958
Koshy, Mridula
Stray Blades of Grass
Dalhousie Review v88 no1 p105-13 Spr 2008
Kosmatka, Ted
The art of alchemy
The Best science fiction and fantasy of the year: volume three; edited by Jonathan Strahan

The prophet of Flores
The Best science fiction and fantasy of the year: volume two; edited by Jonathan Strahan
The Year's best science fiction: twenty-fifth annual collection; edited by Gardner Dozois
Kostival, Ben
Islanders
New England Review v30 no1 p146-51 2009
Kotowicz, Madeline
In Rut
Boston Review v31 no6 p41-3 N/D 2006
Koulack, David
Chess
Dalhousie Review v86 no1 p51-9 Spr 2006
The Clock
Dalhousie Review v87 no1 p119-24 Spr 2007
The Surgeon
Dalhousie Review v86 no2 p221-9 Summ 2006
Koum. Lamb, H.
Koumandareas, Menēs
Seraphim
Angelic & black; contemporary Greek short stories; edited and translated by David Connolly; with an introduction by Vangelis Hatzivassileiou
Koustas, Panagiotis
Athos Emfovos in the temple of sound
The SFWA European hall of fame; sixteen contemporary masterpieces of science fiction from the continent; edited by James Morrow and Kathryn Morrow
Kovar, Vincent
The all-night dentist
Hardcore hardboiled; edited by Todd Robinson; introduction by Otto Penzler
Kowalski's in love. Rollins, J.
Kozak, Harley Jane
Common Prayer
Ms. v15 no3 p66-71 Fall 2005
Kozameh, Alicia
Impression of heights
Díaz, G. J. Women and power in Argentine literature; stories, interviews, and critical essays; [by] Gwendolyn Díaz
Kozlov, Vladimir
Drill and Song Day
Agni no67 p157-63 2008
Kozlowski, Lori
Three times a night, every other night
Las Vegas noir; edited by Jarrett Keene & Todd James Pierce.
Krall, Hanna
The Woman from Hamburg
The New Yorker v80 no40 p52, 54, 56, 58-9 D 20-27 2004
Kramlovsky, Beatrix
Silk road
Passport to crime; the finest mystery stories from International Crime Writers; edited by Janet Hutchings
Kramon, Justin M.
The Way People Act in the World
StoryQuarterly v41 p398-423 2005
Kranes, David
Target Practice
Ploughshares v32 no2/3 p118-25 Fall 2006

Krasikov, Sana
The alternate
  Krasikov, S. One more year; stories
Asal
  Krasikov, S. One more year; stories
  The Virginia Quarterly Review v84 no3 p151-
    67 Summ 2008
Better half
  Krasikov, S. One more year; stories
Companion
  The O. Henry Prize stories 2007; edited and
    with an introduction by Laura Furman; with
    essays on the story they admire most by ju-
    rors Charles D'Ambrosio, Ursula K. Le
    Guin, Lily Tuck
  Krasikov, S. One more year; stories
  The New Yorker v81 no30 p84-93 O 3 2005
Debt
  Krasikov, S. One more year; stories
Maia in Yonkers
  Krasikov, S. One more year; stories
The repatriates
  Krasikov, S. One more year; stories
  The New Yorker v84 no10 p116-25 Ap 21
    2008
There will be no fourth Rome
  Krasikov, S. One more year; stories
Krasznahorkai, László
War and war [excerpt]
  Terrestrial intelligence; international fiction
    now from New Directions; edited by Bar-
    bara Epler
Krause, Erika
Zero
  The dictionary of failed relationships; 26 tales
    of love gone wrong; edited by Meredith
    Broussard
Krause, Jo Neace
A Woman in the News
  The Massachusetts Review v49 no3 p263-78
    Aut 2008
Krauss, Nicole
From the Desk of Daniel Varsky
  Harper's v314 p75-80 Je 2007
Kreativity for kats. Leiber, F.
The **Krells** of Tancras Moor. Stackpole, M. A.
Kremer, Harold
Gelatin
  The Flight of the condor; stories of violence
    and war from Colombia; translated and
    compiled by Jennifer Gabrielle Edwards;
    foreword by Hugo Chaparro Valderrama.
Kress, Nancy
Art of war
  The new space opera; edited by Gardner
    Dozois and Jonathan Strahan
Beggars in Spain
  The Best of the best, volume 2; 20 years of
    the best short science fiction novels; edited
    by Gardner Dozois
By fools like me
  The Best science fiction and fantasy of the
    year: volume two; edited by Jonathan
    Strahan
Computer virus
  Kress, N. Nano comes to Clifford Falls and
    other stories; with a forward by Mike
    Resnck

Ej-es
  The Year's best science fiction: twenty-first
    annual collection; edited by Gardner Dozois
  Kress, N. Nano comes to Clifford Falls and
    other stories; with a forward by Mike
    Resnck
Elevator
  Strahan, J. Eclipse two; new science fiction
    and fantasy; edited by Jonathan Strahan
First flight
  Kress, N. Nano comes to Clifford Falls and
    other stories; with a forward by Mike
    Resnck
Fountain of age
  Nebula Awards showcase 2009; the year's
    best SF and fantasy; selected by the Sci-
    ence Fiction and Fantasy Writers of Ameri-
    ca; edited by Ellen Datlow
Laws of survival
  The Year's best science fiction: twenty-fifth
    annual collection; edited by Gardner Dozois
Mirror image
  Kress, N. Nano comes to Clifford Falls and
    other stories; with a forward by Mike
    Resnck
The most famous little girl in the world
  Kress, N. Nano comes to Clifford Falls and
    other stories; with a forward by Mike
    Resnck
My mother dancing
  Nebula Awards showcase 2007; the year's
    best SF and fantasy; selected by the Sci-
    ence Fiction and Fantasy Writers of Ameri-
    ca; edited by Mike Resnick
  Kress, N. Nano comes to Clifford Falls and
    other stories; with a forward by Mike
    Resnck
Nano comes to Clifford Falls
  Kress, N. Nano comes to Clifford Falls and
    other stories; with a forward by Mike
    Resnck
Patent infringement
  This is my funniest; leading science fiction
    writers present their funniest stories ever;
    edited by Mike Resnick
  Kress, N. Nano comes to Clifford Falls and
    other stories; with a forward by Mike
    Resnck
  [Short story]
  Nature v440 p382 Mr 16 2006
Savior
  Kress, N. Nano comes to Clifford Falls and
    other stories; with a forward by Mike
    Resnck
Shiva in shadow
  The Year's best science fiction: twenty-
    second annual collection; edited by Gardner
    Dozois
  Kress, N. Nano comes to Clifford Falls and
    other stories; with a forward by Mike
    Resnck
Stone man
  Wizards; edited by Jack Dann and Gardner
    Dozois

Kun, Michael—*Continued*

Corrections to my memoirs
Kun, M. Corrections to my memoirs; collected stories

Did she jump or was she pushed
Kun, M. Corrections to my memoirs; collected stories

Does your job application put your company at risk?
Kun, M. Corrections to my memoirs; collected stories

Fresh fruit
Kun, M. Corrections to my memoirs; collected stories

The handwriting patient
Kun, M. Corrections to my memoirs; collected stories

Heaven help me
Kun, M. Corrections to my memoirs; collected stories

Her night classes
Kun, M. Corrections to my memoirs; collected stories

The last chance Texaco
Kun, M. Corrections to my memoirs; collected stories

My wife and my dead wife
Kun, M. Corrections to my memoirs; collected stories

One last story about girls and chocolate
Kun, M. Corrections to my memoirs; collected stories

A place like here, only different
Kun, M. Corrections to my memoirs; collected stories

Steve Smith
Kun, M. Corrections to my memoirs; collected stories

That will be ten cents
Kun, M. Corrections to my memoirs; collected stories

Touched, very touched
Kun, M. Corrections to my memoirs; collected stories

Weight and fortune
Kun, M. Corrections to my memoirs; collected stories

You have made quite a purchase
Kun, M. Corrections to my memoirs; collected stories

Kundera, Milan

The hitchhiking game
My mistress's sparrow is dead; great love stories, from Chekhov to Munro; edited by Jeffrey Eugenides

KUNG FU

Messinger, J. Winged attack

Kunzru, Hari

Magda Mandela
The book of other people; edited by Zadie Smith
The New Yorker v83 no23 p68-71 Ag 13 2007

Raj, Bohemian
The New Yorker v84 no4 p108-15 Mr 10 2008

Kuo, Alex

Free Kick
Ploughshares v30 no4 p67-73 Wint 2004/2005

Kuper, Thorsten

Project 38; or, The game of small causes
The black mirror and other stories; an anthology of science fiction from Germany & Austria; edited & with an introduction & notes by Franz Rottensteiner; translated by Mike Mitchell.

Kuprin, A. I. (Aleksandr Ivanovich)

Liquid sunshine
Worlds apart; an anthology of Russian fantasy and science fiction; edited and with commentary by Alexander Levitsky; translated by Alexander Levitsky and Martha T. Kitchen

A toast
Worlds apart; an anthology of Russian fantasy and science fiction; edited and with commentary by Alexander Levitsky; translated by Alexander Levitsky and Martha T. Kitchen

Kuprin, Aleksandr Ivanovich *See* Kuprin, A. I. (Aleksandr Ivanovich), 1870-1938

Kureishi, Hanif

A meeting, at last
Telling tales; edited by Nadine Gordimer
Something to Tell You
Critical Quarterly v50 no1/2 p43-60 Spr/Summ 2008

Kuris, Gabriel

The Human Atlas of Hackensack
Harvard Review (1992) no32 p139-54 2007

Kurland, Anthony

South of South
Harvard Review (1992) no31 p90-5 2006

Kursk. Suarez, M. E.

Kushner, Ellen

Beauty Sleeping [Includes a commentary]
Parabola v30 no1 p84-5 F 2005

Kuskin, William and Adcock, Justin

Watermark [Graphic novella]
Southern Quarterly v43 no3 p109-18 Spr 2006

Kuskin, William and Slade, Matthew

Into the Book [Graphic story]
English Language Notes v46 no2 p17-21 Fall/Wint 2008

Pilgrimage to the MLA [Graphic story]
English Language Notes v46 no2 p73-5 Fall/Wint 2008

Kuttner, Henry

A cross of centiures
A cross of centuries; twenty-five imaginative tales about the Christ; edited by Michael Bishop

KUWAIT

Hammad, H. a.- . The return of a captive
Salih, L. M. Guns and jasmine
Uthman, L. a.- . The ID card

Kuwari, Widad 'Abd al-Latif al-

Layla
Oranges in the sun; short stories from the Arabian Gulf; edited and translated by Deborah S. Akers, Abubaker A. Bagader

Kvashay-Boyle, K.
Da bomb
Politically inspired; edited by Stephen Elliott; assistant editor, Gabriel Kram; associate editors, Elizabeth Brooks [et al.]

Kwahulé, Koffi
Babyface
From Africa; new francophone stories; edited by Adele King

Kwa'mboka
Birds
Her Majesty; 21 stories by women; edited by Jackie Gay and Emma Hargrave

Kwong, W. Tsung-Yan
All Who Die Share One Breath
New Letters v72 no3/4 p43-64 2006
Kwoon. Johnson, C. R.
Kyle, Aryn
Allegiance
The Best American short stories, 2007; selected from U. S. and Canadian magazines by Stephen King with Heidi Pitlor; with an introduction by Stephen King
Ploughshares v32 no2/3 p126-45 Fall 2006
Femme
The Georgia Review v58 no4 p851-4 Wint 2004
Little Deaths
StoryQuarterly v41 p381-7 2005
KYOTO (JAPAN) *See* Japan—Kyoto
KYRGHYSTAN
Shukman, H. Man with golden eagle
Kyriakidis, Achilleas
Nebraska
Angelic & black; contemporary Greek short stories; edited and translated by David Connolly; with an introduction by Vangelis Hatzivassileiou

L

L.. Gospodinov, G.
L. DeBard and Aliette. Groff, L.
L. DeBard and Aliette: a love story. Groff, L.
L.I.U. My World in the Early 60s. Hagelstein, R.
L. S. Bierce, A.
La Motte-Fouqué, Friedrich Heinrich Karl, Freiherr von
Undine
Tales before Narnia; the roots of modern fantasy and science fiction; edited by Douglas A. Anderson
La Puma, Salvatore
The boys of Bensonhurst
Brooklyn noir 2; the classics; edited by Tim McLoughlin
Laben, Carrie
Something in the mermaid way; y
Realms
LABOR AND LABORING CLASSES
See also Apprentices; Farm workers; Labor unions; Migrant labor; Strikes and lockouts
Cummins, A. Where I work
Halpern, F. Three meetings
Hernandez, L. Autopsy of an engine
Hernandez, L. Death in the sidesaddle
Hernandez, L. Float

Hernandez, L. The last car
Hernandez, L. Manuel, Manuel everywhere
Hernandez, L. Preparing for a strike
Hernandez, L. Thanks to Abbie Wilson
Hernandez, L. This is our song for today
Hernandez, L. Tuesday morning
Hernandez, L. We have a job for you
Hernandez, L. Yes I am a virgin
Lain, D. Instant labor
Libin, Z. All because of a needle
Libin, Z. Mister Buchholtz
London, J. South of the slot
Monk, B. Hocus-pocus
Monk, B. Now you see it
Monk, B. Small fry
Pinski, D. "Our" first of May
Pollack, R. Reflected light
Saunders, G. Christmas
Wendroff, Z. In the textile islands
Labor Day hurricane, 1935. Trevor, D.
Labor days. McLean, S.
LABOR DISPUTES
James, C. L. R. Bad Boo-boo-loo messes up the time
LABOR UNIONS
See also Labor and laboring classes; Strikes and lockouts
Arnow, H. L. S. White collar woman
Bierce, A. Industrial discontent in ancient America
Thomas, J. Union dick
Winn, T. Mrs. Somebody Somebody
Laborde, Karen
Barbecue
Gettysburg Review v18 no4 p569-77 Wint 2005
Labors of the heart. Davis, C.
LABRADOR (NFLD.)
Atwood, M. The Labrador fiasco
The **Labrador** fiasco. Atwood, M.
LaBrie, Aimee
Ducklings
LaBrie, A. Wonderful girl
Encore
LaBrie, A. Wonderful girl
Girls
LaBrie, A. Wonderful girl
In Mem
LaBrie, A. Wonderful girl
The last dead boyfriend
LaBrie, A. Wonderful girl
Look at the sky and tell me what you see
LaBrie, A. Wonderful girl
Our last supper
LaBrie, A. Wonderful girl
Runaway
LaBrie, A. Wonderful girl
Six different ways to die in the windy city!
LaBrie, A. Wonderful girl
Snowball
LaBrie, A. Wonderful girl
Tribute to an optometrist
LaBrie, A. Wonderful girl
Wanted
LaBrie, A. Wonderful girl
What she should do
LaBrie, A. Wonderful girl
Wonderful girl
LaBrie, A. Wonderful girl

LaBrie, Aimee—*Continued*
Words to live by
  LaBrie, A. Wonderful girl
Labrunie, Gérard *See* Nerval, Gérard de, 1808-1855
LaBute, Neil
Boo-boo
  LaBute, N. Seconds of pleasure; stories
Los feliz
  LaBute, N. Seconds of pleasure; stories
Full service
  LaBute, N. Seconds of pleasure; stories
Grand slam
  LaBute, N. Seconds of pleasure; stories
Layover
  LaBute, N. Seconds of pleasure; stories
Look at her
  LaBute, N. Seconds of pleasure; stories
Loose change
  LaBute, N. Seconds of pleasure; stories
Maraschino
  LaBute, N. Seconds of pleasure; stories
Open all night
  LaBute, N. Seconds of pleasure; stories
Opportunity
  LaBute, N. Seconds of pleasure; stories
Perfect
  LaBute, N. Seconds of pleasure; stories
Ravishing
  LaBute, N. Seconds of pleasure; stories
A second of pleasure
  LaBute, N. Seconds of pleasure; stories
Soft target
  LaBute, N. Seconds of pleasure; stories
Some do it naturally
  LaBute, N. Seconds of pleasure; stories
Spring break
  LaBute, N. Seconds of pleasure; stories
Switzerland
  LaBute, N. Seconds of pleasure; stories
Time-share
  LaBute, N. Seconds of pleasure; stories
Wait
  LaBute, N. Seconds of pleasure; stories
Whitecap
  LaBute, N. Seconds of pleasure; stories
LABYRINTHS
Brenchley, C. Going the Jerusalem mile
Evenson, B. Watson's boy
Stevens, F. The labyrinth
Lachrymose and the golden egg. Pratt, T.
Lackey, Mercedes
Aliens ate my pickup
  This is my funniest 2; leading science fiction writers present their funniest stories ever; edited by Mike Resnick
Lacunae. Boswell, R.
Lacunae. Kadesch, M. C.
The **lad** who stared everyone down. Yolen, J.
LADeDeDa. Le Guin, U. K. and McIntyre, V. N.
Ladies in spring. Welty, E.
The **ladies** in the library. Vidal, G.
Ladies' man. Niles, C.
Ladies' man. Nisbet, R.
The **ladies** of Grace Adieu. Clarke, S.
The **Ladies** of Sheung Wan. Han, S.
The **Lady** and the Dragon. Millet, L.
The **lady** and the merman. Yolen, J.
The **lady** and the Tiger. Roberson, J.

Lady Appleton and the Bristol crystals. Emerson, K. L.
Lady Appleton and the cautionary herbal. Emerson, K. L.
Lady Appleton and the Cripplegate chrisoms. Emerson, K. L.
Lady Appleton and the London man. Emerson, K. L.
The **lady** downstairs. Fowler, C.
A **lady** from Redhorse. Bierce, A.
Lady in red. Strout, A. M.
Lady Kate. Auchincloss, L.
The **lady** of the evening. Neera
Lady of the Skulls. McKillip, P. A.
Lady Patterly's lover. MacLeod, C.
Lady Roxanne La Belle. Resnick, L.
A **lady** slipper. Dunbar, P. L.
The **lady** was a tramp. Merril, J.
The **lady** will have the Slug Louie. Hempel, A.
The **lady** with the little dog. Chekhov, A. P.
The **lady** with the pet dog. Chekhov, A. P.
The **lady** with the pet dog. Oates, J. C.
The **lady** with the pet tribble. Brockmeier, K.
The **Lady** with the Pooch. Curbelo, J. D.
The **Lady** with the Red Car. Reeve, F. D.
Lady Yeti and the palace of artificial snows. Russell, K.
The **ladybird** room. Nisbet, R.
Lady's dream. Wolff, T.
LaFarge, Paul
Lamentation over the destruction of Ur
  Politically inspired; edited by Stephen Elliott; assistant editor, Gabriel Kram; associate editors, Elizabeth Brooks [et al.]
  The Year's best fantasy and horror: seventeenth annual collection; edited by Ellen Datlow, Kelly Link and Gavin J. Grant
Lafayette. Kiernan, C. R.
Lafe Halloway's two fights. Dunbar, P. L.
LAFFERTY, R. A., 1914-2002
  Parodies, imitations, etc.
  Di Filippo, P. Shuteye for the timebroker
The **lagerstatte**. Barron, L.
Lagioia, Nicola
Nineteen-ninety-two
  The Literary Review (Madison, N.J.) v49 no1 p119-32 Fall 2005
Lago, Sylvia
Golden days of a queen of diamonds
  Violations; stories of love by Latin American women; edited and with an introduction by Psiche Hughes; foreword by Brian Matthews
LAGOS (NIGERIA) *See* Nigeria—Lagos
Lagrange habitat Jefferson. Bova, B.
Lahiri, Jhumpa
A choice of accommodations
  Lahiri, J. Unaccustomed earth
Going ashore
  Lahiri, J. Unaccustomed earth
Hell-heaven
  Lahiri, J. Unaccustomed earth
Interpreter of maladies
  Children playing before a statue of Hercules; edited and introduced by David Sedaris
Nobody's business
  Lahiri, J. Unaccustomed earth
Once in a lifetime
  Lahiri, J. Unaccustomed earth

Lanagan, Margo—Continued
Singing my sister down
The Year's best fantasy and horror: eighteenth annual collection; edited by Ellen Datlow, Kelly Link & Gavin J. Grant
Under hell, over heaven
Lanagan, M. Red spikes
Winkie
Lanagan, M. Red spikes
The Year's best fantasy and horror: twentieth annual collection; edited by Ellen Datlow and Kelly Link & Gavin J. Grant
Wooden bride
The James Tiptree Award Anthology 3; edited by Karen Joy Fowler [et al.]
LANCASHIRE (ENGLAND) See England—Lancashire
LANCELOT (LEGENDARY CHARACTER)
James, C. L. R. Sir Lancelot and the tack
Lancelotta, Victoria
The Anniversary Trip
Gettysburg Review v21 no1 p103-12 Spr 2008
Everything Is Fine
The Antioch Review v66 no3 p461-70 Summ 2008
Land, Jon
Killing time
Thriller 2; stories you just can't put down; edited by Clive Cussler; [stories by] Kathleen Antrim . . . [et al.]
The **land** beyond the blow. Bierce, A.
Land Divers. Messud, C.
Land of a thousand dances: an R&B fable. Garza, O.
Land of ass and honey. Brown, D.
Land of exile. Cho, C.
Land of oblivion. See Coloane, F. Forgotten land [variant title: Land of oblivion]
The **land** of pain. Richter, S.
The **Land** of Sunshine and Flowers. Rosenberg, J.
Land of the midnight sun. Ohlin, A.
The **land** of youth. Thomas, E.
The **land** shark. Bower, B. M.
LAND SPECULATION See Speculation
The **land** where lemon trees bloom. Connell, E. S.
Landau, Caroline C.
Kessel
Hanging Loose no88 p95-109 2006
Landers, Clifford E.
(tr.) See Fonseca, Rubem
(tr.) See Ribeiro, João Ubaldo
Landfill. Oates, J. C.
Landfill. Rhodes, D.
Landing on Water. Baumgartner, M.
Landis, Geoffrey A.
The eyes of America
The Year's best science fiction: twenty-first annual collection; edited by Gardner Dozois
Lazy Taekos
Best American fantasy; guest editors Ann & Jeff VanderMeer; series editor Matthew Cheney
LANDLADIES See Landlord and tenant
The **landlady**. Dahl, R.
The **landlock**. Massie, E.
The **landlord**. McCabe, E.
LANDLORD AND TENANT
See also Tenant farming
Arjouni, J. The Rudolf family does good works

Bishop, E. Seven-days monologue
Clayton, J. J. Bodies like mouths
Crowther, P. Conundrums to guess
Dahl, R. The landlady
Fulton, A. If it's not too much to ask
Granados, C. Vieja chueca
Hwang, F. Garden city
Kantner, R. Down home blues
Kobrin, L. The calamity of Mottel Hannah-Beyle's
McCollum, M. He ain't Jesus
Naiyer Masud. The big garbage dump
Phillips, G. And what shall we call you?
Porter, J. A. West Baltimore
Purdy, J. Entre dos luces
Rand, N. House envy
Santangelo, E. Eaten alive
Stafford, J. The tea time of stouthearted ladies
Sutton, B. Tenants
Tea, M. Larry's place
Trevor, W. Another Christmas
Ts'an-hsüeh. The spring
Updike, D. Geranium
Vaz, K. Our lady of the artichokes
Wang Ping. The last communist virgin
Yun, H. The man who was left as nine pairs of shoes
LANDLORDS See Landlord and tenant
The **Landmark** Hotel. Connor, J.
Landmark theater may shut down. Higgins, G. V.
Landry, Judith
(tr.) See Comment, Bernard
(tr.) See Desprat, Jean-Paul
(tr.) See Gualdoni, Flaminio
(tr.) See Mencoboni, Marco
(tr.) See Otten, Willem Jan
(tr.) See Riva, Pablo Lentini
(tr.) See Sand, George
LANDSCAPE GARDENING
See also Trees
Porter, J. A. Merrymount
The **landscape** of love. Lott, B.
A **landscape** of shallows. Finch, C.
Landscape portrait. Burke, T.
Landscaping. Geni, A.
Landslide. McGlynn, D.
Landsman, Julie
Suspension
New Letters v71 no2 p77-86 2005
Lane, Joel
Against my ruins
Lane, J. The lost district and other stories
Among the dead
Lane, J. The lost district and other stories
Beth's law
British invasion; edited by Christopher Golden, Tim Lebbon & James A. Moore
Beyond the river
Lane, J. The lost district and other stories
The bootleg heart
Lane, J. The lost district and other stories
The city of love
Summer chills; strangers in stranger lands; edited by Stephen Jones
Coming of age
Lane, J. The lost district and other stories
Contract bridge
Lane, J. The lost district and other stories

LANGUAGE AND LANGUAGES—*Continued*

Gangbo, J. M. "Rometta and Giulieo"
Grimes, C. Making love: a translation
Ìṣ:l'olá, A. The uses of English
Kun, M. That will be ten cents
Lamri, T. "The pilgrimage"
Lamri, T. "You wicked wooden eyes, what are you looking at?"
Lefer, D. How much an ant can carry
Levin, Z. Grammar
Malouf, D. The only speaker of his tongue
Micklem, S. "Eft" or "Epic"
Millhauser, S. History of a disturbance
Rose, A. Ultima thule
Schutt, C. The Duchess of Albany
Stone, E. J. Tabloid reporter to the stars
Swanwick, M. Urdumheim
Tillman, L. The recipe
Vaswani, N. The pelvis series
Wallace, D. Slippered feet
Witt, M. Meaning of ends
Yellin, T. Naphtali
Zoshchenko, M. Monkey language

Language for time travelers. De Camp, L. S.
The **language** of sharks. MacEnulty, P.

Lannes, Roberta

The anguish of departure
  Summer chills; strangers in stranger lands; edited by Stephen Jones
The bandit of sanity
  Dark delicacies; original tales of terror and the macabre by the world's greatest horror writers; edited by Del Howison and Jeff Gelb

Lanoie, Christine

Cities Beneath Them
  The Massachusetts Review v46 no3 p484-93 Fall 2005

Lansdale, Joe R.

The big blow
  Lansdale, J. R. Mad dog summer and other stories
  Lansdale, J. R. Sanctified and chicken-fried; the portable Lansdale
Bill, the little steam shovel
  Lansdale, J. R. The shadows, kith and kin
Bubba Ho-Tep
  Lansdale, J. R. Sanctified and chicken-fried; the portable Lansdale
Deadman's road
  Lansdale, J. R. The shadows, kith and kin
  The living dead; edited by John Joseph Adams
Dirt devils
  Lansdale, J. R. Sanctified and chicken-fried; the portable Lansdale
Dog
  Dark delicacies 2; fear: more original tales of terror and the macabre by the world's greatest horror writers; edited by Del Howison and Jeff Gelb
The events concerning a nude fold-out found in a Harlequin romance
  Lansdale, J. R. The shadows, kith and kin
The fat man and the elephant
  Lansdale, J. R. Sanctified and chicken-fried; the portable Lansdale

A fine dark line [excerpt]
  Lansdale, J. R. Sanctified and chicken-fried; the portable Lansdale
The gentleman's hotel
  Lansdale, J. R. The shadows, kith and kin
God of the Razor
  Lansdale, J. R. The God of the Razor
Incident on and off a mountain road
  Lansdale, J. R. The God of the Razor
Janet finds the razor
  Lansdale, J. R. The God of the Razor
King of shadows
  Lansdale, J. R. The God of the Razor
The long dead day
  Lansdale, J. R. The shadows, kith and kin
Mad dog summer
  Lansdale, J. R. Mad dog summer and other stories
The magic wagon [excerpt]
  Lansdale, J. R. Sanctified and chicken-fried; the portable Lansdale
Mister weed-eater
  Lansdale, J. R. Sanctified and chicken-fried; the portable Lansdale
Mr. Bear
  The Horror Writers Association presents Blood lite; an anthology of humorous horror stories; edited by Kevin J. Anderson
The mule rustlers
  Lansdale, J. R. Mad dog summer and other stories
Night they missed the horror show
  Lansdale, J. R. Sanctified and chicken-fried; the portable Lansdale
Not from Detroit
  Lansdale, J. R. The God of the Razor
The pit
  Lansdale, J. R. Sanctified and chicken-fried; the portable Lansdale
Screwup
  Lansdale, J. R. Mad dog summer and other stories
The shadows, kith and kin
  Lansdale, J. R. The shadows, kith and kin
The shaggy house
  Lansdale, J. R. The God of the Razor
The steam man of the prairie and the dark rider get down
  Lansdale, J. R. Mad dog summer and other stories
The stream man of prairie and the dark rider get down: a dime novel
  Steampunk; edited by Ann & Jeff VanderMeer
Tight little stitches in a dead man's back
  Lansdale, J. R. Sanctified and chicken-fried; the portable Lansdale
The two-bear mambo [excerpt]
  Lone Star sleuths; an anthology of Texas crime fiction; edited and with an introduction by Bill Cunningham, Steven L. Davis, and Rollo K. Newsom.
Veil's visit
  Lansdale, J. R. Mad dog summer and other stories
Way down there
  Lansdale, J. R. Mad dog summer and other stories

Lee, Manfred, 1905-1971

For works written by this author in collaboration with Frederic Dannay see Queen, Ellery

Lee, Marie Myung-Ok

The Strip Mall and the Shaolin Temple

TriQuarterly no130 p41-59 2008

Lee, Mark

Memo to our journalists

Politically inspired; edited by Stephen Elliott; assistant editor, Gabriel Kram; associate editors, Elizabeth Brooks [et al.]

LEE, ROBERT E. (ROBERT EDWARD), 1807-1870

About

Allred, L. East of Appomattox

Harness, C. L. Quarks at Appomattox

Lee, Stewart

The aphid

Perverted by language; fiction inspired by The Fall; edited and introduced by Peter Wild.

Lee, Tanith

Dead yellow

Nature v453 p1284 Je 26 2008

The hill

The Year's best fantasy and horror: twenty-first annual collection; edited by Ellen Datlow and Kelly Link & Gavin J. Grant

Zinder

Wizards; edited by Jack Dann and Gardner Dozois

Lee, Tien-Yi

While We Waited

The Southern Review (Baton Rouge, La.) v45 no2 p214-27 Spr 2009

Lee, Yoon Ha

Eating hearts

Year's best fantasy 6; edited by David G. Hartwell & Kathryn Cramer

Leebron, Fred G.

Baby girl

Before; short stories about pregnancy from our top writers; edited by Emily Franklin and Heather Swain

The Idiot, or Life in Wartime

TriQuarterly no132 p165-85 2008

Leedom-Ackerman, Joanne

The beginning of violence

Short stories of the civil rights movement; an anthology; edited by Margaret Earley Whitt

Lees, Allan M.

The invisible hand

Nature v453 p822 Je 5 2008

Lefer, Diane

Alas, Falada!

Lefer, D. California transit

Angle and grip

Lefer, D. California transit

At the site where vision is most perfect

Lefer, D. California transit

The atlas mountains

Lefer, D. California transit

California transit

Lefer, D. California transit

How much an ant can carry

Lefer, D. California transit

Naked Chinese people

Lefer, D. California transit

The prosperity of cities and desert places

Lefer, D. California transit

Leff, Valerie

Poison

The Antioch Review v64 no3 p493-510 Summ 2006

Leff, Valerie Ann

The Love of My Life

The Antioch Review v66 no3 p434-48 Summ 2008

Metafiction: Reading Lolita Under Book Contract

Southwest Review v93 no1 p31-43 2008

The **left-handed** thief Bendel-Simso, M. M., ed. Early American detective stories; an anthology; edited by LeRoy Lad Panek and Mary M. Bendel-Simso.

Leftover Gonal-F. Brown, L. C.

Lefty. Dufresne, J.

Leg of lamb. Stewart, P.

LEGACIES See Inheritance and succession

Legacies. Fancher, J. and Cherryh, C. J.

Legacies. Murphy, Y.

The **Legacy**. Hendry, R.

The **Legacy** of Bernie the Loser. Curtin, J. M.

The **Legal** Fiction of the Lake Matchimanitou Indian School. Fletcher, M. L. M.

LEGAL PROFESSION See Law and lawyers

LEGAL STORIES See Law and lawyers

The **legend** of Andrea Cerameline. Durtschi, M.

The **legend** of Bayboy and the Mexican surfer. Shannon, J.

A **legend** of good men. Vann, D.

The **legend** of Ngurangurante (the son of the crocodile). De Mazia, V.

Legends. Puchner, E.

LEGENDS AND FOLK TALES

See also Grail; Wandering Jew

Armstrong, M. The boy who chased seagulls

Blades, L. The glumbo glisae

Carew, J. Bra Anancy and Tiger

De Mazia, V. The legend of Ngurangurante (the son of the crocodile)

Eberhardt, I. The tears of the almond tree

Lumley, B. Born of the winds

Lupoff, R. A. Treasure of the red robe men

Wolfe, G. Lord of the land

Yolen, J. The moon ribbon

Africa

Tadjo, V. The legend of Abla Pokou, queen of the Baoulé people

Ireland

Blackford, R. Manannan's children

Russia

Gogol´, N. V. Vyi [abridged]

Valente, C. M. Urchins, while swimming

West Indies

Hopkinson, N. Tan-Tan and Dry Bone

Legion of plotters. Matheson, R.

Legions in time. Swanwick, M.

The **legislation** of sheikh mal-allah. Taha, M. A.

Lego. Nadelson, S.

LeGuin, Ursula See Le Guin, Ursula K., 1929-

Lehane, Dennis

Gone down to Corpus

Lehane, D. Coronado; stories

ICU

Lehane, D. Coronado; stories

Leonard, Elmore—*Continued*

The colonel's lady [variant title: Road to Inspiration]

    Leonard, E. The complete Western stories of Elmore Leonard

The hard way

    Leonard, E. The complete Western stories of Elmore Leonard

    Best stories of the American West, v1; edited by Marc Jaffe

How Carlos Webster changed his name to Carl and became a famous Oklahoma lawman

    McSweeney's mammoth treasury of thrilling tales; edited by Michael Chabon

"Hurrah for Captain Early"

    Leonard, E. The complete Western stories of Elmore Leonard

Jugged [variant title: The boy from Dos Cabezas]

    Leonard, E. The complete Western stories of Elmore Leonard

The kid [variant title: The gift of Regalo]

    Leonard, E. The complete Western stories of Elmore Leonard

The last shot [variant title: A matter of duty]

    Leonard, E. The complete Western stories of Elmore Leonard

Law of the hunted ones [variant title: Outlaw Pass]

    Leonard, E. The complete Western stories of Elmore Leonard

Long night

    Leonard, E. The complete Western stories of Elmore Leonard

The longest day of his life

    Leonard, E. The complete Western stories of Elmore Leonard

Louly and Pretty Boy

    Dangerous women; edited by Otto Penzler

    The Best American Mystery Stories, 2006; edited and with an introduction by Scott Turow; Otto Penzler, series editor

Man with the iron arm [variant title: The one arm man]

    Leonard, E. The complete Western stories of Elmore Leonard

Moment of vengeance [variant title: The waiting man]

    Leonard, E. The complete Western stories of Elmore Leonard

The nagual [variant title: The accident at John Stam's]

    Leonard, E. The complete Western stories of Elmore Leonard

No man's guns

    Leonard, E. The complete Western stories of Elmore Leonard

Only good ones

    Leonard, E. The complete Western stories of Elmore Leonard

The rancher's lady [variant title: The woman from Tascosa]

    Leonard, E. The complete Western stories of Elmore Leonard

Red hell hits Canyon Diablo [variant title: Tizwin]

    Leonard, E. The complete Western stories of Elmore Leonard

The rustlers [variant title: Along the Pecos]

    Leonard, E. The complete Western stories of Elmore Leonard

Saint with a six-gun [variant title: The hanging of Bobby Valdez]

    Leonard, E. The complete Western stories of Elmore Leonard

Three-ten to Yuma

    Leonard, E. The complete Western stories of Elmore Leonard

The Tonto woman

    Leonard, E. The complete Western stories of Elmore Leonard

Trail of the Apache [variant title: Apache agent]

    Leonard, E. The complete Western stories of Elmore Leonard

Trouble at Rindo's station [variant title: Rindo's station]

    Leonard, E. The complete Western stories of Elmore Leonard

Under the friar's ledge

    Leonard, E. The complete Western stories of Elmore Leonard

When the women come out to dance

    A New omnibus of crime; edited by Tony Hillerman and Rosemary Herbert; contributing editors Sue Grafton and Jeffery Deaver

You never see Apaches . . . [variant title: Eight days from Willcox]

    Leonard, E. The complete Western stories of Elmore Leonard

LEONARDO, DA VINCI, 1452-1519

About

Baker, K. Silent Leonardo

Gilchrist, E. You must change your life

Leonardo's baby. Herrmann, M.

Leong, Sandra

Coming of Age in Faheete

    New England Review v26 no1 p96-108 2005

Earthly Delights

    The Antioch Review v63 no3 p539-47 Summ 2005

Ma and Me

    Prairie Schooner v79 no4 p111-24 Wint 2005

The Thousand and One Faces of Mama-san

    New England Review v27 no1 p40-55 2006

Leonor. Kodama, M.

Leopard. Tower, W.

The **leopard.** Uchida, H.

Leopard arms. Zumas, L.

LEOPARDS

Hawes, L. Our lady of sorrows

Tower, W. Leopard

Uchida, H. The leopard

A **leopard's** spots. Forrest, K. V.

LEOPOLD, NATHAN FREUNDENTHAL, 1904 OR 5-1971

About

Orner, P. Dear Mr. Klezcka

The **leper** colony. Howard, C.

The **lepidopterist.** Shepard, L.

LEPRECHAUNS

Wolfe, G. A cabin on the coast

LEPROSY

Tompkins, P. The road to Carville

Lermontov, Mikhail IUr´evich

Shtoss

> Worlds apart; an anthology of Russian fantasy and science fiction; edited and with commentary by Alexander Levitsky; translated by Alexander Levitsky and Martha T. Kitchen

Lermontov. Michaelopoulou, A.

LESBIANISM

> *See also* Homosexuality

Alvarado, B. Comadres in the kitchen

Anders, C. Transfixed, helpless, and out of control

Andreas-Salomé, L. At one, again, with nature

Angel, J. Supplement

Barthelme, D. Henrietta and Alexandra

Bell, J. Help the aged

Belrose, J. L. House built of sticks

Brant, B. E. Swimming upstream

Brown, R. An augury

Brown, R. The last time I saw you

Brown, R. The movie

Brown, R. Other

Brown, R. Trying to say

Brownworth, V. Violation

Bukowski, C. Workout

Burgin, R. My sister's house

Caponegro, M. Ill-timed

Capps, T. Alice

Ch'oe, Y. The last of Hanak'o

Coake, C. We're in trouble

Crozier, O. Murder on Chuckanut Drive

Curtis, R. Hungry self

D'Allesandro, S. Jane and Sam

Donoghue, E. The cost of things

Donoghue, E. Speaking in tongues

Donoghue, E. The welcome

Dourado, A. Bald island

Drury, J. M. The "sound" of music

Faust, C. Cutman

Finch, P. Bethany's wood

Flanagan, E. Goldfish

Freed, L. An error of desire

Gaitskill, M. Tiny, smiling daddy

Gaitskill, M. Today I'm yours

Gottlieb, D. Undone

Gurba, M. Dahlia season

Gurba, M. Primera comunión

Gurba, M. White girl

Harleman, A. Sharks

Harris, J. Let sleeping cats lie

Henry, L. Capital punishment

Hernandez, L. The red curtain

Hoffman, B. I've been waiting for you

Holladay, C. C. The blue monkey

Jay, K. Speeding cars

Jones, N. The bold, the beautiful

July, M. It was romance

July, M. The moves

July, M. Something that needs nothing

July, M. Ten true things

Karlin, K. Bye-bye Larry

Kay, J. You go when you can no longer stay

Kennedy, C. What thou and I did, till we loved

Kennedy, P. Queer

Kercheval, J. L. Alice in Dairyland

Klages, E. Time gypsy

Krughoff, L. Halley's comet

Le Guin, U. K. Mountain ways

Levithan, D. Miss Lucy had a steamboat

Liel, L. The last minute

Lindop, L. Sunday morning

Magee, K. All the America you want

Magee, K. As human as you are standing here

Martin, V. The open door

McRae, D. Never drop by

Meaker, M. Round heels

Mebus, S. Bull in the heather

Mindt, A. Sabor a mi

Mohanraj, M. A. Seven cups of water (Jaffna, 1948)

Newman, L. The best revenge

Newman, L. Flashback

Newman, L. The gift

Newman, L. One Shabbos evening

Newman, L. Only a phase

Newman, L. Something shiny

Newman, L. The world to come

Ockert, J. Mother may I

Olafsson, O. May

Pearlman, E. Signs of life

Porter, A. Connecticut

Porter, A. Merkin

Pratt, T. Living with the harpy

Redmann, J. M. The intersection of camp and St. Mary

Rivera-Valdes, S. The deepest seed of the lemon

Rivera-Valdes, S. Life leads

Rivera-Valdes, S. Like in jail

Roberts, N. This is not skin

Robinson, R. Shame

Rossiter, E. Questions of war

Selke, L. Sex and the married dyke

Shaw, H. Single white farmhouse

Sherman, D. Walpurgis afternoon

Steck, U. Phantoms

Tallent, E. Eros 101

Tea, M. Music from earth

Tomlinson, J. Shadow flag

Treat, J. Dear Dr. Haskell

Treat, J. Little bitches

Trevor, D. The thin tear in the fabric of space

Trezise, R. The brake fluid at Gina's

Westcott, G. The sailor

Wright, P. Looking for Aimee

Zelazny, R. Come to me not in winter's white

Lescroart, John T.

The cover story is always a lie

> Murder at the racetrack; edited by Otto Penzler

A friendly little game

> Dead man's hand; crime fiction at the poker table; edited by Otto Penzler.

Lescroart, John T. and Rose, M. J.

The portal

> Thriller; edited by James Patterson

Leslie, Nathan

A Day in the Park

> *The North American Review* v291 no5 p24-5 S/O 2006

The Fire Pit

> *South Carolina Review* v38 no2 p116-28 Spr 2006

Shaletown

> *The North American Review* v290 no3/4 p22-3 My/Ag 2005

Levi, Primo—[Excerpt from A Tranquil Star]—
Continued
The molecule's defiance
    Levi, P. A tranquil star; unpublished stories
      of Primo Levi; translated by Ann Goldstein
      and Alessandra Bastagli
One night
    Levi, P. A tranquil star; unpublished stories
      of Primo Levi; translated by Ann Goldstein
      and Alessandra Bastagli
The sorcerers
    Levi, P. A tranquil star; unpublished stories
      of Primo Levi; translated by Ann Goldstein
      and Alessandra Bastagli
A tranquil star
    Levi, P. A tranquil star; unpublished stories
      of Primo Levi; translated by Ann Goldstein
      and Alessandra Bastagli
    The New Yorker v82 no49 p72-4 F 12 2007
The TV fans from Delta Cep.
    Levi, P. A tranquil star; unpublished stories
      of Primo Levi; translated by Ann Goldstein
      and Alessandra Bastagli
Leviathan. Wolff, T.
Leviathan wept. Abraham, D.
Levin, Gabriel
Attir
    Raritan v26 no3 p1-24 Wint 2007
Levin, Jennifer
Stand Wherever You Want
    Iowa Review v35 no1 p131-40 Spr 2005
Levin, Zvulen
The country girl
    Shining and shadow; an anthology of early
      Yiddish stories from the Lower East Side;
      edited and translated by Albert Waldinger
Flochne
    Shining and shadow; an anthology of early
      Yiddish stories from the Lower East Side;
      edited and translated by Albert Waldinger
Grammar
    Shining and shadow; an anthology of early
      Yiddish stories from the Lower East Side;
      edited and translated by Albert Waldinger
Honorarium
    Shining and shadow; an anthology of early
      Yiddish stories from the Lower East Side;
      edited and translated by Albert Waldinger
The humorist
    Shining and shadow; an anthology of early
      Yiddish stories from the Lower East Side;
      edited and translated by Albert Waldinger
A hush
    Shining and shadow; an anthology of early
      Yiddish stories from the Lower East Side;
      edited and translated by Albert Waldinger
"Mame"
    Shining and shadow; an anthology of early
      Yiddish stories from the Lower East Side;
      edited and translated by Albert Waldinger
The thought
    Shining and shadow; an anthology of early
      Yiddish stories from the Lower East Side;
      edited and translated by Albert Waldinger
Two girls and one suitor
    Shining and shadow; an anthology of early
      Yiddish stories from the Lower East Side;
      edited and translated by Albert Waldinger

Levin-Scherz, Linda
Driving Lessons
    The North American Review v289 no6 p19-26
    N/D 2004
Levine, David D.
I hold my father's paws
    The Year's best science fiction: twenty-fourth
      annual collection; edited by Gardner Dozois
Titanium Mike saves the day
    Nebula Awards showcase 2009; the year's
      best SF and fantasy; selected by the Sci-
      ence Fiction and Fantasy Writers of Ameri-
      ca; edited by Ellen Datlow
Levine, Norman
By a frozen river
    Contemporary Jewish writing in Canada; an
      anthology; edited by Michael Greenstein
Levine, Paul
Mom is my co-counsel
    Mystery Writers of America presents the
      prosecution rests; new stories about court-
      rooms, criminals, and the law; edited by
      Linda Fairstein.
Levine, Peter
After This, Nothing
    StoryQuarterly v40 p459-73 2004
In Her Sweet Lowlands
    South Carolina Review v38 no1 p72-80 Fall
    2005
Proximal
    Southern Humanities Review v42 no3 p266-75
    Summ 2008
Levine, Stacey and Schneiderman, Davis
Milk and Mary
    Western Humanities Review v63 no2 p34-8
    Summ 2009
Levinson, David Samuel
The Sweet Spot
    Prairie Schooner v83 no1 p111-26 Spr 2009
Levinson, Martin H.
Bucky the Time-Binding Beaver
    Etc. v65 no3 p274-6 Jl 2008
The Wizard of Is
    Etc. v64 no3 p267-70 Jl 2007
Levinson, Robert S.
A Prisoner of memory and 24 of the year's
    finest crime and mystery stories; edited by
    Ed Gorman & Martin H. Greenberg
And the winner is . . .
    Hollywood and crime; original crime stories
    set during the history of Hollywood; edited
    by Robert J. Randisi
Chapter 82: Myrna Lloyd is missing
    The Deadly Bride; and 21 of the year's finest
    crime and mystery stories; including com-
    plete coverage of the year in mystery and
    crime fiction; edited by Ed Gorman and
    Martin H. Greenberg
The hit
    The Adventure of the missing detective and
    19 of the year's finest crime and mystery
    stories!; edited by Ed Gorman and Martin
    H. Greenberg
LEVITATION
Allen, W. To err is human—to float, divine
Dann, J. and Malzberg, B. N. Life in the air
Levitation. Ozick, C.

Levithan, David
The alumni interview
  Levithan, D. How they met, and other stories
Andrew Chang
  Levithan, D. How they met, and other stories
Breaking and entering
  Levithan, D. How they met, and other stories
The escalator, a love story
  Levithan, D. How they met, and other stories
Flirting with waiters
  Levithan, D. How they met, and other stories
The good witch
  Levithan, D. How they met, and other stories
How they met
  Levithan, D. How they met, and other stories
Intersection
  Levithan, D. How they met, and other stories
Lost sometimes
  Levithan, D. How they met, and other stories
Memory dance
  Levithan, D. How they met, and other stories
Miss Lucy had a steamboat
  Levithan, D. How they met, and other stories
The number of people who meet on airplanes
  Levithan, D. How they met, and other stories
Princes
  Levithan, D. How they met, and other stories
A romantic inclination
  Levithan, D. How they met, and other stories
Skipping the prom
  Levithan, D. How they met, and other stories
Starbucks boy
  Levithan, D. How they met, and other stories
What a song can do
  Levithan, D. How they met, and other stories
Without saying
  Levithan, D. How they met, and other stories

Levitin, Alexis
(tr.) See Gospodinov, Georgi
The **levitron**. Oldshue, R.

Levitsky, Ronald
The blue line
  Chicago blues; edited by Libby Fischer Hellmann

Levy, Janice
Cheer for the Laundry
  Confrontation no96/97 p94-107 Fall 2006/Wint 2007
It's All in the Delivery
  StoryQuarterly v40 p483-99 2004

Levy, John
Alberto and Diego Giacometti
  Legal Studies Forum v32 no1 p161-4 2008
Public Pretenders
  Legal Studies Forum v32 no1 p169-71 2008
Signatures
  Legal Studies Forum v32 no1 p165-7 2008

Levy, Magdalena
(tr.) See Gospodinov, Georgi

Lewin, Michael Z.
Cigarettes
  The Best British mysteries, 2006; edited by Maxim Jakubowski

Lewis, Anthony R.
Request for proposal
  This is my funniest 2; leading science fiction writers present their funniest stories ever; edited by Mike Resnick

Lewis, C. S.
The Lion, The Witch, and The Wardrobe [Condensed and adapted for reading aloud]
  The Saturday Evening Post v278 no2 p40-3 Mr/Ap 2006

LEWIS, C. S. (CLIVE STAPLES), 1898-1963
Parodies, imitations, etc.
Gaiman, N. The problem of Susan

Lewis, Clive Staples See Lewis, C. S. (Clive Staples), 1898-1963

Lewis, Jason
Rodolfo and Nélida
  Harvard Review (1992) no33 p6-16 2007

LEWIS, MERIWETHER, 1774-1809
About
Scholes, K. The man with great despair behind his eyes

Lewis, Miles Marshall
Numbers up
  Bronx noir; edited by S. J. Rozan

Lewis, Paul
(jt. auth) See Lockley, Steve and Lewis, Paul

Lewis, Sinclair
The willow walk
  The Penguin book of Gaslight crime; con artists, burglars, rogues, and scoundrels from the time of Sherlock Holmes; edited with an introduction and notes by Michael Sims.

Lewis, Trudy
Homeland Hijab
  Prairie Schooner v81 no1 p149-71 Spr 2007
Limestone Diner
  The Best American short stories, 2004; edited by Lorrie Moore; Katrina Kenison series editor
Queen of Karst
  Southwest Review v89 no2/3 p442-61 2004

Lewis, William Henry
Crusade
  Lewis, W. H. I got somebody in Staunton; stories
For the brothers who ain't here
  Lewis, W. H. I got somebody in Staunton; stories
I got somebody in Staunton
  Lewis, W. H. I got somebody in Staunton; stories
In the swamp
  Lewis, W. H. I got somebody in Staunton; stories
  African American Review v39 no1/2 p5-15 Spr/Summ 2005
Kudzu
  Lewis, W. H. I got somebody in Staunton; stories
Potcake
  Lewis, W. H. I got somebody in Staunton; stories
  The Kenyon Review v27 no1 p93-109 Wint 2005
Rossonian days
  Lewis, W. H. I got somebody in Staunton; stories
Shades
  Lewis, W. H. I got somebody in Staunton; stories
Urban renewal
  Lewis, W. H. I got somebody in Staunton; stories

Like dancing on both feet. McGruder, K.
Like he was just anyone else. Prior, A.
Like in jail. Rivera-Valdes, S.
Like it or not. Eisenberg, D.
Like rabbits. Feeny, P.
Like shattered stone. Lane, J.
Like some old story. Blaeser, K. M.
Like someone in a coma. MacEnulty, P.
Like to die. Aird, C.
Like visiting Joseph Cornell. Ronk, M. C.
Likely Lake. Robison, M.
The **likeness** of Julie. Matheson, R.
Likes of him. Gay, J.
Liking what you see: a documentary. Chiang, T.
Li'l Dickens. Stahl, J.
Lilacs. Fisher, C.
Lila's story. Singer, M.
Liliana. Meloy, M.
LILIES
 Klassen, S. Surprised
LILITH (LEGENDARY CHARACTER)
 Domecq, B. Lillith
 Domecq, B. Sammaël and Lillith
Lillith. Domecq, B.
Lily. McEwan, I.
Lily. Mueenuddin, D.
Lily of the valley. Wunsch, E.
Lily Pad. Wingfield, A.
The **lily-white** boys. Maxwell, W.
Lily, with clouds. Goss, T.
Lim, Thea
 Swish
  Canadian Woman Studies v26 no1 p37-40
   Wint/Spr 2007
LIMA (PERU) *See* Peru—Lima
Lima Barreto, Afonso Henrique de
 The man who knew Javanese
  Oxford anthology of the Brazilian short story;
   edited by K. David Jackson
Lima, Peru; July 28, 1979. Alarcón, D.
Lima, Peru, July 28, 1979 [Reprint] Alarcón, D.
Limber like me . . . Mordecai, P.
LIMBO
 Lanagan, M. Under hell, over heaven
Limbo. Alvarado, B.
Lime pickle. Lasdun, J.
The **Lime** Soda Sea. Stroud, B.
The **Limeroom.** Burnside, J.
Limestone Diner. Lewis, T.
Limit point. Brodsky, M.
The **limitations** of Pambé Serang. Kipling, R.
The **Limner.** Barnes, J.
Limpopo. Tolstaia, T.
Lin, Tao
 Cull the steel heart, melt the ice one, love the
  weak thing; say nothing of consolation, but
  irrelevance, disaster, and nonexistence;
  have no hope or hate—nothing; ruin your-
  self exclusively, completely, and whenever
  possible
  Lin, T. Bed; stories
 Insomnia for a better tomorrow
  Lin, T. Bed; stories
 Love is a thing on sale for more money than
  there exists
  Lin, T. Bed; stories
 Love is the indifferent god of the religion in
  which universe is church
  Lin, T. Bed; stories

 Nine, ten
  Lin, T. Bed; stories
 Sasquatch
  Lin, T. Bed; stories
 Sincerity
  Lin, T. Bed; stories
 Suburban teenage wasteland blues
  Lin, T. Bed; stories
 Three-day cruise
  Lin, T. Bed; stories
Linaweaver, Brad
 A good bag
  Alternate generals III; edited by Harry Turtle-
   dove and Roland J. Green
LINCOLN, ABRAHAM, 1809-1865
 About
  Alarcón, D. Abraham Lincoln has been shot
  Almond, S. Lincoln, arisen
  Bradbury, R. Downwind from Gettysburg
  Card, O. S. The Yazoo Queen
Lincoln, arisen. Almond, S.
The **Lincoln** train. McHugh, M. F.
The **Lindberg** baby. Svoboda, T.
LINDBERGH, CHARLES, 1902-1974
 About
  Waldrop, H. Us
Lindeman, Micki
 Eulogy for a Warrior
  *Tribal College Journal of American Indian
   Higher Education* v19 no1 p57-8 Fall 2007
Lindo y querido. Muñoz, M.
Lindop, Laurie
 Sunday morning
  Before; short stories about pregnancy from
   our top writers; edited by Emily Franklin
   and Heather Swain
Lindsey, Byron
 (tr.) *See* Shklovsky, Yevgeny
Lindsey, David L.
 Heat from another sun [excerpt]
  Lone Star sleuths; an anthology of Texas
   crime fiction; edited and with an introduc-
   tion by Bill Cunningham, Steven L. Davis,
   and Rollo K. Newsom.
Lindskold, Jane
 The travails of Princess Stephen
  Pandora's closet; edited by Jean Rabe and
   Martin H. Greenberg.
 Unlimited
  Future Americas; edited by Martin H.
   Greenberg and John Helferd
Lindskold, Jane and Saberhagen, Fred
 Servant of death
  Man vs. machine; edited by John Helfers and
   Martin H. Greenberg.
The **Line** Fence. Buckler, E.
The **lineaments** of gratified desire. Wilce, Y. S.
Lingua franca. McDonnell, C.
LINGUISTS
 Caponegro, M. The translator
 Grodstein, L. The sisters of St. Misery
 Williams, T. The tenth muse
Link, Kelly
 The cannon
  Link, K. Magic for beginners; illustrated by
   Shelley Jackson
 Catskin
  McSweeney's mammoth treasury of thrilling
   tales; edited by Michael Chabon

The **listeners**. Gunn, J. E.
Listening for the Silences. Bontly, T.
Listening in. Ronk, M. C.
Listening to Billy. Nolan, W. F.
Listening to Brahms. Charnas, S. M.
Listing. Treat, J.
Liston, Charles *See* Liston, Sonny, 1932-1970
LISTON, SONNY, 1932-1970
                          About
  Bear, E. Sonny Liston takes the fall
Lit a shuck for Texas. L'Amour, L.
Litany for the homeland. Hospital, J. T.
LITERACY
  Bahah, M. O. A parting shot
  L'Amour, L. The man who stole Shakespeare
  Luvaas, W. A working man's apocrypha
  Nisbet, R. The ladybird room
A **literary** adventure. Bolaño, R.
LITERARY CRITICS
  Chekhov, A. P. Drama
  Dobozy, T. The Laughing Cat
  Singer, I. B. Vanvild Kava
A **literary** encounter. Bradbury, R.
**LITERARY FORGERIES AND MYSTIFICA-
    TION**
  Dahl, R. The great automatic grammatizator
  Haldeman, J. W. The Hemingway hoax
A **literary** forgery. Johnson, G. C.
LITERARY LIFE
      See also Authors
A **literary** riot. Bierce, A.
Litman, Ellen
  About Kamyshinskiy
    Best New American voices 2007; [edited by
      Sue Miller; series editors, John Kulka and
      Natalie Danford]
    Litman, E. The last chicken in America; a
      novel in stories
    TriQuarterly no121 p97-112 2005
  Among the lilacs and the girls
    Litman, E. The last chicken in America; a
      novel in stories
  Charity
    Litman, E. The last chicken in America; a
      novel in stories
  Dancers
    Best of Tin House; stories; foreword by Dor-
      othy Allison
    Litman, E. The last chicken in America; a
      novel in stories
  Home
    Litman, E. The last chicken in America; a
      novel in stories
  In the man-free zone
    Litman, E. The last chicken in America; a
      novel in stories
  The last chicken in America
    Litman, E. The last chicken in America; a
      novel in stories
  Peculiarities of the national driving
    Litman, E. The last chicken in America; a
      novel in stories
  Russian club
    Litman, E. The last chicken in America; a
      novel in stories
  The trajectory of frying pans
    Litman, E. The last chicken in America; a
      novel in stories
    Ploughshares v33 no2/3 p66-81 Fall 2007

What do you dream of, cruiser Aurora?
    Litman, E. The last chicken in America; a
      novel in stories
When the neighbors love you
    Litman, E. The last chicken in America; a
      novel in stories
Litt, Toby
  The monster
    The book of other people; edited by Zadie
      Smith
Little, Bentley
  We find things old
    The Year's best fantasy and horror: eighteenth
      annual collection; edited by Ellen Datlow,
      Kelly Link & Gavin J. Grant
Little Abrahams. Broches, R.
A **little** advance. Iagnemma, K.
Little Albert's nightmare experience. Libin, Z.
Little Billy. Dunbar, P. L.
Little birds. Van Booy, S.
A **little** bit farther. Quiroga, A.
Little bitches. Treat, J.
Little blue pill. Jordan, R.
The **little** book. Erdrich, L.
The **little** boy. Gaitskill, M.
A **little** boy. Trezise, R.
The **little** boy at the Savior's Christmas tree.
    Dostoyevsky, F.
Little boy blue. McAllister, B.
Little brown bird. Thompson, J.
The **little** cat laughed to see such sport. Swanwick,
    M.
The **little** clock spirit and the lovers. Schwitters,
    K.
A **Little** Collateral Damage. Nelson, R. B.
Little dead girl singing. Gallagher, S.
A **Little** Death. Cheuse, A.
Little Deaths. Kyle, A.
Little Dedo. Holder, N.
Little Drops of Water. Vonnegut, K.
A **little** early in the day. Richardson, M. J.
Little Edens. Moss, B. K.
Little faces. McIntyre, V. N.
Little fool. Bunin, I. A.
Little girl lost. Matheson, R.
The **little** goat. Ornitz, S.
Little goddess. McDonald, I.
Little grains of dust. Mukhopadhyay, T.
A **little** history of modern music. Gass, W. H.
Little horses. Shawl, N.
A **little** knowledge. Merril, J.
Little Larry. Bierce, A.
A **little** learning. Hughes, M.
Little little big man. Julavits, H.
The **little** magic shop. Sterling, B.
Little Man. Horack, S.
A **little** man. Sologub, F.
Little Maria. Palazzeschi, A.
A **little** maverick. Stapleton, P.
The **little** monster. Ts'an-hsüeh
The **Little** Museum of Memory. Slouka, M.
The **little** nugget strike. Merrill, G. E.
The **little** people. Howard, R. E.
Little Pig, Berry Brown, and the hard moon. Lake,
    J.
A **little** present on this dark November day. Hecht,
    J.
LITTLE RED RIDING HOOD
  Strout, A. M. Lady in red

LITTLE RED RIDING HOOD—*Continued*
Parodies, imitations, etc.
Coover, R. Grandmother's nose
Little Red's tango. Straub, P.
LITTLE ROCK (ARK.) *See* Arkansas—Little
Rock
The **Little** Shoemaker from Guanajuato. Garro, E.
Little sins. MacLean, M.
Little sins. Waters, D.
Little sister. Enright, A.
Little Sonja Rosenkranz. Weil, G.
Little Sorrel. Smith, R. T.
Little Star of Bela Lua. Monteiro, L.
Little stones, little pistols, little clash. Rubin, J.
The **little** story. Bierce, A.
A **little** street music. Stern, D.
The **little** that is everything. Parry, E. A.
The **little** things. Malerba-Foran, J.
Little trouble girl. Roiphe, E.
A **little** variety, please. Purdy, J.
The **little** wrens and robins. Kiely, B.
Little Yellow Bird. Downe, K.
Little yellow dogs. Monk, B.
Little Yeses, Little Nos. Crowley, J.
The **littlest** Hitler. Boudinot, R.
The **littlest** Jackal. Silverberg, R.
Litzky, Tsaurah
Purple tulip
Sex for America; politically inspired erotica;
edited by Stephen Elliott
Litzky, Tsaurah
End-of-the-world sex
Politically inspired; edited by Stephen Elliott;
assistant editor, Gabriel Kram; associate ed-
itors, Elizabeth Brooks [et al.]
Liu, Aimee E.
The other side
Meeting across the river; stories inspired by
the haunting Bruce Springsteen song; edited
by Jessica Kaye and Richard J. Brewer
Liu, Marjorie M.
Where the heart lives
My big fat supernatural honeymoon; edited by
P.N. Elrod.
Live-bait. Zoshchenko, M.
The **live** coward. Anderson, P.
Live-in. Ali, M. N.
The **liver** nephew. Ito, S.
LIVERPOOL (ENGLAND). CATHEDRAL
James, C. L. R. The Liverpool cathedral
The **Liverpool** cathedral. James, C. L. R.
Lives. Grant, J.
The **lives** of ordinary superheroes. Haynes, D.
The **lives** of rocks. Bass, R.
The **lives** of the philosophers. Brockmeier, K.
Lives of the Saints. Row, J.
The **living.** Albert, E.
Living at the Chelsea. Bishop, J. P.
Living on the beach. Anderson, B.
The **Living** Portrait. Otten, W. J.
The **living** roots. Adisa, O. P.
A **living** soul. Gospodinov, G.
Living with the gilt. Cutler, J.
Living with the harpy. Pratt, T.

Livings, Jack
The dog
The Best American short stories, 2006; select-
ed from U.S. and Canadian magazines by
Ann Patchett with Katrina Kenison; with an
introduction by Ann Patchett
The Paris Review v47 p245-65 Spr 2005
A Floating Life
StoryQuarterly v42 p385-414 2006
The heir
Pushcart prize XXXIII: best of the small
presses 2009; edited by Bill Henderson
with the Pushcart Prize editors
The **lizard.** Uchida, H.
Lizard man. Poissant, D. J.
The **lizard** of Ooze. Lake, J.
LIZARDS
Shepard, L. The Drive-In Puerto Rico
Lizaveta. Frost, G.
Llah, 'Abd al- and Qadir, 'Abd al-
A bouquet of jasmine
Oranges in the sun; short stories from the
Arabian Gulf; edited and translated by Deb-
orah S. Akers, Abubaker A. Bagader
LOANS
See also Moneylenders
Lobato, José Bento Monteiro
The funnyman who repented
Oxford anthology of the Brazilian short story;
edited by K. David Jackson
Lobo, the king of Currumpaw. Seton, E. T.
Lobsenz, Robert
Boats of Mine a-Boating
The Antioch Review v64 no3 p527-37 Summ
2006
Lobster night. Banks, R.
Lobsters. Stross, C.
Local Honey. Shank, J. A.
Local hospitality. Nye, N. S.
Local news. Ohlin, A.
Local Time. Hemley, R.
Locard's principle. Deaver, J.
Location, location, location. Spiegelman, P.
LOCH NESS MONSTER
Roberson, J. A compromised Christmas
Lochte, Dick
Devil dog
Hollywood and crime; original crime stories
set during the history of Hollywood; edited
by Robert J. Randisi
A Prisoner of memory and 24 of the year's
finest crime and mystery stories; edited by
Ed Gorman & Martin H. Greenberg
Diamond dog
Creature cozies; edited by Jill M. Morgan
Wolf Woman Bay; and nine more of the
finest crime and mystery novellas of the
year; edited by Ed Gorman and Martin H.
Greenberg
Low tide
The Best American mystery stories, 2004; ed-
ited and with an introduction by Nelson
DeMille; Otto Penzler, series editor
The World's finest mystery and crime stories,
fifth annual collection; edited by Ed
Gorman and Martin H. Greenberg
Lock, Norman
The Captain Is Sleeping
New England Review v26 no4 p8-18 2005

The **Long** Road South. Corne, J. S.
Long short short long. Malla, P.
The **long** shot. Martinez, M.
The **long** sunset. Gorman, E.
Long Term. Appel, J. M.
The **long** wait. West, D.
The **long** walk. O'Shaughnessy, P.
A **long** winter. Tóibín, C.
Longabaugh, Harry *See* Sundance Kid, 1861?-1908
The **longest** day of his life. Leonard, E.
The **longest** ladder. Morwood, P.
LONGEVITY
    See also Aging; Rejuvenation
    Silverberg, R. Capricorn games
    Silverberg, R. Going
    Silverberg, R. To be continued
Longhi, Jon
    Fixed
      San Francisco noir; edited by Peter Maravelis
Longhorn, Ryan Amfahr
    Another Body
      The North American Review v293 no3/4 p24-8 My/Ag 2008
Longstreet, Katherine
    The Waters of Xochimilco
      The Antioch Review v66 no4 p747-59 Fall 2008
    Zócalo
      The Massachusetts Review v49 no3 p364-74 Aut 2008
Longworth, Steve
    Succussion [Science fiction]
      Nature v448 p838 Ag 16 2007
Lonigan. L'Amour, L.
Look and feel. Reidy, D.
Look at her. LaBute, N.
Look at the sky and tell me what you see. LaBrie, A.
Look death in the eye. Block, L.
Look ma, I'm breathing. Rivecca, S.
Look out, kids. McKenzie, E.
Look what love is doing to me. James, M.
Looking at animals. Goldfaden, J.
Looking for a female tenet. Brady, C.
Looking for Aimee. Wright, P.
Looking for eight. Fuentes, M.
Looking for Greywolf. Harrison, W.
Looking for love. Woronov, M.
Looking for Mr Goodbug. Malartre, E.
Looking for my keys. Sarah, R.
Looking for Shahbazi. Hamadani, M. R.
Looking for the answers. Ames, J.
Looking for the elephant. Jo Kyung Ran
Looking glass. Kittredge, W.
The **lookout**. Villard, M.
Lookout. Weinman, S.
Looks are deceiving. Stackpole, M. A.
Looney, George
    To Give Ghosts the Finger
      The Southern Review (Baton Rouge, La.) v40 no4 p733-40 Aut 2004
Loonie and Me. Winton, T.
Loophole. Skinner, Q.
Loopy. Rendell, R.
Loose change. LaBute, N.
Loose hair. Taha, M. A.
Loose packaging. Zoshchenko, M.
Loot. Smith, J.

Lopatin, Peter
    Nathan at the Speed of Light
      Commentary v128 no3 p43-52 O 2009
Lopes, Henri
    The advance
      The Anchor book of modern African stories; edited by Nadežda Obradovic; with a foreword by Chinua Achebe
Lopes, Reinaldo José
    Gathering of the clans
      Nature v439 p116 Ja 5 2006
Lopez, Larry
    Hidian
      TriQuarterly no133 p79-84 2009
Lopez, Robert
    Asunder
      New England Review v26 no2 p253-5 2005
Loquat. Keret, E.
Lord, Nancy
    Candace counts coup
      Pushcart prize XXVII; best of the small presses; edited by Bill Henderson with the Pushcart prize editors
Lord Kelvin's machine. Blaylock, J. P.
The **Lord** Moves Us Forward, Forward. Inezian, A. M.
The **lord** of the jungle. Resnick, M.
Lord of the land. Wolfe, G.
Lord of the worms. Lumley, B.
Lordon, Randye
    Like a sore thumb
      Women of mystery; an anthology; Katherine V. Forrest, editor
Lords of imagination. Zebrowski, G.
The **Lorelei**. Irvine, A. C.
Lorenz, Johnny
    (tr.) *See* Tezza, Cristovão
Lorrie, Michael
    Bullheads
      Atlantic Monthly (1993) v295 no3 p117-24, 126-30 Ap 2005
LOS ALAMOS (N.M.) *See* New Mexico—Los Alamos
LOS ANGELES (CALIF.) *See* California—Los Angeles
En **los** parques, al anochecer. Mayoral, M.
Losers in paradise. Clayton, J. J.
Losing. Tabor, M. L.
Losing a Matriarch. McHugh, M.
Losing color. Stern, R. G.
Losing Dolly. Rusch, K. K.
Losing Lars. Richards, J.
Losing the plot. Aird, C.
The **loss**. Báez, A.
Loss prevention. Lange, R.
Lost. Thompson, J.
Lost and found. Bentil, T.
Lost and found. Burke, J.
Lost and found. Romm, R.
Lost and found. Schutz, B. M.
Lost arts. Dedman, S.
The **lost** boy. Hambly, B.
The **lost** boy: a reporter at large. McHugh, M. F.
The **lost** breed. Murphy, Y.
The **lost** brother. Oates, J. C.
Lost causes. Perry, A.
Lost Children. Thon, M. R.
The **lost** coast. Muller, M.
Lost continent. Egan, G.

The **lost** district. Lane, J.
The **lost** eagle. Tremayne, P.
Lost in a field of paper flowers. Rollo, G.
Lost in Dublin. Starr, J.
Lost in Los Angeles. Baingana, D.
Lost in sun and silence. Palermo, V.
Lost in translation. Baumbach, J.
Lost in Uttar Pradesh. Connell, E. S.
Lost Languages of Africa. Libman, D. S.
Lost Places. Ponte, A. J.
The **lost** pony. Holladay, C. C.
The **lost** princess man. Barnes, J.
The **lost** property room. Canavan, T.
The **lost** Sabbath. Molodowsky, K.
Lost sometimes. Levithan, D.
Lost soul. Erison, M. P.
The **lost** Tiki palaces of Detroit. Zadoorian, M.
The **lost** tribe. Gifford, B.
Lost victories. Vollmann, W. T.
Lostronaut. Lethem, J.
LOT (BIBLICAL FIGURE)
About
Douglas, C. N. Strangers in a strange land
Lott, Bret
Appraisal
    Lott, B. The difference between women and men; stories
The difference between women and men
    Lott, B. The difference between women and men; stories
An evening on the cusp of the apocalypse
    Lott, B. The difference between women and men; stories
    The best Christian short stories; edited and with an introduction by Bret Lott
Everything cut will come back
    Lott, B. The difference between women and men; stories
Family
    Lott, B. The difference between women and men; stories
Gesture
    Lott, B. The difference between women and men; stories
Halo
    Lott, B. The difference between women and men; stories
History
    Lott, B. The difference between women and men; stories
The issue of money
    Lott, B. The difference between women and men; stories
The landscape of love
    Good Housekeeping v241 no4 p259-60, 262-7 O 2005
Nostaglia
    Lott, B. The difference between women and men; stories
A part of it
    Lott, B. The difference between women and men; stories
Rose
    Crossroads; tales of the southern literary fantastic; edited by F. Brett Cox and Andy Duncan
    Lott, B. The difference between women and men; stories

Somebody else
    Lott, B. The difference between women and men; stories
Song of the South
    The Georgia Review v58 no4 p765-74 Wint 2004
Th train, the lake, the bridge
    Lott, B. The difference between women and men; stories
A way through this
    Lott, B. The difference between women and men; stories
LOTTERIES
Beard, A. Huddersfield versus Crewe
Capote, T. Jug of silver
Chekhov, A. P. 75 Grand [variant title: 75,000]
Clayton, J. J. Losers in paradise
Harris, J. Come in, Mr. Lowry, your number is up!
Kellerman, F. The luck of the draw
Pohl, F. Spending a day at the lottery fair
Lotto. Solomon, A.
Loud lake. Kenagy, M.
The **loudest** voice. Paley, G.
Louella and the Holy Ghost. Manley, C.
LOUIS, JOE, 1914-1981
About
Mayfield, J. The last days of Duncan Street
Louise's ghost. Link, K.
LOUISIANA
Brite, P. Z. The feast of St. Rosalie
Bukoski, A. The low August fever
Burke, J. L. The convict
Burke, J. L. Mist
Burke, J. L. Water people
Chabon, M. The Martian agent, a planetary romance
Cherry, K. Where she was
Crone, M. Fever
Davis, A. B. The significance of importance
Dean, D. The queen mother
DeGravelles, C. The last man on Earth to play the bones
Donoghue, E. Enchantment
Downs, G. Ain't I a king, too?
Dufresne, J. The freezer Jesus
Ford, R. Calling
Gautreaux, T. Died and gone to Vegas
Gautreaux, T. Good for the soul
Harris, C. Lucky
Hunton, E. R. Who gives himself
Kazumi Stahl, A. Natural disasters
Park, P. A family history
Pizzolatto, N. Two shores
Pizzolatto, N. Wanted man
Richard, N. What you do next
Sherman, D. The fiddler of Bayou Teche
Soileau, S. The boucherie
Stine, R. L. Roomful of witnesses
Straight, S. El ojo de agua
Wynbush, O. B. The noose
Baton Rouge
Moore, D. W. Wide awake in Baton Rouge
Parrish, T. It pours
New Orleans
Adcock, T. Lawyers' tongues
Atkins, A. Angola South
Bear, E. Two dreams on trains
Bensko, J. A spell

LOVE STORIES—*Continued*

Hadley, T. The surrogate
Haldeman, J. W. Heartwired
Handal, N. Umm Kulthoum at midnight
Harrison, W. Two cars on a hillside
Hayes, D. Motormouth
Hayes, D. Shakedown
Hellmann, L. F. Your sweet man
Helprin, M. Last tea with armorers
Helprin, M. Passchendaele
Helprin, M. Prelude
Hempel, A. The most girl part of you
Henriquez, C. The wide, pale ocean
Henriquez, C. Yanina
Hickam, H. Dosie, of Killakeet Island
Hinton, S. E. The girl who loved movies
Hodgson, W. H. The captain of the onion boat
Hodgson, W. H. The girl with the grey eyes
Hodgson, W. H. In the Wailing Gully
Hodgson, W. H. Kind, kind and gentle is she
Hodgson, W. H. The smugglers
Hodgson, W. H. A timely escape
Hodgson, W. H. What happened in the Thunder-
    bolt
Hoffman, A. Black is the color of my true
    love's hair
Hoffman, A. The witch of Truro
Hoffmann, Y. The heart is katmandu [excerpt]
Holladay, C. C. The quick-change artist
Iagnemma, K. On the nature of human romantic
    interaction
Ingalls, R. Last act: the madhouse
Jackson, R. Echo
James, H. A cure for coquettes
James, H. In a circus
James, H. My guardian and I
James, H. My lost darling
James, H. The pair of slippers
James, H. A sealed tear
James, H. A summer adventure
James, H. Woman's influence; or, Incidents of
    a courtship
Johnson, C. R. Cultural relativity
Keane, J. B. Under the sycamore tree
Kelly, J. P. Faith
Keret, E. Knockoff Venus
Kiely, B. A ball of malt and Madame Butterfly
Kiely, B. Bluebell Meadow
Kiely, B. The fairy women of Lisbellaw
Kim, T. The post horse curse
King, L. Five Tuesdays in winter
Kitahara, A. Forget-me-not
Kitahara, A. Innocent in love
Kitahara, A. No time for tears
Knight, M. Birdland
Krysl, M. Welcome to the torture center, love
Kulpa, K. Cristina in another country
Kulpa, K. Elaine, I love you
Kulpa, K. Have you seen her?
Kundera, M. The hitchhiking game
Kwahulé, K. Babyface
La Motte-Fouqué, F. H. K., Freiherr von. Un-
    dine
La Puma, S. The boys of Bensonhurst
L'Amour, L. The cross and the candle
Lanagan, M. A good heart
LaSalle, P. Nocturne
LaSalle, P. Where we last saw time
Lee, H. K. Burning ring of fire

Lehane, D. Until Gwen
Levithan, D. The escalator, a love story
Levithan, D. Flirting with waiters
Levithan, D. Intersection
Levithan, D. Memory dance
Levithan, D. The number of people who meet
    on airplanes
Levithan, D. Skipping the prom
Levithan, D. Without saying
Litman, E. The last chicken in America
Lynn, D. H. Dean of women
MacLaverty, B. Matters of life & death 2: visit-
    ing Takabuti
Martin, C. The best jeweler
Martin, V. His blue period
McClanahan, E. Dog loves Ellie
McGrath, P. Julius
McLean, S. Holland
McNett, M. Ozzie the burro
Meloy, M. Travis, B.
Menger-Anderson, K. Neurasthenia: a Victorian
    love story, 1871
Meno, J. An apple could make you laugh
Meno, J. Astronaut of the year
Minot, E. Berniced
Mitchell, S. The last mortal man
Mohanraj, M. A. Marry in haste (Chicago,
    1964)
Molodowsky, K. Elaine
Molodowsky, K. In the palace
Montgomery, L. Whose world is this?
Morse, D. L. Conceived
Munro, A. Chance
Murakami, H. A folklore for my generation: a
    pre-history of late-stage capitalism
Nadelson, S. Half a day in Halifax
Nisbet, R. Jam jars of seaweed and dreams of
    love
Nisbet, R. Lips
Ohlin, A. Babylon
Ohlin, A. Wonders never cease
O'Shaughnessy, P. The young lady
Ozick, C. At Fumicaro
Pande, M. A kind of love story
Panning, A. Pinned
Parra, E. A. Cuerpo presente/Requiem
Peri Rossi, C. To love or to ingest
Porter, K. A. The martyr
Pratt, T. Hart and Boot
Pratt, T. Impossible dreams
Pratt, T. Romanticore
Rash, R. Dangerous love
Reid, G. After the rain
Reid, G. The champion
Reid, G. Hey, mister!
Reid, G. Irony is . . .
Reid, G. Pavilion 24
Reid, G. The road out of town
Rhodes, D. Beautiful Consuela
Rhodes, D. The Carolingian Period
Rhodes, D. The violoncello
Rickert, M. Cold fires
Rickert, M. The girl who ate butterflies
Rickert, M. You have never been here
Rivas, M. Carmiña
Rivas, M. What do you want with me, love?
Rosenblum, M. H. Home movies
Rupavati. Thayyaal
Sadoff, I. Seven romances

LOVE STORIES—*Continued*

Sargent, P. If ever I should leave you
Scholes, K. The doom of love in small places
Scholes, K. The doom of love is small spaces
Scoville, S. The gift of a car
Shepard, J. Eros 7
Shepard, J. Love and hydrogen
Shepard, J. Piano stops here
Sherman, R. Tag sale
Shibli, A. May God keep love in a cool and dry place
Shields, C. Chemistry
Shinn, S. Bargain with the wind
Silber, J. The high road
Sillitoe, A. The rope trick
Sillitoe, A. A scream of toys
Sillitoe, A. A trip to Southwell
Silverberg, R. Needle in a timestack
Singer, I. B. Burial at sea
Singer, I. B. Dazzled
Singer, I. B. Hershele and Hanele' or, The power of a dream
Singer, I. B. The last gaze
Singer, I. B. Pity
Singer, I. B. Strong as death is love
Singer, N. The killer whispers and prays . . .; or, Like a sledge-hammer to the ribcage
Singleton, G. Recovery
Singleton, G. What attracts us to Gruel
Smith, C. A. The mandrakes
Snyder, S. Blue yodel
Snyder, S. Dumpster Tuesday
Snyder, S. The star attraction of 1919
Snyder, S. Wreck
Sorrentino, G. The moon in its flight
Soueif, A. Chez Milou
Spencer, W. B. The oddskeeper's daughter
Stafford, J. The mountain day
Stamm, P. Through the night
Stern, D. A little street music
Stern, R. G. A short history of love
Straight, S. The Golden Gopher
Strom, D. Mary
Tait, J. Reasons for concern regarding my girlfriend of five days, Monica Garza
Tallent, E. Eight hundred pages
Tallent, E. Eros 101
Thomas, E. The land of youth
Thormahlen, A. Dyke Crest Lane no. 1
Tognazzini, A. Compliments
Tomlinson, J. Birds of Providence
Tomlinson, J. First husband, first wife
Toomer, J. Avey
Trevor, W. Big bucks
Trevor, W. A perfect relationship
Troy, J. The order of things
Troy, M. Falling in love
Vapnyar, L. Salad olivier
Vollmer, M. Future missionaries of America
Vukcevich, R. Jumping
Wald, A. H. The virgin's heart
Ward, R. Chemistry
Weil, J. Sarverville remains
Wendroff, Z. Gretchen of Cemetary Lane
Westcott, G. The sailor
Wideman, J. E. Hunters
Williams, J. New shoes
Willis, C. Blued moon
Winterson, J. O'Brien's first Christmas

Winton, T. Damaged goods
Wolfe, G. Golden city far
Wolff, T. Deep kiss
Woolson, C. F. A Florentine experiment
Working, R. The tin man
Woronov, M. The alligator man
Woronov, M. Jack, part one
Woronov, M. Jack, part two
Yasuoka, S. The glass slipper
Yolen, J. Sans Soleil
Yolen, J. The tree's wife
Zebrowski, G. Takes you back
Zelazny, R. The engine at Heartspring's Center
Zelazny, R. The man who loved the Faioli
Zelazny, R. Recital
Zelazny, R. A very good year
Zumas, L. Handfasting
Zumas, L. Waste no time if this method fails

Love Stories. Morison, S.
A **love** story. Hamer-Jacklyn, S.
Love Story. Kadish, R.
A **love** story. Maxwell, W.
A **Love** Story. Swartz, A.
Love web. Granados, C.

Lovecraft, H. P. (Howard Phillips)

At the mountains of madness
    Lovecraft, H. P. H.P. Lovecraft; tales; edited by Peter Straub
The call of Cthulhu
    Lovecraft, H. P. H.P. Lovecraft; tales; edited by Peter Straub
The case of Charles Dexter Ward
    Lovecraft, H. P. H.P. Lovecraft; tales; edited by Peter Straub
The cats of Ulthar
    Cat tales: fantastic feline fiction; edited by George H. Scithers
The colour out of space
    Lovecraft, H. P. H.P. Lovecraft; tales; edited by Peter Straub
Cool air
    Lovecraft, H. P. H.P. Lovecraft; tales; edited by Peter Straub
Discarded draft of The shadow over Innsmouth
    Weird shadows over Innsmouth; edited by Stephen Jones; illustrated by Randy Broecker [et al.]
The dreams in the Witch House
    Lovecraft, H. P. H.P. Lovecraft; tales; edited by Peter Straub
The Dunwich horror
    Lovecraft, H. P. H.P. Lovecraft; tales; edited by Peter Straub
The haunter of the dark
    Lovecraft, H. P. H.P. Lovecraft; tales; edited by Peter Straub
He
    Lovecraft, H. P. H.P. Lovecraft; tales; edited by Peter Straub
Herbert West—reanimator
    Lovecraft, H. P. H.P. Lovecraft; tales; edited by Peter Straub
Herbert West—reanimator: six shots by moonlight
    Adaptations: from short story to big screen; 35 great stories that have inspired great films; edited by Stephanie Harrison

Lovecraft, H. P. (Howard Phillips)—*Continued*

The horror at Red Hook

Lovecraft, H. P. H.P. Lovecraft; tales; edited by Peter Straub

Brooklyn noir 2; the classics; edited by Tim McLoughlin

The lurking fear

Lovecraft, H. P. H.P. Lovecraft; tales; edited by Peter Straub

The music of Erich Zann

Lovecraft, H. P. H.P. Lovecraft; tales; edited by Peter Straub

The outsider

Lovecraft, H. P. H.P. Lovecraft; tales; edited by Peter Straub

Pickman's model

Lovecraft, H. P. H.P. Lovecraft; tales; edited by Peter Straub

The rats in the walls

Lovecraft, H. P. H.P. Lovecraft; tales; edited by Peter Straub

The shadow out of time

Lovecraft, H. P. H.P. Lovecraft; tales; edited by Peter Straub

The shadow over Innsmouth

Lovecraft, H. P. H.P. Lovecraft; tales; edited by Peter Straub

The shunned house

Lovecraft, H. P. H.P. Lovecraft; tales; edited by Peter Straub

The statement of Randolph Carter

Lovecraft, H. P. H.P. Lovecraft; tales; edited by Peter Straub

The thing on the doorstep

Lovecraft, H. P. H.P. Lovecraft; tales; edited by Peter Straub

The whisperer in darkness

Lovecraft, H. P. H.P. Lovecraft; tales; edited by Peter Straub

LOVECRAFT, H. P. (HOWARD PHILLIPS), 1890-1937

About

Di Filippo, P. A monument to after-thought unveiled

Samuels, M. A gentleman from Mexico

Parodies, imitations, etc.

Bear, E. Shoggoths in bloom

Bear, E. Tiger! Tiger!

Gaiman, N. A study in emerald

Howard, R. E. The fire of Asshurbanipal

Lupoff, R. A. The adventure of the Voorish Sign

Lupoff, R. A. The devil's hop yard

Lupoff, R. A. Documents in the case of Elizabeth Akeley

Lupoff, R. A. The doom that came to Dunwich

Lupoff, R. A. The horror south of Red Hook

Smith, C. A. The seven geases

Zelazny, R. The insider

Lovecraft, Howard Phillips *See* Lovecraft, H. P. (Howard Phillips), 1890-1937

Lovegrove, James

At one

British invasion; edited by Christopher Golden, Tim Lebbon & James A. Moore

Project: Verbivore

Nature v451 p372 Ja 17 2008

Lovelace, Sean

Coffee Pot Tree

River Styx no76/77 p99 2008

Lovell, Glenville

Hit and run

Hard boiled Brooklyn; edited by Reed Farrel Coleman

Out of body

Queens noir; edited by Robert Knightly

Lovely. Straley, J.

Lovely Lily. Davis, J. S.

Lovely Rita. Meloy, M.

The **Lover**. Galgut, D.

Lover boy. Gorman, E.

Lover boy. Mozetič, B.

Lover when you're near me. Matheson, R.

Loverde, Lorin

(tr.) See Laurent, Patricia

LOVERS

Alarcón, D. Third Avenue suicide

Alexander, D. Beneficient diversions from the crackdkins diet

Allende, I. The Guggenheim lovers

Alvarado, B. In box canyon

Amdahl, G. Visigoth

Anapol, B. A stone house

Anaya, R. A. The captain

Anaya, R. A. Children of the desert

Andreas-Salomé, L. Before the awakening

Andreas-Salomé, L. A death

Andreas-Salomé, L. One night

Angel, J. Rounding third

Arnold, G. Hospitality

Barkley, B. Another perfect catastrophe

Barry, R. Grace

Bartels, E. E. Woman is boss

Barthelme, S. Claire

Bass, R. Canoeists

Beltran, R. Shere-Sade/Sheri-Sade

Bender, A. I will pick out your ribs (from my teeth)

Bender, A. The meeting

Bennett, T. Blind faith

Bentham, R. When should we live?

Biller, M. The architect

Biller, M. Aviva's back

Biller, M. Baghdad at seven-thirty

Biller, M. Butterflies

Biller, M. Fearing for Ilana

Biller, M. Happy ending with sticky tape

Biller, M. The mahogany elephant

Biller, M. The maserati years

Biller, M. My name was Singer

Biller, M. The right time of the month

Biller, M. Seven attempts at loving

Biller, M. Two Israelis in Prague

Biller, M. We were sitting in Cibo Matto

Biller, M. Yellow sandals

Billingham, M. Stroke of luck

Bingham, S. His sons

Bingham, S. That winter

Bissell, T. Animals in our lives

Blackshaw, G. Girlfriend

Bolaño, R. Phone calls

Boof, Kola. The one you meet everywhere

Boullosa, C. Impossible story

Boyd, W. Incandescence

Boyle, T. C. The love of my life

Boyle, T. C. The swift passage of the animals

Lowe, Ramona

The woman in the window

"Tell it to us easy" and other stories; a complete short fiction anthology of African American women writers in Opportunity magazine, (1923-1948); edited by Judith Musser.

LOWELL, ROBERT, 1917-1977

About

Boyers, R. The visit

LOWELL (MASS.) *See* Massachusetts—Lowell

Lowell and the Rolling Thunder. Deaver, P. F.

LOWER EAST SIDE (NEW YORK, N.Y.) *See* New York (N.Y.)—Lower East Side

Lower wacker blues. Pinkerton, B.

The **lower** wacker Hilton. D'Amato, B.

Lowndes, Belloc

Popeau intervenes

The Mammoth book of vintage whodunnits; edited by Maxim Jakubowski

Lowry, Malcolm

China

Lowry, M. The voyage that never ends; fictions, poems, drafts, and letters; edited by Michael Hofmann

The forest path to the spring

Lowry, M. The voyage that never ends; fictions, poems, drafts, and letters; edited by Michael Hofmann

June the 30th, 1934

Lowry, M. The voyage that never ends; fictions, poems, drafts, and letters; edited by Michael Hofmann

Kristbjorg's story: in the Black Hills

Lowry, M. The voyage that never ends; fictions, poems, drafts, and letters; edited by Michael Hofmann

Strange comfort afforded by the profession

Lowry, M. The voyage that never ends; fictions, poems, drafts, and letters; edited by Michael Hofmann

Through the Panama

Lowry, M. The voyage that never ends; fictions, poems, drafts, and letters; edited by Michael Hofmann

Under the volcano

Lowry, M. The voyage that never ends; fictions, poems, drafts, and letters; edited by Michael Hofmann

Lowy, Todd Hasak- *See* Hasak-Lowy, Todd, 1969-

Loy, Jamie Lee

Bury your mother

Trinidad noir; edited by Lisa Allen-Agostini & Jeanne Mason.

Loyalty. Turow, S.

Lozar, Tom

(tr.) See Novak, Maja

LSD (DRUG)

D'Allesandro, S. How I came to dinosaur pond

MacEnulty, P. Purple haze

Tenn, W. The lemon-green spaghetti-loud dynamite-dribble day

LSD. Erdrich, L.

Lu, Alvin

Le rouge et le noir

San Francisco noir; edited by Peter Maravelis

Luau. Troy, M.

Lubar, David

Hats off

Orson Scott Card's Intergalctic medicine show; [edited by] Edmund R. Schubert and Orson Scott Card

LUBLIN (POLAND) *See* Poland—Lublin

Lucarelli, Carlo

Beret

Rome noir; edited by Chiara Stangalino & Maxim Jakubowski; translated by Anne Milano Appel, Ann Goldstein, and Kathrine Jason

Lucas, Chad

Gingerbread Ninja

Dalhousie Review v88 no2 p261-72 Summ 2008

Luce, Kelly

Christmas Stories

The North American Review v293 no3/4 p17-21 My/Ag 2008

Lucho. Engel, P.

Lucifer. Zelazny, R.

Lucifer over Lancashire. Blincoe, N.

Luciferase. Sterling, B.

Lucille. Nunez, E.

Lucille's House. Mitchell, E.

The **lucite** cane. Scott, J.

Luck. Kelly, J. P.

Luck. Molodowsky, K.

Luck be a lady. Enright, A.

Luck be a lady. Estep, M.

Luck be a lady. Winn, T.

The **luck** in the head. Harrison, M. J.

The **luck** of the draw. Kellerman, F.

The **Luck** of the Hopeless. Fitch, B.

Lucky. Harris, C.

Lucky. Roeder, K. K.

Lucky. Tuck, L.

Lucky Alan. Lethem, J.

Lucky bastard. Starr, J.

Lucky Chow Fun. Groff, L.

Lucky girls. Freudenberger, N.

Lucky Hans. Schwitters, K.

Lucky seven & Dalloway. Dickinson, S.

Lucky strike. Rees, R.

Lucy—Freer Than I've Ever Been. Funke, T. R.

Lucy had a list. Sandford, J.

Lucy, in her splendor. Finlay, C. C.

Lucy's last hurrah. Barry, R.

Luda and Milena. Vapnyar, L.

LUDDITES

Finger, A. Our Ned

Ludlow. Glatt, L.

Ludwig, Sidura

Holding my breath underwater

Going the distance; edited by Alan Beard

Ludwigsen, Will

A good psycho is hard to find

The Horror Writers Association presents Blood lite; an anthology of humorous horror stories; edited by Kevin J. Anderson

The **luger** is a 9MM automatic handgun with a parabellum action. Mundis, J.

Lukyanenko, Sergei

Destiny, Inc.

The SFWA European hall of fame; sixteen contemporary masterpieces of science fiction from the continent; edited by James Morrow and Kathryn Morrow

Lull. Link, K.

Luloff, Joanna Rae

Galle Road

Confrontation no100 p207-23 Fall 2007/Wint 2008

Lum, Elmo

Baikal

StoryQuarterly v40 p269-74 2004

What I never said

New stories from the Southwest; edited by D. Seth Horton; foreword by Ray Gonzalez. *New England Review* v27 no3 p81-8 2006

Luman, P. T.

Gangster's brand

The Black Lizard big book of pulps; edited by Otto Penzler

LUMBER INDUSTRY

See also Loggers

Rash, R. Pemberton's bride

Lumber land. Pendarvis, J.

LUMBERJACKS *See* Loggers

LUMBERMEN *See* Loggers

Luminous. Egan, G.

Lumley, Brian

Big "C"

Lumley, B. Screaming science fiction; horrors from out of space

Born of the winds

Lumley, B. The taint and other novellas; best Mythos tales, volume one

Deja viewer

Lumley, B. Screaming science fiction; horrors from out of space

End piece: old man with a blade

Lumley, B. Necroscope: Harry and the pirates and other tales from the lost years

The fairground horror

Lumley, B. The taint and other novellas; best Mythos tales, volume one

Feasibility study

Lumley, B. Screaming science fiction; horrors from out of space

For the dead travel slowly

Lumley, B. Necroscope: Harry and the pirates and other tales from the lost years

Gaddy's gloves

Lumley, B. Screaming science fiction; horrors from out of space

Harry and the pirates

Lumley, B. Necroscope: Harry and the pirates and other tales from the lost years

The horror at Oakdeene

Lumley, B. The taint and other novellas; best Mythos tales, volume one

The house of the temple

Lumley, B. The taint and other novellas; best Mythos tales, volume one

Lord of the worms

Lumley, B. The taint and other novellas; best Mythos tales, volume one

The man who felt pain

Lumley, B. Screaming science fiction; horrors from out of space

The man who saw no spiders

Lumley, B. Screaming science fiction; horrors from out of space

My thing Friday

Dark delicacies; original tales of terror and the macabre by the world's greatest horror writers; edited by Del Howison and Jeff Gelb

No way home

Lumley, B. Screaming science fiction; horrors from out of space

Rising with Surtsey

Lumley, B. The taint and other novellas; best Mythos tales, volume one

Snarker's son

Lumley, B. Screaming science fiction; horrors from out of space

The strange years

Lumley, B. Screaming science fiction; horrors from out of space

The sun, the sea and the silent scream

Summer chills; strangers in stranger lands; edited by Stephen Jones

The taint

Weird shadows over Innsmouth; edited by Stephen Jones; illustrated by Randy Broecker [et al.]

Lumley, B. The taint and other novellas; best Mythos tales, volume one

Lummis, Charles Fletcher

Póh-hlaik, the cave boy

Adventures in the West; stories for young readers; edited by Susanne George Bloomfield and Eric Melvin Reed

Luna. Serizawa, A.

Luna. Smith, R. T.

Luna. Stewart, P.

Lunch, Lydia

The spirit of philosophical vitriol

Istanbul noir; edited by Mustafa Ziyalan & Amy Spangler; translated by Amy Spangler & Mustafa Ziyalan.

Lunch at the best restaurant in the world. Gilchrist, E.

Lunch with His Mother. Hubbard, J. R.

LUNCHEONS

Hempel, A. The day I had everything

Lunching with the Antichrist. Moorcock, M.

Lundberg, Jason Erik

Most excellent and lamentable

Text: Ur; the new book of masks; [edited by Forrest Aguirre]

Lundell, Michael

Welcome to Battlesburg

River Styx no71 p21-41 2005

Lundin, Leigh

Quality of mercy

Mystery Writers of America presents the prosecution rests; new stories about courtrooms, criminals, and the law; edited by Linda Fairstein.

Lunstrum, Kirsten Sundberg

Baby love

Lunstrum, K. S. Swimming with strangers; stories

The bath

Lunstrum, K. S. Swimming with strangers; stories

Carmel

Lunstrum, K. S. Swimming with strangers; stories

Lutz, Gary
  People shouldn't have to be the ones to tell you
    The Anchor book of new American short stories; edited by Ben Marcus
Lutz, Jessica
  All quiet
    Istanbul noir; edited by Mustafa Ziyalan & Amy Spangler; translated by Amy Spangler & Mustafa Ziyalan.
Lutz, John
  The laundry room
    Manhattan noir; edited by Lawrence Block
  Mitt's murder
    At the scene of the crime; forensic mysteries from today's best writers; edited by Dana Stabenow
  Nighthawks
    The World's finest mystery and crime stories, fifth annual collection; edited by Ed Gorman and Martin H. Greenberg
  Second story sunlight
    The World's finest mystery and crime stories, fourth annual collection; edited by Ed Gorman and Martin H. Greenberg
Luvaas, William
  Carpentry
    Luvaas, W. A working man's apocrypha; short stories
  Hilltop (an American story)
    Luvaas, W. A working man's apocrypha; short stories
  How I died
    Luvaas, W. A working man's apocrypha; short stories
  Let it snow
    Luvaas, W. A working man's apocrypha; short stories
  Original sin
    Luvaas, W. A working man's apocrypha; short stories
  Rain
    Luvaas, W. A working man's apocrypha; short stories
  Season of limb fall
    Luvaas, W. A working man's apocrypha; short stories
  The sexual revolution
    Luvaas, W. A working man's apocrypha; short stories
  Silver thaw
    Luvaas, W. A working man's apocrypha; short stories
  To the death
    Luvaas, W. A working man's apocrypha; short stories
  Trespass
    Luvaas, W. A working man's apocrypha; short stories
  The woman who was allergic to herself
    Luvaas, W. A working man's apocrypha; short stories
  Word Rage
    The North American Review v289 no6 p33-6 N/D 2004
  A working man's apocrypha
    Luvaas, W. A working man's apocrypha; short stories

Yesterday after the storm . . .
    Luvaas, W. A working man's apocrypha; short stories
LUXEMBURG, ROSA, 1871-1919
      About
  Finger, A. Comrade Luxemburg and Comrade Gramsci pass each other at a Congress of the Second International in Switzerland on the 10th of March, 1912
Luxenberg, Howard
  The photograph
    Best of Tin House; stories; foreword by Dorothy Allison
Luxurious hearses. Akpan, U. C.
Lý Lan
  Accident
    Michigan Quarterly Review v44 no1 p19-26 Wint 2005
Lychack, William
  Calvary
    The Southern Review (Baton Rouge, La.) v45 no2 p308-11 Spr 2009
  The Ghostwriter
    Harvard Review (1992) no32 p88-92 2007
  Stolpestad
    Ploughshares v34 no1 p105-11 Spr 2008
Lydia's body. Kaftan, V.
Lying. Ng, C.
Lying doggo. Mason, B. A.
Lying under the apple tree. Munro, A.
Lynch, Chris
  (jt. auth) See Francisco, Ben and Lynch, Chris
Lynch, Thomas
  Block Island
    The Southern Review (Baton Rouge, La.) v43 no3 p502-20 Summ 2007
  Hunter's Moon
    Granta v98 p233-51 Summ 2007
LYNCHING
  Baldwin, J. Going to meet the man
  Dunbar, P. L. The lynching of Jube Benson
  Dunbar, P. L. The tragedy at Three Forks
  Kalamu ya Salaam. Alabama
  Lewis, W. H. I got somebody in Staunton
  Walker, A. Advancing Luna—and Ida B. Wells
The **lynching** of Jube Benson. Dunbar, P. L.
Lynds, Dennis
  Success of a mission
    Thriller; edited by James Patterson
Lynds, Dennis, 1924-
    For works written by this author under other names see Collins, Michael, 1924-2005
Lynds, Gayle
  The hunt for Dmitri
    Thriller; edited by James Patterson
Lynn, David H.
  Emergency Run
    TriQuarterly no130 p27-40 2008
  A Pair of Muddy Pumps
    Southwest Review v93 no2 p252-63 2008
  Steps Through Sand, Through Fire
    TriQuarterly no123 p124-39 2005
Lynn, David Hayden
  Balked eclogue
    Lynn, D. H. Year of fire; stories
  Birnkrandt and Kamenski
    Lynn, D. H. Year of fire; stories

Lynn, David Hayden—*Continued*
  Children of God
    Lynn, D. H. Year of fire; stories
  Chrysalis
    Lynn, D. H. Year of fire; stories
  Dean of women
    Lynn, D. H. Year of fire; stories
  Deserts and dowries
    Lynn, D. H. Year of fire; stories
  Life sentences
    Lynn, D. H. Year of fire; stories
  Mistaken identity
    Lynn, D. H. Year of fire; stories
  Moving house
    Lynn, D. H. Year of fire; stories
  Mt. Pleasant
    Lynn, D. H. Year of fire; stories
  Muggings
    Lynn, D. H. Year of fire; stories
  Naming the stones
    Lynn, D. H. Year of fire; stories
  Paschal lamb
    Lynn, D. H. Year of fire; stories
  Poetry of the Amish
    Lynn, D. H. Year of fire; stories
  Steps through sand, through fire
    Lynn, D. H. Year of fire; stories
  Tracks
    Lynn, D. H. Year of fire; stories
  Year of fire
    Lynn, D. H. Year of fire; stories
Lynn, Elizabeth A.
  The silver dragon
    The Year's best fantasy and horror: eighteenth annual collection; edited by Ellen Datlow, Kelly Link & Gavin J. Grant
Lynn, raving. Mandelbaum, P.
Lyons, Daniel
  The Greyhound
    Playboy's college fiction; a collection of 21 years of contest winners; edited by Alice K. Turner; foreword by Thom Jones
LYSERGIC ACID DIETHYLAMIDE *See* LSD (Drug)
Lysing toward Bethlehem. Wilson, F. P.
Lystra, Donald
  We're All Adults
    The North American Review v290 no1 p8-12 Ja/F 2005
Lytton, Bulwer
  The house and the brain
    The Mammoth book of vintage whodunnits; edited by Maxim Jakubowski

M

"**M**". Kubati, R.
Ma, Kathryn
  For Sale By Owner
    Prairie Schooner v80 no1 p166-74 Spr 2006
Ma and Me. Leong, S.
Ma Jian
  The eight-fanged roach
    Ma Jian. Stick out your tongue; translated from the Chinese by Flora Drew
  The final initiation
    Ma Jian. Stick out your tongue; translated from the Chinese by Flora Drew

  The golden crown
    Ma Jian. Stick out your tongue; translated from the Chinese by Flora Drew
  The smile of Lake Drolmula
    Ma Jian. Stick out your tongue; translated from the Chinese by Flora Drew
  Where are you running to?
    Words without borders; the world through the eyes of writers; an anthology; edited by Samantha Schnee, Alane Salierno Mason, and Dedi Felman
  The woman and the blue sky
    Ma Jian. Stick out your tongue; translated from the Chinese by Flora Drew
    The Paris Review v47 p161-70 Fall/Wint 2005
Ma Perkins comes to stay. Bradbury, R.
The **maalishwalla**. Shroff, M. F.
Maazel, Fiona
  Inquire Today, Apply Within
    The Yale Review v93 no2 p150-63 Ap 2005
Mabura, Lily
  Elgon
    Callaloo v30 no2 p527-32 Spr 2007
MACABRE STORIES *See* Horror stories
Macaire, Jennifer
  Island
    The dictionary of failed relationships; 26 tales of love gone wrong; edited by Meredith Broussard
MacAlister, Katie
  Cat got your tongue?
    My big fat supernatural honeymoon; edited by P.N. Elrod.
MACARTHUR, DOUGLAS, 1880-1964
        About
  Sanders, W. Not fade away
The **Macauley** circuit. Silverberg, R.
MacBride, Alexander
  The ape man
    The Year's best fantasy and horror: twenty-first annual collection; edited by Ellen Datlow and Kelly Link & Gavin J. Grant
MacCreadle's bike. Williams, C.
MacDonald, George
  The magic mirror
    Tales before Narnia; the roots of modern fantasy and science fiction; edited by Douglas A. Anderson
Macdonald, Ross
  Gone girl
    A New omnibus of crime; edited by Tony Hillerman and Rosemary Herbert; contributing editors Sue Grafton and Jeffery Deaver
Macdonald, Sean
  (tr.) See Mu Shiying
MacDougal, Bonnie
  Out of order [excerpt]
    On the Mason-Dixon line; an anthology of contemporary Delaware writers; edited by Billie Travalini and Fleda Brown.
MACEDONIA
  Fais, M. Halima, Desdemona, Bubu
MacEnulty, Pat
  The bargain
    MacEnulty, P. The language of sharks; stories by Pat MacEnulty

MacEnulty, Pat—*Continued*

Blue abstraction
MacEnulty, P. The language of sharks; stories by Pat MacEnulty

Dancing for Poppa
MacEnulty, P. The language of sharks; stories by Pat MacEnulty

The deep end of the blue sky
MacEnulty, P. The language of sharks; stories by Pat MacEnulty

The end
MacEnulty, P. The language of sharks; stories by Pat MacEnulty

Fire and light
MacEnulty, P. The language of sharks; stories by Pat MacEnulty

Floating on the darkness
MacEnulty, P. The language of sharks; stories by Pat MacEnulty

Giving up the guilt
MacEnulty, P. The language of sharks; stories by Pat MacEnulty

The hawk's shadow
MacEnulty, P. The language of sharks; stories by Pat MacEnulty

The hurricane dance
MacEnulty, P. The language of sharks; stories by Pat MacEnulty

Inside out
MacEnulty, P. The language of sharks; stories by Pat MacEnulty

The language of sharks
MacEnulty, P. The language of sharks; stories by Pat MacEnulty

Like someone in a coma
MacEnulty, P. The language of sharks; stories by Pat MacEnulty

Picture day
MacEnulty, P. The language of sharks; stories by Pat MacEnulty

Purple haze
MacEnulty, P. The language of sharks; stories by Pat MacEnulty

Singing in the free world
MacEnulty, P. The language of sharks; stories by Pat MacEnulty

Some place to live
MacEnulty, P. The language of sharks; stories by Pat MacEnulty

Suburban hunger
MacEnulty, P. The language of sharks; stories by Pat MacEnulty

Viral love
MacEnulty, P. The language of sharks; stories by Pat MacEnulty

MacGowan, John

Fastosous and avaro
Tales before Narnia; the roots of modern fantasy and science fiction; edited by Douglas A. Anderson

MacGregor, Kinley

The wager
Elemental; the Tsunami relief anthology; stories of science fiction and fantasy; [edited by] Steven Savile and Alethea Kontis; introduction by Arthur C. Clarke

Machado, Anibal

The death of the standard-bearer
Oxford anthology of the Brazilian short story; edited by K. David Jackson

The first corpse
Oxford anthology of the Brazilian short story; edited by K. David Jackson

Machado de Assis

Dona Paula
Oxford anthology of the Brazilian short story; edited by K. David Jackson

The fortune-teller
Oxford anthology of the Brazilian short story; edited by K. David Jackson

Life
Oxford anthology of the Brazilian short story; edited by K. David Jackson

The nurse
Oxford anthology of the Brazilian short story; edited by K. David Jackson

The secret heart
Oxford anthology of the Brazilian short story; edited by K. David Jackson

The Siamese academies
Oxford anthology of the Brazilian short story; edited by K. David Jackson

Wallow, swine!
Oxford anthology of the Brazilian short story; edited by K. David Jackson

Wedding song
Oxford anthology of the Brazilian short story; edited by K. David Jackson

A woman's arms
Oxford anthology of the Brazilian short story; edited by K. David Jackson

Machart, Bruce

Among the living amidst the trees
Best stories of the American West, v1; edited by Marc Jaffe

The **machine**. Williams, C.

Machine maid. Lanagan, M.

The **machine** of a religious man. Moore, R. R.

MACHINERY AND CIVILIZATION *See* Technology and civilization

MACHINERY AND MACHINISTS

Davis, R. Engines of desire & despair
Gautreaux, T. The safe
Keith, W. H. Partnership
Kun, M. You have made quite a purchase
Swann, S. A. The historian's apprentice
Veiga, J. J. The misplaced machine

Macho outing. Tognazzini, A.

Machu Picchu. Cisneros, S.

MacInnes, Mairi

Arcady and After
The Sewanee Review v117 no3 p410-24 Summ 2009

Macker, Richard

A deadly joke
Passport to crime; the finest mystery stories from International Crime Writers; edited by Janet Hutchings

Macker, Teddy

Strawberry
Southern Humanities Review v41 no3 p268-78 Summ 2007

The Wild Rubicon
The Antioch Review v66 no3 p563-9 Summ 2008

Macy, Caitlin

Annabel's mother

Macy, C. Spoiled; stories

Bad ghost

Macy, C. Spoiled; stories

Bait and switch

Macy, C. Spoiled; stories

Christie

The O. Henry Prize stories, 2005; edited and with an introduction by Laura Furman

Macy, C. Spoiled; stories

Eden's gate

Macy, C. Spoiled; stories

The red coat

This is not chick lit; original stories by America's best women writers; edited by Elizabeth Merrick

Macy, C. Spoiled; stories

The secret vote

Macy, C. Spoiled; stories

Spoiled

Macy, C. Spoiled; stories

Taroudant

Macy, C. Spoiled; stories

Mad dog summer. Lansdale, J. R.

Mad house. Matheson, R.

Mad Jack. Roberson, J.

Madame Guralnik. Pearlman, E.

Madame President and her first lady. Kirn, W.

Madame Rosette. Dahl, R.

Madame secretary's lover man. Lamar, J.

Madden, David

A Cry of Ice

New Letters v72 no3/4 p81-98 2006

Maddox, Marjorie

A Wave Rushed Over

U.S. Catholic v72 no9 p30-4 S 2007

Made for each other. West, D.

Madeline's version. Cox, F. B.

Mademoiselle Arc-en-ciel. Rhodes, D.

Mademoiselle 'Tasie-a story. Thompson, E. B.

Madison, Bob

Red sunset

Gaslight grimoire; fantastic tales of Sherlock Holmes; edited by J. R. Campbell and Charles Prepolec

Madison at Guignol. Oates, J. C.

The **Madison** Heights syndrome. Wellman, A. M.

The **Madmen's** Ship. Sánchez Piñol, A.

MADNESS *See* Insanity; Mental illness

Madness and folly. Tabor, M. L.

The **Madonna** of Seville. Keithley, G.

Madonna of the maquiladora. Frost, G.

The **Madonna** of the Relics. Smith, G. B.

The **madonna** of turkey season. McInerney, J.

Madrid, Geronimo

Goanna

The Literary Review (Madison, N.J.) v50 no2 p62-75 Wint 2007

What I Did Showed Extremely Bad Judgment

Bomb no97 p120-7 Fall 2006

Madsen, Krista

Bust

River Styx no76/77 p97-8 2008

Maeda Keijiro. Fumiyo, S.

Maelstrom. Baker, K.

Maes, Augustin

Beauty and virtue

New stories from the South: the year's best, 2007; selected from U.S. magazines by Edward P. Jones with Kathy Pories; with an introduction by Edward P. Jones

Maes, Nicholas

Snow Day

Dalhousie Review v85 no1 p63-72 Spr 2005

Maestro. Archer, J.

MAFIA

See also Gangsters

Bova, B. Piker's peek

Everheart, C. Chili dog

Himes, C. Strictly business

Kelley, N. The messenger of soulsville

Kozlowski, L. Three times a night, every other night

Lyons, D. The Greyhound

Pearson, R. Close shave

Picciarelli, P. The prince of Arthur Avenue

Randisi, R. J. The Bocce Ball King of Farragut Road

Rankin, I. Graduation day

Reaves, S. The test

Resnick, L. The capo of darkness

Stella, C. Waiting for Gallo

Tapply, W. G. Unplayable lies

Zafiro, F. Dead even

MAGAZINES *See* Periodicals

Magda Mandela. Kunzru, H.

Magda Maria. Oates, J. C.

Magee, Kelly

All the America you want

Magee, K. Body language

As human as you are standing here

Magee, K. Body language

Body language

Magee, K. Body language

The business of souls

Magee, K. Body language

Fortune

Magee, K. Body language

Heat rises

Magee, K. Body language

Knock them down

Magee, K. Body language

The Niña, the Pinta, the Santa Maria

Magee, K. Body language

Not people, not this

Magee, K. Body language

Straitjacket

Magee, K. Body language

Vertical mile

Magee, K. Body language

Magee, Rosemary M.

A Curious Race

Southern Humanities Review v40 no4 p370-82 Fall 2006

The **Magellan** House. Gardiner, J. R.

Maggie. Stelmok, J.

Maggie Eisner: Frank [Medical Humanities, 31 no1 June 2005] Eisner, M.

Maggie Meriwether's rich experience. Stafford, J.

Maggies. Shawl, N.

MAGI

Stackpole, M. A. The final gift

Willis, C. Epiphany

MAGIC

See also Supernatural phenomena; Witchcraft

Andrews, D. Cold spell
Baingana, D. Passion
Beagle, P. S. Barrens dance
Beagle, P. S. Quarry
Beagle, P. S. El regalo
Berg, C. Unmasking
Bischoff, D. Quoth the screaming chicken
Bradley, D. C. They would only be roads
Brite, P. Z. Crown of thorns
Canavan, T. The lost property room
Card, O. S. Grinning man
Card, O. S. The Yazoo Queen
Cook, G. Filed teeth
Coville, B. The metamorphosis of Justin Jones
Crowther, P. The space between the lines
De Camp, L. S. and Pratt, F. The castle of iron
De Camp, L. S. and Pratt, F. Fletcher and I
De Camp, L. S. and Pratt, F. The green magician
De Camp, L. S. and Pratt, F. The mathematics of magic
DeCandido, K. R. A. A clean getaway
Dowling, T. The magikkers
Frost, G. The girlfriends of Dorian Gray
Green, S. R. The nightside, needless to say
Howard, R. E. Black Canaan
Howard, R. E. Kelly the conjure-man
Hughes, M. Mastermindless
Irvine, A. C. Wizard's six
Johnson, C. R. The gift of the Osuo
Johnson, K. 26 monkeys, also the abyss
Kaftan, V. Lydia's body
Keret, E. Bottle
Klages, E. Basement magic
Klages, E. Flying over water
Klages, E. Travel agency
Kress, N. Stone man
MacDonald, G. The magic mirror
MacGregor, K. The wager
Mamatas, N. Summon bind banish
McCarron, M. The magician's house
Modesitt, L. E., Jr. Black ordermage
Modesitt, L. E., Jr. Sisters of Sarronnyn, sisters of Westwind
Monteleone, T. F. A spell for Jonathan
Moscoe, M. Danny's very long trip
Newman, K. The gypsies in the wood
Nix, G. Beyond the sea gate of the scholar-pirates of Sarsköe
Nix, G. Holly and iron
Pratchett, T. Once and future
Pratchett, T. The sea and little fishes
Pratt, T. Komodo
Rickert, M. Anyway
Rivera-Valdes, S. Ana at four times: Ana and the magic wand
Schwartz, D. J. The somnambulist
Simpson, H. The green room
Smith, C. A. The colossus of Ylourgne
Smith, C. A. The coming of the white worm
Smith, C. A. The holiness of Azédarac
Stackpole, M. A. The Krells of Tancras Moor
Sterling, B. The little magic shop
Van Eekhout, G. The osteomancer's son
Wells, M. The potter's daughter
Wilce, Y. S. The lineaments of gratified desire

Williams, L. Winterborn
Williams, T. The stranger's hands
Wolfe, G. The magic animal
Magic. Porter, K. A.
The **magic** animal. Wolfe, G.
The **magic** barrel. Malamud, B.
The **magic** box. Sillitoe, A.
Magic for beginners. Link, K.
Magic in a certain slant of light. Coates, D.
Magic lantern. Richards, S. S.
Magic lantern show. Miura, T.
The **magic** mirror. MacDonald, G.
The **magic** of your touch. Robinson, P.
The **magic** paint. Levi, P.
The **magic** pony. Sarris, G.
The **magic** touch: a Peter Pansy detective yarn. Robbins, A. B.
The **magic** wagon [excerpt] Lansdale, J. R.
The **magician**. Trezise, R.

MAGICIANS

Allyn, D. Palace in the pines
Bear, E. The chains that you refuse
Beattie, A. Solid wood
Butcher, J. Day off
Butcher, J. Heorot
Butcher, J. It's my birthday, too
Butcher, J. The warrior
Clarke, S. John Uskglass and the Cumbrian charcoal burner
Cook, G. The nights of dreadful silence
Coville, B. Wizard's boy
Dann, J. and others. Afternoon at Schrafft's
Davidson, C. The apprentice's guide to modern magic
Ford, J. The Manticore spell
Gordon, M. The magician's wife
Greenspon, J. Disappear
Holladay, C. C. The quick-change artist
Hubbard, L. R. Battle of wizards
Huff, T. Blood wrapped
Keret, E. Hat trick
Lee, Y. H. Eating hearts
Mahajan, K. The cremation ground
Martin, G. R. R. In the lost lands
McCafferty, J. Embraced
McIlvoy, K. Permission
Meno, J. In the arms of someone you love
Nelson, R. F. Food is fuel
Pratt, T. In a glass casket
Robbins, A. B. The magic touch: a Peter Pansy detective yarn
Rosenblum, M. H. Color vision
Scholes, K. Into the blank where life is hurled
Smith, C. A. The last incantation
Smith, C. A. The maze of Maal Dweb
Smith, C. A. The maze of the enchanter [variant title: The maze of Maal Dweb]
Zelazny, R. The last defender of Camelot
Zelazny, R. Tower of ice
Magicians. Shaw, K. L.
The **magician's** house. McCarron, M.
The **magician's** little joke. Bierce, A.
The **magician's** wife. Gordon, M.
The **magikkers**. Dowling, T.

Magill, Mark
The Horse Thieves of Rockaway Beach
Bomb no92 p116-20 Summ 2005
The **magnetic** boarder. Asch, S.
Magnitude. Daugherty, T.

MAIDS (SERVANTS)—*Continued*
  Sayles, J. Casa de los Babys
  Singer, I. B. Dazzled
  Stafford, J. The hope chest
  Taraqqi, G. The maid
  Trevor, W. The dancing-master's music
The **maids**. Hayden, G. M.
Mail. Stern, R. G.
The **main** event. Crowther, P.
MAINE
  Bear, E. Shoggoths in bloom
  Bowes, R. The mask of the Rex
  Busch, F. The barrens
  Busch, F. Patrols
  Ford, R. Charity
  Hand, E. Echo
  Higgins, G. V. Slowly now the dancer
  Irvine, A. C. Clownfish
  King, O. We're all in this together
  Matheson, R. The children of Noah
  Robinson, L. Cuxabexis, Cuxabexis
  Robinson, L. Finches
  Stelmok, J. Maxfield Ridge
  Stelmok, J. Not your average bear
  Stelmok, J. The samaritan
  Stelmok, J. The three requests
  Swan, G. A garden amid fires
  Swan, G. On the island
  Swan, G. Uncle Lazarus
  Tower, W. Retreat

Farm life
See Farm life—Maine

Maintaining. Kulpa, K.
Maisto, Michelle
  The Day We Exist Again
    Women's Studies Quarterly v36 no1/2 p227-35 Spr/Summ 2008
Maitland, Sara
  Why I became a plumber
    The Year's best fantasy and horror: seventeenth annual collection; edited by Ellen Datlow, Kelly Link and Gavin J. Grant
The **maitre** d'. Bova, B.
Maja-Pearce, Adewale
  Civil War I-VII
    The Anchor book of modern African stories; edited by Nadežda Obradovic; with a foreword by Chinua Achebe
Majesty. July, M.
Majfud, Jorge
  The Age of Barbaria
    The Humanist v68 no4 p28-9 Jl/Ag 2008
  The Walled Society
    The Humanist v68 no4 p25-7 Jl/Ag 2008
Major, Devorah
  Trade winds
    So long been dreaming; postcolonial science fiction & fantasy; Nalo Hopkinson & Uppinder Mehan, eds
Major Spacer in the 21st century!. Waldrop, H.
Majorette. Groff, L.
The **major's** tale. Bierce, A.
Majumdar uncle. Keating, H. R. F.
Majzels, Robert
  Hellman's scrapbook [excerpt]
    Contemporary Jewish writing in Canada; an anthology; edited by Michael Greenstein

Makanin, Vladimir
  A Time of Exchanges
    Agni no67 p164-87 2008
Makdisi, Jean Said
  Pietà
    Qissat; short stories by Palestinian women; edited by Jo Glanville
Make a nest. Treat, J.
Make it sound like a train. McIlvoy, K.
Make straight for the shore. Kiely, B.
Makélé, Caya
  The labors of Arianna
    From Africa; new francophone stories; edited by Adele King
The **maker** of gargoyles. Smith, C. A.
Makeshift memorial. Stewart, P.
Making a fortune. Twain, M.
Making adultery work. Johnson, M. L.
Making amends. Deaver, J.
Making an Elephant.
Making changes. Michaels, L.
Making faces. McDowell, I.
Making Good. Segal, L.
Making It to Thirty. Gangemi, K.
Making love: a translation. Grimes, C.
Making love in 2003. July, M.
Making memories. Frizell, J.
The **making** of the worlds, of gods, and of giants. Thomas, E.
Making the sale. Heeren, F.
The **makin's**. Bonner, M. O.
Makkai, Rebecca
  The Briefcase
    New England Review v29 no2 p59-65 2008
  The World's Last Englishman
    The Sewanee Review v115 no4 p540-51 Fall 2007
Makuchi *See* Nfah-Abbenyi, Juliana Makuchi, 1958-
Maladies of the inner ear. Goliger, G.
MALADJUSTED CHILDREN *See* Emotionally disturbed children
Malae, Peter Nathaniel
  The arms of Brian Flinteraft
    Malae, P. N. Teach the free man; stories
  Before high desert
    Malae, P. N. Teach the free man; stories
  The good nurse
    Malae, P. N. Teach the free man; stories
  Got it one last time
    Malae, P. N. Teach the free man; stories
  Guts and viscera in the chicken farm
    Malae, P. N. Teach the free man; stories
  The once-a-week performance
    Malae, P. N. Teach the free man; stories
  The Paige Renaissance
    Southwest Review v93 no3 p391-411 2008
  Reliable vet dad, reliable con son
    Malae, P. N. Teach the free man; stories
  Smuggling a kiss
    Malae, P. N. Teach the free man; stories
  The story
    Malae, P. N. Teach the free man; stories
  Tags
    Malae, P. N. Teach the free man; stories
  Turning point
    Malae, P. N. Teach the free man; stories
  What you can do after shutdown
    Malae, P. N. Teach the free man; stories

Malamud, Bernard
The magic barrel
Inside the hornet's head; an anthology of Jewish American writing; edited by Jerome Charyn
My mistress's sparrow is dead; great love stories, from Chekhov to Munro; edited by Jeffrey Eugenides

MALARIA
Chilson, P. Tea with soldiers
Smith, M. The white net

Malartre, Elisabeth
Looking for Mr Goodbug
Nature v435 p854 Je 9 2005

MALATESTA, PAOLO, CA. 1246-1285
About
Zelazny, R. The Malatesta collection
The **Malatesta** collection. Zelazny, R.

MALAWI
Lipenga, K. Wainting for a turn

MALAYA
See also Malaysia

MALAYSIA
Sonnenberg, B. Taiping

Malcontenta. Williams, L.
A **male** influence in the house. Tomlinson, J.
Male of the species. Mindt, A.
El **malecon**. Selgin, P.
Malediction. Grubb, J.

Maleeny, Tim
Suspension of disbelief
Thriller 2; stories you just can't put down; edited by Clive Cussler; [stories by] Kathleen Antrim . . . [et al.]
Till death do us part
Mystery Writers of America presents death do us part; new stories about love, lust, and murder; edited by Harlan Coben

Malerba, Luigi
Consuming the View
Harper's v310 p31 Ja 2005

Malerba-Foran, Joan
The little things
The Best of the Bellevue Literary Review; edited by Dannielle Ofri and the staff of the Bellevue Literary Review

MALIBRAN, MARÍA, 1808-1836
About
Green, G. Voices in a mask
Malibu dog. Kellerman, F.

MALICIOUS MISCHIEF
Granados, C. The latchkey chronicles: Goldfinger

Malik, Muhammad 'Abd al-
That winter
Oranges in the sun; short stories from the Arabian Gulf; edited and translated by Deborah S. Akers, Abubaker A. Bagader

Maliszewski, Paul
Contrails
StoryQuarterly v41 p195-8 2005
The Mugging
StoryQuarterly v41 p388-91 2005
The Prayer
StoryQuarterly v41 p303-8 2005
Ted
StoryQuarterly v41 p478-85 2005

Maliszewski, Paul
Prayer against the experts and their ways
Pushcart prize XXVII; best of the small presses; edited by Bill Henderson with the Pushcart prize editors
Malkele Eshman. Molodowsky, K.

Malla, Pasha
Being like bulls
Malla, P. The withdrawal method; stories
Big city girls
Malla, P. The withdrawal method; stories
Dizzy when you look down in
Malla, P. The withdrawal method; stories
The film we made about dads
Malla, P. The withdrawal method; stories
Long short short long
Malla, P. The withdrawal method; stories
The love life of the automation Turk
Malla, P. The withdrawal method; stories
The past composed
Malla, P. The withdrawal method; stories
Pet therapy
Malla, P. The withdrawal method; stories
Pushing oceans in and pulling oceans outs
Malla, P. The withdrawal method; stories
Respite
Malla, P. The withdrawal method; stories
The slough
Malla, P. The withdrawal method; stories
Timber on the wheel of everyone
Malla, P. The withdrawal method; stories
When Jacques Cousteau gave Pablo Picasso a piece of black coral
Malla, P. The withdrawal method; stories

Mallam Sile. Ali, M. N.

Mallcolm-Clarke, Darja
The beacon
Realms

Mallett, Margaret
Never too late to make amends
The Times Educational Supplement p44-7 D 21-28 2007 TES Magazine

Malone, Michael
Raindancer
Murder at the racetrack; edited by Otto Penzler
Red clay
A New omnibus of crime; edited by Tony Hillerman and Rosemary Herbert; contributing editors Sue Grafton and Jeffery Deaver
White trash noir
Murder at the foul line; edited by Otto Penzler

Maloney, Darby
The best laid plans
Trinidad noir; edited by Lisa Allen-Agostini & Jeanne Mason.

Maloney, Geoffrey
Not another black cat story
Cat tales: fantastic feline fiction; edited by George H. Scithers

Malouf, David
At Schindler's
Malouf, D. The complete stories
Bad blood
Malouf, D. The complete stories
Blacksoil country
Malouf, D. The complete stories

Malouf, David—*Continued*
A change of scene
  Malouf, D. The complete stories
Closer
  Malouf, D. The complete stories
The domestic cantata
  Malouf, D. The complete stories
Dream stuff
  Malouf, D. The complete stories
Elsewhere
  Malouf, D. The complete stories
The empty lunch-tin
  Malouf, D. The complete stories
Eustace
  Malouf, D. The complete stories
Every move you make
  Malouf, D. The complete stories
  The O. Henry Prize stories 2008; edited and
    with an introduction by Laura Furman; with
    essays on the stories they admire most by
    jurors Chimamanda Ngozi Adiche, David
    Leavitt, David Means
  Granta no95 p15-36 Fall 2006
Great Day
  Malouf, D. The complete stories
In trust
  Malouf, D. The complete stories
Jacko's ranch
  Malouf, D. The complete stories
Lone Pine
  Malouf, D. The complete stories
A medium
  Malouf, D. The complete stories
Mrs. Porter and the rock
  Malouf, D. The complete stories
Night training
  Malouf, D. The complete stories
The only speaker of his tongue
  Malouf, D. The complete stories
Out of the stream
  Malouf, D. The complete stories
The prowler
  Malouf, D. The complete stories
Sally's story
  Malouf, D. The complete stories
Sorrows and secrets
  Malouf, D. The complete stories
Southern skies
  Malouf, D. The complete stories
The sun in winter
  Malouf, D. The complete stories
That antic Jezebel
  Malouf, D. The complete stories
Towards midnight
  Malouf, D. The complete stories
A traveller's tale
  Malouf, D. The complete stories
A trip to the Grundelsee
  Malouf, D. The complete stories
The Valley of Lagoons
  Malouf, D. The complete stories
War baby
  Malouf, D. The complete stories
Malpede, Karen
On the Train
  Confrontation no92/93 p71-86 Fall 2005/Wint
    2006
Prophecy
  TriQuarterly no123 p178-90 2005

Malthusian's zombie. Ford, J.
Malvu the helmsman: a story of vesta. Scheerbart,
  P.
Malzberg, Barry N.
A delightful comedic premise
  This is my funniest; leading science fiction
    writers present their funniest stories ever;
    edited by Mike Resnick
The interceptor
  Manhattan noir 2; the classics; edited by
    Lawrence Block
The passion of Azazel
  The Del Rey book of science fiction and fan-
    tasy; sixteen original works by speculative
    fiction's finest voices; edited by Ellen
    Datlow
Understanding entropy
  A cross of centuries; twenty-five imaginative
    tales about the Christ; edited by Michael
    Bishop
(jt. auth) See Dann, Jack and Malzberg, Barry
  N.
(jt. auth) See Pronzini, Bill and Malzberg, Barry
  N.
Ma'mami, Sulayman al-
The white dog
  Oranges in the sun; short stories from the
    Arabian Gulf; edited and translated by Deb-
    orah S. Akers, Abubaker A. Bagader
Mama's boy. Nolan, W. F.
Mamatas, Nick
A sudden absence of bees
  Nature v450 p134 N 1 2007
Summon bind banish
  Bandersnatch; edited by Paul Tremblay and
    Sean Wallace
There is a light that never goes out
  Poe's lighthouse; all new collaborations with
    Edgar Allan Poe; edited by Christopher
    Conlon
"**Mame**". Levin, Z.
MAMMALS, FOSSIL *See* Fossils
MAMMOTHS
  Kelly, J. P. Luck
  Waldrop, H. Winter quarters
Mammy (a short story). West, D.
Mammy Peggy's pride. Dunbar, P. L.
Mamzer. Rosen, R. D.
MAN
  Resnick, M. Safari 2103 A.D.
MAN, PREHISTORIC *See* Prehistoric man; Pre-
  historic times
A **man**. Barthelme, D.
The **man**. Bradbury, R.
Man and Boy. Donoghue, E.
The **man** and the snake. Bierce, A.
Man and wife. Chase, K.
Man at the bus stop. Mukhopadhyay, T.
The **man** at the corner of now and forever.
  Zelazny, R.
The **man** back there. Crouse, D.
Man Bites Dog. Nguyen, P.
A **man** called Horse. Johnson, D. M.
Man catch. Rice, C.
Man crawling out of trees. Proulx, A.
Man-eating cats. Murakami, H.
The **man** for the job. Phillips, G.
The **man** from Allston Electric. Kalotay, D.
The **Man** from Nowhere. Mejides, M.

The **man** from Shemhaza. Brust, S.
Man from the South. Dahl, R.
The **man** in Bogota. Hempel, A.
The **man** in the moon. Maxwell, W.
The **man** inside. McAllister, B.
A **Man** Like Him. Li Yiyun
Man-O'-War. Vollmer, M.
A **man** of awesome power. Maḥfūẓ, N.
A **man** of forethought. Burke, K.
A **man** of light. Ford, J.
The **man** of many names. Gospodinov, G.
A **man** of principle. Wendroff, Z.
Man of quiet desperation goes on short vacation. Yu, C.
Man of rock, man of stone. Yolen, J.
Man of steel.
A **man** of talent. Silverberg, R.
Man of the house. Granados, C.
The **man** of the house. Koretsky, J. L.
Man of War. Dickinson, S.
Man oh man — it's Manna Man. Singleton, G.
The **man** on the ceiling. Tem, S. R. and Tem, M.
The **man** on the cross. Crider, B.
The **man** on the ground. Howard, R. E.
The **Man** on the Island. Grady, W.
The **man** on the stairs. July, M.
Man or monster. Kuhoric, J. A.
The **man** out of the nose. Bierce, A.
The **man** outside. Effinger, G. A.
The **man** overboard. Bierce, A.
Man pass man. Ali, M. N.
Man Receives Letter. Gordon, P.
Man throws dog out window. Montemarano, N.
Man walking. Richards, S. S.
The **man** who ate Michael Rockefeller. Stokes, C.
The **man** who became himself. Yu, C.
The **man** who came back. Ferber, E.
The **man** who came early. Anderson, P.
The **man** who came out of the corner of my eye. Dobozy, T.
The **man** who could fly. Anaya, R. A.
The **man** who could see radiance. Clayton, J. J.
The **man** who did nothing. Traviss, K.
The **man** who didn't play golf. Brett, S.
The **man** who fell in love with the stump of a tree. Rohn, R.
The **man** who felt pain. Lumley, B.
The **man** who fought Roland LaStarza. Oates, J. C.
The **man** who found a pistol. Anaya, R. A.
The **man** who had never been sick a day in his life. Maxwell, W.
The **man** who had no friends and didn't want any. Maxwell, W.
The **man** who killed a shadow. Wright, R.
The **man** who killed (and saved) Wall Street. Stein, J.
The **Man** Who Knew Beckett. Gates, D.
The **man** who knew how. Sayers, D. L.
The **man** who knew Javanese. Lima Barreto, A. H. d.
The **man** who lived backwards. Hall, C. F.
The **man** who lost his father. Maxwell, W.
The **man** who loved the Faioli. Zelazny, R.
The **man** who loved to eat. Maxwell, W.
The **man** who made the world. Matheson, R.
The **man** who married a tree. D'Souza, T.
The **man** who never forgot. Silverberg, R.

The **man** who painted the dragon griaule. Shepard, L.
The **man** who ran with deer. Averill, T. F.
The **man** who read a book. Disch, T. M.
The **man** who robbed his own post office. Archer, J.
The **Man** Who Sang So Well. Thompson, L. D.
The **man** who saw no spiders. Lumley, B.
The **man** who sold his mother. Taha, M. A.
The **man** who stole Shakespeare. L'Amour, L.
The **Man** Who Touched Stars. Schenck, E.
The **man** who wanted revenge. Chekhov, A. P.
The **man** who was left as nine pairs of shoes. Yun, H.
The **man** who was made of netting. Vaz, K.
The **man** who wrote on beaches. Donoghue, E.
The **man** whose head expanded. Aylett, S.
Man with a passion. Block, L.
Man with golden eagle. Shukman, H.
The **man** with great despair behind his eyes. Scholes, K.
The **Man** with the Black Hair and the Many Tattoos. Köhlmeier, P.
The **man** with the collecting-box. Daeninckx, D.
The **man** with the glass nose. Schwitters, K.
Man with the iron arm [variant title: The one arm man] Leonard, E.
The **man** with the plug in his nose. Anderson, B.
The **man** with the strange head. Breuer, M. J.
A **man** with two lives. Bierce, A.
Man without a tongue. Goodis, D.
Man, Woman, Gun. Stone, R.
A **Man** You Could Talk To. Brøgger, S.
The **management** of grief. Mukherjee, B.
The **Manager's** Son. Colbert, J. W.
Manannan's children. Blackford, R.
Manasseh. Yellin, T.
MANCHESTER (ENGLAND) *See* England— Manchester
Mancini, Evelina Cattermole *See* Lara, Contessa, 1849-1896
Mandalas. Rustomji, R.
Mandanipour, Shahriar
  Seasons of Purgatory
    The Literary Review (Madison, N.J.) v51 no1 p71-86 Fall 2007
The **mandarin** question. Vaz, K.
Mandel, Steven B.
  Blind man blue
    Chicago blues; edited by Libby Fischer Hellmann
Mandelbaum, Paul
  Changeling
    Mandelbaum, P. Garrett in wedlock; a novel-in-stories
  The explorers
    Mandelbaum, P. Garrett in wedlock; a novel-in-stories
  Garrett in the wild
    Mandelbaum, P. Garrett in wedlock; a novel-in-stories
  Garrett in wedlock
    Mandelbaum, P. Garrett in wedlock; a novel-in-stories
  Lynn, raving
    Mandelbaum, P. Garrett in wedlock; a novel-in-stories

Mandelbaum, Paul—*Continued*
The omelet king
    Mandelbaum, P. Garrett in wedlock; a novel-
        in-stories
Parni's present
    Mandelbaum, P. Garrett in wedlock; a novel-
        in-stories
Pendant
    Mandelbaum, P. Garrett in wedlock; a novel-
        in-stories
Several answers
    Mandelbaum, P. Garrett in wedlock; a novel-
        in-stories
Virtue
    Mandelbaum, P. Garrett in wedlock; a novel-
        in-stories
Yoga is a personal journey
    Mandelbaum, P. Garrett in wedlock; a novel-
        in-stories
Mandelbaum, the Criminal. Shapiro, G.
Mandelberg, John
To Reign After Death
    Southwest Review v90 no4 p555-66 2005
Mandelman, Avner
Black
    Mandelman, A. Talking to the enemy; stories;
        Avner Mandelman
Curse
    Mandelman, A. Talking to the enemy; stories;
        Avner Mandelman
Life in parts
    Mandelman, A. Talking to the enemy; stories;
        Avner Mandelman
Mish-mash
    Mandelman, A. Talking to the enemy; stories;
        Avner Mandelman
Og
    Mandelman, A. Talking to the enemy; stories;
        Avner Mandelman
Pity
    Mandelman, A. Talking to the enemy; stories;
        Avner Mandelman
Talking to the enemy
    Mandelman, A. Talking to the enemy; stories;
        Avner Mandelman
Terror
    Mandelman, A. Talking to the enemy; stories;
        Avner Mandelman
Test
    Mandelman, A. Talking to the enemy; stories;
        Avner Mandelman
Mandel´shtam, Osip *See* Mandelstam, Osip,
    1891-1938
MANDELSTAM, OSIP, 1891-1938
About
Perlman, E. I was only in a childish way con-
    nected to the established order
The **mandrakes.** Smith, C. A.
Mandy. Soueif, A.
Maneki Neko. Sterling, B.
Manfred. Barthelme, D.
Manfredo, Lou
Case closed
    Brooklyn noir; edited by Tim McLoughlin
    The Best American mystery stories, 2005; ed
        ited and with an introduction by Joyce Car-
        ol Oates; Otto Penzler, series editor

Manghnani, Shivani
House of Men
    Boston Review v34 no3 p38-40 My/Je 2009
Mango Red goes to war. Effinger, G. A.
Mangoes with chili (San Francisco, 1983).
    Mohanraj, M. A.
Manguel, Alberto
(tr.) See Martínez, Guillermo
MANHATTAN (NEW YORK, N.Y.) *See* New
    York (N.Y.)—Manhattan
The **Manhattan** Project. Nguyen, P.
A **Manhattan** romance. Oates, J. C.
Manhattan Transfer. Currier, J.
Manhattans. Busch, F.
Manheimer, Jerry
Nice Guys Finish Last (excerpt)
    *Tribal College Journal of American Indian
        Higher Education* v19 no1 p52-3 Fall 2007
The **manhood** test. Ali, M. N.
MANHUNTS
        See also Adventure
    Hammett, D. The road home
    Lehane, D. ICU
    Woolrich, C. New York blues
    Zelazny, R. The naked matador
MANIC-DEPRESSIVE ILLNESS
    Moffett, K. The medicine man
    Palazzeschi, A. Our friend Galletti
Manickchand, Reena Andrea
Dougla
    Trinidad noir; edited by Lisa Allen-Agostini
        & Jeanne Mason.
Manigot, Anthony P.
A French Creole Sunday: Callaloo on a Clear
    Conscience
    Callaloo v30 no1 p369-71 Wint 2007
Manikin. Michaels, L.
MANILA (PHILIPPINES) *See* Philippines—Ma-
    nila
Manila burning. Howard, C.
Manilla, Marie
Childproof
    Calyx v24 no3 p95-104 Summ 2008
MANITOBA *See* Canada—Manitoba
Manjarrez, Hector
Fin del mundo/The end of the world
    Best of contemporary Mexican fiction; Alvaro
        Uribe, editor; Olivia Sears, translation edi-
        tor
Mankind journeys through forests of symbols.
    Chappell, F.
Manley, Carol
Big Bob
    Manley, C. Church booty
Catfish
    Manley, C. Church booty
Church booty
    Manley, C. Church booty
Dearborn and LaSalle
    Manley, C. Church booty
Everything is going to be alright
    Manley, C. Church booty
Felons
    Manley, C. Church booty
Ghosts
    Manley, C. Church booty
Gucci Junior in Iraq
    Manley, C. Church booty

Markovits, Benjamin
  Another Sad, Bizarre Chapter in Human History
    The Paris Review v50 p127-35 Fall 2008
Marks, Neal
  Down and out in Brentwood
    The Deadly Bride; and 21 of the year's finest
      crime and mystery stories; including com-
      plete coverage of the year in mystery and
      crime fiction; edited by Ed Gorman and
      Martin H. Greenberg
Markus, Peter
  And Then, One Day, the Rains
    Chicago Review v53 no2/3 p64-5 Aut 2007
  The dead man's boat
    Detroit noir; edited by E. J. Olsen & John C.
      Hocking
  Fish Heads
    Chicago Review v53 no2/3 p60-2 Aut 2007
  The Hands That Hold the Hammer
    Chicago Review v53 no2/3 p57-8 Aut 2007
  The Moon Is a Fish Eye
    Chicago Review v53 no2/3 p59 Aut 2007
  The Sky at the Bottom of the River
    Chicago Review v53 no2/3 p63 Aut 2007
Marley, Louise
  Absalom's mother
    Marley, L. Absalom's mother & other stories
  Body and blood
    Marley, L. Absalom's mother & other stories
  Deep river
    Marley, L. Absalom's mother & other stories
  Diamond girls
    Marley, L. Absalom's mother & other stories
  Gathering genius
    Marley, L. Absalom's mother & other stories
  Jamie says
    Marley, L. Absalom's mother & other stories
  Night shift
    Marley, L. Absalom's mother & other stories
  P dolce
    Fast forward 1; future fiction from the cutting
      edge; edited by Lou Anders
    Marley, L. Absalom's mother & other stories
  Small in the saddle
    This is my funniest 2; leading science fiction
      writers present their funniest stories ever;
      edited by Mike Resnick
    Marley, L. Absalom's mother & other stories
  Starchild wondersmith
    Marley, L. Absalom's mother & other stories
  Technicolor
    Pandora's closet; edited by Jean Rabe and
      Martin H. Greenberg.
MARLOWE, CHRISTOPHER, 1564-1593
                    About
  Bear, E. L'esprit d'escalier
  Bear, E. This tragic glass
  Waldrop, H. Heart of whitenesse
Maron, Margaret
  You may already be a winner
    Sisters on the case; celebrating twenty years
      of Sisters in Crime; edited by Sara Paretsky
Marooned in Andromeda. Smith, C. A.
Marooned on Ug. Bierce, A.
Márquez, Gabriel García *See* García Márquez,
    Gabriel, 1928-
Marquiss, Twister
  Bill, Wyoming
    Callaloo v32 no2 p421-5 Spr 2009

Marrak, Michael
  Astrosapiens
    The black mirror and other stories; an anthol-
      ogy of science fiction from Germany &
      Austria; edited & with an introduction &
      notes by Franz Rottensteiner; translated by
      Mike Mitchell.
MARRIAGE
    See also Childless marriage; Divorce;
      Family life; Husband and wife; Interfaith
      marriage; Interracial marriage; Marriage
      problems; Weddings
  Abbott, L. K. The human use of inhuman beings
  Abenshushan, V. La cama de Lukin/Lukin's bed
  Agnihotri, S. Avoid agony
  Ali, M. N. Mallam Sile
  Anderson, B. Glorious things
  Apple, M. Talker
  Archer, J. In the eye of the beholder
  Atwood, M. The entities
  Auchincloss, L. The artist's model
  Auchincloss, L. An hour and a lifetime
  Auchincloss, L. Pa's darling
  Barthelme, D. The piano player
  Baxter, C. Saul and Patsy are in labor
  Biller, M. In bed with Sheikh Yassin
  Blackwell, K. What we do for love
  Bova, B. Orchestra(ted) Sam
  Bova, B. Takes two to tangle
  Budnitz, J. Nadia
  Busch, F. One last time for old times' sake
  Busch, F. Something along those lines
  Canty, K. The boreal forest
  Canty, K. No place in this world for you
  Chang, E. Red rose, white rose
  Chase, K. Man and wife
  Clayton, J. J. Aaron, personal
  Clayton, J. J. The man who could see radiance
  Coake, C. A single awe
  Coleman, W. Joy ride
  Connell, E. S. Arcturus
  Cooper, J. C. As time goes by
  Cooper, J. C. The eye of the beholder
  Cozarinsky, E. The bride from Odessa
  Crane, E. Banana love
  Dahl, R. William and Mary
  Daugherty, T. City codes
  Davis, A. B. The significance of importance
  Davis, C. The same sky
  Dean, D. The best man
  DeMarinis, R. Birds of the mountain west
  Dokey, R. Electric dog
  Dorfman, A. Gringos
  Dormen, L. The best place to be
  Downs, G. Snack cakes
  Drosso, A.-M. Heat
  Drosso, A.-M. Pasha, be careful
  Drosso, A.-M. Penance
  Dufresne, J. Epithalamion
  Eldridge, C. The former world record holder
    settles down
  Engberg, S. Above the houses
  Engberg, S. Fortune
  Engberg, S. Moon
  Enright, A. Pale hands I loved, beside the
    Shalimar
  Enright, A. Taking pictures
  Erdrich, L. The butcher's wife
  Faber, M. Bye-bye Natalia

MARRIAGE PROBLEMS—*Continued*

MARRIAGE PROBLEMS—*Continued*

Kennedy, C. The testosterone club
Keret, E. Actually, I've had some phenomenal hard-ons lately
Keret, E. Boomerang
Keret, E. Eight percent of nothing
Keret, E. Ironclad rules
Keret, E. More life
Khan, R. Alms
Kiely, B. Soldier, red soldier
King, O. My second wife
King, S. Mute
Krasikov, S. Asal
Krasikov, S. The repatriates
Kremer, H. Gelatin
Kun, M. Did she jump or was she pushed
Kureishi, H. A meeting, at last
LaBute, N. Loose change
LaBute, N. A second of pleasure
LaBute, N. Time-share
Lago, S. Golden days of a queen of diamonds
Lahiri, J. Interpreter of maladies
Lahiri, J. A temporary matter
Le Guin, U. K. Mountain ways
Lette, K. Justice
Leung, B. Dog sleep
Levin, Z. The country girl
Levin, Z. Flochne
Levin, Z. The thought
Li Yiyun. The arrangement
Link, K. Stone animals
Lippman, L. A good **** spoiled [variant title: A good fuck spoiled]
Lott, B. The difference between women and men
Lott, B. An evening on the cusp of the apocalypse
Lott, B. Family
Lott, B. Halo
Lott, B. A part of it
Lott, B. A way through this
Lunstrum, K. S. Dangerous women
Luongo, M. Glen echo
Luongo, M. What Nina wants
Lupica, M. Mrs. Cash
Luvaas, W. Carpentry
Lynn, D. H. Muggings
Lynn, D. H. Year of fire
MacEnulty, P. Inside out
Machado de Assis. The fortune-teller
Magee, K. Straitjacket
Mandelbaum, P. Virtue
Manjarrez, H. Fin del mundo/The end of the world
Martin, J. Russian lover
Mastretta, A. Aunt Mariana
Matheson, R. No such thing as a vampire
Matheson, R. A visit to Santa Claus
Maxwell, W. The Trojan women
McCafferty, J. Delivered
McCauley, W. The guy you said Joyce is fucking
McCauley, W. Winner
McCollum, M. He ain't Jesus
McGraw, E. Lucky devil
McInerney, J. Getting in touch with Lonnie
McInerney, J. I love you, honey
McInerney, J. Putting Daisy down
McInerney, J. Sleeping with pigs

McIntyre, V. Binge
McIntyre, V. Dunford
McKenzie, E. The possible world
McNally, T. M. Life in the body
McPhee, M. The anthropology of sex
Meacham, R. Good fences
Meacham, R. Let's do
Meacham, R. Simple as that
Means, D. Counterparts
Means, D. Petrouchka [with omissions]
Means, D. The secret goldfish
Meloy, M. The children
Meloy, M. O Tannenbaum
Meloy, M. Two-step
Meno, J. In the arms of someone you love
Meno, J. The sound before the end of the world
Meno, J. Tijuana women
Messina, M. America 1918
Messina, M. Ciancianedda
Messina, M. Her father's house
Messinger, J. Big Doug rides torch
Meyers, A. It's too late, baby
Michalopoulou, A. The firefly hunt
Michalopoulou, A. I'd like
Michalopoulou, A. I'd like (orchestral version)
Millar, M. The couple next door
Miller, A. L. Dimitry Gurov's Dowdy wife
Miller, A. L. My summer of love
Miller, S. G. Old Border Road
Mina, D. An invisible minus sign
Mohanraj, M. A. Other cities (Chicago, 1962)
Mohanraj, M. A. The princess in the forest (Chicago, 1955)
Monk, B. Do not revive
Moore, L. Paper losses
Morris, M. The hall of the meteorites
Morse, D. L. Conceived
Muller, M. Cattails
Muller, M. He said . . . she said
Munro, A. The bear came over the mountain
Munro, A. Circle of prayer
Munro, A. Runaway
Nelson, A. Kansas
Nisbet, R. Marianne
Nisbet, R. The path to Porthgain
Novakovich, J. Night guests
Novakovich, J. Tchaikovsky's bust
Nu'aymi, H. a.- . A woman
Oates, J. C. Bad habits
Oates, J. C. The blind man's sighted daughters
Oates, J. C. The dead
Oates, J. C. Hunger
Oates, J. C. Raven's Wing
Oates, J. C. The tryst
Ochsner, G. Last words of the mynah bird
Ockert, J. Des
Ohlin, A. An analysis of some troublesome recent behavior
Ohlin, A. I love to dance at weddings
Ohlin, A. The King of Kohlrabi
Ohlin, A. Simple exercises for the beginning student
Olafsson, O. February
Olafsson, O. March
Olafsson, O. On the lake
Olafsson, O. September
O'Mahony, M. Every ounce of soul
Opatoshu, J. In the saloon
Opatoshu, J. Morris and his son Philip

MARRIAGE PROBLEMS—*Continued*

Orner, P. Pampkin's lament
O'Shaughnessy, P. The couple behind the curtain
O'Shaughnessy, P. The furnace man
O'Shaughnessy, P. Sandstorm
O'Shaughnessy, P. Tiny angels
O'Shaughnessy, P. To still the beating of her heart
O'Shaughnessy, P. The young lady
Otis, M. Welcome to Yosemite
Otis, M. Yes, yes, cherries
Ozick, C. What happened to the baby?
Panning, A. Freeze
Parker, D. Big blonde
Parker, M. Couple strike it rich on second honeymoon
Parker, M. Go ugly early
Parks, T. After all I gave up for him!
Parks, T. The room
Parks, T. Something odd
Parks, T. Talking about it
Patterson, S. Aground and aloft
Peelle, L. Reasons for and advantages of breathing
Perlman, E. In the time of the dinosaur
Perry, A. Sneaker wave
Phillips, G. Roger Crumbler considered his shave
Pickard, N. Joy ride
Pinkerton, D. Headlock
Pollack, N. Confessions of a dial-up gigolo
Porter, A. Connecticut
Porter, A. Coyotes
Porter, K. A. María Concepción
Porter, K. A. That tree
Potwatka, A. You are not my husband
Qi, S. Big Mama
Qi, S. Love me, love my dog
Queiroz, R. d. Metonymy; or, The husband's revenge
Randolph, L. Billy
Randolph, L. A member of the family
Randolph, L. The shouting woman
Rankin, I. Soft spot
Raphael, L. Fresh air
Reah, D. Glazed
Reed, K. Into the jungle
Reid, G. Irony is . . .
Reinhorn, H. By the time you get this
Reinhorn, H. Golden pioneers
Rendell, R. The fall of a coin
Rheinheimer, K. Homes
Rhodes, S. At the top of his game
Richard, N. What you do next
Richler, M. Barney's version [excerpt]
Roberts, A. Eleanor
Robinson, R. Assez
Romano, T. Confidences
Romano, T. The day of settlement
Romano, T. In motion
Romano, T. Trace
Romano, T. Whistle opera
Row, J. For you
Rust, E. M. God and birds
Rust, E. M. Stealing Yakima
Rust, E. M. The weight of bones
Sallis, J. Wolf
Salter, J. Arlington

Salter, J. Give
Salter, J. My Lord you
Schaap, J. C. Exodus
Schaeffer, S. F. Wolves
Schutt, C. Young
Schwarzschild, E. Drift
Scoville, S. Clara and Ben
Searls, D. Goldenchain
Serao, M. Checchina's virtue
Shabtai, Y. Past continuous
Shamlan, S. a.- . Knowing his secret
Sharratt, M. Taking the bullets out
Shepard, J. The gun lobby
Sherman, R. Two stories; Single family; Scenic view
Shields, C. Block out
Shields, C. Invention
Shields, C. The orange fish
Shrayer-Petrov, D. He, she and the others
Shrayer-Petrov, D. Rusty
Shroff, M. F. Jamal Haddi's revenge
Sikka, M. Uncle Musto takes a mistress
Sillitoe, A. Confrontation
Sillitoe, A. The disgrace of Jim Scarfedale
Sillitoe, A. Enoch's two letters
Sillitoe, A. The fishing-boat picture
Sillitoe, A. The magic box
Sillitoe, A. Revenge
Sillitoe, A. The road
Sillitoe, A. The sniper
Silverberg, R. Needle in a timestack
Simpson, H. If I'm spared
Singer, I. B. Advice
Singer, I. B. Burial at sea
Singer, I. B. The bus
Singer, I. B. Disguised
Singer, I. B. The image
Singer, I. B. The impresario
Singer, I. B. The mathematician
Singer, I. B. The mistake
Singh, V. The wife
Smith, R. T. Tastes like chicken
Smith, R. T. Uke Rivers delivers
Sobott-Mogwe, G. Smile of fortune
Soueif, A. Mandy
Soueif, A. Returning
Soueif, A. Sandpiper
Soueif, A. Satan
Stafford, J. Cops and robbers
Stafford, J. A country love story
Stafford, J. An influx of poets
Stark, C. Getting out more
Stashower, D. A peach of a shot
Stefaniak, M. H. You love that dog
Stern, R. G. Double Charley
Stern, R. G. Troubles
Stevens, J. D. Hunger
Stevens, J. D. Spelling lessons
Stevenson, J. Light my fire
Stevenson, J. Walking with angels
Stewart, P. Shit happens
Strout, E. A different road
Stuckey-French, E. Mudlavia
Sullivan, F. The business of leaving
Swan, G. The death of the cat
Taha, M. A. Family honor
Taha, M. A. A rose to Hafeeza's eyes
Tallent, E. Tabriz
Talley, M. Driven to distraction

MARSHALL ISLANDS
James, C. L. R. The bomb threat—Part 1
James, C. L. R. The bomb threat—Part 2
Marshmallow People. Cummings, J. M.
Marsten, Richard, 1926-2005
> *For works written by this author under other names see* Hunter, Evan, 1926-2005; McBain, Ed, 1926-2005
Marsters, Sage
Bear story
> Pushcart prize XXXII: best of the small presses 2008; edited by Bill Henderson with the Pushcart Prize editors
> *New England Review* v27 no4 p180-7 2006
Marston, Edward
Corpus Christi
> Thou shalt not kill; biblical mystery stories; edited by Anne Perry
The St. Valentine's Day Massacre
> The Best British mysteries, 2005; edited by Maxim Jakubowski
Marston, Rachel
A Necromancer's Guide to Child Rearing
> *The Massachusetts Review* v47 no4 p633-5 Wint 2006
Marta. Lessa, O.
Martel, Yann
The facts behind the Helsinki Roccamatios
> Martel, Y. The facts behind the Helsinki Roccamatios
Manners of dying
> Martel, Y. The facts behind the Helsinki Roccamatios
The time I heard The Private Donald J. Rankin string concerto with one discordant violin, by John Morton
> Martel, Y. The facts behind the Helsinki Roccamatios
The Vita Æterna Mirror Company: mirrors to last till kingdom come
> Martel, Y. The facts behind the Helsinki Roccamatios
Marten, Eugene
Wedding Night
> *The Antioch Review* v66 no3 p471-86 Summ 2008
Martha. Woronov, M.
Martha's streets. Bolger, D.
MARTIAL ARTS
Somerville, P. Trouble and the shadowy death-blow
The **martian** agent, a planetary romance. Chabon, M.
The **Martian** child. Gerrold, D.
The **Martian** crown jewels. Anderson, P.
The **martian** spy. Grunert, C.
MARTIANS
> *See also* Interplanetary visitors; Mars (Planet)
Anderson, P. The Martian crown jewels
Bradbury, R. February 1999: Y11a
Bradbury, R. The Messiah
Brown, S. Empire
Gerrold, D. The Martian child
Gerrold, D. Pickled mongoose
Grunert, C. The martian spy
Lumley, B. My thing Friday
Matheson, R. Trespass
Pohl, F. The day the Martians came

Rich, M. The beauty monster
Rich, M. Foggery
Smith, C. A. Vulthoom
Willis, C. The soul selects her own society: invasion and repulsion
Willis, C. The soul selects her own society: invasion and repulsion: a chronological reinterpretation of two of Emily Dickinson's poems: a Wellsian perspective
Zelazny, R. A rose for Ecclesiastes
Zelazny, R. A rose for Ecclesiasts
Martians. Abbott, L. K.
Martin, Allana
Death of a healing woman [excerpt]
> Lone Star sleuths; an anthology of Texas crime fiction; edited and with an introduction by Bill Cunningham, Steven L. Davis, and Rollo K. Newsom.
Martin, Clancy
The best jeweler
> Pushcart prize XXXII: best of the small presses 2008; edited by Bill Henderson with the Pushcart Prize editors
Martin, Douglas A.
Threshhold
> *The Literary Review (Madison, N.J.)* v48 no3 p116-24 Spr 2005
Martin, George R. R.
And death his legacy
> Martin, G. R. R. Dreamsongs: volume I
And seven times never kill man
> Martin, G. R. R. Dreamsongs: volume I
A beast for Norn
> Martin, G. R. R. Dreamsongs: volume II
Bitterblooms
> Martin, G. R. R. Dreamsongs: volume I
The exit to San Breta
> Martin, G. R. R. Dreamsongs: volume I
The fortress
> Martin, G. R. R. Dreamsongs: volume I
From the journal of Xavier Desmond
> Martin, G. R. R. Dreamsongs: volume II
The glass flower
> Martin, G. R. R. Dreamsongs: volume II
Guardians
> Martin, G. R. R. Dreamsongs: volume II
The hedge knight: a tale of the seven kingdoms
> Martin, G. R. R. Dreamsongs: volume II
The hero
> Martin, G. R. R. Dreamsongs: volume I
The ice dragon
> Martin, G. R. R. Dreamsongs: volume I
In the lost lands
> Martin, G. R. R. Dreamsongs: volume I
The lonely songs of Laren Dorr
> Martin, G. R. R. Dreamsongs: volume I
Meathouse man
> Martin, G. R. R. Dreamsongs: volume I
> The living dead; edited by John Joseph Adams
The monkey treatment
> Martin, G. R. R. Dreamsongs: volume I
Nightflyers
> Martin, G. R. R. Dreamsongs: volume I
Only kids are afraid of the dark
> Martin, G. R. R. Dreamsongs: volume I
The pear-shaped man
> Martin, G. R. R. Dreamsongs: volume I

Martin, George R. R.—*Continued*
Portraits of his children
   Martin, G. R. R. Dreamsongs: volume II
Remembering Melody
   Martin, G. R. R. Dreamsongs: volume I
Sandkings
   Martin, G. R. R. Dreamsongs: volume I
The second kind of loneliness
   Martin, G. R. R. Dreamsongs: volume I
Shell games
   Martin, G. R. R. Dreamsongs: volume II
The skin trade
   Martin, G. R. R. Dreamsongs: volume II
A song for Lya
   Martin, G. R. R. Dreamsongs: volume I
The stone city
   Martin, G. R. R. Dreamsongs: volume I
The tower of ashes
   Martin, G. R. R. Dreamsongs: volume I
Unsound variations
   Martin, G. R. R. Dreamsongs: volume II
The way of cross and dragon
   Martin, G. R. R. Dreamsongs: volume I
With morning comes mistfall
   Martin, G. R. R. Dreamsongs: volume I

Martin, Jana
Belmar
   Martin, J. Russian lover & other stories
Factory
   Martin, J. Russian lover & other stories
The father
   Martin, J. Russian lover & other stories
Galletas
   Martin, J. Russian lover & other stories
Goodbye John Denver
   Martin, J. Russian lover & other stories
Hope
   Martin, J. Russian lover & other stories
I'm not quite finished yet
   Martin, J. Russian lover & other stories
Perforated: a lexicon
   Martin, J. Russian lover & other stories
Rubber days
   Martin, J. Russian lover & other stories
Russian lover
   Martin, J. Russian lover & other stories
Three sisters
   Martin, J. Russian lover & other stories
Tremor
   Martin, J. Russian lover & other stories
Try
   Martin, J. Russian lover & other stories
Why I got fired
   Martin, J. Russian lover & other stories
Work
   Martin, J. Russian lover & other stories

Martin, Lee
Dejá New
   Ms. v15 no2 p78-82 Summ 2005
People Always Going To
   Prairie Schooner v79 no2 p75-9 Summ 2005
The welcome table
   Short stories of the civil rights movement; an
      anthology; edited by Margaret Earley Whitt

Martin, Man
Dollywood
   The Kenyon Review v29 no2 p138-43 Spr
      2007

Martin, Stephen-Paul
Stopping
   Western Humanities Review v63 no1 p109-23
      Wint 2009
Martin, Susan Harper
Giant Things
   Iowa Review v36 no2 p1-15 Fall 2006
Martin, Susan Hubbard
How the parsonage was papered
   Adventures in the West; stories for young
      readers; edited by Susanne George Bloom-
      field and Eric Melvin Reed
Martin, Valerie
Beethoven
   Martin, V. The unfinished novel and other
      stories
The bower
   Martin, V. The unfinished novel and other
      stories
The change
   Martin, V. The unfinished novel and other
      stories
His blue period
   Martin, V. The unfinished novel and other
      stories
The open door
   Martin, V. The unfinished novel and other
      stories
The unfinished novel
   Martin, V. The unfinished novel and other
      stories
Martin Hellinger. Clifton, A.
Martin Sloane [excerpt] Redhill, M.
Martinez, Carlos
The devil's bookkeeper
   The Black Lizard big book of pulps; edited
      by Otto Penzler
Martínez, Guillermo
Vast Hell
   The New Yorker v85 no11 p58-61 Ap 27
      2009
Martinez, Liz
Freddie Prinze is my guardian angel
   Manhattan noir; edited by Lawrence Block
Lights out for Frankie
   Queens noir; edited by Robert Knightly
Martinez, Michele
Ambition
   Politics noir; dark tales from the corridors of
      power; edited by Gary Phillips.
The last honest man in Brooklyn
   Hard boiled Brooklyn; edited by Reed Farrel
      Coleman
The long shot
   Murder at the racetrack; edited by Otto
      Penzler
The mother
   Mystery Writers of America presents the
      prosecution rests; new stories about court-
      rooms, criminals, and the law; edited by
      Linda Fairstein.
Martone, Michael
4H
   Chicago Review v54 no4 p19-23 Spr 2009
Dutch Boy 32-V
   Bomb no107 p supp26-supp27 Spr 2009
Four Ironies
   Chicago Review v54 no4 p24-6 Spr 2009

Martone, Michael—*Continued*
  The safety patrol
    So the story goes; twenty-five years of the
      Johns Hopkins short fiction series; edited
      by John T. Irwin and Jean McGarry; with
      a foreword by John Barth
The **martyr**. Porter, K. A.
MARTYRS
  Ismaeel, D. E. Dates and bitter coffee
  Taha, M. A. Motherhood
Marty's drink or die club. Pollack, N.
Marusek, David
  A boy in Cathyland
    Marusek, D. Getting to know you
  Cabbages and kale or: How we downsized
    North America
    Marusek, D. Getting to know you
  The earth is on the mend
    Marusek, D. Getting to know you
  Getting to know you
    Marusek, D. Getting to know you
  Listen to me
    Marusek, D. Getting to know you
  My morning glory
    Marusek, D. Getting to know you
    Nature v440 p844 Ap 6 2006
  Osama Phone Home
    Technology Review (Cambridge, Mass.: 1998)
      v110 no2 p72-80 Mr/Ap 2007
  VTV
    Marusek, D. Getting to know you
  We were out of our minds with joy
    Marusek, D. Getting to know you
  The wedding album
    Rewired; the post-cyberpunk anthology;
      James Patrick Kelly & John Kessel, editors
    Marusek, D. Getting to know you
  Yurek Rutz, Yurek Rutz, Yurek Rutz
    Marusek, D. Getting to know you
Marut, Ret *See* Traven, B.
Marvellous Madame Mim. With, C.
The **marvelous** brass chessplaying automaton.
  Wolfe, G.
MARX, KARL, 1818-1883
          About
  Arnott, J. Ten lords a-leaping
  Waldrop, H. A better world's in birth!
MARY, BLESSED VIRGIN, SAINT
          About
  Frost, G. Madonna of the maquiladora
  Somers, A. The fall
  Tan, M. Muddy pond
  Tyent, N. Miriam
MARY, QUEEN OF SCOTS, 1542-1587
          About
  Clarke, S. Antickes and frets
Mary. Kercheval, J. L.
Mary. Strom, D.
Mary knew about Marilyn. Parks, T.
Mary, Mary, shut the door. Schutz, B. M.
Maryam's Maze. Ez Eldin, M.
Marybeth and the fish. Ronk, M. C.
MARYLAND
  Barth, J. Assisted living
  Barth, J. The bard award
  Barth, J. The end
  Barth, J. Peeping Tom
  Barth, J. Progressive dinner
  Barth, J. Rebeginning

  Barth, J. Teardown
  Barth, J. Us/Them
  Golden, M. After [excerpt]
  Luongo, M. Cake
  Spencer, M. E. Beyond the years
  Tabor, M. L. The burglar
          Baltimore
  France, L. R. School girl
  Lippman, L. Black-eyed Susan
  Lippman, L. Easy as a-b-c
  Lippman, L. Scratch a woman
  McCafferty, J. Delivered
  Rheinheimer, K. Baltimore
  Scott, J. X number of possibilities
  Steinberg, S. Static
Mary's Visit. Stacey, T.
Maryson, W. J.
  Verstummte musik
    The SFWA European hall of fame; sixteen
      contemporary masterpieces of science fic-
      tion from the continent; edited by James
      Morrow and Kathryn Morrow
Maryville, California, pop. 7. Goldfaden, J.
Marz, Micki
  Miscast
    The International Association of Crime Writ-
      ers presents Murder in Vegas; new crime
      tales of gambling and desperation; edited
      by Michael Connelly
Marzipan. Bender, A.
Mas, Alexandre
  The Color of Darkness
    The Georgia Review v62 no2 p229-44 Summ
      2008
Masdon, Joe
  Jack's mantle
    Pandora's closet; edited by Jean Rabe and
      Martin H. Greenberg.
Masello, Robert
  Where there's a will . . .
    Dark delicacies 2; fear: more original tales of
      terror and the macabre by the world's
      greatest horror writers; edited by Del
      Howison and Jeff Gelb
The **maserati** years. Biller, M.
Mash Turning. Bengal, R.
The **mask**. Stevens, J. D.
The **mask** of '67. Prill, D.
The **mask** of the Rex. Bowes, R.
MASKS (FOR THE FACE)
  Hill, J. My father's mask
  Maxwell, W. The masks
  Walpole, Sir H. The silver mask
MASKS (SCULPTURE)
  Silverberg, R. Not our brother
The **masks**. Maxwell, W.
Masks: a story. Thompson, E. B.
Maso, Carole
  Young H Saved from Infamy
    Harper's v311 p25-8 Jl 2005
MASOCHISM
  Gaitskill, M. A romantic weekend
  Granados, C. Comfort
  Huston, C. Like a lady
  Lane, J. The window
  Levin, Z. Flochne
  Pavlou, S. The strange case of Jarcd Spoon,
    who went to pieces for love
  Villoro, J. Lightweight champ

Mason, Bobbie Ann
  Blue country
    Mason, B. A. Nancy Culpepper; stories
  The heirs
    Mason, B. A. Nancy Culpepper; stories
  Lying doggo
    Mason, B. A. Nancy Culpepper; stories
  Nancy Culpepper
    Mason, B. A. Nancy Culpepper; stories
  The prelude
    Mason, B. A. Nancy Culpepper; stories
  Proper gypsies
    Mason, B. A. Nancy Culpepper; stories
  Spence + Lila
    Mason, B. A. Nancy Culpepper; stories
Mason, Daniel
  1858: East Indies: Alfred Russel Wallace Advances a Theory [Reprint]
    Lapham's Quarterly v1 no3 p143-6 Summ 2008
  Death of the Pugilist
    Harper's v315 p82-8 Jl 2007
  The Ecstasy of Alfred Russel Wallace
    Harper's v316 p78-82 Mr 2008
  A Registry of My Passage upon the Earth
    Harper's v310 p77-83 Ap 2005
Mason, John
  (tr.) See Shklovsky, Yevgeny
Masque. Gorman, E.
MASSACHUSETTS
  See also Nantucket Island (Mass.)
  Barnes, S. Earthquake
  Clayton, J. J. Fantasy for a Friday afternoon
  Clayton, J. J. Voices
  Di Filippo, P. Wikiworld
  Mason, B. A. Blue country
  McInerney, J. Reunion
  Mindt, A. An artist at work
  Okasi, M. T. Salvation army
  Rickert, M. The Christmas witch
  Updike, J. Personal archaeology
Boston
  Bear, E. The chains that you refuse
  Bowes, R. If angels fight
  Clayton, J. J. Glory
  Clayton, J. J. The man who could see radiance
  Haldeman, J. W. Finding my shadow
  James, H. T; or, Summer in the city
  Kalotay, D. Sunshine Cleaners
  Lovecraft, H. P. Pickman's model
  Lyons, D. The Greyhound
  Robinson, K. S. Glacier
  Simmons, P. Night vision
  Sniegoski, T. E. Noah's ophans
  Trevor, D. Central Square
  Trevor, D. Girls I know
  Updike, J. German lessons
  Updike, J. Marching through Boston
  Updike, J. Outage
  West, D. The typewriter
Cambridge
  Bear, E. The chains that you refuse
  Burgin, R. Notes on Mrs. Slaughter
  Clayton, J. J. Cambridge is sinking!
  Clayton, J. J. The company you keep
  Clayton, J. J. Vertigo
  Kalotay, D. Anniversary
  Lahiri, J. Nobody's business
  LaSalle, P. Where we last saw time

Cape Cod
  Boyd, W. The woman on the beach with a dog
  Clayton, J. J. Adult fiction
  Hoffman, A. The conjurer's handbook
  Hoffman, A. The edge of the world
  Hoffman, A. India
  Hoffman, A. Insulting the angels
  Hoffman, A. Lionheart
  Hoffman, A. The pear tree
  Hoffman, A. The summer kitchen
  Hoffman, A. The token
  Hoffman, A. The wedding of snow and ice
  Hoffman, A. Wish you were here
  Hoffman, A. The witch of Truro
Lowell
  Winn, T. Blue tango
  Winn, T. Cantogallo
  Winn, T. Copper leaves waving
  Winn, T. Frankie Floats
  Winn, T. Glass box
  Winn, T. Luck be a lady
  Winn, T. Mrs. Somebody Somebody
  Winn, T. Smoke
Provincetown
  Shrayer-Petrov, D. Hurricane Bob
Salem
  Gallison, K. Spectral evidence
Massacre river [excerpt] Philoctète, R.
MASSACRES
  Abbott, L. K. One of star wars, one of doom
  Cepeda Samudio, A. The soldiers
  Judah, S. Nathoo
  Singer, M. Body count
  Smith, N. Scrapbook
MASSAGE
  Halpern, F. Blessed hands
MASSEURS
  Shroff, M. F. The maalishwalla
The **masseuse**. Wohlforth, T.
Massey, Sujata
  The mayor's movie
    Politics noir; dark tales from the corridors of power; edited by Gary Phillips.
Massie, Elizabeth
  The landlock
    Summer chills; strangers in stranger lands; edited by Stephen Jones
  The next-door collector
    Deadly housewives; edited by Christine Matthews
Massinello Pietro. Bradbury, R.
Masson, David I.
  Traveler's rest
    New worlds; an anthology; edited by Michael Moorcock
The **master**. McCabe, E.
The **master** and Margarita [excerpt] Bulgakov, M. A.
The **master** at St. Bartholomew's hospital, 1914-1916. Oates, J. C.
Master of Ceremonics. Rodríguez, A.
Master of the asteroid. See Smith, C. A. The god of the asteroid [variant title: Master of the asteroid]
Mastermindless. Hughes, M.
The **masterpiece** of death. Lamb, H.
Masters, Andrea
  Dark of the Moon
    Confrontation no101 p116-29 Spr/Summ 2008

Masters, Hilary
Meatloaf
New Letters v71 no1 p184-94 2004/2005
Masterson and the clerks. Sladek, J. T.
Mastretta, Angeles
Aunt Concha Esparza
Colchie, T. A whistler in the nightworld; short fiction from the Latin Americas; edited by Thomas Colchie
Aunt Mariana
Violations; stories of love by Latin American women; edited and with an introduction by Psiche Hughes; foreword by Brian Matthews
MASTURBATION
Edgerton, C. Debra's flap and snap
Hayes, D. This world of ours
McIntyre, V. Dunford
Michaels, L. Getting lucky
Stewart, P. Smile
Ward, A. E. Butte as in beautiful
Welsh, I. Kingdom of Fife
Masud, Naiyer *See* Naiyer Masud
Masuda, Tokisada *See* Amakusa, Shiro, 1621 or 2-1638
Masurel, Pauline
Static
Her Majesty; 21 stories by women; edited by Jackie Gay and Emma Hargrave
Matas, Enrique Vila- *See* Vila-Matas, Enrique, 1948-
The **match**. Sillitoe, A.
The **match**. Zoshchenko, M.
MATCHMAKERS *See* Marriage brokers
MATCHMAKING
Dunbar, P. L. Mammy Peggy's pride
Reisen, A. The experienced bride
Sankaran, L. Bombay this
Mater Dolorosa. Fuentes, C.
Mates. Pearlman, E.
Matesis, Pavlos
Murder's singular taste
Angelic & black; contemporary Greek short stories; edited and translated by David Connolly; with an introduction by Vangelis Hatzivassileiou
The **Mathematician**. Kehlmann, D.
MATHEMATICIANS
Blish, J. FYI
Iagnemma, K. On the nature of human romantic interaction
Margulis, L. The estimator
Michaels, L. Cryptology
Michaels, L. Nachman
Michaels, L. Nachman at the races
Michaels, L. Nachman burning
Michaels, L. Nachman from Los Angeles
Michaels, L. Of mystery there is no end
Michaels, L. The penultimate conjecture
Singer, I. B. The mathematician
Zamíatin, E. I. We [excerpt]
MATHEMATICS
Haringa, J. M. A perfect and unmappable grace
Rucker, R. v. B. Six thought experiments concerning the nature of computation: Experiment 1: Lucky number
Rucker, R. v. B. Six thought experiments concerning the nature of computation: Experiment 6: Hello infinity

Rucker, R. v. B. and Bisson, T. 2+2=5
The **mathematics** of magic. De Camp, L. S. and Pratt, F.
MATHER, COTTON, 1663-1728
About
Di Filippo, P. Observable things
Matheson, Richard
Advance notice
Matheson, R. Collected stories v 1; edited by Stanley Wiater
Being
Matheson, R. Collected stories v2; edited by Stanley Wiater
Big surprise
Matheson, R. Collected stories v3; edited by Stanley Wiater
Blood son
Matheson, R. Collected stories v 1; edited by Stanley Wiater
Born of man and woman
Matheson, R. Collected stories v 1; edited by Stanley Wiater
Brother to the machine
Matheson, R. Collected stories v 1; edited by Stanley Wiater
Buried talents
Matheson, R. Collected stories v3; edited by Stanley Wiater
Button, button
Matheson, R. Collected stories v3; edited by Stanley Wiater
By appointment only
Matheson, R. Collected stories v3; edited by Stanley Wiater
The children of Noah
Matheson, R. Collected stories v2; edited by Stanley Wiater
Clothes make the man
Matheson, R. Collected stories v 1; edited by Stanley Wiater
The conqueror
Matheson, R. Collected stories v2; edited by Stanley Wiater
The creeping terror
Matheson, R. Collected stories v3; edited by Stanley Wiater
Crickets
Matheson, R. Collected stories v3; edited by Stanley Wiater
The curious child
Matheson, R. Collected stories v2; edited by Stanley Wiater
Dance of the dead
Matheson, R. Collected stories v2; edited by Stanley Wiater
Day of reckoning [variant titles: The faces; Graveyard shift]
Matheson, R. Collected stories v3; edited by Stanley Wiater
Deadline
Matheson, R. Collected stories v3; edited by Stanley Wiater
Dear diary
Matheson, R. Collected stories v2; edited by Stanley Wiater
Death ship
Matheson, R. Collected stories v 1; edited by Stanley Wiater

Maxwell, William—*Continued*

The woman who didn't want anything more
  Maxwell, W. Later novels and stories; [edited by Christopher Carduff]

The woman who had no eye for small details
  Maxwell, W. Later novels and stories; [edited by Christopher Carduff]

The woman who never drew breath except to complain
  Maxwell, W. Later novels and stories; [edited by Christopher Carduff]

The woman with a talent for talking
  Maxwell, W. Later novels and stories; [edited by Christopher Carduff]

The woodcutter
  Maxwell, W. Later novels and stories; [edited by Christopher Carduff]

Young Francis Whitehead
  Maxwell, W. Early novels and stories; [edited by Christopher Carduff]

May, Sharon

The monkey king
  Best new American voices 2009; guest editor Mary Gaitskill; series editors John Kulka and Natalie Danford

Through the Water of the Clouds
  StoryQuarterly v41 p75-90 2005

The wizard of Khao-I-Dang
  Best new American voices 2008; guest editor Richard Bausch; series editors John Kulka and Natalie Danford

May. Olafsson, O.

MAY DAY

Kadare, I. Agamemnon's daughter

May Day. Charters, D.

May God keep love in a cool and dry place. Shibli, A.

May there be a road. L'Amour, L.

May We Be Forgiven. Homes, A. M.

Maybe it's racist . . . Lawson, J. E.

Maybe, maybe not. Sutton, B.

Maybe Someone Should Call the Commodores. Holden, M.

Maybe We Ain't That Young Anymore (1979). Shimkin, D.

Mayer, Larry N.

Love for Miss Dottie
  Best new American voices 2009; guest editor Mary Gaitskill; series editors John Kulka and Natalie Danford

Mayfield, Julian

The last days of Duncan Street
  D.C. noir 2; the classics; edited by George Pelecanos.

Mayflower II. Baxter, S.

Mayfly. Watts, P. and Murphy, D.

Mayo, Jim, 1908-1988

For works written by this author under other names see L'Amour, Louis, 1908-1988

The **mayor**. Mozetič, B.

The **mayor** of Mare Tranq. Pohl, F.

Mayoral, Marina

In the Parks, At Nightfall
  StoryQuarterly v41 p161, 163, 165, 167, 169, 171, 173 2005

En los parques, al anochecer
  StoryQuarterly v41 p160, 162, 164, 166, 168, 170, 172 2005

MAYORS

Baraka, I. A. Neo-American
Blish, J. Earthman, come here
Corso, P. Raw egg in beer
Mejia, A. E. The new order
Suescun, N. My father was blue

The **mayor's** movie. Massey, S.

Mayr, Suzette

Toot sweet Matricia
  So long been dreaming; postcolonial science fiction & fantasy; Nalo Hopkinson & Uppinder Mehan, eds

The **maze** of Maal Dweb. Smith, C. A.

The **maze** of the enchanter [variant title: The maze of Maal Dweb] Smith, C. A.

Mazelis, Jo

And you read your Emily Dickinson
  Urban Welsh; new short fiction; edited by Lewis Davies

Mazer in prison. Card, O. S.

Mazor, Julian

Washington
  D.C. noir 2; the classics; edited by George Pelecanos.

Mazza, Cris

Change the world
  Homewrecker: an adultery reader; edited by Daphne Gottlieb

Mazzucato, Francesca

Tiburtina noir blues
  Rome noir; edited by Chiara Stangalino & Maxim Jakubowski; translated by Anne Milano Appel, Ann Goldstein, and Kathrine Jason

MC5 (MUSICAL GROUP)

Wild, P. Radical adults lick godhead style

M'Cabe, James D.

Seventy miles an hour
  Bendel-Simso, M. M., ed. Early American detective stories; an anthology; edited by LeRoy Lad Panek and Mary M. Bendel-Simso.

The telltale eye
  Bendel-Simso, M. M., ed. Early American detective stories; an anthology; edited by LeRoy Lad Panek and Mary M. Bendel-Simso.

McAllister, Bruce

Angels
  McAllister, B. The girl who loved animals and other stories; with an introduction by Harry Harrison and an afterword by Barry N. Malzberg

The ark
  McAllister, B. The girl who loved animals and other stories; with an introduction by Harry Harrison and an afterword by Barry N. Malzberg

Assassin
  McAllister, B. The girl who loved animals and other stories; with an introduction by Harry Harrison and an afterword by Barry N. Malzberg

Benji's pencil
  McAllister, B. The girl who loved animals and other stories; with an introduction by Harry Harrison and an afterword by Barry N. Malzberg

McAllister, Bruce—*Continued*

The boy in Zaquitos
> McAllister, B. The girl who loved animals and other stories; with an introduction by Harry Harrison and an afterword by Barry N. Malzberg
> The Best American short stories, 2007; selected from U. S. and Canadian magazines by Stephen King with Heidi Pitlor; with an introduction by Stephen King

Dream baby
> McAllister, B. The girl who loved animals and other stories; with an introduction by Harry Harrison and an afterword by Barry N. Malzberg

The faces outside
> McAllister, B. The girl who loved animals and other stories; with an introduction by Harry Harrison and an afterword by Barry N. Malzberg

The girl who loved animals
> McAllister, B. The girl who loved animals and other stories; with an introduction by Harry Harrison and an afterword by Barry N. Malzberg

Hero, the movie
> McAllister, B. The girl who loved animals and other stories; with an introduction by Harry Harrison and an afterword by Barry N. Malzberg

Kin
> McAllister, B. The girl who loved animals and other stories; with an introduction by Harry Harrison and an afterword by Barry N. Malzberg
> The Year's best science fiction: twenty-fourth annual collection; edited by Gardner Dozois

Little boy blue
> McAllister, B. The girl who loved animals and other stories; with an introduction by Harry Harrison and an afterword by Barry N. Malzberg

The man inside
> McAllister, B. The girl who loved animals and other stories; with an introduction by Harry Harrison and an afterword by Barry N. Malzberg

Moving on
> McAllister, B. The girl who loved animals and other stories; with an introduction by Harry Harrison and an afterword by Barry N. Malzberg

Poison
> Year's best fantasy 8; edited by David G. Hartwell, Kathryn Cramer

Southpaw
> McAllister, B. The girl who loved animals and other stories; with an introduction by Harry Harrison and an afterword by Barry N. Malzberg

Spell
> McAllister, B. The girl who loved animals and other stories; with an introduction by Harry Harrison and an afterword by Barry N. Malzberg

Stu
> McAllister, B. The girl who loved animals and other stories; with an introduction by Harry Harrison and an afterword by Barry N. Malzberg

World of the wars
> McAllister, B. The girl who loved animals and other stories; with an introduction by Harry Harrison and an afterword by Barry N. Malzberg

McAllister, Laurent

Kapuzine and the wolf: a hortatory tale
> Witpunk; edited by Claude Lalumière and Marty Halpern

McAuley, Paul

Meat
> *Nature* v435 p128 My 5 2005

Shadow Life
> *Discover* v30 no7 p58-9 Jl/Ag 2009

McAuley, Paul J.

Dead men walking
> The Year's best science fiction: twenty-fourth annual collection; edited by Gardner Dozois

Incomers
> The Starry rift; tales of new tomorrows: an original science fiction anthology; edited by Jonathan Strahan

Take me to the river
> Weird shadows over Innsmouth; edited by Stephen Jones; illustrated by Randy Broecker [et al.]

The thought war
> The Best science fiction and fantasy of the year: volume three; edited by Jonathan Strahan

Winning peace
> The new space opera; edited by Gardner Dozois and Jonathan Strahan

McAuley, Paul J. and Newman, Kim

Prisoners of the action
> The Del Rey book of science fiction and fantasy; sixteen original works by speculative fiction's finest voices; edited by Ellen Datlow

McBain, Ed

Accident report
> McBain, E. Learning to kill; stories

Association test
> McBain, E. Learning to kill; stories

Barking at butterflies
> A New omnibus of crime; edited by Tony Hillerman and Rosemary Herbert; contributing editors Sue Grafton and Jeffery Deaver

Bedbug
> McBain, E. Learning to kill; stories

The big day
> McBain, E. Learning to kill; stories

Carrera's woman
> McBain, E. Learning to kill; stories

Chalk [variant title: I killed Jennie]
> McBain, E. Learning to kill; stories

Chinese puzzle
> McBain, E. Learning to kill; stories

Death flight [variant title: Ticket to death]
> McBain, E. Learning to kill; stories

Downpour [variant title: Murder on the Keys]
> McBain, E. Learning to kill; stories

McBain, Ed—_Continued_

Dummy [variant title: The big scream]
  McBain, E. Learning to kill; stories
Every morning
  McBain, E. Learning to kill; stories
Eyewitness
  McBain, E. Learning to kill; stories
First offense
  McBain, E. Learning to kill; stories
Good and dead
  McBain, E. Learning to kill; stories
Improvisation
  Dangerous women; edited by Otto Penzler
  The Best American Mystery Stories, 2006;
    edited and with an introduction by Scott
    Turow; Otto Penzler, series editor
The innocent one
  McBain, E. Learning to kill; stories
Kid kill
  McBain, E. Learning to kill; stories
Kiss me, Dudley
  McBain, E. Learning to kill; stories
The last spin
  McBain, E. Learning to kill; stories
Merely hate
  Transgressions; edited by Ed McBain
  Wolf Woman Bay; and nine more of the
    finest crime and mystery novellas of the
    year; edited by Ed Gorman and Martin H.
    Greenberg
The merry merry Christmas
  McBain, E. Learning to kill; stories
The molested
  McBain, E. Learning to kill; stories
On the sidewalk, bleeding
  McBain, E. Learning to kill; stories
Runaway
  McBain, E. Learning to kill; stories
See him die
  McBain, E. Learning to kill; stories
Small homicide
  McBain, E. Learning to kill; stories
Still life
  McBain, E. Learning to kill; stories

McBain, Ed, 1926-2005

_For works written by this author under oth-
  er names see_ Hunter, Evan, 1926-2005

McBrearty, Robert Garner

Episode
  The North American Review v291 no6 p31-6
    N/D 2006

McCabe, Eugene

Cancer
  McCabe, E. Heaven lies about us; stories
Heaven lies about us
  McCabe, E. Heaven lies about us; stories
Heritage
  McCabe, E. Heaven lies about us; stories
The landlord
  McCabe, E. Heaven lies about us; stories
The master
  McCabe, E. Heaven lies about us; stories
The mother
  McCabe, E. Heaven lies about us; stories
Music at Annahullion
  McCabe, E. Heaven lies about us; stories
The orphan
  McCabe, E. Heaven lies about us; stories

Roma
  McCabe, E. Heaven lies about us; stories
Truth
  McCabe, E. Heaven lies about us; stories
Victims
  McCabe, E. Heaven lies about us; stories
Victorian fields
  McCabe, E. Heaven lies about us; stories

McCafferty, Jane

Berna's place
  McCafferty, J. Thank you for the music
Brother to brother
  McCafferty, J. Thank you for the music
Dear Mr. Springsteen
  McCafferty, J. Thank you for the music
Delivered
  On the Mason-Dixon line; an anthology of
    contemporary Delaware writers; edited by
    Billie Travalini and Fleda Brown.
The dog who saved her
  McCafferty, J. Thank you for the music
Elizabeth Tines
  McCafferty, J. Thank you for the music
Embraced
  McCafferty, J. Thank you for the music
Family on ice
  McCafferty, J. Thank you for the music
Guiding light
  McCafferty, J. Thank you for the music
Light of Lucy
  McCafferty, J. Thank you for the music
The pastor's brother
  McCafferty, J. Thank you for the music
So long, Marianne
  McCafferty, J. Thank you for the music
Stadium hearts
  McCafferty, J. Thank you for the music
Thank you for the music
  McCafferty, J. Thank you for the music
You could never love the clown I love
  McCafferty, J. Thank you for the music

McCaffrey, Anne

The ship who sang
  Nebula Awards showcase 2006; the year's
    best SF and fantasy; selected by the Sci-
    ence Fiction and Fantasy Writers of Ameri-
    ca; edited by Gardner Dozois

McCall, Thomas

MUD
  The Best of the Bellevue Literary Review;
    edited by Dannielle Ofri and the staff of
    the Bellevue Literary Review

McCall Smith, Alexander

He loved to go for drives with his father
  A New omnibus of crime; edited by Tony
    Hillerman and Rosemary Herbert; contrib-
    uting editors Sue Grafton and Jeffery
    Deaver
In the eyes of children
  Dead man's hand; crime fiction at the poker
    table; edited by Otto Penzler.

McCall Smith, R. A. _See_ McCall Smith, Alexander, 1948-

McCandless, D. B.

The corpse in the crystal
  The Black Lizard big book of pulps; edited
    by Otto Penzler

McCandless, D. B.—*Continued*
He got what he asked for
The Black Lizard big book of pulps; edited by Otto Penzler
McCann, Colum
As if there were trees
New Dubliners; edited by Oona Frawley
Phreak
The Paris Review v50 p11-36 Fall 2008
McCann, Richard
Crêpe de chine
McCann, R. Mother of sorrows
Ms. v15 no1 p84-5 Spr 2005
The diarist
McCann, R. Mother of sorrows
The O. Henry Prize stories 2007; edited and with an introduction by Laura Furman; with essays on the story they admire most by jurors Charles D'Ambrosio, Ursula K. Le Guin, Lily Tuck
Dream house
McCann, R. Mother of sorrows
Eduardo's hair
McCann, R. Mother of sorrows
Fugitive light, old photos
McCann, R. Mother of sorrows
My brother in the basement
McCann, R. Mother of sorrows
My mother's clothes: the school of beauty and shame
McCann, R. Mother of sorrows
Snapshots of the visible man
McCann, R. Mother of sorrows
Some threads through the Medina
McCann, R. Mother of sorrows
The universe, concealed
McCann, R. Mother of sorrows
McCarron, Meghan
The flying woman
Best American fantasy; guest editors Ann & Jeff VanderMeer; series editor Matthew Cheney
The magician's house
The Best science fiction and fantasy of the year: volume three; edited by Jonathan Strahan
McCarthy, Ralph
(tr.) See Murakami, Ryu
McCarthy, Robert
I Am the Author of My Own Life
The Paris Review v46 p9-29 Wint 2004
McCarthy, Sean Padraic
Flowers
The Sewanee Review v114 no3 p355-72 Summ 2006
Wade and Todd Figure Things Out
Confrontation no98/99 p11-26 Spr/Summ 2007
McCarthy, Tom
Kool things: or why I want to fuck Patty Hearst
Noise; fiction inspired by Sonic Youth; edited bt Peter Wild; introduction by Lee Ranaldo
McCarty, Henry *See* Billy, the Kid
McCauley, Carole Spearin
Crone's Revenge
Femspec v6 no2 p122-6 2005
Two left shoes
Women of mystery; an anthology; Katherine V. Forrest, editor

McCauley, William
Adultery
McCauley, W. Adulteries, hot tubs & such like matters
Allergies
McCauley, W. Adulteries, hot tubs & such like matters
The ardent admirer
McCauley, W. Adulteries, hot tubs & such like matters
A book for Michael Sama
McCauley, W. Need
Delusions
McCauley, W. Adulteries, hot tubs & such like matters
Edna's mission
McCauley, W. Adulteries, hot tubs & such like matters
Foday
McCauley, W. Need
The gates of Sodom
McCauley, W. Adulteries, hot tubs & such like matters
The guy you said Joyce is fucking
McCauley, W. Adulteries, hot tubs & such like matters
Hungry de catch me
McCauley, W. Need
Mister Henry's trousers
McCauley, W. Need
The mix
McCauley, W. Need
Need
McCauley, W. Need
The offer
McCauley, W. Need
Palaver
McCauley, W. Need
Tradition
McCauley, W. Adulteries, hot tubs & such like matters
The turning over
McCauley, W. Need
Wedding party
McCauley, W. Adulteries, hot tubs & such like matters
Winner
McCauley, W. Adulteries, hot tubs & such like matters
MCCAY, WINSOR, 1871-1934
Parodies, imitations, etc.
Effinger, G. A. Seven nights in Slumberland
McClanahan, Ed
And then I wrote . . .
McClanahan, E. O the clear moment
Another great moment in sports
McClanahan, E. O the clear moment
Dog loves Ellie
McClanahan, E. O the clear moment
Fondelle or The whore with a heart of gold
McClanahan, E. O the clear moment
A foreign correspondence
McClanahan, E. O the clear moment
Great moments in sports
McClanahan, E. O the clear moment
Hey Shoobie!
McClanahan, E. O the clear moment
How's that again?
McClanahan, E. O the clear moment

McDevitt, Jack—*Continued*

The candidate
Nature v440 p580 Mr 23 2006

Deus Tex
This is my funniest; leading science fiction writers present their funniest stories ever; edited by Mike Resnick

Friends in high places
A cross of centuries; twenty-five imaginative tales about the Christ; edited by Michael Bishop

The mission
Crossroads; tales of the southern literary fantastic; edited by F. Brett Cox and Andy Duncan

McDonald, Craig

The last interview
The Deadly Bride; and 21 of the year's finest crime and mystery stories; including complete coverage of the year in mystery and crime fiction; edited by Ed Gorman and Martin H. Greenberg

Rope-a-dope
Dublin noir; the Celtic tiger vs. the ugly American; edited by Ken Bruen

McDonald, Fritz

By the Pool
Confrontation no100 p64-72 Fall 2007/Wint 2008

McDonald, Ian

The Djinn's wife
The Year's best science fiction: twenty-fourth annual collection; edited by Gardner Dozois

The dust assassin
The Starry rift; tales of new tomorrows: an original science fiction anthology; edited by Jonathan Strahan
The Best science fiction and fantasy of the year: volume three; edited by Jonathan Strahan

Little goddess
The Year's best science fiction: twenty-third annual collection; edited by Gardner Dozois

Sanjeev and Robotwallah
Fast forward 1; future fiction from the cutting edge; edited by Lou Anders
The Year's best science fiction: twenty-fifth annual collection; edited by Gardner Dozois

Tendeléo's story
The Best of the best, volume 2; 20 years of the best short science fiction novels; edited by Gardner Dozois

Verthandi's bing
The Year's best science fiction: twenty-fifth annual collection; edited by Gardner Dozois

Verthandi's ring
The new space opera; edited by Gardner Dozois and Jonathan Strahan

McDonald, Roger

The bullock run
The O. Henry Prize stories 2008; edited and with an introduction by Laura Furman; with essays on the stories they admire most by jurors Chimamanda Ngozi Adiche, David Leavitt, David Means

McDonnell, Carole

Lingua franca
So long been dreaming; postcolonial science fiction & fantasy; Nalo Hopkinson & Uppinder Mehan, eds

McDowell, Ian

Making faces
Crossroads; tales of the southern literary fantastic; edited by F. Brett Cox and Andy Duncan

McDuff on the mound. Coover, R.

McElrath, Frances

A native teacher
Adventures in the West; stories for young readers; edited by Susanne George Bloomfield and Eric Melvin Reed

McElroy, Lee *See* Kelton, Elmer, 1926-2009

McEwan, Ian

The Diagnosis
The New Yorker v80 no40 p116, 118-29 D 20-27 2004

Lily
Granta no88 p123-37 Wint 2004

On Chesil Beach
The New Yorker v82 no43 p98-107 D 25 2006/Ja 1 2007

McFadden, Dennis

The House on Denty Road
South Carolina Review v40 no1 p6-18 Fall 2007

Old Grimes
South Carolina Review v39 no1 p3-17 Fall 2006

McFarland, Dennis

Nothing to ask for
The New Granta book of the American short story; edited and introduced by Richard Ford

The Preacher's Wife
The American Scholar v75 no4 p104-16 Aut 2006

McGahan, Jerry

Benediction
The Antioch Review v66 no4 p777-82 Fall 2008

Reclamations
The Georgia Review v62 no1 p135-49 Spr 2008

McGarry, Jean

The Accident
Western Humanities Review v63 no2 p103-9 Summ 2009

The last time
So the story goes; twenty-five years of the Johns Hopkins short fiction series; edited by John T. Irwin and Jean McGarry; with a foreword by John Barth

The Sweetness of Her Name
Ploughshares v31 no4 p96-104 Wint 2005/2006

Transference
The Yale Review v97 no3 p98-112 Jl 2009

McGinn, Judith

Secret Burial
South Carolina Review v37 no1 p112-21 Fall 2004

McGlaughlin, Laura

(tr.) *See* Zabala, Manel

McGlynn, David
Consequences of knowledge
  McGlynn, D. The end of the straight and narrow; stories
Deep in the heart
  McGlynn, D. The end of the straight and narrow; stories
The end of the straight and narrow
  McGlynn, D. The end of the straight and narrow; stories
The eyes to see
  McGlynn, D. The end of the straight and narrow; stories
Landslide
  The best Christian short stories; edited and with an introduction by Bret Lott
  McGlynn, D. The end of the straight and narrow; stories
Moonland on fire
  McGlynn, D. The end of the straight and narrow; stories
Seventeen one-hundredths of a second
  McGlynn, D. The end of the straight and narrow; stories
Sweet Texas angel
  McGlynn, D. The end of the straight and narrow; stories
Testimony
  McGlynn, D. The end of the straight and narrow; stories
McGowan, James T.
Strange Things Can Happen Around Midnight
  The North American Review v291 no6 p10-19 N/D 2006
McGrath, Kristina
In Her Days as a Gentleman: A Decline & Rise in Humours & Fortunes
  Iowa Review v35 no1 p147-55 Spr 2005
McGrath, Patrick
Ground zero
  McGrath, P. Ghost town; tales of Manhattan then and now
Julius
  McGrath, P. Ghost town; tales of Manhattan then and now
The year of the gibbet
  McGrath, P. Ghost town; tales of Manhattan then and now
McGraw, Erin
Appearance of scandal
  McGraw, E. The good life; stories
Aruba
  McGraw, E. The good life; stories
Ax of the apostles
  What are you looking at?; the first fat fiction anthology; edited by Donna Jarrell and Ira Sukrungruang
  McGraw, E. The good life; stories
  The best Christian short stories; edited and with an introduction by Bret Lott
The beautiful Tennessee waltz
  McGraw, E. The good life; stories
The best friend
  McGraw, E. The good life; stories
Citizen of Vienna
  McGraw, E. The good life; stories
Daily affirmations
  McGraw, E. The good life; stories

Lucky devil
  McGraw, E. The good life; stories
One for my baby
  McGraw, E. The good life; stories
The penance practicum
  McGraw, E. The good life; stories
A whole new man
  McGraw, E. The good life; stories
McGregor, Jon
Which Reminded Her, Later
  Granta v99 p85-100 Fall 2007
McGruder, Krista
The bereavement of Eugene Wheeler
  McGruder, K. Beulah land
Beulah land
  McGruder, K. Beulah land
Clan of marsupials
  McGruder, K. Beulah land
Counting coup
  McGruder, K. Beulah land
Dirty laundry
  McGruder, K. Beulah land
Divination
  McGruder, K. Beulah land
Fee simple
  McGruder, K. Beulah land
Host
  McGruder, K. Beulah land
Like dancing on both feet
  McGruder, K. Beulah land
The southernmost point
  McGruder, K. Beulah land
A view from Eagle Rock Mountain
  McGruder, K. Beulah land
McGuane, Thomas
Aliens
  McGuane, T. Gallatin Canyon; stories
Cowboy
  McGuane, T. Gallatin Canyon; stories
  The Best American short stories, 2006; selected from U.S. and Canadian magazines by Ann Patchett with Katrina Kenison; with an introduction by Ann Patchett
  Beha, C. R. The Ecco anthology of contemporary American short fiction; selected by Joyce Carol Oates and Christopher R. Beha.
  The New Yorker v81 no28 p82-4, 86-7 S 19 2005
Gallatin Canyon
  The Best American short stories, 2004; edited by Lorrie Moore; Katrina Kenison series editor
  McGuane, T. Gallatin Canyon; stories
Ice
  McGuane, T. Gallatin Canyon; stories
  The New Yorker v80 no44 p78-83 Ja 24-31 2005
Miracle boy
  McGuane, T. Gallatin Canyon; stories
North Coast
  McGuane, T. Gallatin Canyon; stories
Old friends
  The Best American short stories, 2005; selected from U.S. and Canadian magazines by Michael Chabon with Katrina Kenison; with an introduction by Michael Chabon
  McGuane, T. Gallatin Canyon; stories
  The New Yorker v80 no32 p74-81 O 25 2004

McInerney, Jay—*Continued*

Con doctor

McInerney, J. How it ended; new and collected stories

The debutante's return

McInerney, J. How it ended; new and collected stories

Everything is lost

McInerney, J. How it ended; new and collected stories

Getting in touch with Lonnie

McInerney, J. How it ended; new and collected stories

How it ended

McInerney, J. How it ended; new and collected stories

I love you, honey

McInerney, J. How it ended; new and collected stories

In the north-west frontier province

McInerney, J. How it ended; new and collected stories

Invisible fences

McInerney, J. How it ended; new and collected stories

It's six a.m. do you know where you are?

McInerney, J. How it ended; new and collected stories

The last bachelor

McInerney, J. How it ended; new and collected stories

The madonna of turkey season

McInerney, J. How it ended; new and collected stories

The march

McInerney, J. How it ended; new and collected stories

My public service

McInerney, J. How it ended; new and collected stories

Penelope on the pond

McInerney, J. How it ended; new and collected stories

Philomena

McInerney, J. How it ended; new and collected stories

Putting Daisy down

McInerney, J. How it ended; new and collected stories

The queen and I

McInerney, J. How it ended; new and collected stories

Reunion

McInerney, J. How it ended; new and collected stories

Simple gifts

McInerney, J. How it ended; new and collected stories

Sleeping with pigs

McInerney, J. How it ended; new and collected stories

Smoke

McInerney, J. How it ended; new and collected stories

Story of my life

McInerney, J. How it ended; new and collected stories

Summary judgment

McInerney, J. How it ended; new and collected stories

Third party

Dangerous women; edited by Otto Penzler

McInerney, J. How it ended; new and collected stories

The waiter

McInerney, J. How it ended; new and collected stories

McInerny, Ralph M.

The devil that walks at noonday

The World's finest mystery and crime stories, fourth annual collection; edited by Ed Gorman and Martin H. Greenberg

Fear and trembling: a Father Dowling story

Thou shalt not kill; biblical mystery stories; edited by Anne Perry

McIntosh, K. H.

For works written by this author under other names see Aird, Catherine

McIntosh, Richard

Ready for blast off

The Times Educational Supplement p14-18 Ag 29 2008 TES Magazine supp

McIntosh, Will

Followed

The living dead; edited by John Joseph Adams

McIntyre, Vestal

Binge

McIntyre, V. You are not the one; stories

Disability

McIntyre, V. You are not the one; stories

Dunford

McIntyre, V. You are not the one; stories

Foray

McIntyre, V. You are not the one; stories

Nightwalking

McIntyre, V. You are not the one; stories

Octo

McIntyre, V. You are not the one; stories

ONJ.com

McIntyre, V. You are not the one; stories

Sahara

McIntyre, V. You are not the one; stories

McIntyre, Vonda N.

Little faces

The James Tiptree Award Anthology 3; edited by Karen Joy Fowler [et al.]

The Year's best science fiction: twenty-third annual collection; edited by Gardner Dozois

A modest proposal. . .for the perfection of nature

Nature v434 p122 Mr 3 2005

(jt. auth) See Le Guin, Ursula K. and McIntyre, Vonda N.

McKay, Becka Mara

(tr.) See Epstein, Alex

McKean, James

Bound

Iowa Review v37 no1 p69-72 Spr 2007

McKellar, Christine

Bits and pieces

Las Vegas noir; edited by Jarrett Keene & Todd James Pierce

McKenzie, Elizabeth

Caveat emptor

Stafford, J. The collected stories of Jean Stafford

Hope ranch

McKenzie, E. Stop that girl; a novel in stories

Last of our tribe

McKenzie, E. Stop that girl; a novel in stories

Let me take you down

McKenzie, E. Stop that girl; a novel in stories

Life on Comet

McKenzie, E. Stop that girl; a novel in stories

Look out, kids

McKenzie, E. Stop that girl; a novel in stories

The possible world

McKenzie, E. Stop that girl; a novel in stories

S.O.S.

McKenzie, E. Stop that girl; a novel in stories

Stop that girl

McKenzie, E. Stop that girl; a novel in stories

We know where we are, but not why

McKenzie, E. Stop that girl; a novel in stories

McKiernan, Dennis L.

Pricks and afflictions

Thieves' world; enemies of fortune; edited by Lynn Abbey

McKillip, Patricia A.

Ash, wood, fire

McKillip, P. A. Harrowing the dragon

Baba Yaga and the sorcerer's son

McKillip, P. A. Harrowing the dragon

The fellowship of the dragon

McKillip, P. A. Harrowing the dragon

The harrowing of the dragon of Hoarsbreath

McKillip, P. A. Harrowing the dragon

Lady of the Skulls

McKillip, P. A. Harrowing the dragon

The lion and the lark

McKillip, P. A. Harrowing the dragon

A matter of music

McKillip, P. A. Harrowing the dragon

Naming day

Wizards; edited by Jack Dann and Gardner Dozois

The snow queen

McKillip, P. A. Harrowing the dragon

Star-crossed

McKillip, P. A. Harrowing the dragon

The stranger

McKillip, P. A. Harrowing the dragon

Toad

McKillip, P. A. Harrowing the dragon

Transmutations

McKillip, P. A. Harrowing the dragon

A troll and two roses

McKillip, P. A. Harrowing the dragon

Voyage into the heart

McKillip, P. A. Harrowing the dragon

The witches of Junket

McKillip, P. A. Harrowing the dragon

McKinley, James

Chipmunks

New Letters v71 no2 p111-20 2005

McKinney, Catherine

Traveling with Children

South Carolina Review v38 no1 p173-81 Fall 2005

McKinnon, K. C.

For works written by this author under other names see Pelletier, Cathie

McKinstray, Stefan

No one here says what they mean

Best new American voices 2008; guest editor Richard Bausch; series editors John Kulka and Natalie Danford

McKnight, Maggie

The First Time I Met H.

Iowa Review v38 no1 p13-19 Spr 2008

McLaglen, John J., 1938-

For works written by this author under other names see Harvey, John, 1938-

McLaughlin, Martin

(tr.) See Calvino, Italo

McLean, Anne

(tr.) See Cercas, Javier

McLean, Keith

Barely Human

Dalhousie Review v85 no3 p423-9 Aut 2005

Kindness

Dalhousie Review v87 no2 p275-80 Summ 2007

McLean, Russel D.

Pedro Paul

Expletive deleted; edited by Jen Jordan

McLean, Stuart

"Be-bop-a-lula"

McLean, S. Home from the vinyl cafe; a year of stories

The birthday party

McLean, S. Home from the vinyl cafe; a year of stories

Burd

McLean, S. Home from the vinyl cafe; a year of stories

Dave cooks the turkey

McLean, S. Home from the vinyl cafe; a year of stories

A day off

McLean, S. Home from the vinyl cafe; a year of stories

Driving lessons

McLean, S. Home from the vinyl cafe; a year of stories

Emil

McLean, S. Home from the vinyl cafe; a year of stories

Holland

McLean, S. Home from the vinyl cafe; a year of stories

The housewife and the diva

Good Housekeeping v241 no1 p207-8, 210, 212, 214 Jl 2005

The jockstrap

McLean, S. Home from the vinyl cafe; a year of stories

Labor days

McLean, S. Home from the vinyl cafe; a year of stories

Music lessons

McLean, S. Home from the vinyl cafe; a year of stories

On the roof

McLean, S. Home from the vinyl cafe; a year of stories

McNamara, Shannon
Skyfish Falling
Confrontation no94/95 p114-17 Spr/Summ 2006
McNeely, Thomas H.
Ghost Horse
StoryQuarterly v42 p88-96 2006
Sheep
Best of the South: from the second decade of New stories from the South; selected and introduced by Anne Tyler
McNett, Molly
Alewives
McNett, M. One dog happy
Bactine
McNett, M. One dog happy
Catalog sales
McNett, M. One dog happy
Catalogue Sales
New England Review v25 no4 p66-79 2004
Helping
McNett, M. One dog happy
One dog happy
McNett, M. One dog happy
Ozzie the burro
McNett, M. One dog happy
Rumor's Gift
New Letters v72 no3/4 p21-34 2006
Wishbone
McNett, M. One dog happy
McPhee, Martha
The anthropology of sex
Best of Tin House; stories; foreword by Dorothy Allison
McQuade, Molly
Think, Feel, See
TriQuarterly no125 p212-21 2006
McQueen, Latanya
Coyotes
The North American Review v293 no1 p19-24 Ja/F 2008
McRae, Diana
Never drop by
Women of mystery; an anthology; Katherine V. Forrest, editor
McWhorter, Tom
A tragedy with pigs
New stories from the Southwest; edited by D. Seth Horton; foreword by Ray Gonzalez.
Me and Big Foot. McCorkle, J.
Me and Miss Mandible. Barthelme, D.
Me and Mitch. Pronzini, B. and Malzberg, B. N.
Me and Paul. Wingate, S.
Me and the Bean. Zeises, L. M.
Me, Myself, & I. Reese, R. M.
Me (the bitch) and Bustanji. Dabbagh, S.
Me-topia. Roberts, A.
Meacham, Rebecca
The assignment
Meacham, R. Let's do
Good fences
Meacham, R. Let's do
Hold fast
Meacham, R. Let's do
Let's do
Meacham, R. Let's do
Simple as that
Meacham, R. Let's do

Tom and Georgia come over to swim
Meacham, R. Let's do
Trim & notions
Meacham, R. Let's do
Weights and measures
Meacham, R. Let's do
Worship for shut-ins
Meacham, R. Let's do
Mead, Donald
A thing forbidden
The Year's best fantasy and horror: twenty-first annual collection; edited by Ellen Datlow and Kelly Link & Gavin J. Grant
Meadley, Robert
Conversations at ma maia metron
New worlds; an anthology; edited by Michael Moorcock
Meadowlands. Oates, J. C.
Meaker, Marijane
Round heels
A hell of a woman; an anthology of female noir; edited by Megan Abbott; foreword by Val McDermid
A **mean** and spiteful toad. Maxwell, W.
A **mean** utility. Davidson, C.
Meaney, John
From the heart
The new space opera 2; edited by Gardner Dozois and Jonathan Strahan
Sideways from now
Fast forward 1; future fiction from the cutting edge; edited by Lou Anders
Via Vortex
Sideways in crime; an alternate mystery anthology; edited by Lou Anders
Meaning of ends. Witt, M.
Means, David
The Blade
Harper's v318 p67-70 Ap 2009
Blown from the bridge
Means, D. The secret goldfish; stories
The Botch
Harper's v317 p76-81 N 2008
Carnie
Means, D. The secret goldfish; stories
Counterparts
Means, D. The secret goldfish; stories
Dustman appearances to date
Means, D. The secret goldfish; stories
Elyria Man
Means, D. The secret goldfish; stories
The Gulch
Harper's v312 p79-82 Ap 2006
Hunger
Means, D. The secret goldfish; stories
It counts as seeing
Means, D. The secret goldfish; stories
Lightning man
Means, D. The secret goldfish; stories
Michigan death trip
Means, D. The secret goldfish; stories
The nest
Means, D. The secret goldfish; stories
Petrouchka [with omissions]
Means, D. The secret goldfish; stories
The project
Means, D. The secret goldfish; stories
A River in Egypt
The New Yorker v82 no40 p84-9 D 4 2006

Megan, Carolyn
The Pull of Beauty
The Antioch Review v67 no3 p547-57 Summ 2009
Towards a Language of Desire
The Massachusetts Review v47 no1 p9-19 Spr 2006

Megid, Ibrahim Abdel
The other city
The Anchor book of modern African stories; edited by Nadežda Obradovic; with a foreword by Chinua Achebe

Mehadheb, Imed
"Undertow"
Multicultural literature in contemporary Italy; edited by Marie Orton and Graziella Parati

Mehra, Devika
The garden
Best new American voices 2004; guest editor John Casey; series editors John Kulka and Natalie Danford

Mehringer, Amy
Apartment 1-A
The Best of the Bellevue Literary Review; edited by Dannielle Ofri and the staff of the Bellevue Literary Review

Mehta, Rahul
Quarantine
The Kenyon Review v30 no2 p75-89 Spr 2008

Meins, S. R.
Kafka the Bagger
Gettysburg Review v22 no1 p68-76 Spr 2009

Meissner, Bill
The Car Circle
The North American Review v290 no1 p29-33 Ja/F 2005

Mejia, Arturo Echeverri
The new order
The Flight of the condor; stories of violence and war from Colombia; translated and compiled by Jennifer Gabrielle Edwards; foreword by Hugo Chaparro Valderrama.

Mejia, Michael
The Abjection
Agni no69 p114-19 2009
Report of Ito Sadohara, Head of Tuna, Uokai, Ltd., to the Ministry of Commerce, Regarding Recent Events in the Domestic Fishing Industry
Agni no64 p139-86 2006

Mejía, Rafael Abreu *See* Abreu Mejía, Rafael, 1939-

Mejía Vallejo, Manuel
Fear
The Flight of the condor; stories of violence and war from Colombia; translated and compiled by Jennifer Gabrielle Edwards; foreword by Hugo Chaparro Valderrama.

Mejides, Miguel
The Man from Nowhere
The Review of Contemporary Fiction v26 no3 p46-64 Fall 2006
Nowhere man
Havana noir; edited by Achy Obejas

Mekler, Dovid Leyb
The Dybbuk
No star too beautiful; Yiddish stories from 1382 to the present; compiled and translated by Joachim Neugroschel

Melanie. Hayes, D.
MELBOURNE (AUSTRALIA) *See* Australia—Melbourne
MÉLIÈS, GEORGES, 1861-1938
About
Waldrop, H. Fin de Cyclé
Melissa's plan. Shattuck, J.
Melko, Paul
Alien fantasies
Melko, P. Ten sigmas & other unlikelihoods
Death of the egg king
Melko, P. Ten sigmas & other unlikelihoods
Doctor Mighty & the case of ennui; y
Melko, P. Ten sigmas & other unlikelihoods
Dysfunctional family cat
Melko, P. Ten sigmas & other unlikelihoods
Fallow earth
Melko, P. Ten sigmas & other unlikelihoods
Singletons in love
The Year's best science fiction: twenty-first annual collection; edited by Gardner Dozois
Melko, P. Ten sigmas & other unlikelihoods
Snail stones
Melko, P. Ten sigmas & other unlikelihoods
Strength alone
Melko, P. Ten sigmas & other unlikelihoods
The summer of the seven
Melko, P. Ten sigmas & other unlikelihoods
Ten sigmas
The Year's best science fiction: twenty-second annual collection; edited by Gardner Dozois
Melko, P. Ten sigmas & other unlikelihoods
The teosinthe war
Melko, P. Ten sigmas & other unlikelihoods
Walls of the universe
Melko, P. Ten sigmas & other unlikelihoods

Melley, Timothy
The Prince of Natick
StoryQuarterly v40 p95-125 2004

Mellick, Carlton
City hobgoblins
Perverted by language; fiction inspired by The Fall; edited and introduced by Peter Wild.

Mellis, Miranda F.
The Elephant Man
The Kenyon Review v27 no2 p77-8 Spr 2005

Melnyczuk, Askold
The Dimensions of Silence
Ploughshares v32 no4 p114-22 Wint 2006/2007
The Great Hospital
Gettysburg Review v18 no2 p199-216 Summ 2005
The Translator
Harvard Review (1992) no30 p150-62 2006

Melody. Biller, M.
Melody. Soueif, A.
Meloy, Maile
Agustin
Meloy, M. Both ways is the only way I want it
Ploughshares v34 no1 p125-37 Spr 2008
The children
Meloy, M. Both ways is the only way I want it
The girlfriend
Meloy, M. Both ways is the only way I want it

Meloy, Maile—*Continued*
  Liliana
    Meloy, M. Both ways is the only way I want
      it
    The Paris Review v50 p132-42 Wint 2008
  Lovely Rita
    Meloy, M. Both ways is the only way I want
      it
  Nine
    Meloy, M. Both ways is the only way I want
      it
  Ranch girl
    Beha, C. R. The Ecco anthology of contem-
      porary American short fiction; selected by
      Joyce Carol Oates and Christopher R.
      Beha.
  Red from green
    Meloy, M. Both ways is the only way I want
      it
  Spy vs. spy
    Meloy, M. Both ways is the only way I want
      it
  O Tannenbaum
    Meloy, M. Both ways is the only way I want
      it
  Travis, B.
    Meloy, M. Both ways is the only way I want
      it
  Two-step
    Meloy, M. Both ways is the only way I want
      it
Meloy, Paul
  Alex and the toyceivers
    Sedia, E. Paper cities; an anthology of urban
      fantasy
  The vague
    British invasion; edited by Christopher Gol-
      den, Tim Lebbon & James A. Moore
The **Melrose**. Rheinheimer, K.
Meltdown. Percy, B.
The **melting** pot. Pincio, T.
MELVILLE, HERMAN, 1819-1891
              Parodies, imitations, etc.
  Di Filippo, P. Anselmo Merino
  Di Filippo, P. Billy Budd
  Finger, A. Moby Dick; or, The leg
Melvin in the sixth grade. Johnson, D.
A **member** of the family. Randolph, L.
Membership. Stewart, P.
Memekwesiw. Misha
Memento mori. Haldeman, J. W.
Memento mori. Nolan, J.
Memo and Oblivion. Burgin, R.
Memoirs of a Muse. Vapnyar, L.
The **Memoirs** of Stefan Czarniecki. Gombrowicz,
  W.
Memorial day. Richard, M.
Memorial Day Weekend. Watson, D.
Memories of Uncle Neddy. Bishop, E.
MEMORY
          See also Amnesia
  Anderson, B. The peacocks
  Apple, M. Adventures in dementia
  Báez, A. My daughter's eyes
  Barth, J. As I was saying . . .
  Boyle, T. C. Rastrow's island
  Bradbury, R. If paths must cross again
  Bradbury, R. The pumpernickel
  Brennan, K. The emergence of modernism

  Buentello, J. A certain recollection
  Bunin, I. A. Cold fall
  Bunin, I. A. Late hour
  Busch, F. The barrens
  Cherne, B. The countess
  Clayton, J. J. History lessons
  Cluccellas, Maria Isabel. Tango and feathers
  Cozarinsky, E. Literature
  Crone, M. Pipe smoke
  Dick, P. K. We can remember it for you whole-
    sale
  Disch, T. M. Ringtime
  Fonseca, R. The enemy
  Fonseca, R. Pride
  Ford, J. The scribble mind
  Fuentes, C. Sweethearts
  Gabrielyan, N. Hide and seek
  Gardam, J. The hair of the dog
  Gardam, J. The last reunion
  Gardam, J. The Milly Ming
  Garrett, G. P. Epilogue: my life as a home mov-
    ie
  Ghitany, G. A drowsy haze
  Gifford, B. Johnny Across
  Green, S. R. The difference a day makes
  Grimes, C. Discourse on the sublime and the
    beautiful
  Groff, L. Sir fleeting
  Hadley, T. A card trick
  Hadley, T. Phosphorescence
  Hawes, L. A fine mess
  Helprin, M. Reconstruction
  Hogan, D. Pictures
  Holladay, C. C. The peacock
  Johnson, A. D. Shard of glass
  Jones, E. P. Adam Robinson acquires grandpar-
    ents and a little sister
  Jones, E. P. Blindsided
  Jones, E. P. The Devil swims across the
    Anacostia River
  Lennon, J. R. The Rememberer
  Levi, P. The girl in the book
  Lewis, W. H. Why we jump
  Machado de Assis. Dona Paula
  MacLaverty, B. A Belfast memory
  Malouf, D. The empty lunch-tin
  Malouf, D. Towards midnight
  Martel, Y. The Vita Æterna Mirror Company:
    mirrors to last till kingdom come
  Marusek, D. The wedding album
  McCafferty, J. So long, Marianne
  McLean, S. The birthday party
  Miller, A. Presence
  Miller, A. The turpentine still
  Mingas, D. Memory
  Moffett, K. The fortune teller
  Montgomery, L. Arts and crafts of American
    WASPs
  Montgomery, L. We the girly girls from Massa-
    chusetts
  Munro, A. Messenger
  Naiyer Masud. Allam and son
  Olafsson, O. August
  Olsen, T. I stand here ironing
  Parrish, P. J. One shot
  Porter, A. Hole
  Proulx, A. Family man
  Reed, R. Night of time
  Resnick, M. and Kress, N. Solomon's choice

MEMORY—*Continued*

Reynolds, C. A train to catch
Rivecca, S. Uncle
Rivera-Valdes, S. Ana at four times: Ana and the lemon balm
Rivera-Valdes, S. Blue like bluing
Ronk, M. C. The score
Rosenblum, M. H. Home movies
Sarah, R. Looking for my keys
Shua, A. M. The spinal column
Sillitoe, A. The sniper
Silverberg, R. The man who never forgot
Simpson, H. The tree
Smith, L. The Happy Memories Club
Soueif, A. Returning
Stubblefield, R. Preserves
Sundaresan, I. Shelter of rain
Sutton, B. Maybe, maybe not
Swan, G. Women who don't tell war stories
Swann, M. Return
Swann, S. A. The historian's apprentice
Swanwick, M. A midwinter's tale
Thompson, J. Throw like a girl
Tillman, L. The recipe
Tomlinson, J. The accomplished son
Tomlinson, J. Berliner
Tomlinson, J. Flights
Tomlinson, J. Marathon man
Trevor, W. Folie à deux
Updike, J. The brown chest
Updike, J. My father's tears
Updike, J. Personal archaeology
Updike, J. The road home
Van Booy, S. French artist killed in Sunday's earthquake
Van Booy, S. The reappearance of strawberries
Van Booy, S. The world laughs in flowers
Vidal, G. A moment of green laurel
Walters, A. L. Las Vegas, New Mexico, July 1969
Westcott, G. The wedding march
Williams, C. The burn
Windley, C. What Saffi knows
Wolff, T. Deep kiss
Yellin, T. Strangers on a train
Zelazny, R. The night has 999 eyes
Memory. Mingas, D.
Memory dance. Levithan, D.
Memory in tweed. Burke, T.
Memory lapse at the waterfront. Pflug, U.
The **memory** of Martha. Dunbar, P. L.
Memory Sickness. Nguyen, P.
MEMPHIS (TENN.) *See* Tennessee—Memphis
Memphis, 1825: The Nerve and the Blood. Averill, T. F.

MEN

See also Single men

Barthelme, D. A man
Barthelme, D. Three
Clayton, J. J. Dance to the old words
Fincke, G. Sorry I worried you
Gordon, M. Three men tell me stories about their boyhoods
Jamison, L. Quiet men
Kiely, B. Bloodless Byrne of a Monday
Kiely, B. Mock battle
Luongo, M. Boyfriends
Muramatsu, T. Yumeko
Parker, M. Results for novice males

Shields, C. Love so fleeting, love so fine
Tabor, M. L. Losing
Wallace, D. F. Brief interviews with hideous men
Yoss. The red bridge
Men and angels. Enright, A.
Men and Boys. Delfosse, O. G.
Men and women in love. Bradfield, S.
Men are trouble. Kelly, J. P.
Men at lunch. Baumbach, J.
Men from below. Lamb, H.
The **men** in black raincoats. Hamill, P.
The **men** in the back room at the country club. Rucker, R. v. B.
Men, Monsters, and Mothers. Howard, H.
Men more than mortal. Kadetsky, E.
Men of Ireland. Trevor, W.
Men of rough persuasion. Abbott, L. K.
Men on White Horses. Lenard-Cook, L.
Men sell not such in any town. Hopkinson, N.
Men shoot things to kill them. Barry, R.
The **Men** Went Out to Smoke. P´yetsukh, V. A.
The **men** with the leopard wallpaper. Currans-Sheehan, T.

Menasche, Daniel

The White Bird
The Massachusetts Review v48 no3 p409-19 Fall 2007

MENCKEN, H. L. (HENRY LOUIS), 1880-1956
About

Willis, C. Inside job

Mencken, Henry Louis *See* Mencken, H. L. (Henry Louis), 1880-1956

Mencoboni, Marco

Ad Vesperas
FMR (Black Edition) no16 p20-30 D 2006/Ja 2007
The Cantoria delle Messe by Luca Della Robbia
FMR (Black Edition) no27 p71-84 S/O 2008

Mendes, Bob

Fleeting fashion
The World's finest mystery and crime stories, fourth annual collection; edited by Ed Gorman and Martin H. Greenberg

Méndez, Alberto

First Defeat (1939)
The New Yorker v82 no23 p66-73 Jl 31 2006

Mendoza, Mario *See* Mendoza Zambrano, Mario, 1964-

Mendoza, Plinio

The day we buried our weapons
The Flight of the condor; stories of violence and war from Colombia; translated and compiled by Jennifer Gabrielle Edwards; foreword by Hugo Chaparro Valderrama.

Mendoza-Burke's Reform. LaSalle, P.

Mendoza Zambrano, Mario

A Christmas story
The Flight of the condor; stories of violence and war from Colombia; translated and compiled by Jennifer Gabrielle Edwards; foreword by Hugo Chaparro Valderrama.

Menefee, Joan

Touching Dummies
The North American Review v292 no3/4 p51-8 My/Ag 2007

Menéndez, Ana

Traveling Fools
Bomb no107 p supp4, supp6 Spr 2009

Menéndez Plasecia, Ronaldo

Waiting
The Review of Contemporary Fiction v26 no3 p107-9 Fall 2006

Menger-Anderson, Kirsten

The Baquet
Southwest Review v89 no2/3 p395-413 2004

The baquet, 1850
Menger-Anderson, K. Doctor Olaf van Schuler's brain

The burning, 1725
Menger-Anderson, K. Doctor Olaf van Schuler's brain

Doctor Olaf van Schuler's brain, 1664
Menger-Anderson, K. Doctor Olaf van Schuler's brain

The doctors, 2006
Menger-Anderson, K. Doctor Olaf van Schuler's brain

Happy effects, 1741
Menger-Anderson, K. Doctor Olaf van Schuler's brain

Hysteria, 1820
Menger-Anderson, K. Doctor Olaf van Schuler's brain

My name is Lubbert Das, 1765
Menger-Anderson, K. Doctor Olaf van Schuler's brain

Neurasthenia: a Victorian love story, 1871
Menger-Anderson, K. Doctor Olaf van Schuler's brain

Reading Grandpa's head, 1837
Menger-Anderson, K. Doctor Olaf van Schuler's brain

Salk and Sabin
Ploughshares v34 no2/3 p75-84 Fall 2008

Salk and Sabin, 1955
Menger-Anderson, K. Doctor Olaf van Schuler's brain

The siblings, 1910
Menger-Anderson, K. Doctor Olaf van Schuler's brain

A spoonful makes you fertile, 1931
Menger-Anderson, K. Doctor Olaf van Schuler's brain

The story of her breasts, 1971
Menger-Anderson, K. Doctor Olaf van Schuler's brain

MENNONITES

Johnson, D. Beverly Home

Mennuti, Nicholas D.

Connected
Agni no67 p54-72 2008

Meno, Joe

Airports of light
Meno, J. Demons in the spring

Animals in the zoo
Meno, J. Demons in the spring

An apple could make you laugh
Meno, J. Demons in the spring

The architecture of the moon
Meno, J. Demons in the spring

Art school is boring so
Meno, J. Demons in the spring

Astronaut of the year
Meno, J. Bluebirds used to croon in the choir

Be a good citizen
Meno, J. Bluebirds used to croon in the choir

The boy who was a chirping oriole
Meno, J. Demons in the spring

Frances the ghost
Meno, J. Demons in the spring
TriQuarterly no126 p113-22 2006

Get well, Seymour!
Meno, J. Demons in the spring

Ghost plane
Meno, J. Demons in the spring

Happiness will be yours
Meno, J. Bluebirds used to croon in the choir

Hold on to your hat
Meno, J. Bluebirds used to croon in the choir

How to say good night
Meno, J. Bluebirds used to croon in the choir

I want the quiet moments of a party girl
Meno, J. Demons in the spring

Iceland today
Meno, J. Demons in the spring

I'll be your sailor
Meno, J. Bluebirds used to croon in the choir

In the arms of someone you love
Meno, J. Bluebirds used to croon in the choir

It is romance
Meno, J. Demons in the spring

Like a rocket with a beat
Chicago noir; edited by Neal Pollack

Midway
Meno, J. Bluebirds used to croon in the choir

Miniature elephants are popular
Meno, J. Demons in the spring

Mr. Song
Meno, J. Bluebirds used to croon in the choir

Oceanland
Meno, J. Demons in the spring

Our neck of the woods
Meno, J. Bluebirds used to croon in the choir

People are becoming clouds
Meno, J. Demons in the spring

The sound before the end of the world
Meno, J. Demons in the spring

Stockholm 1973
Meno, J. Demons in the spring

A strange episode of *Aqua Voyage*
Meno, J. Bluebirds used to croon in the choir

Tijuana women
Meno, J. Bluebirds used to croon in the choir

A town of night
Meno, J. Bluebirds used to croon in the choir

A trip to Greek mythology camp
Meno, J. Bluebirds used to croon in the choir

The Unabomber and my brother
Meno, J. Demons in the spring

The use of medicine
Meno, J. Bluebirds used to croon in the choir

What a schoolgirl you are
Meno, J. Demons in the spring

Winter at the world famous ice hotel
Meno, J. Demons in the spring

Menon, Manjula

American Child
The North American Review v291 no2 p27-35 Mr/Ap 2006

Feast
Southern Humanities Review v41 no2 p133-65 Spr 2007

MENOPAUSE

Hawes, L. My last Indian

Martin, V. The change

MENTAL ILLNESS—*Continued*
  Wood, S. Protecting the innocent
MENTAL TELEPATHY *See* Telepathy
MENTALLY HANDICAPPED
        See also Mentally handicapped children
  Berniker, S. J. Aqua Velva Smitty
  Castillon, C. Knots and nuts
  Clarke, B. Geronimo
  Curtis, R. The Sno-Kone Cart
  D'Ambrosio, C., Jr. Drummond & son
  Dobozy, T. Last notes
  Donoghue, E. The sanctuary of hands
  Finger, A. Our Ned
  Grooms, A. Food that pleases, food to take
      home
  Holladay, C. C. The iron road
  Howard, J. East of the sun
  Klassen, S. Adelia
  Lardner, R. Haircut
  Lee, T. Zinder
  Li Yiyun. After a life
  Liebrecht, S. Kibbutz
  Munro, A. Child's play
  Oates, J. C. Heat
  Proulx, A. People in hell just want a drink of
      water
  Puchner, E. Children of God
  Richards, S. S. Grass fires
  Russell, K. The star-gazer's log of summer-time
      crime
  Scott, J. Or else, part II: What will happen
  Scott, J. Or else, part III: Rain on concrete
  Snyder, S. Dumpster Tuesday
  Tolstaia, T. Night
  Weil, J. Sarverville remains
  Williams, J. Congress
MENTALLY HANDICAPPED CHILDREN
        See also Autistic children
  Brau, E. The siesta
  Gallo, L. The king of slack
  Judah, S. The courtship of Naomi Samuel
  Pohl, F. and Kornbluth, C. M. The meeting
  Porter, K. A. He
  Quiroga, H. The decapitated chicken
MENTALLY ILL
        See also Insane, Criminal and dangerous
        Care and treatment
  Anderson, B. Balance
  Bakr, S. Thirty-one beautiful green trees
  D'Ambrosio, C., Jr. Screenwriter
  Duval, P. Spectator sport
  Gomez, R. Electric gods
  Hempel, A. Tumble home
  Lumley, B. The horror at Oakdeene
  Munro, A. Circle of prayer
  Potash, R. The sad house in Talbiye
  Walters, A. L. Buffalo wallow woman
  Welch, N. Mental
  Williams, J. The visiting privilege
  With, C. Pyjamas
  Wolfe, G. The death of Dr. Island
  Zumas, L. Waste no time if this method fails
Mepham, Aimee
  Knuckle Curve
    River Styx no74 p63-4 2007

Mercader, Mercer
  The postponed journey
    English translations of short stories by con-
      temporary Argentine women writers; edited
      by Eliana Cazaubon Hermann; translated by
      Sally Webb Thornton
Mercado, Sergio Ramírez *See* Ramírez Mercado,
    Sergio, 1942-
Mercado, Tununa
  Combatant love
    Díaz, G. J. Women and power in Argentine
      literature; stories, interviews, and critical
      essays; [by] Gwendolyn Díaz
  Delirious love
    Díaz, G. J. Women and power in Argentine
      literature; stories, interviews, and critical
      essays; [by] Gwendolyn Díaz
MERCENARIES *See* Soldiers of fortune
The **merchant** and the alchemist's gate. Chiang,
    T.
MERCHANT MARINE *See* Seamen
The **Merchant** of Mombasa. Kestin, H.
MERCHANTS
        See also Department stores
  Adiga, A. The railway station
  Ali, M. N. Mallam Sile
  Corso, P. Yesterday's news
  Dammaj, Z. M. The corn seller
  Gappah, P. Aunt Juliana's Indian
  Koënings, N. S. Setting up shop
  McGrath, P. Julius
  Mukhopadhyay, T. The corner shop
  Naiyer Masud. Custody
The **merchants** of Venus. Pohl, F.
Mercier, Micheline
  Et au diable les frontières . . .
    Canadian Woman Studies v26 no1 p65
      Wint/Spr 2007
Merciful plunder. Hodgson, W. H.
MERCURY (PLANET)
  Silverberg, R. Sunrise on Mercury
  Smith, C. A. The immortals of Mercury
Mercury. Burgin, R.
Mercury. Henriquez, C.
Mercury. Kiernan, C. R.
Mercy. Benedict, P.
MERCY DEATH *See* Euthanasia
The **Mercy** of the World. Coyne, S.
The **Mere** Act of Motion. Sardar, G.
Meredith, D. R. (Doris R.)
  The sheriff and the Panhandle murders [excerpt]
    Lone Star sleuths; an anthology of Texas
      crime fiction; edited and with an introduc-
      tion by Bill Cunningham, Steven L. Davis,
      and Rollo K. Newsom.
Meredith, Doris R. *See* Meredith, D. R. (Doris
    R.)
Merely hate. McBain, E.
Mergenthal, Terry
  The Practical Heart
    Gettysburg Review v22 no1 p37-51 Spr 2009
Merger. Charters, D.
MERIAN, MARIA SIBYLLA, 1647-1717
        About
  Stevenson, R. P. Insect dreams

Merino, Juan Fernando

The sixth commandment
  The Flight of the condor; stories of violence and war from Colombia; translated and compiled by Jennifer Gabrielle Edwards; foreword by Hugo Chaparro Valderrama.

Merişca, Lucian

Some earthlings' adventures on Outrerria
  The SFWA European hall of fame; sixteen contemporary masterpieces of science fiction from the continent; edited by James Morrow and Kathryn Morrow

Merkin, Daphne

My Sexiest Summer
  Best Life v4 no6 p96-101 Jl/Ag 2007

Merkin. Porter, A.

Merkner, Christopher

In Lapland
  Gettysburg Review v22 no3 p455-61 Aut 2009

MERLIN (LEGENDARY CHARACTER)

Roberson, J. A lesser working
Roberson, J. Shadows in the wood

Mermaid Fire. Cason, P.

MERMAIDS

Beagle, P. S. Salt wine
Laben, C. Something in the mermaid way
Maitland, S. Why I became a plumber

MERMEN

Beagle, P. S. Salt wine
Yolen, J. The lady and the merman

Merridew of abominable memory. Roberson, C.

Merril, Judith

Barrier of dread
  Merril, J. Homecalling and other stories; the complete solo short science fiction of Judith Merril; edited by Elisabeth Carey
Connection completed
  Merril, J. Homecalling and other stories; the complete solo short science fiction of Judith Merril; edited by Elisabeth Carey
Daughters of earth
  Merril, J. Homecalling and other stories; the complete solo short science fiction of Judith Merril; edited by Elisabeth Carey
Dead center
  Merril, J. Homecalling and other stories; the complete solo short science fiction of Judith Merril; edited by Elisabeth Carey
Death is the penalty
  Merril, J. Homecalling and other stories; the complete solo short science fiction of Judith Merril; edited by Elisabeth Carey
The deep down dragon
  Merril, J. Homecalling and other stories; the complete solo short science fiction of Judith Merril; edited by Elisabeth Carey
Exile from space
  Merril, J. Homecalling and other stories; the complete solo short science fiction of Judith Merril; edited by Elisabeth Carey
The future of happiness
  Merril, J. Homecalling and other stories; the complete solo short science fiction of Judith Merril; edited by Elisabeth Carey
Hero's way
  Merril, J. Homecalling and other stories; the complete solo short science fiction of Judith Merril; edited by Elisabeth Carey

Homecalling
  Merril, J. Homecalling and other stories; the complete solo short science fiction of Judith Merril; edited by Elisabeth Carey
The lady was a tramp
  Merril, J. Homecalling and other stories; the complete solo short science fiction of Judith Merril; edited by Elisabeth Carey
A little knowledge
  Merril, J. Homecalling and other stories; the complete solo short science fiction of Judith Merril; edited by Elisabeth Carey
The lonely
  Merril, J. Homecalling and other stories; the complete solo short science fiction of Judith Merril; edited by Elisabeth Carey
Peeping Tom
  Merril, J. Homecalling and other stories; the complete solo short science fiction of Judith Merril; edited by Elisabeth Carey
Pioneer stock
  Merril, J. Homecalling and other stories; the complete solo short science fiction of Judith Merril; edited by Elisabeth Carey
Project nursemaid
  Merril, J. Homecalling and other stories; the complete solo short science fiction of Judith Merril; edited by Elisabeth Carey
Rain check
  Merril, J. Homecalling and other stories; the complete solo short science fiction of Judith Merril; edited by Elisabeth Carey
The Shrine of Temptation
  Merril, J. Homecalling and other stories; the complete solo short science fiction of Judith Merril; edited by Elisabeth Carey
So proudly we hail
  Merril, J. Homecalling and other stories; the complete solo short science fiction of Judith Merril; edited by Elisabeth Carey
Stormy weather
  Merril, J. Homecalling and other stories; the complete solo short science fiction of Judith Merril; edited by Elisabeth Carey
Survival ship
  Merril, J. Homecalling and other stories; the complete solo short science fiction of Judith Merril; edited by Elisabeth Carey
That only a mother
  Merril, J. Homecalling and other stories; the complete solo short science fiction of Judith Merril; edited by Elisabeth Carey
  Femspec v4 no2 p103-14 2004
Whoever you are
  Merril, J. Homecalling and other stories; the complete solo short science fiction of Judith Merril; edited by Elisabeth Carey
Wish upon a star
  Merril, J. Homecalling and other stories; the complete solo short science fiction of Judith Merril; edited by Elisabeth Carey
A woman of the world
  Merril, J. Homecalling and other stories; the complete solo short science fiction of Judith Merril; edited by Elisabeth Carey
Woman's work is never done!
  Merril, J. Homecalling and other stories; the complete solo short science fiction of Judith Merril; edited by Elisabeth Carey

Merrill, George Edmands
The little nugget strike
  Adventures in the West; stories for young
  readers; edited by Susanne George Bloom-
  field and Eric Melvin Reed
Merry Christmas from Navarro Lodge, 1928. Ba-
  ker, K.
Merry go-rounds. Trezise, R.
The **merry** merry Christmas. McBain, E.
Merrymount. Porter, J. A.
Merrymount. Porter, J. A.
Merullo, Roland
Visions of Gerard
  Agni no67 p97-121 2008
The **mescaline** runes. Daughtry, P.
MESOPOTAMIA
Swanwick, M. Urdumheim
A **mess** of pork. Arnow, H. L. S.
A **mess** of pottage. Dunbar, P. L.
The **message**. Pearlman, E.
Message from the Inca. Anaya, R. A.
A **message** from the water. Luongo, M.
Message to Legatee. Frym, G.
Messages. Beagan, G.
Messages. Savory, B. A.
Messenger. Munro, A.
The **messenger**. Wilson, W. L.
The **messenger** of soulsville. Kelley, N.
Messina, Maria
America 1911
  Messina, M. Behind closed doors; Her fa-
  ther's house and other stories of Sicily;
  translated and with an introduction and
  afterword by Elise Magistro; preface by
  Fred Gardaphé
America 1918
  Messina, M. Behind closed doors; Her fa-
  ther's house and other stories of Sicily;
  translated and with an introduction and
  afterword by Elise Magistro; preface by
  Fred Gardaphé
Caterina's loom
  Messina, M. Behind closed doors; Her father's house and other stories of Sicily;
  translated and with an introduction and
  afterword by Elise Magistro; preface by
  Fred Gardaphé
Ciancianedda
  Messina, M. Behind closed doors; Her father's house and other stories of Sicily;
  translated and with an introduction and
  afterword by Elise Magistro; preface by
  Fred Gardaphé
Dainty shoes
  Messina, M. Behind closed doors; Her fa-
  ther's house and other stories of Sicily;
  translated and with an introduction and
  afterword by Elise Magistro; preface by
  Fred Gardaphé
Grace
  Messina, M. Behind closed doors; Her fa-
  ther's house and other stories of Sicily;
  translated and with an introduction and
  afterword by Elise Magistro; preface by
  Fred Gardaphé

Grandmother Lidda
  Messina, M. Behind closed doors; Her father's house and other stories of Sicily;
  translated and with an introduction and
  afterword by Elise Magistro; preface by
  Fred Gardaphé
Her father's house
  Messina, M. Behind closed doors; Her father's house and other stories of Sicily;
  translated and with an introduction and
  afterword by Elise Magistro; preface by
  Fred Gardaphé
I take you out
  Messina, M. Behind closed doors; Her fa-
  ther's house and other stories of Sicily;
  translated and with an introduction and
  afterword by Elise Magistro; preface by
  Fred Gardaphé
Red roses
  Messina, M. Behind closed doors; Her fa-
  ther's house and other stories of Sicily;
  translated and with an introduction and
  afterword by Elise Magistro; preface by
  Fred Gardaphé
Messinger, Jonathan
Between here and there
  Messinger, J. Hiding out; decoys by Jonathan
  Messinger; illustrations by Rob Funderburk
Bicycle kick
  Messinger, J. Hiding out; decoys by Jonathan
  Messinger; illustrations by Rob Funderburk
Big Doug rides torch
  Messinger, J. Hiding out; decoys by Jonathan
  Messinger; illustrations by Rob Funderburk
The birds below
  Messinger, J. Hiding out; decoys by Jonathan
  Messinger; illustrations by Rob Funderburk
Captain Tomorrow
  Messinger, J. Hiding out; decoys by Jonathan
  Messinger; illustrations by Rob Funderburk
Christmas spirit
  Messinger, J. Hiding out; decoys by Jonathan
  Messinger; illustrations by Rob Funderburk
Hiding out
  Messinger, J. Hiding out; decoys by Jonathan
  Messinger; illustrations by Rob Funderburk
Not even the zookeeper can keep control
  Messinger, J. Hiding out; decoys by Jonathan
  Messinger; illustrations by Rob Funderburk
One valve opens
  Messinger, J. Hiding out; decoys by Jonathan
  Messinger; illustrations by Rob Funderburk
Scream in the dark
  Messinger, J. Hiding out; decoys by Jonathan
  Messinger; illustrations by Rob Funderburk
True hero
  Messinger, J. Hiding out; decoys by Jonathan
  Messinger; illustrations by Rob Funderburk
We will all write a poem
  Messinger, J. Hiding out; decoys by Jonathan
  Messinger; illustrations by Rob Funderburk
Winged attack
  Messinger, J. Hiding out; decoys by Jonathan
  Messinger; illustrations by Rob Funderburk
Wrought iron
  Messinger, J. Hiding out; decoys by Jonathan
  Messinger; illustrations by Rob Funderburk

Messinger, Jonathan—*Continued*
  You can never forget
    Messinger, J. Hiding out; decoys by Jonathan
      Messinger; illustrations by Rob Funderburk
Messud, Claire
  Land Divers
    The New York Review of Books v56 no12
      p44, 46-9 Jl 16 2009
Mestre-Reed, Ernesto
  After Elián
    Colchie, T. A whistler in the nightworld;
      short fiction from the Latin Americas; ed-
      ited by Thomas Colchie
  Two Visits
    Southwest Review v90 no3 p476-93 2005
Metafiction: Reading Lolita Under Book Contract.
    Leff, V. A.
Metal Bars [Prize-winning essay in The Writer
    Short-Memoir Contest] Woods, D.
Metal fatigue. Busch, F.
Metamorphoses of Venus. Burke, K.
METAMORPHOSIS
  Auslander, S. The metamorphosis
  Bierce, A. The eyes of the panther
  Bierce, A. L. S.
  Cross, E. The recipe
  DeNiro, A. If I leap
  Gerrold, D. Franz Kafka, superhero!
  Gunn, E. Stable strategies for middle manage-
    ment
  Hill, J. You will hear the locust sing
  Hoffman, N. K. Sea air
  Howard, R. E. Black Canaan
  Howard, R. E. Golnor the Ape
  Howard, R. E. Spectres in the dark
  Howard, R. E. The valley of the lost
  Keret, E. Fatso
  Keret, E. Horsie
  Langelaan, G. The fly
  Nestvold, R. Exit without savings
  Prill, D. The mask of '67
  Rand, K. To dream to be
  Rickert, M. Moorina of the seals
  Shepard, L. Crocodile rock
  Shomer, E. Laws of nature
  Taha, M. A. The freak
  Wang Ping. Maverick
  Yolen, J. Words of power
The **metamorphosis**. Auslander, S.
The **metamorphosis**. Johnson, G.
Metamorphosis. Kardos, M. P.
The **metamorphosis** of Justin Jones. Coville, B.
The **metamorphosis** of the world. Smith, C. A.
The **metaphor** is dead–pass it on. Shields, C.
The **metaphysics** of orange juice. Tognazzini, A.
Metcalfe, William
  Ellie and Eric and Master Ah
    Dalhousie Review v87 no3 p413-23 Aut 2007
Meteorite mountain. Ts'an-hsüeh
METEORITES
  Dowling, T. The suits at Auderlene
  Finlay, C. C. The smackdown outside Dedham
  Franke, H. W. Meteorites
Meteorites. Franke, H. W.
Meter down. Shroff, M. F.
Methadone. Daldorph, B.
The **method**. Fitch, J.
METIS
  Erdrich, L. Jolly Beef, Metis legend

Metonymy; or, The husband's revenge. Queiroz,
    R. d.
Metzger, Robert A.
  Perchance to dream
    Nature v438 p394 N 17 2005
MEXICAN AMERICANS
    See also Mexicans—United States
  Anaya, R. A. Devil deer
  Anaya, R. A. In search of Epifano
  Azevedo, K. d. Together we are lost
  Castillo, R. The battle of the Alamo
  Gurba, M. Dahlia season
  Gurba, M. Just drift
  Gurba, M. Primera comunión
  Gurba, M. White girl
  Hernandez, L. The Catholic girl
  Hernandez, L. Count the raindrops
  Hernandez, L. The cross
  Hernandez, L. Migrations
  Hernandez, L. My little tyrant heart
  Hernandez, L. The neighbor
  Hernandez, L. Ojitos
  Hernandez, L. Pinky Sandoval
  Hernandez, L. The red curtain
  Hernandez, L. Somewhere between Santa Moni-
    ca and incarnacion de Cristo
  Hernandez, L. Manuel, Manuel everywhere
  Hinojosa, R. Partners in crime [excerpt]
  Hinojosa-Smith, Rolando. The Gulf Oil -Can
    Santa Claus
  Jiménez, F. Moving still
  Lefer, D. At the site where vision is most per-
    fect
  Mindt, A. Sabor a mi
  Muñoz, M. Bring brang brung
  Muñoz, M. The comeuppance of Lupe Rivera
  Muñoz, M. The faith healer of Olive Avenue
  Muñoz, M. The good brother
  Muñoz, M. The heart finds its own conclusion
  Muñoz, M. Ida y vuelta
  Muñoz, M. Lindo y querido
  Muñoz, M. Señor X
  Muñoz, M. Tell him about Brother John
  Muñoz, M. When you come into your kingdom
  Murray, Y. M. The conquest [excerpt]
  Paredes, A. The hammon and the beans
  Parra, E. A. The oath
  Raymond, J. The suckling pig
  Rodriguez, L. J. My ride, my revolution
  Saenz, B. A. Exile
  Sanderson, J. Commerce Street
  Shannon, J. The legend of Bayboy and the Mex-
    ican surfer
Mexican Chocolates. Reeve, F. D.
Mexican gatsby. Steiber, R.
MEXICANS
                    New York (N.Y.)
  Lessa, O. Marta
                    United States
  Bradbury, R. I see you never
  Cisneros, S. Machu Picchu
  Duncklee, J. Antonio sings his song
  Duncklee, J. The developers
  Galaviz-Budziszewski, A. Maximillian
  Gifford, B. Rosa Blanca
  Kelton, E. North of the big river
  Puchner, E. Diablo
  Waters, D. The Bulls at San Luis

MEXICANS—*Continued*
Zambia
Smith, M. Pajamas
MEXICO
Anaya, R. A. In search of Epifano
Anaya, R. A. The man who could fly
Bolaño, R. Gómez Palacio
Boyle, T. C. Blinded by the light
Bradbury, R. The lifework of Juan Diaz
Domecq, B. The Judas-tail
Fuentes, C. The armed family
Fuentes, C. Conjugal ties (2)
Fuentes, C. A cousin without charm
Fuentes, C. The discomfiting brother
Fuentes, C. The disobedient son
Fuentes, C. Eternal father
Fuentes, C. A family like any other
Fuentes, C. The father's servant
Fuentes, C. The gay divorcee
Fuentes, C. The mariachi's mother
Fuentes, C. The official family
Fuentes, C. The secret marriage
Fuentes, C. The star's son
Hadley, D. The teachings of Bronc Buster Billy Brown
Hernandez, L. Migrations
Julavits, H. Ambivalence
Kulpa, K. Cristina in another country
Lefer, D. California transit
Lefer, D. How much an ant can carry
Lowry, M. Under the volcano
Parra, E. A. Cuerpo presente/Requiem
Parra, E. A. The darkest night
Parra, E. A. The hunter
Parra, E. A. The well
Porter, K. A. Flowering Judas
Porter, K. A. María Concepción
Porter, K. A. The martyr
Porter, K. A. Virgin Violeta
Richardson, K. The third death of the little clay dog
Sada, D. El fenomeno ominoso/The ominous phenomenon
Stevens, J. D. Mexico is missing
Villoro, J. Lightweight champ
Villoro, J. Mariachi
Waldrop, H. Thin, on the ground
Waters, D. Mr. Epstein and the dealer
Zavala, H. L. A golpe de martillo/Hammering away
18th century
Duncklee, J. Padre Mirandi
Politics
See Politics—Mexico
Prisoners and prisons
See Prisoners and prisons—Mexico
Rural life
Anaya, R. A. Jerónimo's journey
Hernandez, L. Somewhere between Santa Monica and incarnacion de Cristo
Parra, E. A. The Christ of San Buenaventura
Silverberg, R. Not our brother
Acapulco
Bolaño, R. Last evenings on Earth
Cuernavaca
Anaya, R. A. B. Traven is alive and well in Cuernavaca
Guadalajara
Bensko, J. Out from Guadalajara

Juarez
Granados, C. A scenic night
Parra, E. A. The showcase of dreams
Mexico City
Bolaño, R. The grub
Samuels, M. A gentleman from Mexico
White, E. Cinnamon skin
San Cristóbal
Past, A. When I was a man
Tijuana
Meno, J. Tijuana women
Yucatan
Selgin, P. The sea cure
MEXICO, GULF OF *See* Gulf of Mexico
Mexico. Hartglass, C.
MEXICO CITY (MEXICO) *See* Mexico—Mexico City
Mexico is missing. Stevens, J. D.
Meyer, Philipp
One day this will all be yours
  New stories from the South: the year's best, 2007; selected from U.S. magazines by Edward P. Jones with Kathy Pories; with an introduction by Edward P. Jones
The Wolf
  Iowa Review v36 no2 p88-100 Fall 2006
Meyers, Annette
It's too late, baby
  A hell of a woman; an anthology of female noir; edited by Megan Abbott; foreword by Val McDermid
Not just the facts
  Sisters on the case; celebrating twenty years of Sisters in Crime; edited by Sara Paretsky
  For works written by this author in collaboration with Martin Meyers see Meyers, Maan
Meyers, Kent
Rodney Valen's second life
  The Best American mystery stories 2007; edited and with and introduction by Carl Hiaasen; Otto Penzler, series editor
  The Georgia Review v60 no3/4 p480-96 Fall/Wint 2006
Meyers, Maan
The organ grinder
  Manhattan noir; edited by Lawrence Block
Meyers, Martin
Why do they have to hit?
  Manhattan noir; edited by Lawrence Block
  For works written by this author in collaboration with Annette Meyers see Meyers, Maan
Meyers, Michael Kalmes
Monkey head
  Chicago noir; edited by Neal Pollack
MIAMI (FLA.) *See* Florida—Miami
Miami, 1959. Justice, J. R.
MIAMI BEACH (FLA.) *See* Florida—Miami Beach
Miasma. Foltz, C.
Micah's Story. Ducker, B.
MICE
Arnow, H. L. S. An episode in the life of Ezekial Whitmore
Arnow, H. L. S. Zekie, the hill-billy mouse
Beagle, P. S. Gordon, the self-made cat
Grahame, K. First whisper of the wind in the willows

Michel, Maren
Hover
Calyx v24 no2 p14-28 Wint 2008
Michelangelo and the statue of David. James, C.
L. R.
MICHELANGELO BUONARROTI, 1475-1564
About
James, C. L. R. Michelangelo and the statue of
David
MICHIGAN
Allyn, D. Wolf Woman Bay
Brown, D. Ascent
Brown, D. Ask for a convertible
Brown, D. The dangers of salmonella
Brown, D. Descent
Brown, D. Entebbe
Brown, D. How to clean up any stain
Brown, D. On being french
Brown, D. Running
Bukoski, A. The Pulaski guards
Coake, C. Abandon
Deaver, J. Copycat
Irvine, A. C. Gus dreams of biting the mailman
Moceri, M. Eclipse tonight
Moceri, M. The mystery spot
Moceri, M. Sky full of burdens
Monson, A. Freda thinks spring
Monson, A. A huge, old radio
Monson, A. Isle Royale
Monson, A. Other electricities
Monson, A. The sudden possibility of nakedness
Monson, A. We are going to see the oracle of
Apollo in Tapiola, Michigan
Woolson, C. F. Jeannette
Ann Arbor
Gaitskill, M. College town, 1980
Detroit
Abbott, M. Our eyes couldn't stop opening
Bakopoulos, D. Happy
Bernier, C. Migration
Boland, J. The night watchman is asleep
Cooper, D. Night coming
Hernandez, L. Death in the sidesaddle
Hernandez, L. The last car
Hernandez, L. Manuel, Manuel everywhere
Hernandez, L. Over the Belle Isle boundary
Hernandez, L. Thanks to Abbie Wilson
Hernandez, L. This is our song for today
Hernandez, L. Tuesday morning
Hernandez, L. We have a job for you
Hernandez, L. Yes I am a virgin
Holden, C. Red quarters
Irvine, A. C. The golems of Detroit
Johnson, R. K. Hey love
Lynn, D. H. Year of fire
Markus, P. The dead man's boat
Oates, J. C. How I contemplated the world from
the Detroit House of Corrections, and be-
gan my life over again
Oates, J. C. Panic
O'Brien, D. Honesty above all else
Preddy, M. The coffee break
Shawl, N. Little horses
Wild, P. Radical adults lick godhead style
Zadoorian, M. The lost Tiki palaces of Detroit
Michigan death trip. Means, D.
Micklem, Sarah
The Captive Chronologist
TriQuarterly no122 p44-52 2005

"Eft" or "Epic"
The Best of Lady Churchill's rosebud wrist-
let; edited by Kelly Link & Gavin J. Grant;
introduction by Dan Chaon
Micrographia esoterica. Rose, A.
MICROORGANISMS
Reed, K. Precautions
Micus, Edward
Miracle on 3W
Confrontation no92/93 p87-92 Fall 2005/Wint
2006
MIDDLE AGE
See also Aging
Alvarado, B. Comadres in the kitchen
Clayton, J. J. Talking to Charlie
Connell, E. S. The palace of the moorish kings
Connell, E. S. St. Augustine's pigeon
Davis, C. Electric
Dean, D. The afterlife of Lyle Stone
Deaver, P. F. Geneseo
Deaver, P. F. Silent retreats
Fincke, G. Sorry I worried you
Kelby, N. Jubilation, Florida
McLean, S. Labor days
Neera. Aunt Severina
Reinhorn, H. Good to hear you
Sillitoe, A. The chiker
Simpson, H. Constitutional
Simpson, H. Early one morning
Simpson, H. Every third thought
Somerville, P. The Cold War
Tabor, M. L. Proof
Wolff, T. Leviathan
MIDDLE AGES
See also Chivalry; Feudalism; Knights
and knighthood
Allyn, D. The murder ballads
Lanagan, M. A good heart
Resnick, L. Lady Roxanne La Belle
MIDDLE CLASSES
Thompson, J. The family Barcus
MIDDLE EAST
Tidhar, L. Shira
The **middle** of nowhere. Pohl, F.
The **middle** toe of the right foot. Bierce, A.
MIDDLE WESTERN STATES
Connell, E. S. The walls of Avila
MacLaverty, B. Winter storm
Middleton, Nancy
Fruit
South Carolina Review v37 no2 p147-55 Spr
2005
MIDGETS *See* Dwarfs
Midlin, Kansas, jump shot. Averill, T. F.
Midnight at the Hotel California. Gappah, P.
Midnight bowling. Dalton, Q.
Midnight Clear. McCorkle, J.
Midnight grinding. Kelly, R.
Midnight in Silicon Valley. Hamilton, D.
Midnight Thoughts on the Law of Probability.
Black, W.
A **midsummer** day's dream. Bierce, A.
Midtown Pythagoras. Brodsky, M.
Midway. Meno, J.
MIDWEST *See* Middle Western States
A **Midwinter** Night. Wachtel, C.
A **midwinter's** tale. Swanwick, M.
MIDWIVES
Sayles, J. To the light

Miéville, China

Jack
  The new weird; Ann & Jeff VanderMeer, editors
Reports of certain events in London
  McSweeney's enchanted chamber of astonishing stories; edited by Michael Chabon; illustrations by Mike Mignola
  The Year's best fantasy and horror: eighteenth annual collection; edited by Ellen Datlow, Kelly Link & Gavin J. Grant
The tain
  Cities; [by] Paul Di Filippo . . . [et al.]; edited and introduced by Peter Crowther

Miéville, China and others

The ball room
  The Year's best fantasy and horror: nineteenth annual collection; edited by Ellen Datlow and Kelly Link & Gavin J. Grant
The **mighty** manslayer. Lamb, H.
Mighty Mouse and the conceited cowboy. James, C. L. R.
Mighty Mouse and the sinking ship. James, C. L. R.
Mighty Mouse to the rescue—again. James, C. L. R.

MIGRANT LABOR
Nichols, J. Slow monkeys

MIGRANT WORKERS
Duncklee, J. Antonio sings his song
Jiménez, F. Moving still
Migration. Bernier, C.
Migration. Herwitz, D.
Migration over Gruel. Singleton, G.
Migrations. Hernandez, L.
Miguel's theft. Andrade, C. D. d.
Mijo. Alessio, C.
The **Mikado's** favorite song. Moore, M.
Mike. Berry, W.
Mike Beaudry 1950-1988 An Elegy. Hodgen, C.
MILAN (ITALY) See Italy—Milan

Milbrodt, Teresa
To Fill
  The North American Review v292 no1 p8-15 Ja/F 2007
Mildred. Michaels, L.

Miles, Keith
Old bag dad
  The Best British mysteries, 2006; edited by Maxim Jakubowski
Miles. Burgin, R.
The **miles** between Harriet Tubman and Harry Truman. Varallo, A.
Miles to go. Weber, D.
The **Milfinators**. Stella, C.

Milionis, Christophoros
The find
  Angelic & black; contemporary Greek short stories; edited and translated by David Connolly; with an introduction by Vangelis Hatzivassileiou

MILITARY AERONAUTICS
  See also World War, 1939-1945—Aerial operations
Shepard, J. Climb aboard the mighty flea

MILITARY DESERTION
Brenner, Y. H. From A to M

MILITARY INTELLIGENCE
Bear, E. Gone to flowers
McAllister, B. The boy in Zaquitos

MILITARY MANEUVERS
Glasby, J. S. The quest for Y'ha-nthlei
Lupoff, R. A. Brackish waters
Roberts, A. Blindness and invisibility

MILITARY MINES
Joyce, G. An ordinary soldier of the Queen

MILITARY OCCUPATION
Vonnegut, K. The commandant's desk

MILITARY SERVICE, COMPULSORY *See* Draft

Militsa or mid-August reverie. Kalokyris, D.

Milius and Melanie. Stern, R. G.

Milk. Daidō, T.

Milk. Pollack, E.

Milk. Richmond, M.

Milk and Mary. Levine, S. and Schneiderman, D.

Milk bread beer ice. Shields, C.

The **Milk** of Human Kindness. Waldorf, S.

Milkboy. Romano, T.

Milking. Thomas, E.

Milkweed. Ockert, J.

Millar, Kenneth *See* Macdonald, Ross, 1915-1983

Millar, Margaret
The couple next door
  A New omnibus of crime; edited by Tony Hillerman and Rosemary Herbert; contributing editors Sue Grafton and Jeffery Deaver

Millás, Juan José
Vidas al límite: Biografía de una mosca / Lives on the Edge: Biography of a Fly [Part of a special issue: Elogio de la mosca en el arte / In Praise of Flies in Art]
  Artes de Mexico no93 p52-9, 61-4, 88-93 Mr 2009

The **millenium** express. Silverberg, R.

Miller, Alyce
Aftershock
  New England Review v26 no4 p189-91 2005
Tish, Love
  Iowa Review v35 no2 p128-42 Fall 2005

Miller, Alyce L.
Aftershock
  Miller, A. L. Water; nine stories
Cleaning house
  Miller, A. L. Water; nine stories
Dimitry Gurov's Dowdy wife
  Miller, A. L. Water; nine stories
Friends: an elegy
  Miller, A. L. Water; nine stories
Getting to know the world
  Miller, A. L. Water; nine stories
Hawaii
  Miller, A. L. Water; nine stories
Ice
  Miller, A. L. Water; nine stories
My summer of love
  Miller, A. L. Water; nine stories
Swimming
  Miller, A. L. Water; nine stories

Miller, Arthur
The bare manuscript
  Miller, A. Presence; stories
Beavers
  Miller, A. Presence; stories
  Harper's v310 p79-82 F 2005

Millhauser, Steven—*Continued*

The new automaton theater
  Beha, C. R. The Ecco anthology of contemporary American short fiction; selected by Joyce Carol Oates and Christopher R. Beha.

The Next Thing
  Harper's v316 p70-8 My 2008

The other town
  Millhauser, S. Dangerous laughter; thirteen stories

Un précurseur du cinéma
  Cahiers du Musée National d'Art Moderne no94 p3-25 Wint 2005/2006

A precursor of the cinema
  Millhauser, S. Dangerous laughter; thirteen stories

A Report on Our Recent Troubles
  Harper's v315 p76-80 N 2007

The room in the attic
  Millhauser, S. Dangerous laughter; thirteen stories

The tower
  Millhauser, S. Dangerous laughter; thirteen stories

The wizard of West Orange
  Millhauser, S. Dangerous laughter; thirteen stories

Millhiser, Marlys

Had he but known
  Creature cozies; edited by Jill M. Morgan

A **million** dollar story. Gildner, G.

MILLIONAIRES
        See also Capitalists and financiers; Wealth
  Barthelme, D. I bought a little city
  Chase, M. Wheeler-dealer
  Dahl, R. The butler
  Dahl, R. Neck
  Greenman, B. In the air room
  Pohl, F. The merchants of Venus

Millions for defense. Breuer, M. J.

The **millionth** chance. Clouston, J. S.

Mills, Enoch Josiah

The black hero of the ranges
  Adventures in the West; stories for young readers; edited by Susanne George Bloomfield and Eric Melvin Reed

Millwell. Hirshberg, G.

The **Milly** Ming. Gardam, J.

Milofsky, David

Biofeedback
  The Best of the Bellevue Literary Review; edited by Dannielle Ofri and the staff of the Bellevue Literary Review

The Shabbos Goy
  TriQuarterly no129 p178-86 2007

Milt and Moose. Pollack, E.

Milward, Andrew Malan

The Cure for Cancer
  The Literary Review (Madison, N.J.) v48 no4 p91-114 Summ 2005

Skywriting
  The Southern Review (Baton Rouge, La.) v44 no4 p748-61 Aut 2008

Ulysses
  Confrontation no98/99 p156-61 Spr/Summ 2007

Mimi Ungerer and Janet. Ducornet, R.

Mimic. Sillitoe, A.

A **mimicry** of mockingbirds. Carl, L. S.

Mina, Denise

An invisible minus sign
  Deadly housewives; edited by Christine Matthews

Mina, John

I shall return
  Alternate generals III; edited by Harry Turtledove and Roland J. Green

Minal in winter (Chicago, 1999). Mohanraj, M. A.

The **minaret**. Blackwell, K.

The **mind/body** problem. Boyd, W.

MIND AND BODY
  Rose, A. Enchanted looms
  Silverberg, R. Passengers

MIND CONTROL *See* Brainwashing

MIND READING *See* Telepathy

Mindt, Alex

An artist at work
  Mindt, A. Male of the species

Free spirits
  Mindt, A. Male of the species

The gypsy
  Mindt, A. Male of the species

Immigration
  Mindt, A. Male of the species

Karrooo
  Mindt, A. Male of the species

King of America
  Mindt, A. Male of the species

Male of the species
  Mindt, A. Male of the species

Reception
  Mindt, A. Male of the species

Ruby
  Mindt, A. Male of the species

Sabor a mi
  The Pushcart Prize XXX: best of the small presses 2006; edited by Bill Henderson with the Pushcart Prize editors
  Mindt, A. Male of the species

Stories of the hunt
  Mindt, A. Male of the species

Mine. Lane, J.

Mine is the kingdom. Zelazny, R.

Miner, Valerie

Back Home at the Driftwood Lodge
  Southwest Review v89 no2/3 p269-81 2004

Vital signs
  Best stories of the American West, v1; edited by Marc Jaffe

The **miner**. Duncklee, J.

Mineral and steel. Waters, D.

MINERS *See* Coal mines and mining; Gold mines and mining; Mines and mining

MINES, MILITARY *See* Military mines

Mines. Straight, S.

MINES AND MINING
        See also Coal mines and mining; Gold mines and mining
  Bacigalupi, P. The people of sand and slag
  Cowdrey, A. E. The tribes of Bela
  Dunbar, P. L. The tenderfoot
  Duncklee, J. The miner
  Duncklee, J. The mines of Magdalena
  Duncklee, J. Soul of the hob-nailed boot
  Kent, L. T. In common
  Merrill, G. E. The little nugget strike

MINES AND MINING—*Continued*
Ward, A. E. She almost wrote
The **mines** of Magdalena. Duncklee, J.
Mingas, Dimitris
Memory
Angelic & black; contemporary Greek short stories; edited and translated by David Connolly; with an introduction by Vangelis Hatzivassileiou
MINGUS, CHARLES, 1922-1979
About
Luongo, M. What Nina wants
Miniature elephants are popular. Meno, J.
MINIATURE OBJECTS
Hubbard, L. R. The professor was a thief
Millhauser, S. In the reign of Harad IV
The **miniaturist**. Julavits, H.
Minimal damage. Barnes, H. L.
Minimal Indian. Glancy, D.
MINING TOWNS
Bradbury, R. Almost the end of the world
MINISTERS *See* Clergy
The **minister's** missing daughter. Thompson, V.
Mink. Grant, J. A.
Minla's flowers. Reynolds, A.
MINNEAPOLIS (MINN.) *See* Minnesota—Minneapolis
MINNESOTA
Amdahl, G. The free fall
Drosso, A.-M. From Alexandria to Roseville
Erdrich, L. The blue velvet box
O'Brien, T. On the rainy river
Stelmok, J. The north shore
Thayer, S. Hi, I'm God
Weaver, W. Haircut
Weaver, W. You are what you drive
Farm life
See Farm life—Minnesota
Minneapolis
Disch, T. M. The white man
Erickson, K. J. Noir neige
Guest, J. Eminent domain
Hart, E. Blind sided
Hautman, P. The guy
Logue, M. Blasted
Roiphe, E. Little trouble girl
Sharratt, M. Taking the bullets out
Skinner, Q. Loophole
Zellar, B. Better luck next time
St. Paul
Bush, G. If you harm us
Everheart, C. Chili dog
Housewright, D. Mai-Nu's window
Krueger, W. K. Bums
Millett, L. The brewer's son
Murphy, N. The butterfly garden
Murphy, N. The catcher
Murphy, N. Miini-Giizi
Rawson, J. Eleven ways to live in the city
Rawson, J. The interview
Rawson, J. A working history of the alley
Rubenstein, B. Smoke got in my eyes
Singer, Julia Klatt. Chicken
Singer, Julia Klatt. From one window
Singer, Julia Klatt. Translations
Vázquez, D., Jr. The fat-brush painter
Vázquez, D., Jr. The first time I saw St. Paul
Vázquez, D., Jr. My friend Cintia
Minnow. Gautier, A.

Minnow. Waldman, A.
Minoff, Ann
Burgess
The Literary Review (Madison, N.J.) v50 no4 p217-25 Summ 2007
Minor, Kyle
A day meant to do less
The Best American mystery stories, 2008; edited and with an introduction by George Pelecanos; Otto Penzler, series editor
Gettysburg Review v20 no2 p275-320 Summ 2007
Minor key. Harvey, J.
A **minor** personal matter. Ruefle, M.
MINOR PLANETS *See* Asteroids
The **minority** committee. Dunbar, P. L.
The **minority** report. Dick, P. K.
Minors. Rheinheimer, K.
Minot, Eliza
Berniced
The dictionary of failed relationships; 26 tales of love gone wrong; edited by Meredith Broussard
Minot, Susan
Green
The dictionary of failed relationships; 26 tales of love gone wrong; edited by Meredith Broussard
MINSTRELS
Yolen, J. The singer of seeds
Mint in your mouth (San Francisco, 1990). Mohanraj, M. A.
Mintz, Catherine
A nice thought
Nature v456 p140 N 6 2008
Minus, Marian
The fine line: a story of the color line
"Tell it to us easy" and other stories; a complete short fiction anthology of African American women writers in Opportunity magazine, (1923-1948); edited by Judith Musser.
Half-bright: a short story
"Tell it to us easy" and other stories; a complete short fiction anthology of African American women writers in Opportunity magazine, (1923-1948); edited by Judith Musser.
Minutes of the last meeting. Chapman, S.
Mirabella, Angelina
My Heart Is with You in This Sad Time
The Southern Review (Baton Rouge, La.) v41 no4 p781-93 Aut 2005
Mirabelli, Eugene
The woman in Schrödinger's wave equations
Nebula Awards showcase 2008; the year's best SF and fantasy; selected by the Science Fiction and Fantasy Writers of America; edited by Ben Bova
Miracle. Budnitz, J.
The **miracle** at Ballinspittle. Boyle, T. C.
Miracle boy. McGuane, T.
Miracle-Gro. Hyde, M.
Miracle on 3W. Micus, E.
MIRACLES
Barnhill, K. Elegy to Gabrielle, patron saint of healers, whores, and righteous thieves
Boyle, T. C. The miracle at Ballinspittle
Di Filippo, P. Lignum Crucis

MISSING CHILDREN—*Continued*

Nelson, A. Kansas
Ockert, J. Jakob Loomis
Pinborough, S. The nowhere man
Scott, L. Prophet
Tumasonis, D. The swing
Windley, C. What Saffi knows
The **missing** clock hands: an implausible happening. Gail, O. W.
The **missing** line. Singer, I. B.

MISSING PERSONS

See also Missing children

Abbott, L. K. Gravity
Abbott, L. K. Martians
Alvarado, B. Emily's exit
Bakken, K. N. Remains
Barlas, T. A woman, any woman
Bates, J. W. The ungrateful dead
Beattie, A. Fléchette follies
Bierce, A. Whither?
Boswell, R. A walk in winter
Bowes, R. If angels fight
Bradbury, R. The poems
Braunbeck, G. A. Fisherman's delight
Butcher, J. Heorot
Chilson, P. Tea with soldiers
Collins, M. The kidnapping of Xiang Fei
Denevi, M. Victor Scarpazo; or, The end of the pursuit
Donoghue, E. Baggage
Doogan, M. Glamour
Douglass, S. This way to the exit
Ellin, S. The specialty of the house
Gildner, G. Something special
Grimes, C. Drafting the field report
Handler, D. Delmonico
Handler, D. Delmonico
Howard, R. E. The hoofed thing
Hubbard, L. R. The room
King, L. R. The house
Koretsky, J. L. The tormenting eye of God
LaBute, N. Opportunity
Lannes, R. The anguish of departure
Matheson, R. Dying room only
Millhauser, S. The disappearance of Elaine Coleman
Monk, B. Pieces of paper
Monk, B. Writing lesson
Montemarano, N. To fall apart
Munro, A. Silence
Murakami, H. Man-eating cats
Parra, E. A. The showcase of dreams
Pearson, R. Queeny
Reed, K. No two alike
Reinhorn, H. Last seen
Robson, J. Cracklegrackle
Roden, B. Northwest passage
Rust, E. M. Robert Horncroft, naked
Smith, A. N. Find me
Stamm, P. Flotsam
Stavans, I. The disappearance
Thayer, S. Hi, I'm God
Tóibín, C. A long winter
Ts'an-hsüeh. My brother
Van Booy, S. Snow falls and then disappears
Williams, L. The hide
Wolfe, G. Has anybody seen Junie Moon?
Wolven, S. The copper kings
Missing the morning bus. Carcaterra, L.

The **mission**. McDevitt, J.
Mission. Puchner, E.
The **mission** of Mr. Scatters. Dunbar, P. L.
Mission to Siberut. L'Amour, L.
Mission work. Bukoski, A.

MISSIONARIES

Bierce, A. To Fiji and return
Bissell, T. God lives in St. Petersburg
L'Amour, L. Beyond the great snow mountains
Valente, C. M. A dirge for Prester John
Waters, D. Mormons in heat
Wolfe, G. The seraph from its sepulcher
Missionaries. Chamberlin, J.

MISSISSIPPI

Allen, J. R. Mississippi story
Bennett, L. The convert
Faulkner, W. Tomorrow
Kelly, R. Oh, sordid shame!
Lefer, D. California transit
Manley, C. Catfish
Ruffin, P. The day J. P. saved the South
Ruffin, P. The hands of John Merchant
Ruffin, P. Harvey Watson and the angel
Ruffin, P. J. P. and the water tower
Ruffin, P. Jesus in the mist
Ruffin, P. The queen
Ruffin, P. When momma came home for Christmas and Talmidge quoted Frost
Scholes, K. East of Eden and just a little bit south
Scholes, K. That old-time religion
Shirley, P. Charisma
Shirley, P. The Downtown Club
Shirley, P. The story of William B. Greene
Spencer, E. Ship Island: the story of a mermaid
Waldrop, H. A dozen tough jobs
Walker, A. To my young husband
Williams, J. Spring is now

MISSISSIPPI RIVER VALLEY

Bacigalupi, P. Calorie man
Mississippi story. Allen, J. R.
Missolonghi 1824. Crowley, J.

MISSOURI

Bierce, A. The thing at Nolan
Pizzolatto, N. Nepal
Steinberg, S. Hydroplane
Thelwell, M. Direct action

Kansas City

Connell, E. S. Mrs. Proctor Bemis
Pickard, N. I killed

St. Louis

Bierce, A. Concerning balloons
Keene, J. Annotations [excerpt]
McNally, T. M. The gateway
Pizzolatto, N. Ghost birds
Missus, your soup is cold. Gordin, J.
Mist. Burke, J. L.

MISTAKEN IDENTITY

See also Impersonations

Baumbach, J. Bright is innocent: scenes from an imaginary movie
Connell, E. S. Caribbean provedor
Goodis, D. Never too old to burn
Hart, C. G. Murder for lunch
Jones, S. G. Captivity narrative 109
L'Amour, L. A gun for Kilkenny
Lynn, D. H. Mistaken identity
Matheson, R. The edge
Prior, A. Like he was just anyone else

MISTAKEN IDENTITY—*Continued*
Rock, P. Pergrine falcon
Silko, L. Mistaken identity
Silko, L. Old pancakes
Vollmer, M. Bodies
Wignall, K. The death of Jeffers
Mistaken identity. Lynn, D. H.
Mistaken identity. Silko, L.
Mistakes [With commentary] Berger, B. H.
Mister Buchholtz. Libin, Z.
Mister Doctor Batley [Medical Humanities, 32 no1 June 2006] Batley, N. J.
Mister Henry's trousers. McCauley, W.
Mister Jerry Is a Big One. Byers, M.
Mister Magister. Monteleone, T. F.
Mister weed-eater. Lansdale, J. R.
Mistletoe. Barkley, B.
Mistress Morgana
All in a day's work
Politically inspired; edited by Stephen Elliott; assistant editor, Gabriel Kram; associate editors, Elizabeth Brooks [et al.]
The **Mistress** of Leche Island. Conroy-Goldman, M.
The **mistress** of the horse god. Wieland, M.
MISTRESSES
Barbey d'Aurevilly, J. The crimson curtain
Chang, E. Red rose, white rose
Mueenuddin, D. In other rooms, other wonders
Parks, T. The room
Qi, S. Love me, love my dog
Sherman, D. La Fée Verte
Updike, D. Kinds of love
Vapnyar, L. Mistress
Mistrial. Oates, J. C.
The **mists** of time. Purdom, T.
Mitchard, Jacquelyn
"Avery, If It's a Girl"
Good Housekeeping v249 no3 p171-2, 174-6, 179 S 2009
Mitchell, David
Judith Castle
The book of other people; edited by Zadie Smith
What you do not know you want
McSweeney's enchanted chamber of astonishing stories; edited by Michael Chabon; illustrations by Mike Mignola
Mitchell, Emily
Lucille's House
New England Review v28 no2 p189-97 2007
Vanishing Bicycle
Raritan v28 no2 p17-23 Fall 2008
Mitchell, Judith Claire
Unknown donor
Barnstorm; contemporary Wisconsin fiction; edited by Raphael Kadushin
Mitchell, Peter
Gawain
Dalhousie Review v87 no3 p387-96 Aut 2007
Mitchell, Syne
The last mortal man
Elemental; the Tsunami relief anthology; stories of science fiction and fantasy; [edited by] Steven Savile and Alethea Kontis; introduction by Arthur C. Clarke
Mitcov, Anna
Cloud Formations
Calyx v23 no1 p71-80 Wint 2006

Mitosos. Krysl, M.
Mitra, Keya
The Outage
Confrontation no94/95 p60-72 Spr/Summ 2006
Pompeii recreated
Best New American voices 2007; [edited by Sue Miller; series editors, John Kulka and Natalie Danford]
Mitsora, Maria
Halfpastdoom
Angelic & black; contemporary Greek short stories; edited and translated by David Connolly; with an introduction by Vangelis Hatzivassileiou
Mitsotaki, Claire
Pink and black
Angelic & black; contemporary Greek short stories; edited and translated by David Connolly; with an introduction by Vangelis Hatzivassileiou
Mitsuhara, Yuri
Eighteenth summer
Passport to crime; the finest mystery stories from International Crime Writers; edited by Janet Hutchings
Mitt's murder. Lutz, J.
Mitya's love. Bunin, I. A.
Mitzvah. Goldberg, T.
Miura, Tetsuo
And all promenade!
Miura, T. Shame in the blood; a novel; translated by Andrew Driver
Face of death
Miura, T. Shame in the blood; a novel; translated by Andrew Driver
Homecoming
Miura, T. Shame in the blood; a novel; translated by Andrew Driver
Magic lantern show
Miura, T. Shame in the blood; a novel; translated by Andrew Driver
A portrait of Shino
Miura, T. Shame in the blood; a novel; translated by Andrew Driver
Shame in the blood
Miura, T. Shame in the blood; a novel; translated by Andrew Driver
The **mix**. McCauley, W.
MIXED BLOODS
See also Mulattoes
Erdrich, L. The antelope wife
Henry, W. The fourth horseman
Henry, W. Santa Fé passage
Updike, D. Love songs from America
Updike, D. A word with the boy
Mixed Breeding. Solomon, S.
Mlalazi, Christopher
King of Bums
The Literary Review (Madison, N.J.) v52 no2 p217-25 Wint 2009
Mo Yan
Inside Out
World Literature Today v83 no4 p36-7 Jl/Ag 2009
Learning from Pu Songling
World Literature Today v83 no4 p30-1 Jl/Ag 2009

Mo Yan—*Continued*
Wolf
World Literature Today v83 no4 p35 Jl/Ag 2009
Moamrath, M. M.
A study in scarlet herrings
This is my funniest 2; leading science fiction writers present their funniest stories ever; edited by Mike Resnick
MOBILE (ALA.) *See* Alabama—Mobile
Mobility. Rylands, J. T.
Möbius, stripped of a muse. Klages, E.
Mobster. Woronov, M.
The **Moby** Clitoris of his beloved. Watson, I.
Moby Dick fights a strange eagle. James, C. L. R.
Moby Dick; or, The leg. Finger, A.
Moceri, Margaret
Actual seasons
Moceri, M. Sky full of burdens
Eclipse tonight
Moceri, M. Sky full of burdens
Einstein made easy
Moceri, M. Sky full of burdens
Escape velocity
Moceri, M. Sky full of burdens
How to faint
Moceri, M. Sky full of burdens
The mystery spot
Moceri, M. Sky full of burdens
Proper fires
Moceri, M. Sky full of burdens
Sky full of burdens
Moceri, M. Sky full of burdens
There's only one way I can lie
Moceri, M. Sky full of burdens
Mock, Sharon
Attar of roses
Realms
Mock battle. Kiely, B.
The **mocking-bird**. Bierce, A.
Moctezuma *See* Montezuma II, Emperor of Mexico, ca. 1480-1520
Model. Shabtai, Y.
Model rockets. Nadelson, S.
MODELS, ARTISTS' *See* Artists' models
MODELS, FASHION *See* Fashion models
MODELS AND MODELMAKING
Padilla, I. The antipodes and the century
The **modern** age. Hwang, F.
Modern Lovers. Moody, R.
Modern mating. Zakour, J.
Modesitt, L. E., Jr.
Always outside the lines: four battles
Modesitt, L. E., Jr. Viewpoints critical; selected stories; [by] L.E. Modesitt, Jr.
Beyond the obvious wind
Modesitt, L. E., Jr. Viewpoints critical; selected stories; [by] L.E. Modesitt, Jr.
Black ordermage
Modesitt, L. E., Jr. Viewpoints critical; selected stories; [by] L.E. Modesitt, Jr.
The difference
Man vs. machine; edited by John Helfers and Martin H. Greenberg.
Modesitt, L. E., Jr. Viewpoints critical; selected stories; [by] L.E. Modesitt, Jr.
The dock to heaven
Modesitt, L. E., Jr. Viewpoints critical; selected stories; [by] L.E. Modesitt, Jr.

Fallen angel
Modesitt, L. E., Jr. Viewpoints critical; selected stories; [by] L.E. Modesitt, Jr.
Ghost mission
Year's best fantasy 7; edited by David G. Hartwell & Kathryn Cramer
Modesitt, L. E., Jr. Viewpoints critical; selected stories; [by] L.E. Modesitt, Jr.
The great American economy
Modesitt, L. E., Jr. Viewpoints critical; selected stories; [by] L.E. Modesitt, Jr.
Iron man, plastic ships
Modesitt, L. E., Jr. Viewpoints critical; selected stories; [by] L.E. Modesitt, Jr.
News clips recovered from the NYC ruins
Modesitt, L. E., Jr. Viewpoints critical; selected stories; [by] L.E. Modesitt, Jr.
The pilots
Modesitt, L. E., Jr. Viewpoints critical; selected stories; [by] L.E. Modesitt, Jr.
Power to . . . ?
Modesitt, L. E., Jr. Viewpoints critical; selected stories; [by] L.E. Modesitt, Jr.
Precision set
Modesitt, L. E., Jr. Viewpoints critical; selected stories; [by] L.E. Modesitt, Jr.
Rule of law
Modesitt, L. E., Jr. Viewpoints critical; selected stories; [by] L.E. Modesitt, Jr.
Second coming
Modesitt, L. E., Jr. Viewpoints critical; selected stories; [by] L.E. Modesitt, Jr.
Sisters of Sarronnyn, sisters of Westwind
Modesitt, L. E., Jr. Viewpoints critical; selected stories; [by] L.E. Modesitt, Jr.
Spec-ops
Modesitt, L. E., Jr. Viewpoints critical; selected stories; [by] L.E. Modesitt, Jr.
The swan pilot
Modesitt, L. E., Jr. Viewpoints critical; selected stories; [by] L.E. Modesitt, Jr.
Understanding
Modesitt, L. E., Jr. Viewpoints critical; selected stories; [by] L.E. Modesitt, Jr.
A **modest** proposal. Stafford, J.
A **modest** proposal. . .for the perfection of nature. McIntyre, V. N.
Modisane, Bloke
The dignity of begging
The Anchor book of modern African stories; edited by Nadežda Obradovic; with a foreword by Chinua Achebe
The **Moebius** Strip. Douglas, C. V.
Moebius trip. Wurts, J.
Moen, D. S.
A sword called Rhonda
This is my funniest 2; leading science fiction writers present their funniest stories ever; edited by Mike Resnick
Moe's villa. Purdy, J.
Moesta, Rebecca
(jt. auth) See Anderson, Kevin J. and Moesta, Rebecca
Moffett, Judith
The bear's baby
The Year's best science fiction: twenty-first annual collection; edited by Gardner Dozois

Moffett, Kevin
First marriage
New stories from the South; the year's best, 2008; selected from U.S. magazines by ZZ Packer with Kathy Pories; with an introduction by ZZ Packer
The fortune teller
Moffett, K. Permanent visitors
StoryQuarterly v40 p243-56 2004
The gardener of Eden
Moffett, K. Permanent visitors
In the Pines
Harvard Review (1992) no34 p26-41 2008
The medicine man
Moffett, K. Permanent visitors
Pushcart prize XXXI: best of the small presses 2007; edited by Bill Henderson; with the Pushcart Prize editors
The newcomer
Moffett, K. Permanent visitors
Space
Moffett, K. Permanent visitors
A statement of purpose
Moffett, K. Permanent visitors
Tattooizm
The Best American short stories, 2006; selected from U.S. and Canadian magazines by Ann Patchett with Katrina Kenison; with an introduction by Ann Patchett
Moffett, K. Permanent visitors
Ursa, on zoo property and off
Moffett, K. Permanent visitors
The volunteer's friend
Moffett, K. Permanent visitors
Mofina, Rick
Lightning rider
The International Association of Crime Writers presents Murder in Vegas; new crime tales of gambling and desperation; edited by Michael Connelly
The Deadly Bride; and 21 of the year's finest crime and mystery stories; including complete coverage of the year in mystery and crime fiction; edited by Ed Gorman and Martin H. Greenberg
Mogera Wogura. Kawakami, H.
Mogwe, Gaele Sobott- *See* Sobott-Mogwe, Gaele, 1956-
MOHAMMEDANISM *See* Islam
MOHAMMEDANS *See* Muslims
Mohan, Steven
Our flag was still there
Future Americas; edited by Martin H. Greenberg and John Helferd
Mohanraj, Mary Anne
Acts of faith (Chicago, 1963)
Mohanraj, M. A. Bodies in motion; stories
Bodies in motion (Chicago, 1999)
Mohanraj, M. A. Bodies in motion; stories
Challah (Philadelphia, 1998)
Mohanraj, M. A. Bodies in motion; stories
The emigrant (Colombo, 1979)
Mohanraj, M. A. Bodies in motion; stories
A gentle man (Massachusettes, 1979)
Mohanraj, M. A. Bodies in motion; stories
Lakshmi's diary (Chicago, 1969)
Mohanraj, M. A. Bodies in motion; stories
Mangoes with chili (San Francisco, 1983)
Mohanraj, M. A. Bodies in motion; stories

Marry in haste (Chicago, 1964)
Mohanraj, M. A. Bodies in motion; stories
Minal in winter (Chicago, 1999)
Mohanraj, M. A. Bodies in motion; stories
Mint in your mouth (San Francisco, 1990)
Mohanraj, M. A. Bodies in motion; stories
Monsoon day (Colombo, 2002)
Mohanraj, M. A. Bodies in motion; stories
Oceans bright and wide (Colombo, 1939)
Mohanraj, M. A. Bodies in motion; stories
Other cities (Chicago, 1962)
Mohanraj, M. A. Bodies in motion; stories
The princess in the forest (Chicago, 1955)
Mohanraj, M. A. Bodies in motion; stories
Seven cups of water (Jaffna, 1948)
Mohanraj, M. A. Bodies in motion; stories
Sins of the father (Jaffna, 1977)
Mohanraj, M. A. Bodies in motion; stories
Sister Mary (Colombo, 1949)
Mohanraj, M. A. Bodies in motion; stories
Tightness in the chest (Vermont, 1986)
Mohanraj, M. A. Bodies in motion; stories
Wood and flesh (Berkeley, 1999)
Mohanraj, M. A. Bodies in motion; stories
Moise, Lenelle
Cuck(h)olding a stranger
Homewrecker: an adultery reader; edited by Daphne Gottlieb
Mokoso, Ndeley
God of meme
The Anchor book of modern African stories; edited by Nadežda Obradovic; with a foreword by Chinua Achebe
MOLE (DERMATOLOGY)
Brennan, K. The emergence of modernism
The **molecule's** defiance. Levi, P.
Moles, David
Down and out in the Magic Kingdom
Strahan, J. Eclipse two; new science fiction and fantasy; edited by Jonathan Strahan
Finisterra
The Year's best science fiction: twenty-fifth annual collection; edited by Gardner Dozois
Planet of the Amazon women
The Year's best science fiction: twenty-third annual collection; edited by Gardner Dozois
The third party
The Year's best science fiction: twenty-second annual collection; edited by Gardner Dozois
The **molested**. McBain, E.
The **molester**. Burke, J. L.
Moliner, Empar
The Importance of Oral and Dental Hygiene
The Review of Contemporary Fiction v28 no1 p100-3 Spr 2008
Mollel, Tololwa M. (Tololwa Marti)
A night out
The Anchor book of modern African stories; edited by Nadežda Obradovic; with a foreword by Chinua Achebe
Molly's menorah. Gordon, S. J.
Molodowsky, Kadya
Alter Iteleh's and his daughters
Molodowsky, K. A house with seven windows; short stories; translated from the Yiddish by Leah Schoolnik

Molodowsky, Kadya—*Continued*

The meeting
   Molodowsky, K. A house with seven windows; short stories; translated from the Yiddish by Leah Schoolnik

Off the track
   Molodowsky, K. A house with seven windows; short stories; translated from the Yiddish by Leah Schoolnik

An old-country Erev Pesakh
   Molodowsky, K. A house with seven windows; short stories; translated from the Yiddish by Leah Schoolnik

On a day of rest
   Molodowsky, K. A house with seven windows; short stories; translated from the Yiddish by Leah Schoolnik

On the eve of the journey
   Molodowsky, K. A house with seven windows; short stories; translated from the Yiddish by Leah Schoolnik

The queen
   Molodowsky, K. A house with seven windows; short stories; translated from the Yiddish by Leah Schoolnik

The Rafalovitches
   Molodowsky, K. A house with seven windows; short stories; translated from the Yiddish by Leah Schoolnik

The Rashkovitcher wedding
   Molodowsky, K. A house with seven windows; short stories; translated from the Yiddish by Leah Schoolnik

The rich man from Azherkov
   Molodowsky, K. A house with seven windows; short stories; translated from the Yiddish by Leah Schoolnik

Rosele
   Molodowsky, K. A house with seven windows; short stories; translated from the Yiddish by Leah Schoolnik

The shared sukkah
   Molodowsky, K. A house with seven windows; short stories; translated from the Yiddish by Leah Schoolnik

Slander
   Molodowsky, K. A house with seven windows; short stories; translated from the Yiddish by Leah Schoolnik

The son-in-law
   Molodowsky, K. A house with seven windows; short stories; translated from the Yiddish by Leah Schoolnik

Sylvia
   Molodowsky, K. A house with seven windows; short stories; translated from the Yiddish by Leah Schoolnik

To hear the megillah on Purim
   Molodowsky, K. A house with seven windows; short stories; translated from the Yiddish by Leah Schoolnik

Tulia Shor's stories: King Solomon's bride
   Molodowsky, K. A house with seven windows; short stories; translated from the Yiddish by Leah Schoolnik

Tulia Shor's stories: The captain
   Molodowsky, K. A house with seven windows; short stories; translated from the Yiddish by Leah Schoolnik

Tulia Shor's stories: The fourth Mitzvah
   Molodowsky, K. A house with seven windows; short stories; translated from the Yiddish by Leah Schoolnik

Unhappy celebrations
   Molodowsky, K. A house with seven windows; short stories; translated from the Yiddish by Leah Schoolnik

A wedding
   Molodowsky, K. A house with seven windows; short stories; translated from the Yiddish by Leah Schoolnik

The white wedding dress
   Molodowsky, K. A house with seven windows; short stories; translated from the Yiddish by Leah Schoolnik

Zorekh the community's
   Molodowsky, K. A house with seven windows; short stories; translated from the Yiddish by Leah Schoolnik

Molohon, Jason Brady

Vita Vya Uganda
   Callaloo v31 no2 p470-6 Spr 2008

Mom and Mother Teresa. Dorsey, C. J.

Mom is my co-counsel. Levine, P.

Mombasa. Komie, L. B.

A **moment** of green laurel. Vidal, G.

Moment of vengeance [variant title: The waiting man] Leonard, E.

A **moment** of wrong thinking. Block, L.

Momentary. Sanders, T.

Moments of personal adventure. Sallis, J.

Momi watu. Shawl, N.

Mommers, Helmuth W,

Habemus papam
   The black mirror and other stories; an anthology of science fiction from Germany & Austria; edited & with an introduction & notes by Franz Rottensteiner; translated by Mike Mitchell.

Mommy, Daddy, & Mollie. Nolan, W. F.

Mon Desir. Morris, P.

Mon plaisir. July, M.

Mona Retires. Caplow, S.

Mona, Yehya, Basma. Koldys, S.

MONACO

Monte Carlo
   Woollcott, A. Rien ne va plus

The **monarch** of the glen. Gaiman, N.

Monarch, the big bear of Tallac. Seton, E. T.

MONASTICISM AND RELIGIOUS ORDERS
   See also Convent life; Monks

Moncada, Jesús

Provisional Report of Elies Santapau's Sprint
   The Review of Contemporary Fiction v28 no1 p36-9 Spr 2008

Monday. Erdrich, L.

Monday. Helprin, M.

Mondongo. Baraka, I. A.

Monénembo, Tierno

A fistful of groundnuts
   From Africa; new francophone stories; edited by Adele King

Monette, Sarah

Draco campestris
   Best American fantasy; guest editors Ann & Jeff VanderMeer; series editor Matthew Cheney

Monette, Sarah—*Continued*
Drowning Palmer
The Year's best fantasy and horror: twentieth annual collection; edited by Ellen Datlow and Kelly Link & Gavin J. Grant
A light in Troy
Realms
Three letters from the Queen of Elfland
The Best of Lady Churchill's rosebud wrist-let; edited by Kelly Link & Gavin J. Grant; introduction by Dan Chaon
(jt. auth) See Bear, Elizabeth and Monette, Sarah

MONEY
See also Finance
Bonner, M. O. The makin's
Canty, K. Where the money went
Curtis, R. Twenty grand
Donoghue, E. The cost of things
Graham, T. Fortune
Lain, D. The headline trick
Lott, B. The issue of money
Rust, E. M. Rich girls
Yu, C. 401(k)
Zoshchenko, M. Host accountancy
The **money**. Gee, M.
Money, fame, and beautiful women. Segal, L. G.
MONEY LAUNDERING
Archer, J. Charity begins at home
Archer, J. Maestro
Money Makes The Monkey Dance. Rodriguez, A.
Money shot. Banks, R.
The **money** to feed them. Spiegelberg, M.
Money whipped. Harrison, W.
MONEYLENDERS
See also Pawnbrokers
Smith, C. A. The weird of Avoosl Wuthoqquan
Money's worth. Sinor, B. H.
MONGOLIA
Sargent, P. Climb the wind
Sargent, P. Erdeni's tiger
Sargent, P. Spirit brother
MONGOLISM (DISEASE) *See* Down's syn-drome
MONGOLS
See also Tatars
Lamb, H. Ameer of the sea
Lamb, H. Law of fire
Lamb, H. The lion cub
Lamb, H. Prophecy of the blind
Lamb, H. Rose face
Lamb, H. Said Afzel's elephant
Lamb, H. The skull of Shirzad Mir
Monhegan light. Russo, R.
Monis, Virginia Olper
Woes of the middle class
Writing to delight; Italian short stories by nineteenth-century women writers; edited by Antonia Arslan and Gabriella Romani
Monitoring: 10 Spot Samples. Kauffman, J.
Monk, Bathsheba
Annie Kusiak's meaning of life
Monk, B. Now you see it . . .; stories from Cokesville, PA
Congratulations Goldie Katowitz
Monk, B. Now you see it . . .; stories from Cokesville, PA

Do not revive
Monk, B. Now you see it . . .; stories from Cokesville, PA
Epilogue: Excellent sperm
Monk, B. Now you see it . . .; stories from Cokesville, PA
Flying lesson
Monk, B. Now you see it . . .; stories from Cokesville, PA
The great wall
Monk, B. Now you see it . . .; stories from Cokesville, PA
Hocus-pocus
Monk, B. Now you see it . . .; stories from Cokesville, PA
Last call
Monk, B. Now you see it . . .; stories from Cokesville, PA
Little yellow dogs
Monk, B. Now you see it . . .; stories from Cokesville, PA
Mrs. Herbinko's birthday party
Monk, B. Now you see it . . .; stories from Cokesville, PA
Mrs. Szewczak and the rescue dog
Monk, B. Now you see it . . .; stories from Cokesville, PA
Now you don't
Monk, B. Now you see it . . .; stories from Cokesville, PA
Now you see it
Monk, B. Now you see it . . .; stories from Cokesville, PA
Pieces of paper
Monk, B. Now you see it . . .; stories from Cokesville, PA
Slam book
Monk, B. Now you see it . . .; stories from Cokesville, PA
Small fry
Monk, B. Now you see it . . .; stories from Cokesville, PA
Writing lesson
Monk, B. Now you see it . . .; stories from Cokesville, PA

MONK, THELONIOUS, 1917-1982
About
Baraka, I. A. A Monk story
Dobozy, T. Philip's killer hat
Wideman, J. E. The silence of Thelonious Monk
A **Monk** story. Baraka, I. A.
Monkey day. Baker, K.
Monkey head. Meyers, M. K.
Monkey Hill. Theroux, P.
The **monkey** king. May, S.
Monkey language. Zoshchenko, M.
The **monkey** murder. Gardner, E. S.
Monkey say, monkey do. Keret, E.
Monkey shines. Schaller, E.
The **monkey** treatment. Martin, G. R. R.
MONKEYS
See also Baboons
Johnson, K. 26 monkeys, also the abyss
Lanagan, M. Monkey's paternoster
Malla, P. Pet therapy
Martin, G. R. R. The monkey treatment
May, S. The monkey king
Murakami, H. A Shinagawa monkey
Saunders, G. 93990

MONKEYS—*Continued*
  Scholes, K. One small step
  Smith, M. Motorcycles
  Unger, D. Leslie and Sam
Monkey's paternoster. Lanagan, M.
The **monkey's** paw. Jablonski, N.
MONKS
  Gardam, J. The people of Privilege Hill
  Morrell, D. The Abelard sanction
  Remizov, A. The blaze
  Ryman, G. The last ten years in the life of Hero
    Kai
  Smith, C. A. The Beast of Averoigne
  Smith, C. A. The disinterment of Venus
The **monks** of the Abbey Victoria. Holmes, R.
**MONMOUTH, ROBERT CAREY, 1ST EARL
    OF, 1560?-1639**
                    About
  Garrett, G. P. Ghost me what's holy now
Monologue for two. Zelazny, R.
Monopoly. Atwood, M.
MONROE, MARILYN, 1926-1962
                    About
  Oates, J. C. Three girls
Monsieur Kalashnikov. Aciman, A.
Monsieur le Genius. Eggers, P.
Monsó, Imma
  The Window
    The Review of Contemporary Fiction v28 no1
      p66-73 Spr 2008
Monson, Ander
  Big 32
    Monson, A. Other electricities; stories
  Consideration of the force required to break an
    arm
    Monson, A. Other electricities; stories
  Constellations
    Monson, A. Other electricities; stories
  Dream obits for Liz
    Monson, A. Other electricities; stories
  Elsie and Henry
    Monson, A. Other electricities; stories
  Everyone Looks Better When They're Under
    Arrest
    Ploughshares v32 no1 p93-105 Spr 2006
  Forecast
    Monson, A. Other electricities; stories
  Freda thinks spring
    Monson, A. Other electricities; stories
  Get started
    Monson, A. Other electricities; stories
  A huge, old radio
    Monson, A. Other electricities; stories
  Intermittence
    Monson, A. Other electricities; stories
  Isle Royale
    Monson, A. Other electricities; stories
  Other electricities
    Monson, A. Other electricities; stories
  Piñata
    Monson, A. Other electricities; stories
  Residue
    Monson, A. Other electricities; stories
  The sudden possibility of nakedness
    Monson, A. Other electricities; stories
  We are going to see the oracle of Apollo in
    Tapiola, Michigan
    Monson, A. Other electricities; stories
Monsoon. Herrman, H.

Monsoon. Judah, S.
Monsoon day (Colombo, 2002). Mohanraj, M. A.
The **monster**. Haldeman, J. W.
Monster. Link, K.
The **monster**. Litt, T.
The **monster** and the maiden. Zelazny, R.
The **monster** in the park. James, C. L. R.
The **Monster** in Winter. Lock, N.
The **monster** of the prophecy. Smith, C. A.
Monster radio. Roberson, C.
MONSTERS
          See also Yeti
  Ballingrud, N. North American lake monsters
  Berry, J. Inheritance
  Chase, M. Leapers
  Coville, B. My little brother is a monster
  Cully, S. Roadkill
  Curtis, R. Monsters
  David, P. What monsters do
  Erdrich,   L.   Summer   1913/Miskomini-
    Geezis/Raspberry sun
  Ford, J. The Manticore spell
  Frost, G. Lizaveta
  Hodgson, W. H. The derelict
  Howard, R. E. The hoofed thing
  Howard, R. E. The house of Arabu
  Howard, R. E. The little people
  Huberath, M. S. "Yoo retoont, sneogg. Ay noo."
  James, C. L. R. The monster in the park
  Lamsley, T. Walking the dog
  Lanagan, M. She-creatures
  Langan, J. Tutorial
  Link, K. Monster
  Litt, T. The monster
  Lovecraft, H. P. The call of Cthulhu
  Lumley, B. For the dead travel slowly
  Lumley, B. The horror at Oakdeene
  Matheson, R. Born of man and woman
  McNally, J. Creature features
  Nix, G. Read it in the headlines!
  Parker, M. Smoke from Chester leading me
    down to see Dogman
  Powell, M. The abominable ice man
  Pratt, T. Komodo
  Pratt, T. Romanticore
  Rickert, M. The girl who ate butterflies
  Rickert, M. A very little madness goes a long
    way
  Roberson, C. Monster radio
  Russell, K. Children's reminiscences of the
    westward migration
  Shepard, J. Tedford and the megalodon
  Shepard, L. The ease with which we freed the
    beast
  Smith, C. A. The Beast of Averoigne
  Smith, C. A. The dweller in the gulf
  Smith, C. A. The nameless offspring
  Spindler, C. and Nelson, D. E. You were neither
    hot nor cold, but lukewarm, and so I spit
    you out
  Tambour, A. The age of fish, post-flowers
  Ts'an-hsüeh. The little monster
  Ulanski, D. It came from Monkey Skull Creek
  VanderMeer, J. The Third Bear
Monsters. Curtis, R.
The **monsters** of heaven. Ballingrud, N.
Monstrosities. Holladay, C.
Mont Royal. Singh, J.

Montalbetti, Christine

Hotel Komaba Eminence
World Literature Today v82 no2 p53-5 Mr/Ap
2008

MONTANA

Bower, B. M. Big medicine
Bower, B. M. By gollies, yes!
Bower, B. M. Happy Jack, wild man
Bower, B. M. The intervention of almighty
voice
Bower, B. M. The land shark
Bower, B. M. Law on the Flying U
Bower, B. M. On the middle guard
Bower, B. M. The outlaw
Bower, B. M. The tale of a native son
Davis, C. Grounded
Davis, C. Mouse rampant
Davis, C. The same sky
Hirshberg, G. The janus tree
Marsters, S. Bear story
McGuane, T. Aliens
McGuane, T. Cowboy
McGuane, T. Gallatin Canyon
McGuane, T. Old friends
McGuane, T. Vicious circle
Meloy, M. Travis, B.
Meloy, M. Two-step
Nelson, A. Falsetto
Nelson, A. Heart shaped rock
Ward, A. E. Butte as in beautiful

Montanye, C. S.

The perfect crime
The Black Lizard big book of pulps; edited
by Otto Penzler
A shock for the countess
The Black Lizard big book of pulps; edited
by Otto Penzler

MONTE CARLO (MONACO) *See* Monaco—
Monte Carlo

Monteiro, Luana

Antonio de Juvita
Monteiro, L. Little Star of Bela Lua
Curado
Monteiro, L. Little Star of Bela Lua
Little Star of Bela Lua
Monteiro, L. Little Star of Bela Lua
The whirling dove
Monteiro, L. Little Star of Bela Lua

Montejo, Eugenio

The Notebook of Blas Coll
The Southern Review (Baton Rouge, La.) v44
no4 p610-19 Aut 2008

Monteleone, Thomas F.

Camera obscura
Monteleone, T. F. Rough beasts and other
mutations
Changing of the guard
Monteleone, T. F. Rough beasts and other
mutations
A creature of accident
Monteleone, T. F. Rough beasts and other
mutations
The Curandeiro
Monteleone, T. F. Rough beasts and other
mutations
The dancer in the darkness
Monteleone, T. F. Rough beasts and other
mutations

Get it out
Monteleone, T. F. Rough beasts and other
mutations
Group phenomena
Monteleone, T. F. Rough beasts and other
mutations
It's in the bag
Monteleone, T. F. Rough beasts and other
mutations
Just in the niche of time
Monteleone, T. F. Rough beasts and other
mutations
Mister Magister
Monteleone, T. F. Rough beasts and other
mutations
Off to see the wizard
Monteleone, T. F. Rough beasts and other
mutations
Please stand by
Monteleone, T. F. Rough beasts and other
mutations
Present perfect
Monteleone, T. F. Rough beasts and other
mutations
The prisoner's tale
Monteleone, T. F. Rough beasts and other
mutations
A spell for Jonathan
Monteleone, T. F. Rough beasts and other
mutations
Taking the night train
Monteleone, T. F. Rough beasts and other
mutations
The way of the cross
Monteleone, T. F. Rough beasts and other
mutations
The white man
Monteleone, T. F. Rough beasts and other
mutations

Montemarano, Nicholas

The beginning of grief
Montemarano, N. If the sky falls; stories
Giving Up the Ghost
Gettysburg Review v20 no3 p385-411 Aut
2007
If the sky falls, hold up your hands
Montemarano, N. If the sky falls; stories
Man throws dog out window
Montemarano, N. If the sky falls; stories
The Antioch Review v63 no3 p440-55 Summ
2005
Note to future self
Montemarano, N. If the sky falls; stories
The November fifteen
Montemarano, N. If the sky falls; stories
Once Removed
The Southern Review (Baton Rouge, La.) v42
no4 p839-58 Aut 2006
The other man
Montemarano, N. If the sky falls; stories
Poster Child
Agni no62 p112-29 2005
Shift
Montemarano, N. If the sky falls; stories
Story
Montemarano, N. If the sky falls; stories
To fall apart
Montemarano, N. If the sky falls; stories

Mordecai, Pamela

Alvin's ilk

Mordecai, P. Pink icing and other stories

Blood

Mordecai, P. Pink icing and other stories

The burning tree and the balloon man

Mordecai, P. Pink icing and other stories

Chalk it up

Mordecai, P. Pink icing and other stories

Corinthians thirteen thirteen

Mordecai, P. Pink icing and other stories

Crucial concern

Mordecai, P. Pink icing and other stories

The game

Mordecai, P. Pink icing and other stories

Hartstone High

Mordecai, P. Pink icing and other stories

Limber like me . . .

Mordecai, P. Pink icing and other stories

"Once on the shores of the stream, Senegambia . . ."

Mordecai, P. Pink icing and other stories

Pink icing

Mordecai, P. Pink icing and other stories

Shining waters

Mordecai, P. Pink icing and other stories

More Afraid of You. Ferris, J.

More beautiful than you. Rickert, M.

More life. Keret, E.

More than skin deep. Bradford, B.

More than winter or spring. Treat, J.

Moreau. Steele, A. M.

Moreland, Ken

'Into the Wild Blue Yonder' and Other Airplane Stories

Nebraska Life v13 no2 p38-9 Mr/Ap 2009

La **Morena.** Solar, L. A.

MORENGA, JAKOB, D. 1907

About

Timm, U. Morenga [excerpt]

Morenga [excerpt] Timm, U.

Morgan, Alistair

Departure

The Paris Review v50 p132-62 Summ 2008

Icebergs

The PEN/O.Henry Prize stories 2009; chosen and with an introduction by Laura Furman; with essays on the stories They admire most by jurors A. S. Byatt; Anthony Doerr; Tim O'Brien

The Paris Review v49 p11-30 Wint 2007

MORGAN, SIR HENRY, 1635?-1688

About

Baker, K. The maid on the shore

Morgan, Jill M.

Scratch that one

Creature cozies; edited by Jill M. Morgan

Morgan, Seth

Street court

San Francisco noir 2; the classics; edited by Peter Maravelis.

Morgan. Thomas, E.

Morgana, Mistress

An open letter to the Bush administration

Sex for America; politically inspired erotica; edited by Stephen Elliott

MORGUES

Anderson, B. Balance

Morirse está en Hebreo. Stavans, I.

Morison, Neale

All over, Rover

Nature v452 p780 Ap 10 2008

Morison, Stephen, Jr.

Love Stories

South Carolina Review v38 no2 p207-14 Spr 2006

Morita, Ryuji

Fruits of Shinjuku

Morita, R. Tokyo fragments; Ryuji Morita [et al.]; translated by Giles Murray

MORMONISM *See* Mormons and Mormonism

MORMONS AND MORMONISM

Card, O. S. Christmas at Helaman's house

Card, O. S. God plays fair once too often

Card, O. S. Neighbors

Card, O. S. Worthy to be one of us

Self, W. The principle

Udall, B. Buckeye the elder

Waters, D. Mormons in heat

Mormons in heat. Waters, D.

Morning at fifty. Steinberg, A. L.

Morning swimmers. Donovan, G.

Mornington Place. Gee, M.

MOROCCO

Berrada, Mohammed. A life in detail

L'Amour, L. Glorious! Glorious!

Shukman, H. Mortimer of the Maghreb

Morocco. Updike, J.

Morocco Junction 90210. Morrison, P.

Morphine. Erdrich, L.

Morpho sanguinalis. Jansen, J.

Morrell, David

The Abelard sanction

Thriller; edited by James Patterson

The Deadly Bride; and 21 of the year's finest crime and mystery stories; including complete coverage of the year in mystery and crime fiction; edited by Ed Gorman and Martin H. Greenberg

Continental grip

Murder is my racquet; edited by Otto Penzler

Morris, Abigail

The Girl with the Metal Hair

Femspec v5 no2 p204-6 2004

Morris, J. M. *See* Morris, Mark, 1963-

Morris, Keith Lee

The Culvert

The Southern Review (Baton Rouge, La.) v41 no2 p322-32 Spr 2005

The Presidential Suite

New England Review v28 no4 p23-35 2007

Tired heart

New stories from the South: the year's best, 2006; selected from U.S. magazines by Allan Gurganus with Kathy Pories; with an introduction by Allan Gurganus

New England Review v26 no2 p184-99 2005

Morris, Maria

Homing instinct

Going the distance; edited by Alan Beard

Morris, Mark

Puppies for sale

British invasion; edited by Christopher Golden, Tim Lebbon & James A. Moore

Stamps

Fourbodings; [by] Simon Clark . . . [et al.]; edited by Peter Crowther

Morris, Mary
The Dead Woman
TriQuarterly no130 p69-83 2008
The hall of the meteorites
Scribblers on the roof; contemporary American Jewish fiction; edited by Melvin Jules Bukiet and David G. Roskies
Night Dive
Confrontation no94/95 p19-29 Spr/Summ 2006
Slamgram
Bomb no92 p90-2 Summ 2005
Morris, Paula
Mon Desir
Harvard Review (1992) no35 p109-28 2008
Morris, Rebecca
(tr.) See Guo, Xiaolu
Morris, William
A king's lesson
Tales before Narnia; the roots of modern fantasy and science fiction; edited by Douglas A. Anderson
Morris and his son Philip. Opatoshu, J.
Morrison, Arthur
The Lenton Croft robberies
The Mammoth book of vintage whodunnits; edited by Maxim Jakubowski
Morrison, Patt
Morocco Junction 90210
Los Angeles noir; edited by Denise Hamilton
Morrissette, Micaela
Ave Maria
Pushcart prize XXXIII: best of the small presses 2009; edited by Bill Henderson with the Pushcart Prize editors
Morrissey, Donna
Red Carpet Caper
The Walrus v5 no1 p77-8 Ja/F 2008
Morrissey, Thomas
Can't catch me
Brooklyn noir; edited by Tim McLoughlin
Morrow, Bradford
Amazing Grace
Pushcart prize XXVII; best of the small presses; edited by Bill Henderson with the Pushcart prize editors
Gardener of heart
Poe's children; the new horror: an anthology; [edited by] Peter Straub.
The hoarder
Murder in the rough; edited by Otto Penzler
Morrow, James
Auspicious eggs
Witpunk; edited by Claude Lalumière and Marty Halpern
Morse, David Lawrence
Conceived
The O. Henry Prize stories, 2006; edited and with an introduction by Laura Furman; jurors: Kevin Brockmeier, Francine Prose, Colm Toibin
Morse operator. Gardiner, J. R.
Morson, Ian
The moving-picture mystery
The Best British mysteries, 2006; edited by Maxim Jakubowski

Mort, Colin
The Vacationers
The Virginia Quarterly Review v82 no3 p178-201 Summ 2006
Mortal kombat. Wilson, K.
MORTALITY
Silverberg, R. Death do us part
Mortals. Wolff, T.
Mortazavi, Andrew
Stop Six, Ft. Worth
Iowa Review v38 no3 p8-22 Wint 2008/2009
Morte infinita. Crouse, D.
Mortegarde. Williams, L.
MORTICIANS *See* Undertakers and undertaking
The **mortification** of the flesh. Dunbar, P. L.
Mortimer, John
Rumpole and the bubble reputation
A New omnibus of crime; edited by Tony Hillerman and Rosemary Herbert; contributing editors Sue Grafton and Jeffery Deaver
Rumpole and the Christmas break
The Best British mysteries, 2006; edited by Maxim Jakubowski
Rumpole and the scales of justice
The Best British mysteries, 2005; edited by Maxim Jakubowski
Mortis Causa. Chalar, L.
Morton, Lisa
Black Mill Cove
Dark delicacies; original tales of terror and the macabre by the world's greatest horror writers; edited by Del Howison and Jeff Gelb
Sparks fly upward
The living dead; edited by John Joseph Adams
Morton, Oliver
The Albian message
Nature v438 p710 D 1 2005
Morwood, Peter
The longest ladder
The Magic toybox; edited by Denise Little
MOSAD (ISRAEL) *See* Israel. Mossad
La **mosca** que soñaba que era águila / The Fly That Dreamed It Was An Eagle [Part of a special issue: Elogio de la mosca en el arte / In Praise of Flies in Art] Monterroso, A.
Moscoe, Mike
Danny's very long trip
The Magic toybox; edited by Denise Little
MOSCOW (RUSSIA) *See* Russia—Moscow
Moser, Elise
Chocolates from Paris
Dalhousie Review v87 no2 p287-90 Summ 2007
Coral
Dalhousie Review v85 no3 p447-52 Aut 2005
Moser, Elise
The seven-day itch
Witpunk; edited by Claude Lalumière and Marty Halpern
MOSES (BIBLICAL FIGURE)
About
Winsor, C. The last Israelite in the Red Sea

Moses, Jennifer

Child of God

New stories from the South; the year's best, 2008; selected from U.S. magazines by ZZ Packer with Kathy Pories; with an introduction by ZZ Packer

You've Told Me Before

The Antioch Review v63 no2 p373-86 Spr 2005

Mosley, Walter

After the wedding

Mosley, W. The right mistake; the further philosophical investigations of Scrates Fortlow

The apology

Mosley, W. The right mistake; the further philosophical investigations of Scrates Fortlow

Archibald Lawless, anarchist at large: walking the line

Transgressions; edited by Ed McBain

The big nickel

Mosley, W. The right mistake; the further philosophical investigations of Scrates Fortlow

Black dog

Black noir; mystery, crime and suspense stories by African-American writers; edited by Otto Penzler

Breeding ground

Mosley, W. The right mistake; the further philosophical investigations of Scrates Fortlow

Details

Mosley, W. The right mistake; the further philosophical investigations of Scrates Fortlow

Gone fishin' [excerpt]

Lone Star sleuths; an anthology of Texas crime fiction; edited and with an introduction by Bill Cunningham, Steven L. Davis, and Rollo K. Newsom.

Karma

Dangerous women; edited by Otto Penzler

The Best American Mystery Stories, 2006; edited and with an introduction by Scott Turow; Otto Penzler, series editor

Maxie

Mosley, W. The right mistake; the further philosophical investigations of Scrates Fortlow

Mr. In-Between

Dead man's hand; crime fiction at the poker table; edited by Otto Penzler.

The picket

The darker mask; edited by Gary Phillips and Christopher Chambers.

Red caddy

Mosley, W. The right mistake; the further philosophical investigations of Scrates Fortlow

The right mistake

Mosley, W. The right mistake; the further philosophical investigations of Scrates Fortlow

The trail

Mosley, W. The right mistake; the further philosophical investigations of Scrates Fortlow

Traitor

Mosley, W. The right mistake; the further philosophical investigations of Scrates Fortlow

Trifecta

Mosley, W. The right mistake; the further philosophical investigations of Scrates Fortlow

Two women

Mosley, W. The right mistake; the further philosophical investigations of Scrates Fortlow

The **Mosque** at Larabanga. Edugyan, E.

Mosquito incense. Black, C.

MOSQUITOES

Shirley, J. Skeeter junkie

Mosquitoes and mountain ballads. Ts'an-hsüeh

Moss, Barbara Klein

Camping in

Moss, B. K. Little Edens; stories

The consolations of art

Moss, B. K. Little Edens; stories

December birthday

Moss, B. K. Little Edens; stories

Interpreters

Moss, B. K. Little Edens; stories

Little Edens

Moss, B. K. Little Edens; stories

The palm tree of Dilys Cathcart

Moss, B. K. Little Edens; stories

Rug weaver

Moss, B. K. Little Edens; stories

Villaclaudia

Moss, B. K. Little Edens; stories

Moss, Rose Rappoport

Spenser Street

The Antioch Review v64 no3 p438-40 Summ 2006

MOSSAD (ISRAEL) *See* Israel. Mossad

The **most** beautiful apartment in New York. Scott, J.

The **most** beautiful girl. Stamm, P.

The **most** beautiful girl in the world. Troy, M.

The **most** beautiful spot in the world. Weil, G.

Most beloved. Tolstaia, T.

The **most** everything in the world. Crane, E.

Most excellent and lamentable. Lundberg, J. E.

The **most** famous little girl in the world. Kress, N.

The **most** girl part of you. Hempel, A.

Most Livable City. Sayrafiezadeh, S.

The **most** of it. Ruefle, M.

The **most** unwanted. Sundaresan, I.

The **most** wonderful moment. Michalopoulou, A.

Mostre. Beattie, A.

MOTELS

Anderson, B. The westerly

Angel, J. The history of Vegas

Angel, J. Rounding third

Barkley, B. 19 amenities

Bensko, J. The ocean

Boswell, R. Skin deep

Chattin, J. Nowheresville

Gifford, B. After hours at La Chinita

Lott, B. The issue of money

Reinhorn, H. Golden pioneers

Snyder, S. Happy Fish, Plus Coin

Swan, G. Traveling light

Waters, D. Holiday at the Shamrock

Wingate, S. The Balkan House

MOTHERS AND DAUGHTERS—*Continued*

Klimasewiski, M. N. Tanner and Jun Hee
Krasikov, S. The alternate
Krysl, M. Belly
Krysl, M. Cherry Garcia, pistachio cream
Krysl, M. Heraclitus, help us
Kulpa, K. Cartography
Kyle, A. Allegiance
LaBrie, A. Girls
LaBrie, A. In Mem
LaBrie, A. Our last supper
LaBrie, A. Wonderful girl
Lahiri, J. Hell-heaven
Lamsley, T. Running in the family
Lanagan, M. Forever upward
Lewis, T. Limestone Diner
Li Yiyun. The arrangement
Li Yiyun. Love in the marketplace
Link, K. The constable of Abal
Loy, J. L. Bury your mother
Lunstrum, K. S. Familial kindness
Luongo, M. Do that everywhere
Luongo, M. Tea set
Luvaas, W. The woman who was allergic to
    herself
MacEnulty, P. The bargain
MacEnulty, P. Floating on the darkness
MacEnulty, P. Like someone in a coma
Macy, C. Annabel's mother
Macy, C. Bad ghost
Macy, C. Spoiled
Magona, S. It was Easter Sunday the day I went
    to Netreg
Manley, C. Felons
Manley, C. Intensive care
Manley, C. On the bus
Manley, C. Sixty-six Ford Galaxie
Marley, L. Technicolor
Matheson, R. Prey
Matthews, C. The house of deliverance
Mattison, A. I am not your mother
Maxwell, W. The shepherd's wife
McCabe, E. Heaven lies about us
McCafferty, J. The dog who saved her
McCafferty, J. Guiding light
McHugh, M. F. Oversite
McInerney, J. The debutante's return
McKenzie, E. Let me take you down
McKenzie, E. Look out, kids
McKenzie, E. Stop that girl
McKenzie, E. We know where we are, but not
    why
McLean, S. Valentine's Day
McNally, T. M. Skin deep
Meacham, R. Tom and Georgia come over to
    swim
Meacham, R. Trim & notions
Meloy, M. Nine
Menger-Anderson, K. Salk and Sabin, 1955
Mitra, K. Pompeii recreated
Molodowsky, K. In a Jewish home
Molodowsky, K. The Rafalovitches
Molodowsky, K. The son-in-law
Monk, B. Last call
Moon, E. Accidents don't just happen- they're
    caused
Mordecai, P. Chalk it up
Mountford, P. Horizon
Munro, A. Silence

Munro, A. Soon
Murphy, Y. Abalone, Ebony and Tusk
Murphy, Y. The woman in the leopard-spotted
    robe
Nayman, S. The house on Kronenstrasse
Nayman, S. The lamp
Nelson, A. Stitches
Newman, L. Only a phase
Oates, J. C. Angel of wrath
Oates, J. C. The haunting
Oates, J. C. Honor code
Oates, J. C. In hot May
Oates, J. C. The knife
Oates, J. C. Mark of Satan
Oates, J. C. The museum of Dr. Moses
Oates, J. C. Nowhere
Oates, J. C. Tell me you forgive me?
Ockert, J. Mother may I
Olsen, T. I stand here ironing
Otis, M. The straight and narrow
Otis, M. Triage
Palmer, K. Virtuoso mio
Palwick, S. Stormdusk
Paretsky, S. Acid test
Parks, T. The old house
Pearlman, E. Rules
Pelletier, C. The music of angels
Pflug, U. Ramona's baby
Pflug, U. Red velvet dust
Pintado, M. F. The scene
Randolph, L. Hyacinths
Randolph, L. A member of the family
Raphael, L. Big girls don't cry
Raphael, L. Nocturne
Reed, K. Visiting the dead
Rees, R. Ethel Mermaid
Rees, R. Tea leaves
Reinhorn, H. The heights
Reisen, A. The experienced bride
Reisen, A. Mother goes to the library
Rheinheimer, K. Telling Brenda
Richter, S. My mother the rock star
Rickert, M. The chambered fruit
Rickert, M. Evidence of love in a case of aban-
    donment: one daughter's personal account
Rivera-Valdes, S. Life leads
Roberson, J. In his name
Roberts, A. Eleanor
Roberts, A. The time telephone
Rodgers, S. J. Lost spirits
Romano, T. Treading water
Romm, R. The arrival
Romm, R. Weight
Ruffin, P. The natural man
Rusch, K. K. Patriotic gestures
Sankaran, L. Birdie num-num
Schor, L. Coming of age
Scott, J. Or else, part IV: That place
Scott, J. The Queen of Sheba is afraid of snow
Shaffer, A. Dropping the baby
Shawl, N. Momi watu
Shields, C. Family secrets
Shields, C. Sailors lost at sea
Shirley, J. Brittany? Oh: she's in translucent
    blue
Shirley, P. A death in the family
Shomer, E. The other mother
Sillitoe, A. The disgrace of Jim Scarfedale
Smith, A. The history of history

MOTHERS AND SONS—*Continued*

Purdy, J. Geraldine
Purdy, J. Moe's villa
Purdy, J. No stranger to Luke
Rankin, I. The hanged man
Raphael, L. Secret anniversaries of the heart
Raqabah, B. A. New wrinkles
Rash, R. Last rite
Rashid, F. Syra
Reed, K. Playmate
Reisen, A. When does Mame eat?
Richards, S. S. Grass fires
Rickert, M. Anyway
Rivas, M. Vermeer's milkmaid
Rodgers, S. J. Still life
Rohrlich, R. Citizen in the south
Roley, B. A. American son [excerpt]
Romano, T. The day of settlement
Romano, T. If you eat, you never die
Romano, T. On hold
Romano, T. Sundays
Rosa, J. G. Treetops
Rusch, K. K. Defect
Rylands, J. T. Youth
Sankaran, L. Bombay this
Schutt, C. Darkest of all
Schutt, C. The human season
Schutt, C. The life of the palm and the breast
Schwarzschild, E. Drift
Shabtai, Y. Twilight
Shrayer-Petrov, D. David and Goliath
Silverberg, R. There was an old woman
Simpson, H. Early one morning
Simpson, H. The tree
Singleton, G. Director's cut
Smith, A. I know something you don't know
Snee, T. First start
Spencer, E. The boy in the tree
Stelmok, J. The three requests
Stern, R. G. The ideal address
Stevens, J. D. Great myths of our time
Stewart, P. A new day
Stollman, A. L. Die grosse liebe
Strom, D. Husband, wife
Stuckey-French, E. Mudlavia
Swann, S. A. Family photos
Taha, M. A. The bird and the cage
Taha, M. A. The man who sold his mother
Taha, M. A. Motherhood
Taraqqi, G. A mansion in the sky
Tartt, D. The ambush
Tóibín, C. Donal Webster
Tóibín, C. A long winter
Tóibín, C. The name of the game
Tóibín, C. A priest in the family
Tóibín, C. A song
Tolstaia, T. Night
Tomlinson, J. A male influence in the house
Treat, J. Fruits of the dead
Treat, J. Make a nest
Treat, J. Meat Eaters & Plant Eaters
Treat, J. My mom from Budapest
Trevor, D. Saint Francis in Flint
Trevor, W. At Olivehill
Tudish, C. Killer
Twelve, O. Fluff
Uchida, S. My son's lips
Upadhyay, S. The weight of a gun
Vann, D. A legend of good men

Varallo, A. The knot
Varallo, A. Sunday wash
Vollmer, M. Second home
Watkins, S. Desgraciado
Wendroff, Z. Alas–I recovered
West, D. Interlude
Wideman, J. E. Weight
Wieland, M. Swan's home
Williams, C. Wire
Williams, J. Marabou
Wilson, K. Worst-Case Scenario
Wingate, S. Me and Paul
Winton, T. On her knees
Wolfe, G. Hunter Lake
Wolfe, G. The island of Doctor Death and other stories
Wolff, T. Down to bone
Wolff, T. Firelight
Wolff, T. The other Miller
Woolson, C. F. A transplanted boy
Yu, C. My last days as me
Ziyalan, M. Black palace
Zumas, L. Farewell navigator
A **Mother's** Body. Peroni, P.
Mother's day. Stewart, P.
Mother's flowers. Eschbach, A.

MOTHERS-IN-LAW

Arango, A. Murder, according to my mother-in-law
Blackwell, K. Queen of the May
Cutler, J. Doctor's orders
Douglas, C. N. Lawn and order
Gerber, M. J. Latitude
Hamer-Jacklyn, S. A guest
Holthe, T. U. The flame
Ledbetter, S. How to murder your mother-in-law
Linscott, G. Gracious silence
Martin, J. Russian lover
Motz, J. With a little help from your friends
Rodgers, S. J. Bones and flowers
Winton, T. Reunion
Mother's son. Hadley, T.
Mother's Summer Vacation. Taylor, K.
Mothers without children. Desaulniers, J.

MOTHS

Beagle, P. S. The fable of the moth
Nabokov, V. V. Christmas

MOTION PICTURE ACTORS AND AC-TRESSES

Allen, W. Tandoori ransom
Bradbury, R. Darling Adolf
Coleman, W. Winona's choice
Ellison, H. The resurgence of Miss Ankle-strap Wedgie
Farris, J. First born
Fuchs, D. West of the Rockies
Fuentes, C. The star's son
Hallberg, G. R. Early humans
Hammett, D. This little pig
July, M. Roy Spivey
LaBute, N. Soft target
Lane, J. The city of love
Lethem, J. Perkus Tooth
Levinson, R. S.
Matthews, C. For benefit of Mr. Means
Prill, D. The mask of '67
Purdy, J. Easy street
Salter, J. Eyes of the stars
Schor, L. Still the top banana

Mott, Jordan
The Bends
The Kenyon Review v29 no1 p82-96 Wint
2007
Motz, Jutta
With a little help from your friends
Passport to crime; the finest mystery stories
from International Crime Writers; edited by
Janet Hutchings
Mouche. Maupassant, G. d.
Moulessehoul, Mohammed
The wicked tongue
The Anchor book of modern African stories;
edited by Nadežda Obradovic; with a fore-
word by Chinua Achebe
Moulthrop, Robert
How'd It Go?
Confrontation no104 p114-26 Summ 2009
Moulton, Muriel
Canary in the Coal Mine
Harvard Review (1992) no27 p139-53 2004
MOUNTAIN CLIMBING *See* Mountaineering
The **mountain** day. Stafford, J.
Mountain ways. Le Guin, U. K.
MOUNTAINEERING
Andreas-Salomé, L. On their way
Coake, C. Solos
Eggers, D. Up the mountain coming down slow-
ly
Levi, P. Bear meat
Zelazny, R. This mortal mountain
MOUNTAINS
See also Adirondack Mountains (N.Y.);
Catskill Mountains (N.Y.); Himalaya
Mountains; Rocky Mountains; Volcanoes
Eggers, D. Theo
Hwang, S. Mountains
Neggers, C. On the run
Mountains. Hwang, S.
Mountains. O'Brien, S. L.
Mountford, Peter
Barbarians' Fantasies
Boston Review v32 no2 p31-3 Mr/Ap 2007
Horizon
Best new American voices 2008; guest editor
Richard Bausch; series editors John Kulka
and Natalie Danford
Michigan Quarterly Review v46 no4 p559-71
Fall 2007
Mountjoy, Jesse
Her Sunday
Legal Studies Forum v32 no1 p79-86 2008
John Hay
Legal Studies Forum v32 no1 p105-18 2008
The Road to San Sebastian
Legal Studies Forum v32 no1 p76 2008
Mounts, Michelle
Baths
StoryQuarterly v41 p220-42 2005
The **mournful** cry of owls. Golden, C.
A **mournful** property. Bierce, A.
MOURNING *See* Bereavement
Mourning. Staffetti, A.
MOURNING CUSTOMS *See* Funeral rites and
ceremonies
The **mourning** door. Graver, E.
Mouse. Faber, M.
Mouse. McMullin, J.
Mouse maker. Lanagan, M.

Mouse rampant. Davis, C.
The **mouse's** aura. Daughtry, P.
A **Mouthful** of Cut Glass. Hadley, T.
The **movements** of the body. Ebenbach, D. H.
The **moves.** July, M.
The **movie.** Brown, R.
Movie Nights in Rangoon. Wong, K.
MOVING (HOUSEHOLD GOODS)
McIlvoy, K. The people who own pianos
Moving. Kim, Y. H.
Moving. Rock, L.
Moving house. Lynn, D. H.
Moving on. McAllister, B.
MOVING PICTURE INDUSTRY *See* Motion
pictures
The **moving-picture** mystery. Morson, I.
MOVING PICTURES *See* Motion pictures
Moving pictures. Haywood, G. A.
Moving still. Jiménez, F.
Moving the Bees. Schlee, A.
Moving vehicles. Grimes, C.
Moxon's master. Bierce, A.
Moya, Horacio Castellanos
Revulsion [excerpt]
Words without borders; the world through the
eyes of writers; an anthology; edited by
Samantha Schnee, Alane Salierno Mason,
and Dedi Felman
Moyer, Kermit
Slightly Far East
The Hudson Review v57 no4 p593-606 Wint
2005
Moyshe Liar. Opatoshu, J.
**Mozart, Johann Chrysostom Wolfgang
Amadeus** *See* Mozart, Wolfgang Amadeus,
1756-1791
**MOZART, WOLFGANG AMADEUS, 1756-
1791**
About
Frost, G. Divertimento
O'Shaughnessy, P. His master's hand
Tsutsui, Y. Bravo herr Mozart!
Mozart day. Domecq, B.
Mozetič, Brane
Bathroom
Mozetič, B. Passion; translated by Tamara
Soban
The beach
Mozetič, B. Passion; translated by Tamara
Soban
Boy
Mozetič, B. Passion; translated by Tamara
Soban
Cinema
Mozetič, B. Passion; translated by Tamara
Soban
Dancing
Mozetič, B. Passion; translated by Tamara
Soban
Disco
Mozetič, B. Passion; translated by Tamara
Soban
Egghead
Mozetič, B. Passion; translated by Tamara
Soban
G.
Mozetič, B. Passion; translated by Tamara
Soban

Mozetič, Brane—*Continued*

Gym
　Mozetič, B. Passion; translated by Tamara
　　Soban
Gypsies
　Mozetič, B. Passion; translated by Tamara
　　Soban
Hairdresser
　Mozetič, B. Passion; translated by Tamara
　　Soban
Interloper
　Mozetič, B. Passion; translated by Tamara
　　Soban
Ivan
　Mozetič, B. Passion; translated by Tamara
　　Soban
The letter
　Mozetič, B. Passion; translated by Tamara
　　Soban
Library
　Mozetič, B. Passion; translated by Tamara
　　Soban
Lover boy
　Mozetič, B. Passion; translated by Tamara
　　Soban
The mayor
　Mozetič, B. Passion; translated by Tamara
　　Soban
Nino
　Mozetič, B. Passion; translated by Tamara
　　Soban
No. 6
　Mozetič, B. Passion; translated by Tamara
　　Soban
Oblivion
　Mozetič, B. Passion; translated by Tamara
　　Soban
The poem
　Mozetič, B. Passion; translated by Tamara
　　Soban
The poet
　Mozetič, B. Passion; translated by Tamara
　　Soban
Rage
　Mozetič, B. Passion; translated by Tamara
　　Soban
The rails
　Mozetič, B. Passion; translated by Tamara
　　Soban
Rape
　Mozetič, B. Passion; translated by Tamara
　　Soban
Razorblade
　Mozetič, B. Passion; translated by Tamara
　　Soban
The reader
　Mozetič, B. Passion; translated by Tamara
　　Soban
The soldiers
　Mozetič, B. Passion; translated by Tamara
　　Soban
The station
　Mozetič, B. Passion; translated by Tamara
　　Soban
The street
　Mozetič, B. Passion; translated by Tamara
　　Soban

Telephone
　Mozetič, B. Passion; translated by Tamara
　　Soban
The unfortunate
　Mozetič, B. Passion; translated by Tamara
　　Soban
Video
　Mozetič, B. Passion; translated by Tamara
　　Soban
Woman
　Mozetič, B. Passion; translated by Tamara
　　Soban
You
　Mozetič, B. Passion; translated by Tamara
　　Soban
Mozina, Andy
The Arch
　The Massachusetts Review v47 no1 p135-52
　　Spr 2006
Overpass
　The Southern Review (Baton Rouge, La.) v45
　　no1 p117-28 Wint 2009
Quality Snacks
　River Styx no76/77 p6-20 2008
Mozzi, Giulio
A Happy Life
　The Literary Review (Madison, N.J.) v49 no1
　　p155-63 Fall 2005
Mphahlele, Ezekiel
Down the quiet street
　Telling tales; edited by Nadine Gordimer
Mr. Aickman's air rifle. Straub, P.
Mr. and Mrs. Rose. Miller, B.
Mr. Barcle's mill. Bierce, A.
Mr. Barton's head case. Kellerman, F.
Mr. Bear. Lansdale, J. R.
Mr. big deal. Doolittle, S.
Mr. Blandings builds his castle. Hodgins, E.
Mr. Bones. Theroux, P.
Mr Botibol. Dahl, R.
Mr. Boy. Kelly, J. P.
Mr. Clunk!. Domecq, B.
Mr. Cornelius Johnson, office-seeker. Dunbar, P.
　L.
Mr. Epstein and the dealer. Waters, D.
Mr. Fuller's revolt. Zelazny, R.
Mr. Furbush. Spofford, H. E. P.
Mr. Gaunt. Langan, J.
Mr. Goober's show. Waldrop, H.
Mr. Gray's folly. Connolly, J.
Mr. Green. Butler, R. O.
Mr. Groby's slippery gift. Dunbar, P. L.
Mr. In-Between. Mosley, W.
Mr. Jim Beckwourth's adventure. Bierce, A.
Mr. Jock Danplank. Hodgson, W. H.
Mr. Lillicrop's shining moment. Kulpa, K.
Mr. Masthead, journalist. Bierce, A.
Mr. Mitochondria. Stollman, A. L.
Mr. Mix-Up. Hawes, L.
Mr. Nobody at all. Beattie, A. and Mathews, H.
Mr. Poo-Poo. Oliver, R.
Mr. Pope's garden. Bishop, E.
Mr. Rat. Thompson, J.
Mr. Raynor the school-teacher. Sillitoe, A.
Mr. Rubblemeaker's Path. Scott-Fleming, S.
Mr. Sender. Crone, M.
Mr. Sigerson. Beagle, P. S.
Mr Simonelli; or, The fairy widower. Clarke, S.
Mr. Sly stops for a cup of joe. Bull, S. E.

Mr Snip Snip Snip. Enright, A.
Mr. Song. Meno, J.
Mr. Swiddler's flip-flap. Bierce, A.
Mr. Tall. Earley, T.
Mr. Vesey Comes to Work. Weintraub, J.
Mr. Woodchuck. Baum, L. F.
Mrs. Big. Cadnum, M.
Mrs Bixby and the colonel's coat. Dahl, R.
Mrs. Cash. Lupica, M.
Mrs. Cassidy's last year. Gordon, M.
Mrs. Cataki. Karystiani, I.
Mrs Covet. Miller, R.
Mrs. Creel. West, D.
Mrs. Dennison's head. Bierce, A.
Mrs. Dutta writes a letter. Divakaruni, C. B.
Mrs. Ethel Menafee and Mr. Bridie Stoltz. Berg, E.
Mrs. Fargo. Luongo, M.
Mrs. Herbinko's birthday party. Monk, B.
Mrs. Hickey. Miller, B.
Mrs Hyde frolics in the eel pit. Bannister, I.
Mrs Mabb. Clarke, S.
Mrs. Maecenas. Burke, K.
Mrs. Manstey's view. Wharton, E.
Mrs. Millennium. Layer, F. E.
Mrs. Porter and the rock. Malouf, D.
Mrs. Proctor Bemis. Connell, E. S.
Mrs. Saunders writes to the world. Schwartz, L. S.
Mrs. Somebody Somebody. Winn, T.
Mrs. Szewczak and the rescue dog. Monk, B.
Mrs. Turner cutting the grass. Shields, C.
Mrs. Zeno's paradox. Klages, E.
MS found in a minidrive. Rucker, R. v. B.
Ms. found in the abandoned time machine. Silverberg, R.
Ms. Midshipwoman Harrington. Weber, D.
Ms. Puddins. Stewart, P.
Mt. Pisgah's Christmas 'possum. Dunbar, P. L.
Mt. Pleasant. Lynn, D. H.
Mu Shiying
  The Shanghai Foxtrot (a Fragment) by Mu Shiying [With an introduction by Sean Macdonald]
    Modernism/Modernity v11 no4 p797-807 N 2004
Muay Thai. Resnick, R.
Mubayi, Suneela
  (tr.) See Shibli, Adania
Mu'bi, Zahra S. al-
  Suq al-Nada
    Oranges in the sun; short stories from the Arabian Gulf; edited and translated by Deborah S. Akers, Abubaker A. Bagader
Much ado. Rosa, J. G.
Much ado about nothing. Emerson, K. L.
Much have I traveled. Brady, C.
MUD. McCall, T.
Mud. With, C.
La **muda** boca/The muted mouth. Hinojosa, F.
Mudder tongue. Evenson, B.
Muddy pond. Tan, M.
Muddy water, turn to wine. Parker, M.
Mudlavia. Stuckey-French, E.
Mudman. Benedict, P.
Mueenuddin, Daniyal
  About a burning girl
    Mueenuddin, D. In other rooms, other wonders

In other rooms, other wonders
  Mueenuddin, D. In other rooms, other wonders
    The New Yorker v84 no39 p64-73 D 1 2008
Lily
  Mueenuddin, D. In other rooms, other wonders
Nawabdin Electrician
  Mueenuddin, D. In other rooms, other wonders
    The New Yorker v83 no25 p72-7 Ag 27 2007
Our lady of Paris
  Mueenuddin, D. In other rooms, other wonders
Provide, provide
  Mueenuddin, D. In other rooms, other wonders
    Granta no104 p79-111 Wint 2008
Saleema
  Mueenuddin, D. In other rooms, other wonders
A spoiled man
  Mueenuddin, D. In other rooms, other wonders
    The New Yorker v84 no28 p74-83 S 15 2008
Mueller, Craig
  The Pope's Nose
    The Literary Review (Madison, N.J.) v49 no3 p32-62 Spr 2006
Mueller, Daniel
  Connected
    Prairie Schooner v81 no4 p118-33 Wint 2007
  The night my brother worked the header
    Playboy's college fiction; a collection of 21 years of contest winners; edited by Alice K. Turner; foreword by Thom Jones
Mueller, Richard
  And the sea shall give up its dead
    The Year's best fantasy and horror: eighteenth annual collection; edited by Ellen Datlow, Kelly Link & Gavin J. Grant
Mueller, W. E.
  Working the Crossword
    The Writer v122 no2 p24-6 F 2009
Muffaz, Afifah
  Calamansi juice
    Bandersnatch; edited by Paul Tremblay and Sean Wallace
Mugger and Mouse Get Married. Agresta, M.
MUGGING
  Hart, E. Blind sided
  Kellerman, F. Small miracles
  Lynn, D. H. Muggings
  Meacham, R. The assignment
  Mordecai, P. Corinthians thirteen thirteen
  Romano, T. Confidences
  Steinberg, S. To sit, unmoving
  Vallorani, N. Pasolini's shadow
The **Mugging.** Maliszewski, P.
Muggings. Lynn, D. H.
Muirhead, Margaret
  An open letter concerning sponsorship
    The Best of Lady Churchill's rosebud wristlet; edited by Kelly Link & Gavin J. Grant; introduction by Dan Chaon
La **mujer** de la gabardina roja/The woman in the red coat. Samperio, G.

Mukherjee, Bharati
Even Macau Girls Get the Blues
New Letters v71 no4 p51-61 2005
The management of grief
The New Granta book of the American short
story; edited and introduced by Richard
Ford
Mukherjee, Srimati
When It Is Green and Not Blue
Feminist Studies v32 no3 p620-31 Fall 2006
Mukherji, Sandip
The Gift
Confrontation no94/95 p73-82 Spr/Summ
2006
Mukhopadhyay, Tito
The broken mirror
Mukhopadhyay, T. The gold of the sunbeams
and other stories; introduction by Soma
Mukhopadhyay
The calendar
Mukhopadhyay, T. The gold of the sunbeams
and other stories; introduction by Soma
Mukhopadhyay
The climb
Mukhopadhyay, T. The gold of the sunbeams
and other stories; introduction by Soma
Mukhopadhyay
The corner shop
Mukhopadhyay, T. The gold of the sunbeams
and other stories; introduction by Soma
Mukhopadhyay
The field
Mukhopadhyay, T. The gold of the sunbeams
and other stories; introduction by Soma
Mukhopadhyay
The gold of the sunbeams
Mukhopadhyay, T. The gold of the sunbeams
and other stories; introduction by Soma
Mukhopadhyay
Grey, apple green, and white
Mukhopadhyay, T. The gold of the sunbeams
and other stories; introduction by Soma
Mukhopadhyay
Impressive people
Mukhopadhyay, T. The gold of the sunbeams
and other stories; introduction by Soma
Mukhopadhyay
Just a smile
Mukhopadhyay, T. The gold of the sunbeams
and other stories; introduction by Soma
Mukhopadhyay
Little grains of dust
Mukhopadhyay, T. The gold of the sunbeams
and other stories; introduction by Soma
Mukhopadhyay
Man at the bus stop
Mukhopadhyay, T. The gold of the sunbeams
and other stories; introduction by Soma
Mukhopadhyay
The showers
Mukhopadhyay, T. The gold of the sunbeams
and other stories; introduction by Soma
Mukhopadhyay
MULATTOES
Bonner, M. O. A sealed pod
Hughes, L. Spanish blood
Nelson, A. We and they
Thompson, E. B. Masks: a story
The **muldoon**. Hirshberg, G.

Mule killers. Peelle, L.
The **mule** rustlers. Lansdale, J. R.
Mules. Brown, E.
Mulholland dive. Connelly, M.
Mull, Helen Faw
Excess baggage
"Tell it to us easy" and other stories; a com-
plete short fiction anthology of African
American women writers in Opportunity
magazine, (1923-1948); edited by Judith
Musser.
Uncle Ben
"Tell it to us easy" and other stories; a com-
plete short fiction anthology of African
American women writers in Opportunity
magazine, (1923-1948); edited by Judith
Musser.
White only: a story of the color line
"Tell it to us easy" and other stories; a com-
plete short fiction anthology of African
American women writers in Opportunity
magazine, (1923-1948); edited by Judith
Musser.
Mullan, Nick
Todd's Dad
The North American Review v290 no2 p41-2
Mr/Ap 2005
Mullan, Pat
Tribunal
Dublin noir; the Celtic tiger vs. the ugly
American; edited by Ken Bruen
Muller, Eddie
The grand inquisitor
A hell of a woman; an anthology of female
noir; edited by Megan Abbott; foreword by
Val McDermid
Kid's last fight
San Francisco noir; edited by Peter Maravelis
Last call
Meeting across the river; stories inspired by
the haunting Bruce Springsteen song; edited
by Jessica Kaye and Richard J. Brewer
Muller, Marcia
Benny's space
Muller, M. Somewhere in the city
Cattails
Muller, M. Somewhere in the city
Cave of ice
Muller, M. Somewhere in the city
The cracks in the sidewalk
Muller, M. Somewhere in the city
The cyaniders
Muller, M. Somewhere in the city
Deceptions
Muller, M. Somewhere in the city
San Francisco noir 2; the classics; edited by
Peter Maravelis.
Dust to dust
Muller, M. Somewhere in the city
Final resting place
Muller, M. Somewhere in the city
Forbidden things
Muller, M. Somewhere in the city
He said . . . she said
Deadly housewives; edited by Christine Mat-
thews
The holes in the system
Muller, M. Somewhere in the city

Munro, Alice—*Continued*
Face
  The New Yorker v84 no27 p58-67 S 8 2008
Fathers
  Munro, A. The view from Castle Rock; stories
Fiction
  Harper's v315 p71-80 Ag 2007
Free radicals
  The Best American mystery stories, 2009; edited and with an introduction by Jeffery Deaver
  The New Yorker v84 no1 p136-43 F 11-18 2008
Half a grapefruit
  Children playing before a statue of Hercules; edited and introduced by David Sedaris
Hired girl
  Munro, A. The view from Castle Rock; stories
Home
  Munro, A. The view from Castle Rock; stories
  The Virginia Quarterly Review v82 no3 p108-28 Summ 2006
Illinois
  Munro, A. The view from Castle Rock; stories
Lying under the apple tree
  Munro, A. The view from Castle Rock; stories
Messenger
  Munro, A. The view from Castle Rock; stories
No advantages
  Munro, A. The view from Castle Rock; stories
Passion
  Munro, A. Runaway; stories
  The O. Henry Prize stories, 2006; edited and with an introduction by Laura Furman; jurors: Kevin Brockmeier, Francine Prose, Colm Toibin
Powers
  Munro, A. Runaway; stories
Runaway
  Munro, A. Runaway; stories
  The Best American short stories, 2004; edited by Lorrie Moore; Katrina Kenison series editor
Silence
  Munro, A. Runaway; stories
  The Best American short stories, 2005; selected from U.S. and Canadian magazines by Michael Chabon with Katrina Kenison; with an introduction by Michael Chabon
Some Women
  The New Yorker v84 no42 p69-77 D 22-29 2008
Soon
  Munro, A. Runaway; stories
The ticket
  Munro, A. The view from Castle Rock; stories
Trespasses
  Munro, A. Runaway; stories
Tricks
  Munro, A. Runaway; stories

The turkey season
  The Ecco book of Christmas stories; edited by Alberto Manguel
The view from Castle Rock
  The Best American short stories, 2006; selected from U.S. and Canadian magazines by Ann Patchett with Katrina Kenison; with an introduction by Ann Patchett
  Munro, A. The view from Castle Rock; stories
  The O. Henry Prize stories 2007; edited and with an introduction by Laura Furman; with essays on the story they admire most by jurors Charles D'Ambrosio, Ursula K. Le Guin, Lily Tuck
  The New Yorker v81 no25 p64-77 Ag 29 2005
Wenlock Edge
  The New Yorker v81 no39 p80-91 D 5 2005
What do you want to know for?
  Munro, A. The view from Castle Rock; stories
  The O. Henry Prize stories 2008; edited and with an introduction by Laura Furman; with essays on the stories they admire most by jurors Chimamanda Ngozi Adiche, David Leavitt, David Means
  The American Scholar v75 no3 p94-105 Summ 2006
The wilds of Morris Township
  Munro, A. The view from Castle Rock; stories
Working for a living
  Munro, A. The view from Castle Rock; stories

The **Mupandawana** dancing champion. Gappah, P.

Murakami, Haruki
Airplane; or, How he talked to himself as if reciting poetry
  Murakami, H. Blind willow, sleeping woman; twenty-four stories; translated from the Japanese by Philip Gabriel and Jay Rubin
Birthday girl
  Murakami, H. Blind willow, sleeping woman; twenty-four stories; translated from the Japanese by Philip Gabriel and Jay Rubin
Blind willow, sleeping woman
  Murakami, H. Blind willow, sleeping woman; twenty-four stories; translated from the Japanese by Philip Gabriel and Jay Rubin
Chance traveler
  Murakami, H. Blind willow, sleeping woman; twenty-four stories; translated from the Japanese by Philip Gabriel and Jay Rubin
  Harper's v311 p78-84 Jl 2005
Crabs
  Murakami, H. Blind willow, sleeping woman; twenty-four stories; translated from the Japanese by Philip Gabriel and Jay Rubin
Dabchick
  Murakami, H. Blind willow, sleeping woman; twenty-four stories; translated from the Japanese by Philip Gabriel and Jay Rubin
Firefly
  Murakami, H. Blind willow, sleeping woman; twenty-four stories; translated from the Japanese by Philip Gabriel and Jay Rubin

MURDER STORIES—*Continued*

Arango, A. Murder, according to my mother-in-law
Archer, J. The alibi
Ardai, C. The good samaritan
Ardai, C. The home front
Arnott, J. Ten lords a-leaping
Arnott, M. Dollface
Aydinoglu, Y. One among us
Ayres, N. J. Rust
Bacigalupi, P. Softer
Baker, K. Running the snake
Baker, K. The cheers like waves
Bangkok, J. Counterfeit love
Banks, L. E. What the devil won't take . . .
Banks, R. Money shot
Banks, R. Lobster night
Barnard, R. Everybody's girl
Barnard, R. The hangman's beautiful daughter
Barnard, R. The path to the shroud
Barr, M. W. Kolchak & the cult murders
Barr, N. GDMFSOB
Barrett, L. Blue vandas
Battles, B. Perfect gentleman
Baxter, S. Fate and the fire-lance
Belrose, J. L. House built of sticks
Bender, A. The case of the salt and pepper shakers
Benford, G. Dark heaven
Benjamin, C. L. The last supper
Bennett, A. Murder!
Berkeley, A. Dark journey
Berliner, J. The road to Rachel
Bierce, A. An adventure at Brownville
Bierce, A. Authenticating a ghost
Bierce, A. "By her own hand"
Bierce, A. The haunted valley
Bierce, A. An imperfect conflagration
Bierce, A. The moonlit road
Bierce, A. A mournful property
Bierce, A. The thing at Nolan
Bilal, M. The stepson
Billingham, M. Stroke of luck
Bishop, T. The fragile commandment
Black, M. A. Articulation of murder
Blackwell, K. What we do for love
Block, L. Bargain in blood
Block, L. Bride of violence
Block, L. The burning fury
Block, L. The dope
Block, L. Frozen stiff
Block, L. Hate goes courting
Block, L. I don't fool around
Block, L. If you can't stand the heat
Block, L. Lie back and enjoy it
Block, L. Look death in the eye
Block, L. One night of death
Block, L. Pseudo identity
Block, L. Ride a white horse
Block, L. A shroud for the damned
Block, L. Terrible Tommy Terhune
Bolaño, R. Phone calls
Born, J. O. The drought
Born, J. O. Tourist trade
Bowes, R. Dust devil on a quiet street
Bowker, D. Johnny Seven
Bradbury, R. The Finnegan
Bradbury, R. The fruit at the bottom of the bowl
Bradbury, R. The illustrated man

Bradbury, R. Ma Perkins comes to stay
Bradbury, R. The murder
Bradbury, R. The smiling people
Brennan, A. Killing justice
Brett, S. Cain was innocent
Breuer, M. J. On board the martian liner
British horror weekend
Brod, D. C. My heroes have always been short-stops
Brown, E. The touch of angels
Brown, F. The wench is dead
Browne, R. G. Bottom deal
Bruen, K. Nora B.
Bruen, K. Spittin iron
Buckell, T. S. The people's machine
Budavari, S. Medium risk
Bull, W. Heidegger's cat
Bunin, I. A. Light breathing
Burke, T. The hands of Mr. Ottermole
Busch, F. The rescue mission
Cadnum, M. Hungry
Cadnum, M. Or be to not
Cain, J. M. Pastorale
Campbell, F. Murder is academic
Carcaterra, L. A thousand miles from nowhere
Carl, L. S. Way down in Egypt's land
Carrington, T. Last stop, Ditmars
Carroll, W. J. Height advantage
Carron, H. B. A favor for the mayor
Castaneda, R. Coyote hunt
Catt, D. Evil comes
Cavell, B. Evolution
Cetin, I. The bloody horn
Chabon, M. The god of dark laughter
Chekhov, A. P. Assignment
Chekhov, A. P. A crime: a double murder case
Chekhov, A. P. Drama
Chekhov, A. P. The drama at the hunt
Chekhov, A. P. Murder (abridged)
Cheng, T. Gold mountain
Chesnutt, C. W. The sheriff's children
Child, L. Safe enough
Christie, A. Philomel cottage
Coake, C. All through the house
Coake, C. His mission
Coben, H. Entrapped
Cody, L. In those days
Cody, L. Reconstruction
Cody, L. Turning it round
Cody, L. Walking blues
Cody, L. Woke up this morning
Coelen, I. The best time for planting
Coleman, R. F. Pearls
Coleman, R. F. Portrait of the killer as a young man
Collins, M. A. and Clemens, M. V. The high life: a heartland homicide story
Collins, W. The diary of Ann Rodway
Coloane, F. The empty bottle [variant title: Bottle of cana]
Connelly, M. Coroner's inquest
Connelly, M. Mulholland dive
Connolly, J. Mr. Gray's folly
Cooper, D. Graduate seminar
Cooper, D. The guro artists
Cooper, D. Knife/Tape/Rope
Correa, A. Olúo
Costa, S. Black heart and cabin girl
Coward, M. Offenders

MURDER STORIES—*Continued*

Lippman, L. A good **** spoiled [variant title: A good fuck spoiled]

Lippman, L. Pony girl

Lippman, L. Scratch a woman

Lippman, L. What he needed

Lispector, C. The body

Lobato, J. B. M. The funnyman who repented

Lordon, R. Like a sore thumb

Lott, B. Rose

Lovesey, P. The field

Lovesey, P. Needle match

Lumley, B. For the dead travel slowly

Lupoff, R. A. The Golden Saint meets the Scorpion Queen

Lupoff, R. A. Streamliner

Lutz, J. The laundry room

Lutz, J. Mitt's murder

Lutz, J. Nighthawks

Machado, A. The death of the standard-bearer

Machado de Assis. The fortune-teller

Machado de Assis. The nurse

Macker, R. A deadly joke

MacLaverty, B. The wedding ring

MacLeod, C. Lady Patterly's lover

Magee, K. Vertical mile

Maḥfūz, N. The seventh heaven

Maleeny, T. Suspension of disbelief

Maleeny, T. Till death do us part

Malone, M. Red clay

Malone, M. White trash noir

Maloney, D. The best laid plans

Malouf, D. Blacksoil country

Malouf, D. Lone Pine

Malzberg, B. N. The interceptor

Mandel, S. B. Blind man blue

Manickchand, R. A. Dougla

Marston, E. The St. Valentine's Day Massacre

Martinez, M. The mother

Marz, M. Miscast

Massie, E. The next-door collector

Matheson, R. Button, button

Matheson, R. The conqueror

Matheson, R. The near departed

Matthews, C. For benefit of Mr. Means

McBain, E. Accident report

McBain, E. Barking at butterflies

McBain, E. Bedbug

McBain, E. Chinese puzzle

McBain, E. Death flight [variant title: Ticket to death]

McBain, E. Downpour [variant title: Murder on the Keys]

McBain, E. Dummy [variant title: The big scream]

McBain, E. Eyewitness

McBain, E. Improvisation

McBain, E. Kid kill

McBain, E. Still life

McDermid, V. The consolation blonde

McDermid, V. The wagon mound

McDevitt, J. The adventure of the southsea trunk

McDonald, C. The last interview

McInerney, J. Con doctor

McLean, R. D. Pedro Paul

McMahan, R. The cold, hard truth

McMullen, S. The constant past

McNeely, T. H. Sheep

Means, D. Carnie

Means, D. The spot

Means, D. A visit from Jesus

Medina, P. Bennie Rojas and the rough riders

Melko, P. Death of the egg king

Meloy, M. The girlfriend

Meyers, A. It's too late, baby

Meyers, K. Rodney Valen's second life

Meyers, M. The organ grinder

Miles, K. Old bag dad

Millhiser, M. Had he but known

Mokoso, N. God of meme

Monson, A. Forecast

Moorcock, M. The case of the Nazi canary

Moore, D. Bumping uglies

Mootoo, S. The funeral party

Mordecai, P. Shining waters

Morrell, D. Continental grip

Morrow, B. The hoarder

Mortimer, J. Rumpole and the Christmas break

Mosley, W. Mr. In-Between

Mosley, W. The picket

Motz, J. With a little help from your friends

Mullan, P. Tribunal

Muller, M. He said . . . she said

Munro, A. Child's play

Murphy, D. R. Sounds of silence

Murphy, Y. The only light to see by

Myers, A. Murder by ghost

Myers, A. Murder, the missing heir and the boiled egg

Nelsen, G. The one

Nelson, K. Public trouble

Nelson, P. Burying Mr. Henry

Nelson, R. F. Refiner's fire

Neri, K. Hocus-pocus on Friday the 13th

Nevins, F. M., Jr. A nightcap of Hemlock

Nolan, J. Open mike

Nolan, J. Memento mori

Nolan, W. F. In real life

Nolan, W. F. Killing Charlie

Nolan, W. F. Poetic justice

Nolan, W. F. Silk and fire

Noll, I. Fisherman's friend

Nutman, P. The misadventure of Eat Man and Little Boy, or, How I made a monster

Oates, J. C. Angel of wrath

Oates, J. C. Doll: a romance of the Mississippi

Oates, J. C. The fish factory

Oates, J. C. The gathering squall

Oates, J. C. Heat

Oates, J. C. Hi! Howya doin!

Oates, J. C. Honor code

Oates, J. C. Hunger

Oates, J. C. Last days

Oates, J. C. Manslaughter

Oates, J. C. Meadowlands

Oates, J. C. Strip poker

Oates, J. C. Tell me you forgive me?

Oates, J. C. The twins: a mystery

Oates, J. C. Valentine, July heat wave

Oates, J. C. Will you always love me?

Oates, N. The empty house

Obejas, A. Zenzizenzic

O'Brien, D. Honesty above all else

O'Brien, J. The tik

Ochsner, G. When the dark is light enough

Ockert, J. Deviated septum

Orozco, D. Officers weep

MURDER STORIES—*Continued*

MURDER STORIES—*Continued*

Stirling, S. M. A murder in Eddsford

Straley, J. Weight of the world

Streukens, N. Emerald green

Sussex, L. Robots & Zombies, Inc.

Sweazy, L. D. The promotion

Swierczynski, D. Death runs faster

Swierczynski, D. The replacement

Sykes, J. Closer to the flame

Talley, M. Driven to distraction

Talley, M. The queen is dead, long live the queen

Talley, M. Safety first

Talley, M. Too many cooks

Taylor, E. A pinch of snuff

Tel, J. Bola de la fortuna

Templeton, P. Eight guns over a dead girl

Thomson, M. F. Occam's Razor

Tinker, H. Entanglement

Toomey, M. Ten dimes

Trevor, W. Bravado

Trezise, R. The brake fluid at Gina's

Tsutsui, Y. The very edge of happiness

Turnbull, P. Max Winner's shadow

Turow, S. Loyalty

Twelve, O. Fluff

Uchida, H. The lieutenant's killer

Valley, R. Shadows from the screen

Varley, John. The Bellman

Vaz, K. The mandarin question

Vermeulen, J. The corpse that lost its head

Vernon, G. Mattie in the middle

Viets, E. Red meat

Vollmer, M. Bodies

Vonnegut, K. Just you and me, Sammy

Waldrop, H. Flatfeet!

Walker, P. Such a lucky, pretty girl

Walsh, T. Double check

Watson, B. Water dog God: a ghost story

Weinberg, R. Genius Loci

Welty, E. Where is the voice coming from?

Wentworth, K. D. Cat call

Westlake, D. E. Never shake a family tree

Westwood, K. Nightship

Wheat, C. The only good judge

White, D. Righteous son

White, L. T. Chosen to die

Whiteley, A. Geoffrey says

Whitfield, R. About kid Deth

Wignall, K. The death of Jeffers

Williams, C. Edge

Williams, J. R. Rose

Williams, T. Something about Teddy

Wilson, L. Best eaten cold

Winchell, P. Kindly omit flowers

With, C. Drive Uncle Randy

Wohlforth, T. Juanita

Wolfe, G. Redbeard

Woodrell, D. Uncle

Woods, P. L. I'll be doggone

Woolrich, C. 3 kills for 1

Woolrich, C. Angel face [variant title: Murder in wax]

Woolrich, C. The case of the killer-diller

Woolrich, C. Death in the Yoshiwara

Woolrich, C. Detective William Brown

Woolrich, C. The dilemma of the dead lady

Woolrich, C. Endicott's girl

Woolrich, C. The fatal footlights

Woolrich, C. Rear window [variant title: It had to be murder]

Woolrich, C. Two murders, one crime

Woolrich, C. You bet your life

Wright, R. The man who killed a shadow

Yeaman, R. N. A world more real

Yemni, S. Burn and go

Young, D. Housework

Zafiro, F. Dead even

Zelazny, R. Final dining

Zelazny, R. Home is the hangman

Ziyalan, M. Black palace

Murder, the missing heir and the boiled egg. Myers, A.

MURDER TRIALS *See* Trials

The **murderer**. Schnitzler, A.

The **murderer,** the pony, and Miss Brown to you. Richards, S. S.

MURDERERS

See also Murder stories

Ashwin, K. Something out of the ordinary

Barnes, H. L. A pulling thing

Barnes, H. L. Punishment

Berniker, S. J. Aqua Velva Smitty

Bierce, A. The hypnotist

Bierce, A. My favorite murder

Bisson, T. The old rugged cross

Block, L. Rude awakening

Bradbury, R. At midnight, in the month of June

Breen, J. L. Serial killer

Bukoski, A. Twelve below zero

Burgin, R. The urn

Cho, C. Land of exile

Cody, L. K. K.

Cohen, P. Designer justice

Coleman, R. F. Accidentally, like a Martyr

Cooper, D. The hostage drama

Cooper, D. Jerk

Deaver, J. Interrogation

Depestre, Y. Abikú

Dufresne, J. Based on a true story

Dufresne, J. The timing of unfelt smiles

Fisher, S. You'll always remember me

Formetta, C. D. Last summer together

Franceschini, E. Roman holidays

Fuentes, C. Mater Dolorosa

Gaiman, N. Keepsakes and treasures

Gerber, M. J. Night stalker

Glatt, L. What Milton heard

Goldman, J. Knife fight

Gomez, D. R. Bitter sorrows

Gorman, E. Masque

Irby, L. God don't like ugly

Johnson, G. Who, what, when, where

Kelly, R. Breakfast serial

Kessel, J. Every angel is terrifying

Kremer, H. Gelatin

L'Amour, L. Monument Rock

Lansdale, J. R. Incident on and off a mountain road

Lansdale, J. R. The shadows, kith and kin

Leonard, E. Three-ten to Yuma

Lescroart, J. T. A friendly little game

Lippman, L. ARM and the woman

Ludwigsen, W. A good psycho is hard to find

Marston, E. Corpus Christi

Masdon, J. Jack's mantle

Matesis, P. Murder's singular taste

Mazzucato, F. Tiburtina noir blues

Murphy, Yannick—*Continued*

In a bear's eye

The O. Henry Prize stories 2007; edited and with an introduction by Laura Furman; with essays on the story they admire most by jurors Charles D'Ambrosio, Ursula K. Le Guin, Lily Tuck

Murphy, Y. In a bear's eye: stories

Into the arms of the man on the moon

Murphy, Y. In a bear's eye: stories

Is this a land, a continent, can it be conquered?

Murphy, Y. In a bear's eye: stories

Jesus of the snow

Murphy, Y. In a bear's eye: stories

Kato and the Indians from here

Murphy, Y. In a bear's eye: stories

Lake Mohican

Murphy, Y. In a bear's eye: stories

Legacies

Murphy, Y. In a bear's eye: stories

Lester

Murphy, Y. In a bear's eye: stories

The lost breed

Murphy, Y. In a bear's eye: stories

The only light to see by

Murphy, Y. In a bear's eye: stories

Our underwater mother

Murphy, Y. In a bear's eye: stories

Pan, pan, pan

Murphy, Y. In a bear's eye: stories

Ready in the night

Murphy, Y. In a bear's eye: stories

Real enough

Murphy, Y. In a bear's eye: stories

Story of the spirit

Murphy, Y. In a bear's eye: stories

The Un-son

TriQuarterly no133 p269-79 2009

Walls

Murphy, Y. In a bear's eye: stories

Whitely on the tips

Murphy, Y. In a bear's eye: stories

The woman in the leopard-spotted robe

Murphy, Y. In a bear's eye: stories

Murr, Muhammad al-

An idyllic world

Oranges in the sun; short stories from the Arabian Gulf; edited and translated by Deborah S. Akers, Abubaker A. Bagader

Murray, Alice I.

The simple one

"Tell it to us easy" and other stories; a complete short fiction anthology of African American women writers in Opportunity magazine, (1923-1948); edited by Judith Musser.

Murray, Annie

SeaSky

Her Majesty; 21 stories by women; edited by Jackie Gay and Emma Hargrave

The tonsil machine

Going the distance; edited by Alan Beard

Murray, Peter, 1952-

See also Hautman, Pctc, 1952-

Murray, Sabina

Balboa

Southwest Review v92 no1 p132-7 2007

Murray, Sheila

Going Home

Dalhousie Review v88 no1 p69-82 Spr 2008

Murray, Yxta Maya

The conquest [excerpt]

California uncovered; stories for the 21st century; edited by Chitra Banerjee Divakaruni, William E. Justice, and James Quay

Muscles. Clayton, J. J.

Muse. Gorman, E.

Muse in overalls. Buckler, E.

Muse of fire. Simmons, D.

A **muse** with burning eyes. Resnick, M. and Faw, B.

The **museum** of Dr. Moses. Oates, J. C.

The **Museum** of Lost and Found. Pokwatka, A.

The **museum** of unconditional surrender [excerpt] Ugrešic, D.

The **museum** of whatnot. Wilson, K.

The **Museum** of Wooden Architecture. Chapman, J. D.

A **museum** piece. Zelazny, R.

MUSEUMS

See also Waxworks

Allende, I. The Guggenheim lovers

Bear, E. Orm the beautiful

Hadley, T. The card trick

Hill, J. Last breath

Jurado, A. Saying goodbye through twenty-five centuries

Millhauser, S. Here at the Historical Society

Monette, S. Draco campestris

Smith, R. T. Little Sorrel

Williams, C. Perhaps the last

Wilson, K. The museum of whatnot

The **mushroom** Duchess. Roggie, D.

The **mushroom** moon. Calvino, I.

MUSHROOMS

Roggie, D. The mushroom Duchess

Mushrooms. Lehane, D.

Mushrooms. Maxwell, W.

Mushrooms of Freedom. Kurkov, A.

MUSIC

See also Popular music

Baraka, I. A. Rhythm travel

Brockmeier, K. A fable ending in the sound of a thousand parakeets

Frost, G. Divertimento

Gass, W. H. A little history of modern music

Harrison, J. The accompanist

Martel, Y. The time I heard The Private Donald J. Rankin string concerto with one discordant violin, by John Morton

Naslund, S. J. The perfecting of the Chopin Valse no. 14 in E Minor

Orullian, P. Beats of seven

Palmer, K. Virtuoso mio

Rose, A. The musical illusionist

Silverberg, R. The Macauley circuit

Stern, D. Fabrikant's way

Ts'an-hsüeh. Mosquitoes and mountain ballads

MUSIC, POPULAR *See* Popular music

Music at Annahullion. McCabe, E.

Music from earth. Tea, M.

MUSIC HALL ENTERTAINERS *See* Entertainers

MUSIC HALLS (VARIETY THEATERS, CABARETS, ETC.)

See also Vaudeville

MUSIC LESSONS

McCafferty, J. Guiding light
McLean, S. Music lessons
McMullin, J. Mouse
Music lessons. Lain, D.
Music lessons. McLean, S.
The **music** of angels. Pelletier, C.
The **music** of Erich Zann. Lovecraft, H. P.

MUSIC TEACHERS

Bakken, K. N. The body/love problem
Bellows, N. First four measures
Burke, K. Olympians
Crouse, T. Sphinxes
Gordon, M. Eleanor's music
Kalotay, D. Serenade
Lasdun, J. The half sister
McCuaig, A. Across the universe
McGraw, E. One for my baby
McIlvoy, K. Make it sound like a train
Moss, B. K. The palm tree of Dilys Cathcart
Ohlin, A. Simple exercises for the beginning student
Pande, M. A kind of love story
Treat, J. Violin lessons
Veríssimo, É. The house of the melancholy angel
The **music** you never hear. Dalton, Q.
The **musical** genius of Moscow, Kansas. Averill, T. F.
The **musical** illusionist. Rose, A.

MUSICAL INSTRUMENTS

Gaiman, N. Good boys deserve favors
Haldeman, J. W. Diminished chord
Levi, J. The scrimshaw violin
A **musical** interlude. Charnas, S. M.

MUSICALS

Allen, W. Sing, you sacher tortes

MUSICIANS

See also Cellists; Conductors (Music); Drummers; Flutists; Guitarists; Harpists; Organists; Pianists; Saxophonists; Trumpet players; Violinists
Ali, M. N. The true Aryan
Arjouni, J. Self-defense
Boudinot, R. The flautist
Brady, C. Looking for a female tenet
Burke, J. L. Jesus out to sea
Burke, J. L. The night Johnny Ace died
Coake, C. In the event
Cody, L. Walking blues
Cody, L. Woke up this morning
Coleman, W. Jazz at twelve
Dunbar, P. L. How George Johnson "won out"
Faber, M. Beyond pain
Gordimer, N. Alternative endings: the second sense
Gorman, E. Riff
Harvey, J. Drummer unknown
Hernández, F. The crocodile
Lewis, W. H. Rossonian days
Lowry, M. The forest path to the spring
Lupoff, R. A. The whisperers
Machado de Assis. Wedding song
Moon, E. Hand to hand
Moon, E. New world symphony
Murakami, H. Tony Takitani
Olafsson, O. October
Rivera-Valdés, S. The eighth fold
Robinson, P. The magic of your touch

Royle, N. Iceland
Rubin, J. Little stones, little pistols, little clash
Serros, M. Worship
Shawl, N. But she's only a dream
Shields, C. Chemistry
Shrayer-Petrov, D. Jonah and Sarah
Smith, R. T. Uke Rivers delivers
Stern, D. The Altman sonata
Stern, D. The condom and the clarinet
Stern, D. A little street music
Strom, D. Walruses
Tóibín, C. A song
Woolson, C. F. The South Devil
Zumas, L. Thieves and mapmakers

Musil, Robert
Tonka
My mistress's sparrow is dead; great love stories, from Chekhov to Munro; edited by Jeffrey Eugenides

MUSLIM WOMEN

Badr, L. Other cities
Dabbagh, S. Me (the bitch) and Bustanji
Gee, M. The good hope
Habayeb, H. A thread snaps
Jarrar, R. Barefoot bridge
Moulessehoul, M. The wicked tongue
Taha, R. A single metre
Takrouri, B. Tales from the azzinar quarter, 1984-1987

MUSLIMS

See also Islam; Muslim women
Adichie, C. N. A private experience
Apple, M. Indian giver
Berrada, Mohammed. A life in detail
Fowler, C. The threads
Gee, M. What was important
Liebrecht, S. Munich
Lutz, J. All quiet
Raboteau, E. Kavita through glass
Ṣālih, a.- A handful of dates
Taha, M. A. The birth
Taha, M. A. Family honor
Taha, M. A. Loose hair
Taha, M. A. Satan
Toer, P. A. Circumcision
Toer, P. A. The rewards of marriage
India
Adiga, A. The railway station
Sundaresan, I. Fire
Italy
Dekhis, A. "Salvation"
Mussels in the flower vase. Skabardonis, Y.
Mustecaplioglu, Baris
An extra body
Istanbul noir; edited by Mustafa Ziyalan & Amy Spangler; translated by Amy Spangler & Mustafa Ziyalan.
The **mutant** season. Silverberg, R.

MUTATION (BIOLOGY)

See also Albinos
Anderson, P. Logic
Anderson, P. The sharing of flesh
Anderson, P. Tomorrow's children
Dooling, R. Roe #5
Finlay, C. C. A game of chicken
Huberath, M. S. "Yoo retoont, sneogg. Ay noo."
Kelly, R. The cerebral passion
Roberts, A. The question of [?query term]
Silverberg, R. The mutant season

MUTATION (BIOLOGY)—*Continued*

Silverberg, R. This is the road
Van Pelt, J. The last of the o-forms
Wolfe, G. Seven American nights

Mute. King, S.

Mute. Matheson, R.

Mute. Wolfe, G.

MUTE PERSONS

Akins, E. Her book
Brockmeier, K. A fable ending in the sound of a thousand parakeets
Helprin, M. Passchendaele
LaValle, V. The angel of loneliness
McBain, E. Dummy [variant title: The big scream]
Reid, G. Soon we will be blind
Russell, K. Accident brief, occurrence # 00/422
Van Booy, S. Distant ships
The **mute** witness Bendel-Simso, M. M., ed. Early American detective stories; an anthology; edited by LeRoy Lad Panek and Mary M. Bendel-Simso.

MUTILATION

Barrett, M. Grip
Butler, R. O. Severance
Harstad, J. Vietnam. Thursday
Rhodes, D. Glass eyes
Sprinkle, P. For the common good

MUTINY

Hodgson, W. H. The getting even of Tommy Dodd
Hodgson, W. H. The 'prentices' mutiny
Lake, J. To raise a mutiny betwixt yourselves

Mutiny. Burke, K. P.

Muttsy. Hurston, Z. N.

Muza. Bunin, I. A.

Muzungu. Serpell, N.

My adventures with the SPCA. Di Filippo, P.

My Aeschylus. Shepard, J.

My amendment. Saunders, G.

My aunt from twelfth street. Weidman, J.

My aunt Gold Teeth. Naipaul, V. S.

My baby . . . West, D.

My best friend. Castillon, C.

My best friend. Keret, E.

My black Rachmaninoff. Burgin, R.

My bones here are waiting for yours. Vaz, K.

My brain's too tired to think. Coleman, W.

My Brother. Schaefer, W. D.

My brother. Ts'an-hsüeh

My brother Eli. Epstein, J.

My brother in the basement. McCann, R.

My brother, mine. Chattin, J.

My brother's keeper. Hale, D. J.

My catechism. Gifford, B.

My chaos theory. Watkins, S.

My Cousin Coyote, as Told by Dog. Addison, M.

My cousin Rachel's uncle Murray. Isaacs, S.

My cousin-sister Rambanai. Gappah, P.

My credentials. Bierce, A.

My dad's not a monster, mom. Castillon, C.

My daughter's eyes. Báez, A.

My day with Judy. D'Allesandro, S.

My dear Mrs. Wurtelbach. Burke, K.

My dear Shura. See Tolstaia, T. Sweet Shura

My decorous pornography. Greenman, B.

My Doppelganger's Arms. Buckingham, P.

My ex-classmates' Kids. Thorne, M.

My Ex-Husband. Rawlins, P.

My ex, the moral philosopher. Stern, R. G.

My Father in All Seasons. Zakrewsky, J.

My father was blue. Suescun, N.

My father's friends. Maxwell, W.

My Father's Land. Lim, C.-W.

My father's mask. Hill, J.

My father's tears. Updike, J.

My favorite murder. Bierce, A.

My First Job after the War. Kistler, D.

My first wedding. Blackwell, K.

My first world. Zebrowski, G.

My flamboyant grandson. Saunders, G.

My Flame. Tuck, L.

My Fourth. Cotsirilos, T.

My friend Flicka. O'Hara, M.

My friend goo. Jackson, S.

My friend Joseph. Judah, S.

My Friend Petey. Elliott, S.

My friend Zarathustra. Sallis, J.

My general. Emshwiller, C.

My girlfriend Bobbi. Granados, C.

My girlfriend's naked. Keret, E.

My grandfather's river. Cooper, B.

My guardian and I. James, H.

My Heart. Ward, D.

My heart is a snake farm. Gurganus, A.

My Heart Is with You in This Sad Time. Mirabella, A.

My heroes have always been shortstops. Brod, D. C.

My high, squeaky voice. Pendarvis, J.

My house shall be called the house of prayer. Hodgson, W. H.

My interview with the Avenger. Bissell, T.

My lady Green Sleeves. Pohl, F.

My lady love, my dove. Dahl, R.

My lady of the diodes. Zelazny, R.

My last days as me. Yu, C.

My last Duchess. Atwood, M.

My last Indian. Hawes, L.

My life. Gaiman, N.

My life is awesome! and great!. Crane, E.

My life is good. Edelman, S.

My little brother is a monster. Coville, B.

My little tyrant heart. Hernandez, L.

My Lord you. Salter, J.

My lost darling. James, H.

My Love and My Sugarcane. Quintana Veiga, J. A.

My man came by the crib the other day . . . Baraka, I. A.

My mom from Budapest. Treat, J.

My morning glory. Marusek, D.

My most memorable encounter. O'Doherty, S.

My mother dancing. Kress, N.

My mother never dies. Castillon, C.

My mother the rock star. Richter, S.

My Mother the Writer. Fernández de Jaun, A.

My mother's clothes: the school of beauty and shame. McCann, R.

My mother's lover. Stevens, J. D.

My Mother's War. Pham, T. M.

My muse. Bierce, A.

My name. Reinhorn, H.

My name is Helen. Woronov, M.

My name is Lubbert Das, 1765. Menger-Anderson, K.

My name was Singer. Biller, M.

My nap. Tognazzini, A.

MYSTERY AND DETECTIVE STORIES—

France—*Continued*

Lowndes, B. Popeau intervenes
M'Cabe, J. D. The telltale eye
Morson, I. The moving-picture mystery
O'Shaughnessy, P. Gertrude Stein solves a mystery
Poe, E. A. The purloined letter
Vidocq; or, The charcoal burner of France
Written in blood

Germany

Rippen, C. Barefoot
Rosavo, N. The wounded hand
Rykena, S. Cold-blooded
Schuster, F. German summer

Haiti

Thomas, E. The adventure of voodoo moon

India

Keating, H. R. F. Majumdar uncle

Ireland

Jeffers, H. P. The adventure of the blarney stone
Orczy, E., Baroness. The Dublin mystery
Tremayne, P. The astrologer who predicted his own murder
Tremayne, P. The banshee
Tremayne, P. The blemish
Tremayne, P. Corpse on a holy day
Tremayne, P. Cry "wolf!"
Tremayne, P. Dark moon rising
Tremayne, P. Death of an icon
Tremayne, P. Does God obey his own law?: A Sister Fidelma story
Tremayne, P. The fosterer
Tremayne, P. The heir-apparent
Tremayne, P. Like a dog returning . . .
Tremayne, P. The lost eagle
Tremayne, P. Sanctuary!
Tremayne, P. Scattered thorns
Tremayne, P. Whispers of the dead
Tremayne, P. Who stole the fish?

Italy

Jeffers, H. P. The accidental murderess
Thomas, D. S. The case of the Portuguese sonnets

Japan

Mitsuhara, Y. Eighteenth summer
Norizuki, R. An urban legend puzzle

Netherlands

Baantjer. DeKok and the hammer blow

Norway

Scheen, K. Moonglow

Rome

Rowe, R. Caveat emptor

Russia

Akunin, B. Table talk, 1882
Chekhov, A. P. The Swedish match
The twisted ring

Scotland

Aird, C. Cold comfort
Aird, C. Dead letters
Aird, C. Handsel Monday
Knight, A. Faro and the bogus inspector
Rankin, I. Tell me who to kill

United States

Abbott, J. Do unto others [excerpt]
After a clew
Albert, S. W. Bloom where you're planted
Albert, S. W. A deadly chocolate valentine
Albert, S. W. Death of a Rose Rustler

Albert, S. W. Ivy's wild, wonderful weeds
Albert, S. W. The knat who became a hero
Albert, S. W. Mustard madness
Albert, S. W. The pennyroyal plot
Albert, S. W. The Rosemary caper
Albert, S. W. Rosemary remembered [excerpt]
Albert, S. W. An unthymely death
Albert, S. W. A violet death
Allen, W. How deadly your taste buds, my sweet
Allen, W. Pinchuck's law
Allison, H. Corollary
Anderson, L. Black Legion
Arnold, G. "C.S.A."
Ayres, N. J. Black Zak and the heart attack
Barr, N. Track of the cat [excerpt]
Barreaux, A. Sally the sleuth
Bland, E. T. The canasta club
Block, L. By dawn's early light
Block, L. A moment of wrong thinking
Block, L. The naked and the deadly
Block, L. Stag party girl
Block, L. Twin call girls
Blown upon: or, The sagacious reporter
Booth, C. G. Stag party
Borthwick, J. S. The case of the hooked-billed kites [excerpt]
Boyd, P. Hot enough to kill [excerpt]
Breen, J. L. The adventure of the missing three quarters
Breen, J. L. All-star team
Breen, J. L. The Babe Ruth murder case
Breen, J. L. The body in the bullpen
Breen, J. L. Designated murderer
Breen, J. L. Diamond Dick
Breen, J. L. Fall of a hero
Breen, J. L. Horsehide sleuth
Breen, J. L. Insider trading
Breen, J. L. Instant replay
Breen, J. L. Kill the umpire
Breen, J. L. Malice at the mike
Breen, J. L. The Mother's-Day doubleheader
Breen, J. L. The number 12 jinx
Breen, J. L. Old-timers' game
Breen, J. L. Streak to death
Breen, J. L. Throw out the first ax
Burke, J. Lost and found
Cain, P. One, two, three
Carter, N. Nick Carter, detective
Chambers, W. The duchess pulls a fast one
Chandler, R. Finger man
Chandler, R. Killer in the rain
Chandler, R. Red wind
Chercover, S. The non compos mentis blues
Chercover, S. One serving of bad luck
Clubnose
Cohen, P. Recalled to life
Collins, M. A. Scrap
Collins, M. A. That kind of nag
Collins, M. A. and Clemens, M. V. Murderlized
Connelly, M. Cielo Azul
Connelly, M. Father's day
Connelly, M. One–dollar jackpot
Connelly, M. Suicide run
Cooper, S. R. Funny as a dead relative [excerpt]
The costly kiss: a New York detective experience
Crider, B. The adventure of the White City
Crider, B. The man on the cross

MYSTERY AND DETECTIVE STORIES—

United States—*Continued*

Crider, B. Winning can be murder [excerpt]

Crumley, J. Bordersnakes [excerpt]

Dain, C. Dreams of Jeannie

D'Amato, B. The lower wacker Hilton

Davis, N. The price of a dime

DeAndrea, W. L. Snowy reception

Deaver, J. Locard's principle

The detective

The detective from Baltimore

The detective story

A detective's story

A detective's story [2]

Dold, G. Bay of sorrows [excerpt]

Douglas, C. N. Bogieman

Douglas, C. N. Junior partner in crime

DuBois, B. Country manners

Dymmoch, M. A. A shade of blue

Elrod, P. N. Grave-robbed

Elrod, P. N. Her mother's daughter

Estleman, L. D. The adventure of the coughing
    dentist

Estleman, L. D. Kill the cat

Estleman, L. D. The profane angel

Faherty, T. Closing credits

Faye, L. The case of Colonel Warburton's mad-
    ness

The first case

Freeman, M. E. W. and Chamberlin, J. E. The
    long arm

Friedman, K. Armadillos and old lace [excerpt]

Gardner, E. S. The cat-woman

Garrett, P. The knotted handkerchief

The girl detective

Goodis, D. The case of the laughing queen

Goodis, D. Man without a tongue

Grafton, S. A poison that leaves no trace

The Gramercy Park mystery

Greer, R. O. Oprah's song

Grissom, K. Drowned man's key [excerpt]

Guyot, P. Barry of Hollywood

Hall, P. Deal me in

Hammett, D. The creeping Siamese

Hammett, D. The girl with the silver eyes

Hammett, D. Laughing masks

Hammett, D. The scorched face

Hammett, D. The Thin Man and the Flack

Hart, C. G. Death on the river walk [excerpt]

Healy, J. F. Aftermath

Healy, J. F. I/M-print: a Tess Cassidy short sto-
    ry

Healy, J. F. A matter of honor

Healy, J. F. Prayers for the dying

Herndon, N. Time bombs [excerpt]

Herron, D. Knives in the dark

Hillerman, T. Chee's witch

The hob-nailed shoes

Hockensmith, S. Excerpts from an unpublished
    memoir found in the basement of the home
    for retired actors

Hockensmith, S. Gustav Amlingmeyer, Holmes
    of the range

Hopkins, P. E. Talma Gordon

Howard, C. C. An old offender

Kaminsky, S. M. Evangeline

Kellerman, F. Bull's-eye

Kellerman, F. Discards

Kellerman, F. The garden of Eden

Kellerman, F. Open house

Kellerman, F. A woman of mystery

Konrath, J. A. Overproof

Kuhlken, K. Too sweet

Lansdale, J. R. The two-bear mambo [excerpt]

The left-handed thief

Lindsey, D. L. Heat from another sun [excerpt]

Linscott, G. The case of Colonel Crockett's vio-
    lin

Lippman, L. The accidental detective

Lippman, L. Ropa Vieja

Lippman, L. The shoeshine man's regrets

Lochte, D. Devil dog

Lutz, J. Second story sunlight

Macdonald, R. Gone girl

MacLean, M. Little sins

Martin, A. Death of a healing woman [excerpt]

Matthews, B. The twinkling of an eye

M'Cabe, J. D. Seventy miles an hour

McBain, E. Good and dead

McBain, E. Kiss me, Dudley

McCandless, D. B. The corpse in the crystal

McCandless, D. B. He got what he asked for

McCoy, H. Frost rides alone

McInerny, R. M. Fear and trembling: a Father
    Dowling story

McNab, C. Animal act

Meredith, D. R. The sheriff and the Panhandle
    murders [excerpt]

Millett, L. The brewer's son

Mosley, W. Gone fishin' [excerpt]

Mosley, W. Karma

Muller, M. Benny's space

Muller, M. Deceptions

Muller, M. Final resting place

Muller, M. The holes in the system

Muller, M. The lost coast

Muller, M. The place that time forgot

Muller, M. Season of sharing

Muller, M. Silent night

Muller, M. Somewhere in the city

Muller, M. Up at the Riverside

Muller, M. The wall

The mute witness

Nelscott, K. Guarding Lacey

O'Callaghan, M. Going to the dogs

O'Shaughnessy, P. Dead money

O'Shaughnessy, P. The long walk

O'Shaughnessy, P. O'Shay's special case

O'Shaughnessy, P. Success without college

Paretsky, S. A family Sunday in the park: V. I.
    Warshawski's first case

Paretsky, S. Photo finish

Paretsky, S. Publicity stunts

Parker, P. S. Letter from a dead man

Paul, P. The Jane from Hell's Kitchen

Pearl, M. The adventure of the Boston Dromio

Pearson, R. Boldt's broken angel

Perelman, S. J. Farewell, my lovely appetizer

Phillips, G. The accomplice

Pohle, R. W. The flowers of Utah

Pronzini, B. The bughouse caper

Pronzini, B. The cloud cracker

Pronzini, B. Medium rare

Pronzini, B. Quincannon in paradise

Pronzini, B. Souls burning

Pronzini, B. The winning ticket

Redman, B. R. The perfect crime

Rehder, B. Buck fever [excerpt]

MYSTERY AND DETECTIVE STORIES—
United States—*Continued*
  Riordan, R. The last king of Texas [excerpt]
  Rose, L. Ghosts and the machine
  Rubenstein, B. Smoke got in my eyes
  Russell, W. Hunting rogues
  Sanderson, J. El Camino del Rio [excerpt]
  Schutz, B. M. The black eyed blonde
  Schutz, B. M. Lost and found
  Schutz, B. M. Mary, Mary, shut the door
  Schutz, B. M. Til death do us part
  Schutz, B. M. What goes around
  Schutz, B. M. Whatever it takes
  The secret cipher: a detective story
  Spofford, H. E. P. Mr. Furbush
  Stabenow, D. On the evidence: a Liam Camp-
    bell short story
  Standish, H. L. Five thousand dollars reward
  Stashower, D. The seven walnuts
  Strange stories of a detective; or, Curiosities of
    crime
  Sublett, J. Rock critic murders [excerpt]
  Swanson, D. J. Umbrella man [excerpt]
  Swierczynski, D. The last case of Hilly Palmer
  A tell-tale ink mark
  The tell-tales key; or, A woman as a detective
  Thompson, J. The killer inside me [excerpt]
  Thompson, V. The minister's missing daughter
  Torrey, R. Concealed weapon
  Torrey, R. Mansion of death
  Tracing a murderer
  Treat, L. H as in homicide
  Twain, M. Making a fortune
  Walker, M. W. The red scream [excerpt]
  Walsh, M. The song at twilight
  Wheat, C. The case of the rival queens
  Wilson, F. P. Interlude at Duane's
  Yorke, C. B. Snowbound
The **mystery** of Captain Chappel. Hodgson, W. H.
The **mystery** of missing ships. Hodgson, W. H.
The **mystery** of the derelict. Hodgson, W. H.
The **mystery** of the five hundred diamonds. Barr,
  R.
The **mystery** of the poisoned kipper. Benchley, R.
The **mystery** of the water-logged ship. Hodgson,
  W. H.
The **mystery** spot. Moceri, M.
Myth Manners' Guide to Greek Missology #1:
  Andromeda and Perseus. Turtledove, H.
Myth milk. Keret, E.
A **Myth** of Recovery. Brown, R.
Myth of the Americans. Sarsanedas, J.
MYTHICAL ANIMALS
        See also Dragons; Griffins; Unicorns;
    Vampires; Werewolves
  Bear, E. Ice
  Cadnum, M. Bite the hand
  Cadnum, M. Hungry
  Cadnum, M. P-bird
  Gaiman, N. Sunbird
  Martin, G. R. R. A beast for Norn
  Wolfe, G. The magic animal
  Zelazny, R. The horses of Lir
  Zelazny, R. Unicorn variation
MYTHOLOGY
        See also Mythical animals; Sirens (My-
    thology)
  Cadnum, M. Arrival
  Cadnum, M. Daphne

  Cadnum, M. Give him the eye
  Cadnum, M. Medusa
  De Camp, L. S. and Pratt, F. The roaring trum-
    pet
  De Camp, L. S. and Pratt, F. The wall of ser-
    pents
  Gaiman, N. The monarch of the glen
  Gilman, G. I. Unleaving
  Hughes, M. Inner huff
  Khankhoje, M. Journey into the vortex
  Pratt, T. Living with the harpy
  Pratt, T. Romanticore
  Pratt, T. Terrible ones
  Rickert, M. Leda
  Roberson, J. A wolf upon the wind
  Russell, K. Children's reminiscences of the
    westward migration
  Scutt, C. Europa
  Silverberg, R. After the myths went home
  Silverberg, R. Breckenridge and the continuum
  Turtledove, H. Myth Manners' Guide to Greek
    Missology #1: Andromeda and Perseus
  Vidal, G. The ladies in the library

N

N.. King, S.
N0072-JK1. Fusco, A. C.
Nabakov, Vladimir
  The Word
    The New Yorker v81 no42 p76, 78 D 26
    2005/Ja 2 2006
Nabokov, Vladimir Vladimirovich
  Christmas
    The Ecco book of Christmas stories; edited
    by Alberto Manguel
  Natasha
    The New Yorker v84 no17 p54-6, 58-60 Je
    9-16 2008
  Spring in Fialta
    My mistress's sparrow is dead; great love sto-
    ries, from Chekhov to Munro; edited by
    Jeffrey Eugenides
**NABOKOV, VLADIMIR VLADIMIROVICH,
  1899-1977**
                About
  Gospodinov, G. L.
Nachman, of Bratslav *See* Naḥman, of Bratslav,
    1772-1811
Nachman. Michaels, L.
Nachman at the races. Michaels, L.
Nachman ben Simchah *See* Naḥman, of Bratslav,
    1772-1811
Nachman burning. Michaels, L.
Nachman from Los Angeles. Michaels, L.
Nádas, Péter
  A Tale of Fire and Knowledge
    The Virginia Quarterly Review v83 no1
    p170-7 Wint 2007
Nadasi, Mia
  (tr.) *See* Örkény, István
Nadelson, Scott
  The cantor's daughter
    Nadelson, S. The cantor's daughter; stories
  Half a day in Halifax
    Nadelson, S. The cantor's daughter; stories
  The headhunter
    Nadelson, S. The cantor's daughter; stories

Nadelson, Scott—*Continued*

Lego
Nadelson, S. The cantor's daughter; stories

Model rockets
Nadelson, S. The cantor's daughter; stories

Rehearsal
Nadelson, S. The cantor's daughter; stories

Return
Nadelson, S. The cantor's daughter; stories

Walter's girls
Nadelson, S. The cantor's daughter; stories

Nadia. Budnitz, J.

Nadia's nectar. Watson, I.

Nadzam, Bonnie

This Road
Callaloo v30 no3 p730-7 Summ 2007

Nagata, Linda

Goddesses
Nebula awards showcase 2002; edited by Kim Stanley Robinson

The **nagual** [variant title: The accident at John Stam's] Leonard, E.

Nahai, Gina B.

The Pearl Canon
TriQuarterly no133 p307-17 2009

Nahariya. Lauterbach, B.

Nahman

The Spinning Top
Parabola v30 no3 p86-7 Fall 2005

Nahman, of Bratslav

A tale of a king's son who was switched at birth with a maidservant's son
No star too beautiful; Yiddish stories from 1382 to the present; compiled and translated by Joachim Neugroschel

Nahrung, Jason

Smoking, waiting for the dawn
Dreaming again; thirty-five new stories celebrating the wild side of Australian fiction; edited by Jack Dann

Naiads, Sirens, Mermaids, Nymphs. Stanton, M.

Nail. Michalopoulou, A.

Naipaul, V. S. (Vidiadhar Surajprasad)

My aunt Gold Teeth
The Paris review book for planes, trains, elevators, and waiting rooms; by the editors of the Paris review; with an introduction by Richard Powers

Naipaul, Vidiadhar Surajprasad *See* Naipaul, V. S. (Vidiadhar Surajprasad), 1932-

Nairobi. Oates, J. C.

Naiyer Masud

Allam and son
Naiyer Masud. Snake catcher; translated from Urdu by Muhammad Umar Memon

The big garbage dump
Naiyer Masud. Snake catcher; translated from Urdu by Muhammad Umar Memon

Custody
Naiyer Masud. Snake catcher; translated from Urdu by Muhammad Umar Memon

Epistle
Naiyer Masud. Snake catcher; translated from Urdu by Muhammad Umar Memon

Ganjefa
Naiyer Masud. Snake catcher; translated from Urdu by Muhammad Umar Memon

Lamentation
Naiyer Masud. Snake catcher; translated from Urdu by Muhammad Umar Memon

Obscure domains of fear and desire
Naiyer Masud. Snake catcher; translated from Urdu by Muhammad Umar Memon

Resting place
Naiyer Masud. Snake catcher; translated from Urdu by Muhammad Umar Memon

Snake catcher
Naiyer Masud. Snake catcher; translated from Urdu by Muhammad Umar Memon

Weather vane
Naiyer Masud. Snake catcher; translated from Urdu by Muhammad Umar Memon

The woman in black
Naiyer Masud. Snake catcher; translated from Urdu by Muhammad Umar Memon

Najjar, Taghreed A.

Who Hid the Eid Lamb?
World Literature Today v79 no1 p75-7 Ja/Ap 2005

The **naked** and the deadly. Block, L.

Naked Chinese people. Lefer, D.

The **Naked** Circus. Wuori, G. K.

The **naked** face of God. Finch, S.

The **naked** juror. Nunez, S.

Naked little men. Cadnum, M.

The **Naked** Man. Becker, G.

The **naked** matador. Zelazny, R.

Naked woman playing chopin. Erdrich, L.

The **naked** year [excerpt] Pil'niàk, B.

Nakhman *See* Nahman, of Bratslav, 1772-1811

The **name** of the game. Tóibín, C.

The **nameless** offspring. Smith, C. A.

NAMES, PERSONAL *See* Personal names

Names. Hanway, N. S.

The **names** of the lost. Currey, R.

NAMIBIA

Jafta, M. The home-coming
Timm, U. Morenga [excerpt]

Naming day. McKillip, P. A.

Naming the stones. Lynn, D. H.

Nan and Claude. Ward, A. E.

Nan Madol. Connell, E. S.

Nancy Culpepper. Mason, B. A.

NANNIES *See* Governesses; Nursemaids

Nanny dearest. Allen, W.

Nano comes to Clifford Falls. Kress, N.

NANOTECHNOLOGY

Chapman, S. Minutes of the last meeting
Kosmatka, T. The art of alchemy
Kress, N. Nano comes to Clifford Falls

Nantes Notes. Firebrace, W.

NANTUCKET ISLAND (MASS.)

Hecht, J. Being and nothingness
Hecht, J. Cramp bark
Hecht, J. Get money
Hecht, J. Happy trails to you
Hecht, J. A little present on this dark November day
Levi, J. The scrimshaw violin
Wilson, F. P. Anna

Nap time. Franklin, T.

Naphtali. Yellin, T.

NAPLES (ITALY) *See* Italy—Naples

NAPOLEON I, EMPEROR OF THE FRENCH, 1769-1821

About

Zebrowski, G. Nappy

Nappy. Zebrowski, G.

Narayanan, Vivek

Encounters with the Kodambakkam Hyena

Agni no61 p35-49 2005

NARCISSISM

Gabrielyan, N. Master of the grass

Gordon, C. Emmanuele! Emmanuele!

NARCOTIC HABIT *See* Drug addiction

NARCOTICS, CONTROL OF *See* Drug traffic

NARCOTICS AGENTS *See* Drug traffic

The **Narrow** Jet. Byatt, A. S.

Narrow road to the deep north. Amdahl, G.

The **narrow** straw mat. Uchida, H.

NARWHAL

Duval, P. Fun with mammals

Nash, Roger

The camera and the cobra

The PEN/O.Henry Prize stories 2009; chosen and with an introduction by Laura Furman; with essays on the stories They admire most by jurors A. S. Byatt; Anthony Doerr; Tim O'Brien

NASHVILLE (TENN.) *See* Tennessee—Nashville

Nashville. Hauser, E.

Nashville gone to ashes. Hempel, A.

Naslund, Sena Jester

The perfecting of the Chopin Valse no. 14 in E Minor

Crossroads; tales of the southern literary fantastic; edited by F. Brett Cox and Andy Duncan

Nason, Riel

The Prom

Dalhousie Review v87 no2 p233-40 Summ 2007

Natalie. Enright, A.

Natasha. Bezmozgis, D.

Natasha. Nabokov, V. V.

Nate Pinckney-Alderson, superhero. Crane, E.

Nathan at the Speed of Light. Lopatin, P.

Nathoo. Judah, S.

NATION, CARRY AMELIA MOORE, 1846-1911

About

Bierce, A. The maid of Podunk

The **national** anthem. Lethem, J.

NATIONAL SOCIALISM

See also Germany—1918-1945

Bowen, R. Doppelganger

Bradbury, R. Darling Adolf

Gorman, E. Crystal's big night

Henkel, O. Hitler on the campaign trail in America

Klages, E. Triangle

Mandelman, A. Pity

Moorcock, M. The case of the Nazi canary

Nayman, S. The house on Kronenstrasse

Nayman, S. The lamp

Rachel, D. The last man I killed

Shaw, I. Sailor off the Bremen

Shepard, J. Ancestral legacies

Sherez, S. God-box

Stackpole, M. A. Seamless

Stavans, I. The disappearance

Tidhar, L. 304, Adolph Hitler Strasse

Vapnyar, L. There are Jews in my house

Wilson, F. P. Aryans and Absinthe

Wolfe, G. Donovan sent us

NATIONALISM

Toer, P. A. Acceptence

The **nationalist** and the American girl. Reisen, A.

Native aliens. Van Eekhout, G.

Native Language. Harmon, A. G.

A **native** teacher. McElrath, F.

Nativity. Hospital, J. T.

Natural/(1978-2004). Song, D. K.

Natural color. Updike, J.

A **natural** death. Frankel-Zaltzman, P.

Natural disasters. Kazumi Stahl, A.

The **natural** man. Ruffin, P.

The **natural** order. Lasdun, J.

Natural paradises. Solá, M.

NATURALISTS

See also Paleontologists

Stafford, J. The lippia lawn

NATURE

Hand, E. Winter's wife

Lowry, M. The forest path to the spring

Nausea 1979. Murakami, H.

Nautical intervention. Goldfaden, J.

NAVAHO INDIANS *See* Navajo Indians

NAVAJO INDIANS

Allen, P. G. Burned alive in the blues

Crow, L. Cowboys and Indians

Gorman, E. and Starr, R. D. The shadow that shapes the light

Hillerman, T. Chee's witch

Koretsky, J. L. A delicate balance

Koretsky, J. L. A stranger among them

Stoddard, J. The elephant ironclads

NAVAL BATTLES

See also Sea stories; World War, 1914-1918—Naval operations; World War, 1939-1945—Naval operations

L'Amour, L. Voyage to Tobolai

Purdom, T. The mists of time

Weber, D. The Captain from Kirkbean

Weber, D. In the Navy

Naval History. Kelman, J.

Nawabdin Electrician. Mueenuddin, D.

Nawaz, Saleema

Scar Tissue

Dalhousie Review v88 no2 p205-17 Summ 2008

Nayman, Shira

Dark urgings of the blood

Nayman, S. Awake in the dark; stories

The house on Kronenstrasse

Nayman, S. Awake in the dark; stories

The lamp

Nayman, S. Awake in the dark; stories

The porcelain monkey

Nayman, S. Awake in the dark; stories

NAZIS *See* National socialism

NAZISM *See* National socialism

Ndebele, Njabulo S. (Njabulo Simakahle)

Death of a son

Telling tales; edited by Nadine Gordimer

The prophetess

The Anchor book of modern African stories; edited by Nadežda Obradovic; with a foreword by Chinua Achebe

Ndongo-Bidyogo, Donato
  The Dream
    Iowa Review v36 no2 p75-9 Fall 2006
Neal, Andrea
  Tecumseh and Rebekah
    The Saturday Evening Post v277 no4 p68-9, 90, 92 Jl/Ag 2005
Neal, Larry
  Our bright tomorrows
    D.C. noir 2; the classics; edited by George Pelecanos.
Neal, Lawrence P. *See* Neal, Larry, 1937-1981
NEANDERTHAL RACE
    See also Prehistoric man
  Card, O. S. Heal thyself
  De Camp, L. S. The gnarly man
  Lake, J. and Nestvold, R. Incipit
  Richter, S. The cavemen in the hedges
  Roberts, A. Me-topia
Near Banbridge town. Kiely, B.
NEAR-DEATH EXPERIENCES
  Pearlman, E. Signs of life
The **near** departed. Matheson, R.
NEAR EAST *See* Middle East
Near-extinct birds of the central cordillera. Fountain, B.
The **near** remote. Allen, J. R.
The **near-son**. Curtis, R.
Nearby, the Edge of Europe. Oates, N.
The **nearest** thing in the world. Chattin, J.
Nearly people. Williams, C.
Nebel, Frederick
  Wise guy
    The Black Lizard big book of pulps; edited by Otto Penzler
NEBRASKA
  Breuer, M. J. The man with the strange head
  Breuer, M. J. The oversight
  Flanagan, E. Every sad detail
  Gorman, E. Different kinds of dead
  Rheinheimer, K. Dogs
  Wheeler, T. Welcome home
Nebraska. Kyriakidis, A.
Necahual. Buckell, T. S.
Necessary lies. Bakken, K. N.
Necessary noise. Donoghue, E.
The **necessity** of certain behaviors. Cain, S.
Neck. Dahl, R.
Neck and Neck. Friedman, B. J.
The **necklace**. Holthe, T. U.
NECKLACES
  Holthe, T. U. The necklace
  Lara, Contessa. The coral necklace
The **necromancer's** apprentice. Carl, L. S.
A **Necromancer's** Guide to Child Rearing. Marston, R.
Necromancy in Naat. Smith, C. A.
The **necromantic** tale. Smith, C. A.
NECROPHILIA
  Bear, E. The dying of the light
  Lamb, J. Esprit de corpse
  Lane, J. The bootleg heart
  Shirley, J. War and peace
  Swanwick, M. The dead
The **necropolis** of Thebes. Sterling, B.
Nectarine Love. Gustine, A.
Need. McCauley, W.
Need. Sallis, J.
Needle. Cheon, W. Y.

Needle in a timestack. Silverberg, R.
Needle match. Lovesey, P.
Needlepoint. Bael, S.
Neera
  Aunt Severina
    Writing to delight; Italian short stories by nineteenth-century women writers; edited by Antonia Arslan and Gabriella Romani
  The lady of the evening
    Writing to delight; Italian short stories by nineteenth-century women writers; edited by Antonia Arslan and Gabriella Romani
  Paolina
    Writing to delight; Italian short stories by nineteenth-century women writers; edited by Antonia Arslan and Gabriella Romani
Neff, Ondrej
  The fourth day to eternity
    The SFWA European hall of fame; sixteen contemporary masterpieces of science fiction from the continent; edited by James Morrow and Kathryn Morrow
Negative Nixons. Davis, M.
Neggers, Carla
  On the run
    Thriller 2; stories you just can't put down; edited by Clive Cussler; [stories by] Kathleen Antrim . . . [et al.]
The **neglected** garden. Koja, K.
A **negligible** game on the journey. Ts'an-hsüeh
The **negotiated** settlement. Gappah, P.
Negro progress. Grooms, A.
NEGROES *See* African Americans
Negrón-Muntaner, Frances
  The ugly dyckling
    Centro Journal v19 no1 p351-9 Spr 2007
The **neighbor**. Hernandez, L.
Neighbor. Silverberg, R.
The **neighborhood**. Gordon, M.
NEIGHBORS
  Akmakjian, H. Sunday
  Angel, J. Supplement
  Angel, J. Whistle pig
  Barth, J. The end
  Barth, J. Progressive dinner
  Barth, J. Rebeginning
  Barth, J. Teardown
  Barth, J. Us/Them
  Bensko, J. Painted animals
  Bishop, E. The housekeeper
  Boudinot, R. Newholly
  Bradbury, R. Massinello Pietro
  Brant, B. E. Turtle gal
  Brazaitis, M. Air conditioning and heat
  Clarke, B. The apology
  Clarke, B. The reason was us
  Cooper, J. C. Rushing nowhere
  Cooper, J. C. Wait a minute, world!
  Coverson, M. Dance with me
  Crane, E. Varieties of loudness in Chicago
  Crone, M. Where what gets into people comes from
  Currans-Sheehan, T. The wild club
  Curtis, R. Solicitation
  Dahl, R. The great switcheroo
  Dean, D. What the left hand is saying
  DeNiro, A. The friendly giants
  DuBois, B. The dark snow
  Dunbar, P. L. Jethro's garden

NEW YORK (N.Y.)—Manhattan—*Continued*

Oates, J. C. Nairobi
Olafsson, O. January
Orner, E. Fear and loathing in Chelsea
Ozick, C. Actors
Pendarvis, J. Outsiders
Rahman, I. Here come the dog people
Resnick, M. Two hunters in Manhattan
Saunders, G. My flamboyant grandson
Schulman, H. The revisionist
Scott, J. The most beautiful apartment in New York
Selgin, P. Wednesday at the bagel shop
Shepard, L. Only partly here
Shomer, E. Fill in the blank
Stamm, P. The experiment
Stamm, P. Through the night
Stamm, P. The true pure land
Sullivan, C. J. The last round
Sutton, B. Tra il devoto et profano
Thompson, J. How we brought the good news
Tower, W. Executors of important energies
Ward, A. E. The way the sky changed
Wilson, F. P. When he was fab
Woolrich, C. The death rose
Woolrich, C. The fatal footlights
Woolrich, C. The heavy sugar
Woolrich, C. New York blues

Queens

Abbott, J. Jihad sucks; or, The conversion of the Jews
Byrne, M. Only the strong survive
Carrington, T. Last stop, Ditmars
Eisenstadt, J. Golden venture
Eng, V. The flower of flushing
Farley, B. The investigation
Fusilli, J. The guardians
Guglielmelli, J. Buckner's error
Ha Jin. The house behind a weeping cherry
Hamill, D. Under the Throg Neck Bridge
Lovell, G. Out of body
Martinez, L. Lights out for Frankie
McIntyre, V. Disability
Montemarano, N. Story
Norton, V. Dirty heaven
Selgin, P. My search for red and gray wide-striped pajamas
Stamm, P. In the outer suburbs
Wishnia, K. J. A. Dissed
Wishnia, K. J. A. Viernes loco

NEW YORK (N.Y.). STATUE OF LIBERTY
See Statue of Liberty (New York, N.Y.)

NEW YORK (STATE)
See also Adirondack Mountains (N.Y.); Long Island (N.Y.)

Banks, R. Lobster night
Barry, R. Lucy's last hurrah
Bass, R. Field events
Bear, E. Old leatherwings
Berry, J. To measure the earth
Busch, F. Frost line
Child, L. Safe enough
Clarke, B. The Hotel Utica
Farmer, P. J. The volcano
Gates, D. The bad thing
Groff, L. Lucky Chow Fun
Moody, R. The Mansion on the Hill
Oates, J. C. The corn maiden: a love story
Oates, J. C. Honor code

Oates, J. C. The museum of Dr. Moses
Oates, J. C. Nowhere
Scott, J. Everybody loves somebody
Thompson, J. Applause, applause
Wolff, T. The deposition
Wolven, S. The high iron

Long Island

Watkins, S. Bocky-Bocky

New York City
See New York (N.Y.)

Niagara Falls

Holladay, C. C. The interview
Means, D. The spot
Snyder, S. Blue yodel

Syracuse

Busch, F. The rescue mission

Troy

Fulton, A. Centrally isolated
Fulton, A. L'Air du Temps
Fulton, A. The nightingales of Troy

Westchester County

Collins, S. Water hazard
Marcus, J. S. It's freezing here in Milwaukee
New York, 2007. Comment, B.
New York blues. Woolrich, C.
New York mining disaster. Murakami, H.
The **New** York Times at special bargain rates. King, S.

NEW YORK YANKEES (BASEBALL TEAM)
Helprin, M. Perfection

NEW YORK ZOOLOGICAL PARK See Bronx Zoo

NEW ZEALAND

Anderson, B. Day out
Anderson, B. The girls
Anderson, B. The man with the plug in his nose
Anderson, B. Poojah
Anderson, B. Tuataras
Anderson, B. Up the river with Mrs Gallant
Gifford, B. Murder at the Swordfish Club
Svoboda, T. '80s lilies

NEW ZEALANDERS

Italy

Anderson, B. Fast post
Parks, T. Changing address
Newbie wrangler. Anderson, T. J.
The **newcomer**. Moffett, K.
Newholly. Boudinot, R.

Newland, Peggy
Clowns
Daedalus v136 no2 p127-37 Spr 2007

Newlydeads. Kittredge, C.

Newman, Kim
Another fish story
Weird shadows over Innsmouth; edited by Stephen Jones; illustrated by Randy Broecker [et al.]
The gypsies in the wood
The Year's best fantasy and horror: nineteenth annual collection; edited by Ellen Datlow and Kelly Link & Gavin J. Grant
The red planet league
Gaslight grimoire; fantastic tales of Sherlock Holmes; edited by J. R. Campbell and Charles Prepolec
Richard Riddle, boy detective, in "The case of the French spy"
Summer chills; strangers in stranger lands; edited by Stephen Jones

NIAGARA FALLS (N.Y.) *See* New York (State)—Niagara Falls

NIAGARA FALLS (N.Y. AND ONT.)
Malla, P. Being like bulls

NICARAGUANS
Germany
Ramírez Mercado, S. Saint Nikolaus

Nicastro, Laura
Haguit
English translations of short stories by contemporary Argentine women writers; edited by Eliana Cazaubon Hermann; translated by Sally Webb Thornton

Nice Guys. Adcock, S.

Nice Guys Finish Last (excerpt). Manheimer, J.

A **nice** place to visit. Deaver, J.

A **nice** thought. Mintz, C.

Nichols, Jim
Slow monkeys
Contemporary Maine fiction; an anthology of short stories; edited by Wesley McNair

Nichols, John
Spoon Mountain or Bust
Orion v26 no4 p40-7 Jl/Ag 2007

Nichols, Laura D.
Prodigal
"Tell it to us easy" and other stories; a complete short fiction anthology of African American women writers in Opportunity magazine, (1923-1948); edited by Judith Musser.

Nichols, Robert
Six ways of looking at farming
So the story goes; twenty-five years of the Johns Hopkins short fiction series; edited by John T. Irwin and Jean McGarry; with a foreword by John Barth

Nicholson, Annalise
To Devotion
Seventeen v65 no6 p154-6, 158 Je 2006

Nicholson, Margaret Beda *See* Yorke, Margaret

Nicholson, Scott
Dog person
The Year's best fantasy and horror: twentieth annual collection; edited by Ellen Datlow and Kelly Link & Gavin J. Grant
Last writes
Poe's lighthouse; all new collaborations with Edgar Allan Poe; edited by Christopher Conlon

Nick Carter, detective. Carter, N.

Nickels, Tim
England and nowhere
The Year's best fantasy and horror: twenty-first annual collection; edited by Ellen Datlow and Kelly Link & Gavin J. Grant

Nickels. Lombardo, B.

Nickels and dimes. Klaskin, R.

Nickless, Barbara
Suffer the children
Future Americas; edited by Martin H. Greenberg and John Helferd

NICKNAMES
Keret, E. Teddy Trunk
Kun, M. Steve Smith

NICO, 1938-1988
About
Lane, J. An unknown past

Nicobar Lane—the soul eater's story. Resnick, M.

NIECES
Fuentes, C. The father's servant
Hammett, D. Laughing masks
Johnson, G. Schadenfreude
Krasikov, S. Debt
MacLaverty, B. The wedding ring
Malouf, D. Closer
Masurel, P. Static
McLean, S. Summer camp
Watson, B. Water dog God: a ghost story
West, D. Summer setting

Niels Bohr and the sleeping dane. Sullivan, J.

NIETZSCHE, FRIEDRICH WILHELM, 1844-1900
Parodies, imitations, etc.
Allen, W. Thus ate Zarathustra

Niewenhuis, Loreen
Years and Months
The Antioch Review v66 no3 p503-7 Summ 2008

NIGER
Chilson, P. Tea with soldiers

NIGERIA
Adichie, C. N. Cell one
Adichie, C. N. Ghosts
Adichie, C. N. The headstrong historian
Adichie, C. N. A private experience
Adichie, C. N. Tomorrow is too far
Aiyejina, F. The one-handed hero
Akpan, U. C. Luxurious hearses
Aniebo, I. N. C. Four dimensions
Civil War, 1967-1970
Achebe, C. Sugar baby
Maja-Pearce, A. Civil War I-VII
Lagos
Adichie, C. N. The American Embassy

NIGERIANS
South africa
Adichie, C. N. Jumping Monkey Hill
United States
Adichie, C. N. The arrangers of marriage
Adichie, C. N. Imitation
Adichie, C. N. On Monday of last week
Adichie, C. N. The shivering
Adichie, C. N. The thing around your neck

NIGHT
Chekhov, A. P. A night of horror [variant title: Dreadful night]
Matheson, R. Finger prints
Zelazny, R. Is there a demon lover in the house?

Night. Tolstaia, T.

Hen **night**. Weinman, S.

A **night** at the cemetery [variant title: In the cemetery; In the graveyard] Chekhov, A. P.

A **Night** at the Opera. Frame, J.

A **night** at Wagon Camp. L'Amour, L.

The **Night** Before. Lustig, A.

The **night** before. Williams, C.

The **night** before Christmas. Odrach, T.

Night blossoms. Rickert, M.

NIGHT CLUBS
Cooper, J. C. The party
Finn, P. M. Where beautiful ladies dance for you
Fonseca, R. The flesh and the bones
Fredrickson, J. Good evenin', blues
Gardam, J. The virgins of Bruges
Gifford, B. After hours at La Chinita

Nine points of the law. Hornung, E. W.
Nine starships waiting. Zelazny, R.
Nine, ten. Lin, T.
Nine-Tenths of the Law. George, S.
Nineteen-ninety-two. Lagioia, N.
Nineteen seconds. Shirley, J.
Ninety-eight point six. Deaver, J.
Ninety nights on Mercury. Abbott, L. K.
Nini, Matthew Charles
  La Vie En Rose
    Dalhousie Review v88 no2 p257-60 Summ
    2008
Ninjettes. Flora, K.
Nino. Mozetič, B.
The **ninth** skeleton. Smith, C. A.
Niranjana, Anupama
  A day with Charulata
    Gibson, M. E. Separate journeys; short stories
    by contemporary Indian women; edited by
    Geeta Dharmarajan; introduction by Mary
    Ellis Gibson
Nirvana High. Gunn, E.
Nirvana High. Gunn, E. and What, L.
Nisbet, Euan
  Photons do not lie
    Nature v439 p762 F 9 2006
Nisbet, Jim
  Facilis descensus averno
    Paris noir; capital crime fiction; edited by
    Maxim Jakubowski
  Weight less than shadow
    San Francisco noir; edited by Peter Maravelis
Nisbet, Robert
  An April story
    Nisbet, R. Downtrain
  Barber shop blues
    Nisbet, R. Downtrain
  Birthdays
    Nisbet, R. Downtrain
  Dors, mon petit, dors
    Nisbet, R. Downtrain
  Infidel
    Nisbet, R. Downtrain
  Jam jars of seaweed and dreams of love
    Nisbet, R. Downtrain
  Ladies' man
    Nisbet, R. Downtrain
  The ladybird room
    Nisbet, R. Downtrain
  Lips
    Nisbet, R. Downtrain
  Marianne
    Nisbet, R. Downtrain
  Miss Grey of Market Street
    Nisbet, R. Downtrain
  Nightingale
    Nisbet, R. Downtrain
  Ocky Boxer
    Nisbet, R. Downtrain
  Our father
    Nisbet, R. Downtrain
  The path to Porthgain
    Nisbet, R. Downtrain
  Reconnaissance
    Nisbet, R. Downtrain
  Sounds of the town
    Nisbet, R. Downtrain
  Time to go home
    Nisbet, R. Downtrain

  Wheelerdealer
    Nisbet, R. Downtrain
  When the sun went down
    Nisbet, R. Downtrain
Nissen, Thisbe
  The Church of the Fellowship of Something
    StoryQuarterly v42 p117-33 2006
  Etiquette
    The dictionary of failed relationships; 26 tales
    of love gone wrong; edited by Meredith
    Broussard
  Win's girl
    The Best American mystery stories, 2008; ed-
    ited and with an introduction by George
    Pelecanos; Otto Penzler, series editor
Nister *See* Der Nister, 1884-1950
Niven, Larry
  Breeding maze
    This is my funniest 2; leading science fiction
    writers present their funniest stories ever;
    edited by Mike Resnick
  The solipsist at dinner
    Elemental; the Tsunami relief anthology; sto-
    ries of science fiction and fantasy; [edited
    by] Steven Savile and Alethea Kontis; in-
    troduction by Arthur C. Clarke
Niven, Larry and Cooper, Brenda
  The terror bard
    Fast forward 1; future fiction from the cutting
    edge; edited by Lou Anders
Nivira
  Etsò
    Confrontation no98/99 p210-13 Spr/Summ
    2007
Nix, Garth
  Bad luck, trouble, death, and vampire sex
    Eclipse one; new science fiction and fantasy;
    edited by Jonathan Strahan
  Beyond the sea gate of the scholar-pirates of
    Sarsköe
    Fast ships, black sails; edited by Ann & Jeff
    VanderMeer
    The Best science fiction and fantasy of the
    year: volume three; edited by Jonathan
    Strahan
  Holly and iron
    Wizards; edited by Jack Dann and Gardner
    Dozois
  Infestation
    The Starry rift; tales of new tomorrows: an
    original science fiction anthology; edited by
    Jonathan Strahan
  Old friends
    Dreaming again; thirty-five new stories cele-
    brating the wild side of Australian fiction;
    edited by Jack Dann
  Punctuality
    The new space opera 2; edited by Gardner
    Dozois and Jonathan Strahan
  Read it in the headlines!
    Year's best fantasy 6; edited by David G.
    Hartwell & Kathryn Cramer
  Sir Hereward and Mister Fitz go to war again
    The Year's best fantasy and horror: twenty-
    first annual collection; edited by Ellen
    Datlow and Kelly Link & Gavin J. Grant
    Year's best fantasy 8; edited by David G.
    Hartwell, Kathryn Cramer

Nolan, William F.—*Continued*
Depompa
> Dark delicacies; original tales of terror and the macabre by the world's greatest horror writers; edited by Del Howison and Jeff Gelb
>> Nolan, W. F. Nightshadows; the best new horror fiction by a living legend in dark fantasy

The ex
> Nolan, W. F. Nightshadows; the best new horror fiction by a living legend in dark fantasy

The Fasterfaster affair
> Nolan, W. F. Wild galaxy; selected science fiction stories; introduction by the author

Freak
> Nolan, W. F. Wild galaxy; selected science fiction stories; introduction by the author

The Grackel question
> Nolan, W. F. Wild galaxy; selected science fiction stories; introduction by the author

Happily ever after
> Nolan, W. F. Wild galaxy; selected science fiction stories; introduction by the author

Hopping for Abe
> Nolan, W. F. Nightshadows; the best new horror fiction by a living legend in dark fantasy

How do I know you're real?
> Nolan, W. F. Wild galaxy; selected science fiction stories; introduction by the author

In real life
> Nolan, W. F. Nightshadows; the best new horror fiction by a living legend in dark fantasy

Jenny among the zeebs
> Nolan, W. F. Wild galaxy; selected science fiction stories; introduction by the author

The joy of living
> Nolan, W. F. Wild galaxy; selected science fiction stories; introduction by the author

Kelly, Frederic Michael
> Nolan, W. F. Wild galaxy; selected science fiction stories; introduction by the author

Killing Charlie
> Nolan, W. F. Nightshadows; the best new horror fiction by a living legend in dark fantasy

Listening to Billy
> Nolan, W. F. Nightshadows; the best new horror fiction by a living legend in dark fantasy

Lone star traveler
> Nolan, W. F. Wild galaxy; selected science fiction stories; introduction by the author

Mama's boy
> Nolan, W. F. Nightshadows; the best new horror fiction by a living legend in dark fantasy

The mating of Thirdburt
> Nolan, W. F. Wild galaxy; selected science fiction stories; introduction by the author

Mommy, Daddy, & Mollie
> Nolan, W. F. Nightshadows; the best new horror fiction by a living legend in dark fantasy

On becoming immortal
> Nolan, W. F. Nightshadows; the best new horror fiction by a living legend in dark fantasy

Once upon a time
> Nolan, W. F. Nightshadows; the best new horror fiction by a living legend in dark fantasy

Papa's planet
> Nolan, W. F. Wild galaxy; selected science fiction stories; introduction by the author

Poetic justice
> Nolan, W. F. Nightshadows; the best new horror fiction by a living legend in dark fantasy

Ripper!
> Nolan, W. F. Nightshadows; the best new horror fiction by a living legend in dark fantasy

Scotch on the rocks
> Nolan, W. F. Nightshadows; the best new horror fiction by a living legend in dark fantasy

Silk and fire
> Nolan, W. F. Nightshadows; the best new horror fiction by a living legend in dark fantasy

The small world of Lewis Stillman
> Nolan, W. F. Wild galaxy; selected science fiction stories; introduction by the author

Starblood
> Nolan, W. F. Wild galaxy; selected science fiction stories; introduction by the author

Stuntman
> Nolan, W. F. Wild galaxy; selected science fiction stories; introduction by the author

To serve the ship
> Nolan, W. F. Wild galaxy; selected science fiction stories; introduction by the author

Toe to tip, tip to toe, pip-pop as you go
> Nolan, W. F. Wild galaxy; selected science fiction stories; introduction by the author

The tragic narrative of Arthur Bedford Addison
> Poe's lighthouse; all new collaborations with Edgar Allan Poe; edited by Christopher Conlon
>> Nolan, W. F. Nightshadows; the best new horror fiction by a living legend in dark fantasy

An unlucky encounter
> Nolan, W. F. Nightshadows; the best new horror fiction by a living legend in dark fantasy

Violation
> Nolan, W. F. Wild galaxy; selected science fiction stories; introduction by the author

Wolf song
> Nolan, W. F. Nightshadows; the best new horror fiction by a living legend in dark fantasy

Year of the witch
> Nolan, W. F. Nightshadows; the best new horror fiction by a living legend in dark fantasy

Noll, Ingrid
Fisherman's friend
> Passport to crime; the finest mystery stories from International Crime Writers; edited by Janet Hutchings

The **Noll** dynasty. Cooper, D.

Nollas, Dimitris
The old enemy
Angelic & black; contemporary Greek short stories; edited and translated by David Connolly; with an introduction by Vangelis Hatzivassileiou

Nom de guerre. Thomas, J.

Nomberg, Hersh Dovid
In the mountains
No star too beautiful; Yiddish stories from 1382 to the present; compiled and translated by Joachim Neugroschel

The **non** compos mentis blues. Chercover, S.

Non-existent cats. Richards, T.

Nonstop to Portales. Willis, C.

NONVIOLENCE
James, C. L. R. Emperor Jones and the African drums
Martin, L. The welcome table

Noon wine. Porter, K. A.

The **noonday** pool. MacLeod, I.

The **noose**. Wynbush, O. B.

Nor iron bars a cage. Block, L.

Nora. Just, W. S.

Nora B. Bruen, K.

Nord's gambit. Buckell, T. S.

Nor'easter. DeMartini, B.

Noriega, Chon A.
A Slice of the Pie
Aztlán v30 no2 p1-2 Fall 2005

Norizuki, Rintarō
An urban legend puzzle
Passport to crime; the finest mystery stories from International Crime Writers; edited by Janet Hutchings

Normal insanity. Schwitters, K.

A **normal** life. Thompson, J.

Norman, David
The Cliffs
Southern Humanities Review v42 no1 p70-80 Wint 2008

Norman, Howard
Church Owl
Ploughshares v31 no4 p105-10 Wint 2005/2006
Derringer
Salmagundi no144/145 p81-7 Fall 2004/Wint 2005

NORMANDY (FRANCE) *See* France—Normandy

NORMANS
England
Cutler, J. Living with the gilt

Norman's date. Baraka, I. A.

Norment, Lee
Long Gone Daddy
The Southern Review (Baton Rouge, La.) v41 no3 p547-51 Summ 2005

Norrby, Erling
From Loneliness to Ubiquitousness
The Kenyon Review v28 no1 p7-12 Wint 2006

Norris, Benjamin Franklin *See* Norris, Frank, 1870-1902

Norris, Frank
The third circle
San Francisco noir 2; the classics; edited by Peter Maravelis.

North, Anna
A Record Book for Small Farmers
Atlantic Monthly (1993) v295 no1 p183-6, 188-92 Ja/F 2005

NORTH AFRICA
See also Sahara
Gordon, C. Emmanuele! Emmanuele!
L'Amour, L. By the ruins of "El Walarieh"
Sterling, B. Dinner in Audoghast
Wald, A. H. The virgin's heart

North American lake monsters. Ballingrud, N.

NORTH CAROLINA
Blackwell, K. My first wedding
Butner, R. Ash city stomp
Chapman, J. D. Amanuensis
Chattin, J. Outer banks
Crone, M. The ice garden
Crone, M. It
Crone, M. Pipe smoke
Crone, M. Salvage
Crone, M. Where what gets into people comes from
Fountain, B. The good ones are already taken
Gurganus, A. Fourteen feet of water in my house
Hickam, H. Dosie, of Killakeet Island
Parker, M. Couple strike it rich on second honeymoon
Parker, M. Off island
Porter, J. A. Merrymount
Porter, J. A. Pending
Rash, R. Deep Gap
Rash, R. Last rite
Rash, R. Pemberton's bride
Singleton, G. Scotch and Dr Pepper
Vollmer, M. Freebleeders
Watkins, S. Driver's ed
Watts, S. P. Unassigned territory
Raleigh
Orner, P. The last socialist

North Coast. McGuane, T.

NORTH DAKOTA
Boswell, R. A walk in winter
Butler, R. O. Christmas 1910
DeMarinis, R. The missile gypsies
Disch, T. M. The Wall of America
Erdrich, L. Night train
Erdrich, L. Still life with "marigold" & the blue mumbled earth
Erdrich, L. The butcher's wife
Erdrich, L. Disaster stamps of Pluto
Erdrich, L. Fleur
Erdrich, L. Naked woman playing chopin
Erdrich, L. Scales
Erdrich, L. Tales of burning love
Erdrich, L. The world's greatest fishermen
Gifford, B. Ball lighting
Grimes, C. The inspection

North of. Bertino, M.

North of Diddy-Wah-Diddy. Swanwick, M.

North of nowhere. Hospital, J. T.

North of ordinary. Gardiner, J. R.

North of the Faro. Bluestein, E.

North of the port. Bukoski, A.

The **north** shore. Stelmok, J.

NORTHERN IRELAND
See also Ulster (Ireland and Northern Ireland)
Bruen, K. Dead right

NORTHERN IRELAND—*Continued*
Kiely, B. The night we rode with Sarsfield
McCabe, E. Heritage
McCabe, E. Victims
Perry, A. Hostages
Politics
See Politics—Northern Ireland
Belfast
Kiely, B. Make straight for the shore
Kiely, B. Rich and rare were the gems she wore
Kiely, B. Ten pretty girls
MacLaverty, B. A Belfast memory
MacLaverty, B. On the roundabout
MacLaverty, B. The Trojan sofa
MacLaverty, B. A trusted neighbour
NORTHERN RHODESIA *See* Zambia
NORTHMEN *See* Vikings
NORTHWEST, PACIFIC *See* Pacific Northwest
Northwest passage. Roden, B.
Norton, Vanessa
Dirty heaven
Sex for America; politically inspired erotica; edited by Stephen Elliott
NORWAY
Macker, R. A deadly joke
VanderMeer, J. The farmer's cat
Bergen
Barnard, R. The life-lie
The **Norwegian** Captain. Gold, H.
NORWEGIANS
See also Vikings
United States
Mirrielees, E. R. A matter of nationality
NOSE
Barreto, P. The baby in rose tarlatan
The **nose**. Gogol´, N. V.
Nose dive. Corso, P.
The **noseless** horror. Howard, R. E.
Nostaglia. Lott, B.
NOSTALGIA
Hempel, A. The rest of God
Hempel, A. Tom-rock through the eels
Komla-Ebri, K. "Home . . . sickness"
Molodowsky, K. Eliahu Zalkind's bookkeeping
Molodowsky, K. A glimmer of youth
Molodowsky, K. Home for Passover
Oates, J. C. Where is here?
Weaver, W. Sheetrock
Nostalgia/Nostalgia. Rivera-Garza, C.
Nostalgia. Goto, H.
Not a matter of love. Alvarado, B.
Not all fingers are equal. Homenidis, C.
Not another black cat story. Maloney, G.
Not at home to visitors. Wright, J.
Not enough monkeys. Schutz, B. M.
Not even the zookeeper can keep control. Messinger, J.
Not fade away. Sanders, W.
Not from Detroit. Lansdale, J. R.
Not human beings. Keret, E.
Not in the record. Reeves, E. W.
Not just the facts. Meyers, A.
Not much is new here. Barry, R.
Not our brother. Silverberg, R.
Not people, not this. Magee, K.
Not Quite a Murder Mystery. Hanson, K. M.
Not the Ocean. Ehle, R.
Not the same shoes. Van Booy, S.
Not Too Frail for Love.

Not waving but drowning. Rash, R.
Not your average bear. Stelmok, J.
Note to future self. Montemarano, N.
The **notebook**. Fonseca, R.
Notebook no. 9. Boyd, W.
The **Notebook** of Blas Coll. Montejo, E.
Notes. Sallis, J.
Notes for a story about people with weird phobias. Crane, E.
Notes for a story of a man who will not die alone. Eggers, D.
Notes from a Forgotten War, So-called. Hinojosa-Smith, R.
Notes of the writing of horror: a story. Ligotti, T.
Notes on Mrs. Slaughter. Burgin, R.
Notes on redevelopment. Moody, R.
Nothing. Keret, E.
Nothing bad happens here. Tognazzini, A.
Nothing but net. Deaver, J.
Nothing changes. Bohanon, M. L.
Nothing ever happens in white America. Ebenbach, D. H.
Nothing ever just disappears. D'Allesandro, S.
Nothing like an ocean. Tomlinson, J.
Nothing Like That. Freeman, C.
Nothing personal. Cadigan, P.
Nothing right. Nelson, A.
Nothing to ask for. McFarland, D.
Notini, Sylvia
(tr.) *See* Mencoboni, Marco
Nottamun town. Maguire, G.
NOTTINGHAM (ENGLAND) *See* England—Nottingham
NOVA SCOTIA *See* Canada—Nova Scotia
Novack, Carol
Better Than Court TV: Sensational Cases from the NYC Courts
Legal Studies Forum v32 no1 p175-6 2008
Novack, Sandra
A Good Woman's Love
South Carolina Review v37 no1 p179-84 Fall 2004
White Trees in Summer
Gettysburg Review v19 no3 p395-408 Aut 2006
Novak, Maja
The Fall of the House of Pirnat
Agni no63 p48-60 2006
Novakovich, Josip
59th parallel
Novakovich, J. Infidelities; stories of war and lust
The bridge under the Danube
Novakovich, J. Infidelities; stories of war and lust
Hail
Novakovich, J. Infidelities; stories of war and lust
Neighbors
Novakovich, J. Infidelities; stories of war and lust
Night guests
Novakovich, J. Infidelities; stories of war and lust
A purple story
Novakovich, J. Infidelities; stories of war and lust

Novakovich, Josip—_Continued_

Ribs
  Novakovich, J. Infidelities; stories of war and lust

Snow powder
  Novakovich, J. Infidelities; stories of war and lust

Spleen
  Novakovich, J. Infidelities; stories of war and lust

The stamp
  Novakovich, J. Infidelities; stories of war and lust

Tchaikovsky's bust
  Novakovich, J. Infidelities; stories of war and lust

A **novel** failure: an interview with Nobel candidate Sylvia Solas. Grimes, C.

NOVELISTS _See_ Authors

The **novels** of Raymond Carver. Singleton, G.

November. Olafsson, O.

The **November** fifteen. Montemarano, N.

The **November** game. Wilson, F. P.

November May Day. Watrous, M.

November Storm. Oldshue, R.

Novik, Naomi

Araminta, or, The wreck of the Amphidrake
  Fast ships, black sails; edited by Ann & Jeff VanderMeer

Now I am married. Gordon, M.

(Now + n, now – n). Silverberg, R.

Now that it's spring. Busch, F.

Now you don't. Monk, B.

Now you see it. Monk, B.

Nowarian blues. Espinet, R.

Nowhere. Oates, J. C.

Nowhere man. Mejides, M.

The **nowhere** man. Pinborough, S.

Nowheresville. Chattin, J.

Nowlin-O'Banion, Amanda

Rent-a-Gang
  Callaloo v32 no2 p438-9 Spr 2009

Nu'aymi, Huda al-

A woman
  Oranges in the sun; short stories from the Arabian Gulf; edited and translated by Deborah S. Akers, Abubaker A. Bagader

NUCLEAR BOMB _See_ Atomic bomb

NUCLEAR ENERGY

Kalfus, K. Pu-239

NUCLEAR POWER _See_ Nuclear energy

NUCLEAR POWER PLANTS

Percy, B. Meltdown

NUCLEAR WARFARE

See also Atomic bomb

Benioff, D. De composition
Bradbury, R. The garbage collector
Hasak-Lowy, T. The end of Larry's wallet
Lain, D. I read the news today
Liebrecht, S. A good place for the night
Moorcock, M. Crossing into Cambodia
Moorcock, M. Going to Canada
Moorcock, M. Leaving Pasadena
Pohl, F. Fermi and frost
Pohl, F. The knights of Arthur
Polyak, S. and Polyak, C. The prophecy: a Red Sox alternate history
Sallis, J. Jeremiad
Van Pelt, J. The long way home

NUCLEAR WEAPONS

L'Amour, L. The Goose flies South
L'Amour, L. Tailwind to Tibet
Margulis, L. Sunday morning with J. Robert Oppenheimer

A **Nude** in the Rain. Portela, E. L.

Nudist Exposed. Homes, A. M.

NUDITY

Averill, T. F. The man who ran with deer
Barthelme, D. Presents
Duval, P. Rear view
Keret, E. My girlfriend's naked
Reid, G. Lollipop
Ruffin, P. The natural man
Rust, E. M. Robert Horncroft, naked
Shields, C. Dressing down
Weaver, W. Blaze of glory

Number 19. Hirahara, N.

The **number** of people who meet on airplanes. Levithan, D.

The **numbers** game. Clevenger, C.

Numbers up. Lewis, M. M.

Nunc dimittis. Dahl, R.

Nunez, Elizabeth

Lucille
  Trinidad noir; edited by Lisa Allen-Agostini & Jeanne Mason.

Nunez, Sigrid

The naked juror
  Daedalus v134 no1 p118-25 Wint 2005

The Poor Girl [Reprint]
  Harper's v314 p31-3 My 2007

NUNS

See also Ex-nuns

Brite, P. Z. Henry goes shopping
Brown, E. Mules
Bukowski, C. Hard without music
Burke, J. L. Texas City, 1947
Burke, T. Visitation
Erdrich, L. Saint Marie
Finlay, C. C. After the gaud chrysalis
Fulton, A. Happy dust
Gardam, J. The virgins of Bruges
Gifford, B. African adventure story
Gordon, M. The blind spot
Gordon, M. The deacon
Hodgson, W. H. The captain of the onion boat
Jones, L. B. The epicurean
Kennedy, C. Habit
Marley, L. Body and blood
Mohanraj, M. A. Sister Mary (Colombo, 1949)
Morrissette, M. Ave Maria
Oates, J. C. In the region of ice
Ochsner, G. A darkness held
Phan, A. The Delta
Riley, P. Damping down the road
Russell, K. St. Lucy's home for girls raised by wolves
Russo, R. The whore's child
Scoville, S. The pin collectors
Shepard, J. Eustace
Sundaresan, I. Shelter of rain
Zelazny, R. The last Inn on the road with Dannie Plachta

The **nurse**. Machado de Assis

NURSEMAIDS

Brady, C. Slender little thing
Rosen, N. What must I say to you?
Wendroff, Z. Pavlik's mysterious disappearance

NURSERIES (HORTICULTURE)
Lunstrum, K. S. The nursery
Moffett, K. The gardener of Eden
The **nursery**. Lunstrum, K. S.
NURSERY RHYMES
Lanagan, M. Winkie
Nursery Sam. Bova, B.
NURSERY SCHOOLS
Allen, W. The rejection
NURSES AND NURSING
See also Orderlies
Abrams, L. Taj Mahal
Ali, M. N. Live-in
Andreas-Salomé, L. Unit for "Men, internal"
Brady, C. Slender little thing
Cohen, M. The sins of Tomas Benares
Fonseca, R. The book of panegyrics
Fonseca, R. The dwarf
Fulton, A. The nightingales of Troy
Gaitskill, M. An old virgin
Iarovici, D. Tap dance
King, O. We're all in this together
LaValle, V. The angel of loneliness
Lins, O. Easter Sunday
Lunstrum, K. S. The bath
Lynn, D. H. Birnkrandt and Kamenski
Machado de Assis. The nurse
Malae, P. N. The good nurse
Marley, L. Night shift
McAllister, B. Dream baby
McIlvoy, K. Ice
Oates, J. C. Angel of Mercy
Potash, R. The sad house in Talbiye
Randolph, L. The boy in the band uniform
Rash, R. Cold Harbor
Sayles, J. Casa de los Babys
Silver, M. The visitor
Welk, M. V. Code blue
NURSING HOMES
Bolger, D. Martha's streets
Boyers, R. Secrets and sons
Duval, P. Wheatback
Guista, M. A walk outside
MacLaverty, B. The assessment
Mestre-Reed, E. After Elián
Muñoz, M. Ida y vuelta
Munro, A. The bear came over the mountain
Oldshue, R. The levitron
Reed, K. Old soldiers
Reynolds, C. A train to catch
Sayles, J. Dillinger in Hollywood
Scholes, K. Action team-ups number thirty-seven
Schutt, C. See amid the winter's snow
Smith, L. The Happy Memories Club
Steinberg, A. L. Morning at fifty
Nussbaum, Mia
Of Course It's Always the End of Time
Iowa Review v38 no2 p178-9 Fall 2008
Nut-cracking. Bierce, A.
Nutman, Philip
The misadventure of Eat Man and Little Boy, or, How I made a monster
British invasion; edited by Christopher Golden, Tim Lebbon & James A. Moore
Nye, Jody Lynn
Consequences
Thieves' world; enemies of fortune; edited by Lynn Abbey

The growling
This is my funniest; leading science fiction writers present their funniest stories ever; edited by Mike Resnick
The revenge of Chatty Cathy
The Magic toybox; edited by Denise Little
Nye, Naomi Shihab
Local hospitality
Qissat; short stories by Palestinian women; edited by Jo Glanville
Nylund, Eric S.
Butterflies like jewels
Elemental; the Tsunami relief anthology; stories of science fiction and fantasy; [edited by] Steven Savile and Alethea Kontis; introduction by Arthur C. Clarke
Nymph & faun. Templeton, E.
The **nymph's** child. Vaughn, C.

O

O, Chonghui
The bronze mirror
Land of exile: contemporary Korean fiction; translated and edited by Marshall Pihl, Bruce Fulton, and Ju-Chan Fulton
OAKLAND (CALIF.) See California—Oakland
Oakley, Ryan
Jack Jaw and the Arab's ape
Hardcore hardboiled; edited by Todd Robinson; introduction by Otto Penzler
The **oakthing**. Maguire, G.
Oasis of Hope. Coleman, L.
Oates, Joyce Carol
Angel of Mercy
Oates, J. C. The female of the species; tales of mystery and suspense
Angel of wrath
Oates, J. C. The female of the species; tales of mystery and suspense
At the seminary
Oates, J. C. High lonesome; new & selected stories, 1966-2006
Bad habits
Oates, J. C. The museum of Dr. Moses; tales of mystery and suspense
The banshee
Oates, J. C. The female of the species; tales of mystery and suspense
The Adventure of the missing detective and 19 of the year's finest crime and mystery stories!; edited by Ed Gorman and Martin H. Greenberg
BD 11 1 87
Oates, J. C. High lonesome; new & selected stories, 1966-2006
The blind man's sighted daughters
The Best American mystery stories, 2008; edited and with an introduction by George Pelecanos; Otto Penzler, series editor
Oates, J. C. Dear husband,
Bonobo Momma
Michigan Quarterly Review v48 no1 p70-81 Wint 2009
Concerning the case of Bobby T.
Oates, J. C. High lonesome; new & selected stories, 1966-2006

Ochsner, Gina—*Continued*

Last words of the mynah bird

Ochsner, G. People I wanted to be

Signs and markings

Ochsner, G. People I wanted to be

Song of the selkie

Best American fantasy; guest editors Ann & Jeff VanderMeer; series editor Matthew Cheney

Thicker Than Water

The New Yorker v81 no24 p56-63 Ag 22 2005

When the dark is light enough

Ochsner, G. People I wanted to be

Ockert, Jason

Adrift and distant

Ockert, J. Rabbit punches; stories

Des

Ockert, J. Rabbit punches; stories

Deviated septum

Ockert, J. Rabbit punches; stories

Horseshoes

Ockert, J. Rabbit punches; stories

Infants and men

Ockert, J. Rabbit punches; stories

Jakob Loomis

New stories from the South: the year's best, 2007; selected from U.S. magazines by Edward P. Jones with Kathy Pories; with an introduction by Edward P. Jones

The Best American mystery stories 2007; edited and with and introduction by Carl Hiaasen; Otto Penzler, series editor

Leaving

Ockert, J. Rabbit punches; stories

Milkweed

Ockert, J. Rabbit punches; stories

Mother may I

Ockert, J. Rabbit punches; stories

Scarecrowed

Ockert, J. Rabbit punches; stories

Slight

Ockert, J. Rabbit punches; stories

Some storm

Ockert, J. Rabbit punches; stories

Terrified by raisins

Ockert, J. Rabbit punches; stories

Ocky Boxer. Nisbet, R.

O'Connell, Jack

The swag from Doc Hawthorne's

The Best American mystery stories, 2004; edited and with an introduction by Nelson DeMille; Otto Penzler, series editor

O'Connell, Shaun

Paper Route

The Massachusetts Review v48 no3 p392-406 Fall 2007

O'Connor, Flannery

1955: Georgia: Flannery O'Connor Stages a Moral [Excerpt from Good Country People]

Lapham's Quarterly v2 no1 p168-73 Wint 2009

The artificial nigger

The New Granta book of the American short story; edited and introduced by Richard Ford

The displaced person

The best American Catholic short stories; a Sheed & Ward collection; edited by Daniel McVeigh and Patricia Schnapp

Revelation

Children playing before a statue of Hercules; edited and introduced by David Sedaris

About

Duncan, A. Unique chicken goes in reverse

Johnson, G. Last encounter with the enemy

Parodies, imitations, etc.

Effinger, G. A. Put your hands together

O'Connor, Joseph

Two little clouds

New Dubliners; edited by Oona Frawley

O'Connor, Mary Flannery *See* O'Connor, Flannery

O'Connor, Stephen

Bestiary

New England Review v27 no4 p8-11 2006

Love Is the Crooked Thing

The Massachusetts Review v50 no1-2 p244-56 Spr/Summ 2009

Powers and Principalities

The Massachusetts Review v46 no3 p418-37 Fall 2005

Trouble

New England Review v29 no3 p88-104 2008

White Fire

TriQuarterly no132 p186-99 2008

Ziggurat

The New Yorker v85 no19 p66-71 Je 29 2009

Octo. McIntyre, V.

October. Olafsson, O.

October in the chair. Gaiman, N.

Octobers. Sallis, J.

OCTOPUS

Beagle, P. S. The fable of the octopus

Hodgson, W. H. From the tideless sea (first part)

McIntyre, V. Octo

Octopus, the Sausalito quarterly of new writing, art & ideas. Connell, E. S.

The **odd** fellow. Crone, M.

The **odds**. Cook, T. H.

The **odds** it would be you. Mattison, A.

The **oddskeeper's** daughter. Spencer, W. B.

Oddsmaker. Wellen, E.

Ode to Katan Amano. Kiernan, C. R.

O'Dea, Lori

Shame

The Massachusetts Review v46 no4 p627-47 Wint 2005/2006

ODESSA (UKRAINE) *See* Ukraine—Odessa

Odessa. DeMarinis, R.

Odoevskiĭ, V. F. (Vladimir Fedorovich), kniaz´

The year 4338. Letters from St. Petersburg [abridged]

Worlds apart; an anthology of Russian fantasy and science fiction; edited and with commentary by Alexander Levitsky; translated by Alexander Levitsky and Martha T. Kitchen

Odoevskiĭ, Vladimir Fedorovich *See* Odoevskiĭ, V. F. (Vladimir Fedorovich), kniaz´, 1803-1869

O'Doherty, Susan
My most memorable encounter
Sex for America; politically inspired erotica;
edited by Stephen Elliott
Odom, Mel
The affair of the wooden boy
The Magic toybox; edited by Denise Little
O'Donoghue, Mary
Motocross
Agni no62 p96-108 2005
Odrach, Theodore
The night before Christmas
The Ecco book of Christmas stories; edited
by Alberto Manguel
O'Driscoll, Mike
13 O'clock
Inferno; new tales of terror and the supernatu-
ral; edited by Ellen Datlow.
The silence of the falling stars
The Year's best fantasy and horror: seven-
teenth annual collection; edited by Ellen
Datlow, Kelly Link and Gavin J. Grant
ODYSSEUS (LEGENDARY CHARACTER)
James, C. L. R. Ulysses—a great hero
Ōe, Kenzaburō
Abandoned children of this planet
Telling tales; edited by Nadine Gordimer
OEDIPUS (LEGENDARY CHARACTER)
Disch, T. M. In praise of older women
Of a sweet slow dance in the wake of temporary
dogs. Castro, A.-T.
Of all the insatiable human urges. Rust, E. M.
Of cheese and Christ. Domecq, B.
Of Course It's Always the End of Time.
Nussbaum, M.
Of honor and the lion. Roberson, J.
Of Jimmie Harris. Bonner, M. O.
Of late I dreamt of Venus. Van Pelt, J.
Of love and other monsters. Singh, V.
Of Love and Radishes. Manley, C. B.
Of metal men and scarlet thread and dancing with
the sunrise. Scholes, K.
Of Music, Painting and Other Matters. Riva, P. L.
Of mystery there is no end. Michaels, L.
Of soil and climate. Wolfe, G.
Of time and the yan. Zelazny, R.
Off. Bender, A.
Off island. Parker, M.
Off-site. Charters, D.
Off the mangrove coast. L'Amour, L.
Off the rack. Vaughan, E. A.
Off the track. Molodowsky, K.
Off to see the wizard. Monteleone, T. F.
Offenders. Coward, M.
The **offer.** McCauley, W.
An **offering** to the moon. Smith, C. A.
Offertory. Hempel, A.
OFFICE WORKERS
Adameșteanu, G. Provisional [excerpt]
Boudinot, R. Bee beard
Brodsky, M. Closure
Clayton, J. J. Losers in paradise
Crouse, D. Code
Dokey, R. The mouse
Extavour, R. M. Eric's turn
Faiz, J. The prize
Granados, C. Love web
Kun, M. Touched, very touched
Lane, J. Among the dead

Lange, R. Dead boys
Levi, P. Bureau of vital statistics
Luongo, M. Pretty
Meno, J. An apple could make you laugh
Messinger, J. Hiding out
Michalopoulou, A. What will you do next?
Moffett, K. Ursa, on zoo property and off
Molodowsky, K. A letter
Moore, M. The Mikado's favorite song
Mukhopadhyay, T. The calendar
Rich, M. Foggery
Sankaran, L. Mysore coffee
Searls, D. The cubicles
Shiina, M. The yellow tent on the roof
Shomer, E. The summer of questions
Sladek, J. T. Masterson and the clerks
Sterling, B. Code
Thompson, J. Mr. Rat
Upadhyay, S. The wedding hero
Wild, P. Cruiser's Creek
Officers weep. Orozco, D.
The **official** family. Fuentes, C.
Offit, Sidney
No time for senior's
Brooklyn noir; edited by Tim McLoughlin
Offshore. Wilson, F. P.
Offutt, Andrew
Dark of the moon
Thieves' world; enemies of fortune; edited by
Lynn Abbey
Offutt, Chris
Chuck's bucket
McSweeney's mammoth treasury of thrilling
tales; edited by Michael Chabon
Cutting the Gut
Gettysburg Review v19 no3 p479-86 Aut
2006
Second hand
Best of the South: from the second decade of
New stories from the South; selected and
introduced by Anne Tyler
O'Flynn, Catherine
Snare, girl
Noise; fiction inspired by Sonic Youth; edited
bt Peter Wild; introduction by Lee Ranaldo
Og. Mandelman, A.
Ogawa, Yoko
Pregnancy Diary
The New Yorker v81 no42 p98-107 D 26
2005/Ja 2 2006
Ogden, George Washington
McCoy's stampede
Adventures in the West; stories for young
readers; edited by Susanne George Bloom-
field and Eric Melvin Reed
OGLALA INDIANS
Urrea, L. A. Bid farewell to her many horses
Oh, death. Lasdun, J.
Oh, false young man!. Baker, K.
Oh, hum. Baumbach, J.
Oh, Joseph, I'm so tired. Yates, R.
Oh land of national paradise, how glorious are thy
bounties. Vollmer, M.
Oh Lord! Why not? Greenman, B.
Oh My Darling. Davenport, S.
Oh, sordid shame!. Kelly, R.
O'Hagan, Andrew
Foreigners
The New Yorker v80 no38 p92-100 D 6 2004

O'Hagan, Andrew—*Continued*
Gordon
   The book of other people; edited by Zadie
      Smith
O'Hanlon, Shane
A Helpful Nurse
   Journal of the American Geriatrics Society
      v56 no11 p2139 N 2008
O'Hara, Craig
A Strange Case
   Confrontation no100 p154-66 Fall 2007/Wint
      2008
O'Hara, Mary
My friend Flicka
   Adaptations: from short story to big screen;
      35 great stories that have inspired great
      films; edited by Stephanie Harrison
OHIO
Barthelme, D. Up, aloft in the air
Dunbar, P. L. Nelse Hatton's vengeance
Magee, K. Straitjacket
Miller, A. L. My summer of love
Pollock, D. R. Discipline
Pollock, D. R. Hair's fate
Pollock, D. R. Lard
Pollock, D. R. Real life
Rahman, I. Eating, Ohio
Rahman, I. I dream of microwaves
Rahman, I. Real, actual life
Weaver, W. Bad blood
Welch, N. Thanatology
Wieland, M. Swan's home
   Frontier and pioneer life
   See Frontier and pioneer life—Ohio
   Cincinnati
Jones, N. Half the story
   Cleveland
Brazaitis, M. Coming home
Ohlin, Alix
An analysis of some troublesome recent behav-
   ior
   Ohlin, A. Babylon and other stories
Babylon
   Ohlin, A. Babylon and other stories
Edgewater
   Ohlin, A. Babylon and other stories
Ghostwriting
   Ohlin, A. Babylon and other stories
I love to dance at weddings
   Ohlin, A. Babylon and other stories
The Idea Man
   Southwest Review v92 no3 p345-53 2007
In trouble with the Dutchman
   Ohlin, A. Babylon and other stories
   The Massachusetts Review v47 no4 p767-82
      Wint 2006
The King of Kohlrabi
   Ohlin, A. Babylon and other stories
Land of the midnight sun
   Ohlin, A. Babylon and other stories
Local news
   Ohlin, A. Babylon and other stories
Meeting Uncle Bob
   Ohlin, A. Babylon and other stories
The Only Child
   Ploughshares v33 no2/3 p94-105 Fall 2007

Simple exercises for the beginning student
   The Best American short stories, 2005; select-
      ed from U.S. and Canadian magazines by
      Michael Chabon with Katrina Kenison;
      with an introduction by Michael Chabon
   Ohlin, A. Babylon and other stories
The swanger blood
   Ohlin, A. Babylon and other stories
   Southwest Review v89 no2/3 p335-45 2004
The Teacher
   Daedalus v137 no3 p126-34 Summ 2008
The tennis partner
   Ohlin, A. Babylon and other stories
A theory of entropy
   Ohlin, A. Babylon and other stories
Transcription
   Best new American voices 2004; guest editor
      John Casey; series editors John Kulka and
      Natalie Danford
   Ohlin, A. Babylon and other stories
Vigo Park
   TriQuarterly no129 p250-7 2007
Wonders never cease
   Ohlin, A. Babylon and other stories
You are here
   Ohlin, A. Babylon and other stories
OIL INDUSTRY *See* Petroleum industry
Oil of dog. Bierce, A.
OIL WELLS *See* Petroleum industry
OJIBWA INDIANS *See* Chippewa Indians
Ojikutu, Bayo
The gospel of moral ends
   Chicago noir; edited by Neal Pollack
Ojitos. Hernandez, L.
El **ojo** de agua. Straight, S.
Okanoggan Falls. Gilman, C.
Okasi, Mehdi Tavana
Salvation army
   Best new American voices 2009; guest editor
      Mary Gaitskill; series editors John Kulka
      and Natalie Danford
O'Keefe, Michael
The Proposal
   Bomb no92 p102-3 Summ 2005
O'Keitinn, Risteard
Dogged
   Pushcart prize XXXI: best of the small press-
      es 2007; edited by Bill Henderson; with the
      Pushcart Prize editors
   The Antioch Review v63 no3 p548-62 Summ
      2005
Okkervil River. Tolstaia, T.
OKLAHOMA
Daugherty, T. Lamplighter
Daugherty, T. The standoff
Leonard, E. How Carlos Webster changed his
   name to Carl and became a famous Okla-
   homa lawman
Okorafor, Nnedimma
When scarabs multiply
   So long been dreaming; postcolonial science
      fiction & fantasy; Nalo Hopkinson &
      Uppinder Mehan, eds
Okorafor-Mbachu, Nnedimma *See* Okorafor,
   Nnedimma

Okri, Ben
What the tapster saw
  The Anchor book of modern African stories;
    edited by Nadežda Obradovic; with a fore-
    word by Chinua Achebe
Olafsson, Olaf
April
  Olafsson, O. Valentines; stories
August
  Olafsson, O. Valentines; stories
December
  Olafsson, O. Valentines; stories
February
  Olafsson, O. Valentines; stories
January
  Olafsson, O. Valentines; stories
July
  Olafsson, O. Valentines; stories
June
  Olafsson, O. Valentines; stories
March
  Olafsson, O. Valentines; stories
May
  Olafsson, O. Valentines; stories
November
  Olafsson, O. Valentines; stories
October
  Olafsson, O. Valentines; stories
On the lake
  The O. Henry Prize stories 2008; edited and
    with an introduction by Laura Furman; with
    essays on the stories they admire most by
    jurors Chimamanda Ngozi Adiche, David
    Leavitt, David Means
September
  Olafsson, O. Valentines; stories
Olchváry, Paul
(tr.) See Dragomán, György
Olczak, Martin
T H Jacobson
  The Literary Review (Madison, N.J.) v48 no4
    p247-9 Summ 2005
An **old** 3 a.m. story. Clayton, J. J.
Old Abe's conversion. Dunbar, P. L.
OLD AGE
        See also Aging; Elderly
Adichie, C. N. Ghosts
Aird, C. Exit strategy
Anaya, R. A. In search of Epifano
Anderson, B. Living on the beach
Apple, M. The Jew of Home Depot
Arjouni, J. At peace
Asch, S. A surrendered home
Atwood, M. The bad news
Atwood, M. The boys at the Lab
Auchincloss, L. Due process
Barthelme, D. Belief
Barthelme, D. This newspaper here
Barthelme, D. You are cordially invited
Baum, L. F. Aunt 'Phroney's boy
Beattie, A. The last odd day in L. A.
Beattie, A. The rabbit hole as likely explanation
Beattie, A. The rabbitt hole as likely
    explanantion
Bender, K. E. Theft
Berg, E. Over the hill and into the woods
Berniker, S. J. Aqua Velva Smitty
Bierce, A. The applicant
Bierce, A. Infernia

Bolger, D. Martha's streets
Bradbury, R. Arrival and departure
Bradbury, R. A far-away guitar
Bradbury, R. Junior
Bradbury, R. Miss Appletree and I
Bradbury, R. Season of disbelief
Bradbury, R. The swan
Bradbury, R. Time intervening/interim
Broches, R. Little Abrahams
Buckler, E. The snowman
Bulushi, S. Sounds of the sea
Bunin, I. A. Old and young
Burgin, R. Notes on Mrs. Slaughter
Capote, T. Preacher's legend
Carofiglio, G. Christmas Eves
Corso, P. Raw egg in beer
Cozarinsky, E. View of dawn over the lake
Crouse, D. Copy Kats
Crowther, P. Days of the wheel
Davidson, R. Twilight in Caeli-Amur
Davis, J. S. Ava Bean
Davis, J. S. Lovely Lily
DeMarinis, R. Bête noire
Déry, T. Philemon and Baucis
Doran, M. M. End October
Downs, G. Between states
Downs, G. Black pork
Ducornet, R. La Goulue in retirement
Dunbar, P. L. The brief cure of Aunt Fanny
Durban, P. Gravity
Duval, P. Wheatback
Eisenberg, D. Someone to talk to
Erdrich, L. Disaster stamps of Pluto
Erpenbeck, J. Light a fire or leave
Fonseca, R. The book of panegyrics
Fox, P. The broad estates of death
Fulton, A. Queen Wintergreen
Gabrielyan, N. Bee heaven
Garcia-Aguilera, C. The dinner
Gardam, J. Babette
Gardam, J. The last reunion
Gardam, J. The latter days of Mr. Jones
Gardam, J. The Milly Ming
Gardam, J. The people of Privilege Hill
Gilbert, A. The invisible witness
Gordon, C. The presence
Gordon, M. Mrs. Cassidy's last year
Gordon, M. Out of the fray
Greer, A. S. Darkness
Groff, L. Sir fleeting
Hamer-Jacklyn, S. A guest
Hamer-Jacklyn, S. A love story
Harris, J. Faith and Hope go shopping
Hatoum, M. The truth is a seven-headed animal
Hawes, L. Halcyon House
Hecht, J. Over there
Helprin, M. Sail shining in white
Henry, S. Sister death
Holthe, T. U. The necklace
Husayn, 'A. A. An encounter
Hwang, F. The old gentleman
Jones, E. P. Marie
Jones, N. What you call winter
Jordan, P. The hustle
Judah, S. Dreams
Judah, S. Old man Moses
July, M. The sister
Kaisaridis, Y. The old man and the tree

OLD AGE—*Continued*

Walters, A. L. Las Vegas, New Mexico, July 1969

Waters, D. Mr. Epstein and the dealer

West, D. Mrs. Creel

Wharton, E. Mrs. Manstey's view

Williams, J. R. Rose

Yates, D. Bring everybody

Old age. Opatoshu, J.

OLD AGE HOMES

See also Nursing homes; Retirement communities

Barnes, J. Knowing French

Fonseca, R. The eleventh of May

Hale, J. C. Claire

Hamer-Jacklyn, S. A love story

Harris, J. Faith and Hope go shopping

Klassen, S. Ending with poetry

Reinhorn, H. My name

Thormahlen, A. Visiting hour

Old Ages. Pariani, L.

Old and young. Bunin, I. A.

The old badger game. Proulx, A.

Old bag dad. Miles, K.

Old batteries. Qi, S.

Old Border Road. Miller, S. G.

Old boys, old girls. Jones, E. P.

The old country. Guista, M.

An old-country Erev Pesakh. Molodowsky, K.

The old dictionary. Davis, L.

Old Doc Yak. L'Amour, L.

Old Earl died pulling traps. Higgins, G. V.

The old economy husband. Dormen, L.

The old enemy. Nollas, D.

An old fairy tale. Schwitters, K.

Old flame. Trevor, W.

The Old Friend. Furman, L.

An old friend. Kiely, B.

Old friends. Clayton, J. J.

Old friends. McGuane, T.

Old friends. Nix, G.

Old Garfield's heart. Howard, R. E.

The old gentleman. Hwang, F.

Old girlfriends. Updike, D.

Old glory. Coville, B.

"Old Glory" in the desert. Paine, R. D.

Old Golly. Hodgson, W. H.

Old Grimes. McFadden, D.

Old Hacker. Kelly, R.

Old Haunts. Gray, V.

Old haunts. Matheson, R.

The old house. Parks, T.

Old house. Tognazzini, A.

The Old Impossible. Bloom, A.

Old joy. Raymond, J.

OLD LADIES *See* Old age

Old leatherwings. Bear, E.

OLD MAIDS *See* Single women

The old man. Lasdun, J.

The old man and the tree. Kaisaridis, Y.

The old man at the railroad crossing. Maxwell, W.

Old man Moses. Judah, S.

The old man who was afraid of falling. Maxwell, W.

OLD MEN *See* Old age

Old mortality. Porter, K. A.

Old nylon bathrobes. Ronk, M. C.

An old offender. Howard, C. C.

Old pancakes. Silko, L.

Old Providence. Shukman, H.

Old Red. Gordon, C.

The old rugged cross. Bisson, T.

Old school. Onspaugh, M.

Old Sins. Swan, M.

Old soldiers. Reed, K.

An old-time Christmas. Dunbar, P. L.

An old virgin. Gaitskill, M.

Old Virginia. Barron, L.

Old Waitresses. Almond, S.

The old woman whose house was beside a running stream. Maxwell, W.

OLD WOMEN *See* Old age

The old world. Palwick, S.

Old Wounds. O'Brien, E.

An older lover etc. Williams, J.

The oldest rivalry. Arndorfer, J.

Oldshue, Robert

The levitron

The Best of the Bellevue Literary Review; edited by Dannielle Ofri and the staff of the Bellevue Literary Review

November Storm

New England Review v29 no2 p71-83 2008

Summer Friend

Gettysburg Review v21 no4 p638-61 Wint 2008

Ole Conju'in Joe. Dunbar, P. L.

Oleša, Jurij *See* Olesha, IUriĭ Karlovich, 1899-1960

Olesha, IUriĭ Karlovich

Love

Worlds apart; an anthology of Russian fantasy and science fiction; edited and with commentary by Alexander Levitsky; translated by Alexander Levitsky and Martha T. Kitchen

Oleson, Lee

Charles and Manuel

Confrontation no100 p55-63 Fall 2007/Wint 2008

Olive. Rees, R.

Oliver, Diane

Neighbors

Short stories of the civil rights movement; an anthology; edited by Margaret Earley Whitt

Oliver, Frances

Dancing on air

The Year's best fantasy and horror: eighteenth annual collection; edited by Ellen Datlow, Kelly Link & Gavin J. Grant

Oliver, Reggie

Among the tombs

The Year's best fantasy and horror: nineteenth annual collection; edited by Ellen Datlow and Kelly Link & Gavin J. Grant

Mr. Poo-Poo

The Year's best fantasy and horror: twenty-first annual collection; edited by Ellen Datlow and Kelly Link & Gavin J. Grant

Oliver Twink. Cooper, D.

Olivia and Xania. Fonseca, R.

"Ollie, oh . . .". Chute, C.

Olmos, Gabriela

El Gran Enano / The Great Dwarf

Artes de Mexico no83 p32-3, 71 2007

O'Loughlin, Jim
  I'm on Fire
    The North American Review v290 no2 p33
    Mr/Ap 2005
Olsen, E. J.
  Snow angel
    Detroit noir; edited by E. J. Olsen & John C.
    Hocking
Olsen, Gregg
  The crime of my life
    Killer year; stories to die for . . . from the
    hottest new crime writers; edited by Lee
    Child
Olsen, Lance
  Six questions for an alien
    Text: Ur; the new book of masks; [edited by
    Forrest Aguirre]
Olsen, Sondra Spatt
  When We Were Virgins
    The Antioch Review v65 no4 p744-57 Fall
    2007
Olsen, Tillie
  I stand here ironing
    Inside the hornet's head; an anthology of
    Jewish American writing; edited by Jerome
    Charyn
Olson, Richard J.
  A Curious Assignment
    The Advocate (Vancouver, B.C.) v66 no3
    p366-70 My 2008
Oltion, Jerry
  The great Martian pyramid hoax
    Fourth planet from the sun; tales of Mars
    from The Magazine of Fantasy & Science
    Fiction; edited by Gordon Van Gelder
Olúo. Correa, A.
Olympians. Burke, K.
OLYMPIC GAMES
  Clarke, B. Carrying the torch
The **Olympic** Sleep Event. Lehner, C.
Olympic talent. Lovett, R. A.
O'Mahony, Michael
  Every ounce of soul
    Expletive deleted; edited by Jen Jordan
Omari, Ifemu
  Obeah catastrophe
    Her Majesty; 21 stories by women; edited by
    Jackie Gay and Emma Hargrave
The **Omega** Force. Moody, R.
The **omelet** king. Mandelbaum, P.
The **omelette** and the egg. Auchincloss, L.
OMENS
  Rust, E. M. The prisoner pear
The **ominous** philologist. Ducornet, R.
Omphalosphere: New York 2057. Cohen, J.
On a bad day you can see forever. Allen, W.
On a cold, dark night. Biller, M.
On a day of rest. Molodowsky, K.
On a scale of one to three. Lain, D.
On becoming immortal. Nolan, W. F.
On being french. Brown, D.
On board the martian liner. Breuer, M. J.
On Chesil Beach. McEwan, I.
On her knees. Winton, T.
On hold. Romano, T.
On Junius Bridge. Pearlman, E.
On Messalonskee Lake. Ward, A. E.
On Monday Last Week. Adichie, C. N.
On Monday of last week. Adichie, C. N.

On Mrs. Willie Masters. Coover, R.
On Not Growing Up [Excerpt from Conjunctions:
    50] Marcus, B.
On one familiar street. Bunin, I. A.
On Riding a Death Train. Peña, D.
On Saturday afternoon. Sillitoe, A.
On Saturday the siren sounds at noon. Petry, A. L.
On sex and relationships. Boudinot, R.
On Skua Isalnd. Langan, J.
On sleepless roads. Davidson, C.
On the bank of an alien stream. Asch, S.
On the bridge. Hodgson, W. H.
On the brink of that bright new world. Reed, R.
On the bus. Manley, C.
On the cliff by the river. Rosenbaum, B.
On the Decline of Sparrows. Cobb, W. J.
On the eve of the journey. Molodowsky, K.
On the evidence: a Liam Campbell short story.
    Stabenow, D.
On the Ferry to St Christophe. Young, B.
On the front. Burke, T.
On the golden porch. Tolstaia, T.
On the grounds of the complex commemorating
    the Nazis' treatment of the Jews. Hasak-
    Lowy, T.
On the high frontier. Flynn, M.
On the horse of dawn. Coloane, F.
On the Importance of the Lesbian Continuum at
    Daytona Beach, 2004: A Scale of One
    Young Woman's Sexuality. Doench, M.
On the island. Jacobsen, J.
On the island. Swan, G.
On the lake. Olafsson, O.
On the middle guard. Bower, B. M.
On the Mourning Customs of Elephants. Epstein,
    A.
On the nature of human romantic interaction.
    Iagnemma, K.
On the nutritional value of dreams. Keret, E.
On the other side of the bridge. Opatoshu, J.
On the rainy river. O'Brien, T.
On the road to Amurang. L'Amour, L.
On the road to new Egypt. Ford, J.
On the road to Splenoba. Zelazny, R.
On the roof. McLean, S.
On the roundabout. MacLaverty, B.
On the run. Neggers, C.
On the sea: a sailor's story [variant title: At sea]
    Chekhov, A. P.
On the show. Tower, W.
On the sidewalk, bleeding. McBain, E.
On the stealing of stories. Gospodinov, G.
On the streets. Trevor, W.
On the strip. Trezise, R.
On the taste of names. Gospodinov, G.
On the Train. Malpede, K.
On the train. Wolfe, G.
On the way to my father's funeral, he tells me his
    story. Baumbach, J.
On the way to Wonderland. Wendroff, Z.
On their way. Andreas-Salomé, L.
On twilight. Ruefle, M.
On vision. Brennan, K.
O'Nan, Stewart
  The great Rushdie
    Politically inspired; edited by Stephen Elliott;
    assistant editor, Gabriel Kram; associate ed-
    itors, Elizabeth Brooks [et al.]
Once a cowboy. Evans, M.

The **once-a-week** performance. Malae, P. N.
Once and future. Pratchett, T.
Once in a lifetime. Lahiri, J.
Once more, Lazarus. Tobar, H.
"**Once** on the shores of the stream, Senegambia . . .". Mordecai, P.
Once Removed. Montemarano, N.
Once the shore. Yoon, P.
Once Upon a Fishing Trip. Carter, W. B.
Once upon a time. Nolan, W. F.
Once upon a time there was a tiny mouse. Schwitters, K.
Once You Find Passion . . . How Can You Let It Go? Porter, J.
One. Effinger, G. A.
One. Moran, A.
The **one**. Nelsen, G.
One Act. Apple, J.
One among us. Aydinoglu, Y.
The **one** arm man. See Leonard, E. Man with the iron arm [variant title: The one arm man]
One blue star. Miller, M.
One charge of powder. Le May, A.
One Christmas at Shiloh. Dunbar, P. L.
One day this will all be yours. Meyer, P.
One death to go. Auslander, S.
One dog happy. McNett, M.
One–dollar jackpot. Connelly, M.
One Endless English Evening. White, E.
One evening's work. James, H.
One-Eyed Jack and the Suicide King. Bear, E.
One fast Packard. Hamilton, S.
One for the books. Matheson, R.
One good one. Hogan, C.
One Hundred Four. Chase, A.
One hundred percent. Keret, E.
One Hundred Rubies of a Pomegranate. Roy, R.
One kind of officer. Bierce, A.
One kiss on the mouth in Mombasa. Keret, E.
One Last Chinese Zinger. Phillian, G. S.
One last game. Reed, R.
One last gun notch. L'Amour, L.
One last story about girls and chocolate. Kun, M.
One last tale of the nineties. Gospodinov, G.
One last time for old times' sake. Busch, F.
One leg. Gifford, B.
One less concern. Thijssen, V.
The **one** marvelous thing. Ducornet, R.
One Million B.C., The Prehistory of Love. Nelson, V.
One Minus One. Toíbín, C.
One Mississippi. Raiche, J.
One more for the road. Knightly, R.
One night. Andreas-Salomé, L.
One night. Levi, P.
One night in 1979 I did too much coke and couldn't sleep and had what I thought was a million-dollar idea to write the definitive tell-all book about glam rock based on my own personal experience but this is as far as I got. Cooper, D.
One night in Africa. Eberhardt, I.
One night of death. Block, L.
One night on Riga's train. Taha, M. A.
One night; or, Scheherazade's bare minimum. Disch, T. M.
One of Our Whales Is Missing. Buckley, C.
One of star wars, one of doom. Abbott, L. K.

One of the missing. Bierce, A.
One of twins. Bierce, A.
One of us. Jablonski, N.
One officer, one man. Bierce, A.
One person. Rand, K.
One Pink, One Black. Goyette, M. E.
One potato two potato. Anderson, B.
One red rose on a new black dress. Bukoski, A.
One serving of bad luck. Chercover, S.
One Shabbos evening. Newman, L.
One She Once. Unferth, D. O.
One shot. Parrish, P. J.
One shot difference. DuBois, B.
One small step. Scholes, K.
One stick: both ends sharpened. Shirley, J.
One Summer Night. Lipman, E.
One swallow doesn't make a summer. Thomas, E.
The **one** that got away. Smith, J.
The **one** that got away. Teppo, M.
The **One** Thing She Would Not Do. Stern, D.
The **one** thing that she would not do. Stern, D.
One Time. Carey, E.
One true love. Lippman, L.
One, two, three. Cain, P.
One up. Romano, T.
One valve opens. Messinger, J.
One way journey. Silverberg, R.
One, Whispering Pines. Fallon, M.
One year. Brenner, Y. H.
One Year in Paradise. Klyuchareva, N.
One year later. Hayashi, M.
O'Neill, Heather
  The End of Pinky
  The Walrus v5 no1 p73-4 Ja/F 2008
O'Neill, Joseph
  Promises, promises
  The American Scholar v78 no2 p109 Spr 2009
  The World of Cheese
  Harper's v318 p61-8 F 2009
O'Neill, R.
  Fighting man [Medical Humanities, v30 no2 December 2004]
  Journal of Medical Ethics v30 no2 p95 D 2004 supp
The **ones** without visas. Harleman, A.
Oness, Elizabeth
  Underwater Adventure
  Gettysburg Review v19 no4 p597-605 Wint 2006
Ong, Yi-Ping
  Marriages are Made in Heaven
  Harvard Review (1992) no25 p174-86 Fall 2003
The **onion** and I. Averill, T. F.
ONJ.com. McIntyre, V.
Only a phase. Newman, L.
Only a thing. Nelson, A.
Only Afternoon in Granada. Ponte, A. J.
The **Only** Child. Ohlin, A.
The **only** game. Lane, J.
The **only** good judge. Wheat, C.
Only good ones. Leonard, E.
Only goodness. Lahiri, J.
Only in your dreams. Frood, A.
Only kids are afraid of the dark. Martin, G. R. R.
The **only** light to see by. Murphy, Y.
The **only** man. Maḥfūẓ, N.
The **only** meaning of the oil-wet water. Eggers, D.

Only on a Sunday morning. Dunn, G.
The **only** one of millions just like him. Berg, E.
The **Only** Part Left. Bukai, Z.
Only partly here. Shepard, L.
The **only** son of the doctor. Gordon, M.
The **only** speaker of his tongue. Malouf, D.
Only the dead know Brooklyn. Wolfe, T.
Only the strong survive. Byrne, M.
Only the words are different. Sallis, J.
Only this. Dahl, R.
The **only** way out. Chekhov, A. P.
The **only** word I know in Spanish. Francis, P.
Onspaugh, Mark
  Old school
    The Horror Writers Association presents Blood lite; an anthology of humorous horror stories; edited by Kevin J. Anderson
ONTARIO *See* Canada—Ontario
Ool Athag. Webb, D.
Oops. Donoghue, E.
Oops!. Ducornet, R.
The **Oort** crowd. MacLeod, K.
Opatoshu, Joseph
  The evil urge
    Shining and shadow; an anthology of early Yiddish stories from the Lower East Side; edited and translated by Albert Waldinger
  A house on Gorek Street
    Shining and shadow; an anthology of early Yiddish stories from the Lower East Side; edited and translated by Albert Waldinger
  In the saloon
    Shining and shadow; an anthology of early Yiddish stories from the Lower East Side; edited and translated by Albert Waldinger
  Morris and his son Philip
    Shining and shadow; an anthology of early Yiddish stories from the Lower East Side; edited and translated by Albert Waldinger
  Moyshe Liar
    Shining and shadow; an anthology of early Yiddish stories from the Lower East Side; edited and translated by Albert Waldinger
  Old age
    Shining and shadow; an anthology of early Yiddish stories from the Lower East Side; edited and translated by Albert Waldinger
  On the other side of the bridge
    Shining and shadow; an anthology of early Yiddish stories from the Lower East Side; edited and translated by Albert Waldinger
  The saloon keeper's girl
    Shining and shadow; an anthology of early Yiddish stories from the Lower East Side; edited and translated by Albert Waldinger
  Saloon—night
    Shining and shadow; an anthology of early Yiddish stories from the Lower East Side; edited and translated by Albert Waldinger
Open all night. LaBute, N.
Open and shut. Schutz, B. M.
The **open** door. Martin, V.
Open doors. Smith, M. M.
Open heart. Schwarzschild, E.
Open-heart surgery. Clayton, J. J.
Open house. Collins, M. A.
Open house. D'Ambrosio, C., Jr.
Open house. Kellerman, F.
Open House. Seigel, A.

An **open** letter concerning sponsorship. Muirhead, M.
An **open** letter to Doctor X. Prose, F.
An **open** letter to the Bush administration. Morgana, M.
Open mike. Nolan, J.
Open my heart. McNally, T. M.
Open–Source Science. Sterling, B.
Open Up and Say Ow. Almond, S.
Openclose. Bisson, T.
Opening day. Geary, T. M.
Opening Her Text. Hahn, K.
Opening One Eye at a Time. Twitty, A.
OPERA
  Charnas, S. M. A musical interlude
  Cross, E. Appearances
  Disch, T. M. A knight at the opera
  Gordon, M. Eleanor's music
  Green, G. Creatures of the mind
  Green, G. A flood of memories
  Green, G. "Such dear ecstasy"
  Green, G. "This very vivd morn"
  Green, G. Voices in a mask
  Green, G. "Your sister and some wine!"
  Helprin, M. Il colore ritrovato
  Ingalls, R. Last act: the madhouse
  Robinson, R. A perfect stranger
Opera. Galloway, J.
OPERATION DESERT STORM *See* Persian Gulf War, 1991
Operation northwoods. Grippando, J.
Operation Tesla. Hecht, J.
OPERATIONS, SURGICAL *See* Surgery
Opie, James
  The Hunters, the Hunted
    Parabola v32 no1 p41 Spr 2007
The **opium** general. Moorcock, M.
Oppel, Jean-Hugues
  Paris calling
    Paris noir; capital crime fiction; edited by Maxim Jakubowski
Oppenheim, Edward Phillips
  The case of Mr and Mrs Stetson
    The Mammoth book of vintage whodunnits; edited by Maxim Jakubowski
OPPENHEIMER, J. ROBERT, 1904-1967
About
  Margulis, L. Sunday morning with J. Robert Oppenheimer
Oppenheimer, Robert *See* Oppenheimer, J. Robert, 1904-1967
Opportunity. LaBute, N.
The **opposite** field. Parenti, J.
The **opposite** of solid. Baker, L. P.
The **opposite** of zero. Singleton, G.
Oprah's song. Greer, R. O.
OPTOMETRISTS
  Lethem, J. The glasses
Or be to not. Cadnum, M.
Or else. Nelson, A.
Or else, part I: In the automat. Scott, J.
Or else, part II: What will happen. Scott, J.
Or else, part III: Rain on concrete. Scott, J.
Or else, part IV: That place. Scott, J.
The **oracle** spoke. Phillips, H.
ORACLES
  Phillips, H. The oracle spoke
  Silverberg, R. In the House of Double Minds
Oral Histories. Schwarz, G.

ORANGE

Mundhri, Y. b. S. a.- . Oranges in the sun

Orange. Gaiman, N.

The **orange**. Rosenbaum, B.

The **orange** bird. Swan, G.

The **orange** fish. Shields, C.

Oranges in the sun. Mundhri, Y. b. S. a.- .

Oranges, Patas, Puddles. Griner, P.

ORANGUTANS

Willis, C. Samaritan

The **orchard**. Buckler, E.

Orchestra(ted) Sam. Bova, B.

The **orchid**. Roque, M. V.

Orczy, Emmuska, Baroness

The Dublin mystery

The Mammoth book of vintage whodunnits; edited by Maxim Jakubowski

The **ordeal** at Mt. Hope. Dunbar, P. L.

Order of the day. Cony, C. H.

The **order** of things. Troy, J.

ORDERLIES

Jablonski, N. Big guy

Johnson, D. Emergency

Orderly: how I spent that year after high school. Bradford, A.

An **Ordinary** Death. Hussein, A.

Ordinary facts. Kirac, R.

Ordinary Life. Bean, B.

An **ordinary** soldier of the Queen. Joyce, G.

ORDNANCE

Ruffin, P. Crows

OREGON

Bierce, A. How to saw bears

Chilson, P. American food

Chilson, P. Toumani Ogun

Daughtry, P. The centaur's son

Doerr, A. The caretaker

Hwang, F. Intruders

Judson, T. The thief catcher

Kalotay, D. Snapshots

Lain, D. The suburbs of the citadel of thought

Le Guin, U. K. Ether, Or

Nolan, W. F. Scotch on the rocks

Percy, B. The caves in Oregon

Percy, B. Crash

Percy, B. The faulty builder

Percy, B. Meltdown

Percy, B. Refresh, refresh

Percy, B. Somebody is going to have to pay for this

Percy, B. Unearthed

Percy, B. When the bear came

Percy, B. Whisper

Percy, B. The woods

Raymond, J. Benny

Raymond, J. Old joy

Raymond, J. Train choir

Reinhorn, H. Charlotte

Reinhorn, H. Golden pioneers

Romm, R. The arrival

Rusch, K. K. Patriotic gestures

Rust, E. M. Moon over water

Shayla, H. Himmelen

Stubblefield, R. Preserves

Tognazzini, A. Gainesville, Oregon—1962

Eugene

Packer, A. Her firstborn

Portland

Lain, D. I read the news today

Lain, D. Instant labor

Lain, D. Shopping at the end of the world

Lain, D. The subliminal son

Puchner, E. Children of God

Raymond, J. Words and things

ORGAN

Matheson, R. Shockwave

The **organ** grinder. Meyers, M.

Organic Shrapnel and Other Stories. Trudell, D.

ORGANISTS

Reidy, D. Dancing man

ORGASM

Brodkey, H. Innocence

Steinke, D. Orgasm

Orgasm. Steinke, D.

ORIENTALS *See* Asians

Origami Aeroplane. Komie, L. B.

Origin story. Link, K.

Original sin. Luvaas, W.

Originals. Sargent, P.

Orion. Austin, K.

Örkény, István

Prayer

The Times Literary Supplement no5396 p12-13 S 1 2006

ORKNEY (SCOTLAND)

Brown, G. M. The burning harp

Brown, G. M. The cinquefoil

Brown, G. M. The drowned rose

Brown, G. M. The fight at Greenay

Brown, G. M. The fires of Christmas

Brown, G. M. The girl

Brown, G. M. Hawkfall

Brown, G. M. The interrogator

Brown, G. M. Tithonus

The **Orkney** Island Lobster Theft. Brooks, J.

The **Orlov-Sokolovs**. Ulitskaya, L.

Orm the beautiful. Bear, E.

Orner, Eric

Fear and loathing in Chelsea

Sex for America; politically inspired erotica; edited by Stephen Elliott

Orner, Peter

Dear Mr. Klezcka

Chicago noir; edited by Neal Pollack

Everybody Serves Caesar: Chicago Stories

Ploughshares v33 no2/3 p106-16 Fall 2007

Jake Arvey in the Lobby of The Standard Club of Chicago, December 1976

StoryQuarterly v42 p41-4 2006

Last Car over the Sagamore Bridge

Harvard Review (1992) no28 p67-9 2005

The last socialist

Sex for America; politically inspired erotica; edited by Stephen Elliott

Pampkin's lament

Pushcart prize XXXII: best of the small presses 2008; edited by Bill Henderson with the Pushcart Prize editors

She's Not Here

Bomb no92 p107 Summ 2005

Spokane

Bomb no92 p104-7 Summ 2005

ORNITHOLOGISTS

Fountain, B. Near-extinct birds of the central cordillera

Knight, M. Birdland

Ornitz, Samuel
The little goat
Inside the hornet's head; an anthology of Jewish American writing; edited by Jerome Charyn
Orozco, Daniel
Officers weep
The Best American mystery stories, 2005; edited and with an introduction by Joyce Carol Oates; Otto Penzler, series editor
Shakers
StoryQuarterly v42 p45-59 2006
The **orphan**. McCabe, E.
The **orphan**. Wendroff, Z.
ORPHANS
Averill, T. F. The Bocce brothers
Bierce, A. A baby tramp
Bissell, T. Aral
Bova, B. Selene city
Caponegro, M. Junior achievement
Crone, M. The odd fellow
Crowther, P. We're all bozos on this bus!
Dahl, R. Katina
Fincke, G. Rip his head off
Gerrold, D. Dancer in the dark
Gifford, B. African adventure story
Gordimer, N. The ultimate safari
Gorriti, J. M. A year in California
Hoffman, A. The witch of Truro
James, H. My guardian and I
James, H. Unto the least of these
Jones, L. B. The epicurean
Judah, S. My son, Jude Paul
Judah, S. Nathoo
Klages, E. In the house of the seven librarians
Lam, V. A long migration
Lansdale, J. R. King of shadows
Michaels, A. Fugitive pieces [excerpt]
Percoto, C. The caning
Phan, A. Bound
Phan, A. The Delta
Phan, A. Gates of Saigon
Phan, A. Miss Lien
Phan, A. Motherland
Phan, A. We should never meet
Saunders, G. Jon
Stapleton, P. A little maverick
Tolstaia, T. Sweet dreams, son
Vanbeck, M. Given her history
Verolin, Irma. The stairway in the gray patio
Wald, A. H. The virgin's heart
Wendroff, Z. The orphan
Yoon, P. And we will be here
Orphans. Rosenbaum, B.
Orphée, Elvira
The journey of Amatista and the dirty prince
English translations of short stories by contemporary Argentine women writers; edited by Eliana Cazaubon Hermann; translated by Sally Webb Thornton
Justice shall be done
Díaz, G. J. Women and power in Argentine literature; stories, interviews, and critical essays; [by] Gwendolyn Díaz
Orquidea. Valdés, J.
Orr, Elaine Neil
Buffalo Gals
Southern Cultures v14 no1 p97-106 Spr 2008

Orr, Mary
The wisdom of Eve
Adaptations: from short story to big screen; 35 great stories that have inspired great films; edited by Stephanie Harrison
Orrin Lindsay's Plan of Aerial Navigation, with a Narrative of His Explorations in the Higher Regions of the Atmosphere, and His Wonderful Voyage round the Moon!. Riddell, J. L.
Orringer, Julie
Pilgrims
Pushcart prize XXVII; best of the small presses; edited by Bill Henderson with the Pushcart prize editors
Stars of Motown shining bright
The New Granta book of the American short story; edited and introduced by Richard Ford
Orson Welles' Blue Brocade Vest. Blackwood, S.
Ortiz, Oscar F.
Settling of scores
Havana noir; edited by Achy Obejas
Orullian, Peter
Beats of seven
Orson Scott Card's Intergalctic medicine show; [edited by] Edmund R. Schubert and Orson Scott Card
Orvieto dominos, bolsena eels. Stern, R. G.
OSAMA BIN LADEN
About
Krysl, M. Dinner with Osama
Osama Phone Home. Marusek, D.
Osborn, Carolyn
The Father
The Antioch Review v64 no2 p339-49 Spr 2006
My brother is a cowboy
Lone Star literature; from the Red River to the Rio Grande; edited by Don Graham
Osborn, Marijane
Afterword: Amlæd (Hamlet) [With introduction]
ANQ v20 no3 p74-7 Summ 2007
Oscar and Hypatia. Stern, R. G.
O'Shaughnessy, Mary
For works written by this author in collaboration with Pamela O'Shaughnessy see O'Shaughnessy, Perri
O'Shaughnessy, Pamela
For works written by this author in collaboration with Mary O'Shaughnessy see O'Shaughnessy, Perri
O'Shaughnessy, Perri
Chocolate milkshake
O'Shaughnessy, P. Sinister shorts
The couple behind the curtain
O'Shaughnessy, P. Sinister shorts
Dead money
O'Shaughnessy, P. Sinister shorts
The furnace man
O'Shaughnessy, P. Sinister shorts
Gertrude Stein solves a mystery
O'Shaughnessy, P. Sinister shorts
A grandmother's tale
O'Shaughnessy, P. Sinister shorts
His master's hand
O'Shaughnessy, P. Sinister shorts
House afire
O'Shaughnessy, P. Sinister shorts

Our friend Galletti. Palazzeschi, A.
Our Friend Max. Peterson, P. W.
Our lady of Paris. Mueenuddin, D.
Our Lady of Sorrows. Davis, S.
Our lady of sorrows. Hawes, L.
Our lady of the artichokes. Vaz, K.
Our last garage sale. Wingate, S.
Our last supper. LaBrie, A.
Our little lone star. Feitell, M.
Our Lives Are the Rivers. Manrique, J.
Our man in Geneva wins a million euros. Gappah,
  P.
Our men and women. Shields, C.
Our mortal span. Waldrop, H.
Our neck of the woods. Meno, J.
Our Ned. Finger, A.
Our neural Chernobyl. Sterling, B.
Our own little Kakadu. Hospital, J. T.
Our point of view. Stewart, P.
Our spring catalog. Pendarvis, J.
Our underwater mother. Murphy, Y.
Our wall. Oates, J. C.
Our War. Pàmies, S.
Ousmane, Sembène
  Her three days
    The Anchor book of modern African stories;
    edited by Nadežda Obradovic; with a fore-
    word by Chinua Achebe
Out in the open. Ebenbach, D. H.
Out of body. Lovell, G.
Out of order [excerpt] MacDougal, B.
Out of phase. Haldeman, J. W.
Out of place. Sargent, P.
Out of sync. Begamudré, V.
Out of the Blue. Denton, E.
Out of the deep. Howard, R. E.
Out of the depths. Brenner, Y. H.
Out of the fray. Gordon, M.
Out of the mouths. Finch, S.
Out of the storm. Hodgson, W. H.
Out of the stream. Malouf, D.
Out of these convertites; or, Richard goes to pris-
  on. Granville-Barker, H.
Out of Time, Out of Place. Bernard, K.
Out to sea. Russell, K.
Out twelve-steppin, summer of AA. Holder, N.
The **Outage**. Mitra, K.
Outage. Updike, J.
The **outbreeders**. Silverberg, R.
The **Outcast**. Harrison, J.
OUTDOOR LIFE
    See also Country life; Wilderness surviv-
  al
Outer banks. Chattin, J.
The **outer** darkness. Lamsley, T.
OUTER SPACE
    See also Space flight
  Gerrold, D. Riding Janis
  Irvine, A. C. Volunteers
  Rich, M. The asking place
  Rich, M. Forever down the ringing groves
  Rich, M. Impossible alone
  Rich, M. The never-winner
  Wright, J. C. The far end of history
            Communication
        See Interstellar communication
            Exploration
  Benford, G. The worm turns
  Blish, J. How beautiful with banners

Di Filippo, P. Beyond Mao
  Efremov, I. A. The Andromeda Nebula
    [abridged]
  Franke, H. W. Meteorites
  Merril, J. Daughters of earth
  Silverberg, R. Ozymandias
  Silverberg, R. Sunrise on Mercury
  Silverberg, R. Why?
  Stanchfield, J. Beyond the wall
The **outermost** borough. Wilson, G.
The **outlaw**. Bower, B. M.
Outlaw Pass. See Leonard, E. Law of the hunted
    ones [variant title: Outlaw Pass]
OUTLAWS
        See also Brigands and robbers
  Duncklee, J. The last breakfast
  Gorman, E. Junior
  Henry, W. A bullet for Billy the Kid
  Henry, W. The fourth horseman
  L'Amour, L. Jackson of Horntown
  Leonard, E. Law of the hunted ones [variant ti-
    tle: Outlaw Pass]
  Leonard, E. The longest day of his life
  Leonard, E. No man's guns
  Leonard, E. The Tonto woman
  Leonard, E. Trouble at Rindo's station [variant
    title: Rindo's station]
The **outlaws**. Swann, M.
Outnumbering the best. Pohl, F.
The **outrider**. Lamb, H.
Outside. Rodgers, S. J.
Outside work detail. Wolven, S.
The **outside** world. Lane, J.
The **outsider**. Lovecraft, H. P.
Outsiders. Pendarvis, J.
The **outward** sign. Zelazny, R.
Over by the river. Maxwell, W.
Over the Belle Isle boundary. Hernandez, L.
Over the child. Reisen, A.
Over the hill and into the woods. Berg, E.
Over the river. Lamb, H.
Over the sea from Skye. Carl, L. S.
Over there. Hecht, J.
Over there. Resnick, M.
Over thirty. Rice, C.
Overburden. Tomlinson, J.
Overcome. Michalopoulou, A.
Overdue. Rich, M.
OVERLAND JOURNEYS
  Anderson, B. The man with the plug in his nose
  Chuculate, E. Galveston Bay, 1826
  Munro, A. Illinois
  Scott, J. Everybody loves somebody
  Smith, M. Imagine this!
Overmyer, Eric
  Marigny triangle
    New Orleans noir; edited by Julie Smith
Overpass. Mozina, A.
Overproof. Konrath, J. A.
The **oversight**. Breuer, M. J.
Oversite. McHugh, M. F.
The **oversoul**. Joyce, G.
Overtime. Rash, R.
Overture. Green, G.
Overture to the Twentieth Century. Baricco, A.
Ovid
  Daedalus and Icarus
    Parabola v33 no3 p24 Fall 2008

OVITZ, MICHAEL
About
Allen, W. Surprise rocks Disney trial
Owens, Gareth
A new note for Nat
Nature v448 p1080 Ag 30 2007
Tick-tock curly-wurly
Nature v443 p120 S 7 2006
The **owl**. Williams, C.
The **owl** and the pussycat. Disch, T. M.
OWLS
Disch, T. M. The owl and the pussycat
Martin, V. The change
OwnzOreo. Doctorow, C.
Oyeyemi, Helen
Pie-Kah
Granta v100 p341-9 Wint 2007
Oysters. Cronin, J.
Oz, Amos
Heirs
The New Yorker v82 no46 p74-9 Ja 22 2007
Waiting
The New Yorker v84 no40 p82-9 D 8 2008
The way of the wind
Telling tales; edited by Nadine Gordimer
OZ (IMAGINARY PLACE)
De Camp, L. S. and Pratt, F. Sir Harold and the gnome king
Ozark Lake. Connell, N.
Ozick, Cynthia
Actors
Ozick, C. Dictation; a quartet
At Fumicaro
Ozick, C. Dictation; a quartet
Dictation
Ozick, C. Dictation; a quartet
Levitation
Inside the hornet's head; an anthology of Jewish American writing; edited by Jerome Charyn
Stone
Scribblers on the roof; contemporary American Jewish fiction; edited by Melvin Jules Bukiet and David G. Roskies
What happened to the baby?
Ozick, C. Dictation; a quartet
Ozymandias. Silverberg, R.
Ozzie the burro. McNett, M.

P

P-bird. Cadnum, M.
P dolce. Marley, L.
Pa Wars. Grace, P.
Pace. Roderick, D.
Pachter, Adam Emerson
Green monster
Fenway fiction; short stories from Red Sox nation; edited by Adam Emerson Pachter
The **Pacific**. Helprin, M.
The **pacific** mystery. Baxter, S.
PACIFIC NORTHWEST
Patterson, S. Aground and aloft
Shawl, N. Cruel Sistah
PACIFIC OCEAN
World War, 1939-1945
See World War, 1939-1945—Pacific Ocean

The **pacing** mustang. Seton, E. T.
Package. Dalton, Q.
Package deal. Block, L.
Packages. Stern, R. G.
Packer, Ann
Her firstborn
Before; short stories about pregnancy from our top writers; edited by Emily Franklin and Heather Swain
Packer, Nancy Huddleston
Her Men
The Sewanee Review v117 no3 p425-39 Summ 2009
Regulars
The Sewanee Review v115 no1 p68-76 Wint 2007
Packer, Vin *See* Meaker, Marijane, 1927-
Packer, ZZ
The ant of the self
The New Granta book of the American short story; edited and introduced by Richard Ford
Doris is coming
Short stories of the civil rights movement; an anthology; edited by Margaret Earley Whitt
Gideon
The book of other people; edited by Zadie Smith
Where Eric fell
Politically inspired; edited by Stephen Elliott; assistant editor, Gabriel Kram; associate editors, Elizabeth Brooks [et al.]
Packing. Wilson, R.
Padilla, Ignacio
The antipodes and the century
Colchie, T. A whistler in the nightworld; short fiction from the Latin Americas; edited by Thomas Colchie
Padre Mirandi. Duncklee, J.
Padura Fuentes, Leonardo
The Happy Death of Alborada Almanza
The Review of Contemporary Fiction v26 no3 p65-8 Fall 2006
Staring at the sun
Havana noir; edited by Achy Obejas
Paedomorphosis. Kiernan, C. R.
Paffgen, Christa *See* Nico, 1938-1988
PAGANISM
Hawes, L. Summerlands
Pagano, Mabel
A death in June
English translations of short stories by contemporary Argentine women writers; edited by Eliana Cazaubon Hermann; translated by Sally Webb Thornton
Pagans. Bass, R.
Page 42. Ronk, M. C.
The **Pager**. Kim, Y. H.
Pagès, Vicenç
Continental
The Review of Contemporary Fiction v28 no1 p79-89 Spr 2008
Pages from a journal found in a shoebox left in a Greyhound bus somewhere between Tulsa, Oklahoma, and Louisville, Kentucky. Gaiman, N.
Pages from a Life. Whitley, S. J.
Pages from an abandoned journal. Vidal, G.
Pages from the annual report. Barthelme, D.

Pages from the Textbook of Alternate History: Columbus Discovers Asia. Nguyen, P.
Pages from the Textbook of Alternate History: Joan of Arc, Patron Saint of Mothers and Soldiers [Excerpt from the writings of Jean d'Aulon] Nguyen, P.
Paging Daryl and Java Man. Redekop, F.
The **Paige** Renaissance. Malae, P. N.

PAIN

See also Suffering

Dixon, S. Pain
Lane, J. The pain barrier
Luongo, M. If the heart is lean
Meacham, R. Worship for shut-ins
Montemarano, N. The beginning of grief
Richter, S. The land of pain
Silverberg, R. The pain peddlers
Totton, S. Bluecoat Jack

Pain. Dixon, S.
Pain. Pietrzyk, L.
Le **pain**. Stewart, P.
The **pain** barrier. Lane, J.
The **pain** peddlers. Silverberg, R.

Paine, Ralph Delahaye

"Old Glory" in the desert

Adventures in the West; stories for young readers; edited by Susanne George Bloomfield and Eric Melvin Reed

PAINT

Levi, P. The magic paint
The **painted** drum. Erdrich, L.
A **Painted** Face. Tran, V.
The **Painted** Snake. Bensko, J.

Painter, Pamela

Reading in his wake

The Pushcart Prize XXIX: best of the small presses 2005; edited by Bill Henderson with the Pushcart Prize editors

Painter. Ducornet, R.

PAINTERS

See also Women painters

Anderson, B. Subalpine meadow
Baraka, I. A. Norman's date
Crone, M. It
Crouse, D. Retreat
Dahl, R. Skin
Đoàn, L. The venus of Chua village
Dobozy, T. The inert landscapes of György Ferenc
Ducornet, R. Painter
Gee, M. Into the blue
Gorodischer, A. How to succeed in life
Greenman, B. Black, gray, green, red, blue: a letter from a famous painter on the moon
Greenman, B. In the air room
Henry, O. Art and the bronco
Irvine, A. C. The Lorelei
Keret, E. Cheerful colors
Khalifah, 'A. A. The dogs
Lovecraft, H. P. Pickman's model
Porter, K. A. The leaning tower
Shukman, H. Old Providence
Stern, R. G. In a word, Trowbridge
Swan, G. The orange bird

PAINTERS, INDUSTRIAL *See* Industrial painters

The **Painter's** Wife. Nesset, K.
Painting. Keret, E.
The **painting**. Rhodes, D.

Painting By Numbers. Corkum, D.
Painting eggplants. Disch, T. M.
Painting Haiti. Jasper, M.
Painting the baby's room. Watkins, S.

PAINTINGS

Bradbury, R. The smile
Denevi, M. Victor Scarpazo; or, The end of the pursuit
Erdrich, L. The plunge of the brave
Ford, J. The scribble mind
Fountain, B. Rêve Haitien
Hodgson, W. H. Captain Gunbolt Charity and the painted lady
Hornung, E. W. Nine points of the law
Jasper, M. Painting Haiti
Keret, E. Painting
King, S. Stationary bike
Lannes, R. The anguish of departure
Palazzeschi, A. The portrait of the queen
Rhodes, D. The painting
Rickert, M. Cold fires
Shields, C. The orange fish
Singer, I. B. The painting
Smith, C. A. The willow landscape
Steinberg, S. Lifelike
Stevens, J. D. Love in a straight line
Tóibín, C. The use of reason
Wilson, G. The outermost borough
Zelazny, R. Final dining

A **Pair** of Muddy Pumps. Lynn, D. H.
The **pair** of slippers. James, H.
The **paisley** arms. Yates, D.

PAJAMAS

With, C. Pyjamas
Pajamas. Smith, M.

Pak, Wanso

Winter outing

Land of exile: contemporary Korean fiction; translated and edited by Marshall Pihl, Bruce Fulton, and Ju-Chan Fulton

PAKISTAN

Hillhouse, R. Diplomatic constraints
Massey, S. The mayor's movie
Mueenuddin, D. Lily
Mueenuddin, D. Provide, provide
Mueenuddin, D. Saleema
Mueenuddin, D. A spoiled man
Rahman, I. I, Claudius
Rashid, F. Syra

Lahore

Mueenuddin, D. About a burning girl
Mueenuddin, D. In other rooms, other wonders
Mueenuddin, D. Nawabdin Electrician

PAKISTANI AMERICANS

Rahman, I. All roads lead to flesh and bone
Rahman, I. Call me Manny
Rahman, I. Eating, Ohio
Rahman, I. From Kilgore to Kurtz, at the Steak 'n' Stage
Rahman, I. Here come the dog people
Rahman, I. I dream of microwaves
Rahman, I. Real, actual life

PAKISTANIS

France

Mueenuddin, D. Our lady of Paris

England

Davies, L. The fare
Holland, B. Sinners

Paley, Grace—*Continued*

Goodbye and good luck

Inside the hornet's head; an anthology of Jewish American writing; edited by Jerome Charyn

Justice—A Beginning

The Massachusetts Review v49 no4 p423-4 Wint 2008

The loudest voice

The Ecco book of Christmas stories; edited by Alberto Manguel

Love

My mistress's sparrow is dead; great love stories, from Chekhov to Munro; edited by Jeffrey Eugenides

Wants

The Massachusetts Review v49 no4 p443-4 Wint 2008

Palimpest. Gilman, L. A.

Palimpsest. Connor, J.

Palimpsest. Stross, C.

Palimpsest. Valente, C. M.

Pallas at noon. Marchand, J.

PALM BEACH (FLA.) *See* Florida—Palm Beach

Palm court. Salter, J.

PALM SPRINGS (CALIF.) *See* California—Palm Springs

The **palm** tree of Dilys Cathcart. Moss, B. K.

Palmer, Daniel

(jt. auth) See Palmer, Michael and Palmer, Daniel

Palmer, Karen

Virtuoso mio

The Pushcart Prize XXIX: best of the small presses 2005; edited by Bill Henderson with the Pushcart Prize editors

Palmer, Michael and Palmer, Daniel

Disfigured

Thriller; edited by James Patterson

Palmer, Søren G.

Per Nietzche's Instructions

The North American Review v291 no3/4 p60-8 My/Ag 2006

Palochky. DeMarinis, R.

Palwick, Susan

Beautiful stuff

Palwick, S. The fate of mice

The living dead; edited by John Joseph Adams

Elephant

Palwick, S. The fate of mice

Ever after

Palwick, S. The fate of mice

The fate of mice

Palwick, S. The fate of mice

Gestella

Palwick, S. The fate of mice

GI Jesus

Palwick, S. The fate of mice

Going after Bobo

Palwick, S. The fate of mice

Jo's hair

Palwick, S. The fate of mice

The old world

Palwick, S. The fate of mice

Sorrel's heart

Palwick, S. The fate of mice

The Best science fiction and fantasy of the year: volume two; edited by Jonathan Strahan

Stormdusk

Palwick, S. The fate of mice

Pam calls her mother on five-cent Sundays. Jablonski, N.

Pàmies, Sergi

Our War

The Review of Contemporary Fiction v28 no1 p74-8 Spr 2008

Pampkin's lament. Orner, P.

Pamuk, Orhan

The View

The New Yorker v83 no2 p44-5 Mr 5 2007

Pan-Fried. Jensen, B.

Pan, pan, pan. Murphy, Y.

PANAMA

Henriquez, C. Ashes

Henriquez, C. Beautiful

Henriquez, C. The box house and the snow

Henriquez, C. Drive

Henriquez, C. Gabriella, my heart

Henriquez, C. Mercury

Henriquez, C. The wide, pale ocean

Henriquez, C. Yanina

Shukman, H. Darien dogs

Panama City

Henriquez, C. Come together, fall apart

PANAMA CANAL

Auchincloss, L. An hour and a lifetime

PANAMA CITY (PANAMA) *See* Panama—Panama City

The **Panama** hen. Schulz, G.

Panayotopoulos, Nikos

The strength of materials

Angelic & black; contemporary Greek short stories; edited and translated by David Connolly; with an introduction by Vangelis Hatzivassileiou

Pancake, Ann

Arsonists

The Georgia Review v63 no2 p320-34 Summ 2009

Dog song

The Pushcart Prize XXIX: best of the small presses 2005; edited by Bill Henderson with the Pushcart Prize editors

Panciera, Carla

All of a Sudden

New England Review v25 no3 p115-20 2004

No Sooner

New England Review v27 no4 p15-24 2006

PANDAS

McAllister, B. The ark

Pande, Mrinal

A kind of love story

Gibson, M. E. Separate journeys; short stories by contemporary Indian women; edited by Geeta Dharmarajan; introduction by Mary Ellis Gibson

Pandemonium. Barthelme, D.

Pandemonium [Three stories from Flying to America: 45 More Stories] Barthelme, D.

Pandora's box. Auchincloss, L.

Pangbourne. Gardam, J.

Panic. Oates, J. C.

Panna cotta. Ducornet, R.

Parra, Eduardo Antonio—*Continued*
How life goes
  Parra, E. A. No man's land; selected stories;
  translated by Christopher Winks
The hunter
  Parra, E. A. No man's land; selected stories;
  translated by Christopher Winks
Just don't take the little I got
  Parra, E. A. No man's land; selected stories;
  translated by Christopher Winks
The oath
  Parra, E. A. No man's land; selected stories;
  translated by Christopher Winks
Real life
  Parra, E. A. No man's land; selected stories;
  translated by Christopher Winks
The showcase of dreams
  Parra, E. A. No man's land; selected stories;
  translated by Christopher Winks
Traveler Hotel
  Parra, E. A. No man's land; selected stories;
  translated by Christopher Winks
The well
  Parra, E. A. No man's land; selected stories;
  translated by Christopher Winks
Parrella, Valeria
Things I've Forgotten
  The Literary Review (Madison, N.J.) v49 no1
  p8-17 Fall 2005
Parrett, Aaron
The Stars Threw Down Their Spears
  The Massachusetts Review v48 no2 p217-24
  Summ 2007
Parrish, P. J.
One shot
  Mystery Writers of America presents death do
  us part; new stories about love, lust, and
  murder; edited by Harlan Coben
Pride
  Detroit noir; edited by E. J. Olsen & John C.
  Hocking
Parrish, Tim
It pours
  Wide awake in the Pelican State; stories by
  contemporary Louisiana writers; edited by
  Ann Brewster Dobie; with a foreword by
  Ernest J. Gaines
PARROTS
Butler, R. O. Mr. Green
Chaon, D. I demand to know where you're tak-
  ing me
Gordimer, N. History
Parry, Elsie A.
The little that is everything
  "Tell it to us easy" and other stories; a com-
  plete short fiction anthology of African
  American women writers in Opportunity
  magazine, (1923-1948); edited by Judith
  Musser.
Parry, Owen
Appearences
  Parry, O. Strike the harp!; American Christ-
  mas stories
The Christmas Joe
  Parry, O. Strike the harp!; American Christ-
  mas stories
Coal and iron
  Parry, O. Strike the harp!; American Christ-
  mas stories

How Jimmy Mulvaney astonished the world for
  Christmas
  Parry, O. Strike the harp!; American Christ-
  mas stories
The lie of the land
  Parry, O. Strike the harp!; American Christ-
  mas stories
Parsons, Ron
Big Blue
  Gettysburg Review v22 no3 p483-7 Aut 2009
Hezekiah Number Three
  Gettysburg Review v21 no1 p33-47 Spr 2008
Parson's pleasure. Dahl, R.
Part Bat. Miller, L. E.
Part light, part memory. Hill, B. H.
A **part** of it. Lott, B.
Part of the game. Wilson, F. P.
Part of the pack: another view of night life in
  Harlem. Campbell, H. V.
Part-time father. Clayton, J. J.
The **part-time** job. James, P. D.
PARTIES
        See also Dinners
Abbott, L. K. As fate would have it
Anderson, B. It is necessary I have a balloon
Barth, J. Toga party
Barthelme, D. Florence Green is 81
Barthelme, D. The question party
Barthelme, D. The Viennese Opera Ball
Beattie, A. Tending something
Bender, A. Off
Berg, E. The party
Bolaño, R. Days of 1978
Boswell, R. In a foreign land
Burgin, R. Mercury
Capote, T. The walls are cold
Clarke, B. The fund-raiser's dance card
Clarke, B. The reason was us
Coake, C. A single awe
Dolores, C. Aunt Zézé's tears
Dunbar, P. L. The lion tamer
Ebenbach, D. H. Between Camelots
Erdrich, L. Fuck with Kayla and you die
Fowler, C. The univited
Fuchs, D. The golden West
Fuchs, D. Triplicate
Gaiman, N. How to talk to girls at parties
Gardam, J. The people of Privilege Hill
Gee, M. What was important
Hardy, T. The three strangers
Hinton, S. E. After the party
Hunt, H. Sovietski!
James, H. One evening's work
James, H. The story of a ribbon bow
Jones, N. The crow and the monkey
Joyce, J. The dead
Kalotay, D. Serenade
LaBrie, A. In Mem
Lahiri, J. A choice of accommodations
Mansfield, K. The garden party
McGraw, E. The beautiful Tennessee waltz
McInerney, J. Everything is lost
McIntyre, V. Binge
McLean, S. Polly Anderson's Christmas party
Messinger, J. True hero
Michaels, L. The captain
Michaels, L. Fingers and toes
Michaels, L. Making changes
Monk, B. Pieces of paper

Patino, Martha Elvira
"Shipwreck"
Multicultural literature in contemporary Italy; edited by Marie Orton and Graziella Parati
Patio nights. Glavin, A.
Patriotic gestures. Rusch, K. K.
PATRIOTISM
Downs, G. The hired man
Parker, D. Song of the shirt, 1941
Percoto, C. The caning
Patrols. Busch, F.
The **patter** of tiny feet. Riddihough, G.
Pattern for survival. Matheson, R.
The **patterns** of life. Maxwell, W.
Patterson, Caroline
Hunters and Gatherers
Southwest Review v91 no2 p242-57 2006
Patterson, Steven
Aground and aloft
Best stories of the American West, v1; edited by Marc Jaffe
A Good Pig
Iowa Review v38 no2 p144-60 Fall 2008
Patterson, Victoria
Winter Formal
The Southern Review (Baton Rouge, La.) v45 no1 p61-72 Wint 2009
Patton, Jim
Capital of the world
D. C. noir; edited by George Pelecanos
Paul, Annie
Cock Soup
Callaloo v30 no1 p48-50 Wint 2007
Paul, Jacob
From A Song of Ilan (a novel)
Western Humanities Review v62 no2 p49-65 Spr/Summ 2008
Paul, Julie
Boring Baby
Dalhousie Review v87 no2 p249-58 Summ 2007
Paul, Perry
The Jane from Hell's Kitchen
The Black Lizard big book of pulps; edited by Otto Penzler
Paulsell, Stephanie
Annunciation
The Literary Review (Madison, N.J.) v50 no2 p46-52 Wint 2007
Pavane for a prince of the air. Hand, E.
The **pavement** artist. Hutchinson, D.
Pavilion 24. Reid, G.
Pavlik's mysterious disappearance. Wendroff, Z.
Pavlou, Stel
The strange case of Jared Spoon, who went to pieces for love
Elemental; the Tsunami relief anthology; stories of science fiction and fantasy; [edited by] Steven Savile and Alethea Kontis; introduction by Arthur C. Clarke
Pavol Hudák, the poet, is talking. Gildner, G.
Pawar, Urmila
Justice
Gibson, M. E. Separate journeys; short stories by contemporary Indian women; edited by Geeta Dharmarajan; introduction by Mary Ellis Gibson

Pawel, Rebecca
The kiss of death
A hell of a woman; an anthology of female noir; edited by Megan Abbott; foreword by Val McDermid
PAWNBROKERS
Johnston, B. A. Republican
Offutt, C. Second hand
Rash, R. Back of beyond
Paxson, Diana L. and Grey, Ian
The ghost in the phoenix
Thieves' world; enemies of fortune; edited by Lynn Abbey
Payback. DeMarinis, R.
Payday. Seranella, B.
Paying my dues. Coleman, V.
Payment in kind. Duffy, S.
Payne, Roberta
Henry
Gettysburg Review v20 no2 p195-207 Summ 2007
Paz Soldán, Edmundo
Dochera
Colchie, T. A whistler in the nightworld; short fiction from the Latin Americas; edited by Thomas Colchie
Peace, David
Tokyo Year Zero
Granta no96 p133-56 Wint 2006
Peace. Apple, M.
PEACE CORPS (U.S.)
Bissell, T. Animals in our lives
Chilson, P. Disturbance-loving species
McCauley, W. A book for Michael Sama
Peace on Suburbia. Rickert, M.
Peace rituals. Speegle, D.
The **peaceable** land; or, The unbearable vision of Harriet Beecher Stowe. Wilson, R. C.
Peacekeeper. Heathcock, A.
A **peach** of a shot. Stashower, D.
The **peach** stone. Horgan, P.
Peaches. Ciaccia, J.
Peaches. Simmons, G.
The **peacock**. Holladay, C. C.
Peacock blue. Capildeo, V.
Peacock from Heaven. Bobrinsky
PEACOCKS
Anderson, B. The peacocks
The **peacocks**. Anderson, B.
Peake, Mervyn Laurence
The party at lady cusp-canine's
New worlds; an anthology; edited by Michael Moorcock
PEANUTS (COMIC STRIP)
Auslander, S. Smite the heathens, Charlie Brown
The **pear-shaped** man. Martin, G. R. R.
The **pear** tree. Hoffman, A.
Pearce, Adewale Maja- *See* Maja-Pearce, Adewale
Pearl, Matthew
The adventure of the Boston Dromio
Sherlock Holmes in America; edited by Martin H. Greenberg, Jon L. Lellenberg, and Daniel Stashower
The **Pearl** Canon. Nahai, G. B.
The **pearl** diver. Kiernan, C. R.
PEARL DIVING
Rashid, 'A. M. A crisis at sea

Pearlman, Edith
Aunt Telephone
  The Antioch Review v64 no3 p420-31 Summ
    2006
The coat
  Pearlman, E. How to fall; stories
Cul-De-Sac
  Agni no65 p97-110 2007
Elder Jinks
  Pushcart prize XXXIII: best of the small
    presses 2009; edited by Bill Henderson
    with the Pushcart Prize editors
  The Antioch Review v65 no4 p689-98 Fall
    2007
Eyesore
  Pearlman, E. How to fall; stories
Granski
  The Antioch Review v63 no3 p429-39 Summ
    2005
Home schooling
  Pearlman, E. How to fall; stories
How to fall
  Pearlman, E. How to fall; stories
If love were all
  Pearlman, E. How to fall; stories
The large lady
  Pearlman, E. How to fall; stories
Madame Guralnik
  Pearlman, E. How to fall; stories
Mates
  Pearlman, E. How to fall; stories
The message
  Pearlman, E. How to fall; stories
On Junius Bridge
  Agni no61 p186-97 2005
Purim night
  Pearlman, E. How to fall; stories
Rules
  Pearlman, E. How to fall; stories
Self-reliance
  The Best American short stories, 2006; select-
    ed from U.S. and Canadian magazines by
    Ann Patchett with Katrina Kenison; with an
    introduction by Ann Patchett
Shenanigans
  Pearlman, E. How to fall; stories
Signs of life
  Pearlman, E. How to fall; stories
The story
  Pearlman, E. How to fall; stories
Trifle
  Pearlman, E. How to fall; stories
Pearls. Coleman, R. F.
Pearls to swine. Koënings, N. S.
Pearson, Ridley
Boldt's broken angel
  Thriller 2; stories you just can't put down;
    edited by Clive Cussler; [stories by] Kath-
    leen Antrim . . . [et al.]
Close shave
  Murder is my racquet; edited by Otto Penzler
Queeny
  Mystery Writers of America presents death do
    us part; new stories about love, lust, and
    murder; edited by Harlan Coben
  The Best American mystery stories 2007; ed-
    ited and with and introduction by Carl
    Hiaasen; Otto Penzler, series editor
Peas. Gross, C.

PEASANT LIFE
China
Li Yiyun. Persimmons
Italy
Percoto, C. The bread of the departed
Peattie, Elia Wilkinson
The McCulloughs of the Bluff
  Adventures in the West; stories for young
    readers; edited by Susanne George Bloom-
    field and Eric Melvin Reed
Pecado. Granados, C.
Peck, Dale
Dues
  The O. Henry Prize stories, 2005; edited and
    with an introduction by Laura Furman
  The Pushcart Prize XXIX: best of the small
    presses 2005; edited by Bill Henderson
    with the Pushcart Prize editors
Peck, Louisa
Rachmaninoff Lives
  Calyx v22 no3 p74-89 Summ 2005
Peculiarities of the national driving. Litman, E.
Ped-o-Matique. Rogers, J.
Pedagogy. Luongo, M.
PEDDLERS AND PEDDLING
Andrews, R. Solomon's alley
Dybek, S. The Palatski Man
Hwang, S. A dream of good fortune
Kim, T. The post horse curse
Mukhopadhyay, T. Little grains of dust
Peden, Margaret Sayers
(tr.) See Allende, Isabel
PEDIATRICIANS *See* Physicians
PEDOPHILIA
Báez, A. Aura
Báez, A. The Pinocchio
Kiernan, C. R. Anamorphosis
McLean, R. D. Pedro Paul
Rees, R. Iodine
Siegel, J. Empathy
Trevor, W. An afternoon
Pedro Paul. McLean, R. D.
Peebles, Frances de Pontes
The drowned woman
  The O. Henry Prize stories, 2005; edited and
    with an introduction by Laura Furman
Peek, Ben
The funeral, ruined
  Sedia, E. Paper cities; an anthology of urban
    fantasy
Peek-a-moose. Ruefle, M.
Peeling. Sayles, J.
Peelle, Lydia
Kidding Season
  Orion v28 no2 p52-63 Mr/Ap 2009
Mule killers
  The O. Henry Prize stories, 2006; edited and
    with an introduction by Laura Furman; ju-
    rors: Kevin Brockmeier, Francine Prose,
    Colm Toibin
Phantom Pain
  Granta no102 p130-51 Summ 2008
Reasons for and advantages of breathing
  Pushcart prize XXXIII: best of the small
    presses 2009; edited by Bill Henderson
    with the Pushcart Prize editors

PENGUINS
Bradfield, S. Penguins for lunch
Penguins for lunch. Bradfield, S.
PENIS
Clarke, B. Carrying the torch
McCauley, W. Allergies
Stevens, J. D. The President's penis
Welsh, I. Rattlesnakes
Penkov, Miroslav
Buying Lenin
The Southern Review (Baton Rouge, La.) v43
no4 p742-54 Aut 2007
Devshirmeh
The Southern Review (Baton Rouge, La.) v41
no3 p479-92 Summ 2005
Penn, Arthur *See* Matthews, Brander, 1852-1929
Penn, Vinnie
Trim
Hardcore hardboiled; edited by Todd Robinson; introduction by Otto Penzler
PENNSYLVANIA
DeNiro, A. Quiver
DeNiro, A. Skinny dipping in the Lake of the Dead
Monk, B. Annie Kusiak's meaning of life
Monk, B. The great wall
Monk, B. Hocus-pocus
Monk, B. Last call
Monk, B. Now you don't
Monk, B. Now you see it
Monk, B. Slam book
Monk, B. Small fry
Porter, A. Departure
Schwarzschild, E. Drift
Schwarzschild, E. Irreversible
Schwarzschild, E. Spring Garden
Shepard, L. Stars seen through stone
Tudish, C. Dog stories
Tudish, C. The dowry
Tudish, C. The infusion suite
Tudish, C. Jordan's stand
Tudish, C. Killer
Tudish, C. Pigeon
Tudish, C. The springhouse
Updike, D. Shining so nicely in the sun
Updike, J. My father's tears
Updike, J. The road home

Coal mines and mining
See Coal mines and mining—Pennsylvania

Erie
DeNiro, A. Home of the

Philadelphia
Adichie, C. N. Imitation
Burgin, R. Ghost parks
Burgin, R. Vacation
De los Santos, M. Cornelia
Dozois, G. R. The hanging curve
Goodis, D. Black pudding
Malla, P. The love life of the automation Turk
Schwarzschild, E. No rest for the middleman
Schwarzschild, E. Open heart
Schwarzschild, E. Reunion
Swierczynski, D. Death runs faster
Weiner, J. League of Justice (Philadelphia Division)

Pittsburgh
Hill, J. Bobby Conroy comes back from the dead

Litman, E. About Kamyshinskiy
Litman, E. Among the lilacs and the girls
Litman, E. Charity
Litman, E. Dancers
Litman, E. Home
Litman, E. In the man-free zone
Litman, E. The last chicken in America
Litman, E. Peculiarities of the national driving
Litman, E. Russian club
Litman, E. The trajectory of frying pans
Litman, E. What do you dream of, cruiser Aurora?
Litman, E. When the neighbors love you
PENNSYLVANIA DUTCH
Bierce, A. Four jacks and a knave
Penny in the dust. Buckler, E.
"Penny" Joe Crane died for my sins. Rand, K.
The **pentecostal** home for flying children. Clarke, W.
PENTECOSTALISM
Rash, R. Chemistry
The **penultimate** conjecture. Michaels, L.
Peonies and forget-me-nots. Gospodinov, G.
People Always Going To. Martin, L.
People are becoming clouds. Meno, J.
People in hell just want a drink of water. Proulx, A.
People like that. Chattin, J.
People like that are the only people here. Moore, L.
People like us. Valdés, J.
People, Not Places. Brown, S.
The **people** of Privilege Hill. Gardam, J.
The **people** of sand and slag. Bacigalupi, P.
People of the dark. Howard, R. E.
The **people** outside. Edwards, M.
People people. Nelson, A.
People shouldn't have to be the ones to tell you. Lutz, G.
The **people** who own pianos. McIlvoy, K.
People's choice. Hyde, M.
The **people's** machine. Buckell, T. S.
The **people's** wat. Sandstrom, E. K.
Pepper. Coleman, W.
Pepper hunt. Blackwell, K.
Peppermint frogs. Anderson, B.
Per Nietzche's Instructions. Palmer, S. G.
Perabo, Susan
Shelter
Iowa Review v39 no1 p69-80 Spr 2009
PERCEVAL (LEGENDARY CHARACTER)
Finlay, C. C. Wild thing
Perchance to dream. Carmody, I.
Perchance to dream. Metzger, R. A.
Perchance to dream. Stackpole, M. A.
Percoto, Caterina
The bread of the departed
Writing to delight; Italian short stories by nineteenth-century women writers; edited by Antonia Arslan and Gabriella Romani
The caning
Writing to delight; Italian short stories by nineteenth-century women writers; edited by Antonia Arslan and Gabriella Romani
Percy, Benjamin
April 20, 2008
Esquire v149 no5 p85-6, 88, 90, 92 My 2008
The caves in Oregon
Percy, B. Refresh, refresh; stories

708 SHORT STORY INDEX, 2005-2009

Percy, Benjamin—*Continued*
Crash
    Percy, B. Refresh, refresh; stories
The faulty builder
    Percy, B. Refresh, refresh; stories
In the Rough
    The Antioch Review v65 no3 p524-46 Summ 2007
The killing
    Percy, B. Refresh, refresh; stories
Meltdown
    Percy, B. Refresh, refresh; stories
Refresh, refresh
    The Best American short stories, 2006; selected from U.S. and Canadian magazines by Ann Patchett with Katrina Kenison; with an introduction by Ann Patchett
    Percy, B. Refresh, refresh; stories
    Pushcart prize XXXI: best of the small presses 2007; edited by Bill Henderson; with the Pushcart Prize editors
    The Paris Review v47 p87-100 Fall/Wint 2005
Somebody is going to have to pay for this
    Percy, B. Refresh, refresh; stories
    The Paris Review v49 p56-71 Spr 2007
Unearthed
    Poe's children; the new horror: an anthology; [edited by] Peter Straub.
When the bear came
    Percy, B. Refresh, refresh; stories
Whisper
    Percy, B. Refresh, refresh; stories
The woods
    Percy, B. Refresh, refresh; stories
Perec, Georges
The runaway
    Paris tales; stories; translated by Helen Constantine
Peregrines. Charnas, S. M.
Perelman, S. J. (Sidney Joseph)
Farewell, my lovely appetizer
    The vicious circle; mystery and crime stories by members of the Algonquin Round Table; edited by Otto Penzler
Four-and-twenty blackjacks
    The vicious circle; mystery and crime stories by members of the Algonquin Round Table; edited by Otto Penzler
Up the close and down the stair
    The vicious circle; mystery and crime stories by members of the Algonquin Round Table; edited by Otto Penzler
Perelman, Sidney Joseph *See* Perelman, S. J. (Sidney Joseph), 1904-1979
Peretz, Isaac Leib
Cabalists
    No star too beautiful; Yiddish stories from 1382 to the present; compiled and translated by Joachim Neugroschel
Hear, o Israel; or, The bassist
    No star too beautiful; Yiddish stories from 1382 to the present; compiled and translated by Joachim Neugroschel
On the stagecoach
    No star too beautiful; Yiddish stories from 1382 to the present; compiled and translated by Joachim Neugroschel

Stories
    No star too beautiful; Yiddish stories from 1382 to the present; compiled and translated by Joachim Neugroschel
Perez, Rene S., II
Last Primer
    Callaloo v30 no3 p921-8 Summ 2007
Perez, Yoel
Two Friends
    Parabola v31 no3 p93 Fall 2006
Perfect. LaBute, N.
A **perfect** and unmappable grace. Haringa, J. M.
The **perfect** crime. Montanye, C. S.
The **perfect** crime. Redman, B. R.
A **perfect** day for kangaroos. Murakami, H.
Perfect gentleman. Battles, B.
A **perfect** location. Klassen, S.
The **perfect** marriage. Woronov, M.
A **perfect** relationship. Trevor, W.
A **Perfect** Rotation of the Earth. Fitzgerald, S. F.
Perfect Rush. Jacobs, M.
A **perfect** stranger. Boyers, R.
A **perfect** stranger. Garrett, G. P.
A **perfect** stranger. Robinson, R.
The **perfecting** of the Chopin Valse no. 14 in E Minor. Naslund, S. J.
PERFECTION
    Anderson, B. Feeding the sparrows
    Molodowsky, K. The Amsterdams
    Rhodes, D. The painting
Perfection. Berwin, M.
Perfection. Flewelling, L.
Perfection. Helprin, M.
Perfection. Maxwell, W.
Perfection: A Story. Helprin, M.
Perforated: a lexicon. Martin, J.
The **performance**. Miller, A.
PERFORMANCE ART
    Boyd, W. Beulah Berlin, an A-Z
    Cooper, D. Jerk
    Disch, T. M. The first annual performance art festival at the Slaughter Rock Battlefield
    Grimes, C. Subdivisions of space
    Thomas, J. Heart for heart's sake
PERFORMERS *See* Entertainers
PERFUMES
    Dahl, R. Bitch
Pergrine falcon. Rock, P.
Perhaps a miracle. Gilchrist, E.
Perhaps the last. Williams, C.
Peri Rossi, Cristina
To love or to ingest
    Violations; stories of love by Latin American women; edited and with an introduction by Psiche Hughes; foreword by Brian Matthews
Périgord, Charles Maurice de Talleyrand- *See* Talleyrand-Périgord, Charles Maurice de, prince de Bénévent, 1754-1838
The **perimeter**. Chase, M.
PERIODICALS
    Connell, E. S. Octopus, the Sausalito quarterly of new writing, art & ideas
    Gabriele, L. Don't let the 100 percent divorce rate spoil your wedding!
    Nelson, R. F. Pulp life
Perjury. Working, R.

Perkins-Valdez, Dolen
  The Clipping
    The Kenyon Review v29 no3 p56-67 Summ
    2007
Perkus Tooth. Lethem, J.
Perle, Yeshue
  A legend
    No star too beautiful; Yiddish stories from
    1382 to the present; compiled and translat-
    ed by Joachim Neugroschel
Perlman, Elliot
  Good morning, again
    Perlman, E. The reasons I won't be coming;
    stories
  The Hong Kong Fir doctrine
    Perlman, E. The reasons I won't be coming;
    stories
  I was only in a childish way connected to the
    established order
    Perlman, E. The reasons I won't be coming;
    stories
  In the time of the dinosaur
    Perlman, E. The reasons I won't be coming;
    stories
  Manslaughter
    Perlman, E. The reasons I won't be coming;
    stories
  Spitalnic's last year
    Perlman, E. The reasons I won't be coming;
    stories
  A tale in two cities
    Perlman, E. The reasons I won't be coming;
    stories
  Your niece's speech night
    Perlman, E. The reasons I won't be coming;
    stories
Permanent position. Gilbey, J.
Permission. McIlvoy, K.
Pernicketty's fright. Bierce, A.
Peroni, Paula
  A Mother's Body
    The Antioch Review v66 no4 p760-3 Fall
    2008
The **Perp** [Excerpt from The Bridegroom] Ha Jin
Perpetua. Barthelme, D.
Perpetua. Reed, K.
Perpetual mobile [variant title: Perpetuum mobile]
    Chekhov, A. P.
Perrotta, Tom
  The Bittersweet Salvation . . . of Tim Mason
    Best Life v4 no8 p114-19, 144-5 O 2007
  Kiddie Pool
    Best Life v3 no6 p102-7, 121 Jl/Ag 2006
  The smile on Happy Chang's face
    The Best American short stories, 2005; select-
    ed from U.S. and Canadian magazines by
    Michael Chabon with Katrina Kenison;
    with an introduction by Michael Chabon
Perry, Anne
  Ere I killed thee
    The World's finest mystery and crime stories,
    fourth annual collection; edited by Ed
    Gorman and Martin H. Greenberg
  Hostages
    Transgressions; edited by Ed McBain
  The judgement
    Powers of detection; stories of mystery &
    fantasy; edited by Dana Stabenow

  Lost causes
    Thou shalt not kill; biblical mystery stories;
    edited by Anne Perry
    The Deadly Bride; and 21 of the year's finest
    crime and mystery stories; including com-
    plete coverage of the year in mystery and
    crime fiction; edited by Ed Gorman and
    Martin H. Greenberg
  Sneaker wave
    Dangerous women; edited by Otto Penzler
  A tale of one city
    The Best British mysteries, 2006; edited by
    Maxim Jakubowski
Perry, George Sessions
  Hold autumn in your hand
    Lone Star literature; from the Red River to
    the Rio Grande; edited by Don Graham
Perry, Princess
  Color Struck
    African American Review v42 no2 p331-8
    Summ 2008
Perry, Rachael
  The Rhein
    Prairie Schooner v81 no2 p138 Summ 2007
  The Stunt Couple Fight
    Prairie Schooner v81 no2 p137 Summ 2007
Perry Chumly's eclipse. Bierce, A.
PERSECUTION
      See also Atrocities; Jews—Persecutions;
      Martyrs
    Goss, T. Csilla's story
    Mahajan, K. The cremation ground
    Steck, U. Phantoms
    Stevens, J. D. Burn
PERSIA *See* Iran
PERSIAN GULF WAR, 1991
    Joyce, G. An ordinary soldier of the Queen
    Kiesbye, S. Islanders
    Stern, R. G. The Anaximander fragment
    Swofford, A. Will they kill you in Iraq?
PERSIAN WARS, 500-449 B.C. *See* Greece—
    Persian Wars, 500-449 B.C.
Persimmons. Li Yiyun
Persimmons. Yates, D.
The **persistence** of ice. Tomlinson, J.
Personal archaeology. Updike, J.
PERSONAL BEAUTY
    Chekhov, A. P. Curved mirror [variant title:
    Crooked mirror (a Christmas story)]
    Chiang, T. Liking what you see: a documentary
    Donoghue, E. Pluck
    Harris, J. Eau de toilette
    Harris, J. A place in the sun
    Hernandez, L. Preparing for a strike
    Leigh, S. Transformation
    Pearlman, E. Eyesore
    Rhodes, D. Beautiful Consuela
    Stafford, J. The end of a career
Personal effects. Kalman, J.
A **personal** magnet. Henry, O.
PERSONAL NAMES
    Domecq, B. Mr. Clunk!
    Dunbar, P. L. Johnsonham, Junior
    Dunlap, S. Hearing her name
    Langer, A. The book of names
    Manley, C. Piranha
    McKillip, P. A. Naming day
    Murakami, H. A Shinagawa monkey
    Romano, T. City Hall

PERSONAL NAMES—*Continued*
    Singleton, G. The opposite of zero
    Stamm, P. The most beautiful girl
PERSONALITY DISORDERS
        See also Dual personality; Hallucinations
        and illusions; Insane, Criminal and danger-
        ous; Multiple personality
    Burgin, R. Aerialist
    Burgin, R. The spirit of New York
    Chute, C. "Ollie, oh . . ."
    Oates, J. C. At the seminary
    Pollock, D. R. Lard
    Sarris, G. The magic pony
    Silverberg, R. Counterpart
    Silverberg, R. Ringing the changes
    Stafford, J. The echo and the nemesis
    Stern, R. G. East, West . . . Midwest
    Wolfe, G. Kevin Malone
    Wolff, T. The other Miller
PERU
    Alarcón, D. The visitor
    Alarcón, D. War by candlelight
            Lima
    Alarcón, D. City of clowns
    Alarcón, D. Flood
    Alarcón, D. Lima, Peru; July 28, 1979
    Alarcón, D. A science for being alone
    Taylor, Nick. The smell of despair
PERUVIANS
          United States
    Alarcón, D. Absence
Pervert. Finlay, C. C.
The **pessimistic** fortune-teller. Maxwell, W.
PESTS
           Control
    Grimes, C. Glue trap
    Sanders, W. The scuttling; or, Down by the sea
      with Marvin and Pamela
    Silverberg, R. Sundance
Pet therapy. Malla, P.
PETER, THE APOSTLE, SAINT
           About
    Linney, R. Early marvels
Peter Kahn's third wife. Lasdun, J.
Peter Skilling. Irvine, A. C.
Peters, Doris
    "Faith"
        "Tell it to us easy" and other stories; a com-
        plete short fiction anthology of African
        American women writers in Opportunity
        magazine, (1923-1948); edited by Judith
        Musser.
Peters, Ralph, 1952-
        See also Parry, Owen, 1952-
Peters. Tolstaia, T.
Petersburg [excerpt] Bely, A.
Petersen, Kate
    Denver by Morning
        Iowa Review v35 no2 p115-18 Fall 2005
Peterson, Paula W.
    Our Friend Max
        Iowa Review v35 no2 p1-13 Fall 2005
    Shelter
        Prairie Schooner v82 no1 p9-31 Spr 2008
Peterson, Quintin
    Cold as ice
        D. C. noir; edited by George Pelecanos
The **Peterson** fire. Gifford, B.

Petesch, Natalie L. M.
    Selma
        Short stories of the civil rights movement; an
        anthology; edited by Margaret Earley Whitt
Les **Petites** Ménagè res [With photograph by
    Masao Gozu] Grainville, P.
Petrie, Graham
    The Voyage Home
        Confrontation no102/103 p74-95 Wint
        2008/Spr 2009
Petrin, Jas R.
    Car trouble
        The Best American mystery stories, 2008; ed-
        ited and with an introduction by George
        Pelecanos; Otto Penzler, series editor
PETROLEUM INDUSTRY
    'Arimi, S. a.- . Ghomran's oil field
    Burke, J. L. Water people
    Karlin, K. Bye-bye Larry
    L'Amour, L. Pirates with wings
    Silko, L. Storyteller
    Swofford, A. Freedom Oil
Petronio, B.
    The Substitute Plumber
        Frontiers v25 no3 p35-46 2004
Petrouchka [with omissions]. Means, D.
Petrov, David Shrayer- *See* Shrayer-Petrov, Da-
    vid, 1936-
Petrushevskaya, Ludmilla
    The Fountain House
        The New Yorker v85 no26 p66-9 Ag 31 2009
Petry, Ann
    Marie of the Cabin Club [With introduction by
      Gene Jarrett]
        PMLA v121 no1 p245-54 Ja 2006
Petry, Ann Lane
    The bones of Louella Brown
        "Tell it to us easy" and other stories; a com-
        plete short fiction anthology of African
        American women writers in Opportunity
        magazine, (1923-1948); edited by Judith
        Musser.
    On Saturday the siren sounds at noon
        Black noir; mystery, crime and suspense sto-
        ries by African-American writers; edited by
        Otto Penzler
PETS
        See also names of individual pets
    Brockmeier, K. The lady with the pet tribble
    Day, A. In the darkness
    Donoghue, E. The cost of things
    Donoghue, E. Do they know it's Christmas?
    Fonseca, R. Betsy
    Fulton, A. If it's not too much to ask
    Grimes, C. Vivisection
    Hempel, A. At the gates of the animal kingdom
    Hempel, A. The lady will have the Slug Louie
    Hempel, A. Today will be a quiet day
    Lackey, M. Aliens ate my pickup
    Martin, G. R. R. Sandkings
    Massie, E. The next-door collector
    Meloy, P. Alex and the toyceivers
    Rand, K. The teddy's touch
    Ruefle, M. My pet, my clock

Petsetidis, Dimitris
Away ground
　　Angelic & black; contemporary Greek short stories; edited and translated by David Connolly; with an introduction by Vangelis Hatzivassileiou
Petting zoo. Wolfe, G.
Petty, Audrey
Soundtrack
　　The Massachusetts Review v47 no3 p426-38 Fall 2006
Pezzullo, Ralph
Step up
　　Hard boiled Brooklyn; edited by Reed Farrel Coleman
Pflug, Ursula
Basement alembic
　　Pflug, U. After the fires; stories
Blue gloves
　　Pflug, U. After the fires; stories
Border crossings
　　Bandersnatch; edited by Paul Tremblay and Sean Wallace
A dog's life
　　Pflug, U. After the fires; stories
The exit
　　Pflug, U. After the fires; stories
The eyes of Horus
　　Pflug, U. After the fires; stories
Fires
　　Pflug, U. After the fires; stories
Memory lapse at the waterfront
　　Pflug, U. After the fires; stories
Python
　　Pflug, U. After the fires; stories
Ramona's baby
　　Pflug, U. After the fires; stories
Red velvet dust
　　Pflug, U. After the fires; stories
The wizard of Wardenclyffe
　　Pflug, U. After the fires; stories
Pham, Thu Minh
My Mother's War
　　Amerasia Journal v31 no2 p147-52 2005
Phan, Aimee
Bound
　　Phan, A. We should never meet; stories
The Delta
　　Phan, A. We should never meet; stories
　　Michigan Quarterly Review v43 no4 p485-506 Fall 2004
Emancipation
　　Phan, A. We should never meet; stories
Gates of Saigon
　　Phan, A. We should never meet; stories
Miss Lien
　　Phan, A. We should never meet; stories
Motherland
　　Phan, A. We should never meet; stories
Visitors
　　Phan, A. We should never meet; stories
We should never meet
　　Phan, A. We should never meet; stories
Phan Thanh Hao
(tr.) See Le Minh Khue
The **phantom** bandit. Bonham, F.
The **phantom** caravan. Lamb, H.
The **Phantom** of the Sewers. Farmer, P. J.
Phantom Pain. Peelle, L.

Phantoms. Steck, U.
The **Phantoms** [abridged] Turgenev, I. S.
The **phantoms** of the fire. Smith, C. A.
Pharisees. Fincke, G.
PHARMACEUTICAL INDUSTRY
Kress, N. Patent infringement
PHARMACISTS
Anderson, B. The daggy end
Apple, M. Proton decay
Boudinot, R. Drugs and toys
Duval, P. Rear view
Oates, J. C. Objects in mirror are closer than they appear
Parker, M. Everything was paid for
Waters, D. Mr. Epstein and the dealer
Phelan, Twist
Strange bedfellows
　　Politics noir; dark tales from the corridors of power; edited by Gary Phillips.
Time will tell
　　Mystery Writers of America presents the prosecution rests; new stories about courtrooms, criminals, and the law; edited by Linda Fairstein.
Phil in the Marketplace. Lethem, J.
PHILADELPHIA (PA.) *See* Pennsylvania—Philadelphia
PHILANTHROPISTS
Budnitz, J. Elephant and boy
Henry, O. The chair of philanthromathematics
Singer, I. B. There are no coincidences
PHILANTHROPY *See* Endowments; Philanthropists
Philanthropy. Simon, B.
Philemon and Baucis. Déry, T.
PHILIPPINES
Battles, B. Perfect gentleman
Hammett, D. Ber-Lulu
　　　　　　　　Manila
Carron, H. B. A favor for the mayor
Howard, C. Manila burning
Philip's killer hat. Dobozy, T.
Phillian, G. S.
The Killing
　　Prairie Schooner v82 no3 p45-57 Fall 2008
One Last Chinese Zinger
　　River Styx no72 p53-69 2006
Phillips, Gary
The accomplice
　　Creature cozies; edited by Jill M. Morgan
And what shall we call you?
　　The darker mask; edited by Gary Phillips and Christopher Chambers.
Disco zombies
　　The cocaine chronicles; edited by Gary Phillips and Jervey Tervalon
House of tears
　　Black noir; mystery, crime and suspense stories by African-American writers; edited by Otto Penzler
The man for the job
　　Dublin noir; the Celtic tiger vs. the ugly American; edited by Ken Bruen
Roger Crumbler considered his shave
　　Los Angeles noir; edited by Denise Hamilton

Phillips, Gary—*Continued*

Searching for Cisa

Kolchak: the night stalker chronicles; 26 original tales of the surreal, the bizarre, the macabre; edited by Joe Gentile, Garrett Anderson, Lori Gentile; Kolchak created by Jeff Rice

Swift boats for Jesus

Politics noir; dark tales from the corridors of power; edited by Gary Phillips.

Where all our dreams come true

Hollywood and crime; original crime stories set during the history of Hollywood; edited by Robert J. Randisi

Phillips, Holly

The oracle spoke

Realms

Queen of the butterfly kingdom

Interfictions; an anthology of interstitial writing; edited by Delia Sherman and Theodora Goss

The small door

The Best science fiction and fantasy of the year: volume three; edited by Jonathan Strahan

Phillips, Jayne Anne

Solly and Lark: Winfield, West Virginia, 1965

Granta v100 p17-28 Wint 2007

Termite, 1959

The Southern Review (Baton Rouge, La.) v41 no1 p60-76 Wint 2005

Phillips, Rowan Ricardo

(tr.) See Pagès, Vicenç

(tr.) See Sánchez Piñol, Albert

Phillips, Scott

Babs

Las Vegas noir; edited by Jarrett Keene & Todd James Pierce.

The Emerson, 1950

The Best American mystery stories, 2008; edited and with an introduction by George Pelecanos; Otto Penzler, series editor

The girl who kissed Barnaby Jones

Los Angeles noir; edited by Denise Hamilton

Nocturne le jeudi

Paris noir; capital crime fiction; edited by Maxim Jakubowski

Philoctète, René

Massacre river [excerpt]

Terrestrial intelligence; international fiction now from New Directions; edited by Barbara Epler

PHILOLOGISTS

Ducornet, R. The ominous philologist

Philomel cottage. Christie, A.

Philomena. McInerney, J.

The **Philosopher** and the Checkout Girl: A Story. Epstein, J.

PHILOSOPHERS

Ballantyne, T. Aristotle OS

Brockmeier, K. The lives of the philosophers

Gospodinov, G. The man of many names

Wilson, R. C. The Cartesian theater

The **philosophy** lesson. Stafford, J.

PHILOSOPHY OF LIFE *See* Life (Philosophy of life)

Phinn, Gervase

"Anyone could have done it. But only James had a crisp £5 note, a stepladder, a key to the chemistry cupboard marked 'Flammable' and a misdirected sense of curiosity..."

The Times Educational Supplement p14-18 Jl 25 2008 TES Magazine supp

Phipps-Kettlewell, Marilène

Dame-Marie

Callaloo v30 no3 p788-92 Summ 2007

The **phlebotomist's** love life. Simpson, H.

Phoebe and the Character of Happiness. Fraser, R.

Phoebe with Impending Frost. Appel, J. M.

Phoel, Cynthia Morrison

Galia

Gettysburg Review v19 no3 p363-81 Aut 2006

Satisfactory Proof

Harvard Review (1992) no28 p146-61 2005

PHOENIX (ARIZ.) *See* Arizona—Phoenix

Phoenix. Alvarado, B.

The **Phone** Call. Solzhenitsyn, A.

Phone calls. Bolaño, R.

Phone Man. Weible, K.

Phone Ring Two. Dixon, S.

Phosphorescence. Hadley, T.

Photo finish. Paretsky, S.

The **Photograph**. Doyle, R.

The **photograph**. Luxenberg, H.

The **Photograph**. Redwood, J. D.

The **photograph**. Zoshchenko, M.

The **Photographer**. Yuknavitch, L.

PHOTOGRAPHERS

See also Women photographers

Akmakjian, H. Sunday

Auster, P. Auggie Wren's Christmas story

Barron, L. The imago sequence

Bennett, T. Blind faith

Bissell, T. Death defies

Block, L. Man with a passion

Brady, C. Scissors, paper, rock

Brennan, K. On vision

Butner, R. The wounded

Cheuse, A. Moonrise, Hernandez, New Mexico, 1941

Chilson, P. Freelancing

Cortázar, J. Blow-up

Coxe, G. H. Murder picture

Crane, E. You must be this happy to enter

Crouse, D. Click

Efoui, K. A hunting scene as observed by a sentimental photographer

Goldfaden, J. Looking at animals

Greer, A. S. Newton Wicks

Harrison, W. The shadow that lost its man

Hawes, L. My last Indian

Hodge, B. With acknowledgements to Sun Tzu

Holthe, T. U. Weightless

Hospital, J. T. Frames and wonders

Jo Kyung Ran. Looking for the elephant

Lahiri, J. Going ashore

L'Amour, L. By the ruins of "El Walarieh"

Lunstrum, K. S. Carmel

Meacham, R. The assignment

Monteleone, T. F. Camera obscura

Nelson, R. F. Cutters

Olafsson, O. July

Phillips, S. The Emerson, 1950

Reid, G. Hey, mister!

Pizzolatto, Nic—*Continued*

The guild of thieves, lost women, and sunrise palms

    Pizzolatto, N. Between here and the yellow sea; stories

Haunted earth

    Pizzolatto, N. Between here and the yellow sea; stories

    Iowa Review v35 no2 p14-24 Fall 2005

Nepal

    Pizzolatto, N. Between here and the yellow sea; stories

Two shores

    Pizzolatto, N. Between here and the yellow sea; stories

Wanted man

    The Best American mystery stories, 2009; edited and with an introduction by Jeffery Deaver

Pizzolatto, Nicolas

Between Here and the Yellow Sea

    Atlantic Monthly (1993) v294 no4 p159-72 N 2004

Place, Vanessa

A Parable, I Suppose

    Western Humanities Review v62 no2 p142-9 Spr/Summ 2008

A **Place** for Fine Hats. Gullard, P.

A **Place** in Time: Some Chapters of a Telling Story. Berry, W.

A **place** like here, only different. Kun, M.

A **place** of comfort, light and hope. Higgins, G. V.

A **Place** of Serenity. Hanson, R.

The **place** of the swallows. Anaya, R. A.

The **place** that time forgot. Muller, M.

Places Down Below. Smith, J.

The **places** of Aache. Zelazny, R.

Plager, Silvia

A change of heart

    English translations of short stories by contemporary Argentine women writers; edited by Eliana Cazaubon Hermann; translated by Sally Webb Thornton

The **plagiarist**. Seamon, H.

PLAGUE

    See also Disasters

Aguirre, F. Andretto walks the king's way

Anderson, B. The last escape

Evenson, B. Fugue–state

Holder, N. Passion play

Hubbard, L. R. Danger in the dark

Lanagan, M. The goosle

McAllister, B. The boy in Zaquitos

Rajaniemi, H. Deus ex homine

Rand, K. Ice folly

Yolen, J. Green plague

Zelazny, R. Stowaway

The **plague** of doves. Erdrich, L.

The **Plaid** Shoes. Farnsworth, V.

Plain Women Speaking Beautifully. Wuori, G. K.

Plainface. Ball, J.

Plan of occupancy. Echenoz, J.

Planck time. Iwoleit, M. K.

Planet Big Zero. Lethem, J.

Planet of the Amazon women. Moles, D.

The **planet** of the dead. Smith, C. A.

Planet of the Yids. Shteyngart, G.

PLANETS, MINOR *See* Asteroids

The **plans** they made. Lane, J.

PLANTATION LIFE

Carl, L. S. Way down in Egypt's land

Dunbar, P. L. Anner 'Lizer's stumblin' block

Dunbar, P. L. Ash-Cake Hannah and her Ben

Dunbar, P. L. Aunt Tempe's revenge

Dunbar, P. L. Aunt Tempe's triumph

Dunbar, P. L. A blessed deceit

Dunbar, P. L. The brief cure of Aunt Fanny

Dunbar, P. L. Cahoots

Dunbar, P. L. The colonel's awakening

Dunbar, P. L. The conjuring contest

Dunbar, P. L. Dandy Jim's conjure scare

Dunbar, P. L. Dizzy-headed Dick

Dunbar, P. L. The Easter wedding

Dunbar, P. L. A family feud

Dunbar, P. L. How Brother Parker fell from grace

Dunbar, P. L. The intervention of Peter

Dunbar, P. L. Jim's probation

Dunbar, P. L. A lady slipper

Dunbar, P. L. The last fiddling of Mordaunt's Jim

Dunbar, P. L. The memory of Martha

Dunbar, P. L. Mr. Groby's slippery gift

Dunbar, P. L. The strength of Gideon

Dunbar, P. L. A supper by proxy

Dunbar, P. L. The trouble about Sophiny

Dunbar, P. L. Uncle Simon's Sundays out

Dunbar, P. L. The walls of Jericho

Dunbar, P. L. Who stand for the gods

Frost, G. Attack of the jazz giants

Jeffers, H. F. A plate of mojo

Planting Happiness. Heeger, S.

PLANTS

Goldfaden, J. King of the ferns

Maxwell, W. The shepherd's wife

Raphael, L. The story of a plant

PLASTIC SURGERY

Berwin, M. Perfection

Cody, L. Solar zits

Menger-Anderson, K. The story of her breasts, 1971

Palmer, M. and Palmer, D. Disfigured

Reed, K. No two alike

Snyder, S. Wreck

Plate, Peter

Genesis to revelation

    San Francisco noir; edited by Peter Maravelis

A **plate** of mojo. Jeffers, H. F.

PLATH, SYLVIA

About

Johnson, G. Double exposure

Platinum. Salter, J.

PLATONIC LOVE *See* Love

Platonov, Andrei

Among Animals and Plants

    The New Yorker v83 no32 p117-19, 122-8, 135, 137 O 22 2007

The sun, the moon, and the ether channel

    Worlds apart; an anthology of Russian fantasy and science fiction; edited and with commentary by Alexander Levitsky; translated by Alexander Levitsky and Martha T. Kitchen

Plato's Bruise. Gray, V. K.

Platt, Charles

The disaster story

    New worlds; an anthology; edited by Michael Moorcock

Plattner, Andrew
　A Marriage of Convenience
　　New Letters v74 no1 p17-26 2007/2008
　Runaway
　　The Sewanee Review v116 no1 p29-47 Wint
　　2008
A **play** for a boy and sock puppets. Sedia, E.
Playdate. Walbert, K.
The **players** and the kings. Kiely, B.
PLAYGROUNDS
　Jones, S. G. To run without falling
PLAYING CARDS *See* Cards
Playing house. Coover, R.
Playing the game. Charters, D.
Playing the game. Dann, J. and Dozois, G. R.
Playing the joker. Simpson, P.
Playing the odds. Claire, A.
Playing with Fire [Part III]
Playland. Hansen, R.
Playmate. Reed, K.
PLAYWRIGHTS *See* Dramatists
Plaza Mauá. Lispector, C.
Pleasant drugs and terminal liquors. Kulpa, K.
Please don't hurt me. Wilson, F. P.
Please, Leave a Message. Powell, N.
Please stand by. Monteleone, T. F.
PLEASURE *See* Happiness; Hedonism
Pleasure boating in Lituya Bay. Shepard, J.
The **pleasure** garden of Felipe Sagittarius.
　　Moorcock, M.
The **pleasure** of their company. Silverberg, R.
Pletzinger, Thomas
　Bruck on the Floor Sings as Quietly as Monk
　　Plays
　　Iowa Review v37 no2 p105-10 Fall 2007
Pleyben. Bingham, S.
The **plight**. Hamid Ahmad, 'A. a.- .
Ploetz, Steven
　In love with Rachel
　　Playboy's college fiction; a collection of 21
　　years of contest winners; edited by Alice
　　K. Turner; foreword by Thom Jones
The **Plot**. Gallagher, S.
Plot Theory. Cusumano, C.
Plot twist. Schow, D. J.
Plotters and shooters. Baker, K.
Pluck. Donoghue, E.
Plum Creek. Furman, L.
The **plunderer**. Dimitriou, S.
The **plunge**. Goodis, D.
The **plunge** of the brave. Erdrich, L.
**Plunkett, Edward John Moreton Drax, Baron
　　Dunsany** *See* Dunsany, Edward John More-
　　ton Drax Plunkett, Baron, 1878-1957
PLUTO (PLANET)
　Lovecraft, H. P. The whisperer in darkness
The **Plutonian** drug. Smith, C. A.
Pneuman, Angela
　All Saints Day
　　The Best American short stories, 2004; edited
　　by Lorrie Moore; Katrina Kenison series
　　editor
　The Beachcomber
　　StoryQuarterly v42 p209-39 2006
Pneumonia. Keith, J.
POACHING
　　　See also Hunting
　Bishop, T. A Hoover steak
　Dahl, R. The champion of the world

Poaching. Shields, C.
Poch, John
　Blade
　　Callaloo v32 no2 p447-53 Spr 2009
Poché, Reggie
　Sunshine Money
　　River Styx no73 p12-24 2006
Pocket Dog. Vestal, S.
Pocketful of dharma. Bacigalupi, P.
Pockets. Rucker, R. v. B. and Shirley, J.
Poe, David R.
　An Easy Day at Easy Red
　　The Literary Review (Madison, N.J.) v49 no4
　　p100-14 Summ 2006
Poe, Edgar Allan
　The black cat
　　Murder short & sweet; edited by Paul D.
　　Staudohar
　The purloined letter
　　The Mammoth book of vintage whodunnits;
　　edited by Maxim Jakubowski
POE, EDGAR ALLAN, 1809-1849
　　　　　　About
　Frost, G. In the sunken museum
　Oates, J. C. Poe posthumous; or, The light-
　　house
　　　　Parodies, imitations, etc.
　Arnzen, M. A. The dead lantern
　Baker, K. So this guy walks into a lighthouse—
　Braunbeck, G. A. Fisherman's delight
　Castle, M. The watcher at the window
　Conlon, C. Darkness, and she was alone
　Di Filippo, P. The days of other light
　Douglas, C. N. The riches there that lie
　Engstrom, E. Deep into the darkness peering
　Hamner, E. A passion for solitude
　Hoffman, B. I've been waiting for you
　Johnson, G. C. A literary forgery
　Kassak, F. Who's afraid of Ed Garpo?
　Lebbon, T. The flames beneath the light
　Lodi, E. Salamander scrimshander
　Lupoff, R. A. Fourth Avenue interlude
　Mamatas, N. There is a light that never goes out
　Nicholson, S. Last writes
　Nolan, W. F. The tragic narrative of Arthur
　　Bedford Addison
　Resnick, M. and Faw, B. A muse with burning
　　eyes
　Rock, P. Disentangling
　Rucker, R. v. B. MS found in a minidrive
　Schlich, S. Inside the Iron Maiden
　Shirley, J. Blind eye
　Tham, H. The seventh day
　Yarbro, C. Q. A new interpretation of the
　　Liggerzun Text
Poe posthumous; or, The light-house. Oates, J. C.
The **poem**. Brau, E.
The **poem**. Mozetič, B.
Poems and Reflections. Bucknam, T.
Poet. Ducornet, R.
The **poet**. Mozetič, B.
The **poet** and the general. Brazaitis, M.
The **poet** and the muse. Tolstaia, T.
Poetic justice. Nolan, W. F.
POETRY
　Beagle, P. S. Spook
　Boudinot, R. Written by machines
　Bradbury, R. The poems
　Bradfield, S. Angry duck

POETRY—*Continued*

    Fowler, K. J. The last worders
    Groff, L. Blythe
    Kiely, B. The night we rode with Sarsfield
    Klassen, S. Ending with poetry
    Marchand, J. Pallas at noon
    Messinger, J. One valve opens
    Shabtai, Y. True tenderness
    Shields, C. Purple blooms
    Stern, R. G. Dying

Poetry and Prose. Poupart, L.

Poetry of the Amish. Lynn, D. H.

POETS

        See also Troubadours; Women poets
    Anderson, B. The right sort of ears
    Arnason, E. Knapsack poems
    Auchincloss, L. The young Apollo
    Bishop, K. J. The art of dying
    Blish, J. The oath
    Bolaño, R. Enrique Martin
    Brazaitis, M. The poet and the general
    Bukowski, C. The night nobody believed I was
        Allen Ginsberg
    Burke, K. Scherzando
    Daughtry, P. The mouse's aura
    de Caldas Brito, C. "The beggar"
    DeMarinis, R. Birds of the mountain west
    Dimitriou, S. The plunderer
    Đoàn, L. The clone
    Dobson, J. Hey, girlie
    Ducornet, R. Poet
    Fulton, A. If it's not too much to ask
    Groff, L. L. DeBard and Aliette
    Groff, L. L. DeBard and Aliette: a love story
    Groff, L. Surfacing
    Hays, D. Ackerman in Eden
    Hemon, A. American commando
    Hemon, A. The conductor
    Hemon, A. Szmura's room
    Johnson, G. Double exposure
    Kiely, B. Blackbird on a bramble bough
    Levi, P. The fugitive
    Lynn, D. H. Mistaken identity
    Martin, V. The open door
    Matheson, R. When day is dun
    Milofsky, D. Biofeedback
    Monk, B. Epilogue: Excellent sperm
    Moore, L. The Jewish hunter
    Oates, J. C. The heart sutra
    Panselinos, A. Arrogance
    Perlman, E. I was only in a childish way connected to the established order
    Ruefle, M. A minor personal matter
    Ruefle, M. A romantic poet and his destiny
    Sallis, J. Jeremiad
    Salter, J. Give
    Salter, J. My Lord you
    Segal, L. G. Money, fame, and beautiful women
    Shirley, J. The word "random", deliberately repeated
    Silverberg, R. A man of talent
    Smith, C. A. The monster of the prophecy
    Soueif, A. Mandy
    Stafford, J. An influx of poets
    Stern, R. G. Mail
    Stevens, J. D. Why I married the porn star
    Taylor, P. E. Leaping Leo
    Thomas, E. One swallow doesn't make a summer

    Tidhar, L. Shira
    Tolstaia, T. Limpopo
    Tolstaia, T. The poet and the muse
    Windley, C. The joy of life
    Zimmer, P. The mechanics

POGROMS *See* Jews—Persecutions

Póh-hlaik, the cave boy. Lummis, C. F.

Pohl, Frederik

    The celebrated no-hit inning
        Pohl, F. Platinum Pohl; the collected best stories
    Creation myths of the recently extinct
        Pohl, F. Platinum Pohl; the collected best stories
    Criticality
        Pohl, F. Platinum Pohl; the collected best stories
    Day million
        Pohl, F. Platinum Pohl; the collected best stories
    The day the icicle works closed
        Pohl, F. Platinum Pohl; the collected best stories
    The day the Martians came
        Pohl, F. Platinum Pohl; the collected best stories
    Fermi and frost
        Pohl, F. Platinum Pohl; the collected best stories
    The gold at the starbow's end
        Pohl, F. Platinum Pohl; the collected best stories
    The greening of Bed-Stuy
        Pohl, F. Platinum Pohl; the collected best stories
    Growing up in Edge City
        Pohl, F. Platinum Pohl; the collected best stories
    The high test
        Pohl, F. Platinum Pohl; the collected best stories
    I remember a winter
        Pohl, F. Platinum Pohl; the collected best stories
    The kindly isle
        Pohl, F. Platinum Pohl; the collected best stories
    The knights of Arthur
        Pohl, F. Platinum Pohl; the collected best stories
    Let the ants try
        Pohl, F. Platinum Pohl; the collected best stories
    The mapmakers
        Pohl, F. Platinum Pohl; the collected best stories
    The mayor of Mare Tranq
        Pohl, F. Platinum Pohl; the collected best stories
    The merchants of Venus
        Pohl, F. Platinum Pohl; the collected best stories
    The middle of nowhere
        Pohl, F. Platinum Pohl; the collected best stories
    My lady Green Sleeves
        Pohl, F. Platinum Pohl; the collected best stories

Pokwatka, Aimee

The Museum of Lost and Found

The Literary Review (Madison, N.J.) v49 no4 p35-49 Summ 2006

Pol Pot's beautiful daughter (fantasy). Ryman, G.

POLAND

See also Auschwitz (Poland: Concentration camp)

Biller, M. 80 centimeters of bad temper

Card, O. S. The elephant of Poznan

Singer, I. B. The bond

Singer, I. B. The conference

Singer, I. B. Dazzled

Singer, I. B. The interview

Singer, I. B. The pocket remembered

Yarbrough, S. Two dogs

Communism

See Communism—Poland

Rural life

Singer, I. B. The divorce

Singer, I. B. The litigants

Singer, I. B. Strong as death is love

Krakow

Michaels, L. Nachman

Lodz

Wendroff, Z. In the textile islands

Lublin

Singer, I. B. Hershele and Hanele' or, The power of a dream

Singer, I. B. A nest egg for paradise

Warsaw

Oates, J. C. My Warszawa: 1980

Singer, I. B. Between shadows

Singer, I. B. The bitter truth

Singer, I. B. Loshikl

POLAR REGIONS *See* Antarctic regions; Arctic regions

POLES

Ireland

Doyle, R. The pram

Italy

Serdakowski, B. "Elsewhere"

United States

Gordon, M. Temporary shelter

O'Connor, F. The displaced person

Singer, I. B. The smuggler

POLICE

Alarcón, D. Lima, Peru; July 28, 1979

Allen, J. R. The near remote

Armstrong, M. The Duh Vice

Baraka, I. A. The pig detector

Barnes, H. L. A pulling thing

Barrett, M. Suspects wanted

Barthelme, D. The police band

Baumbach, J. Bright is innocent: scenes from an imaginary movie

Blish, J. Beep

Breen, J. L. Serial killer

Bruen, K. Nora B.

Buentello, J. A certain recollection

Cadigan, P. Nothing personal

Chekhov, A. P. The drama at the hunt

Coxe, G. H. Murder picture

Davis, F. C. The sinister sphere

Deaver, J. Chapter and verse

DeCandido, K. R. A. A clean getaway

Dee, E. The tailman

DeMarinis, R. Nightwork, 1973

Dexter, C. The double crossing

Doolittle, S. Mr. big deal

DuBois, B. One shot difference

Dufresne, J. Died and gone to heaven

Estleman, L. D. Smart aleck

Fiorillo, H. The aroma of death

Fredrickson, J. A change in his heart

Fujino, C. The housewife and the police box

Gallagher, S. Jailbird for Jesus

Gardner, E. S. The monkey murder

Glass, L. The Herald

Gomez, D. R. Bitter sorrows

Goodis, D. The dead laugh last

Goodis, D. The plunge

Guyot, P. What a wonderful world

Hajiri, M. a.- . The checkpoint

Harvey, J. Snow, snow, snow

Higgins, G. V. The habits of the animals: the progress of the seasons

Hoch, E. D. Friday night luck

Hogan, C. Two thousand volts

Howard, C. The leper colony

Jackson, L. Vintage death

James, C. L. R. Police proclamation

Kiely, B. Secondary top

Kirac, R. Ordinary facts

Lam, V. Eli

Lescroart, J. T. A friendly little game

Liparulo, R. Kill zone

McCauley, W. Palaver

Meno, J. The sound before the end of the world

Nebel, F. Wise guy

Orozco, D. Officers weep

Parker, T. J. Skinhead central

Parra, E. A. Just don't take the little I got

Preston, D. and Child, L. Gone fishing

Quertermous, B. Cadaver dog

Rusch, K. K. The power of human reason

Scottoline, L. Love match

Slavin, J. Squatters

Walsh, T. Double check

White, L. T. The city of hell!

Wolven, S. Barracuda

Woolrich, C. 3 kills for 1

Woolrich, C. Blue is for bravery

Woolrich, C. Detective William Brown

Woolrich, C. Double feature

Woolrich, C. Endicott's girl

Woolrich, C. Two murders, one crime

Argentina

Brau, E. The siesta

Arizona

Alvarado, B. Limbo

Sierra, J. The fifth world

Atlanta (Ga.)

Kelly, R. Romicide

Kelly, R. The winds within

Kiernan, C. R. Anamorphosis

Australia

Winton, T. Commission

Winton, T. Fog

Bombay (India)

Archer, J. The commissioner

Shroff, M. F. Busy Sunday

California

See also Police—Los Angeles (Calif.); Police—San Francisco (Calif.)

Deaver, J. Surveillance

Shirley, J. War and peace

Woods, P. L. Divine droplets

POLICE—*Continued*

Chicago (Ill.)

Allen, J. R. Holding pattern

Allen, J. R. The near remote

Black, M. A. Chasing the blues

Carlson, P. M. Frighted out of fear; or, the bombs bursting in air

D'Amato, B. The lower wacker Hilton

Guilfoile, K. Zero zero day

Hellmann, L. F. The whole world is watching

Howard, C. Under suspicion

Mandel, S. B. Blind man blue

Walker, D. J. A weekend in the country

Welk, M. V. Code blue

China

Qi, S. The evidence

Denver (Colo.)

Stein, J. C. Better lucky than good

Detroit (Mich.)

Olsen, E. J. Snow angel

Parrish, P. J. Pride

England

See also Police—London (England)

Harvey, J. The sun, the moon and the stars

Lane, J. Beth's law

Robinson, P. The price of love

Turnbull, P. Max Winner's shadow

Florida

Born, J. O. The drought

France

Manotti, D. Zero tolerance

Hawaii

Hansen-Young, D. Oaths, Ohana, and everything

Hollywood (Calif.)

See Police—Los Angeles (Calif.)

Houston (Tex.)

Vincent, B. Rule number one

Iowa

Collins, M. A. and Clemens, M. V. The high life: a heartland homicide story

Ireland

Rickards, J. Wish

Italy

Lucarelli, C. Beret

Kentucky

McMahan, R. The cold, hard truth

Las Vegas (Nev.)

Tran, V. This or any desert

Trans, V. This or any desert

London (England)

Bierce, A. A representative inquest

Cody, L. The uniform

Collins, W. Who is the thief?

Harvey, J. Drummer unknown

Harvey, J. Sack o' woe

Updike, D. A word with the boy

Los Angeles (Calif.)

Coleman, W. Shark liver oil

Connelly, M. Mulholland dive

Holmes, E. Dangerous days

Lochte, D. Diamond dog

Waldrop, H. Flatfeet!

Wilson, F. P. Sex slaves of the dragon tong

Woods, P. L. I'll be doggone

Malawi

Chaponda, D. Heroic proportions

Maryland

Golden, M. After [excerpt]

Michigan

Deaver, J. Copycat

Johnson, B. Michiganders, 1979

Minnesota

Bush, G. If you harm us

Logue, M. Blasted

Mobile (Ala.)

Benford, G. Dark heaven

Nevada

Hornsby, W. Dust up

New Hampshire

DuBois, B. A trace of a trace

New Orleans (La.)

Atkins, A. Angola South

McLoughlin, T. Scared rabbit

Overmyer, E. Marigny triangle

Smith, J. Loot

New York (N.Y.)

Ardai, C. The good samaritan

Block, L. I don't fool around

Block, L. The way to power

Cohen, G. Right is right

Deaver, J. Nothing but net

Dee, E. Ernie K.'s gelding

Fairstein, L. Going under

Fusilli, J. Brenda, my star

Fusilli, J. The guardians

Goodis, D. The case of the laughing queen

Goodis, D. Man without a tongue

Guerriero, L. Eating Italian

Jasper, K. Thursday

Knightly, R. One more for the road

Knightly, R. Take the man's pay

Lovecraft, H. P. The horror at Red Hook

Manfredo, L. Case closed

Martinez, L. Freddie Prinze is my guardian angel

Martinez, M. The last honest man in Brooklyn

McBain, E. Accident report

McBain, E. Chinese puzzle

McBain, E. First offense

McBain, E. Kid kill

McBain, E. Merely hate

McBain, E. See him die

McBain, E. Small homicide

McBain, E. Still life

McInerney, J. The march

McLoughlin, T. When all this was Bay Ridge

Meyers, A. Not just the facts

Morrissey, T. Can't catch me

Schuyler, G. S. The shoemaker murder

Solomita, S. Crazy Jill saves the slinky

Walker, P. Such a lucky, pretty girl

Westlake, D. E. The best friend-murder

Woolrich, C. The fatal footlights

New York (State)

Deaver, J. Forever

Oregon

Chilson, P. American food

Crozier, O. Murder on Chuckanut Drive

Paris (France)

Ravalec, V. Feeding the hungry

Sylvain, D. Heatwave

Pennsylvania

Ayres, N. J. Rust

Russia

Zoshchenko, M. A hasty business

San Francisco (Calif.)

Twain, M. The black hole of San Francisco

POLICE—*Continued*
Texas
See also Police—Houston (Tex.)
Flaig, S. Texas toast
Sweazy, L. D. The promotion
Toronto (Ont.)
Stewart, P. Makeshift memorial
United States
Baldwin, J. Going to meet the man
Deaver, J. The poker lesson
Garrett, G. P. Empty bed blues
Garrett, G. P. Pornographers
Oates, J. C. High lonesome
Twain, M. The stolen white elephant
Vermont
Wolven, S. Taciturnity
Washington (D.C.)
Castaneda, R. Coyote hunt
Pelecanos, G. P. String music
Peterson, Q. Cold as ice
The **police** band. Barthelme, D.
Police proclamation. James, C. L. R.
Policeman Bluejay. Baum, L. F.
POLICEWOMEN
Ayres, N. J. Rust
Burke, A. Winning
Fairstein, L. Going under
Huston, C. Interrogation B
King, L. R. The fool
Margolin, P. The house on Pine Terrace
Parrish, P. J. Pride
Quiroga, A. A little bit farther
Rucka, G. Contact and cover
Winchell, P. Kindly omit flowers
POLIOMYELITIS
Bukoski, A. The wand of youth
Groff, L. L. DeBard and Aliette
Groff, L. L. DeBard and Aliette: a love story
Groff, L. Surfacing
Menger-Anderson, K. Salk and Sabin, 1955
Waldrop, H. The king of where-I-go
Polish. Singleton, G.
POLISH AMERICANS
Bukoski, A. Antoni Kosmatka resists the goddess of love
Bukoski, A. The case for bread and sausage
Bukoski, A. Gossamer bloom
Bukoski, A. A guide to American trees
Bukoski, A. The low August fever
Bukoski, A. North of the port
Bukoski, A. One red rose on a new black dress
Bukoski, A. The Pulaski guards
Bukoski, A. Report of the guardian of the sick
Bukoski, A. The shadow players
Bukoski, A. A walk down lonely street
Bukoski, A. The Wally na Zdrowie show
Bukoski, A. The wand of youth
POLISH REFUGEES
Singer, I. B. Runners to nowhere
Polite conversation. Stafford, J.
POLITICAL CAMPAIGNS *See* Politics
POLITICAL CORRUPTION *See* Corruption (in politics)
POLITICAL CRIMES AND OFFENSES
See also Assassination; Political prisoners; Terrorism
POLITICAL DEFECTORS *See* Defectors
Political Economy. Twain, M.

POLITICAL ETHICS
See also Power (Social sciences)
POLITICAL INTRIGUE *See* International intrigue; Politics
The **political** officer. Finlay, C. C.
Political Parties in China's Judiciary. Suli, Z.
POLITICAL PRISONERS
Déry, T. Love
Déry, T. Two women
Evangelisti, V. Sepultura
Kozameh, A. Impression of heights
Moss, B. K. Rug weaver
Roberson, C. The sky is large and the earth is small
Silverberg, R. Hawksbill Station
Zebrowski, G. My first world
POLITICIANS *See* Politics
POLITICS
See also Suffrage; Utopias; Women in politics
Baraka, I. A. From war stories
Baraka, I. A. Neo-American
Bierce, A. Corrupting the press
Bierce, A. Mr. Masthead, journalist
García Márquez, G. Death constant beyond love
Mejia, A. E. The new order
Modesitt, L. E., Jr. The difference
Silverberg, R. Counterpart
Singer, I. B. Sabbath in Gehanna
Tallent, E. Tabriz
Africa
Serna, E. Tesoro viviente/Living treasure
Argentina
Gorriti, J. M. The black glove
Gorriti, J. M. The dead man's fiancée
Gorriti, J. M. The mazorquero's daughter
Valenzuela, L. The key
China
Qi, S. The tenants
Greece
Galanaki, R. An almost-blue arm
Illinois
Orner, P. Pampkin's lament
Indonesia
Toer, P. A. Acceptence
Toer, P. A. In twilight born
Toer, P. A. Independence Day
Mexico
Stavans, I. Morirse está en Hebreo
Northern Ireland
McCabe, E. Heritage
Russia
Zoshchenko, M. An incident on the Volga
Zoshchenko, M. Monkey language
Texas
Brammer, B. L. The Gay Place [excerpt]
United States
Bender, K. E. Candidate
Bowes, R. If angels fight
Brennan, A. Killing justice
Connell, E. S. Election eve
Cooper, J. C. Just-life politics
Coville, B. Old glory
Davis, M. Negative Nixons
Dunbar, P. L. A council of state
Dunbar, P. L. A mess of pottage
Dunbar, P. L. The scapegoat
Grady, J. The bottom line
MacDougal, B. Out of order [excerpt]

POLITICS—United States—*Continued*
Martin, G. R. R. And death his legacy
McInerney, J. My public service
McInerney, J. Penelope on the pond
Molodowsky, K. Brothers
Morton, L. Sparks fly upward
Norton, V. Dirty heaven
Pohl, F. Servant of the people
Porter, K. A. A day's work
Rich, M. The never-winner
Sargent, P. A smaller government
Steele, A. M. Hail to the chief
Wolfe, G. Hour of trust
              1900-
Connell, E. S. Election eve
King, O. We're all in this together
Landis, G. A. The eyes of America
         Zimbabwe
Marechera, D. Thought tracks in the snow
Politics. Moon, E.
Pollack, Eileen
Beached in Boca
    Pollack, E. In the mouth; stories and novellas
The bris
    The Best American short stories, 2007; select-
      ed from U. S. and Canadian magazines by
      Stephen King with Heidi Pitlor; with an in-
      troduction by Stephen King
    Pollack, E. In the mouth; stories and novellas
Milk
    Pollack, E. In the mouth; stories and novellas
Milt and Moose
    Pollack, E. In the mouth; stories and novellas
The safe
    Pollack, E. In the mouth; stories and novellas
Uno
    Pollack, E. In the mouth; stories and novellas
    Prairie Schooner v81 no1 p191-207 Spr 2007
Pollack, Neal
City of commerce
    Los Angeles noir; edited by Denise Hamilton
Confessions of a dial-up gigolo
    Homewrecker: an adultery reader; edited by
      Daphne Gottlieb
Jewy Jew
    Stumbling and raging; more politically in-
      spired fiction; edited by Stephen Elliott;
      with associate editors Greg Larson [et al.]
Marty's drink or die club
    Chicago noir; edited by Neal Pollack
Scavenger hunt
    Brooklyn noir; edited by Tim McLoughlin
Pollack, Rachel
Burning Beard: the dreams and visions of Jo-
    seph Ben Jacob, Lord Viceroy of Egypt
    Interfictions; an anthology of interstitial writ-
      ing; edited by Delia Sherman and Theodora
      Goss
Reflected light
    Steampunk; edited by Ann & Jeff
      VanderMeer
Pollock, Donald Ray
Assailants
    Pollock, D. R. Knockemstiff
Bactine
    Pollock, D. R. Knockemstiff
Blessed
    Pollock, D. R. Knockemstiff

Discipline
    Pollock, D. R. Knockemstiff
Dynamite hole
    Pollock, D. R. Knockemstiff
The fights
    Pollock, D. R. Knockemstiff
Fish sticks
    Pollock, D. R. Knockemstiff
Giganthomachy
    Pollock, D. R. Knockemstiff
Hair's fate
    Pollock, D. R. Knockemstiff
Honolulu
    Pollock, D. R. Knockemstiff
Hooler
    Pollock, D. R. Knockemstiff
I start over
    Pollock, D. R. Knockemstiff
Knockemstiff
    Pollock, D. R. Knockemstiff
Lard
    Pollock, D. R. Knockemstiff
Pills
    Pollock, D. R. Knockemstiff
Rainy Sunday
    Pollock, D. R. Knockemstiff
Real life
    Pollock, D. R. Knockemstiff
Schott's Bridge
    Pollock, D. R. Knockemstiff
Hoi **Polloi:** Three Views. Reynolds, C.
POLLUTION
Bacigalupi, P. Pump six
Bacigalupi, P. Small offerings
Kelly, R. Tyrophex-fourteen
Pohl, F. Creation myths of the recently extinct
Williams, C. Slitten gorge
Polly Anderson's Christmas party. McLean, S.
Polyak, Christina
(jt. auth) See Polyak, Sam and Polyak, Christina
Polyak, Sam and Polyak, Christina
The prophecy: a Red Sox alternate history
    Fenway fiction; short stories from Red Sox
      nation; edited by Adam Emerson Pachter
POLYGAMY
    See also Mormons and Mormonism
Bilal, A. A voice from the earth
Hamid Ahmad, 'A. a.- . The plight
Ousmane, Sembène. Her three days
Singer, I. B. The betrayer of Israel
Pomerantz, Sharon
The Virgin of Upper Broadway
    Prairie Schooner v81 no1 p12-41 Spr 2007
Pomfret, Scott
Chicken
    Homewrecker: an adultery reader; edited by
      Daphne Gottlieb
Pomo basuto. Burke, T.
Pompeii recreated. Mitra, K.
Pompeo, Anthony
Role Model
    Critical Quarterly v49 no1 p96-103 Spr 2007
PONDS
Moceri, M. Proper fires
Selgin, P. The wolf house

Porter, Andrew—*Continued*

The Antioch Review v63 no1 p65-78 Wint 2005

Coyotes

Porter, A. The theory of light and matter

Departure

Pushcart prize XXXII: best of the small presses 2008; edited by Bill Henderson with the Pushcart Prize editors

Porter, A. The theory of light and matter

Hole

Porter, A. The theory of light and matter

Merkin

Porter, A. The theory of light and matter

River dog

Porter, A. The theory of light and matter

Skin

Porter, A. The theory of light and matter

Storms

Porter, A. The theory of light and matter

The theory of light and matter

Porter, A. The theory of light and matter

Prairie Schooner v80 no2 p159-77 Summ 2006

Porter, Joe Ashby

Merrymount

The Yale Review v94 no1 p136-46 Ja 2006

Solstice

Michigan Quarterly Review v45 no4 p655-74 Fall 2006

Porter, Joseph Ashby

Dream on

Porter, J. A. All aboard; stories; [by] Joe Ashby Porter

Forgotten coast

Porter, J. A. All aboard; stories; [by] Joe Ashby Porter

Merrymount

Porter, J. A. All aboard; stories; [by] Joe Ashby Porter

Pending

Porter, J. A. All aboard; stories; [by] Joe Ashby Porter

Reunion eve

Porter, J. A. All aboard; stories; [by] Joe Ashby Porter

Solstice

Porter, J. A. All aboard; stories; [by] Joe Ashby Porter

West Baltimore

So the story goes; twenty-five years of the Johns Hopkins short fiction series; edited by John T. Irwin and Jean McGarry; with a foreword by John Barth

Porter, Katherine Anne

The circus

Porter, K. A. Collected stories and other writings

The cracked looking-glass

Porter, K. A. Collected stories and other writings

A day's work

Porter, K. A. Collected stories and other writings

The downward path to wisdom

Porter, K. A. Collected stories and other writings

The fig tree

Porter, K. A. Collected stories and other writings

Flowering Judas

Porter, K. A. Collected stories and other writings

The grave

Lone Star literature; from the Red River to the Rio Grande; edited by Don Graham

Porter, K. A. Collected stories and other writings

Hacienda

Porter, K. A. Collected stories and other writings

He

Porter, K. A. Collected stories and other writings

Holiday

Porter, K. A. Collected stories and other writings

The jilting of Granny Weatherall

Porter, K. A. Collected stories and other writings

The journey

Porter, K. A. Collected stories and other writings

The last leaf

Porter, K. A. Collected stories and other writings

The leaning tower

Porter, K. A. Collected stories and other writings

Magic

Porter, K. A. Collected stories and other writings

María Concepción

Porter, K. A. Collected stories and other writings

The martyr

Porter, K. A. Collected stories and other writings

Noon wine

Porter, K. A. Collected stories and other writings

Old mortality

Porter, K. A. Collected stories and other writings

Pale horse, pale rider

Porter, K. A. Collected stories and other writings

Rope

Porter, K. A. Collected stories and other writings

The source

Porter, K. A. Collected stories and other writings

That tree

Porter, K. A. Collected stories and other writings

Theft

Porter, K. A. Collected stories and other writings

Virgin Violeta

Porter, K. A. Collected stories and other writings

The witness

Porter, K. A. Collected stories and other writings

POVERTY—*Continued*

Bogary, A. Bloodstains on the wall
Bonner, M. O. Tin can
Boudinot, R. So little time
Brau, E. The blessing
Cho, C. Land of exile
Collins, W. The diary of Ann Rodway
Davis, J. S. Detritus
Déry, T. Behind the brick wall
Drosso, A.-M. Heat
Fox, P. The broad estates of death
Garcia-Aguilera, C. The dinner
Gauss, M. A life like Maggy's
Gordimer, N. The ultimate safari
Gordin, J. Door number 279
Granados, C. Small time
Hernández, J. J. For Christmas
Hwang, S. A dream of good fortune
Inglis, T. M. Fairy "Spuds"
James, H. The rainy day
James, H. The sacrifice
Judah, S. The funeral
Krysl, M. Mitosos
Libin, Z. Little Albert's nightmare experience
Libin, Z. Mister Buchholtz
Lopes, H. The advance
Lynn, D. H. Children of God
McCabe, E. The landlord
McCabe, E. The master
McCabe, E. The mother
McCabe, E. The orphan
McCauley, W. Foday
McCauley, W. Mister Henry's trousers
Miura, T. Homecoming
Mollel, T. M. A night out
Molodowsky, K. Hinde the gardener
Monis, V. O. Woes of the middle class
Opatoshu, J. A house on Gorek Street
Palazzeschi, A. Bistino and the Marquis
Percoto, C. The bread of the departed
Raymond, J. Train choir
Rebelo, M. Down our street
Richard, M. Gentleman's agreement
Sada, D. El fenomeno ominoso/The ominous phenomenon
Sankaran, L. The red carpet
Saunders, G. Puppy
Scliar, M. The last poor man
Scott, J. The Queen of Sheba is afraid of snow
Shepard, J. Spending the night with the poor
Thon, M. R. Confession for Raymond Good Bird
Van Booy, S. No greater gift
Weaver, W. The gleaners
Zoshchenko, M. Classy lady
Zoshchenko, M. Electrification
Powder. Wolff, T.
The **powder** monkey. Bell, T.
Powell, Garry Craig
Kamila and the king of kandy
   The Best American mystery stories, 2009; edited and with an introduction by Jeffery Deaver
Powell, Mark
Snodgrass Hill
   South Carolina Review v37 no2 p197-203 Spr 2005

Powell, Martin
The abominable ice man
   Kolchak: the night stalker chronicles; 26 original tales of the surreal, the bizarre, the macabre; edited by Joe Gentile, Garrett Anderson, Lori Gentile; Kolchak created by Jeff Rice
Sherlock Holmes in the lost world
   Gaslight grimoire; fantastic tales of Sherlock Holmes; edited by J. R. Campbell and Charles Prepolec
Powell, Padgett
Horses
   The Paris Review v46 p79-84 Wint 2004
The Interrogative Mood
   The Paris Review v50 p153-67 Wint 2008
Scarliotti and the sinkhole
   The Anchor book of new American short stories; edited by Ben Marcus
Powell, Todd
Please, Leave a Message
   The Writer v121 no4 p27-9 Ap 2008
Power, Henriette Lazaridis
Chess Lessons
   New England Review v27 no3 p164-73 2006
POWER (SOCIAL SCIENCES)
Zelazny, R. King Solomon's ring
Power complex. Haldeman, J. W.
Power lines. Daugherty, T.
The **power** of human reason. Rusch, K. K.
Powerless. Kessel, J.
Powerman. Chenoweth, A.
Powers, J. F. (James Farl)
Dawn
   The best American Catholic short stories; a Sheed & Ward collection; edited by Daniel McVeigh and Patricia Schnapp
Lions, harts, leaping does
   The best American Catholic short stories; a Sheed & Ward collection; edited by Daniel McVeigh and Patricia Schnapp
Powers, James Farl *See* Powers, J. F. (James Farl), 1917-1999
Powers, Richard
The Seventh Event
   Granta no90 p57-74 Summ 2005
Powers, Tim
The better boy
   Powers, T. Strange itineraries
Fifty cents
   Powers, T. Strange itineraries
Itinerary
   Powers, T. Strange itineraries
Night moves
   Powers, T. Strange itineraries
Pat Moore
   Powers, T. Strange itineraries
Through and through
   Powers, T. Strange itineraries
The way down the hill
   Powers, T. Strange itineraries
We traverse afar
   Powers, T. Strange itineraries
Where they are hid
   Powers, T. Strange itineraries
Powers, William
Zero
   Iowa Review v37 no3 p107-13 Wint 2007/2008

The **prison**. Stansberry, D.
PRISON CAMPS *See* World War, 1939-1945—
Prisoners and prisons
PRISON ESCAPES *See* Escapes
Prison ships. Lane, J.
The **prisoner**. Brau, E.
Prisoner 2412. Horowitz, A.
The **Prisoner** of Mount Warning. Wilding, M.
The **prisoner** pear. Rust, E. M.
PRISONERS, POLITICAL *See* Political prison-
ers
PRISONERS AND PRISONS
> *See also* Ex-convicts; Political prisoners;
> Prisoners of war
Aydinoglu, Y. One among us
Bishop, E. In prison
Brau, E. The prisoner
Bukowski, C. 20 tanks from Kasseldown
Disch, T. M. Nights in the garden of the
Kerhonkson prison for the aged and infirm
Frankel-Zaltzman, P. A natural death
Hamid Ahmad, 'A. a.- . The plight
Herbert, B. and Anderson, K. J. Sea Child: a
tale of Dune
Hinton, S. E. Different shorelines
Hinton, S. E. Homecoming
Hinton, S. E. Sentenced
Hinton, S. E. Visit
Hodgson, W. H. Judge Barclay's wife
Howard, C. Blues in the Kabul night
Hurwitz, G. Dirty weather
Kim, M. Scarlet fingernails
Kozameh, A. Impression of heights
Lefer, D. At the site where vision is most per-
fect
Manickchand, R. A. Dougla
McAuley, P. J. Dead men walking
McAuley, P. J. and Newman, K. Prisoners of
the action
Monk, B. Do not revive
Piñón, N. Procession of love
Pohl, F. My lady Green Sleeves
Reed, R. Winemaster
Rivas, M. The coming of wisdom with time
Shawl, N. Deep end
Shepard, L. Jailwise
Singer, I. B. Loshikl
Smith, R. T. Blaze
Snyder, S. Voodoo heart
Solomita, S. Bubba
Stewart, P. Heirloom
Thomas, J. Wakizashi
Thompson, J. His own time
Varon, P. The feast
Waggoner, T. All in the execution
Waldrop, H. A dozen tough jobs
Wideman, J. E. What we cannot speak about we
must pass over in silence
Wilson, F. P. The November game
Zelazny, R. Dismal light
China
Ma Jian. Where are you running to?
Cuba
Betancourt, L. A. Guilty
Rivera-Valdes, S. Like in jail
England
Archer, J. The alibi
Archer, J. It can't be October already
Waites, M. Just pretend

Mexico
Fuentes, C. Mater Dolorosa
Peru
Alarcón, D. Flood
Russia
Brenner, Y. H. From A to M
Hummel, E. The fish of Berlin [excerpt]
Kolendo, A. Wintering
United States
Atkins, A. Angola South
Barnes, H. L. Punishment
Burke, J. L. Big midnight special
Capote, T. A diamond guitar
Chaon, D. I demand to know where you're tak-
ing me
Coleman, W. Purgatory
Grady, J. Kiss the sky
Jones, E. P. Old boys, old girls
MacEnulty, P. Singing in the free world
Malae, P. N. The arms of Brian Flinteraft
Malae, P. N. Before high desert
Malae, P. N. The good nurse
Malae, P. N. Guts and viscera in the chicken
farm
Malae, P. N. The once-a-week performance
Malae, P. N. Reliable vet dad, reliable con son
Malae, P. N. Smuggling a kiss
Malae, P. N. The story
Malae, P. N. Tags
Malae, P. N. What you can do after shutdown
Marion, S. Dogs with human faces
McInerney, J. Con doctor
Menger-Anderson, K. Hysteria, 1820
Oates, J. C. How I contemplated the world from
the Detroit House of Corrections, and be-
gan my life over again
Pohl, F. The greening of Bed-Stuy
Sayles, J. The Halfway Diner
Seranella, B. Misdirection
Straight, S. Mines
Thompson, J. The woman at the well
Tobin, P. passage
Wolven, S. Outside work detail
Zafiro, F. Rescuing Isaac
Prisoners of the action. McAuley, P. J. and New-
man, K.
PRISONERS OF WAR
> *See also* Concentration camps; World
> War, 1939-1945—Prisoners and prisons
Emshwiller, C. My general
Monteleone, T. F. The prisoner's tale
Phan, A. Gates of Saigon
PRISONS *See* Prisoners and prisons
Pritchard, Sara
Two Studies in Entropy
New Letters v74 no2 p33-56 2008
Pritchett, Jenny
Thieves
Southwest Review v93 no4 p513-22 2008
Pritchett, Michael
Reason to Believe He Hath Deserted
New Letters v73 no1 p61-84 2006/2007
Pritchett, V. S.
A New World
Harper's v309 p30-2 D 2004
Private. Barnes, H. L.
A **private** and very awesome leopard. Shabtai, Y.
PRIVATE DETECTIVES *See* Detectives, Private
A **private experience**. Adichie, C. N.

PRIVATE EYE STORIES *See* Detectives, Private; Mystery and detective stories
PRIVATE SCHOOLS *See* School life
Private tuition with Mr. Bose. Desai, A.
The **private** war of Private Jacob. Haldeman, J. W.
The **prize**. Faiz, J.
Probability. Rylands, J. T.
The **problem** child. Maxwell, W.
PROBLEM CHILDREN *See* Emotionally disturbed children
A **problem** in communication. Breuer, M. J.
The **Problem** of Evil in Hauberk, Missouri. Davis, M.
The **problem** of human consumption. Almond, S.
The **problem** of Susan. Gaiman, N.
The **problem** of the sore bridge–among others. Farmer, P. J.
The **Problem** with Bright Fires. Sainte Croix, S.
Problems for self-study. Yu, C.
Proboscis. Barron, L.
Probst, Mark
  Daytrip
    The Yale Review v95 no4 p129-40 O 2007
Procedure. Magson, A.
The **procession** of shadows. Santamaria, G.
Proctor Bemis. Connell, E. S.
PROCURERS *See* Pimps
Prodigal. Nichols, L. D.
Prodigal me. Ellison, J. T.
The **prodigal** son. Wieland, M.
Product development. Kress, N.
Product development [Short story] Kress, N.
The **profane** angel. Estleman, L. D.
Professional killer. Block, L.
Professional man. Goodis, D.
Professor Arecibo. Kalfus, K.
The **professor** was a thief. Hubbard, L. R.
PROFESSORS *See* Teachers
La profonde. Dowling, T.
PROGERIA
  Ryan, P. So much for Artemis
PROGRAMMING (COMPUTERS)
  Boudinot, R. Written by machines
  Silverberg, R. Enter a soldier. Later: enter another
  Zhu Wen. Ah, Xiao Xie
A **progression**. Burke, K.
Progressive dinner. Barth, J.
Prohibition. Westcott, G.
The **project**. Means, D.
Project 38; or, The game of small causes. Kuper, T.
Project nursemaid. Merril, J.
Project: Verbivore. Lovegrove, J.
The **projectionist's** wife. Rash, R.
Prologue to a life. West, D.
Prologue to the Law Faculty Tales. Fridman, G. H. L.
Prologue (two lives in letters). Tomlinson, J.
The **Prom**. Nason, R.
Prom season. Kalotay, D.
PROMETHEUS (LEGENDARY FIGURE)
  Brau, E. The forgotten god
  Machado de Assis. Life
Prometheus unbound, at last. Robinson, K. S.
PROMISCUITY
  Bradfield, S. Penguins for lunch
  Brown, K. Unction

Gilchrist, E. The Double Happiness Bun
Kiely, B. A great god's angel standing
Luongo, M. Do that everywhere
McGlynn, D. Sweet Texas angel
Monteiro, L. The whirling dove
Stern, R. G. The girl who loves Schubert
Umansky, E. Crew cut
Promise. Crane, E.
Promise. Harvey, J.
The **promise**. Hodgson, W. H.
The **promise**. Yolen, J.
Promise Breaker. Adrian, C.
The **promised** land. Clayton, J. J.
Promises; a tale of the city Imperishable. Lake, J.
Promises, promises. O'Neill, J.
The **promoter**. Dunbar, P. L.
The **promotion**. Sweazy, L. D.
Pronzini, Bill
  The bughouse caper
    Pronzini, B. Quincannon's game; western stories
  The cloud cracker
    Pronzini, B. Quincannon's game; western stories
  I wasn't there
    Hollywood and crime; original crime stories set during the history of Hollywood; edited by Robert J. Randisi
  Medium rare
    Pronzini, B. Quincannon's game; western stories
  Quincannon in paradise
    Pronzini, B. Quincannon's game; western stories
  Souls burning
    San Francisco noir 2; the classics; edited by Peter Maravelis
  The winning ticket
    A Prisoner of memory and 24 of the year's finest crime and mystery stories; edited by Ed Gorman & Martin H. Greenberg
  Wrong place, wrong time
    The World's finest mystery and crime stories, fourth annual collection; edited by Ed Gorman and Martin H. Greenberg
Pronzini, Bill and Malzberg, Barry N.
  Me and Mitch
    The Adventure of the missing detective and 19 of the year's finest crime and mystery stories!; edited by Ed Gorman and Martin H. Greenberg
Proof. Sherman, R.
Proof. Tabor, M. L.
Proof of God. Jones, H. G.
Proof of Heirship. Homer, P.
PROPAGANDA
  Bulgakov, M. A. The fatal eggs
Proper fires. Moceri, M.
Proper gypsies. Mason, B. A.
The **properties** of stainless steel. Barkley, B.
PROPERTY
    See also Real estate
  Cozarinsky, E. Real estate
  Keane, J. B. The Fort Field
  Maxwell, W. The woman who didn't want anything more
  Naiyer Masud. The big garbage dump
PROPERTY, REPOSSESSION OF *See* Repossession

The **Property** of Water. Flaherty, K.
PROPHECIES
   Ali, M. N. Ward G-4
   Collins, W. Nine o'clock
   Dunbar, P. L. A prophesy of fate
   Roberts, A. And tomorrow and
   Sherman, D. La Fée Verte
Prophecy. Anderson, P.
Prophecy. Malpede, K.
The **prophecy:** a Red Sox alternate history.
   Polyak, S. and Polyak, C.
Prophecy of the blind. Lamb, H.
A **prophesy** of fate. Dunbar, P. L.
Prophet. Scott, L.
The **prophet** of Flores. Kosmatka, T.
The **prophet** of Zongo Street. Ali, M. N.
PROPHETS
   Ali, M. N. The prophet of Zongo Street
   Rhine, R. S. The seer
   Silverberg, R. Thomas the Proclaimer
   Sterling, B. Dinner in Audoghast
Prophet's dilemma. Auslander, S.
Proportionate response. Healy, J. F.
The **Proposal**. O'Keefe, M.
Proposals and advice. Schwarzschild, E.
The **Proposition**. Bezmozgis, D.
Prose, Francine
   An open letter to Doctor X
      This is not chick lit; original stories by Amer-
      ica's best women writers; edited by Eliza-
      beth Merrick
      The Virginia Quarterly Review v82 no2
      p140-9 Spr 2006
Prospect. Rapaport, J.
PROSPECTORS
   Dunbar, P. L. The case of Cadwallader
   Swanwick, M. Tin marsh
The **prosperity** of cities and desert places. Lefer,
   D.
PROSTITUTES
      See also Courtesans; Escorts (Dating ser-
      vice); Pimps
   Abella, A. Shanghai
   Amado, J. How Porciúncula the mulatto got the
      corpse off his back
   Angel, J. The history of Vegas
   Barnes, J. Hygiene
   Bennett, T. All the same
   Biller, M. Happy ending with sticky tape
   Biller, M. The sweet whore
   Bishop, T. Bootleggers
   Bluestein, E. The artist's story
   Boyd, W. Fantasia on a favorite waltz
   Burgin, R. Simone
   Burgin, R. The urn
   Burgin, R. Vacation
   Burke, T. Edie's nod
   Carew, J. The burial
   Cohen, S. A girl named Charlie
   Crouse, D. Click
   Crumley, J. Whores
   Dahl, R. Madame Rosette
   Danticat, E. Night women
   Díaz, J. The brief wondrous life of Oscar Wao
   Erdrich, L. The world's greatest fishermen
   Frost, G. Lizaveta
   Garrett, G. P. Empty bed blues
   Gifford, B. After hours at La Chinita
   Gogol', N. V. Nevsky Prospekt

   Grady, J. The bottom line
   Granados, C. Vieja chueca
   Guthrie, A. Call me, I'm dying
   Ha Jin. The house behind a weeping cherry
   Haycox, E. Stage to Lordsburg
   Hernandez, L. The red curtain
   Irsfeld, J. H. Stop, rewind, and play
   James, M. Look what love is doing to me
   Johnson, D. Xmas in Las Vegas
   Jones, E. P. Old boys, old girls
   Jones, E. P. Resurrecting Methuselah
   Kellerman, F. Bonding
   Kennedy, C. The correct names of things
   Kiely, B. A ball of malt and Madame Butterfly
   LaBute, N. Ravishing
   Lane, J. Mine
   Lippman, L. One true love
   Lippman, L. Scratch a woman
   MacEnulty, P. Like someone in a coma
   Malouf, D. Sally's story
   Mandelman, A. Life in parts
   Martinez, M. The last honest man in Brooklyn
   Matheson, R. A flourish of strumpets
   Matthews, C. And then she was gone
   McGuane, T. The zombie
   McInerney, J. The queen and I
   Means, D. The spot
   Michaels, L. A girl with a monkey
   Montemarano, N. The usual human disabilities
   Morita, R. Fruits of Shinjuku
   Muroi, Y. Piss
   Neera. The lady of the evening
   Norris, F. The third circle
   Parra, E. A. Just don't take the little I got
   Patton, J. Capital of the world
   Pincio, T. The melting pot
   Porter, K. A. Magic
   Powell, G. C. Kamila and the king of kandy
   Qi, S. The girl in blue jeans
   Rivera-Valdes, S. Life leads
   Rodriguez, A. Jaguar
   Romano, T. Silences
   Selby, H. Tralala
   Sherman, D. La Fée Verte
   Shroff, M. F. The queen guards her own
   Singer, I. B. On the way to the poorhouse
   Soracco, S. Double espresso
   Sterry, D. H. Confessions of a sex maniac
   Stewart, P. Swallow me whole
   Tea, M. Larry's place
   Theodore, J. Dark nights
   Torres, S. Early fall
   Trezise, R. On the strip
   Valdés, J. Cornelia
   Valenzuela, L. End of millenium
   Vallorani, N. Pasolini's shadow
   Vapnyar, L. Borscht
   Varble, V. Bat
   Vidal, G. Three stratagems
   Waters, D. Blood management
   With, C. Angel's house of ice
   With, C. Mud
   Zhu Wen. I love dollars
PROSTITUTION
      See also Prostitutes
   Baraka, I. A. Mondongo
   Black, M. A. Chasing the blues
   Boosta. Silence is golden
   Bova, B. The show must go on!

PUERTO RICO—_Continued_
Steinberg, S. To sit, unmoving
Puffed rice and meatballs. Vapnyar, L.
PUGILISM _See_ Boxing
The **pugilist** at rest. Jones, T.
Puig's wife. Connell, E. S.
Pukallus, Horst
The age of the burning mountains
The black mirror and other stories; an anthology of science fiction from Germany & Austria; edited & with an introduction & notes by Franz Rottensteiner; translated by Mike Mitchell.
Pulaski, Jack
The Matinee
Agni no60 p47-62 2004
The **Pulaski** guards. Bukoski, A.
Pull!. Amsden, D.
The **Pull** of Beauty. Megan, C.
Pulled up. Brown, R.
A **pulling** thing. Barnes, H. L.
Pulp alibis. Di Filippo, P.
Pulp and Paper. Rolnick, J.
Pulp cover. Wolfe, G.
Pulp life. Nelson, R. F.
Pump six. Bacigalupi, P.
PUMPING IRON _See_ Weight lifting
Pumpkin Head. Oates, J. C.
Punch. Coover, R.
PUNCH AND JUDY
Coover, R. Punch
Pratchett, T. Theatre of cruelty
Punches. Venturini, F.
Punching bag. Castillon, C.
Punctuality. Nix, G.
PUNIC WAR, 2D, 218-201 B.C.
Friesner, E. M. First, catch your elephant
PUNISHMENT
Edwards, M. The people outside
Hemon, A. The liar
Lawson, J. E. Whipped on the face with a length of thorn bush: yes, directly on the face
Nelson, R. F. Pulp life
Percoto, C. The caning
Pratt, T. Terrible ones
Silverberg, R. To see the invisible man
Trezise, R. Chickens
Zoshchenko, M. Thieves
Punishment. Barnes, H. L.
Punishment. Zucker, G.
The **punishment** fits the crime. Berreby, D.
Puntí, Jordi
A Fire
The Review of Contemporary Fiction v28 no1 p104-8 Spr 2008
PUPPETS AND PUPPET PLAYS
Kasper, C. The theater spectacular
Nix, G. Beyond the sea gate of the scholar-pirates of Sarsköe
Sedia, E. A play for a boy and sock puppets
Wolfe, G. The toy theater
Puppies for sale. Morris, M.
Puppy. Saunders, G.
The **puppy**. West, D.
Purdom, Tom
The mists of time
The Year's best science fiction: twenty-fifth annual collection; edited by Gardner Dozois

Purdy, B.
Anniversary VE day [Medical Humanities, v30 no2 December 2004]
Journal of Medical Ethics v30 no2 p92-3 D 2004 supp
Purdy, James
Bonnie
Purdy, J. Moe's villa & other stories
Brawith
Purdy, J. Moe's villa & other stories
The Antioch Review v67 no3 p583-92 Summ 2009
Easy street
Purdy, J. Moe's villa & other stories
Entre dos luces
Purdy, J. Moe's villa & other stories
Geraldine
Purdy, J. Moe's villa & other stories
Gertude's hand
Purdy, J. Moe's villa & other stories
Kitty place
Purdy, J. Moe's villa & other stories
A little variety, please
Purdy, J. Moe's villa & other stories
Moe's villa
Purdy, J. Moe's villa & other stories
No stranger to Luke
Purdy, J. Moe's villa & other stories
Reaching rose
Purdy, J. Moe's villa & other stories
The white blackbird
Purdy, J. Moe's villa & other stories
Pure Love. Bordiuk, A.
Pure products. Buckman, D.
Purgatory. Coleman, W.
Purgatory. Daniells, R. C.
Purgatory, Nevada. Daugherty, T.
PURIM
Molodowsky, K. To hear the megillah on Purim
Purim night. Pearlman, E.
Purity. Ligotti, T.
The **purloined** letter. Poe, E. A.
Purple Bamboo Park. Slate, E. V.
Purple blooms. Shields, C.
Purple haze. MacEnulty, P.
Purple priestess of the mad moon. Brackett, L.
A **purple** story. Novakovich, J.
Purple tulip. Litzky, T.
Purrz, baby. Hendricks, V.
The **pursued**. Quiroga, H.
Purvis, Mark
Mark Purvis: Bonfire night 1969 [Medical Humanities, 31 no1 June 2005]
Journal of Medical Ethics v31 no6 p44 Je 2005 supp
Push. Angel, J.
Push. Kern, N.
Push no more. Silverberg, R.
Pushed or was fell. Brandon, J.
Pushers. Hearon, S.
Pushing oceans in and pulling oceans outs. Malla, P.
Pushkin, Aleksandr Sergeevich
The queen of spades
The Mammoth book of vintage whodunnits; edited by Maxim Jakubowski

Pushkin, Aleksandr Sergeevich—*Continued*
    Worlds apart; an anthology of Russian fantasy
    and science fiction; edited and with com-
    mentary by Alexander Levitsky; translated
    by Alexander Levitsky and Martha T.
    Kitchen
**PUSHKIN, ALEKSANDR SERGEEVICH,
    1799-1837**
                    About
    Shrayer-Petrov, D. Lanskoy Road
    Zoshchenko, M. The Pushkin Centenary Cele-
    brations
Pushkin. Zoshchenko, M.
The **Pushkin** Centenary Celebrations. Zoshchenko,
    M.
Put your hands together. Effinger, G. A.
Putre, John Walter
    The evil we do
        Mystery Writers of America presents the
        prosecution rests; new stories about court-
        rooms, criminals, and the law; edited by
        Linda Fairstein.
Putting Daisy down. McInerney, J.
Putting Things Together. Porto, M. A.
P'yetsukh, V. A.
    Killer Miller
        The Paris review book for planes, trains, ele-
        vators, and waiting rooms; by the editors of
        the Paris review; with an introduction by
        Richard Powers
    The Men Went Out to Smoke
        The Antioch Review v63 no3 p584-9 Summ
        2005
PYGMIES
    Lispector, C. The smallest woman in the world
Pyjamas. With, C.
PYRAMIDS
    Anaya, R. A. The village that the gods painted
        yellow
The **pyre** and others. Schow, D. J.
The **python**. Kiely, B.
Python. Pflug, U.

Q

QABBĀNĪ, NIZĀR, 1923-1998
                    About
    Nu'aymi, H. a.- . A woman
Qadir, 'Abd al-
    (jt. auth) See Llah, 'Abd al- and Qadir, 'Abd al-
Qadir 'Aqil, 'Abd al-
    The siege
        Oranges in the sun; short stories from the
        Arabian Gulf; edited and translated by Deb-
        orah S. Akers, Abubaker A. Bagader
Qi, Shouhua
    Big Mama
        Qi, S. Red Guard fantasies and other stories
    Buddha's feet
        Qi, S. Red Guard fantasies and other stories
    The evidence
        Qi, S. Red Guard fantasies and other stories
        Feminist Studies v31 no2 p400-15 Summ
        2005
    Fatherhood
        Qi, S. Red Guard fantasies and other stories
    The girl in blue jeans
        Qi, S. Red Guard fantasies and other stories

How was your dance today?
    Qi, S. Red Guard fantasies and other stories
The long march, sort of
    Qi, S. Red Guard fantasies and other stories
Love me, love my dog
    Qi, S. Red Guard fantasies and other stories
Old batteries
    Qi, S. Red Guard fantasies and other stories
Red Guard fantasies
    Qi, S. Red Guard fantasies and other stories
The swallow: not exactly an interlude
    Qi, S. Red Guard fantasies and other stories
Teacher Yu
    Qi, S. Red Guard fantasies and other stories
The tenants
    Qi, S. Red Guard fantasies and other stories
The test; or, The little rice wine pot
    Qi, S. Red Guard fantasies and other stories
QUADROONS *See* Mulattoes
Quality merchandise. Zoshchenko, M.
Quality of Life. Sneed, C.
Quality of mercy. Lundin, L.
Quality Snacks. Mozina, A.
Quanta. Keret, E.
The **Quantum** before Christmas. Gee, H.
Quantum erat demonstrandum. Simms, C. N.
Quarantine. Mehta, R.
Quarks at Appomattox. Harness, C. L.
The **quarrel**. Buckler, E.
The **Quarrel** in the Strong-Box [Story to be pub-
    lished in Who is Mark Twain?] Twain, M.
QUARRELING
    Bennett, T. Filigree
    Bennett, T. Matinee
    Fincke, G. The history of staying awake
    Greenman, B. Contemplating a thing about a
        person
    Hughes, M.-B. Honeymoon
    Iarovici, D. If wishes were horses
    Ïṣ:l'olá, A. The uses of English
    Judah, S. Hephzibah
    Julavits, H. Ambivalence
    Kalotay, D. Snapshots
    Kun, M. My wife and my dead wife
    Maxted, A. Dagenham
    McCafferty, J. You could never love the clown
        I love
    Molodowsky, K. Charter members
    Molodowsky, K. Family life
    Molodowsky, K. Malkele Eshman
    Nisbet, R. Birthdays
    Olafsson, O. October
    Parks, T. Lebensraum
    Robinson, R. At the beach
    Smith, M. Motorcycles
    Wolff, T. Hunters in the snow
    Zoshchenko, M. A glass
Quarry, Justin
    Heart Farm
        TriQuarterly no132 p250-77 2008
    Test-Drive Baby
        The Southern Review (Baton Rouge, La.) v45
        no1 p136-43 Wint 2009
Quarry. Beagle, P. S.
Quarry's luck. Collins, M. A.
Quartermaster returns. Wilce, Y. S.

Quatro, Jamie
  Holy Ground
    The Antioch Review v67 no3 p566-80 Summ
    2009
Qubit conflicts. De Vries, J.
Que-Linda takes the rite aid. Akins, M.
Queen, Ellery
  The adventure of the needle's eye
    Murder short & sweet; edited by Paul D.
    Staudohar
The **queen**. Molodowsky, K.
The **queen**. Ruffin, P.
The **queen** and I. McInerney, J.
The **queen** and the philosopher. Johnson, C. R.
The **queen** guards her own. Shroff, M. F.
The **queen** is dead, long live the queen. Talley, M.
The **queen** mother. Dean, D.
The **Queen** of Hearts. Wright, B.
Queen of Karst. Lewis, T.
The **Queen** of Sheba is afraid of snow. Scott, J.
The **queen** of spades. Pushkin, A. S.
The **queen** of spades. Ulitskaya, L.
Queen of the Apocalypse. Bradfield, S.
Queen of the butterfly kingdom. Phillips, H.
Queen of the groupies. Kihn, G.
Queen of the May. Blackwell, K.
The **queen** of the night. Thomas, D. S.
Queen Wintergreen. Fulton, A.
QUEENS
    See also names of queens
  Smith, C. A. The death of Ilalotha
QUEENS (NEW YORK, N.Y.) *See* New York
  (N.Y.)—Queens
Queeny. Pearson, R.
Queer. Kennedy, P.
The **Queer** Zoo. Cain, S.
Queiroz, Rachel de
  Metonymy; or, The husband's revenge
    Oxford anthology of the Brazilian short story;
    edited by K. David Jackson
Quénum, Olympe Bhêly- *See* Bhêly-Quénum,
  Olympe
Quertermous, Bryon
  Cadaver dog
    A Prisoner of memory and 24 of the year's
    finest crime and mystery stories; edited by
    Ed Gorman & Martin H. Greenberg
  Murder boy
    Hardcore hardboiled; edited by Todd Robin-
    son; introduction by Otto Penzler
Quesada, Uriel
  Spoken Portrait
    Iowa Review v36 no2 p68-74 Fall 2006
The **quest** for Y'ha-nthlei. Glasby, J. S.
Question 62. Boyle, T. C.
A **question** mark for God. Đoàn, L.
The **question** of [?query term]. Roberts, A.
The **question** party. Barthelme, D.
Questions of home. Baingana, D.
Questions of war. Rossiter, E.
The **quick-change** artist. Holladay, C. C.
Quick draw. Parkin, S.
The **quick** stop 5®. Weller, S.
Quiescent. King, S.
Quiet. Eggers, D.
Quiet. Watel, L. K.
The **quiet** hours. Lane, J.
Quiet men. Jamison, L.
A **Quiet** Mind. Barbee, L.

Quigley, Edward A.
  Sundown at Trimble
    New Letters v73 no3 p72-9 2007
Quijada, Carmelo
  "Back alleys"
    Multicultural literature in contemporary Italy;
    edited by Marie Orton and Graziella Parati
  "Vendettas"
    Multicultural literature in contemporary Italy;
    edited by Marie Orton and Graziella Parati
Quill, Monica, 1929-
    *For works written by this author under oth-
    er names see* McInerny, Ralph M., 1929-
Quin-Harkin, Janet, 1941-
    See also Bowen, Rhys, 1941-
Quincannon in paradise. Pronzini, B.
Quintana Veiga, José Antonio
  My Love and My Sugarcane
    The Review of Contemporary Fiction v26 no3
    p17-32 Fall 2006
Quiroga, Ana
  A little bit farther
    Díaz, G. J. Women and power in Argentine
    literature; stories, interviews, and critical
    essays; [by] Gwendolyn Díaz
Quiroga, Horacio
  Anaconda
    Quiroga, H. The decapitated chicken and oth-
    er stories; selected and translated by Mar-
    garet Sayers Peden; introduction by George
    D. Schade; illustrations by Ed Lindlof; new
    foreword by Jean Franco
  The dead man
    Quiroga, H. The decapitated chicken and oth-
    er stories; selected and translated by Mar-
    garet Sayers Peden; introduction by George
    D. Schade; illustrations by Ed Lindlof; new
    foreword by Jean Franco
  The decapitated chicken
    Quiroga, H. The decapitated chicken and oth-
    er stories; selected and translated by Mar-
    garet Sayers Peden; introduction by George
    D. Schade; illustrations by Ed Lindlof; new
    foreword by Jean Franco
  Drifting
    Quiroga, H. The decapitated chicken and oth-
    er stories; selected and translated by Mar-
    garet Sayers Peden; introduction by George
    D. Schade; illustrations by Ed Lindlof; new
    foreword by Jean Franco
  The feather pillow
    Quiroga, H. The decapitated chicken and oth-
    er stories; selected and translated by Mar-
    garet Sayers Peden; introduction by George
    D. Schade; illustrations by Ed Lindlof; new
    foreword by Jean Franco
  In the middle of the night
    Quiroga, H. The decapitated chicken and oth-
    er stories; selected and translated by Mar-
    garet Sayers Peden; introduction by George
    D. Schade; illustrations by Ed Lindlof; new
    foreword by Jean Franco
  The incense tree roof
    Quiroga, H. The decapitated chicken and oth-
    er stories; selected and translated by Mar-
    garet Sayers Peden; introduction by George
    D. Schade; illustrations by Ed Lindlof; new
    foreword by Jean Franco

Quiroga, Horacio—*Continued*
  Juan Darien
    Quiroga, H. The decapitated chicken and oth-
      er stories; selected and translated by Mar-
      garet Sayers Peden; introduction by George
      D. Schade; illustrations by Ed Lindlof; new
      foreword by Jean Franco
  The pursued
    Quiroga, H. The decapitated chicken and oth-
      er stories; selected and translated by Mar-
      garet Sayers Peden; introduction by George
      D. Schade; illustrations by Ed Lindlof; new
      foreword by Jean Franco
  A slap in the face
    Quiroga, H. The decapitated chicken and oth-
      er stories; selected and translated by Mar-
      garet Sayers Peden; introduction by George
      D. Schade; illustrations by Ed Lindlof; new
      foreword by Jean Franco
  The son
    Quiroga, H. The decapitated chicken and oth-
      er stories; selected and translated by Mar-
      garet Sayers Peden; introduction by George
      D. Schade; illustrations by Ed Lindlof; new
      foreword by Jean Franco
  Sunstroke
    Quiroga, H. The decapitated chicken and oth-
      er stories; selected and translated by Mar-
      garet Sayers Peden; introduction by George
      D. Schade; illustrations by Ed Lindlof; new
      foreword by Jean Franco
QUISLINGS *See* World War, 1939-1945—Collab-
  orationists
Quite normal. Burke, T.
Quiver. DeNiro, A.
Quoth the screaming chicken. Bischoff, D.
Quotidian. Erdrich, L.

R

R.M.S. "Empress of Australia". Hodgson, W. H.
R&R. Shepard, L.
RABBIS
  Apple, M. The Jew of Home Depot
  Apple, M. Stabbing an elephant
  Auslander, S. The metamorphosis
  Beagle, P. S. The rabbi's hobby
  Goldberg, T. Mitzvah
  Hamer-Jacklyn, S. No more rabbi!
  Helprin, M. Jacob Bayer and the telephone
  Kellerman, F. Holy water
  Levi, J. The scrimshaw violin
  Malamud, B. The magic barrel
  Mandelman, A. Mish-mash
  Michaels, L. Murderers
  Opatoshu, J. The evil urge
  Rosen, J. First date
  Singer, I. B. A boy knows the truth
  Singer, I. B. A cage for Satan
  Singer, I. B. The recluse
  Spark, D. A short wedding story
The **rabbi's** hobby. Beagle, P. S.
The **rabbit** hole as likely explanation. Beattie, A.
Rabbit-in-the-Moon. Dinh, V.
Rabbit punch. Sutton, B.
RABBITS
  Kennedy, C. Cold snap
  Link, K. Stone animals

  Marshall, P. Bunnymoon
  Murphy, Y. Lake Mohican
  Tomlinson, J. Angel, his rabbit, and Kyle
    McKell
The **rabbitt** hole as likely explanantion. Beattie,
  A.
Rabe, Jean
  Better guns
    Future Americas; edited by Martin H.
      Greenberg and John Helferd
  Hang ten
    Places to be, people to kill; edited by Martin
      H. Greenberg and Brittianey A. Koren
  Roadshow
    The Magic toybox; edited by Denise Little
  Stalking old John Bull
    Man vs. machine; edited by John Helfers and
      Martin H. Greenberg.
Rabids. Jensen, T.
Rabin, Arnold
  Brahms Second, in Color
    New England Review v26 no3 p110-16 2005
Rabinovitch, Sholem *See* Sholem Aleichem,
  1859-1916
Rabinowitz, Sholem Yakov *See* Sholem
  Aleichem, 1859-1916
Rabinowitz, Solomon *See* Sholem Aleichem,
  1859-1916
Raboteau, Emily
  The Eye of Horus
    StoryQuarterly v40 p433-58 2004
  Kavita through glass
    Pushcart Prize XXVIII: best of the small
      presses 2004; edited by Bill Henderson and
      the Pushcart prize editors
  Smile
    The Best American Mystery Stories, 2006;
      edited and with an introduction by Scott
      Turow; Otto Penzler, series editor
    Gettysburg Review v18 no3 p387-8 Aut 2005
RACCOONS
  Kim, J. Yangban
  Rust, E. M. Raccoons
Raccoons. Rust, E. M.
The **race**. Brazaitis, M.
The **race** at Left Bower. Bierce, A.
RACE PROBLEMS *See* Race relations
RACE RELATIONS
    See also African Americans; African
      Americans—Relations with Jews;
      Antisemitism; Culture conflict; Interracial
      marriage; Miscegenation; Prejudices
  Bradbury, R. And the rock cried out
  Effinger, G. A. All the last wars at once
  Howard, R. E. Black Canaan
  Irsfeld, J. H. Ambivalence Hardy Fire
          India
    See India—Race relations
        South Africa
    See South Africa—Race relations
        United States
    See United States—Race relations
RACEHORSES *See* Horses
Rachel, David
  The last man I killed
    The Best American mystery stories, 2005; ed-
      ited and with an introduction by Joyce Car-
      ol Oates; Otto Penzler, series editor
Rachel. Lai, L.

Rachel in love. Murphy, P.
Rachel in Rome. Czerniawski, A.
Rachlin, Nahid
  Bound Woman
    New Letters v71 no1 p11-21 2004/2005
Rachmaninoff Lives. Peck, L.
Rachmaninov. Ali, M. N.
The **Racial** Colorist / Der rassistische Kolorist.
  Okri, B.
RACIAL INTERMARRIAGE *See* Interracial
  marriage
RACING
      See also Automobile races; Bicycle rac-
      ing; Dog racing; Horse racing
RACISM *See* Antisemitism; Prejudices; Race rela-
  tions
RACKETEERS *See* Crime and criminals; Gang-
  sters; Mafia
RACKETS *See* Gambling
Radiant doors. Swanwick, M.
Radiant green star. Shepard, L.
Radiant Health. Joseph, S.
RADIATION
  Anaya, R. A. Devil deer
  De Camp, L. S. The isolinguals
  DeMarinis, R. Apocalypse then
    Physiological effect
  Del Rey, L. Nerves
  Merril, J. That only a mother
  Shepard, J. The Zero Meter Diving Team
  Zeman, A. Bang
Radical adults lick godhead style. Wild, P.
RADICALISM *See* Radicals and radicalism
RADICALS AND RADICALISM
      See also Anarchism and anarchists
  Gardiner, J. R. Leaving Port McHair
  Hadley, T. The enemy
  Kiesbye, S. Islanders
  Lu, A. Le rouge et le noir
  Upadhyay, S. Supreme pronouncements
RADIO
  Betancourt, J. G. Invasion of the Jack Benny
    snatchers
  Bradbury, R. Ma Perkins comes to stay
  Dobozy, T. Radio Blik
  Ely, S. Talk radio
  Guilfoile, K. Zero zero day
  Marcus, B. The least you need to know about
    radio
  Monson, A. Other electricities
  Roberson, C. Monster radio
  Sillitoe, A. The magic box
Radio Blik. Dobozy, T.
RADIO BROADCASTING
  Barthelme, D. The big broadcast of 1938
  Bukoski, A. Your hit parade
RADIO PROGRAMS
  Boyle, T. C. The kind assassin
  Libaire, J. Pirate Daddy's lonely hearts club
    call-in show
  Schulberg, B. Your Arkansas traveler
Radio waves. Swanwick, M.
RADIOACTIVITY
  Steinmuller, A. and Steinmuller, K. The eye that
    never weeps
Radius, Anna Zuccari *See* Neera, 1846-1918

Radojcic, Natasha
  Shades of mango
    Best of Tin House; stories; foreword by Dor-
      othy Allison
Radzinsky, Oleg
  He Himself and His Wife Alena
    The Literary Review (Madison, N.J.) v48 no3
      p143-6 Spr 2005
Raeff, Anne
  The Buchovskys on Their Own
    New England Review v26 no2 p143-58 2005
The **Rafalovitches**. Molodowsky, K.
Raffel, Dawn
  Beyond All Blessing and Song, Praise and Con-
    solation
    The Antioch Review v66 no3 p449-52 Summ
      2008
  Up the Old Goat Road
    The Anchor book of new American short sto-
      ries; edited by Ben Marcus
The **raffle**. Currans-Sheehan, T.
The **Raft**. Hicok, B.
The **raft**. Hodgson, W. H.
Rafters. McIlvoy, K.
RAFTING (SPORTS)
  Olafsson, O. June
Rage. Mozetič, B.
The **raggle** taggle gypsy-o. Swanwick, M.
Ragman. Wangerin, W.
The **Ragman's** daughter. Sillitoe, A.
Raharimanana, Jean-Luc
  Fahavalo
    From Africa; new francophone stories; edited
      by Adele King
Rahman, Imad
  All roads lead to flesh and bone
    Rahman, I. I dream of microwaves; stories
  Call me Manny
    Rahman, I. I dream of microwaves; stories
  Eating, Ohio
    Rahman, I. I dream of microwaves; stories
  From Kilgore to Kurtz, at the Steak 'n' Stage
    Rahman, I. I dream of microwaves; stories
  Here come the dog people
    Rahman, I. I dream of microwaves; stories
  I, Claudius
    Rahman, I. I dream of microwaves; stories
  I dream of microwaves
    Rahman, I. I dream of microwaves; stories
  Real, actual life
    Rahman, I. I dream of microwaves; stories
Rahoo. Wolfe, F.
Raiche, Joseph
  One Mississippi
    The Best American mystery stories, 2005; ed-
      ited and with an introduction by Joyce Car-
      ol Oates; Otto Penzler, series editor
Raider nation. Hasak-Lowy, T.
RAILROAD ACCIDENTS
  Lott, B. Th train, the lake, the bridge
  Simmons, G. Peaches
RAILROADS
      See also Subways
  Bierce, A. Across the continent
  Bierce, A. An upper class misdemeanant
  Bierce, A. The wizard of Bumbassa
  Holladay, C. C. The broken lake
  Holladay, C. C. The iron road
  Holladay, C. C. Syrup and feather

Rand, Ken—*Continued*
Last vision
    Rand, K. Where angels fear
Medicine
    Rand, K. Where angels fear
No wine before its time
    Rand, K. Where angels fear
One person
    Rand, K. Where angels fear
"Penny" Joe Crane died for my sins
    Rand, K. Where angels fear
Refuge
    Rand, K. Where angels fear
Sawk
    Rand, K. Where angels fear
Song of mother jungle
    Rand, K. Where angels fear
Soul taster
    Rand, K. Where angels fear
The stranger at Gunnison's camp
    Rand, K. Where angels fear
The swimmer
    Rand, K. Where angels fear
The teddy's touch
    Rand, K. Where angels fear
Through these eyes
    Rand, K. Where angels fear
To dream to be
    Rand, K. Where angels fear
Trophy kill
    Rand, K. Where angels fear
Where angels fear
    Rand, K. Where angels fear
Rand, Naomi
House envy
    Hard boiled Brooklyn; edited by Reed Farrel Coleman
Randall, Scott
The Gifted Class
    Dalhousie Review v87 no1 p85-94 Spr 2007
Law School
    Dalhousie Review v85 no3 p431-45 Aut 2005
Randisi, Robert J.
The Bocce Ball King of Farragut Road
    Hard boiled Brooklyn; edited by Reed Farrel Coleman
Upon my soul
    Greatest hits; original stories of assassins, hitmen, and hired guns; edited by Robert J. Randisi
Randolph, Ladette
After Canaan
    Randolph, L. This is not the tropics; stories
Billy
    Randolph, L. This is not the tropics; stories
The blue room
    Randolph, L. This is not the tropics; stories
The boy in the band uniform
    Randolph, L. This is not the tropics; stories
Dill
    Randolph, L. This is not the tropics; stories
The girls
    Randolph, L. This is not the tropics; stories
Hyacinths
    Randolph, L. This is not the tropics; stories
It's cheaper to live in the dark
    Randolph, L. This is not the tropics; stories
A member of the family
    Randolph, L. This is not the tropics; stories

Miss Kielbasa
    Randolph, L. This is not the tropics; stories
The picture in her dream
    Randolph, L. This is not the tropics; stories
The sensitive man
    Randolph, L. This is not the tropics; stories
The shouting woman
    Randolph, L. This is not the tropics; stories
This is not the tropics
    Randolph, L. This is not the tropics; stories
What she knows
    Randolph, L. This is not the tropics; stories
Rani, T. Janaki
The decision
    Gibson, M. E. Separate journeys; short stories by contemporary Indian women; edited by Geeta Dharmarajan; introduction by Mary Ellis Gibson
Rankin, Ian
Graduation day
    Murder in the rough; edited by Otto Penzler
The hanged man
    A New omnibus of crime; edited by Tony Hillerman and Rosemary Herbert; contributing editors Sue Grafton and Jeffery Deaver
Soft spot
    Dangerous women; edited by Otto Penzler
Tell me who to kill
    The Best British mysteries, 2005; edited by Maxim Jakubowski
Ransom, A'lelia
Incident
    "Tell it to us easy" and other stories; a complete short fiction anthology of African American women writers in Opportunity magazine, (1923-1948); edited by Judith Musser.
The **Ransome** women. Farris, J.
Rapaport, Jennifer
Prospect
    Fenway fiction; short stories from Red Sox nation; edited by Adam Emerson Pachter
RAPE
Baldeosingh, K. The rape
Block, L. Bride of violence
Block, L. Lie back and enjoy it
Campbell, B. J. Family reunion
Chabon, M. Son of the wolfman
Coleman, W. Darkness
Cuesta, M. Virgins of Regla
Dalton, Q. Back on earth
D'Ambrosio, C., Jr. Up North
Fais, M. Halima, Desdemona, Bubu
Gaitskill, M. The girl on the plane
Hamill, D. Under the Throg Neck Bridge
Harper, J. Johnny Cash is dead
Hempel, A. The uninvited
Hwang, S. Mountains
Johnson, G. Who, what, when, where
Jones, H. G. Proof of God
Kiernan, C. R. To this water (Johnstown, Pennsylvania 1889)
Lane, J. Prison ships
Lange, R. Fuzzyland
Leigh, S. Transformation
Lethem, J. The happy man
Lutz, J. All quiet
MacEnulty, P. Purple haze

Rash, Ron
  Back of beyond
    New stories from the South; the year's best,
      2008; selected from U.S. magazines by ZZ
      Packer with Kathy Pories; with an introduc-
      tion by ZZ Packer
  Blackberries in June
    Rash, R. Chemistry and other stories
  Chemistry
    Rash, R. Chemistry and other stories
  Cold Harbor
    Rash, R. Chemistry and other stories
  Dangerous love
    Rash, R. Chemistry and other stories
  Deep Gap
    Rash, R. Chemistry and other stories
  Hard Times
    The Sewanee Review v115 no1 p46-55 Wint
      2007
  Honesty
    Rash, R. Chemistry and other stories
  Into the Gorge
    The Southern Review (Baton Rouge, La.) v44
      no4 p628-37 Aut 2008
  Last rite
    Rash, R. Chemistry and other stories
  Not waving but drowning
    Rash, R. Chemistry and other stories
  Overtime
    Rash, R. Chemistry and other stories
  Pemberton's bride
    Rash, R. Chemistry and other stories
  The projectionist's wife
    Rash, R. Chemistry and other stories
  Redfish, Possums, and the New South
    South Carolina Review v41 no2 p3-10 Spr
      2009
  Speckle trout
    The O. Henry Prize stories, 2005; edited and
      with an introduction by Laura Furman
  Speckled trout
    Rash, R. Chemistry and other stories
  Their ancient, glittering eyes
    Rash, R. Chemistry and other stories
    The Kenyon Review v28 no2 p102-17 Spr
      2006
Rashid, 'Ali Muhammad
  A crisis at sea
    Oranges in the sun; short stories from the
      Arabian Gulf; edited and translated by Deb-
      orah S. Akers, Abubaker A. Bagader
Rashid, Fatima
  Syra
    Best New American voices 2007; [edited by
      Sue Miller; series editors, John Kulka and
      Natalie Danford]
Rashid, Hasan
  The storyteller
    Oranges in the sun; short stories from the
      Arabian Gulf; edited and translated by Deb-
      orah S. Akers, Abubaker A. Bagader
The **Rashkovitcher** wedding. Molodowsky, K.
Rasmussen, Rebecca
  The Bird Sisters
    TriQuarterly no130 p118-39 2008
Rastrow's island. Boyle, T. C.
Rat Beach. Styron, W.
The **Rat** Hunt. Baldwin, D. N.

Rath, Tina
  A trick of the dark
    The Year's best fantasy and horror: eighteenth
      annual collection; edited by Ellen Datlow,
      Kelly Link & Gavin J. Grant
Rathbun, Jennie
  Kidney Season
    The Virginia Quarterly Review v81 no3 p196-
      213 Summ 2005
RATS
  Alphonsus, J. Sardanapalo
  Cadnum, M. Elf trap
  Coover, R. The return of the dark children
  Dahl, R. Claud's dog: The ratcatcher
  Flint, E. A soldier's complaint
  Fowler, C. Seven feet
  Grimes, C. Glue trap
  Hamner, E. A passion for solitude
  Hodgson, W. H. The albatross
  Hodgson, W. H. The mystery of the derelict
  Lovecraft, H. P. The rats in the walls
  Sallis, J. Season premiere
  Swirsky, R. The adventures of Captain Black
    Heart Wentworth: a nautical tail
Rats. Schanoes, V.
Rats and cobras. Judah, S.
The **rats** in the walls. Lovecraft, H. P.
Rats live on no evil star. Kiernan, C. R.
Rattler. Wolfe, G. and Hopkins, B.
Rattles of bones. Howard, R. E.
RATTLESNAKES
  Averill, T. F. The summer grandma was sup-
    posed to die
  Smith, C. A. The resurrection of the rattlesnake
  Welsh, I. Rattlesnakes
Rattlesnakes. Welsh, I.
Ravalec, Vincent
  Feeding the hungry
    Paris tales; stories; translated by Helen Con-
      stantine
Ravanipour, Moniro
  Remote Control
    World Literature Today v83 no3 p18-21
      My/Je 2009
Raven. Bunin, I. A.
RAVENS
  Straley, J. Lovely
Raven's Wing. Oates, J. C.
"**Ravi's** wedding". Wadia, L.-A. L.
Ravishing. LaBute, N.
Raw egg in beer. Corso, P.
Rawlings, Wendy
  The Skeleton
    The Massachusetts Review v48 no4 p547-56
      Wint 2007
Rawlins, Paul
  My Ex-Husband
    Confrontation no101 p53-75 Spr/Summ 2008
Rawson, JoAnna
  Eleven ways to live in the city
    Murphy, N. Twelve branches; stories from St.
      Paul; [by] Nora Murphy ... {et al.}
  The interview
    Murphy, N. Twelve branches; stories from St.
      Paul; [by] Nora Murphy ... {et al.}
  A working history of the alley
    Murphy, N. Twelve branches; stories from St.
      Paul; [by] Nora Murphy ... {et al.}

Ray, Janisse
Pilgrimage
The Georgia Review v61 no3 p587-601 Fall 2007
Ray, Rebbecca
I can hear the grass grow
Perverted by language; fiction inspired by The Fall; edited and introduced by Peter Wild.
Ray, Shann
The Dark Between Them
StoryQuarterly v41 p458-77 2005
Ray and Sheila have a day. Rubin, E.
Raymond, Jonathan
Benny
Raymond, J. Livability; stories; [by] Jon Raymond
The coast
Raymond, J. Livability; stories; [by] Jon Raymond
New shoes
Raymond, J. Livability; stories; [by] Jon Raymond
Old joy
Raymond, J. Livability; stories; [by] Jon Raymond
The suckling pig
Raymond, J. Livability; stories; [by] Jon Raymond
Train choir
Raymond, J. Livability; stories; [by] Jon Raymond
The wind
Raymond, J. Livability; stories; [by] Jon Raymond
Words and things
Raymond, J. Livability; stories; [by] Jon Raymond
Young bodies
Raymond, J. Livability; stories; [by] Jon Raymond
Rayner, Richard
After the Movie
The New Yorker v83 no10 p72-5 Ap 30 2007
Razing Temples. Baldwin, D. N.
Razorblade. Mozetič, B.
Razorhead the axeman. Smith, R. T.
The **re-education** of M. Grooms. Greenman, B.
Rea, Amanda
Helping
Iowa Review v36 no3 p145-56 Wint 2006/2007
The **reach**. King, S.
Reaching you through the letter carrier. Aziz Mishri, 'A. a.- .
Read, Cornelia
Hungry enough
A hell of a woman; an anthology of female noir; edited by Megan Abbott; foreword by Val McDermid
Read it in the headlines!. Nix, G.
The **reader**. Mozetič, B.
Readers Digest. Horn, D.
The **reading** Elvis. Windley, C.
Reading Erica Jong. Yates, D.
Reading Grandpa's head, 1837. Menger-Anderson, K.
Reading his heart. King, L.
Reading in his wake. Painter, P.
Reading Lessons. Danticat, E.

A **reading** problem. Stafford, J.
Reading the bones. Finch, S.
Ready for blast off. McIntosh, R.
Ready in the night. Murphy, Y.
Reah, Danuta
Glazed
Getting even; revenge stories; edited by Mitzi Szereto
Real, actual life. Rahman, I.
Real beach weather. Anderson, B.
The **Real** Brooklyn. Wolitzer, H.
The **real** Eleanor Rigby. Fulton, A.
Real enough. Murphy, Y.
REAL ESTATE
See also Speculation
Atwood, M. The entities
Boyle, T. C. Rastrow's island
Daugherty, T. City codes
Đoàn, L. The real estate of Chua village
Haldeman, J. W. Foreclosure
Higgins, G. V. Old Earl died pulling traps
Leung, B. Good company
Lippman, L. ARM and the woman
Magee, K. All the America you want
Peelle, L. Shadow on a weary land
Scott, J. The most beautiful apartment in New York
Singer, I. B. The litigants
Trevor, W. At Olivehill
Updike, J. Personal archaeology
REAL ESTATE BUSINESS
Canty, K. No place in this world for you
Duncklee, J. The developers
Harrison, W. Texas heat
Keret, E. Eight percent of nothing
Spiegelman, P. Location, location, location
Ward, A. E. The stars are bright in Texas
REAL ESTATE DEVELOPMENT
Crone, M. Paradise
The **real** estate of Chua village. Đoàn, L.
Real grief. Fulton, J.
Real life. Parra, E. A.
Real life. Pollock, D. R.
Real Life is Really Real. Pinkerton, D.
Real love. Desaulniers, J.
REAL PROPERTY *See* Real estate
The **real** thing. Hurwitz, G.
The **real** thing. Rich, M.
The **real** thing: 'S.O.S'. Hodgson, W. H.
The **real** winner of the preliminary games. Keret, E.
The **real** world. Pierce, T. J.
Realism. Yu, C.
The **reality** trip. Silverberg, R.
Really happy day. Tognazzini, A.
The **realm** of the unreal. Bierce, A.
The **reaper**. Sherman, R.
The **reappearance** of strawberries. Van Booy, S.
Rear view. Nelson, A.
Rear window [variant title: It had to be murder] Woolrich, C.
Reason to Believe He Hath Deserted. Pritchett, M.
Reason to Blame. De Sa, A.
The **reason** was us. Clarke, B.
The **reason** we were so afraid. Tognazzini, A.
Reasons for and advantages of breathing. Peelle, L.
Reasons for concern regarding my girlfriend of five days, Monica Garza. Tait, J.

Reasons for Living. Mann, R.

Reaves, Sam
  The test
    Chicago blues; edited by Libby Fischer Hellmann

Rebbetzin. Ebenbach, D. H.

Rebeginning. Barth, J.

REBELLIONS See Revolutions

Rebelo, Marquês
  Down our street
    Oxford anthology of the Brazilian short story; edited by K. David Jackson

Recalled to life. Cohen, P.

The receivers. Reynolds, A.

Reception. Mindt, A.

The reception hall. Maḥfūẓ, N.

The receptionist. Donovan, G.

Rechner, Mary
  Teeth
    The Kenyon Review v27 no2 p88-101 Spr 2005

The recipe. Cross, E.

The recipe. Tillman, L.

Recital. Zelazny, R.

A recital for the Pope. Stern, R. G.

Rècits. Sallis, J.

Reckoning. Déry, T.

The reckoning. Harjo, J.

Reclamations. McGahan, J.

Recluse. Gaffney, E.

RECLUSES
  Anaya, R. A. The silence of the Llano
  Doerr, A. The caretaker
  Faulkner, W. A rose for Emily
  Li Yiyun. Death is not a bad joke if told the right way
  Pollock, D. R. Dynamite hole

Recompense. Shell, L.

RECONCILIATION
  Mason, B. A. The prelude

Reconnaissance. Nisbet, R.

RECONSTRUCTION
    See also United States—1865-1898

Reconstruction. Helprin, M.

Reconstruction. Shaw, S.

Recoper: Breathing life into the revolution. Asher, N.

A Record Book for Small Farmers. North, A.

The recording. Wolfe, G.

Recover. With, C.

Recovery. Scott, A. J.

Recovery. Singleton, G.

Recruitment. Wisker, G.

RECTORS See Anglican and Episcopal clergy; Catholic priests

Recuperation. Doyle, R.

RECYCLING INDUSTRY
  Qi, S. Old batteries

Red. Larsson, B.

Red. Yuan-Innes, M.

RED ARMY (SOVIET UNION) See Russia—Army

The red bow. Saunders, G.

The red bridge. Yoss

Red butte showdown. L'Amour, L.

Red caddy. Mosley, W.

Red car. Bingham, S.

The red carpet. Sankaran, L.

Red Carpet Caper. Morrissey, D.

Red clay. Malone, M.

The Red Coat. D'Souza, T.

The red coat. Macy, C.

The red convertible. Erdrich, L.

The red curtain. Hernandez, L.

The red dress: a short story. Tompkins, G. W.

Red-eyed helldriver. Erdrich, L.

Red from green. Meloy, M.

RED GUARD
  Qi, S. Red Guard fantasies

Red Guard fantasies. Qi, S.

Red hands. Lamb, H.

Red hell hits Canyon Diablo [variant title: Tizwin] Leonard, E.

The red herring. Hodgson, W. H.

The red king. Archer, J.

Red leather tassels. Rosenbaum, B.

Red means stop. Stewart, P.

Red meat. Viets, E.

The red Mercedes. Capel, T.

A Red Pen. Henion, K.

The red phone. Kessel, J.

The red planet league. Newman, K.

Red quarters. Holden, C.

Red River Crossing. Boggs, J. D.

Red River Valley. Averill, T. F.

Red rose, white rose. Chang, E.

Red roses. Messina, M.

Red Ryder nails the Hammond kid. Shepherd, J.

The red scream [excerpt] Walker, M. W.

RED SEA
  Winsor, C. The last Israelite in the Red Sea

The red shoes. Báez, A.

The red shoes. Zettel, S.

Red Sonja and Lessingham in Dreamland. Jones, G. A.

RED SOX (BASEBALL TEAM) See Boston Red Sox (Baseball team)

Red star. Bogdanov, A. A.

Red summer. Heer, L.

Red sunset. Madison, B.

Red tape. Zoshchenko, M.

Red velvet dust. Pflug, U.

Red wind. Chandler, R.

The red world of Polaris. Smith, C. A.

Réda, Jacques
  Rue du Commerce
    Paris tales; stories; translated by Helen Constantine

Redbeard. Wolfe, G.

Redchapel. Resnick, M.

Reddi, Rishi P.
  Justice Shiva Ram Murthy
    The Best American short stories, 2005; selected from U.S. and Canadian magazines by Michael Chabon with Katrina Kenison; with an introduction by Michael Chabon
    Harvard Review (1992) no27 p118-33 2004

Reddick, D. B.
  Murders off the wall
    Medium of murder; edited by Susan Budavari and Suzanne Flaig

Redekop, Fred
  Paging Daryl and Java Man
    New England Review v28 no1 p194-8 2007

Redel, Victoria
  And Grace, Friday
    The Massachusetts Review v49 no4 p505 Wint 2008

REDEMPTION *See* Atonement

Redfish, Possums, and the New South. Rash, R.

The **redhead**. Black, C.

Redhill, Michael

The Getaway
The Walrus v5 no6 p40-1 Jl/Ag 2008

Martin Sloane [excerpt]
Contemporary Jewish writing in Canada; an anthology; edited by Michael Greenstein

Redhorn-Chamberlain, Sharon

Broken Promises
Tribal College Journal of American Indian Higher Education v19 no1 p56 Fall 2007

Redman, Ben Ray

The perfect crime
Murder short & sweet; edited by Paul D. Staudohar

Redmann, J. M. (Jean M.)

The intersection of camp and St. Mary
Women of mystery; an anthology; Katherine V. Forrest, editor

Redmann, Jean M. *See* Redmann, J. M. (Jean M.), 1955-

REDUCING

Allen, W. Thus ate Zarathustra

Berg, E. The day I ate nothing I even remotely wanted

Berg, E. The day I ate whatever I wanted

Berg, E. Double diet

Hasak-Lowy, T. Will Power, Inc.

McCorkle, J. Crash diet

McGraw, E. Ax of the apostles

Solwitz, S. Ballerina

Redwood, James D.

The Photograph
The Kenyon Review v26 no4 p85-97 Fall 2004

The Stamp Collector
TriQuarterly no125 p159-69 2006

Reed, Ernesto Mestre- *See* Mestre-Reed, Ernesto, 1964-

Reed, James

Enough People Hate You
Gettysburg Review v21 no2 p287-328 Summ 2008

Reed, Kit

Captive kong
Reed, K. Dogs of truth; new and uncollected stories

Escape from shark island
Reed, K. Dogs of truth; new and uncollected stories

Focus group
Reed, K. Dogs of truth; new and uncollected stories

Getting it back
Reed, K. Dogs of truth; new and uncollected stories

Grand opening
Reed, K. Dogs of truth; new and uncollected stories

High rise high
Reed, K. Dogs of truth; new and uncollected stories

Incursions
Reed, K. Dogs of truth; new and uncollected stories

Into the jungle
Reed, K. Dogs of truth; new and uncollected stories

No two alike
Reed, K. Dogs of truth; new and uncollected stories

Old soldiers
Reed, K. Dogs of truth; new and uncollected stories

Perpetua
Reed, K. Dogs of truth; new and uncollected stories

Playmate
Reed, K. Dogs of truth; new and uncollected stories

Precautions
Reed, K. Dogs of truth; new and uncollected stories

The shop of little horrors
Reed, K. Dogs of truth; new and uncollected stories

Visiting the dead
Reed, K. Dogs of truth; new and uncollected stories

Yard sale
Reed, K. Dogs of truth; new and uncollected stories

The zombie prince
Reed, K. Dogs of truth; new and uncollected stories

Reed, Lillian Craig *See* Reed, Kit, 1932-

Reed, Philip

Claustrophobia
Meeting across the river; stories inspired by the haunting Bruce Springsteen song; edited by Jessica Kaye and Richard J. Brewer

Reed, Robert

Abducted souls
Reed, R. The cuckoo's boys

A billion eves
Science fiction: the best of the year 2007 edition; edited by Rich Horton

Camouflage
The Year's best science fiction: twenty-third annual collection; edited by Gardner Dozois

The children's crusade
Reed, R. The cuckoo's boys

Coelacanths
Reed, R. The cuckoo's boys

The cuckoo's boys
Reed, R. The cuckoo's boys

Dewey Smith and the meaning of All
Nature v455 p1148 O 23 2008

The dragons of Summer Gulch
The Year's best science fiction: twenty-second annual collection; edited by Gardner Dozois

Eight episodes
Asimov's science fiction: 30th anniversary anthology; edited by Sheila Williams

First Tuesday
Reed, R. The cuckoo's boys

Five thrillers
The Best science fiction and fantasy of the year: volume three; edited by Jonathan Strahan

Good mountain
The Year's best science fiction: twenty-fourth annual collection; edited by Gardner Dozois

Reinhorn, Holiday—*Continued*
Fuck you
    Reinhorn, H. Big cats; stories
Gabe
    This is not chick lit; original stories by America's best women writers; edited by Elizabeth Merrick
Get away from me, David
    Reinhorn, H. Big cats; stories
Golden pioneers
    Reinhorn, H. Big cats; stories
Good to hear you
    Reinhorn, H. Big cats; stories
The heights
    Reinhorn, H. Big cats; stories
Last seen
    Reinhorn, H. Big cats; stories
My name
    Reinhorn, H. Big cats; stories
Seashell
    Reinhorn, H. Big cats; stories
The white dog
    Reinhorn, H. Big cats; stories

Reisen, Abraham
The barber's bride
    Shining and shadow; an anthology of early Yiddish stories from the Lower East Side; edited and translated by Albert Waldinger
Brother and beau
    Shining and shadow; an anthology of early Yiddish stories from the Lower East Side; edited and translated by Albert Waldinger
"A couple of words"
    Shining and shadow; an anthology of early Yiddish stories from the Lower East Side; edited and translated by Albert Waldinger
The experienced bride
    Shining and shadow; an anthology of early Yiddish stories from the Lower East Side; edited and translated by Albert Waldinger
He laughed
    Shining and shadow; an anthology of early Yiddish stories from the Lower East Side; edited and translated by Albert Waldinger
His trip to America
    Shining and shadow; an anthology of early Yiddish stories from the Lower East Side; edited and translated by Albert Waldinger
The holy pair
    Shining and shadow; an anthology of early Yiddish stories from the Lower East Side; edited and translated by Albert Waldinger
In a Yiddish cabaret
    Shining and shadow; an anthology of early Yiddish stories from the Lower East Side; edited and translated by Albert Waldinger
In disguise
    Shining and shadow; an anthology of early Yiddish stories from the Lower East Side; edited and translated by Albert Waldinger
Irrelevance
    Shining and shadow; an anthology of early Yiddish stories from the Lower East Side; edited and translated by Albert Waldinger
Mother goes to the library
    Shining and shadow; an anthology of early Yiddish stories from the Lower East Side; edited and translated by Albert Waldinger

The nationalist and the American girl
    Shining and shadow; an anthology of early Yiddish stories from the Lower East Side; edited and translated by Albert Waldinger
Over the child
    Shining and shadow; an anthology of early Yiddish stories from the Lower East Side; edited and translated by Albert Waldinger
A shopgirl
    Shining and shadow; an anthology of early Yiddish stories from the Lower East Side; edited and translated by Albert Waldinger
Show-windows
    Shining and shadow; an anthology of early Yiddish stories from the Lower East Side; edited and translated by Albert Waldinger
They're afraid
    Shining and shadow; an anthology of early Yiddish stories from the Lower East Side; edited and translated by Albert Waldinger
The two mothers
    Shining and shadow; an anthology of early Yiddish stories from the Lower East Side; edited and translated by Albert Waldinger
When does Mame eat?
    Shining and shadow; an anthology of early Yiddish stories from the Lower East Side; edited and translated by Albert Waldinger

Reisman, Nancy
Tea
    The O. Henry Prize stories, 2005; edited and with an introduction by Laura Furman
Reiteration. Brown, S.
The **rejected** buppie. Baraka, I. A.
The **rejection**. Allen, W.
REJUVENATION
    Bradbury, R. Death and the maiden
    Stafford, J. The end of a career
The **Relation**. Klonimos, S.
The **relationship**. Baumbach, J.
Relationship Resume. Davis, L. S.
RELATIVES *See* Family life
RELATIVITY (PHYSICS)
    See also Space and time
    Breuer, M. J. The gostak and the doshes
Reliable vet dad, reliable con son. Malae, P. N.
RELICS
    Di Filippo, P. Lignum Crucis
Relics of the Thim. Hughes, M.
RELIEF, PUBLIC *See* Public welfare
RELIGION
    See also Biblical stories; Buddhism; Catholic faith; Christianity; Clergy; Conversion; Faith; God; Jehovah's Witnesses; Judaism; Mormons and Mormonism; Paganism; Santeria
    Almond, S. Blue messiah
    Alvarado, B. Emily's exit
    Auslander, S. Startling revelations from the lost book of Stan
    Bestwick, S. Hazy shade of winter
    Bierce, A. The conflagration in Ghargaroo
    Bierce, A. The dog in Ganegwag
    Blish, J. This earth of hours
    Chekhov, A. P. Murder (abridged)
    Chiang, T. Hell is the absence of God
    Crowther, P. Even beggars would ride
    Daniells, R. C. Purgatory
    Davis, J. S. Detritus

RELIGION—*Continued*

Frost, G. Madonna of the maquiladora

Glancy, D. Minimal Indian

Gorman, E. Moral imperative

Grimsley, J. Jesus is sending you this message

Haldeman, J. W. Angel of light

Kelly, R. Bookmarks

Lain, D. How to stop selling Jesus

MacLaverty, B. A trusted neighbour

MacLeod, K. A case of consilience

Malouf, D. Closer

Martin, G. R. R. And seven times never kill man

Martin, G. R. R. A song for Lya

Martin, G. R. R. The way of cross and dragon

McGlynn, D. Moonland on fire

Modesitt, L. E., Jr. Second coming

Nelson, R. F. Cutters

Oates, J. C. Mark of Satan

Pendarvis, J. Your body is changing

Pneuman, A. All Saints Day

Prather, P. The faithful

Rees, R. The first letter of Rosalind to the four churches of the village Bellevue

Rosenbaum, B. The house beyond your sky

Rowe, C. Another word for map is faith

Ruffin, P. Harvey Watson and the angel

Ruffin, P. Jesus in the mist

Rust, E. M. God and birds

Scholes, K. Invisible empire of ascending light

Silverberg, R. The Pope of the chimps

Singer, I. B. The accuser and the accused

Smith, C. Ask him if he knows Jesus

Smith, R. T. Jesus wept

Stavans, I. Xerox man

Stevens, J. D. The mask

Trevor, D. Saint Francis in Flint

Valdés, J. Orquidea

Vollmer, M. Future missionaries of America

Wilson, R. C. Julian, a Christmas story

Woolson, C. F. St. Clair Flats

Yates, D. A certain samaritan

RELIGION, PRIMITIVE *See* Religion

RELIGIOUS LIFE *See* Convent life

RELIGIOUS PERSECUTION *See* Persecution

Remains. Bakken, K. N.

Remains of the night. McNally, J.

Remaking. Crouch, B.

A **remarkable** adventure. Bierce, A.

REMARQUE, ERICH MARIA, 1898-1970

About

Grass, G. Witnesses of an era

REMARRIAGE

Clayton, J. J. Part-time father

Singer, I. B. The power of darkness

Singer, I. B. Strangers

Thompson, J. A normal life

Trevor, W. The children

The **rematch**. Lupica, M.

Rember, John

Sudden death, over time

Best stories of the American West, v1; edited by Marc Jaffe

Remedies. Hwang, F.

Remember. Valaitis-Heflin, R. L.

Remember me. Silman, D.

Remember me with kindness. Jakubowski, M.

Remember the Time. Burgess, M.

The **Rememberer**. Lennon, J. R.

Remembering Las Cartoneras. Castillo, A.

Remembering Melody. Martin, G. R. R.

Remembrance. Baxter, S.

Remembrance, Ohio. Bradbury, R.

Remizov, Alekseï

The Bear cub

Worlds apart; an anthology of Russian fantasy and science fiction; edited and with commentary by Alexander Levitsky; translated by Alexander Levitsky and Martha T. Kitchen

The blaze

Worlds apart; an anthology of Russian fantasy and science fiction; edited and with commentary by Alexander Levitsky; translated by Alexander Levitsky and Martha T. Kitchen

Remote Control. Ravanipour, M.

The **Remotes**. Boswell, M.

RENAISSANCE

See also Italy—16th century

Rendall, Penny

Flowers for Doña Alicia

Going the distance; edited by Alan Beard

Rendall, Steven

(tr.) *See* Lichberg, Heinz von

Rendell, Ruth

The fall of a coin

Murder short & sweet; edited by Paul D. Staudohar

Loopy

A New omnibus of crime; edited by Tony Hillerman and Rosemary Herbert; contributing editors Sue Grafton and Jeffery Deaver

Rendezvous. DeMille, N.

A **rendezvous** in Averoigne. Smith, C. A.

Renewal. Shiner, L.

Rennie, Alistair

The Gutter sees the light that never shines

The new weird; Ann & Jeff VanderMeer, editors

Reno, Nicki

Sliver

Confrontation no92/93 p219-29 Fall 2005/Wint 2006

RENOIR, AUGUSTE, 1841-1919

About

Steele, A. M. An incident at the luncheon of the boating party

Rent-a-Gang. Nowlin-O'Banion, A.

Renter's guide to the Hamptons. Bakken, K. N.

Repair kit. Baxter, S.

The **repatriates**. Krasikov, S.

Repeating the past. Watts, P.

REPENTANCE

See also Sin

Repko, Sue

Deliverance

Gettysburg Review v18 no1 p110-22 Spr 2005

Replacement. Li, S.

The **replacement**. Swierczynski, D.

The **Replacements**. Reed, W. D. M.

Replica. Hunton, E. R.

Repo. Manley, C.

Report from the near future: crystallization. Gerrold, D.

Report of Ito Sadohara, Head of Tuna, Uokai, Ltd., to the Ministry of Commerce, Regarding Recent Events in the Domestic Fishing Industry. Mejia, M.

Report of the guardian of the sick. Bukoski, A.

A **Report** on Our Recent Troubles. Millhauser, S.

Report on Performance Art in One Province of the Empire Especially in Regard to Three Exhibitions Involving Swine. Yates, S.

Reportage. Shields, C.

REPORTERS *See* Journalists

Reports of certain events in London. Miéville, C.

REPOSSESSION

    Davidson, C. On sleepless roads

    Rahman, I. Real, actual life

A **representative** inquest. Bierce, A.

Representing Doris. Walpole, P.

REPRODUCTION, ASEXUAL *See* Asexual reproduction

The **Reptile** Garden. Erdrich, L.

The **Republic** of George's Island. McMahon, D.

The **Republic** of Southern Cross. Bryusov, V. Y.

República and Grau. Alarcón, D.

Republican. Johnston, B. A.

A **reputation**. Connell, R. E.

Request for proposal. Lewis, A. R.

Requiem. Barnes, Z. L.

Requiem for Sammy the magic cat. Altschul, A. F.

The **Requirement**. Berry, W.

Rerst stop. Erdrich, L.

The **rescue** mission. Busch, F.

RESCUES

    Anderson, P. Starfog

    Busch, F. The hay behind the house

    Busch, F. Patrols

    DeAndrea, W. L. Prince Charming

    Deaver, J. Tunnel girl

    Gurganus, A. Fourteen feet of water in my house

    Holladay, C. C. The peacock

    James, H. A cure for coquettes

    Messinger, J. Wrought iron

    Molodowsky, K. Tulia Shor's stories: King Solomon's bride

    Muller, M. Cave of ice

    Nelson, R. F. The cave

    Olafsson, O. April

    Olafsson, O. On the lake

    Reid, G. Hey, mister!

Rescuing Isaac. Zafiro, F.

RESEARCH

    Fulton, J. The animal girl

    Lain, D. The Sea Monkey conspiracy

    Nelson, R. F. Mechanical men

    Richter, S. Twin study

    Waters, M. Y. Mirror studies

    Zelazny, R. Dismal light

RESEARCH WORKERS

    Just, W. S. Nora

    Tsutsui, Y. Bad for the heart

    Tsutsui, Y. Salmonella men on planet porno

Resemblance. Senna, D.

Reservoir. Lane, J.

A **Resident** of Dresden. Netzband, D. H.

Resident priest. Hassler, J.

Residue. Monson, A.

RESISTANCE MOVEMENTS (WORLD WAR, 1939-1945) *See* World War, 1939-1945—Underground movements

RESISTANCE TO GOVERNMENT

    James, C. L. R. Children in the resistance

    James, C. L. R. Emperor Jones and the African drums

    Keeble, J. The cross

    Roberts, A. The siege of Fadiman

Resize. Kennedy, C.

Resnick, Laura

    The capo of darkness

        This is my funniest; leading science fiction writers present their funniest stories ever; edited by Mike Resnick

    Lady Roxanne La Belle

        The Magic toybox; edited by Denise Little

Resnick, Mike

    A better mousetrap

        Nature v450 p456 N 15 2007

    The Bull Moose at bay

        Resnick, M. The other Teddy Roosevelts

    Bully!

        Resnick, M. The other Teddy Roosevelts

    The burning spear at twilight

        Alternate generals III; edited by Harry Turtledove and Roland J. Green

    Bwana

        Resnick, M. Dreamwish beasts and snarks; with a foreword by Kristine Kathryn Rusch

    Catastrophe Baker and a canticle for Leibowitz

        The new space opera 2; edited by Gardner Dozois and Jonathan Strahan

    Catastrophe baker and the cold equations

        This is my funniest 2; leading science fiction writers present their funniest stories ever; edited by Mike Resnick

    Great unreported discoveries no. 163

        Nature v441 p906 Je 15 2006

    Hunting the snark

        Resnick, M. Dreamwish beasts and snarks; with a foreword by Kristine Kathryn Rusch

    The light that binds, hte claws that catch

        Resnick, M. The other Teddy Roosevelts

    The lord of the jungle

        Resnick, M. Dreamwish beasts and snarks; with a foreword by Kristine Kathryn Rusch

    Nicobar Lane—the soul eater's story

        Resnick, M. Dreamwish beasts and snarks; with a foreword by Kristine Kathryn Rusch

    Over there

        Asimov's science fiction: 30th anniversary anthology; edited by Sheila Williams

        Resnick, M. The other Teddy Roosevelts

    The pale, thin god

        A cross of centuries; twenty-five imaginative tales about the Christ; edited by Michael Bishop

    Redchapel

        Resnick, M. The other Teddy Roosevelts

    Revolt of the Sugar Plum Fairies

        This is my funniest; leading science fiction writers present their funniest stories ever; edited by Mike Resnick

    The Roosevelt dispatches

        Resnick, M. The other Teddy Roosevelts

    Safari 2103 A.D.

        Resnick, M. Dreamwish beasts and snarks; with a foreword by Kristine Kathryn Rusch

RESTAURANTS, LUNCHROOMS, ETC.—
Continued

Schor, L. Collateral damage
Selgin, P. Our cups are bottomless
Sillitoe, A. Uncle Ernest
Soueif, A. Chez Milou
Stewart, P. All day breakfast
Thorne, M. Disappearer
Tierce, M. Suck it
Tognazzini, A. The story of our lives
Tóibín, C. The name of the game
Tomlinson, J. So exotic
Treat, J. Waiting
Trevor, W. Cheating at canasta
Ulitskaya, L. Zurich
Resting place. Naiyer Masud
Restless waters. Howard, R. E.
Restoration. Rylands, J. T.
RESTORATION ENGLAND *See* England—17th century
Restraint. Gallagher, S.
Restraint. Inezian, A. M. L.
Restrepo, Laura
The scent of invisible roses
Colchie, T. A whistler in the nightworld; short fiction from the Latin Americas; edited by Thomas Colchie
RESTROOMS
King, S. Rest stop
Results for novice males. Parker, M.
The **results** of a dog going blind. Schmuck, R.
A **resumed** identity. Bierce, A.
The **resurgence** of Miss Ankle-strap Wedgie. Ellison, H.
Resurrecting Methuselah. Jones, E. P.
RESURRECTION
Blish, J. A work of art
Bradbury, R. The wish
Cadnum, M. Gravity
Hodgson, W. H. The promise
Irvine, A. C. Peter Skilling
Moorcock, M. A dead singer
Santamaria, G. The procession of shadows
Smith, C. A. The empire of the necromancers
Swan, G. Uncle Lazarus
Resurrection. Crucet, J. C.
Resurrection. Sapira, P.
Resurrection hockey. Schumacher, J.
The **resurrection** man. McCrumb, S.
The **resurrection** of the rattlesnake. Smith, C. A.
Resurrection Sunday. Manley, C.
Retail Therapy. Ferber, A.
The **retired** arsonist. Hoch, E. D.
RETIREMENT
See also Old age
Anderson, B. So lovely of them
Dee, E. The tailman
Gurganus, A. My heart is a snake farm
Harris, J. Fule's gold
McGruder, K. The southernmost point
Pearlman, E. Self-reliance
Pollack, E. Milt and Moose
Shomer, E. Tourist season
Weaver, W. Blaze of glory
RETIREMENT COMMUNITIES
Schwarzschild, E. Irreversible
Schwarzschild, E. Spring Garden
Retreat. Crouse, D.
The **Retreat**. Schrager, L.

Retreat. Tower, W.
Retrospection. Baraka, I. A.
Retrospective. Jones, H. G.
Retrospective. Wignall, K.
RETROSPECTIVE STORIES
Anderson, B. Discontinuous lives
Bass, R. Her first elk
Bass, R. Titan
Bunin, I. A. Rusya
Busch, F. Sense of direction
Connell, E. S. The walls of Avila
Crouse, D. Swimming in the dark
Cutler, J. Judith
Eisenberg, D. The custodian
Ellin, S. The day of the bullet
Gaiman, N. The Flints of memory lane
Garrett, G. P. Gator bait
Gordon, C. Old Red
Irby, L. God don't like ugly
Johnson, G. Escalators
O'Brien, T. On the rainy river
Pohl, F. I remember a winter
Shukman, H. The garden of God: 1976
Shukman, H. The garden of God: 1988
Stafford, J. In the zoo
Swan, G. The death of the cat
Trevor, D. Labor Day hurricane, 1935
Valtinos, T. Addiction to nicotine
Wolff, T. The liar
"**Return**". Ahmed, F.
Return. Matheson, R.
Return. Nadelson, S.
Return. Swann, M.
The **return** of a captive. Hammad, H. a.- .
The **return** of service. Baumbach, J.
The **Return** of the BBQ Killers. Foltz, C.
The **return** of the dark children. Coover, R.
The **Return** of the Prisoner. Al Nasiri, B.
The **return** of the sorcerer. Smith, C. A.
The **return** of the thin white dude . . . screaming. Bruen, K.
Return to Port William. Berry, W.
Return trip to Christmas. Buckler, E.
Returning. Soueif, A.
Returning from rubber gathering. Verissimo, J.
Returns & Exchanges. Berg, E.
Returns and exchanges. Berg, E.
Reuben, David B.
The Greatest Loss
Journal of the American Geriatrics Society v54 no7 p1144 Jl 2006
Reuben. Yellin, T.
Reunification. Singer, M.
A **reunion**. Andreas-Salomé, L.
Reunion. Bender, K. E.
Reunion. Cheever, J.
Reunion. Engberg, S.
Reunion. Ford, R.
Reunion. McInerney, J.
Reunion. Schwarzschild, E.
Reunion. Winton, T.
Reunion eve. Porter, J. A.
REUNIONS
Andreas-Salomé, L. A reunion
Barnes, J. Hygiene
Connell, E. S. The walls of Avila
Frost, G. Some things are better left
Fuentes, C. Sweethearts
Garcia-Aguilera, C. The dinner

REVENGE—*Continued*

Lane, J. Prison ships
Lee, H. K. Burning ring of fire
Lehane, D. Mushrooms
Leonard, E. The boy who smiled
Leonard, E. Moment of vengeance [variant title: The waiting man]
Link, K. Catskin
Lippman, L. Femme fatale
Lochte, D. Low tide
Lowachee, K. The forgotten ones
Lupica, M. The rematch
Lustbader, E. V. The uncertainty principle
MacLaverty, B. Up the coast
MacLean, M. McHenry's gift
Magson, A. Procedure
Malouf, D. Blacksoil country
Mandelman, A. Pity
Matthews, C. The house of deliverance
McCauley, W. Winner
McDonald, C. Rope-a-dope
Modesitt, L. E., Jr. Understanding
Murphy, D. R. Sounds of silence
Nolan, W. F. The ex
Nye, J. L. The revenge of Chatty Cathy
Oates, J. C. Give me your heart
Oates, J. C. High lonesome
Oates, J. C. Vigilante
O'Bryan, J. The unlikely redemption of Jared Pearce
Olafsson, O. December
Ortiz, O. F. Settling of scores
Ozick, C. Actors
Paretsky, S. Acid test
Parra, E. A. The hunter
Perry, A. A tale of one city
Porter, K. A. María Concepción
Powell, G. C. Kamila and the king of kandy
Puchner, E. Mission
Queiroz, R. d. Metonymy; or, The husband's revenge
Quijada, C. "Vendettas"
Quiroga, H. A slap in the face
Rabe, J. Stalking old John Bull
Rand, K. Eye of the assassin
Reed, R. Show me yours
Reeves, R. Dance macabre
Resnick, M. The soul eater
Richardson, K. The third death of the little clay dog
Robbins, T. Spurs
Roberts, A. Eleanor
Roley, B. A. Kinship
Rollo, G. Lost in a field of paper flowers
Rosa, J. G. Those Lopes
Rylands, J. T. Mobility
Sale, M. Estelle is dead
Sargent, P. Spirit brother
Segal, L. G. The reverse bug
Sharp, Z. Served cold
Shaw, I. Sailor off the Bremen
Shirley, J. Seven knives
Sholer, L. Imitate the sun
Silman, D. Remember me
Slater, D. Stiffed
Smith, C. A. The justice of the elephant
Smith, J. Hotwalking
Smith, N. Jaybird
Smith, R. T. Razorhead the axeman

Solá, M. Natural paradises
Solomita, S. Crazy Jill saves the slinky
Spencer, B. The true history
Spencer, W. B. The death of the novel
Spiegelman, P. Location, location, location
Spinosa, T. Killing O'Malley
Stackpole, M. A. The Krells of Tancras Moor
Steck, U. Phantoms
Stella, C. Tainted goods
Sterns, A. The rest is silence
Stewart, M. Justice served
Stine, R. L. Wifey
Szereto, M. Hell is where the heart is
Taylor, E. A pinch of snuff
Thomas, E. The adventure of voodoo moon
Thomas, J. Wakizashi
Thorne, M. My ex-classmates' Kids
Tomlinson, J. The accomplished son
Tran, V. This or any desert
Trans, V. This or any desert
Uchida, H. Afterglow
Updike, J. Bech noir
Vermeulen, J. Chalele
Viets, E. Vampire hours
Waldrop, H. The lions are asleep this night
Wallace, J. Custom sets
Waterman, F. Best man wins
Welk, M. V. Code blue
Wells, M. The potter's daughter
White, D. Righteous son
Wilhelm, K. Rules of the game
Wilson, F. P. Please don't hurt me
Wingate, S. Our last garage sale
Wolff, T. The chain
Wolven, S. Atomic supernova
Wolven, S. Taciturnity
Woodrell, D. Uncle
Woolrich, C. 3 kills for 1
Woolrich, C. Two murders, one crime
Yemni, S. Burn and go
Young, H. 1%
Zebrowski, G. Black pockets
Zelazny, R. My lady of the diodes
Zelazny, R. Recital
Ziyalan, M. Black palace
Zumas, L. Blotilla takes the cake
Revenge. Enright, A.
Revenge. Sillitoe, A.
Revenge. Toer, P. A.
The **revenge** of Chatty Cathy. Nye, J. L.
The **revenge** of the callico cat. Chapman, S.
Revenge of the dinosaurs. Eisenberg, D.
Reverie. Baumbach, J.
The **Reversal**. Friedman, B. J.
A **reversal** of fortune. Black, H.
The **reverse** bug. Segal, L. G.
Reviews. Bova, B.
The **revisionist**. Schulman, H.
Revival Road. Erdrich, L.
The **Revived** Art of the Toy Theatre. Spark, D.
A **revolt** of the gods. Bierce, A.
Revolt of the Sugar Plum Fairies. Resnick, M.
A **Revolting** Character. Tran, B.
REVOLUTION, AMERICAN, 1775-1783 *See* United States—Revolution, 1775-1783
Revolution: number 9. Rohrig, J.
REVOLUTIONARIES *See* Revolutionists
Revolutionaries. Abbott, L. K.

REVOLUTIONARY WAR, 1775-1783 *See* United States—Revolution, 1775-1783

REVOLUTIONISTS

Alarcón, D. Lima, Peru; July 28, 1979
Baraka, I. A. New & old
Bercovitch, B. Becoming revolutionary
Chase, M. The terminal project
Coloane, F. How the Chilote Otey died
Fountain, B. Near-extinct birds of the central cordillera
Head, B. The coming of the Christ-Child
Libin, Z. Two shrines
Lowachee, K. The forgotten ones
Neal, L. Our bright tomorrows
Porter, K. A. Flowering Judas
Samara, N. The tables outlived Amin
Wolfe, G. Hour of trust

REVOLUTIONS

See also Coups d'état; Revolutionists

Abella, A. Shanghai
Carey, P. The fat man in history
Fonseca, R. The eleventh of May
Hughes, M. Help wonted
Nganang, P. Our neighborhood fool
Raharimanana, J.-L. Fahavalo
Sallis, J. The good in men
Silverberg, R. The pleasure of their company
Téllez, H. Prelude

Revolutions. Row, J.
Revolver. Roberts, J.

Revoyr, Nina

Golden Pacific
The cocaine chronicles; edited by Gary Phillips and Jervey Tervalon

Revulsion [excerpt] Moya, H. C.
The **rewards** of marriage. Toer, P. A.
El **Rey**. Wolven, S.

Rey Rosa, Rodrigo

The good cripple [excerpt]
Terrestrial intelligence; international fiction now from New Directions; edited by Barbara Epler

Reynolds, Alastair

Beyond the Aquila rift
The Year's best science fiction: twenty-third annual collection; edited by Gardner Dozois
Feeling rejected
Nature v437 p788 S 29 2005
Fury
Strahan, J. Eclipse two; new science fiction and fantasy; edited by Jonathan Strahan
Minla's flowers
The new space opera; edited by Gardner Dozois and Jonathan Strahan
Nightingale
The Year's best science fiction: twenty-fourth annual collection; edited by Gardner Dozois
The receivers
Other earths; edited by Nick Gevers and Jay Lake.
Signal to noise
The Year's best science fiction: twenty-fourth annual collection; edited by Gardner Dozois
The sledge-maker's daughter
The Year's best science fiction: twenty-fifth annual collection; edited by Gardner Dozois

The star surgeon's apprentice
The Starry rift; tales of new tomorrows: an original science fiction anthology; edited by Jonathan Strahan
Turquoise days
The Best of the best, volume 2; 20 years of the best short science fiction novels; edited by Gardner Dozois
Zima blue
The Year's best science fiction: twenty-third annual collection; edited by Gardner Dozois

Reynolds, Brad

The twin
The World's finest mystery and crime stories, fourth annual collection; edited by Ed Gorman and Martin H. Greenberg

Reynolds, Clay

Agatite [excerpt]
Lone Star sleuths; an anthology of Texas crime fiction; edited and with an introduction by Bill Cunningham, Steven L. Davis, and Rollo K. Newsom.
Hoi Polloi: Three Views
Callaloo v32 no2 p454-64 Spr 2009
A train to catch
Lone Star literature; from the Red River to the Rio Grande; edited by Don Graham

Reyzen, Avrom

The Jew who destroyed the temple
No star too beautiful; Yiddish stories from 1382 to the present; compiled and translated by Joachim Neugroschel

Rheda, Regina

Dona Carminda e o príncipe
Meridians v5 no1 p27-33 2004
Miss Carminda and the Prince
Meridians v5 no1 p34-9 2004

The **Rhein**. Perry, R.

Rheinheimer, Kurt

The B & W
Reinheimer, K. Little criminals; Kurt Reinheimer
Baltimore
Reinheimer, K. Little criminals; Kurt Reinheimer
Debut
Reinheimer, K. Little criminals; Kurt Reinheimer
Dogs
Reinheimer, K. Little criminals; Kurt Reinheimer
The fabulous Greens
Reinheimer, K. Little criminals; Kurt Reinheimer
FLA
Reinheimer, K. Little criminals; Kurt Reinheimer
Grand Strand
Reinheimer, K. Little criminals; Kurt Reinheimer
Homes
Reinheimer, K. Little criminals; Kurt Reinheimer
Hooks
Reinheimer, K. Little criminals; Kurt Reinheimer
The Melrose
South Carolina Review v38 no1 p158-68 Fall 2005

Rheinheimer, Kurt—*Continued*
   Minors
      Reinheimer, K. Little criminals; Kurt
      Reinheimer
   Moon Beach
      Reinheimer, K. Little criminals; Kurt
      Reinheimer
   Shoes
      Reinheimer, K. Little criminals; Kurt
      Reinheimer
   St. Louis
      Reinheimer, K. Little criminals; Kurt
      Reinheimer
   The stop
      Reinheimer, K. Little criminals; Kurt
      Reinheimer
   Telling Brenda
      Reinheimer, K. Little criminals; Kurt
      Reinheimer
   Umpire
      Reinheimer, K. Little criminals; Kurt
      Reinheimer
Rhine, Robert Steven
   The seer
      Dark delicacies; original tales of terror and
      the macabre by the world's greatest horror
      writers; edited by Del Howison and Jeff
      Gelb
The **rhino** in the barn. McIlvoy, K.
RHINOCEROS
   McIlvoy, K. The rhino in the barn
Rhoda. Foer, J. S.
Rhoda. Vann, D.
RHODE ISLAND
   Harleman, A. Thoreau's laundry
   Kulpa, K. How the light walks
   Ohlin, A. Local news
                  Block Island
      See Block Island (R.I.)
                     Newport
   Auchincloss, L. Lady Kate
   Gordon, M. Rosecliff
                    Providence
   Harleman, A. Autumn, 1911
   Lovecraft, H. P. The haunter of the dark
   Solomon, A. Lotto
Rhodes, Dan
   Beautiful Consuela
      Rhodes, D. Don't tell me the truth about love;
      stories
   The Carolingian Period
      Rhodes, D. Don't tell me the truth about love;
      stories
   Glass eyes
      Rhodes, D. Don't tell me the truth about love;
      stories
   Landfill
      Rhodes, D. Don't tell me the truth about love;
      stories
   Mademoiselle Arc-en-ciel
      Rhodes, D. Don't tell me the truth about love;
      stories
   The painting
      Rhodes, D. Don't tell me the truth about love;
      stories
   The violoncello
      Rhodes, D. Don't tell me the truth about love;
      stories

Rhodes, Roberta Pantal
   Two Arms Holding Me
      Confrontation no90/91 p216-23 Spr/Summ
      2005
Rhodes, Stephen
   At the top of his game
      The Best American mystery stories, 2008; ed-
      ited and with an introduction by George
      Pelecanos; Otto Penzler, series editor
RHODESIA
   Clark, G. M. The center of the world
RHODESIA, NORTHERN *See* Zambia
RHODESIA, SOUTHERN *See* Zimbabwe
Rhythm travel. Baraka, I. A.
Ribbeck, Bernhard
   A blue and cloudless sky
      The SFWA European hall of fame; sixteen
      contemporary masterpieces of science fic-
      tion from the continent; edited by James
      Morrow and Kathryn Morrow
Ribbons Then Fever. Lehner, C.
Ribeiro, Edgard Telles
   The turn in the river
      Colchie, T. A whistler in the nightworld;
      short fiction from the Latin Americas; ed-
      ited by Thomas Colchie
Ribeiro, João Ubaldo
   Fortunate Buddhas
      Bomb no102 p109-12 Wint 2008
Ribs. Novakovich, J.
Rice, Christopher
   Man catch
      Thriller; edited by James Patterson
   Over thirty
      Los Angeles noir; edited by Denise Hamilton
Rich, Mark
   Across the sky
      Rich, M. Across the sky
   The apples of Venus
      Rich, M. Across the sky
   The asking place
      Rich, M. Across the sky
   The beauty monster
      Rich, M. Across the sky
   Foggery
      Rich, M. Across the sky
   Forever down the ringing groves
      Rich, M. Across the sky
   Impossible alone
      Rich, M. Across the sky
   The never-winner
      Rich, M. Across the sky
   Overdue
      Rich, M. Across the sky
   The real thing
      Rich, M. Across the sky
   Smoking gun
      Rich, M. Across the sky
   The suckers
      Rich, M. Across the sky
   To hunt in fields
      Rich, M. Across the sky
   Whenever they go out
      Rich, M. Across the sky
Rich, Simon
   Strong and Mighty Men
      Best Life v3 no9 p110-13, 127 N 2006
Rich. Gilchrist, E.
Rich and rare were the gems she wore. Kiely, B.

The **rich** brother. Wolff, T.

Rich girls. Rust, E. M.

A **rich** man. Jones, E. P.

The **rich** man from Azherkov. Molodowsky, K.

Rich Miller's hand. See Leonard, E. Blood money
    [variant title: Rich Miller's hand]

RICH PEOPLE *See* Wealth

Richar, Gustav A.
    (tr.) See Dörrie, Doris

Richard, Mark
    Gentleman's agreement
        The Anchor book of new American short sto-
          ries; edited by Ben Marcus
    Memorial day
        Best of the South: from the second decade of
          New stories from the South; selected and
          introduced by Anne Tyler

Richard, Nancy
    What you do next
        Wide awake in the Pelican State; stories by
          contemporary Louisiana writers; edited by
          Ann Brewster Dobie; with a foreword by
          Ernest J. Gaines

Richard Riddle, boy detective, in "The case of the
    French spy". Newman, K.

Richards, Jeff
    Losing Lars
        Southern Humanities Review v39 no4 p328-37
        Fall 2005

Richards, Susan Starr
    The ape in the face
        Richards, S. S. The hanging in the foaling
          barn; stories
    Clarence Cummins and the semi-permanent loan
        Richards, S. S. The hanging in the foaling
          barn; stories
    Gawain and the horsewoman
        Richards, S. S. The hanging in the foaling
          barn; stories
    Grass fires
        Richards, S. S. The hanging in the foaling
          barn; stories
    The hanging in the foaling barn
        Richards, S. S. The hanging in the foaling
          barn; stories
    Magic lantern
        Richards, S. S. The hanging in the foaling
          barn; stories
    Man walking
        Richards, S. S. The hanging in the foaling
          barn; stories
    The murderer, the pony, and Miss Brown to you
        Richards, S. S. The hanging in the foaling
          barn; stories
    The screened porch
        Richards, S. S. The hanging in the foaling
          barn; stories

Richards, Tim
    Isnis
        The Review of Contemporary Fiction v27 no3
        p109-25 Fall 2007

Richards, Tony
    Birchiam pier
        British invasion; edited by Christopher Gol-
          den, Tim Lebbon & James A. Moore
    Non-existent cats
        Cat tales: fantastic feline fiction; edited by
          George H. Scithers

Richardson, Kat
    The third death of the little clay dog
        Butcher, J. Mean streets; [by] Jim Butcher ...
        [et al]

Richardson, Michael John
    A little early in the day
        Meeting across the river; stories inspired by
          the haunting Bruce Springsteen song; edited
          by Jessica Kaye and Richard J. Brewer

The **richer,** the poorer. West, D.

The **riches** there that lie. Douglas, C. N.

The **Richest** Girl in the World. Young, R. C.

Richler, Mordecai
    Barney's version [excerpt]
        Contemporary Jewish writing in Canada; an
          anthology; edited by Michael Greenstein

Richmond, Michelle
    Milk
        Sex for America; politically inspired erotica;
          edited by Stephen Elliott

Richter, Joan
    The gambling master of Shanghai
        The International Association of Crime Writ-
          ers presents Murder in Vegas; new crime
          tales of gambling and desperation; edited
          by Michael Connelly

Richter, Stacey
    Blackout
        Richter, S. Twin study; stories
    A case study of emergency room procedure and
        risk management by hospital staff members
        in the urban facility
        Richter, S. Twin study; stories
        The Year's best fantasy and horror: nineteenth
          annual collection; edited by Ellen Datlow
          and Kelly Link & Gavin J. Grant
    The cavemen in the hedges
        Richter, S. Twin study; stories
    Christ, their Lord
        Best of Tin House; stories; foreword by Dor-
          othy Allison
        Richter, S. Twin study; stories
    Duet
        Richter, S. Twin study; stories
    Habits and habitat of the southwestern bad boy
        Richter, S. Twin study; stories
    The land of pain
        Richter, S. Twin study; stories
        Pushcart prize XXXI: best of the small press-
          es 2007; edited by Bill Henderson; with the
          Pushcart Prize editors
    The long hall
        Richter, S. Twin study; stories
    My mother the rock star
        Richter, S. Twin study; stories
    Twin study
        Richter, S. Twin study; stories
    Velvet
        Richter, S. Twin study; stories
    Young people today
        Richter, S. Twin study; stories

Rickards, John
    Twenty dollar future
        Expletive deleted; edited by Jen Jordan
    Wish
        Dublin noir; the Celtic tiger vs. the ugly
          American; edited by Ken Bruen

Rickert, M.
Angel face
Rickert, M. Map of dreams; with a foreword
by Christopher Barzak ; and an afterword
by Gordon Van Gelder
Anyway
Rickert, M. Map of dreams; with a foreword
by Christopher Barzak ; and an afterword
by Gordon Van Gelder
Art is not a violent subject
Rickert, M. Map of dreams; with a foreword
by Christopher Barzak ; and an afterword
by Gordon Van Gelder
Bread and bombs
The Year's best fantasy and horror: seven-
teenth annual collection; edited by Ellen
Datlow, Kelly Link and Gavin J. Grant
Rickert, M. Map of dreams; with a foreword
by Christopher Barzak ; and an afterword
by Gordon Van Gelder
The chambered fruit
Rickert, M. Map of dreams; with a foreword
by Christopher Barzak ; and an afterword
by Gordon Van Gelder
The Christmas witch
Year's best fantasy 7; edited by David G.
Hartwell & Kathryn Cramer
Cold fires
Rickert, M. Map of dreams; with a foreword
by Christopher Barzak ; and an afterword
by Gordon Van Gelder
The Year's best fantasy and horror: eighteenth
annual collection; edited by Ellen Datlow,
Kelly Link & Gavin J. Grant
Don't ask
Year's best fantasy 8; edited by David G.
Hartwell, Kathryn Cramer
Evidence of love in a case of abandonment: one
daughter's personal account
The Best science fiction and fantasy of the
year: volume three; edited by Jonathan
Strahan
The girl who ate butterflies
Rickert, M. Map of dreams; with a foreword
by Christopher Barzak ; and an afterword
by Gordon Van Gelder
The harrowing
Rickert, M. Map of dreams; with a foreword
by Christopher Barzak ; and an afterword
by Gordon Van Gelder
Holiday
The Best science fiction and fantasy of the
year: volume two; edited by Jonathan
Strahan
The Year's best fantasy and horror: twenty-
first annual collection; edited by Ellen
Datlow and Kelly Link & Gavin J. Grant
Journey into the kingdom
The Year's best fantasy and horror: twentieth
annual collection; edited by Ellen Datlow
and Kelly Link & Gavin J. Grant
Leda
Rickert, M. Map of dreams; with a foreword
by Christopher Barzak ; and an afterword
by Gordon Van Gelder
Poe's children; the new horror: an anthology;
[edited by] Peter Straub.

Many voices
Rickert, M. Map of dreams; with a foreword
by Christopher Barzak ; and an afterword
by Gordon Van Gelder
Map of dreams
Rickert, M. Map of dreams; with a foreword
by Christopher Barzak ; and an afterword
by Gordon Van Gelder
Moorina of the seals
Rickert, M. Map of dreams; with a foreword
by Christopher Barzak ; and an afterword
by Gordon Van Gelder
More beautiful than you
Rickert, M. Map of dreams; with a foreword
by Christopher Barzak ; and an afterword
by Gordon Van Gelder
Night blossoms
Rickert, M. Map of dreams; with a foreword
by Christopher Barzak ; and an afterword
by Gordon Van Gelder
Peace on Suburbia
Rickert, M. Map of dreams; with a foreword
by Christopher Barzak ; and an afterword
by Gordon Van Gelder
The super hero saves the world
Rickert, M. Map of dreams; with a foreword
by Christopher Barzak ; and an afterword
by Gordon Van Gelder
A very little madness goes a long way
Rickert, M. Map of dreams; with a foreword
by Christopher Barzak ; and an afterword
by Gordon Van Gelder
You have never been here
Feeling very strange; the Slipstream antholo-
gy; James Patrick Kelly & John Kessel, ed-
itors
Rickert, Mary *See* Rickert, M., 1959-
RICKSHAW MEN
Adiga, A. Umbrella Street
Rickshaw runner. Williams, N. J.
The **Ricus** Adams. Gardiner, J. R.
Riddell, J. L.
Orrin Lindsay's Plan of Aerial Navigation, with
a Narrative of His Explorations in the
Higher Regions of the Atmosphere, and His
Wonderful Voyage round the Moon!
Science-Fiction Studies v36 pt2 p300-20 Jl
2009
Riddihough, Guy
The patter of tiny feet
Nature v449 p1088 O 25 2007
Riddle. Coover, R.
The **riddle** of the woolsack. Emerson, K. L.
RIDDLES
Bierce, A. A literary riot
Coover, R. Riddle
Ride a white horse. Block, L.
Ride me like a wave. Yolen, J.
The **ride** of the Gabbleratchet. Swainston, S.
Ride or start shootin'. L'Amour, L.
Ride the Peter Pan. Whittenberg, A.
The **rider** of the gray horse. Lamb, H.
Ridge weather. Weil, J.
Riding bitch. Jeter, K. W.
Riding for the brand. L'Amour, L.
Riding Janis. Gerrold, D.
Riding on the q-ball. Love, R.
Riding the crocodile. Egan, G.
Riding the doghouse. DeVita, R.

Riding the white bull. Kiernan, C. R.

Ridpath, Michael

Partnership track

The Detection collection; edited by Simon Brett

Rien ne va plus. Woollcott, A.

RIF REVOLT, 1921-1926

L'Amour, L. Glorious! Glorious!

Rifaat, Alifa

At the time of the Jasmine

The Anchor book of modern African stories; edited by Nadežda Obradovic; with a foreword by Chinua Achebe

Rifai, Talib al-

Bashrawi

Oranges in the sun; short stories from the Arabian Gulf; edited and translated by Deborah S. Akers, Abubaker A. Bagader

Riff. Gorman, E.

Riff-raff. Charters, D.

The **rifleman**. Davidson, C.

Right is right. Cohen, G.

The **right** mistake. Mosley, W.

The **right** of young men. Biller, M.

The **right** sort of ears. Anderson, B.

The **right** time of the month. Biller, M.

The **right** to remain. Parker, M.

The **right** tool for the job. Pelegrimas, M.

Righteous son. White, D.

Righteousness. Gee, M.

Rigney, Mark

The facts

The Best of the Bellevue Literary Review; edited by Dannielle Ofri and the staff of the Bellevue Literary Review

A **Rigor** Mortis of the Tongue & Other Earthly Things. Chikwava, B.

Rikki *See* Ducornet, Rikki

Riley, Ali

Hag

The Walrus v5 no4 p80-1 My 2008

Riley, Ethel

Dark Laughter

"Tell it to us easy" and other stories; a complete short fiction anthology of African American women writers in Opportunity magazine, (1923-1948); edited by Judith Musser.

Riley, Gwendoline

Au pont du font

Riley, G. Tuesday nights and Wednesday mornings

Children

Riley, G. Tuesday nights and Wednesday mornings

I thought about you

Riley, G. Tuesday nights and Wednesday mornings

La la land

Riley, G. Tuesday nights and Wednesday mornings

Narcissism

Riley, G. Tuesday nights and Wednesday mornings

One more cup of coffee

Riley, G. Tuesday nights and Wednesday mornings

Perpetual Piccadilly

Riley, G. Tuesday nights and Wednesday mornings

Sad love

Riley, G. Tuesday nights and Wednesday mornings

September

Riley, G. Tuesday nights and Wednesday mornings

Sick notes

Riley, G. Tuesday nights and Wednesday mornings

War story

Riley, G. Tuesday nights and Wednesday mornings

Riley, Patricia

Damping down the road

Reckonings; contemporary short fiction by Native American women; edited by Hertha D. Sweet Wong, Lauren Stuart Muller, Jana Sequoya Magdaleno

Wisteria

Reckonings; contemporary short fiction by Native American women; edited by Hertha D. Sweet Wong, Lauren Stuart Muller, Jana Sequoya Magdaleno

RIMBAUD, ARTHUR, 1854-1891

About

Hand, E. Wonderwall

Rimbaud, Jean Nicolas Arthur *See* Rimbaud, Arthur, 1854-1891

Rinaldi, Nicholas

An Insanity, a Madness, a Furor

Prairie Schooner v82 no2 p29-35 Summ 2008

Rindo's station. See Leonard, E. Trouble at Rindo's station [variant title: Rindo's station]

The **ring**. Ronk, M. C.

The **ring**. Zahn, T.

The **Ring** and the Box It Came In. Gillette, J.

Ring-barking. Gee, M.

Ringing the changes. Silverberg, R.

Ringing the changes. Somers, J.

Ringing up baby. Klages, E.

RINGS

Bowes, R. Dust devil on a quiet street

Howard, R. E. The haunter of the ring

Kennedy, C. Resize

Ronk, M. C. The ring

Shirley, P. The consequence of summer heat

Zahn, T. The ring

Rings. Guerrero, L.

The **rings** of Saturn [excerpt] Sebald, W. G.

Ringtime. Disch, T. M.

RIO DE JANEIRO (BRAZIL) *See* Brazil—Rio de Janeiro

Riordan, Rick

The last king of Texas [excerpt]

Lone Star sleuths; an anthology of Texas crime fiction; edited and with an introduction by Bill Cunningham, Steven L. Davis, and Rollo K. Newsom.

Riordan's fiftieth. Stern, R. G.

Riot at the Calc Exam. Adams, C.

RIOTS

Adichie, C. N. A private experience

Castaneda, R. Coyote hunt

Edwards, M. The people outside

Hellmann, L. F. The whole world is watching

RIOTS—*Continued*

Oppel, J.-H. Paris calling

Roman, C. Vendors of peculiar objects

Shukman, H. The garden of God: 1988

Rip his head off. Fincke, G.

Ripp, Victor

Paris, July or August 1940

The Antioch Review v64 no3 p554-67 Summ 2006

Rippen, Chris

Barefoot

The World's finest mystery and crime stories, fourth annual collection; edited by Ed Gorman and Martin H. Greenberg

The best

The World's finest mystery and crime stories, fifth annual collection; edited by Ed Gorman and Martin H. Greenberg

Ripper!. Nolan, W. F.

Riptide. Tabor, M. L.

The **rise** and fall. Woronov, M.

The **rise** and fall of Sharpie Cakes. Murakami, H.

Rising with Surtsey. Lumley, B.

A **risk** for Father Christmas. Lenz, S.

Risk merchants. Sutton, B.

Rite of passage. Roberson, J.

Rite of spring. Lanagan, M.

RITES AND CEREMONIES

Barthelme, D. Pandemonium

Chadbourn, M. Farewell to the 21st century girl

Disch, T. M. Jour de fête

Dybek, S. The Palatski Man

Ma Jian. The final initiation

Mamatas, N. Summon bind banish

Onspaugh, M. Old school

Poirier, M. J. I, Maggot

Silverberg, R. The feast of St. Dionysus

Singer, I. B. Two

Skinner, J. All about balls

Ritsou, Ery

An Interview that Didn't Happen

Michigan Quarterly Review v46 no2 p251-6 Spr 2007

Riva, Lesley

(tr.) See Malerba, Luigi

Riva, Pablo Lentini

Beau Séjour

FMR (Black Edition) no25 p153-64 My/Je 2008

Of Music, Painting and Other Matters

FMR (Black Edition) no12 p59-80 Ap/My 2006

The **rival**. Anderle, H.

Rivas, Manuel

Butterfly's tongue

Rivas, M. Vermeer's milkmaid and other stories; translated from the Galician by Jonathan Dunne

Carmiña

Rivas, M. Vermeer's milkmaid and other stories; translated from the Galician by Jonathan Dunne

Cartoons

Rivas, M. Vermeer's milkmaid and other stories; translated from the Galician by Jonathan Dunne

The coming of wisdom with time

Rivas, M. Vermeer's milkmaid and other stories; translated from the Galician by Jonathan Dunne

Conga, conga

Rivas, M. Vermeer's milkmaid and other stories; translated from the Galician by Jonathan Dunne

The gaffer and iron maiden

Rivas, M. Vermeer's milkmaid and other stories; translated from the Galician by Jonathan Dunne

The girl with the pirate trousers

Rivas, M. Vermeer's milkmaid and other stories; translated from the Galician by Jonathan Dunne

Havana's vast cemetery

Rivas, M. Vermeer's milkmaid and other stories; translated from the Galician by Jonathan Dunne

Here and there

Rivas, M. Vermeer's milkmaid and other stories; translated from the Galician by Jonathan Dunne

The objects

Rivas, M. Vermeer's milkmaid and other stories; translated from the Galician by Jonathan Dunne

Saxophone in the mist

Rivas, M. Vermeer's milkmaid and other stories; translated from the Galician by Jonathan Dunne

Vermeer's milkmaid

Rivas, M. Vermeer's milkmaid and other stories; translated from the Galician by Jonathan Dunne

What do you want with me, love?

Rivas, M. Vermeer's milkmaid and other stories; translated from the Galician by Jonathan Dunne

A white flower for bats

Rivas, M. Vermeer's milkmaid and other stories; translated from the Galician by Jonathan Dunne

Yoko's light

Rivas, M. Vermeer's milkmaid and other stories; translated from the Galician by Jonathan Dunne

You'll both be very happy

Rivas, M. Vermeer's milkmaid and other stories; translated from the Galician by Jonathan Dunne

Rivecca, Suzanne

It Sounds Like You're Feeling . . .

StoryQuarterly v42 p353-74 2006

Look ma, I'm breathing

Best new American voices 2009; guest editor Mary Gaitskill; series editors John Kulka and Natalie Danford

Uncle

Best new American voices 2008; guest editor Richard Bausch; series editors John Kulka and Natalie Danford

Pushcart prize XXXIII: best of the small presses 2009; edited by Bill Henderson with the Pushcart Prize editors

New England Review v28 no1 p10-21 2007

The **riven** night. Hodgson, W. H.

The **river**. Trevor, D.

River dog. Porter, A.
River hills. Engberg, S.
A **River** in Egypt. Means, D.
The **river** maid. Yolen, J.
A **river** man goes to war. Bonham, F.
River of the queen. Reed, R.
River story. Nelson, R. F.
River Swim. Widner, J.
Rivera, Frida Kahlo *See* Kahlo, Frida, 1907-1954
Rivera, Tomás
  The portrait
    Lone Star literature; from the Red River to the Rio Grande; edited by Don Graham
Rivera-Garza, Cristina
  Nostalgia/Nostalgia
    Best of contemporary Mexican fiction; Alvaro Uribe, editor; Olivia Sears, translation editor
Rivera-Valdes, Sonia
  Ana at four times: Ana and the lemon balm
    Rivera-Valdés, S. Stories of little women & grown-up girls; translated by Emily Maguire
  Ana at four times: Ana and the magic wand
    Rivera-Valdés, S. Stories of little women & grown-up girls; translated by Emily Maguire
  Ana at four times: Ana and the moon
    Rivera-Valdés, S. Stories of little women & grown-up girls; translated by Emily Maguire
  Ana at four times: Ana and the snow
    Rivera-Valdés, S. Stories of little women & grown-up girls; translated by Emily Maguire
  Blue like bluing
    Rivera-Valdés, S. Stories of little women & grown-up girls; translated by Emily Maguire
  The deepest seed of the lemon
    Rivera-Valdés, S. Stories of little women & grown-up girls; translated by Emily Maguire
  The eighth fold
    Rivera-Valdés, S. Stories of little women & grown-up girls; translated by Emily Maguire
  Life leads
    Rivera-Valdés, S. Stories of little women & grown-up girls; translated by Emily Maguire
  Like in jail
    Rivera-Valdés, S. Stories of little women & grown-up girls; translated by Emily Maguire
  Sunday at the same time
    Rivera-Valdés, S. Stories of little women & grown-up girls; translated by Emily Maguire
RIVERBOATS *See* Steamboats
RIVERS
    See also Thames River (England)
  Copper, B. Voices in the water
  Johnson, K. At the mouth of the river of bees
  Parks, T. In defiance of club rules
  Quiroga, H. In the middle of the night
  Wang Ping. Maverick
  Yolen, J. The river maid
Rivers to Gilead. Davenport, S.

Riverside. Bradburd, R.
RIVIERA (FRANCE AND ITALY)
  Templeton, E. The blue hour
The **Road**. Buchanan, C.
The **road**. Sillitoe, A.
The **Road** Back to Destruction Bay. White, L. M.
The **road** es traveled. Fisher, C.
The **road** from prosperity. Welch, N.
The **road** home. Hammett, D.
The **road** home. Updike, J.
The **Road** On. Wright, D.
The **road** out of town. Reid, G.
The **road** to Carville. Tompkins, P.
The **road** to endless sleep. Fiscus, J.
The **Road** to Hofuf. Johnson, N.
Road to Inspiration. See Leonard, E. The colonel's lady [variant title: Road to Inspiration]
Road to nightfall. Silverberg, R.
The **road** to Platero. Anaya, R. A.
The **road** to Rachel. Berliner, J.
The **road** to recovery. Frost, G.
The **Road** to San Sebastian. Mountjoy, J.
Road trip. McLean, S.
Roadkill. Cully, S.
ROADS
  Clark, S. Langthwaite Road
The **Roads** of Home. Updike, J.
Roadshow. Rabe, J.
The **roaming** forest. Moorcock, M.
The **roaring** ground. Finch, S.
The **roaring** trumpet. De Camp, L. S. and Pratt, F.
Robb, Donna Marie
  Soul Spinner
    Femspec v4 no2 p281-92 2004
ROBBER BARONS *See* Capitalists and financiers
ROBBERS *See* Brigands and robbers; Robbery
ROBBERY
    See also Bank robbers; Theft
  Alessio, Carolyn. Casualidades
  Angel, J. Whistle pig
  Brady, C. The dazzling world
  Bruen, K. Black stuff
  Bukowski, C. Just passing time
  Clevenger, C. The numbers game
  Ferrigno, R. The hour when the ship comes in
  Fonseca, R. Happy New Year
  Ford, E. Elwood's last job
  Gilchrist, E. The famous poll at Jody's Bar
  Hammett, D. The green elephant
  Hinton, S. E. No white light no tunnel
  Hodgson, W. H. Diamond cut diamond with a vengeance
  King, J. Snake eyes
  Kinman, G. T. Catnapping
  Knight, M. Smash and grab
  Lange, R. Loss prevention
  Larsen, T. Lids
  Lupoff, R. A. The Crimson Wizard and the jewels of Lemuria
  Magee, K. Straitjacket
  Mendes, B. Fleeting fashion
  Mofina, R. Lightning rider
  Morgan, S. Street court
  Mueenuddin, D. Nawabdin Electrician
  Muller, E. Kid's last fight
  Oates, J. C. The knife
  O'Brien, T. What's the score?
  Phan, A. Visitors

ROBBERY—*Continued*

Phillips, G. House of tears

Pinter, J. The point guard

Rock, P. Stranger

Shomer, E. Fill in the blank

Smith, M. M. Fair exchange

Téllez, H. Prelude

Treat, J. Trail

Vincent, B. Rule number one

Zelazny, R. My lady of the diodes

Zoshchenko, M. Love

Robbins, A. B.

The magic touch: a Peter Pansy detective yarn

The International Association of Crime Writers presents Murder in Vegas; new crime tales of gambling and desperation; edited by Michael Connelly

Robbins, Tod

Spurs

Adaptations: from short story to big screen; 35 great stories that have inspired great films; edited by Stephanie Harrison

Roberson, Chris

And such small deer

Year's best fantasy 8; edited by David G. Hartwell, Kathryn Cramer

Death on the crosstime express

Sideways in crime; an alternate mystery anthology; edited by Lou Anders

Gold mountain

The Year's best science fiction: twenty-third annual collection; edited by Gardner Dozois

Merridew of abominable memory

Gaslight grimoire; fantastic tales of Sherlock Holmes; edited by J. R. Campbell and Charles Prepolec

Monster radio

This is my funniest 2; leading science fiction writers present their funniest stories ever; edited by Mike Resnick

The sky is large and the earth is small

The Best science fiction and fantasy of the year: volume two; edited by Jonathan Strahan

The Year's best science fiction: twenty-fifth annual collection; edited by Gardner Dozois

Roberson, Jennifer

Blood of sorcery

Roberson, J. Guinevere's truth and other tales

By the time I get to Phoenix

Roberson, J. Guinevere's truth and other tales

A compromised Christmas

Roberson, J. Guinevere's truth and other tales

Ending, and beginning

Roberson, J. Guinevere's truth and other tales

Fair play

Roberson, J. Guinevere's truth and other tales

Garden of glories

Roberson, J. Guinevere's truth and other tales

Guinevere's truth

Roberson, J. Guinevere's truth and other tales

In his name

Roberson, J. Guinevere's truth and other tales

Jesus freaks

Roberson, J. Guinevere's truth and other tales

The lady and the Tiger

Roberson, J. Guinevere's truth and other tales

A lesser working

Roberson, J. Guinevere's truth and other tales

Mad Jack

Roberson, J. Guinevere's truth and other tales

Of honor and the lion

Roberson, J. Guinevere's truth and other tales

Piece of mind

Roberson, J. Guinevere's truth and other tales

Rite of passage

Roberson, J. Guinevere's truth and other tales

Shadows in the wood

Roberson, J. Guinevere's truth and other tales

Sleeping dogs

Roberson, J. Guinevere's truth and other tales

Spoils of war

Roberson, J. Guinevere's truth and other tales

Valley of the shadow

Roberson, J. Guinevere's truth and other tales

A wolf upon the wind

Roberson, J. Guinevere's truth and other tales

Robert, Marc

Erzählungenlied

The Kenyon Review ns27 no3 p36-7 Summ 2005

Robert Earl and W. C. Shirley, P.

Robert Horncroft, naked. Rust, E. M.

Roberts, Adam

Allen met the Devil

Roberts, A. Swiftly; stories that never were and might not be

And tomorrow and

Elemental; the Tsunami relief anthology; stories of science fiction and fantasy; [edited by] Steven Savile and Alethea Kontis; introduction by Arthur C. Clarke

Blindness and invisibility

Roberts, A. Swiftly; stories that never were and might not be

Dantesque

Roberts, A. Swiftly; stories that never were and might not be

Eleanor

Roberts, A. Swiftly; stories that never were and might not be

Jupiter magnified

Roberts, A. Swiftly; stories that never were and might not be

Me-topia

Science fiction: the best of the year 2007 edition; edited by Rich Horton

New model computer

Roberts, A. Swiftly; stories that never were and might not be

The question of [?query term]

Roberts, A. Swiftly; stories that never were and might not be

The siege of Fadiman

Roberts, A. Swiftly; stories that never were and might not be

Stationary acceleration

Roberts, A. Swiftly; stories that never were and might not be

Swiftly

Roberts, A. Swiftly; stories that never were and might not be

The time telephone

Roberts, A. Swiftly; stories that never were and might not be

Tour de Lune

Roberts, A. Swiftly; stories that never were and might not be

Roberts, Jason

7C

    McSweeney's enchanted chamber of astonishing stories; edited by Michael Chabon; illustrations by Mike Mignola

Roberts, Joshua

Revolver

    Agni no61 p92-106 2005

Roberts, Nathan

This is not skin

    Best new American voices 2004; guest editor John Casey; series editors John Kulka and Natalie Danford

Roberts, Peter

The trial of Jeremy Owens

    Nature v443 p244 S 14 2006

Roberts, Ralph

The flim-flam alien

    This is my funniest; leading science fiction writers present their funniest stories ever; edited by Mike Resnick

Roberts, Scott M.

Eviction notice

    Orson Scott Card's Intergalctic medicine show; [edited by] Edmund R. Schubert and Orson Scott Card

Roberts, Amy Sayre- *See* Sayre-Roberts, Amy

Robin, Régine

The wanderer [excerpt]

    Contemporary Jewish writing in Canada; an anthology; edited by Michael Greenstein

The **robin**. Vidal, G.

Robinson, Eden

Terminal Avenue

    So long been dreaming; postcolonial science fiction & fantasy; Nalo Hopkinson & Uppinder Mehan, eds

Robinson, Frank M.

The Santa Claus planet

    This is my funniest 2; leading science fiction writers present their funniest stories ever; edited by Mike Resnick

Robinson, John

Walking after Dark

    The Sewanee Review v113 no3 p388-403 Summ 2005

Robinson, Kim Stanley

Glacier

    Asimov's science fiction: 30th anniversary anthology; edited by Sheila Williams

Prometheus unbound, at last

    Nature v436 p888 Ag 11 2005

Robinson, Lewis

Cuxabexis, Cuxabexis

    Before; short stories about pregnancy from our top writers; edited by Emily Franklin and Heather Swain

Finches

    Contemporary Maine fiction; an anthology of short stories; edited by Wesley McNair

Robinson, Marilynne

Jack

    Harper's v317 p62-72 Ag 2008

Robinson, Peter

Birthday dance

    Thou shalt not kill; biblical mystery stories; edited by Anne Perry

The cherub affair

    The World's finest mystery and crime stories, fifth annual collection; edited by Ed Gorman and Martin H. Greenberg

The Eastvale Ladies' Poker Circle

    Dead man's hand; crime fiction at the poker table; edited by Otto Penzler.

The magic of your touch

    The Best British mysteries, 2006; edited by Maxim Jakubowski

The price of love

    Mystery Writers of America presents the blue religion; new stories about cops, criminals, and the chase; edited by Michael Connelly

Shadow on the water

    The Best British mysteries, 2005; edited by Maxim Jakubowski

Robinson, Roxana

Assez

    Robinson, R. A perfect stranger; and other stories; Roxana Robinson

Assistance

    Robinson, R. A perfect stranger; and other stories; Roxana Robinson

At the beach

    Robinson, R. A perfect stranger; and other stories; Roxana Robinson

Blind man

    Robinson, R. A perfect stranger; and other stories; Roxana Robinson

Choosing sides

    Robinson, R. A perfect stranger; and other stories; Roxana Robinson

Embrace

    This is not chick lit; original stories by America's best women writers; edited by Elizabeth Merrick

The face-lift

    Robinson, R. A perfect stranger; and other stories; Roxana Robinson

Family Christmas

    Robinson, R. A perfect stranger; and other stories; Roxana Robinson

The Finish Line

    Good Housekeeping v247 no4 p187-8, 190-1, 194, 196-8 O 2008

The football game

    Robinson, R. A perfect stranger; and other stories; Roxana Robinson

Intersection

    Robinson, R. A perfect stranger; and other stories; Roxana Robinson

The Leap

    The American Scholar v77 no1 p92-100 Wint 2008

A perfect stranger

    Robinson, R. A perfect stranger; and other stories; Roxana Robinson

Pilgrimage

    Robinson, R. A perfect stranger; and other stories; Roxana Robinson

Shame

    Robinson, R. A perfect stranger; and other stories; Roxana Robinson

The treatment

    Robinson, R. A perfect stranger; and other stories; Roxana Robinson

Robinson, Spider
Too hot to hoot
  This is my funniest; leading science fiction
    writers present their funniest stories ever;
    edited by Mike Resnick
Robison, Carol
Sharks
  Calyx v22 no3 p8-12 Summ 2005
Robison, Mary
Likely Lake
  Pushcart Prize XXVIII: best of the small
    presses 2004; edited by Bill Henderson and
    the Pushcart prize editors
Yours
  My mistress's sparrow is dead; great love sto-
    ries, from Chekhov to Munro; edited by
    Jeffrey Eugenides
Robot dreams. Asimov, I.
The **robot** who came to dinner. Goulart, R.
ROBOTS
Aldiss, B. W. Supertoys last all summer long
Anderson, P. The immortal game
Anderson, P. Kings who die
Asimov, I. Robot dreams
Baker, K. Oh, false young man!
Barthelme, D. Subpoena
Barton, W. Off on a starship
Bear, E. Tideline
Bear, G. Ram shift phase 2
Beaulieu, B. P. Chasing humanity
Bierce, A. Moxon's master
Bluestein, E. Abio or love at first sight
Bradbury, R. April 2026: The long years
Bradbury, R. A blade of grass
Bradbury, R. Changeling
Bradbury, R. Downwind from Gettysburg
Bradbury, R. G.B.S.- Mark V
Chase, M. Brothers
Cohen, J. Last transmission; or, Man with a
  robotic ermine
Davis, R. Engines of desire & despair
Doctorow, C. I, robot
Evans, R. Touch sensitive
Ford, J. The seventh expression of the robot
  general
Goulart, R. The robot who came to dinner
Hubbard, L. R. Battle of wizards
Hunt, S. Love machine
Iagnemma, K. The upgrade
Kelly, J. P. Bernardo's house
Kelly, J. P. The best Christmas ever
Lai, L. Rachel
Lain, D. "Identity is a construct"
Lanagan, M. Machine maid
Martin, G. R. R. Meathouse man
Marusek, D. The wedding album
Matheson, R. Brother to the machine
Matheson, R. Lazarus II
Matheson, R. Steel
McDonald, I. Sanjeev and Robotwallah
Millhauser, S. The new automaton theater
Modesitt, L. E., Jr. Precision set
Mommers, H. W. Habemus papam
Moore, C. L. No woman born
Nestvold, R. Exit without savings
Nolan, W. F. Freak
Nolan, W. F. The mating of Thirdburt
Oates, J. C. EDickinsonRepliLuxe
Pohl, F. The celebrated no-hit inning

Pohl, F. Servant of the people
Pratt, T. and Van Eekhout, G. Robots and fall-
  ing hearts
Reynolds, A. Zima blue
Roberts, A. And tomorrow and
Scholes, K. Of metal men and scarlet thread and
  dancing with the sunrise
Silverberg, R. Going down smooth
Silverberg, R. Good news from the Vatican
Silverberg, R. The Iron Chancellor
Silverberg, R. Ozymandias
Silverberg, R. The sixth palace
Sterling, B. Green days in Brunei
Stross, C. Down on the farm
Stross, C. Trunk and disorderly
Swanwick, M. Ancient engines
Thomas, J. Precious metal
Thomas, J. The pressman
Tiptree, J. The girl who was plugged in
Waldrop, H. Our mortal span
Weber, D. Miles to go
Weber, D. The traitor
Williamson, J. With folded hands
Wolfe, G. The marvelous brass chessplaying au-
  tomaton
Zelazny, R. Devil car (Jenny/Murdoch)
Zelazny, R. The engine at Heartspring's Center
Zelazny, R. The force that through the circuit
  drives the current
Zelazny, R. The great slow kings
Zelazny, R. Halfjack
Zelazny, R. Home is the hangman
Zelazny, R. The last of the wild ones
Zelazny, R. Passion play
Zelazny, R. The stainless steel leech
Robots & Zombies, Inc. Sussex, L.
Robots and falling hearts. Pratt, T. and Van
  Eekhout, G.
Robson, Justina
Cracklegrackle
  The new space opera 2; edited by Gardner
    Dozois and Jonathan Strahan
Dreadnought
  Nature v434 p680 Mr 31 2005
The girl hero's mirror says he's not the one
  Fast forward 1; future fiction from the cutting
    edge; edited by Lou Anders
Robson, L. L. (Leslie Lloyd)
Chupa mi pena, baby
  Urban Welsh; new short fiction; edited by
    Lewis Davies
Robson, Leslie Lloyd *See* Robson, L. L. (Leslie
  Lloyd), 1931-
Rock, Laura
Moving
  Dalhousie Review v87 no1 p101-8 Spr 2007
Rock, Peter
Balancing genius
  Politically inspired; edited by Stephen Elliott;
    assistant editor, Gabriel Kram; associate ed-
    itors, Elizabeth Brooks [et al.]
Blooms
  Rock, P. The unsettling; stories
Disappeared girls
  Rock, P. The unsettling; stories
Disentangling
  Rock, P. The unsettling; stories
Gold firebird
  Rock, P. The unsettling; stories

Rock, Peter—*Continued*
New stories from the Southwest; edited by D. Seth Horton; foreword by Ray Gonzalez.
Halo effect
Rock, P. The unsettling; stories
Johnson Creek
StoryQuarterly v42 p159-75 2006
Lights
Rock, P. The unsettling; stories
Pergrine falcon
Rock, P. The unsettling; stories
Shaken
Rock, P. The unsettling; stories
The sharpest knife
Rock, P. The unsettling; stories
Signal mirror
Rock, P. The unsettling; stories
The silent men
Rock, P. The unsettling; stories
Western Humanities Review v59 no2 p145-63 Fall 2005
Stranger
Rock, P. The unsettling; stories
Thrill
Rock, P. The unsettling; stories
The **rock**. Gildner, G.
Rock Brake. Schwartz, J.
ROCK CLIMBING
Haschemeyer, O. The fantome of Fatma
Proulx, A. Testimony of the donkey
Rock critic murders [excerpt] Sublett, J.
ROCK MUSIC
Allen, P. G. Burned alive in the blues
Bates, J. W. The ungrateful dead
Benioff, D. When the nines roll over
Boudinot, R. The flautist
Burke, J. L. The night Johnny Ace died
Cadigan, P. The final remake of *The return of Little Latin Larry,* with a completely remastered soundtrack and the original audience
Cooper, D. One night in 1979 I did too much coke and couldn't sleep and had what I thought was a million-dollar idea to write the definitive tell-all book about glam rock based on my own personal experience but this is as far as I got
De Lint, C. That was radio clash
Di Filippo, P. Slowhand and Little Sister
Faber, M. Beyond pain
Gischler, V. Kill posse
Holder, N. I know who you ate last summer
Holder, N. Out twelve-steppin, summer of AA
July, M. I kiss a door
Kelly, R. Blood suede shoes
Kihn, G. Queen of the groupies
Kun, M. The blue engines
Lane, J. An unknown past
MacEnulty, P. Purple haze
McAuley, P. J. Take me to the river
McCafferty, J. Dear Mr. Springsteen
Mellick, C. City hobgoblins
Moorcock, M. A dead singer
Nolan, W. F. Jenny among the zeebs
Phillips, G. Where all our dreams come true
Puchner, E. Essay #3: Leda and the swan
Reidy, D. Dancing man
Reidy, D. Look and feel
Richter, S. The long hall

Rubin, J. Little stones, little pistols, little clash
Shepard, J. Won't get fooled again
Shepard, L. Stars seen through stone
Sterling, B. Are you for 86?
Trezise, R. Merry go-rounds
Waldrop, H. Flying saucer rock and roll
Zumas, L. Thieves and mapmakers
ROCK MUSICIANS *See* Rock music
Rock Star. Conroy-Goldman, M.
ROCKEFELLER, MICHAEL CLARK, 1938-1961?
About
Stokes, C. The man who ate Michael Rockefeller
Rocket ride. Davidson, C.
Rocklynne, Ross
Time wants a skeleton
The Mammoth book of golden age science fiction; edited by Isaac Asimov, Charles G. Waugh and Martin H. Greenberg
ROCKS
Zelazny, R. Collector's fever
Rockwood, Lucas
That's How She Says Goodbye
Confrontation no92/93 p171-81 Fall 2005/Wint 2006
ROCKY MOUNTAINS
Bacigalupi, P. The tamarisk hunter
Roden, Barbara
Northwest passage
The Year's best fantasy and horror: nineteenth annual collection; edited by Ellen Datlow and Kelly Link & Gavin J. Grant
The things that shall come upon them
Gaslight grimoire; fantastic tales of Sherlock Holmes; edited by J. R. Campbell and Charles Prepolec
RODEOS
Fuentes, M. Looking for eight
Roderick, David
Pace
Prairie Schooner v79 no3 p94-105 Fall 2005
Rodgers, Susan Jackson
Beautiful things
Rodgers, S. J. The trouble with you is and other stories
Bones and flowers
Rodgers, S. J. The trouble with you is and other stories
Bust
Rodgers, S. J. The trouble with you is and other stories
Delivery
Rodgers, S. J. The trouble with you is and other stories
Fits and starts
Rodgers, S. J. The trouble with you is and other stories
Green beans
Rodgers, S. J. The trouble with you is and other stories
How I spent my summer vacation
Rodgers, S. J. The trouble with you is and other stories
I've Looked Everywhere
StoryQuarterly v41 p454-7 2005
Lost spirits
Rodgers, S. J. The trouble with you is and other stories

Rohrlich, Ruby
Citizen in the south
"Tell it to us easy" and other stories; a complete short fiction anthology of African American women writers in Opportunity magazine, (1923-1948); edited by Judith Musser.

Roiphe, Emily
Little trouble girl
Noise; fiction inspired by Sonic Youth; edited bt Peter Wild; introduction by Lee Ranaldo
Role Model. Pompeo, A.

Roley, Brian Ascalon
American son [excerpt]
California uncovered; stories for the 21st century; edited by Chitra Banerjee Divakaruni, William E. Justice, and James Quay
Anesthesia
The North American Review v291 no3/4 p45-50 My/Ag 2006
Blood of Jose Rizal
Prairie Schooner v80 no1 p91-100 Spr 2006
Kinship
Los Angeles noir; edited by Denise Hamilton
Roll. Desaulniers, J.
Roll your owns. Fisher, C.
Rolling over. Angel, J.
Rolling the bones. Savage, T.

Rollins, James
Kowalski's in love
Thriller; edited by James Patterson

Rollins, William
Chicago confetti
The Black Lizard big book of pulps; edited by Otto Penzler

Rollo, Gord
Lost in a field of paper flowers
British invasion; edited by Christopher Golden, Tim Lebbon & James A. Moore
Rollo's dairy (Jake and Deedee). Anderson, B.

Rolnick, Josh
Big River
Western Humanities Review v61 no2 p85-110 Spr/Summ 2007
Pulp and Paper
Harvard Review (1992) no34 p137-47 2008
Roma. McCabe, E.

Roman, Celso
Vendors of peculiar objects
The Flight of the condor; stories of violence and war from Colombia; translated and compiled by Jennifer Gabrielle Edwards; foreword by Hugo Chaparro Valderrama.
Roman arches. Corso, P.
ROMAN CATHOLIC CHURCH *See* Catholic faith
ROMAN CATHOLIC RELIGION *See* Catholic faith
ROMAN EMPIRE *See* Rome
Roman holidays. Franceschini, E.
Roman holidays; or, SPQ-arrrrrr. Caine, R.
ROMAN SOLDIERS *See* Soldiers—Rome
A **romance**. Romm, R.
Romance in the blue bathroom. Kalpakian, L.
Romance manual. Dean, D.
ROMANCES (LOVE STORIES) *See* Love affairs; Love stories
ROMANIA
Adameşteanu, G. Provisional [excerpt]

Matheson, R. No such thing as a vampire
Toganov, B. The children
ROMANIANS
United States
Iarovici, D. Practical
Iarovici, D. Waiting for power
Romano, Clarissa
Predicting the Weather
South Carolina Review v39 no1 p196-200 Fall 2006
Romano, Tony
America
Romano, T. If you eat, you never die; chicago tales
Bllod lines
Romano, T. If you eat, you never die; chicago tales
The casket
Romano, T. If you eat, you never die; chicago tales
City Hall
Romano, T. If you eat, you never die; chicago tales
Comic books
Romano, T. If you eat, you never die; chicago tales
Confidences
Romano, T. If you eat, you never die; chicago tales
The day of settlement
Romano, T. If you eat, you never die; chicago tales
Deep left
Romano, T. If you eat, you never die; chicago tales
Fixing a hole
Romano, T. If you eat, you never die; chicago tales
Hungers
Romano, T. If you eat, you never die; chicago tales
If you eat, you never die
Romano, T. If you eat, you never die; chicago tales
In motion
Romano, T. If you eat, you never die; chicago tales
Milkboy
Romano, T. If you eat, you never die; chicago tales
New neighborhood
Romano, T. If you eat, you never die; chicago tales
No balls
Romano, T. If you eat, you never die; chicago tales
On hold
Romano, T. If you eat, you never die; chicago tales
One up
Romano, T. If you eat, you never die; chicago tales
Silences
Romano, T. If you eat, you never die; chicago tales
Sulfur memories
Romano, T. If you eat, you never die; chicago tales

Romano, Tony—*Continued*

Sundays
 Romano, T. If you eat, you never die; chicago tales
Trace
 Romano, T. If you eat, you never die; chicago tales
Treading water
 Romano, T. If you eat, you never die; chicago tales
When the rains come
 Romano, T. If you eat, you never die; chicago tales
Whistle opera
 Romano, T. If you eat, you never die; chicago tales

Romantic fever. Harleman, A.

A **romantic** inclination. Levithan, D.

A **romantic** poet and his destiny. Ruefle, M.

A **romantic** weekend. Gaitskill, M.

Romanticore. Pratt, T.

ROME

De Camp, L. S. Lest darkness fall
Duane, D. The fix
Fiscus, J. The road to endless sleep
Howard, R. E. Worms of the earth
Linscott, G. Gracious silence
Pohl, F. Waiting for the Olympians
Silverberg, R. With Caesar in the underworld

30 B.C.-476 A.D.

Shepard, J. Hadrian's wall

History

30 B.C.-476 A.D., Empire
Auchincloss, L. The grandeur that was Byzantium

ROME (ITALY) *See* Italy—Rome

Rome, Autumn 1510. Gualdoni, F.

Romero, Pedro Jorge

(jt. auth) See De la Casa, Ricard and Romero, Pedro Jorge

"**Rometta** and Giulieo". Gangbo, J. M.

Romicide. Kelly, R.

Romm, Robin

The arrival
 Romm, R. The mother garden; stories
The beads
 Romm, R. The mother garden; stories
Celia's fish
 Romm, R. The mother garden; stories
The egg game
 Romm, R. The mother garden; stories
Family epic
 Romm, R. The mother garden; stories
Lost and found
 Romm, R. The mother garden; stories
The mother garden
 Romm, R. The mother garden; stories
No small feat
 Romm, R. The mother garden; stories
A romance
 Romm, R. The mother garden; stories
The tilt
 Romm, R. The mother garden; stories
Weight
 Romm, R. The mother garden; stories
Where nothing is
 Romm, R. The mother garden; stories

Roncagliolo, Santiago

Internal Affairs
 The Virginia Quarterly Review v83 no4 p224-39 Fall 2007

Ronk, Martha Clare

La Belle Dame
 Ronk, M. C. Glass grapes; and other stories; [by] Martha Ronk.
Blue/Green
 Ronk, M. C. Glass grapes; and other stories; [by] Martha Ronk.
Cones
 Ronk, M. C. Glass grapes; and other stories; [by] Martha Ronk.
The flea market
 Ronk, M. C. Glass grapes; and other stories; [by] Martha Ronk.
The gift
 Ronk, M. C. Glass grapes; and other stories; [by] Martha Ronk.
Glass grapes
 Ronk, M. C. Glass grapes; and other stories; [by] Martha Ronk.
Hands
 Ronk, M. C. Glass grapes; and other stories; [by] Martha Ronk.
Her subject/his subject
 Ronk, M. C. Glass grapes; and other stories; [by] Martha Ronk.
The letter
 Ronk, M. C. Glass grapes; and other stories; [by] Martha Ronk.
The lightbulb
 Ronk, M. C. Glass grapes; and other stories; [by] Martha Ronk.
Like visiting Joseph Cornell
 Ronk, M. C. Glass grapes; and other stories; [by] Martha Ronk.
Listening in
 Ronk, M. C. Glass grapes; and other stories; [by] Martha Ronk.
Marybeth and the fish
 Ronk, M. C. Glass grapes; and other stories; [by] Martha Ronk.
My son and the bicycle wheel
 Ronk, M. C. Glass grapes; and other stories; [by] Martha Ronk.
Myopia
 Ronk, M. C. Glass grapes; and other stories; [by] Martha Ronk.
Old nylon bathrobes
 Ronk, M. C. Glass grapes; and other stories; [by] Martha Ronk.
Page 42
 Ronk, M. C. Glass grapes; and other stories; [by] Martha Ronk.
The photograph
 Ronk, M. C. Glass grapes; and other stories; [by] Martha Ronk.
The ring
 Ronk, M. C. Glass grapes; and other stories; [by] Martha Ronk.
The score
 Ronk, M. C. Glass grapes; and other stories; [by] Martha Ronk.
The sofa
 Ronk, M. C. Glass grapes; and other stories; [by] Martha Ronk.

Ronk, Martha Clare—*Continued*

Soft conversation

Ronk, M. C. Glass grapes; and other stories; [by] Martha Ronk.

The tattoo

Ronk, M. C. Glass grapes; and other stories; [by] Martha Ronk.

The tea bowl

Ronk, M. C. Glass grapes; and other stories; [by] Martha Ronk.

Their calendar

Ronk, M. C. Glass grapes; and other stories; [by] Martha Ronk.

The watch

Ronk, M. C. Glass grapes; and other stories; [by] Martha Ronk.

The **Roof** of the World. Buckner, D.

Roof of the world. Lamb, H.

ROOFS

McLean, S. On the roof

Quiroga, H. The incense tree roof

The **room**. Hubbard, L. R.

The **room**. Parks, T.

The **room**. Trevor, W.

Room for a fourth. Hamilton, S.

A **room** in Linden. Kiely, B.

The **room** in the attic. Millhauser, S.

A **room** in Tsukiji. Yasuoka, S.

Room no. 12. Maḥfūẓ, N.

The **room** outside. Maxwell, W.

Room to move. Coward, M.

A **roomful** of Christmas. Temple, S.

Roomful of witnesses. Stine, R. L.

The **rooming** house. Wolven, S.

ROOMING HOUSES *See* Boarding houses

ROOMMATES

Barkley, B. Another perfect catastrophe

Barrett, M. Grip

Eisenberg, D. Twilight of the superheroes

Enright, A. Pale hands I loved, beside the Shalimar

Enright, A. Pillow

Gaitskill, M. College town, 1980

Jackson, S. Egg

Keret, E. Bottle

Martin, G. R. R. Remembering Melody

Meno, J. Art school is boring so

Mohanraj, M. A. Mint in your mouth (San Francisco, 1990)

Nevill, A. L. G. Yellow teeth

Pratt, T. Living with the harpy

Riley, G. Sick notes

Romm, R. A romance

The **rooms** of fear. Hodgson, W. H.

Rooney, Frank

Cyclists' raid

Adaptations: from short story to big screen; 35 great stories that have inspired great films; edited by Stephanie Harrison

Roorbach, Bill

Harbinger Hall

Atlantic Monthly (1993) v294 no5 p147-50, 152-4, 156-62, 164-6 D 2004

A job at Little Henry's

Contemporary Maine fiction; an anthology of short stories; edited by Wesley McNair

ROOSEVELT, ALICE HATHAWAY LEE, 1861-1884

About

Resnick, M. The light that binds, hte claws that catch

Roosevelt, Teddy *See* Roosevelt, Theodore, 1858-1919

ROOSEVELT, THEODORE, 1858-1919

About

Bierce, A. An ancient hunter

Bierce, A. A leaf blown in from days to be

Resnick, M. The Bull Moose at bay

Resnick, M. Bully!

Resnick, M. The light that binds, hte claws that catch

Resnick, M. Over there

Resnick, M. Redchapel

Resnick, M. The Roosevelt dispatches

Resnick, M. Two hunters in Manhattan

The **Roosevelt** dispatches. Resnick, M.

Rooster, pollard, cricket, goose. Holland, N.

ROOSTERS

Winn, T. Cantogallo

Root, Amy

Solstice

Southern Humanities Review v41 no4 p342-50 Fall 2007

Root, Mary

The Darkest Skies in North America

South Carolina Review v41 no2 p32-42 Spr 2009

Root. Koretsky, J. L.

The **root** of Ampoi. Smith, C. A.

The **Root** of the Problem. Abbey, L. J.

Root worker. Jones, E. P.

The **roots** of Western civilization. Gildner, G.

Ropa Vieja. Lippman, L.

Rope. Porter, K. A.

Rope-a-dope. McDonald, C.

The **rope** trick. Sillitoe, A.

The **ropedancer:** an introduction. Gifford, B.

The **Ropewalk**. Brown, K.

Roque, Mariela Varona

The orchid

Havana noir; edited by Achy Obejas

Roripaugh, Lee Ann

Amphibious Life

The North American Review v290 no3/4 p45-9 My/Ag 2005

Sugar Plum Fairy

River Styx no69/70 p70-84 2005

Rosa, João Guimarães

The girl from beyond

Oxford anthology of the Brazilian short story; edited by K. David Jackson

The jaguar

Oxford anthology of the Brazilian short story; edited by K. David Jackson

Much ado

Oxford anthology of the Brazilian short story; edited by K. David Jackson

Sorôco, his mother, his daughter

Oxford anthology of the Brazilian short story; edited by K. David Jackson

The third bank of the river

Oxford anthology of the Brazilian short story; edited by K. David Jackson

Rosenbaum, Benjamin—*Continued*
Sense and sensibility
Rosenbaum, B. The ant king and other stories
A siege of cranes
The Year's best fantasy and horror: twentieth annual collection; edited by Ellen Datlow and Kelly Link & Gavin J. Grant
Rosenbaum, B. The ant king and other stories
Start the clock
The Year's best science fiction: twenty-second annual collection; edited by Gardner Dozois
Rosenbaum, B. The ant king and other stories
The valley of giants
The Year's best fantasy and horror: seventeenth annual collection; edited by Ellen Datlow, Kelly Link and Gavin J. Grant
Rosenbaum, B. The ant king and other stories
(jt. auth) See Ackert, David and Rosenbaum, Benjamin
Rosenbaum, Benjamin and Ackert, David
Stray
The Year's best science fiction: twenty-fifth annual collection; edited by Gardner Dozois
Rosenbaum, Stephen A.
An Abalone Opportunity
Thomas M. Cooley Journal of Practical & Clinical Law v8 no1 p15-23 2006
Rosenberg, Jill
The Land of Sunshine and Flowers
South Carolina Review v38 no1 p62-71 Fall 2005
Rosenberg, Yudel
The Golem; or, The miraculous deeds of Rabbi Liva [excerpt]
No star too beautiful; Yiddish stories from 1382 to the present; compiled and translated by Joachim Neugroschel
Rosenblatt, Roger
Death Explains Himself
The Kenyon Review v27 no2 p14 Spr 2005
Rosenblum, Mary Helene
Color vision
Wizards; edited by Jack Dann and Gardner Dozois
Home movies
The Year's best science fiction: twenty-fourth annual collection; edited by Gardner Dozois
Sacrifice
Sideways in crime; an alternate mystery anthology; edited by Lou Anders
Search engine
The Year's best science fiction: twenty-third annual collection; edited by Gardner Dozois
Rewired; the post-cyberpunk anthology; James Patrick Kelly & John Kessel, editors
Skin deep
The Year's best science fiction: twenty-second annual collection; edited by Gardner Dozois
Splinters of glass
The new space opera; edited by Gardner Dozois and Jonathan Strahan
Rosenfarb, Chava
A Friday in the life of Sarah Zonabend
Contemporary Jewish writing in Canada; an anthology; edited by Michael Greenstein

Letters to God
Arguing with the storm; stories by Yiddish women writers; edited and with a preface by Rhea Tregebov; introduction by Kathryn Hellerstein.
Rosenfarb, Chava
Bociany
No star too beautiful; Yiddish stories from 1382 to the present; compiled and translated by Joachim Neugroschel
Rosenfeld, Lucinda
Yuppie
The dictionary of failed relationships; 26 tales of love gone wrong; edited by Meredith Broussard
Rosenfeld, Yoyne
Miss Bertha
No star too beautiful; Yiddish stories from 1382 to the present; compiled and translated by Joachim Neugroschel
Rosenthal, Lucy
Solid food
Scribblers on the roof; contemporary American Jewish fiction; edited by Melvin Jules Bukiet and David G. Roskies
Rosenvall's Cage. Tuttle, S.
Rosenwaike, Polly
Catcalling: A Desire Story in Nine Parts
River Styx no74 p18-28 2007
ROSES
Marshall, A. J. By any other name
Porter, J. A. Merrymount
ROSH HA-SHANAH
Molodowsky, K. From Leyb the shoemaker
Rosie Little in the Mother Country. Wood, D.
Rosie Little joins the dots. Wood, D.
Rosie Little's brilliant career. Wood, D.
Ross, Gary Earl
Dead reckoning
Medium of murder; edited by Susan Budavari and Suzanne Flaig
Rossberger. Hagelstein, C.
Rossi, Cristina Peri *See* Peri Rossi, Cristina, 1941-
Rossi, Jeri Cain
And hell walked in
New Orleans noir; edited by Julie Smith
Rossiter, Ellen
Questions of war
Stumbling and raging; more politically inspired fiction; edited by Stephen Elliott; with associate editors Greg Larson [et al.]
Rossonian days. Lewis, W. H.
Roszak, Theodore
The Devil's Playground
Film Comment v40 no6 p64, 67-70 N/D 2004
The **rotator**. Sargent, P.
Roth, Henry
The cellar
Inside the hornet's head; an anthology of Jewish American writing; edited by Jerome Charyn
Freight
The New Yorker v82 no30 p100, 102-4, 106-13 S 25 2006
God the Novelist
The New Yorker v82 no15 p72-5 My 29 2006

Roth, Matthue

Beating around the burning bush
  Homewrecker: an adultery reader; edited by
    Daphne Gottlieb

Roth, Philip

Cunt crazy
  Inside the hornet's head; an anthology of
    Jewish American writing; edited by Jerome
    Charyn

Epstein
  The Paris review book for planes, trains, ele-
    vators, and waiting rooms; by the editors of
    the Paris review; with an introduction by
    Richard Powers

Rothenberger, Michele

Damon and Pythias
  Parabola v29 no4 p79-80 Wint 2004

Le rouge et le noir. Lu, A.

Round heels. Meaker, M.

Roundheads and Cavaliers. James, C. L. R.

Rounding third. Angel, J.

The **Roup**. Frame, R.

"Rovera". Grossman, J.

Row, Jess

The American girl
  Row, J. The train to Lo Wu; stories
The ferry
  Row, J. The train to Lo Wu; stories
For you
  Row, J. The train to Lo Wu; stories
Heaven Lake
  Row, J. The train to Lo Wu; stories
Lives of the Saints
  Ploughshares v35 no1 p126-41 Spr 2009
Revolutions
  Row, J. The train to Lo Wu; stories
The secrets of bats
  Row, J. The train to Lo Wu; stories
The train to Lo Wu
  Row, J. The train to Lo Wu; stories
  Ploughshares v30 no4 p112-32 Wint
    2004/2005

Rowe, Christopher

Another word for map is faith
  The Year's best fantasy and horror: twentieth
    annual collection; edited by Ellen Datlow
    and Kelly Link & Gavin J. Grant
  Science fiction: the best of the year 2007 edi-
    tion; edited by Rich Horton
Gather
  The Del Rey book of science fiction and fan-
    tasy; sixteen original works by speculative
    fiction's finest voices; edited by Ellen
    Datlow
The voluntary state
  The Year's best science fiction: twenty-
    second annual collection; edited by Gardner
    Dozois
  Nebula Awards showcase 2006; the year's
    best SF and fantasy; selected by the Sci-
    ence Fiction and Fantasy Writers of Ameri-
    ca; edited by Gardner Dozois
  Rewired; the post-cyberpunk anthology;
    James Patrick Kelly & John Kessel, editors

Rowe, Rosemary

Caveat emptor
  The Best British mysteries, 2005; edited by
    Maxim Jakubowski

Roxie. Reed, R.

Roy, Reena

One Hundred Rubies of a Pomegranate
  Frontiers v27 no1 p116-29 2006

Roy Spivey. July, M.

Royal Blue. Baxter, C.

The **Royal** Flush Saga. Hunault, A.

The **royal** ghosts. Upadhyay, S.

Royal jelly. Dahl, R.

Royle, Nicholas

The goldfinch
  British invasion; edited by Christopher Gol-
    den, Tim Lebbon & James A. Moore
Iceland
  Perverted by language; fiction inspired by The
    Fall; edited and introduced by Peter Wild.

Roy's Jewish problem. Raphael, L.

Rozan, S. J.

Building
  Manhattan noir; edited by Lawrence Block
Hothouse
  Bronx noir; edited by S. J. Rozan
  The Best American mystery stories, 2008; ed-
    ited and with an introduction by George
    Pelecanos; Otto Penzler, series editor
The last kiss
  Dangerous women; edited by Otto Penzler
The next nice day
  Deadly housewives; edited by Christine Mat-
    thews
Night court
  Mystery Writers of America presents the
    prosecution rests; new stories about court-
    rooms, criminals, and the law; edited by
    Linda Fairstein.
Passline
  The International Association of Crime Writ-
    ers presents Murder in Vegas; new crime
    tales of gambling and desperation; edited
    by Michael Connelly
Shots
  Murder at the foul line; edited by Otto
    Penzler
Sunset
  Hard boiled Brooklyn; edited by Reed Farrel
    Coleman
Undocumented
  A hell of a woman; an anthology of female
    noir; edited by Megan Abbott; foreword by
    Val McDermid

Ruark, Ellen

In a Way It's Something Glamorous
  Southwest Review v89 no2/3 p390-4 2004

The **rubaiyat** of Nicholas Baldwin. Emerson, K.
L.

Rubber days. Martin, J.

RUBBER INDUSTRY

Verissimo, J. Going after rubber
Verissimo, J. Returning from rubber gathering

Rubenstein, Bruce

Smoke got in my eyes
  Twin cities; edited by Julie Schaper & Steven
    Horwitz

Rubenstein, Carol and Ress, Regina

Love at First Sight [With commentary]
  Parabola v30 no2 p86-9 My 2005

Ruefle, Mary—*Continued*

If all the world were paper
    Ruefle, M. The most of it
Lichen
    Ruefle, M. The most of it
A minor personal matter
    Ruefle, M. The most of it
Monument
    Ruefle, M. The most of it
The most of it
    Ruefle, M. The most of it
My pet, my clock
    Ruefle, M. The most of it
My search among the birds
    Ruefle, M. The most of it
    Iowa Review v38 no1 p3-7 Spr 2008
On twilight
    Ruefle, M. The most of it
Peek-a-moose
    Ruefle, M. The most of it
A romantic poet and his destiny
    Ruefle, M. The most of it
Sleep
    Ruefle, M. The most of it
Snow
    Ruefle, M. The most of it
Some nondescript autumn weekend
    Ruefle, M. The most of it
Suburb of long suffering
    Ruefle, M. The most of it
The taking of Moundville by zoom
    Ruefle, M. The most of it
University of the Limitless Mouse
    Ruefle, M. The most of it
What woman
    Ruefle, M. The most of it
Woman with a yellow scarf
    Ruefle, M. The most of it
    Iowa Review v38 no1 p1-2 Spr 2008

Ruffin, Paul

Crows
    Ruffin, P. Jesus in the mist; stories
The day J. P. saved the South
    Ruffin, P. Jesus in the mist; stories
The hands of John Merchant
    Ruffin, P. Jesus in the mist; stories
Harvey Watson and the angel
    Ruffin, P. Jesus in the mist; stories
Hunters
    Ruffin, P. Jesus in the mist; stories
In search of the tightrope walker
    Ruffin, P. Jesus in the mist; stories
J. P. and the water tower
    Ruffin, P. Jesus in the mist; stories
Jesus in the mist
    Ruffin, P. Jesus in the mist; stories
The natural man
    Ruffin, P. Jesus in the mist; stories
The queen
    Ruffin, P. Jesus in the mist; stories
Teaching her about catfish
    Ruffin, P. Jesus in the mist; stories
Time of the panther
    Ruffin, P. Jesus in the mist; stories
The well
    Ruffin, P. Jesus in the mist; stories
When momma came home for Christmas and
    Talmidge quoted Frost
    Ruffin, P. Jesus in the mist; stories

Rug weaver. Moss, B. K.
Rugalach. Tabor, M. L.
RUGENDAS, JOHANN MORITZ, 1802-1858
    About
    Aira, C. An episode in the life of a landscape
        painter [excerpt]
RUGS
    Moss, B. K. Rug weaver
A **ruined** world. Bluestein, E.
The **Ruins**. Rajbanshi, R.
Ruiz Rosas, Teresa
    Santa Catalina, Arequipa
        Violations; stories of love by Latin American
        women; edited and with an introduction by
        Psiche Hughes; foreword by Brian Mat-
        thews
Rule number one. Vincent, B.
Rules. Pearlman, E.
Rules of the game. Wilhelm, K.
RUMANIA *See* Romania
Rumford, Julia
    Elise
        "Tell it to us easy" and other stories; a com-
        plete short fiction anthology of African
        American women writers in Opportunity
        magazine, (1923-1948); edited by Judith
        Musser
Rumiya and the shofar. Potash, R.
Rumor City. Isozaki, A.
Rumor's Gift. McNett, M.
Rumours about me. Tsutsui, Y.
Rumpole and the bubble reputation. Mortimer, J.
Rumpole and the Christmas break. Mortimer, J.
Rumpole and the scales of justice. Mortimer, J.
Run, Dad! [Part of a special section on Korean
    author Kim Aeran] Kim, A.
Run Run Run Run Run Run Away. Bank, M.
Run silent, run deep. Goldsworthy, P.
The **run** to Hardscrabble Station. Dietz, W. C.
Runaway. Giberga, J. S.
Runaway. LaBrie, A.
Runaway. McBain, E.
Runaway. Munro, A.
Runaway. Nikitas, D.
The **runaway**. Perec, G.
Runaway. Plattner, A.
Runaway. Zuras, R. L.
The **Runaway** Bear Trap. Demuth, V.
The **Runaway** Stagecoach. Holladay, C.
RUNAWAYS (CHILDREN)
    Nelson, A. Dick
    Scott, J. Worry
    Thon, M. R. Heavenly creatures: for wandering
        children and their delinquent mother
    Ts'an-hsüeh. Helin
RUNAWAYS (YOUTH)
    Alvarado, B. Not a matter of love
    Bowes, R. Aka St. Mark's place
    Curtis, R. To the Interstate
    Davis, C. Grounded
    Erdrich, L. The plague of doves
    Irvine, A. C. The uterus garden
    Jones, E. P. A new man
    July, M. Something that needs nothing
    LaBrie, A. Runaway
    Nelson, A. Eminent domain
    Nikitas, D. Runaway
    Oates, J. C. Spider Boy
    Pizzolatto, N. Between here and the yellow sea

RUSSIA—*Continued*
Leningrad
See Russia—St. Petersburg
Moscow
Blackwood, G. Sacrificial lion
Bulgakov, M. A. The fatal eggs
Bulgakov, M. A. The master and Margarita [excerpt]
Bunin, I. A. Caucasus
Bunin, I. A. Cleansing Monday
Bunin, I. A. Muza
Bunin, I. A. On one familiar street
Chekhov, A. P. Ivan the cabman
Chekhov, A. P. A night of horror [variant title: Dreadful night]
Harleman, A. Biscuit baby
Harleman, A. Stalin dreaming
Harleman, A. Street of swans
Krasikov, S. The repatriates
Krasikov, S. There will be no fourth Rome
Miller, A. L. Dimitry Gurov's Dowdy wife
Perlman, E. A tale in two cities
Pinborough, S. The Bohemian of the Arbat
Shepard, L. Eternity and afterward
Shrayer-Petrov, D. Apple cider vinegar
Shrayer-Petrov, D. Rusty
Shrayer-Petrov, D. Tsukerman and his children
Tolstaia, T. The fakir
Tolstaia, T. Fire and dust
Tolstaia, T. Sweet Shura
Ulitskaya, L. Angel
Ulitskaya, L. The queen of spades
Vapnyar, L. Lydia's Grove
Wendroff, Z. Homeless
Wendroff, Z. A secure lodging
St. Petersburg
Archer, J. Don't drink the water
Bely, A. Petersburg [excerpt]
Gogol´, N. V. Nevsky Prospekt
Lermontov, M. I. Shtoss
Tolstaia, T. Loves me, loves me not
Tolstaia, T. Okkervil River
Tolstaia, T. Peters
Tolstaia, T. Sonya
Zamîàtin, E. I. The dragon
Vladivostok
Working, R. Slava
The **Russian**. Coen, E.
RUSSIAN AMERICANS
Ochsner, G. A blessing
Russian club. Litman, E.
Russian lover. Martin, J.
RUSSIAN REFUGEES
Brenner, Y. H. Impressions of a journey
The **Russian** Riviera. Bezmozgis, D.
RUSSIAN SECRET POLICE *See* Police—Russia
RUSSIAN SOLDIERS *See* Soldiers—Russia
RUSSIANS
Argentina
Cozarinsky, E. Literature
Austria
Andreas-Salomé, L. Incognito
Andreas-Salomé, L. A reunion
Canada
Moorcock, M. Going to Canada
China
L'Amour, L. Shanghai, not without gestures
Czech Republic
Templeton, E. A coffeehouse acquaintance

England
Harvey, J. The sun, the moon and the stars
Thirlwell, A. Nigora
Europe
Zoshchenko, M. A trap
France
Bunin, I. A. In Paris
Harleman, A. Biscuit baby
Germany
Arjouni, J. The Rudolf family does good works
Italy
Tolstaia, T. See the other side
Japan
Yasuoka, S. The house guard
Mexico
Porter, K. A. Hacienda
Switzerland
Ulitskaya, L. Zurich
United States
Bear, E. Botticelli
DeMarinis, R. Palochky
Hammett, D. Laughing masks
Kalotay, D. Sunshine Cleaners
Krasikov, S. The alternate
Krasikov, S. Asal
Krasikov, S. Better half
Krasikov, S. Companion
Krasikov, S. Debt
Krasikov, S. Maia in Yonkers
Krasikov, S. There will be no fourth Rome
Litman, E. About Kamyshinskiy
Litman, E. Among the lilacs and the girls
Litman, E. Charity
Litman, E. Dancers
Litman, E. Home
Litman, E. In the man-free zone
Litman, E. The last chicken in America
Litman, E. Peculiarities of the national driving
Litman, E. Russian club
Litman, E. The trajectory of frying pans
Litman, E. What do you dream of, cruiser Aurora?
Litman, E. When the neighbors love you
Monk, B. Epilogue: Excellent sperm
Ohlin, A. Land of the midnight sun
Otis, M. The next door girl
Shepard, L. Larissa Miusov
Shrayer-Petrov, D. Hände hoch!
Shrayer-Petrov, D. Hurricane Bob
Shrayer-Petrov, D. Old writer Foreman
Silver, L. Fish
Ulitskaya, L. Dauntless women of the Russian steppe
Van Booy, S. Apples
Van Booy, S. As much below as up above
Vapnyar, L. Borscht
Vapnyar, L. A bunch of broccoli and the third shelf
Vapnyar, L. Luda and Milena
Vapnyar, L. Mistress
Vapnyar, L. Puffed rice and meatballs
Vapnyar, L. Salad olivier
Wallace, J. Custom sets
Russo, Richard
Horseman
> The Best American short stories, 2007; selected from U. S. and Canadian magazines by Stephen King with Heidi Pitlor; with an introduction by Stephen King

Russo, Richard—*Continued*

Monhegan light

Contemporary Maine fiction; an anthology of short stories; edited by Wesley McNair

The whore's child

The best American Catholic short stories; a Sheed & Ward collection; edited by Daniel McVeigh and Patricia Schnapp

RUSSO-JAPANESE WAR, 1904-1905

Uchida, H. Triumphant march into Port Arthur

Rust, Elissa Minor

Crabwise

Rust, E. M. The prisoner pear; stories from the lake

God and birds

Rust, E. M. The prisoner pear; stories from the lake

Iris and Megan imagine alternatives

Rust, E. M. The prisoner pear; stories from the lake

Moon over water

Rust, E. M. The prisoner pear; stories from the lake

Of all the insatiable human urges

Rust, E. M. The prisoner pear; stories from the lake

The prisoner pear

Rust, E. M. The prisoner pear; stories from the lake

Raccoons

Rust, E. M. The prisoner pear; stories from the lake

Rich girls

Rust, E. M. The prisoner pear; stories from the lake

Robert Horncroft, naked

Rust, E. M. The prisoner pear; stories from the lake

Stealing Yakima

Rust, E. M. The prisoner pear; stories from the lake

Vital organs

Rust, E. M. The prisoner pear; stories from the lake

The weight of bones

Rust, E. M. The prisoner pear; stories from the lake

Rust. Ayres, N. J.

Rust and bone. Davidson, C.

The **rusted** gates of heaven. Thomas, J.

RUSTLERS, CATTLE *See* Cattle thieves

The **rustlers** [variant title: Along the Pecos] Leonard, E.

Rustomji, Roshni

American Dhansak and the Holy Man of Oaxaca

The Massachusetts Review v45 no3 p309-18 Aut 2004

Mandalas

Ms. v19 no1 p64-9 Wint 2009

Rusya. Bunin, I. A.

Ruta, Suzanne

(tr.) *See* Benmalek, Anouar

Ruy Sánchez, Alberto

Nijara, o las Tres Pistas del Cuerpo Cuando Ama / Nijara, or the Three Rings of a Body in Love

Artes de Mexico no83 p50-7, 77-8 2007

Las Tres Pasiones de un Ceramista / A Potter's Three Passions

Artes de Mexico no74 p38-46, 86-7 2005

RWANDA

Akpan, U. C. My parent's bedroom

Sehene, B. Dead girl walking

Ryan, Patrick

So much for Artemis

The Best American short stories, 2006; selected from U.S. and Canadian magazines by Ann Patchett with Katrina Kenison; with an introduction by Ann Patchett

Rybicki, Ed

All of me

Nature v454 p1028 Ag 21 2008

Rybicki, John

Burning Down in His Belly and Other Short-Shorts

The North American Review v293 no6 p10-11 N/D 2008

Rycraft, R. A.

Covenant

Calyx v24 no3 p82-9 Summ 2008

RYDER, ALBERT PINKHAM, 1847-1917

About

Irvine, A. C. The Lorelei

Rykena, Stephan

Cold-blooded

The World's finest mystery and crime stories, fourth annual collection; edited by Ed Gorman and Martin H. Greenberg

Rylands, Jane Turner

Art

Rylands, J. T. Across the bridge of sighs; more Venetian stories

Design

Rylands, J. T. Across the bridge of sighs; more Venetian stories

Enterprise

Rylands, J. T. Across the bridge of sighs; more Venetian stories

Finish

Rylands, J. T. Across the bridge of sighs; more Venetian stories

Fortune

Rylands, J. T. Across the bridge of sighs; more Venetian stories

Integration

Rylands, J. T. Across the bridge of sighs; more Venetian stories

Mobility

Rylands, J. T. Across the bridge of sighs; more Venetian stories

Probability

Rylands, J. T. Across the bridge of sighs; more Venetian stories

Restoration

Rylands, J. T. Across the bridge of sighs; more Venetian stories

Service

Rylands, J. T. Across the bridge of sighs; more Venetian stories

Vocation

Rylands, J. T. Across the bridge of sighs; more Venetian stories

Youth

Rylands, J. T. Across the bridge of sighs; more Venetian stories

Ryman, Geoff
  Birth days
    The Year's best science fiction: twenty-first annual collection; edited by Gardner Dozois
  Have not have
    The James Tiptree Award Anthology 3; edited by Karen Joy Fowler [et al.]
  The last ten years in the life of Hero Kai
    The Year's best fantasy and horror: nineteenth annual collection; edited by Ellen Datlow and Kelly Link & Gavin J. Grant
  Pol Pot's beautiful daughter (fantasy)
    Year's best fantasy 7; edited by David G. Hartwell & Kathryn Cramer
    The Year's best fantasy and horror: twentieth annual collection; edited by Ellen Datlow and Kelly Link & Gavin J. Grant
    Nebula Awards showcase 2009; the year's best SF and fantasy; selected by the Science Fiction and Fantasy Writers of America; edited by Ellen Datlow
  V.A.O.
    Cities; [by] Paul Di Filippo . . . [et al.]; edited and introduced by Peter Crowther
Ryunosuke, Akutagawa
  Autumn
    New England Review v28 no1 p75-84 2007
  An Evening Conversation
    New England Review v28 no1 p85-90 2007
Rzetelny, Harriet
  Shaking the dead geranium
    The Best of the Bellevue Literary Review; edited by Dannielle Ofri and the staff of the Bellevue Literary Review

S

S.O.S.. McKenzie, E.
Saadat, Rhian
  Uncle Mehdi's carpet deal
    Urban Welsh; new short fiction; edited by Lewis Davies
Saavedra, Miguel de Cervantes *See* Cervantes Saavedra, Miguel de, 1547-1616
SABBATH
  Judah, S. The courtship of Naomi Samuel
  Molodowsky, K. The lost Sabbath
  Molodowsky, K. On a day of rest
  Weaver, W. Flax
  Wendroff, Z. Around the great Samovar
  Wendroff, Z. Zorekh and Bulani
Saberhagen, Fred
  (jt. auth) See Lindskold, Jane and Saberhagen, Fred
Sabor a mi. Mindt, A.
SABOTAGE
  Garrett, G. P. A story goes with it
  Rabe, J. Stalking old John Bull
  Silverberg, R. Delivery guaranteed
SABOTEURS *See* Sabotage
Sack o' woe. Harvey, J.
The **Sackman** Street Boys. Besserman, P.
Sacred statues. Trevor, W.
SACRIFICE
  Niven, L. and Cooper, B. The terror bard
  Rickert, M. Anyway
  Rogers, B. H. Cross carriers
  Rozan, S. J. Building

SACRIFICE, HUMAN *See* Human sacrifice
The **sacrifice**. James, H.
Sacrifice. Rosenblum, M. H.
Sacrificial lion. Blackwood, G.
A **Sad** and Simple Story. Pratt, D.
The **sad** house in Talbiye. Potash, R.
Sad, Lady? Stanton, M.
The **sad** Serbian. Gruber, F.
Sada, Daniel
  El fenomeno ominoso/The ominous phenomenon
    Best of contemporary Mexican fiction; Alvaro Uribe, editor; Olivia Sears, translation editor
Sadastor. Smith, C. A.
SADISM
        See also Cruelty
  Baldwin, J. Going to meet the man
  Bender, A. Motherfucker
  Bierce, A. My favorite murder
  Brau, E. Bárcena's dog
  Burgin, R. With all my heart
  Cooper, D. The hostage drama
  Cooper, D. Knife/Tape/Rope
  Deaver, J. Afraid
  Elliott, S. Social contract
  Gaitskill, M. A romantic weekend
  Jordan, R. Little blue pill
  Machado de Assis. The secret heart
  Malouf, D. Night training
  Valdés, J. Flidia
  Yu, F. S. Social contract
Sadler, Mark, 1924-
        For works written by this author under other names see Collins, Michael, 1924-2005; Lynds, Dennis, 1924-2005
The **sadness** of detail. Carroll, J.
Sadoff, Ira
  Seven romances
    The Paris review book for planes, trains, elevators, and waiting rooms; by the editors of the Paris review; with an introduction by Richard Powers
Sáenz, Andrea
  A Candle for Chema
    Calyx v23 no2 p75-83 Summ 2006
Saenz, Benjamin Alire
  Exile
    Lone Star literature; from the Red River to the Rio Grande; edited by Don Graham
Saer, Juan José
  Baked mud
    Words without borders; the world through the eyes of writers; an anthology; edited by Samantha Schnee, Alane Salierno Mason, and Dedi Felman
Safari 2103 A.D. Resnick, M.
The **safe**. Gautreaux, T.
Safe. Gordon, M.
Safe. Keegan, C.
The **safe**. Pollack, E.
Safe enough. Child, L.
The **safehouse**. Faber, M.
Safekeeping. Hallowell, J.
SAFES
  Gautreaux, T. The safe
Safety. Sanow, A.
Safety critical. Gilbey, J.
Safety first. Talley, M.
The **safety** patrol. Martone, M.

Safety procedures. Gordimer, N.
The **Saffron** gatherers. Hand, E.
The **Saga** of the Irish in America. LaSalle, P.
The **sagebrush** kid. Proulx, A.
Sagebrush Schoolhouse. Fanning, E.
Sagesse. Bingham, S.
The **Sagging** Marx. Warkentin, A.
Saguaro arms. Sallis, J.
SAHARA
   Shukman, H. The garden of God: 1976
   Shukman, H. The garden of God: 1996 (2)
   Shukman, H. Mortimer of the Maghreb
Sahara. McIntyre, V.
Sahn, Seung
   Stopping the Torrent
      Parabola v30 no4 p92-5 Wint 2005
SAID, EDWARD W.
                           About
   Gordimer, N. Dreaming of the dead
Said Afzel's elephant. Lamb, H.
Saidi, William
   The garden of evil
      The Anchor book of modern African stories;
      edited by Naděžda Obradović; with a fore-
      word by Chinua Achebe
SAIGON (VIETNAM) *See* Vietnam—Ho Chi
   Minh City
Saikaku, Ihara
   1688: Osaka: Ihara Saikaku Tells a Cautionary
      Tale [From The ten virtues of tea that all
      disappeared at once]
      Lapham's Quarterly v1 no2 p71-2 Spr 2008
Sail shining in white. Helprin, M.
Sailing to Byzantium. Silverberg, R.
SAILING VESSELS
   Hodgson, W. H. The crew of the Lancing
   Hodgson, W. H. The storm
   McGuane, T. The refugee
   Yellin, T. Simeon
The **sailor**. Westcott, G.
Sailor off the Bremen. Shaw, I.
SAILORS *See* Seamen
Sailors lost at sea. Shields, C.
Sailor's valentine. Holladay, C. C.
The **Saint**. Daugherty, T.
Saint-Aubin, Horace de *See* Balzac, Honoré de,
   1799-1850
Saint Francis in Flint. Trevor, D.
Saint George and the translator. Tawada, Y.
Saint Helene. Hoffman, A.
SAINT KITTS (SAINT KITTS-NEVIS)
   Grilley, K. Maubi and Jumbies
Saint Marie. Erdrich, L.
Saint Nathan. Lee, J. C.
Saint Nikolaus. Ramírez Mercado, S.
SAINT PETERSBURG (RUSSIA) *See* Russia—
   St. Petersburg
SAINT VALENTINE'S DAY *See* Valentine's
   Day
Saint with a six-gun [variant title: The hanging of
   Bobby Valdez] Leonard, E.
Saintcrow, Lilith
   Half of being married
      My big fat supernatural honeymoon; edited by
      P.N. Elrod.
Sainte Croix, Stuart
   The Problem with Bright Fires
      The Massachusetts Review v48 no1 p134-42
      Spr 2007

SAINTS
   Hemley, R. The warehouse of saints
   Molodowsky, K. Zorekh the community's
Sakey, Marcus
   The desert here and the desert far away
      Thriller 2; stories you just can't put down;
      edited by Clive Cussler; [stories by] Kath-
      leen Antrim . . . [et al.]
   Gravity and need
      Killer year; stories to die for . . . from the
      hottest new crime writers; edited by Lee
      Child
   No one
      Chicago blues; edited by Libby Fischer
      Hellmann
Saknussemm, Kris
   Time of the End
      The Antioch Review v64 no3 p406-19 Summ
      2006
Saks, Andy
   My night at Fenway
      Fenway fiction; short stories from Red Sox
      nation; edited by Adam Emerson Pachter
Sakura. Misha
Sala, Toni
   Barren
      The Review of Contemporary Fiction v28 no1
      p120-4 Spr 2008
Salaam, Kalamu ya *See* Kalamu ya Salaam,
   1947-
Salaam, Kiini Ibura
   K-Ush: The Legend of the Last Wero
      Femspec v6 no1 p122-34 2005
Salad olivier. Vapnyar, L.
Salak, Kira
   Turning of the Dead
      The Massachusetts Review v46 no1 p154-81
      Spr 2005
The **Salamander**. Rodoreda, M.
Salamander scrimshander. Lodi, E.
Salammbô. Kiernan, C. R.
Salammbô redux (2007). Kiernan, C. R.
Sale, Medora
   Estelle is dead
      Sisters on the case; celebrating twenty years
      of Sisters in Crime; edited by Sara Paretsky
Sale, Richard
   The house of Kaa
      The Black Lizard big book of pulps; edited
      by Otto Penzler
   Three wise men of Babylon
      The Black Lizard big book of pulps; edited
      by Otto Penzler
Saleema. Mueenuddin, D.
SALEM (MASS.) *See* Massachusetts—Salem
SALES PERSONNEL AND SELLING
   Boudinot, R. The sales team
   Budnitz, J. Sales
   Dann, J. and others. Golden apples of the sun
   Donovan, G. Harry Dietz
   Edgerton, C. The great speckled bird
   Eldridge, C. Thieves
   Faber, M. The eyes of the soul
   Gifford, B. What happened in Japan
   Gorman, E. Different kinds of dead
   Hemon, A. Good living
   Kremer, H. Gelatin
   Lain, D. How to stop selling Jesus
   Lange, R. Fuzzyland

Sánchez, José Miguel *See* Yoss, 1969-
Sánchez Piñol, Albert
  The Madmen's Ship
    The Review of Contemporary Fiction v28 no1
    p95-9 Spr 2008
Sanctity: All life is here. Bradshaw, H.
The **sanctity** of an oath. Bierce, A.
Sanctuary!. Tremayne, P.
The **sanctuary** of hands. Donoghue, E.
Sand, George
  La dernière Aldini
    FMR (Black Edition) no21 p157-60 S/O 2007
Sand. Erpenbeck, J.
Sand. Winton, T.
Sand and frost. Windley, C.
Sandcastles: a dystopia. Cramer, K.
Sanders, Gregory
  Good witch, bad witch
    Best of the South: from the second decade of
    New stories from the South; selected and
    introduced by Anne Tyler
    New stories from the South: the year's best,
    2005; edited by Shannon Ravenel; with a
    preface by Jill McCorkle
    South Carolina Review v37 no1 p40-8 Fall
    2004
Sanders, Scott Russell
  Four Winds
    Michigan Quarterly Review v48 no1 p15-32
    Wint 2009
  Heart Woods
    The North American Review v293 no1 p25-32
    Ja/F 2008
Sanders, Ted
  Flounder
    Gettysburg Review v21 no2 p257-65 Summ
    2008
  Momentary
    The Massachusetts Review v47 no4 p727-54
    Wint 2006
Sanders, William
  Amba
    The Year's best science fiction: twenty-third
    annual collection; edited by Gardner Dozois
  Dry bones
    Nebula Awards showcase 2006; the year's
    best SF and fantasy; selected by the Sci-
    ence Fiction and Fantasy Writers of Ameri-
    ca; edited by Gardner Dozois
  Not fade away
    Alternate generals III; edited by Harry Turtle-
    dove and Roland J. Green
  The scuttling; or, Down by the sea with Marvin
    and Pamela
    Witpunk; edited by Claude Lalumière and
    Marty Halpern
  Sitka
    The Year's best science fiction: twenty-
    second annual collection; edited by Gardner
    Dozois
Sanderson, Jim
  El Camino del Rio [excerpt]
    Lone Star sleuths; an anthology of Texas
    crime fiction; edited and with an introduc-
    tion by Bill Cunningham, Steven L. Davis,
    and Rollo K. Newsom.
  Commerce Street
    Lone Star literature; from the Red River to
    the Rio Grande; edited by Don Graham

Sandford, John
  Lucy had a list
    Murder in the rough; edited by Otto Penzler
    The Best American mystery stories 2007; ed-
    ited and with and introduction by Carl
    Hiaasen; Otto Penzler, series editor
Sandkings. Martin, G. R. R.
Sandlot. Hall, W. D.
Sandor, Marjorie
  A Lesser Sonata
    The Georgia Review v63 no2 p203-15 Summ
    2009
Sandpiper. Soueif, A.
Sandstorm. O'Shaughnessy, P.
SANDSTORMS *See* Storms
Sandstrom, Eve K.
  The people's wat
    Sisters on the case; celebrating twenty years
    of Sisters in Crime; edited by Sara Paretsky
Sangar. Lamb, H.
SANITATION
  Blish, J. A dusk of Idols
  Bradbury, R. The garbage collector
Sanity. Wolff, T.
Sanjeev and Robotwallah. McDonald, I.
Sankaran, Lavanya
  Alphabet soup
    Sankaran, L. The red carpet; Bangalore stories
  Apple pie, one by two
    Sankaran, L. The red carpet; Bangalore stories
  Birdie num-num
    Sankaran, L. The red carpet; Bangalore stories
  Bombay this
    Sankaran, L. The red carpet; Bangalore stories
  Closed curtains
    Sankaran, L. The red carpet; Bangalore stories
  Mysore coffee
    Sankaran, L. The red carpet; Bangalore stories
  The red carpet
    Sankaran, L. The red carpet; Bangalore stories
  Two four six eight
    Sankaran, L. The red carpet; Bangalore stories
Sanny Tranny is alive and well and living on
    Davie. With, C.
Sanow, Anne
  Safety
    The Kenyon Review v30 no1 p118-35 Wint
    2008
Sans farine. Shepard, J.
Sans Soleil. Yolen, J.
Sansal, Boualem
  After Rach'el
    The Paris Review v51 p102-22 Summ 2009
SANSON, CHARLES-HENRI
            About
    Shepard, J. Sans farine
The **Santa**. Hope, T. G.
SANTA BARBARA (CALIF.) *See* California—
    Santa Barbara
SANTA CLAUS
    Bradfield, S. The anti-Santa
    Lenz, S. A risk for Father Christmas
    Matheson, R. A visit to Santa Claus
    Pratchett, T. FTB
    Ramírez Mercado, S. Saint Nikolaus
    Scholes, K. The Santaman cycle
    Straley, J. Weight of the world
The **Santa** Claus planet. Robinson, F. M.
Santa Claus vs. Johnny Crawford. Cooper, D.

SANTA CRUZ (CALIF.) *See* California—Santa Cruz

SANTA FE (N.M.) *See* New Mexico—Santa Fe

Santa Fé passage. Henry, W.

SANTA MONICA (CALIF.) *See* California—Santa Monica

The **Santaman** cycle. Scholes, K.

Santamaria, German
The procession of shadows
The Flight of the condor; stories of violence and war from Colombia; translated and compiled by Jennifer Gabrielle Edwards; foreword by Hugo Chaparro Valderrama.

Santangelo, Evelina
Eaten alive
Rome noir; edited by Chiara Stangalino & Maxim Jakubowski; translated by Anne Milano Appel, Ann Goldstein, and Kathrine Jason

SANTERIA
Correa, A. Olúo
Depestre, Y. Abikú

Santo Kyoden. Uchida, H.

Santoliquido. Ricuperati, G.

Santos, John Phillip
A Book of Swoons
Bomb no98 p106-12 Wint 2007

Santos, Tomas N.
Seeing Miss Saigon
Amerasia Journal v31 no1 p111-21 2005

Santos-Febres, Mayra
Flight
Colchie, T. A whistler in the nightworld; short fiction from the Latin Americas; edited by Thomas Colchie

The **Santosbrazzi** Killer. Julavits, H.

Sapers, Jonathan
Good Samaritans
Confrontation no96/97 p59-78 Fall 2006/Wint 2007

Sapira, Peter
Resurrection
The Literary Review (Madison, N.J.) v49 no3 p123-32 Spr 2006

SAPPHIRES
Goodis, D. The blue sweetheart

Sara Beltrame. Beltrame, S.

Sara in the Apartments of the Countess. Bradway, B.

Sara Sage [excerpt] Bosco, M.

Sarah, Robyn
Looking for my keys
Contemporary Jewish writing in Canada; an anthology; edited by Michael Greenstein

SARAJEVO (BOSNIA AND HERCEGOVINA)
See Bosnia and Hercegovina—Sarajevo

Saramago, José
The centaur
Telling tales; edited by Nadine Gordimer

Sarat, Lauren
Stitching
Confrontation no96/97 p187-97 Fall 2006/Wint 2007

Sardanapalo. Alphonsus, J.

Sardar, Gian
The Mere Act of Motion
Confrontation no101 p162-72 Spr/Summ 2008

The **sardonic** star of Tom Doody. Hammett, D.

Sargent, Pamela
Amphibians
Sargent, P. Thumbprints; with an introduction by James Morrow
Climb the wind
Sargent, P. Thumbprints; with an introduction by James Morrow
Erdeni's tiger
Sargent, P. Thumbprints; with an introduction by James Morrow
Gather blue roses
Sargent, P. Thumbprints; with an introduction by James Morrow
If ever I should leave you
Sargent, P. Thumbprints; with an introduction by James Morrow
Originals
Sargent, P. Thumbprints; with an introduction by James Morrow
Out of place
Sargent, P. Thumbprints; with an introduction by James Morrow
The rotator
Future Americas; edited by Martin H. Greenberg and John Helferd
Shrinker
Sargent, P. Thumbprints; with an introduction by James Morrow
A smaller government
Fast forward 1; future fiction from the cutting edge; edited by Lou Anders
Spirit brother
Sargent, P. Thumbprints; with an introduction by James Morrow
Thumbprints
Sargent, P. Thumbprints; with an introduction by James Morrow
Utmost bones
Sargent, P. Thumbprints; with an introduction by James Morrow
Venus flowers at night
Sargent, P. Thumbprints; with an introduction by James Morrow

Saro-Wiwa, Ken
Africa kills her sun
The Anchor book of modern African stories; edited by Nadežda Obradovic; with a foreword by Chinua Achebe

Sarris, Greg
The magic pony
California uncovered; stories for the 21st century; edited by Chitra Banerjee Divakaruni, William E. Justice, and James Quay

Sarsanedas, Jordi
Myth of the Americans
The Review of Contemporary Fiction v28 no1 p32-5 Spr 2008

Sartor, Colette
Lamb
Prairie Schooner v82 no1 p56-73 Spr 2008

Sarverville remains. Weil, J.

SASKATCHEWAN *See* Canada—Saskatchewan

SASQUATCH
Greenman, B. A field guide to the North American Bigfoot
Gunn, E. Up the fire road

Sasquatch. Lin, T.

Satan. Soueif, A.

Satan. Taha, M. A.

Satan Takes 12 Steps. Glasser, P.
SATANISM
      See also Demoniac possession
  Howard, R. E. Casonetto's last song
  Kelly, R. Devil's Creek
Satan's on Euclid Just off Juniper. Fredd, D. E.
Satan's Snakes, Vanilla Cokes. McCormick, K. Z.
Satelmajer, Ingrid
  They Keep Falling
    The Massachusetts Review v49 no3 p376-84
    Aut 2008
SATI
  Sundaresan, I. The faithful wife
Satifka, Erica
  Automatic
    Realms
Satija, Ron
  The Undertaker
    Texas Bar Journal v72 no6 p458-61 Je 2009
SATIRE
      See also Humor; Irony; Parodies
  Almond, S. Blue messiah
  Andrade, C. D. d. Miguel's theft
  Arnow, H. L. S. Zekie, the hill-billy mouse
  Auslander, S. Bobo the self-hating chimp
  Auslander, S. God is a big happy chicken
  Auslander, S. Holocaust tips for kids
  Auslander, S. Prophet's dilemma
  Auslander, S. Somebody up there likes you
  Auslander, S. Startling revelations from the lost
    book of Stan
  Auslander, S. They're all the same
  Baker, K. Maelstrom
  Baraka, I. A. The rejected buppie
  Barnes, H. L. Groundwork
  Barthelme, D. I bought a little city
  Barthelme, D. Me and Miss Mandible
  Barthelme, D. The new member
  Barthelme, D. The question party
  Barthelme, D. Tickets
  Bear, G. Ram shift phase 2
  Bender, A. Job's jobs
  Benford, G. How to write a scientific paper
  Bierce, A. Across the continent
  Bierce, A. An ancient hunter
  Bierce, A. The applicant
  Bierce, A. Ashes of the beacon
  Bierce, A. Banking at Mexican Hill
  Bierce, A. A bottomless grave
  Bierce, A. "The bubble reputation"
  Bierce, A. Burbank's crime
  Bierce, A. A champion of the sex
  Bierce, A. The City of the Gone Away
  Bierce, A. The civil service in Florida
  Bierce, A. The conflagration in Ghargaroo
  Bierce, A. Converting a prodigal
  Bierce, A. The dog in Ganegwag
  Bierce, A. An execution in Batrugia
  Bierce, A. The fall of the Republic
  Bierce, A. Feodora
  Bierce, A. The Golampians
  Bierce, A. The great strike of 1895
  Bierce, A. Hades in trouble
  Bierce, A. His Waterloo
  Bierce, A. The hypnotist
  Bierce, A. An imperfect conflagration
  Bierce, A. Industrial discontent in ancient Amer-
    ica
  Bierce, A. Insurance in ancient America

  Bierce, A. The jury in ancient America
  Bierce, A. The kingdom of Tortirra
  Bierce, A. The land beyond the blow
  Bierce, A. Largo al Gapperino
  Bierce, A. The late John Sweetbosh, Esq.
  Bierce, A. A leaf blown in from days to be
  Bierce, A. Letters from a Hdkhoite
  Bierce, A. The lion at bay
  Bierce, A. Little Larry
  Bierce, A. The maid of Podunk
  Bierce, A. Marooned on Ug
  Bierce, A. A mournful property
  Bierce, A. The new church that was not built
  Bierce, A. A providential intimation
  Bierce, A. A representative inquest
  Bierce, A. The Scolliver pig
  Bierce, A. Sons of the fair star
  Bierce, A. Storm and sunshine
  Bierce, A. The Tamtonians
  Bierce, A. Trustland: a tale of a traveler
  Bierce, A. An upper class misdemeanant
  Bierce, A. The war with Wug
  Bierce, A. The wizard of Bumbassa
  Bishop, M. The Yukio Mishima Cultural Asso-
    ciation of Kudzu Valley, Georgia
  Boswell, R. In a foreign land
  Boudinot, R. Blood relatives I: My mother was
    a monster
  Boudinot, R. Blood relatives II: Profession
  Boudinot, R. Civilization
  Boudinot, R. Contaminant
  Boudinot, R. Drugs and toys
  Boudinot, R. The sales team
  Boyden, A. The eleventh
  Bradbury, R. The watchful poker chip of H.
    Matisse
  Bradfield, S. Angry duck
  Bradfield, S. The anti-Santa
  Bradfield, S. Pig paradise
  Bradfield, S. The reflection once removed
  Breuer, M. J. The fingers of the past
  Brockmeier, K. Home videos
  Butler, R. O. 18 1/2
  Card, O. S. God plays fair once too often
  Card, O. S. Neighbors
  Chekhov, A. P. What you usually find in novels
    [variant title: Elements most often found in
    novels, short stories, etc.]
  Ch'oe, Y. The thirteen-scent flower
  Cony, C. H. Order of the day
  Coover, R. The Presidents
  Cosper, D. Love, American style, 2033
  Cox, A. M. Tabloids bring back family values!
  Crane, E. Clearview
  Dahl, R. Pig
  Dann, J. and Dozois, G. R. Slow dancing with
    Jesus
  Derby, M. The sound gun
  Di Filippo, P. Pulp alibis
  Di Filippo, P. Science fiction
  Di Filippo, P. Shake it to the West
  Disch, T. M. The abduction of Bunny Steiner;
    or, A shameless lie
  Disch, T. M. A family of the post-apocalypse
  Disch, T. M. The first annual performance art
    festival at the Slaughter Rock Battlefield
  Disch, T. M. The man who read a book
  Đoàn, L. The real estate of Chua village
  Dostoyevsky, F. Bobok

SATIRE—*Continued*

Dozois, G. R. and Dann, J. Slow dancing with Jesus

Dufresne, J. The freezer Jesus

Effinger, G. A. All the last wars at once

Effinger, G. A. Solo in the spotlight

Effinger, G. A. Target: Berlin! The role of the Air Force four-door hardtop

Farmer, P. J. The Jungle Rot Kid on the nod

Farmer, P. J. The Phantom of the Sewers

Ford, J. On the road to new Egypt

Frost, G. Touring Jesusworld

Gabriele, L. Don't let the 100 percent divorce rate spoil your wedding!

Gerrold, D. Franz Kafka, superhero!

Gerrold, D. The Kennedy enterprise

Gerrold, D. Report from the near future: crystallization

Giudice, V. The file cabinet

Grimes, C. The inspection

Gunn, E. Fellow Americans

Gunn, E. Nirvana High

Gunn, E. and What, L. Nirvana High

Hallberg, G. R. Early humans

Harris, C. An evening with Al Gore

Hodgins, E. Mr. Blandings builds his castle

Hodgson, W. H. Date 1965: modern warfare

Kaftan, V. Godivy

Kelly, J. P. Serpent

Koënings, N. S. Pearls to swine

Kress, N. Patent infringement

Krysl, M. Are we dwelling deep yet?

Krysl, M. Dinner with Osama

Kun, M. The handwriting patient

Kun, M. Steve Smith

L'Amour, L. Author's tea

Lanagan, M. Wooden bride

Lawson, J. E. The ankle–biter's guide to slithering

Lawson, J. E. Deface the nation

Lawson, J. E. Maybe it's racist . . .

Lawson, J. E. A serenade to beauty everlasting

Levi, P. Censorship in Bitinia

Levi, P. Knall

Levin, Z. Honorarium

Lewis, A. R. Request for proposal

Libin, Z. A refurbished play

MacLeod, K. Jesus Christ, reanimator

Malzberg, B. N. The passion of Azazel

Matheson, R. The man who made the world

McInerney, J. Sleeping with pigs

McInerney, J. Smoke

Michaels, L. Some laughed

Molodowsky, K. Married off

Montemarano, N. The November fifteen

Moody, R. Notes on redevelopment

Moorcock, M. Firing the cathedral

Morrow, J. Auspicious eggs

Muirhead, M. An open letter concerning sponsorship

Murakami, H. The rise and fall of Sharpie Cakes

Nix, G. Read it in the headlines!

Orozco, D. Officers weep

Palazzeschi, A. Dagobert

Parashuram. The scripture read backward

Pelevin, V. The life and adventures of shed Number XII

Pendarvis, J. Courageous blast: the legacy of America's most radical gum

Pendarvis, J. Final remarks

Perlman, E. Spitalnic's last year

Pierce, T. J. Columbine: the musical

Pierce, T. J. Wrestling Al Gore

Polyak, S. and Polyak, C. The prophecy: a Red Sox alternate history

Richter, S. A case study of emergency room procedure and risk management by hospital staff members in the urban facility

Rucker, R. v. B. Jenna and me

Rushkoff, D. 70 is the new 30!

Rylands, J. T. Design

Rylands, J. T. Enterprise

Rylands, J. T. Service

Salles Gomes, P. E. Her times two

Sargent, P. The rotator

Sargent, P. Thumbprints

Saunders, G. Brad Carrigan, American

Saunders, G. CivilWarLand in bad decline

Saunders, G. I can speak!

Saunders, G. In persuasion nation

Saunders, G. Jon

Saunders, G. My amendment

Saunders, G. My flamboyant grandson

Saunders, G. The 400-pound CEO

Schor, L. Collateral damage

Schor, L. Interviewing Barbie

Schor, L. The scalp agency

Schor, L. Still the top banana

Scliar, M. The last poor man

Searls, D. The cubicles

Self, W. The principle

Sherman, J. The usurper memos

Shields, C. Good manners

Shields, C. The next best kiss

Shirley, J. My victim

Shukert, R. The Paris Hilton International Fellowship

Silverberg, R. Good news from the Vatican

Silverberg, R. The littlest Jackal

Singleton, G. Soldiers in Gruel

Skeet, M. I love Paree

Sologub, F. A little man

Stackpole, M. A. Absolutely charming

Stackpole, M. A. Let me call you sweetheart

Stahl, J. Li'l Dickens

Steele, A. M. Hail to the chief

Steele, A. M. The teb hunter

Stein, J. The man who killed (and saved) Wall Street

Stern, R. G. Dying

Stern, R. G. Good morrow, swine

Stern, R. G. Lesson for the day

Stevens, J. D. The mask

Stevens, J. D. The President's penis

Stevens, J. D. What we sell in the room today

Stevens, J. D. When the President prays

Swanwick, M. The last geek

Tambour, A. The shoe in SHOES window

Tolstaia, T. Limpopo

Trimm, M. Climbing redemption mountain

Twain, M. The stolen white elephant

Valdés, J. Neighbors

Vonnegut, K. Armageddon in retrospect

Waldrop, H. Ilcirs of the perisphere

Wilde, H. Bringing up baby

Willis, C. Ado

Sayre-Roberts, Amy
Death mouth
Chicago noir; edited by Neal Pollack
The **scab's** progress. Sterling, B. and Di Filippo, P.
Scale. Pourciau, G.
Scales. Erdrich, L.
The **scalp** agency. Schor, L.
Scalzi, John
The tale of the wicked
The new space opera 2; edited by Gardner Dozois and Jonathan Strahan
Scan. Simpson, H.
SCANDAL
Oates, J. C. Spider Boy
Vidal, G. The Zenner trophy
A **scandal** in Drury Lane; or, The vampire trap. Wheat, C.
SCANDINAVIA
Martin, G. R. R. The fortress
The **scapegoat**. Dunbar, P. L.
Scar stories. Kaftan, V.
Scar Tissue. Nawaz, S.
Scarborough, Dorothy
From the wind [excerpt]
Lone Star literature; from the Red River to the Rio Grande; edited by Don Graham
Scarce. Kercheval, J. L.
Scarecrow. Boyd, B.
Scarecrow. Brennan, T.
The **scarecrow**. Schwitters, K.
Scarecrowed. Ockert, J.
SCARECROWS
Lovesey, P. The field
Maxwell, W. The French scarecrow
Scared rabbit. McLoughlin, T.
The **Scared** Teenaged Boy. Mulligan, S.
A **scarf**. Shields, C.
Scarlet fingernails. Kim, M.
Scarliotti and the sinkhole. Powell, P.
SCARS
Crouse, D. The ugliest boy
Kaftan, V. Scar stories
Scarsbrook, Richard
Brown is Not a Colour
Dalhousie Review v88 no2 p299-309 Summ 2008
Scattered thorns. Tremayne, P.
Scavenger hunt. Pollack, N.
Scego, Igiaba
"Faduma & Barni (April, 2003)"
Multicultural literature in contemporary Italy; edited by Marie Orton and Graziella Parati
The **scene**. Pintado, M. F.
Scene of the crime. Johnson, G.
Scenes. Shields, C.
Scenes from the life of Margaret. Sillitoe, A.
Scenes from the life of the only girl in Water Shield, Alaska. Tulathimutte, T.
Scenes inside the dilapidated walls. Ts'an-hsüeh
A **scenic** night. Granados, C.
The **scent** of apples. Bunin, I. A.
The **scent** of cinnamon. Lambert, C.
Schaap, James C.
Exodus
The best Christian short stories; edited and with an introduction by Bret Lott

Schaap, James Calvin
Silent Night, Merciful Night
Christianity Today v49 no12 p46-9 D 2005
Schadenfreude. Johnson, G.
Schaefer, Margaret
(tr.) See Schnitzler, Arthur
Schaefer, William D.
In the Annex
The Literary Review (Madison, N.J.) v52 no1 p111-19 Fall 2008
My Brother
The North American Review v293 no6 p25-8 N/D 2008
Schaeffer, Susan Fromberg
Wolves
The O. Henry Prize stories, 2006; edited and with an introduction by Laura Furman; jurors: Kevin Brockmeier, Francine Prose, Colm Toibin
Schafer, Mark
(tr.) See Piñera, Virgilio
Schafer, William
The Inheritors
Arizona Attorney v43 no8 p36, 38-9 Ap 2007
Schall, Joe
Domestic Relations
Confrontation no102/103 p37-49 Wint 2008/Spr 2009
Schaller, Eric
Monkey shines
Text: Ur; the new book of masks; [edited by Forrest Aguirre]
Schanoes, Veronica
Rats
Interfictions; an anthology of interstitial writing; edited by Delia Sherman and Theodora Goss
The Year's best fantasy and horror: twenty-first annual collection; edited by Ellen Datlow and Kelly Link & Gavin J. Grant
Serpents
The Best of Lady Churchill's rosebud wristlet; edited by Kelly Link & Gavin J. Grant; introduction by Dan Chaon
Schappell, Elissa
That sort of woman
On the Mason-Dixon line; an anthology of contemporary Delaware writers; edited by Billie Travalini and Fleda Brown.
Schattschneider, P. (Peter)
A letter from the other side
The black mirror and other stories; an anthology of science fiction from Germany & Austria; edited & with an introduction & notes by Franz Rottensteiner; translated by Mike Mitchell.
Schattschneider, Peter See Schattschneider, P. (Peter), 1950-
Schear, Elaine
Her last week in their paradise
The Best of the Bellevue Literary Review; edited by Dannielle Ofri and the staff of the Bellevue Literary Review
Scheen, Kjersti
Moonglow
Passport to crime; the finest mystery stories from International Crime Writers; edited by Janet Hutchings

Scheerbart, Paul
Malvu the helmsman: a story of vesta
The black mirror and other stories; an anthology of science fiction from Germany & Austria; edited & with an introduction & notes by Franz Rottensteiner; translated by Mike Mitchell.

Scheid, Susan
The Cancer Patient's Book of Grammar
Prairie Schooner v80 no4 p159-69 Wint 2006
The **scheme** of things. D'Ambrosio, C., Jr.

Scherder, Ralph
Hot Spots
The Literary Review (Madison, N.J.) v48 no4 p214-24 Summ 2005

Scherzando. Burke, K.
Scherzo with Tyrannosaur. Swanwick, M.
Schevoski. Vernon, O.

SCHIAVO, TERRI, 1963-2005
About
Greenman, B. How little we know about cast polymers, and about life

Schiffman, Carl
Curly Hamson and the Lucky Couple
The Antioch Review v64 no2 p350-62 Spr 2006

Schille, Candy B. K.
Danger Dog and I Are Going In
Calyx v23 no1 p49-53 Wint 2006

SCHIZOPHRENIA
See also Dual personality; Personality disorders
Blish, J. Testament of Andros
Fulton, A. Dorothy Loves maleman
Guista, M. Secrets
Hill, J. Voluntary committal
Mazzucato, F. Tiburtina noir blues
Oates, J. C. Last days
Upadhyay, S. The weight of a gun

Schlee, Ann
Moving the Bees
Confrontation no104 p150-60 Summ 2009

Schleef, Debra
From the Archives of Drs. Placek and Arriola
. . .
Femspec v7 no1 p97-105 2006

Schlich, Steve
Inside the Iron Maiden
Poe's lighthouse; all new collaborations with Edgar Allan Poe; edited by Christopher Conlon

Schmeidler, Lynn
The Speed of Dark
The Georgia Review v63 no2 p277-86 Summ 2009

Schmuck, Rebecca
The results of a dog going blind
The best Christian short stories; edited and with an introduction by Bret Lott

Schneiderman, Davis
(jt. auth) See Levine, Stacey and Schneiderman, Davis

Schnitzler, Arthur
Casanova's homecoming
Schnitzler, A. Bachelors; stories and novellas; selected and translated from the German by Margret Schaefer

Doctor Graesler
Schnitzler, A. Bachelors; stories and novellas; selected and translated from the German by Margret Schaefer
Lieutenant Gustl
Schnitzler, A. Bachelors; stories and novellas; selected and translated from the German by Margret Schaefer
New England Review v27 no4 p72-92 2006
The murderer
Schnitzler, A. Bachelors; stories and novellas; selected and translated from the German by Margret Schaefer

Schoffstall, John
Fourteen experiments in postal delivery
The Year's best fantasy and horror: twentieth annual collection; edited by Ellen Datlow and Kelly Link & Gavin J. Grant

SCHOLARS
See also Intellectuals
Adichie, C. N. The headstrong historian
Baumbach, J. The Villa Mondare
Brockmeier, K. The lives of the philosophers
Burke, K. Mrs. Maecenas
Hadley, T. A card trick
Hoffman, A. Lionheart
Johnson, G. Shameless
Kiely, B. The heroes in the dark house
Lahiri, J. Going ashore
Langan, J. Mr. Gaunt
Malouf, D. A traveller's tale
Marley, L. P dolce
Molodowsky, K. The Amsterdams
Segal, L. Other people's deaths
Segal, L. G. An absence of cousins
Segal, L. G. At whom the dog barks
Segal, L. G. Fatal wish
Segal, L. G. Other people's deaths
Segal, L. G. The talk in Eliza's kitchen
Segal, L. G. Yom Kippur card
Shomer, E. The hottest spot on earth
Sutton, B. Rabbit punch

Scholes, Ken
Action team-ups number thirty-seven
Scholes, K. Long walks, last flights & other strange journeys
The doom of love in small places
Scholes, K. Long walks, last flights & other strange journeys
The doom of love is small spaces
The Best science fiction and fantasy of the year: volume three; edited by Jonathan Strahan
East of Eden and just a little bit south
Scholes, K. Long walks, last flights & other strange journeys
Edward Bear
Scholes, K. Long walks, last flights & other strange journeys
Fearsome Jones' discarded love collection
Scholes, K. Long walks, last flights & other strange journeys
A good hairy day in Anarchy
Scholes, K. Long walks, last flights & other strange journeys
Hibakusha dreaming in the shadowy land of death
Scholes, K. Long walks, last flights & other strange journeys

Scholes, Ken—*Continued*

Into the blank where life is hurled
  Scholes, K. Long walks, last flights & other strange journeys
Invisible empire of ascending light
  Strahan, J. Eclipse two; new science fiction and fantasy; edited by Jonathan Strahan
Last flight of the Goddess
  Scholes, K. Long walks, last flights & other strange journeys
The man with great despair behind his eyes
  Scholes, K. Long walks, last flights & other strange journeys
Of metal men and scarlet thread and dancing with the sunrise
  Scholes, K. Long walks, last flights & other strange journeys
One small step
  Scholes, K. Long walks, last flights & other strange journeys
The Santaman cycle
  Scholes, K. Long walks, last flights & other strange journeys
So sang the girl who had no name
  Scholes, K. Long walks, last flights & other strange journeys
Soon we shall all be Saunders
  Scholes, K. Long walks, last flights & other strange journeys
Summer on Paris, light from the sky
  Scholes, K. Long walks, last flights & other strange journeys
That old-time religion
  Scholes, K. Long walks, last flights & other strange journeys

Schonfeld, Yael

The collection treatment
  Playboy's college fiction; a collection of 21 years of contest winners; edited by Alice K. Turner; foreword by Thom Jones

School days. McLean, S.

School gate mums. Gray, M.

School girl. France, L. R.

SCHOOL LIFE

Abbott, L. K. One of star wars, one of doom
Altschul, A. F. Requiem for Sammy the magic cat
Alvarado, B. What Lydia thinks of roses
Anaya, R. A. The apple orchard
Boudinot, R. The littlest Hitler
Dunbar, P. L. The boy and the bayonet
Fonseca, R. The enemy
Gardiner, J. R. The head of Farnham Hall
Granados, C. My girlfriend Bobbi
Heker, L. Far away
Herman, M. El fin del mundo
Holladay, C. C. Jane's hat
Houser, N. First kisses from beyond the grave
Inglis, T. M. Fairy "Spuds"
Jiménez, F. Moving still
Johnson, D. Melvin in the sixth grade
Kun, M. The blue engines
LaBrie, A. Snowball
Lennon, J. R. Eight pieces for the left hand
Luongo, M. Pedagogy
Marley, L. Starchild wondersmith
Martone, M. The safety patrol
McLean, S. School days
Oates, J. C. *BD* 11 1 87

Packer, Z. Doris is coming
Pierce, T. J. Columbine: the musical
Pierce, T. J. Newsworld II
Reed, K. High rise high
Riley, P. Damping down the road
Romano, T. New neighborhood
Russell, K. St. Lucy's home for girls raised by wolves
Soueif, A. 1964
Trevor, W. Traditions
Uthman, L. a.- . The homeland is far away, the roads are many
Varallo, A. Be true to your school
Vidal, G. The Zenner trophy
Vollmer, M. The digging
Weaver, W. Marked for death
Williams, J. Spring is now
Willis, C. All my darling daughters
Wyss, G. Kids make their own houses

Australia

Malouf, D. Eustace

Canada

Rees, R. Ethel Mermaid

China

Qi, S. Teacher Yu

England

Dahl, R. Galloping Foxley
Sillitoe, A. Mr. Raynor the school-teacher

India

Adiga, A. Lighthouse Hill (the foot of the hill)
Adiga, A. St. Alfonso's Boys' High School and Junior College

Iran

Taraqqi, G. The unfinished game

Ireland

Doyle, R. New boy
Kiely, B. The shortest way home
Kiely, B. A view from the treetop

Jamaica

Mordecai, P. Alvin's ilk
Mordecai, P. Hartstone High

Japan

Kitahara, A. Love's chill wind
Yasuoka, S. Homework

Uganda

Baingana, D. Hunger
Baingana, D. Passion

United States

Barry, R. Instructions for a substitute bus driver
Baxter, C. Gryphon
Capotosto, M. The souls of white children
Castillo, R. The battle of the Alamo
DeNymme, S. Poker and shooter
Eisenberg, D. The girl who left her sock on the floor
Friedmann, P. Two-story brick houses
Gurba, M. Just drift
Hernandez, L. The Catholic girl
Hunton, E. R. Who gives himself
Jones, E. P. A poor Guatemalan dreams of a Downtown in Peru
Jones, E. P. Spanish in the morning
Kulpa, K. Elaine, I love you
Kyle, A. Allegiance
Levithan, D. Breaking and entering
Levithan, D. The good witch
Levithan, D. Lost sometimes
Levithan, D. Miss Lucy had a steamboat
Levithan, D. A romantic inclination

Schuitema, Adam
Debts and Debtors
TriQuarterly no125 p133-50 2006
Schulberg, Budd
Your Arkansas traveler
Adaptations: from short story to big screen;
35 great stories that have inspired great
films; edited by Stephanie Harrison
Schulman, Helen
The revisionist
The Paris review book for planes, trains, ele-
vators, and waiting rooms; by the editors of
the Paris review; with an introduction by
Richard Powers
Schultz, Christopher
End State
Esquire v147 no5 p122-7 My 2007
Schultz, James Willard
The buffalo hunt
Adventures in the West; stories for young
readers; edited by Susanne George Bloom-
field and Eric Melvin Reed
Schulz, Gesine
The Panama hen
The World's finest mystery and crime stories,
fourth annual collection; edited by Ed
Gorman and Martin H. Greenberg
Schulze, Ingo
Cell phone
Telling tales; edited by Nadine Gordimer
Estonia, Out in the Country
Granta v100 p295-311 Wint 2007
Schumacher, Julie
Resurrection hockey
On the Mason-Dixon line; an anthology of
contemporary Delaware writers; edited by
Billie Travalini and Fleda Brown.
Schuman, David
Enemy
River Styx no75 p11-20 2007
Stay
Pushcart prize XXXI: best of the small press-
es 2007; edited by Bill Henderson; with the
Pushcart Prize editors
SCHUMANN, CLARA, 1819-1896
About
Marley, L. P dolce
SCHUMANN-HEINK, ERNESTINE, 1861-1936
About
Marley, L. Deep river
Schuster, Frauke
African Christmas
The World's finest mystery and crime stories,
fifth annual collection; edited by Ed
Gorman and Martin H. Greenberg
German summer
Passport to crime; the finest mystery stories
from International Crime Writers; edited by
Janet Hutchings
Two sisters
The World's finest mystery and crime stories,
fourth annual collection; edited by Ed
Gorman and Martin H. Greenberg
Schutt, Christine
The blood jet
Schutt, C. A day, a night, another day, sum-
mer; stories

Darkest of all
Schutt, C. A day, a night, another day, sum-
mer; stories
Do you think I am who I will be?
Schutt, C. A day, a night, another day, sum-
mer; stories
The Duchess of Albany
The O. Henry Prize stories 2007; edited and
with an introduction by Laura Furman; with
essays on the story they admire most by ju-
rors Charles D'Ambrosio, Ursula K. Le
Guin, Lily Tuck
The human season
Schutt, C. A day, a night, another day, sum-
mer; stories
In The Classroom
The Massachusetts Review v49 no4 p494
Wint 2008
The life of the palm and the breast
Schutt, C. A day, a night, another day, sum-
mer; stories
See amid the winter's snow
Schutt, C. A day, a night, another day, sum-
mer; stories
They turn their bodies into spears
Schutt, C. A day, a night, another day, sum-
mer; stories
Unrediscovered, unrenameable
Schutt, C. A day, a night, another day, sum-
mer; stories
Weather is here, wish you were beautiful
Schutt, C. A day, a night, another day, sum-
mer; stories
Winterreise
Schutt, C. A day, a night, another day, sum-
mer; stories
You drive
The Anchor book of new American short sto-
ries; edited by Ben Marcus
Young
Schutt, C. A day, a night, another day, sum-
mer; stories
Schutz, Benjamin M.
The black eyed blonde
Schutz, B. M. Mary, Mary, shut the door and
other stories
Christmas in Dodge City
Schutz, B. M. Mary, Mary, shut the door and
other stories
D.C. noir 2; the classics; edited by George
Pelecanos.
Expert opinion
Schutz, B. M. Mary, Mary, shut the door and
other stories
Lost and found
Schutz, B. M. Mary, Mary, shut the door and
other stories
Mary, Mary, shut the door
Schutz, B. M. Mary, Mary, shut the door and
other stories
Meeting of the minds
Schutz, B. M. Mary, Mary, shut the door and
other stories
Not enough monkeys
Schutz, B. M. Mary, Mary, shut the door and
other stories
Open and shut
Schutz, B. M. Mary, Mary, shut the door and
other stories

SCIENCE FICTION—*Continued*

Effinger, G. A. In the wings
Effinger, G. A. Mango Red goes to war
Effinger, G. A. One
Effinger, G. A. Posterity
Effinger, G. A. The thing from the slush
Effinger, G. A. The wicked old witch
Egan, G. Crystal nights
Egan, G. Luminous
Egan, G. Oceanic
Egan, G. Riding the crocodile
Eklund, G. and Benford, G. Hellas is Florida
Emshwiller, C. All washed up while looking for a better world
Emshwiller, C. Grandma
Eschbach, A. Mother's flowers
Eschbach, A. Wonders of the universe
Evenson, B. Body
Farmer, P. J. The last rise of Nick Adams
Farmer, P. J. The volcano
Fawcett, B. Last of the fourth
Finch, C. A landscape of shallows
Finch, S. Reading the bones
Finlay, C. C. The factwhore proposition
Finlay, C. C. A game of chicken
Finlay, C. C. Lucy, in her splendor
Finlay, C. C. The smackdown outside Dedham
Flynn, M. On the high frontier
Ford, J. The dismantled invention of fate
Ford, J. The dreaming wind
Ford, J. The seventh expression of the robot general
Francisco, B. and Lynch, C. This is my blood
Franke, H. W. Meteorites
Franke, H. W. Thought control
Franke, H. W. Welcome home
Friedell, E. Is the earth inhabited?
Friesner, E. M. The fraud
Frost, G. A day in the life of Justin Argento Morrel
Frost, G. The road to recovery
Fusco, A. C. N0072-JK1
Gaiman, N. Goliath
Gaiman, N. How to talk to girls at parties
Gaiman, N. The monarch of the glen
Gaiman, N. Orange
Gentle, M. A sun in the attic
Gerrold, D. Chess with a dragon
Gerrold, D. Dancer in the dark
Gerrold, D. The diamond sky
Gerrold, D. Digging in Gehenna
Gerrold, D. It needs salt
Gerrold, D. Riding Janis
Gerrold, D. The strange death of Orson Welles
Goonan, K. A. Sundiver day
Green, D. Clockwork atom bomb
Green, Dominic. Send me a mentagram
Gregory, D. The illustrated biography of Lord Grimm
Gunn, E. Computer friendly
Gunn, E. Green fire
Gunn, E. Nirvana High
Gunn, E. What are friends for?
Gunn, E. and What, L. Nirvana High
Gunn, J. E. The listeners
Haldeman, J. W. Brochure
Haldeman, J. W. Expedition, with recipes
Haldeman, J. W. Faces

Haldeman, J. W. Fantasy for six electrodes and one adrenaline drip
Haldeman, J. W. For White Hill
Haldeman, J. W. Foreclosure
Haldeman, J. W. Giza
Haldeman, J. W. Graves
Haldeman, J. W. Heartwired
Haldeman, J. W. Memento mori
Haldeman, J. W. The monster
Haldeman, J. W. Out of phase
Haldeman, J. W. The private war of Private Jacob
Haldeman, J. W. A separate war
Haldeman, J. W. Time piece
Haldeman, J. W. To Howard Hughes: a modest proposal
Hamilton, P. F. Blessed by an angel
Hamilton, P. F. Footvote
Hand, E. Cleopatra Brimstone
Harness, C. L. Quarks at Appomattox
Harris, C. W. The fate of the Poseidonia
Harris, J. The G-SUS gene
Harris, J. The spectator
Harrison, H. Space rats of the CCC
Harrison, M. J. Tourism
Harty, R. Why the sky turns red when the sun goes down
Henkel, O. Hitler on the campaign trail in America
Hodge, B. With acknowledgements to Sun Tzu
Hodgson, W. H. "The dream of x"
Hoffman, N. K. Sea air
Huberath, M. S. "Yoo retoont, sneogg. Ay noo."
Hughes, M. Falberoth's ruin
Hughes, M. Finding Sajessarian
Hughes, M. The gist hunter
Hughes, M. Go tell the Phoenicians
Hughes, M. Help wonted
Hughes, M. Inner huff
Hughes, M. A little learning
Hughes, M. Mastermindless
Hughes, M. Relics of the Thim
Hughes, M. Thwarting Jabbi Gloond
Hutchinson, D. The pavement artist
Irvine, A. C. Gus dreams of biting the mailman
Irvine, A. C. Peter Skilling
Irvine, A. C. Pictures from an expedition
Irvine, A. C. Reformation
Irvine, A. C. Shepherded by Galatea
Irvine, A. C. The uterus garden
Irvine, A. C. Volunteers
Iwoleit, M. K. Planck time
Jeschke, W. Partners for life
Johnson, K. 26 monkeys, also the abyss
Jones, A. E. Created he them
Keith, W. H. Partnership
Kelly, J. P. The best Christmas ever
Kelly, J. P. Faith
Kelly, J. P. Itsy bitsy spider
Kelly, J. P. Men are trouble
Kelly, J. P. Mr. Boy
Kessel, J. Events preceding the Helvetican renaissance
Kiernan, C. R. In view of nothing
Klages, E. Ringing up baby
Kosmatka, T. The art of alchemy
Kosmatka, T. The prophet of Flores
Koustas, P. Athos Emfovos in the temple of sound

SCIENCE FICTION—*Continued*

Merril, J. The future of happiness
Merril, J. Hero's way
Merril, J. Homecalling
Merril, J. The lady was a tramp
Merril, J. A little knowledge
Merril, J. The lonely
Merril, J. Pioneer stock
Merril, J. Project nursemaid
Merril, J. Rain check
Merril, J. So proudly we hail
Merril, J. Stormy weather
Merril, J. Survival ship
Merril, J. That only a mother
Merril, J. Whoever you are
Merril, J. Wish upon a star
Merril, J. A woman of the world
Merril, J. Woman's work is never done!
Miéville, C. The tain
Mirabelli, E. The woman in Schrödinger's wave
   equations
Modesitt, L. E., Jr. The difference
Modesitt, L. E., Jr. Iron man, plastic ships
Modesitt, L. E., Jr. Power to . . . ?
Modesitt, L. E., Jr. Precision set
Modesitt, L. E., Jr. Second coming
Modesitt, L. E., Jr. The swan pilot
Moffett, J. The bear's baby
Moles, D. Planet of the Amazon women
Mommers, H. W. Habemus papam
Monteleone, T. F. Camera obscura
Monteleone, T. F. A creature of accident
Monteleone, T. F. The Curandeiro
Monteleone, T. F. Group phenomena
Monteleone, T. F. Mister Magister
Monteleone, T. F. Present perfect
Monteleone, T. F. The way of the cross
Moon, E. Accidents don't just happen- they're
   caused
Moon, E. Hand to hand
Moon, E. If nudity offends you
Moon, E. New world symphony
Moon, E. Say cheese
Moorcock, M. Behold the man
Moorcock, M. The Cairene Purse
Moorcock, M. Colour
Moorcock, M. The deep fix
Moorcock, M. Ironface
Moore, C. L. No woman born
Murphy, P. Inappropriate behavior
Murphy, P. Wild girls
Neff, O. The fourth day to eternity
Nestvold, R. Exit without savings
Nisbet, J. Weight less than shadow
Niven, L. Breeding maze
Niven, L. and Cooper, B. The terror bard
Nix, G. Infestation
Nolan, W. F. And miles to go before I sleep
Nolan, W. F. The day the Gorf took over
Nolan, W. F. The Fasterfaster affair
Nolan, W. F. Freak
Nolan, W. F. The Grackel question
Nolan, W. F. Happily ever after
Nolan, W. F. Hopping for Abe
Nolan, W. F. How do I know you're real?
Nolan, W. F. Jenny among the zeebs
Nolan, W. F. The joy of living
Nolan, W. F. Kelly, Frederic Michael
Nolan, W. F. Lone star traveler

Nolan, W. F. The mating of Thirdburt
Nolan, W. F. Papa's planet
Nolan, W. F. The small world of Lewis Stillman
Nolan, W. F. Starblood
Nolan, W. F. Stuntman
Nolan, W. F. To serve the ship
Nolan, W. F. Toe to tip, tip to toe, pip-pop as
   you go
Nolan, W. F. The tragic narrative of Arthur
   Bedford Addison
Nolan, W. F. Violation
Olsen, L. Six questions for an alien
Oltion, J. The great Martian pyramid hoax
Palwick, S. Going after Bobo
Pavlou, S. The strange case of Jared Spoon,
   who went to pieces for love
Pelland, J. Captive girl
Platt, C. The disaster story
Pohl, F. Creation myths of the recently extinct
Pohl, F. Criticality
Pohl, F. The day the icicle works closed
Pohl, F. Growing up in Edge City
Pohl, F. The knights of Arthur
Pohl, F. Let the ants try
Pohl, F. The mapmakers
Pohl, F. The mayor of Mare Tranq
Pohl, F. The middle of nowhere
Pohl, F. My lady Green Sleeves
Pohl, F. Shaffery among the immortals
Pohl, F. Some joys under the star
Pohl, F. Spending a day at the lottery fair
Pohl, F. To see another mountain
Pohl, F. Waiting for the Olympians
Popkes, S. Great Caruso
Popkes, S. The ice
Pratchett, T. The sea and little fishes
Pratt, T. Impossible dreams
Pukallus, H. The age of the burning mountains
Rand, K. Big bird
Rand, K. Bridge O' doom
Rand, K. Buzzards of Oz
Rand, K. Desperate times
Rand, K. Eye of the assassin
Rand, K. The find
Rand, K. Gone fishin'
Rand, K. Good dog
Rand, K. The Henry and the Martha
Rand, K. Here there be humans
Rand, K. One person
Rand, K. Song of mother jungle
Rand, K. The teddy's touch
Rand, K. Trophy kill
Reed, K. Captive kong
Reed, K. Focus group
Reed, K. Grand opening
Reed, K. High rise high
Reed, K. Perpetua
Reed, R. Abducted souls
Reed, R. A billion eves
Reed, R. The children's crusade
Reed, R. The cuckoo's boys
Reed, R. First Tuesday
Reed, R. Good mountain
Reed, R. Hatch
Reed, R. Night of time
Reed, R. On the brink of that bright new world
Reed, R. One last game
Reed, R. River of the queen
Reed, R. Savior

SCIENCE FICTION—*Continued*

Reed, R. Winemaster

Resnick, M. Catastrophe Baker and a canticle for Leibowitz

Resnick, M. Catastrophe baker and the cold equations

Resnick, M. Hunting the snark

Resnick, M. Nicobar Lane—the soul eater's story

Resnick, M. Safari 2103 A.D.

Resnick, M. The soul eater

Resnick, M. and Kress, N. Solomon's choice

Reynolds, A. Fury

Reynolds, A. Minla's flowers

Reynolds, A. Signal to noise

Reynolds, A. The star surgeon's apprentice

Reynolds, A. Turquoise days

Reynolds, A. Zima blue

Ribbeck, B. A blue and cloudless sky

Rich, M. Across the sky

Rich, M. The apples of Venus

Rich, M. Forever down the ringing groves

Rich, M. Smoking gun

Rich, M. To hunt in fields

Richter, S. The land of pain

Rickert, M. Evidence of love in a case of abandonment: one daughter's personal account

Rickert, M. Map of dreams

Roberson, C. Death on the crosstime express

Roberson, C. Gold mountain

Roberson, J. Jesus freaks

Roberts, A. Blindness and invisibility

Roberts, A. Jupiter magnified

Roberts, A. Me-topia

Roberts, A. New model computer

Roberts, A. The question of [?query term]

Roberts, A. The siege of Fadiman

Roberts, A. The time telephone

Roberts, A. Tour de Lune

Robinson, F. M. The Santa Claus planet

Robson, J. The girl hero's mirror says he's not the one

Rosenbaum, B. The house beyond your sky

Rosenbaum, B. Start the clock

Rosenblum, M. H. Skin deep

Rosenblum, M. H. Splinters of glass

Rowe, C. The voluntary state

Rucker, R. v. B. Cobb wakes up

Rucker, R. v. B. Jenna and me

Rucker, R. v. B. The men in the back room at the country club

Rucker, R. v. B. Panpsychism proved

Rucker, R. v. B. Six thought experiments concerning the nature of computation: Experiment 1: Lucky number

Rucker, R. v. B. Six thought experiments concerning the nature of computation: Experiment 2: The million chakras

Rucker, R. v. B. Six thought experiments concerning the nature of computation: Experiment 3: Aint paint

Rucker, R. v. B. Six thought experiments concerning the nature of computation: Experiment 4: Terry's talker

Rucker, R. v. B. Six thought experiments concerning the nature of computation: Experiment 5: The kind rain

Rucker, R. v. B. Six thought experiments concerning the nature of computation: Experiment 6: Hello infinity

Rucker, R. v. B. Visions of the metanovel

Rucker, R. v. B. and Bisson, T. 2+2=5

Rucker, R. v. B. and Di Filippo, P. Elves of the subdimensions

Rucker, R. v. B. and Shirley, J. Pockets

Rucker, R. v. B. and Sterling, B. Junk DNA

Rusch, K. K. Defect

Rusch, K. K. June Sixteenth at Anna's

Ryman, G. Have not have

Sanders, W. Amba

Sanders, W. The scuttling; or, Down by the sea with Marvin and Pamela

Sargent, P. A smaller government

Sargent, P. Utmost bones

Sargent, P. Venus flowers at night

Satifka, E. Automatic

Sawyer, R. J. Identity theft

Scalzi, J. The tale of the wicked

Schattschneider, P. A letter from the other side

Scholes, K. Invisible empire of ascending light

Schroeder, K. The hero

Scliar, M. The last poor man

Shawl, N. Deep end

Shawl, N. Good boy

Shawl, N. Maggies

Shepard, J. The creature from the Black Lagoon

Shunn, W. Inclination

Silverberg, R. The artifact business

Silverberg, R. Born with the dead

Silverberg, R. Bride 91

Silverberg, R. Collecting team

Silverberg, R. Death do us part

Silverberg, R. The emperor and the maula

Silverberg, R. Gorgon planet

Silverberg, R. Halfway house

Silverberg, R. A man of talent

Silverberg, R. The man who never forgot

Silverberg, R. Ringing the changes

Silverberg, R. The Science Fiction Hall of Fame

Silverberg, R. A sea of faces

Silverberg, R. The songs of summer

Silverberg, R. The time of the burning

Silverberg, R. To be continued

Silverberg, R. Warm man

Silverberg, R. We know who we are

Silverberg, R. With Caesar in the underworld

Simmons, D. Muse of fire

Sinisalo, J. Baby doll

Skillingstead, J. Life on the preservation

Skillingstead, Jack. Dead worlds

Smith, C. A. The demon of the flower

Smith, C. A. The eternal world

Smith, C. A. From the crypts of memory

Smith, C. A. Marooned in Andromeda

Smith, C. A. The planet of the dead

Smith, C. A. The Plutonian drug

Smith, C. A. The red world of Polaris

Smith, C. A. A star-change

Smith, D. W. In search of the perfect orgasm

Smith, M. M. The compound

Spencer, W. B. The lights of Armageddon

Spencer, W. B. Your faithful servant

Stableford, B. The great chain of being

Stackpole, M. A. Let me call you sweetheart

Stackpole, M. A. Tip-off

Stanchfield, J. In the river

SCIENCE FICTION—*Continued*

Steele, A. M. The last science fiction writer
Steele, A. M. The teb hunter
Steele, A. M. World without end, amen
Steinmuller, A. and Steinmuller, K. The eye that never weeps
Stephenson, N. Excerpt from the third and last volume of Tribes of the Pacific Coast
Sterling, B. Bicycle repairman
Sterling, B. Cicada Queen
Sterling, B. The compassionate, the digital
Sterling, B. The growthing
Sterling, B. Homo sapiens declared extinct
Sterling, B. Ivory tower
Sterling, B. Kiosk
Sterling, B. Taklamakan
Sterling, B. and Di Filippo, P. The scab's progress
Sterling, B. and Rucker, R. v. B. Junk DNA
Stoddard, J. The elephant ironclads
Stone, L. F. The conquest of Gola
Strieber, W. Kaddish
Stross, C. Antibodies
Stross, C. Bear trap
Stross, C. Big brother iron
Stross, C. A colder war
Stross, C. Dechlorinating the moderator
Stross, C. Down on the farm
Stross, C. Extracts from the club diary
Stross, C. Lobsters
Stross, C. Missile gap
Stross, C. Ship of fools
Stross, C. Toast: a con report
Stross, C. Yellow snow
Sussex, L. Ardent clouds
Sussex, L. Robots & Zombies, Inc.
Swann, S. A. The historian's apprentice
Swanwick, M. The dead
Swanwick, M. From Babel's fall'n glory we fled
Swanwick, M. A great day for brontosaurs
Swanwick, M. Griffin's egg
Swanwick, M. King dragon
Swanwick, M. A midwinter's tale
Swanwick, M. Mother grasshopper
Swanwick, M. Radiant doors
Swanwick, M. Scherzo with Tyrannosaur
Swanwick, M. Tin marsh
Swanwick, M. The very pulse of the machine
Swanwick, M. Wild minds
Tambour, A. The age of fish, post-flowers
Thomas, J. The ballad of Moosecock Lip
Thomas, J. Dissecting the soul
Thomas, J. Heart for heart's sake
Thomas, J. Immolation
Thomas, J. The library of sorrows
Thomas, J. Nom de guerre
Thomas, J. The palace of nothingness
Thomas, J. Pink pills
Thomas, J. Precious metal
Thomas, J. The rusted gates of heaven
Thomas, J. Sisters of no mercy
Thomas, J. Union dick
Thomas, J. Unlimited daylight
Thomas, J. Wakizashi
Tidhar, L. Shira
Tiptree, J. And I awoke and found me here on the cold hill's side
Van Eekhout, G. Far as you can go

Van Eekhout, G. Native aliens
Van Pelt, J. The last of the o-forms
Van Pelt, J. Of late I dreamt of Venus
VanderMeer, J. Fixing Hanover
Varley, J. Air raid
Varley, J. In the hall of the Martian kings
Vinge, V. The cookie monster
Vlcek, E. Say it with flowers
Waldrop, H. Calling your name
Waldrop, H. D = R x T
Waldrop, H. Heirs of the perisphere
Waldrop, H. London, Paris, Banana . . .
Waldrop, H. Major Spacer in the 21st century!
Waldrop, H. Mr. Goober's show
Waldrop, H. The other real world
Watson, I. Saving for a sunny day, or the benefits of reincarnation
Watts, P. The island
Watts, P. and Murphy, D. Mayfly
Weber, D. A certain talent
Weber, D. In the Navy
Weber, D. Miles to go
Weber, D. Ms. Midshipwoman Harrington
Weber, D. Sir George and the dragon
Weber, D. The traitor
Wilce, Y. S. Quartermaster returns
Wilhelm, K. No light in the window
Williams, S. and Dix, S. Night of the dolls
Williams, T. The tenth muse
Williams, W. J. Daddy's world
Williams, W. J. Incarnation day
Williams, W. J. Ligdan and the young pretender
Williams, W. J. Send them flowers
Willingham, B. Fearless space pirates of the outer rings
Willis, C. Blued moon
Willis, C. The curse of kings
Willis, C. Even the queen
Willis, C. Inn
Willis, C. Jack
Willis, C. Newsletter
Willis, C. Nonstop to Portales
Wilson, R. C. The Cartesian theater
Wilson, R. C. YFL–500
Wolfe, G. Calamity warps
Wolfe, G. The death of Dr. Island
Wolfe, G. Forlesen
Wolfe, G. From the cradle
Wolfe, G. The god and his nman
Wolfe, G. Graylord Man's last words
Wolfe, G. Has anybody seen Junie Moon?
Wolfe, G. In glory like their star
Wolfe, G. Pulp cover
Wolfe, G. The seraph from its sepulcher
Wolfe, G. Shields of Mars
Wolfe, G. Viewpoint
Wurts, J. Moebius trip
Young, R. F. The first Mars mission
Yu, C. Florence
Zebrowski, G. Lords of imagination
Zebrowski, G. My first world
Zebrowski, G. The soft terrible music
Zelazny, R. ...And call me Conrad, part one
Zelazny, R. ...And call me Conrad, part two
Zelazny, R. Angel, dark angel
Zelazny, R. Auto-da-fé
Zelazny, R. Circe has her problems
Zelazny, R. The eve of RUMOKO
Zelazny, R. For a breath I tarry

SCIENCE FICTION—*Continued*

Zelazny, R. The furies
Zelazny, R. He that moves
Zelazny, R. The hounds of sorrow
Zelazny, R. The injured
Zelazny, R. 'Kjwalll'kje'k'koothaïlll'kje'k
Zelazny, R. The Malatesta collection
Zelazny, R. Mine is the kingdom
Zelazny, R. Moonless in byzantium
Zelazny, R. Nine starships waiting
Zelazny, R. Song of the blue baboon
Zelazny, R. Sun's trophy stirring
Zelazny, R. A thing of terrible beauty
Zelazny, R. This mortal mountain
Zelazny, R. Threshold of the prophet
Zelazny, R. Walpurgisnacht
Zelazny, R. The Year of the Good Seed with Dannie Plachta

Science fiction. Di Filippo, P.
The **Science** Fiction Hall of Fame. Silverberg, R.
A **science** for being alone. Alarcón, D.
The **Scientific** Ape. Stevenson, R. L.
A **scientific** dream. Bierce, A.

SCIENTIFIC EXPEDITIONS

Grimes, C. Drafting the field report
Lovecraft, H. P. At the mountains of madness
Silverberg, R. Breckenridge and the continuum
Smith, C. A. A captivity in Serpens [variant title: The amazing planet]
Tsutsui, Y. Bad for the heart
Tsutsui, Y. Salmonella men on planet porno

SCIENTIFIC EXPERIMENTS

Bailey, H. Dr. Gelabius
Bierce, A. Perry Chumly's eclipse
Bulgakov, M. A. The fatal eggs
Carey, P. The fat man in history
Dahl, R. William and Mary
Dooling, R. Roe #5
Fusco, A. C. N0072-JK1
Hubbard, L. R. The dangerous dimension
Hubbard, L. R. The professor was a thief
Kosmatka, T. The prophet of Flores
Kuprin, A. I. Liquid sunshine
Langelaan, G. The fly
Pohl, F. The gold at the starbow's end
Rowe, C. Gather
Saunders, G. 93990
Silverberg, R. There was an old woman
Sterling, B. Swarm
Williams, W. J. Surfacing
Wilson, R. C. The Cartesian theater

SCIENTIFIC RESEARCH *See* Research

SCIENTISTS

See also Anthropologists; Archeologists; Astronomers; Bacteriologists; Biologists; Chemists; Inventors; Paleontologists; Physicists; Women scientists

Bear, E. Shoggoths in bloom
Bear, E. When you visit the Magoebaskloof Hotel, be certain not to miss the samango monkeys
Blaylock, J. P. Lord Kelvin's machine
Boyle, T. C. Blinded by the light
Cadnum, M. Hungry
Chiang, T. Exhalation
Coates, D. Magic in a certain slant of light
Cornell, P. Michael Laurits is: drowning
De Camp, L. S. The gnarly man
Egan, G. Glory

Egan, G. Steve fever
Fulton, J. The animal girl
Grimes, C. A novel failure: an interview with Nobel candidate Sylvia Solas
Hubbard, L. R. The dangerous dimension
Hubbard, L. R. The professor was a thief
Klages, E. The green glass sea
Kosmatka, T. The art of alchemy
Kress, N. Shiva in shadow
Langelaan, G. The fly
Lovecraft, H. P. Cool air
Lumley, B. Deja viewer
MacLeod, I. New light on the Drake equation
Maleeny, T. Till death do us part
Margulis, L. The estimator
Margulis, L. Meeting
Margulis, L. Sunday morning with J. Robert Oppenheimer
McLeod, I. New light on the Drake equation
Nelson, A. People people
Ohlin, A. An analysis of some troublesome recent behavior
Ohlin, A. A theory of entropy
Pohl, F. Speed trap
Rich, M. Impossible alone
Roberts, A. Stationary acceleration
Shepard, J. Ancestral legacies
Silverberg, R. To the dark star
Somerville, P. Trouble and the shadowy deathblow
Sterling, B. Homo sapiens declared extinct
Sterling, B. Ivory tower
Stevens, F. Unseen—unfeared
Swanwick, M. Girls and boys, come out to play
Waters, M. Y. Mirror studies

Scissors, paper, rock. Brady, C.

Scliar, Moacyr
The cow
    Oxford anthology of the Brazilian short story; edited by K. David Jackson
The last poor man
    Oxford anthology of the Brazilian short story; edited by K. David Jackson

Scofield, Sandra
Swim
    Callaloo v32 no2 p468-82 Spr 2009

The **Scolliver** pig. Bierce, A.

Scoppettone, Sandra
Everybody loves somebody
    A hell of a woman; an anthology of female noir; edited by Megan Abbott; foreword by Val McDermid
    A Prisoner of memory and 24 of the year's finest crime and mystery stories; edited by Ed Gorman & Martin H. Greenberg

The **scorched** face. Hammett, D.
The **score.** Ronk, M. C.
Scoring. Vollmer, M.
Scorn for life. Sperani, B.
Scotch and Dr Pepper. Singleton, G.
Scotch on the rocks. Nolan, W. F.

SCOTLAND

See also Orkney (Scotland)

Boyle, T. C. Swept away
Faber, M. All black
Faber, M. A hole with two ends
Link, K. Flying lessons
Munro, A. No advantages
O'Hagan, A. Gordon

SCRAP METAL INDUSTRY
   Gautreaux, T. The safe
Scrapbook. Smith, N.
Scratch. Lane, J.
Scratch a woman. Lippman, L.
Scratch that one. Morgan, J. M.
The **Scratchboard** Project. Cummings, J. M.
Scream. Gordon, G.
Scream in the dark. Messinger, J.
A **scream** of toys. Sillitoe, A.
Scream queen. Kelly, R.
The **screened** porch. Richards, S. S.
Screens. Lamsley, T.
The **screenwriter**. Brown, J.
Screenwriter. D'Ambrosio, C., Jr.
Screwup. Lansdale, J. R.
The **scribble** mind. Ford, J.
Scribner, Keith
   Paradise in a Cup
      TriQuarterly no121 p206-20 2005
The **scrimshaw** violin. Levi, J.
The **scripture** read backward. Parashuram
SCRIPTWRITERS *See* Authors
SCULPTORS
         See also Women sculptors
   Bova, B. A can of worms
   Busch, F. Sense of direction
   Ducornet, R. Giulia on her knees
   Hutchinson, D. The pavement artist
   Lane, J. Like shattered stone
   Rickert, M. Art is not a violent subject
   Rivera-Valdes, S. Ana at four times: Ana and
      the lemon balm
   Singleton, G. Director's cut
   Unger, D. Cuban nights
The **sculptor's** son. Gifford, B.
SCULPTURE
         See also Masks (Sculpture); Monuments;
      Statues; Wood carving
Scurati, Antonio
   Eternal Rome
      Rome noir; edited by Chiara Stangalino &
      Maxim Jakubowski; translated by Anne Mi-
      lano Appel, Ann Goldstein, and Kathrine
      Jason
Scutt, Cecily
   Europa
      Dreaming again; thirty-five new stories cele-
      brating the wild side of Australian fiction;
      edited by Jack Dann
SEA *See* Ocean
Sea air. Hoffman, N. K.
The **sea** and its shore. Bishop, E.
The **sea** and little fishes. Pratchett, T.
Sea burial. Kennedy, C.
SEA CAPTAINS *See* Seamen; Shipmasters
Sea change. McCormack, U.
Sea Child: a tale of Dune. Herbert, B. and Ander-
   son, K. J.
The **sea** cure. Selgin, P.
Sea Dogs. Fayer, S.
The **sea** horses. Hodgson, W. H.
The **Sea** Monkey conspiracy. Lain, D.
SEA MONSTERS
         See also Loch Ness monster
   Beagle, P. S. Chandail
   Campbell, R. Raised by the moon
   Hodgson, W. H. An adventure of the deep wa-
      ters

Hodgson, W. H. Demons of the sea
Hodgson, W. H. The haunted *Pampero*
Hodgson, W. H. The sea horses
Hodgson, W. H. A tropical horror
Hodgson, W. H. The voice in the dawn
Kiernan, C. R. From cabinet 34, drawer 6
Lumley, B. The taint
McAuley, P. J. Take me to the river
Sea Oak. Saunders, G.
The **sea** of clouds. Bova, B.
A **sea** of faces. Silverberg, R.
The **sea** of hesitation. Barthelme, D.
SEA STORIES
         See also Seamen names of wars with the
      subdivision Naval operations
   Birmingham, J. Heere be monsters
   Bunn, A. The ledge
   Chandler, A. B. Grimes and the Gaijin Daimyo
   Hodgson, W. H. An adventure of the deep wa-
      ters
   Hodgson, W. H. The albatross
   Hodgson, W. H. Bullion
   Hodgson, W. H. Captain Dang
   Hodgson, W. H. Demons of the sea
   Hodgson, W. H. A fight with a submarine
   Hodgson, W. H. The finding of the *Graiken*
   Hodgson, W. H. The getting even of Tommy
      Dodd
   Hodgson, W. H. The ghost pirates
   Hodgson, W. H. The homecoming of Captain
      Dan
   Hodgson, W. H. In the danger zone
   Hodgson, W. H. The island of the crossbones
   Hodgson, W. H. Jack Grey, second mate
   Hodgson, W. H. The mystery of Captain
      Chappel
   Hodgson, W. H. The mystery of missing ships
   Hodgson, W. H. The 'prentices' mutiny
   Hodgson, W. H. The raft
   Hodgson, W. H. The real thing: 'S.O.S'
   Hodgson, W. H. The regeneration of Captain
      Bully Keller
   Hodgson, W. H. The riven night
   Hodgson, W. H. The *Shamraken* homeward-
      bounder
   Hodgson, W. H. The sharks of the St. Elmo
   Hodgson, W. H. The silent ship
   Hodgson, W. H. The storm
   Hodgson, W. H. Through the vortex of a cy-
      clone
   Hodgson, W. H. A tropical horror
   Hodgson, W. H. We two and Bully Dunkan
   Hodgson, W. H. What happened in the Thunder-
      bolt
   Lupoff, R. A. Treasure of the red robe men
   Purdom, T. The mists of time
   Rashid, 'A. M. A crisis at sea
   Shepard, J. Tedford and the megalodon
   Wolfe, G. A cabin on the coast
The **sea** was wet as wet can be. Shirley, J.
The **Seafarer**. Calbert, C.
Seafaring. Bierce, A.
The **seal** hunter. Finlay, C. C.
A **sealed** pod. Bonner, M. O.
A **sealed** tear. James, H.
SEALS (ANIMALS)
   Bierce, A. L. S.
   Ochsner, G. Song of the selkie
   Rickert, M. Moorina of the seals

See no evil, feel no joy. Emshwiller, C.
See the girl. Cooney, E.
See the other side. Tolstaia, T.
See the Other Side. Tolstaya, T.
See what tomorrow brings. Thompson, J. W.
Seebohm's cap. Schweighofer, P.
The **seed** from the sepulcher. Smith, C. A.
Seedling of Mars. Smith, C. A.
Seeing Miss Saigon. Santos, T. N.
Seeing the world. Campbell, R.
The **seer.** Rhine, R. S.
Sefarim, Mendele Mokher
The little man; or, The life story of Yitsik-Avrom the power broker
No star too beautiful; Yiddish stories from 1382 to the present; compiled and translated by Joachim Neugroschel
Shem and Japeth on a train
No star too beautiful; Yiddish stories from 1382 to the present; compiled and translated by Joachim Neugroschel
Segal, Lore
The Arbus Factor
The New Yorker v83 no41 p78, 81 D 24-31 2007
Making Good
The American Scholar v77 no4 p90-7 Aut 2008
Other people's deaths
The O. Henry Prize stories 2008; edited and with an introduction by Laura Furman; with essays on the stories they admire most by jurors Chimamanda Ngozi Adiche, David Leavitt, David Means
The New Yorker v82 no31 p80-5 O 2 2006
Segal, Lore Groszmann
An absence of cousins
Segal, L. G. Shakespeare's kitchen; stories; [by] Lore Segal
At whom the dog barks
Segal, L. G. Shakespeare's kitchen; stories; [by] Lore Segal
Fatal wish
Segal, L. G. Shakespeare's kitchen; stories; [by] Lore Segal
Garbage thief
Segal, L. G. Shakespeare's kitchen; stories; [by] Lore Segal
A gated community
Segal, L. G. Shakespeare's kitchen; stories; [by] Lore Segal
Leslie's shoes
Segal, L. G. Shakespeare's kitchen; stories; [by] Lore Segal
Money, fame, and beautiful women
Segal, L. G. Shakespeare's kitchen; stories; [by] Lore Segal
Other people's deaths
Segal, L. G. Shakespeare's kitchen; stories; [by] Lore Segal
The reverse bug
Scribblers on the roof; contemporary American Jewish fiction; edited by Melvin Jules Bukiet and David G. Roskies
Segal, L. G. Shakespeare's kitchen; stories; [by] Lore Segal
The talk in Eliza's kitchen
Segal, L. G. Shakespeare's kitchen; stories; [by] Lore Segal

Yom Kippur card
Segal, L. G. Shakespeare's kitchen; stories; [by] Lore Segal
SEGREGATION *See* Race relations
Segue. Shields, C.
Sehene, Benjamin
Dead girl walking
From Africa; new francophone stories; edited by Adele King
Seidel, Dena
Good Times
The Hudson Review v58 no1 p47-62 Spr 2005
Seigel, Andrea
Open House
The Kenyon Review v28 no4 p67-79 Fall 2006
Seikoh, Itoh
God is nowhere; God is now here
The Ecco book of Christmas stories; edited by Alberto Manguel
Seizure. Kennedy, C.
Sekaran, Shanthi
Stalin
Best new American voices 2004; guest editor John Casey; series editors John Kulka and Natalie Danford
Selby, Hubert
Tralala
Brooklyn noir 2; the classics; edited by Tim McLoughlin
Selden's tale. Stashower, D.
Selene city. Bova, B.
Selene city [2] Bova, B.
Selene city [3] Bova, B.
The **Selene** Gardening Society. Brown, M.
Self, Will
The principle
2033; the future of misbehavior: interplanetary dating, Madame President, socialized plastic surgery, and other good news from the future; from the editors of Nerve.com; instigated by Svedka
SELF-DEFENSE *See* Martial arts
Self-defense. Arjouni, J.
SELF-MADE MEN
See also Success
Self-Portrait with Beach [Reprint] Tuten, F.
Self-reliance. Pearlman, E.
SELF-SACRIFICE
Colombi, M. Learn a trade for a rainy day
Goodis, D. Professional man
Kipling, R. The wish house
Lindskold, J. and Saberhagen, F. Servant of death
Petesch, N. L. M. Selma
Reisen, A. When does Mame eat?
Resnick, M. and Kress, N. Solomon's choice
Silverberg, R. Blaze of glory
Smith, C. A. Beyond the singing flame
Smith, C. A. The city of the singing flame
SELF-SERVICE
Preece, S. Agoraphobix
SELF-SERVICE LAUNDRIES
Ford, E. Elwood's last job
Panning, A. Five reasons I miss the laundromat
The **selfish** giant. Wilde, O.
SELFISHNESS
Reed, K. Getting it back

Shabtai, Yaakov—*Continued*
Uncle Peretz takes off
Shabtai, Y. Uncle Peretz takes off; short sto-ries; translated from the Hebrew by Dalya Bilu
Uncle Shmuel
Shabtai, Y. Uncle Peretz takes off; short sto-ries; translated from the Hebrew by Dalya Bilu
The visit
Shabtai, Y. Uncle Peretz takes off; short sto-ries; translated from the Hebrew by Dalya Bilu
The voyage to Mauritius
Shabtai, Y. Uncle Peretz takes off; short sto-ries; translated from the Hebrew by Dalya Bilu

Shade, Eric
Youghiogeny
River Styx no69/70 p6-16 2005
The **Shade**. Dixon, S.
A **shade** of blue. Dymmoch, M. A.
Shades. Lewis, W. H.
Shades. Shepard, L.
Shades of mango. Radojcic, N.
The **Shadow**. Lee, H.-K.
Shadow flag. Tomlinson, J.
The **Shadow** from the Wall. Nelson, R. B.
Shadow Life. McAuley, P.
Shadow man. Hughes, M.
The **shadow** man. Tawada, Y.
Shadow of a doubt. Godfrey, R.
The **Shadow** of Doubt. Tillman, L.
The **Shadow** of Love. Lee, K.
The **shadow** of Manny Ramirez. Solar, R.
The **shadow** of the beast. Howard, R. E.
The **shadow** of the orchid. Takagi, N.
Shadow of Turning. Turner, C.
Shadow on a weary land. Peelle, L.
Shadow on the water. Robinson, P.
The **shadow** out of time. Lovecraft, H. P.
The **shadow** over Innsmouth. Lovecraft, H. P.
The **shadow** players. Bukoski, A.
A **shadow** table. Fulton, A.
The **shadow** that lost its man. Harrison, W.
The **shadow** that shapes the light. Gorman, E. and Starr, R. D.
Shadowboxer. Di Filippo, P.
Shadowjack. Zelazny, R.
The **shadows**. Smith, C. A.
Shadows from the screen. Valley, R.
Shadows in the wood. Roberson, J.
The **shadows**, kith and kin. Lansdale, J. R.
Shafak, Elif
The Bastard of Istanbul
Granta no96 p157-74 Wint 2006
Shaffer, Ann
Dropping the baby
Barnstorm; contemporary Wisconsin fiction; edited by Raphael Kadushin
Shaffer, Catherine H.
The charge-up man
Nature v444 p652 N 30 2006
Shaffery among the immortals. Pohl, F.
Shafi'i, Muna al-
The age of pain
Oranges in the sun; short stories from the Arabian Gulf; edited and translated by Deb-orah S. Akers, Abubaker A. Bagader

Hunger
Oranges in the sun; short stories from the Arabian Gulf; edited and translated by Deb-orah S. Akers, Abubaker A. Bagader
Shaft. Enright, A.
A **shaggy** dog story. Gerrold, D.
The **shaggy** house. Lansdale, J. R.
Shah, Biren
From the desk of Jarrod Foster
Nature v442 p328 Jl 20 2006
Shahan, Sherry
Jesus Rides Shotgun
Confrontation no98/99 p167-71 Spr/Summ 2007
Shake it to the West. Di Filippo, P.
Shaken. Rock, P.
Shakers. Orozco, D.
Shakespeare, Nicholas
The White Hole of Bombay
Granta v100 p275-88 Wint 2007
SHAKESPEARE, WILLIAM, 1564-1616
About
Bear, E. L'esprit d'escalier
Klassen, S. Eye of the moon
Ozick, C. Actors
Rahman, I. I, Claudius
Ward, A. E. Shakespeare.com
Zelazny, R. Exeunt omnes
Parodies, imitations, etc.
Cadnum, M. Or be to not
Douglas, C. N. Those are pearls that were his eyes
McKillip, P. A. Star-crossed
Roberts, A. And tomorrow and
Talley, M. Too many cooks
Shakespeare.com. Ward, A. E.
Shaking the dead geranium. Rzetelny, H.
Shaletown. Leslie, N.
Shallaballah. Samuels, M.
Shallow Breaths. Primbs, J.
Shambles: A new career for the home help. Hay, A.
A **shambles** in Belgravia. Newman, K.
Shame. Castillon, C.
Shame. O'Dea, L.
Shame. Robinson, R.
The **Shame**. Sprow, V.
Shame. West, K. E.
Shame in the blood. Miura, T.
Shame under the chuppah. Judah, S.
Shameless. Johnson, G.
Shamengwa. Erdrich, L.
Shami, Janset Berkok
Coffee Time
New Letters v74 no3 p61-5 2008
Delivery
The Massachusetts Review v48 no1 p80-7 Spr 2007
Shamlan, Sharifah al-
Knowing his secret
Oranges in the sun; short stories from the Arabian Gulf; edited and translated by Deb-orah S. Akers, Abubaker A. Bagader
La **shampouineuse**. Charyn, J.
The **Shamraken** homeward-bounder. Hodgson, W. H.
Shandy takes the hook. L'Amour, L.
SHANGHAI (CHINA) *See* China—Shanghai
Shanghai. Abella, A.

The **Shanghai** Foxtrot (a Fragment) by Mu
  Shiying [With an introduction by Sean
  Macdonald] Mu Shiying
Shanghai, not without gestures. L'Amour, L.
Shank, J. Alicia
  Local Honey
    Michigan Quarterly Review v44 no2 p318-30
    Spr 2005
Shannon, Harry
  A host of shadows
    Dark delicacies 2; fear: more original tales of
    terror and the macabre by the world's
    greatest horror writers; edited by Del
    Howison and Jeff Gelb
Shannon, John
  The legend of Bayboy and the Mexican surfer
    Politics noir; dark tales from the corridors of
    power; edited by Gary Phillips.
Shannon, Ray *See* Haywood, Gar Anthony
Shanties. Anderson, B.
The **shape** of the past. Gardiner, J. R.
Shapiro, Gerald
  Mandelbaum, the Criminal
    Ploughshares v34 no1 p153-79 Spr 2008
Shapiro, Lamed
  The cross
    No star too beautiful; Yiddish stories from
    1382 to the present; compiled and translat-
    ed by Joachim Neugroschel
Shard of glass. Johnson, A. D.
SHARECROPPERS *See* Tenant farming
A **shared** journey. Im, C.
The **shared** patio. July, M.
The **shared** sukkah. Molodowsky, K.
Sharing. Wideman, J. E.
The **sharing** of flesh. Anderson, P.
Sharing the Musical Experience of a Lifetime.
  Tanabe, M. K. G.
The **shark** fight—Second installment. James, C. L.
  R.
Shark liver oil. Coleman, W.
SHARKS
  James, C. L. R. Bad Boo-boo-loo and the shark
    fight
  James, C. L. R. The shark fight—Second install-
    ment
  Murakami, H. Hanalei Bay
  Shepard, J. Astounding stories
  Winton, T. Family
Sharks. Harleman, A.
Sharks. Robison, C.
The **sharks** of the St. Elmo. Hodgson, W. H.
Sharma, Akhil
  Cosmopolitan
    Children playing before a statue of Hercules;
    edited and introduced by David Sedaris
Sharp, Zoe
  Served cold
    A hell of a woman; an anthology of female
    noir; edited by Megan Abbott; foreword by
    Val McDermid
Sharpe, Matthew
  (jt. auth) See Simon, Adam and Sharpe, Mat-
    thew
The **sharpest** knife. Rock, P.
SHARPSHOOTERS
  Liparulo, R. Kill zone

Sharratt, Mary
  Taking the bullets out
    Twin cities; edited by Julie Schaper & Steven
    Horwitz
Shauntrelle. Nelson, A.
SHAVING
  Téllez, H. Lather and nothing else
Shaw, Andrea
  Jus' a Pinch of the Yellow Powder
    Femspec v6 no1 p135-44 2005
SHAW, BERNARD, 1856-1950
                  About
  Bradbury, R. G.B.S.- Mark V
Shaw, George Bernard *See* Shaw, Bernard, 1856-
  1950
Shaw, Heather
  Single white farmhouse
    Year's best fantasy 6; edited by David G.
    Hartwell & Kathryn Cramer
Shaw, Irwin
  Borough of cemeteries
    Brooklyn noir 2; the classics; edited by Tim
    McLoughlin
  Sailor off the Bremen
    Manhattan noir 2; the classics; edited by
    Lawrence Block
SHAW, KAREN
                  About
  Barthelme, D. Manfred
Shaw, Kendra Langford
  Magicians
    The Antioch Review v67 no3 p524-36 Summ
    2009
Shaw, Patricia Hearst *See* Hearst, Patricia Camp-
  bell
Shaw, Sam
  Reconstruction
    The Best American mystery stories, 2005; ed-
    ited and with an introduction by Joyce Car-
    ol Oates; Otto Penzler, series editor
    StoryQuarterly v40 p302-23 2004
Shawl, Nisi
  At the huts of Ajala
    Shawl, N. Filter house; short fiction
  The beads of Ku
    Shawl, N. Filter house; short fiction
  Bird day
    Shawl, N. Filter house; short fiction
  But she's only a dream
    Shawl, N. Filter house; short fiction
  Cruel Sistah
    The Year's best fantasy and horror: nineteenth
    annual collection; edited by Ellen Datlow
    and Kelly Link & Gavin J. Grant
  Deep end
    So long been dreaming; postcolonial science
    fiction & fantasy; Nalo Hopkinson &
    Uppinder Mehan, eds
    Shawl, N. Filter house; short fiction
  Good boy
    Shawl, N. Filter house; short fiction
  Little horses
    Detroit noir; edited by E. J. Olsen & John C.
    Hocking
    Shawl, N. Filter house; short fiction
  Maggies
    Shawl, N. Filter house; short fiction
  Momi watu
    Shawl, N. Filter house; short fiction

Shawl, Nisi—*Continued*
The pragmatical princess
 Shawl, N. Filter house; short fiction
The Raineses´
 Shawl, N. Filter house; short fiction
Shiomah's land
 Shawl, N. Filter house; short fiction
Wallamelon
 Shawl, N. Filter house; short fiction
The water museum
 Shawl, N. Filter house; short fiction
The **shawl**. Erdrich, L.
Shayla, Heidi
Himmelen
 Pushcart prize XXXII: best of the small
 presses 2008; edited by Bill Henderson
 with the Pushcart Prize editors
 The Georgia Review v60 no1 p130-43 Spr
 2006
She almost wrote. Ward, A. E.
She couldn't help wondering. Brodsky, M.
She-creatures. Lanagan, M.
She is a Woman; I am Also a Woman. Bikwan,
 W.
(She owns) Every thing. Enright, A.
She sees my monsters now. Reed, R.
She thinks dots. Ducornet, R.
Sheard, Timothy
All bleeding stops . . . eventually
 Hard boiled Brooklyn; edited by Reed Farrel
 Coleman
Sheckley, Robert
Cordle to onion to carrot
 This is my funniest; leading science fiction
 writers present their funniest stories ever;
 edited by Mike Resnick
Shed this life. Dalton, Q.
Sheehan, Aurelie
Horse, Girl, Landscape
 New England Review v26 no3 p67-72 2005
Spin
 Ploughshares v34 no2/3 p114-26 Fall 2008
Sheehan, Tricia Currans- *See* Currans-Sheehan,
 Tricia
Sheehy, Hugh
Harold Plays the Pauper
 Southwest Review v90 no4 p596-619 2005
The invisibles
 The Best American mystery stories, 2008; ed-
 ited and with an introduction by George
 Pelecanos; Otto Penzler, series editor
 The Kenyon Review v29 no4 p45-67 Fall
 2007
Swallowfly
 The Antioch Review v65 no3 p454-68 Summ
 2007
Sheena McMain: Boxing Catfish Blues [Medical
 Humanities, 31 no1 June 2005] McMain, S.
SHEEP
Bierce, A. Jo Dornan and the ram
Bierce, A. My favorite murder
Coloane, F. Passage to Puerto Edén
Sheep. McNeely, T. H.
SHEEP FARMING *See* Sheep
Sheetrock. Weaver, W.
Sheets, Nicole
By Now It Should Sound Like Music
 Western Humanities Review v61 no2 p12-21
 Spr/Summ 2007

Sheets. Waters, D.
Sheigetz. Stavans, I.
The **Sheika's** condition. Bellatin, M.
Sheldon, Alice Hastings Bradley *See* Tiptree,
 James, 1916-1987
Sheldon, Raccoona, 1916-1987
 See also Tiptree, James, 1916-1987
Shelf life. Corso, P.
Shell, Lilith
Recompense
 "Tell it to us easy" and other stories; a com-
 plete short fiction anthology of African
 American women writers in Opportunity
 magazine, (1923-1948); edited by Judith
 Musser.
Shell game. Asher, N.
Shell games. Martin, G. R. R.
**SHELLEY, MARY WOLLSTONECRAFT,
1797-1851**
     About
Zelazny, R. There shall be no moon!
   Parodies, imitations, etc.
Kessel, J. Pride and Prometheus
SHELLEY, PERCY BYSSHE, 1792-1822
     About
Zelazny, R. There shall be no moon!
SHELLS
Bradbury, R. The sea shell
Russell, K. The City of Shells
Shells. Roscoe, P.
The **Shelter**. Gildner, G.
The **shelter**. Humaydan, I. N. a.- .
Shelter. Mun, N.
Shelter. Perabo, S.
Shelter. Peterson, P. W.
Shelter of rain. Sundaresan, I.
The **Shelter** of the World. Rushdie, S.
Shenanigans. Pearlman, E.
Shepard, B.H.
Sweet Benny and the Sanchez penitentiary band
 Hardcore hardboiled; edited by Todd Robin-
 son; introduction by Otto Penzler
Shepard, Jim
The Academy of Chaos and Self-Command
 The Virginia Quarterly Review p31-42 2006
 supp
Ajax is all about attack
 Shepard, J. Love and hydrogen; new and se-
 lected stories
Alicia and Emmett with the 17th Lancers at Ba-
 laclava
 Shepard, J. Love and hydrogen; new and se-
 lected stories
Ancestral legacies
 Shepard, J. Like you'd understand, anyway;
 stories
The assassination of Reinhard Heydrich
 Shepard, J. Love and hydrogen; new and se-
 lected stories
Astounding stories
 Shepard, J. Love and hydrogen; new and se-
 lected stories
Batting against Castro
 Shepard, J. Love and hydrogen; new and se-
 lected stories
Climb aboard the mighty flea
 Shepard, J. Love and hydrogen; new and se-
 lected stories

Shepard, Jim—*Continued*

Courtesy for beginners
Shepard, J. Like you'd understand, anyway; stories

The creature from the Black Lagoon
Shepard, J. Love and hydrogen; new and selected stories

Dade County, November 2000
Politically inspired; edited by Stephen Elliott; assistant editor, Gabriel Kram; associate editors, Elizabeth Brooks [et al.]

Descent into perpetual night
Shepard, J. Love and hydrogen; new and selected stories

Eros 7
Shepard, J. Like you'd understand, anyway; stories

Eustace
Shepard, J. Love and hydrogen; new and selected stories

The First South Central Australian Expedition
Shepard, J. Like you'd understand, anyway; stories

Glut your soul on my accursed ugliness
Shepard, J. Love and hydrogen; new and selected stories

The gun lobby
Shepard, J. Love and hydrogen; new and selected stories

Hadrian's wall
The Pushcart Prize XXX: best of the small presses 2006; edited by Bill Henderson with the Pushcart Prize editors
Shepard, J. Like you'd understand, anyway; stories

Happy with Crocodiles
The American Scholar v77 no3 p110-23 Summ 2008

In cretaceous seas
Burnham, C. Who can save us now?; brand-new superheroes and their amazing [short] stories; edited by Owen King and John McNally; [illustrations by Chris Burnham]

John Ashcroft: more important things than me
Shepard, J. Love and hydrogen; new and selected stories
Stumbling and raging; more politically inspired fiction; edited by Stephen Elliott; with associate editors Greg Larson [et al.]
Best of Tin House; stories; foreword by Dorothy Allison

Krakatau
Shepard, J. Love and hydrogen; new and selected stories

Love and hydrogen
Shepard, J. Love and hydrogen; new and selected stories

Mars attacks
Shepard, J. Love and hydrogen; new and selected stories

Messiah
Shepard, J. Love and hydrogen; new and selected stories

The mortality of parents
Shepard, J. Love and hydrogen; new and selected stories

My Aeschylus
Shepard, J. Like you'd understand, anyway; stories

Piano stops here
Shepard, J. Love and hydrogen; new and selected stories

Pleasure boating in Lituya Bay
Shepard, J. Like you'd understand, anyway; stories
Ploughshares v33 no1 p184-201 Spr 2007

Proto-scorpions of the silurian
Shepard, J. Like you'd understand, anyway; stories

Reach for the sky
Shepard, J. Love and hydrogen; new and selected stories

Resolution: The First South Central Australian Expedition Jim Shepard
Granta no95 p219-42 Fall 2006

Runway
Shepard, J. Love and hydrogen; new and selected stories

Sans farine
Shepard, J. Like you'd understand, anyway; stories
The Best American short stories, 2007; selected from U. S. and Canadian magazines by Stephen King with Heidi Pitlor; with an introduction by Stephen King

Spending the night with the poor
Shepard, J. Love and hydrogen; new and selected stories

Tedford and the megalodon
McSweeney's mammoth treasury of thrilling tales; edited by Michael Chabon

Trample the dead, hurdle the weak
Shepard, J. Like you'd understand, anyway; stories
Harper's v311 p72-4, 76-8 S 2005

Won't get fooled again
Shepard, J. Love and hydrogen; new and selected stories

The Zero Meter Diving Team
Shepard, J. Like you'd understand, anyway; stories
Bomb no101 p98-104 Fall 2007

Shepard, Karen

Light as a Feather
Ploughshares v33 no2/3 p117-31 Fall 2007

Shepard, Lucius

The arcevoalo
Shepard, L. The best of Lucius Shepard

Beast of the heartland
Shepard, L. The best of Lucius Shepard

Crocodile rock
Shepard, L. Eternity and other stories

Dead money
Shepard, L. The best of Lucius Shepard

Delta Sly Honey
Shepard, L. The best of Lucius Shepard

Dog-eared paperback of my life
Other earths; edited by Nick Gevers and Jay Lake.

The Drive-In Puerto Rico
Shepard, L. Eternity and other stories

The ease with which we freed the beast
Inferno; new tales of terror and the supernatural; edited by Ellen Datlow.

Eternity and afterward
Shepard, L. Eternity and other stories

Hands up! Who wants to die?
Shepard, L. Eternity and other stories

Sherman, Rachel—*Continued*

Two stories; Single family; Scenic view

Sherman, R. The first hurt; stories

Sherrard, Cherene

A Woman's Ambition

Feminist Studies v33 no3 p591-605 Fall 2007

Sherred, T. L.

E for effort

The Mammoth book of golden age science fiction; edited by Isaac Asimov, Charles G. Waugh and Martin H. Greenberg

Sherrill, Steven

Flower

Noise; fiction inspired by Sonic Youth; edited bt Peter Wild; introduction by Lee Ranaldo

Sherwood, Frances

History

So the story goes; twenty-five years of the Johns Hopkins short fiction series; edited by John T. Irwin and Jean McGarry; with a foreword by John Barth

She's Not Here. Orner, P.

She's taking her tits to the grave. Cheek, C.

She's the One. Hadley, T.

Shibli, Adania

Dust

Iowa Review v37 no2 p93-104 Fall 2007

Faint hints of tranquillity

Words without borders; the world through the eyes of writers; an anthology; edited by Samantha Schnee, Alane Salierno Mason, and Dedi Felman

May God keep love in a cool and dry place

Qissat; short stories by Palestinian women; edited by Jo Glanville

We Are All Equally Far from Love

World Literature Today v83 no2 p57-61 Mr/Ap 2009

Shiel, Matthew Phipps

The stone of the Edmundsbury Monks

The Mammoth book of vintage whodunnits; edited by Maxim Jakubowski

Shields, Carol

Absence

Shields, C. Collected stories

Accidents

Shields, C. Collected stories

Block out

Shields, C. Collected stories

Chemistry

Shields, C. Collected stories

Collision

Shields, C. Collected stories

Death of an artist

Shields, C. Collected stories

Dolls, dolls, dolls, dolls

Shields, C. Collected stories

Dressing down

Shields, C. Collected stories

Dressing up for the carnival

Shields, C. Collected stories

Dying for love

Shields, C. Collected stories

Edith-Esther

Shields, C. Collected stories

Eros

Shields, C. Collected stories

Family secrets

Shields, C. Collected stories

Flatties: their various forms and uses

Shields, C. Collected stories

Flitting behavior

Shields, C. Collected stories

Fragility

Shields, C. Collected stories

Fuel for the fire

Shields, C. Collected stories

Good manners

Shields, C. Collected stories

The harp

Shields, C. Collected stories

Hazel

Shields, C. Collected stories

Hinterland

Shields, C. Collected stories

Home

Shields, C. Collected stories

Ilk

Shields, C. Collected stories

Invention

Shields, C. Collected stories

Invitations

Shields, C. Collected stories

The journal

Shields, C. Collected stories

Keys

Shields, C. Collected stories

Love so fleeting, love so fine

Shields, C. Collected stories

The metaphor is dead–pass it on

Shields, C. Collected stories

Milk bread beer ice

Shields, C. Collected stories

Mirrors

Shields, C. Collected stories

Mrs. Turner cutting the grass

Shields, C. Collected stories

New music

Shields, C. Collected stories

The next best kiss

Shields, C. Collected stories

The orange fish

Shields, C. Collected stories

Others

Shields, C. Collected stories

Our men and women

Shields, C. Collected stories

Pardon

Shields, C. Collected stories

Poaching

Shields, C. Collected stories

Purple blooms

Shields, C. Collected stories

Reportage

Shields, C. Collected stories

Sailors lost at sea

Shields, C. Collected stories

Salt

Shields, C. Collected stories

A scarf

Shields, C. Collected stories

Scenes

Shields, C. Collected stories

Segue

The Virginia Quarterly Review v81 no1 p143-55 Wint 2005

Soup du jour

Shields, C. Collected stories

SHIPWRECKS AND CASTAWAYS—*Continued*

Hodgson, W. H. Out of the storm
Hodgson, W. H. The real thing: 'S.O.S'
Hodgson, W. H. The voice in the dawn
Hodgson, W. H. The voice in the night
L'Amour, L. The Dancing Kate
Scliar, M. The cow
Smith, C. A. The uncharted isle
Stevens, F. Friend island

SHIPYARDS

Knight, M. Gerald's monkey

Shira. Tidhar, L.

Shirley, John

Ash
  San Francisco noir 2; the classics; edited by Peter Maravelis.
Blind eye
  Poe's lighthouse; all new collaborations with Edgar Allan Poe; edited by Christopher Conlon
  Shirley, J. Living shadows; stories: new and preowned
Brittany? Oh: she's in translucent blue
  Shirley, J. Living shadows; stories: new and preowned
Buried in the sky
  Shirley, J. Living shadows; stories: new and preowned
The gunshot
  Shirley, J. Living shadows; stories: new and preowned
In the road
  Shirley, J. Living shadows; stories: new and preowned
Isolation Point, California
  Shirley, J. Living shadows; stories: new and preowned
Jody and Annie on TV
  Shirley, J. Living shadows; stories: new and preowned
Miss singularity
  Shirley, J. Living shadows; stories: new and preowned
My victim
  Shirley, J. Living shadows; stories: new and preowned
Nineteen seconds
  Shirley, J. Living shadows; stories: new and preowned
One stick: both ends sharpened
  Shirley, J. Living shadows; stories: new and preowned
The sea was wet as wet can be
  Shirley, J. Living shadows; stories: new and preowned
Seven knives
  Shirley, J. Living shadows; stories: new and preowned
The sewing room
  Shirley, J. Living shadows; stories: new and preowned
Skeeter junkie
  Shirley, J. Living shadows; stories: new and preowned
Sleepwalkers
  Shirley, J. Living shadows; stories: new and preowned

Sweet armageddon
  Shirley, J. Living shadows; stories: new and preowned
War and peace
  Shirley, J. Living shadows; stories: new and preowned
What would you do for love?
  Shirley, J. Living shadows; stories: new and preowned
The word "random", deliberately repeated
  Shirley, J. Living shadows; stories: new and preowned
(jt. auth) See Rucker, Rudy von Bitter and Shirley, John

Shirley, Philip

Charisma
  Shirley, P. Oh don't you cry for me
The consequence of summer heat
  Shirley, P. Oh don't you cry for me
A death in the family
  Shirley, P. Oh don't you cry for me
The Downtown Club
  Shirley, P. Oh don't you cry for me
Robert Earl and W. C.
  Shirley, P. Oh don't you cry for me
The story of William B. Greene
  Shirley, P. Oh don't you cry for me
To be loved in Skyline
  Shirley, P. Oh don't you cry for me
The trust Jesus society
  Shirley, P. Oh don't you cry for me
The turkey hunt
  Shirley, P. Oh don't you cry for me

Shirley Brierley: Screaming and Shouting [Medical Humanities, 31 no1 June 2005] Brierley, S.

The **shirt**. Connell, M.

Shirts against skins. Singleton, G.

Shishin, Alex

Counterparts
  Prairie Schooner v80 no1 p191-7 Spr 2006

Shit happens. Stewart, P.

The **Shiva**. Schottenfeld, S.

Shiva in shadow. Kress, N.

Shivani, Anis

Anatolia
  Confrontation no98/99 p27-50 Spr/Summ 2007
Go Sell it on the Mountain
  Dalhousie Review v88 no3 p337-56 Aut 2008
Jealousy
  Confrontation no92/93 p105-25 Fall 2005/Wint 2006
Manzanar
  Agni no68 p111-29 2008

The **shivering**. Adichie, C. N.

Shivnan, Sally

Dicking the Buddha
  The Antioch Review v65 no3 p424-36 Summ 2007

Shklovsky, Yevgeny

A Cup of Coffee in the Café on Ostozhenka
  Agni no58 p105-11 2003

Shlesinger, Miriam

(tr.) See Keret, Etgar

Shock and awe. Turtledove, H.

A **shock** for the countess. Montanyc, C. S.

Shockwave. Matheson, R.

The **shoe** in SHOES window. Tambour, A.

Shoeless Joe Jackson comes to Iowa. Kinsella, W. P.

The **shoemaker** murder. Schuyler, G. S.

SHOEMAKERS

Cadnum, M. Naked little men

Molodowsky, K. From Leyb the shoemaker

Molodowsky, K. Godl the shoemaker of Rehovot

Van Booy, S. Apples

Shoes. Rheinheimer, K.

The **shoeshine** man's regrets. Lippman, L.

Shoggoths in bloom. Bear, E.

Sholem Aleichem

Seventy-five thousand (a pack of tsoris)

No star too beautiful; Yiddish stories from 1382 to the present; compiled and translated by Joachim Neugroschel

Sholer, Luke

Imitate the sun

The Adventure of the missing detective and 19 of the year's finest crime and mystery stories!; edited by Ed Gorman and Martin H. Greenberg

Sholom Aleichem *See* Sholem Aleichem, 1859-1916

Shomer, Enid

Chosen

Shomer, E. Tourist season; stories

Crash course

Shomer, E. Tourist season; stories

Fill in the blank

New stories from the South: the year's best, 2006; selected from U.S. magazines by Allan Gurganus with Kathy Pories; with an introduction by Allan Gurganus

Shomer, E. Tourist season; stories

The hottest spot on earth

Shomer, E. Tourist season; stories

Prairie Schooner v79 no4 p63-79 Wint 2005

Laws of nature

Shomer, E. Tourist season; stories

The other mother

Shomer, E. Tourist season; stories

Rapture

Shomer, E. Tourist season; stories

The summer of questions

Shomer, E. Tourist season; stories

Sweethearts

Shomer, E. Tourist season; stories

Tourist season

Shomer, E. Tourist season; stories

SHOOTING

Alvarado, B. Bastille Day

Arnow, H. L. S. The two hunters

Currans-Sheehan, T. The last trapshoot

Fulmer, D. Algiers

Golden, M. After [excerpt]

Hinton, S. E. No white light no tunnel

McLoughlin, T. Scared rabbit

Tudish, C. Killer

Williams, J. Anodyne

Wilson, K. The shooting man

Shooting Booth. Smith, R. T.

The **shooting** man. Wilson, K.

The **shooting** of John Roy Worth. Kaminsky, S. M.

Shooting Snakes. Cokal, S.

Shooting Tuvia. Keret, E.

The **shop** of little horrors. Reed, K.

A **shopgirl**. Reisen, A.

SHOPKEEPERS *See* Merchants

SHOPLIFTING

Anderson, B. Rollo's dairy (Jake and Deedee)

McHugh, M. F. Frankenstein's daughter

Stafford, J. Bad characters

Shoplifting in the USA. Donovan, G.

Shoppers: No purchase necessary. Kelly, J. P.

SHOPPING

Bannister, I. Mrs Hyde frolics in the eel pit

Crane, E. Donovan's closet

Ducornet, R. The one marvelous thing

Harris, J. Come in, Mr. Lowry, your number is up!

Harris, J. Faith and Hope go shopping

Klassen, S. The seven steps

Sherman, R. Tag sale

Sotiropoulou, E. The assistants

Shopping. Averill, T. F.

Shopping. Seller-Mason, S.

Shopping at the end of the world. Lain, D.

SHOPPING BAG LADIES *See* Homeless persons

Short Bull, Jesse

The Wildman

Tribal College Journal of American Indian Higher Education v19 no1 p44-5 Fall 2007

The **short** history of a prince [excerpt] Hamilton, J.

A **short** history of love. Stern, R. G.

A **short** history of the Civil War. Garrett, G. P.

The **short** night. Uchida, H.

Short talks. Carson, A.

A **short** wedding story. Spark, D.

The **shortest** way home. Kiely, B.

The **shot** tower. Bingham, S.

The **Shotgun** Situation. Sylvester, L.

Shotgun wedding. Almond, S.

Shots. Rozan, S. J.

Should I be scared? Ward, A. E.

Shoulders, Felicity

Ashes

Calyx v25 no2 p110-19 Summ 2009

Shouting Nazarene. Pruett, L.

The **shouting** woman. Randolph, L.

Shouts of joy. Raphael, L.

Shovel work. Bukoski, A.

Show & tell. Crouse, D.

Show me the way to go home. L'Amour, L.

Show me yours. Reed, R.

Show Me Yours . . . Van Camp, R.

The **show** must go on!. Bova, B.

Show-windows. Reisen, A.

The **showcase** of dreams. Parra, E. A.

Showdown at Anchor. Dawson, P.

The **showers**. Mukhopadhyay, T.

Shraer-Petrov, David *See* Shrayer-Petrov, David, 1936-

Shrake, Bud

Strange peaches [excerpt]

Lone Star literature; from the Red River to the Rio Grande; edited by Don Graham

Shrake, Edwin *See* Shrake, Bud, 1931-2009

Shrayer-Petrov, David

Apple cider vinegar

Shrayer-Petrov, D. and Shrayer, M. Jonah and Sarah; Jewish stories of Russia and America; edited by Maxim D. Shrayer

Shrayer-Petrov, David—*Continued*

David and Goliath
  Shrayer-Petrov, D. and Shrayer, M. Jonah and Sarah; Jewish stories of Russia and America; edited by Maxim D. Shrayer
Dismemberers
  Shrayer-Petrov, D. and Shrayer, M. Jonah and Sarah; Jewish stories of Russia and America; edited by Maxim D. Shrayer
Hände hoch!
  Shrayer-Petrov, D. and Shrayer, M. Jonah and Sarah; Jewish stories of Russia and America; edited by Maxim D. Shrayer
He, she and the others
  Shrayer-Petrov, D. and Shrayer, M. Jonah and Sarah; Jewish stories of Russia and America; edited by Maxim D. Shrayer
Hurricane Bob
  Shrayer-Petrov, D. and Shrayer, M. Jonah and Sarah; Jewish stories of Russia and America; edited by Maxim D. Shrayer
In the reeds
  Shrayer-Petrov, D. and Shrayer, M. Jonah and Sarah; Jewish stories of Russia and America; edited by Maxim D. Shrayer
Jonah and Sarah
  Shrayer-Petrov, D. and Shrayer, M. Jonah and Sarah; Jewish stories of Russia and America; edited by Maxim D. Shrayer
Lanskoy Road
  Shrayer-Petrov, D. and Shrayer, M. Jonah and Sarah; Jewish stories of Russia and America; edited by Maxim D. Shrayer
Old writer Foreman
  Shrayer-Petrov, D. and Shrayer, M. Jonah and Sarah; Jewish stories of Russia and America; edited by Maxim D. Shrayer
Rusty
  Shrayer-Petrov, D. and Shrayer, M. Jonah and Sarah; Jewish stories of Russia and America; edited by Maxim D. Shrayer
Tsukerman and his children
  Shrayer-Petrov, D. and Shrayer, M. Jonah and Sarah; Jewish stories of Russia and America; edited by Maxim D. Shrayer
Young Jews and two gymnasium girls
  Shrayer-Petrov, D. and Shrayer, M. Jonah and Sarah; Jewish stories of Russia and America; edited by Maxim D. Shrayer

Shriki. Keret, E.
The **Shrine** of Temptation. Merril, J.
SHRINES
Di Filippo, P. Lignum Crucis
Shrinker. Sargent, P.
Shroff, Murzban
The great divide
  Shroff, M. F. Breathless in Bombay; stories
Shroff, Murzban F.
Babu Barrah Takka
  Shroff, M. F. Breathless in Bombay; stories
Breathless in Bombay
  Shroff, M. F. Breathless in Bombay; stories
  Gettysburg Review v18 no2 p259-88 Summ 2005
Busy Sunday
  Shroff, M. F. Breathless in Bombay; stories
  Southwest Review v91 no3 p428-43 2006
Dhobi ghat
  Shroff, M. F. Breathless in Bombay; stories

A different bhel
  Shroff, M. F. Breathless in Bombay; stories
Haraami
  Shroff, M. F. Breathless in Bombay; stories
Jamal Haddi's revenge
  Shroff, M. F. Breathless in Bombay; stories
Love in the time of AIDS
  Shroff, M. F. Breathless in Bombay; stories
The maalishwalla
  Shroff, M. F. Breathless in Bombay; stories
Meter down
  Shroff, M. F. Breathless in Bombay; stories
  South Carolina Review v37 no2 p132-42 Spr 2005
The queen guards her own
  Shroff, M. F. Breathless in Bombay; stories
This house of mine
  Shroff, M. F. Breathless in Bombay; stories
Traffic
  Shroff, M. F. Breathless in Bombay; stories
A **shroud** for the damned. Block, L.
The **shrug** of Atlas. Gentile, J.
Shrunk. Grimes, C.
Shteyngart, Gary
A Love Letter
  The New Yorker v82 no6 p66-77 Mr 27 2006
Planet of the Yids
  Granta no93 p69-81 Spr 2006
Shtok, Fradel
The archbishop
  No star too beautiful; Yiddish stories from 1382 to the present; compiled and translated by Joachim Neugroschel
Shtoss. Lermontov, M. I.
Shua, Ana María
Death as a side effect
  Díaz, G. J. Women and power in Argentine literature; stories, interviews, and critical essays; [by] Gwendolyn Díaz
Farewell, my love
  Violations; stories of love by Latin American women; edited and with an introduction by Psiche Hughes; foreword by Brian Matthews
The spinal column
  Díaz, G. J. Women and power in Argentine literature; stories, interviews, and critical essays; [by] Gwendolyn Díaz
The white Guanaco in the middle of France
  English translations of short stories by contemporary Argentine women writers; edited by Eliana Cazaubon Hermann; translated by Sally Webb Thornton
Shugaar, Antony
(tr.) See Parrella, Valeria
Shukert, Rachel
The Paris Hilton International Fellowship
  2033; the future of misbehavior: interplanetary dating, Madame President, socialized plastic surgery, and other good news from the future; from the editors of Nerve.com; instigated by Svedka
Shukman, Henry
Castaway
  Shukman, H. Mortimer of the Maghreb; stories
Darien dogs
  Shukman, H. Mortimer of the Maghreb; stories

Shukman, Henry—*Continued*

The garden of God: 1976
  Shukman, H. Mortimer of the Maghreb; stories

The garden of God: 1988
  Shukman, H. Mortimer of the Maghreb; stories

The garden of God: 1996
  Shukman, H. Mortimer of the Maghreb; stories

The garden of God: 1996 (2)
  Shukman, H. Mortimer of the Maghreb; stories

Man with golden eagle
  Shukman, H. Mortimer of the Maghreb; stories

Mortimer of the Maghreb
  Shukman, H. Mortimer of the Maghreb; stories

Old Providence
  Shukman, H. Mortimer of the Maghreb; stories

Shuman, Shirley Nelson

Concerto
  "Tell it to us easy" and other stories; a complete short fiction anthology of African American women writers in Opportunity magazine, (1923-1948); edited by Judith Musser.

Shunn, William

Inclination
  Science fiction: the best of the year 2007 edition; edited by Rich Horton

Strong medicine
  The Year's best science fiction: twenty-first annual collection; edited by Gardner Dozois

The **shunned** house. Lovecraft, H. P.

Shuter, Susan

The West Highland Line
  Dalhousie Review v86 no3 p435-47 Aut 2006

Shuteye for the timebroker. Di Filippo, P.

The **Siamese** academies. Machado de Assis

SIAMESE TWINS

Jablonski, N. One of us

Jablonski, N. Pam calls her mother on five-cent Sundays

Lazellari, E. The date

Pollack, E. Uno

Siba'i, Ahmad al-

Auntie Kadrajan
  Oranges in the sun; short stories from the Arabian Gulf; edited and translated by Deborah S. Akers, Abubaker A. Bagader

SIBERIA (RUSSIA)

Goss, T. The rapid advance of sorrow

Kolendo, A. Wintering

L'Amour, L. Coast patrol

L'Amour, L. Flight to the north

Sanders, W. Amba

Siberia. Erpenbeck, J.

Siblings. Woon, Y.

The **siblings**, 1910. Menger-Anderson, K.

SIBYLS *See* Oracles

SICILY

Messina, M. America 1911

Messina, M. America 1918

Messina, M. Caterina's loom

Messina, M. Ciancianedda

Messina, M. Dainty shoes

Messina, M. Grace

Messina, M. Grandmother Lidda

Messina, M. Her father's house

Messina, M. I take you out

Messina, M. Red roses

SICK CHILDREN

Adrian, C. The vision of Peter Damien

Brown, E. Thursday's child

Hasak-Lowy, T. The end of Larry's wallet

Hoffman, A. The summer kitchen

McIlvoy, K. Cascade Lake

Moore, L. People like that are the only people here

Murray, A. SeaSky

Shepard, J. Alicia and Emmett with the 17th Lancers at Balaclava

Sherman, R. Two stories; Single family; Scenic view

Taraqqi, G. The Shemiran bus

Ts'an-hsüeh. Helin

Sick days. Stewart, P.

Sick in London. Gordon, M.

Sick Play. Searle, E.

Sidewalks. Keret, E.

Sideways from now. Meaney, J.

The **sidewinders**. Ellis, S.

Sidney Balbion. Helprin, M.

Siegal, Lisa

The Dark Part of the Road
  Georgia Bar Journal v13 no7 p46-55 Je 2008

The **siege**. Qadir 'Aqil, 'A. a.-

A **siege** of cranes. Rosenbaum, B.

The **siege** of Fadiman. Roberts, A.

Siegel, Gail Louise

The Dog Ate My . . .
  StoryQuarterly v40 p300-1 2004

Siegel, James

Empathy
  Thriller; edited by James Patterson

Sierra, Javier

The fifth world
  Thriller 2; stories you just can't put down; edited by Clive Cussler; [stories by] Kathleen Antrim . . . [et al.]

SIERRA LEONE

Fountain, B. The lion's mouth

McCauley, W. Foday

McCauley, W. Hungry de catch me

McCauley, W. Mister Henry's trousers

McCauley, W. Need

McCauley, W. The offer

The **siesta**. Brau, E.

Sightings. Spencer, E.

Sightings. Wideman, J. E.

Sightseeing. Lapcharoensap, R.

The **Sightseer**. Wilson, S.

Signal mirror. Rock, P.

Signal to noise. Reynolds, A.

Signaling for rescue. Herrmann, M.

Signatures. Levy, J.

The **significance** of importance. Davis, A. B.

Signing ceremony. Charters, D.

Signor, Randy Michael

Crossing over
  Meeting across the river; stories inspired by the haunting Bruce Springsteen song; edited by Jessica Kaye and Richard J. Brewer

SIGNS (OMENS) *See* Omens

Signs. Greenman, B.

Signs and markings. Ochsner, G.
SIGNS AND SIGNBOARDS
    Greenman, B. Signs
Signs of life. Pearlman, E.
SIKHS
    Mukherjee, B. The management of grief
Sikka, Mohan
    Uncle Musto takes a mistress
        The PEN/O.Henry Prize stories 2009; chosen
        and with an introduction by Laura Furman;
        with essays on the stories They admire
        most by jurors A. S. Byatt; Anthony Doerr;
        Tim O'Brien
Silas Jackson. Dunbar, P. L.
Silber, Joan
    Allegiance
        Ploughshares v33 no2/3 p132-48 Fall 2007
    The high road
        Pushcart Prize XXVIII: best of the small
        presses 2004; edited by Bill Henderson and
        the Pushcart prize editors
    War buddies
        The O. Henry Prize stories 2007; edited and
        with an introduction by Laura Furman; with
        essays on the story they admire most by ju-
        rors Charles D'Ambrosio, Ursula K. Le
        Guin, Lily Tuck
SILENCE
    Brockmeier, K. The year of silence
Silence. Albright, J.
Silence. Munro, A.
Silence. Palazzeschi, A.
Silence is golden. Boosta
The **silence** of angels. Báez, A.
The **silence** of the falling stars. O'Driscoll, M.
The **silence** of the Llano. Anaya, R. A.
The **silence** of Thelonious Monk. Wideman, J. E.
Silences. Romano, T.
Silent Bianca. Yolen, J.
The **silent** colony. Silverberg, R.
Silent Leonardo. Baker, K.
The **silent** men. Rock, P.
Silent night. Muller, M.
Silent Night, Merciful Night. Schaap, J. C.
Silent retreats. Deaver, P. F.
Silent Sam'el. Dunbar, P. L.
The **silent** ship. Hodgson, W. H.
Siler, Jenny
    For sale by owner
        Greatest hits; original stories of assassins,
        hitmen, and hired guns; edited by Robert J.
        Randisi
Silhol, Lea
    Emblemata (reciting the heart sutra)
        Interfictions; an anthology of interstitial writ-
        ing; edited by Delia Sherman and Theodora
        Goss
Silk and fire. Nolan, W. F.
Silk road. Kramlovsky, B.
Silko, Leslie
    Mistaken identity
        Reckonings; contemporary short fiction by
        Native American women; edited by Hertha
        D. Sweet Wong, Lauren Stuart Muller, Jana
        Sequoya Magdaleno

Old pancakes
    Reckonings; contemporary short fiction by
    Native American women; edited by Hertha
    D. Sweet Wong, Lauren Stuart Muller, Jana
    Sequoya Magdaleno
Storyteller
    Reckonings; contemporary short fiction by
    Native American women; edited by Hertha
    D. Sweet Wong, Lauren Stuart Muller, Jana
    Sequoya Magdaleno
The **Silkworms**. Frame, J.
Sillitoe, Alan
    Before snow comes
        Sillitoe, A. New and collected stories
    The bike
        Sillitoe, A. New and collected stories
    Brothers
        Sillitoe, A. New and collected stories
    The caller
        Sillitoe, A. New and collected stories
    Canals
        Sillitoe, A. New and collected stories
    Chicken
        Sillitoe, A. New and collected stories
    The chiker
        Sillitoe, A. New and collected stories
    Confrontation
        Sillitoe, A. New and collected stories
    The decline and fall of Frankie Buller
        Sillitoe, A. New and collected stories
    The devil's almanack
        Sillitoe, A. New and collected stories
    The disgrace of Jim Scarfedale
        Sillitoe, A. New and collected stories
    The end of Enoch?
        Sillitoe, A. New and collected stories
    Enoch's two letters
        Sillitoe, A. New and collected stories
    The fiddle
        Sillitoe, A. New and collected stories
    The firebug
        Sillitoe, A. New and collected stories
    The fishing-boat picture
        Sillitoe, A. New and collected stories
    The gate of a great mansion
        Sillitoe, A. New and collected stories
    Guzman, go home
        Sillitoe, A. New and collected stories
    The loneliness of the long distance runner
        Sillitoe, A. New and collected stories
    The magic box
        Sillitoe, A. New and collected stories
    The match
        Sillitoe, A. New and collected stories
    The meeting
        Sillitoe, A. New and collected stories
    Mimic
        Sillitoe, A. New and collected stories
    Mr. Raynor the school-teacher
        Sillitoe, A. New and collected stories
    No name in the street
        Sillitoe, A. New and collected stories
    Noah's Ark
        Sillitoe, A. New and collected stories
    On Saturday afternoon
        Sillitoe, A. New and collected stories
    The other John Peel
        Sillitoe, A. New and collected stories

Silverberg, Robert—*Continued*
Thomas the Proclaimer
  Silverberg, R. Something wild is loose 1969-
    72
The time of the burning
  Asimov's science fiction: 30th anniversary an-
    thology; edited by Sheila Williams
To be continued
  Silverberg, R. To be continued
To see the invisible man
  Silverberg, R. Phases of the moon; stories of
    six decades
  Silverberg, R. To the dark star 1962-1969
To the dark star
  Silverberg, R. To the dark star 1962-1969
Trips
  Silverberg, R. Trips, 1972-73
Warm man
  Silverberg, R. Phases of the moon; stories of
    six decades
  Silverberg, R. To be continued
We know who we are
  Silverberg, R. To the dark star 1962-1969
What we learned from this morning's newspaper
  Silverberg, R. Something wild is loose 1969-
    72
When we went to see the end of the world
  Silverberg, R. Something wild is loose 1969-
    72
Why?
  Silverberg, R. To be continued
The wind and the rain
  Silverberg, R. Something wild is loose 1969-
    72
With Caesar in the underworld
  Silverberg, R. Phases of the moon; stories of
    six decades
World of a thousand colors
  Silverberg, R. To be continued
  (jt. auth) See Ellison, Harlan and Silverberg,
    Robert
Silverheels. Cook, G.
Silverston, Sondra
  (tr.) See Keret, Etgar
Simeon. Yellin, T.
Simmons, Dan
Muse of fire
  The new space opera; edited by Gardner
    Dozois and Jonathan Strahan
This year's class picture
  The living dead; edited by John Joseph Ad-
    ams
Simmons, Glori
Peaches
  Stumbling and raging; more politically in-
    spired fiction; edited by Stephen Elliott;
    with associate editors Greg Larson [et al.]
Simmons, Philip
Night vision
  Playboy's college fiction; a collection of 21
    years of contest winners; edited by Alice
    K. Turner; foreword by Thom Jones
Simms, C. N.
After the snow
  Nature v452 p912 Ap 17 2008
Quantum erat demonstrandum
  Nature v456 p280 N 13 2008

Simms, Eleanor
Tell it to us easy
  "Tell it to us easy" and other stories; a com-
    plete short fiction anthology of African
    American women writers in Opportunity
    magazine, (1923-1948); edited by Judith
    Musser.
Simms, Laura
The Ears of the Eyes in the Heart
  Parabola v31 no1 p74-8 Spr 2006
The Nightingale
  Parabola v30 no3 p83-6 Fall 2005
Simo, Erik
The black mirror
  The black mirror and other stories; an anthol-
    ogy of science fiction from Germany &
    Austria; edited & with an introduction &
    notes by Franz Rottensteiner; translated by
    Mike Mitchell.
Simon, Adam and Sharpe, Matthew
Seconds [With introduction and reproductions of
  paintings]
  Bomb no108 p supp24-supp27 Summ 2009
Simon, Beth
Beachhead
  Southwest Review v91 no4 p604-10 2006
Philanthropy
  Southwest Review v93 no4 p586-92 2008
Simon, Daniel
(tr.) See Montalbetti, Christine
SIMONE, NINA
                    About
Jackson, S. Here is the church
Luongo, M. What Nina wants
Simone. Burgin, R.
Simple as that. Meacham, R.
Simple exercises for the beginning student. Ohlin,
  A.
Simple gifts. McInerney, J.
The **simple** one. Murray, A. I.
Simpson, Helen
Constitutional
  Simpson, H. In the driver's seat; stories
  Granta no90 p193-215 Summ 2005
The door
  Simpson, H. In the driver's seat; stories
Early one morning
  Simpson, H. In the driver's seat; stories
  Granta no87 p87-100 Fall 2004
Every third thought
  Simpson, H. In the driver's seat; stories
The green room
  Simpson, H. In the driver's seat; stories
Greensleeves
  The New Yorker v82 no37 p84-7 N 13 2006
Homework
  The New Yorker v83 no17 p82-6 Je 25 2007
If I'm spared
  Simpson, H. In the driver's seat; stories
In-Flight Entertainment
  Granta v100 p89-101 Wint 2007
In the driver's seat
  Simpson, H. In the driver's seat; stories
The phlebotomist's love life
  Simpson, H. In the driver's seat; stories
Scan
  Granta v98 p85-92 Summ 2007
The tree
  Simpson, H. In the driver's seat; stories

Singer, Isaac Bashevis—*Continued*

The litigants
    Singer, I. B. Collected stories: One night in
        Brazil to The death of Methuselah
Logorihims
    Singer, I. B. Collected stories: One night in
        Brazil to The death of Methuselah
Loshikl
    Singer, I. B. Collected stories: One night in
        Brazil to The death of Methuselah
The manuscript
    Singer, I. B. Collected stories: One night in
        Brazil to The death of Methuselah
The mathematician
    Singer, I. B. Collected stories: One night in
        Brazil to The death of Methuselah
Miracles
    Singer, I. B. Collected stories: One night in
        Brazil to The death of Methuselah
The mirror
    No star too beautiful; Yiddish stories from
        1382 to the present; compiled and translat-
        ed by Joachim Neugroschel
The missing line
    Singer, I. B. Collected stories: One night in
        Brazil to The death of Methuselah
The mistake
    Singer, I. B. Collected stories: One night in
        Brazil to The death of Methuselah
Moon and madness
    Singer, I. B. Collected stories: One night in
        Brazil to The death of Methuselah
Morris and Timna
    Singer, I. B. Collected stories: One night in
        Brazil to The death of Methuselah
My adventures 25 as an idealist
    Singer, I. B. Collected stories: One night in
        Brazil to The death of Methuselah
A nest egg for paradise
    Singer, I. B. Collected stories: One night in
        Brazil to The death of Methuselah
A night in the poorhouse
    Singer, I. B. Collected stories: One night in
        Brazil to The death of Methuselah
Not for the Sabbath
    Singer, I. B. Collected stories: One night in
        Brazil to The death of Methuselah
On the way to the poorhouse
    Singer, I. B. Collected stories: One night in
        Brazil to The death of Methuselah
One day of happiness
    Singer, I. B. Collected stories: One night in
        Brazil to The death of Methuselah
One night in Brazil
    Singer, I. B. Collected stories: One night in
        Brazil to The death of Methuselah
The painting
    Singer, I. B. Collected stories: One night in
        Brazil to The death of Methuselah
A party in Miami Beach
    Singer, I. B. Collected stories: One night in
        Brazil to The death of Methuselah
A peephole in the gate
    Singer, I. B. Collected stories: One night in
        Brazil to The death of Methuselah
Pity
    Singer, I. B. Collected stories: One night in
        Brazil to The death of Methuselah

The pocket remembered
    Singer, I. B. Collected stories: One night in
        Brazil to The death of Methuselah
The power of darkness
    Singer, I. B. Collected stories: One night in
        Brazil to The death of Methuselah
The psychic journey
    Singer, I. B. Collected stories: One night in
        Brazil to The death of Methuselah
The recluse
    Singer, I. B. Collected stories: One night in
        Brazil to The death of Methuselah
The reencounter
    Singer, I. B. Collected stories: One night in
        Brazil to The death of Methuselah
Remnants
    Singer, I. B. Collected stories: One night in
        Brazil to The death of Methuselah
Runners to nowhere
    Singer, I. B. Collected stories: One night in
        Brazil to The death of Methuselah
Sabbath in Gehanna
    Singer, I. B. Collected stories: One night in
        Brazil to The death of Methuselah
The safe deposit
    Singer, I. B. Collected stories: One night in
        Brazil to The death of Methuselah
The secret
    Singer, I. B. Collected stories: One night in
        Brazil to The death of Methuselah
The smuggler
    Singer, I. B. Collected stories: One night in
        Brazil to The death of Methuselah
Strangers
    Singer, I. B. Collected stories: One night in
        Brazil to The death of Methuselah
Strong as death is love
    Singer, I. B. Collected stories: One night in
        Brazil to The death of Methuselah
Tanhum
    Singer, I. B. Collected stories: One night in
        Brazil to The death of Methuselah
A telephone call on Yom Kippur
    Singer, I. B. Collected stories: One night in
        Brazil to The death of Methuselah
There are no coincidences
    Singer, I. B. Collected stories: One night in
        Brazil to The death of Methuselah
The trap
    Singer, I. B. Collected stories: One night in
        Brazil to The death of Methuselah
Two
    Singer, I. B. Collected stories: One night in
        Brazil to The death of Methuselah
Two weddings and one divorce
    Singer, I. B. Collected stories: One night in
        Brazil to The death of Methuselah
Vanvild Kava
    Singer, I. B. Collected stories: One night in
        Brazil to The death of Methuselah
Why Heisherik was born
    Singer, I. B. Collected stories: One night in
        Brazil to The death of Methuselah
Yochna and Schmelke
    Singer, I. B. Collected stories: One night in
        Brazil to The death of Methuselah

SINGER, ISAAC BASHEVIS, 1904-1991
About
    Biller, M. My name was Singer

Singer, Israel Joshua

Magda

No star too beautiful; Yiddish stories from 1382 to the present; compiled and translated by Joachim Neugroschel

Singer, Jon

Willow pattern

Interfictions; an anthology of interstitial writing; edited by Delia Sherman and Theodora Goss

Singer, Margot

Body count

Singer, M. The pale of settlement; stories
Prairie Schooner v81 no3 p71-85 Fall 2007

Borderland

Singer, M. The pale of settlement; stories
Gettysburg Review v20 no4 p551-68 Wint 2007

Deir Yassin

Singer, M. The pale of settlement; stories
Western Humanities Review v59 no1 p43-63 Spr 2005

Expatriate

Singer, M. The pale of settlement; stories

Hazor

Singer, M. The pale of settlement; stories

Helicopter days

Singer, M. The pale of settlement; stories

Lila's story

Singer, M. The pale of settlement; stories

The pale of settlement

Singer, M. The pale of settlement; stories
The North American Review v290 no1 p18-26 Ja/F 2005

Reunification

Singer, M. The pale of settlement; stories
Agni no60 p166-76 2004

Singer, Nathan

The killer whispers and prays . . .; or, Like a sledge-hammer to the ribcage

Expletive deleted; edited by Jen Jordan

Singer, Sean

Franz Kafka—Serious About Your Safety
Salmagundi no150/151 p78-84 Spr/Summ 2006

Singer, Julia Klatt

Chicken

Murphy, N. Twelve branches; stories from St. Paul; [by] Nora Murphy ... {et al.}

From one window

Murphy, N. Twelve branches; stories from St. Paul; [by] Nora Murphy ... {et al.}

Translations

Murphy, N. Twelve branches; stories from St. Paul; [by] Nora Murphy ... {et al.}

The **singer** of seeds. Yolen, J.

SINGERS

Averill, T. F. The musical genius of Moscow, Kansas

Benioff, D. When the nines roll over

Bennett, T. Saving Grace

Coleman, W. Dunny

Crone, M. Fever

Cross, E. Appearances

Earley, T. Yard art

Faber, M. The courage consort

Freed, L. Songbird

Fusilli, J. Brenda, my star

Gifford, B. After hours at La Chinita

Green, G. "This very vivd morn"

Green, G. Voices in a mask

Hellmann, L. F. Your sweet man

Helprin, M. Il colore ritrovato

Hodgson, W. H. Kind, kind and gentle is she

July, M. I kiss a door

Kitahara, A. No time for tears

Kozlowski, L. Three times a night, every other night

McCracken, E. Some terpsichore

McIlvoy, K. Make it sound like a train

Meno, J. Mr. Song

Muller, M. The cracks in the sidewalk

Popkes, S. Great Caruso

Purdy, J. Kitty place

Rand, K. "Penny" Joe Crane died for my sins

Rickert, M. Moorina of the seals

Russell, K. Accident brief, occurrence # 00/422

Shepard, L. Stars seen through stone

Snyder, S. Dumpster Tuesday

Strom, D. Husband, wife

Tóibín, C. Famous blue raincoat

Tóibín, C. A song

Tomlinson, J. Berliner

Villoro, J. Mariachi

With, C. Sanny Tranny is alive and well and living on Davie

Zelazny, R. Recital

Singh, Jaspreet

Mont Royal
The Walrus v4 no7 p83-5 S 2007

Singh, Vandana

Delhi

So long been dreaming; postcolonial science fiction & fantasy; Nalo Hopkinson & Uppinder Mehan, eds

The Year's best science fiction: twenty-second annual collection; edited by Gardner Dozois

Hunger

Interfictions; an anthology of interstitial writing; edited by Delia Sherman and Theodora Goss

Of love and other monsters

The Year's best science fiction: twenty-fifth annual collection; edited by Gardner Dozois

The wife

The Year's best fantasy and horror: seventeenth annual collection; edited by Ellen Datlow, Kelly Link and Gavin J. Grant

SINGING AND VOICE CULTURE

Badib, 'A. 'A. Trilling cries of joy

Beaumont, M. Contraflow

Maxwell, W. The fisherman who had nobody to go out in his boat with him

Pendarvis, J. My high, squeaky voice

Singing girl. Lamb, H.

Singing in the free world. MacEnulty, P.

Singing my sister down. Lanagan, M.

Singing of Mount Abora. Goss, T.

Singing second part. Tomlinson, J.

Singing Worm. Chin, M.

A **single** awe. Coake, C.

A **Single** Fact Can Spoil a Good Argument. Priddy, J.

The **single** girl's guide to compromising homeland security. Kirkman, J.

SINGLE MEN
See also Widowers
Allen, D., Jr. The green suit
Buckler, E. Just like everyone else
Bunin, I. A. Antigone
Burgin, R. Aerialist
Burke, K. Olympians
Canty, K. Sleeping beauty
Chaon, D. Shepherdess
Connell, M. The shirt
Crouse, D. The forgotten kingdom
Dahl, R. Georgy Porgy
Duncklee, J. The miner
Ebenbach, D. H. Between Camelots
Ebenbach, D. H. Bridesmaid
Fox, P. Grace
Hayes, D. Twenty-six hours, twenty-five minutes
Jones, N. Home for a short time
Kalotay, D. Rehearsal dinner
Keane, J. B. Under the sycamore tree
Kiely, B. The green lanes
Krasikov, S. The alternate
Lasdun, J. The half sister
Levin, Z. A hush
McInerney, J. The last bachelor
Murakami, H. The year of spaghetti
Ozick, C. At Fumicaro
Sillitoe, A. No name in the street
Tolstaia, T. Okkervil River
Treat, J. Listing
Upadhyay, S. Chintamani's women
Updike, D. Geranium
Updike, D. Old girlfriends
Wilson, K. Worst-Case Scenario
Wingate, S. Beaching it
Working, R. The tin man
A **single** metre. Taha, R.

SINGLE-PARENT FAMILY
Eisenberg, D. Window
Keeble, J. I could love you (if I wanted)
Nisbet, R. Dors, mon petit, dors
Ockert, J. Mother may I
Rust, E. M. Stealing Yakima
Single white farmhouse. Shaw, H.

SINGLE WOMEN
See also Unmarried mothers; Widows
Adichie, C. N. The shivering
Adichie, C. N. The thing around your neck
Almond, S. The evil B. B. Chow
Almond, S. Shotgun wedding
Anderson, B. The daggy end
Andreas-Salomé, L. Before the awakening
Andreas-Salomé, L. Incognito
Andreas-Salomé, L. Maidens' roundelay
Apple, M. Yao's chick
Asch, S. A mannequin
Atwood, M. The age of lead
Atwood, M. The other place
Beattie, A. Tending something
Benioff, D. Neversink
Bingham, S. The shot tower
Bluestein, E. Tea
Boswell, R. City bus
Boyers, R. The French lesson
Bradbury, R. Death and the maiden
Bradbury, R. The whole town's sleeping
Brady, C. Looking for a female tenet
Brady, C. Wait for instructions

Brady, C. Wicked stepmother
Brockmeier, K. The view from the seventh layer
Brown, D. Entebbe
Brown, D. Land of ass and honey
Brown, D. On being french
Brown, D. Thanksgiving
Brown, D. Your own private America
Buckler, E. Long, long after school
Cain, S. The necessity of certain behaviors
Canty, K. The birthday girl
Capote, T. Among the paths to Eden
Coffman, L. H. The dream lover
Coleman, W. Hibernation
Colombi, M. Learn a trade for a rainy day
Cooper, J. C. Success
Corso, P. Nose dive
Crane, E. Donovan's closet
Cummins, A. Where I work
Curtis, R. Hungry self
Curtis, R. The Sno-Kone Cart
Curtis, R. Summer, with twins
Curtis, R. The wolf at the door
Dolores, C. Aunt Zézé's tears
Donoghue, E. Touchy subjects
Dufresne, J. Epithalamion
Ebenbach, D. H. Bridesmaid
Ellison, J. The company of men
Engberg, S. Mother of chartres
Engberg, S. River hills
Enright, A. Indifference
Enright, A. (She owns) Every thing
Erdrich, L. Morphine
Erdrich, L. Knives
Espinet, R. Nowarian blues
Faber, M. The hundred and ninety-nine steps
Feitell, M. The marrying kind
Freed, L. The curse of the appropriate man
Fuentes, C. The father's servant
Fulton, A. A shadow table
Fulton, J. The animal girl
Gabrielyan, N. The studio apartment
Gaitskill, M. Don't cry
Gappah, P. My cousin-sister Rambanai
Gay, J. Likes of him
Gay, J. A walk across the rooftops
Gerber, M. J. Night stalker
Gerber, M. J. Tell me your secret
Gifford, B. Ball lighting
Gilchrist, E. Jade Buddhas, red bridges, fruits of love
Glatt, L. Tag
Gordon, M. Bishop's house
Gordon, M. Eleanor's music
Gordon, M. The Epiphany Branch
Gordon, M. Walt
Gough, J. Julia
Graham, T. The blue book of dogs
Graham, T. Eyes of glass
Graham, T. Heaven's gate
Graham, T. Ultrasaurus
Graham, T. Waiting for Elvis
Granville-Barker, H. Georgiana
Guo, S. Clover
Hasegawa, J. The unfertilized egg
Hawes, L. Salinger's mistress
Hayes, D. Hope
Hempel, A. The new lodger
Hirahara, N. Tat Master
Hukumenoglu, H. The smell of fish

Siscar, Cristina
  Hoop, thread, and canvas
      Díaz, G. J. Women and power in Argentine
      literature; stories, interviews, and critical
      essays; [by] Gwendolyn Díaz
The **Sister**. Boyers, R.
The **sister**. July, M.
Sister Anne and the cowboy. Vaile, C. M.
Sister death. Henry, S.
Sister Jackson's superstitions. Dunbar, P. L.
Sister Mary (Colombo, 1949). Mohanraj, M. A.
SISTERS
      See also Brothers and sisters; Half-
      sisters; Stepsisters; Twins
  Albert, E. We have trespassed
  Alvarado, B. Emily's exit
  Anderson, B. The girls
  Angel, J. Portions
  Atwood, M. The headless horseman
  Bakken, K. N. Eggs
  Bakken, K. N. Vigil
  Barnes, S. Calling home
  Barnes, S. Earthquake
  Barth, J. As I was saying . . .
  Boswell, R. Almost not beautiful
  Brady, C. The dazzling world
  Brandon, J. Pushed or was fell
  Budnitz, J. Flush
  Cadnum, M. Ella and the canary prince
  Cooper, J. C. As time goes by
  Corso, P. Freezer burn
  Corso, P. Unraveled
  Curtis, R. The Sno-Kone Cart
  Davis, D. S. By the scruff of the soul
  Davis, D. S. Dies Irae
  Desaulniers, J. Where we all should have been
  Desaulniers, J. Who knows more than you
  Donoghue, E. Necessary noise
  Enright, A. Little sister
  Enright, A. Natalie
  Erdrich, L. F-M
  Estleman, L. D. Smart aleck
  Feitell, M. It couldn't be more beautiful
  Fowler, K. J. The last worders
  Fulton, A. Centrally isolated
  Fulton, A. Dorothy Loves maleman
  Gerber, M. J. I don't believe this
  Gifford, B. Havana Moon
  Gilchrist, E. The brown cape
  Gordon, M. Delia
  Goss, T. Lily, with clouds
  Granados, C. The bride
  Groff, L. Lucky Chow Fun
  Hadley, T. Buckets of blood
  Harleman, A. The angel of Entropy
  Harris, J. Hello, goodbye
  Hawes, L. The knack
  Hempel, A. San Francisco
  Hernandez, L. The cross
  Herrmann, M. Leonardo's baby
  Herrmann, M. Signaling for rescue
  Highsmith, P. Where the door is always open
      and the welcome mat is out
  Holland, N. Someone is always missing
  Holland, N. What begins with bird
  Hyde, M. Second-hand
  Johnson, G. Schadenfreude
  Jones, C. Irregularities
  Kiely, B. Wild rover no more

  Koretsky, J. L. Alligator story
  Krughoff, L. Halley's comet
  Kwa'mboka. Birds
  LaBrie, A. Our last supper
  LaBute, N. Opportunity
  Lam, D. The seventy-two-ounce steak challenge
  Leung, B. Desdemona's ruins
  Lunstrum, K. S. Familial kindness
  Lutz, G. People shouldn't have to be the ones
      to tell you
  Luvaas, W. Silver thaw
  Macaire, J. Island
  MacLaverty, B. The wedding ring
  Macy, C. Bait and switch
  Maron, M. You may already be a winner
  Martin, J. Three sisters
  Mason, B. A. The heirs
  Masurel, P. Static
  McInerney, J. Reunion
  McKenzie, E. Last of our tribe
  McNett, M. Catalog sales
  McPhee, M. The anthropology of sex
  Meacham, R. Trim & notions
  Michalopoulou, A. Light
  Michalopoulou, A. A slight, controlled unease
  Miller, A. L. Getting to know the world
  Mohanraj, M. A. Sister Mary (Colombo, 1949)
  Molodowsky, K. Unhappy celebrations
  Moorcock, M. The Cairene Purse
  Morábito, F. Los crucigramas/Crosswords
  Nadelson, S. Walter's girls
  Nelson, A. Party of one
  Nelson, A. People people
  Oates, J. C. The blind man's sighted daughters
  Oates, J. C. Heat
  Oates, J. C. Soft-core
  Oates, J. C. Special
  Oates, J. C. Will you always love me?
  Ohlin, A. The swanger blood
  Orphée, E. The journey of Amatista and the
      dirty prince
  Palmer, K. Virtuoso mio
  Palwick, S. GI Jesus
  Panning, A. All-U-Can-Eat
  Panning, A. Cravings
  Pearlman, E. Home schooling
  Perry, A. Sneaker wave
  Pflug, U. Red velvet dust
  Phillips, H. The small door
  Pinborough, S. The nowhere man
  Redmann, J. M. The intersection of camp and
      St. Mary
  Richards, S. S. The screened porch
  Richter, S. The long hall
  Rozan, S. J. Undocumented
  Russell, K. Ava wrestles the alligator
  Schuster, F. Two sisters
  Singer, I. B. The power of darkness
  Stafford, J. In the zoo
  Sundaresan, I. Fire
  Swann, M. Secret
  Tabor, M. L. Sine die
  Talley, M. The queen is dead, long live the
      queen
  Tóibín, C. Famous blue raincoat
  Tomlinson, J. Things kept
  Trevor, W. Sitting with the dead
  Ts'an-hsüeh. Meteorite mountain
  Varallo, A. The houses left behind

SISTERS—*Continued*

Wang Ping. Crush

Wang Ping. Where the poppies blow

Welch, N. Running to Ethiopia

West, D. The long wait

West, D. The richer, the poorer

Wildgen, M. Healer

Windley, C. Home schooling

SISTERS AND BROTHERS *See* Brothers and sisters

Sisters for Shama. Koënings, N. S.

SISTERS-IN-LAW

Holladay, C. C. Hollyhocks

Keane, J. B. A tale of two furs

Moceri, M. There's only one way I can lie

Naiyer Masud. Obscure domains of fear and desire

Percy, B. Whisper

Sisters of Langham. Leckie, B.

Sisters of no mercy. Thomas, J.

The **sisters** of St. Misery. Grodstein, L.

Sisyphus and the stranger. Di Filippo, P.

Sitka. Sanders, W.

Sittenfeld, Curtis

Volunteers are shining stars

This is not chick lit; original stories by America's best women writers; edited by Elizabeth Merrick

SITTING BULL, DAKOTA CHIEF, 1831-1890

About

Duncklee, J. The last breakfast

Sitting pretty. Crowther, P.

The **sitting** tenant. King, F.

Sitting with the dead. Trevor, W.

Six different ways to die in the windy city!. LaBrie, A.

The **Six-dollar** Box of Cereal. Wortman, D.

Six-gun stampede. L'Amour, L.

Six love. Hall, J. W.

Six questions for an alien. Olsen, L.

Six stories. Kluge, A.

Six thought experiments concerning the nature of computation: Experiment 1: Lucky number. Rucker, R. v. B.

Six thought experiments concerning the nature of computation: Experiment 2: The million chakras. Rucker, R. v. B.

Six thought experiments concerning the nature of computation: Experiment 3: Aint paint. Rucker, R. v. B.

Six thought experiments concerning the nature of computation: Experiment 4: Terry's talker. Rucker, R. v. B.

Six thought experiments concerning the nature of computation: Experiment 5: The kind rain. Rucker, R. v. B.

Six thought experiments concerning the nature of computation: Experiment 6: Hello infinity. Rucker, R. v. B.

Six ways of looking at farming. Nichols, R.

The **sixteen** parts. Greene, M.

The **Sixteenth** Section. Yarbrough, S.

The **sixth** commandment. Merino, J. F.

The **sixth** palace. Silverberg, R.

Sixty-six Ford Galaxie. Manley, C.

Sized up. Apple, M.

Sizer, Bridget Bentz

Snow Blind

The Kenyon Review v28 no3 p38-49 Summ 2006

Sizzle Island [Part II] Law, S. K.

Skabardonis, Yorgos

Mussels in the flower vase

Angelic & black; contemporary Greek short stories; edited and translated by David Connolly; with an introduction by Vangelis Hatzivassileiou

SKATEBOARDING

Cooper, D. The brainiacs

Skeet, Michael

I love Paree

Witpunk; edited by Claude Lalumière and Marty Halpern

Skeeter junkie. Shirley, J.

The **Skeleton**. Rawlings, W.

SKELETONS

Bhêly-Quénum, O. A child in the bush of ghosts

Connolly, J. Mr. Gray's folly

Howard, R. E. Rattles of bones

Kelly, R. The dark tribe

Rust, E. M. The weight of bones

Sanders, W. Dry bones

Smith, C. A. The ninth skeleton

A **sketch** of highway on the nap of a mountain. Boswell, R.

Sketch with Two Cucumbers and Two Adams in It. Lomke, E.

Skiffington, Brian Baldi

Pints and Quarts: An Oral History Collected and Conveyed

The Massachusetts Review v48 no3 p380-9 Fall 2007

Skillet and saber. Howe, J.

Skillingstead, Jack

Life on the preservation

The Year's best science fiction: twenty-fourth annual collection; edited by Gardner Dozois

Science fiction: the best of the year 2007 edition; edited by Rich Horton

Skillingstead, Jack

Dead worlds

The Year's best science fiction: twenty-first annual collection; edited by Gardner Dozois

SKIN

Kelly, R. Dead skin

Malla, P. The slough

Parks, R. Skin deep

Rosenblum, M. H. Skin deep

Singleton, G. Shirts against skins

Diseases

Sherman, R. The first hurt

Skin. Dahl, R.

Skin. Porter, A.

Skin deep. Bluestein, E.

Skin deep. Boswell, R.

Skin deep. McNally, T. M.

Skin deep. Parks, R.

Skin deep. Rosenblum, M. H.

The **skin** from the muscle. Angel, J.

The **skin** of the world. Clegg, D.

The **skin** trade. Martin, G. R. R.

Skinhead central. Parker, T. J.

Skinner, José
All about balls
Las Vegas noir; edited by Jarrett Keene & Todd James Pierce.
Skinner, Quinton
Loophole
Twin cities; edited by Julie Schaper & Steven Horwitz
Skinny dipping in the Lake of the Dead. DeNiro, A.
Skipping the prom. Levithan, D.
Skippy. West, D.
SKIS AND SKIING
Olafsson, O. March
Somerville, P. The Cold War
Somerville, P. The future, the future, the future
Skitter. Szilágyi, A. L.
Skull. Almond, S.
The **skull-faced** boy. Kirtley, D. B.
The **Skull** Hunter. Day, R.
The **skull** of Shirzad Mir. Lamb, H.
The **Skunk**. Difalco, S.
Sky above a wall. Bunin, I. A.
The **Sky** at the Bottom of the River. Markus, P.
Sky full of burdens. Moceri, M.
The **sky** is large and the earth is small. Roberson, C.
The **sky** ranch. Working, R.
Sky Woman's Grandchildren [With commentary by the author] Bruchac, J.
SKYDIVING
Working, R. The sky ranch
Skyfish Falling. McNamara, S.
Skyliner. Barrett, M.
The **skysailor's** tale. Swanwick, M.
Skywriting. Milward, A. M.
Slackened caprice. Graham, O. B.
Slade, Matthew
(jt. auth) See Kuskin, William and Slade, Matthew
Sladek, John Thomas
Masterson and the clerks
New worlds; an anthology; edited by Michael Moorcock
Slam book. Monk, B.
Slamgram. Morris, M.
Slander. Molodowsky, K.
A **slap** in the face. Quiroga, H.
Slate, E. V.
Purple Bamboo Park
The PEN/O.Henry Prize stories 2009; chosen and with an introduction by Laura Furman; with essays on the stories They admire most by jurors A. S. Byatt; Anthony Doerr; Tim O'Brien
New England Review v28 no2 p25-34 2007
Slater, David
Stiffed
D. C. noir; edited by George Pelecanos
Slater, Judith
A Benevolence of Ladybugs
StoryQuarterly v40 p392-412 2004
Slatter, Angela
The jacaranda wife
Dreaming again; thirty-five new stories celebrating the wild side of Australian fiction; edited by Jack Dann
Slaughter house. Matheson, R.

SLAUGHTERING AND SLAUGHTER-HOUSES
Dahl, R. Pig
Slava. Working, R.
A **slave** for life: a story of the long ago. Cook, C. F.
Slave Quarters. Dickinson, S.
SLAVE TRADE
Stevenson, R. P. Insect dreams
SLAVERY
See also African Americans; Fugitive slaves; Slave trade
Adisa, O. P. The living roots
Akpan, U. C. Fattening for Gabon
Arnow, H. L. S. No lady
Ball, P. M. The last great house of Isla Tortuga
Carl, L. S. Way down in Egypt's land
Dunbar, P. L. Ash-Cake Hannah and her Ben
Dunbar, P. L. Aunt Tempe's revenge
Dunbar, P. L. Cahoots
Dunbar, P. L. The conjuring contest
Dunbar, P. L. Dandy Jim's conjure scare
Dunbar, P. L. The Easter wedding
Dunbar, P. L. The ingrate
Dunbar, P. L. Mr. Groby's slippery gift
Dunbar, P. L. The strength of Gideon
Dunbar, P. L. A supper by proxy
Dunbar, P. L. Viney's free papers
Finlay, C. C. We come not to praise Washington
Hayden, G. M. The maids
Hill, B. H. Part light, part memory
Holladay, C. C. The burning
Kelly, R. Oh, sordid shame!
Kobayashi, T. Panopte's eye
McHugh, M. F. The Lincoln train
McHugh, M. F. Nekropolis
Monette, S. A light in Troy
Nickless, B. Suffer the children
Purdom, T. The mists of time
Swanwick, M. Legions in time
Westwood, K. Nightship
Wilson, R. C. The peaceable land; or, The unbearable vision of Harriet Beecher Stowe
York, R. Huntress moon
SLAVES *See* Slavery
Slavin, Julia
Squatters
Best of Tin House; stories; foreword by Dorothy Allison
Slay, Jack, Jr.
Murmur's laws
A cross of centuries; twenty-five imaginative tales about the Christ; edited by Michael Bishop
SLED DOG RACING
Amdahl, G. The barber-chair
The **sledge-maker's** daughter. Reynolds, A.
SLEEP
Ali, M. N. The manhood test
Bierce, A. The civil service in Florida
Boyle, T. C. The kind assassin
Kress, N. Beggars in Spain
Ruefle, M. Sleep
Russell, K. Z.Z.'s sleep-away camp for disordered dreamers
Yates, D. The sleep machine
Sleep. Doyle, R.
Sleep. Ruefle, M.

The **sleep** machine. Yates, D.
A **sleep** not unlike death. Chercover, S.
Sleeping Arthur [Includes a commentary] Yolen, J.
Sleeping beauty. Canty, K.
Sleeping dogs. Roberson, J.
Sleeping dogs lie. Bear, E.
Sleeping with pigs. McInerney, J.
The **sleeping** woman. Fulton, J.
Sleepwalk. Sayers, V.
Sleepwalker in a fog. Tolstaia, T.
Sleepwalkers. Shirley, J.
Sleepy time Gal. Gildner, G.
Slender little thing. Brady, C.
Slice of pie. Cameron, B.
A **Slice** of the Pie. Noriega, C. A.
Slicing sautéed spinach. Vapnyar, L.
Slight. Ockert, J.
A **slight,** controlled unease. Michalopoulou, A.
Slighted. Bankole, O. G.
Slightly Far East. Moyer, K.
Slimy Shlomo is a homo. Keret, E.
Slingin'. Artemis, B.
Slippered feet. Wallace, D.
Slipping into darkness. Sullivan, C. J.
Slipping sideways through eternity. Yolen, J.
Slitten gorge. Williams, C.
Sliver. Reno, N.
Slocombe, Romain
    Guy Georges' final crime
        Paris noir; capital crime fiction; edited by
        Maxim Jakubowski
Slomski, Heather A.
    The Allure of All This
        TriQuarterly no126 p123-30 2006
Sloss, Aria Beth
    We Were Hardly Angels
        Harvard Review (1992) no36 p30-49 2009
The **slough**. Malla, P.
Slouka, Mark
    August
        Harper's v313 p79-82 Ag 2006
    Dominion
        The Best American short stories, 2006; select-
        ed from U.S. and Canadian magazines by
        Ann Patchett with Katrina Kenison; with an
        introduction by Ann Patchett
        TriQuarterly no121 p58-67 2005
    The Little Museum of Memory
        Granta no96 p213-25 Wint 2006
SLOVAKIA
    Hunt, H. Sovietski!
Slow burn. Hilaire
Slow dancing with Jesus. Dozois, G. R. and Dann,
    J.
Slow drink. Singleton, G.
Slow life. Swanwick, M.
Slow monkeys. Nichols, J.
A **slow** Saturday night at the Surrealist Sporting
    Club. Moorcock, M.
Slowhand and Little Sister. Di Filippo, P.
Slowik, Mary
    Teeth
        Iowa Review v37 no1 p124-41 Spr 2007
Slowly now the dancer. Higgins, G. V.
The **Slows**. Hareven, G.
SLUM LIFE
    McCabe, E. Truth
    Pizzolatto, N. Cryptograph

Sillitoe, A. The decline and fall of Frankie
    Buller
Stableford, B. The immortals of Atlantis
Theroux, P. The gateway of India
Waberi, A. A. A woman and a half
Slumber Party. Wortman, J.
The **Slump** Buster. Carlson, R.
SLUMS *See* Slum life
The **smackdown** outside Dedham. Finlay, C. C.
Smaglik, Paul
    For he on honeydew hath fed. . .
        Nature v439 p368 Ja 19 2006
Small avalanches. Oates, J. C.
Small Deaths. Kearns, K.
The **small** door. Phillips, H.
Small fry. Monk, B.
Small hands. Hawes, L.
Small homicide. McBain, E.
Small Humilitations. Leslie, N.
Small in the saddle. Marley, L.
The **small** machine. Barkley, B.
A **small** matter. Fulton, J.
Small mercies. Winton, T.
Small miracles. Kellerman, F.
Small offerings. Bacigalupi, P.
A **small** room in Koboldtown. Swanwick, M.
Small Rotations of the Earth. Edelglass, E.
The **small** salvation. Busch, F.
Small time. Granados, C.
SMALL TOWN LIFE
    Aisemberg, I. Ramón Acuña's time
    Bachelder, C. Blue Knights bounced from CVD
        Tourney
    Barrett, M. Cadillac
    Barrett, M. It's Saturday
    Barry, R. Instructions for a substitute bus driver
    Barry, R. Love him, Petaluma
    Bensko, J. Summer girls
    Boast, W. Weather enough
    Boudinot, R. Drugs and toys
    Bradbury, R. Colonel Stonesteel's genuine
        home-made truly Egyptian mummy
    Buckler, E. The quarrel
    Burke, J. L. The burning of the flag
    Capote, T. Children on their birthdays
    Capote, T. Jug of silver
    Card, O. S. Feed the baby of love
    Carey, J. In the matter of fallen angels
    Clarke, W. The pentecostal home for flying
        children
    Clayton, J. J. Fantasy for a Friday afternoon
    Crone, M. The ice garden
    Crone, M. Where what gets into people comes
        from
    Davis, C. Electric
    Doran, M. M. Showdown
    Doran, M. M. Wedding at the Gormay Cafe
    Dowling, T. The fooly
    Downs, G. Between states
    DuBois, B. The dark snow
    Dunbar, P. L. The independence of Silas
        Bollender
    Dunbar, P. L. The minority committee
    Dunbar, P. L. The mortification of the flesh
    Dunbar, P. L. The ordeal at Mt. Hope
    Duval, P. Rear view
    Erdrich, L. Disaster stamps of Pluto
    Erdrich, L. A wedge of shade
    Faulkner, W. A rose for Emily

Smith, Clark Ashton—*Continued*

The dweller in the gulf

Smith, C. A. The maze of the enchanter; edited by Scott Connors and Ron Hilger; with an introduction by Gahan Wilson

The empire of the necromancers

Smith, C. A. Lost worlds; introduction to the Bison Books edition by Jeff Vandermeer

Smith, C. A. A vintage from Atlantis; edited by Scott Connors and Ron Hilger; with an introduction by Michael Dirda

The end of the story

Smith, C. A. Out of space and time; introduction to the Bison Books edition by Jeff Vandermeer

Smith, C. A. The end of the story; edited by Scott Connors and Ron Hilger; with an introduction by Ramsey Campbell

The epiphany of death

Smith, C. A. The end of the story; edited by Scott Connors and Ron Hilger; with an introduction by Ramsey Campbell

The eternal world

Smith, C. A. A vintage from Atlantis; edited by Scott Connors and Ron Hilger; with an introduction by Michael Dirda

The face by the river

Smith, C. A. The door to Saturn; edited by Scott Connors and Ron Hilger; with an introduction by Tim Powers

The flower-women

Smith, C. A. Lost worlds; introduction to the Bison Books edition by Jeff Vandermeer

Smith, C. A. The maze of the enchanter; edited by Scott Connors and Ron Hilger; with an introduction by Gahan Wilson

From the crypts of memory

Smith, C. A. Out of space and time; introduction to the Bison Books edition by Jeff Vandermeer

Genius Loci

Smith, C. A. The maze of the enchanter; edited by Scott Connors and Ron Hilger; with an introduction by Gahan Wilson

The ghoul

Smith, C. A. The door to Saturn; edited by Scott Connors and Ron Hilger; with an introduction by Tim Powers

The god of the asteroid [variant title: Master of the asteroid]

Smith, C. A. A vintage from Atlantis; edited by Scott Connors and Ron Hilger; with an introduction by Michael Dirda

A good embalmer

Smith, C. A. The door to Saturn; edited by Scott Connors and Ron Hilger; with an introduction by Tim Powers

The Gorgon

Smith, C. A. Lost worlds; introduction to the Bison Books edition by Jeff Vandermeer [Variant title: Symposium of the Gorgon]

Smith, C. A. The door to Saturn; edited by Scott Connors and Ron Hilger; with an introduction by Tim Powers

The holiness of Azédarac

Smith, C. A. Lost worlds; introduction to the Bison Books edition by Jeff Vandermeer

Smith, C. A. A vintage from Atlantis; edited by Scott Connors and Ron Hilger; with an introduction by Michael Dirda

The hunters from beyond

Smith, C. A. Lost worlds; introduction to the Bison Books edition by Jeff Vandermeer

Smith, C. A. The door to Saturn; edited by Scott Connors and Ron Hilger; with an introduction by Tim Powers

The ice demon

Smith, C. A. The maze of the enchanter; edited by Scott Connors and Ron Hilger; with an introduction by Gahan Wilson

The immeasurable horror

Smith, C. A. The end of the story; edited by Scott Connors and Ron Hilger; with an introduction by Ramsey Campbell

The immortals of Mercury

Smith, C. A. A vintage from Atlantis; edited by Scott Connors and Ron Hilger; with an introduction by Michael Dirda

The invisible city

Smith, C. A. A vintage from Atlantis; edited by Scott Connors and Ron Hilger; with an introduction by Michael Dirda

The isle of the torturers

Smith, C. A. Lost worlds; introduction to the Bison Books edition by Jeff Vandermeer

Smith, C. A. The maze of the enchanter; edited by Scott Connors and Ron Hilger; with an introduction by Gahan Wilson

The justice of the elephant

Smith, C. A. The door to Saturn; edited by Scott Connors and Ron Hilger; with an introduction by Tim Powers

The kingdom of the worm

Smith, C. A. The door to Saturn; edited by Scott Connors and Ron Hilger; with an introduction by Tim Powers

The kiss of Zoraida

Smith, C. A. The door to Saturn; edited by Scott Connors and Ron Hilger; with an introduction by Tim Powers

The last hieroglyph

Smith, C. A. Out of space and time; introduction to the Bison Books edition by Jeff Vandermeer

The last incantation

Smith, C. A. Lost worlds; introduction to the Bison Books edition by Jeff Vandermeer

Smith, C. A. The end of the story; edited by Scott Connors and Ron Hilger; with an introduction by Ramsey Campbell

The letter from Mohaun Los

Smith, C. A. Lost worlds; introduction to the Bison Books edition by Jeff Vandermeer

Smith, C. A. The door to Saturn; edited by Scott Connors and Ron Hilger; with an introduction by Tim Powers

The light from beyond

Smith, C. A. Lost worlds; introduction to the Bison Books edition by Jeff Vandermeer

The maker of gargoyles

Smith, C. A. The maker of gargolyes and other stories; introduction by Darrell Schweitzer

Smith, C. A. A vintage from Atlantis; edited by Scott Connors and Ron Hilger; with an introduction by Michael Dirda

Smith, Clark Ashton—[Variant title: Symposium of the Gorgon]—*Continued*

The mandrakes
    Smith, C. A. The maze of the enchanter; edited by Scott Connors and Ron Hilger; with an introduction by Gahan Wilson
Marooned in Andromeda
    Smith, C. A. The end of the story; edited by Scott Connors and Ron Hilger; with an introduction by Ramsey Campbell
The maze of Maal Dweb
    Smith, C. A. Lost worlds; introduction to the Bison Books edition by Jeff Vandermeer
The maze of the enchanter [variant title: The maze of Maal Dweb]
    Smith, C. A. The maze of the enchanter; edited by Scott Connors and Ron Hilger; with an introduction by Gahan Wilson
The metamorphosis of the world
    Smith, C. A. The end of the story; edited by Scott Connors and Ron Hilger; with an introduction by Ramsey Campbell
The monster of the prophecy
    Smith, C. A. Out of space and time; introduction to the Bison Books edition by Jeff Vandermeer
    Smith, C. A. The end of the story; edited by Scott Connors and Ron Hilger; with an introduction by Ramsey Campbell
A murder in the fourth dimension
    Smith, C. A. The end of the story; edited by Scott Connors and Ron Hilger; with an introduction by Ramsey Campbell
The nameless offspring
    Smith, C. A. The maker of gargolyes and other stories; introduction by Darrell Schweitzer
    Smith, C. A. A vintage from Atlantis; edited by Scott Connors and Ron Hilger; with an introduction by Michael Dirda
Necromancy in Naat
    Smith, C. A. Lost worlds; introduction to the Bison Books edition by Jeff Vandermeer
The necromantic tale
    Smith, C. A. The end of the story; edited by Scott Connors and Ron Hilger; with an introduction by Ramsey Campbell
A night in Malnéant
    Smith, C. A. Out of space and time; introduction to the Bison Books edition by Jeff Vandermeer
    Smith, C. A. The end of the story; edited by Scott Connors and Ron Hilger; with an introduction by Ramsey Campbell
The ninth skeleton
    Smith, C. A. The end of the story; edited by Scott Connors and Ron Hilger; with an introduction by Ramsey Campbell
An offering to the moon
    Smith, C. A. The door to Saturn; edited by Scott Connors and Ron Hilger; with an introduction by Tim Powers
The phantoms of the fire
    Smith, C. A. The end of the story; edited by Scott Connors and Ron Hilger; with an introduction by Ramsey Campbell
The planet of the dead
    Smith, C. A. Lost worlds; introduction to the Bison Books edition by Jeff Vandermeer

Smith, C. A. The end of the story; edited by Scott Connors and Ron Hilger; with an introduction by Ramsey Campbell
The Plutonian drug
    Smith, C. A. Lost worlds; introduction to the Bison Books edition by Jeff Vandermeer
    Smith, C. A. A vintage from Atlantis; edited by Scott Connors and Ron Hilger; with an introduction by Michael Dirda
The red world of Polaris
    Smith, C. A. The door to Saturn; edited by Scott Connors and Ron Hilger; with an introduction by Tim Powers
A rendezvous in Averoigne
    Smith, C. A. Out of space and time; introduction to the Bison Books edition by Jeff Vandermeer
    Smith, C. A. The door to Saturn; edited by Scott Connors and Ron Hilger; with an introduction by Tim Powers
The resurrection of the rattlesnake
    Smith, C. A. The maker of gargolyes and other stories; introduction by Darrell Schweitzer
    Smith, C. A. The end of the story; edited by Scott Connors and Ron Hilger; with an introduction by Ramsey Campbell
The return of the sorcerer
    Smith, C. A. Out of space and time; introduction to the Bison Books edition by Jeff Vandermeer
    Smith, C. A. The door to Saturn; edited by Scott Connors and Ron Hilger; with an introduction by Tim Powers
The root of Ampoi
    Smith, C. A. The end of the story; edited by Scott Connors and Ron Hilger; with an introduction by Ramsey Campbell
Sadastor
    Smith, C. A. Out of space and time; introduction to the Bison Books edition by Jeff Vandermeer
    Smith, C. A. The end of the story; edited by Scott Connors and Ron Hilger; with an introduction by Ramsey Campbell
The satyr
    Smith, C. A. The end of the story; edited by Scott Connors and Ron Hilger; with an introduction by Ramsey Campbell
The second interment
    Smith, C. A. Out of space and time; introduction to the Bison Books edition by Jeff Vandermeer
    Smith, C. A. A vintage from Atlantis; edited by Scott Connors and Ron Hilger; with an introduction by Michael Dirda
The secret of the cairn [variant title: The light from beyond]
    Smith, C. A. The maze of the enchanter; edited by Scott Connors and Ron Hilger; with an introduction by Gahan Wilson
The seed from the sepulcher
    Smith, C. A. A vintage from Atlantis; edited by Scott Connors and Ron Hilger; with an introduction by Michael Dirda
Seedling of Mars
    Smith, C. A. A vintage from Atlantis; edited by Scott Connors and Ron Hilger; with an introduction by Michael Dirda

Smith, Clark Ashton—[Variant title: Symposium of the Gorgon]—*Continued*

The seven geases

Smith, C. A. Lost worlds; introduction to the Bison Books edition by Jeff Vandermeer

The shadows

Smith, C. A. Out of space and time; introduction to the Bison Books edition by Jeff Vandermeer

A star-change

Smith, C. A. The maze of the enchanter; edited by Scott Connors and Ron Hilger; with an introduction by Gahan Wilson

The supernumerary corpse

Smith, C. A. A vintage from Atlantis; edited by Scott Connors and Ron Hilger; with an introduction by Michael Dirda

The tale of Satampra Zeiros

Smith, C. A. Lost worlds; introduction to the Bison Books edition by Jeff Vandermeer

Smith, C. A. The end of the story; edited by Scott Connors and Ron Hilger; with an introduction by Ramsey Campbell

The testament of Athammaus

Smith, C. A. The maker of gargolyes and other stories; introduction by Darrell Schweitzer

Smith, C. A. Out of space and time; introduction to the Bison Books edition by Jeff Vandermeer

Smith, C. A. The door to Saturn; edited by Scott Connors and Ron Hilger; with an introduction by Tim Powers

The third episode of Vathek

Smith, C. A. The maker of gargolyes and other stories; introduction by Darrell Schweitzer

The third episode of Vathek: the story of the princess Zulkaïs and the prince Kalilah

Smith, C. A. The maze of the enchanter; edited by Scott Connors and Ron Hilger; with an introduction by Gahan Wilson

Thirteen phantasms

Smith, C. A. The maker of gargolyes and other stories; introduction by Darrell Schweitzer

Smith, C. A. The end of the story; edited by Scott Connors and Ron Hilger; with an introduction by Ramsey Campbell

Told in the desert

Smith, C. A. The door to Saturn; edited by Scott Connors and Ron Hilger; with an introduction by Tim Powers

The treader of the dust

Smith, C. A. Lost worlds; introduction to the Bison Books edition by Jeff Vandermeer

Ubbo-Sathla

Smith, C. A. Out of space and time; introduction to the Bison Books edition by Jeff Vandermeer

Smith, C. A. A vintage from Atlantis; edited by Scott Connors and Ron Hilger; with an introduction by Michael Dirda

The uncharted isle

Smith, C. A. Out of space and time; introduction to the Bison Books edition by Jeff Vandermeer

Smith, C. A. The end of the story; edited by Scott Connors and Ron Hilger; with an introduction by Ramsey Campbell

The vaults of Yoh-Vombis

Smith, C. A. Out of space and time; introduction to the Bison Books edition by Jeff Vandermeer

Smith, C. A. A vintage from Atlantis; edited by Scott Connors and Ron Hilger; with an introduction by Michael Dirda

The venus of Azombeii

Smith, C. A. The end of the story; edited by Scott Connors and Ron Hilger; with an introduction by Ramsey Campbell

A vintage from Atlantis

Smith, C. A. A vintage from Atlantis; edited by Scott Connors and Ron Hilger; with an introduction by Michael Dirda

The voyage of King Euvoran

Smith, C. A. The maze of the enchanter; edited by Scott Connors and Ron Hilger; with an introduction by Gahan Wilson

A voyage to Sfanomoë

Smith, C. A. Lost worlds; introduction to the Bison Books edition by Jeff Vandermeer

Smith, C. A. The end of the story; edited by Scott Connors and Ron Hilger; with an introduction by Ramsey Campbell

Vulthoom

Smith, C. A. The maze of the enchanter; edited by Scott Connors and Ron Hilger; with an introduction by Gahan Wilson

The weaver in the vault

Smith, C. A. The maze of the enchanter; edited by Scott Connors and Ron Hilger; with an introduction by Gahan Wilson

The weird of Avoosl Wuthoqquan

Smith, C. A. Out of space and time; introduction to the Bison Books edition by Jeff Vandermeer

Smith, C. A. A vintage from Atlantis; edited by Scott Connors and Ron Hilger; with an introduction by Michael Dirda

The White Sybil

Smith, C. A. The maze of the enchanter; edited by Scott Connors and Ron Hilger; with an introduction by Gahan Wilson

The willow landscape

Smith, C. A. The door to Saturn; edited by Scott Connors and Ron Hilger; with an introduction by Tim Powers

Xeethra

Smith, C. A. Lost worlds; introduction to the Bison Books edition by Jeff Vandermeer

Smith, Cordelia T.

Black brother

"Tell it to us easy" and other stories; a complete short fiction anthology of African American women writers in Opportunity magazine, (1923-1948); edited by Judith Musser.

Smith, D. Lynn

The charnel house

Summer chills; strangers in stranger lands; edited by Stephen Jones

Smith, Neil—*Continued*
Green fluorescent protein
Smith, N. Bang crunch; stories
Isolettes
Smith, N. Bang crunch; stories
Jaybird
Smith, N. Bang crunch; stories
Scrapbook
Smith, N. Bang crunch; stories
Smith, R. A. McCall *See* McCall Smith, Alexander, 1948-
Smith, R. T.
Bitterwolf
Smith, R. T. Uke Rivers delivers; stories
Blaze
Smith, R. T. Uke Rivers delivers; stories
Docent
The Best American short stories, 2004; edited by Lorrie Moore; Katrina Kenison series editor
Smith, R. T. Uke Rivers delivers; stories
I have lost my right
Smith, R. T. Uke Rivers delivers; stories
Ina Grove
The Best American Mystery Stories, 2006; edited and with an introduction by Scott Turow; Otto Penzler, series editor
The Virginia Quarterly Review v81 no4 p230-53 Fall 2005
Jesus wept
The Pushcart Prize XXX: best of the small presses 2006; edited by Bill Henderson with the Pushcart Prize editors
Smith, R. T. Uke Rivers delivers; stories
Little Sorrel
Smith, R. T. Uke Rivers delivers; stories
Luna
TriQuarterly no130 p112-17 2008
Razorhead the axeman
Smith, R. T. Uke Rivers delivers; stories
Shooting Booth
Smith, R. T. Uke Rivers delivers; stories
Story
New stories from the South: the year's best, 2007; selected from U.S. magazines by Edward P. Jones with Kathy Pories; with an introduction by Edward P. Jones
Prairie Schooner v80 no1 p8-16 Spr 2006
Tastes like chicken
New stories from the South: the year's best, 2006; selected from U.S. magazines by Allan Gurganus with Kathy Pories; with an introduction by Allan Gurganus
Trousseau
Smith, R. T. Uke Rivers delivers; stories
Tube Rose
Smith, R. T. Uke Rivers delivers; stories
Uke Rivers delivers
Smith, R. T. Uke Rivers delivers; stories
Wretch like me
New stories from the South; the year's best, 2008; selected from U.S. magazines by ZZ Packer with Kathy Pories; with an introduction by ZZ Packer
The Virginia Quarterly Review v83 no2 p156-77 Spr 2007
Smith, Richie
Graft vs. Host
Confrontation no104 p213-26 Summ 2009

Smith, Rob McClure
Disasters of War
Confrontation no90/91 p48-57 Spr/Summ 2005
Smith, Rosamond, 1938-
See also Oates, Joyce Carol, 1938-
Smith, Sybil
Hound of Heaven
Harvard Review (1992) no33 p116-22 2007
Smith, Tyler
A troop [sic] of baboons
Best American fantasy; guest editors Ann & Jeff VanderMeer; series editor Matthew Cheney
Smith, Zadie
Hanwell in Hell
The New Yorker v80 no28 p113-14, 116-23 S 27 2004
Hanwell Senior
The New Yorker v83 no12 p138-42 My 14 2007
Hanwell Snr
The book of other people; edited by Zadie Smith
Smith, Debbie *See* Smith, D. Lynn
Smith, Sarah
The woman in chains [excerpt]
No star too beautiful; Yiddish stories from 1382 to the present; compiled and translated by Joachim Neugroschel
Smither, Elizabeth
The Girl Who Proposed
Harvard Review (1992) no31 p6-15 2006
Smoke. Boswell, R.
Smoke. Heathcock, A.
Smoke. McIlvoy, K.
Smoke. McInerney, J.
Smoke. Winn, T.
Smoke from Chester leading me down to see Dogman. Parker, M.
Smoke got in my eyes. Rubenstein, B.
SMOKING
Ford, J. The fat one
Hempel, A. Du jour
Lewin, M. Z. Cigarettes
McInerney, J. Smoke
Popkes, S. Great Caruso
Tsutsui, Y. The last smoker
Smoking gun. Rich, M.
Smoking, waiting for the dawn. Nahrung, J.
Smolazh, Yoysef
The open grave
No star too beautiful; Yiddish stories from 1382 to the present; compiled and translated by Joachim Neugroschel
A **smooth** hero. Tang, J.
Smorgasbord. Wolff, T.
Smother. Oates, J. C.
SMUGGLERS *See* Smuggling
The **smugglers**. Hodgson, W. H.
SMUGGLING
Archer, J. Know what I mean?
Byrne, M. Only the strong survive
Connell, E. S. Caribbean provedor
Daughtry, P. French letters
Eisenstadt, J. Golden venture
Fountain, B. The lion's mouth
Hodgson, W. H. The red herring
Hodgson, W. H. Senator Sandy MacGhee

SMUGGLING—*Continued*

Hodgson, W. H. The smugglers
Kennedy, C. Habit
L'Amour, L. East of Gorontalo
Lanagan, M. She-creatures
Pendarvis, J. Tollbooth confidential
Trezise, R. Coney Island
Waters, D. Mr. Epstein and the dealer

Smuggling a kiss. Malae, P. N.

Smyles, Iris

The Great Lawn
Bomb no99 p102-3 Spr 2007

Snack cakes. Downs, G.

Snail stones. Melko, P.

Snake. King, O.

Snake boy. Barnes, H. L.

Snake catcher. Naiyer Masud

Snake eyes. King, J.

The **snake** girl. Kessel, J.

Snake Island. Ts'an-hsüeh

Snake Oil. McMullan, M.

SNAKES

Barnes, H. L. Snake boy
Bierce, A. The man and the snake
Bierce, A. Snaking
Bishop, T. Courting Miss Ellen
Dahl, R. Poison
Domecq, B. The Judas-tail
Doyle, Sir A. C. The Adventure of the Speckled Band
Gurganus, A. My heart is a snake farm
Harjo, J. The crow and the snake
Harjo, J. The flood
Honwana, L. B. Papa, snake & I
Johnston, B. A. Anything that floats
Kelly, R. Miss Abigail's delicate condition
Kessel, J. The snake girl
Kiely, B. The python
King, J. Snake eyes
Malla, P. Pet therapy
Meyers, K. Rodney Valen's second life
Monteiro, L. Curado
Naiyer Masud. Snake catcher
Quiroga, H. Anaconda
Smith, R. T. Tastes like chicken

Snakes. Zakrewsky, J.

Snaking. Bierce, A.

Snap. Gardam, J.

Snapper. Funkhouser, E.

Snapshot. Koretsky, J. l.

Snapshots. Kalotay, D.

Snapshots of the visible man. McCann, R.

Snare, girl. O'Flynn, C.

Snares. Erdrich, L.

Snarker's son. Lumley, B.

Sneaker wave. Perry, A.

Snee, Tom

First start
Fenway fiction; short stories from Red Sox nation; edited by Adam Emerson Pachter

Sneed, Christine

Quality of Life
New England Review v28 no2 p14-23 2007

SNEEZE

Chekhov, A. P. Death of an office worker [variant titles: Death of a government clerk; Death of an official]

Sneezing Lessons. Hannaham, J.

Snell, D. L.

Love seat solitaire
The Horror Writers Association presents Blood lite; an anthology of humorous horror stories; edited by Kevin J. Anderson

Snicket, Lemony, 1970-

See also Handler, Daniel, 1970-

Sniegoski, Thomas E.

Noah's ophans
Butcher, J. Mean streets; [by] Jim Butcher ... [et al]

The **sniper**. Sillitoe, A.

Snipers. Singleton, G.

The **snipper**. Jablonski, N.

The **Sno-Kone** Cart. Curtis, R.

SNOBS AND SNOBBISHNESS

Binchy, M. All that matters
Dunbar, P. L. The lion tamer
King, S. Graduation afternoon
Koënings, N. S. Pearls to swine
Macy, C. Christie
Molodowsky, K. The daughter-in-law
Molodowsky, K. The meeting
Molodowsky, K. The Rafalovitches
Molodowsky, K. The son-in-law
Rendall, P. Flowers for Doña Alicia
Robinson, R. Family Christmas
Williams, J. ACK

Snodgrass Hill. Powell, M.

SNOW

See also Avalanches
Barry, R. Lucy's last hurrah
Battersby, L. In from the sow
Fromm, P. Snow cave
Henriquez, C. The box house and the snow
Malla, P. Big city girls
Marusek, D. The earth is on the mend
Monson, A. Freda thinks spring
Monson, A. Intermittence
Olafsson, O. February
Rich, M. To hunt in fields
Rivera-Valdes, S. Ana at four times: Ana and the snow
Ruefle, M. Snow
Russell, K. Lady Yeti and the palace of artificial snows
Wieland, M. God's dogs

Snow. Ruefle, M.

Snow. Stewart, P.

Snow angel. Olsen, E. J.

Snow angels. Stewart, P.

Snow blind. Guo, S.

Snow Blind. Sizer, B. B.

Snow cave. Fromm, P.

Snow day. Holladay, C. C.

Snow Day. Maes, N.

Snow falls and then disappears. Van Booy, S.

Snow fever. Barry, R.

Snow in summer. Yolen, J.

Snow powder. Novakovich, J.

The **Snow** Queen. Andersen, H. C.

The **snow** queen. McKillip, P. A.

Snow, snow, snow. Harvey, J.

SNOW STORMS *See* Storms

SNOW WHITE (LEGENDARY CHARACTER)

Coover, R. The dead queen
Nolan, W. F. Once upon a time

Snowball. Green, C.

Snowball. LaBrie, A.

Snowball's chance. Stross, C.
Snowbound. Ward, L.
Snowbound. Yorke, C. B.
The **snowman**. Buckler, E.
SNOWSTORMS *See* Storms
Snub. Pourciau, G.
Snyder, Scott
　The 13th Egg
　　The Virginia Quarterly Review v84 no2 p4-27
　　Spr 2008
　About face
　　Snyder, S. Voodoo heart; stories
　Blue yodel
　　Snyder, S. Voodoo heart; stories
　Dumpster Tuesday
　　Snyder, S. Voodoo heart; stories
　Happy Fish, Plus Coin
　　Snyder, S. Voodoo heart; stories
　The star attraction of 1919
　　Snyder, S. Voodoo heart; stories
　The thirteenth egg
　　Burnham, C. Who can save us now?; brand-
　　new superheroes and their amazing [short]
　　stories; edited by Owen King and John
　　McNally; [illustrations by Chris Burnham]
　Voodoo heart
　　Snyder, S. Voodoo heart; stories
　Wreck
　　Snyder, S. Voodoo heart; stories
So exotic. Tomlinson, J.
So far from the stage. Chattin, J.
So good. Keret, E.
So help me God. Oates, J. C.
So It Is in Life. Kharms, D.
So little time. Boudinot, R.
So long. Albert, E.
So long, anyway. Somerville, P.
So long Gerry. Lamsley, T.
So lovely of them. Anderson, B.
So much for Artemis. Ryan, P.
So much rain, so much thirst. Chattin, J.
So On. Wright, D.
So proudly we hail. Merril, J.
So sang the girl who had no name. Scholes, K.
So this guy walks into a lighthouse—. Baker, K.
So this is permanence. Soileau, S.
So this is writing! Episode one: The poet I know.
　Pendarvis, J.
So this is writing! Episode two: The consultants.
　Pendarvis, J.
So very familiar. Celik, B.
Soap opera. Clayton, J. J.
Sob in the silence. Wolfe, G.
Sobeloff, Judy
　Missing
　　South Carolina Review v41 no2 p43-6 Spr
　　2009
Sober second thought. James, H.
Sobering Thoughts. Zoshchenko, M.
Sobott-Mogwe, Gaele
　Smile of fortune
　　The Anchor book of modern African stories;
　　edited by Nadežda Obradovic; with a fore-
　　word by Chinua Achebe
Sobre la muerte del autor/On the death of the au-
　thor. Enrigue, A.
SOCCER
　Alem, K. The spider's fart
　Crees, S. What friction? What factions?

　Donoghue, E. Team men
　Harvey, J. Chance
　MacLaverty, B. A Belfast memory
　Messinger, J. Bicycle kick
　Nisbet, R. Ocky Boxer
　O'Brien, T. What's the score?
　Rippen, C. The best
　Shepard, J. Ajax is all about attack
SOCIAL CLASSES
　　See also Class distinction
　Baker, K. Where the golden apples grow
　Blackwell, K. What we do for love
　Dunbar, P. L. Jimmy Weedon's contretemps
　Gordon, M. The neighborhood
　Gurganus, A. Fourteen feet of water in my
　　house
　Harty, R. What can I tell you about my brother?
　Holladay, C. C. Snow day
　Iagnemma, K. A little advance
　James, H. The rainy day
　James, H. The rose-colored silk
　James, H. The sacrifice
　James, H. The sprite tranformed
　Jones, E. P. Bad neighbors
　Judah, S. Hannah and Benjamin
　Kirshenbaum, B. Faith is a girl's name
　Klimasewiski, M. N. The third house
　Leigh, S. Transformation
　Magee, K. All the America you want
　Monk, B. Do not revive
　Monk, B. Pieces of paper
　Munro, A. The ticket
　Oates, J. C. How I contemplated the world from
　　the Detroit House of Corrections, and be-
　　gan my life over again
　Parker, M. Everything was paid for
　Pizzolatto, N. Nepal
　Roberts, A. Eleanor
　Sankaran, L. The red carpet
　Somerville, P. The future, the future, the future
　Swan, G. On the island
　Thomas, E. A third-class carriage
SOCIAL CONDITIONS *See* Social problems
Social contract. Elliott, S.
Social contract. Yu, F. S.
Social games. Ebenbach, D. H.
SOCIAL GROUPS
　Barthelme, D. Tickets
　Silverberg, R. In the group
SOCIAL ISOLATION
　Fujino, C. Her room
　Houliaras, N. The body
　Kenagy, M. Loud lake
　L'Amour, L. And proudly die
　Lin, T. Suburban teenage wasteland blues
　Molodowsky, K. The Amsterdams
　Molodowsky, K. Slander
　Reinhorn, H. Gabe
　Richter, S. Christ, their Lord
　Silverberg, R. To see the invisible man
　Simmons, P. Night vision
　Singleton, G. Lickers
　Smith, M. The witchcraft decree
　Stamm, P. All that's missing
　Stamm, P. In strange gardens
　Ts'an-hsüeh. My brother
　Tsutsui, Y. Bad for the heart
　Weaver, W. Marked for death

SOCIAL ISOLATION—*Continued*
Wellman, A. M. The Madison Heights syndrome

SOCIAL PROBLEMS
See also Child labor; Crime and criminals; Divorce; Drug abuse; Drug addiction; Homeless persons; Juvenile delinquency; Poverty; Prejudices; Prostitution; Race relations; Slum life; Suicide; Technology and civilization; Unemployed; Violence

Bachelder, C. Blue Knights bounced from CVD Tourney

Ducornet, R. The butcher's comics

Ducornet, R. Chi Gong

Gordon, M. Separation

Hart, E. Blind sided

Hospital, J. T. Credit repair

Jones, E. P. Adam Robinson acquires grandparents and a little sister

Meno, J. Our neck of the woods

SOCIAL SATIRE *See* Satire

SOCIAL STATUS
Asch, S. Leybel is dead—Leybel lives

Bierce, A. Feodora

Bierce, A. An upper class misdemeanant

Dunbar, P. L. The mission of Mr. Scatters

Dunbar, P. L. The scapegoat

Luongo, M. Chestnut season

Maxwell, W. The two women friends

Molodowsky, K. The daughter-in-law

Molodowsky, K. A long journey

Munro, A. Hired girl

Munro, A. Lying under the apple tree

Rylands, J. T. Design

SOCIAL WORKERS
Bingham, S. Doing good

Busch, F. The rescue mission

Chase, M. Dawn

Johnson, B. Michiganders, 1979

Troy, M. Group home

SOCIALISM
Finger, A. The blind marksman

Resnick, M. The lord of the jungle

SOCIALISTS
Libin, Z. A Yiddish-speaking socialist

SOCIETY NOVELS
See also Aristocracy

The **sock** story. Gunn, E.

The **sofa**. Ronk, M. C.

Soft conversation. Ronk, M. C.

Soft-core. Oates, J. C.

Soft spot. Rankin, I.

Soft target. LaBute, N.

The **soft** terrible music. Zebrowski, G.

A **soft** voice whispers nothing. Ligotti, T.

SOFTBALL
Downs, G. Black pork

Lewis, T. Limestone Diner

Ruffin, P. Jesus in the mist

Softer. Bacigalupi, P.

Softly spoke the gabbleduck. Asher, N.

Sohn, Amy
Call-hell

The dictionary of failed relationships; 26 tales of love gone wrong; edited by Meredith Broussard

Soileau, Stephanie
The boucherie

Best of the South: from the second decade of New stories from the South; selected and introduced by Anne Tyler

New stories from the South: the year's best, 2005; edited by Shannon Ravenel; with a preface by Jill McCorkle

StoryQuarterly v40 p35-62 2004

So this is permanence

New stories from the South; the year's best, 2008; selected from U.S. magazines by ZZ Packer with Kathy Pories; with an introduction by ZZ Packer

Sojka, Carole
Art can be murder

Medium of murder; edited by Susan Budavari and Suzanne Flaig

Sokoloff, Alexandra
The edge of seventeen

The darker mask; edited by Gary Phillips and Christopher Chambers.

Solá, Marcela
Kind's silence [excerpt]

Words without borders; the world through the eyes of writers; an anthology; edited by Samantha Schnee, Alane Salierno Mason, and Dedi Felman

Díaz, G. J. Women and power in Argentine literature; stories, interviews, and critical essays; [by] Gwendolyn Díaz

Natural paradises

Díaz, G. J. Women and power in Argentine literature; stories, interviews, and critical essays; [by] Gwendolyn Díaz

Solace. Antrim, D.

Solange. Dumas, A.

Solange. Rees, R.

Solar, Liz A.
La Morena

Thomas M. Cooley Journal of Practical & Clinical Law v8 no1 p25-6 2006

Solar, Rachel
The shadow of Manny Ramirez

Fenway fiction; short stories from Red Sox nation; edited by Adam Emerson Pachter

SOLAR ENERGY
Kuprin, A. I. Liquid sunshine

Solar News headquarters, Selene. Bova, B.

Solar news offices, Selene city. Bova, B.

Soldán, Edmundo Paz *See* Paz Soldán, Edmundo, 1967-

The **soldier**. Dahl, R.

The **soldier** as a boy. Haschemeyer, O.

The **Soldier** in My Throat. Fitzgerald, D.

Soldier of an empire unacquainted with defeat. Cook, G.

A **soldier** of the queen. Aird, C.

Soldier, red soldier. Kiely, B.

SOLDIERS
See also Women soldiers

Amdahl, G. Narrow road to the deep north

Baker, K. The Briscian saint

Bear, E. Tideline

Bierce, A. Two military executions

Botero, J. C. The execution

Bradbury, R. By the numbers!

Brazaitis, M. Defending the woman

Cepeda Samudio, A. The soldiers

SOLDIERS—*Continued*

Chambers, C. Avatar
Chercover, S. A sleep not unlike death
Dansky, R. E. Killer App
DeNiro, A. The centaur
Erdrich, L. Father's milk
Finlay, C. C. After the gaud chrysalis
Haldeman, J. W. The private war of Private Jacob
Haldeman, J. W. Time piece
Hammad, H. a.- . The return of a captive
Hodgson, W. H. Kind, kind and gentle is she
Hwang, S. Mountains
James, H. The blue handkerchief
James, H. A cure for coquettes
Kang, M. S. A fearful symmetry
L'Amour, L. Glorious! Glorious!
L'Amour, L. Where there's fighting
Maguire, G. Nottamun town
Martin, G. R. R. The fortress
Mejia, A. E. The new order
Mejía Vallejo, M. Fear
Mendoza, P. The day we buried our weapons
Moon, E. Politics
Novakovich, J. Hail
Peek, B. The funeral, ruined
Phillips, H. The oracle spoke
Rand, K. The glass army
Reed, R. Savior
Rickards, J. Twenty dollar future
Roberts, A. The siege of Fadiman
Schnitzler, A. Lieutenant Gustl
Shepard, J. Hadrian's wall
Shepard, J. My Aeschylus
Shepard, L. The arcevoalo
Singer, I. B. Why Heisherik was born
Spencer, B. The true history
Swanwick, M. "Hello," said the stick
Téllez, H. Lather and nothing else
Thomas, E. Home
Toer, P. A. Independence Day
Toer, P. A. Revenge
Vonnegut, K. Great day
Walbert, K. Do something
Warner, J. Tough day for the army
Zelazny, R. Passage to Dilfar (Dilvish 1 of 11)

Africa

Enekwe, O. O. The last battle
Maja-Pearce, A. Civil War I-VII

Argentina

Brau, E. Bárcena's dog

Australia

Malouf, D. At Schindler's
Malouf, D. Night training

Brazil

Monteiro, L. Antonio de Juvita

Canada

Bear, E. Gone to flowers

France

Barbey d'Aurevilly, J. The crimson curtain

Germany

Maguire, G. The oakthing

Great Britain

Aird, C. A soldier of the queen
Granville-Barker, H. Picket, July 1916
Joyce, G. An ordinary soldier of the Queen
McCabe, E. Victims
Robinson, P. Shadow on the water
Sillitoe, A. The sniper

India

Judah, S. The horoscope never lies

Israel

Keret, E. Loquat
Keret, E. Not human beings
Keret, E. The tits on an eighteen-year-old
Keret, E. Vacuum seal
Oz, A. The way of the wind
Singer, M. Borderland

Italy

Colombi, M. Dear hope
Levi, P. Fra Diavolo on the Po

Japan

James, C. L. R. Children in the resistance
Tsutsui, Y. Commuter army
Uchida, H. The lieutenant's killer
Uchida, H. The war museum

Nigeria

Aiyejina, F. The one-handed hero

Rome

Howard, R. E. Worms of the earth

Russia

See also Cossacks

Benioff, D. The devil comes to Orekhovo
Brenner, Y. H. One year
Bunin, I. A. Cold fall
Bunin, I. A. Sunstroke
Pushkin, A. S. The queen of spades

United States

See also African American soldiers The shape of things

Amsden, D. Pull!
Baraka, I. A. Mondongo
Barnes, H. L. Private
Bear, E. Botticelli
Bierce, A. Killed at Resaca
Bierce, A. A son of the gods
Bierce, A. A tough tussle
Bunch, C. Murdering Uncle Ho
DeMille, N. Rendezvous
Doogan, M. War can be murder
Fountain, B. The good ones are already taken
Garrett, G. P. Heroes
Garrett, G. P. Tanks
Irsfeld, J. H. Ambivalence Hardy Fire
Irsfeld, J. H. Death of a soldier
Irsfeld, J. H. It's fun to say yes, but sometimes you just got to say no
Irsfeld, J. H. Puerto Rico '61
Jones, T. The pugilist at rest
Leonard, E. The last shot [variant title: A matter of duty]
Manley, C. Gucci Junior in Iraq
Parry, O. Appearences
Shepard, L. Salvador
Shepard, L. A walk in the garden
Sherman, R. The reaper
Silver, M. The visitor
Singer, N. The killer whispers and prays . . .; or, Like a sledge-hammer to the ribcage
Smith, R. T. Wretch like me
Stansberry, D. The prison
Tea, M. Music from earth
Thompson, J. It would not make me tremble to see ten thousand fall
Vonnegut, K. Brighten up
Vonnegut, K. The commandant's desk
Vonnegut, K. Guns before butter
Vonnegut, K. Just you and me, Sammy

SOUTH AFRICA—*Continued*
Morgan, A. Icebergs
Mphahlele, E. Down the quiet street
Ndebele, N. S. The prophetess
Smith, T. A troop [sic] of baboons
Sobott-Mogwe, G. Smile of fortune
Race relations
Head, B. The coming of the Christ-Child
Ndebele, N. S. Death of a son
Johannesburg
Gordimer, N. Alternative endings: the first sense
Modisane, B. The dignity of begging
SOUTH AFRICANS
France
Kohler, S. The transitional object
SOUTH AMERICA
See also Amazon River Valley
SOUTH CAROLINA
Clarke, B. The reason was us
Flanagan, E. Intervention
Lehane, D. Running out of dog
Rheinheimer, K. Grand Strand
Rheinheimer, K. Moon Beach
Ruffin, P. Crows
Singleton, G. Assurance
Singleton, G. Christmas in Gruel
Singleton, G. Migration over Gruel
Singleton, G. Polish
Singleton, G. Soles in Gruel
Singleton, G. Which rocks we choose
Charleston
Durban, P. Gravity
Hospital, J. T. South of loss
SOUTH DAKOTA
Baum, L. F. Aunt 'Phroney's boy
Lowry, M. Kristbjorg's story: in the Black Hills
Meyers, K. Rodney Valen's second life
Seton, E. T. Badlands Billy, the wolf that won
Seton, E. T. Tito, the story of the coyote that learned how
Farm life
See Farm life—South Dakota
Frontier and pioneer life
See Frontier and pioneer life—South Dakota
The **South** Devil. Woolson, C. F.
SOUTH KOREA
Yoon, P. Once the shore
South of Lookout Mountain. Fowler, J.
South of loss. Hospital, J. T.
South of South. Kurland, A.
South of Suez. L'Amour, L.
South of the slot. London, J.
SOUTH SEA ISLANDS *See* Islands of the Pacific
SOUTHEAST ASIA
Blue, E. The cut the crap machine
Bluestein, E. Abio or love at first sight
Bluestein, E. The blanks
Bluestein, E. Hamburger School
Bluestein, E. North of the Faro
Bluestein, E. Pineapple wars
Bluestein, E. A ruined world
Bluestein, E. Skin deep
Bluestein, E. Tea
Shepard, L. Dog-eared paperback of my life
Southern circumstance. Fowler, M.
SOUTHERN RHODESIA *See* Zimbabwe
Southern skies. Malouf, D.

SOUTHERN STATES
See also Confederate States of America names of individual states
Bachelder, C. Blue Knights bounced from CVD Tourney
Billingslea-Brown, A. J. Moonshot
Fowler, M. Southern circumstance
Garrett, G. P. Gator bait
Gordon, C. Old Red
Howard, R. E. Pigeons from hell
Johnson, G. Alliances of youth
Johnson, G. Crazy ladies
McCrumb, S. The resurrection man
Morris, K. L. Tired heart
O'Connor, F. The displaced person
O'Connor, F. Revelation
Porter, K. A. Old mortality
Roberts, R. The flim-flam alien
Ruffin, P. In search of the tightrope walker
Singleton, G. Soldiers in Gruel
Singleton, G. Which rocks we choose
Waldrop, H. The Sawing Boys
Waldrop, H. The ugly chickens
Woolson, C. F. Rodman the keeper
Farm life
See Farm life—Southern States
The **southernmost** point. McGruder, K.
Southpaw. McAllister, B.
Southward, Christopher
(tr.) See Tsuji, Hitonari
SOUTHWEST, NEW *See* Southwestern States
SOUTHWESTERN STATES
Barnes, H. L. Snake boy
Effgen, R. The inappropriate behavior of our alleged loved ones
Elyshevitz, A. Hermano
Horgan, P. The devil in the desert
Kemnitz, C. The fifth daughter
Lum, E. What I never said
Miller, S. G. Old Border Road
Tait, J. Reasons for concern regarding my girlfriend of five days, Monica Garza
Souvenir. Steinberg, S.
A **souvenir** to remember. DuBois, B.
SOVIET UNION *See* Russia
Crimea
See Ukraine—Crimea
Sovietski!. Hunt, H.
A **Sow** of Violence. Jackson, M. O.
The **sow,** the mare, and the cow. Yolen, J.
Space. Moffett, K.
SPACE AND TIME
See also Relativity (Physics); Time travel
Bisson, T. The edge of the universe
Bisson, T. Get me to the church on time
Blish, J. Common time
Crowther, P. The space between the lines
Gerrold, D. In the quake zone
Hughes, R. Castor on troubled waters
Irvine, A. C. Gus dreams of biting the mailman
Iwoleit, M. K. Planck time
Klages, E. Mrs. Zeno's paradox
Lake, J. and Nestvold, R. Canadian who came almost all the way back from the stars
Lumley, B. Deja viewer
Moorcock, M. The visible men
Neff, O. The fourth day to eternity
Rocklynne, R. Time wants a skeleton
Silverberg, R. Breckenridge and the continuum

SPACE TRAVEL *See* Space flight
Space University. Bova, B.
The **spaces** in our lives. Ashley, A.
The **spaces** inside sleep. LaSalle, P.
The **spacetime** pit. Brown, E.
SPAIN
  Card, O. S. Pretty boy
  Claire, A. Playing the odds
  Connell, E. S. The walls of Avila
  Daughtry, P. Street of wounded Mercedes
  De la Casa, R. and Romero, P. J. The day we
    went through the transition
  Lamri, T. "Elevenzerothreetwothousandfour"
  Murphy, Y. Jesus of the snow
  Rivas, M. Butterfly's tongue
  Rivas, M. Carmiña
  Rivas, M. Here and there
  Rivas, M. Saxophone in the mist
  Rivas, M. Vermeer's milkmaid
  Rivas, M. You'll both be very happy
  Sillitoe, A. Guzman, go home
  Singer, I. B. The bus
  Swan, G. Exiles
Colonies
  Duncklee, J. Two gold coins
Rural life
  Tóibín, C. A long winter
Spaldin, Nicola
  Schrödinger's mousetrap. Part 7: Lessons from
    the past
    Nature v434 p25 Mr 3 2005
Spamface. Hayes, M.
SPANIARDS
Egypt
  Posadas, Carmen. The Nubian lover
Spanish blood. Hughes, L.
Spanish in the morning. Jones, E. P.
SPANISH INQUISITION *See* Inquisition
A **Spanish** lesson. Shepard, L.
Spanish prelude to a second marraige. Updike, J.
Spargo, R. Clifton
  The Empty Center
    The Antioch Review v66 no3 p523-36 Summ
    2008
Spark, Debra
  Conservation
    The Massachusetts Review v47 no2 p209-34
    Summ 2006
  The Revived Art of the Toy Theatre
    Agni no58 p165-90 2003
  A short wedding story
    Contemporary Maine fiction; an anthology of
    short stories; edited by Wesley McNair
Spark, Muriel
  The leaf-sweeper
    The Ecco book of Christmas stories; edited
    by Alberto Manguel
  The Portobello Road
    Terrestrial intelligence; international fiction
    now from New Directions; edited by Bar-
    bara Epler
Sparks, Cat
  Sammarynda deep
    Sedia, E. Paper cities; an anthology of urban
    fantasy
Sparks, Timothy *See* Dickens, Charles, 1812-1870
Sparks fly upward. Morton, L.

Sparling, Bret
  Buying In: Views from Entry Level
    Chicago Review v53 no4/54 no1/2 p160-82
    Summ 2008
Sparrow, Katherine
  Pirate solutions
    Fast ships, black sails; edited by Ann & Jeff
    VanderMeer
SPAS *See* Health resorts
Spatz, Gregory
  Any Landlord's Dream
    New England Review v26 no3 p44-62 2005
  Happy for You
    New England Review v27 no4 p165-76 2006
  Stay Away
    New England Review v30 no1 p117-26 2009
Speak, Dorothy
  Authenticity
    Dalhousie Review v88 no3 p383-93 Aut 2008
Speak, geek. Gunn, E.
Speak No Evil. Iweala, U.
Speaking in tongues. Donoghue, E.
Spears, John R.
  Smiley Hewitt and the prairie-wolf
    Adventures in the West; stories for young
    readers; edited by Susanne George Bloom-
    field and Eric Melvin Reed
Specht, Mary Helen
  Texas Night-Blooming
    Southwest Review v93 no3 p448-60 2008
Special. Oates, J. C.
A **Special** City. Brautigan, I.
Special economics. McHugh, M. F.
Special strength. Mahar, A.
Special Terms. Frame, R.
The **specialist.** Smith, A.
The **specialist's** hat. Link, K.
The **specialty** of the house. Ellin, S.
Speckle trout. Rash, R.
Speckled trout. Rash, R.
Spectators. Laken, V.
Spector, Mordkhe
  The Jewish muzhik [excerpt]
    No star too beautiful; Yiddish stories from
    1382 to the present; compiled and translat-
    ed by Joachim Neugroschel
Spectral evidence. Gallison, K.
Spectres in the dark. Howard, R. E.
Spectrography. Murphy, R.
SPECULATION
  Duncklee, J. The developers
  Rozan, S. J. Sunset
Speech sounds. Butler, O. E.
SPEECHES, ADDRESSES, ETC.
      See also Lectures and lecturing
  Bierce, A. Concerning balloons
  Cony, C. H. Order of the day
  DiChario, N. Alien radio
  Kun, M. Fresh fruit
  Kun, M. Touched, very touched
  Shields, C. The metaphor is dead–pass it on
  Zoshchenko, M. The Pushkin Centenary Cele-
    brations
The **Speed** of Dark. Schmeidler, L.
The **speed** of dark [excerpt] Moon, E.
Speed trap. Pohl, F.
Speeding cars. Jay, K.

SPIES—*Continued*

Gorman, E. Crystal's big night

Greenman, B. How little we know about cast polymers, and about life

Hodgson, W. H. The diamond spy

Keret, E. Yordan

Kessel, J. Events preceding the Helvetican renaissance

Klimasewiski, M. N. Tyrants

L'Amour, L. The Goose flies South

L'Amour, L. West from Singapore

L'Amour, L. Wings over Khabarovsk

LaSalle, P. Tunis and time

Lustbader, E. V. The other side of the mirror

Lynds, G. The hunt for Dmitri

Meaney, J. From the heart

Morrell, D. The Abelard sanction

Rusch, K. K. Defect

Schweighofer, P. Seebohm's cap

Steinberg, S. Caught

Sterling, B. Taklamakan

Thomas, R. Cast a yellow shadow [excerpt]

Thor, B. The Athens solution

Wolfe, G. Donovan sent us

York, R. Huntress moon

Spillane, Frank Morrison *See* Spillane, Mickey, 1918-2006

SPILLANE, MICKEY, 1918-2006

Parodies, imitations, etc.

DeAndrea, W. L. The adventure of the cripple parade

Spilling the beans: a letter to Linda Evangelista. Garrett, G. P.

Spilman, Richard

At the Concert of Alternative Music

The Massachusetts Review v45 no4 p756-67 Wint 2004/2005

Pie

River Styx no76/77 p105-14 2008

Spice

Hanging Loose no93 p73-7 2008

Spin. Sheehan, A.

The **spinal** column. Shua, A. M.

Spindler, Cara and Nelson, David Erik

You were neither hot nor cold, but lukewarm, and so I spit you out

The Best of Lady Churchill's rosebud wristlet; edited by Kelly Link & Gavin J. Grant; introduction by Dan Chaon

Spinning. Coberly, J.

The **Spinning** Top. Nahman

Spinosa, Tony

Killing O'Malley

Hard boiled Brooklyn; edited by Reed Farrel Coleman

Spinrad, Norman

The Brown Revolution

Nature v455 p564 S 25 2008

No direction home

New worlds; an anthology; edited by Michael Moorcock

SPINSTERS *See* Single women

The **Spirit** Bird. Nelson, K.

Spirit brother. Sargent, P.

The **spirit** of New York. Burgin, R.

The **spirit** of philosophical vitriol. Lunch, L.

The **spirit** of Tom Molyneaux. Howard, R. E.

Spirit Over Water. Swan, G.

Spirit walker. Dun, D.

Spirited away. Gordin, J.

SPIRITUALISM

Báez, A. Aura

Báez, A. The awakening

Budavari, S. Medium risk

Carl, L. S. The necromancer's apprentice

Chekhov, A. P. A night of horror [variant title: Dreadful night]

Granados, C. The latchkey chronicles: Séance

Koënings, N. S. Wondrous strange

Lane, J. Exposure

Malouf, D. A medium

Neri, K. Hocus-pocus on Friday the 13th

Rodgers, S. J. Lost spirits

Thompson, J. Do not deny me

Willis, C. Inside job

Spit. Bruen, K.

The **Spit**. Goldenthal, J.

Spit baths. Downs, G.

Spitalnic's last year. Perlman, E.

Spitfire. Sillitoe, A.

Spittin iron. Bruen, K.

Spivack, Kathleen

Biology

Confrontation no96/97 p54-8 Fall 2006/Wint 2007

Spleen. Novakovich, J.

The **splendid** source. Matheson, R.

A **Splendid** Wife. Dermont, A.

Splinters of glass. Rosenblum, M. H.

The **split**. Chattin, J.

A **Split-Level** Life. Berger, S. B.

SPLIT PERSONALITY *See* Dual personality

Split Up on a Dark Sad Night, Agreeing It Was Best. Passaro, V.

Splitfoot. Walter, P.

Spofford, Harriet Elizabeth Prescott

Mr. Furbush

Bendel-Simso, M. M., ed. Early American detective stories; an anthology; edited by LeRoy Lad Panek and Mary M. Bendel-Simso.

Spoiled. Macy, C.

Spoiled Brat. Cusset, C.

A **spoiled** man. Mueenuddin, D.

Spoils. Vonnegut, K.

Spoils of war. Roberson, J.

Spokane. Orner, P.

SPOKANE INDIANS

Alexie, S. The toughest Indian in the world

Alexie, S. The toughnest Indian in the world

Spoken Portrait. Quesada, U.

SPONTANEOUS COMBUSTION *See* Combustion, Spontaneous

Spook. Beagle, P. S.

Spooked. Albert, E.

Spooky in Florida. Baumbach, J.

Spoon Mountain or Bust. Nichols, J.

A **spoonful** makes you fertile, 1931. Menger-Anderson, K.

Sportfishing with Cameron. German, N.

SPORTS

See also Athletes; Coaching (Athletics); Games; Swimming; Track (Athletics)

Fisher, C. Hurdles

Sportsman. Hempel, A.

The **spot**. Means, D.

Stacey, Tom—*Continued*

Mary's Visit

Confrontation no100 p84-105 Fall 2007/Wint
2008

The Swap

Confrontation no92/93 p11-32 Fall 2005/Wint
2006

Stackpole, Michael A.

Absolutely charming

Stackpole, M. A. Perchance to dream, and
other stories

Asgard unlimited

Stackpole, M. A. Perchance to dream, and
other stories

Blood duty

Stackpole, M. A. Perchance to dream, and
other stories

The final gift

Stackpole, M. A. Perchance to dream, and
other stories

It's the thought that counts

Stackpole, M. A. Perchance to dream, and
other stories

Kid binary and the two-bit gang

Stackpole, M. A. Perchance to dream, and
other stories

The Krells of Tancras Moor

Stackpole, M. A. Perchance to dream, and
other stories

Let me call you sweetheart

Stackpole, M. A. Perchance to dream, and
other stories

Looks are deceiving

Unusual suspects; stories of mystery & fantasy; edited by Dana Stabenow.

The Parker panic

Stackpole, M. A. Perchance to dream, and
other stories

Peer review

Stackpole, M. A. Perchance to dream, and
other stories

Perchance to dream

Stackpole, M. A. Perchance to dream, and
other stories

Seamless

Pandora's closet; edited by Jean Rabe and
Martin H. Greenberg.

Shepherd

Stackpole, M. A. Perchance to dream, and
other stories

Tip-off

Stackpole, M. A. Perchance to dream, and
other stories

When you're dead

Stackpole, M. A. Perchance to dream, and
other stories

Wind tiger

Stackpole, M. A. Perchance to dream, and
other stories

Stacy and her idiot. Atkins, P.

Stadium. LaSalle, P.

Staffel, Megan

Salt

Ploughshares v34 no4 p104-14 Wint
2008/2009

Staffetti, Al

Mourning

Dalhousie Review v88 no1 p97-102 Spr 2008

Stafford, Jean

Bad characters

Stafford, J. The collected stories of Jean Stafford

Beatrice Trueblood's story

Stafford, J. The collected stories of Jean Stafford

Between the porch and the altar

Stafford, J. The collected stories of Jean Stafford

The bleeding heart

Stafford, J. The collected stories of Jean Stafford

The captain's gift

Stafford, J. The collected stories of Jean Stafford

Children are bored on Sunday

Stafford, J. The collected stories of Jean Stafford

The children's game

Stafford, J. The collected stories of Jean Stafford

Cops and robbers

Stafford, J. The collected stories of Jean Stafford

A country love story

Stafford, J. The collected stories of Jean Stafford

The darkening moon

Stafford, J. The collected stories of Jean Stafford

The echo and the nemesis

Stafford, J. The collected stories of Jean Stafford

The end of a career

Stafford, J. The collected stories of Jean Stafford

The healthiest girl in town

Stafford, J. The collected stories of Jean Stafford

The hope chest

Stafford, J. The collected stories of Jean Stafford

I love someone

Stafford, J. The collected stories of Jean Stafford

In the zoo

Stafford, J. The collected stories of Jean Stafford

An influx of poets

Stafford, J. The collected stories of Jean Stafford

The interior castle

Stafford, J. The collected stories of Jean Stafford

The liberation

Stafford, J. The collected stories of Jean Stafford

Life is no abyss

Stafford, J. The collected stories of Jean Stafford

The lippia lawn

Stafford, J. The collected stories of Jean Stafford

Maggie Meriwether's rich experience

Stafford, J. The collected stories of Jean Stafford

Start the clock. Rosenbaum, B.
Starting at last. Gee, M.
Starting over. Davis, C. A.
Startling revelations from the lost book of Stan. Auslander, S.
STARVATION
  Williams, C. Nearly people
Stashower, Daniel
  The adventure of the agitated actress
    The World's finest mystery and crime stories, fourth annual collection; edited by Ed Gorman and Martin H. Greenberg
  A peach of a shot
    Murder is my racquet; edited by Otto Penzler
  Selden's tale
    Ghosts in Baker Street; edited by Martin H. Greenberg, Jon Lellenberg, Daniel Stashower
  The seven walnuts
    Sherlock Holmes in America; edited by Martin H. Greenberg, Jon L. Lellenberg, and Daniel Stashower.
The **State** Newscast at Ten. Lowe, C.
State of Siege. Poniatowska, E.
The **State** versus Adam Shelley. Schutz, B. M.
Statehood. Gonzalez, K. A.
A **statement** in the case. Goss, T.
The **statement** of Amos Oz. Biller, M.
Statement of Juanita Carlotta Maria Rivera y Queveda. Bova, B.
A **statement** of purpose. Moffett, K.
The **statement** of Randolph Carter. Lovecraft, H. P.
Static. Masurel, P.
Static. Steinberg, S.
The **station**. Mozetič, B.
Station story. Gospodinov, G.
Stationary acceleration. Roberts, A.
Stationary bike. King, S.
Statler pulchrifex. Weber, M.
STATUE OF LIBERTY (NEW YORK, N.Y.)
  Bensko, J. Sea dogs
STATUES
  Bierce, A. A bit of chivalry
  Biguenet, J. The work of art
  Bova, B. The sea of clouds
  Brau, E. The Buddha's eyes
  Drury, D. Things we knew when the house caught fire
  Earley, T. Yard art
  James, C. L. R. The Nobbie stories for children and adults
  Langan, J. Laocöon, or the singularity
  Olafsson, O. September
  Smith, C. A. The disinterment of Venus
  Smith, C. A. The venus of Azombeii
  Trevor, W. Sacred statues
  Vaz, K. The night longs for the ruby
STATUETTES *See* Art objects; Statues
Stavans, Ilan
  The disappearance
    Stavans, I. The disappearance; a novella and stories
    The Massachusetts Review v47 no2 p329-43 Summ 2006
  Morirse está en Hebreo
    Stavans, I. The disappearance; a novella and stories

Sheigetz
  The Literary Review (Madison, N.J.) v49 no3 p114-22 Spr 2006
Xerox man
  Stavans, I. The disappearance; a novella and stories
Stay. Schuman, D.
Stay Away. Spatz, G.
Staying. Gregory, R. B.
The **Staying** Freight. Heathcock, A.
Stazinski, John
  Just Because I Said So
    The Southern Review (Baton Rouge, La.) v45 no2 p233-44 Spr 2009
Steak tartare. D'Amato, B.
Steal Small. Horrocks, C.
Stealing Yakima. Rust, E. M.
The **steam** man of the prairie and the dark rider get down. Lansdale, J. R.
STEAMBOATS
  Bierce, A. My muse
  Bunin, I. A. Calling cards
  Greenleaf, F. Our first well in Nebraska
  Zhu Wen. A boat crossing
The **steamship** Friesland. Calamai, P.
Steck, Ursula
  Phantoms
    Women of mystery; an anthology; Katherine V. Forrest, editor
Steel. Matheson, R.
The **steel** general. Zelazny, R.
STEEL INDUSTRY
  Kosmatka, T. The art of alchemy
Steele, Allen M.
  Escape from earth
    Steele, A. M. The last science fiction writer
  Hail to the chief
    Steele, A. M. The last science fiction writer
  High roller
    Steele, A. M. The last science fiction writer
  An incident at the luncheon of the boating party
    Steele, A. M. The last science fiction writer
  The last science fiction writer
    Steele, A. M. The last science fiction writer
  Moreau
    Steele, A. M. The last science fiction writer
  Take me back to old Tennessee
    Steele, A. M. The last science fiction writer
  The teb hunter
    Witpunk; edited by Claude Lalumière and Marty Halpern
    Steele, A. M. The last science fiction writer
  The war of dogs and boids
    Steele, A. M. The last science fiction writer
  World without end, amen
    Steele, A. M. The last science fiction writer
Steele, Max
  The unripe heart
    Best of the South: from the second decade of New stories from the South; selected and introduced by Anne Tyler
Steelwork. Sorrentino, G.
Steen, Edla van
  Carol head Lina heart
    Oxford anthology of the Brazilian short story; edited by K. David Jackson
STEEPLECHASING *See* Horse racing

Steeves, Rafael Franco
The couple and the stranger
  Colchie, T. A whistler in the nightworld;
    short fiction from the Latin Americas; ed-
    ited by Thomas Colchie
Stefaniak, Mary Helen
You love that dog
  New stories from the South: the year's best,
    2006; selected from U.S. magazines by Al-
    lan Gurganus with Kathy Pories; with an
    introduction by Allan Gurganus
Šteger, Aleš
Doctor Benn's Astrolabe
  The Antioch Review v67 no3 p300-2 Spr 2009
Steiber, Raymond
Mexican gatsby
  The World's finest mystery and crime stories,
    fourth annual collection; edited by Ed
    Gorman and Martin H. Greenberg
Steimberg, Alicia
Young Amatista
  Violations; stories of love by Latin American
    women; edited and with an introduction by
    Psiche Hughes; foreword by Brian Mat-
    thews
STEIN, GERTRUDE, 1874-1946
About
McGarry, J. The last time
Parodies, imitations, etc.
O'Shaughnessy, P. Gertrude Stein solves a mys-
  tery
Stein, Jeanne C.
Better lucky than good
  At the scene of the crime; forensic mysteries
    from today's best writers; edited by Dana
    Stabenow
The witch and the wicked
  Many bloody returns; edited by Charlaine
    Harris and Toni L. P. Kelner
Stein, Joel
The man who killed (and saved) Wall Street
  2033; the future of misbehavior: interplane-
    tary dating, Madame President, socialized
    plastic surgery, and other good news from
    the future; from the editors of Nerve.com;
    instigated by Svedka
STEINBECK, JOHN, 1902-1968
Parodies, imitations, etc.
Effinger, G. A. The man outside
Steinberg, Alan L.
Morning at fifty
  The Best of the Bellevue Literary Review;
    edited by Dannielle Ofri and the staff of
    the Bellevue Literary Review
Steinberg, Susan
Caught
  Steinberg, S. Hydroplane
Court
  Steinberg, S. Hydroplane
The garage
  Steinberg, S. Hydroplane
How it starts
  Steinberg, S. Hydroplane
Hydroplane
  Steinberg, S. Hydroplane
Invitation
  Steinberg, S. Hydroplane
The last guest
  Steinberg, S. Hydroplane

Lifelike
  Steinberg, S. Hydroplane
Souvenir
  Steinberg, S. Hydroplane
Static
  Steinberg, S. Hydroplane
To sit, unmoving
  Steinberg, S. Hydroplane
The walk
  Steinberg, S. Hydroplane
Steiner, George
At five in the afternoon
  Pushcart Prize XXVIII: best of the small
    presses 2004; edited by Bill Henderson and
    the Pushcart prize editors
Steinfeld, J. J.
A Glass Shard and Memory
  Dalhousie Review v86 no1 p71-7 Spr 2006
Steinhauer, Olen
Hungarian lessons
  Expletive deleted; edited by Jen Jordan
The piss-stained Czech
  Dublin noir; the Celtic tiger vs. the ugly
    American; edited by Ken Bruen
Steinitz, Hilary Jerrill
In the Foyer
  New England Review v27 no2 p143-53 2006
Steinke, Darcey
Orgasm
  The dictionary of failed relationships; 26 tales
    of love gone wrong; edited by Meredith
    Broussard
Steinmuller, Angela and Steinmuller, Karlheinz
The eye that never weeps
  The black mirror and other stories; an anthol-
    ogy of science fiction from Germany &
    Austria; edited & with an introduction &
    notes by Franz Rottensteiner; translated by
    Mike Mitchell.
Steinmuller, Karlheinz
(jt. auth) See Steinmuller, Angela and
  Steinmuller, Karlheinz
Stella, Charlie
Father Diodorus
  The Adventure of the missing detective and
    19 of the year's finest crime and mystery
    stories!; edited by Ed Gorman and Martin
    H. Greenberg
The Milfinators
  Hardcore hardboiled; edited by Todd Robin-
    son; introduction by Otto Penzler
Tainted goods
  Dublin noir; the Celtic tiger vs. the ugly
    American; edited by Ken Bruen
Waiting for Gallo
  Hard boiled Brooklyn; edited by Reed Farrel
    Coleman
Stella nova. Bear, E.
Stelmok, Jerry
Maggie
  Stelmok, J. Not your average bear & other
    Maine stories
Maxfield Ridge
  Stelmok, J. Not your average bear & other
    Maine stories
The north shore
  Stelmok, J. Not your average bear & other
    Maine stories

Stern, Richard G.—*Continued*

Dying
Stern, R. G. Almonds to zhoof; [by] Richard Stern

East, West . . . Midwest
Stern, R. G. Almonds to zhoof; [by] Richard Stern

Gaps
Stern, R. G. Almonds to zhoof; [by] Richard Stern

Gardiner's legacy
Stern, R. G. Almonds to zhoof; [by] Richard Stern

Gifts
Stern, R. G. Almonds to zhoof; [by] Richard Stern

The girl who loves Schubert
Stern, R. G. Almonds to zhoof; [by] Richard Stern

The good European
Stern, R. G. Almonds to zhoof; [by] Richard Stern

Good morrow, swine
Stern, R. G. Almonds to zhoof; [by] Richard Stern

The ideal address
Stern, R. G. Almonds to zhoof; [by] Richard Stern

Idylls of Dugan and Strunk
Stern, R. G. Almonds to zhoof; [by] Richard Stern

The illegibility of this world
Stern, R. G. Almonds to zhoof; [by] Richard Stern

In a word, Trowbridge
Stern, R. G. Almonds to zhoof; [by] Richard Stern

In return
Stern, R. G. Almonds to zhoof; [by] Richard Stern

In the dock
Stern, R. G. Almonds to zhoof; [by] Richard Stern

Ins and outs
Stern, R. G. Almonds to zhoof; [by] Richard Stern

Introductory
Stern, R. G. Almonds to zhoof; [by] Richard Stern

Lesson for the day
Stern, R. G. Almonds to zhoof; [by] Richard Stern

Losing color
Stern, R. G. Almonds to zhoof; [by] Richard Stern

Mail
Stern, R. G. Almonds to zhoof; [by] Richard Stern

Milius and Melanie
Stern, R. G. Almonds to zhoof; [by] Richard Stern

My ex, the moral philosopher
Stern, R. G. Almonds to zhoof; [by] Richard Stern

Nine letters, twenty days
Stern, R. G. Almonds to zhoof; [by] Richard Stern

Orvieto dominos, bolsena eels
Stern, R. G. Almonds to zhoof; [by] Richard Stern

Oscar and Hypatia
Stern, R. G. Almonds to zhoof; [by] Richard Stern

Packages
Stern, R. G. Almonds to zhoof; [by] Richard Stern

La pourriture noble
Stern, R. G. Almonds to zhoof; [by] Richard Stern

A recital for the Pope
Stern, R. G. Almonds to zhoof; [by] Richard Stern

Riordan's fiftieth
Stern, R. G. Almonds to zhoof; [by] Richard Stern

A short history of love
Stern, R. G. Almonds to zhoof; [by] Richard Stern

The sorrows of Captain Schreiber
Stern, R. G. Almonds to zhoof; [by] Richard Stern

Story making
Stern, R. G. Almonds to zhoof; [by] Richard Stern

Sylvan and Agnes
Stern, R. G. Almonds to zhoof; [by] Richard Stern

Teeth
Stern, R. G. Almonds to zhoof; [by] Richard Stern

Troubles
Stern, R. G. Almonds to zhoof; [by] Richard Stern

Veni, vidi . . . wendt
Stern, R. G. Almonds to zhoof; [by] Richard Stern

Wanderers
Stern, R. G. Almonds to zhoof; [by] Richard Stern

Wissler remembers
Stern, R. G. Almonds to zhoof; [by] Richard Stern

Wool
Stern, R. G. Almonds to zhoof; [by] Richard Stern

Zhoof
Stern, R. G. Almonds to zhoof; [by] Richard Stern

Stern, Steve

Lazar Malkin enters heaven
Scribblers on the roof; contemporary American Jewish fiction; edited by Melvin Jules Bukiet and David G. Roskies

Sternberg, Shelly A.

Life Is a Dream
Journal of the American Geriatrics Society v57 no6 p1115 Je 2009

Sterns, Aaron

The rest is silence
Dreaming again; thirty-five new stories celebrating the wild side of Australian fiction; edited by Jack Dann

STEROIDS

Pollock, D. R. Discipline

Stevenson, Robert Louis—*Continued*
The Scientific Ape
The Times Literary Supplement no5364 p13
Ja 20 2006
The Waif woman: a cue–from a saga
Tales before Narnia; the roots of modern fan-
tasy and science fiction; edited by Douglas
A. Anderson
Stevenson, Rosalind Palermo
Insect dreams
Poe's children; the new horror: an anthology;
[edited by] Peter Straub.
Stew. Dorfman, A.
Stewards of the earth. Vollmer, M.
Stewart, David
The Country House
The Sewanee Review v116 no4 p525-41 Fall
2008
Stewart, Ian
Schrödinger's mousetrap. Part 1: The trap is
primed
Nature v433 p200-1 Ja 20 2005
What I did on my holidays
Nature v448 p726 Ag 9 2007
Stewart, Maria W.
The First Stage of Life
PMLA v123 no1 p162-5 Ja 2008
Stewart, Mariah
Justice served
Thriller 2; stories you just can't put down;
edited by Clive Cussler; [stories by] Kath-
leen Antrim . . . [et al.]
Stewart, Pamela
All day breakfast
Stewart, P. Elysium & other stories
Ash Wednesday
Stewart, P. Elysium & other stories
Avoiding penance
Stewart, P. Elysium & other stories
Black
Stewart, P. Elysium & other stories
Elysium
Stewart, P. Elysium & other stories
Ham
Stewart, P. Elysium & other stories
Heirloom
Stewart, P. Elysium & other stories
Horsey ride
Stewart, P. Elysium & other stories
Infinity pool
Stewart, P. Elysium & other stories
Leg of lamb
Stewart, P. Elysium & other stories
Luna
Stewart, P. Elysium & other stories
Makeshift memorial
Stewart, P. Elysium & other stories
Membership
Stewart, P. Elysium & other stories
Mother's day
Stewart, P. Elysium & other stories
Ms. Puddins
Stewart, P. Elysium & other stories
A new day
Stewart, P. Elysium & other stories
Our point of view
Stewart, P. Elysium & other stories
Le pain
Stewart, P. Elysium & other stories

Park
Stewart, P. Elysium & other stories
Pregnant
Stewart, P. Elysium & other stories
Red means stop
Stewart, P. Elysium & other stories
Shit happens
Stewart, P. Elysium & other stories
Sick days
Stewart, P. Elysium & other stories
Smile
Stewart, P. Elysium & other stories
Snow
Stewart, P. Elysium & other stories
Snow angels
Stewart, P. Elysium & other stories
Swallow me whole
Stewart, P. Elysium & other stories
Vacation
Stewart, P. Elysium & other stories
Walk left stand right
Stewart, P. Elysium & other stories
Stick Man. Coover, R.
The **stickball** witch. Beagle, P. S.
Sticks and stones. Michaels, L.
Stiefel, Babette
Dark quarry
"Tell it to us easy" and other stories; a com-
plete short fiction anthology of African
American women writers in Opportunity
magazine, (1923-1948); edited by Judith
Musser.
Stiff soup. Davis, C.
Stiffed. Slater, D.
The **still** but falling world. Van Booy, S.
Still Life. Coyne, S.
Still-life. DeLillo, D.
Still Life. Keithley, G.
Still life. Klassen, S.
Still life. McBain, E.
Still life with action figure. Finlay, C. C.
Still life with boobs. Harris, A. L.
Still life with "marigold" & the blue mumbled
earth. Erdrich, L.
Still Life with Poppies. Van den Berg, L.
The **still** point. Peelle, L.
Still the top banana. Schor, L.
Stilled life. Cadigan, P.
Stillman Wing. Weil, J.
Stine, Jovial Bob, 1943-
*For works written by this author under oth-
er names see* Stine, R. L., 1943-
Stine, R. L.
Roomful of witnesses
Thriller 2; stories you just can't put down;
edited by Clive Cussler; [stories by] Kath-
leen Antrim . . . [et al.]
Wifey
Mystery Writers of America presents death do
us part; new stories about love, lust, and
murder; edited by Harlan Coben
The **stinky** princess. Coville, B.
Stirling, S. M.
A murder in Eddsford
Sideways in crime; an alternate mystery an-
thology; edited by Lou Anders
Stitches. Nelson, A.
Stitching. Sarat, L.

Stock, Raymond
(tr.) See Wali, Najem
STOCK EXCHANGE
Higgins, G. V. Life was absolutely swell
Lasdun, J. An anxious man
Olafsson, O. September
Rhodes, S. At the top of his game
Woronov, M. Wall Street
STOCKHOLM (SWEDEN) *See* Sweden—Stockholm
Stockholm 1973. Meno, J.
Stockholm syndrome. Tallerman, D.
StockingS. Ciaccia, J.
Stockton, C. Rush
Kingfish
StoryQuarterly v40 p275-99 2004
Stoddard, Florence Jackson
Street of the mortar and pestle: a story of color in the capital
"Tell it to us easy" and other stories; a complete short fiction anthology of African American women writers in Opportunity magazine, (1923-1948); edited by Judith Musser.
Stoddard, Jason
The elephant ironclads
The Del Rey book of science fiction and fantasy; sixteen original works by speculative fiction's finest voices; edited by Ellen Datlow
Stoddy Awchaw. Goodwin, G. H.
STOKER, BRAM, 1847-1912
Parodies, imitations, etc.
Roberson, C. And such small deer
Stokes, Christopher
The man who ate Michael Rockefeller
Best new American voices 2008; guest editor Richard Bausch; series editors John Kulka and Natalie Danford
Stokes, Randall
In Mexico
Arizona Attorney v44 no9 p14-16, 18-19 My 2008
The **stolen** father. Roe, E.
The **Stolen** Heart. Oates, J. C.
The **Stolen** Pigeons. Duras, M.
The **stolen** white elephant. Twain, M.
Stollman, Aryeh Lev
Die grosse liebe
Contemporary Jewish writing in Canada; an anthology; edited by Michael Greenstein
Mr. Mitochondria
Scribblers on the roof; contemporary American Jewish fiction; edited by Melvin Jules Bukiet and David G. Roskies
Stolpestad. Lychack, W.
Stolz, Karen
A beau for Aunt Sheree
Good Housekeeping v241 no5 p233-9 N 2005
Stone, Eric James
PR problems
The Horror Writers Association presents Blood lite; an anthology of humorous horror stories; edited by Kevin J. Anderson
Tabloid reporter to the stars
Orson Scott Card's Intergalctic medicine show; [edited by] Edmund R. Schubert and Orson Scott Card

Taint of treason
Orson Scott Card's Intergalctic medicine show; [edited by] Edmund R. Schubert and Orson Scott Card
Stone, Leslie F.
The conquest of Gola
Daughters of earth; feminist science fiction in the twentieth century; edited by Justine Larbalestier
Cosmic Joke
Femspec v4 no2 p90-102 2004
Stone, Nick
Papal visit
Perverted by language; fiction inspired by The Fall; edited and introduced by Peter Wild.
Stone, Robert
Helping
The New Granta book of the American short story; edited and introduced by Richard Ford
Stone, Ruth
Clearwater
Thomas M. Cooley Journal of Practical & Clinical Law v8 no1 p5-14 2006
Stone, Ryan
Man, Woman, Gun
South Carolina Review v41 no2 p110-15 Spr 2009
Stone, Sarah
News of the World
Ploughshares v33 no2/3 p149-63 Fall 2007
Stone. Ozick, C.
Stone animals. Link, K.
Stone Boat. Kittredge, W.
The **stone** city. Martin, G. R. R.
A **stone** house. Anapol, B.
Stone man. Kress, N.
The **stone** of the Edmundsbury Monks. Shiel, M. P.
The **stone** pavement. Uchida, H.
The **stone** ship. Hodgson, W. H.
The **stone** woman. Lamb, H.
STONECUTTERS
Smith, C. A. The maker of gargoyles
Stonefather. Card, O. S.
Stones. Bruen, K.
Stones. Herrmann, M.
Stones. Otis, M.
Stonewall and Jackson. Schottenfeld, S.
Stonewalls. Bowman, J. R.
STONING
Sundaresan, I. Fire
The **stop**. Rheinheimer, K.
Stop!. Shields, C.
The **stop**. Stamm, P.
Stop me—if you've heard this one. Lardner, R.
Stop Six, Ft. Worth. Mortazavi, A.
Stop that girl. McKenzie, E.
Stopping. Martin, S.-P.
Stopping the Torrent. Sahn, S.
Storekeeper (A Romance). Dedora, J.
STORES
Akins, M. Que-Linda takes the rite aid
Anderson, B. Rollo's dairy (Jake and Deedee)
Bennett, T. Checkout #5
Bishop, T. Courting Miss Ellen
Brite, P. Z. Henry goes shopping
Currey, R. The names of the lost
Faber, M. Less than perfect

STORY WITHIN A STORY—*Continued*

Miller, A. The performance

Mitsora, M. Halfpastdoom

Molodowsky, K. Tulia Shor's stories: King Solomon's bride

Molodowsky, K. Tulia Shor's stories: The captain

Molodowsky, K. Tulia Shor's stories: The fourth Mitzvah

Muller, M. The Indian witch

Muller, M. Time of the wolves

Murakami, H. A folklore for my generation: a pre-history of late-stage capitalism

Murphy, Y. Aunt Germaine

Murphy, Y. Story of the spirit

Naiyer Masud. The woman in black

Nelson, D. E. Bay

Nisbet, R. An April story

Nisbet, R. The path to Porthgain

Nollas, D. The old enemy

O'Shaughnessy, P. A grandmother's tale

Rickert, M. Cold fires

Rickert, M. The harrowing

Rickert, M. Journey into the kingdom

Robinson, P. Shadow on the water

Russo, R. The whore's child

Scholes, K. A good hairy day in Anarchy

Singer, I. B. The enemy

Singer, I. B. Loshikl

Singer, I. B. The manuscript

Singer, I. B. Moon and madness

Singer, I. B. A night in the poorhouse

Singer, I. B. Not for the Sabbath

Singer, I. B. Runners to nowhere

Singer, I. B. The secret

Singer, I. B. Two weddings and one divorce

Smith, C. A. Told in the desert

Sterling, B. User-centric

Swanwick, M. A midwinter's tale

Wolfe, G. Black shoes

Wolfe, G. From the cradle

The **storyteller**. Báez, A.

The **storyteller**. Rashid, H.

Storyteller. Silko, L.

Storytellers, liars, and bores. Michaels, L.

STORYTELLING

Abbott, L. K. When our dream world finds us, and these hard times are gone

Ali, M. N. The story of day and night

Anaya, R. A. The man who could fly

Anaya, R. A. The place of the swallows

Báez, A. The storyteller

Baraka, I. A. Norman's date

Barth, J. I've been told: a story's story

Barthelme, D. And then

Beagle, P. S. Chandail

Bierce, A. A story at the club

Bolaño, R. Dentist

Clark, G. M. The center of the world

Colfer, E. A fowl tale

Connell, E. S. The land where lemon trees bloom

Dimitriou, S. The plunderer

Disch, T. M. One night; or, Scheherazade's bare minimum

Dobozy, T. The Laughing Cat

Dobozy, T. Tales of Hungarian resistance

Doyle, R. The pram

Dunbar, P. L. A family feud

Erdrich, L. The plague of doves

Faqih, Z. S. a.- . The veiled one

Ferrell, C. Documents of passion love

Ford, J. Under the bottom of the lake

Gaiman, N. October in the chair

Garrett, G. P. A story goes with it

Garrett, G. P. Tanks

Gautreaux, T. Died and gone to Vegas

Hemon, A. The bees, part 1

Hempel, A. Offertory

Holladay, C. C. Snow day

Hwang, F. The modern age

Koënings, N. S. Sisters for Shama

Kun, M. One last story about girls and chocolate

Lamri, T. "The pilgrimage"

Lynn, D. H. Chrysalis

Malouf, D. A traveller's tale

Martel, Y. The facts behind the Helsinki Roccamatios

Molodowsky, K. Tulia Shor's stories: King Solomon's bride

Molodowsky, K. Tulia Shor's stories: The captain

Molodowsky, K. Tulia Shor's stories: The fourth Mitzvah

Montemarano, N. Story

Parker, M. What happens next

Parks, R. Courting the Lady Scythe

Ploetz, S. In love with Rachel

Rashid, H. The storyteller

Riley, P. Damping down the road

Rivera-Valdes, S. Ana at four times: Ana and the magic wand

Rock, P. Lights

Roe, E. The stolen father

Rosenbaum, B. On the cliff by the river

Silko, L. Storyteller

Silverberg, R. The emperor and the maula

Singleton, G. Which rocks we choose

Smith, A. End of story

Stevens, J. D. The death of the short story

Stevens, J. D. Fish story

Stevens, J. D. The joke

Swanwick, M. The skysailor's tale

Theroux, P. Twenty-two stories

Toganov, B. The children

Troy, M. Talk story

Ts'an-hsüeh. A negligible game on the journey

Tuma, H. The Waldiba story

Wang Ping. Crush

Yarbrough, S. Two dogs

Yellin, T. Dan

Yellin, T. Reuben

Storytelling. Gordon, M.

Stowaway. Zelazny, R.

Stowe, Rebecca

The Big Picture

Michigan Quarterly Review v46 no4 p635-51 Fall 2007

Straight, Susan

The Golden Gopher

Los Angeles noir; edited by Denise Hamilton

Mines

Pushcart Prize XXVIII; best of the small presses 2004; edited by Bill Henderson and the Pushcart prize editors

Strickley, Sarah A.
A Dark Turn
Harvard Review (1992) no36 p180-209 2009
Strictly business. Himes, C.
Strieber, Whitley
Kaddish
Dark delicacies; original tales of terror and
the macabre by the world's greatest horror
writers; edited by Del Howison and Jeff
Gelb
Strike anywhere. Nelson, A.
STRIKES AND LOCKOUTS
Bierce, A. The great strike of 1895
Cepeda Samudio, A. The soldiers
Dunbar, P. L. At Shaft 11
Gordin, J. I'm going on strike
Hernandez, L. Preparing for a strike
Parry, O. Coal and iron
String-driven thing. Stanger, V.
String music. Pelecanos, G. P.
String Theory. Troy, M.
Stringing a bear. Bierce, A.
The **Strip** Mall and the Shaolin Temple. Lee, M.
M.-O.
Strip poker. Oates, J. C.
Stripping. Oates, J. C.
STRIPTEASERS
Battles, B. Perfect gentleman
Fonseca, R. The flesh and the bones
Glatt, L. The body shop
Martin, J. Why I got fired
Parra, E. A. The hunter
Saunders, G. Sea Oak
Wishnia, K. J. A. The dope show
Xu Xi. Crying with Audrey Hepburn
Stroby, Wallace
Lovers in the cold
Meeting across the river; stories inspired by
the haunting Bruce Springsteen song; edited
by Jessica Kaye and Richard J. Brewer
Strock, Ian Randal
Mars is the wrong colour
Nature v455 p706 O 2 2008
STROKE *See* Cerebrovascular disease
Stroke of luck. Billingham, M.
Strokes. Henningsen, G. R.
Strom, Dao
Grass roof, tin roof [excerpt]
California uncovered; stories for the 21st cen-
tury; edited by Chitra Banerjee Divakaruni,
William E. Justice, and James Quay
Husband, wife
Strom, D. The gentle order of girls and boys;
four stories
Mary
Strom, D. The gentle order of girls and boys;
four stories
Neighbors
Strom, D. The gentle order of girls and boys;
four stories
Walruses
Strom, D. The gentle order of girls and boys;
four stories
Strong and Mighty Men. Rich, S.
A **strong** dead man. Alarcón, D.
Strong Girls. Miscolta, D.
Stross, Charles
Antibodies
Stross, C. Toast

Bear trap
Stross, C. Toast
Big brother iron
Stross, C. Toast
A colder war
Stross, C. Toast
Stross, C. Wireless
Dechlorinating the moderator
Stross, C. Toast
Down on the farm
Stross, C. Wireless
Extracts from the club diary
Stross, C. Toast
Lobsters
Stross, C. Toast
Asimov's science fiction: 30th anniversary an-
thology; edited by Sheila Williams
Rewired; the post-cyberpunk anthology;
James Patrick Kelly & John Kessel, editors
MAXO signals
Nature v436 p1206 Ag 25 2005
MAXOS
Stross, C. Wireless
Missile gap
Stross, C. Wireless
Palimpsest
Stross, C. Wireless
Pimpf
Year's best fantasy 7; edited by David G.
Hartwell & Kathryn Cramer
Rogue farm
The Year's best science fiction: twenty-first
annual collection; edited by Gardner Dozois
Stross, C. Wireless
Ship of fools
Stross, C. Toast
Snowball's chance
Stross, C. Wireless
Toast: a con report
Stross, C. Toast
Trunk and disorderly
The Best science fiction and fantasy of the
year: volume two; edited by Jonathan
Strahan
Stross, C. Wireless
Unwirer
Stross, C. Wireless
Yellow snow
Stross, C. Toast
Stroud, Ben
The Lime Soda Sea
Michigan Quarterly Review v48 no3 p440-52
Summ 2009
Strout, A. M.
Lady in red
Pandora's closet; edited by Jean Rabe and
Martin H. Greenberg.
Strout, Elizabeth
A different road
The Best American mystery stories, 2008; ed-
ited and with an introduction by George
Pelecanos; Otto Penzler, series editor
Structure. DeMarinis, R.
Strung out. Allen, W.
Strung Out in Suburbia. Hall, H. P.
Stu. McAllister, B.
Stuart, Charles Edward *See* Charles Edward,
Prince, grandson of James II, King of En-
gland, 1720-1788

SUBURBAN LIFE—*Continued*

Cadigan, P. Jimmy
Cheever, J. The swimmer
Clarke, B. For those of us who need such things
Clarke, B. The fund-raiser's dance card
Clarke, B. The reason was us
Coover, R. Suburban jigsaw
DeNiro, A. The friendly giants
Douglas, C. N. Lawn and order
Drury, D. Things we knew when the house caught fire
Frost, G. Collecting dust
Fujino, C. The housewife and the police box
Glavin, A. Patio nights
Grant, G. J. Yours, etc.
Greenland, C. Timothy
Hill, J. In the rundown
Hodgins, E. Mr. Blandings builds his castle
Kun, M. A place like here, only different
Lin, T. Suburban teenage wasteland blues
Lippman, L. One true love
Lippman, L. Scratch a woman
MacEnulty, P. Suburban hunger
McInerney, J. Putting Daisy down
Means, D. The secret goldfish
Mindt, A. An artist at work
Moss, B. K. Little Edens
Nikitas, D. Runaway
Oates, J. C. The hair
Orozco, D. Officers weep
Perrotta, T. The smile on Happy Chang's face
Reed, K. Playmate
Sherman, D. Walpurgis afternoon
Silverberg, R. What we learned from this morning's newspaper
Thompson, J. Her untold story
Thompson, J. The woman taken in adultery

Suburban teenage wasteland blues. Lin, T.

SUBURBS *See* Suburban life

The **suburbs** of the citadel of thought. Lain, D.

SUBVERSIVE ACTIVITIES

See also Terrorism

SUBWAYS

Blauner, P. Going, going, gone
Dann, J. and Zebrowski, G. Yellowhead
Di Filippo, P. Underground
Gran, S. The token booth clerk
McBain, E. The molested
Michaels, L. Getting lucky
Monteleone, T. F. Taking the night train
Novakovich, J. 59th parallel
Raiche, J. One Mississippi
Sayers, V. Walker Evans is a spy on the Lexington Avenue local
Schanoes, V. Serpents
Van Booy, S. No greater gift
Willis, C. The winds of Marble Arch

SUCCESS

See also Ambition

Báez, A. Como se dice success in Spanish?
Brockmeier, K. A fable with a photograph of a glass mobile on the wall
Cooper, J. C. The eye of the beholder
Cooper, J. C. Success
Dahl, R. Mr Botibol
Epstein, J. My brother Eli
Giudice, V. The file cabinet
Hernández, F. The crocodile
Keret, E. Shriki

Klam, M. Issues I dealt with in therapy
Molodowsky, K. A letter
Molodowsky, K. Luck
Mullan, P. Tribunal
Rylands, J. T. Design
Sankaran, L. Apple pie, one by two
Schulberg, B. Your Arkansas traveler
Wolff, T. The rich brother

Success. Cooper, J. C.

Success of a mission. Lynds, D.

Success without college. O'Shaughnessy, P.

The **successes** of Jimmy Sylvester. Smith, L. K.

SUCCESSION *See* Inheritance and succession

Succor. Jablonski, N.

Succussion [Science fiction] Longworth, S.

Such a big Mr. England. Feitell, M.

Such a lucky, pretty girl. Walker, P.

"**Such** dear ecstasy". Green, G.

Such fun. Salter, J.

Suck it. Tierce, M.

The **suckers.** Rich, M.

The **suckling** pig. Raymond, J.

SUDAN

Krysl, M. Mitosos
Krysl, M. Welcome to the torture center, love

SUDANESE

United States

Soileau, S. The boucherie

A **sudden** absence of bees. Mamatas, N.

Sudden death, over time. Rember, J.

SUDDEN INFANT DEATH SYNDROME

Clarke, B. The apology
Herrmann, M. Ducklings
Packer, A. Her firstborn
Poissant, D. J. Venn diagram

The **sudden** possibility of nakedness. Monson, A.

Suderman, Michelle

(tr.) *See* Millás, Juan José
(tr.) *See* Olmos, Gabriela
(tr.) *See* Ruy Sánchez, Alberto
(tr.) *See* Torres Bodet, Jaime

Sue the Audit Committee: The Case of the Sabre Rattling Lawyer. Zinski, C. J.

Suescun, Nicolas

My father was blue
    The Flight of the condor; stories of violence and war from Colombia; translated and compiled by Jennifer Gabrielle Edwards; foreword by Hugo Chaparro Valderrama.

Suet Soot Suit. Yepsen, R.

Suffer the children. Nickless, B.

SUFFERING

See also Good and evil; Pain

Maxwell, W. The woman who never drew breath except to complain
Montgomery, L. We Americans
Perlman, E. Spitalnic's last year
Sargent, P. Gather blue roses
Silverberg, R. Flies

SUFFRAGE

Resnick, M. The Bull Moose at bay

SUFISM

Bellatin, M. The Sheika's condition

SUGAR

Achebe, C. Sugar baby

Sugar. Chapman, J. D.

Sugar. Hensley, J.

Sugar baby. Achebe, C.

Sugar Bowl. Senna, D.

SUICIDE—*Continued*

Shannon, J. The legend of Bayboy and the Mexican surfer

Shields, C. Dying for love

Shirley, J. Miss singularity

Shirley, J. Seven knives

Shirley, J. Sweet armageddon

Shua, A. M. Death as a side effect

Sillitoe, A. On Saturday afternoon

Sillitoe, A. The second chance

Silverberg, R. Sunrise on Mercury

Singer, I. B. One day of happiness

Smith, C. A. A night in Malnéant

Smith, G. B. Presently in ruins

Spencer, W. B. The death of the novel

Stafford, J. The philosophy lesson

Steinberg, S. The garage

Stevens, J. D. The suicide

Sutton, B. Tenants

Swann, M. Secret

Thomas, E. The attempt

Uchida, H. The bowler hat

Vann, D. The higher blue

Waters, D. What to do with the dead

Weil, G. The most beautiful spot in the world

Weil, J. Ridge weather

Welch, N. Texas sounds like an easy place to leave

Wideman, J. E. Sightings

Williams, C. The suicide pit

Williams, J. Marabou

Williams, J. Substance

Wilson, R., Jr. Hard times

Winton, T. Small mercies

Wolven, S. Tigers

Xu Xi. Crying with Audrey Hepburn

Zumas, L. The everything hater

The **suicide**. Biller, M.

A **suicide**. Ducornet, R.

The **suicide**. Stevens, J. D.

The **suicide**. Tognazzini, A.

Suicide by fitness center. Oates, J. C.

Suicide Note #1 . . . Or 12 Good Reasons Not to Kill Yourself. Houston, P.

The **suicide** pit. Williams, C.

Suicide run. Connelly, M.

Suicide watch. Oates, J. C.

The **Suit** Continued. Mahala, S.

The **suitable** surroundings. Bierce, A.

The **suits** at Auderlene. Dowling, T.

Sukhodol. Bunin, I. A.

SUKKOTH

Molodowsky, K. The shared sukkah

Sukkwam Island. Vann, D.

Sulaitis, D. S.

Concerning the Correct Way to Make Cabbage
Boston Review v34 no2 p31-3 Mr/Ap 2009

Sulfur memories. Romano, T.

Suli, Zhu

Political Parties in China's Judiciary
Duke Journal of Comparative & International Law v17 no2 p533-60 Spr 2007

Sullivan, C. J.

Alex Pinto hears the bell
Chicago noir; edited by Neal Pollack

The last round
Manhattan noir; edited by Lawrence Block

Slipping into darkness
Brooklyn noir; edited by Tim McLoughlin

Sullivan, Felicia

The business of leaving
Homewrecker: an adultery reader; edited by Daphne Gottlieb

Sullivan, Jonathon

Niels Bohr and the sleeping dane
Year's best fantasy 6; edited by David G. Hartwell & Kathryn Cramer

Sullivan, May Miller *See* Miller, May, 1899-1995

Sullivan, Tricia

Post-ironic stress syndrome
The Starry rift; tales of new tomorrows: an original science fiction anthology; edited by Jonathan Strahan

The **sultan's** emissary. Judson, T.

The **Sultans's** Battery. Adiga, A.

The **sum** of our parts. Adrian, C.

SUMATRA (INDONESIA)

Schmuck, R. The results of a dog going blind

SUMERIANS

Howard, R. E. The house of Arabu

Summary judgment. McInerney, J.

SUMMER

Curtis, R. The alpine slide

Hempel, A. The rest of God

Kiely, B. The python

Peelle, L. Sweethearts of the rodeo

Steele, M. The unripe heart

Welch, N. The Good Humor man

Summer 1913/Miskomini-Geezis/Raspberry sun. Erdrich, L.

A **summer** adventure. James, H.

Summer afternoon. Ford, J.

Summer, as in love. Almond, S.

A **summer** break. Zoshchenko, M.

Summer camp. McLean, S.

SUMMER CAMPS

Allen, W. Calisthenics, poison ivy, final cut

Atwell, M. S. Blue night, Clover Lake

Gordon, M. The thorn

Hadley, T. The eggy stone

Kenagy, M. Loud lake

Lunstrum, K. S. The drowning

McLean, S. Summer camp

Meno, J. A trip to Greek mythology camp

Munro, A. Child's play

Shepard, J. Courtesy for beginners

Sherman, R. Keeping time

Summer Crossing. Capote, T.

Summer day. Bunin, I. A.

A **summer** day. Stafford, J.

Summer Friend. Oldshue, R.

The **summer** grandma was supposed to die. Averill, T. F.

The **Summer** Guest. Juska, E.

SUMMER HOMES

Bakken, K. N. Renter's guide to the Hamptons

Flanagan, E. Burn

Hempel, A. The children's party

Hempel, A. Weekend

Hoffman, A. The pear tree

Hoffman, A. The summer kitchen

Hoffman, A. Wish you were here

Martin, J. Belmar

Olafsson, O. April

Perry, A. Sneaker wave

Shields, C. Mirrors

Swan, G. A garden amid fires

Swan, G. On the island

SUPERNATURAL PHENOMENA—See also—
Continued

The **supernumerary** corpse. Smith, C. A.
SUPERSTITION
    See also Occultism; Omens; Vampires;
      Voodooism; Werewolves
  Alem, K. The spider's fart
  Ali, M. N. Man pass man
  Baker, K. The Briscian saint
  Barlow, J. The possession of Thomas-Bessie: a
    Victorian melodrama
  Bierce, A. A fowl witch
  Bierce, A. The man and the snake
  Bierce, A. The suitable surroundings
  Blades, L. The glumbo glisae
  Dunbar, P. L. The brief cure of Aunt Fanny
  Dunbar, P. L. Dandy Jim's conjure scare
  Dunbar, P. L. The hoodooing of Mr. Bill Simms
  Dunbar, P. L. The interference of Patsy Ann
  Dunbar, P. L. Ole Conju'in Joe
  Dunbar, P. L. Sister Jackson's superstitions
  Fisher, R. John Archer's nose
  Goswami, M. R. The empty chest
  Granville-Barker, H. The fire that burned in the
    corner
  Hoffman, A. The token
  Mahāsvetā Debī. Bayen
  Mahrus, H. 'I. a.- . Al-Assadiah
  Monk, B. Hocus-pocus
  Naipaul, V. S. My aunt Gold Teeth
  Smith, C. A. The colossus of Ylourgne
Supertoys last all summer long. Aldiss, B. W.
The **supervisor's** tale. Bova, B.
A **supper** by proxy. Dunbar, P. L.
Supple bodies. Williams, C.
Supplement. Angel, J.
Supplying Audubon. Durham, F.
Supreme beings. Boswell, R.
SUPREME COURT (U.S.) *See* United States. Su-
    preme Court
Supreme pronouncements. Upadhyay, S.
Suq al-Nada. Mu'bi, Z. S. a.- .
Sure We Do. Solomon, S.
SÛRETÉ, FRENCH *See* Police—Paris (France)
Surface tension. Blish, J.
Surfacing. Groff, L.
Surfacing. Williams, W. J.
The **surfer**. Link, K.
SURFERS
  Cooper, D. Brian aka "Bear"
  Murakami, H. Hanalei Bay
  Yates, D. Oceanside, 1985
Surge. Soros, E.
The **surgeon**. Dahl, R.
The **Surgeon**. Koulack, D.
SURGEONS
    See also Physicians; Women physicians
  Caponegro, M. Junior achievement
  Chon, K. Kapitan Ri
  Coleman, A. S. The eternal quest
  Egan, G. Yeyuka
  Engberg, S. Moon
  Randolph, L. The boy in the band uniform
  Shua, A. M. The spinal column
  Stamm, P. Deep furrows
SURGERY
    See also Amputation; Brain—Surgery;
    Plastic surgery; Transplantation of organs,
    tissues, etc.
  Fincke, G. The serial plagiarist
  Garrett, G. P. Feeling good, feeling fine

  Jones, N. The bold, the beautiful
  Kiernan, C. R. Faces in revolving souls
  McIlvoy, K. Maraschinos
  Naiyer Masud. The woman in black
  O'Shaughnessy, P. The second head
  Schwarzschild, E. Open heart
  Shua, A. M. Death as a side effect
  Silverberg, R. The pain peddlers
  Stafford, J. The interior castle
  Sutton, B. The brotherhood of healing
  Tabor, M. L. Trouble with kitchens
SURINAME
  Stevenson, R. P. Insect dreams
Surprise at the airport. Zar'uni, A. a.- .
Surprise egg. Keret, E.
SURPRISE ENDINGS
  Barthelme, D. The new member
  Bierce, A. A remarkable adventure
  Bierce, A. A story at the club
  Bunin, I. A. The hunchback's affair
  Deaver, J. Afraid
  Deaver, J. Chapter and verse
  Deaver, J. The commuter
  Deaver, J. Double jeopardy
  Deaver, J. Interrogation
  Deaver, J. Ninety-eight point six
  Deaver, J. The Westphalian ring
  Dokey, R. Never trust the weatherman
  DuBois, B. The unplug war
  Flewelling, L. Perfection
  Grilley, K. Maubi and Jumbies
  Hautala, R. The hum
  Johnson, C. R. Cultural relativity
  Keane, J. B. Protocol
  Kun, M. Weight and fortune
  Machado de Assis. The fortune-teller
  Niven, L. The solipsist at dinner
  Pickard, N. I killed
  Shinn, S. The double-edged sword
  Smith, C. A. A good embalmer
  Smith, M. M. The compound
  Wallace, J. Dead man
  Wolff, T. The other Miller
Surprise rocks Disney trial. Allen, W.
Surprise, surprise. Bova, B.
Surprised. Klassen, S.
The **surprising** weight of the body's organs.
  Trevor, D.
SURREALISM
  Allen, J. R. Holding pattern
  Allen, J. R. It shall be again
  Anderson, B. Clockmaker's requiem
  Barthelme, D. Pandemonium
  Barthelme, D. Presents
  Barzak, C. The guardian of the egg
  Baumbach, J. Drool
  Baumbach, J. The fell of love
  Baumbach, J. Spooky in Florida
  Bayley, B. J. The four-color problem
  Bellatin, M. The Sheika's condition
  Bender, A. Dearth
  Bender, A. End of the line
  Bender, A. Hymn
  Bender, A. Ironhead
  Bender, A. The leading man
  Benedict, P. Mudman
  Budnitz, J. Miracle
  Budnitz, J. Where we come from
  Burke, K. In quest of Olympus

The **surrogate**. Hadley, T.
SURROGATE MOTHERS
Li Yiyun. Prison
McAllister, B. The girl who loved animals
Surveillance. Deaver, J.
SURVEYORS
Berry, J. To measure the earth
**SURVIVAL (AFTER AIRPLANE ACCI-
    DENTS, SHIPWRECKS, ETC.)**
        See also Shipwrecks and castaways; Wil-
        derness survival
Bass, R. The hermit's story
Bierce, A. A psychological shipwreck
Bierce, A. A shipwreckollection
Bova, B. The supervisor's tale
Bova, B. Two years before the mast
Butler, O. E. Speech sounds
Connell, E. S. Yellow raft
Emshwiller, C. Al
Gee, M. Good people
Jones, E. P. A poor Guatemalan dreams of a
    Downtown in Peru
L'Amour, L. Survival
L'Amour, L. With these hands
Lansdale, J. R. Tight little stitches in a dead
    man's back
Stevens, F. Friend island
Willis, C. A letter from the Clearys
Survival. Gorman, E.
Survival. L'Amour, L.
Survival. Wistow, G.
Survival of the fittest. Edelman, S.
Survival ship. Merril, J.
Surviving Toronto. Vogt, M. D.
The **Survivor**. Lang, J.
SURVIVORS, HOLOCAUST *See* Holocaust sur-
    vivors
Survivors. Thon, M. R.
Sushis & Chips [With photograph by Joel
    Sternfeld] Egloff, J.
Suspects wanted. Barrett, M.
SUSPENSE STORIES
        See also Adventure; Conspiracies; Horror
        stories; Kidnapping; Murder stories; Mys-
        tery and detective stories; Secret service;
        Spies; Terrorism

Bell, T. The powder monkey
Berry, S. The devils' due
Blackwood, G. Sacrificial lion
Child, L. James Penney's new identity
Connell, N. Ozark Lake
Deaver, J. The weapon
Dun, D. Spirit walker
Graham, H. The face in the window
Grippando, J. Operation northwoods
Hamilton, D. At the drop of a hat
Hillhouse, R. Diplomatic constraints
Hurwitz, G. Dirty weather
Kava, A. Goodnight, sweet mother
Konrath, J. A. Epitaph
Lescroart, J. T. and Rose, M. J. The portal
Liparulo, R. Kill zone
Liss, D. The double dealer
Lustbader, E. V. The other side of the mirror
Lynds, D. Success of a mission
Lynds, G. The hunt for Dmitri
Mooney, C. Falling
Morrell, D. The Abelard sanction

Neville, K. The Tuesday club
Palmer, M. and Palmer, D. Disfigured
Preston, D. and Child, L. Gone fishing
Reich, C. Assassins
Rice, C. Man catch
Rollins, J. Kowalski's in love
Siegel, J. Empathy
Thor, B. The Athens solution
Vogt, M. D. Surviving Toronto
Suspension. Landsman, J.
Suspension of disbelief. Maleeny, T.
Suspicion. Sayers, D. L.
Sussex, Lucy
Ardent clouds
    The Del Rey book of science fiction and fan-
    tasy; sixteen original works by speculative
    fiction's finest voices; edited by Ellen
    Datlow
Frozen Charlottes
    The Year's best fantasy and horror: eighteenth
    annual collection; edited by Ellen Datlow,
    Kelly Link & Gavin J. Grant
Robots & Zombies, Inc.
    Dreaming again; thirty-five new stories cele-
    brating the wild side of Australian fiction;
    edited by Jack Dann
SUSSEX (ENGLAND) *See* England—Sussex
Sutherland, Romy
(tr.) *See* Vargas Llosa, Mario
Sutton, Barbara
The art of getting real
    Sutton, B. The send-away girl; stories; by
    Barbara Sutton
The brotherhood of healing
    Sutton, B. The send-away girl; stories; by
    Barbara Sutton
The empire of light
    Sutton, B. The send-away girl; stories; by
    Barbara Sutton
Maybe, maybe not
    Sutton, B. The send-away girl; stories; by
    Barbara Sutton
Rabbit punch
    Sutton, B. The send-away girl; stories; by
    Barbara Sutton
The rest of Esther
    Sutton, B. The send-away girl; stories; by
    Barbara Sutton
Risk merchants
    Sutton, B. The send-away girl; stories; by
    Barbara Sutton
The send-away girl
    Sutton, B. The send-away girl; stories; by
    Barbara Sutton
Tenants
    Sutton, B. The send-away girl; stories; by
    Barbara Sutton
Tra il devoto et profano
    Sutton, B. The send-away girl; stories; by
    Barbara Sutton
Svengali. DeMarinis, R.
Svoboda, Terese
'80s lilies
    The O. Henry Prize stories, 2006; edited and
    with an introduction by Laura Furman; ju-
    rors: Kevin Brockmeier, Francine Prose,
    Colm Toibin

Svoboda, Terese—*Continued*
The Egg Trick
The Literary Review (Madison, N.J.) v48 no3 p69-75 Spr 2005
Endangered Species
Prairie Schooner v81 no1 p212-16 Spr 2007
The Lindberg baby
Text: Ur; the new book of masks; [edited by Forrest Aguirre]
The **swag** from Doc Hawthorne's. O'Connell, J.
Swails, Kelly
Cake and candy
Pandora's closet; edited by Jean Rabe and Martin H. Greenberg.
Swain, Heather
What you won't read in books
Before; short stories about pregnancy from our top writers; edited by Emily Franklin and Heather Swain
Swain, James
The sunshine tax
The International Association of Crime Writers presents Murder in Vegas; new crime tales of gambling and desperation; edited by Michael Connelly
Swainston, Steph
The ride of the Gabbleratchet
The new weird; Ann & Jeff VanderMeer, editors
Swallow me whole. Stewart, P.
The **swallow:** not exactly an interlude. Qi, S.
Swallowfly. Sheehy, H.
SWALLOWS
Qi, S. The swallow: not exactly an interlude
Swamp mischief. Proulx, A.
The **Swamp** Mussel God's Song.
SWAMPS
Ferrigno, R. Can you help me out here?
Howard, R. E. Black Canaan
Koretsky, J. L. Alligator story
Kress, N. Wetlands preserve
Russell, K. Ava wrestles the alligator
Sherman, D. The fiddler of Bayou Teche
Woolson, C. F. The South Devil
Swan, Gladys
Cochise
Swan, G. A garden amid fires
The death of the cat
Swan, G. A garden amid fires
Exiles
Swan, G. A garden amid fires
The Literary Review (Madison, N.J.) v48 no1 p130-60 Fall 2004
A garden amid fires
Swan, G. A garden amid fires
On the island
Swan, G. A garden amid fires
The orange bird
Swan, G. A garden amid fires
Search and Rescue
StoryQuarterly v41 p486-95 2005
Spirit Over Water
The Sewanee Review v117 no3 p440-55 Summ 2009
Traveling light
Swan, G. A garden amid fires
New Letters v71 no1 p108-19 2004/2005
Uncle Lazarus
Swan, G. A garden amid fires

The Sewanee Review v114 no4 p481-94 Fall 2006
Women who don't tell war stories
Swan, G. A garden amid fires
Swan, Mary
Long Exposure
Harvard Review (1992) no29 p51-65 2005
Old Sins
Ploughshares v34 no2/3 p155-68 Fall 2008
Swan in retreat. Wieland, M.
The **Swan** Princess. Upton, L.
The **swanger** blood. Ohlin, A.
Swann, Maxine
Creeping
Swann, M. Flower children
Dressing up
Swann, M. Flower children
Ploughshares v33 no1 p202-12 Spr 2007
Flower children
Swann, M. Flower children
I may look dumb
Swann, M. Flower children
Intervention
Swann, M. Flower children
The outlaws
Swann, M. Flower children
Return
Swann, M. Flower children
Secret
The Best American short stories, 2006; selected from U.S. and Canadian magazines by Ann Patchett with Katrina Kenison; with an introduction by Ann Patchett
Swann, M. Flower children
Ploughshares v31 no4 p157-73 Wint 2005/2006
Swann, S. Andrew
Family photos
Future Americas; edited by Martin H. Greenberg and John Helferd
Fealty
Places to be, people to kill; edited by Martin H. Greenberg and Brittianey A. Koren
The historian's apprentice
Man vs. machine; edited by John Helfers and Martin H. Greenberg.
Swan's home. Wieland, M.
Swan's song. Wieland, M.
SWANSEA (WALES) *See* Wales—Swansea
Swanson, Doug J.
Umbrella man [excerpt]
Lone Star sleuths; an anthology of Texas crime fiction; edited and with an introduction by Bill Cunningham, Steven L. Davis, and Rollo K. Newsom.
Swanson, Fritz
For the love of Paul Bunyan
Best American fantasy; guest editors Ann & Jeff VanderMeer; series editor Matthew Cheney
Swanwick, Michael
Ancient engines
Asimov's science fiction: 30th anniversary anthology; edited by Sheila Williams
The bordello in faerie
Swanwick, M. The dog said bow-wow
The changeling's tale
Swanwick, M. The best of Michael Swanwick

SWINDLERS AND SWINDLING—*Continued*

Opatoshu, J. Morris and his son Philip

O'Shaughnessy, P. O'Shay's special case

Rankin, I. Soft spot

Ruffin, P. J. P. and the water tower

Shabtai, Y. A private and very awesome leopard

Simpson, H. The tree

Singleton, G. Lickers

Smith, J. The one that got away

Somers, J. Ringing the changes

Starr, J. Lost in Dublin

Stevens, J. D. Love in a straight line

Troy, M. Beach dogs

Unger, D. The perfect wife

Verissimo, J. Returning from rubber gathering

Westermann, J. The secret

Willis, C. Inside job

The **Swineherd** and the Great, illustrious writer. Schwitters, K.

The **swing**. Tumasonis, D.

Swingle, H. Morley *See* Swingle, Morley

Swingle, Morley

Hard blows

    Mystery Writers of America presents the prosecution rests; new stories about courtrooms, criminals, and the law; edited by Linda Fairstein.

Swirsky, Rachel

The adventures of Captain Black Heart Wentworth: a nautical tail

    Fast ships, black sails; edited by Ann & Jeff VanderMeer

Marry the sun

    The Best science fiction and fantasy of the year: volume three; edited by Jonathan Strahan

Swish. Lim, T.

SWISS

England

Stamm, P. All that's missing

Italy

Stamm, P. Passion

Latvia

Stamm, P. Like a child, like an angel

United States

Stamm, P. Flotsam

Stamm, P. In the outer suburbs

Stamm, P. The true pure land

Switchback. Nocenti, A.

Switching off the lights. Crowther, P.

SWITZERLAND

Stamm, P. Ice lake

Stamm, P. The kiss

Tremain, R. A game of cards

Zurich

Reich, C. Assassins

Switzerland. Enright, A.

Switzerland. LaBute, N.

Swofford, Anthony

Escape and evasion

    Sex for America; politically inspired erotica; edited by Stephen Elliott

Freedom Oil

    Politically inspired; edited by Stephen Elliott; assistant editor, Gabriel Kram; associate editors, Elizabeth Brooks [et al.]

Will they kill you in Iraq?

    Best of Tin House; stories; foreword by Dorothy Allison

Sword brother. Weber, D.

A **sword** called Rhonda. Moen, D. S.

The **sword** dance. Yasuoka, S.

The **sword** of Damocles. Sterling, B.

SWORDS

Bishop, K. J. The art of dying

Moen, D. S. A sword called Rhonda

Wolfe, G. The hour of the sheep

Yolen, J. Evian steel

SYDNEY (AUSTRALIA) *See* Australia—Sydney

Sykes, Jerry

Closer to the flame

    The World's finest mystery and crime stories, fourth annual collection; edited by Ed Gorman and Martin H. Greenberg

    The Best British mysteries, 2005; edited by Maxim Jakubowski

Sykes, Kim

Arrivederci, Aldo

    Queens noir; edited by Robert Knightly

Sylvain, Dominique

Heatwave

    Paris noir; capital crime fiction; edited by Maxim Jakubowski

Sylvan and Agnes. Stern, R. G.

Sylvester, Louis

The Shotgun Situation

    Confrontation no102/103 p22-36 Wint 2008/Spr 2009

Sylvia. Molodowsky, K.

SYMBIOSIS

McIntyre, V. N. Little faces

SYMBOLISM

    See also Allegories; Parables

Chappell, F. Mankind journeys through forests of symbols

Dumas, H. The marchers

Hempel, A. Pool night

Kadare, I. The Great Wall

Lispector, C. The breaking of the bread

Panayotopoulos, N. The strength of materials

Rosa, J. G. The third bank of the river

Veiga, J. J. The misplaced machine

Symbols. Kohler, S.

Symons, Julian

Flowers that bloom in the spring

    A New omnibus of crime; edited by Tony Hillerman and Rosemary Herbert; contributing editors Sue Grafton and Jeffery Deaver

SYMPATHY

    See also Empathy

Angel, J. Rolling over

Hospital, J. T. South of loss

McLean, S. Emil

Singer, I. B. Moon and madness

Sympathy. Furman, L.

SYNAGOGUES

Majzels, R. Hellman's scrapbook [excerpt]

SYNCOPE (PSYCHOLOGY)

Moceri, M. How to faint

Synthetic serendipity. Vinge, V.

SYPHILIS

Sallis, J. Syphilis: a synopsis

Syphilis: a synopsis. Sallis, J.

Syra. Rashid, F.

SYRIA

Damascus

Smith, C. A. The kiss of Zoraida

Syrup and feather. Holladay, C. C.

Szereto, Mitzi
  Hell is where the heart is
    Getting even; revenge stories; edited by Mitzi
    Szereto

Szilágyi, Anca
  The Boarder
    Western Humanities Review v62 no1 p26-32
    Wint 2008

Szilágyi, Anca L.
  Skitter
    The Massachusetts Review v48 no3 p364-9
    Fall 2007

Szmura's room. Hemon, A.

Szporluk, Mary Ann
  (tr.) See Makanin, Vladimir

T

T H Jacobson. Olczak, M.

T; or, Summer in the city. James, H.

The **Tab**. Hutchins, F. F.

TABERNACLES, FEAST OF *See* Sukkoth

Tabitha Warren. Faber, M.

The **Table**. Toledo Paz, N.

Table 16. Frame, R.

Table talk, 1882. Akunin, B.

The **tables** outlived Amin. Samara, N.

Tabloid reporter to the stars. Stone, E. J.

Tabloids bring back family values!. Cox, A. M.

TABOO *See* Superstition

Tabor, Mary L.
  The burglar
    Tabor, M. L. The woman who never cooked;
    stories
  Guarding the pie
    Tabor, M. L. The woman who never cooked;
    stories
  Losing
    Tabor, M. L. The woman who never cooked;
    stories
  Madness and folly
    Tabor, M. L. The woman who never cooked;
    stories
  Proof
    Tabor, M. L. The woman who never cooked;
    stories
  Riptide
    Tabor, M. L. The woman who never cooked;
    stories
  Rugalach
    Tabor, M. L. The woman who never cooked;
    stories
  Sine die
    Tabor, M. L. The woman who never cooked;
    stories
  To swim?
    Tabor, M. L. The woman who never cooked;
    stories
  Trouble with kitchens
    Tabor, M. L. The woman who never cooked;
    stories
  The woman who never cooked
    Tabor, M. L. The woman who never cooked;
    stories

Tabriz. Tallent, E.

Tabucchi, Antonio
  Letter from Casablanca
    Terrestrial intelligence; international fiction
    now from New Directions; edited by Bar-
    bara Epler

Taciturnity. Wolven, S.

Taddeo, Lisa
  The Last Days of Heath Ledger
    Esquire v149 no4 p126-31 Ap 2008

Tadjo, Véronique
  The legend of Abla Pokou, queen of the Baoulé
  people
    From Africa; new francophone stories; edited
    by Adele King

Tag. Glatt, L.

Tag sale. Sherman, R.

Tagatac, Geronimo G.
  Stretched toward him like a dark wake
    Best stories of the American West, v1; edited
    by Marc Jaffe

Tags. Malae, P. N.

Taha, Muhammad 'Ali
  The bird
    Taha, M. A. Mohammad Ali Taha's "A rose
    to Hafeeza's eyes" and other stories; trans-
    lated by Jamal Assadi
  The bird and the cage
    Taha, M. A. Mohammad Ali Taha's "A rose
    to Hafeeza's eyes" and other stories; trans-
    lated by Jamal Assadi
  The birth
    Taha, M. A. Mohammad Ali Taha's "A rose
    to Hafeeza's eyes" and other stories; trans-
    lated by Jamal Assadi
  A boy who picked the sun
    Taha, M. A. Mohammad Ali Taha's "A rose
    to Hafeeza's eyes" and other stories; trans-
    lated by Jamal Assadi
  The dinosaur
    Taha, M. A. Mohammad Ali Taha's "A rose
    to Hafeeza's eyes" and other stories; trans-
    lated by Jamal Assadi
  Family honor
    Taha, M. A. Mohammad Ali Taha's "A rose
    to Hafeeza's eyes" and other stories; trans-
    lated by Jamal Assadi
  The fear
    Taha, M. A. Mohammad Ali Taha's "A rose
    to Hafeeza's eyes" and other stories; trans-
    lated by Jamal Assadi
  The freak
    Taha, M. A. Mohammad Ali Taha's "A rose
    to Hafeeza's eyes" and other stories; trans-
    lated by Jamal Assadi
  The legislation of sheikh mal-allah
    Taha, M. A. Mohammad Ali Taha's "A rose
    to Hafeeza's eyes" and other stories; trans-
    lated by Jamal Assadi
  Loose hair
    Taha, M. A. Mohammad Ali Taha's "A rose
    to Hafeeza's eyes" and other stories; trans-
    lated by Jamal Assadi
  The man who sold his mother
    Taha, M. A. Mohammad Ali Taha's "A rose
    to Hafeeza's eyes" and other stories; trans-
    lated by Jamal Assadi

Taha, Muhammad 'Ali—*Continued*
Motherhood
Taha, M. A. Mohammad Ali Taha's "A rose to Hafeeza's eyes" and other stories; translated by Jamal Assadi
One night on Riga's train
Taha, M. A. Mohammad Ali Taha's "A rose to Hafeeza's eyes" and other stories; translated by Jamal Assadi
A rose to Hafeeza's eyes
Taha, M. A. Mohammad Ali Taha's "A rose to Hafeeza's eyes" and other stories; translated by Jamal Assadi
Satan
Taha, M. A. Mohammad Ali Taha's "A rose to Hafeeza's eyes" and other stories; translated by Jamal Assadi
Separation
Taha, M. A. Mohammad Ali Taha's "A rose to Hafeeza's eyes" and other stories; translated by Jamal Assadi
The wild honey
Taha, M. A. Mohammad Ali Taha's "A rose to Hafeeza's eyes" and other stories; translated by Jamal Assadi

Taha, Raeda
A single metre
Qissat; short stories by Palestinian women; edited by Jo Glanville

TAHOE, LAKE (CALIF. AND NEV.) *See* Lake Tahoe (Calif. and Nev.)

Taiga, taiga, burning bright. DeNiro, A.
The **tailman**. Dee, E.

TAILORS
Allen, W. Sam, you made the pants too fragrant
Lipenga, K. Wainting for a turn
Maxwell, W. The industrious tailor
Singer, I. B. The power of darkness

Tails. Grant, J.
Tailwind to Tibet. L'Amour, L.
The **tain**. Miéville, C.
The **taint**. Lumley, B.
Taint of treason. Stone, E. J.
Tainted goods. Stella, C.
TAIPEI (TAIWAN) *See* Taiwan—Taipei
Taiping. Sonnenberg, B.
Tairlidhe. MacLeod, K.

Tait, John
Jane from Cameroon
Michigan Quarterly Review v46 no2 p316-27 Spr 2007
Lisbon
TriQuarterly no129 p169-77 2007
Reasons for concern regarding my girlfriend of five days, Monica Garza
New stories from the Southwest; edited by D. Seth Horton; foreword by Ray Gonzalez.

TAIWAN
Guo, S. Snow blind
              Taipei
Guo, S. Moon seal

TAIWANESE
          United States
Guo, S. Clover
Guo, S. Snow blind
Hwang, F. Remedies
Hwang, F. A visit to the suns

Taj Mahal. Abrams, L.

Takagi, Nobuko
The shadow of the orchid
Inside and other short fiction; Japanese women by Japanese women; with a foreword by Ruth Ozeki; compiled by Cathy Layne

Take all of Murphy. Lam, V.
Take It from Me. Canning, R.
Take me back to old Tennessee. Steele, A. M.
Take me to the river. McAuley, P. J.
Take over. Grimwood, J. C.
Take That. Taylor, L.
Take the man's pay. Knightly, R.
Takeaway. Ballantyne, T.
Taken. Holmes, C.
Takenaka Hanbei. Fumiyo, S.
Takeover. Charters, D.
The **taker**. Fonseca, R.
Takes two to tangle. Bova, B.
Takes you back. Zebrowski, G.
Taking a Statement. Chalar, J. C.
Taking a stitch in a dead man's arm. Vaz, K.
Taking good care of myself. MacLeod, I. R.
Taking Inventory. Harris, J.
The **taking** of Moundville by zoom. Ruefle, M.
Taking on PJ. Colfer, E.
Taking pictures. Enright, A.
Taking the bullets out. Sharratt, M.
Taking the night train. Monteleone, T. F.
Taking the train. Shields, C.
Taklamakan. Sterling, B.

Takrouri, Basima
Tales from the azzinar quarter, 1984-1987
Qissat; short stories by Palestinian women; edited by Jo Glanville

Tal, Gila
Spider Places
Dalhousie Review v86 no2 p231-6 Summ 2006

Tal Taulai Khan. Lamb, H.
A **tale** in two cities. Perlman, E.
A **Tale** of a Disguise That Worked. Johnston, P. D.
The **tale** of a native son. Bower, B. M.
A **tale** of Christmas and love. West, D.
A **Tale** of Fire and Knowledge. Nádas, P.
The **tale** of Junko and Sayuri. Beagle, P. S.
The **Tale** of Kim Takbo. Yi, M.-G.
A **tale** of one city. Perry, A.
The **tale** of Satampra Zeiros. Smith, C. A.
A **tale** of Spanish vengeance. Bierce, A.
A **tale** of the bosphorus. Bierce, A.
The **tale** of the seventeenth eunuch. Yolen, J.
Tale of the Teahouse. Tharoor, K.
The **tale** of the wicked. Scalzi, J.
A **tale** of two furs. Keane, J. B.
Tales from the azzinar quarter, 1984-1987. Takrouri, B.
Tales of burning love. Erdrich, L.
Tales of Hungarian resistance. Dobozy, T.
Tales of the Swedish army. Barthelme, D.
Thc **Talibé**. Cross, B. P.
Talk. Beattie, A.
Talk. Lesser, E.
The **talk** in Eliza's kitchen. Segal, L. G.
Talk radio. Ely, S.
Talk story. Troy, M.
Talk talk talk. Dufresne, J.
The **talk** talked between worms. Abbott, L. K.

"**Talk** to Me": The Case of the Auditor as Great Communicator. Zinski, C. J.
Talk with Men. Gough, T.
A **talk** with Thomas. Thormahlen, A.
Talker. Apple, M.
Talking about it. Parks, T.
Talking to Charlie. Clayton, J. J.
Talking to the enemy. Mandelman, A.
TALL STORIES *See* Improbable stories
The **tall** T. See Leonard, E. The captives [variant title: The tall T]
Tallent, Elizabeth
  Eight hundred pages
    Politically inspired; edited by Stephen Elliott; assistant editor, Gabriel Kram; associate editors, Elizabeth Brooks [et al.]
  Eros 101
    Best of Tin House; stories; foreword by Dorothy Allison
  Tabriz
    Pushcart prize XXXIII: best of the small presses 2009; edited by Bill Henderson with the Pushcart Prize editors
Taller. Bullock, J.
Tallerman, David
  Stockholm syndrome
    The living dead; edited by John Joseph Adams
Talley, Marcia
  Driven to distraction
    The Deadly Bride; and 21 of the year's finest crime and mystery stories; including complete coverage of the year in mystery and crime fiction; edited by Ed Gorman and Martin H. Greenberg
  The queen is dead, long live the queen
    Thou shalt not kill; biblical mystery stories; edited by Anne Perry
  Safety first
    The World's finest mystery and crime stories, fifth annual collection; edited by Ed Gorman and Martin H. Greenberg
  Too many cooks
    The World's finest mystery and crime stories, fourth annual collection; edited by Ed Gorman and Martin H. Greenberg
TALLEYRAND-PÉRIGORD, CHARLES MAURICE DE, PRINCE DE BÉNÉVENT, 1754-1838
    About
  L'Amour, L. Meeting at Falmouth
Talma Gordon. Hopkins, P. E.
Tamalpais. Almond, S.
Tamarack State. Barrett, A.
The **tamarisk** hunter. Bacigalupi, P.
Tamar's prayers. Gad-Cykman, A.
Tambour, Anna
  The age of fish, post-flowers
    Sedia, E. Paper cities; an anthology of urban fantasy
  Gladiolus ezposed
    The Del Rey book of science fiction and fantasy; sixteen original works by speculative fiction's finest voices; edited by Ellen Datlow
  The shoe in SHOES window
    Interfictions; an anthology of interstitial writing; edited by Delia Sherman and Theodora Goss

Tamburlaine *See* Timur, the Great, 1336-1405
Tamerlane *See* Timur, the Great, 1336-1405
TAMPA (FLA.) *See* Florida—Tampa
The **Tamtonians**. Bierce, A.
Tan, Cecilia
  Bambino road, chapter one
    Fenway fiction; short stories from Red Sox nation; edited by Adam Emerson Pachter
Tan, Maureen
  Muddy pond
    New Orleans noir; edited by Julie Smith
Tan-Tan and Dry Bone. Hopkinson, N.
Tandoori ransom. Allen, W.
Tang, Irwin
  Cheese
    Callaloo v32 no2 p488-97 Spr 2009
Tang, Julian
  From Mars with love
    Nature v456 p544 N 27 2008
  A smooth hero
    Nature v458 p114 Mr 5 2009
TANGO (DANCE)
  Valenzuela, L. Tango
Tango. McGuane, T.
Tango. Valenzuela, L.
The **tank** trapeze. Moorcock, M.
TANKS (MILITARY SCIENCE)
  Vonnegut, K. Happy birthday, 1951
Tanks. Garrett, G. P.
O **Tannenbaum**. Meloy, M.
Tanner, Les
  Fillmore's Magic Elixir
    Idaho Magazine v6 no12 p43-7 S 2007
  Incident at Morgan Creek
    Idaho Magazine v3 no9 p9-12 Je 2004
Tanner, Ron
  Cats as Tuna
    Iowa Review v39 no1 p53-5 Spr 2009
Tanner. Klimasewiski, M. N.
Tanner and Jun Hee. Klimasewiski, M. N.
The **Tanteth**. Raphael, L.
Tantimedh, Adisakdi
  Kali's final cut
    Kolchak: the night stalker chronicles; 26 original tales of the surreal, the bizarre, the macabre; edited by Joe Gentile, Garrett Anderson, Lori Gentile; Kolchak created by Jeff Rice
Tanya. Bunin, I. A.
Tap. Davis, C.
Tap dance. Iarovici, D.
TAPE AND WIRE RECORDERS *See* Tape recordings
Tape measure. Gordimer, N.
Tape Measure [Excerpt from Beethoven Was One-Sixteenth Black and Other Stories] Gordimer, N.
TAPE RECORDINGS
  Ochsner, G. How one carries another
A **Taper's** Tale. DeMott, B.
The **Tapestried** Chamber; or, The lady in the sacque. Scott, Sir W.
Tapestry. Jones, E. P.
TAPEWORMS *See* Cestoda
Tapply, William G.
  Unplayable lies
    Murder in the rough; edited by Otto Penzler
Taraghi, Goli *See* Taraqqi, Gulī
Taraqqi, Goli *See* Taraqqi, Gulī

Taraqqi, Gulï

The bizarre comportment of Mr. Alpha in exile
  Taraqqï, G. A mansion in the sky; and other short stories

Father
  Taraqqï, G. A mansion in the sky; and other short stories

Grandma's house
  Taraqqï, G. A mansion in the sky; and other short stories

The maid
  Taraqqï, G. A mansion in the sky; and other short stories

A mansion in the sky
  Taraqqï, G. A mansion in the sky; and other short stories

My little friend
  Taraqqï, G. A mansion in the sky; and other short stories

The Shemiran bus
  Taraqqï, G. A mansion in the sky; and other short stories

The unfinished game
  Words without borders; the world through the eyes of writers; an anthology; edited by Samantha Schnee, Alane Salierno Mason, and Dedi Felman

Targan, Barry

Frolic and Banter
  The Sewanee Review v115 no1 p56-61 Wint 2007

When Lovely Woman Stoops to Folly
  Confrontation no90/91 p68-86 Spr/Summ 2005

The **Target**. Centner, C. M.

Target: Berlin! The role of the Air Force four-door hardtop. Effinger, G. A.

Target Practice. Kranes, D.

The **tarn** and the rosary. Brown, G. M.

Tarnawsky, Yuriy

The Yellow Streetcar with No Name
  Western Humanities Review v62 no2 p38-40 Spr/Summ 2008

TAROT

Báez, A. Como se dice success in Spanish?
Gaiman, N. Fifteen painted cards from a vampire tarot

Taroudant. Macy, C.

Tarr, Judith

Measureless to man
  Alternate generals III; edited by Harry Turtledove and Roland J. Green

TARTARS *See* Tatars

Tartt, Donna

The ambush
  The Best American short stories, 2006; selected from U.S. and Canadian magazines by Ann Patchett with Katrina Kenison; with an introduction by Ann Patchett

TARZAN (FICTITIOUS CHARACTER)

MacBride, A. The ape man

Taser. Reese, J.

Task. Chekhov, A. P.

The **task**. Tognazzini, A.

The **task** of this translator. Hasak-Lowy, T.

Taste. Dahl, R.

A **taste** of dust. Schwartz, L. S.

The **Taste** of Life. Fan Wu

The **taste** of silver. DuBois, B.

A **taste** of summer. Klages, E.

The **taste** of wheat. Sedia, E.

Tastes like chicken. Smith, R. T.

Tastes Like Regular. Goldstein, Y.

Tat Master. Hirahara, N.

Tatanka Iyotake *See* Sitting Bull, Dakota Chief, 1831-1890

TATARS

Lamb, H. Alamut
Lamb, H. Chang Nor
Lamb, H. The mighty manslayer
Lamb, H. Roof of the world
Lamb, H. The star of evil omen
Lamb, H. Tal Taulai Khan
Lamb, H. The white Khan

Tate, James

Terminix [Reprint]
  Harper's v314 p25-6 Je 2007

Tatsopoulos, Petros

A smelly weakness
  Angelic & black; contemporary Greek short stories; edited and translated by David Connolly; with an introduction by Vangelis Hatzivassileiou

The **tattoo**. Ronk, M. C.

TATTOOING

Bennett, T. Filigree
Biller, M. Butterflies
Bradbury, R. The illustrated man
Bradford, B. More than skin deep
Carcache, M. The moon and the stars
Dahl, R. Skin
Erdrich, L. The bingo van
Flanagan, E. The usual mistakes
Gallagher, S. The back of his hand
Hand, E. The least Trumps
Hirahara, N. Tat Master
Moffett, K. Tattooizm
Nolan, J. Memento mori
Ronk, M. C. The tattoo

Tattooizm. Moffett, K.

TAVERNS *See* Hotels, taverns, etc.

Tawada, Yoko

Hair Tax
  World Literature Today v82 no3 p31 My/Je 2008

In front of Trang Tien Bridge
  Tawada, Y. Facing the bridge; translated from the Japanese by Margaret Mitsutani

Saint George and the translator
  Tawada, Y. Facing the bridge; translated from the Japanese by Margaret Mitsutani

The shadow man
  Tawada, Y. Facing the bridge; translated from the Japanese by Margaret Mitsutani

Where Europe begins
  Terrestrial intelligence; international fiction now from New Directions; edited by Barbara Epler

TAXATION

Hurd, D. L. Guadalupe and the taxman
Moon, E. And ladies of the club

TAXICABS

Ali, M. N. The true Aryan
De Silva, D. Don't talk to the passenger
Shroff, M. F. Meter down
Uchida, S. My son's lips
Wiltz, C. Night taxi

TAXIDERMY
Davis, C. Mouse rampant
Lecompte, D. Three tepid shots, two decapitated gulls, and a crippled taxidermist

Taylor, Ed
Grendel
Southwest Review v94 no3 p411-13 2009
Hymn to Kalliope
Southwest Review v91 no4 p521-9 2006

Taylor, Eric.
A pinch of snuff
The Black Lizard big book of pulps; edited by Otto Penzler

Taylor, Katherine
Crying and Smoking
Southwest Review v89 no4 p553-65 2004
The Heiress from Horn Lake
Ploughshares v31 no4 p174-90 Wint 2005/2006
Mother's Summer Vacation
Prairie Schooner v80 no3 p60-73 Fall 2006

Taylor, Lois
Are You There
Southwest Review v92 no1 p82-8 2007
Take That
South Carolina Review v37 no1 p142-6 Fall 2004
We Waken in Paradise
The Literary Review (Madison, N.J.) v49 no2 p160-7 Wint 2006

Taylor, Marianne
Creepy World
Ms. v15 no1 p72-6 Spr 2005

Taylor, Pat Ellis
Leaping Leo
Lone Star literature; from the Red River to the Rio Grande; edited by Don Graham

Taylor, Seth
Chicks Love Scars
The North American Review v290 no2 p34-40 Mr/Ap 2005

Taylor, Stephen
Bloomsbury Nights: Being, Food, and Love
The Antioch Review v65 no1 p161-72 Wint 2007
Is Your Figure Less than Greek?
The Antioch Review v63 no4 p745-54 Fall 2005

Taylor, Nick
The smell of despair
Politically inspired; edited by Stephen Elliott; assistant editor, Gabriel Kram; associate editors, Elizabeth Brooks [et al.]

Tchaikovsky's bust. Novakovich, J.

Tea, Michelle
9/11 L.A. bookstore
Politically inspired; edited by Stephen Elliott; assistant editor, Gabriel Kram; associate editors, Elizabeth Brooks [et al.]
Larry's place
San Francisco noir; edited by Peter Maravelis
Music from earth
Sex for America; politically inspired erotica; edited by Stephen Elliott

TEA
Mukhopadhyay, T. Little grains of dust
Nisbet, R. Miss Grey of Market Street
Tea. Bluestein, E.
Tea. Reisman, N.

The **tea** bowl. Ronk, M. C.
Tea leaves. Rees, R.
Tea set. Luongo, M.
The **tea** time of stouthearted ladies. Stafford, J.
Tea with soldiers. Chilson, P.
Teachable Moment. Hauser, P.
The **Teacher**. Jhabvala, R. P.
The **Teacher**. Ohlin, A.
The **teacher** who feared rats. James, C. L. R.
Teacher Yu. Qi, S.

TEACHERS
See also Students; Tutors
Abbott, L. K. The eldest of things
Abbott, L. K. One of star wars, one of doom
Abbott, L. K. The way sin is said in wonderland
Adichie, C. N. Jumping Monkey Hill
Adiga, A. Lighthouse Hill (the foot of the hill)
Adrian, C. High speeds
Allen, J. R. Mississippi story
Amdahl, G. Visigoth
Anaya, R. A. The apple orchard
Anderson, B. Peppermint frogs
Anderson, B. School story
Anderson, B. Tuataras
Arnow, H. L. S. Interruptions to school at home
Arnow, H. L. S. The un-American activities of Miss Prink
Atwood, M. The other place
Auchincloss, L. L'ami des femmes
Baingana, D. Passion
Bakken, K. N. Necessary lies
Barry, R. How to save a wounded bird
Barthelme, D. Me and Miss Mandible
Bass, R. Penetrations
Baxter, C. Gryphon
Baxter, C. Saul and Patsy are in labor
Beattie, A. Duchais
Bender, K. E. Candidate
Bennett, T. All the same
Bishop, M. The Yukio Mishima Cultural Association of Kudzu Valley, Georgia
Bissell, T. God lives in St. Petersburg
Bolaño, R. Gómez Palacio
Boyers, R. Samantha
Boyle, T. C. Up against the wall
Bradbury, R. Let's play poison
Bradfield, S. Men and women in love
Braver, G. Ghost writer
Brown, G. M. The drowned rose
Buckell, T. S. Nord's gambit
Buckler, E. Long, long after school
Buckler, E. A present for Miss Merriam
Bynum, S. S.-L. Accomplice
Campbell, F. Murder is academic
Canin, E. The palace thief
Canty, K. The boreal forest
Carr, P. M. An El Paso Idyll
Chilson, P. Tea with soldiers
Chilson, P. Toumani Ogun
Clark, M. The secret heart of Christ
Clark, M. R. Her neighbor's claim
Clayton, J. J. Fantasy for a Friday afternoon
Coffman, L. H. The dream lover
Cozarinsky, E. The bride from Odessa
Crane, E. What happens when the mipods leave their milieu
Crouse, D. Dear
Day, C. B. The pink hat
Déry, T. Reckoning

TEACHERS—*Continued*

Rhodes, D. The Carolingian Period
Rich, M. Smoking gun
Richard, N. What you do next
Rivas, M. Butterfly's tongue
Robinson, R. Blind man
Row, J. Heaven Lake
Row, J. The secrets of bats
Rucker, R. v. B. and Di Filippo, P. Elves of the subdimensions
Ruffin, P. Teaching her about catfish
Russo, R. Horseman
Russo, R. The whore's child
Rust, E. M. Moon over water
Sanders, W. Dry bones
Schow, D. J. The pyre and others
Schutt, C. Do you think I am who I will be?
Scott, J. Or else, part III: Rain on concrete
Seamon, H. The plagiarist
Segal, L. Other people's deaths
Segal, L. G. An absence of cousins
Segal, L. G. At whom the dog barks
Segal, L. G. Fatal wish
Segal, L. G. Garbage thief
Segal, L. G. Leslie's shoes
Segal, L. G. Other people's deaths
Segal, L. G. The talk in Eliza's kitchen
Segal, L. G. Yom Kippur card
Selgin, P. Boy b
Selgin, P. Sawdust
Shaffer, A. Dropping the baby
Sherman, R. The neutered bulldog
Shirley, J. What would you do for love?
Sierra, J. The fifth world
Sillitoe, A. Mr. Raynor the school-teacher
Simmons, D. This year's class picture
Singer, I. B. The safe deposit
Singleton, G. The opposite of zero
Smith, L. The Happy Memories Club
Smith, M. The Tonga
Spencer, M. E. Beyond the years
Spencer, W. B. The death of the novel
Stafford, J. The liberation
Steinberg, S. Lifelike
Stern, D. The fellowship
Stern, D. The future
Stern, R. G. A counterfactual proposition
Stern, R. G. Good morrow, swine
Stern, R. G. Lesson for the day
Stern, R. G. Wissler remembers
Strom, D. Husband, wife
Tait, J. Reasons for concern regarding my girlfriend of five days, Monica Garza
Taraqqi, G. The bizarre comportment of Mr. Alpha in exile
Thompson, J. Soldiers of Spiritos
Tillman, L. The recipe
Toer, P. A. In twilight born
Tognazzini, A. Gainesville, Oregon—1962
Tolstaia, T. The moon came out
Tolstaia, T. Most beloved
Tomlinson, J. Nothing like an ocean
Tomlinson, J. The persistence of ice
Trevor, D. The thin tear in the fabric of space
Trevor, W. A perfect relationship
Uchida, H. The bowler hat
Ulitskaya, L. Angel
Updike, D. Adjunct
Updike, D. The last of the Caribs

Updike, J. German lessons
Vapnyar, L. Love lessons — Mondays, 9 A.M.
Varallo, A. In the age of automobiles
Varallo, A. A tiny raft
Wideman, J. E. Sightings
Williams, J. Anodyne
Williams, J. Congress
Windley, C. The reading Elvis
Windley, C. Sand and frost
Wolfe, G. The toy theater
Wolff, T. Firelight
Wolff, T. In the garden of North American martyrs
Wolff, T. A mature student
Wolff, T. A white bible
Working, R. The sky ranch
Wyss, G. Kids make their own houses
Yates, D. Gisela
Yellin, T. Ephraim
Yellin, T. Issachar
Yellin, T. Naphtali
Yellin, T. Zebulun

The **teachers** rode a wheel of fire. Zelazny, R.

Teaching. Doyle, R.

Teaching her about catfish. Ruffin, P.

The teachings of Bronc Buster Billy Brown. Hadley, D.

Teacup. Treat, J.

Team men. Donoghue, E.

Team move. Charters, D.

Teardown. Barth, J.

Teardown. Lecard, M.

Tearjerker. Berman, S.

The **tears** of the almond tree. Eberhardt, I.

Tears seven times salt. Kiernan, C. R.

The **teb** hunter. Steele, A. M.

Technicolor. Marley, L.

TECHNOLOGY AND CIVILIZATION

Anderson, P. Turning point
Breuer, M. J. Mechanocracy
Derby, M. The sound gun
DuBois, B. The unplug war
Roberts, A. The time telephone
Sterling, B. Kiosk

Tecumseh and Rebekah. Neal, A.

Ted. Maliszewski, P.

TEDDY BEARS

Scholes, K. Edward Bear
Steele, A. M. The teb hunter

Teddy Trunk. Keret, E.

The **teddy's** touch. Rand, K.

Teef. Michalopoulou, A.

Teele, Elinor

The Dead of Winter
The Massachusetts Review v48 no2 p309-12 Summ 2007

TEENAGERS *See* Adolescence; Youth

TEETH

Wilson, K. The choir director affair (The baby's teeth)

Teeth. Rechner, M.

Teeth. Slowik, M.

Teeth. Stern, R. G.

TEHRAN (IRAN) *See* Iran—Tehran

Tehran calling. Le, N.

Teigeler, Piet
Flying fast
The World's finest mystery and crime stories, fourth annual collection; edited by Ed Gorman and Martin H. Greenberg
TEKAKWITHA, KATERI, 1656-1680
About
Cohen, L. The history of them all
Tekulve, Susan
Ostriches
New Letters v73 no1 p9-22 2006/2007
Tel, Jonathan
Bola de la fortuna
The Best American mystery stories, 2009; edited and with an introduction by Jeffery Deaver
The Yale Review v96 no1 p120-37 Ja 2008
TEL AVIV (ISRAEL) *See* Israel—Tel Aviv
Tel Aviv. Liebrecht, S.
TELECOMMUNICATION
See also Telephone; Television
Telegrams of the Soul: A Selection. Altenberg, P.
TELEGRAPHERS
Gardiner, J. R. Morse operator
TELEKINESIS *See* Psychokinesis
TELEPATHY
Anderson, P. Call me Joe
Anderson, P. Journey's end
Bear, E. The something-dreaming game
Elrod, P. N. The way of the matter
Franke, H. W. Thought control
Franke, H. W. Welcome home
Lain, D. The subliminal son
Martin, G. R. R. Nightflyers
Martin, G. R. R. A song for Lya
Matheson, R. Lover when you're near me
Matheson, R. Mute
Matheson, R. Witch war
Meaney, J. Sideways from now
Merril, J. Peeping Tom
Nocenti, A. Switchback
Rich, M. Forever down the ringing groves
Sargent, P. Out of place
Silverberg, R. Ship-sister, star-sister
Silverberg, R. Something wild is loose
Stackpole, M. A. It's the thought that counts
Weber, D. A beautiful friendship
Zelazny, R. Comes now the power
Zelazny, R. King Solomon's ring
Zelazny, R. No award
TELEPHONE
Bausch, R. 1-900
Biller, M. It's a sad story
Bisson, T. He loved Lucy
Bolaño, R. Phone calls
Budnitz, J. Visitors
Bukoski, A. The woman who ate cat food
Card, O. S. Inventing lovers on the phone
Eldridge, C. Becky
Espinosa, G. Family birthday wishes
Garrett, G. P. A perfect stranger
Ghermandi, G. "The village telephone"
Hecht, J. Happy trails to you
Helprin, M. Jacob Bayer and the telephone
Hill, J. The black phone
Kessel, J. The red phone
King, S. The New York Times at special bargain rates
Laidlaw, M. Cell call

Luongo, M. Cake
Matheson, R. Long distance call
Moore, M. The Mikado's favorite song
Oates, J. C. So help me God
Portela, E. L. The last passenger
Roberts, A. The time telephone
Schulze, I. Cell phone
Sterling, B. In paradise
Tognazzini, A. Answering machine
Telephone. Mozetič, B.
Telephone bird. Lange, R.
A **telephone** conversation with my father. Tognazzini, A.
TELEPORTATION
Meaney, J. Via Vortex
TELEVISION
Bradbury, R. Almost the end of the world
Cadigan, P. The day the Martels got the cable
Canty, K. They were expendable
Crane, E. The glistening head of Ricky Ricardo begs further experimentation
Dalton, Q. Back on earth
Davis, L. Television
Gerrold, D. The Kennedy enterprise
LaBute, N. Los feliz
Marusek, D. VTV
Monteleone, T. F. Please stand by
Pierce, T. J. Studio sense
Rivas, M. A white flower for bats
Saunders, G. In persuasion nation
Schulberg, B. Your Arkansas traveler
Shukman, H. Man with golden eagle
Zelazny, R. The new pleasure
Television. Davis, L.
TELEVISION ANNOUNCERS *See* Television announcing
TELEVISION ANNOUNCING
Ohlin, A. Local news
Pearlman, E. Eyesore
TELEVISION BROADCASTING *See* Television announcing
TELEVISION PRODUCERS AND DIRECTORS
Greenman, B. The re-education of M. Grooms
Richler, M. Barney's version [excerpt]
TELEVISION PROGRAMS
Atwood, M. The age of lead
Barnes, H. L. Groundwork
Bradford, R. Carolina live
Brockmeier, K. Home videos
Collins, B. Trailer trashed
Crane, E. Betty the zombie
Crane, E. My life is awesome! and great!
Crane, E. Notes for a story about people with weird phobias
Davis, L. Something spooky on Geophys
Deaver, J. Bump
Gower, J. TV land
Haywood, G. A. Moving pictures
Henderson, C. J. What every coin has
Kelly, J. P. The Leila Torn Show
Klages, E. Be prepared
Lawson, J. E. Deface the nation
Link, K. Magic for beginners
McGraw, E. A whole new man
Meno, J. A strange episode of *Aqua Voyage*
Monteleone, T. F. It's in the bag
Pearlman, E. How to fall
Pierce, T. J. The real world

TELEVISION PROGRAMS—*Continued*
Reed, K. Focus group
Reed, R. Eight episodes
Saunders, G. Brad Carrigan, American
Schor, L. The exercise machine
Silverberg, R. The pain peddlers
Tsutsui, Y. Rumours about me
Volk, S. 31/10
Waldrop, H. Mr. Goober's show
Yu, C. My last days as me
TELL, WILLIAM
About
James, C. L. R. Ghana independence
Tell Borges if you see him. LaSalle, P.
Tell him about Brother John. Muñoz, M.
Tell it to us easy. Simms, E.
Tell me. Barth, J.
Tell Me. Leidinger, L.
Tell Me about Your Brother. Godsave, B.
Tell Me Again. Bosworth, B.
Tell me everything. Michaels, L.
Tell me who to kill. Rankin, I.
Tell me you forgive me? Oates, J. C.
Tell me your secret. Gerber, M. J.
A **tell-tale** ink mark Bendel-Simso, M. M., ed.
Early American detective stories; an anthology; edited by LeRoy Lad Panek and Mary M. Bendel-Simso.
The **tell-tales** key; or, A woman as a detective Bendel-Simso, M. M., ed. Early American detective stories; an anthology; edited by LeRoy Lad Panek and Mary M. Bendel-Simso.
Telles, Lygia Fagundes
Just a saxophone
Oxford anthology of the Brazilian short story; edited by K. David Jackson
Téllez, Hernando
Lather and nothing else
The Flight of the condor; stories of violence and war from Colombia; translated and compiled by Jennifer Gabrielle Edwards; foreword by Hugo Chaparro Valderrama.
Prelude
The Flight of the condor; stories of violence and war from Colombia; translated and compiled by Jennifer Gabrielle Edwards; foreword by Hugo Chaparro Valderrama.
Telling Brenda. Rheinheimer, K.
A **Telling** of the Love of Winnedumah for Pahwanike. Austin, M.
The **telltale** eye. M'Cabe, J. D.
Tem, Melanie
(jt. auth) See Tem, Steve Rasnic and Tem, Melanie
Tem, Steve Rasnic
Eggs
Weird shadows over Innsmouth; edited by Stephen Jones; illustrated by Randy Broecker [et al.]
Tem, Steve Rasnic and Tem, Melanie
The man on the ceiling
Poe's children; the new horror: an anthology; [edited by] Peter Straub.
TEMPERANCE
Zoshchenko, M. Lemonade
The **temperate** family. Garrett, C.
TEMPERATURES, LOW *See* Low temperatures

Temple, Scott
A roomful of Christmas
The Best of the Bellevue Literary Review; edited by Dannielle Ofri and the staff of the Bellevue Literary Review
TEMPLES, BUDDHIST *See* Buddhist temples
Templeton, Edith
The blue hour
Templeton, E. The darts of Cupid and other stories
A coffeehouse acquaintance
Templeton, E. The darts of Cupid and other stories
The darts of Cupid
Templeton, E. The darts of Cupid and other stories
The dress rehearsal
Templeton, E. The darts of Cupid and other stories
Equality cake
Templeton, E. The darts of Cupid and other stories
Irresistibly
Templeton, E. The darts of Cupid and other stories
Nymph & faun
Templeton, E. The darts of Cupid and other stories
Templeton, Patty
Eight guns over a dead girl
Hardcore hardboiled; edited by Todd Robinson; introduction by Otto Penzler
A **temporary** crown. Pike, S.
Temporary Lives. D., R.
A **temporary** matter. Lahiri, J.
Temporary shelter. Gordon, M.
The **temptation** of King David. DuBois, B.
Ten dimes. Toomey, M.
Ten keys. Child, L.
Ten lords a-leaping. Arnott, J.
Ten operations in ten years. Castillon, C.
Ten pretty girls. Kiely, B.
Ten sigmas. Melko, P.
Ten true things. July, M.
TENANT FARMING
O'Connor, F. The displaced person
The **tenants**. Qi, S.
Tenants. Sutton, B.
Tendeléo's story. McDonald, I.
Tender foot. Welch, N.
The **tenderfoot**. Dunbar, P. L.
Tending something. Beattie, A.
Tendrils of love. Kellerman, F.
Tenenboim, Yoysef
Hear, O Israel
No star too beautiful; Yiddish stories from 1382 to the present; compiled and translated by Joachim Neugroschel
Tenhoff, S. P.
Ichiban
Confrontation no90/91 p125-42 Spr/Summ 2005
Tenn, William
The lemon-green spaghetti-loud dynamite-dribble day
This is my funniest; leading science fiction writers present their funniest stories ever; edited by Mike Resnick

TERMINAL ILLNESS—*Continued*
  Williams, J. Honored guest
  Wood, M. Ernie's ark
Terminal lounge. Sayles, J.
The **terminal** project. Chase, M.
Terminix [Reprint] Tate, J.
Termite, 1959. Phillips, J. A.
Terrible ones. Pratt, T.
A **terrible** thing. Wallace, D.
Terrible Tommy Terhune. Block, L.
A **terribly** strange bed. Collins, W.
Terrified by raisins. Ockert, J.
Terror. Mandelman, A.
The **terror** bard. Niven, L. and Cooper, B.
The **terror** of the water-tank. Hodgson, W. H.
TERRORISM
        See also Violence
  Abbott, J. Jihad sucks; or, The conversion of the
    Jews
  Abbott, L. K. Revolutionaries
  Abraham, D. Leviathan wept
  Bagi, Y. 'A. a.- . Bus #99
  Bear, E. Gone to flowers
  Boudinot, R. Absolut Boudinot
  Brown, R. Means and ends
  Castro, A.-T. Of a sweet slow dance in the
    wake of temporary dogs
  DeAndrea, W. L. Snowy reception
  Di Filippo, P. Lignum Crucis
  Doctorow, C. When sysadmins ruled the earth
  Fitzhugh, B. The neighbors
  Genna, G. Caput Mundi
  Gilchrist, E. Götterdämmerung, in which Nora
    Jane and Freddy Harwood confront evil in
    a world they never made
  Goonan, K. A. Electric rains
  Hewson, D. The circle
  Hoch, E. D. The face of Ali Baba
  Kadetsky, E. The poison that purifies you
  Keret, E. Surprise egg
  Krysl, M. Dinner with Osama
  Lamri, T. "Elevenzerothreetwothousandfour"
  Lin, T. Love is a thing on sale for more money
    than there exists
  Lutz, J. All quiet
  Mandelman, A. Talking to the enemy
  Martinez, L. Lights out for Frankie
  McCabe, E. Victims
  Milionis, C. The find
  Mitsora, M. Halfpastdoom
  Moorcock, M. The flaneur of les arcades de
    l'opera
  Mukherjee, B. The management of grief
  Pizzolatto, N. Cryptograph
  Rusch, K. K. Craters
  Sholer, L. Imitate the sun
  Silverberg, R. The littlest Jackal
  Singer, M. Body count
  Singer, M. The pale of settlement
  Sterling, B. Join the navy and see the worlds
  Taylor, Nick. The smell of despair
  Thor, B. The Athens solution
  Tidhar, L. My travels with Al-Qaeda
  Updike, J. Varieties of religious experience
  Ward, A. E. Should I be scared ?
  Williams, S. Inevitable
  Working, R. The Irish martyr
TERRORISTS *See* Terrorism

Terry, James
  The Wildcat Massacre
    The Georgia Review v62 no3 p533-50 Fall
    2008
Tervalon, Jervey
  The battling priests of Corpus Christi
    New Orleans noir; edited by Julie Smith
  Serving monster
    The cocaine chronicles; edited by Gary Phil-
    lips and Jervey Tervalon
TESLA, NIKOLA, 1856-1943
            About
  Landis, G. A. The eyes of America
  Pflug, U. The wizard of Wardenclyffe
Tesoro viviente/Living treasure. Serna, E.
Tessier, Thomas
  In praise of folly
    Poe's children; the new horror: an anthology;
    [edited by] Peter Straub.
Test. Mandelman, A.
The **test.** Matheson, R.
The **test.** Reaves, S.
Test-Drive Baby. Quarry, J.
The **test;** or, The little rice wine pot. Qi, S.
TEST PILOTS *See* Air pilots
TEST TUBE FERTILIZATION *See* Fertilization
  in vitro
Testament of Andros. Blish, J.
The **testament** of Athammaus. Smith, C. A.
Testimony. McGlynn, D.
Testimony of the donkey. Proulx, A.
The **testosterone** club. Kennedy, C.
Tetanus. Oates, J. C.
Teternikov, Fedor Kuz´mich *See* Sologub,
      Fyodor, 1863-1927
Teternikov, Fyodor Kuzmich *See* Sologub,
      Fyodor, 1863-1927
TEXAS
  Abbott, L. K. The view of me from Mars
  Abrams, L. Taj Mahal
  Apple, M. The Jew of Home Depot
  Bass, R. Goats
  Berry, Betsy. Family and flood
  Castillo, R. The battle of the Alamo
  Crumley, J. Whores
  Daugherty, T. Power lines
  DeMarinis, R. The life and times of a forty-
    nine-pound man
  Doctorow, E. L. Child, dead, in the rose garden
  Feitell, M. Our little lone star
  Flaig, S. Texas toast
  Fuentes, M. Looking for eight
  Garrett, G. P. The misery and the glory of Tex-
    as Pete
  Graves, J. The last running
  Greene, A. C. The girl at Cabe ranch
  Guthridge, M. The host
  Harrison, W. Texas heat
  Hearon, S. A prince of a fellow [excerpt]
  Hempel, A. Cotton Flat Road
  Henry, O. Art and the bronco
  Hickey, D. I'm bound to follow the longhorn
    cows
  Hinojosa, R. Partners in crime [excerpt]
  Hinojosa-Smith, Rolando. The Gulf Oil -Can
    Santa Claus
  Howard, C. To live and die in Midland, Texas
  Howard, R. E. The man on the ground
  Howard, R. E. Old Garfield's heart

Thelwell, Michael
  Direct action
    Short stories of the civil rights movement; an anthology; edited by Margaret Earley Whitt
Them old cowboy songs. Proulx, A.
Then came the poor. Bishop, E.
Theo. Eggers, D.
Theodore, Judith
  Dark nights
    Trinidad noir; edited by Lisa Allen-Agostini & Jeanne Mason.
A **theory** of entropy. Ohlin, A.
The **theory** of light and matter. Porter, A.
Theory of Realty. Jones, H. G.
Theory of relity. Jones, H. G.
Theotokopoulos, Domenikos *See* El Greco, 1541-1614
There a petal silently falls. Ch'oe, Y.
There are meadows in Lanark. Kiely, B.
There are no pockets in our graveclothes. Falk, B.
There are some things he should keep to himself. Eggers, D.
There is a light that never goes out. Mamatas, N.
There is no crime on Easter Island. Pickard, N.
There Is No Place That Does Not See You. Irby, L.
There shall be no darkness. Blish, J.
There shall be no moon!. Zelazny, R.
There shall your heart be also. Hambly, B.
There was an old woman. Silverberg, R.
There were three. Bonner, M. O.
There will be no fourth Rome. Krasikov, S.
There's a ghost in my house. Dudman, C.
There's a pill for that. Castillon, C.
There's a Place for Fun in Your Life. Voedisch, R.
There's always a trail. L'Amour, L.
There's no light between floors. Tremblay, P. G.
There's only one way I can lie. Moceri, M.
Therese. Matheson, R.
Theroux, Paul
  The Best Year of My Life
    The New Yorker v81 no36 p82-4, 86-9 N 14 2005
  The elephant god
    Theroux, P. The Elephanta suite
  The gateway of India
    Theroux, P. The Elephanta suite
  Monkey Hill
    Theroux, P. The Elephanta suite
    The New Yorker v82 no43 p108-15, 117-27 D 25 2006/Ja 1 2007
  Mr. Bones
    The New Yorker v83 no27 p82-9 S 17 2007
  Twenty-two stories
    The PEN/O.Henry Prize stories 2009; chosen and with an introduction by Laura Furman; with essays on the stories They admire most by jurors A. S. Byatt; Anthony Doerr; Tim O'Brien
  Warm dogs
    Telling tales; edited by Nadine Gordimer
These Are My Arms. Jaeger, T.
These are my last words. Grimes, C.
These are the names I know. Jones, S. G.
These hours. Montgomery, L.
These Moments Brief as Clouds of Breath in Cold Air. Angus, K.
These Things Happen. Kenny, M.

These Wildernesses. Solomon, A.
They Decide No More Death. Eggers, D.
They Don't Ring at the Bernardines'. Ficowski, J.
They drank champagne at the restaurant. Castillon, C.
They Keep Falling. Satelmajer, I.
They shall not grow old. Dahl, R.
They took everything. Drosso, A.-M.
They turn their bodies into spears. Schutt, C.
They were expendable. Canty, K.
They would only be roads. Bradley, D. C.
They're afraid. Reisen, A.
They're all the same. Auslander, S.
Thicker than blood. L'Amour, L.
Thicker Than Water. Ochsner, G.
A **thief**. Chekhov, A. P.
The **Thief**. Furman, L.
The **thief**. Ramos, G.
The **thief**. Zoshchenko, M.
The **thief** catcher. Judson, T.
THIEVES
    See also Cattle thieves; Horse thieves; Theft
  Anderson, F. I. Blind man's buff
  Barr, R. The mystery of the five hundred diamonds
  Brodsky, M. Limit point
  Carew, J. Tilson Ezekiel alias Ti - Zek
  Carey, P. The fat man in history
  Charyn, J. Young Isaac
  Chekhov, A. P. A confession
  Chekhov, A. P. A thief
  Collins, W. The biter bit
  Collins, W. Who is the thief?
  Coward, M. Room to move
  Dahl, R. The hitchhiker
  Dahl, R. The surgeon
  Dahl, R. The umbrella man
  Davis, F. C. The sinister sphere
  Deaver, J. Surveillance
  Dexter, C. Between the lines
  Doerr, A. The caretaker
  Donovan, G. Shoplifting in the USA
  Edgerton, C. The great speckled bird
  Erdrich, L. The little book
  Etchison, D. The dark country
  Faber, M. Less than perfect
  Gallagher, S. Jailbird for Jesus
  Gardner, E. S. The monkey murder
  Gildner, G. Pavol Hudák, the poet, is talking
  Green, A. Food stamp
  Hodgson, W. H. The getting even of "Parson" Guyles
  Hodgson, W. H. Jem Binney and the safe at Lockwood Hall
  Holthe, T. U. The five-forty-five to Cannes
  Holthe, T. U. The last bullfight
  Holthe, T. U. The pointer
  Ibn Sayf Rahabi, M. The disaster
  Judson, T. The thief catcher
  Kadetsky, E. Men more than mortal
  Kempadoo, O. Standing on thin skin
  Knight, M. Smash and grab
  Langer, A. Bobby Kagan knows everything
  Larsen, T. Lids
  LaSalle, P. Tell Borges if you see him
  Lecard, M. Teardown
  MacLaverty, B. The Trojan sofa
  McDevitt, J. Deus Tex

This nib for hire. Allen, W.

THIS OLD HOUSE (TELEVISION PRO-GRAM)

Weaver, W. Sheetrock

This or any desert. Tran, V.

This or any desert. Trans, V.

This person. July, M.

This Road. Nadzam, B.

This tragic glass. Bear, E.

"This very vivd morn". Green, G.

This way to the exit. Douglass, S.

This year's class picture. Simmons, D.

Thisted, Valdemar

Letters from hell: letter III

Tales before Narnia; the roots of modern fantasy and science fiction; edited by Douglas A. Anderson

The thistles in Sweden. Maxwell, W.

THOMAS, AQUINAS, SAINT, 1225?-1274

About

Thormahlen, A. A talk with Thomas

Thomas, Alberta

Gold is where you find it

"Tell it to us easy" and other stories; a complete short fiction anthology of African American women writers in Opportunity magazine, (1923-1948); edited by Judith Musser.

Thomas, Donald Serrell

The case of Peter the painter

Thomas, D. S. Sherlock Holmes and the king's evil and other new adventures of the great detective; [by] Donald Thomas

The case of the Greek key

Thomas, D. S. The execution of Sherlock Holmes; [by] Donald Thomas

The case of the king's evil

Thomas, D. S. Sherlock Holmes and the king's evil and other new adventures of the great detective; [by] Donald Thomas

The case of the Peasenhall murder

Thomas, D. S. The execution of Sherlock Holmes; [by] Donald Thomas

The case of the phantom chambermaid

Thomas, D. S. The execution of Sherlock Holmes; [by] Donald Thomas

The case of the Portuguese sonnets

Thomas, D. S. Sherlock Holmes and the king's evil and other new adventures of the great detective; [by] Donald Thomas

The case of the tell-tale hands

Thomas, D. S. Sherlock Holmes and the king's evil and other new adventures of the great detective; [by] Donald Thomas

The case of the Zimmermann telegram

Thomas, D. S. Sherlock Holmes and the king's evil and other new adventures of the great detective; [by] Donald Thomas

The execution of Sherlock Holmes

Thomas, D. S. The execution of Sherlock Holmes; [by] Donald Thomas

The queen of the night

Thomas, D. S. The execution of Sherlock Holmes; [by] Donald Thomas

Thomas, Edward

The artist

Thomas, E. The ship of swallows; a selection of short stories; edited and introduced by Jeremy Hooker; preface by Myfanwy Thomas

The attempt

Thomas, E. The ship of swallows; a selection of short stories; edited and introduced by Jeremy Hooker; preface by Myfanwy Thomas

Birds of a feather flock together

Thomas, E. The ship of swallows; a selection of short stories; edited and introduced by Jeremy Hooker; preface by Myfanwy Thomas

The first of spring

Thomas, E. The ship of swallows; a selection of short stories; edited and introduced by Jeremy Hooker; preface by Myfanwy Thomas

The flower-gatherer

Thomas, E. The ship of swallows; a selection of short stories; edited and introduced by Jeremy Hooker; preface by Myfanwy Thomas

The friend of the blackbird

Thomas, E. The ship of swallows; a selection of short stories; edited and introduced by Jeremy Hooker; preface by Myfanwy Thomas

Hawthornden

Thomas, E. The ship of swallows; a selection of short stories; edited and introduced by Jeremy Hooker; preface by Myfanwy Thomas

Home

Thomas, E. The ship of swallows; a selection of short stories; edited and introduced by Jeremy Hooker; preface by Myfanwy Thomas

The land of youth

Thomas, E. The ship of swallows; a selection of short stories; edited and introduced by Jeremy Hooker; preface by Myfanwy Thomas

The making of the worlds, of gods, and of giants

Thomas, E. The ship of swallows; a selection of short stories; edited and introduced by Jeremy Hooker; preface by Myfanwy Thomas

Milking

Thomas, E. The ship of swallows; a selection of short stories; edited and introduced by Jeremy Hooker; preface by Myfanwy Thomas

Morgan

Thomas, E. The ship of swallows; a selection of short stories; edited and introduced by Jeremy Hooker; preface by Myfanwy Thomas

One swallow doesn't make a summer

Thomas, E. The ship of swallows; a selection of short stories; edited and introduced by Jeremy Hooker; preface by Myfanwy Thomas

Thomas, Edward—*Continued*
The pilgrim
　Thomas, E. The ship of swallows; a selection
　　of short stories; edited and introduced by
　　Jeremy Hooker; preface by Myfanwy
　　Thomas
The ship of swallows
　Thomas, E. The ship of swallows; a selection
　　of short stories; edited and introduced by
　　Jeremy Hooker; preface by Myfanwy
　　Thomas
Sunday afternoon
　Thomas, E. The ship of swallows; a selection
　　of short stories; edited and introduced by
　　Jeremy Hooker; preface by Myfanwy
　　Thomas
A third-class carriage
　Thomas, E. The ship of swallows; a selection
　　of short stories; edited and introduced by
　　Jeremy Hooker; preface by Myfanwy
　　Thomas
Thomas, Eugene
The adventure of voodoo moon
　The Black Lizard big book of pulps; edited
　　by Otto Penzler
Thomas, James Ellis
Triumph of the Southside Ladyjacks
　The New Yorker v80 no35 p96-103 N 15
　2004
Thomas, Jeffrey
The ballad of Moosecock Lip
　Thomas, J. Punktown
Dissecting the soul
　Thomas, J. Punktown
Face
　Thomas, J. Punktown
The flaying season
　Thomas, J. Punktown
Heart for heart's sake
　Thomas, J. Punktown
Immolation
　Thomas, J. Punktown
　The new weird; Ann & Jeff VanderMeer, edi-
　　tors
The library of sorrows
　Thomas, J. Punktown
Nom de guerre
　Thomas, J. Punktown
The palace of nothingness
　Thomas, J. Punktown
Pink pills
　Thomas, J. Punktown
Precious metal
　Thomas, J. Punktown
The pressman
　Thomas, J. Punktown
The reflections of ghosts
　Thomas, J. Punktown
The rusted gates of heaven
　Thomas, J. Punktown
Sisters of no mercy
　Thomas, J. Punktown
Union dick
　Thomas, J. Punktown
Unlimited daylight
　Thomas, J. Punktown
Wakizashi
　Thomas, J. Punktown

Thomas, Lee
An apiary of white bees
　Inferno; new tales of terror and the supernatu-
　　ral; edited by Ellen Datlow.
Thomas, Ross
Cast a yellow shadow [excerpt]
　D.C. noir 2; the classics; edited by George
　　Pelecanos.
Thomas, Scarlett
Paratext
　Nature v441 p548 My 25 2006
Thomas, Sheree R.
The grassdreaming tree
　So long been dreaming; postcolonial science
　　fiction & fantasy; Nalo Hopkinson &
　　Uppinder Mehan, eds
Thomas the Proclaimer. Silverberg, R.
Thompson, Aida
Thanksgiving Day
　Femspec v7 no1 p106-7 2006
Thompson, Brian
Geezers
　The Best British mysteries, 2005; edited by
　　Maxim Jakubowski
Thompson, Chandler
(tr.) See Roncagliolo, Santiago
Thompson, Eloise Bibb
Mademoiselle 'Tasie-a story
　"Tell it to us easy" and other stories; a com-
　　plete short fiction anthology of African
　　American women writers in Opportunity
　　magazine, (1923-1948); edited by Judith
　　Musser.
Masks: a story
　"Tell it to us easy" and other stories; a com-
　　plete short fiction anthology of African
　　American women writers in Opportunity
　　magazine, (1923-1948); edited by Judith
　　Musser.
Thompson, Isabel M.
Ebony-a story
　"Tell it to us easy" and other stories; a com-
　　plete short fiction anthology of African
　　American women writers in Opportunity
　　magazine, (1923-1948); edited by Judith
　　Musser.
Thompson, James W.
See what tomorrow brings
　Short stories of the civil rights movement; an
　　anthology; edited by Margaret Earley Whitt
Thompson, Jean
Applause, applause
　Children playing before a statue of Hercules;
　　edited and introduced by David Sedaris
The brat
　Thompson, J. Throw like a girl; stories
Do not deny me
　Thompson, J. Do not deny me; stories
Escape
　Thompson, J. Do not deny me; stories
The family Barcus
　Thompson, J. Throw like a girl; stories
The five senses
　Thompson, J. Throw like a girl; stories
Her untold story
　Thompson, J. Do not deny me; stories
Holy Week
　Thompson, J. Throw like a girl; stories

Through the night. Donoghue, E.
Through the night. Stamm, P.
Through the Panama. Lowry, M.
Through the vortex of a cyclone. Hodgson, W. H.
Through the Water of the Clouds. May, S.
Through these eyes. Rand, K.
Through walls. Keret, E.
Throw like a girl. Thompson, J.
Thug Life. Foundation, L.
The thumb. Bishop, E.
Thumbprints. Sargent, P.
Thumbtacks. Ducornet, R.
THURBER, JAMES, 1894-1961
Parodies, imitations, etc.
Effinger, G. A. The day the invaders came
THURMAN, UMA
About
Watkins, S. Bocky-Bocky
Thursday. Jasper, K.
Thursday at Agape Table. Klassen, S.
Thursday's child. Brown, E.
Thurston, Michael
And Learn by Going
Confrontation no94/95 p166-76 Spr/Summ 2006
Thus ate Zarathustra. Allen, W.
Thúy, Lê Thi Diem
The Americans
The Massachusetts Review v50 no1-2 p17-23 Spr/Summ 2009
Thwarting Jabbi Gloond. Hughes, M.
TIBBETT, LAWRENCE, 1896-1960
About
Green, G. "This very vivd morn"
TIBET (CHINA) *See* China—Tibet
Tibet, New York. Cantor, R.
Tiburtina noir blues. Mazzucato, F.
Tice, Bradford
The Art of Human Surveillance
The American Scholar v78 no1 p98-110 Wint 2009
Tick-tock curly-wurly. Owens, G.
The ticket. Munro, A.
Ticket to death. See McBain, E. Death flight [variant title: Ticket to death]
Tickets. Barthelme, D.
Tickets to nowhere. Harrison, W.
Ticknor, Beginning. Heti, S.
Tidal wave wedding. Panning, A.
Tideline. Bear, E.
Tidhar, Lavie
304, Adolph Hitler Strasse
Realms
My travels with Al-Qaeda
Salon fantastique; edited and with an introduction by Ellen Datlow and Terri Windling
Shira
The Del Rey book of science fiction and fantasy; sixteen original works by speculative fiction's finest voices; edited by Ellen Datlow
The **Tie-Down**. Rogers, D.
Tien-Mei Lin, Christine
(tr.) See Bikwan, Wong

Tierce, Merritt
Suck it
New stories from the South; the year's best, 2008; selected from U.S. magazines by ZZ Packer with Kathy Pories; with an introduction by ZZ Packer
Southwest Review v92 no3 p434-45 2007
TIERRA DEL FUEGO (ARGENTINA AND CHILE)
Coloane, F. Tierra del Fuego
Tierra del Fuego. Coloane, F.
Tiger. Luongo, M.
Tiger in the night. Aldiss, B. W.
Tiger Lilies. Gildner, G.
Tiger! Tiger!. Bear, E.
TIGERS
Aldiss, B. W. Tiger in the night
Kinman, G. T. Catnapping
Lee, Y. H. Eating hearts
Quiroga, H. Juan Darien
Rosenbaum, B. On the cliff by the river
Tigers. Wolven, S.
The Tiger's Wife. Obreht, T.
Tight little stitches in a dead man's back. Lansdale, J. R.
Tightness in the chest (Vermont, 1986). Mohanraj, M. A.
Tihanyi, Eva
Body and Soul
Dalhousie Review v86 no1 p99-102 Spr 2006
Green is the Most Difficult Colour
Dalhousie Review v87 no1 p95-100 Spr 2007
TIJUANA (MEXICO) *See* Mexico—Tijuana
Tijuana women. Meno, J.
The tik. O'Brien, J.
'Til death do us part. Matheson, R.
Til death do us part. Schutz, B. M.
Tilghman, Christopher
Aerial Bombardment
The Virginia Quarterly Review p85-103 2006 supp
Change of Address
Ploughshares v33 no2/3 p164-83 Fall 2007
Till death do us part. Maleeny, T.
Tiller Family Soup. Wilson, K.
Tillman, Lynne
The recipe
This is not chick lit; original stories by America's best women writers; edited by Elizabeth Merrick
The Shadow of Doubt
The Literary Review (Madison, N.J.) v49 no3 p6-14 Spr 2006
Tilmac, Feryal
Hitching in the lodos
Istanbul noir; edited by Mustafa Ziyalan & Amy Spangler; translated by Amy Spangler & Mustafa Ziyalan.
Tilson Ezekiel alias Ti - Zek. Carew, J.
The tilt. Romm, R.
Timber on the wheel of everyone. Malla, P.
TIME
See also Clocks and watches
Anderson, P. Flight to forever
Anderson, P. Time lag
Bierce, A. Mr. Barcle's mill
Bradbury, R. Season of disbelief
Gail, O. W. The missing clock hands: an implausible happening

To fit the crime. Matheson, R.
To Give Ghosts the Finger. Looney, G.
To go boldly. Doctorow, C.
To hang me high. L'Amour, L.
To have been. Magris, C.
To hear the megillah on Purim. Molodowsky, K.
To Howard Hughes: a modest proposal. Haldeman, J. W.
To hunt in fields. Rich, M.
To know all things that are in the earth. Maxey, J.
To live and die in Midland, Texas. Howard, C.
To London and Rome. Barthelme, D.
To look too closely. Grainger, P.
To measure the earth. Berry, J.
To my young husband. Walker, A.
To raise a mutiny betwixt yourselves. Lake, J.
To Reign After Death. Mandelberg, J.
To return by foot. Ahdal, W. a.- .
To run without falling. Jones, S. G.
To see another mountain. Pohl, F.
To see the invisible man. Silverberg, R.
To serve the ship. Nolan, W. F.
To sit, unmoving. Steinberg, S.
To still the beating of her heart. O'Shaughnessy, P.
To swim? Tabor, M. L.
To tell the truth. Báez, A.
To the absolute zero of existence: a story from 2371. Lasswitz, K.
To the City. Aw, T.
To the dark star. Silverberg, R.
To the death. Luvaas, W.
To the Interstate. Curtis, R.
To the Lady that Thinks She Knows. Im, M.
To the land beyond the sunset. Baker, K.
To the light. Sayles, J.
To the madhouse. Johnson, G.
To the poet's wife. Stevens, J. D.
To this water (Johnstown, Pennsylvania 1889). Kiernan, C. R.
To those of you who missed your connecting flights out of O'Hare. Hempel, A.
Toad. McKillip, P. A.
Toad-rich. Cadnum, M.
A **toast**. Kuprin, A. I.
Toast. West, P.
Toast: a con report. Stross, C.
The **Toaster**. Pierce, G.
TOBACCO HABIT *See* Smoking
TOBACCO INDUSTRY
Tsutsui, Y. The last smoker
Tobar, Héctor
Once more, Lazarus
Los Angeles noir; edited by Denise Hamilton
Tobin, Patrick
Cake
The Kenyon Review v29 no1 p30-43 Wint 2007
Passage
New stories from the Southwest; edited by D. Seth Horton; foreword by Ray Gonzalez.
The Literary Review (Madison, N.J.) v49 no3 p135-46 Spr 2006
That Kind of Nonsense
Agni no58 p75-88 2003
Today I'm yours. Gaitskill, M.
Today is the day. Shields, C.
Today will be a quiet day. Hempel, A.

Todd, Caroline
See also Todd, Charles
Todd, Charles
Home coming
Mystery Writers of America presents death do us part; new stories about love, lust, and murder; edited by Harlan Coben
Todd, Marilyn
Thoroughly modern millinery
The Best British mysteries, 2006; edited by Maxim Jakubowski
Todd, Penelope
from On This Island
Iowa Review v38 no2 p88-91 Fall 2008
Todd, René L.
Vinegar
Best new American voices 2004; guest editor John Casey; series editors John Kulka and Natalie Danford
The **toddler**. Lamsley, T.
Todd's Dad. Mullan, N.
Toe to tip, tip to toe, pip-pop as you go. Nolan, W. F.
Toer, Pramoedya Ananta
Acceptence
Toer, P. A. All that is gone; translated from the Indonesian by Willem Samuels
All that is gone
Toer, P. A. All that is gone; translated from the Indonesian by Willem Samuels
Circumcision
Toer, P. A. All that is gone; translated from the Indonesian by Willem Samuels
In twilight born
Toer, P. A. All that is gone; translated from the Indonesian by Willem Samuels
Independence Day
Toer, P. A. All that is gone; translated from the Indonesian by Willem Samuels
Inem
Toer, P. A. All that is gone; translated from the Indonesian by Willem Samuels
Revenge
Toer, P. A. All that is gone; translated from the Indonesian by Willem Samuels
The rewards of marriage
Toer, P. A. All that is gone; translated from the Indonesian by Willem Samuels
Toes, Jac.
Lead . . . follow
The World's finest mystery and crime stories, fourth annual collection; edited by Ed Gorman and Martin H. Greenberg
Toews, Miriam
The Double Knot
The Walrus v5 no6 p70-1 Jl/Ag 2008
Toga party. Barth, J.
Toganov, Bogdan
The children
Bandersnatch; edited by Paul Tremblay and Sean Wallace
Together again. Cadnum, M.
Together we are lost. Azevedo, K. d.
Together We Are Lost. De Azevedo, K.

Tognazzini, Anthony—*Continued*

The suicide
  Tognazzini, A. I carry a hammer in my pocket for occasions such as these; stories

The task
  Tognazzini, A. I carry a hammer in my pocket for occasions such as these; stories

A telephone conversation with my father
  Tognazzini, A. I carry a hammer in my pocket for occasions such as these; stories

Teresa's second dream
  Tognazzini, A. I carry a hammer in my pocket for occasions such as these; stories

That which I should have done, I did not do
  Tognazzini, A. I carry a hammer in my pocket for occasions such as these; stories

True confessions of the bat-fonz
  Tognazzini, A. I carry a hammer in my pocket for occasions such as these; stories

The unfortunate poker game
  Tognazzini, A. I carry a hammer in my pocket for occasions such as these; stories

The weather retires
  Tognazzini, A. I carry a hammer in my pocket for occasions such as these; stories

Westminster march
  Tognazzini, A. I carry a hammer in my pocket for occasions such as these; stories

What comes of conversation
  Tognazzini, A. I carry a hammer in my pocket for occasions such as these; stories

What I'm doing after this
  Tognazzini, A. I carry a hammer in my pocket for occasions such as these; stories

Woodpecker
  Tognazzini, A. I carry a hammer in my pocket for occasions such as these; stories

Working out with Kafka
  Tognazzini, A. I carry a hammer in my pocket for occasions such as these; stories

Tóibín, Colm

The Color of Shadows
  The New Yorker v85 no9 p64-71 Ap 13 2009

Donal Webster
  The book of other people; edited by Zadie Smith

Famous blue raincoat
  Tóibín, C. Mothers and sons; stories

A journey
  Tóibín, C. Mothers and sons; stories

A long winter
  Tóibín, C. Mothers and sons; stories

The name of the game
  Tóibín, C. Mothers and sons; stories

One Minus One
  The New Yorker v83 no11 p68-73 My 7 2007

A priest in the family
  Tóibín, C. Mothers and sons; stories

A song
  Tóibín, C. Mothers and sons; stories

A summer job
  Tóibín, C. Mothers and sons; stories

Three friends
  Tóibín, C. Mothers and sons; stories

The use of reason
  Tóibín, C. Mothers and sons; stories

Toilet training. Allen, J. R.

TOILETS

Gospodinov, G. A fly in the urinal

Gospodinov, G. Station story

Prabhaker, S. A hard truth about waste management

The **token**. Hoffman, A.

The **token** booth clerk. Gran, S.

TOKLAS, ALICE B.

About

McGarry, J. The last time

TOKYO (JAPAN) *See* Japan—Tokyo

Tokyo Story. Tyree, W.

Tokyo Year Zero. Peace, D.

Told in the desert. Smith, C. A.

Toledo Paz, Natalia

The Table
  Bomb no98 p100 Wint 2007

Tollbooth confidential. Pendarvis, J.

Tolstaia, Tat´iana

The circle
  Tolstaia, T. White walls; collected stories; [by] Tatyana Tolstaya; translated by Antonina W. Bouis [and] Jamey Gambrell

A clean sheet
  Tolstaia, T. White walls; collected stories; [by] Tatyana Tolstaya; translated by Antonina W. Bouis [and] Jamey Gambrell

Date with a bird
  Tolstaia, T. White walls; collected stories; [by] Tatyana Tolstaya; translated by Antonina W. Bouis [and] Jamey Gambrell

The fakir
  Tolstaia, T. White walls; collected stories; [by] Tatyana Tolstaya; translated by Antonina W. Bouis [and] Jamey Gambrell

Fire and dust
  Tolstaia, T. White walls; collected stories; [by] Tatyana Tolstaya; translated by Antonina W. Bouis [and] Jamey Gambrell

Heavenly flame
  Tolstaia, T. White walls; collected stories; [by] Tatyana Tolstaya; translated by Antonina W. Bouis [and] Jamey Gambrell

Hunting the wooly mammoth
  Tolstaia, T. White walls; collected stories; [by] Tatyana Tolstaya; translated by Antonina W. Bouis [and] Jamey Gambrell

Limpopo
  Tolstaia, T. White walls; collected stories; [by] Tatyana Tolstaya; translated by Antonina W. Bouis [and] Jamey Gambrell

Loves me, loves me not
  Tolstaia, T. White walls; collected stories; [by] Tatyana Tolstaya; translated by Antonina W. Bouis [and] Jamey Gambrell

The moon came out
  Tolstaia, T. White walls; collected stories; [by] Tatyana Tolstaya; translated by Antonina W. Bouis [and] Jamey Gambrell

Most beloved
  Tolstaia, T. White walls; collected stories; [by] Tatyana Tolstaya; translated by Antonina W. Bouis [and] Jamey Gambrell

Night
  Tolstaia, T. White walls; collected stories; [by] Tatyana Tolstaya; translated by Antonina W. Bouis [and] Jamey Gambrell

Okkervil River
  Tolstaia, T. White walls; collected stories; [by] Tatyana Tolstaya; translated by Antonina W. Bouis [and] Jamey Gambrell

Tompkins, Grace W.
Across the line
"Tell it to us easy" and other stories; a complete short fiction anthology of African American women writers in Opportunity magazine, (1923-1948); edited by Judith Musser.
The fugitive
"Tell it to us easy" and other stories; a complete short fiction anthology of African American women writers in Opportunity magazine, (1923-1948); edited by Judith Musser.
The red dress: a short story
"Tell it to us easy" and other stories; a complete short fiction anthology of African American women writers in Opportunity magazine, (1923-1948); edited by Judith Musser.

Tompkins, Pat
The road to Carville
The Best of the Bellevue Literary Review; edited by Dannielle Ofri and the staff of the Bellevue Literary Review

The **Tonga**. Smith, M.
The **tongues** of the flames. Güzelsoy, I.
Tonight is a favor to Holly. Hempel, A.
Tonka. Musil, R.
Tonopah Range. Le May, A.
The **tonsil** machine. Murray, A.
The **Tonto** woman. Leonard, E.
Tony Rollo's conclusion. Bierce, A.
Tony Takitani. Murakami, H.
Too hot to hoot. Robinson, S.
Too many cooks. Talley, M.
Too much pigment. Carrow, E.
Too much talking! (abridged). Chekhov, A. P.
Too sweet. Kuhlken, K.
Too Young for Funerals. Crace, J.

Toomer, Jean
Avey
D.C. noir 2; the classics; edited by George Pelecanos.

Toomey, Mike
Ten dimes
Hardcore hardboiled; edited by Todd Robinson; introduction by Otto Penzler

Toot sweet Matricia. Mayr, S.
Tooth and claw. Boyle, T. C.
A **toothbrush**. Keating, H. R. F.
Toother. Dowling, T.
Top floor. Ts'an-hsüeh
Top of the list. Goldfaden, J.
Top of the world. Crider, B.
Topeka underground. Averill, T. F.
Torah! Torah! Torah!: three Bible tales for the third millennium. Disch, T. M.
Torch ship Hermes. Bova, B.
Torch ship Hermes [continued] Bova, B.

Torday, Daniel
Undress
The Kenyon Review v29 no3 p125-36 Summ 2007

Torelli-Viollier, Antonietta *See* Colombi, Marchesa, 1840-1920
The **tormenting** eye of God. Koretsky, J. L.

TORNADOES
Erdrich, L. Summer 1913/Miskomini-Geezis/Raspberry sun

Feitell, M. Our little lone star
Gildner, G. Tornadoes
Luvaas, W. Yesterday after the storm . . .
Magee, K. Not people, not this
Tornadoes. Gildner, G.
Toro. Varallo, A.

Torockio, Christopher
Beach Ball
Gettysburg Review v17 no4 p527-45 Wint 2004
Sayings of Confucius
The Antioch Review v63 no2 p351-72 Spr 2005

TORONTO (ONT.) *See* Canada—Toronto

Torres, Justin
Lessons
Granta no104 p248-55 Wint 2008

Torres, Steven
Early fall
Bronx noir; edited by S. J. Rozan

Torres Bodet, Jaime
Apólogo del Juglar y de la Domadora / Apologue of the Juggler and the Lion Tamer
Artes de Mexico no83 p26-31, 68-71 2007

Torrey, Roger
Concealed weapon
The Black Lizard big book of pulps; edited by Otto Penzler
Mansion of death
The Black Lizard big book of pulps; edited by Otto Penzler

Torriani, Antonietta *See* Colombi, Marchesa, 1840-1920
Torriani, Maria *See* Colombi, Marchesa, 1840-1920
Torso. Boyers, R.
Torsvan, Berick Traven *See* Traven, B.
Torsvan, Traven *See* Traven, B.
The **Tortoise** That Refused to Leave Home.

TORTURE
Bender, A. End of the line
Brau, E. The prisoner
Brownworth, V. Violation
Fais, M. Halima, Desdemona, Bubu
Kadare, I. The blinding order
Montemarano, N. The November fifteen
Pascoe, J. The kidnapper bell
Reed, R. Savior
Smith, C. A. The isle of the torturers
Toer, P. A. Revenge
Working, R. Inmates
Torture me. Crouse, D.
The **Torturer's** Wife. Glave, T.
Total Lunar Eclipse. Dintino, T.

TOTALITARIANISM
See also Communism; Dictators; National socialism
Andahazi, F. The sleep of the just
Eisenberg, D. Someone to talk to
Emshwiller, C. The general
Groff, L. The wife of the dictator
James, C. L. R. Michelangelo and the statue of David
Kadare, I. Agamemnon's daughter
Kadare, I. The blinding order
Shields, C. Collision
Stross, C. Big brother iron
Wolff, T. A mature student
Zamiâtin, E. I. We [excerpt]

Totally wired. Jackson, M.
Totton, Sarah
  Bluecoat Jack
    Text: Ur; the new book of masks; [edited by
    Forrest Aguirre]
Totty. Lasdun, J.
Touch. Zentner, A.
Touch not the cat. Aird, C.
The **touch** of angels. Brown, E.
The **touch** of death. Howard, R. E.
Touch sensitive. Evans, R.
Touched, very touched. Kun, M.
Touching bottom. Hildebrand, J.
Touching Dummies. Menefee, J.
Touchy subjects. Donoghue, E.
Tough day for the army. Warner, J.
Tough Love. Bryant, D.
Tough love 3001. Marillier, J.
A **tough** tussle. Bierce, A.
The **toughest** Indian in the world. Alexie, S.
The **toughnest** Indian in the world. Alexie, S.
Toumani Ogun. Chilson, P.
Toupee for a bald tyre. Goddard, R.
Tour de Lune. Roberts, A.
A **Tour** of the Country. Browder, C.
TOURETTE SYNDROME
  Lethem, J. Tugboat syndrome
Touring. Dann, J. and others
Touring Jesus World. Frost, G.
Touring Jesusworld. Frost, G.
Tourism. Harrison, M. J.
TOURIST COURTS *See* Motels
Tourist Sam. Bova, B.
Tourist season. Shomer, E.
TOURIST TRADE
    See also Travel agents
  Albert, E. The living
  Anaya, R. A. The village that the gods painted
    yellow
  Bluestein, E. The blanks
  Born, J. O. Tourist trade
  Bova, B. Isolation area
  Bova, B. Tourist Sam
  Donoghue, E. Enchantment
  Gildner, G. The roots of Western civilization
  Irsfeld, J. H. The tourist
  Klassen, S. Beyond the border
  Koënings, N. S. Theft
  Lahiri, J. Interpreter of maladies
  Lapcharoensap, R. Farangs
  Maxwell, W. The gardens of Mount-Saint-
    Michel
  Parker, M. Couple strike it rich on second hon-
    eymoon
  Russell, K. Ava wrestles the alligator
  Russell, K. The City of Shells
  Shields, C. Reportage
  Singer, I. B. The bus
  Stamm, P. Fado
  Stern, R. G. Orvieto dominos, bolsena eels
  Updike, J. The apparition
Tourist trade. Born, J. O.
TOURISTS *See* Tourist trade
Tournier, Michel
  The ass and the ox
    Telling tales; edited by Nadine Gordimer
  Mother Christmas
    The Ecco book of Christmas stories; edited
    by Alberto Manguel

Tow. McDermott, M.
Towards a better life. Burke, K.
Towards a Language of Desire. Megan, C.
Towards Midnight. Gilmour, P.
Towards midnight. Malouf, D.
Tower, Wells
  The brown coast
    Tower, W. Everything ravaged, everything
    burned
  Door in your eye
    Tower, W. Everything ravaged, everything
    burned
  Down through the valley
    Tower, W. Everything ravaged, everything
    burned
  Everything ravaged, everything burned
    The Anchor book of new American short sto-
    ries; edited by Ben Marcus
    Tower, W. Everything ravaged, everything
    burned
  Executors of important energies
    Tower, W. Everything ravaged, everything
    burned
  Leopard
    Tower, W. Everything ravaged, everything
    burned
    The New Yorker v84 no36 p74-9 N 10 2008
  On the show
    Tower, W. Everything ravaged, everything
    burned
    Harper's v314 p80-6 My 2007
  Retreat
    Pushcart prize XXXIII: best of the small
    presses 2009; edited by Bill Henderson
    with the Pushcart Prize editors
    Tower, W. Everything ravaged, everything
    burned
  Wild America
    Tower, W. Everything ravaged, everything
    burned
The **tower**. Millhauser, S.
The **tower** of ashes. Martin, G. R. R.
Tower of ice. Zelazny, R.
The **tower** of morning's bones. Duncan, H.
Tower, Wells
  Everything ravaged, everything burned
    Pushcart prize XXVII; best of the small
    presses; edited by Bill Henderson with the
    Pushcart prize editors
TOWERS
  Duval, P. Cellular
  Millhauser, S. The tower
A **town** of night. Meno, J.
The **town** on blighted sea. Dellamonica, A. M.
Toxic Life. Wang, K.
Toxoplasmosis or the Beginning of Things You
    Can't Take Back. FitzGerald, M. A.
Toy planes. Buckell, T. S.
The **toy** theater. Wolfe, G.
TOYS
    See also Teddy bears
  Bischoff, D. Quoth the screaming chicken
  Chapman, S. The revenge of the callico cat
  Crouse, D. Show & tell
  Duane, D. The fix
  Dunning, C. Dolls, revenge, dolls again
  Everson, K. The what-not doll
  Friesner, E. M. Cubby Grumbles makes a
    change

TOYS—*Continued*

Gee, M. Righteousness
Greer, A. S. Newton Wicks
Knightly, R. First calvary
Lake, J. Little Pig, Berry Brown, and the hard moon
Lanagan, M. Baby Jane
Morwood, P. The longest ladder
Moscoe, M. Danny's very long trip
Nadelson, S. Lego
Odom, M. The affair of the wooden boy
Rabe, J. Roadshow
Resnick, L. Lady Roxanne La Belle
Rosa, J. G. Treetops
Selinger, G. Jack Tar
Smith, D. W. The call of the track ahead

Tra il devoto et profano. Sutton, B.

Trace. Romano, T.

A **trace** of a trace. DuBois, B.

Tracing a murderer Bendel-Simso, M. M., ed.
Early American detective stories; an anthology; edited by LeRoy Lad Panek and Mary M. Bendel-Simso.

TRACK (ATHLETICS)

Apple, M. Stepdaughters
Reinhorn, H. Last seen
Sillitoe, A. The loneliness of the long distance runner

Track of the cat [excerpt] Barr, N.

Tracks. Lynn, D. H.

Trade winds. Major, D.

TRADERS

DeNiro, A. The exchanges
Martin, G. R. R. A beast for Norn
Martin, G. R. R. Guardians
Moon, E. Say cheese
Nisbet, R. Sounds of the town

Trading corners. Bennett, T.

Tradition. McCauley, W.

Tradition. Moon, E.

The **traditional** story returns. Baumbach, J.

Traditions. Trevor, W.

TRAFALGAR, BATTLE OF, 1805

Brown, S. Reiteration

Traffic. Shroff, M. F.

TRAFFIC ACCIDENTS

See also Hit-and-run drivers

Abbott, L. K. The final proof of fate and circumstance
Abbott, M. Hollywood lanes
Baxter, C. Innocent
Beattie, A. Fléchette follies
Bogary, A. Bloodstains on the wall
Boyle, T. C. Balto
Boyle, T. C. Chicxulub
Boyle, T. C. The swift passage of the animals
Campbell, B. J. The inventor, 1972
Canty, K. The emperor of ice cream
Coake, C. In the event
Coake, C. We're in trouble
Coleman, W. Joy ride
Connelly, M. Mulholland dive
Cooper, J. C. Rushing nowhere
Dammaj, H. The nightmare
Davis, C. The same sky
Davis, J. S. Giving up the ghost
Dean, D. Confessions of a falling woman
Dufresne, J. The dead of night
Enright, A. Until the girl died

Flanagan, E. Honda people
Fonseca, R. Account of the incident
Fonseca, R. The dwarf
Glatt, L. Dirty Hannah gets hit by a car
Graham, T. Twins
Grimes, C. Moving vehicles
Hempel, A. The harvest
Hinton, S. E. The missed trip
Holthe, T. U. The five-forty-five to Cannes
Kava, A. Goodnight, sweet mother
King, S. The New York Times at special bargain rates
Kulpa, K. In the land of mars
Kun, M. The last chance Texaco
Lewis, T. Limestone Diner
Ma'mami, S. a.- . The white dog
Manley, C. Intensive care
Martin, J. Goodbye John Denver
McClanahan, E. A foreign correspondence
McGuane, T. Gallatin Canyon
McInerney, J. Third party
Means, D. Blown from the bridge
Monson, A. Elsie and Henry
Muñoz, M. Lindo y querido
Munro, A. Dimension
Nelson, A. Falsetto
Nelson, R. F. Pulp life
Nolan, W. F. Behind the curtain
Nolan, W. F. Depompa
O'Bryan, J. The unlikely redemption of Jared Pearce
Olafsson, O. November
Otis, M. Stones
Panning, A. Freeze
Panning, A. What happened
Parra, E. A. How life goes
Percy, B. The faulty builder
Powell, P. Scarliotti and the sinkhole
Qi, S. The long march, sort of
Rylands, J. T. Restoration
Shirley, P. Robert Earl and W. C.
Shomer, E. Crash course
Shua, A. M. The spinal column
Sillitoe, A. A time to keep
Stewart, P. Ham
Stewart, P. Makeshift memorial
Thompson, J. Smash
Trezise, R. The brake fluid at Gina's
Van Booy, S. Distant ships
Weil, G. Don't touch me
Wieland, M. Swan's home
Williams, J. The farm
Winton, T. Damaged goods
Yanique, T. Gita Pinky Manachandi

The **tragedy** at Three Forks. Dunbar, P. L.

A **tragedy** with pigs. McWhorter, T.

The **tragic** narrative of Arthur Bedford Addison. Nolan, W. F.

The **trail**. Mosley, W.

Trail. Treat, J.

Trail of the Apache [variant title: Apache agent] Leonard, E.

TRAILER PARKS

Anderson, B. Shanties
Collins, B. Trailer trashed
Duval, P. Welcome wagon
Moon, E. If nudity offends you
Waters, D. Mineral and steel
Worley, E. B. Grove

Trailer trashed. Collins, B.
TRAILERPARKS *See* Trailer parks
The **Train**. Boilard, J.
The **train**. Somerville, P.
The **Train**. Walden, G. R.
Train choir. Raymond, J.
Train Delayed Due to Horrible, Horrible Accident. Booker, B.
The **train** going back. Pendarvis, J.
The **Train** to Ghent. Wald, A. H.
The **train** to Lo Wu. Row, J.
TRAIN TRAVEL *See* Railroads—Travel
Trainor, Kim
  The Four Species of Sorrow
    Dalhousie Review v86 no1 p113-21 Spr 2006
TRAINS *See* Railroads—Trains
Traitor. Mosley, W.
The **traitor**. Weber, D.
TRAITORS *See* Treason
The **trajectory** of frying pans. Litman, E.
Tralala. Selby, H.
Trammell, Robert
  Ingrained
    Southwest Review v89 no4 p593-601 2004
Trample the dead, hurdle the weak. Shepard, J.
TRAMPS *See* Homeless persons
Tran, Ben
  A Revolting Character
    Michigan Quarterly Review v44 no1 p120-9 Wint 2005
Tran, Qui-Phiet
  (tr.) See Tran Dieu Hang
Tran, Vu
  The gift of years
    The O. Henry Prize stories 2007; edited and with an introduction by Laura Furman; with essays on the story they admire most by jurors Charles D'Ambrosio, Ursula K. Le Guin, Lily Tuck
  The Other Country
    Harvard Review (1992) no28 p8-23 2005
  A Painted Face
    The Southern Review (Baton Rouge, La.) v41 no1 p27-43 Wint 2005
  This or any desert
    The Best American mystery stories, 2009; edited and with an introduction by Jeffery Deaver
  Vagaries
    Michigan Quarterly Review v43 no4 p545-70 Fall 2004
Tran Dieu Hang
  Farewell to Douala
    Michigan Quarterly Review v43 no4 p665-78 Fall 2004
A **tranquil** star. Levi, P.
Trans, Vu
  This or any desert
    Las Vegas noir; edited by Jarrett Keene & Todd James Pierce.
Transaction. Dybek, S.
TRANSCENDENTALISM
    See also Idealism
Transcription. Ohlin, A.
Transference. McGarry, J.
The **Transfiguration** of Alessandro Comi. Lock, N.
Transfixed, helpless, and out of control. Anders, C.

Transformation. Leigh, S.
The **transformation** of Targ. Brandon, P. and Dann, J.
The **Transformation** of Uncle Bert. Ziegler, D.
Transformations. Schwitters, K.
Transfusion. Wintrebert, J.
The **transitional** object. Kohler, S.
Transitory Cities. Viswanathan, P.
The **translator**. Brkic, C. A.
The **translator**. Caponegro, M.
The **Translator**. Melnyczuk, A.
TRANSLATORS
  Baxter, S. Fate and the fire-lance
  Brkic, C. A. The translator
  Gordon, M. The translator's husband
  Hasak-Lowy, T. The task of this translator
  Kubati, R. "Leaving with no return"
  May, S. The wizard of Khao-I-Dang
  Micklem, S. "Eft" or "Epic"
  Singer, I. B. My adventures 25 as an idealist
  Smith, N. Isolettes
  Stern, R. G. Cooley's version
  Tawada, Y. Saint George and the translator
The **translator's** husband. Gordon, M.
TRANSMIGRATION
    See also Reincarnation
  Fais, M. Halima, Desdemona, Bubu
  Machado de Assis. The Siamese academies
  Marley, L. P dolce
The **transmission**. Keeble, J.
Transmission. McDermott, M.
Transmutations. McKillip, P. A.
Transparency. Hwang, F.
Transparent. Bernstein, S. D.
Transplant. Banks, R.
TRANSPLANTATION OF ORGANS, TISSUES, ETC.
  Bradbury, R. The visit
  Ito, S. The liver nephew
  Jeschke, W. Partners for life
  Klassen, S. Eye of the moon
  Pohl, F. The merchants of Venus
  Pohl, F. and Kornbluth, C. M. The meeting
  Silverberg, R. Caught in the organ draft
  Trevor, D. The surprising weight of the body's organs
  With, C. Sanny Tranny is alive and well and living on Davie
A **transplanted** boy. Woolson, C. F.
Transport of delight. Denison, R.
TRANSSEXUALS
  Kiernan, C. R. Mercury
  Obejas, A. Destiny returns
  Tenorio, L. The brothers
Transtexting pose. Speegle, D.
TRANSVESTISM
  Akins, M. Que-Linda takes the rite aid
  Bilal, M. The stepson
  Burgin, R. Vacation
  Donoghue, E. The welcome
  Jablonski, N. The end of everything
  Jablonski, N. The monkey's paw
  Lispector, C. Plaza Mauá
  Luxenberg, H. The photograph
  Magee, K. As human as you are standing here
  McCann, R. My mother's clothes: the school of beauty and shame
  McInerney, J. The queen and I
  Michaels, L. Getting lucky

Treat, Jessica—*Continued*

Teacup
Treat, J. Meat eaters & plant eaters; stories
Trail
Treat, J. Meat eaters & plant eaters; stories
Violin lessons
Treat, J. Meat eaters & plant eaters; stories
A visit
Treat, J. Meat eaters & plant eaters; stories
The voix humaine
Treat, J. Meat eaters & plant eaters; stories
Waiting
Treat, J. Meat eaters & plant eaters; stories

Treat, Lawrence
H as in homicide
Murder short & sweet; edited by Paul D. Staudohar
The **treatment**. Robinson, R.

Tree, Matthew
(tr.) See Puntí, Jordi
(tr.) See Sala, Toni
(tr.) See Serra, Màrius
The **tree**. Simpson, H.

TREE HOUSES
Hawes, L. Dawson's folly
The **tree** is my hat. Wolfe, G.
Tree Thieves. Weil, J.
Tree Trimming. Whitcomb, G.
Treehouse. Thompson, J.

TREES
See also Apple trees; Christmas trees
Blaeser, K. M. Growing things
Gee, M. Ring-barking
Hill, J. Dead-wood
Kaisaridis, Y. The old man and the tree
Mahrus, H. 'I. a.- . Al-Assadiah
Murphy, Y. Whitely on the tips
O'Shaughnessy, P. Lemons
Rich, M. To hunt in fields
Silverberg, R. The fangs of the trees
Slatter, A. The jacaranda wife
Steinberg, S. Lifelike
Webb, J. Paradise design'd
Williams, C. Other skins
Yolen, J. The tree's wife
The **trees**. Edwinson, W.
The **tree's** wife. Yolen, J.
Treetops. Rosa, J. G.

Treglia, Jessica
Canceled
Boston Review v34 no4 p35-7 Jl/Ag 2009

Treisman, Deborah
(tr.) See Duras, Marguerite
(tr.) See Jelloun, Tahar Ben
(tr.) See Le Clézio, J. M. G.

Tremain, Rose
A game of cards
The O. Henry Prize stories 2008; edited and with an introduction by Laura Furman; with essays on the stories they admire most by jurors Chimamanda Ngozi Adiche, David Leavitt, David Means
The Paris Review v48 p36-42 Summ 2006

Tremayne, Peter
The astrologer who predicted his own murder
Tremayne, P. Whispers of the dead; fifteen Sister Fidelma mysteries

The banshee
Tremayne, P. Whispers of the dead; fifteen Sister Fidelma mysteries
The Best British mysteries, 2006; edited by Maxim Jakubowski
The blemish
Tremayne, P. Whispers of the dead; fifteen Sister Fidelma mysteries
Corpse on a holy day
Tremayne, P. Whispers of the dead; fifteen Sister Fidelma mysteries
Cry "wolf!"
Tremayne, P. Whispers of the dead; fifteen Sister Fidelma mysteries
Dark moon rising
Tremayne, P. Whispers of the dead; fifteen Sister Fidelma mysteries
Death of an icon
Tremayne, P. Whispers of the dead; fifteen Sister Fidelma mysteries
Does God obey his own law?: A Sister Fidelma story
Thou shalt not kill; biblical mystery stories; edited by Anne Perry
The fosterer
Tremayne, P. Whispers of the dead; fifteen Sister Fidelma mysteries
Gold at night
Tremayne, P. Whispers of the dead; fifteen Sister Fidelma mysteries
The heir-apparent
Tremayne, P. Whispers of the dead; fifteen Sister Fidelma mysteries
Like a dog returning . . .
Tremayne, P. Whispers of the dead; fifteen Sister Fidelma mysteries
The lost eagle
Tremayne, P. Whispers of the dead; fifteen Sister Fidelma mysteries
Sanctuary!
The Deadly Bride; and 21 of the year's finest crime and mystery stories; including complete coverage of the year in mystery and crime fiction; edited by Ed Gorman and Martin H. Greenberg
Scattered thorns
Tremayne, P. Whispers of the dead; fifteen Sister Fidelma mysteries
Whispers of the dead
Tremayne, P. Whispers of the dead; fifteen Sister Fidelma mysteries
The World's finest mystery and crime stories, fourth annual collection; edited by Ed Gorman and Martin H. Greenberg
Who stole the fish?
Tremayne, P. Whispers of the dead; fifteen Sister Fidelma mysteries

Tremblay, Paul G.
There's no light between floors
Realms
Tremor. Martin, J.
The **Trench**. DeLuca, E.
The **trenches**. Brown, R.
The **Trentino** kid. Ford, J.
Las **Tres** Pasiones de un Ceramista / A Potter's Three Passions. Ruy Sánchez, A.

TRESPASS
Campbell, B. J. The trespasser
Simpson, H. Up at a villa

Trespass. Luvaas, W.
Trespass. Matheson, R.
The **trespasser**. Campbell, B. J.
Trespasses. Munro, A.
Trethewey, Eric
  By the Wolf
    Southern Humanities Review v43 no2 p143-51
      Spr 2009
Treuer, David
  Hard Body
    TriQuarterly no133 p24-36 2009
Trevisan, Dalton
  The corpse in the parlor
    Oxford anthology of the Brazilian short story;
      edited by K. David Jackson
  The vampire of Curitiba
    Oxford anthology of the Brazilian short story;
      edited by K. David Jackson
Trevor, Douglas
  Central Square
    Trevor, D. The thin tear in the fabric of space
  Fellowship of the bereaved
    Trevor, D. The thin tear in the fabric of space
  Girls I know
    Trevor, D. The thin tear in the fabric of space
    The O. Henry Prize stories, 2006; edited and
      with an introduction by Laura Furman; ju-
      rors: Kevin Brockmeier, Francine Prose,
      Colm Toibin
  Haircuts
    Trevor, D. The thin tear in the fabric of space
  Labor Day hurricane, 1935
    Trevor, D. The thin tear in the fabric of space
  The river
    Trevor, D. The thin tear in the fabric of space
  Saint Francis in Flint
    Trevor, D. The thin tear in the fabric of space
  The surprising weight of the body's organs
    Trevor, D. The thin tear in the fabric of space
  The thin tear in the fabric of space
    Trevor, D. The thin tear in the fabric of space
Trevor, William
  An afternoon
    Trevor, W. Cheating at canasta
    The New Yorker v82 no11 p76-81 My 1 2006
  Another Christmas
    The Ecco book of Christmas stories; edited
      by Alberto Manguel
  At Olivehill
    Trevor, W. Cheating at canasta
    The Sewanee Review v114 no3 p341-54
      Summ 2006
  Big bucks
    Trevor, W. A bit on the side
  A bit on the side
    Trevor, W. A bit on the side
  Bravado
    Trevor, W. Cheating at canasta
    The New Yorker v82 no45 p68-73 Ja 15 2007
  Cheating at canasta
    Trevor, W. Cheating at canasta
  The children
    Trevor, W. Cheating at canasta
    The New Yorker v81 no34 p74-81 O 31 2005
  The dancing-master's music
    Trevor, W. A bit on the side

The dressmaker's child
  The O. Henry Prize stories, 2006; edited and
    with an introduction by Laura Furman; ju-
    rors: Kevin Brockmeier, Francine Prose,
    Colm Toibin
  Trevor, W. Cheating at canasta
An evening out
  Trevor, W. A bit on the side
Faith
  Trevor, W. Cheating at canasta
  The New Yorker v83 no15 p82-7 Je 4 2007
Folie à deux
  Trevor, W. Cheating at canasta
  The O. Henry Prize stories 2008; edited and
    with an introduction by Laura Furman; with
    essays on the stories they admire most by
    jurors Chimamanda Ngozi Adiche, David
    Leavitt, David Means
  The New Yorker v82 no22 p60-5 Jl 24 2006
Graillis's legacy
  Trevor, W. A bit on the side
Justina's priest
  Trevor, W. A bit on the side
Lovers of their time
  My mistress's sparrow is dead; great love sto-
    ries, from Chekhov to Munro; edited by
    Jeffrey Eugenides
Men of Ireland
  Trevor, W. Cheating at canasta
  The New Yorker v81 no5 p72-7 Mr 21 2005
Old flame
  Trevor, W. Cheating at canasta
On the streets
  Trevor, W. A bit on the side
A perfect relationship
  Trevor, W. Cheating at canasta
The room
  Trevor, W. Cheating at canasta
  The O. Henry Prize stories 2007; edited and
    with an introduction by Laura Furman; with
    essays on the story they admire most by ju-
    rors Charles D'Ambrosio, Ursula K. Le
    Guin, Lily Tuck
  The New Yorker v81 no13 p76-81 My 16
    2005
Rose wept
  Trevor, W. A bit on the side
Sacred statues
  Trevor, W. A bit on the side
Sitting with the dead
  Trevor, W. A bit on the side
Solitude
  Trevor, W. A bit on the side
Traditions
  Trevor, W. A bit on the side
The Woman of the House
  The New Yorker v84 no41 p74-81 D 15 2008
Trezise, Rachel
  The brake fluid at Gina's
    Trezise, R. Fresh apples
  But not really
    Trezise, R. Fresh apples
  Chickens
    Trezise, R. Fresh apples
  Coney Island
    Trezise, R. Fresh apples
  Fresh apples
    Urban Welsh; new short fiction; edited by
      Lewis Davies

Troll bridge. Pratchett, T.
TROLLEYS
  Bradbury, R. The trolley
TROLLS *See* Fairies
Trolls' night out. Blackford, J.
A **troop** [sic] of baboons. Smith, T.
Trophy kill. Rand, K.
Tropical fish. Baingana, D.
A **tropical** horror. Hodgson, W. H.
Tropp, Girija
  Feeling Satisfactory
    Agni no61 p107-14 2005
TROTSKY, LEON, 1879-1940
                About
  Michaels, L. Trotsky's garden
  Zoshchenko, M. An unpleasant story
Trotsky's garden. Michaels, L.
TROUBADOURS
  Monteiro, L. Little Star of Bela Lua
Trouble. O'Connor, S.
The **trouble** about Sophiny. Dunbar, P. L.
The **trouble** and strife. Aird, C.
Trouble and the shadowy deathblow. Somerville,
  P.
Trouble at Rindo's station [variant title: Rindo's
  station] Leonard, E.
Trouble with kitchens. Tabor, M. L.
Trouble with the angels. Hughes, L.
Troubles. Stern, R. G.
Trouillot, Evelyne
  The Chareron inheritance
    Words without borders; the world through the
      eyes of writers; an anthology; edited by
      Samantha Schnee, Alane Salierno Mason,
      and Dedi Felman
TROUSERS
  Stone, N. Papal visit
The **trousers**. Dunbar, P. L.
Trousseau. Smith, R. T.
Troy, Judy
  Harold Carlisle
    The Kenyon Review v29 no2 p60-8 Spr 2007
  The order of things
    The PEN/O.Henry Prize stories 2009; chosen
      and with an introduction by Laura Furman;
      with essays on the stories They admire
      most by jurors A. S. Byatt; Anthony Doerr;
      Tim O'Brien
  Ramone
    Best of the South: from the second decade of
      New stories from the South; selected and
      introduced by Anne Tyler
Troy, Mary
  Beach dogs
    Troy, M. Cookie Lily; stories
  Cookie Lily
    Troy, M. Cookie Lily; stories
  Dormez Vous?
    River Styx no73 p98-109 2006
  Falling in love
    Troy, M. Cookie Lily; stories
  Fantasy
    Troy, M. Cookie Lily; stories
  Group home
    Troy, M. Cookie Lily; stories
  Happy birthday Gerald Meatloaf
    Troy, M. Cookie Lily; stories
  Island entertainment
    Troy, M. Cookie Lily; stories

Luau
    Troy, M. Cookie Lily; stories
The most beautiful girl in the world
    Troy, M. Cookie Lily; stories
String Theory
    New Letters v71 no4 p111-32 2005
Talk story
    Troy, M. Cookie Lily; stories
Troyan, Sasha
  Hidden Works
    Ploughshares v35 no1 p142-62 Spr 2009
TRUCK DRIVERS
  Archer, J. Know what I mean?
  Arnow, H. L. S. Marigolds and mules
  Azevedo, K. d. Together we are lost
  Ch'oe, Y. The thirteen-scent flower
  DeVita, R. Riding the doghouse
  Duval, P. Fun with mammals
  Fitch, S. The end of Indian summer
  Matheson, R. Duel
  Mofina, R. Lightning rider
  Pollock, D. R. Hair's fate
  Roberson, J. By the time I get to Phoenix
  Scholes, K. So sang the girl who had no name
  Sillitoe, A. A time to keep
  Waldrop, H. Wild, wild horses
  Wishnia, K. J. A. The dope show
  Wolfe, G. and Hopkins, B. Rattler
Truck Stop. Fletcher, M. L. M.
TRUCKS
                Accidents
            See Traffic accidents
Trudell, Dennis
  Organic Shrapnel and Other Stories
    The North American Review v293 no2 p18-23
      Mr/Ap 2008
The **True** American. Wadholm, T.
The **true** Aryan. Ali, M. N.
True confessions of the bat-fonz. Tognazzini, A.
True Crime. Gansworth, E.
The **true** daughter. Wood, D.
True friendship. Hernandez, J. F.
True hero. Messinger, J.
The **true** history. Spencer, B.
True Illusion. Epstein, A.
The **true** pure land. Stamm, P.
The **true** republic. Almond, S.
True short story. Smith, A.
True tenderness. Shabtai, Y.
Trumpet blues. Rudel, A.
TRUMPET PLAYERS
  Elkin, S. The guest
  Snyder, S. About face
Trunk and disorderly. Stross, C.
Trunk, Y. Y.
  A Roman philosopher writes a letter
    No star too beautiful; Yiddish stories from
      1382 to the present; compiled and translat-
      ed by Joachim Neugroschel
The **trust** Jesus society. Shirley, P.
A **trusted** neighbour. MacLaverty, B.
The **trustfulness** of Polly. Dunbar, P. L.
Trustland: a tale of a traveler. Bierce, A.
Truth. McCabe, E.
The **Truth** About Sammy. Woody, M.
The **Truth** in Dreams. Scott, J.
The **truth** is a seven-headed animal. Hatoum, M.
Truth or dare. Berg, E.

Truth window: a tale of the bedlam rose. Dowling, T.

TRUTHFULNESS AND FALSEHOOD

See also Honesty

Abbott, L. K. The view of me from Mars

Auchincloss, L. L'ami des femmes

Báez, A. To tell the truth

Bakhsawayn, 'A. A. The silver polisher

Bender, A. Two days

Benioff, D. Neversink

Bennett, L. The convert

Blackwell, K. George, Nadia, Blaise

Blackwell, K. The secret life of peonies

Burgin, R. The liar

Clarke, B. The fund-raiser's dance card

Crouse, D. Crybaby

Dobozy, T. Tales of Hungarian resistance

Donoghue, E. Expecting

Flanagan, E. The story of Gladys

Fonseca, R. The notebook

Hawes, L. Salinger's mistress

Hayashi, M. One year later

Hemon, A. The liar

James, C. L. R. The dirty snowball and white raincoat

James, C. L. R. Police proclamation

Knight, M. Gerald's monkey

Kun, M. Corrections to my memoirs

Martin, V. The unfinished novel

Michaelopoulou, A. Lermontov

Mitchell, D. Judith Castle

Monk, B. Mrs. Szewczak and the rescue dog

Moulessehoul, M. The wicked tongue

Nelson, A. People people

O'Connor, J. Two little clouds

Olafsson, O. February

Olafsson, O. July

Opatoshu, J. Moyshe Liar

Otis, M. Welcome to Yosemite

Parker, M. Muddy water, turn to wine

Pifer, D. Fruitcakes and fiction

Ploetz, S. In love with Rachel

Randolph, L. The sensitive man

Rash, R. Honesty

Rashid, H. The storyteller

Singer, I. B. The bitter truth

Spiegelman, P. In Vino, Veritas

Stafford, J. The healthiest girl in town

Turow, S. Loyalty

Wolff, T. The liar

Try. Martin, J.

Try and kill it. Wolfe, G.

Trying again. Gaskell, W.

Trying to Find a Corndog In Tompkins County. Urban, M.

Trying to say. Brown, R.

The **tryst**. Oates, J. C.

Ts'an-hsüeh

The bizarre wooden building

Ts'an-hsüeh. Blue light in the sky & other stories; [by] Can Xue; translated by Karen Gernant and Chen Zeping

Blue light in the sky

Ts'an-hsüeh. Blue light in the sky & other stories; [by] Can Xue; translated by Karen Gernant and Chen Zeping

Burial

Ts'an-hsüeh. Blue light in the sky & other stories; [by] Can Xue; translated by Karen Gernant and Chen Zeping

Helin

Ts'an-hsüeh. Blue light in the sky & other stories; [by] Can Xue; translated by Karen Gernant and Chen Zeping

The little monster

Ts'an-hsüeh. Blue light in the sky & other stories; [by] Can Xue; translated by Karen Gernant and Chen Zeping

The lure of the sea

Ts'an-hsüeh. Blue light in the sky & other stories; [by] Can Xue; translated by Karen Gernant and Chen Zeping

Meteorite mountain

Words without borders; the world through the eyes of writers; an anthology; edited by Samantha Schnee, Alane Salierno Mason, and Dedi Felman

Mosquitoes and mountain ballads

Ts'an-hsüeh. Blue light in the sky & other stories; [by] Can Xue; translated by Karen Gernant and Chen Zeping

My brother

Ts'an-hsüeh. Blue light in the sky & other stories; [by] Can Xue; translated by Karen Gernant and Chen Zeping

A negligible game on the journey

Ts'an-hsüeh. Blue light in the sky & other stories; [by] Can Xue; translated by Karen Gernant and Chen Zeping

Night in the mountain village

Ts'an-hsüeh. Blue light in the sky & other stories; [by] Can Xue; translated by Karen Gernant and Chen Zeping

Scenes inside the dilapidated walls

Ts'an-hsüeh. Blue light in the sky & other stories; [by] Can Xue; translated by Karen Gernant and Chen Zeping

Snake Island

Terrestrial intelligence; international fiction now from New Directions; edited by Barbara Epler

Ts'an-hsüeh. Blue light in the sky & other stories; [by] Can Xue; translated by Karen Gernant and Chen Zeping

The spring

Ts'an-hsüeh. Blue light in the sky & other stories; [by] Can Xue; translated by Karen Gernant and Chen Zeping

Top floor

Ts'an-hsüeh. Blue light in the sky & other stories; [by] Can Xue; translated by Karen Gernant and Chen Zeping

The **Tsar's** boots. Zoshchenko, M.

Tsiaboussis, Vassilis

The doll

Angelic & black; contemporary Greek short stories; edited and translated by David Connolly; with an introduction by Vangelis Hatzivassileiou

Tsuji, Hitonari

Tomorrow's Promises

The Literary Review (Madison, N.J.) v51 no1 p135-64 Fall 2007

TSUNAMIS

Bierce, A. Following the sea

TSUNAMIS—*Continued*

Di Filippo, P. Femaville 29

Panning, A. Tidal wave wedding

Shepard, J. Pleasure boating in Lituya Bay

Tsutsui, Yasutaka

Bad for the heart

    Tsutsui, Y. Salmonella men on planet porno and other stories; translated by Andrew Driver

Bear's Wood Main Line

    Tsutsui, Y. Salmonella men on planet porno and other stories; translated by Andrew Driver

Bravo herr Mozart!

    Tsutsui, Y. Salmonella men on planet porno and other stories; translated by Andrew Driver

Commuter army

    Tsutsui, Y. Salmonella men on planet porno and other stories; translated by Andrew Driver

The Dabba Dabba Tree

    Tsutsui, Y. Salmonella men on planet porno and other stories; translated by Andrew Driver

Don't laugh

    Tsutsui, Y. Salmonella men on planet porno and other stories; translated by Andrew Driver

Farmer airlines

    Tsutsui, Y. Salmonella men on planet porno and other stories; translated by Andrew Driver

Hello, hello, hello!

    Tsutsui, Y. Salmonella men on planet porno and other stories; translated by Andrew Driver

The last smoker

    Tsutsui, Y. Salmonella men on planet porno and other stories; translated by Andrew Driver

Rumours about me

    Tsutsui, Y. Salmonella men on planet porno and other stories; translated by Andrew Driver

Salmonella men on planet porno

    Tsutsui, Y. Salmonella men on planet porno and other stories; translated by Andrew Driver

The very edge of happiness

    Tsutsui, Y. Salmonella men on planet porno and other stories; translated by Andrew Driver

The world is tilting

    Tsutsui, Y. Salmonella men on planet porno and other stories; translated by Andrew Driver

T̀sypkin, Leonid

Summer in Baden-Baden [excerpt]

    Terrestrial intelligence; international fiction now from New Directions; edited by Barbara Epler

Tu B'Shvat: for the Drowned and the Saved. Thon, M. R.

Tú dile a Sarabia que digo yo que la nombre y que la comisione aquí o en donde quiera, que después le explico / You Tell Sarabia That I Said He Shoud Hire Her Here or Wherever, That I'll Explain Later [Part of a special issue: Elogio de la mosca en el arte / In Praise of Flies in Art] Monterroso, A.

TUAMOTU ISLANDS *See* Islands of the Pacific

TUAREGS

Shukman, H. The garden of God: 1976

Tuataras. Anderson, B.

Tube Rose. Smith, R. T.

TUBERCULOSIS

Fulton, A. Happy dust

Guo, S. Moon seal

McIlvoy, K. The rhino in the barn

Stamm, P. Black ice

Tuck, Lily

The House at Belle Fontaine

    The American Scholar v76 no3 p98-107 Summ 2007

Lucky

    The Kenyon Review v27 no4 p131-45 Fall 2005

My Flame

    The Yale Review v96 no4 p138-52 O 2008

Tudish, Catherine

Dog stories

    Tudish, C. Tenney's Landing

The dowry

    Tudish, C. Tenney's Landing

The infusion suite

    Tudish, C. Tenney's Landing

Jordan's stand

    Tudish, C. Tenney's Landing

Killer

    Tudish, C. Tenney's Landing

Pigeon

    Tudish, C. Tenney's Landing

The springhouse

    Tudish, C. Tenney's Landing

Where the devil lost his blanket

    Tudish, C. Tenney's Landing

TUDOR ENGLAND *See* England—16th century

The **Tuesday** club. Neville, K.

Tuesday morning. Hernandez, L.

Tugboat syndrome. Lethem, J.

Tulathimutte, Tony

Scenes from the life of the only girl in Water Shield, Alaska

    The O. Henry Prize stories 2008; edited and with an introduction by Laura Furman; with essays on the stories they admire most by jurors Chimamanda Ngozi Adiche, David Leavitt, David Means

Tulia Shor's stories: King Solomon's bride. Molodowsky, K.

Tulia Shor's stories: The captain. Molodowsky, K.

Tulia Shor's stories: The fourth Mitzvah. Molodowsky, K.

Tulli, Magdalena

Parts of Speech

    Agni no61 p208-22 2005

Tuma, Hama

The Waldiba story

    The Anchor book of modern African stories; edited by Nadežda Obradovic; with a foreword by Chinua Achebe

Tuttle, Lisa
  The Year's best fantasy and horror: twenty-first annual collection; edited by Ellen Datlow and Kelly Link & Gavin J. Grant
  Wives
    Daughters of earth; feminist science fiction in the twentieth century; edited by Justine Larbalestier
Tuttle, Stephen
  Hagiography
    Western Humanities Review v59 no1 p38-42 Spr 2005
  Rosenvall's Cage
    Gettysburg Review v19 no3 p460-8 Aut 2006
'Tutto bene?'. Wright, P.
The **TV** fans from Delta Cep. Levi, P.
TV land. Gower, J.
Twain, Mark
  1905: New York: War Prayer [Reprint]
    Lapham's Quarterly v1 no1 p170-2 Wint 2008
  The black hole of San Francisco
    San Francisco noir 2; the classics; edited by Peter Maravelis.
  An Encounter with an Interviewer
    New England Review v26 no2 p259-62 2005
  Making a fortune
    Bendel-Simso, M. M., ed. Early American detective stories; an anthology; edited by LeRoy Lad Panek and Mary M. Bendel-Simso.
  Political Economy
    Monthly Review (New York, N.Y.) v56 no10 p43-7 Mr 2005
  The Quarrel in the Strong-Box [Story to be published in Who is Mark Twain?]
    Harper's v318 p17-19 Ap 2009
  The stolen white elephant
    The Mammoth book of vintage whodunnits; edited by Maxim Jakubowski
TWAIN, MARK, 1835-1910
            About
  Oates, J. C. Grandpa Clemens & Angelfish, 1906
            Parodies, imitations, etc.
  Effinger, G. A. The wisdom of having money
'Twas the Fight Before Christmas. McCallum, J. and others
Tweddell, Steven
  Max Gehrig, an American Résumé
    The North American Review v293 no3/4 p40-5 My/Ag 2008
Twelve, Otis
  Fluff
    Expletive deleted; edited by Jen Jordan
Twelve beer blues. Hughes, T.
Twelve below zero. Bukoski, A.
Twelve Monthly Devotions. Cunningham, M. A.
The **twentieth** arrondissement. Fargue, L.-P.
Twenty dollar future. Rickards, J.
Twenty evocations. Sterling, B.
Twenty grand. Curtis, R.
Twenty pence with envelope and seasonal greeting. Pratchett, T.
Twenty-two flamingos. Yates, D.
Twenty-two stories. Theroux, P.
Twenty2. The city without secrets. Balding, N.
Twilight. Armstrong, K.
Twilight. Shabtai, Y.

Twilight in Caeli-Amur. Davidson, R.
Twilight of the stooges. Stahl, J.
Twilight of the superheroes. Eisenberg, D.
Twilight states. Cowdrey, A. E.
The **twin.** Reynolds, B.
Twin call girls. Block, L.
Twin study. Richter, S.
Twinkle's enchantment. Baum, L. F.
The **twinkling** of an eye. Matthews, B.
TWINS
        See also Siamese twins
  Adrian, C. Stab
  Barthelme, D. Heather
  Bierce, A. The mocking-bird
  Bierce, A. One of twins
  Blackford, J. Trolls' night out
  Castillon, C. I said one
  Engberg, S. Fortune
  Estleman, L. D. Smart aleck
  Faber, M. The Fahrenheit twins
  Fowler, K. J. The last worders
  Holladay, C. C. The biggest and the best
  Johnson, J. Birthright
  Keret, E. More life
  Kiernan, C. R. Postcards from the King of Tides
  Kress, N. Beggars in Spain
  Lewis, S. The willow walk
  McHugh, M. F. In the air
  Meno, J. The use of medicine
  Morrow, B. Gardener of heart
  Oates, J. C. Heat
  Ochsner, G. Halves of a whole
  Powers, T. Where they are hid
  Richter, S. Twin study
  Selgin, P. Boy b
  Sherman, R. Two stories; Single family; Scenic view
Twins Graham, T.
The **twins:** a mystery. Oates, J. C.
Twinspeak. Fuentes, K.
Twist. Drosso, A.-M.
A **twist** at the end [excerpt] Saylor, S.
The **twisted** ring Bendel-Simso, M. M., ed. Early American detective stories; an anthology; edited by LeRoy Lad Panek and Mary M. Bendel-Simso.
The **Twister.** Boles, P. D.
Twitty, Anne
  Freely, from Chuang Tzu
    Parabola v30 no2 p78-80 My 2005
  Opening One Eye at a Time
    Parabola v30 no1 p81-4 F 2005
Two Arms Holding Me. Rhodes, R. P.
Two Backyards. Giraldi, W.
The **two-bear** mambo [excerpt] Lansdale, J. R.
Two-bit piece. Boehm, L.
Two bits. Effinger, G. A.
The **two** bottles of relish. Dunsany, E. J. M. D. P., Baron
Two boys and a girl. Wolff, T.
Two brothers. Evenson, B.
The **two** brothers. Schwitters, K.
Two cars on a hillside. Harrison, W.
Two Cosmicomics [Story from Cosmicomics] Calvino, I.
Two days. Bender, A.
Two dogs. Yarbrough, S.
Two dreams on trains. Bear, E.

Two Fictions: Chicken Little Goes Too Far. Atwood, M.

Two Fictions: The Tent. Atwood, M.

Two four six eight. Sankaran, L.

Two Friends. Perez, Y.

Two girls and one suitor. Levin, Z.

Two gold coins. Duncklee, J.

Two haunted houses. Bierce, A.

Two hearts. Beagle, P. S.

Two Hours, Two People, and a Box. Weekes, C.

The two hunters. Arnow, H. L. S.

Two hunters in Manhattan. Resnick, M.

Two in the same boat. Gebert, A.

Two Israelis in Prague. Biller, M.

Two left shoes. McCauley, C. S.

Two little clouds. O'Connor, J.

Two military executions. Bierce, A.

The two mothers. Reisen, A.

Two murders, one crime. Woolrich, C.

The Two of Us. Justice, J. R.

Two old men. Baker, K.

The two old women. Baker, K.

Two over easy. Isaacs, S.

Two-player infinitely iterated simultaneous semi-cooperative game with spite and reputation. Yu, C.

Two sadnesses. Effinger, G. A.

The two Sams. Hirshberg, G.

Two shores. Pizzolatto, N.

Two shrines. Libin, Z.

Two sisters. Schuster, F.

Two-step. Meloy, M.

Two stories about Johnson. Bierce, A.

Two stories; Single family; Scenic view. Sherman, R.

Two stories: Telling lives. Sallis, J.

Two stories: The museum of last week. Sallis, J.

Two-story brick houses. Friedmann, P.

Two Studies in Entropy. Pritchard, S.

The two swords of Genghis Khan. Lamb, H.

Two thousand volts. Hogan, C.

Two Tickets for "Turandot". Bloom, S.

Two Virgins. Haverty, C.

Two Visits. Mestre-Reed, E.

Two women. Déry, T.

Two women. Mosley, W.

Two women. Vollmer, M.

The two women friends. Maxwell, W.

Two worlds. Anthony, H. B.

Two years before the mast. Bova, B.

Twopenny novel about an ugly girl. Schwitters, K.

Two's Company. Franzen, J.

TYCOONS *See* Millionaires

Tyent, Nõni

> Miriam
>> A cross of centuries; twenty-five imaginative tales about the Christ; edited by Michael Bishop

Tyge *See* Brahe, Tycho, 1546-1601

Tyler, Alison

> Measure A, B, or me?
>> Sex for America; politically inspired erotica; edited by Stephen Elliott

The typewriter. West, D.

TYPEWRITERS

> Shrayer-Petrov, D. Dismemberers

Typhoid Mary's Proposal. Ford, K.

TYPHOONS

> Murakami, H. The seventh man

Typical Native Scene. Frame, R.

The tyrant in love. Pratt, T.

Tyrants. Klimasewiski, M. N.

Tyree, William

> Tokyo Story
>> *Harvard Review (1992)* no25 p88-97 Fall 2003

Tyrophex-fourteen. Kelly, R.

U

U-BOATS *See* Submarines

U.F.O.'S *See* Flying saucers

Ubbo-Sathla. Smith, C. A.

Uchida, Hyakken

> Afterglow
>> Uchida, H. Realm of the dead; translation by Rachel DiNitto
> The albino
>> Uchida, H. Realm of the dead; translation by Rachel DiNitto
> The ascension
>> Uchida, H. Realm of the dead; translation by Rachel DiNitto
> The banquet
>> Uchida, H. Realm of the dead; translation by Rachel DiNitto
> The bowler hat
>> Uchida, H. Realm of the dead; translation by Rachel DiNitto
> The carp
>> Uchida, H. Realm of the dead; translation by Rachel DiNitto
> The cat
>> Uchida, H. Realm of the dead; translation by Rachel DiNitto
> Chrysanthemum
>> Uchida, H. Realm of the dead; translation by Rachel DiNitto
> The companion
>> Uchida, H. Realm of the dead; translation by Rachel DiNitto
> Driftwood
>> Uchida, H. Realm of the dead; translation by Rachel DiNitto
> Envoy to Tang China
>> Uchida, H. Realm of the dead; translation by Rachel DiNitto
> Fireworks
>> Uchida, H. Realm of the dead; translation by Rachel DiNitto
> The forerunner
>> Uchida, H. Realm of the dead; translation by Rachel DiNitto
> Jintoshi
>> Uchida, H. Realm of the dead; translation by Rachel DiNitto
> Kudan
>> Uchida, H. Realm of the dead; translation by Rachel DiNitto
> The leopard
>> Uchida, H. Realm of the dead; translation by Rachel DiNitto
> The lieutenant's killer
>> Uchida, H. Realm of the dead; translation by Rachel DiNitto

Uchida, Hyakken—*Continued*

The lizard
  Uchida, H. Realm of the dead; translation by Rachel DiNitto
Magnolia
  Uchida, H. Realm of the dead; translation by Rachel DiNitto
The narrow straw mat
  Uchida, H. Realm of the dead; translation by Rachel DiNitto
The pier
  Uchida, H. Realm of the dead; translation by Rachel DiNitto
The reflection
  Uchida, H. Realm of the dead; translation by Rachel DiNitto
Santo Kyoden
  Uchida, H. Realm of the dead; translation by Rachel DiNitto
Seaweed
  Uchida, H. Realm of the dead; translation by Rachel DiNitto
The short night
  Uchida, H. Realm of the dead; translation by Rachel DiNitto
Spring fever
  Uchida, H. Realm of the dead; translation by Rachel DiNitto
The stone pavement
  Uchida, H. Realm of the dead; translation by Rachel DiNitto
The tiny double
  Uchida, H. Realm of the dead; translation by Rachel DiNitto
Triumphant march into Port Arthur
  Uchida, H. Realm of the dead; translation by Rachel DiNitto
The war museum
  Uchida, H. Realm of the dead; translation by Rachel DiNitto
The water bird
  Uchida, H. Realm of the dead; translation by Rachel DiNitto

Uchida, Shungiku

My son's lips
  Inside and other short fiction; Japanese women by Japanese women; with a foreword by Ruth Ozeki; compiled by Cathy Layne

Udall, Brady

Buckeye the elder
  Playboy's college fiction; a collection of 21 years of contest winners; edited by Alice K. Turner; foreword by Thom Jones

Udechukwu, Ada

God's Blessings
  Callaloo v28 no2 p393-402 Spr 2005

UFOs. Lee, D.

UGANDA

Baingana, D. First kiss
Baingana, D. Green stones
Baingana, D. Hunger
Baingana, D. Passion
Baingana, D. Questions of home
Baingana, D. A thank-you note
Baingana, D. Tropical fish
Egan, G. Yeyuka
Gee, M. Good people
Gee, M. The money

Ugarte, Michael

(tr.) See Ndongo-Bidyogo, Donato

The **ugliest** boy. Crouse, D.

UGLINESS

Brennan, K. The emergence of modernism
Cooper, J. C. The eye of the beholder
Harris, J. The Ugly Sister
Pearlman, E. Eyesore
Rhodes, D. Beautiful Consuela
Shepard, J. Glut your soul on my accursed ugliness
Silverberg, R. Caliban
Singleton, G. Shirts against skins

The **ugly** chickens. Waldrop, H.

The **Ugly** Duckling. Andersen, H. C.

The **ugly** dyckling. Negrón-Muntaner, F.

Ugly man. Cooper, D.

The **ugly** young woman: a fairy tale. Schwitters, K.

Ugrešic, Dubravka

The museum of unconditional surrender [excerpt]
  Terrestrial intelligence; international fiction now from New Directions; edited by Barbara Epler

UIGHUR (TURKIC PEOPLE)

Livings, J. The heir

Uke Rivers delivers. Smith, R. T.

UKRAINE

Klassen, S. The Carpathians
Klassen, S. Saved

Crimea

Zoshchenko, M. A workshop for health

Odessa

Faber, M. Bye-bye Natalia

UKRAINIANS

United States

Macy, C. The red coat

Ulanski, Dave

It came from Monkey Skull Creek
  Kolchak: the night stalker chronicles; 26 original tales of the surreal, the bizarre, the macabre; edited by Joe Gentile, Garrett Anderson, Lori Gentile; Kolchak created by Jeff Rice

Ulitskaya, Ludmila

Angel
  Ulitskaya, L. Sonechka; a novella and stories; translated from the Russian by Arch Tait
The beast
  Ulitskaya, L. Sonechka; a novella and stories; translated from the Russian by Arch Tait
Dauntless women of the Russian steppe
  Ulitskaya, L. Sonechka; a novella and stories; translated from the Russian by Arch Tait
The Orlov-Sokolovs
  Ulitskaya, L. Sonechka; a novella and stories; translated from the Russian by Arch Tait
  The New Yorker v81 no9 p174-80, 184-5 Ap 18 2005
The queen of spades
  Ulitskaya, L. Sonechka; a novella and stories; translated from the Russian by Arch Tait
Sonechka
  Ulitskaya, L. Sonechka; a novella and stories; translated from the Russian by Arch Tait
Zurich
  Ulitskaya, L. Sonechka; a novella and stories; translated from the Russian by Arch Tait

Ulla, ulla. Brown, E.
Ulman, Abigail
    Chagall's Wife
        New England Review v28 no4 p46-52 2007
Ulmer, James
    The Copper Bell
        The North American Review v290 no6 p28-9
        N/D 2005
ULSTER (IRELAND AND NORTHERN IRE-LAND)
    Kiely, B. Proxopera
Ultima thule. Rose, A.
Ultima Thule. Smith, L.
The **ultimate** safari. Gordimer, N.
Ultralight. Libman, D. S.
Ultrasaurus. Graham, T.
Ulysses. Milward, A. M.
Ulysses—a great hero. James, C. L. R.
Umansky, Ellen
    Crew cut
        Playboy's college fiction; a collection of 21
            years of contest winners; edited by Alice
            K. Turner; foreword by Thom Jones
The **umbrella** man. Dahl, R.
Umbrella man [excerpt] Swanson, D. J.
Umbrella Street. Adiga, A.
UMBRELLAS
    Canavan, T. The lost property room
    Dahl, R. The umbrella man
Umm Kulthoum at midnight. Handal, N.
Umminger, Alison
    Alien Life
        Prairie Schooner v79 no1 p6-24 Spr 2005
Umpire. Rheinheimer, K.
UN *See* United Nations
The **un-American** activities of Miss Prink. Arnow,
    H. L. S.
Un-pillow talk. Bradbury, R.
The **Un-son**. Murphy, Y.
The **Unabomber** and my brother. Meno, J.
Unaccustomed earth. Lahiri, J.
Unaddressed. Bankole, O. G.
Unassigned territory. Watts, S. P.
The **unblinking** eye. Baxter, S.
UNBORN CHILD *See* Fetus
The **uncertainty** principle. Lustbader, E. V.
Unchain My Heart. Soli, T.
The **uncharted** isle. Smith, C. A.
Uncle. Rivecca, S.
Uncle. Woodrell, D.
Uncle Ben. Mull, H. F.
Uncle Chaim and Aunt Rifke and the angel. Bea-
    gle, P. S.
Uncle Ernest. Sillitoe, A.
Uncle Gus. Hemingway, J.
Uncle Lazarus. Swan, G.
Uncle Mehdi's carpet deal. Saadat, R.
Uncle Musto takes a mistress. Sikka, M.
Uncle Peretz takes off. Shabtai, Y.
Uncle Shmuel. Shabtai, Y.
Uncle Simon's Sundays out. Dunbar, P. L.
UNCLES
    See also Nephews
    Akpan, U. C. Fattening for Gabon
    Amdahl, G. The bouncers
    Amdahl, G. Narrow road to the deep north
    Angel, J. The history of Vegas
    Bakhsawayn, 'A. A. The silver polisher

    Beagle, P. S. Uncle Chaim and Aunt Rifke and
        the angel
    Beattie, A. Just going out
    Berliner, J. High kicks and misdemeanors
    Bhêly-Quénum, O. A child in the bush of ghosts
    Bishop, E. Memories of Uncle Neddy
    Burke, T. Basutoland Christmas
    Burke, T. Memory in tweed
    Clayton, J. J. Muscles
    Clayton, J. J. Waiting for Polly Adler
    Connell, E. S. Lost in Uttar Pradesh
    Connell, E. S. Nan Madol
    Crone, M. Paradise
    DeMarinis, R. Why the tears, Miss Earhart?
    DeNiro, A. The caliber
    Dobozy, T. Four uncles
    Drosso, A.-M. Next on the list?
    Dunbar, P. L. From impulse
    Erdrich, L. The crest
    Evans, M. I learned when I was older
    Fisher, C. The road es traveled
    Flanagan, E. Any ordinary uncle
    Garrett, G. P. Feeling good, feeling fine
    Gifford, B. Wanted man
    Grooms, A. Negro progress
    Hammett, D. Laughing masks
    Hernandez, L. The cross
    Hwang, F. A visit to the suns
    Ito, S. The liver nephew
    Kiely, B. Eton Crop
    Langer, A. Bobby Kagan knows everything
    Lewis, W. H. I got somebody in Staunton
    Li Yiyun. The princess of Nebraska
    Luxenberg, H. The photograph
    Lynn, D. H. Paschal lamb
    Malouf, D. Bad blood
    Mandelman, A. Curse
    Mandelman, A. Mish-mash
    Maxwell, W. The man in the moon
    Michaels, L. Viva la Tropicana
    Monk, B. Congratulations Goldie Katowitz
    Mull, H. F. Uncle Ben
    Nisbet, R. Dors, mon petit, dors
    Oates, J. C. The swimmers
    Ohlin, A. Meeting Uncle Bob
    Omari, I. Obeah catastrophe
    Paine, R. D. "Old Glory" in the desert
    Pendarvis, J. Your body is changing
    Pinski, D. At the attorney's
    Richter, J. The gambling master of Shanghai
    Rivas, M. Havana's vast cemetery
    Rivecca, S. Uncle
    Ruffin, P. The well
    Saadat, R. Uncle Mehdi's carpet deal
    Selgin, P. My search for red and gray wide-
        striped pajamas
    Shabtai, Y. A private and very awesome leopard
    Shabtai, Y. Uncle Peretz takes off
    Shabtai, Y. Uncle Shmuel
    Singer, M. Deir Yassin
    Steinberg, S. Static
    Tolstaia, T. On the golden porch
    Tomlinson, J. A male influence in the house
    Tower, W. The brown coast
    Ts'an-hsüeh. Mosquitoes and mountain ballads
    Ts'an-hsüeh. Snake Island
    Verghese, A. If brains was gas
    Veríssimo, É. The guerrilla
    Walsh, M. O. The Freddies

Unger, Douglas—*Continued*

Matisse
    Unger, D. Looking for war and other stories;
      Douglas Unger
The perfect wife
    Unger, D. Looking for war and other stories;
      Douglas Unger
Second Chances
    Southwest Review v93 no1 p66-81 2008
Tide pool
    Unger, D. Looking for war and other stories;
      Douglas Unger
The writer's widow
    Unger, D. Looking for war and other stories;
      Douglas Unger

The **ungrateful** dead. Armstrong, K.
The **ungrateful** dead. Bates, J. W.
Unhappy celebrations. Molodowsky, K.
Unicorn tapestry. Charnas, S. M.
The **Unicorn** trap. Vonnegut, K.
Unicorn variation. Zelazny, R.

UNICORNS

Black, H. Virgin
Coville, B. Guardian of memory
Friesner, E. M. The fraud
Resnick, M. Stalking the unicorn with guns and
    camera
Vonnegut, K. The Unicorn trap
Yolen, J. The boy who drew unicorns
Zelazny, R. Unicorn variation

UNIDENTIFIED FLYING OBJECTS

DeMarinis, R. Hell's cartoonist

UNIDENTIFIED FLYING SAUCERS *See* Flying saucers

The **uniform**. Cross, H.
The **uninvited**. Hempel, A.
Union dick. Thomas, J.
Unique chicken goes in reverse. Duncan, A.
Unit for "Men, internal". Andreas-Salomé, L.

UNITED ARAB EMIRATES

Dubai

Powell, G. C. Kamila and the king of kandy

UNITED NATIONS

Van Lente, F. Don't even blink

UNITED STATES

    See also Middle Western States; South-
    ern States; Southwestern States; Western
    States names of individual states

18th century

Finlay, C. C. We come not to praise Washington

Revolution, 1775-1783

McGrath, P. The year of the gibbet

19th century

Bierce, A. The fall of the Republic
Bierce, A. The kingdom of Tortirra
Bierce, A. The Tamtonians
Munro, A. Illinois
Wilson, R. C. The peaceable land; or, The un-
    bearable vision of Harriet Beecher Stowe

Civil War, 1861-1865

Adrian, C. A hero of Chickamauga
Allred, L. East of Appomattox
Arnow, H. L. S. Interruptions to school at home
Bierce, A. The affair at Coulter's Notch
Bierce, A. An affair of outposts
Bierce, A. The coup de grâce
Bierce, A. George Thurston
Bierce, A. A horseman in the sky

Bierce, A. Jupiter Doke, Brigadier-General
Bierce, A. Killed at Resaca
Bierce, A. The major's tale
Bierce, A. The mocking-bird
Bierce, A. An occurrence at Owl Creek Bridge
Bierce, A. One kind of officer
Bierce, A. One of the missing
Bierce, A. One officer, one man
Bierce, A. Parker Adderson, philosopher
Bierce, A. A resumed identity
Bierce, A. A son of the gods
Bierce, A. The story of a conscience
Bierce, A. Three and one are one
Bierce, A. A tough tussle
Bierce, A. Two military executions
Bowman, J. R. Stonewalls
Bradbury, R. The drummer boy of Shiloh
Garrett, G. P. A short history of the Civil War
Harness, C. L. Quarks at Appomattox
Holladay, C. C. The interview
James, H. My lost darling
James, H. A sealed tear
Moorcock, M. Colour
Smith, R. T. I have lost my right
Smith, R. T. Trousseau
Smith, R. T. Wretch like me

1865-1898

McHugh, M. F. The Lincoln train

College life

    See College life—United States

Communism

    See Communism—United States

Politics

    See Politics—United States

Presidents

    See Presidents—United States

Prisoners and prisons

    See Prisoners and prisons—United States

Race relations

Arnow, H. L. S. Blessed—blessed
Baraka, I. A. The rejected buppie
Beatty, P. The white boy shuffle [excerpt]
Burke, J. L. The burning of the flag
Burke, J. L. The convict
Capotosto, M. The souls of white children
Cassill, R. V. The first day of school
Chesnutt, C. W. The sheriff's children
Coleman, V. Paying my dues
Cooper, J. C. Wait a minute, world!
Crone, M. Pipe smoke
Dalton, Q. The music you never hear
Di Filippo, P. Shake it to the West
Downs, G. Black pork
Dunbar, P. L. A council of state
Dunbar, P. L. One man's fortunes
Dunbar, P. L. The tragedy at Three Forks
Dunbar, P. L. The wisdom of silence
Durban, P. Gravity
Fowler, M. Southern circumstance
Garrett, G. P. Gator bait
Grooms, A. Flora Devine
Hammett, D. Night shade
Holladay, C. C. Jane's hat
Hughes, L. Trouble with the angels
Hunter, S. Stephen Longacre's greatest match
Kincaid, N. The currency of love
Lawson, J. E. The ankle–biter's guide to slither-
    ing
Lefer, D. Naked Chinese people

UNITED STATES—Race relations—*Continued*
Lewis, W. H. I got somebody in Staunton
Lewis, W. H. Urban renewal
Lieberman, R. A change of scenery
Martin, L. The welcome table
Minus, M. The fine line: a story of the color line
Monk, B. Mrs. Szewczak and the rescue dog
Montemarano, N. Story
Mull, H. F. White only: a story of the color line
O'Brien, T. What's the score?
O'Connor, F. Revelation
Oliver, D. Neighbors
Packer, Z. Doris is coming
Ruffin, P. The day J. P. saved the South
Shawl, N. The Raineses'
Smith, J. Loot
Stoddard, F. J. Street of the mortar and pestle: a story of color in the capital
Straight, S. El ojo de agua
Tervalon, J. The battling priests of Corpus Christi
Thelwell, M. Direct action
Thon, M. R. Confession for Raymond Good Bird
Urrea, L. A. Bid farewell to her many horses
Vega Yunqué, E. Eight morenos
Walker, A. Advancing Luna—and Ida B. Wells
West, D. Mammy (a short story)
Wideman, J. E. Hunters
Wideman, J. E. Sharing
Wideman, J. E. Who invented the jump shot
Williams, J. Spring is now

UNITED STATES. AIR FORCE
Baraka, I. A. Mondongo
DeMarinis, R. A hot day in January
Saunders, G. CommComm

UNITED STATES. ARMY
Ruffin, P. Crows

Officers
Bierce, A. The affair at Coulter's Notch
Bierce, A. One kind of officer
Bierce, A. The story of a conscience
James, H. The story of a ribbon bow
Jones, E. P. Resurrecting Methuselah
Wolff, T. Awaiting orders

UNITED STATES. CONGRESS. HOUSE
Dunbar, P. L. Mr. Cornelius Johnson, office-seeker

UNITED STATES. CONGRESS. SENATE
Crouse, D. Posterity
McInerney, J. My public service

UNITED STATES. DEPT. OF JUSTICE. FEDERAL BUREAU OF INVESTIGATION *See* United States. Federal Bureau of Investigation

UNITED STATES. DEPT. OF JUSTICE. IMMIGRATION AND NATURALIZATION SERVICE *See* United States. Immigration and Naturalization Service

UNITED STATES. FEDERAL BUREAU OF INVESTIGATION
DeNiro, A. The caliber
Doctorow, E. L. Child, dead, in the rose garden
DuBois, B. Country manners
Hunt, S. Love machine
LaSalle, P. Tunis and time
Mohan, S. Our flag was still there
Mooney, C. Falling

O'Shaughnessy, P. Tiny angels
Pearson, R. Close shave
Rusch, K. K. G-Men
Russell, J. Ding-dong-bell
Shepard, L. Hands up! Who wants to die?

UNITED STATES. FEDERAL EMERGENCY MANAGEMENT AGENCY
Lewis, W. H. Crusade

UNITED STATES. IMMIGRATION AND NATURALIZATION SERVICE
Lefer, D. At the site where vision is most perfect

UNITED STATES. MARINE CORPS
Busch, F. I am the news
Connell, E. S. Guadalcanal [variant title: The Marine]
Swofford, A. Escape and evasion
Swofford, A. Will they kill you in Iraq?

UNITED STATES. NAVY
Capote, T. The walls are cold
Connell, E. S. Yellow raft
Green, R. J. "It isn't every day of the week . . ."
Haschemeyer, O. The designated marksman
Lain, D. The word "Mermaid" written on an index card

UNITED STATES. PEACE CORPS *See* Peace Corps (U.S.)

UNITED STATES. SUPREME COURT
Zebrowski, G. Jesus runs

UNITED STATES. WORKS PROGRESS ADMINISTRATION
Arnow, H. L. S. Sugar Tree Holler

Unity Cloud. Dickinson, S.

UNIVERSE
Bisson, T. The edge of the universe
Bisson, T. Get me to the church on time
Card, O. S. Angles
Iwoleit, M. K. Planck time

The **universe,** concealed. McCann, R.

UNIVERSITY LIFE *See* College life
University of the Limitless Mouse. Ruefle, M.
UNIVERSITY STUDENTS *See* College life
The **univited.** Fowler, C.
Unknown donor. Mitchell, J. C.
The **Unknown** Known. Amis, M.
An **unknown** past. Lane, J.
Unknown soldier. Vonnegut, K.
Unleaving. Gilman, G. I.
Unless Alex. Brookhouse, C.
The **unlikely** redemption of Jared Pearce. O'Bryan, J.
Unlimited. Lindskold, J.
Unlimited daylight. Thomas, J.
An **unlucky** encounter. Nolan, W. F.
Unmade bed. Coake, C.

UNMARRIED COUPLES
Anderson, B. Fast post
Anderson, B. I thought there'd be a couch
Anderson, B. We could celebrate
Atwood, M. The bad news
Atwood, M. The entities
Atwood, M. Monopoly
Atwood, M. Moral disorder
Atwood, M. White horse
Bennett, T. Filigree
Bingham, S. Sweet peas
Brady, C. The dazzling world
Brockmeier, K. The lives of the philosophers

UNMARRIED COUPLES—*Continued*

Erdrich, L. Naked woman playing chopin
Goldfaden, J. Documentary
Greenman, B. Batting cleanup
Greenman, B. The duck knows how to make the most of things
Hawes, L. Anteaters don't dream
Hwang, F. Sonata for the left hand
Johnson, D. Threesome
Judah, S. Old man Moses
July, M. The man on the stairs
Kelts, R. N. Equilibrium
Kennedy, C. Seizure
Kennedy, C. Wheelbarrow thief
Macy, C. Eden's gate
Maxted, A. Dagenham
McGruder, K. Clan of marsupials
McGuane, T. Gallatin Canyon
McInerney, J. Everything is lost
Meno, J. I want the quiet moments of a party girl
Moffett, K. A statement of purpose
Moffett, K. Tattooizm
Offutt, C. Second hand
Ohlin, A. Meeting Uncle Bob
Ohlin, A. A theory of entropy
Parker, M. Muddy water, turn to wine
Parker, M. What happens next
Pearlman, E. Mates
Proulx, A. Testimony of the donkey
Romm, R. Where nothing is
Shirley, P. The consequence of summer heat
Simpson, H. In the driver's seat
Simpson, H. The phlebotomist's love life
Snyder, S. Voodoo heart
Stevens, J. D. JFK's shoes
Tillman, L. The recipe
Tognazzini, A. Jane and I at home one Sunday
Updike, J. Spanish prelude to a second marriage
Varallo, A. Sunday wash
Williams, C. Edge
Wingate, S. Bill
Wingate, S. Dig for dollars
Wingate, S. Inside the hole
Wingate, S. Meeting Grace
Wingate, S. Our last garage sale
Wood, D. The wardrobe
Zhu Wen. A hospital night
Zhu Wen. Pounds, ounces, meat

UNMARRIED MOTHERS

Alvarado, B. Phoenix
Baxter, C. Ghosts
Desaulniers, J. After Rosa Parks
Desaulniers, J. Mothers without children
Feeny, P. Like rabbits
Gardam, J. The Milly Ming
Green, A. Food stamp
Hendricks, V. The big O
Hospital, J. T. Nativity
Lunstrum, K. S. The nursery
Manley, C. Dearborn and LaSalle
Meacham, R. Trim & notions
Mohanraj, M. A. Sister Mary (Colombo, 1949)
Mueenuddin, D. Saleema
Munro, A. Soon
Pizzolatto, N. Two shores
Proulx, A. Tits-up in a ditch
Soileau, S. So this is permanence
Troy, M. Cookie Lily

Unmasking. Berg, C.
The **Unnecessary** Cat. Holden, M.
The **unnecessary** man. Drummond, R.
Uno. Pollack, E.
Unperformed experiments have no results. Hospital, J. T.
Unplayable lies. Tapply, W. G.
An **unpleasant** story. Zoshchenko, M.
The **unplug** war. DuBois, B.
Unplugged. del Llano, E.
Unpossible. Gregory, D.
Unraveled. Corso, P.
Unrediscovered, unrenameable. Schutt, C.
The **unripe** heart. Steele, M.
The **unsinkable** Mr. Raft. Woronov, M.
Unsound variations. Martin, G. R. R.
Unstruck. Otis, M.
Until Gwen. Lehane, D.
Until the girl died. Enright, A.
Untitled fragment. Howard, R. E.
[**Untitled** short story]. Ritchie, M.
Unto the least of these. James, H.
Unwanted gold. Dawson, P.
UNWED MOTHERS *See* Unmarried mothers
An **unwelcome** guest. Papernick, J.
Unwin, Brian K.
  The Fountain of Youth
    Journal of the American Geriatrics Society v53 no9 p1630 S 2005
Unwirer. Stross, C.
Up!. Di Filippo, P.
Up against the wall. Boyle, T. C.
Up, aloft in the air. Barthelme, D.
Up at a villa. Simpson, H.
Up at the Riverside. Muller, M.
Up High in the Air. Van den Berg, L.
Up North. D'Ambrosio, C.
Up North. D'Ambrosio, C., Jr.
Up the close and down the stair. Perelman, S. J.
Up the coast. MacLaverty, B.
Up the fire road. Gunn, E.
Up the mountain coming down slowly. Eggers, D.
Up the Old Goat Road. Raffel, D.
Up the river with Mrs Gallant. Anderson, B.
Upadhyay, Samrat
  Chintamani's women
    Upadhyay, S. The royal ghosts; stories
  Father, daughter
    Upadhyay, S. The royal ghosts; stories
  A refugee
    Upadhyay, S. The royal ghosts; stories
  The royal ghosts
    Upadhyay, S. The royal ghosts; stories
  A servant in the city
    Upadhyay, S. The royal ghosts; stories
  Supreme pronouncements
    Upadhyay, S. The royal ghosts; stories
  The third stage
    Upadhyay, S. The royal ghosts; stories
  The wedding hero
    Upadhyay, S. The royal ghosts; stories
  The weight of a gun
    Upadhyay, S. The royal ghosts; stories
  What Will Happen to the Sharma Family
    Ploughshares v32 no1 p169-79 Spr 2006
Updike, David
  Adjunct
    Updike, D. Old girlfriends

Updike, David—*Continued*

Geranium

Updike, D. Old girlfriends

In the age of convertibles

Updike, D. Old girlfriends

Kinds of love

Updike, D. Old girlfriends

The last of the Caribs

Updike, D. Old girlfriends

Love songs from America

Updike, D. Old girlfriends

Old girlfriends

Updike, D. Old girlfriends

Shining so nicely in the sun

Updike, D. Old girlfriends

Good Housekeeping v249 no2 p163-6, 169-71 Ag 2009

The woman from out of town

Updike, D. Old girlfriends

A word with the boy

Updike, D. Old girlfriends

Updike, John

The accelerating expansion of the universe

Updike, J. My father's tears and other stories

The apparition

Updike, J. My father's tears and other stories

Bech noir

Murder short & sweet; edited by Paul D. Staudohar

Blue light

Updike, J. My father's tears and other stories

The brown chest

Beha, C. R. The Ecco anthology of contemporary American short fiction; selected by Joyce Carol Oates and Christopher R. Beha.

Delicate wives

Updike, J. My father's tears and other stories

Free

Updike, J. My father's tears and other stories

The Full Glass

The New Yorker v84 no15 p66-71 My 26 2008; y

Updike, J. My father's tears and other stories

German lessons

Updike, J. My father's tears and other stories

The guardians

Updike, J. My father's tears and other stories

The journey to the dead

Telling tales; edited by Nadine Gordimer

Kinderscenen

Harper's v313 p79-84 D 2006

Kinderszenen

Updike, J. My father's tears and other stories

The laughter of the gods

Updike, J. My father's tears and other stories

Marching through Boston

Short stories of the civil rights movement; an anthology; edited by Margaret Earley Whitt

Morocco

Updike, J. My father's tears and other stories

My father's tears

Updike, J. My father's tears and other stories

The New Yorker v82 no2 p70-6 F 27 2006

Natural color

The New Granta book of the American short story; edited and introduced by Richard Ford

Nessus at Noon

The American Scholar v78 no1 p96-7 Wint 2009

Outage

Updike, J. My father's tears and other stories

The New Yorker v83 no42 p66-70 Ja 7 2008

Personal archaeology

Updike, J. My father's tears and other stories

The road home

Updike, J. My father's tears and other stories

The Roads of Home

The New Yorker v80 no45 p74-81 F 7 2005

Spanish prelude to a second marraige

Updike, J. My father's tears and other stories

Varieties of religious experience

Updike, J. My father's tears and other stories

The walk with Elizanne

The Best American short stories, 2004; edited by Lorrie Moore; Katrina Kenison series editor

Updike, J. My father's tears and other stories

The **upgrade**. Iagnemma, K.

Upon my soul. Randisi, R. J.

Upon the sweeping flood. Oates, J. C.

An **upper** class misdemeanant. Bierce, A.

Upson, William Hazlett

Botts in the Islands

The Saturday Evening Post v280 no1 p71-6, 88 Ja/F 2008

Botts Runs for His Life

The Saturday Evening Post v278 no5 p84-6, 88-92, 94, 96 S/O 2006

Upstairs. Rees, R.

Upton, Lee

The Swan Princess

Confrontation no104 p73-81 Summ 2009

You Know You've Made It When They Hate You

The Antioch Review v63 no1 p124-34 Wint 2005

Urban, Misty

Trying to Find a Corndog In Tompkins County

New Letters v73 no2 p65-81 2007

An **urban** legend puzzle. Norizuki, R.

Urban renewal. Lewis, W. H.

Urchins, while swimming. Valente, C. M.

Urdumheim. Swanwick, M.

The **urn**. Burgin, R.

Urrea, Luis Alberto

Bid farewell to her many horses

Best stories of the American West, v1; edited by Marc Jaffe

Ursa, on zoo property and off. Moffett, K.

Ursu, Anne

The president's new clothes

Politically inspired; edited by Stephen Elliott; assistant editor, Gabriel Kram; associate editors, Elizabeth Brooks [et al.]

Us/Them. Barth, J.

Us. Waldrop, H.

USAF *See* United States. Air Force

Use me. Stern, D.

The **use** of medicine. Meno, J.

The **use** of reason. Tóibín, C.

The **use** of the ellipse, the catalog, the meter & the vibrating plane. Rucker, R. v. B.

Use the Stars to Get Your Bearings. Cognetti, P.

The **used** saver. Baraka, I. A.

Uselton, Ron
  Bliz the Blizzard Queen
    Texas Bar Journal v72 no6 p450-3 Je 2009
User-centric. Sterling, B.
User Interface Stories from the Real World. Blinn, J. F.
The **uses** of English. Íṣ̣ːl'olá, A.
Ussama bin Laden *See* Osama bin Laden
The **usual** human disabilities. Montemarano, N.
The **usual** mistakes. Flanagan, E.
The **usurper** memos. Sherman, J.
UTAH
  McGlynn, D. Seventeen one-hundredths of a
    second
  Richter, S. The long hall
The **uterus** garden. Irvine, A. C.
Uthman, Layla al-
  The homeland is far away, the roads are many
    Oranges in the sun; short stories from the
      Arabian Gulf; edited and translated by Deb-
      orah S. Akers, Abubaker A. Bagader
  The ID card
    Oranges in the sun; short stories from the
      Arabian Gulf; edited and translated by Deb-
      orah S. Akers, Abubaker A. Bagader
Utmost bones. Sargent, P.
UTOPIAS
  Bierce, A. The land beyond the blow
  Bulgarin, F. V. [Im-] Plausible fantasies, or A
    journey in the 29th century [abridged]
  Chernyshevsky, N. G. Vera Pavlovna's fourth
    dream
  Kelly, J. P. Burn
  Odoevskiĭ, V. F., knıaz´ The year 4338. Letters
    from St. Petersburg [abridged]
  Roberts, A. Me-topia
Utriusque cosmi. Wilson, R. C.
The **utter** proximity of God. DeLuca, M. J.
UXMAL SITE (MEXICO)
  Anaya, R. A. The village that the gods painted
    yellow

V

V.A.O.. Ryman, G.
Vaca, Nicolás C.
  El Borrachito
    California Lawyer v27 no4 p26-31, 66 Ap
    2007
Vacation. Burgin, R.
Vacation. Stewart, P.
Vacation. Wallace, D.
The **Vacationers**. Mort, C.
VACATIONS
  Albert, E. When you say you're a Jew
  Beattie, A. Apology for a journey not taken:
    how to write a story
  Bennett, T. Antioxidants
  Bensko, J. Flying St. Croix
  Bolaño, R. Last evenings on Earth
  Brazaitis, M. Iris, thirty years later
  Ch'oe, S. Conviction
  Donoghue, E. The dormition of the virgin
  Ebenbach, D. H. Searching the reef in the off-
    season
  Enright, A. Caravan
  Enright, A. The cruise
  Gee, M. The good hope

Hadley, T. A card trick
Hempel, A. Daylight come
Henriquez, C. Chasing birds
Herrmann, M. Cooking lessons
Herrmann, M. Stones
Howard, R. E. Pigeons from hell
Jacobsen, J. On the island
Julavits, H. Ambivalence
Macaire, J. Island
Maxted, A. Dagenham
McGraw, E. Aruba
McIntyre, V. Foray
McLean, S. Road trip
Mercader, Mercer. The postponed journey
Moceri, M. How to faint
Murphy, Y. Pan, pan, pan
Nisbet, R. Jam jars of seaweed and dreams of
  love
Novakovich, J. Tchaikovsky's bust
Pak, W. Winter outing
Porter, K. A. Holiday
Rabe, J. Hang ten
Robinson, R. Assez
Sheckley, R. Cordle to onion to carrot
Shepard, L. R&R
Shields, C. Accidents
Smith, M. M. Being right
Stamm, P. Passion
Wallace, D. Vacation
Williams, C. Edge
Wright, P. 'Tutto bene?'
Zoshchenko, M. A workshop for health
VACCINES
  Daniells, R. C. Purgatory
Vacuum cleaner. Bova, B.
Vacuum seal. Keret, E.
Vagabond in France and Belgium. Bolaño, R.
Vagaries. Tran, V.
VAGRANTS *See* Homeless persons
The **vague**. Meloy, P.
Vaile, Charlotte M.
  Sister Anne and the cowboy
    Adventures in the West; stories for young
      readers; edited by Susanne George Bloom-
      field and Eric Melvin Reed
Valaitis-Heflin, Robin L.
  Remember
    Idaho Magazine v4 no11 p22-5 Ag 2005
Valdés, Javier
  Beat me to death
    Valdés, J. People like us; short stories; trans-
      lated by Stephen Lytle
  Cornelia
    Valdés, J. People like us; short stories; trans-
      lated by Stephen Lytle
  Flidia
    Valdés, J. People like us; short stories; trans-
      lated by Stephen Lytle
  Neighbors
    Valdés, J. People like us; short stories; trans-
      lated by Stephen Lytle
  Orquidea
    Valdés, J. People like us; short stories; trans-
      lated by Stephen Lytle
  People like us
    Colchie, T. A whistler in the nightworld;
      short fiction from the Latin Americas; ed-
      ited by Thomas Colchie

Valdés, Javier—*Continued*

Valdés, J. People like us; short stories; translated by Stephen Lytle

Valdés, Sonia Rivera- *See* Rivera-Valdés, Sonia

Valdez Quade, Kirstin

The Five Wounds

The New Yorker v85 no22 p60-9 Jl 27 2009

The **vale** of the white horse. McCrumb, S.

Valencia (to the first crossroads). Adiga, A.

Valente, Catherynne M.

A dirge for Prester John

Interfictions; an anthology of interstitial writing; edited by Delia Sherman and Theodora Goss

A gray and soundless tide

Salon fantastique; edited and with an introduction by Ellen Datlow and Terri Windling

Palimpsest

Sedia, E. Paper cities; an anthology of urban fantasy

Urchins, while swimming

Realms

Valentine for Elvis. McCray, B.

Valentine, July heat wave. Oates, J. C.

VALENTINE'S DAY

Gaiman, N. Harlequin Valentine

Singleton, G. Snipers

Valentine's Day. McLean, S.

Valentino, Russell Scott

(tr.) See Bychkov, Andrey

Valenzuela, Luisa

End of millenium

Violations; stories of love by Latin American women; edited and with an introduction by Psiche Hughes; foreword by Brian Matthews

The key

Díaz, G. J. Women and power in Argentine literature; stories, interviews, and critical essays; [by] Gwendolyn Díaz

Tango

Díaz, G. J. Women and power in Argentine literature; stories, interviews, and critical essays; [by] Gwendolyn Díaz

The **Valetudinarian.** Ferris, J.

Valiunas, Algis

In Another Country

The Sewanee Review v115 no4 p552-71 Fall 2007

Vallejo, Manuel Mejía *See* Mejía Vallejo, Manuel, 1923-

Vallese, Joe

Diorama

The North American Review v293 no3/4 p50-8 My/Ag 2008

Valley, Richard

Shadows from the screen

Kolchak: the night stalker chronicles; 26 original tales of the surreal, the bizarre, the macabre; edited by Joe Gentile, Garrett Anderson, Lori Gentile; Kolchak created by Jeff Rice

Valley lines. Trezise, R.

The **valley** of giants. Rosenbaum, B.

The **Valley** of Lagoons. Malouf, D.

The **Valley** of Lost Children. Hodgson, W. H.

The **valley** of sin. Abbott, L. K.

The **Valley** of the Gardens. Daniel, T.

The **valley** of the lost. Howard, R. E.

Valley of the shadow. Roberson, J.

Valley of the sun. L'Amour, L.

VALLEYS

Coloane, F. Forgotten land [variant title: Land of oblivion]

Vallianatos, Corinna

Examination

Gettysburg Review v20 no4 p605-14 Wint 2007

Vallorani, Nicoletta

Pasolini's shadow

Rome noir; edited by Chiara Stangalino & Maxim Jakubowski; translated by Anne Milano Appel, Ann Goldstein, and Kathrine Jason

Valtinos, Thanasēs

Addiction to nicotine

Angelic & black; contemporary Greek short stories; edited and translated by David Connolly; with an introduction by Vangelis Hatzivassileiou

The **value** of money. Maxwell, W.

The **valve** transcript. Zoss, J.

Vampire hours. Viets, E.

The **vampire** of Curitiba. Trevisan, D.

The **vampire** of Khor. Lamb, H.

The **vampire** theme. Hoch, E. D.

VAMPIRES

Armstrong, K. Twilight

Baker, K. Portrait, with flames

Bestwick, S. Hushabye

Bruen, K. Brant bites back

Butcher, J. It's my birthday, too

Caine, R. The first day of the rest of your life

Charnas, S. M. Advocates

Charnas, S. M. A musical interlude

Charnas, S. M. Unicorn tapestry

Crider, B. I was a teenage vampire

Crowther, P. The last vampyre

Dann, J. and Dozois, G. R. Down among the dead men

Dawidziak, M. Interview with a vampire?

Disch, T. M. The white man

Elrod, P. N. Grave-robbed

Elrod, P. N. Her mother's daughter

Frost, G. Some things are better left

Gaiman, N. Fifteen painted cards from a vampire tarot

Golden, C. The mournful cry of owls

Haines, C. The wish

Hallaway, T. Fire and ice and linguini for two

Hambly, B. Sunrise on running water

Harris, C. Dracula night

Harris, C. Lucky

Harris, J. Never give a sucker . . .

Hill, J. Abraham's boys

Howard, R. E. The hills of the dead

Howard, R. E. The horror from the mound

Huff, T. Blood wrapped

Kaminsky, S. M. The night talker

Kelly, R. The boxcar

Kelner, T. L. P. How Stella got her grave back

Kiernan, C. R. Bela's plot

Kilpatrick, N. Bitches of the night

Kovar, V. The all-night dentist

Lansdale, J. R. The steam man of the prairie and the dark rider get down

Van Name, Mark L.
Boar Lake
    Crossroads; tales of the southern literary fantastic; edited by F. Brett Cox and Andy Duncan

Van Pelt, James
The boy behind the gate
The last of the o-forms
    Nebula Awards showcase 2005; the year's best SF and fantasy; selected by the Science Fiction and Fantasy Writers of America; edited by Jack Dann
The long way home
    The Year's best science fiction: twenty-first annual collection; edited by Gardner Dozois
Of late I dreamt of Venus
    The Year's best science fiction: twenty-fifth annual collection; edited by Gardner Dozois

Van Steen, Edla *See* Steen, Edla van

Van Vogt, A. E. (Alfred Elton)
The weapons shop
    The Mammoth book of golden age science fiction; edited by Isaac Asimov, Charles G. Waugh and Martin H. Greenberg

Van Vogt, Alfred Elton *See* Van Vogt, A. E. (Alfred Elton), 1912-2000

Van Winckel, Nance
Black Fields, Black Horses
    Agni no58 p132-41 2003

Vanbeck, Melissa
Given her history
    The Best American mystery stories, 2008; edited and with an introduction by George Pelecanos; Otto Penzler, series editor

VANCOUVER ISLAND (B.C.)
Hughes, M. Bearing up
Windley, C. The reading Elvis
Windley, C. Sand and frost
Windley, C. What Saffi knows

VANDALISM
Currey, R. The names of the lost
Johnson, D. Work
King, O. We're all in this together
Lehane, D. Gone down to Corpus

VanderMeer, Jeff
Exhibit H: torn pages discovered in the vest pocket of an unidentified tourist
    Feeling very strange; the Slipstream anthology; James Patrick Kelly & John Kessel, editors
The farmer's cat
    Year's best fantasy 6; edited by David G. Hartwell & Kathryn Cramer
Fixing Hanover
    The Best science fiction and fantasy of the year: volume three; edited by Jonathan Strahan
The goat variations
    Other earths; edited by Nick Gevers and Jay Lake.
A new face in hell
    Perverted by language; fiction inspired by The Fall; edited and introduced by Peter Wild.
The Third Bear
Realms

Vandevere's house. Helprin, M.

Vandiver, E. B.
Fast like That
    South Carolina Review v38 no2 p233-40 Spr 2006

Vanilla bright like Eminem. Faber, M.

Vanishing Bicycle. Mitchell, E.

VANITY *See* Egoism

Vankin, Deborah
Viki, Flash, and the Pied-Piper of Shoebies
    The cocaine chronicles; edited by Gary Phillips and Jervey Tervalon

Vann, David
The higher blue
    Vann, D. Legend of a suicide
Ichthyology
    Vann, D. Legend of a suicide
Ketchikan
    Vann, D. Legend of a suicide
    StoryQuarterly v42 p262-80 2006
A legend of good men
    Vann, D. Legend of a suicide
Rhoda
    Vann, D. Legend of a suicide
Sukkwam Island
    Vann, D. Legend of a suicide

vanNamen, Kristin S.
The Weight of Grief
    Boston Review v33 no6 p29-32 N/D 2008

Vanquishing the infidel. Dreyer, E.

VANUATU
L'Amour, L. Pirates of the sky

Vapnyar, Lara
Borscht
    Vapnyar, L. Broccoli and other tales of food and love
    Harper's v312 p77-82 F 2006
A bunch of broccoli and the third shelf
    Vapnyar, L. Broccoli and other tales of food and love
Cinderella School
    The New Yorker v82 no14 p68-75 My 22 2006
Love lessons — Mondays, 9 A.M.
    Vapnyar, L. There are Jews in my house
Luda and Milena
    Vapnyar, L. Broccoli and other tales of food and love
    The New Yorker v83 no26 p118-25 S 3-10 2007
Lydia's Grove
    Vapnyar, L. There are Jews in my house
Memoirs of a Muse
    The New Yorker v80 no33 p92-6, 98-9 N 1 2004
Mistress
    Vapnyar, L. There are Jews in my house
Ovrashki's trains
    Vapnyar, L. There are Jews in my house
Puffed rice and meatballs
    The O. Henry Prize stories, 2006; edited and with an introduction by Laura Furman; jurors: Kevin Brockmeier, Francine Prose, Colm Toibin
    Vapnyar, L. Broccoli and other tales of food and love
A question for Vera
    Vapnyar, L. There are Jews in my house

Vapnyar, Lara—_Continued_
Salad olivier
    Vapnyar, L. Broccoli and other tales of food
        and love
Slicing sautéed spinach
    Vapnyar, L. Broccoli and other tales of food
        and love
There are Jews in my house
    Vapnyar, L. There are Jews in my house
The **vapor** of darkness. Maḥfūẓ, N.
Varallo, Anthony
Be true to your school
    Varallo, A. This day in history
A dictionary of saints
    Varallo, A. This day in history
Dummy
    StoryQuarterly v40 p520-1 2004
The eyes of Dr. T. J. Eckleburg
    Varallo, A. This day in history
The Girl at the Station
    Gettysburg Review v21 no3 p383-95 Aut
        2008
The houses left behind
    Varallo, A. This day in history
In the age of automobiles
    On the Mason-Dixon line; an anthology of
        contemporary Delaware writers; edited by
        Billie Travalini and Fleda Brown.
The knot
    Varallo, A. This day in history
The miles between Harriet Tubman and Harry
    Truman
    Varallo, A. This day in history
Parade Rest
    New England Review v28 no2 p125-33 2007
The pines
    Varallo, A. This day in history
Pool season
    Varallo, A. This day in history
Sometimes I'm Becky Macomber
    Varallo, A. This day in history
Sunday wash
    Varallo, A. This day in history
This day in history
    Varallo, A. This day in history
A tiny raft
    Varallo, A. This day in history
Toro
    Harvard Review (1992) no30 p46-52 2006
Varble, Valery
Bat
    New stories from the Southwest; edited by D.
        Seth Horton; foreword by Ray Gonzalez.
Canyons
    Prairie Schooner v81 no2 p121-31 Summ
        2007
Varengeville. Boyd, W.
Varga, Michael
The Crossing
    Dalhousie Review v87 no1 p109-13 Spr 2007
Vargas Llosa, Mario
The Chilean Girls
    The Virginia Quarterly Review v83 no3 p94-
        105 Summ 2007
Three Character Sketches
    Granta v100 p71-83 Wint 2007
VARIATION (BIOLOGY) _See_ Mutation (Biolo-
    gy)
Varieties of loudness in Chicago. Crane, E.

Varieties of religious experience. Updike, J.
Various miracles. Shields, C.
Varley, John
Air raid
    Asimov's science fiction: 30th anniversary an-
        thology; edited by Sheila Williams
In the hall of the Martian kings
    Fourth planet from the sun; tales of Mars
        from The Magazine of Fantasy & Science
        Fiction; edited by Gordon Van Gelder
Varley, John
The Bellman
    The Year's best science fiction: twenty-first
        annual collection; edited by Gardner Dozois
Varon, Policarpo
The feast
    The Flight of the condor; stories of violence
        and war from Colombia; translated and
        compiled by Jennifer Gabrielle Edwards;
        foreword by Hugo Chaparro Valderrama.
Vasco Da Gama's Pigeons. Hardy, M.
VASECTOMY
Romano, T. Deep left
Vast Hell. Martínez, G.
Vaswani, Neela
The pelvis series
    The O. Henry Prize stories, 2006; edited and
        with an introduction by Laura Furman; ju-
        rors: Kevin Brockmeier, Francine Prose,
        Colm Toibin
VAUDEVILLE
Waldrop, H. The horse of a different color (That
    you rode in on)
Vaughan, Elizabeth A.
Off the rack
    Pandora's closet; edited by Jean Rabe and
        Martin H. Greenberg.
VAUGHAN WILLIAMS, RALPH, 1872-1958
About
Reynolds, A. The receivers
Vaughn, Carrie
The nymph's child
    Fast ships, black sails; edited by Ann & Jeff
        VanderMeer
The **vaults** of Yoh-Vombis. Smith, C. A.
Vaysenberg, I. M.
A father and his sons
    No star too beautiful; Yiddish stories from
        1382 to the present; compiled and translat-
        ed by Joachim Neugroschel
Vaz, Katherine
All riptides roar with sand from opposing shores
    Vaz, K. Our lady of the artichokes and other
        Portuguese-American stories
Lisbon story
    Vaz, K. Our lady of the artichokes and other
        Portuguese-American stories
    Harvard Review (1992) no30 p8-32 2006
The man who was made of netting
    Vaz, K. Our lady of the artichokes and other
        Portuguese-American stories
The mandarin question
    Vaz, K. Our lady of the artichokes and other
        Portuguese-American stories
My bones here are waiting for yours
    Vaz, K. Our lady of the artichokes and other
        Portuguese-American stories

VERMEER, JOHANNES, 1632-1675
About
Baker, K. Standing in his light
Vermeer van Delft, Jan *See* Vermeer, Johannes, 1632-1675
Vermeer's milkmaid. Rivas, M.
Vermeulen, John
  Chalele
    The World's finest mystery and crime stories, fourth annual collection; edited by Ed Gorman and Martin H. Greenberg
  The corpse that lost its head
    The World's finest mystery and crime stories, fifth annual collection; edited by Ed Gorman and Martin H. Greenberg

VERMONT
Ohlin, A. Meeting Uncle Bob
Steele, A. M. Escape from earth
Swanwick, M. Triceratops summer
Wolven, S. Ball lightning reported
Wolven, S. El Rey
Wolven, S. Tigers
VERMOUTH *See* Wine and wine making

VERNE, JULES, 1828-1905
About
Hevesi, L. Jules Verne in hell: a letter to the editor from the late writer
Parodies, imitations, etc.
Brown, M. The Selene Gardening Society
Di Filippo, P. The mysterious Iowans
Lupoff, R. A. The secret of the Sahara
Vernon, Gigi
  Mattie in the middle
    Medium of murder; edited by Susan Budavari and Suzanne Flaig
Vernon, Olympia
  And So
    Women's Studies Quarterly v35 no1/2 p271-6 Spr/Summ 2007
  Schevoski
    New Orleans noir; edited by Julie Smith
Verolin, Irma
  The stairway in the gray patio
    English translations of short stories by contemporary Argentine women writers; edited by Eliana Cazaubon Hermann; translated by Sally Webb Thornton
The **Veronese** circle. Goldfaden, J.
Versace Enthroned with Saints Margaret, Jerome, Alex, and the Angel Donatella. Anastas, B.
Verstummte musik. Maryson, W. J.
Verthandi's bing. McDonald, I.
Verthandi's ring. McDonald, I.
Vertical mile. Magee, K.
Vertigo. Clayton, J. J.
Vertigo: A Story. Clayton, J. J.
The **very** edge of happiness. Tsutsui, Y.
A **very** good year. Zelazny, R.
The **very** last days of Boston. Sallis, J.
A **very** little madness goes a long way. Rickert, M.
The **very** pulse of the machine. Swanwick, M.
A **very** special girl. Resnick, M.
A **very** tight place. King, S.
Vessel. Card, O. S.
Vestal, Shawn
  Pocket Dog
    The Southern Review (Baton Rouge, La.) v44 no4 p705-16 Aut 2008

VETERANS
Anderson, B. Balance
Baker, K. Calamari Curls
Barnes, H. L. The first hunger
Barnes, H. L. A pulling thing
Barnes, J. Hygiene
Bear, E. Botticelli
Brown, D. Entebbe
Edwards, J. Liars don't qualify
Purdy, J. Brawith
Silver, M. The visitor

VETERANS (AMERICAN CIVIL WAR, 1861-1865)
Woolson, C. F. Rodman the keeper

VETERANS (AMERICAN INVASION OF PANAMA, 1989)
Barnes, H. L. Punishment

VETERANS (IRAQ WAR, 2003-)
Busch, F. Good to go
Erian, A. Camp whitehorse
Gaitskill, M. The arms and legs of the lake
Percy, B. Meltdown
Percy, B. Somebody is going to have to pay for this
Proulx, A. Tits-up in a ditch
Sakey, M. The desert here and the desert far away
Tomlinson, J. The accomplished son
Tomlinson, J. Angel, his rabbit, and Kyle McKell
Wheeler, T. Welcome home

VETERANS (KOREAN WAR, 1950-1953)
Busch, F. I am the news
Butner, R. The wounded
Hannah, B. Get some young
Ingalls, R. Veterans
Jones, E. P. All Aunt Hagar's children
Rash, R. Cold Harbor
Winn, T. Blue tango

VETERANS (PERSIAN GULF WAR, 1991)
Barnes, H. L. Minimal damage
Piatote, B. H. Life-size Indian

VETERANS (VIETNAMESE WAR, 1961-1975)
Abbott, L. K. Category Z
Abbott, L. K. The way sin is said in wonderland
Abbott, L. K. When our dream world finds us, and these hard times are gone
Alvarado, B. In box canyon
Barnes, H. L. Into the silence
Barnes, H. L. Snake boy
Bukoski, A. The Pulaski guards
Bukoski, A. Report of the guardian of the sick
Bukoski, A. The shadow players
Connell, E. S. Assassin
DeMarinis, R. Handyman
Desaulniers, J. After Rosa Parks
DuBois, B. An empire's reach
Ely, S. Talk radio
Gerrold, D. Thirteen o'clock
Hinton, S. E. No white light no tunnel
Hinton, S. E. The sweetest sound
Johnson, G. Wildfires
Jones, T. The pugilist at rest
Lehane, D. Running out of dog
Malae, P. N. Reliable vet dad, reliable con son
Malouf, D. War baby
Martel, Y. The time I heard The Private Donald J. Rankin string concerto with one discordant violin, by John Morton

VETERANS (VIETNAMESE WAR, 1961-1975)—*Continued*

McAllister, B. Little boy blue
Moceri, M. Actual seasons
Monk, B. Writing lesson
Percy, B. The killing
Pizzolatto, N. The guild of thieves, lost women, and sunrise palms
Pizzolatto, N. Haunted earth
Reinhorn, H. My name
Shepard, L. Shades
Stone, R. Helping
Thompson, J. Lost
Unger, D. Looking for war

VETERANS (WORLD WAR, 1914-1918)

Bradbury, R. Lafayette, farewell
Chapman, J. D. Amanuensis
Graham, O. B. Slackened caprice
Hansen, R. Playland
Kiely, B. The white wild bronco
Sillitoe, A. Uncle Ernest

VETERANS (WORLD WAR, 1939-1945)

Buckler, E. Thanks for listening
Coake, C. Pitch black
Connell, E. S. The land where lemon trees bloom
Dahl, R. The soldier
DeMarinis, R. The horse dealer's lovers
DuBois, B. The last flight
Fusilli, J. Chellini's solution
Lenz, S. A risk for Father Christmas
Martin, J. The father
Nayman, S. The porcelain monkey
Snyder, S. The thirteenth egg
Swan, G. Women who don't tell war stories
Yasuoka, S. The sword dance

Veterans. Ingalls, R.

VETERINARIANS

Doran, M. M. The giver
Glatt, L. Animals
Hubbard, L. R. The room
McLean, S. The pig
Smith, J. Hotwalking

Via Vortex. Meaney, J.
Vicious circle. McGuane, T.
A **victim** of the revolution. Zoshchenko, M.
The **victims**. Burgin, R.
Victims. McCabe, E.
Victor Scarpazo; or, The end of the pursuit. Denevi, M.

VICTORIA, QUEEN OF GREAT BRITAIN, 1819-1901

About

Di Filippo, P. Victoria

Victoria. Di Filippo, P.
VICTORIAN ENGLAND *See* England—19th century
Victorian fields. McCabe, E.
Victory at Sea. Carlson, R.
Victory garden. Attenberg, J.
Vida, Vendela

Soleil
The book of other people; edited by Zadie Smith

Vidal, Gore

Clouds and eclipses
Vidal, G. Clouds and eclipses; the collected short stories

[With an afterword by the author]
Harvard Review (1992) no29 p74-83 2005
Erlinda and Mr. Coffin
Vidal, G. Clouds and eclipses; the collected short stories
The ladies in the library
Vidal, G. Clouds and eclipses; the collected short stories
A moment of green laurel
Vidal, G. Clouds and eclipses; the collected short stories
Pages from an abandoned journal
Vidal, G. Clouds and eclipses; the collected short stories
The robin
Vidal, G. Clouds and eclipses; the collected short stories
Three stratagems
Vidal, G. Clouds and eclipses; the collected short stories
The Zenner trophy
Vidal, G. Clouds and eclipses; the collected short stories

VIDAL, GORE, 1925-

About

Zebrowski, G. The coming of Christ the joker

Vidas al límite: Biografía de una mosca / Lives on the Edge: Biography of a Fly [Part of a special issue: Elogio de la mosca en el arte / In Praise of Flies in Art] Millás, J. J.
Video. Mozetič, B.

VIDEO ART

Lain, D. The subliminal son
Magee, K. Straitjacket

VIDEO GAMES

Abbott, L. K. Men of rough persuasion
Dansky, R. E. Killer App
Doctorow, C. Anda's game
Wilson, K. Mortal kombat

Videos of the Dead. Moody, R.
Viderman, Anne

A fiddle
Arguing with the storm; stories by Yiddish women writers; edited and with a preface by Rhea Tregebov; introduction by Kathryn Hellerstein.

Vidocq; or, The charcoal burner of France Bendel-Simso, M. M., ed. Early American detective stories; an anthology; edited by LeRoy Lad Panek and Mary M. Bendel-Simso.
La **Vie** En Rose. Nini, M. C.
Vieja chueca. Granados, C.
VIENNA (AUSTRIA) *See* Austria—Vienna
The **Viennese** Opera Ball. Barthelme, D.
Viernes loco. Wishnia, K. J. A.

VIETNAM

Đoàn, L. Achieving flyhood
Đoàn, L. The cemetery of Chua village
Đoàn, L. The clone
Đoàn, L. The double bed of Chua village
Đoàn, L. Guot's love
Đoàn, L. A question mark for God
Đoàn, L. The real estate of Chua village
Đoàn, L. Sesame seed
Đoàn, L. The venus of Chua village
Đoàn, L. The wooden cottage
Phan, A. The Delta
Phan, A. Miss Lien
Phan, A. Motherland

VIETNAM—*Continued*

Rhodes, D. The violoncello
Shepard, L. Radiant green star

Communism
See Communism—Vietnam

Ho Chi Minh City
Dinh, V. Substitutes
Phan, A. Bound
Phan, A. Gates of Saigon

Saigon
See Vietnam—Ho Chi Minh City

Vietnam. Thursday. Harstad, J.

VIETNAM VETERANS MEMORIAL (WASH-INGTON, D.C.)
Card, O. S. 50 WPM
Modesitt, L. E., Jr. The pilots
Swanwick, M. Dirty little war

VIETNAMESE
Australia
Kennedy, C. Angel
Norway
Harstad, J. Vietnam. Thursday
United States
Butler, R. O. Crickets
Butler, R. O. Mr. Green
Ely, S. Talk radio
Le, N. Love and honor and pity and pride and compassion and sacrifice
Le, T. D. T. The gangster we are all looking for [excerpt]
Nguyen, V. T. A correct life
Rucker, R. v. B. Six thought experiments concerning the nature of computation: Experiment 3: Aint paint
Strom, D. Grass roof, tin roof [excerpt]
Tan, M. Muddy pond

VIETNAMESE AMERICANS
Mindt, A. King of America
Vietnamese Americans
Phan, A. Emancipation
Vietnamese Americans
Phan, A. Visitors
Vietnamese Americans
Phan, A. We should never meet
Vietnamese Americans
Strom, D. Husband, wife
Vietnamese Americans
Strom, D. Mary
Vietnamese Americans
Strom, D. Neighbors
Vietnamese Americans
Strom, D. Walruses

VIETNAMESE REFUGEES
Le, N. The boat

VIETNAMESE SOLDIERS *See* Soldiers—Vietnam

VIETNAMESE WAR, 1961-1975
Abbott, L. K. Category Z
Abbott, L. K. When our dream world finds us, and these hard times are gone
Bunch, C. Murdering Uncle Ho
Burke, J. L. The village
Card, O. S. 50 WPM
Daugherty, T. Power lines
DeMille, N. Rendezvous
Glancy, D. An American proverb
Haldeman, J. W. DX
Haldeman, J. W. Graves
Haldeman, J. W. The monster

Haldeman, J. W. War year
Harstad, J. Vietnam. Thursday
Hellmann, L. F. The whole world is watching
Irsfeld, J. H. Death of a soldier
Jones, T. The pugilist at rest
McAllister, B. Dream baby
McAllister, B. Little boy blue
McIlvoy, K. Ice
Mindt, A. King of America
Modesitt, L. E., Jr. The pilots
O'Brien, T. On the rainy river
Shepard, L. Delta Sly Honey
Shepard, L. Shades
Silber, J. War buddies
Stevens, J. D. Flying
Swanwick, M. Dirty little war
Tartt, D. The ambush
Tran, V. The gift of years

Viets, Elaine
Red meat
The World's finest mystery and crime stories, fifth annual collection; edited by Ed Gorman and Martin H. Greenberg
Sex and bingo
The World's finest mystery and crime stories, fifth annual collection; edited by Ed Gorman and Martin H. Greenberg
Vampire hours
Many bloody returns; edited by Charlaine Harris and Toni L. P. Kelner

The **View**. Pamuk, O.
The **view** from Castle Rock. Munro, A.
A **view** from Eagle Rock Mountain. McGruder, K.
The **view** from the seventh layer. Brockmeier, K.
A **view** from the treetop. Kiely, B.
The **View** from Yves Hill.
The **view** from Yves Hill. Boyd, W.
The **view** of me from Mars. Abbott, L. K.
Viewpoint. Wolfe, G.
Vigil. Bakken, K. N.
Vigil. Pope, D.
Vigilance. Wolven, S.
Vigilante. Oates, J. C.

VIGILANTES
Parra, E. A. The Christ of San Buenaventura
Stevens, J. D. Burn
Valdés, J. Beat me to death
Zoshchenko, M. Live-bait

Vigna, John
Gas Bar
Dalhousie Review v89 no1 p125-33 Spr 2009

Vigo Park. Ohlin, A.

VIGODA, ABE, 1921-
About
Reidy, D. In memoriam

Viki, Flash, and the Pied-Piper of Shoebies. Vankin, D.

VIKINGS
Howard, R. E. Delenda est
Tower, W. Everything ravaged, everything burned
Tower, Wells. Everything ravaged, everything burned

Vila-Matas, Enrique
Bartleby & Co. [excerpt]
Terrestrial intelligence; international fiction now from New Directions; edited by Barbara Epler

The **Villa** Mondare. Baumbach, J.

VIRTUAL REALITY—*Continued*

Beckett, C. Piccadilly circus

Cadigan, P. The final remake of *The return of Little Latin Larry,* with a completely remastered soundtrack and the original audience

Collins, P. Lure

Di Filippo, P. The emperor of Gondwanaland

Esquivel, L. Blessed reality

Gorman, E. Lover boy

Halam, A. Cheats

Jones, G. A. Red Sonja and Lessingham in Dreamland

Kelly, J. P. The dark side of town

Lethem, J. Access fantasy

Lethem, J. How we got in town and out again

MacLeod, K. Cyndonia

MacLeod, K. Lighting out

McMullen, S. The constant past

Moles, D. Down and out in the Magic Kingdom

Rosenblum, M. H. Home movies

Ryman, G. Have not have

Spencer, W. B. Downloading midnight

Spencer, W. B. The halfway house at the heart of darkness

Vinge, V. Synthetic serendipity

Williams, W. J. Incarnation day

Virtue. Mandelbaum, P.

Virtuoso mio. Palmer, K.

VIRUSES

Collins, P. Lure

Daniells, R. C. Purgatory

Egan, G. Steve fever

Eschbach, A. Mother's flowers

Finch, S. No brighter glory

Finch, S. A world waiting

Kiernan, C. R. Riding the white bull

Kiernan, C. R. Zero summer

Martin, G. R. R. From the journal of Xavier Desmond

Martin, G. R. R. Shell games

Rosenbaum, B. Start the clock

Schow, D. J. Blossom

Wilson, F. P. Lysing toward Bethlehem

The **visible** men. Moorcock, M.

Visigoth. Amdahl, G.

VISION

See also Eye

Vision. Gordon, M.

The **vision**. Lethem, J.

A **vision** in white. Block, L.

Vision in white. Wood, D.

The **vision** of Hehaka 'To. Bishop, T.

The **vision** of Peter Damien. Adrian, C.

VISIONS

See also Dreams; Hallucinations and illusions

Bierce, A. A midsummer day's dream

Bishop, T. The vision of Hehaka 'To

Boyle, T. C. The miracle at Ballinspittle

Bradbury, R. The Messiah

Bulushi, S. Sounds of the sea

Carmody, I. Perchance to dream

Dalton, Q. Lennie remembers the angels

Dammaj, H. The nightmare

Lovecraft, H. P. The shadow out of time

Mosley, W. The picket

Rand, K. Last vision

Rickert, M. Many voices

Rucker, R. v. B. The use of the ellipse, the catalog, the meter & the vibrating plane

Rylands, J. T. Probability

Scurati, A. Eternal Rome

Sokoloff, A. The edge of seventeen

Williams, C. Et in Sempiternum pereant

Winsor, C. Three mediums in San Francisco

Visions fugitives. Boyd, W.

Visions of Gerard. Merullo, R.

Visions of the metanovel. Rucker, R. v. B.

The **visit**. Boyers, R.

The **visit**. Bradbury, R.

The **visit**. Carew, J.

Visit. Donovan, G.

Visit. Hinton, S. E.

The **visit**. Shabtai, Y.

The **visit**. Stamm, P.

A **visit**. Treat, J.

The **Visit,** 1946. Foster, P.

A **visit** from Jesus. Means, D.

A **visit** to Morin. Greene, G.

A **visit** to Parsimonia: a scientific report (1981). Braun, J. and Braun, G.

A **visit** to Santa Claus. Matheson, R.

A **visit** to St. Nick's. Hughes, R. J.

A **visit** to the cockpit. Keret, E.

A **visit** to the suns. Hwang, F.

Visitation. Burke, T.

Visitation. Watson, B.

VISITING

Dahl, R. Neck

Erdrich, L. Destiny

Gordon, M. Bishop's house

Hwang, F. A visit to the suns

Hyde, M. What are you afraid of?

Keane, J. B. Protocol

Keane, J. B. 'The teapots are out'

Newman, L. Sunday afternoon

Niranjana, A. A day with Charulata

Oates, J. C. Nairobi

Oates, J. C. Where is here?

Parks, T. Lebensraum

Shabtai, Y. The visit

Vida, V. Soleil

The **Visiting** Child. Bender, K. E.

Visiting hour. Thormahlen, A.

The **visiting** of Mother Danbury. Dunbar, P. L.

The **visiting** privilege. Williams, J.

Visiting the dead. Reed, K.

The **visitor**. Alarcón, D.

The **visitor**. Dahl, R.

The **visitor**. Silver, M.

VISITORS

Barthelme, D. Tales of the Swedish army

Malouf, D. The domestic cantata

VISITORS, FOREIGN *See* Foreign visitors

Visitors. Budnitz, J.

Visitors. Phan, A.

VISITORS FROM OUTER SPACE *See* Interplanetary visitors

The **Visual** Equivalent of Pain. Fincke, G.

Viswanathan, Padma

Dharnakarna

New Letters v73 no3 p8-36 2007

Transitory Cities

Boston Review v32 no3 p35-6 My/Je 2007

Vita Vya Uganda. Molohon, J. B.

Vital organs. Rust, E. M.

Vital signs. Miner, V.

Vitamin V. Ferrey, A.
VITICULTURE *See* Wine and wine making
Vitriol. Jackson, S.
Viva Deluxe. Schwarzschild, E.
Viva la Tropicana. Michaels, L.
Vivian, E. Charles
Locked in
 The Mammoth book of vintage whodunnits;
  edited by Maxim Jakubowski
Vivian Relf. Lethem, J.
VIVISECTION *See* Medicine—Research
Vivisection. Grimes, C.
Vladimir Hussein. Keret, E.
Vlcek, Ernst
Say it with flowers
 The black mirror and other stories; an anthol-
  ogy of science fiction from Germany &
  Austria; edited & with an introduction &
  notes by Franz Rottensteiner; translated by
  Mike Mitchell.
Vocation. Rylands, J. T.
Voedisch, Robert
There's a Place for Fun in Your Life
 The North American Review v292 no1 p25-9
  Ja/F 2007
Vogau, Boris Andreevich *See* Pil´nı´àk, Boris,
 1894-1937
Vogel, Lisa
The Bone Spa
 The Massachusetts Review v48 no3 p337-45
  Fall 2007
The Door Man
 The Massachusetts Review v50 no1-2 p183-91
  Spr/Summ 2009
Vogrin, Valerie
The hotel-motel bar & grill
 Playboy's college fiction; a collection of 21
  years of contest winners; edited by Alice
  K. Turner; foreword by Thom Jones
The Next Thing: A Story with Chorus
 Ploughshares v34 no4 p129-43 Wint
  2008/2009
things we'll need for the coming difficulties
 Agni no69 p193-215 2009
Vogt, M. Diane
Surviving Toronto
 Thriller; edited by James Patterson
Voice. Nelson, K.
A **voice** from the earth. Bilal, A.
The **voice** in the dawn. Hodgson, W. H.
The **voice** in the night. Hodgson, W. H.
The **voice** of the beach. Campbell, R.
Voices. Clayton, J. J.
Voices in a mask. Green, G.
Voices in the water. Copper, B.
Voices of the kill. Disch, T. M.
The **voix** humaine. Treat, J.
The **volcano**. Farmer, P. J.
VOLCANOES
Farmer, P. J. The volcano
Scoville, S. Ulu's dog
Sussex, L. Ardent clouds
Volk, Stephen
31/10
 The Year's best fantasy and horror: twentieth
  annual collection; edited by Ellen Datlow
  and Kelly Link & Gavin J. Grant

Indicator
 The Best British mysteries, 2005; edited by
  Maxim Jakubowski
The **Volkswagen** Prophecy. Burrell, M. W.
Vollmann, William T.
Breakout
 Grand Street no71 p123-54 Spr 2003
Lost victories
 The Pushcart Prize XXIX: best of the small
  presses 2005; edited by Bill Henderson
  with the Pushcart Prize editors
The woman who laughed
 San Francisco noir 2; the classics; edited by
  Peter Maravelis.
Vollmer, Matthew
Bodies
 Vollmer, M. Future missionaries of America;
  stories by Matthew Vollmer
The digging
 Vollmer, M. Future missionaries of America;
  stories by Matthew Vollmer
Freebleeders
 Vollmer, M. Future missionaries of America;
  stories by Matthew Vollmer
Future missionaries of America
 Vollmer, M. Future missionaries of America;
  stories by Matthew Vollmer
The gospel of Mark Schneider
 Vollmer, M. Future missionaries of America;
  stories by Matthew Vollmer
Man-O'-War
 Vollmer, M. Future missionaries of America;
  stories by Matthew Vollmer
Oh land of national paradise, how glorious are
 thy bounties
 Vollmer, M. Future missionaries of America;
  stories by Matthew Vollmer
Scoring
 The Antioch Review v66 no3 p508-22 Summ
  2008
Second home
 Vollmer, M. Future missionaries of America;
  stories by Matthew Vollmer
Stewards of the earth
 Vollmer, M. Future missionaries of America;
  stories by Matthew Vollmer
Straightedge
 Vollmer, M. Future missionaries of America;
  stories by Matthew Vollmer
Thinking of You
 Confrontation no94/95 p99-113 Spr/Summ
  2006
Two women
 Vollmer, M. Future missionaries of America;
  stories by Matthew Vollmer
Will & testament
 Vollmer, M. Future missionaries of America;
  stories by Matthew Vollmer
Volpi, Jorge
Ars poetica
 Colchie, T. A whistler in the nightworld;
  short fiction from the Latin Americas; ed-
  ited by Thomas Colchie
Volpurno—or the Student. Collins, W.
Voluntary committal. Hill, J.
The **voluntary** state. Rowe, C.
The **volunteer**. Amdahl, G.
Volunteer. Huddle, D.

VOLUNTEER WORKERS

Duval, P. Spectator sport
Fonseca, R. Angels of the marquees
Klassen, S. Ending with poetry
Klassen, S. Thursday at Agape Table
Moffett, K. The volunteer's friend
Pearlman, E. Rules
Sittenfeld, C. Volunteers are shining stars
Volunteers. Irvine, A. C.
Volunteers are shining stars. Sittenfeld, C.
The **volunteer's** friend. Moffett, K.
Von Manstein, Erich *See* Manstein, Erich von, 1887-1973
Vonnegut, Kurt

Armageddon in retrospect
Vonnegut, K. Armageddon in retrospect; and other new and unpublished writings on war and peace; [illustrations by the author; introduction by Mark Vonnegut]

Brighten up
Vonnegut, K. Armageddon in retrospect; and other new and unpublished writings on war and peace; [illustrations by the author; introduction by Mark Vonnegut]

The commandant's desk
Vonnegut, K. Armageddon in retrospect; and other new and unpublished writings on war and peace; [illustrations by the author; introduction by Mark Vonnegut]

Great day
Vonnegut, K. Armageddon in retrospect; and other new and unpublished writings on war and peace; [illustrations by the author; introduction by Mark Vonnegut]

Guns before butter
Vonnegut, K. Armageddon in retrospect; and other new and unpublished writings on war and peace; [illustrations by the author; introduction by Mark Vonnegut]

Happy birthday, 1951
Vonnegut, K. Armageddon in retrospect; and other new and unpublished writings on war and peace; [illustrations by the author; introduction by Mark Vonnegut]

Just you and me, Sammy
Vonnegut, K. Armageddon in retrospect; and other new and unpublished writings on war and peace; [illustrations by the author; introduction by Mark Vonnegut]

Little Drops of Water
Harper's v318 p64-9 Je 2009

Spoils
Vonnegut, K. Armageddon in retrospect; and other new and unpublished writings on war and peace; [illustrations by the author; introduction by Mark Vonnegut]

The Unicorn trap
Vonnegut, K. Armageddon in retrospect; and other new and unpublished writings on war and peace; [illustrations by the author; introduction by Mark Vonnegut]

Unknown soldier
Vonnegut, K. Armageddon in retrospect; and other new and unpublished writings on war and peace; [illustrations by the author; introduction by Mark Vonnegut]

Voodoo heart. Snyder, S.

VOODOOISM

See also Zombies
Bates, J. W. The ungrateful dead
Fazi, M. The cajun knot
Fountain, B. Bouki and the cocaine
Fountain, B. The good ones are already taken
Kelman, J. No strings
Kiernan, C. R. Lafayette
Matheson, R. By appointment only
Matheson, R. From shadowed places
Matheson, R. Therese
Shepard, L. Dead money

VOTING

Edwards, J. Liars don't qualify
Macy, C. The secret vote
Tyler, A. Measure A, B, or me?
The **Voyage** [Medical Humanities, 32 no1 June 2006] Papadimos, T. J.
The **Voyage** Home. Petrie, G.
Voyage into the heart. McKillip, P. A.
The **voyage** of King Euvoran. Smith, C. A.
Voyage of the Iguana. Aylett, S.
The **voyage** out. Gardiner, J. R.
The **Voyage** Over. Bynum, S. S.-l.
The **voyage** to Mauritius. Shabtai, Y.
A **voyage** to Sfanomoë. Smith, C. A.
Voyage to Tobolai. L'Amour, L.

VOYAGES AND TRAVELS

See also Adventure; Air travel; Railroads—Travel; Sea stories; Tourist trade; Travelers
Bierce, A. The captain of the Camel
Bierce, A. How I came to like dogs
Bierce, A. The man overboard
Bierce, A. Seafaring
Lapcharoensap, R. Sightseeing
Lowry, M. Through the Panama
Morris, K. L. Tired heart
Munro, A. The view from Castle Rock
Shabtai, Y. The voyage to Mauritius
Silverberg, R. Trips
Strasser, D. Conquist
Zhu Wen. A boat crossing
The **voyeur**. Deaver, J.

VOYEURS

Barth, J. Peeping Tom
Block, L. Just window shopping
Castle, M. The watcher at the window
Deaver, J. The voyeur
Goldfaden, J. Disorder destroyers
Goldfaden, J. Looking at animals
Johnson, D. Beverly Home
July, M. Something that needs nothing
Laymon, R. The diving girl
McInerney, J. Invisible fences
Michaels, L. Murderers
Mukhopadhyay, T. The corner shop
Rock, P. Thrill
Sallis, J. An ascent of the moon
Sillitoe, A. The chiker
Snyder, S. Voodoo heart
Woolrich, C. Rear window [variant title: It had to be murder]
Vroom. Erdrich, L.
VTV. Marusek, D.
Vukcevich, Ray

Jumping
Witpunk; edited by Claude Lalumière and Marty Halpern

WAITRESSES—*Continued*

Benioff, D. Garden of no

Brady, C. Looking for a female tenet

Bruen, K. Nora B.

Carver, R. Fat

Coats, Y. Irresistible

Corbett, D. Pretty little parasite

Curtis, R. Hungry self

Fitch, S. The end of Indian summer

Fowler, C. American waitress

Fulton, A. A shadow table

Goldfaden, J. Top of the list

Harris, J. Breakfast at Tescos

Hospital, J. T. The end-of-the-world disco

Johnson, T. G. Winter never quits

Krasikov, S. Better half

Kun, M. My wife and my dead wife

Lange, R. Culver City

Lessa, O. Marta

Macy, C. Eden's gate

Martinez, M. The long shot

Minot, E. Berniced

Miura, T. A portrait of Shino

Murakami, H. Birthday girl

Parker, M. Muddy water, turn to wine

Parry, O. The Christmas Joe

Pearlman, E. Trifle

Preddy, M. The coffee break

Rees, R. Hand of a thief

Rock, P. The silent men

Romano, T. Trace

Scoppettone, S. Everybody loves somebody

Scott, J. Freeze-out

Sharp, Z. Served cold

Stamm, P. The kiss

Strom, D. Walruses

Tierce, M. Suck it

Tognazzini, A. The story of our lives

Vernon, G. Mattie in the middle

Welsh, I. If you liked school, you'll love work

. . .

Wake. Dixon, K. H.

Wake. González, K. A.

Wake. Jensen, B.

Wake. Meany, R.

Wakefield. Doctorow, E. L.

Waking the bishop. Doyle, B.

Waking Up. Byrne, J.

Wakizashi. Thomas, J.

Wakkas, Yousef

"The Egyptian lover"

Multicultural literature in contemporary Italy; edited by Marie Orton and Graziella Parati

Walbert, Kate

Conversation

The Yale Review v97 no2 p98-111 Ap 2009

Do something

The Best American short stories, 2007; selected from U. S. and Canadian magazines by Stephen King with Heidi Pitlor; with an introduction by Stephen King

Ploughshares v32 no4 p157-68 Wint 2006/2007

Playdate

The New Yorker v83 no5 p74-81 Mr 26 2007

Walbrook, Louise *See* Templeton, Edith, 1916-

Wald, A. H.

Into the Woods

The North American Review v291 no2 p14-19 Mr/Ap 2006

The Train to Ghent

The Southern Review (Baton Rouge, La.) v43 no3 p652-60 Summ 2007

The virgin's heart

The best Christian short stories; edited and with an introduction by Bret Lott

Walden, Gale Renée

The Train

The Antioch Review v64 no1 p140-50 Wint 2006

Waldman, Amy

Freedom

Boston Review v34 no4 p39-42 Jl/Ag 2009

Waldman, Ayelet

Minnow

McSweeney's enchanted chamber of astonishing stories; edited by Michael Chabon; illustrations by Mike Mignola

Waldorf, Saral

In the Infield Was Patty Peccavi

The Southern Review (Baton Rouge, La.) v43 no2 p358-65 Spr 2007

The Milk of Human Kindness

The Hudson Review v60 no1 p47-67 Spr 2007

Waldrop, Howard

Avast, abaft!

Fast ships, black sails; edited by Ann & Jeff VanderMeer

A better world's in birth!

Waldrop, H. Other worlds, better lives: a Howard Waldrop reader; selected long fiction 1989-2003

Calling your name

The Year's best science fiction: twenty-first annual collection; edited by Gardner Dozois

Waldrop, H. Things will never be the same: a Howard Waldrop reader; selected short fiction 1980-2005

D = R x T

Waldrop, H. Heart of whitenesse

Do ya, do ya, wanna dance?

Waldrop, H. Things will never be the same: a Howard Waldrop reader; selected short fiction 1980-2005

A dozen tough jobs

Waldrop, H. Other worlds, better lives: a Howard Waldrop reader; selected long fiction 1989-2003

The dynasters

Waldrop, H. Heart of whitenesse

Waldrop, H. Things will never be the same: a Howard Waldrop reader; selected short fiction 1980-2005

Fin de Cyclé

Waldrop, H. Other worlds, better lives: a Howard Waldrop reader; selected long fiction 1989-2003

Flatfeet!

Waldrop, H. Other worlds, better lives: a Howard Waldrop reader; selected long fiction 1989-2003

Flying saucer rock and roll

Waldrop, H. Things will never be the same: a Howard Waldrop reader; selected short fiction 1980-2005

Waldrop, Howard—*Continued*

French scenes
  Waldrop, H. Things will never be the same: a Howard Waldrop reader; selected short fiction 1980-2005
Heart of whitenesse
  Waldrop, H. Heart of whitenesse
  Waldrop, H. Things will never be the same: a Howard Waldrop reader; selected short fiction 1980-2005
Heirs of the perisphere
  Waldrop, H. Things will never be the same: a Howard Waldrop reader; selected short fiction 1980-2005
The horse of a different color (That you rode in on)
  The Year's best fantasy and horror: nineteenth annual collection; edited by Ellen Datlow and Kelly Link & Gavin J. Grant
Household words; or, The powers-that-be
  Waldrop, H. Things will never be the same: a Howard Waldrop reader; selected short fiction 1980-2005
The king of where-I-go
  Waldrop, H. Things will never be the same: a Howard Waldrop reader; selected short fiction 1980-2005
The lions are asleep this night
  Feeling very strange; the Slipstream anthology; James Patrick Kelly & John Kessel, editors
  Waldrop, H. Things will never be the same: a Howard Waldrop reader; selected short fiction 1980-2005
London, Paris, Banana . . .
  Waldrop, H. Heart of whitenesse
Major Spacer in the 21st century!
  Waldrop, H. Heart of whitenesse
  Waldrop, H. Other worlds, better lives: a Howard Waldrop reader; selected long fiction 1989-2003
Mr. Goober's show
  Waldrop, H. Heart of whitenesse
  Waldrop, H. Things will never be the same: a Howard Waldrop reader; selected short fiction 1980-2005
Night of the cooters
  This is my funniest; leading science fiction writers present their funniest stories ever; edited by Mike Resnick
  Waldrop, H. Things will never be the same: a Howard Waldrop reader; selected short fiction 1980-2005
The other real world
  Waldrop, H. Heart of whitenesse
  Waldrop, H. Other worlds, better lives: a Howard Waldrop reader; selected long fiction 1989-2003
Our mortal span
  Waldrop, H. Heart of whitenesse
The Sawing Boys
  Waldrop, H. Things will never be the same: a Howard Waldrop reader; selected short fiction 1980-2005
Thin, on the ground
  Year's best fantasy 7; edited by David G. Hartwell & Kathryn Cramer

The ugly chickens
  Waldrop, H. Things will never be the same: a Howard Waldrop reader; selected short fiction 1980-2005
Us
  Waldrop, H. Heart of whitenesse
  Waldrop, H. Things will never be the same: a Howard Waldrop reader; selected short fiction 1980-2005
Wild, wild horses
  Waldrop, H. Things will never be the same: a Howard Waldrop reader; selected short fiction 1980-2005
Winter quarters
  Waldrop, H. Heart of whitenesse
You could go home again
  Waldrop, H. Other worlds, better lives: a Howard Waldrop reader; selected long fiction 1989-2003

WALES

Griffiths, N. Freshers' week
Hughes, T. Twelve beer blues
Nisbet, R. The path to Porthgain
Nisbet, R. Sounds of the town
Nisbet, R. Time to go home
Nisbet, R. Wheelerdealer
Trezise, R. The brake fluid at Gina's
Trezise, R. Fresh apples
Trezise, R. The Joneses
Van Booy, S. Conception
Van Booy, S. Distant ships

Cardiff

Trezise, R. Valley lines

Swansea

Nisbet, R. Nightingale

Wali, Najem

Wars in Distant Lands
  Harper's v316 p75-80 F 2008

The **walk**. Steinberg, S.
A **walk** across the rooftops. Gay, J.
A **walk** down lonely street. Bukoski, A.
A **walk** in the garden. Shepard, L.
A **walk** in the wheat. Kiely, B.
A **walk** in winter. Boswell, R.
Walk left stand right. Stewart, P.
The **Walk** of Light. Yun, D.-N.
A **walk** outside. Guista, M.
The **walk** with Elizanne. Updike, J.

Walker, Alice

Advancing Luna—and Ida B. Wells
  Short stories of the civil rights movement; an anthology; edited by Margaret Earley Whitt
To my young husband
  Short stories of the civil rights movement; an anthology; edited by Margaret Earley Whitt

Walker, David J.

A weekend in the country
  Chicago blues; edited by Libby Fischer Hellmann

Walker, Mary Willis

The red scream [excerpt]
  Lone Star sleuths; an anthology of Texas crime fiction; edited and with an introduction by Bill Cunningham, Steven L. Davis, and Rollo K. Newsom.

Walker, Persia

Such a lucky, pretty girl

Mystery Writers of America presents the blue religion; new stories about cops, criminals, and the chase; edited by Michael Connelly

Walker Evans is a spy on the Lexington Avenue local. Sayers, V.

WALKING

Ahdal, W. a.- . To return by foot

Bradbury, R. The pedestrian

Burgin, R. Notes on Mrs. Slaughter

Celik, B. So very familiar

Copper, B. The cave

Dixon, S. Down the road

James, H. T; or, Summer in the city

Simpson, H. Constitutional

Steinberg, S. The walk

Walking after Dark. Robinson, J.

Walking around money. Westlake, D. E.

Walking Circles. Diehn, A.

Walking the dog. Lamsley, T.

Walking the great road. Di Filippo, P.

Walking with angels. Stevenson, J.

Walking with Caesar. Carew, J.

The **wall**. Muller, M.

The **Wall** of America. Disch, T. M.

The **wall** of fire. Stamm, P.

The **wall** of serpents. De Camp, L. S. and Pratt, F.

WALL STREET (NEW YORK, N.Y.)

See also Stock exchange

Wall Street. Woronov, M.

Wallace, Daniel

The girls

New stories from the South; the year's best, 2008; selected from U.S. magazines by ZZ Packer with Kathy Pories; with an introduction by ZZ Packer

Justice

New stories from the South: the year's best, 2006; selected from U.S. magazines by Allan Gurganus with Kathy Pories; with an introduction by Allan Gurganus

The Georgia Review v59 no1 p93-101 Spr 2005

Slippered feet

Crossroads; tales of the southern literary fantastic; edited by F. Brett Cox and Andy Duncan

A terrible thing

New stories from the South: the year's best, 2007; selected from U.S. magazines by Edward P. Jones with Kathy Pories; with an introduction by Edward P. Jones

The Georgia Review v60 no1 p184-94 Spr 2006

Vacation

The Year's best fantasy and horror: nineteenth annual collection; edited by Ellen Datlow and Kelly Link & Gavin J. Grant

Wallace, David Foster

Brief interviews with hideous men

The Anchor book of new American short stories; edited by Ben Marcus

Good People

The New Yorker v82 no48 p66-9 F 5 2007

Incarnations of burned children

Beha, C. R. The Ecco anthology of contemporary American short fiction; selected by Joyce Carol Oates and Christopher R. Beha.

Wiggle Room

The New Yorker v85 no4 p62-6 Mr 9 2009

Wallace, Edgar

Four Square Jane

The Penguin book of Gaslight crime; con artists, burglars, rogues, and scoundrels from the time of Sherlock Holmes; edited with an introduction and notes by Michael Sims.

Wallace, Joseph

The big five

Bronx noir; edited by S. J. Rozan

Custom sets

Mystery Writers of America presents the prosecution rests; new stories about courtrooms, criminals, and the law; edited by Linda Fairstein.

Dead man

Hard boiled Brooklyn; edited by Reed Farrel Coleman

Wallace, Ron

Logjam

Barnstorm; contemporary Wisconsin fiction; edited by Raphael Kadushin

Wallaert, Josh

The Failing

Gettysburg Review v22 no1 p107-12 Spr 2009

Wallamelon. Shawl, N.

The **Walled** Society. Majfud, J.

The **wallet**. Chekhov, A. P.

Wallow, swine!. Machado de Assis

WALLS

Disch, T. M. The Wall of America

Kadare, I. The Great Wall

Murphy, Y. Walls

Walls. Murphy, Y.

The **walls** of Avila. Connell, E. S.

The **walls** of Jericho. Dunbar, P. L.

Walls of the universe. Melko, P.

The **Wally** na Zdrowie show. Bukoski, A.

Walpole, Sir Hugh

The silver mask

Murder short & sweet; edited by Paul D. Staudohar

Walpole, Peter

Representing Doris

The Virginia Quarterly Review v84 no4 p160-78 Fall 2008

Walpurgis afternoon. Sherman, D.

Walpurgisnacht. Zelazny, R.

Walruses. Strom, D.

Walser, Robert

The Great Talent [Story originally published in German in 1915]

Harper's v316 p23-4 Ja 2008

WALSER, ROBERT, 1878-1956

About

Davenport, G. A field of snow on a slope of the Rosenberg

Walsh, Helen

The city never sleeps

Perverted by language; fiction inspired by The Fall; edited and introduced by Peter Wild.

Walsh, Kieran M.
Getting to Yes
Journal of the American Geriatrics Society
v53 no6 p1072 Je 2005
Walsh, M. O.
The Freddies
Best New American voices 2007; [edited by
Sue Miller; series editors, John Kulka and
Natalie Danford]
Walsh, Michael
The song at twilight
Sherlock Holmes in America; edited by Mar-
tin H. Greenberg, Jon L. Lellenberg, and
Daniel Stashower.
Walsh, Thomas
Double check
The Black Lizard big book of pulps; edited
by Otto Penzler
Walsh, Timothy
If on Thursday the Crows
The North American Review v292 no3/4 p3-7
My/Ag 2007
Walt. Gordon, M.
WALT DISNEY COMPANY
Allen, W. Surprise rocks Disney trial
See also Walt Disney Company
Walter, Jess
Rain on tin
Noise; fiction inspired by Sonic Youth; edited
bt Peter Wild; introduction by Lee Ranaldo
Walter, Paul
Splitfoot
The Year's best fantasy and horror: twenty-
first annual collection; edited by Ellen
Datlow and Kelly Link & Gavin J. Grant
Walters, Anna Lee
Apparitions
Reckonings; contemporary short fiction by
Native American women; edited by Hertha
D. Sweet Wong, Lauren Stuart Muller, Jana
Sequoya Magdaleno
Buffalo wallow woman
Reckonings; contemporary short fiction by
Native American women; edited by Hertha
D. Sweet Wong, Lauren Stuart Muller, Jana
Sequoya Magdaleno
Las Vegas, New Mexico, July 1969
Reckonings; contemporary short fiction by
Native American women; edited by Hertha
D. Sweet Wong, Lauren Stuart Muller, Jana
Sequoya Magdaleno
Walter's girls. Nadelson, S.
The **Wamsutter** wolf. Proulx, A.
The **wand**. Chattin, J.
The **wand** of youth. Bukoski, A.
The **wanderer** [excerpt] Robin, R.
Wanderers. Stern, R. G.
WANDERING JEW
Robin, R. The wanderer [excerpt]
WANDERING JEW (LEGENDARY FIGURE)
Machado de Assis. Life
The **wandering** minstrel. Yasuoka, S.
Wang, Jen
A Cold War Story
Women's Studies Quarterly v34 no3/4 p204-
18 Fall/Wint 2006
Wang, Kirsten
Toxic Life
Idaho Magazine v3 no11 p51-3 Ag 2004

Wang, Shao
The Pianist in the Wal-Mart Parking Lot
Michigan Quarterly Review v47 no2 p345-68
Spr 2008
Wang Ping
All Roads to Lhasa
TriQuarterly no133 p95-7 2009
Crush
Wang Ping. The last communist virgin; sto-
ries
Forage
Wang Ping. The last communist virgin; sto-
ries
The homecoming of an old Beijing man
Wang Ping. The last communist virgin; sto-
ries
House of anything you wish
Wang Ping. The last communist virgin; sto-
ries
The last communist virgin
Wang Ping. The last communist virgin; sto-
ries
Luosang's Dream
TriQuarterly no133 p98-9 2009
Maverick
Wang Ping. The last communist virgin; sto-
ries
Where the poppies blow
Wang Ping. The last communist virgin; sto-
ries
Wang Xiaobo
2015
TriQuarterly no123 p26-79 2005
Wangerin, Walter
Ragman
A cross of centuries; twenty-five imaginative
tales about the Christ; edited by Michael
Bishop
Wanted!. Bonham, F.
Wanted. LaBrie, A.
Wanted man. Gifford, B.
Wanted man. Pizzolatto, N.
Wanting out. Jablonski, N.
Wants. Paley, G.
WAR
See also Armaments; Imaginary wars and
battles; Interplanetary wars; Nuclear war-
fare names of individual wars
Anderson, P. Kings who die
Anderson, P. The live coward
Attenberg, J. Victory garden
Barthelme, D. A picture history of the war
Beagle, P. S. King Pelles the sure
Benioff, D. The devil comes to Orekhovo
Bierce, A. One of the missing
Bierce, A. The war with Wug
Bissell, T. Death defier
Brkic, C. A. The translator
Cho, C. Land of exile
Clark, G. M. The center of the world
Daniel, T. The Valley of the Gardens
Doctorow, C. After the siege
Douglas, C. N. Strangers in a strange land
Emshwiller, C. Boys
Emshwiller, C. The library
Ford, J. The seventh expression of the robot
general
Gad-Cykman, A. Tamar's prayers
Gad-Cykman, A. War chain

WAR—*Continued*

Grant, G. J. Heads down, thumbs up

Gregory, D. The illustrated biography of Lord Grimm

Haldeman, J. W. For White Hill

Haldeman, J. W. The private war of Private Jacob

Haldeman, J. W. A separate war

Hodge, B. With acknowledgements to Sun Tzu

Hodgson, W. H. Date 1965: modern warfare

Ingalls, R. No love lost

Kelly, J. P. Burn

Koustas, P. Athos Emfovos in the temple of sound

LaFarge, P. Lamentation over the destruction of Ur

Lee, M. Memo to our journalists

Marley, L. Absalom's mother

Mendoza, P. The day we buried our weapons

Mohanraj, M. A. Sins of the father (Jaffna, 1977)

Moon, E. Hand to hand

Mordecai, P. The game

Novakovich, J. The bridge under the Danube

Novakovich, J. Hail

Novakovich, J. Neighbors

Novakovich, J. Ribs

Novakovich, J. Snow powder

Pak, W. Winter outing

Rachel, D. The last man I killed

Rajaniemi, H. Deus ex homine

Randolph, L. The boy in the band uniform

Reid, G. Hey, mister!

Reynolds, A. Minla's flowers

Reynolds, A. The receivers

Reynolds, A. The sledge-maker's daughter

Richmond, M. Milk

Rickards, J. Twenty dollar future

Rickert, M. Anyway

Roberson, J. Spoils of war

Roberson, J. A wolf upon the wind

Roberts, A. The siege of Fadiman

Roberts, A. Swiftly

Rossiter, E. Questions of war

Ruefle, M. Monument

Shepard, L. R&R

Shepard, L. Salvador

Shibli, A. Faint hints of tranquillity

Shukman, H. The garden of God: 1976

Shukman, H. Man with golden eagle

Shukman, H. Mortimer of the Maghreb

Silverberg, R. The time of the burning

Smith, C. A. The dimension of change

Stevens, J. D. Some notes on the war

Stross, C. A colder war

Stross, C. Missile gap

Stumacher, A. The Neon desert

Swanwick, M. "Hello," said the stick

Swofford, A. Freedom Oil

Thompson, J. Pie of the month

Turtledove, H. Shock and awe

Williams, C. Excuse the unusual approach

Casualties

Bierce, A. Chickamauga

McAllister, B. Dream baby

WAR AND CHILDREN

James, C. L. R. Children in the resistance

War and peace. Shirley, J.

War and war [excerpt] Krasznahorkai, L.

War baby. Malouf, D.

War buddies. Silber, J.

War by candlelight. Alarcón, D.

War can be murder. Doogan, M.

War chain. Gad-Cykman, A.

WAR CORRESPONDENTS *See* Journalists

WAR CRIME TRIALS

Liebrecht, S. Munich

WAR CRIMINALS

Chilson, P. Toumani Ogun

Segal, L. G. The reverse bug

War Dances. Alexie, S.

The **war** museum. Uchida, H.

The **war** of dogs and boids. Steele, A. M.

The **war** of the Bernsteins. Auslander, S.

The **War** of the Ears. Isegawa, M.

WAR OF THE ROSES *See* England—15th century

WAR ON TERRORISM, 2001-

Singer, N. The killer whispers and prays . . .; or, Like a sledge-hammer to the ribcage

Ward, A. E. Should I be scared?

War stories. Raphael, L.

The **War** Widow. Williams, E.

The **war** with Wug. Bierce, A.

War Wounds. Furr, D.

War year. Haldeman, J. W.

Ward, Amanda Eyre

The blue flame

Ward, A. E. Love stories in this town

Butte as in beautiful

Ward, A. E. Love stories in this town

Grandpa Fred in love

Ward, A. E. Love stories in this town

Miss Montana's wedding day

Ward, A. E. Love stories in this town

Motherhood and terrorism

Stumbling and raging; more politically inspired fiction; edited by Stephen Elliott; with associate editors Greg Larson [et al.]

Ward, A. E. Love stories in this town

Nan and Claude

Ward, A. E. Love stories in this town

On Messalonskee Lake

Ward, A. E. Love stories in this town

Shakespeare.com

Ward, A. E. Love stories in this town

She almost wrote

Ward, A. E. Love stories in this town

Should I be scared ?

Politically inspired; edited by Stephen Elliott; assistant editor, Gabriel Kram; associate editors, Elizabeth Brooks [et al.]

Ward, A. E. Love stories in this town

The stars are bright in Texas

Ward, A. E. Love stories in this town

The way the sky changed

Best of Tin House; stories; foreword by Dorothy Allison

Ward, A. E. Love stories in this town

Ward, Dan

My Heart

The Massachusetts Review v47 no4 p673-91 Wint 2006

Ward, Liza

Dancing lessons

Best new American voices 2004; guest editor John Casey; series editors John Kulka and Natalie Danford

WATCHMEN
Bensko, J. Sea dogs
Boland, J. The night watchman is asleep
Chekhov, A. P. Bad business
Lange, R. Loss prevention
Yasuoka, S. The glass slipper

Watel, Lauren K.
Quiet
Ploughshares v33 no4 p130-45 Wint 2007/2008

WATER
See also Wells
Bacigalupi, P. The tamarisk hunter
Murphy, Y. Our underwater mother
Shawl, N. The water museum
Ts'an-hsüeh. The spring

Water. Abdoh, S.
Water babies. Brown, S.
The **water** bird. Uchida, H.
Water Buffalo Boy (First Shoot). Weigl, B.
Water Damage. Wagner, D.
Water dog God: a ghost story. Watson, B.
Water Everywhere, 1982. Moore, L.
Water hazard. Collins, S.
Water Memories. Gad-Cykman, A.
The **water** museum. Shawl, N.
Water people. Burke, J. L.
Water Spider. Boyagoda, R.
Water sports. Zoshchenko, M.
The **water** tower. Thormahlem, A.
Waterbaby. Card, O. S.
Waterfast. Acampora, L.

Waterman, Fred
Best man wins
The Best American mystery stories, 2004; edited and with an introduction by Nelson DeMille; Otto Penzler, series editor

Watermark [Graphic novella] Kuskin, W. and Adcock, J.

Waters *See* Russell, William

Waters, Don
Blood management
Waters, D. Desert gothic
The Bulls at San Luis
Waters, D. Desert gothic
Dan Buck
Waters, D. Desert gothic
Holiday at the Shamrock
Waters, D. Desert gothic
Little sins
Waters, D. Desert gothic
Mineral and steel
Waters, D. Desert gothic
Mormons in heat
Waters, D. Desert gothic
Pushcart prize XXXIII: best of the small presses 2009; edited by Bill Henderson with the Pushcart Prize editors
The Kenyon Review v29 no4 p140-56 Fall 2007
Mr. Epstein and the dealer
Waters, D. Desert gothic
Southwest Review v90 no2 p271-85 2005
Sheets
Waters, D. Desert gothic
What to do with the dead
Waters, D. Desert gothic
Southwest Review v92 no1 p30-43 2007

Waters, Mary Yukari
Mirror studies
The Best American short stories, 2004; edited by Lorrie Moore; Katrina Kenison series editor

Waters, Thomas *See* Russell, William
Waters. Aguilar, A.
Waters of Forgetfulness. Swartz, M.
The **Waters** of Xochimilco. Longstreet, K.
Watershed. Groff, L.

Watkins, Steve
Adam's house
Watkins, S. My chaos theory; stories
Bocky-Bocky
Watkins, S. My chaos theory; stories
Camouflage
Watkins, S. My chaos theory; stories
Critterworld
Watkins, S. My chaos theory; stories
Desgraciado
Watkins, S. My chaos theory; stories
Driver's ed
Watkins, S. My chaos theory; stories
Family of man
Watkins, S. My chaos theory; stories
Ice age
Watkins, S. My chaos theory; stories
A jelly of light
Watkins, S. My chaos theory; stories
Kafka's sister
Watkins, S. My chaos theory; stories
My chaos theory
Watkins, S. My chaos theory; stories
Painting the baby's room
Watkins, S. My chaos theory; stories

Watrous, Malena
Mummy
StoryQuarterly v42 p415-30 2006
November May Day
TriQuarterly no123 p224-37 2005

Watson, Brad
Visitation
The New Yorker v85 no8 p62-9 Ap 6 2009
Water dog God: a ghost story
Crossroads; tales of the southern literary fantastic; edited by F. Brett Cox and Andy Duncan

Watson, Don
Memorial Day Weekend
Confrontation no90/91 p194-215 Spr/Summ 2005

Watson, Ian
The Moby Clitoris of his beloved
Realms
Nadia's nectar
Nature v441 p666 Je 1 2006
Saving for a sunny day, or the benefits of reincarnation
Science fiction: the best of the year 2007 edition; edited by Rich Horton

Watson, Larry
Doctor's Boys
The North American Review v292 no6 p29-37 N/D 2007

Watson, Patricia
A Fine Looking Man
Canadian Woman Studies v26 no1 p26-30 Wint/Spr 2007

Watson's boy. Evenson, B.

WEAPONS *See* Armaments; Arms and armor; Nuclear weapons

The **weapons** shop. Van Vogt, A. E.

WEATHER

    See also Storms

Bradbury, R. The cold wind and the warm

Ford, J. The dreaming wind

Shields, C. Weather

Sillitoe, A. The devil's almanack

Thomas, E. Milking

Weather. Shields, C.

Weather enough. Boast, W.

Weather is here, wish you were beautiful. Schutt, C.

The **weather** retires. Tognazzini, A.

Weather vane. Naiyer Masud

WEATHER VANES

Naiyer Masud. Weather vane

Weatherwax, Annie

Eating Cake

    Calyx v23 no3 p26-38 Wint 2007

Second Coming

    The Southern Review (Baton Rouge, La.) v44 no4 p727-36 Aut 2008

Weaver, Will

Bad blood

    Weaver, W. Sweet land; new and selected stories

Blaze of glory

    Weaver, W. Sweet land; new and selected stories

Dispersal

    Weaver, W. Sweet land; new and selected stories

Flax

    Weaver, W. Sweet land; new and selected stories

The gleaners

    Weaver, W. Sweet land; new and selected stories

A gravestone made of wheat

    Weaver, W. Sweet land; new and selected stories

Haircut

    Weaver, W. Sweet land; new and selected stories

Heart of the fields

    Weaver, W. Sweet land; new and selected stories

The last farmer

    Weaver, W. Sweet land; new and selected stories

Marked for death

    Weaver, W. Sweet land; new and selected stories

Sheetrock

    Weaver, W. Sweet land; new and selected stories

You are what you drive

    Weaver, W. Sweet land; new and selected stories

The **weaver** in the vault. Smith, C. A.

WEAVERS

Moss, B. K. Rug weaver

The **weavers** at the mill. Kiely, B.

The **web** of La Sanguinaire. Kelly, R.

Webb, Don

Diary from an empty studio

    Witpunk; edited by Claude Lalumière and Marty Halpern

The great white bed

    Year's best fantasy 8; edited by David G. Hartwell, Kathryn Cramer

Ool Athag

    Crossroads; tales of the southern literary fantastic; edited by F. Brett Cox and Andy Duncan

WEBB, JACK, 1920-1982

About

Goldberg, L. Jack Webb's star

Webb, Janeen

Paradise design'd

    Dreaming again; thirty-five new stories celebrating the wild side of Australian fiction; edited by Jack Dann

(jt. auth) See Dann, Jack and Webb, Janeen

Webb, Don

Metamorphosis no. 5

    Lone Star literature; from the Red River to the Rio Grande; edited by Don Graham

Weber, David

A beautiful friendship

    Weber, D. Worlds of Weber: Ms. Midshipwoman Harrington and other stories

The Captain from Kirkbean

    Weber, D. Worlds of Weber: Ms. Midshipwoman Harrington and other stories

A certain talent

    Weber, D. Worlds of Weber: Ms. Midshipwoman Harrington and other stories

In the Navy

    Weber, D. Worlds of Weber: Ms. Midshipwoman Harrington and other stories

Miles to go

    Weber, D. Worlds of Weber: Ms. Midshipwoman Harrington and other stories

Ms. Midshipwoman Harrington

    Weber, D. Worlds of Weber: Ms. Midshipwoman Harrington and other stories

Sir George and the dragon

    Weber, D. Worlds of Weber: Ms. Midshipwoman Harrington and other stories

Sword brother

    Weber, D. Worlds of Weber: Ms. Midshipwoman Harrington and other stories

The traitor

    Weber, D. Worlds of Weber: Ms. Midshipwoman Harrington and other stories

Weber, Matt

Statler pulchrifex

    Nature v442 p718 Ag 10 2006

Webster, Bud

Christus destitutus

    Crossroads; tales of the southern literary fantastic; edited by F. Brett Cox and Andy Duncan

    A cross of centuries; twenty-five imaginative tales about the Christ; edited by Michael Bishop

The **wedding**. Matheson, R.

A **wedding**. Molodowsky, K.

The **wedding** album. Marusek, D.

WEDDING ANNIVERSARIES

Barkley, B. The small machine

McIlvoy, K. Maraschinos

WEDDING ANNIVERSARIES—_Continued_
  Mindt, A. Immigration
Wedding at Rockport. Kalotay, D.
A **wedding** by the sea. Gilchrist, E.
The **wedding** hero. Upadhyay, S.
Wedding in Voerde. Gerlach, G.
The **wedding** march. Westcott, G.
Wedding Night. Marten, E.
The **wedding** of snow and ice. Hoffman, A.
Wedding party. McCauley, W.
Wedding Reception. Clary, R.
The **wedding** ring. MacLaverty, B.
Wedding song. Machado de Assis
WEDDINGS
  Abraham, P. The seven fat brides
  Amado, J. How Porciúncula the mulatto got the
    corpse off his back
  Archer, J. A Greek tragedy
  Barlow, J. The donkey wedding at Gomersal, re-
    counted by an inhabitant of that place
  Barry, R. Not much is new here
  Blackwell, K. My first wedding
  Brazaitis, M. Before the wedding
  Caponegro, M. The father's blessing
  Dixon, S. Time to go
  Doran, M. M. Wedding at the Gormay Cafe
  Douka, M. Carré fix
  Dunbar, P. L. The Easter wedding
  Dymond, J. Cherubs
  Feitell, M. The marrying kind
  Gilchrist, E. A wedding by the sea
  Graham, T. Here and now
  Granados, C. The bride
  Judah, S. Shame under the chuppah
  Kalotay, D. Calamity
  Kalotay, D. Wedding at Rockport
  Kerslake, L. Death of a whale in the Church of
    Elvis
  Klam, M. Issues I dealt with in therapy
  Lahiri, J. A choice of accommodations
  Lunstrum, K. S. Familial kindness
  Ma'mami, S. a.- . The white dog
  Mandelbaum, P. Garrett in wedlock
  Mandelbaum, P. The omelet king
  Marusek, D. The wedding album
  Mason, B. A. Blue country
  Matheson, R. The wedding
  McCauley, W. Wedding party
  Minot, S. Green
  Molodowsky, K. A wedding
  Molodowsky, K. The white wedding dress
  Monson, A. The sudden possibility of nakedness
  Moody, R. The Mansion on the Hill
  Newman, S. The deadly bride
  Ockert, J. Horseshoes
  Ohlin, A. I love to dance at weddings
  Scott, J. Heaven and Hell
  Shroff, M. F. Breathless in Bombay
  Singer, I. B. Yochna and Schmelke
  Snyder, S. The star attraction of 1919
  Steinberg, S. Invitation
  Swirsky, R. Marry the sun
  Upadhyay, S. The wedding hero
  Ward, A. E. Miss Montana's wedding day
  Westcott, G. The wedding march
  Wood, D. Vision in white
A **wedge** of shade. Erdrich, L.
Wednesday at the bagel shop. Selgin, P.
Wednesday is adoration. Klassen, S.

A **week** in South Dakota. Gildner, G.
Weekend. Chase, M.
Weekend. Hempel, A.
A **weekend** in the country. Walker, D. J.
Weekes, Carol
  Two Hours, Two People, and a Box
    Dalhousie Review v86 no1 p103-12 Spr 2006
WEEMS, JOHN EDWARD
          About
  Garrett, G. P. A story goes with it
Weems, Richard K.
  From Now On, You're Back
    The North American Review v291 no3/4 p10-
    15 My/Ag 2006
  John & Xenia
    The North American Review v293 no2 p28-35
    Mr/Ap 2008
WEEPING _See_ Crying
Wegman, Jacob
  This Charming Man
    The Massachusetts Review v48 no2 p234-48
    Summ 2007
Weible, Kennedy
  Phone Man
    Hanging Loose no89 p76-85 2006
Weidman, Jerome
  My aunt from twelfth street
    Manhattan noir 2; the classics; edited by
    Lawrence Block
Weight. Romm, R.
Weight. Wideman, J. E.
Weight and fortune. Kun, M.
Weight less than shadow. Nisbet, J.
WEIGHT LIFTING
  Boyd, W. The mind/body problem
  Pollock, D. R. Discipline
The **weight** of a gun. Upadhyay, S.
The **weight** of bones. Rust, E. M.
The **Weight** of Grief. vanNamen, K. S.
The **Weight** of Me. Kearns, K.
Weight of the world. Straley, J.
The **weight** of words. Ford, J.
Weightless. Holthe, T. U.
Weights and measures. Meacham, R.
Weigl, Bruce
  Water Buffalo Boy (First Shoot)
    Michigan Quarterly Review v43 no4 p608-17
    Fall 2004
Weil, Grete
  And I? witness to pain
    Weil, G. Aftershocks; stories; translated from
      the German by John S. Barrett.
  Don't touch me
    Weil, G. Aftershocks; stories; translated from
      the German by John S. Barrett.
  Finish what you started
    Weil, G. Aftershocks; stories; translated from
      the German by John S. Barrett.
  Guernica
    Weil, G. Aftershocks; stories; translated from
      the German by John S. Barrett.
  The house in the desert
    Weil, G. Aftershocks; stories; translated from
      the German by John S. Barrett.
  Little Sonja Rosenkranz
    Weil, G. Aftershocks; stories; translated from
      the German by John S. Barrett.

Weller, Sam

The quick stop 5®

Burnham, C. Who can save us now?; brand-new superheroes and their amazing [short] stories; edited by Owen King and John McNally; [illustrations by Chris Burnham]

Welles, Harvey

(jt. auth) See Raines, Philip and Welles, Harvey

WELLES, ORSON, 1915-1985

About

Gerrold, D. The strange death of Orson Welles

Kessel, J. It's all true

Wellman, A. M.

The Madison Heights syndrome

Playboy's college fiction; a collection of 21 years of contest winners; edited by Alice K. Turner; foreword by Thom Jones

Wells, Elizabeth

The Afternoon Visit

Dalhousie Review v87 no1 p115-18 Spr 2007

WELLS, H. G. (HERBERT GEORGE), 1866-1946

Parodies, imitations, etc.

Roberson, C. And such small deer

Wells, Herbert George *See* Wells, H. G. (Herbert George), 1866-1946

Wells, Martha

The potter's daughter

Elemental; the Tsunami relief anthology; stories of science fiction and fantasy; [edited by] Steven Savile and Alethea Kontis; introduction by Arthur C. Clarke

Year's best fantasy 7; edited by David G. Hartwell & Kathryn Cramer

WELLS

Bukoski, A. Shovel work

Molodowsky, K. An old-country Erev Pesakh

Parra, E. A. The well

Ruffin, P. The well

Welsch, Gabriel

Beautiful for a Day

New Letters v71 no1 p79-99 2004/2005

Welsh, Irvine

The DOGS of Lincoln Park

Welsh, I. If you liked school, you'll love work . . .

If you liked school, you'll love work . . .

Welsh, I. If you liked school, you'll love work . . .

Kingdom of Fife

Welsh, I. If you liked school, you'll love work . . .

Miss Arizona

Welsh, I. If you liked school, you'll love work . . .

Rattlesnakes

Welsh, I. If you liked school, you'll love work . . .

WELSH

England

Trezise, R. Merry go-rounds

United States

Trezise, R. Coney Island

Welty, Eudora

Ladies in spring

The New Granta book of the American short story; edited and introduced by Richard Ford

Where is the voice coming from?

Short stories of the civil rights movement; an anthology; edited by Margaret Earley Whitt

Wen Huang

(tr.) See Yang Xianhui

The **wench** is dead. Brown, F.

Wenderoth, Joe

Letters to Wendy's

The Anchor book of new American short stories; edited by Ben Marcus

Wendroff, Zalman

The abduction

Wendroff, Z. When it comes to living; selected stories by Zalman Vendrof; [by] Zalman Vendrof; translated by Irene Jerison

Alas–I recovered

Wendroff, Z. When it comes to living; selected stories by Zalman Vendrof; [by] Zalman Vendrof; translated by Irene Jerison

Around the great Samovar

Wendroff, Z. When it comes to living; selected stories by Zalman Vendrof; [by] Zalman Vendrof; translated by Irene Jerison

Blacksmith street

Wendroff, Z. When it comes to living; selected stories by Zalman Vendrof; [by] Zalman Vendrof; translated by Irene Jerison

Caesar and Nero

Wendroff, Z. When it comes to living; selected stories by Zalman Vendrof; [by] Zalman Vendrof; translated by Irene Jerison

The club and the circle

Wendroff, Z. When it comes to living; selected stories by Zalman Vendrof; [by] Zalman Vendrof; translated by Irene Jerison

Gretchen of Cemetary Lane

Wendroff, Z. When it comes to living; selected stories by Zalman Vendrof; [by] Zalman Vendrof; translated by Irene Jerison

Herr Schulz destroys my career

Wendroff, Z. When it comes to living; selected stories by Zalman Vendrof; [by] Zalman Vendrof; translated by Irene Jerison

Homeless

Wendroff, Z. When it comes to living; selected stories by Zalman Vendrof; [by] Zalman Vendrof; translated by Irene Jerison

I am important

Wendroff, Z. When it comes to living; selected stories by Zalman Vendrof; [by] Zalman Vendrof; translated by Irene Jerison

In the textile islands

Wendroff, Z. When it comes to living; selected stories by Zalman Vendrof; [by] Zalman Vendrof; translated by Irene Jerison

A man of principle

Wendroff, Z. When it comes to living; selected stories by Zalman Vendrof; [by] Zalman Vendrof; translated by Irene Jerison

On the way to Wonderland

Wendroff, Z. When it comes to living; selected stories by Zalman Vendrof; [by] Zalman Vendrof; translated by Irene Jerison

The orphan

Wendroff, Z. When it comes to living; selected stories by Zalman Vendrof; [by] Zalman Vendrof; translated by Irene Jerison

Wendroff, Zalman—*Continued*

Pavlik's mysterious disappearance

Wendroff, Z. When it comes to living; selected stories by Zalman Vendrof; [by] Zalman Vendrof; translated by Irene Jerison

A secure lodging

Wendroff, Z. When it comes to living; selected stories by Zalman Vendrof; [by] Zalman Vendrof; translated by Irene Jerison

When it comes to living

Wendroff, Z. When it comes to living; selected stories by Zalman Vendrof; [by] Zalman Vendrof; translated by Irene Jerison

Zlatte's misfortune

Wendroff, Z. When it comes to living; selected stories by Zalman Vendrof; [by] Zalman Vendrof; translated by Irene Jerison

Zorekh and Bulani

Wendroff, Z. When it comes to living; selected stories by Zalman Vendrof; [by] Zalman Vendrof; translated by Irene Jerison

Wenlock Edge. Munro, A.

Wentworth, K. D.

Cat call

Cat tales: fantastic feline fiction; edited by George H. Scithers

We're All Adults. Lystra, D.

We're all bozos on this bus!. Crowther, P.

We're all in this alone. Di Filippo, P.

We're all in this together. King, O.

We're in trouble. Coake, C.

WEREWOLVES

Armstrong, K. Stalked

Blackford, J. Trolls' night out

Blish, J. There shall be no darkness

Howard, R. E. In the forest of Villefère

Howard, R. E. Wolfshead

Kelly, R. Thinning the herd

Link, K. Pretty monsters

Martin, G. R. R. In the lost lands

Martin, G. R. R. The skin trade

McHugh, M. F. Laika comes back safe

Nolan, W. F. Wolf song

Palwick, S. Gestella

Russell, K. St. Lucy's home for girls raised by wolves

Saintcrow, L. Half of being married

Sherman, D. The fiddler of Bayou Teche

Stackpole, M. A. The Krells of Tancras Moor

Thompson, R. A Wulf in groom's clothing

Wolfe, G. The hero as werwolf

WERWOLVES *See* Werewolves

Wesolewski, Hedwig room 301 [variant title: Harry and the dancer] Bukoski, A.

Wessel, John

Neighbors

The International Association of Crime Writers presents Murder in Vegas; new crime tales of gambling and desperation; edited by Michael Connelly

Wesselmann, Douglas

Life Among the Bean Bugs

The North American Review v290 no3/4 p9-16 My/Ag 2005

Wesson, Matianne

Dunya

UMKC Law Review v76 no3 p795-802 Spr 2008

West, Dorothy

Babe

West, D. The last leaf of Harlem; selected and newly discovered fiction by the author of The Wedding; edited by Lionel C. Bascom.

Bent twig

West, D. The last leaf of Harlem; selected and newly discovered fiction by the author of The Wedding; edited by Lionel C. Bascom.

Bessie

West, D. The last leaf of Harlem; selected and newly discovered fiction by the author of The Wedding; edited by Lionel C. Bascom.

The birthday party

West, D. The last leaf of Harlem; selected and newly discovered fiction by the author of The Wedding; edited by Lionel C. Bascom.

The black dress: a short short story

"Tell it to us easy" and other stories; a complete short fiction anthology of African American women writers in Opportunity magazine, (1923-1948); edited by Judith Musser.

A boy in the house

West, D. The last leaf of Harlem; selected and newly discovered fiction by the author of The Wedding; edited by Lionel C. Bascom.

Cook

West, D. The last leaf of Harlem; selected and newly discovered fiction by the author of The Wedding; edited by Lionel C. Bascom.

The cottagers and Mrs. Carmody

West, D. The last leaf of Harlem; selected and newly discovered fiction by the author of The Wedding; edited by Lionel C. Bascom.

The five dollar bill

West, D. The last leaf of Harlem; selected and newly discovered fiction by the author of The Wedding; edited by Lionel C. Bascom.

Hannah Byde

West, D. The last leaf of Harlem; selected and newly discovered fiction by the author of The Wedding; edited by Lionel C. Bascom.

Homecoming

West, D. The last leaf of Harlem; selected and newly discovered fiction by the author of The Wedding; edited by Lionel C. Bascom.

Interlude

West, D. The last leaf of Harlem; selected and newly discovered fiction by the author of The Wedding; edited by Lionel C. Bascom.

Jack in the pot

West, D. The last leaf of Harlem; selected and newly discovered fiction by the author of The Wedding; edited by Lionel C. Bascom.

WEST INDIES

See also Trinidad and Tobago

Baker, K. The maid on the shore

Stafford, J. A modest proposal

WEST INDIES REGION See Caribbean region

West of Dodge. L'Amour, L.

West of Dry Creek. L'Amour, L.

West of the Rockies. Fuchs, D.

WEST VIRGINIA

Bierce, A. The mocking-bird

Bierce, A. A tough tussle

WESTCHESTER COUNTY (N.Y.) See New York (State)—Westchester County

Westcott, Glenway

Adolescence

Wescott, G. Goodbye, Wisconsin; with an introduction by Jerry Rosco; illustrated by Steve Chappell

The dove came down

Wescott, G. Goodbye, Wisconsin; with an introduction by Jerry Rosco; illustrated by Steve Chappell

Goodbye, Wisconsin

Wescott, G. Goodbye, Wisconsin; with an introduction by Jerry Rosco; illustrated by Steve Chappell

A guilty woman

Wescott, G. Goodbye, Wisconsin; with an introduction by Jerry Rosco; illustrated by Steve Chappell

In a thicket

Wescott, G. Goodbye, Wisconsin; with an introduction by Jerry Rosco; illustrated by Steve Chappell

Like a lover

Wescott, G. Goodbye, Wisconsin; with an introduction by Jerry Rosco; illustrated by Steve Chappell

Prohibition

Wescott, G. Goodbye, Wisconsin; with an introduction by Jerry Rosco; illustrated by Steve Chappell

The runaways

Wescott, G. Goodbye, Wisconsin; with an introduction by Jerry Rosco; illustrated by Steve Chappell

The sailor

Wescott, G. Goodbye, Wisconsin; with an introduction by Jerry Rosco; illustrated by Steve Chappell

The wedding march

Wescott, G. Goodbye, Wisconsin; with an introduction by Jerry Rosco; illustrated by Steve Chappell

The whistling swan

Wescott, G. Goodbye, Wisconsin; with an introduction by Jerry Rosco; illustrated by Steve Chappell

Westerfeld, Scott

Ass-hat magic spider

The Starry rift; tales of new tomorrows: an original science fiction anthology; edited by Jonathan Strahan

The **westerly**. Anderson, B.

Westermann, John

The secret

Murder in the rough; edited by Otto Penzler

The **western** campaign. Sallis, J.

WESTERN STATES

Bierce, A. Across the continent

Bishop, T. I cain't go

Bishop, T. The vision of Hehaka 'To

Evans, M. Once a cowboy

Hadley, D. The teachings of Bronc Buster Billy Brown

Haynes, M. M. M. Meantime, Quentin Ghlee

Kittredge, W. Looking glass

Porter, J. A. Solstice

Farm life

See Farm life—Western States

Frontier and pioneer life

See Frontier and pioneer life—Western States

WESTERN STORIES

See also Adventure; Cowboys; Frontier and pioneer life—Western States; Ranch life; Western States

Askins, C. Kit

Austin, M. H. The girls at Overtown

Baker, O. Where the buffaloes begin

Barron, L. Bulldozer

Boggs, J. D. Red River Crossing

Bonham, F. Death Valley silver

Bonham, F. Freeze-out

Bonham, F. Hell in Dakota

Bonham, F. Hurry call for hangin' Gus

Bonham, F. I'll take the high road

Bonham, F. The phantom bandit

Bonham, F. A river man goes to war

Bonham, F. Wanted!

Bower, B. M. Big medicine

Bower, B. M. By gollies, yes!

Bower, B. M. Happy Jack, wild man

Bower, B. M. The intervention of almighty voice

Bower, B. M. The land shark

Bower, B. M. Law on the Flying U

Bower, B. M. On the middle guard

Bower, B. M. The outlaw

Bower, B. M. The tale of a native son

Bradbury, R. The beautiful shave

Cook, W. Bell's station

Cook, W. Blood sky

Cook, W. The contest

Cook, W. The far-travelin' man

Cook, W. The fight at Renegade Basin

Cook, W. Let's all go kill the scared old man

Cook, W. Wildcat on the prod

Dawson, P. Back-trail betrayal

Dawson, P. Hell for homesteaders

Dawson, P. Showdown at Anchor

Dawson, P. A tinhorn takes a tank town

Dawson, P. Unwanted gold

Garland, H. The doctor's visit

Gates, D. Aces & eights

Gauss, M. A life like Maggy's

Gorman, E. Junior

Greenleaf, F. Our first well in Nebraska

Haycox, E. Stage to Lordsburg

Henry, W. A bullet for Billy the Kid

Henry, W. The fourth horseman

Henry, W. Santa Fé passage

Hockensmith, S. Gustav Amlingmeyer, Holmes of the range

Inglis, T. M. Fairy "Spuds"

Johnson, D. M. A man called Horse

Kent, L. T. In common

Wet dog of Galveston. Henderson, J.
Wet straw. Matheson, R.
Wetherall, William
    (tr.) See Akiko, Sugimoto
Wetlands preserve. Kress, N.
Wexelblatt, Robert
    The Artist Wears Rough Clothing and Carries Jade Inside
        The Massachusetts Review v48 no4 p618-34 Wint 2007
    Tinder Box
        The Massachusetts Review v46 no4 p588-610 Wint 2005/2006
Whale. Ramos, G.
The whale below. Blaschke, J. L.
The whaleblimp herder. Butler, C.
Whalen, Tom
    Conversations with Godard
        Agni no62 p191-7 2005
    The Effect
        The Literary Review (Madison, N.J.) v51 no2 p109-15 Wint 2008
WHALES
    James, C. L. R. Moby Dick fights a strange eagle
    Morse, D. L. Conceived
    Raines, P. and Welles, H. The fishie
    Tolstaia, T. Yorick
    Watson, I. The Moby Clitoris of his beloved
    Williams, W. J. Surfacing
The whales. Somerville, P.
Wharton, Edith
    Mrs. Manstey's view
        Manhattan noir 2; the classics; edited by Lawrence Block
    The Verdict
        FMR (Black Edition) no19 p155-64 Je 2007
What, Leslie
    Is that hard science; or, Are you just happy to see me
        Witpunk; edited by Claude Lalumière and Marty Halpern
    Post hoc
        Interfictions; an anthology of interstitial writing; edited by Delia Sherman and Theodora Goss
    (jt. auth) See Gunn, Eileen and What, Leslie
What a schoolgirl you are. Meno, J.
What a song can do. Levithan, D.
What a wonderful world. Guyot, P.
What about that thing, they called. Montgomery, L.
What are cicadas? Enright, A.
What Are Friends For? Epstein, J.
What are friends for? Gunn, E.
What Are the Odds? Singleton, G.
What are you afraid of? Hyde, M.
What attracts us to Gruel. Singleton, G.
What begins with bird. Holland, N.
What can I tell you about my brother? Harty, R.
What Coal Tastes Like. Babic, M. J.
What comes of conversation. Tognazzini, A.
What do you dream of, cruiser Aurora? Litman, E.
What do you want to know for? Munro, A.
What do you want with me, love? Rivas, M.
What ever happened to Frank Snake Church? Alexie, S.
What every boy should know. Maxwell, W.

What every coin has. Henderson, C. J.
What Floats. Nolan, J.
What for, this burden. Encinosa Fú, M.
What friction? What factions? Crees, S.
What generosity. Zoshchenko, M.
What goes around. Schutz, B. M.
What goes on in Saint-Germain. Gavalda, A.
What happened. Panning, A.
What Happened Between Us. Galchen, R.
What happened in Japan. Gifford, B.
What happened in the Thunderbolt. Hodgson, W. H.
What happened to the baby? Ozick, C.
What happens next. Parker, M.
What Happens Next. Rodgers, S. J.
What happens when the mipods leave their milieu. Crane, E.
What he needed. Lippman, L.
What He Saw. Winter, M.
What he saw at the Yiddish theater. Kobrin, L.
What he was like. Maxwell, W.
What I did on my holidays. Stewart, I.
What I Did Showed Extremely Bad Judgment. Madrid, J.
What I didn't see. Fowler, K. J.
What I Found Out About Her. LaSalle, P.
What I have been doing lately. Kincaid, J.
What I never said. Lum, E.
What I Want to Know Is When Did Charlotte McIntosh Get to Be So Jealous? McMullen, M.
What I Won't Tell You. Eck, M.
What if we leave? Singleton, G.
What I'm doing after this. Tognazzini, A.
What is happiness. Schwitters, K.
What is now proved was once only imagined. Hyde, M.
What Is "Son"? Otto, J.
What is undug will be. Baraka, I. A.
What it is. Connor, J.
What it Takes to Spice Up a Haircut. Jernigan, R. K.
What kind of furniture would Jesus pick? Proulx, A.
What language is that? Akpan, U. C.
What Lydia thinks of roses. Alvarado, B.
What Madame Lipsky Wanted. Kalotay, D.
What Manner of Light? Chacón, D.
What Milton heard. Glatt, L.
What monsters do. David, P.
What must I say to you? Rosen, N.
What Nina wants. Luongo, M.
The what-not doll. Everson, K.
What our week was like. Crane, E.
What Quig found. Pierson, C.
What Saffi knows. Windley, C.
What Seems to Move Is Still. Hay, J.
What she knows. Randolph, L.
What she needed. Weiner, J.
What she offered. Cook, T. H.
What she should do. LaBrie, A.
What the Bird Says. Almond, S.
What the Cat Said. Bender, K. E.
What the devil won't take . . . Banks, L. E.
What the left hand is saying. Dean, D.
What the tyger told her. Baker, K.
What thou and I did, till we loved. Kennedy, C.
What to do with the dead. Waters, D.
What to expect. Schwarzschild, E.

What was important. Gee, M.

What Was Left Behind. Barya, M. K.

What we can do. Stamm, P.

What we cannot speak about we must pass over in silence. Wideman, J. E.

What we do for love. Blackwell, K.

What we know about the lost families of — house. Barzak, C.

What we learned from this morning's newspaper. Silverberg, R.

What We Make. Mathews, B.

What we own. Crouse, D.

What we sell in the room today. Stevens, J. D.

What we talk about when we talk about love. Carver, R.

What were the white things? Hempel, A.

What Will Happen to the Sharma Family. Upadhyay, S.

What will people say? Gordin, J.

What will you do next? Michalopoulou, A.

What woman. Ruefle, M.

What would you do for love? Shirley, J.

What Y was. Abbott, L. K.

What you call winter. Jones, N.

What you can do after shutdown. Malae, P. N.

What you can't hang on to. Maxwell, W.

What you do next. Richard, N.

What you do not know you want. Mitchell, D.

What you pawn I will redeem. Alexie, S.

What you pawn I will return. Alexie, S.

What you see. Wagman, D.

What you usually find in novels [variant title: Elements most often found in novels, short stories, etc.] Chekhov, A. P.

What you want. Enright, A.

What you won't read in books. Swain, H.

Whates, Ian
   The key
      Nature v442 p1076 Ag 31 2006
   A piratical sabbatical
      Nature v448 p224 Jl 12 2007

Whatever happened to Sébastien Grosjean? Liddell, R.

Whatever it takes. Schutz, B. M.

What's expected of us. Chiang, T.

What's sure to come. Ford, J.

What's the Price of Passion? Porter, J.

What's the score? O'Brien, T.

What's up, Tiger Lily? Di Filippo, P.

What's your poison? Hinton, S. E.

What's Yours, What's Mine. Eggers, P.

Wheat, Carolyn
   The case of the rival queens
      Sherlock Holmes in America; edited by Martin H. Greenberg, Jon L. Lellenberg, and Daniel Stashower.
   The only good judge
      Brooklyn noir 2; the classics; edited by Tim McLoughlin
   A scandal in Drury Lane; or, The vampire trap
      Ghosts in Baker Street; edited by Martin H. Greenberg, Jon Lellenberg, Daniel Stashower

Wheat, Carrie
   A Constant History
      Confrontation no94/95 p149-65 Spr/Summ 2006

The **Wheelbarrow** Man. Elliott, S.

Wheelbarrow thief. Kennedy, C.

Wheeler, Richard S.
   Hearts
      Best stories of the American West, v1; edited by Marc Jaffe

Wheeler, Theodore
   Welcome home
      Best new American voices 2009; guest editor Mary Gaitskill; series editors John Kulka and Natalie Danford

Wheeler-dealer. Chase, M.

Wheelerdealer. Nisbet, R.

Wheeling. Beattie, A.

Wheels. Zhu Wen

The **wheels** of if. De Camp, L. S.

Wheels of Progress. Wahhaj, G.

Wheelwright, Tess
   An American Story; or, What Unfortunately Happened
      The Yale Review v96 no2 p117-35 Ap 2008

When all this was Bay Ridge. McLoughlin, T.

When Britney Spears comes to my lab. LiCata, V.

When day is dun. Matheson, R.

When Does He Come? Shin, K.-S.

When does Mame eat? Reisen, A.

When he was fab. Wilson, F. P.

When I Fall in Love. Fitch, B.

When I Last Saw Him.

When I was a horse. Domecq, B.

When I was a man. Past, A.

When I was mortal. Marías, J.

When I woke up this morning, everything I had was gone. Boyle, T. C.

When Is a Wall not a Wall? Johnston, P. D.

When it comes to living. Wendroff, Z.

When It Is Green and Not Blue. Mukherjee, S.

When it rains, you'd better get out of Ulga. Ferrero, A.

When it's human instead of when it's dog. Hempel, A.

When Jacques Cousteau gave Pablo Picasso a piece of black coral. Malla, P.

When Jennie saved the windmill. Dobson, C. L.

When Johnny comes marching home. Brenchley, C.

When Leslie Got the Call. Brammer, S.

When Life Gives You Lemons. Yáñez, M.

When Lovely Woman Stoops to Folly. Targan, B.

When momma came home for Christmas and Talmidge quoted Frost. Ruffin, P.

When Mr. Pirzada came to dine. Lahiri, J.

When our dream world finds us, and these hard times are gone. Abbott, L. K.

When scarabs multiply. Okorafor, N.

When She Was Small. Gibb, C.

When should we live? Bentham, R.

When sysadmins ruled the earth. Doctorow, C.

When the bear came. Percy, B.

When the bough breaks. Bradbury, R.

When the dark is light enough. Ochsner, G.

When the heroes came to town. Czyzniejewski, M.

When the neighbors love you. Litman, E.

When the Nell Goes Dry. Obenchain, P.

When the President prays. Stevens, J. D.

When the rains come. Romano, T.

When the Stars Begin to Fall. Gilbreth, J.

When the sun went down. Nisbet, R.

When the Toasts Stopped Being Funny. Almond, S.

When the waker sleeps. Matheson, R.

When the women come out to dance. Leonard, E.

When they learned to yelp. Eggers, D.

When Thou Art King. Stuber, A.

When we went to see the end of the world. Silverberg, R.

When We Were Virgins. Olsen, S. S.

When you come into your kingdom. Muñoz, M.

When you say you're a Jew. Albert, E.

When you visit the Magoebaskloof Hotel, be certain not to miss the samango monkeys. Bear, E.

When you're dead. Stackpole, M. A.

Whenever they go out. Rich, M.

Where all our dreams come true. Phillips, G.

Where angels come in. Nevill, A. L. G.

Where angels fear. Rand, K.

Where angels fear to tread. Kenyon, S.

Where are you going, where have you been? Oates, J. C.

Where are you running to? Ma Jian

Where beautiful ladies dance for you. Finn, P. M.

Where Europe begins. Tawada, Y.

Where Has Your Lover Gone? Champion, L.

Where I work. Cummins, A.

Where I'm likely to find it. Murakami, H.

Where is here? Oates, J. C.

Where is home? Burke, T.

Where is the voice coming from? Welty, E.

Where nothing is. Romm, R.

Where she was. Cherry, K.

Where the buffaloes begin. Baker, O.

Where the devil lost his blanket. Tudish, C.

Where the door is always open and the welcome mat is out. Highsmith, P.

Where the golden apples grow. Baker, K.

Where the heart lives. Liu, M. M.

Where the money went. Canty, K.

Where the poppies blow. Wang Ping

Where the Water Runs Uphill. Davenport, S.

Where there's a will . . . Masello, R.

Where there's fighting. L'Amour, L.

Where they are hid. Powers, T.

Where they hide. Van Booy, S.

Where we all should have been. Desaulniers, J.

Where we come from. Budnitz, J.

Where we last saw time. LaSalle, P.

Where what gets into people comes from. Crone, M.

Where will you go when your skin cannot contain you? Gay, W.

Where You Most Expect It. Rodriguez, J. P.

Which Reminded Her, Later. McGregor, J.

Which rocks we choose. Singleton, G.

Which Tribe Do You Belong To? Pierce, B.

Whicker Island. Brooks, J.

While horse and hero fell. Hoyt, S. A.

While Jane Writes. Serravalle, D.

While We Waited. Lee, T.-Y.

Whipped on the face with a length of thorn bush: yes, directly on the face. Lawson, J. E.

The **Whipping**. Elliot, J.

The **whipping**. Elliott, J.

The **whirling** dove. Monteiro, L.

WHISKEY

Dalton, Q. How to clean your apartment

Whisman, Albert Samuel

(tr.) See Montalbetti, Christine

Whisnant, Luke

How to build a house

New stories from the South: the year's best, 2006; selected from U.S. magazines by Allan Gurganus with Kathy Pories; with an introduction by Allan Gurganus

Whisper. Percy, B.

Whisper yet. Ch'oe, Y.

The **whisperer** in darkness. Lovecraft, H. P.

The **whisperers**. Lupoff, R. A.

Whispers of the dead. Tremayne, P.

Whistle opera. Romano, T.

Whistle pig. Angel, J.

Whistle While You Work: The Case of the Inevitable Internal Investigation. Zinski, C. J.

The **whistling** room. Hodgson, W. H.

The **whistling** swan. Westcott, G.

Whitbeck, William C.

In the Market

The Michigan Bar Journal v86 no8 p20-3 Ag 2007

Whitcomb, Gordy

Tree Trimming

Nebraska Life v12 no5 p32-3 S/O 2008

White, Bill

Carousel

South Dakota Magazine v21 no1 p89-92 My/Je 2005

White, Dave

God's dice

The Adventure of the missing detective and 19 of the year's finest crime and mystery stories!; edited by Ed Gorman and Martin H. Greenberg

Righteous son

Killer year; stories to die for . . . from the hottest new crime writers; edited by Lee Child

White, Edmund

Cinnamon skin

Beha, C. R. The Ecco anthology of contemporary American short fiction; selected by Joyce Carol Oates and Christopher R. Beha.

A Good Sport

The Yale Review v95 no3 p73-101 Jl 2007

One Endless English Evening

The Virginia Quarterly Review p125-32 2006 supp

White, Jacob

The Days Down Here

The Georgia Review v62 no3 p484-505 Fall 2008

Night Miles

The Sewanee Review v117 no3 p456-74 Summ 2009

White, Leslie T.

Chosen to die

The Black Lizard big book of pulps; edited by Otto Penzler

The city of hell!

The Black Lizard big book of pulps; edited by Otto Penzler

White, Lori

Postcards from the Road

The Kenyon Review v29 no3 p79-81 Summ 2007

White, Lowell Mick
Five Things
Callaloo v29 no1 p96-108 Wint 2006
The Road Back to Destruction Bay
Callaloo v32 no2 p498-504 Spr 2009
White, Maya
Eating Earth
Southwest Review v92 no2 p249-54 2007
White, Phyllis Dorothy James *See* James, P. D.
The **white** beast. Zelazny, R.
A **white** bible. Wolff, T.
The **White** Bird. Menasche, D.
The **white** blackbird. Purdy, J.
The **white** boy shuffle [excerpt] Beatty, P.
White-Bread Jesus. Coover, R.
White Bull. Busch, L.
White collar woman. Arnow, H. L. S.
The **white** counterpane. Dunbar, P. L.
The **white** dog. Ma'mami, S. a.- .
The **white** dog. Reinhorn, H.
White falcon. Lamb, H.
White Fire. O'Connor, S.
A **white** flower for bats. Rivas, M.
The **White** Garden. Nelson, R. F.
White girl. Gurba, M.
The **White** Hart Inn. McNally, T. M.
The **White** Hole of Bombay. Shakespeare, N.
White horse. Atwood, M.
White Irish. Bruen, K.
The **white** Khan. Lamb, H.
The **white** man. Disch, T. M.
The **white** man. Monteleone, T. F.
White mule, spotted pig. Lansdale, J. R.
The **white** net. Smith, M.
White only: a story of the color line. Mull, H. F.
The **white** oxen. Burke, K.
The **white** pants of history. Gospodinov, G.
The **white** plains of Western Avenue. Woronov, M.
White Rice. Larochelle, M.-M.
White Sands. Dyer, G.
The **white** seal maid. Yolen, J.
White sky in May. Crone, M.
The **White** Sybil. Smith, C. A.
White trash. Charyn, J.
White trash noir. Malone, M.
White Trees in Summer. Novack, S.
White walls. Tolstaia, T.
The **white** wedding dress. Molodowsky, K.
The **white** wild bronco. Kiely, B.
White Wing. Sherman, J.
Whitecap. LaBute, N.
Whitefoot. Berry, W.
Whitehead, Colson
The all-night bodega of souls
Brooklyn noir 2; the classics; edited by Tim McLoughlin
The Gangsters
The New Yorker v84 no42 p90-8, 100-3 D 22-29 2008
Whiteley, Aliya
Geoffrey says
The Adventure of the missing detective and 19 of the year's finest crime and mystery stories!; edited by Ed Gorman and Martin H. Greenberg
Whitely on the tips. Murphy, Y.

Whitfield, Raoul
About kid Deth
The Black Lizard big book of pulps; edited by Otto Penzler
Whither?. Bierce, A.
Whitley, Stuart J.
Pages from a Life
The Advocate (Vancouver, B.C.) v63 pt3 p347-51 My 2005
Whitney, Heather M.
The Godmother Protocols
Nature v444 p970 D 14 2006
Whittenberg, Allison
Ride the Peter Pan
Feminist Studies v31 no1 p186-93 Spr 2005
WHITTLING *See* Wood carving
WHO (MUSICAL GROUP)
Shepard, J. Won't get fooled again
Who are they who are like clouds? Dufresne, J.
Who Done. Guerra, T.
Who gives himself. Hunton, E. R.
Who Goes Up the Mountain. Hagkull, J.
Who Hid the Eid Lamb? Najjar, T. A.
Who invented the jump shot. Wideman, J. E.
Who is the thief? Collins, W.
Who knows more than you. Desaulniers, J.
Who Occupies this House. Hill, K.
Who shall escape whipping. Baumbach, J.
Who slays the gyant, wounds the beast. Chadbourn, M.
Who stand for the gods. Dunbar, P. L.
Who stole the fish? Tremayne, P.
The **who**, the what, and the why. Abbott, L. K.
Who weeps when one of us goes down blues. Wideman, J. E.
Who, what, when, where. Johnson, G.
WHODUNITS *See* Mystery and detective stories
Whoever you are. Merril, J.
The **Whole** Story. Humphreys, H.
The **whole** world is watching. Hellmann, L. F.
The **whole** world's guilt. Guista, M.
Whorehouse Hollow. Kelly, R.
The **whore's** child. Russo, R.
The **whores** of Onyx City. Gonzales, M. A.
Who's afraid of Ed Garpo? Kassak, F.
Who's afraid of Wolf 359? MacLeod, K.
Who's there? Ducornet, R.
Whose world is this? Montgomery, L.
Why?. Silverberg, R.
Why antichrist? Adrian, C.
Why Bugsy Siegel was a friend of mine. Burke, J. L.
Why do they have to hit? Meyers, M.
Why don't you dance? Carver, R.
Why I am not editing "The stinger". Bierce, A.
Why I became a plumber. Maitland, S.
Why I got fired. Martin, J.
Why I Hate Alaska. Johnson, M.
Why I married the porn star. Stevens, J. D.
Why I'm here. Hempel, A.
Why must it sound like a cowboy song? Buckler, E.
Why the sky turns red when the sun goes down. Harty, R.
Why the tears, Miss Earhart? DeMarinis, R.
Why Wagon Wheels Go Backwards. Edwards, P. K.
Why We Are in Iraq. Wuori, G. K.
Why we jump. Lewis, W. H.

Why'd you bring me here? Cohen, S.
Whyman, Paula
Driver's Education
The Hudson Review v58 no2 p241-54 Summ 2005
Whyte Avenue Blue. Hollingshead, G.
Wi-Jun-Jon. Erdrich, L.
The **wicked** old witch. Effinger, G. A.
Wicked stepmother. Brady, C.
Wickersham, Joan
Psychological Impact
The Hudson Review v58 no4 p603-16 Wint 2006
The Woodwork
Ploughshares v32 no2/3 p196-201 Fall 2006
Wicks, Brandon
The Oubliette
South Carolina Review v40 no2 p84-97 Spr 2008
Wide awake in Baton Rouge. Moore, D. W.
The **wide,** pale ocean. Henriquez, C.
Wideman, John Edgar
Are dreams faster than the speed of light
Wideman, J. E. God's gym; John Edgar Wideman
Fanon
Wideman, J. E. God's gym; John Edgar Wideman
Hunters
Wideman, J. E. God's gym; John Edgar Wideman
Sharing
Wideman, J. E. God's gym; John Edgar Wideman
Sightings
Wideman, J. E. God's gym; John Edgar Wideman
The Paris Review v46 p243-57 Fall 2004
The silence of Thelonious Monk
Wideman, J. E. God's gym; John Edgar Wideman
Weight
Wideman, J. E. God's gym; John Edgar Wideman
What we cannot speak about we must pass over in silence
Wideman, J. E. God's gym; John Edgar Wideman
The Best American short stories, 2004; edited by Lorrie Moore; Katrina Kenison series editor
Who invented the jump shot
Wideman, J. E. God's gym; John Edgar Wideman
Beha, C. R. The Ecco anthology of contemporary American short fiction; selected by Joyce Carol Oates and Christopher R. Beha.
Who weeps when one of us goes down blues
Wideman, J. E. God's gym; John Edgar Wideman
Wolf Whistle [Excerpt from As You Were Saying: American Writers Respond to Their French Contemporaries]
Harper's v314 p35 Ap 2007
Widner, Jill
River Swim
The North American Review v291 no3/4 p33-5 My/Ag 2006

The **widow**. Buckler, E.
Widow. Latiolais, M.
The **widow** Joy. Brown, R.
The **widower** Turmore. Bierce, A.
WIDOWERS
Bensko, J. The robber
Bensko, J. Sirens
Block, L. Welcome to the real world
Busch, F. The small salvation
Canty, K. They were expendable
Capote, T. Among the paths to Eden
Carcaterra, L. Missing the morning bus
Card, O. S. Missed
Crowther, P. Stand-by
Dokey, R. The shopper
Dunbar, P. L. Little Billy
Edelman, S. Survival of the fittest
Elyshevitz, A. Hermano
Engberg, S. Beginning
Engberg, S. Time's body
Erdrich, L. The butcher's wife
Fadanelli,   G.   Interroguen   a Samantha/Questioning Samantha
Flanagan, E. Burn
Fonseca, R. Angels of the marquees
Formetta, C. D. Last summer together
Fuentes, C. The disobedient son
Gardiner, J. R. The shape of the past
Gorman, E. Yesterday's dreams
Hawes, L. A fine mess
Hempel, A. The afterlife
Hodgson, W. H. The riven night
Hyde, M. Second-hand
Jones, E. P. A rich man
Lasdun, J. Cleanness
Lasdun, J. The old man
Lunstrum, K. S. Familial kindness
Mandelman, A. Curse
Matheson, R. Wet straw
Maxwell, W. Homecoming
McCafferty, J. Stadium hearts
Mehringer, A. Apartment 1-A
Meloy, M. Agustin
Mindt, A. Reception
Moffett, K. The volunteer's friend
Molodowsky, K. The Rashkovitcher wedding
Molodowsky, K. Rosele
Murakami, H. Tony Takitani
Olafsson, O. June
Percy, B. Crash
Porter, J. A. Forgotten coast
Raymond, J. The coast
Romm, R. The beads
Romm, R. Family epic
Russo, R. Monhegan light
Schwarzschild, E. What to expect
Shabtai, Y. A marriage proposal
Sillitoe, A. The devil's almanack
Singer, I. B. The power of darkness
Somerville, P. The Cold War
Stelmok, J. Maxfield Ridge
Swan, G. Uncle Lazarus
Trevor, W. Cheating at canasta
Trevor, W. The children
Trevor, W. Graillis's legacy
Updike, J. Free
Vapnyar, L. Luda and Milena
Vollmer, M. Man-O'-War
Watkins, S. Bocky-Bocky

WIDOWERS—*Continued*

Weaver, W. A gravestone made of wheat

Windley, C. The reading Elvis

Wingate, S. Bill

Winton, T. Small mercies

Wunsch, E. Lily of the valley

Widowmaker. Cherryh, C. J. and Fancher, J.

WIDOWS Miriam

Abbott, L. K. Love is the crooked thing

Adichie, C. N. The headstrong historian

Aird, C. The widow's might

Auchincloss, L. Other times, other ways

Barlow, J. The donkey wedding at Gomersal, recounted by an inhabitant of that place

Barnes, J. The things you know

Barron, L. The lagerstatte

Beattie, A. Find and replace

Benbow, M. Egyptian

Bensko, J. Summer girls

Berg, E. Mrs. Ethel Menafee and Mr. Bridie Stoltz

Berg, E. Sin city

Bishop, T. The contest

Blackwell, K. Heartbeatland

Boswell, R. No river wide

Brodsky, M. She couldn't help wondering

Buckler, E. Nettles into orchids

Buckler, E. The widow

Burke, J. L. Mist

Burke, K. Mrs. Maecenas

Cherne, B. The conversion

Cherne, B. Exile

Cherne, B. A holocaust in my breakfast room

Coleman, W. Winona's choice

Dahl, R. The last act

De Marcken, A. Ashes

Divakaruni, C. B. Mrs. Dutta writes a letter

Dobozy, T. Dead letters

Donovan, G. Another life

Duffy, S. Payment in kind

Engberg, S. Beginning

Flanagan, E. The usual mistakes

Fulton, A. Queen Wintergreen

Gappah, P. At the sound of the last post

Gee, M. Beautiful things

Gee, M. Ring-barking

Gildner, G. The inheritance

Glatt, L. Soup

Gordimer, N. Allesverloren

Gordon, M. Death in Naples

Guo, S. Wailing moon

Halpern, F. Goodbye, honey

Helprin, M. Monday

Hempel, A. Nashville gone to ashes

Higgins, G. V. The last wash of the teapot

Hodgson, W. H. Jack Grey, second mate

Hoffman, A. The token

Holthe, T. U. Homecoming

Holthe, T. U. The three widows of Signor Alberto Moretti

Iyengar, V. L. The widows of Tithhoor

Keeble, J. Nocturnal America

Kennedy, C. Sea burial

King, S. The New York Times at special bargain rates

Lambert, C. The scent of cinnamon

Lippman, L. Femme fatale

Lott, B. History

McCafferty, J. Stadium hearts

McGlynn, D. Seventeen one-hundredths of a second

Michalopoulou, A. Light

Moceri, M. Escape velocity

Moorcock, M. Winter Admiral

Munro, A. Free radicals

Novakovich, J. Ribs

Panning, A. What happened

Parks, T. The old house

Perlman, E. Manslaughter

Purdy, J. Moe's villa

Raqabah, B. A. New wrinkles

Roden, B. Northwest passage

Salter, J. Eyes of the stars

Saunders, G. Bohemians

Schutt, C. The Duchess of Albany

Schwartz, L. S. Mrs. Saunders writes to the world

Shabtai, Y. A marriage proposal

Shabtai, Y. True tenderness

Shields, C. Hazel

Shields, C. Mrs. Turner cutting the grass

Shirley, P. The Downtown Club

Singer, I. B. The bus

Singer, I. B. The painting

Smith, N. Funny weird or funny ha ha?

Stamm, P. The visit

Stevenson, J. Garden guerrillas

Stollman, A. L. Die grosse liebe

Swails, K. Cake and candy

Swan, G. Exiles

Templeton, E. Nymph & faun

Thompson, J. Pie of the month

Tóibín, C. The name of the game

Trevor, W. At Olivehill

Trevor, W. Sitting with the dead

Tudish, C. Jordan's stand

Ulitskaya, L. The beast

Unger, D. The writer's widow

Upadhyay, S. A refugee

Ward, A. E. The way the sky changed

Weaver, W. Bad blood

Welsh, I. Miss Arizona

West, D. The cottagers and Mrs. Carmody

West, D. Homecoming

West, D. The lean and the plenty

West, D. A matter of money

West, D. Mrs. Creel

Westlake, D. E. Never shake a family tree

Williams, J. Anodyne

Wingate, S. Knuckles

Xu Xi. Crying with Audrey Hepburn

Yates, D. Gophers

Yoon, P. Once the shore

The **widow's** breakfast. Hill, J.

The **widow's** might. Aird, C.

The **widows** of Tithhoor. Iyengar, V. L.

Widows' Walk. Frame, R.

Widow's Weeds. Vollmann, W. T.

Wieland, Mitch

Beware the pale horse comes riding

Wieland, M. God's dogs; a novel in stories

The bones of hagerman

Wieland, M. God's dogs; a novel in stories

TriQuarterly no125 p195-211 2006

God's dogs

Wieland, M. God's dogs; a novel in stories

The Sewanee Review v116 no4 p509-24 Fall 2008

Wilder, April
Three Men
Southwest Review v91 no4 p530-43 2006
Wilder, Thornton
Précautions Inutiles
The American Scholar v78 no3 p82-4 Summ
2009
WILDER, THORNTON, 1897-1975
Parodies, imitations, etc.
Langan, J. How the day runs down
The **wilderness**. Bradbury, R.
Wilderness. Thompson, J.
WILDERNESS AREAS
Peelle, L. Shadow on a weary land
Smith, M. Game drive
WILDERNESS SURVIVAL
Bukoski, A. Twelve below zero
Fromm, P. Snow cave
Haldeman, J. W. Expedition, with recipes
Proulx, A. Testimony of the donkey
Vann, D. Sukkwam Island
Wildfires. Johnson, G.
Wildflow. Báez, A.
The **Wildflower**. Huntington, C.
Wildgen, Michelle
The Butter Sculptor
StoryQuarterly v40 p324-40 2004
Cooperative
StoryQuarterly v42 p97-116 2006
Healer
Best new American voices 2004; guest editor
John Casey; series editors John Kulka and
Natalie Danford
You're Not You
Prairie Schooner v78 no4 p156-77 Wint 2004
Wilding, Michael
The Prisoner of Mount Warning
The Review of Contemporary Fiction v27 no3
p177-204 Fall 2007
The **Wildman**. Short Bull, J.
The **wilds** of Morris Township. Munro, A.
Wildwood. Díaz, J.
Wildwood. Sumner, M.
Wilhelm, Kate
No light in the window
Daughters of earth; feminist science fiction in
the twentieth century; edited by Justine
Larbalestier
Rules of the game
The World's finest mystery and crime stories,
fourth annual collection; edited by Ed
Gorman and Martin H. Greenberg
Wilhelm, Vinnie
Fauntleroy's Ghost
The Virginia Quarterly Review v85 no1 p180-
201 Wint 2009
In the Absence of Predators
Harvard Review (1992) no34 p70-84 2008
Wilking, Joan
Proper dress
Politically inspired; edited by Stephen Elliott;
assistant editor, Gabriel Kram; associate ed-
itors, Elizabeth Brooks [et al.]
Wilkins, Joe
Anniversary
The Georgia Review v63 no2 p265-6 Summ
2009

Wilkins, Kim
The forest
Dreaming again; thirty-five new stories cele-
brating the wild side of Australian fiction;
edited by Jack Dann
Wilkins, Mary Eleanor, 1852-1930 *See* Freeman,
Mary Eleanor Wilkins, 1852-1930
WILKINSON, JAMES, 1757-1825
About
Hambly, B. There shall your heart be also
The **will**. Hinton, S. E.
Will & testament. Vollmer, M.
Will build to suit. Harleman, A.
Will Power, Inc. Hasak-Lowy, T.
Will they kill you in Iraq? Swofford, A.
Will you always love me? Oates, J. C.
Willa. King, S.
Willett, Jincy
The best of Betty
Children playing before a statue of Hercules;
edited and introduced by David Sedaris
WILLIAM, PRINCE OF GREAT BRITAIN,
1982-
About
July, M. Majesty
William and Mary. Dahl, R.
WILLIAM AUGUSTUS, DUKE OF CUMBER-
LAND, 1721-1765
About
Carl, L. S. Over the sea from Skye
William Blake. Wormser, B.
Williams, Ann Joslin
Cascom Mountain Road
StoryQuarterly v42 p240-56 2006
Cold-Fire
Iowa Review v35 no3 p148-64 Wint
2005/2006
Williams, Charles
Et in Sempiternum pereant
Tales before Narnia; the roots of modern fan-
tasy and science fiction; edited by Douglas
A. Anderson
Williams, Conrad
68° 07' 15N, 31° 36' 44W
Fast ships, black sails; edited by Ann & Jeff
VanderMeer
The burn
Williams, C. Use once, then destroy
City in aspic
Williams, C. Use once, then destroy
Edge
Williams, C. Use once, then destroy
Excuse the unusual approach
Williams, C. Use once, then destroy
Known
Williams, C. Use once, then destroy
The light that passes through you
Williams, C. Use once, then destroy
MacCreadle's bike
Williams, C. Use once, then destroy
The machine
Williams, C. Use once, then destroy
Nearly people
Williams, C. Use once, then destroy
Nest of salt
Williams, C. Use once, then destroy
The night before
Williams, C. Use once, then destroy

Williams, Sean and Dix, Shane

Night of the dolls

Elemental; the Tsunami relief anthology; stories of science fiction and fantasy; [edited by] Steven Savile and Alethea Kontis; introduction by Arthur C. Clarke

Williams, Skye

PiP

Idaho Magazine v4 no10 p42-5 Jl 2005

Williams, Tad

The stranger's hands

Wizards; edited by Jack Dann and Gardner Dozois

Year's best fantasy 8; edited by David G. Hartwell, Kathryn Cramer

The tenth muse

The new space opera 2; edited by Gardner Dozois and Jonathan Strahan

Williams, Timothy

Something about Teddy

The Best American mystery stories, 2004; edited and with an introduction by Nelson DeMille; Otto Penzler, series editor

Williams, Walter Jon

Daddy's world

Nebula awards showcase 2002; edited by Kim Stanley Robinson

Rewired; the post-cyberpunk anthology; James Patrick Kelly & John Kessel, editors

The Green Leopard Plague

The Year's best science fiction: twenty-first annual collection; edited by Gardner Dozois

Nebula Awards showcase 2006; the year's best SF and fantasy; selected by the Science Fiction and Fantasy Writers of America; edited by Gardner Dozois

Incarnation day

The Year's best science fiction: twenty-fourth annual collection; edited by Gardner Dozois

Science fiction: the best of the year 2007 edition; edited by Rich Horton

Investments

The Year's best science fiction: twenty-second annual collection; edited by Gardner Dozois

Ligdan and the young pretender

This is my funniest; leading science fiction writers present their funniest stories ever; edited by Mike Resnick

Pinocchio

The Starry rift; tales of new tomorrows: an original science fiction anthology; edited by Jonathan Strahan

Send them flowers

The new space opera; edited by Gardner Dozois and Jonathan Strahan

Surfacing

The Best of the best, volume 2; 20 years of the best short science fiction novels; edited by Gardner Dozois

Williams, William

Levers

The Massachusetts Review v48 no2 p314-24 Summ 2007

WILLIAMS, WILLIAM CARLOS, 1883-1963
Parodies, imitations, etc.

Stevens, J. D. To the poet's wife

Williamson, Jack

A Christmas carol

Cat tales: fantastic feline fiction; edited by George H. Scithers

With folded hands

The Mammoth book of golden age science fiction; edited by Isaac Asimov, Charles G. Waugh and Martin H. Greenberg

WILLIAMSON, JACK, 1908-2006
About

Pohl, F. The mayor of Mare Tranq

Willis, C. Nonstop to Portales
Parodies, imitations, etc.

Di Filippo, P. Going abo

Weber, D. A certain talent

Williford, Lex

A Cross for Sister Mary Joseph

River Styx no68 p76-8 2004

Willingham, Bill

Fearless space pirates of the outer rings

The new space opera 2; edited by Gardner Dozois and Jonathan Strahan

Willis, Connie

Ado

Willis, C. The winds of Marble Arch and other stories; a Connie Willis compendium in which may be found personal correspondence, travel guides, references to royalty, weather reports, parking fines, and other violations, including matters of life and death (and afterwards), an epiphany or two, and an appendix

All my darling daughters

Willis, C. The winds of Marble Arch and other stories; a Connie Willis compendium in which may be found personal correspondence, travel guides, references to royalty, weather reports, parking fines, and other violations, including matters of life and death (and afterwards), an epiphany or two, and an appendix

At the Rialto

Willis, C. The winds of Marble Arch and other stories; a Connie Willis compendium in which may be found personal correspondence, travel guides, references to royalty, weather reports, parking fines, and other violations, including matters of life and death (and afterwards), an epiphany or two, and an appendix

Blued moon

Willis, C. The winds of Marble Arch and other stories; a Connie Willis compendium in which may be found personal correspondence, travel guides, references to royalty, weather reports, parking fines, and other violations, including matters of life and death (and afterwards), an epiphany or two, and an appendix

Cash crop

Willis, C. The winds of Marble Arch and other stories; a Connie Willis compendium in which may be found personal correspondence, travel guides, references to royalty, weather reports, parking fines, and other violations, including matters of life and death (and afterwards), an epiphany or two, and an appendix

Willis, Connie—*Continued*

Samaritan

> Willis, C. The winds of Marble Arch and other stories; a Connie Willis compendium in which may be found personal correspondence, travel guides, references to royalty, weather reports, parking fines, and other violations, including matters of life and death (and afterwards), an epiphany or two, and an appendix

Service for the burial of the dead

> Willis, C. The winds of Marble Arch and other stories; a Connie Willis compendium in which may be found personal correspondence, travel guides, references to royalty, weather reports, parking fines, and other violations, including matters of life and death (and afterwards), an epiphany or two, and an appendix

The soul selects her own society: invasion and repulsion

> This is my funniest; leading science fiction writers present their funniest stories ever; edited by Mike Resnick

The soul selects her own society: invasion and repulsion: a chronological reinterpretation of two of Emily Dickinson's poems: a Wellsian perspective

> Willis, C. The winds of Marble Arch and other stories; a Connie Willis compendium in which may be found personal correspondence, travel guides, references to royalty, weather reports, parking fines, and other violations, including matters of life and death (and afterwards), an epiphany or two, and an appendix

The winds of Marble Arch

> Willis, C. The winds of Marble Arch and other stories; a Connie Willis compendium in which may be found personal correspondence, travel guides, references to royalty, weather reports, parking fines, and other violations, including matters of life and death (and afterwards), an epiphany or two, and an appendix

Willis, Mary

> *See also* Walker, Mary Willis

Willoughby, Dale

Wrestling with Shadows

> *Dalhousie Review* v89 no1 p97-104 Spr 2009

Willow. Chekhov, A. P.

The **willow** landscape. Smith, C. A.

Willow pattern. Singer, J.

The **willow** walk. Lewis, S.

Willows Village. Gilb, D.

Wills, Aurelia

Wasps

> *The Kenyon Review* v30 no3 p167-77 Summ 2008

WILLS

Bierce, A. The famous Gilson bequest

Bilal, A. A voice from the earth

Bradbury, R. One for his lordship, and one for the road

Fuentes, C. Eternal father

Hinton, S. E. The will

Machado de Assis. The nurse

Maxwell, W. A final report

Nevins, F. M., Jr. A nightcap of Hemlock

Rand, K. Kisses sweeter than wine

Sutton, B. The rest of Esther

Swan, G. Uncle Lazarus

Vollmer, M. Will & testament

Wilson, Antoine

Everyone Else

> *The Paris Review* v46 p175-89 Fall 2004

Wilson, Caleb

Directions

> The Year's best fantasy and horror: twentieth annual collection; edited by Ellen Datlow and Kelly Link & Gavin J. Grant

Wilson, F. Paul (Francis Paul)

Aftershock

> Wilson, F. P. Aftershock & others; 19 oddities

Anna

> Wilson, F. P. Aftershock & others; 19 oddities

Aryans and Absinthe

> Wilson, F. P. Aftershock & others; 19 oddities

Dreams

> Wilson, F. P. Aftershock & others; 19 oddities

Foet

> Wilson, F. P. Aftershock & others; 19 oddities

Interlude at Duane's

> Thriller; edited by James Patterson

> The Deadly Bride; and 21 of the year's finest crime and mystery stories; including complete coverage of the year in mystery and crime fiction; edited by Ed Gorman and Martin H. Greenberg

> Wilson, F. P. Aftershock & others; 19 oddities

Itsy bitsy spider

> Wilson, F. P. Aftershock & others; 19 oddities

Lysing toward Bethlehem

> Wilson, F. P. Aftershock & others; 19 oddities

The November game

> Wilson, F. P. Aftershock & others; 19 oddities

Offshore

> Wilson, F. P. Aftershock & others; 19 oddities

Part of the game

> Dark delicacies; original tales of terror and the macabre by the world's greatest horror writers; edited by Del Howison and Jeff Gelb

> Wilson, F. P. Aftershock & others; 19 oddities

Please don't hurt me

> Wilson, F. P. Aftershock & others; 19 oddities

RAPED

> Wilson, F. P. Aftershock & others; 19 oddities

Sex slaves of the dragon tong

> Wilson, F. P. Aftershock & others; 19 oddities

Sole custody

> Wilson, F. P. Aftershock & others; 19 oddities

Winter, Douglas E.
Less than zombies
The living dead; edited by John Joseph Adams

Winter, Michael
Beyond the Overpass
The Walrus v5 no1 p78-9 Ja/F 2008
The Incinerator Incident
The Walrus v5 no8 p46-9 O/N 2008
What He Saw
The Walrus v3 no5 p80-3 Je 2006

WINTER
Luvaas, W. Silver thaw
Monson, A. Isle Royale
Novakovich, J. Snow powder
Watkins, S. Ice age
Winter. Dixon, S.
Winter, 1979. Chuculate, E.
Winter Admiral. Moorcock, M.
Winter at the world famous ice hotel. Meno, J.
Winter dog. MacLeod, A.
Winter Dogs. Barbarese, J. T.
Winter evenings. Colombi, M.
Winter Formal. Patterson, V.
Winter Honeymoon. Appel, J. M.
Winter life. Campbell, B. J.
Winter light. Burke, J. L.
Winter Light. Wolff, T.
Winter never quits. Johnson, T. G.
Winter outing. Pak, W.
Winter quarters. Waldrop, H.
Winter storm. MacLaverty, B.
A **winter** story. James, H.
Winter Worm, Summer Weed. Guo, X.
Winterborn. Williams, L.
Wintering. Kolendo, A.
Winterreise. Schutt, C.
Winter's king. Yolen, J.
Winter's wife. Hand, E.
Winterson, Jeanette
O'Brien's first Christmas
The Ecco book of Christmas stories; edited by Alberto Manguel
Winton, Tim
Abbreviation
Winton, T. The turning; new stories
Aquifer
Winton, T. The turning; new stories
Big world
Winton, T. The turning; new stories
Boner McPharlin's moll
Winton, T. The turning; new stories
Cockleshell
Winton, T. The turning; new stories
Harvard Review (1992) no27 p15-27 2004
Commission
Winton, T. The turning; new stories
Damaged goods
Winton, T. The turning; new stories
Defender
Winton, T. The turning; new stories
Family
Winton, T. The turning; new stories
Fog
Winton, T. The turning; new stories
Immunity
Winton, T. The turning; new stories
Long, clear view
Winton, T. The turning; new stories

Loonie and Me
The Paris Review v50 p13-22 Spr 2008
On her knees
Winton, T. The turning; new stories
Reunion
Winton, T. The turning; new stories
Sand
Winton, T. The turning; new stories
Small mercies
Winton, T. The turning; new stories
The turning
Winton, T. The turning; new stories
Wintrebert, Joëlle
Transfusion
The SFWA European hall of fame; sixteen contemporary masterpieces of science fiction from the continent; edited by James Morrow and Kathryn Morrow
Wira ni Wira. Kisia, A.
Wire. Williams, C.
Wired for life. Almond, S.
Wire's wire, until it's a body. Fincke, G.
WISCONSIN
Boast, W. Weather enough
Bukoski, A. Antoni Kosmatka resists the goddess of love
Bukoski, A. The case for bread and sausage
Bukoski, A. Gossamer bloom
Bukoski, A. Mission work
Bukoski, A. North of the port
Bukoski, A. One red rose on a new black dress
Bukoski, A. Report of the guardian of the sick
Bukoski, A. The shadow players
Bukoski, A. The Wally na Zdrowie show
Bukoski, A. Your hit parade
Ebenbach, D. H. Nothing ever happens in white America
Gilman, C. Okanoggan Falls
Hamilton, J. The short history of a prince [excerpt]
Herrmann, M. Stones
Hildebrand, J. Touching bottom
Kercheval, J. L. Alice in Dairyland
Kercheval, J. L. New rooms
Westcott, G. Goodbye, Wisconsin
Westcott, G. The whistling swan
Wisdom, Robert
The light and the dark
D. C. noir; edited by George Pelecanos
WISDOM
Singer, I. B. Logorihims
The **wisdom** of Eve. Orr, M.
The **wisdom** of having money. Effinger, G. A.
The **wisdom** of silence. Dunbar, P. L.
The **wisdom** of Solomon. Archer, J.
The **Wisdom** of Solomon. Margoshes, D.
Wise guy. Nebel, F.
Wisenberg, S. L.
Big Ruthie imagines sex without pain
What are you looking at?; the first fat fiction anthology; edited by Donna Jarrell and Ira Sukrungruang
The **wish**. Dahl, R.
The **wish**. Haines, C.
Wish. Rickards, J.
Wish fulfillment. Gaitskill, M.
The **wish** house. Kipling, R.
The **wish** in the fear. Zebrowski, G.
Wish upon a star. Merril, J.

Wolfe, Gene—*Continued*

Viewpoint

Wolfe, G. Starwater strains

Westwind

Wolfe, G. The best of Gene Wolfe; a definitive retrospective of his finest short fiction

Wolfe, Gene and Hopkins, B. (Brian)

Rattler

Wolfe, G. Starwater strains

This is my funniest 2; leading science fiction writers present their funniest stories ever; edited by Mike Resnick

Wolfe, Thomas

Only the dead know Brooklyn

Brooklyn noir 2; the classics; edited by Tim McLoughlin

WOLFE, THOMAS, 1900-1938

About

Bradbury, R. Forever and the Earth

Waldrop, H. You could go home again

Wolfe-Suarez, Ginger

A Trilogy in Form

N.Paradoxa v20 p21-5 2007

Wolff, Tobias

Awaiting orders

The Best American short stories, 2006; selected from U.S. and Canadian magazines by Ann Patchett with Katrina Kenison; with an introduction by Ann Patchett

Wolff, T. Our story begins; new and selected stories

Awake

The New Yorker v84 no25 p66-9 Ag 25 2008

The benefit of the doubt

Wolff, T. Our story begins; new and selected stories

Bullet in the brain

Children playing before a statue of Hercules; edited and introduced by David Sedaris

Wolff, T. Our story begins; new and selected stories

Beha, C. R. The Ecco anthology of contemporary American short fiction; selected by Joyce Carol Oates and Christopher R. Beha.

The chain

Wolff, T. Our story begins; new and selected stories

Deep kiss

Wolff, T. Our story begins; new and selected stories

The deposition

Wolff, T. Our story begins; new and selected stories

The New Yorker v81 no46 p74-9 F 6 2006

Desert breakdown, 1968

Wolff, T. Our story begins; new and selected stories

Down to bone

Wolff, T. Our story begins; new and selected stories

Firelight

The New Granta book of the American short story; edited and introduced by Richard Ford

Wolff, T. Our story begins; new and selected stories

Flyboys

Wolff, T. Our story begins; new and selected stories

Her dog

Wolff, T. Our story begins; new and selected stories

The Walrus v3 no9 p78-81 N 2006

Hunters in the snow

What are you looking at?; the first fat fiction anthology; edited by Donna Jarrell and Ira Sukrungruang

Wolff, T. Our story begins; new and selected stories

In the garden of North American martyrs

Wolff, T. Our story begins; new and selected stories

Lady's dream

Wolff, T. Our story begins; new and selected stories

Leviathan

Wolff, T. Our story begins; new and selected stories

The liar

Wolff, T. Our story begins; new and selected stories

A mature student

Wolff, T. Our story begins; new and selected stories

Mortals

Wolff, T. Our story begins; new and selected stories

Next door

Wolff, T. Our story begins; new and selected stories

The night in question

Wolff, T. Our story begins; new and selected stories

Nightingale

Wolff, T. Our story begins; new and selected stories

The other Miller

Wolff, T. Our story begins; new and selected stories

Powder

Wolff, T. Our story begins; new and selected stories

The rich brother

The best American Catholic short stories; a Sheed & Ward collection; edited by Daniel McVeigh and Patricia Schnapp

Wolff, T. Our story begins; new and selected stories

Sanity

Wolff, T. Our story begins; new and selected stories

Say yes

Wolff, T. Our story begins; new and selected stories

Smorgasbord

Wolff, T. Our story begins; new and selected stories

Soldier's joy

Wolff, T. Our story begins; new and selected stories

That room

Wolff, T. Our story begins; new and selected stories

WOMEN—*Continued*

Samperio, G. La mujer de la gabardina roja/The woman in the red coat

Scott, J. Stumble

Scott, J. Worry

Serao, M. Checchina's virtue

Shawl, N. Bird day

Shawl, N. But she's only a dream

Shepard, L. Larissa Miusov

Shields, C. Dying for love

Shields, C. Scenes

Shields, C. Times of sickness and health

Shields, C. Today is the day

Shomer, E. The hottest spot on earth

Soueif, A. Chez Milou

Tognazzini, A. Teresa's second dream

Valenzuela, L. The key

Wood, D. Vision in white

Yellin, T. Asher

Zoline, P. The heat death of the universe

Zoshchenko, M. A forgotten slogan

Employment

Sayles, J. Peeling

Psychology

Anapol, B. A stone house

Anderson, B. Real beach weather

Atwood, M. Monopoly

Bannister, I. Mrs Hyde frolics in the eel pit

Baxter, C. Ghosts

Bender, A. Dearth

Bender, A. The girl in the flammable skirt

Berg, E. Truth or dare

Boyle, T. C. Dogology

Braverman, K. Histories of the undead

Budnitz, J. Flush

Burgin, R. My black Rachmaninoff

Burnside, J. The bell ringer

Castillon, C. A pink baby

Clarke, B. The fund-raiser's dance card

Coleman, W. Backcity transit by day

Coleman, W. My brain's too tired to think

Coleman, W. Purgatory

Crane, E. My life is awesome! and great!

Davis, J. S. Rapture

De Varennes, Monique. Cabeza

Domecq, B. Gift of the jaguar

Engberg, S. Above the houses

Enright, A. Felix

Enright, A. Pale hands I loved, beside the Shalimar

Faber, M. The courage consort

Flora, K. Ninjettes

Fulton, J. The sleeping woman

Gabrielyan, N. Happiness

Gardam, J. Pangbourne

Gerber, M. J. The Cleopatra birds

Gildner, G. The great depression

Gordimer, N. Mother tongue

Gordon, M. City life

Graham, T. Fortune

Graham, T. Guest

Graham, T. In the realm of the senses

Graham, T. Kilter

Graham, T. Twins

Graver, E. The mourning door

Groff, L. Sir fleeting

Hadley, T. The enemy

Hayes, D. Hope

Hecht, J. Being and nothingness

Hecht, J. Happy trails to you

Heker, L. Spick and span

Hempel, A. The dog of the marriage

Hempel, A. Jesus is waiting

Hempel, A. The uninvited

Hempel, A. What were the white things?

Henriquez, C. Ashes

Henriquez, C. Yanina

Herrmann, M. Leonardo's baby

Holladay, C. C. The broken lake

Jamison, L. Quiet men

Johnson, G. Wildfires

Johnston, B. A. Anything that floats

Kasischke, L. If a stranger approaches you about carrying a foreign object with you onto the plane . . .

Kennedy, C. Dark roots

Kennedy, C. What thou and I did, till we loved

Kennedy, C. Wheelbarrow thief

Kercheval, J. L. Scarce

Kōno, T. Bone meat

Krasikov, S. Companion

Lago, S. Golden days of a queen of diamonds

Liebrecht, S. America

Liebrecht, S. Hiroshima

MacEnulty, P. The end

MacEnulty, P. The language of sharks

MacEnulty, P. Suburban hunger

Machado de Assis. A woman's arms

Macy, C. The secret vote

Macy, C. Taroudant

Malouf, D. Towards midnight

Martin, V. The change

Mason, B. A. Nancy Culpepper

McCafferty, J. Delivered

McGlynn, D. Sweet Texas angel

McGrath, P. Ground zero

McNett, M. Ozzie the burro

Messina, M. America 1911

Messina, M. Her father's house

Michalopoulou, A. Pointe

Miller, A. L. Swimming

Mitchell, J. C. Unknown donor

Molodowsky, K. The queen

Monis, V. O. Woes of the middle class

Munro, A. Runaway

Nayman, S. The house on Kronenstrasse

Oates, J. C. The instructor

Oates, J. C. Madison at Guignol

Oates, J. C. Suicide by fitness center

Oates, J. C. Tell me you forgive me?

Oates, J. C. Will you always love me?

Panning, A. Five reasons I miss the laundromat

Pflug, U. The wizard of Wardenclyffe

Ray, R. I can hear the grass grow

Reinhorn, H. Seashell

Riley, G. War story

Rivera-Valdés, S. The eighth fold

Robinson, R. Intersection

Rodgers, S. J. Bust

Ronk, M. C. Listening in

Ronk, M. C. Marybeth and the fish

Ronk, M. C. Old nylon bathrobes

Ronk, M. C. The photograph

Rosenfarb, C. A Friday in the life of Sarah Zonabend

Salter, J. My Lord you

Sampsell, K. Swimsuit issue

Schwarzschild, E. Drift

WOMEN—Psychology—*Continued*

Simpson, H. In the driver's seat
Simpson, H. The phlebotomist's love life
Smith, A. Writ
Solwitz, S. Ballerina
Stern, R. G. In a word, Trowbridge
Stewart, P. Snow angels
Stewart, P. Walk left stand right
Strom, D. Husband, wife
Strom, D. Neighbors
Strom, D. Walruses
Taha, M. A. A rose to Hafeeza's eyes
Tawada, Y. In front of Trang Tien Bridge
Tawada, Y. Saint George and the translator
Thompson, J. Wilderness
Thompson, J. The woman taken in adultery
Treat, J. Close your eyes
Treat, J. Make a nest
Trevor, W. Solitude
Tudish, C. The springhouse
Ulitskaya, L. Sonechka
Weiner, C. Boyfriends
West, D. Hannah Byde
Williams, J. The other week
Woronov, M. My name is Helen

Relation to other women

Alvarado, B. Comadres in the kitchen
Anderson, B. Day out
Berg, E. Mrs. Ethel Menafee and Mr. Bridie Stoltz
Boswell, R. No river wide
Brady, C. Scissors, paper, rock
Braverman, K. The neutral zone
Budnitz, J. Nadia
Cadigan, P. Stilled life
Capote, T. The bargain
Coleman, W. Darkness
Currans-Sheehan, T. The wild club
Dalton, Q. Dinner at Josette's
Davis, J. S. Blue moon
Davis, J. S. Witnessing
Desaulniers, J. Mothers without children
Divakaruni, C. B. The lives of strangers
Eisenberg, D. The custodian
Erdrich, L. Anna
Erdrich, L. Scales
Erpenbeck, J. Hale and hallowed
Feitell, M. And then you stand up
Flanagan, E. The last girlfriend
Franklin, E. In the herd of elephants
Fujino, C. Her room
Gaskell, W. Trying again
Gordon, M. The baby
Gordon, M. Conversations in prosperity
Gordon, M. Vision
Green, A. Food stamp
Hecht, J. Thank you for the mittens
Helms, B. Oysters
Hempel, A. The annex
Hempel, A. The day I had everything
Hempel, A. Rapture of the deep
Holthe, T. U. The three widows of Signor Alberto Moretti
Íṣ̣ọ̀l'olá, A. The uses of English
Johnson, G. Alliances of youth
Krysl, M. Belly
Le, N. Tehran calling
Lessing, D. M. The grandmothers
Levin, Z. Two girls and one suitor

Lunstrum, K. S. The bath
Macy, C. Annabel's mother
Macy, C. The red coat
Malouf, D. A trip to the Grundelsee
McGraw, E. The best friend
McGruder, K. Dirty laundry
Miller, A. L. Friends: an elegy
Miller, L. E. Kind
Miller, M. Elsie Riley
Molodowsky, K. Brayndl
Munro, A. Powers
Nayman, S. Dark urgings of the blood
Nelson, A. Shauntrelle
Nixon, C. Lunch at the Blacksmith
Noll, I. Fisherman's friend
Otis, M. The next door girl
Otis, M. Yes, yes, cherries
Paley, G. Friends
Richter, S. Duet
Robinson, R. The face-lift
Ronk, M. C. Hands
Salter, J. Such fun
Sayles, J. Casa de los Babys
Sayles, J. The Halfway Diner
Scego, I. "Faduma & Barni (April, 2003)"
Schumacher, J. Resurrection hockey
Schutt, C. Winterreise
Shields, C. Taking the train
Smith, M. Game drive
Soueif, A. I think of you
Soueif, A. Mandy
Stern, R. G. Troubles
Tabor, M. L. Rugalach
Thompson, J. Throw like a girl
Treat, J. Little bitches
Ulitskaya, L. Dauntless women of the Russian steppe
Vernon, O. Schevoski
Vollmer, M. Two women
Wang Ping. Forage
Weinman, S. Hen night
Welch, N. The cheating kind
Windley, C. The joy of life
Woronov, M. The perfect marriage
Woronov, M. The white plains of Western Avenue

Social conditions

See also Feminism

Baum, L. F. Aunt 'Phroney's boy
Bierce, A. "A bad woman"
Billingslea-Brown, A. J. Moonshot
Bluestein, E. Hamburger School
Cherry, K. Where she was
Douglas, C. N. Strangers in a strange land
Gauss, M. A life like Maggy's
Gordon, M. The dancing party
Holladay, C. C. The burning
Irvine, A. C. Pictures from an expedition
Judah, S. Hannah and Benjamin
Judah, S. Shame under the chuppah
L'Amour, L. By the ruins of "El Walarieh"
Levin, Z. "Mame"
Ma Jian. The woman and the blue sky
Machado de Assis. Dona Paula
Messina, M. Caterina's loom
Messina, M. Dainty shoes
Molodowsky, K. Unhappy celebrations
Monk, B. Flying lesson
Mordecai, P. Crucial concern

WOMEN—Social conditions—*Continued*
  Mueenuddin, D. In other rooms, other wonders
  Mueenuddin, D. Saleema
  Nunez, E. Lucille
  Okorafor, N. When scarabs multiply
  Opatoshu, J. A house on Gorek Street
  Pinski, D. At the attorney's
  Reisen, A. The experienced bride
  Resnick, M. The Bull Moose at bay
  Rosa, J. G. Those Lopes
  Rushdie, S. The firebird's nest
  Soueif, A. Melody
  Sundaresan, I. The faithful wife
  Sundaresan, I. Hunger
  Waberi, A. A. A woman and a half
  Zoshchenko, M. Domestic bliss
WOMEN, BLACK *See* African American women
WOMEN, JEWISH *See* Jewish women
WOMEN, MUSLIM *See* Muslim women
WOMEN AIR PILOTS
  Patterson, S. Aground and aloft
WOMEN ARCHEOLOGISTS
  Kiernan, C. R. From cabinet 34, drawer 6
WOMEN ARTISTS
  Boyd, W. Beulah Berlin, an A-Z
  Colombi, M. Learn a trade for a rainy day
  Gabrielyan, N. Bee heaven
  Gabrielyan, N. Master of the grass
  Kitahara, A. Forget-me-not
  Lord, N. Candace counts coup
  MacLaverty, B. Up the coast
  Raymond, J. Words and things
WOMEN ASTRONAUTS
  Swanwick, M. Ginungagap
WOMEN AUTHORS
  Adichie, C. N. Jumping Monkey Hill
  Auchincloss, L. The omelette and the egg
  Bingham, S. That winter
  Blackwell, K. My first wedding
  Chekhov, A. P. Drama
  Finch, P. Bethany's wood
  Gaitskill, M. The agonized face
  Gaitskill, M. Today I'm yours
  Gardam, J. Babette
  Gordon, M. The translator's husband
  Guest, J. Eminent domain
  Hand, E. The Saffron gatherers
  Klassen, S. A perfect location
  Lane, J. Beyond the river
  Macy, C. Bad ghost
  Muller, M. The cracks in the sidewalk
  Niranjana, A. A day with Charulata
  Oates, J. C. Dear Joyce Carol,
  Oates, J. C. My Warszawa: 1980
  Oates, J. C. A Princeton idyll
  Samuels, M. Ghorla
  Serna, E. Tesoro viviente/Living treasure
  Stern, R. G. Cooley's version
WOMEN CLERGY
  Rosen, J. First date
Women I have made cry.
WOMEN IN BUSINESS *See* Businesswomen
WOMEN IN POLITICS
  Singer, I. B. The conference
Women I've known. Johnson, G.
WOMEN JOURNALISTS
  Groff, L. Delicate edible birds
  Higgins, G. V. Warm for September
  Just, W. S. Nora

  Kiely, B. The weavers at the mill
  Lee, A. Anthropology
  Porter, K. A. Pale horse, pale rider
  Shibli, A. Faint hints of tranquillity
  Singer, M. Body count
  Wood, D. Rosie Little's brilliant career
WOMEN LAWYERS
  O'Shaughnessy, P. Juggernaut
  Vogt, M. D. Surviving Toronto
  Wheat, C. The only good judge
Women of Impeccable Wit. Donohue, M.
Women of the Federation. García González, F.
WOMEN PAINTERS
  Martin, J. Work
WOMEN PHOTOGRAPHERS
  Hecht, J. Being and nothingness
  Hecht, J. Happy trails to you
WOMEN PHYSICIANS
  Fincke, G. Sorry I worried you
  Goliger, G. Maladies of the inner ear
  Jones, E. P. Root worker
  Ohlin, A. Transcription
  Sundaresan, I. Shelter of rain
  Tolstaia, T. The poet and the muse
  Working, R. Slava
WOMEN POETS
  Kiely, B. The little wrens and robins
  Singer, I. B. The interview
WOMEN SCIENTISTS
  Apple, M. Proton decay
  Klages, E. Time gypsy
  Margulis, L. Gases
  Unger, D. Leslie and Sam
  Vaswani, N. The pelvis series
WOMEN SCULPTORS
  Yates, R. Oh, Joseph, I'm so tired
WOMEN SOLDIERS
  DeMille, N. Rendezvous
  Dietz, W. C. The run to Hardscrabble Station
  Emshwiller, C. Boys
  Moon, E. Hand to hand
Women who don't tell war stories. Swan, G.
WOMEN'S CLUBS *See* Clubs
WOMEN'S LIBERATION MOVEMENT *See*
  Feminism
Wonder. Driscoll, J.
Wonderful girl. LaBrie, A.
Wonders. King, O.
Wonders never cease. Ohlin, A.
Wonders of the universe. Eschbach, A.
Wonderwall. Hand, E.
Wondrous strange. Koënings, N. S.
Wong, Kenneth
  Movie Nights in Rangoon
    Agni no65 p134-43 2007
Won't You Stay, Please? Eggers, P.
Wood, Anne-E.
  The Flood
    New Letters v74 no2 p19-23 2008
Wood, Danielle
  The anatomy of wolves
    Wood, D. Rosie Little's cautionary tales for
      girls
  The deflowering of Rosie Little
    Wood, D. Rosie Little's cautionary tales for
      girls
  The depthlessness of soup
    Wood, D. Rosie Little's cautionary tales for
      girls

Woolrich, Cornell—*Continued*
Death in the Yoshiwara
    Woolrich, C. Night and fear; a centenary collection of stories by Cornell Woolrich; edited with an introduction by Francis M. Nevins
The death rose
    Woolrich, C. Night and fear; a centenary collection of stories by Cornell Woolrich; edited with an introduction by Francis M. Nevins
Detective William Brown
    Woolrich, C. Night and fear; a centenary collection of stories by Cornell Woolrich; edited with an introduction by Francis M. Nevins
The dilemma of the dead lady
    The Black Lizard big book of pulps; edited by Otto Penzler
Double feature
    Woolrich, C. Night and fear; a centenary collection of stories by Cornell Woolrich; edited with an introduction by Francis M. Nevins
Endicott's girl
    Woolrich, C. Night and fear; a centenary collection of stories by Cornell Woolrich; edited with an introduction by Francis M. Nevins
The fatal footlights
    Woolrich, C. Night and fear; a centenary collection of stories by Cornell Woolrich; edited with an introduction by Francis M. Nevins
The heavy sugar
    Woolrich, C. Night and fear; a centenary collection of stories by Cornell Woolrich; edited with an introduction by Francis M. Nevins
New York blues
    Woolrich, C. Night and fear; a centenary collection of stories by Cornell Woolrich; edited with an introduction by Francis M. Nevins
    Manhattan noir 2; the classics; edited by Lawrence Block
Rear window [variant title: It had to be murder]
    Adaptations: from short story to big screen; 35 great stories that have inspired great films; edited by Stephanie Harrison
Through a dead man's eye
    Woolrich, C. Night and fear; a centenary collection of stories by Cornell Woolrich; edited with an introduction by Francis M. Nevins
Two murders, one crime
    The Black Lizard big book of pulps; edited by Otto Penzler
You bet your life
    Woolrich, C. Night and fear; a centenary collection of stories by Cornell Woolrich; edited with an introduction by Francis M. Nevins
Woolson, Constance Fenimore
Dorothy
    Woolson, C. F. Constance Fenimore Woolson: selected stories & travel narratives; edited by Victoria Brehm and Sharon L. Dean

A Florentine experiment
    Woolson, C. F. Constance Fenimore Woolson: selected stories & travel narratives; edited by Victoria Brehm and Sharon L. Dean
Jeannette
    Woolson, C. F. Constance Fenimore Woolson: selected stories & travel narratives; edited by Victoria Brehm and Sharon L. Dean
"Miss Grief"
    Woolson, C. F. Constance Fenimore Woolson: selected stories & travel narratives; edited by Victoria Brehm and Sharon L. Dean
Rodman the keeper
    Woolson, C. F. Constance Fenimore Woolson: selected stories & travel narratives; edited by Victoria Brehm and Sharon L. Dean
The South Devil
    Woolson, C. F. Constance Fenimore Woolson: selected stories & travel narratives; edited by Victoria Brehm and Sharon L. Dean
St. Clair Flats
    Woolson, C. F. Constance Fenimore Woolson: selected stories & travel narratives; edited by Victoria Brehm and Sharon L. Dean
A transplanted boy
    Woolson, C. F. Constance Fenimore Woolson: selected stories & travel narratives; edited by Victoria Brehm and Sharon L. Dean
Woon, Yvonne
Siblings
    Boston Review v31 no5 p43-4 S/O 2006
The **word**. Chase, M.
The **Word**. Nabakov, V.
The **word** "Mermaid" written on an index card. Lain, D.
The **Word** of the Day Is "Trust". Kitchen, M.
Word Rage. Luvaas, W.
The **word** "random", deliberately repeated. Shirley, J.
A **word** that rhymes with hair. Hawes, L.
A **word** with the boy. Updike, D.
Words. Charters, D.
Words. Shields, C.
Words and things. Raymond, J.
Words of power. Yolen, J.
Words to live by. LaBrie, A.
Words, words, words!. Brandner, G.
WORDSWORTH, DOROTHY, 1771-1855
                    About
    Mason, B. A. The prelude
WORDSWORTH, WILLIAM, 1770-1850
                    About
    Mason, B. A. The prelude
Wordwatching. James, G.
WORK
    Brown, K. Unction
    Monk, B. Flying lesson
Work. Johnson, D.
Work. Martin, J.
Work and Industry in the Northern Midwest. Magnussen, L.
The **work** of art. Biguenet, J.
A **work** of art. Blish, J.
Working, Russell
Dear leader
    Working, R. The Irish martyr
Halloween, via dolorosa
    Working, R. The Irish martyr

Working, Russell—*Continued*
Help
  Working, R. The Irish martyr
Inmates
  Working, R. The Irish martyr
The Irish martyr
  The Pushcart Prize XXIX: best of the small presses 2005; edited by Bill Henderson with the Pushcart Prize editors
  Working, R. The Irish martyr
Perjury
  Working, R. The Irish martyr
The sky ranch
  Working, R. The Irish martyr
Slava
  Working, R. The Irish martyr
The tin man
  Working, R. The Irish martyr
The world in the first year of the wire
  Working, R. The Irish martyr
Working for a living. Munro, A.
A **working** man's apocrypha. Luvaas, W.
Working out with Kafka. Tognazzini, A.
The **working** slob's prayer. Brite, P. Z.
Working the Crossword. Mueller, W. E.
Workout. Bukowski, C.
WORKS PROGRESS ADMINISTRATION (U.S.) *See* United States. Works Progress Administration
A **workshop** for health. Zoshchenko, M.
World champion. Keret, E.
The **world** in the first year of the wire. Working, R.
The **world** is tilting. Tsutsui, Y.
The **world** laughs in flowers. Van Booy, S.
A **world** more real. Yeaman, R. N.
World of a thousand colors. Silverberg, R.
The **World** of Cheese. O'Neill, J.
World of gas. Campbell, B. J.
World of the wars. McAllister, B.
The **world** to come. Newman, L.
A **world** waiting. Finch, S.
WORLD WAR, 1914-1918
Porter, K. A. Pale horse, pale rider
Resnick, M. Over there
Sillitoe, A. The sniper
Todd, C. Home coming
Vonnegut, K. Great day
  Casualties
Oates, J. C. The master at St. Bartholomew's hospital, 1914-1916
  Naval operations
Moon, E. Tradition
  Belgium
Robinson, P. Shadow on the water
  France
Boyd, W. Visions fugitives
Foxwell, E. No man's land
Maguire, G. The oakthing
  Germany
Parry, O. Appearences
  United States
Working, R. The world in the first year of the wire
WORLD WAR, 1939-1945
Auchincloss, L. An hour and a lifetime
Boyd, W. The ghost of a bird
Bradbury, R. Bang! You're dead!
Connell, E. S. Proctor Bemis

Effinger, G. A. Target: Berlin! The role of the Air Force four-door hardtop
Gardiner, J. R. Morse operator
Garrett, G. P. A story goes with it
Gordimer, N. A frivolous woman
Helprin, M. Charlotte of the Utrechtseweg
Helprin, M. Reconstruction
Hughes, M. The devil you don't
Irvine, A. C. The golems of Detroit
L'Amour, L. Flight to the north
L'Amour, L. Mission to Siberut
L'Amour, L. South of Suez
L'Amour, L. Where there's fighting
L'Amour, L. Wings over Brazil
Lupoff, R. A. Brackish waters
Mina, J. I shall return
Swan, G. Women who don't tell war stories
Vonnegut, K. Happy birthday, 1951
Vonnegut, K. Spoils
  Aerial operations
Dahl, R. An African story
Dahl, R. Beware of the dog
Dahl, R. Death of an old man
Dahl, R. Only this
Dahl, R. A piece of cake
Dahl, R. Someone like you
Dahl, R. They shall not grow old
  Atrocities
    See also Holocaust, Jewish (1933-1945)
Levi, J. The scrimshaw violin
  Collaborationists
Chon, K. Kapitan Ri
  Jews
    See also Holocaust, Jewish (1933-1945)
Charyn, J. Letter from Mogilev
Frankel-Zaltzman, P. A natural death
Singer, I. B. The manuscript
  Naval operations
L'Amour, L. West from Singapore
  Prisoners and prisons
    See also Concentration camps
Daughtry, P. Tinker's turn
Levi, P. The death of Marinese
Vonnegut, K. Brighten up
Vonnegut, K. Guns before butter
  Secret service
L'Amour, L. Down Paagumene way
L'Amour, L. East of Gorontalo
L'Amour, L. From here to Banggai
L'Amour, L. The house of Qasavara
L'Amour, L. On the road to Amurang
L'Amour, L. Voyage to Tobolai
L'Amour, L. Well of the unholy light
Schweighofer, P. Seebohm's cap
  Underground movements
Black, C. The redhead
Bolaño, R. Henry Simon Leprince
Levi, P. The death of Marinese
Shepard, J. The assassination of Reinhard Heydrich
Weil, G. Little Sonja Rosenkranz
  Australia
Malouf, D. At Schindler's
Malouf, D. Sally's story
  Belgium
McNally, T. M. Bastogne
  England
Gardam, J. The flight path
MacLeod, I. The chop girl

WORLD WAR, 1939-1945—England—*Continued*
Pearlman, E. If love were all
Sillitoe, A. A scream of toys
Templeton, E. The darts of Cupid
Willis, C. Fire watch
Willis, C. Jack

France
Black, C. The redhead
Dymond, J. Cherubs
Groff, L. Delicate edible birds

Germany
Anaya, R. A. The captain
Vonnegut, K. Just you and me, Sammy

Greece
Dahl, R. Katina
Dahl, R. Yesterday was beautiful
Michaels, A. Fugitive pieces [excerpt]
Valtinos, T. Addiction to nicotine

Hungary
Déry, T. Games of the underworld
Déry, T. Philemon and Baucis
Dobozy, T. Tales of Hungarian resistance

Italy
Helprin, M. A brilliant idea and his own

Japan
L'Amour, L. Flight to Enbetu
Yasuoka, S. The king's ears
Yasuoka, S. The medal

Pacific Ocean
Helprin, M. The Pacific
L'Amour, L. Night over the Solomons
L'Amour, L. West from Singapore

Philippines
Abbott, L. K. The end of grief
Sanders, W. Not fade away

Russia
Klimasewiski, M. N. Tyrants

Solomon Islands
Connell, E. S. Guadalcanal [variant title: The Marine]

Ukraine
Odrach, T. The night before Christmas

United States
Ardai, C. The home front
Burke, J. L. The burning of the flag
Doogan, M. War can be murder
Gorman, E. Crystal's big night
Sayers, V. Walker Evans is a spy on the Lexington Avenue local
Wilson, R., Jr. Hard times

World War II Holiday Memories. Edwinson, W.
World without end, amen. Steele, A. M.
Worlds Apart. Fitzgerald, P.
The **world's** greatest fishermen. Erdrich, L.
The **World's** Last Englishman. Makkai, R.
Worlds of possibilities. Cadigan, P.
The **world's** worst fairy godmother. Coville, B.
Worley, Erin Brooks
Grove
New stories from the South: the year's best, 2006; selected from U.S. magazines by Allan Gurganus with Kathy Pories; with an introduction by Allan Gurganus
Gettysburg Review v18 no1 p65-70 Spr 2005
The **worm** turns. Benford, G.
Worms of the earth. Howard, R. E.

Wormser, Baron
Weldon's Song
The Sewanee Review v114 no4 p535-50 Fall 2006
William Blake
Southwest Review v91 no1 p61-77 2006
Woronov, Mary
The alligator man
Woronov, M. Blind love
The Amazon
Woronov, M. Blind love
Jack, part one
Woronov, M. Blind love
Jack, part two
Woronov, M. Blind love
Looking for love
Woronov, M. Blind love
Martha
Woronov, M. Blind love
Mobster
Woronov, M. Blind love
My name is Helen
Woronov, M. Blind love
The perfect marriage
Woronov, M. Blind love
The rise and fall
Woronov, M. Blind love
The unsinkable Mr. Raft
Woronov, M. Blind love
Wall Street
Woronov, M. Blind love
We were Jewish for a little while
Woronov, M. Blind love
The white plains of Western Avenue
Woronov, M. Blind love
Worry. Scott, J.
Worship. Serros, M.
Worship for shut-ins. Meacham, R.
The **worst** (1960-1971). Cooper, D.
Worst-Case Scenario. Wilson, K.
The **worst** degree of unforgivable. Montemarano, N.
The **Worst** Poison. Oberman, S.
Worthy to be one of us. Card, O. S.
Wortman, David
The Six-dollar Box of Cereal
Southern Humanities Review v42 no3 p250-62 Summ 2008
Wortman, Jennifer
Seminar
The Massachusetts Review v46 no1 p48-61 Spr 2005
Slumber Party
The North American Review v290 no5 p18-23 S/O 2005
Wortsman, Peter
(tr.) See Altenberg, Peter
Wound Man and horned melon go to Hell. Brite, P. Z.
The **wounded**. Butner, R.
The **wounded** hand. Rosavo, N.
WOUNDS AND INJURIES
Almond, S. I am as I am
Bear, E. Gone to flowers
Crowther, P. Even beggars would ride
Déry, T. Philemon and Baucis
Grimes, C. Discourse on the sublime and the beautiful
Haringa, J. M. A perfect and unmappable grace

Wynbush, Octavia B.
The noose
    "Tell it to us easy" and other stories; a complete short fiction anthology of African American women writers in Opportunity magazine, (1923-1948); edited by Judith Musser.

Wynne, Frank
(tr.) See Sansal, Boualem

WYOMING
Bishop, T. Bootleggers
Bishop, T. Courting Miss Ellen
Bishop, T. The great Mormon cricket fly-fishing festival
Bishop, T. A Hoover steak
Duncklee, J. Soul of the hob-nailed boot
King, S. Willa
McKinstray, S. No one here says what they mean
Proulx, A. The contest
Proulx, A. Deep-blood-greasy-bowl
Proulx, A. Dump junk
Proulx, A. Family man
Proulx, A. Florida rental
Proulx, A. The great divide
Proulx, A. The half-skinned steer
Proulx, A. The hellhole
Proulx, A. The Indian wars refought
Proulx, A. Man crawling out of trees
Proulx, A. The old badger game
Proulx, A. People in hell just want a drink of water
Proulx, A. The sagebrush kid
Proulx, A. Summer of the hot tubs
Proulx, A. Testimony of the donkey
Proulx, A. Them old cowboy songs
Proulx, A. Tits-up in a ditch
Proulx, A. The trickle down effect
Proulx, A. The Wamsutter wolf
Proulx, A. What kind of furniture would Jesus pick?
Rand, K. Bridge O' doom
Rand, K. Crickets everywhere
Troy, J. The order of things
Wingate, S. Me and Paul
      Frontier and pioneer life
    See Frontier and pioneer life—Wyoming

Wyss, Geoff
Kids make their own houses
    New stories from the South: the year's best, 2006; selected from U.S. magazines by Allan Gurganus with Kathy Pories; with an introduction by Allan Gurganus

X

X. Abbott, L. K.
X. Finnamore, S.
X number of possibilities. Scott, J.
Xarms, Daniil *See* Kharms, Daniil, 1905-1942
Xeethra. Smith, C. A.
Xerox man. Stavans, I.
Xmas in Las Vegas. Johnson, D.
Xu Xi
Crying with Audrey Hepburn
    Manhattan noir; edited by Lawrence Block

Famine
    The O. Henry Prize stories, 2006; edited and with an introduction by Laura Furman; jurors: Kevin Brockmeier, Francine Prose, Colm Toibin
    Ploughshares v30 no4 p166-79 Wint 2004/2005
XXXL. Erdrich, L.

Y

Y. Erdrich, L.
The **Y** incision. Niles, S.
y = mx+b. Altschul, A. F.
YACHTS AND YACHTING
Clayton, J. J. The promised land
Mooney, C. Falling
Yamada, Amy *See* Yamada, Eimi, 1959-
Yamada, Eimi
Fiesta
    Inside and other short fiction; Japanese women by Japanese women; with a foreword by Ruth Ozeki; compiled by Cathy Layne
Yanagida Kakunoshin.
Yáñez, Mirta
When Life Gives You Lemons
    The Review of Contemporary Fiction v26 no3 p110-13 Fall 2006
Yang Xianhui
I Hate the Moon
    The Literary Review (Madison, N.J.) v51 no1 p31-52 Fall 2007
Yangban. Kim, J.
YANGTZE RIVER VALLEY (CHINA)
Zhu Wen. A boat crossing
Yanina. Henriquez, C.
Yanique, Tiphanie
The bridge
    Pushcart prize XXXII: best of the small presses 2008; edited by Bill Henderson with the Pushcart Prize editors
Gita Pinky Manachandi
    Trinidad noir; edited by Lisa Allen-Agostini & Jeanne Mason.
How to Escape from a Leper Colony
    Boston Review v31 no3 p37-40 My/Je 2006
YANKEE STADIUM (NEW YORK, N.Y.)
Baker, K. The cheers like waves
YANKEES (BASEBALL TEAM) *See* New York Yankees (Baseball team)
Yankele's dream. Gordin, J.
Yankelevich, Matvei
(tr.) See Kharms, Daniil
YAO MING, 1980-
      About
Apple, M. Yao's chick
Yao's chick. Apple, M.
YAQUI INDIANS
Endrezze, A. Grandfather sun falls in love with a moon-faced woman
Yarbro, Chelsea Quinn
A gentleman of the old school
    Dark delicacies; original tales of terror and the macabre by the world's greatest horror writers; edited by Del Howison and Jeff Gelb

Yellin, Tamar—*Continued*
  Issachar
    Yellin, T. Tales of the ten lost tribes
  Manasseh
    Yellin, T. Tales of the ten lost tribes
  Naphtali
    Yellin, T. Tales of the ten lost tribes
  Reuben
    Yellin, T. Tales of the ten lost tribes
  Simeon
    Yellin, T. Tales of the ten lost tribes
  Strangers on a train
    Text: Ur; the new book of masks; [edited by
      Forrest Aguirre]
  Zebulun
    Yellin, T. Tales of the ten lost tribes
Yellow card man. Bacigalupi, P.
Yellow Mama's long weekend. Carcaterra, L.
Yellow raft. Connell, E. S.
Yellow sandals. Biller, M.
Yellow snow. Stross, C.
The **Yellow** Streetcar with No Name. Tarnawsky,
  Y.
Yellow teeth. Nevill, A. L. G.
The **yellow** tent on the roof. Shiina, M.
Yellowhead. Dann, J. and Zebrowski, G.
Yellowjack's game of craps. Dunbar, P. L.
Yellowstone. Harper, B.
YELLOWSTONE NATIONAL PARK
  Bierce, A. Mr. Jim Beckwourth's adventure
  Seton, E. T. Johnny Bear
  Vollmer, M. Oh land of national paradise, how
    glorious are thy bounties
Yemni, Sadik
  Burn and go
    Istanbul noir; edited by Mustafa Ziyalan &
      Amy Spangler; translated by Amy Spangler
      & Mustafa Ziyalan.
Yepsen, Roger
  Suet Soot Suit
    The Southern Review (Baton Rouge, La.) v41
      no2 p427-43 Spr 2005
Yes I am a virgin. Hernandez, L.
Yes, yes, cherries. Otis, M.
Yesterday. Wilbur, E.
Yesterday after the storm . . . Luvaas, W.
Yesterday was beautiful. Dahl, R.
Yesterday's dreams. Gorman, E.
Yesterday's news. Corso, P.
Yesterday's weather. Enright, A.
YETI
  Schwartz, D. J. The ichthyomancer writes his
    friend with an account of the Yeti's birth-
    day party
  Shepard, J. Ancestral legacies
Yeyuka. Egan, G.
Yezierska, Anzia
  Hester Street
    Inside the hornet's head; an anthology of
      Jewish American writing; edited by Jerome
      Charyn
YFL–500. Wilson, R. C.
A **Yiddish-speaking** socialist. Libin, Z.
YOGA
  Cherne, B. The conversion
  Mandelbaum, P. Yoga is a personal journey
  Watkins, S. Bocky-Bocky
Yoga is a personal journey. Mandelbaum, P.
YOKOHAMA (JAPAN) *See* Japan—Yokohama

Yoko's light. Rivas, M.
Yolen, Jane
  Allerleirauh
    Yolen, J. Once upon a time (she said); edited
      by Priscilla Olson
  The barbarian and the queen: thirteen views
    Yolen, J. Once upon a time (she said); edited
      by Priscilla Olson
  Become a warrior
    Yolen, J. Once upon a time (she said); edited
      by Priscilla Olson
  The bird of time
    Yolen, J. Once upon a time (she said); edited
      by Priscilla Olson
  The boy who drew unicorns
    Yolen, J. Once upon a time (she said); edited
      by Priscilla Olson
  The boy who sang for death
    Yolen, J. Once upon a time (she said); edited
      by Priscilla Olson
  Brother Hart
    Yolen, J. Once upon a time (she said); edited
      by Priscilla Olson
  The cat bride
    Yolen, J. Once upon a time (she said); edited
      by Priscilla Olson
  Dawn-strider
    Yolen, J. Once upon a time (she said); edited
      by Priscilla Olson
  Dick W. and his Pussy, or Tess and her Ade-
    quate Dick
    This is my funniest; leading science fiction
      writers present their funniest stories ever;
      edited by Mike Resnick
  Evian steel
    Yolen, J. Once upon a time (she said); edited
      by Priscilla Olson
  The face in the cloth
    Yolen, J. Once upon a time (she said); edited
      by Priscilla Olson
  The faery flag
    Yolen, J. Once upon a time (she said); edited
      by Priscilla Olson
  The fisherman's wife
    Yolen, J. Once upon a time (she said); edited
      by Priscilla Olson
  Flight
    Yolen, J. Once upon a time (she said); edited
      by Priscilla Olson
  The foxwife
    Yolen, J. Once upon a time (she said); edited
      by Priscilla Olson
  The girl who cried flowers
    Yolen, J. Once upon a time (she said); edited
      by Priscilla Olson
  The golden balls
    Yolen, J. Once upon a time (she said); edited
      by Priscilla Olson
  Green plague
    Yolen, J. Once upon a time (she said); edited
      by Priscilla Olson
  The gwynhfar
    Yolen, J. Once upon a time (she said); edited
      by Priscilla Olson
  Happy dens; or, A day in the old wolves' home
    Yolen, J. Once upon a time (she said); edited
      by Priscilla Olson

Yorke, Margaret
The woman from Marlow
The Detection collection; edited by Simon Brett
YORKSHIRE (ENGLAND) *See* England—Yorkshire
The **Yoshi** Compound: a story of post-Waco Texas. Pierce, T. J.
Yoss
The red bridge
Havana noir; edited by Achy Obejas
Yost, David
Stumpy
South Carolina Review v40 no1 p33-8 Fall 2007
You. Mozetič, B.
You are as brave as Vincent Van Gogh. Barthelme, D.
You are cordially invited. Barthelme, D.
You are here. Ohlin, A.
You are not my husband. Potwatka, A.
You Are So Mine. Debeljak, E. J.
You are what you drive. Weaver, W.
You Are Your Own Very Unique Snowflake. Clegg, S. A.
You Be Wing. Davenport, S.
You bet your life. Woolrich, C.
You Can Have It All. Bundy, C.
You can never forget. Messinger, J.
You can't lose. Block, L.
You Can't Not Feel It. Guixà, P.
You could go anywhere now. Buckler, E.
You could go home again. Waldrop, H.
You could have it all. Lane, J.
You drive. Schutt, C.
You Girls Have the Loveliest Legs. Cook, R.
You go when you can no longer stay. Kay, J.
You go where it takes you. Ballingrud, N.
You have made quite a purchase. Kun, M.
You have never been here. Rickert, M.
You Know You've Made It When They Hate You. Upton, L.
You love that dog. Stefaniak, M. H.
You may already be a winner. Maron, M.
You must be this happy to enter. Crane, E.
You must change your life. Gilchrist, E.
You never see Apaches . . . [variant title: Eight days from Willcox] Leonard, E.
You only want to scare her. Herrmann, M.
You want I should whack monkey boy? Adcock, T.
You were neither hot nor cold, but lukewarm, and so I spit you out. Spindler, C. and Nelson, D. E.
"**You** wicked wooden eyes, what are you looking at?". Lamri, T.
You will hear the locust sing. Hill, J.
You won't remember this. Blackwell, K.
Youghiogeny. Shade, E.
You'll always remember me. Fisher, S.
You'll be a woman, my girl. Castillon, C.
You'll both be very happy. Rivas, M.
You'll catch your death of colds. Fawcett, B.
You'll die laughing. Davis, N.
Youmans, Marly
Concealment shoes
Salon fantastique; edited and with an introduction by Ellen Datlow and Terri Windling

An incident at Agate Beach
The Year's best fantasy and horror: nineteenth annual collection; edited by Ellen Datlow and Kelly Link & Gavin J. Grant
Young, Bryan
On the Ferry to St Christophe
Dalhousie Review v88 no3 p359-70 Aut 2008
Young, Doselle
Housework
The darker mask; edited by Gary Phillips and Christopher Chambers.
Young, Hardin
1%
Playboy's college fiction; a collection of 21 years of contest winners; edited by Alice K. Turner; foreword by Thom Jones
Young, Mark Leiren- *See* Leiren-Young, Mark
Young, Robert Clark
The Richest Girl in the World
Southern Humanities Review v39 no2 p143-65 Spr 2005
Young, Robert F.
The first Mars mission
Fourth planet from the sun; tales of Mars from The Magazine of Fantasy & Science Fiction; edited by Gordon Van Gelder
Young. Schutt, C.
The **young** Apollo. Auchincloss, L.
Young bodies. Raymond, J.
Young Body Dream. Almond, S.
Young Francis Whitehead. Maxwell, W.
Young H Saved from Infamy. Maso, C.
Young Invention. Beebe, L.
Young Isaac. Charyn, J.
The **young** lady. O'Shaughnessy, P.
The **young** man who surprised the watchman. Kharms, D.
A **young** man with prospects. Card, O. S.
Young people today. Richter, S.
Young Waitresses. Almond, S.
Youngblood, Shay
The Crying Bride
Callaloo v32 no2 p513-16 Spr 2009
YOUNGER, COLE, 1844-1916
About
Duncklee, J. The last breakfast
YOUNGHUSBAND, SIR FRANCIS EDWARD, 1863-1942
About
Linaweaver, B. A good bag
Your Arkansas traveler. Schulberg, B.
Your body is changing. Pendarvis, J.
Your faithful servant. Spencer, W. B.
Your gold teeth, pt. 2. Di Filippo, P.
Your hit parade. Bukoski, A.
Your Husband's Money. Bonaldo, J.
Your left foot is crazy. Kiely, B.
Your man. Keret, E.
Your mother and I. Eggers, D.
Your niece's speech night. Perlman, E.
Your own private America. Brown, D.
Your papers, please. Raphael, L.
"**Your** sister and some wine!". Green, G.
Your sweet man. Hellmann, L. F.
You're at Macy's, killing time, when it hits you. Dufresne, J.
You're breaking my heart!. Raphael, L.
You're Greta. Biller, M.
You're Not You. Wildgen, M.

'Your're on next Sunday'. Keane, J. B.
Yours. Robison, M.
Yours, etc. Grant, G. J.
YOUTH
  See also Adolescence; Boys; Girls; Students
 Angel, J. Donny
 Angel, J. The history of Vegas
 Angel, J. Portions
 Angel, J. Seconds
 Angel, J. The skin from the muscle
 Averill, T. F. Midlin, Kansas, jump shot
 Báez, A. Amor sucks
 Baingana, D. A thank-you note
 Ball, P. M. The last great house of Isla Tortuga
 Bass, R. Pagans
 Beatty, P. The white boy shuffle [excerpt]
 Benioff, D. The barefoot girl in clover
 Bishop, S. Crosstown traffic
 Boswell, R. The heyday of the insensitive bastards
 Boswell, R. Supreme beings
 Bradbury, R. Hopscotch
 Chase, M. Weekend
 Curtis, R. The alpine slide
 Curtis, R. The witches
 Ellison, J. The company of men
 Franklin, T. Those good days
 Harrison, W. Two cars on a hillside
 Hinton, S. E. Different shorelines
 Hodgen, C. A jeweler's eye for flaw
 Hospital, J. T. Litany for the homeland
 Hughes, T. Twelve beer blues
 Hunt, H. Sovietski!
 Hwang, F. Blue hour
 Hwang, F. A visit to the suns
 Irsfeld, J. H. The horse fountain
 Kalokyris, D. Militsa or mid-August reverie
 Kiely, B. Make straight for the shore
 Kiely, B. The pilgrims
 Kiely, B. The weavers at the mill
 Klassen, S. Ending with poetry
 Klassen, S. Eye of the moon
 Klassen, S. The seven steps
 Langer, A. Bobby Kagan knows everything
 Luongo, M. Do that everywhere
 MacLaverty, B. Up the coast
 Malouf, D. Jacko's ranch
 McHugh, M. F. Interview: on any given day
 McIntyre, V. Sahara
 Meno, J. A trip to Greek mythology camp
 Monk, B. Slam book
 Mukhopadhyay, T. The gold of the sunbeams
 Mukhopadhyay, T. The showers
 Munro, A. Hired girl
 Ohlin, A. The tennis partner
 Pollock, D. R. Pills
 Purdy, J. The white blackbird
 Reed, K. High rise high
 Richter, S. Young people today
 Riley, G. La la land
 Savage, T. Cyberdate.com
 Sayers, V. Walker Evans is a spy on the Lexington Avenue local
 Shomer, E. Laws of nature
 Sillitoe, A. A scream of toys
 Silverberg, R. Caught in the organ draft
 Smith, B. Broken arrow
 Snyder, S. About face

 Spencer, E. Ship Island: the story of a mermaid
 Stamm, P. The kiss
 Straight, S. Mines
 Thomas, E. The land of youth
 Tomlinson, J. Prologue (two lives in letters)
 Trevor, W. Bravado
 Trezise, R. Fresh apples
 Unger, D. Autobiography
 Unger, D. Matisse
 Waldrop, H. The other real world
 Williams, J. Fortune
 With, C. Angel's house of ice
 With, C. Detox
 Yates, D. Oceanside, 1985
Youth. Rylands, J. T.
Youth eternal. Zelazny, R.
You've Been a Wonderful Volunteer. Gage, A.
You've Told Me Before. Moses, J.
Yu, Charles
 32.05864991%
  Yu, C. Third class superhero
 401(k)
  Yu, C. Third class superhero
 Autobiographical raw material unsuitable for the mining of fiction
  Yu, C. Third class superhero
 Florence
  Yu, C. Third class superhero
 Man of quiet desperation goes on short vacation
  Yu, C. Third class superhero
 The man who became himself
  Yu, C. Third class superhero
 My last days as me
  Yu, C. Third class superhero
 Problems for self-study
  Yu, C. Third class superhero
 Realism
  Yu, C. Third class superhero
 Third class superhero
  Yu, C. Third class superhero
 Two-player infinitely iterated simultaneous semi-cooperative game with spite and reputation
  Yu, C. Third class superhero
Yu, F. S.
 Social contract
  Stumbling and raging; more politically inspired fiction; edited by Stephen Elliott; with associate editors Greg Larson [et al.]

 The shield
  Politically inspired; edited by Stephen Elliott; assistant editor, Gabriel Kram; associate editors, Elizabeth Brooks [et al.]
Yuan-Innes, Melissa
 Red
  Nature v449 p946 O 18 2007
YUCATAN (MEXICO) *See* Mexico—Yucatan
YUGOSLAVIA
  See also Bosnia and Hercegovina; Croatia; Serbia
    Sarajevo
  See Bosnia and Hercegovina—Sarajevo
YUGOSLAVS
    Cuba
 Radojcic, N. Shades of mango
    Netherlands
 Shepard, J. Ajax is all about attack

Zelazny, Roger—*Continued*

The Borgia hand
  Zelazny, R. Threshold; edited by David G. Grubbs, Christopher S. Kovacs, Ann Crimmins

But not the Herald
  Zelazny, R. Power & light; edited by David G. Grubbs, Christopher S. Kovacs, Ann Crimmins

Circe has her problems
  Zelazny, R. Threshold; edited by David G. Grubbs, Christopher S. Kovacs, Ann Crimmins

A city divided
  Zelazny, R. Last exit to Babylon; edited by David G. Grubbs, Christopher S. Kovacs, Ann Crimmins

Collector's fever
  Zelazny, R. Threshold; edited by David G. Grubbs, Christopher S. Kovacs, Ann Crimmins

Come to me not in winter's white
  Zelazny, R. This mortal mountain; edited by David G. Grubbs, Christopher S. Kovacs, Anne Crimmins

Comes now the power
  Zelazny, R. Power & light; edited by David G. Grubbs, Christopher S. Kovacs, Ann Crimmins

Corrida
  Zelazny, R. This mortal mountain; edited by David G. Grubbs, Christopher S. Kovacs, Anne Crimmins

Damnation alley
  Zelazny, R. This mortal mountain; edited by David G. Grubbs, Christopher S. Kovacs, Anne Crimmins

Death and the executioner
  Zelazny, R. Power & light; edited by David G. Grubbs, Christopher S. Kovacs, Ann Crimmins

Devil car (Jenny/Murdoch)
  Zelazny, R. Power & light; edited by David G. Grubbs, Christopher S. Kovacs, Ann Crimmins

Dismal light
  Zelazny, R. This mortal mountain; edited by David G. Grubbs, Christopher S. Kovacs, Anne Crimmins

Divine madness
  Zelazny, R. Power & light; edited by David G. Grubbs, Christopher S. Kovacs, Ann Crimmins

The doors of his face, the lamps of his mouth
  Zelazny, R. Threshold; edited by David G. Grubbs, Christopher S. Kovacs, Ann Crimmins

The drawing
  Zelazny, R. Power & light; edited by David G. Grubbs, Christopher S. Kovacs, Ann Crimmins

The engine at Heartspring's Center
  Zelazny, R. This mortal mountain; edited by David G. Grubbs, Christopher S. Kovacs, Anne Crimmins

The eve of RUMOKO
  Zelazny, R. Last exit to Babylon; edited by David G. Grubbs, Christopher S. Kovacs, Ann Crimmins

Exeunt omnes
  Zelazny, R. Last exit to Babylon; edited by David G. Grubbs, Christopher S. Kovacs, Ann Crimmins

Final dining
  Zelazny, R. Threshold; edited by David G. Grubbs, Christopher S. Kovacs, Ann Crimmins

Fire and/or ice
  Zelazny, R. Last exit to Babylon; edited by David G. Grubbs, Christopher S. Kovacs, Ann Crimmins

For a breath I tarry
  Zelazny, R. Power & light; edited by David G. Grubbs, Christopher S. Kovacs, Ann Crimmins

The force that through the circuit drives the current
  Zelazny, R. This mortal mountain; edited by David G. Grubbs, Christopher S. Kovacs, Anne Crimmins

The furies
  Zelazny, R. Power & light; edited by David G. Grubbs, Christopher S. Kovacs, Ann Crimmins

The game of blood and dust
  Zelazny, R. This mortal mountain; edited by David G. Grubbs, Christopher S. Kovacs, Anne Crimmins

The George business
  Zelazny, R. Last exit to Babylon; edited by David G. Grubbs, Christopher S. Kovacs, Ann Crimmins

Go starless in the night
  Zelazny, R. Last exit to Babylon; edited by David G. Grubbs, Christopher S. Kovacs, Ann Crimmins

The graveyard heart
  Zelazny, R. Threshold; edited by David G. Grubbs, Christopher S. Kovacs, Ann Crimmins

The great slow kings
  Zelazny, R. Threshold; edited by David G. Grubbs, Christopher S. Kovacs, Ann Crimmins

Halfjack
  Zelazny, R. Last exit to Babylon; edited by David G. Grubbs, Christopher S. Kovacs, Ann Crimmins

A hand across the galaxy
  Zelazny, R. This mortal mountain; edited by David G. Grubbs, Christopher S. Kovacs, Anne Crimmins

He that moves
  Zelazny, R. This mortal mountain; edited by David G. Grubbs, Christopher S. Kovacs, Anne Crimmins

He who shapes
  Zelazny, R. Threshold; edited by David G. Grubbs, Christopher S. Kovacs, Ann Crimmins

Here there be dragons
  Zelazny, R. This mortal mountain; edited by David G. Grubbs, Christopher S. Kovacs, Anne Crimmins

Heritage
  Zelazny, R. This mortal mountain; edited by David G. Grubbs, Christopher S. Kovacs, Anne Crimmins

Zelazny, Roger—*Continued*

Home is the hangman
  Zelazny, R. Last exit to Babylon; edited by David G. Grubbs, Christopher S. Kovacs, Ann Crimmins
Horseman!
  Zelazny, R. Threshold; edited by David G. Grubbs, Christopher S. Kovacs, Ann Crimmins
The horses of Lir
  Zelazny, R. Last exit to Babylon; edited by David G. Grubbs, Christopher S. Kovacs, Ann Crimmins
The hounds of sorrow
  Zelazny, R. This mortal mountain; edited by David G. Grubbs, Christopher S. Kovacs, Anne Crimmins
The House of the Hanged Man
  Zelazny, R. Power & light; edited by David G. Grubbs, Christopher S. Kovacs, Ann Crimmins
The injured
  Zelazny, R. Power & light; edited by David G. Grubbs, Christopher S. Kovacs, Ann Crimmins
The insider
  Zelazny, R. This mortal mountain; edited by David G. Grubbs, Christopher S. Kovacs, Anne Crimmins
Is there a demon lover in the house?
  Zelazny, R. This mortal mountain; edited by David G. Grubbs, Christopher S. Kovacs, Anne Crimmins
The Juan's thousandth
  Zelazny, R. Power & light; edited by David G. Grubbs, Christopher S. Kovacs, Ann Crimmins
The keys to December
  Zelazny, R. Power & light; edited by David G. Grubbs, Christopher S. Kovacs, Ann Crimmins
King Solomon's ring
  Zelazny, R. Threshold; edited by David G. Grubbs, Christopher S. Kovacs, Ann Crimmins
'Kjwalll'kje'k'koothaïlll'kje'k
  Zelazny, R. Last exit to Babylon; edited by David G. Grubbs, Christopher S. Kovacs, Ann Crimmins
A knight for Merytha (Dilvish 4 of 11)
  Zelazny, R. Power & light; edited by David G. Grubbs, Christopher S. Kovacs, Ann Crimmins
The last defender of Camelot
  Zelazny, R. Last exit to Babylon; edited by David G. Grubbs, Christopher S. Kovacs, Ann Crimmins
The last Inn on the road with Dannie Plachta
  Zelazny, R. This mortal mountain; edited by David G. Grubbs, Christopher S. Kovacs, Anne Crimmins
The last of the wild ones
  Zelazny, R. Last exit to Babylon; edited by David G. Grubbs, Christopher S. Kovacs, Ann Crimmins
Late, late show
  Zelazny, R. Power & light; edited by David G. Grubbs, Christopher S. Kovacs, Ann Crimmins

Love is an imaginary number
  Zelazny, R. Power & light; edited by David G. Grubbs, Christopher S. Kovacs, Ann Crimmins
Lucifer
  Zelazny, R. Power & light; edited by David G. Grubbs, Christopher S. Kovacs, Ann Crimmins
The Malatesta collection
  Zelazny, R. Threshold; edited by David G. Grubbs, Christopher S. Kovacs, Ann Crimmins
The man at the corner of now and forever
  Zelazny, R. This mortal mountain; edited by David G. Grubbs, Christopher S. Kovacs, Anne Crimmins
The man who loved the Faioli
  Zelazny, R. This mortal mountain; edited by David G. Grubbs, Christopher S. Kovacs, Anne Crimmins
Mine is the kingdom
  Zelazny, R. Threshold; edited by David G. Grubbs, Christopher S. Kovacs, Ann Crimmins
The misfit
  Zelazny, R. Threshold; edited by David G. Grubbs, Christopher S. Kovacs, Ann Crimmins
Monologue for two
  Zelazny, R. Threshold; edited by David G. Grubbs, Christopher S. Kovacs, Ann Crimmins
The monster and the maiden
  Zelazny, R. Power & light; edited by David G. Grubbs, Christopher S. Kovacs, Ann Crimmins
Moonless in byzantium
  Zelazny, R. Threshold; edited by David G. Grubbs, Christopher S. Kovacs, Ann Crimmins
Mr. Fuller's revolt
  Zelazny, R. Threshold; edited by David G. Grubbs, Christopher S. Kovacs, Ann Crimmins
A museum piece
  Zelazny, R. Threshold; edited by David G. Grubbs, Christopher S. Kovacs, Ann Crimmins
My lady of the diodes
  Zelazny, R. This mortal mountain; edited by David G. Grubbs, Christopher S. Kovacs, Anne Crimmins
The naked matador
  Zelazny, R. Last exit to Babylon; edited by David G. Grubbs, Christopher S. Kovacs, Ann Crimmins
The new pleasure
  Zelazny, R. Power & light; edited by David G. Grubbs, Christopher S. Kovacs, Ann Crimmins
The night has 999 eyes
  Zelazny, R. Threshold; edited by David G. Grubbs, Christopher S. Kovacs, Ann Crimmins
Nine starships waiting
  Zelazny, R. Threshold; edited by David G. Grubbs, Christopher S. Kovacs, Ann Crimmins

Zelazny, Roger—*Continued*

The Year of the Good Seed with Dannie Plachta
    Zelazny, R. This mortal mountain; edited by
    David G. Grubbs, Christopher S. Kovacs,
    Anne Crimmins

Youth eternal
    Zelazny, R. Threshold; edited by David G.
    Grubbs, Christopher S. Kovacs, Ann
    Crimmins

Zellar, Brad

Better luck next time
    Twin cities; edited by Julie Schaper & Steven
    Horwitz

Zeman, Angela

Bang
    Mystery Writers of America presents the
    prosecution rests; new stories about court-
    rooms, criminals, and the law; edited by
    Linda Fairstein.

Green heat
    The Best American mystery stories, 2004; ed-
    ited and with an introduction by Nelson
    DeMille; Otto Penzler, series editor

ZEN BUDDHISM

Oates, J. C. The heart sutra

The **Zenner** trophy. Vidal, G.

Zentner, Alexi

The Adjuster
    Southwest Review v91 no3 p397-410 2006

Touch
    The O. Henry Prize stories 2008; edited and
    with an introduction by Laura Furman; with
    essays on the stories they admire most by
    jurors Chimamanda Ngozi Adiche, David
    Leavitt, David Means

Zenzizenzic. Obejas, A.

ZEPPELINS *See* Airships

Zero. Krause, E.

Zero. Powers, W.

The **Zero** Meter Diving Team. Shepard, J.

Zero summer. Kiernan, C. R.

Zero tolerance. Manotti, D.

Zero zero day. Guilfoile, K.

Zeroville. Erikson, S.

Zeta's house. Keeble, J.

Zettel, Sarah

The red shoes
    Pandora's closet; edited by Jean Rabe and
    Martin H. Greenberg.

Zhang, Hongling

(tr.) *See* Wang Xiaobo

Zhang Ailing *See* Chang, Eileen, 1920-1995

Zhoof. Stern, R. G.

Zhu Wen

Ah, Xiao Xie
    Zhu Wen. I love dollars and other stories of
    China; translated from the Chinese by Julia
    Lovell

A boat crossing
    Zhu Wen. I love dollars and other stories of
    China; translated from the Chinese by Julia
    Lovell

A hospital night
    Zhu Wen. I love dollars and other stories of
    China; translated from the Chinese by Julia
    Lovell

I love dollars
    Zhu Wen. I love dollars and other stories of
    China; translated from the Chinese by Julia
    Lovell

Pounds, ounces, meat
    Zhu Wen. I love dollars and other stories of
    China; translated from the Chinese by Julia
    Lovell

Wheels
    Zhu Wen. I love dollars and other stories of
    China; translated from the Chinese by Julia
    Lovell

Ziegler, Don

The Transformation of Uncle Bert
    Nebraska Life v11 no6 p34-5 N/D 2007

Ziemelis, K. Erik

Pigs on the wing
    Nature v436 p752 Ag 4 2005

Ziggurat. O'Connor, S.

Ziggy stardust. Biller, M.

Zima blue. Reynolds, A.

ZIMBABWE

Gappah, P. The annex shuffle

Gappah, P. At the sound of the last post

Gappah, P. Aunt Juliana's Indian

Gappah, P. The cracked, pink lips of Rosie's
    bridegroom

Gappah, P. An elegy for Easterly

Gappah, P. In the heart of the golden triangle

Gappah, P. The maid from Lalapanzi

Gappah, P. Midnight at the Hotel California

Gappah, P. The Mupandawana dancing champi-
    on

Gappah, P. The negotiated settlement

Gappah, P. Something nice from London

Marechera, D. Thought tracks in the snow

Politics

See Politics—Zimbabwe

ZIMBABWEANS

England

Gappah, P. My cousin-sister Rambanai

Switzerland

Gappah, P. Our man in Geneva wins a million
    euros

United States

Gappah, P. My cousin-sister Rambanai

Zimmer, Paul

Chicory
    New Letters v75 no1 p73-9 2008/2009

George Washington
    Gettysburg Review v21 no2 p215-17 Summ
    2008

The mechanics
    The Pushcart Prize XXX: best of the small
    presses 2006; edited by Bill Henderson
    with the Pushcart Prize editors

Tommy Henrich's a Prick
    New Letters v73 no1 p142-7 2006/2007

Zimmerman, Robert Allen *See* Dylan, Bob,
1941-

Zinder. Lee, T.

Zinski, Christopher J.

A Strategy Heads for the Rocks: A Bank Direc-
    tor Who Can't Find the Lighthouse
    The Banking Law Journal v124 no10 p931-43
    N/D 2007

Zinski, Christopher J.—*Continued*
Sue the Audit Committee: The Case of the
Sabre Rattling Lawyer
The Banking Law Journal v122 no10 p1019-
32 N/D 2005
"Talk to Me": The Case of the Auditor as Great
Communicator
The Banking Law Journal v122 no7 p751-61
Jl/Ag 2005
Three Years Later: The Case of the Maturing
Audit Committee
The Banking Law Journal v123 no2 p177-92
F 2006
Whistle While You Work: The Case of the In-
evitable Internal Investigation
The Banking Law Journal v122 no8 p855-66
S 2005

ZIONISM
Molodowsky, K. Married off
Molodowsky, K. On the eve of the journey

ZIONISTS
Asch, S. On the bank of an alien stream
Reisen, A. The holy pair

Ziti Motlog. Ducornet, R.

Ziyalan, Mustafa
Black palace
Istanbul noir; edited by Mustafa Ziyalan &
Amy Spangler; translated by Amy Spangler
& Mustafa Ziyalan.

Zlatte's misfortune. Wendroff, Z.

Zoanthropy. Benioff, D.

Zócalo. Longstreet, K.

Zoilo Hashimoto. Bova, B.

Zola, Émile
Squares
Paris tales; stories; translated by Helen Con-
stantine

Zolaria. Horrocks, C.

Zoline, Pamela
The heat death of the universe
New worlds; an anthology; edited by Michael
Moorcock
Daughters of earth; feminist science fiction in
the twentieth century; edited by Justine
Larbalestier

The **zombie**. McGuane, T.

The **zombie** pit. D'Allesandro, S.

The **zombie** prince. Reed, K.

ZOMBIES
Armstrong, K. The ungrateful dead
Ball, P. M. The last great house of Isla Tortuga
Barker, C. Sex, death and starshine
Birmingham, J. Heere be monsters
Bowen, H. W. Everything is better with zombies
Brite, P. Z. Calcutta, lord of nerves
Brooks, M. Great wall: a story from the zombie
war
Castro, A.-T. Dead like me
Crane, E. Betty the zombie
Duncan, A. Zora and the zombie
Edelman, S. Almost the last story by almost the
last man
Ellison, H. and Silverberg, R. The song the
zombie sang
Evenson, B. Prairie
Farris, J. Hunting meth zombies in the great Ne-
braskan wasteland
Finlay, C. C. Fading Quayle, dancing Quayle
Fischer, J. Undead camels ate their flesh

Ford, J. Malthusian's zombie
Gaiman, N. Bitter grounds
Griffiths, N. Never die
Kilpatrick, N. The age of sorrow
Kirtley, D. B. The skull-faced boy
Langan, J. How the day runs down
Link, K. The hortlak
Link, K. Some zombie contingency plans
Link, K. Some zombies contingency plans
McAuley, P. J. The thought war
McIntosh, W. Followed
Morton, L. Sparks fly upward
Nahrung, J. Smoking, waiting for the dawn
Partridge, N. In beauty, like the night
Reed, K. The zombie prince
Rucker, R. v. B. The men in the back room at
the country club
Schow, D. J. Blossom
Schweitzer, D. The dead kid
Shepard, L. Dead money
Simmons, D. This year's class picture
Swanwick, M. The dead
Tallerman, D. Stockholm syndrome
Wilce, Y. S. Quartermaster returns
Winter, D. E. Less than zombies

The **zoo** at Christmas. Gardam, J.

ZOOLOGICAL GARDENS *See* Zoos

ZOOLOGISTS
Bulgakov, M. A. The fatal eggs

ZOOS
Aldiss, B. W. Tiger in the night
Burke, K. The white oxen
Gardam, J. Pangbourne
Jardim, K. The jaguar
Lefer, D. Alas, Falada!
Lispector, C. The buffalo
Malla, P. Pet therapy
McAllister, B. The ark
Meno, J. Animals in the zoo
Messinger, J. Not even the zookeeper can keep
control
Moffett, K. Ursa, on zoo property and off
Murakami, H. A perfect day for kangaroos
Rand, K. The Henry and the Martha
Reinhorn, H. Big cats
Seton, E. T. Monarch, the big bear of Tallac
Silverberg, R. Collecting team
Van Pelt, J. The last of the o-forms
Watkins, S. Critterworld

Zora and the zombie. Duncan, A.

Zorekh and Bulani. Wendroff, Z.

Zorekh the community's. Molodowsky, K.

Zornoza, Andrew
Restaurant Roundup
Gastronomica (Berkeley, Calif.) v9 no2 p74-9
Spr 2009

Zorro. Barthelme, S.

Zoshchenko, Mikhail
The actor
Zoshchenko, M. The galosh and other stories;
translated from the Russian with an introduction by Jeremy Hicks
An anonymous friend
Zoshchenko, M. The galosh and other stories;
translated from the Russian with an introduction by Jeremy Hicks

Zoshchenko, Mikhail—*Continued*

Pushkin

Zoshchenko, M. The galosh and other stories; translated from the Russian with an introduction by Jeremy Hicks

The Pushkin Centenary Celebrations

Zoshchenko, M. The galosh and other stories; translated from the Russian with an introduction by Jeremy Hicks

Quality merchandise

Zoshchenko, M. The galosh and other stories; translated from the Russian with an introduction by Jeremy Hicks

Red tape

Zoshchenko, M. The galosh and other stories; translated from the Russian with an introduction by Jeremy Hicks

Sobering Thoughts

The Paris Review v48 p126-7 Spr 2006

The story of an illness

Zoshchenko, M. The galosh and other stories; translated from the Russian with an introduction by Jeremy Hicks

A summer break

Zoshchenko, M. The galosh and other stories; translated from the Russian with an introduction by Jeremy Hicks

The thief

Zoshchenko, M. The galosh and other stories; translated from the Russian with an introduction by Jeremy Hicks

Thieves

Zoshchenko, M. The galosh and other stories; translated from the Russian with an introduction by Jeremy Hicks

A trap

Zoshchenko, M. The galosh and other stories; translated from the Russian with an introduction by Jeremy Hicks

The Tsar's boots

Zoshchenko, M. The galosh and other stories; translated from the Russian with an introduction by Jeremy Hicks

An unpleasant story

Zoshchenko, M. The galosh and other stories; translated from the Russian with an introduction by Jeremy Hicks

A victim of the revolution

Zoshchenko, M. The galosh and other stories; translated from the Russian with an introduction by Jeremy Hicks

Water sports

Zoshchenko, M. The galosh and other stories; translated from the Russian with an introduction by Jeremy Hicks

What generosity

Zoshchenko, M. The galosh and other stories; translated from the Russian with an introduction by Jeremy Hicks

A workshop for health

Zoshchenko, M. The galosh and other stories; translated from the Russian with an introduction by Jeremy Hicks

Zoss, Joel

The valve transcript

New worlds; an anthology; edited by Michael Moorcock

Zoyka and Valeriya. Bunin, I. A.

Zuber, Isabel

Annie Taylor and the Horse from the Sea

The Southern Review (Baton Rouge, La.) v40 no4 p724-32 Aut 2004

Zuccari, Anna *See* Neera, 1846-1918

Zucker, Gina

Punishment

Before; short stories about pregnancy from our top writers; edited by Emily Franklin and Heather Swain

Zuelke, Karl

A Field of Gray Houses

The Antioch Review v66 no1 p75-91 Wint 2008

Zulieka. Báez, A.

Zulkey, Claire

The great Billik

Chicago noir; edited by Neal Pollack

Zumas, Leni

Blotilla takes the cake

Zumas, L. Farewell navigator; stories

Dragons may be the way forward

Zumas, L. Farewell navigator; stories

The everything hater

Zumas, L. Farewell navigator; stories

Farewell navigator

Zumas, L. Farewell navigator; stories

Handfasting

Zumas, L. Farewell navigator; stories

Heart sockets

Zumas, L. Farewell navigator; stories

How he was a wicked son

Zumas, L. Farewell navigator; stories

Leopard arms

Zumas, L. Farewell navigator; stories

Thieves and mapmakers

Zumas, L. Farewell navigator; stories

Waste no time if this method fails

Zumas, L. Farewell navigator; stories

Zuppa Inglese. Burke, J.

Zuras, Richard Lee

Runaway

StoryQuarterly v41 p432-43 2005

ZURICH (SWITZERLAND) *See* Switzerland—Zurich

Zurich. Ulitskaya, L.

PART II

List of Collections Indexed

20th century ghosts. Hill, J.

2033; the future of misbehavior: interplanetary dating, Madame President, socialized plastic surgery, and other good news from the future; from the editors of Nerve.com; instigated by Svedka. Chronicle Books 2007 197p ISBN 978-0-8118-5940-0; 0-8118-5940-0 LC 2006-30991

A

Abbey, Lynn
(ed) Thieves' world. *See* Thieves' world
Abbott, Lee K.
All things, all at once; new and selected stories. Norton 2006 365p ISBN 0-393-06137-X LC 2005-27348
Abbott, Megan E., 1971-
(ed) A hell of a woman. *See* A hell of a woman
Above the houses. Engberg, S.
Absalom's mother & other stories. Marley, L.
Across the bridge of sighs. Rylands, J. T.
Across the sky. Rich, M.
Adams, John Joseph, 1976-
(ed) The living dead. *See* The living dead
Adaptations: from short story to big screen; 35 great stories that have inspired great films; edited by Stephanie Harrison. Three Rivers Press 2005 619p il ISBN 1-4000-5314-5 LC 2005-3441
Adichie, Chimamanda Ngozi, 1977-
The thing around your neck. Alfred A. Knopf 2009 240p ISBN 978-0-307-27107-5; 0-307-27107-2 LC 2008-41271
Adiga, Aravind
Between the assassinations. Free Press 2009 339p ISBN 978-1-4391-5292-8; 1-4391-5292-6 LC 2009-08525
Originally published in India in 2008 by Picador India.
Adrian, Chris, 1970-
A better angel; stories. Farrar, Straus & Giroux 2008 227p ISBN 978-0-374-28990-4; 0-374-28990-5 LC 2008-7875
Adrift on the haunted seas. Hodgson, W. H.
Adulteries, hot tubs & such like matters. McCauley, W.
The **Adventure** of the missing detective and 19 of the year's finest crime and mystery stories!; edited by Ed Gorman and Martin H. Greenberg. Carroll & Graf Publishers 2005 568p ISBN 0-7867-1643-6; 978-0-78671-643-2
Adventures in the West; stories for young readers; edited by Susanne George Bloomfield and Eric Melvin Reed. University of Nebraska Press 2007 280p ISBN 978-0-8032-5974-4; 0-8032-5974-3 LC 2007-7343
After the fires. Pflug, U.
Aftershock & others. Wilson, F. P.
Aftershocks. Weil, G.
Agamemnon's daughter. Kadare, I.
Aguirre, Forrest
(ed) Text: Ur. *See* Text: Ur
Aird, Catherine
Chapter and hearse. St. Martin's Minotaur 2004 293p ISBN 0-312-29084-5 LC 2003-66820
Akers, Deborah S., 1955-
(ed) Oranges in the sun. *See* Oranges in the sun

Akpan, Uwem Celestine
  Say you're one of them; [by] Uwem Akpan. Little, Brown and Company 2008 358p map ISBN 978-0-316-11378-6; 0-316-11378-6 LC 2008-11340

Alarcón, Daniel, 1977-
  War by candlelight; stories. HarperCollins 2005 188p ISBN 0-06-059478-0 LC 2004-47537

Albert, Elisa, 1978-
  How this night is different; stories. Free Press 2006 208p ISBN 9780743291279; 0-7432-9127-1 LC 2006-47597

Albert, Susan Wittig
  An unthymely death and other garden mysteries. Berkley Books 2003 254p ISBN 0-425-19002-1 LC 2002-43933

Ali, Mohammed Naseehu
  The prophet of Zongo Street; stories. Amistad 2005 212p ISBN 0-06-052354-9 LC 2004-62722

The **Alice** stories. Kercheval, J. L.

All aboard. Porter, J. A.

All Aunt Hagar's children. Jones, E. P.

All fall down. Caponegro, M.

All that is gone. Toer, P. A.

All things, all at once. Abbott, L. K.

Allen, Jeffery Renard, 1962-
  Holding pattern; stories. Graywolf Press 2008 227p ISBN 978-1-55597-509-8; 1-55597-509-7 LC 2008-92846

Allen, Woody
  Mere anarchy. Random House 2007 160p ISBN 978-1-4000-6641-4; 1-4000-6641-7 LC 2006-51880

Allen-Agostini, Lisa
  (ed) Trinidad noir. *See* Trinidad noir

Almond, Steve
  The evil B. B. Chow and other stories. Algonquin Books of Chapel Hill 2005 233p ISBN 1-56512-422-7 LC 2004-58564

Almonds to zhoof. Stern, R. G.

Alternate generals III; edited by Harry Turtledove and Roland J. Green. Baen 2005 306p ISBN 0-7434-9897-6 LC 2004-29942

Alvarado, Beth
  Not a matter of love. New Rivers Press 2006 183p ISBN 0-89823-233-3

Amdahl, Gary
  Visigoth; stories. Milkweed Editions 2006 212p ISBN 978-15-7131-051-4; 1-57131-051-7 LC 2005-27264

An **American** affair. Brazaitis, M.

American dreaming and other stories. Iarovici, D.

American salvage. Campbell, B. J.

American wives. Helms, B.

Anaya, Rudolfo A.
  The man who could fly and other stories. University of Oklahoma Press 2006 197p (Chicana & Chicano visions of the Américas) ISBN 0-8061-3738-X LC 2005-51426

The **Anchor** book of modern African stories; edited by Nadežda Obradovic; with a foreword by Chinua Achebe. Anchor Books 2002 xxiv, 375p ISBN 0-385-72240-0 LC 2002-74441

The **Anchor** book of new American short stories; edited by Ben Marcus. Anchor Books 2004 480p ISBN 1-400-03482-5 LC 2003-70896

And other stories. Gospodinov, G.

Anders, Lou
  (ed) Fast forward 1. *See* Fast forward 1
  (ed) Sideways in crime. *See* Sideways in crime

Anderson, Alison
  (tr) My mother never dies. *See* Castillon, Claire, 1975-. My mother never dies

Anderson, Barbara, 1926-
  Collected stories. Victoria University Press 2006 c2005 379p ISBN 0-86473-498-0 LC 2006-373296

Anderson, Douglas A. (Douglas Allen), 1959-
  (ed) Tales before Narnia. *See* Tales before Narnia

Anderson, Garrett J.
(ed) Kolchak: the night stalker chronicles. *See* Kolchak: the night stalker chronicles
Anderson, Kevin J., 1962-
(ed) The Horror Writers Association presents Blood lite. *See* The Horror Writers Association presents Blood lite
Anderson, Poul, 1926-2001
Call me Joe; edited by Rick Katze and Lis Carey. NESFA Press 2009 510p (The collected short works of Poul Anderson, v 1) ISBN 978-1-886778-75-7; 1-886778-75-2
Andreas-Salomé, Lou, 1861-1937
The human family; stories; translated and with an introduction by Raleigh Whitinger. University of Nebraska Press 2005 202p (European women writers series) ISBN 978-0-8032-5952-2; 978-0-8032-1071-4 (pa) LC 2005-43719
Andrews, Chris
(tr) Last evenings on Earth. *See* Bolaño, Roberto, 1953-2003. Last evenings on Earth
Angel, Jodi, 1971-
The history of Vegas; stories. Chronicle Books 2005 187p ISBN 0-8118-4625-3 LC 2004-29774
Angelic & black; contemporary Greek short stories; edited and translated by David Connolly; with an introduction by Vangelis Hatzivassileiou. Cosmos Publishing 2006 261p ISBN 978-1-932455-11-3; 1-932455-11-6 LC 2006-4248
The **animal** girl. Fulton, J.
Another perfect catastrophe. Barkley, B.
The **ant** king and other stories. Rosenbaum, B.
Anteaters don't dream and other stories. Hawes, L.
Antediluvian tales. Brite, P. Z.
Antioxidants and other stories. Bennett, T.
Apocalypse then. DeMarinis, R.
Apple, Max
The Jew of Home Depot and other stories. Johns Hopkins University Press 2007 170p ISBN 978-0-8018-8738-3; 0-8018-8738-0 LC 2007-18864
The **apple's** bruise. Glatt, L.
Archer, Jeffrey, 1940-
Cat o'nine tales and other stories; drawings by Ronald Searle. St. Martin's Press 2007 254p ISBN 978-0-312-36264-5; 0-312-36264-1 LC 2007-20901
Arguing with the storm; stories by Yiddish women writers; edited and with a preface by Rhea Tregebov; introduction by Kathryn Hellerstein. Feminist Press 2008 xxvi, 169p il (The Reuben/Rifkin Jewish women writers series) ISBN 978-1-55861-558-5; 1-55861-558-8; 978-1-55861-559-8 (pa); 1-55861-559-X (pa) LC 2007-21441
First published 2007 in Canada
Arjouni, Jakob
Idiots; five fairy tales and other stories; translated from the German by Anthea Bell. Other Press 2005 269p ISBN 1-59051-157-3 LC 2004-22638
Armageddon in retrospect. Vonnegut, K.
Arnow, Harriette Louisa Simpson, 1908-1986
The collected short stories of Harriette Simpson Arnow; Sandra L. Ballard & Haeja K. Chung, editors. Michigan State University Press 2005 259p ISBN 0-87013-756-5 LC 2005-14237
Arslan, Antonia
(ed) Writing to delight. *See* Writing to delight
Ascendancies. Sterling, B.
Asimov, Isaac, 1920-1992
(ed) The Mammoth book of golden age science fiction. *See* The Mammoth book of golden age science fiction
Asimov's science fiction: 30th anniversary anthology; edited by Sheila Williams. Tachyon Publications 2007 349p ISBN 978-1-892391-47-6; 1-892391-47-3
Ask for a convertible. Brown, D.

Assadi, Jamal, 1960-
(tr) Mohammad Ali Taha's "A rose to Hafeeza's eyes" and other stories. *See* Taha, Muhammad 'Ali, 1942-. Mohammad Ali Taha's "A rose to Hafeeza's eyes" and other stories
At the scene of the crime; forensic mysteries from today's best writers; edited by Dana Stabenow. Running Press 2008 267p ISBN 978-0-7867-2055-2 LC 2008-928969
Attack of the jazz giants and other stories. Frost, G.
Atwood, Margaret, 1939-
Moral disorder; stories. Nan A. Talese 2006 225p ISBN 978-0-385-50384-6; 0-385-50384-9 LC 2006-44589
Auchincloss, Louis
The friend of women and other stories. Houghton Mifflin 2007 ISBN 978-0-618-71866-5; 0-618-71866-4
Analyzed for short stories only
The young Apollo and other stories. Houghton Mifflin 2006 237p ISBN 0-618-55115-8; 978-0-618-55115-6 LC 2005-19899
Auslander, Shalom
Beware of God; stories. Simon & Schuster 2005 194p ISBN 0-7432-6456-8 LC 2004-51352
Autopsy of an engine and other stories from the Cadillac plant. Hernandez, L.
Averill, Thomas Fox, 1949-
Ordinary genius. University of Nebraska Press 2004 148p (Flyover fiction) ISBN 0-8032-1068-X LC 2004-18195
Awake in the dark. Nayman, S.

B

Babylon and other stories. Ohlin, A.
Bachelors. Schnitzler, A.
Bacigalupi, Paolo
Pump six and other stories. Night Shade Books 2008 239p ISBN 978-1-59780-133-1
Bad dirt. Proulx, A.
Báez, Annecy
My daughter's eyes, and other stories. Curbstone Press 2007 176p ISBN 978-1-931896-38-2; 1-931896-38-0 LC 2006-28832
Baingana, Doreen
Tropical fish; tales from Entebbe. Harlem Moon 2006 183p ISBN 0-7679-2510-6 LC 2005-46770
Baker, Kage
Dark Mondays; stories. Night Shade Books 2006 231p ISBN 1-59780-051-1
Gods and pawns. Tor 2007 335p ISBN 978-0-765-31552-6; 0-765-31552-1 LC 2006-25841
"A Tom Doherty Associates book"
Mother Aegypt and other stories. Night Shade Books 2004 249p ISBN 1-892389-75-4
Bakken, Kerry Neville, 1972-
Necessary lies. BkMk Press 2006 199p ISBN 1-886157-56-1 (pa) LC 2006-14739
Balcom, John
(ed) Running mother and other stories. *See* Guo, Songfen, 1938-2005. Running mother and other stories
Bandersnatch; edited by Paul Tremblay and Sean Wallace. Prime Books 2007 185p ISBN 978-0-8095-7266-3; 0-8095-7266-4
Bang crunch. Smith, N.
Baqadir, Abu Bakr Ahmad
(ed) Oranges in the sun. *See* Oranges in the sun
Baraka, Imamu Amiri, 1934-
Tales of the out & the gone. Akashic Books 2007 221p ISBN 978-1-933354-12-5; 1-933354-12-7
Barkley, Brad
Another perfect catastrophe. Thomas Dunne Books 2004 206p ISBN 0-312-29147-7

Bendel-Simso, Mary M., ed, 1965-
Early American detective stories. *See* Early American detective stories
Bender, Aimee
Willful creatures; stories. Doubleday 2005 208p ISBN 0-385-50113-7
LC 2004-65515
Benioff, David
When the nines roll over and other stories. Viking 2004 223p ISBN
0-670-03339-1 LC 2004-49613
Bennett, Terry, 1948-
Antioxidants and other stories. The Toby Press 2004 305p ISBN
1-59264-084-2
Bensko, John, 1949-
Sea dogs. Graywolf Press 2004 185p ISBN 1-555-97399-X (pa)
LC 2003-112160
Berg, Elizabeth, 1948-
The day I ate whatever I wanted; and other small acts of liberation.
Random House 2008 242p ISBN 978-1-4000-6509-7
LC 2007-34704
The **best** American Catholic short stories; a Sheed & Ward collection;
edited by Daniel McVeigh and Patricia Schnapp. Rowman &
Littlefield Publishers 2007 346p ISBN 978-1-58051-210-7;
1-58051-210-0 LC 2006-24056
"A Sheed & Ward book"
Best American fantasy; guest editors Ann & Jeff VanderMeer; series
editor Matthew Cheney. Prime Books 2007 459p ISBN
978-0-8095-6280-0
The **Best** American mystery stories, 2004; edited and with an
introduction by Nelson DeMille; Otto Penzler, series editor.
Houghton Mifflin 2004 432p ISBN 0-618-32968-4; 0-618-32967-6
(pa)
The **Best** American mystery stories, 2005; edited and with an
introduction by Joyce Carol Oates; Otto Penzler, series editor.
Houghton Mifflin Company 2005 324p ISBN 0-618-51745-6;
0-618-51744-8 (pa)
The **Best** American Mystery Stories, 2006; edited and with an
introduction by Scott Turow; Otto Penzler, series editor. Houghton
2006   384p   ISBN   978-0-618-51746-6;   0-618-51747-4;
978-0-618-51747-3 (pa); 0-618-51747-2 (pa)
The **Best** American mystery stories 2007; edited and with and
introduction by Carl Hiaasen; Otto Penzler, series editor. Houghton
Mifflin   Company   2007   326p   ISBN   978-0-618-81263-9;
0-618-81263-6; 978-0-618-81265-3 (pa); 0-618-81265-2 (pa)
The **Best** American mystery stories, 2008; edited and with an
introduction by George Pelecanos; Otto Penzler, series editor.
Houghton Mifflin Company 2008 423p ISBN 978-0-618-81266-0;
978-0-618-81267-7 (pa) ISSN 1094-8384
The **Best** American mystery stories, 2009; edited and with an
introduction by Jeffery Deaver. Houghton Mifflin Harcourt 2009
384p ISBN 978-0-547-23750-3
"A Mariner original"
The **Best** American short stories, 2004; edited by Lorrie Moore; Katrina
Kenison series editor. 2004 462p ISBN 0-618-19734-6;
0-618-19735-4 (pa)
The **Best** American short stories, 2005; selected from U.S. and Canadian
magazines by Michael Chabon with Katrina Kenison; with an
introduction by Michael Chabon. Houghton Mifflin Company 2005
411p ISBN 0-618-42349-4; 0-618-42705-8 (pa)
The **Best** American short stories, 2006; selected from U.S. and Canadian
magazines by Ann Patchett with Katrina Kenison; with an
introduction by Ann Patchett. Houghton Mifflin Company 2006
xxii, 388p ISBN 0-618-54351-1; 0-618-54352-X (pa)
The **Best** American short stories, 2007; selected from U. S. and
Canadian magazines by Stephen King with Heidi Pitlor; with an
introduction by Stephen King. Houghton Mifflin Company 2007
428p ISBN 978-0-618-71347-9; 0-618-71347-6; 978-0-618-71348-6
(pa); 0-618-71348-4 (pa) LC 2007299831
The **Best** British mysteries, 2005; edited by Maxim Jakubowski. Allison
& Busby 2004 345p ISBN 0-7490-8336-0

The **Best** British mysteries, 2006; edited by Maxim Jakubowski. Allison & Busby 2005 349p ISBN 0-7490-8226-7; 0-7490-8259-3

The **best** Christian short stories; edited and with an introduction by Bret Lott. WestBow Press 2006 xx, 252p ISBN 978-1-59554-077-5; 1-59554-077-6 LC 2006-9607

Best New American voices 2007; [edited by Sue Miller; series editors, John Kulka and Natalie Danford] Harcourt 2006 336p ISBN 978-0-15-603155-4; 0-15-603155-8 ISSN 1536-7908
> "A Harvest original"

Best new American voices 2004; guest editor John Casey; series editors John Kulka and Natalie Danford. Harcourt 2003 306p ISBN 0-15600722-3 ISSN 1536-7908
> "A Harvest Original"

Best new American voices 2008; guest editor Richard Bausch; series editors John Kulka and Natalie Danford. Harcourt 2007 406p ISBN 978-0-15-603149-3 ISSN 1536-7908
> "A Harvest original"

Best new American voices 2009; guest editor Mary Gaitskill; series editors John Kulka and Natalie Danford. Harcourt 2008 343p ISBN 978-0-15-603431-9 ISSN 1536-7908

Best of contemporary Mexican fiction; Alvaro Uribe, editor; Olivia Sears, translation editor. Dalkey Archive Press 2009 xxxi, 529p (Latin American Literature Series) ISBN 978-1-56478-515-2; 1-56478-515-7; 978-1-56478-514-5 (pa); 1-56478-514-9 (pa) LC 2008-18443

The **best** of Gene Wolfe. Wolfe, G.

The **Best** of Lady Churchill's rosebud wristlet; edited by Kelly Link & Gavin J. Grant; introduction by Dan Chaon. Ballantine Books 2007 387p ISBN 978-0-345-49913-4 LC 2007-15118

The **best** of Lucius Shepard. Shepard, L.

The **best** of Michael Moorcock. Moorcock, M.

The **best** of Michael Swanwick. Swanwick, M.

The **Best** of the Bellevue Literary Review; edited by Dannielle Ofri and the staff of the Bellevue Literary Review. Bellevue Literary Press 2008 320p ISBN 978-1-934-13704-8; 1-934-13704-9
> Analyzed for Short Stories only

The **Best** of the best, volume 2; 20 years of the best short science fiction novels; edited by Gardner Dozois. St. Martin's Press 2007 642p ISBN 978-0-312-36341-3; 0-312-36341-9

Best of the South: from the second decade of New stories from the South; selected and introduced by Anne Tyler. Algonquin Books of Chapel Hill 2005 342p ISBN 1-56512-470-7
> "A Shannon Ravenel book"

Best of Tin House; stories; foreword by Dorothy Allison. Tin House Books 2006 445p ISBN 0-9773127-1-2

The **best** place to be. Dormen, L.

The **Best** science fiction and fantasy of the year: volume three; edited by Jonathan Strahan. Night Shade Books 2009 510p ISBN 978-1-59780-149-2

The **Best** science fiction and fantasy of the year: volume two; edited by Jonathan Strahan. Night Shade Books 2008 459p ISBN 978-1-59780-124-9

Best stories of the American West, v1; edited by Marc Jaffe. Forge 2007 316p ISBN 978-0-765-31089-7; 0-765-31089-9
> "A Tom Doherty Associates book"

A **better** angel. Adrian, C.

Between Camelots. Ebenbach, D. H.

Between here and the yellow sea. Pizzolatto, N.

Between the assassinations. Adiga, A.

Beulah land. McGruder, K.

Beware of God. Auslander, S.

Bierce, Ambrose, 1842-1914?
> The short fiction of Ambrose Bierce, volume 1; edited by S. T. Joshi, Lawrence I. Berkove, and David E. Schultz. a comprehensive edition. University of Tennessee Press 2006 ISBN 1-57233-536-X
> Partially analyzed

Bierce, Ambrose, 1842-1914?—*Continued*

The short fiction of Ambrose Bierce, volume 2; edited by S. T. Joshi, Lawrence I. Berkove, and David E. Schultz. a comprehensive edition. University of Tennessee Press 2006 ISBN 1-57233-537-8

Partially analyzed

The short fiction of Ambrose Bierce, volume 3; edited by S. T. Joshi, Lawrence I. Berkove, and David E. Schultz. a comprehensive edition. University of Tennessee Press 2006 ISBN 1-57233-538-6

Partially analyzed

Big cats. Reinhorn, H.

Biller, Maxim, 1960-

Love today; translated from the German by Anthea Bell. Simon & Schuster 2008 216p ISBN 978-1-4165-7265-1; 1-4165-7265-1 LC 2008-11027

Bingham, Sallie

Red car; stories. Sarabande Books 2008 181p ISBN 978-1-932511-59-8; 978-1-932511-60-4 (pa) LC 2007-22454

Bishop, Elizabeth, 1911-1979

Poems, prose, and letters; [selected and edited by Robert Giroux and Lloyd Schwartz] Library of America 2008 979p ISBN 978-1-59853-017-9; 1-59853-017-8 LC 2007-935885

Analyzed for short stories only

Bishop, Michael, 1945-

(ed) A cross of centuries. *See* A cross of centuries

Bishop, Tom, 1937-

The great Mormon cricket fly-fishing festival and other western stories. University of New Mexico Press 2007 201p ISBN 978-0-8263-3928-7 LC 2006-29417

Bissell, Tom

God lives in St. Petersburg; and other stories. Pantheon Books 2005 212p ISBN 0-375-42264-1 LC 2004-52232

Bisson, Terry

Greetings. Tachyon Publications 2005 384p ISBN 1-892391-24-4

Numbers don't lie. Tachyon Publications 2005 163p ISBN 1-892391-32-5

A **bit** on the side. Trevor, W.

Black Friday and other stories. Goodis, D.

The **Black** Lizard big book of pulps; edited by Otto Penzler. Vintage Crime/Black Lizard 2007 1150p ISBN 978-0-307-28048-0 LC 2007-21103

The **black** mirror and other stories.

Black noir; mystery, crime and suspense stories by African-American writers; edited by Otto Penzler. Pegasus Books 2009 349p ISBN 978-1-60598-039-3; 978-1-60598-057-7 (pa)

Black pockets and other dark thoughts. Zebrowski, G.

Blackbird house. Hoffman, A.

Blackwell, Kate, 1941-

You won't remember this; stories. Southern Methodist University Press 2007 229p ISBN 978-0-87074-515-7; 0-87074-515-8 LC 2006-51261

Bleed into me. Jones, S. G.

Blind love. Woronov, M.

Blind willow, sleeping woman. Murakami, H.

Blish, James, 1921-1975

Works of art; selected short fiction of James Blish; edited by James A. Mann. NESFA Press 2008 c2007 524p ISBN 978-1-886778-70-2; 1-886778-70-1

Block, Lawrence, 1938-

(ed) Manhattan noir. *See* Manhattan noir

(ed) Manhattan noir 2. *See* Manhattan noir 2

One night stands and lost weekends. Harper 2008 366p ISBN 978-0-06-158214-1 LC 2008-03500

The stories were originally published as One Night Stands in 1999 and the novellas as The Lost Cases of Ed London in 2001 by Crippen & Landru Publishers

Blood sky. Cook, W.

Bloodletting & miraculous cures. Lam, V.

The **blue**. Gee, M.

Blue light in the sky & other stories. Ts'an-hsüeh

Breen, Jon L., 1943-
Kill the umpire; the calls of Ed Gorgon. Crippen & Landru Publishers 2003 181p ISBN 1-932009-19-1

Brennan, Karen, 1941-
The garden in which I walk. FC2 2004 144p ISBN 1-573-66116-3 LC 2004-4924

Brenner, Yosef Haim
Out of the depths & other stories; [by] Y. H. Brenner; translated and with introductions by David Patterson & Ezra Spicehandler. Toby Press 2008 450p ISBN 978-1-59264-135-2

Brett, Simon, 1945-
(ed) The Detection collection. *See* The Detection collection

Breuer, Miles John, 1889-1945
The man with the strange head and other early science fiction stories; [by] Miles J. Breuer; edited and with an introduction by Michael R. Page. University of Nebraska Press 2008 431p ISBN 978-0-8032-1587-0 LC 2008-8625
Analyzed for Short Stories only

Brewer, Richard J.
(ed) Meeting across the river. *See* Meeting across the river
The **bride** from Odessa. Cozarinsky, E.

Brides and sinners in El Chuco. Granados, C.

Brief encounters with Che Guevara. Fountain, B.

Bring everybody. Yates, D.

Brite, Poppy Z.
Antediluvian tales. Subterranean Press 2007 116p ISBN 978-1-59606-116-3

British invasion; edited by Christopher Golden, Tim Lebbon & James A. Moore. Cemetery Dance Publications 2008 441p ISBN 978-1-58767-175-3; 1-58767-175-1

Broccoli and other tales of food and love. Vapnyar, L.

Brockmeier, Kevin
The view from the seventh layer. Pantheon Books 2008 267p ISBN 978-0-375-42530-1; 0-375-42530-6 LC 2007-23404

Brodsky, Michael, 1948-
Limit point. Six Gallery Press 2007 270p ISBN 978-0-9782961-6-2

Bronx noir; edited by S. J. Rozan. Akashic Books 2007 361p ISBN 978-1-933354-25-5 LC 2006-936535

Brooklyn noir; edited by Tim McLoughlin. Akashic Books 2004 216p ISBN 1-888451-58-0 LC 2003-116590

Brooklyn noir 2; the classics; edited by Tim McLoughlin. Akashic Books 2005 309p ISBN 1-888451-76-9 LC 2004-115735

Broussard, Meredith
(ed) The dictionary of failed relationships. *See* The dictionary of failed relationships

Brown, Danit
Ask for a convertible; stories. Pantheon Books 2008 302p ISBN 978-0-375-42454-0 LC 2007-39745

Brown, Eric, 1960-
Threshold shift; with a foreword by Stephen Baxter. Golden Gryphon Press 2006 218p ISBN 1-930846-43-6 LC 2006-5440

Brown, Fleda, 1944-
(ed) On the Mason-Dixon line. *See* On the Mason-Dixon line

Brown, George Mackay
Hawkfall; introduction by Andrew Greig. New ed. Polygon 2004 212p ISBN 1-904598-18-8 (pa)

Brown, Rebecca, 1956-
The last time I saw you. City Lights Books 2006 97p ISBN 978-0-87286-447-4; 0-87286-447-2 LC 2005-32726

Bruen, Ken
(ed) Dublin noir. *See* Dublin noir

Buckler, Ernest, 1908-1984
Thanks for listening; stories and short fictions by Ernest Buckler; selected and edited by Marta Dvořak. Wilfrid Laurier University Press 2004 302p ISBN 0-88920-438-1

Budavari, Susan
(ed) Medium of murder. *See* Medium of murder
The **budding** tree. Kitahara, A.

Budnitz, Judy

Nice big American baby; stories; Judy Budnitz. Knopf 2005 285p
ISBN 0-375-41242-5 LC 2004-48567

Bukiet, Melvin Jules

(ed) Scribblers on the roof. *See* Scribblers on the roof

Bukoski, Anthony

North of the port; stories. Southern Methodist University Press 2008
176p ISBN 978-0-87074-521-8 LC 2007-49803

Twelve below zero: new and expanded edition; stories. Holy Cow!
Press 2008 161p ISBN 978-0-9779458-7-0; 0-9779458-7-1
LC 2008-27628

Bukowski, Charles

Portions from a wine-stained notebook; uncollected stories and essays,
1944-1990; edited and with an introduction by David Stephen
Calonne. City Lights Books 2008 255p ISBN 978-0-87286-496-2;
978-0-87286-492-4 (pa) LC 008-20485

Analyzed for Short Stories only

Bull by the tale. Duncklee, J.

A **bullet** for Billy the Kid. Henry, W.

Bulletproof girl. Dalton, Q.

Bunin, Ivan Alekseevich, 1870-1953

The collected stories of Ivan Bunin; translated from the Russian, and
with an introduction by Graham Hettlinger. Ivan R. Dee 2007 377p
ISBN 9781566637589; 1-56663-758-9 LC 2007-11830

The Elagin affair and other stories; translated from the Russian, with
an introduction, by Graham Hettlinger. Ivan R. Dee 2005 254p
ISBN 1-56663-641-8 LC 2005-12806

Burgin, Richard

The identity club; new and selected stories. Ontario Review Press
2005 330p ISBN 0-86538-115-1 LC 2005-40669

Burke, James Lee, 1936-

Jesus out to sea; stories. Simon & Schuster 2007 240p ISBN
978-1-4165-4856-0; 1-4165-4856-4 LC 2006-100977

Burke, Kenneth, 1897-1993

Here & elsewhere; the collected fiction of Kenneth Burke;
introduction by Denis Donoghue. Godine 2005 415p ISBN
1-57423-202-9; 1-57423-201-0 (pa) LC 2004-17236

A Black Sparrow book

Burke, Thomas, 1886-1945

Where is home and other stories. Fithian Press 2005 93p ISBN
1-56474-443-4 LC 2004-6958

Busch, Frederick, 1941-2006

Rescue missions; stories. W.W. Norton & Co. 2006 316p ISBN
978-0-393-06252-6; 0-393-06252-X LC 2006-13011

C

Cadnum, Michael

Can't catch me and other twice-told tales. Tachyon Publications 2006
181p ISBN 1-892391-33-3; 978-1-892391-33-3

Cairo stories. Drosso, A.-M.

Calamity and other stories. Kalotay, D.

California transit. Lefer, D.

California uncovered; stories for the 21st century; edited by Chitra
Banerjee Divakaruni, William E. Justice, and James Quay.
California Council for the Humanities 2005 379p ISBN
1-890771-97-X LC 2004-18365

Analyzed for short stories only

Call me Ahab. Finger, A.

Call me Joe. Anderson, P.

Campbell, Bonnie Jo, 1962-

American salvage; stories. Wayne State University Press 2009 170p
ISBN 978-0-8143-3412-6; 0-8143-3412-1 LC 2008-51203

Campbell, J. R., 1963-

(ed) Gaslight grimoire. *See* Gaslight grimoire

Can't catch me and other twice-told tales. Cadnum, M.

The **cantor's** daughter. Nadelson, S.

Canty, Kevin

Where the money went; stories. Nan A. Talese/Doubleday 2009 191p ISBN 978-0-385-52585-5 LC 2008-37480

Caponegro, Mary, 1956-

All fall down; stories. Coffee House Press 2009 214p ISBN 978-1-56689-226-1; 1-56689-206-6 LC 2008-52723

Capote, Truman, 1924-1984

The complete stories of Truman Capote; introduction by Reynolds Price. Random House 2004 300p ISBN 0-679-64310-9 LC 2004-46876

Captive audience. Reidy, D.

Card, Orson Scott

Keeper of dreams. TOR 2008 656p ISBN 978-0-7653-0497-1; 0-7653-0497-X LC 2007-46720

"A Tom Doherty Associates book"

(ed) Orson Scott Card's Intergalctic medicine show. *See* Orson Scott Card's Intergalctic medicine show

Carduff, Christopher

(ed) Early novels and stories. *See* Maxwell, William, 1908-2000. Early novels and stories

(ed) Later novels and stories. *See* Maxwell, William, 1908-2000. Later novels and stories

Carew, Jan, 1925-

The Guyanese wanderer; stories. Sarabande Books 2007 107p ISBN 978-1-932511-50-5; 1-932511-50-4 LC 2006-29427

Carrying the torch. Clarke, B.

Cars go fast. Chattin, J.

Casablanca and other stories. Brau, E.

Casey, John, 1939-

(ed) Best new American voices 2004. *See* Best new American voices 2004

Castillon, Claire, 1975-

My mother never dies; stories; translated from the French by Alison Anderson. Houghton Mifflin Harcourt 2009 163p ISBN 978-0-15-101426-2; 0-15-101426-4 LC 2008-11544

Cat o'nine tales and other stories. Archer, J.

Cat tales: fantastic feline fiction; edited by George H. Scithers. Wildside Press 2008 175p ISBN 978-0-8095-7321-9

The **cemetery** of Chua village and other stories. Đoàn, L.

The **centaur's** son. Daughtry, P.

Chabon, Michael

(ed) The Best American short stories, 2005. *See* The Best American short stories, 2005

(ed) McSweeney's enchanted chamber of astonishing stories. *See* McSweeney's enchanted chamber of astonishing stories

(ed) McSweeney's mammoth treasury of thrilling tales. *See* McSweeney's mammoth treasury of thrilling tales

The **chains** that you refuse. Bear, E.

Chambers, Christopher, 1963-

(ed) The darker mask. *See* The darker mask

Chapter and hearse. Aird, C.

Charnas, Suzy McKee

Stagestruck vampires and other phantasms. Tachyon Publications 2004 328p ISBN 1-892391-21-X

Charters, David

The insiders; a portfolio of stories from high finance. St. Martin's Press 2004 c2002 175p ISBN 0-312-33381-1 LC 2004-50315

Charyn, Jerome, 1937-

(ed) Inside the hornet's head. *See* Inside the hornet's head

Chase, Melvyn, 1938-

The terminal project and other voyages of discovery; stories. Sunstone Press 2005 199p ISBN 0-86534-462-0 LC 2005-12391

Chattin, John

Cars go fast; stories. New Rivers Press 2007 143p ISBN 978-0-89823-234-9; 0-89823-234-1 LC 2006-928667

'Winner of the Many Voices Project.'

Cheating at canasta. Trevor, W.

Chekhov, Anton Pavlovich, 1860-1904
A night in the cemetery and other stories of crime & suspense; translated by Peter Sekirin. Pegasus Books 2008 321p ISBN 978-1-933648-86-6

Chemistry and other stories. Rash, R.

Cherne, Barbara, 1940-
Devora in exile; stories. Fithian Press 2009 94p ISBN 978-1-56474-848-5; 1-56474-848-0 LC 2008-51344

Chicago blues; edited by Libby Fischer Hellmann. Bleak House Books 2007 456p ISBN 978-1-932557-49-7

Chicago noir; edited by Neal Pollack. Akashic Books 2005 252p ISBN 978-1-888451-89-4; 1-888451-89-0 LC 2005-925468

Child, Lee
(ed) Killer year. *See* Killer year

A **child** again. Coover, R.

Children playing before a statue of Hercules; edited and introduced by David Sedaris. Simon & Schuster Paperbacks 2005 344p ISBN 0-7432-7394-x LC 2005-42532

Chilson, Peter
Disturbance-loving species; a novella and stories. Houghton Mifflin 2007 229p ISBN 978-0-618-85870-5; 0-618-85870-9 LC 2007-4210
"A Mariner original"

Ch'oe, Yun, 1953-
There a petal silently falls; three stories; by Ch'oe Yun; translated by Bruce and Ju-Chan Fulton. Columbia University Press 2008 192p (Weatherhead books on Asia) ISBN 978-0-231-14296-0; 0-231-14296-X LC 2007-37906

Church booty. Manley, C.

A **circle** is a balloon and compass both. Greenman, B.

Cities; [by] Paul Di Filippo . . . [et al.]; edited and introduced by Peter Crowther. Four Walls Eight Windows 2004 292p ISBN 1-56858-304-4 (pa)

Clarke, Brock
Carrying the torch; stories. University of Nebraska Press 2005 170p (Prairie Schooner book prize in fiction) ISBN 978-0-8032-1551-1 LC 2004-29038

Clarke, Susanna, 1959-
The ladies of Grace Adieu and other stories; illustrated by Charles Vess. Bloomsbury 2006 235p il ISBN 978-159691-251-9; 1-59691-251-0 LC 2006-14197

Clayton, John Jacob
Wrestling with angels; new and collected stories; [by] John J. Clayton. The Toby Press 2007 616p ISBN 978-1-59264-202-1; 1-59264-202-0

Cloud & ashes. Gilman, G. I.

Clouds and eclipses. Vidal, G.

Coake, Christopher
We're in trouble; stories. Harcourt 2005 306p ISBN 0-15-101094-3 LC 2004-17419

Coben, Harlan, 1962-
(ed) Mystery Writers of America presents death do us part. *See* Mystery Writers of America presents death do us part

The **cocaine** chronicles; edited by Gary Phillips and Jervey Tervalon. Akashic Books 2005 269p ISBN 1-888451-75-0 (pa) LC 2004-115619

Cody, Liza
Lucky dip and other stories. Crippen & Landru Publishers 2003 182p ISBN 1-932009-08-6

Coleman, Reed Farrel, 1956-
(ed) Hard boiled Brooklyn. *See* Hard boiled Brooklyn

Coleman, Wanda
Jazz & twelve o'clock tales; new stories. David R. Godine 2007 147p ISBN 978-1-57423-212-7; 1-57423-212-6 LC 2007-30237
"A Black Sparrow book"

The **collected** short stories of Harriette Simpson Arnow. Arnow, H. L. S.

The **Collected** short stories of Louis L'Amour. L'Amour, L.

The **Collected** short stories of Louis L'Amour: the adventure stories: v4. L'Amour, L.

Collected stories. Anderson, B.

Collected stories. Dahl, R.

The **collected** stories. Michaels, L.

Collected stories. Shields, C.

Collected stories and other writings. Porter, K. A.

The **collected** stories of Amy Hempel. Hempel, A.

The **collected** stories of Benedict Kiely. Kiely, B.

The **collected** stories of Ivan Bunin. Bunin, I. A.

The **collected** stories of Jean Stafford. Stafford, J.

Collected stories: One night in Brazil to The death of Methuselah. Singer, I. B.

Collected stories v 1. Matheson, R.

Collected stories v2. Matheson, R.

Collected stories v3. Matheson, R.

Collins, Wilkie, 1824-1889
Sensation stories; tales of mystery and suspense; edited and introduced by Peter Haining. Peter Owen 2004 240p ISBN 0-7206-1220-9

Coloane, Francisco, 1910-
Tierra del Fuego; translated from the Spanish by Howard Curtis. Europa Editions 2008 187p ISBN 978-1-933372-63-1

Come together, fall apart. Henriquez, C.

The **complete** history of New Mexico. McIlvoy, K.

The **complete** stories. Malouf, D.

The **complete** stories of Paul Laurence Dunbar. Dunbar, P. L.

The **complete** stories of Truman Capote. Capote, T.

The **complete** Western stories of Elmore Leonard. Leonard, E.

Conference with the dead. Lamsley, T.

Confessions of a falling woman. Dean, D.

Conlon, Christopher
(ed) Poe's lighthouse. *See* Poe's lighthouse

Connell, Evan S., 1924-
Lost in Uttar Pradesh; new and selected stories. Counterpoint 2008 359p ISBN 978-1-59376-175-2; 1-59376-175-9 LC 2007-43829

Connelly, Michael, 1956-
(ed) The International Association of Crime Writers presents Murder in Vegas. *See* The International Association of Crime Writers presents Murder in Vegas

(ed) Mystery Writers of America presents the blue religion. *See* Mystery Writers of America presents the blue religion

Connolly, David, 1954-
(ed) Angelic & black. *See* Angelic & black

Constance Fenimore Woolson: selected stories & travel narratives. Woolson, C. F.

Constantine, Helen
(tr) Paris tales. *See* Paris tales

Contemporary Jewish writing in Canada; an anthology; edited by Michael Greenstein. University of Nebraska Press 2004 232p (Jewish writing in the contemporary world) ISBN 0-8032-2185-1 LC 2003-23399

Contemporary Maine fiction; an anthology of short stories; edited by Wesley McNair. Down East Books 2005 295p ISBN 0-89272-693-8 LC 2005-9464

Controlled burn. Wolven, S.

Cook, Glen
An empire unacquainted with defeat; stories of the Dread Empire. Night Shade Books 2009 248p ISBN 978-1-59780-140-9

Cook, Will
Blood sky; western stories; edited by Bill Pronzini. Five Star 2006 207p ISBN 1-59414-403-6 LC 2006-13249

Cookie Lily. Troy, M.

Cooper, Dennis, 1953-
Ugly man; stories. Harper Perennial 2009 238, 22p ISBN 978-0-06-171544-0

Cooper, J. California
Wild stars seeking midnight suns. Doubleday 2006 209p ISBN 0-385-51133-7 LC 2005-56004

Coover, Robert
A child again. McSweeney's Books 2005 276p ISBN 1-932416-22-6

Copy cats. Crouse, D.

D'Allesandro, Sam
  The wild creatures; collected stories of Sam D'Allesandro; edited by Kevin Killian. Suspect Thoughts Press 2005 157p ISBN 0-9763411-1-5 LC 2005-19468
Dalton, Quinn
  Bulletproof girl; stories. Washington Square Press 2005 207p ISBN 0-7434-7055-9 LC 2005-278350
D'Ambrosio, Charles, Jr.
  The dead fish museum. Knopf 2006 236p ISBN 1-4000-4286-0 LC 2005-44672
Danger in the dark. Hubbard, L. R.
Dangerous laughter. Millhauser, S.
Dangerous women; edited by Otto Penzler. Mysterious Press 2005 363p ISBN 0-89296-004-3 LC 2004-49870
Dann, Jack
  (ed) Dreaming again. *See* Dreaming again
  The fiction factory; by Jack Dann with Susan Casper . . . [et al.] Golden Gryphon Press 2005 310p ISBN 1-930846-36-3 LC 2005-7098
  (ed) Nebula Awards showcase 2005. *See* Nebula Awards showcase 2005
  (ed) Wizards. *See* Wizards
Dark delicacies; original tales of terror and the macabre by the world's greatest horror writers; edited by Del Howison and Jeff Gelb. Carroll & Graf 2005 274p ISBN 0-7867-1586-3; 0-7867-1676-2 (pa)
Dark delicacies 2; fear: more original tales of terror and the macabre by the world's greatest horror writers; edited by Del Howison and Jeff Gelb. Carroll & Graf: Distributed by Publishers Group West 2007 269p ISBN 978-0-7867-1950-1; 978-0-7867-1951-8 (pa) LC 2007-15515
Dark integers and other stories. Egan, G.
Dark Mondays. Baker, K.
Dark roots. Kennedy, C.
The **darker** mask; edited by Gary Phillips and Christopher Chambers. TOR 2008 388p il ISBN 978-0-7653-1850-3; 0-7653-1850-4; 978-0-7653-1851-0 (pa); 0-7653-1851-2 (pa) LC 2008-30244
The **darts** of Cupid and other stories. Templeton, E.
Datlow, Ellen
  (ed) The Del Rey book of science fiction and fantasy. *See* The Del Rey book of science fiction and fantasy
  (ed) Inferno. *See* Inferno
  (ed) Nebula Awards showcase 2009. *See* Nebula Awards showcase 2009
  (ed) Salon fantastique. *See* Salon fantastique
  (ed) The Year's best fantasy and horror: eighteenth annual collection. *See* The Year's best fantasy and horror: eighteenth annual collection
  (ed) The Year's best fantasy and horror: nineteenth annual collection. *See* The Year's best fantasy and horror: nineteenth annual collection
  (ed) The Year's best fantasy and horror: seventeenth annual collection. *See* The Year's best fantasy and horror: seventeenth annual collection
  (ed) The Year's best fantasy and horror: twentieth annual collection. *See* The Year's best fantasy and horror: twentieth annual collection
  (ed) The Year's best fantasy and horror: twenty-first annual collection. *See* The Year's best fantasy and horror: twenty-first annual collection
Daugherty, Tracy
  Late in the standoff; stories and a novella. Southern Methodist University Press 2005 177p ISBN 0-87074-498-4 LC 2005-45147
Daughters of earth; feminist science fiction in the twentieth century; edited by Justine Larbalestier. Wesleyan University Press 2006 397p ISBN 978-0-8195-6675-1; 0-8195-6675-6; 978-0-8195-6676-8 (pa); 0-8195-6676-4 (pa) LC 2005-30647
    Analyzed for short stories only
Daughtry, Philip
  The centaur's son. Mercury House 2008 218p ISBN 978-1-56279-131-5

Davidson, Craig, 1976-
  Rust and bone; stories. Norton 2005 239p ISBN 0-393-06129-9
    LC 2005-27727
Davies, Lewis
  (ed) Urban Welsh. *See* Urban Welsh
Davis, Claire, 1949-
  Labors of the heart; stories. St. Martin's Press 2006 228p ISBN
    978-0-312-33284-6; 0-312-33284-X LC 2006-40633
Davis, Jennifer S., 1973-
  Our former lives in art; (stories). Random House 2007 194p ISBN
    978-1-4000-6329-1; 1-4000-6329-9 LC 2006-49228
Dawson, Peter, 1907-1957
  Showdown at Anchor; a western quintet. Five Star 2005 230p ISBN
    1-59414-168-1 LC 2005-12057
A **day,** a night, another day, summer. Schutt, C.
The **day** I ate whatever I wanted. Berg, E.
De Camp, L. Sprague, 1907-2000
  Years in the making; the time-travel stories of L. Sprague de Camp;
    edited by Mark L. Olson. The NESFA Press 2005 377p (L. Sprague
    de Camp, volume 1) ISBN 1-886778-47-7
      Analyzed for short stories only
De Camp, L. Sprague, 1907-2000, and Pratt, Fletcher, 1897-1956
  The mathematics of magic; the Enchanter stories of L. Sprague de
    Camp and Fletcher Pratt; edited by Mark L. Olson. The NESFA
    Press 2007 507p (L. Sprague de Camp, volume 2) ISBN
    978-1-886778-65-8; 1-886778-65-5
De Lint, Charles, 1951-
  The hour before dawn; and two other stories from Newford.
    Subterranean Press 2005 114p ISBN 1-59606-027-1
Dead boys. Lange, R.
The **dead** fish museum. D'Ambrosio, C., Jr.
Dead man's hand; crime fiction at the poker table; edited by Otto
    Penzler. Harcourt 2007 384p ISBN 978-0-15-101277-0
    LC 2007-9583
The **Deadly** Bride; and 21 of the year's finest crime and mystery stories;
    including complete coverage of the year in mystery and crime
    fiction; edited by Ed Gorman and Martin H. Greenberg. Carroll &
    Graf Publishers 2007 553p ISBN 978-0-7867-1917-4;
    0-7867-1917-6
Deadly housewives; edited by Christine Matthews. Avon Trade 2006
    283p ISBN 978-0-06-085327-3 LC 2005-55877
Dean, Debra, 1957-
  Confessions of a falling woman; and other stories. HarperCollins
    Publishers 2008 224p ISBN 978-0-060-82532-4 LC 2007-48212
DeAndrea, William L.
  Murder-all kinds; introduction by Jane Haddam. Crippen & Landru
    Publishers 2003 208p ISBN 1-932009-12-4; 1-932009-13-2 (pa)
Dear husband, Oates, J. C.
Deaver, Jeff
  (ed) The Best American mystery stories, 2009. *See* The Best American
    mystery stories, 2009
  More twisted; collected stories, v2; [by] Jeffery Deaver. Simon &
    Schuster 2006 433p ISBN 978-1-4165-4118-9; 1-4165-4118-7
    LC 2006-52243
  (ed) A New omnibus of crime. *See* A New omnibus of crime
The **decapitated** chicken and other stories. Quiroga, H.
The **Del** Rey book of science fiction and fantasy; sixteen original works
    by speculative fiction's finest voices; edited by Ellen Datlow. Del
    Rey Books 2008 400p ISBN 978-0-345-49632-4 LC 2008-4948
      "A Del Rey trade paperback original"
Delicate edible birds and other stories. Groff, L.
DeMarinis, Rick, 1934-
  Apocalypse then. Seven Stories Press 2004 271p ISBN 1-58322-637-0
    LC 2004-12305
DeMille, Nelson
  (ed) The Best American mystery stories, 2004. *See* The Best American
    mystery stories, 2004
Demons in the spring. Meno, J.

DeNiro, Alan
    Skinny dipping in the Lake of the Dead; stories. Small Beer Press 2006 215p ISBN 1-931520-17-8; 978-1-931520-17-1 LC 2006-4977

The **deportees** and other stories. Doyle, R.

Dery, Tibor
    Love and other stories; introduction by George Szirtes. New Directions 2005 254p ISBN 0-8112-1625-X LC 2005-00995

Desaulniers, Janet, 1954-
    What you've been missing; by Janet Desaulniers. University of Iowa 2004 125p (The John Simmons short fiction award) ISBN 0-87745-910-X (pa) LC 2004-46068

Desert gothic. Waters, D.

The **Detection** collection; edited by Simon Brett. St. Martin's Minotaur 2006 195p ISBN 0-312-35763-X; 978-0-312-35763-4 LC 2006-40430

Detroit noir; edited by E. J. Olsen & John C. Hocking. Akashic Books 2007 280p ISBN 978-1-933354-39-2 LC 2007-926098

The **development**. Barth, J.

Devora in exile. Cherne, B.

Dharmarajan, Geeta
    (ed) Separate journeys. *See* Separate journeys

Di Filippo, Paul
    The emperor of Gondwanaland and other stories. Thunder's Mouth Press 2005 370p ISBN 1-56025-665-6
    Shuteye for the timebroker; stories. Thunder's Mouth Press 2006 312p ISBN 1-56025-817-9; 978-1-56025-817-9

Díaz, Gwendolyn Josie
    Women and power in Argentine literature; stories, interviews, and critical essays; [by] Gwendolyn Díaz. University of Texas Press 2007 376p (Texas Pan American literature in translation series) ISBN 978-0-2927-1648-3; 0-2927-1648-6; 978-0-2927-1649-0 (pa); 0-2927-1649-4 (pa) LC 2006-23555

Dictation. Ozick, C.

The **dictionary** of failed relationships; 26 tales of love gone wrong; edited by Meredith Broussard. Three Rivers Press 2003 294p ISBN 0-609-81009-X (pa) LC 2002-152193

The **difference** between women and men. Lott, B.

Different kinds of dead and other tales. Gorman, E.

Dillinger in Hollywood. Sayles, J.

Dinner with Osama. Krysl, M.

The **disappearance**. Stavans, I.

Disch, Thomas M., 1940-2008
    The wall of America. Tachyon Publications 2008 245p ISBN 978-1-892391-82-7; 1-892391-82-1

Discouraging at best. Lawson, J. E.

Disturbance-loving species. Chilson, P.

Divakaruni, Chitra Banerjee, 1956-
    (ed) California uncovered. *See* California uncovered

Do not deny me. Thompson, J.

Do the blind dream? Gifford, B.

Đoàn, Lê
    The cemetery of Chua village and other stories; by Doan Le; chief translator, Rosemary Nguyen, with additional translations by Duong Tuong and Wayne Karlin. Curbstone Press 2005 189p (Voices from Vietnam) ISBN 1-931896-12-7 LC 2004-21258

Dobie, Ann B.
    (ed) Wide awake in the Pelican State. *See* Wide awake in the Pelican State

Dobozy, Tamas, 1969-
    Last notes and other stories. Arcade Publishing 2006 c2005 181p ISBN 1-55970-808-5 LC 2005-29603
        First published 2005 in Canada

Doctor Olaf van Schuler's brain. Menger-Anderson, K.

Doctorow, Cory
    Overclocked; stories of the future present. Thunder's Mouth Press 2007 285p ISBN 978-1-56025-981-7; 1-56025-981-7

The **dog** of the marriage. Hempel, A.

The **dog** said bow-wow. Swanwick, M.

Dogs of truth. Reed, K.

Dokey, Richard
   Pale morning dun; stories. University of Missouri Press 2004 164p
      ISBN 0-8262-1511-4 LC 2003-22909
Domecq, Brianda, 1942-
   When I was a horse; translated by Kay (Kayla) S. Garcia. TCU Press
      2006   203p   ISBN   0-87565-325-1;   978-0-87565-325-9
      LC 2005-24862
Donoghue, Emma, 1969-
   Touchy   subjects;   stories.   Harcourt   2006   280p   ISBN
      978-0-15-101386-9; 0-15-101386-1 LC 2005-26170
Donovan, Gerard
   Young Irelanders; stories. Overlook Press 2008 223p ISBN
      978-1-59020-030-8
Don't cry. Gaitskill, M.
Don't make me stop now. Parker, M.
Don't tell me the truth about love. Rhodes, D.
The **door** to Saturn. Smith, C. A.
Doran, Maggie Morgan
   Gentle hearts, guilty sins. TripleTree Publishing 2003 187p ISBN
      0-9716638-3-1 LC 2002109712
Dormen, Lesley
   The best place to be. Simon & Schuster 2007 176p ISBN
      978-1-4165-3261-3; 1-4165-3261-7 LC 2006-50184
Downs, Greg, 1971-
   Spit baths; stories. University of Georgia Press 2006 174p (Flannery
      O'Connor Award for Short Fiction) ISBN 978-0-8203-2846-1;
      0-8203-2846-4 LC 2005-37602
Downtrain. Nisbet, R.
Doyle, Roddy
   The deportees and other stories. Viking 2008 c2007 242p ISBN
      978-0-670-01845-1 LC 2007-17659
Dozois, Gardner R.
   (ed) The Best of the best, volume 2. *See* The Best of the best, volume
      2
   (ed) Nebula Awards showcase 2006. *See* Nebula Awards showcase
      2006
   (ed) The new space opera. *See* The new space opera
   (ed) The new space opera 2. *See* The new space opera 2
   (ed) Wizards. *See* Wizards
   (ed) The Year's best science fiction: twenty-fifth annual collection.
      See The Year's best science fiction: twenty-fifth annual collection
   (ed) The Year's best science fiction: twenty-first annual collection. *See*
      The Year's best science fiction: twenty-first annual collection
   (ed) The Year's best science fiction: twenty-fourth annual collection.
      See The Year's best science fiction: twenty-fourth annual collection
   (ed) The Year's best science fiction: twenty-second annual collection.
      See The Year's best science fiction: twenty-second annual collection
   (ed) The Year's best science fiction: twenty-third annual collection.
      See The Year's best science fiction: twenty-third annual collection
Dr. King's refrigerator and other bedtime stories. Johnson, C. R.
The **dream** of X and other fantastic visions. Hodgson, W. H.
Dreaming again; thirty-five new stories celebrating the wild side of
      Australian fiction; edited by Jack Dann. HarperCollins 2008 566p
      ISBN 978-0-06-136408-2 LC 2009-275002
Dreams and realities. Gorriti, J. M.
Dreamsongs: volume I. Martin, G. R. R.
Dreamsongs: volume II. Martin, G. R. R.
Dreamwish beasts and snarks. Resnick, M.
Driver, Andrew
   (tr) Shame in the blood. *See* Miura, Tetsuo, 1931-. Shame in the blood
Dropped from heaven. Judah, S.
Drosso, Anne-Marie, 1951-
   Cairo stories. Telegram 2007 208p ISBN 978-1-84659-025-2;
      1-84659-025-6
The **drowned** life. Ford, J.
Drowning in Gruel. Singleton, G.
Drowning lessons. Selgin, P.

Dublin noir; the Celtic tiger vs. the ugly American; edited by Ken Bruen. Akashic Books 2006 228p ISBN 978-1-888451-92-4; 1-888451-92-0 LC 2005-925466

Ducornet, Rikki

The one marvelous thing; decorated by T. Motley. Dalkey Archive Press 2008 161p il ISBN 978-1-56478-519-0 LC 2008-14617

Dufresne, John, 1948-

Johnny too bad; stories. Norton 2005 247p ISBN 0-393-05789-5 LC 2004-22794

Dunbar, Paul Laurence, 1872-1906

The complete stories of Paul Laurence Dunbar; edited by Gene Andrew Jarrett and Thomas Lewis Morgan; foreword by Shelley Fisher Fishkin. Ohio University Press 2005 542p ISBN 0-8214-1644-8 LC 2005-25267

Duncan, Andy, 1964-

(ed) Crossroads. *See* Crossroads

Duncklee, John, 1929-

Bull by the tale. University of New Mexico Press 2006 287p ISBN 978-0-8263-3889-1; 0-8263-3889-5 LC 2006-10481

Duval, Pete

Rear view. Houghton Mifflin Company 2004 151p ISBN 0-618-44140-9 (pa) LC 2004-47341

E

Early American detective stories; an anthology; edited by LeRoy Lad Panek and Mary M. Bendel-Simso. McFarland & Co. 2008 349p ISBN 978-0-7864-3711-5; 0-7864-3711-1 LC 2008-1849

Early novels and stories. Maxwell, W.

Earthquake. Barnes, S.

The **easiest** thing in the world. Higgins, G. V.

Eating mammals. Barlow, J.

Ebenbach, David Harris

Between Camelots. University of Pittsburgh Press 2005 157p ISBN 0-8229-4268-2 LC 2005-14145

Partially analyzed

The **Ecco** anthology of contemporary American short fiction; selected by Joyce Carol Oates and Christopher R. Beha. HarperCollins 2008 759p ISBN 978-0-06-166158-7 LC 2008-36467

The **Ecco** book of Christmas stories; edited by Alberto Manguel. Ecco 2006 335p ISBN 978-0-06-088848-0; 0-06-088848-2 LC 2006-48165

Eclipse one; new science fiction and fantasy; edited by Jonathan Strahan. Night Shade Books 2007 263p ISBN 978-1-59780-117-1

Eclipse two; new science fiction and fantasy; edited by Jonathan Strahan. Night Shade Books 2008 287p ISBN 978-1-59780-136-2

Edwards, Jennifer Gabrielle, 1971-

(tr and comp.) The Flight of the condor. *See* The Flight of the condor

Effinger, George Alec, 1947-2002

George Alec Effinger live! from planet Earth; featuring contributions by Neal Barrett Jr. ... {et al.}. Golden Gryphon Press 2005 360p ISBN 1-930846-32-0 LC 2004016935

A thousand deaths; with an introduction by Mike Resnick and an afterword by Andrew Fox. Golden Gryphon Press 2007 340p ISBN 978-1-930846-47-0; 1-930846-47-9 LC 2006-100695

Analyzed for short stories only

Egan, Greg, 1961-

Dark integers and other stories. Subterranean Press 2008 232p ISBN 978-1-5906-155-2

The **egg** lady and other neighbors. Currans-Sheehan, T.

Eggers, Dave, 1970-

How we are hungry. McSweeney's Books [2004] 224p ISBN 1-932416-13-7

Partially analyzed

Eisenberg, Deborah

Twilight of the superheroes. Farrar, Straus & Giroux 2006 225p ISBN 978-0-374-29941-5; 0-374-29941-2 LC 2005-42659

The **Elagin** affair and other stories. Bunin, I. A.

F

Faber, Michel

Vanilla bright like Eminem; stories. Harcourt 2007 246p ISBN 978-0-15-101314-2 LC 2006-103560

First published 2005 in the United Kingdom with title: The Fahrenheit twins

Facing the bridge. Tawada, Y.

The **facts** behind the Helsinki Roccamatios. Martel, Y.

The **Fahrenheit** twins. *See* Faber, M. Vanilla bright like Eminem

Fairstein, Linda

(ed) Mystery Writers of America presents the prosecution rests. *See* Mystery Writers of America presents the prosecution rests

The **faith** healer of Olive Avenue. Muñoz, M.

The **family** Diamond. Schwarzschild, E.

Farewell navigator. Zumas, L.

Farmer, Philip José, 1918-2009

Venus on the half-shell and others; edited by Christopher Paul Carey. Subterranean Press 2008 323p ISBN 978-1-59606-142-2

Analyzed for short stories only

Fascination. Boyd, W.

Fast forward 1; future fiction from the cutting edge; edited by Lou Anders. Pyr 2007 409p ISBN 978-1-59102-486-6 LC 2006-35269

Fast ships, black sails; edited by Ann & Jeff VanderMeer. Night Shade Books 2008 241p ISBN 978-1-59780-094-5

The **fate** of mice. Palwick, S.

A **feast** of longing. Klassen, S.

Feeling very strange; the Slipstream anthology; James Patrick Kelly & John Kessel, editors. Tachyon Publications 2006 288p ISBN 978-1-892391-35-X; 1-892391-35-X

Feitell, Merrill, 1971-

Here beneath low-flying planes. University of Iowa Press 2004 123p (The Iowa short fiction award) ISBN 0-87745-911-8 LC 2004-45979

Felman, Dedi

(ed) Words without borders. *See* Words without borders

The **female** of the species. Oates, J. C.

Fenway fiction; short stories from Red Sox nation; edited by Adam Emerson Pachter. Rounder Books 2005 231p ISBN 1-57940-119-8

The **fiction** factory. Dann, J.

Filter house. Shawl, N.

Finch, Sheila, 1935-

The guild of xenolinguists; with a foreword by Ian Watson. Golden Gryphon Press 2007 281p ISBN 978-1-930846-48-7; 1-930846-48-7 LC 2007-6550

Fincke, Gary

Sorry I worried you; stories. University of Georgia Press 2004 217p (Flannery O'Connor Award for short fiction) ISBN 0-8203-2656-9 LC 2004-07413

Fine just the way it is. Proulx, A.

Finger, Anne

Call me Ahab; a short story collection. University of Nebraska Press 2009 192p ISBN 978-0-8032-2533-6 LC 2009-04673

Finlay, Charles Coleman

Wild things. Subterranean Press 2005 230p ISBN 1-59606-030-1

The **first** hurt. Sherman, R.

The **first** person and other stories. Smith, A.

Fisher, Chris, 1957-

Third and long. Coteau Books 2004 271p ISBN 1-55050-290-5

The **five-forty-five** to Cannes. Holthe, T. U.

Flaig, Suzanne

(ed) Medium of murder. *See* Medium of murder

Flanagan, Erin

The usual mistakes. University of Nebraska Press 2005 202p (Flyover fiction) ISBN 0-8032-2029-4 LC 2005-4224

The **Flight** of the condor; stories of violence and war from Colombia; translated and compiled by Jennifer Gabrielle Edwards; foreword by Hugo Chaparro Valderrama. University of Wisconsin Press 2007 xxvii, 156p ISBN 0-299-22360-4; 0-299-22364-7 LC 2007-11784

Flower children. Swann, M.

Flying to America. Barthelme, D.

Follies. Beattie, A.

Fonseca, Rubem
   The taker and other stories; translated from the Portuguese by Clifford E. Landers. Open Letter 2008 166p ISBN 978-1-934824-02-3; 1-934824-02-X LC 2008-926609

Ford, Jeffrey, 1955-
   The drowned life. Harper Perennial 2008 290, 16p ISBN 978-0-06-143506-5; 0-06-143506-6 LC 2008-13181
   The empire of ice cream; with an introduction by Jonathan Carroll. Golden Gryphon Press 2006 319p ISBN 1-930846-39-8 LC 2005-24035

Ford, Richard, 1944-
   (ed) The New Granta book of the American short story. *See* The New Granta book of the American short story

The **forgotten** adventures of Sherlock Holmes. Jeffers, H. P.

Forrest, Katherine V., 1939-
   (ed) Women of mystery. *See* Women of mystery

Fountain, Ben
   Brief encounters with Che Guevara; stories. Ecco 2006 229p ISBN 978-0-06-088558-8; 0-06-088558-0 LC 2005-49507

Fourbodings; [by] Simon Clark . . . [et al.]; edited by Peter Crowther. Cemetery Dance 2005 384p ISBN 1-58767-090-9

Fourth planet from the sun; tales of Mars from The Magazine of Fantasy & Science Fiction; edited by Gordon Van Gelder. Thunder's Mouth Press 2005 307p ISBN 1-56025-666-4 LC 2005-277759

Fowler, Karen Joy
   (ed) The James Tiptree Award Anthology 2. *See* The James Tiptree Award Anthology 2
   (ed) The James Tiptree Award Anthology 3. *See* The James Tiptree Award Anthology 3

Fragile things. Gaiman, N.

Franklin, Emily
   (ed) Before. *See* Before

Frawley, Oona
   (ed) New Dubliners. *See* New Dubliners

Freed, Lynn
   The curse of the appropriate man. Harcourt 2004 188p ISBN 0-15-602994-4 LC 2004-5914
      "A Harvest original"

Fresh apples. Trezise, R.

The **friend** of women and other stories. Auchincloss, L.

From Africa; new francophone stories; edited by Adele King. University of Nebraska Press 2004 150p ISBN 0-8032-2758-2; 0-8032-7810-1 (pa) LC 2003-53347

Frost, Gregory
   Attack of the jazz giants and other stories; with a foreword by Karen Joy Fowler and an afterword by John Kessel. Golden Gryphon Press 2004 344p ISBN 1-930846-34-7 LC 2004-26627

Fuchs, Daniel, 1909-1993
   The golden West; Hollywood stories; selected by Christopher Carduff; introduction by John Updike. Godine 2005 256p ISBN 1-57423-205-3 LC 2004-29888
      "A Black Sparrow book"
      Analyzed for short stories only

Fuentes, Carlos, 1928-
   Happy families; stories; translated by Edith Grossman. Random House 2008 331p ISBN 978-1-4000-6688-9; 1-4000-6688-3 LC 2008-02335
      Original Spanish edition, 2006

Fulton, Alice, 1952-
   The nightingales of Troy; stories of one family's century. W.W. Norton 2008 254p ISBN 978-0-393-04887-2; 0-393-04887-X LC 2008-13206

Fulton, Bruce, 1942-
   (tr & ed) Land of exile: contemporary Korean fiction. *See* Land of exile: contemporary Korean fiction

Fulton, Bruce, 1942-—*Continued*

(tr) There a petal silently falls. *See* Ch'oe, Yun, 1953-. There a petal silently falls

Fulton, John, 1967-

The animal girl; two novellas and three stories. Louisiana State University Press 2007 174p (Yellow shoe fiction) ISBN 978-0-8071-3294-4; 0-8071-3294-2 LC 2007-15679

Fulton, Ju-Chan

(tr & ed) Land of exile: contemporary Korean fiction. *See* Land of exile: contemporary Korean fiction

(tr) There a petal silently falls. *See* Ch'oe, Yun, 1953-. There a petal silently falls

Furman, Laura

(ed) The O. Henry Prize stories, 2005. *See* The O. Henry Prize stories, 2005

(ed) The O. Henry Prize stories, 2006. *See* The O. Henry Prize stories, 2006

(ed) The O. Henry Prize stories 2008. *See* The O. Henry Prize stories 2008

(ed) The PEN/O.Henry Prize stories 2009. *See* The PEN/O.Henry Prize stories 2009

Future Americas; edited by Martin H. Greenberg and John Helferd. Daw Books 2008 312p ISBN 978-0-7564-0508-3

Future missionaries of America. Vollmer, M.

G

Gabrielyan, Nina

Master of the grass; translated by Kathleen Cook, Joanne Turnbull, Jean MacKenzie, and Sofi Cook. GLAS Pubs 2004 208p ISBN 5-7172-0066-8

Gaiman, Neil, 1960-

Fragile things; short fictions and wonders. William Morrow 2006 xxxi, 360p ISBN 978-0-06-051522-5; 0-06-051522-8 LC 2006-48135

Gaitskill, Mary, 1954-

(ed) Best new American voices 2009. *See* Best new American voices 2009

Don't cry; stories. Pantheon Books 2009 226p ISBN 978-0-375-42419-9; 0-375-42419-9 LC 2008-25231

Gallagher, Stephen

Plots and misadventures. Subterranean Press 2007 260p ISBN 978-1-59606-114-9

Gallatin Canyon. McGuane, T.

The **galosh** and other stories. Zoshchenko, M.

Gappah, Petina, 1971-

An elegy for easterly; stories. Faber and Faber 2009 224p ISBN 978-0-86547-906-7; 0-86547-906-2 LC 2008-49219

Gardam, Jane

The people on Privilege Hill and other stories. Europa Editions 2008 196p ISBN 978-1-933372-56-3

A **garden** amid fires. Swan, G.

The **garden** in which I walk. Brennan, K.

The **garden** of Eden and other criminal delights. Kellerman, F.

Gardiner, John Rolfe

The Magellan House; stories; illustrations by Joan Gardiner. Counterpoint 2004 297p il ISBN 1-582-43233-3 LC 2004-4932

Garrett, George P., 1929-2008

Empty bed blues. University of Missouri Press 2006 179p ISBN 0-8262-1630-7; 978-0-8262-1630-4 LC 2005-32955

Garrett in wedlock. Mandelbaum, P.

Gaslight grimoire; fantastic tales of Sherlock Holmes; edited by J. R. Campbell and Charles Prepolec. EDGE 2008 317p ISBN 978-1-8964063-17-3

The **gateway**. McNally, T. M.

Gay, Jackie

(ed) Her Majesty. *See* Her Majesty

God's gym. Wideman, J. E.

Going the distance; edited by Alan Beard. Tindall Street Press 2003 267p ISBN 0-9541303-5-9

The **gold** of the sunbeams and other stories. Mukhopadhyay, T.

Golden, Christopher
 (ed) British invasion. *See* British invasion

The **golden** West. Fuchs, D.

Goldfaden, Josh, 1972-
 Human resources; stories. Tin House Books 2007 236p (Tin House new voice) ISBN 978-0-9776989-1-2; 0-9776989-1-2 LC 2006-100130

The **good** life. McGraw, E.

A **good** place for the night. Liebrecht, S.

Good women. Stevenson, J.

Goodbye, Wisconsin. Wescott, G.

Goodis, David, 1917-1967
 Black Friday and other stories; edited and introduced by Adrian Wootton. Serpent's Tail 2006 434p ISBN 1-85242-469-9; 978-1-85242-469-5 LC 2006-494189
   Analyzed for short stories only

Gordimer, Nadine, 1923-
 Beethoven was one-sixteenth black; and other stories. Farrar, Straus and Giroux 2007 177p ISBN 978-0-374-10982-0; 0-374-10982-6 LC 2007-33474
 (ed) Telling tales. *See* Telling tales

Gordon, Mary, 1949-
 The stories of Mary Gordon. Pantheon Books 2006 457p ISBN 0-375-42316-8 LC 2006-44275

Gorman, Edward
 (ed) The Adventure of the missing detective and 19 of the year's finest crime and mystery stories! *See* The Adventure of the missing detective and 19 of the year's finest crime and mystery stories!
 (ed) The Deadly Bride. *See* The Deadly Bride
 Different kinds of dead and other tales. Five Star 2005 320p ISBN 1-59414-213-0 LC 2005005998
 (ed) A Prisoner of memory and 24 of the year's finest crime and mystery stories. *See* A Prisoner of memory and 24 of the year's finest crime and mystery stories
 (ed) Wolf Woman Bay. *See* Wolf Woman Bay
 (ed) The World's finest mystery and crime stories, fifth annual collection. *See* The World's finest mystery and crime stories, fifth annual collection
 (ed) The World's finest mystery and crime stories, fourth annual collection. *See* The World's finest mystery and crime stories, fourth annual collection

Gorriti, Juana Manuela, 1818-1892
 Dreams and realities; selected fiction of Juana Manuela Gorriti; translated from the Spanish by Sergio Waisman; edited, with an introduction and notes by Francine Masiello. Oxford University Press 2003 lxiii, 270p (Library of Latin America) ISBN 0-19-511737-9; 0-19-511738-7 (pa) LC 2002-31175

Gospodinov, Georgi, 1968-
 And other stories; translated from the Bulgarian by Alexis Levitin and Magdalena Levy. Northwestern University Press 2007 81p (Writings from an unbound Europe) ISBN 978-0-8101-2431-8; 0-8101-2431-9; 978-0-8101-2432-5 (pa); 0-8101-2432-7 (pa) LC 2007-12841

Goss, Theodora
 (ed) Interfictions. *See* Interfictions

Gottlieb, Daphne, 1968-
 (ed) Homewrecker: an adultery reader. *See* Homewrecker: an adultery reader

Grafton, Sue
 (ed) A New omnibus of crime. *See* A New omnibus of crime

Graham, Don, 1940-
 (ed) Lone Star literature. *See* Lone Star literature

Graham, Toni, 1945-
 Waiting for Elvis; stories. Leapfrog Press 2005 214p ISBN 0-9728984-4-1 LC 2004-10610

Granados, Christine, 1969-
 Brides and sinners in El Chuco; short stories. University of Arizona
 Press 2006 120p (Camino del sol) ISBN 978-0-8165-2492-1;
 0-8165-2492-0 LC 2005-17333

Grant, Gavin J.
 (ed) The Best of Lady Churchill's rosebud wristlet. *See* The Best of
 Lady Churchill's rosebud wristlet
 (ed) The Year's best fantasy and horror: eighteenth annual collection.
 See The Year's best fantasy and horror: eighteenth annual collection
 (ed) The Year's best fantasy and horror: nineteenth annual collection.
 See The Year's best fantasy and horror: nineteenth annual collection
 (ed) The Year's best fantasy and horror: seventeenth annual collection.
 See The Year's best fantasy and horror: seventeenth annual
 collection
 (ed) The Year's best fantasy and horror: twentieth annual collection.
 See The Year's best fantasy and horror: twentieth annual collection
 (ed) The Year's best fantasy and horror: twenty-first annual collection.
 See The Year's best fantasy and horror: twenty-first annual
 collection

Granville-Barker, Harley, 1877-1946
 Richard goes to prison, and other stories; edited and with a critical
 appreciation by Eric Salmon. Fairleigh Dickinson University Press
 2004 136p ISBN 0-8386-4025-7 LC 2004-05452

The **great** Mormon cricket fly-fishing festival and other western stories.
 Bishop, T.

Greatest hits; original stories of assassins, hitmen, and hired guns;
 edited by Robert J. Randisi. Carroll & Graf 2005 318p ISBN
 978-0-7867-1581-7; 0-78671-581-2 LC 2006-297413

Green, Geoffrey, 1951-
 Voices in a mask; stories. Northwestern University Press 2008 236p
 ISBN 978-0-8101-5209-0; 0-8101-5209-6 LC 2008-9853

Green, Roland J.
 (ed) Alternate generals III. *See* Alternate generals III

Greenberg, Martin Harry
 (ed) The Adventure of the missing detective and 19 of the year's
 finest crime and mystery stories! *See* The Adventure of the missing
 detective and 19 of the year's finest crime and mystery stories!
 (ed) The Deadly Bride. *See* The Deadly Bride
 (ed) Future Americas. *See* Future Americas
 (ed) Ghosts in Baker Street. *See* Ghosts in Baker Street
 (ed) The Mammoth book of golden age science fiction. *See* The
 Mammoth book of golden age science fiction
 (ed) Man vs. machine. *See* Man vs. machine
 (ed) Pandora's closet. *See* Pandora's closet
 (ed) Places to be, people to kill. *See* Places to be, people to kill
 (ed) A Prisoner of memory and 24 of the year's finest crime and
 mystery stories. *See* A Prisoner of memory and 24 of the year's
 finest crime and mystery stories
 (ed) Sherlock Holmes in America. *See* Sherlock Holmes in America
 (ed) Wolf Woman Bay. *See* Wolf Woman Bay
 (ed) The World's finest mystery and crime stories, fifth annual
 collection. *See* The World's finest mystery and crime stories, fifth
 annual collection
 (ed) The World's finest mystery and crime stories, fourth annual
 collection. *See* The World's finest mystery and crime stories, fourth
 annual collection

Greenman, Ben, 1969-
 A circle is a balloon and compass both; stories about human love.
 MacAdam Cage 2007 273p il ISBN 978-1-59692-207-5;
 1-59692-207-9 LC 2006-103280

Greenstein, Michael
 (ed) Contemporary Jewish writing in Canada. *See* Contemporary
 Jewish writing in Canada

Greetings. Bisson, T.

Grimes, Christopher
 Public works. Fiction Collective Two 2005 200p ISBN 1-57366-124-4
 LC 2005-13409
  Partially analyzed

Groff, Lauren
  Delicate edible birds and other stories. Hyperion 2009 306p ISBN
    978-1-4013-4086-5 LC 2008-44002
Grossman, Edith
  (tr) Happy families. *See* Fuentes, Carlos, 1928-. Happy families
The **guild** of xenolinguists. Finch, S.
Guinevere's truth and other tales. Roberson, J.
Guista, Michael
  Brain work; stories. Houghton Mifflin 2005 178p ISBN 0-618-54672-3
    LC 2005-8776
      "A Mariner original"
Gunn, Eileen
  Stable strategies and others. Tachyon Publications 2004 206p ISBN
    1-892391-18-X (pa)
Guo, Songfen, 1938-2005
  Running mother and other stories; edited and with an introduction by
    John Balcom. Columbia University Press 2009 259p (Modern
    Chinese literature from Taiwan) ISBN 978-0-231-14734-7;
    978-0-231-51930-4 (electronic) LC 2008-11613
Gurba, Myriam
  Dahlia season; stories & a novella. Manic D Press 2007 190p (Future
    tense series) ISBN 978-1-933149-16-5; 1-933149-16-7
    LC 2007-10565
Gurganus, Allan
  (ed) New stories from the South: the year's best, 2006. *See* New
    stories from the South: the year's best, 2006
The **Guyanese** wanderer. Carew, J.

H

H.P. Lovecraft. Lovecraft, H. P.
Hadley, Tessa
  Sunstroke and other stories. Picador 2007 177p ISBN
    978-0-312-42599-9; 0-312-42599-6 LC 2007-13103
Haining, Peter, 1940-2007
  Sensation stories. See Collins, Wilkie, 1824-1889
Haldeman, Joe W., 1943-
  A separate war and other stories. Ace Books 2006 269p ISBN
    0-441-01407-0 LC 2006-6120
  War stories. Night Shade Books 2005 398p ISBN 1-59780-022-8
    Analyzed for short stories only
Halpern, Marty
  (ed) Witpunk. *See* Witpunk
Hamilton, Denise
  (ed) Los Angeles noir. *See* Los Angeles noir
Hammett, Dashiell, 1894-1961
  Lost stories; 21 long-lost stories from the best selling creator of Sam
    Spade, The Maltese Falcon, and The Thin Man; introduction by
    3-time Edgar Award winner Joe Gores; edited by Vince Emery.
    Vince Emery Productions 2005 342p ISBN 0-9725898-1-3;
    978-0-9725898-1-9
      Partially analyzed
Hand, Elizabeth, 1957-
  Saffron and Brimstone; strange stories; a collection. M Press 2006
    240p ISBN 1-59582-096-5; 978-1-59582-096-9 LC 2006-37134
The **hanging** in the foaling barn. Richards, S. S.
Happy families. Fuentes, C.
A **happy** man and other stories, or/oder, Der Glückliche und andere
    Erzählungen. Thormählen, A.
Happy trails to you. Hecht, J.
Hard boiled Brooklyn; edited by Reed Farrel Coleman. Bleak House
    Books 2006 219p il ISBN 1-932557-17-2 LC 2005-936203
Hardcore hardboiled; edited by Todd Robinson; introduction by Otto
    Penzler. Kensington Books 2008 308p ISBN 978-0-7582-2266-4;
    0-7582-2266-1
Hardly knew her. Lippman, L.
Hargrave, Emma
  (ed) Her Majesty. *See* Her Majesty

Henderson, Bill, 1941-—*Continued*

(ed) The Pushcart Prize XXX: best of the small presses 2006. *See* The Pushcart Prize XXX: best of the small presses 2006

(ed) Pushcart prize XXXI: best of the small presses 2007. *See* Pushcart prize XXXI: best of the small presses 2007

(ed) Pushcart prize XXXII: best of the small presses 2008. *See* Pushcart prize XXXII: best of the small presses 2008

(ed) Pushcart prize XXXIII: best of the small presses 2009. *See* Pushcart prize XXXIII: best of the small presses 2009

Henriquez, Cristina, 1977-

Come together, fall apart; a novella and stories. Riverhead Books 2006 306p ISBN 1-59448-915-7 LC 2005-50848

Henry, Will, 1912-1991

A bullet for Billy the Kid; a western trio. Five Star 2009 251p ISBN 978-1-59414-725-8; 1-59414-725-6 LC 2008-39750

"A Five Star western"

Her Majesty; 21 stories by women; edited by Jackie Gay and Emma Hargrave. Tindal Street Press 2003 2002 223p ISBN 0-9535895-7-9

Herbert, Rosemary

(ed) A New omnibus of crime. *See* A New omnibus of crime

Here & elsewhere. Burke, K.

Here beneath low-flying planes. Feitell, M.

Hermann, Eliana Cazaubon, 1930-

(ed) English translations of short stories by contemporary Argentine women writers. *See* English translations of short stories by contemporary Argentine women writers

Hernandez, Lisa

Migrations and other stories. Arte Público Press 2007 167p ISBN 978-1-55885-499-4 LC 2006-51735

Hernandez, Lolita, 1947-

Autopsy of an engine and other stories from the Cadillac plant. Coffee House Press 2004 175p ISBN 1-566-89161-2 LC 2004-12787

Herrmann, Marianne

Signaling for rescue. New Rivers Press 2007 193p ISBN 978-0-89823-235-6; 0-89823-235-X LC 2006-928668

Many Voices Project winner

Herzinger, Kim A., 1946-

(ed) Flying to America. *See* Barthelme, Donald. Flying to America

The **heyday** of the insensitive bastards. Boswell, R.

Hiaasen, Carl, 1953-

(ed) The Best American mystery stories 2007. *See* The Best American mystery stories 2007

Hiding out. Messinger, J.

Higgins, George V., 1939-1999

The easiest thing in the world; the uncollected fiction of George V. Higgins; edited by Matthew J. Bruccoli. Carroll & Graf Publishers 2004 ISBN 0-7867-1474-3 LC 2005-278785

High lonesome. Oates, J. C.

Hill, Joe

20th century ghosts; introduction by Christopher Golden. William Morrow 2007 316p ISBN 978-0-06-114797-5; 0-06-114797-4

First published 2005 in the United Kingdom

Hillerman, Tony

(ed) A New omnibus of crime. *See* A New omnibus of crime

Hinton, S. E.

Some of Tim's stories. University of Oklahoma Press 2007 151p ISBN 978-0-8061-3835-0; 0-8061-3835-1 LC 2006-33610

The **history** of Vegas. Angel, J.

Hocking, John C.

(ed) Detroit noir. *See* Detroit noir

Hodgson, William Hope, 1877-1918

Adrift on the haunted seas; the best short stories of William Hope Hodgson; edited and with an introduction by Douglas A. Anderson. Gold Spring Press 2005 243p ISBN 1-59360-049-6 LC 2005-925490

The dream of X and other fantastic visions; being the fifth volume of The collected fiction of William Hope Hodgson; edited by Douglas A. Anderson. Night Shade Books 2009 449p ISBN 978-1-892389-43-5

Howard, Robert Ervin, 1906-1936
   The horror stories of Robert E. Howard; illustrated by Greg Staples. Ballantine Books/Del Rey 2008 xxv, 523p il ISBN 978-0-345-49020-9 LC 2008-28474
Howison, Del, 1953-
   (ed) Dark delicacies. *See* Dark delicacies
   (ed) Dark delicacies 2. *See* Dark delicacies 2
Hubbard, L. Ron (La Fayette Ron), 1911-1986
   Danger in the dark. Galaxy Press 2008 121p ISBN 978-1-59212-367-4; 1-59212-367-8 LC 2007-927517
   The professor was a thief. Galaxy Press 2008 137p ISBN 978-1-59212-351-3; 1-59212-351-1 LC 2007-927522
Hughes, Matthew, 1949-
   The gist hunter and other stories. Night Shade Books 2005 245p ISBN 1-59780-020-1
Hughes, Psiche
   (ed) Violations. *See* Violations
The **human** family. Andreas-Salomé, L.
Human oddities. Jablonski, N.
Human resources. Goldfaden, J.
Hutchings, Janet
   (ed) Passport to crime. *See* Passport to crime
Hwang, Frances
   Transparency; stories. Back Bay Books/Little, Brown, and Co. 2007 219, 8p ISBN 978-0-316-16693-5; 0-316-16693-6 LC 2006-28395
Hyde, Michael, 1965-
   What are you afraid of? University of North Texas Press 2005 172p (Katherine Anne Porter Prize in Short Fiction series) ISBN 978-1-57441-201-7; 1-57441-201-9 LC 2005-17593
Hydroplane. Steinberg, S.

I

I carry a hammer in my pocket for occasions such as these. Tognazzini, A.
I dream of microwaves. Rahman, I.
I got somebody in Staunton. Lewis, W. H.
I live with you. Emshwiller, C.
I love dollars and other stories of China. Zhu Wen
I think of you. Soueif, A.
Iarovici, Doris
   American dreaming and other stories. Novello Festival Press 2005 166p ISBN 0-9760963-4-X LC 2005-16292
I'd like. Michalopoulou, A.
The **identity** club. Burgin, R.
Idiots. Arjouni, J.
If the heart is lean. Luongo, M.
If the sky falls. Montemarano, N.
If you eat, you never die. Romano, T.
If you liked school, you'll love work . . . Welsh, I.
The **imaginary** lives of mechanical men. Nelson, R. F.
In a bear's eye: stories. Murphy, Y.
In other rooms, other wonders. Mueenuddin, D.
In persuasion nation. Saunders, G.
In strange gardens and other stories. Stamm, P.
In the Convent of Little Flowers. Sundaresan, I.
In the driver's seat. Simpson, H.
In the mouth. Pollack, E.
Inferno; new tales of terror and the supernatural; edited by Ellen Datlow. TOR 2007 381p ISBN 978-0-7653-1558-8; 0-7653-1558-0; 978-0-7653-1559-5 (pa); 0-7653-1559-9 (pa) LC 2007-26073
   "A Tom Doherty Associates book"
Infidelities. Novakovich, J.
Ingalls, Rachel
   Times like these; stories. Graywolf Press 2005 316p ISBN 1-55597-431-7 LC 2005-925169

Inside and other short fiction; Japanese women by Japanese women; with a foreword by Ruth Ozeki; compiled by Cathy Layne. Kodansha International 2006 237p ISBN 978-4-7700-3006-1; 4-7700-3006-1 LC 2005-57722

Inside the hornet's head; an anthology of Jewish American writing; edited by Jerome Charyn. Thunder's Mouth Press 2005 306p ISBN 1-56025-740-7; 978-1-56025-740-0

The **insiders**. Charters, D.

Interfictions; an anthology of interstitial writing; edited by Delia Sherman and Theodora Goss. Interstitial Arts Foundation: Distributed to the trade by Small Beer Press through Consortium 2007 291p ISBN 978-1-9315-2024-9; 1-9315-2024-0 LC 2007-2129

The **International** Association of Crime Writers presents Murder in Vegas; new crime tales of gambling and desperation; edited by Michael Connelly. Forge 2005 351p ISBN 0-7653-0739-1 LC 2004056263

    "A Tom Doherty Associates book"

The **involuntary** human. Gerrold, D.

The **Irish** martyr. Working, R.

Irsfeld, John H., 1937-
    Radio Elvis and other stories. TCU Press 2002 197p ISBN 0-87565-265-4 LC 2002-1242

Irvine, Alexander C.
    Pictures from an expedition; stories. Night Shade Books 2006 227p ISBN 978-1-59780-049-5; 1-59780-049-X

Irwin, John T.
    (ed) So the story goes. *See* So the story goes

A **is** for alien. Kiernan, C. R.

Istanbul noir; edited by Mustafa Ziyalan & Amy Spangler; translated by Amy Spangler & Mustafa Ziyalan. Akashic Books 2008 277p ISBN 978-1-933354-62-0 LC 2008-925932

It's beginning to hurt. Lasdun, J.

It's Saturday. Barrett, M.

J

Jablonski, Noria
    Human oddities; stories. Shoemaker & Hoard 2005 142p ISBN 978-1-59376-084-7; 1-59376-084-1 LC 2005-10498

Jackson, K. David (Kenneth David)
    (ed) Oxford anthology of the Brazilian short story. *See* Oxford anthology of the Brazilian short story

Jaffe, Marc
    (ed) Best stories of the American West, v1. *See* Best stories of the American West, v1

Jakubowski, Maxim
    (ed) The Best British mysteries, 2005. *See* The Best British mysteries, 2005

    (ed) The Best British mysteries, 2006. *See* The Best British mysteries, 2006

    (ed) The Mammoth book of vintage whodunnits. *See* The Mammoth book of vintage whodunnits

    (ed) Paris noir. *See* Paris noir

    (ed) Rome noir. *See* Rome noir

James, C. L. R. (Cyril Lionel Robert), 1901-1989
    The Nobbie stories for children and adults; edited and introduced by Constance Webb; foreword by Anna Grimshaw. University of Nebraska Press 2006 119p ISBN 978-0-8032-2608-1; 0-8032-2608-X LC 2005-26398

James, Henry, 1843-1916
    The uncollected Henry James; newly discovered stories; edited by Floyd R. Horowitz. Carroll & Graf 2004 319p ISBN 0-7867-1272-4

The **James** Tiptree Award Anthology 2; edited by Karen Joy Fowler [et al.] Tachyon Publications 2006 252p ISBN 978-1-892391-31-7; 1-892391-31-7

    Partially analyzed

The **James** Tiptree Award Anthology 3; edited by Karen Joy Fowler [et al.] Tachyon Publications 2007 274p ISBN 978-1-892391-31-7

Jarrell, Donna

(ed) What are you looking at? *See* What are you looking at?

Jazz & twelve o'clock tales. Coleman, W.

Jeffers, H. Paul (Harry Paul), 1934-

The forgotten adventures of Sherlock Holmes; based on the original radio plays by Anthony Boucher and Denis Green. Carroll & Graf Publishers 2005 236p ISBN 0-7867-1587-1

Jesus in the mist. Ruffin, P.

Jesus out to sea. Burke, J. L.

The **Jew** of Home Depot and other stories. Apple, M.

Jigs & reels. Harris, J.

Johnny too bad. Dufresne, J.

Johnson, Charles Richard, 1948-

Dr. King's refrigerator and other bedtime stories; [by] Charles Johnson. Scribner 2005 123p ISBN 0-7432-6453-3 LC 2004-56642

Johnson, Greg, 1953-

Women I've known; new and selected stories. W.W. Norton & Co. 2007 358p ISBN 0-86538-119-4 LC 2006-53271

Jonah and Sarah. Shrayer-Petrov, D. and Shrayer, M.

Jones, Edward P.

All Aunt Hagar's children. Amistad 2006 399p ISBN 978-0-06-055756-0; 0-06-055756-7 LC 2006-42746

(ed) New stories from the South: the year's best, 2007. *See* New stories from the South: the year's best, 2007

Jones, Nalini, 1971-

What you call winter; stories. Alfred A. Knopf 2007 251p ISBN 978-1-4000-4276-0 LC 2007-1464

Jones, Stephen, 1953-

(ed) Summer chills. *See* Summer chills

(ed) Weird shadows over Innsmouth. *See* Weird shadows over Innsmouth

Jones, Stephen Graham, 1972-

Bleed into me; a book of stories. University of Nebraska Press 2005 142p (Native stories) ISBN 0-8032-2605-5; 0-8032-0516-3 LC 2004-20657

Jordan, Jen

(ed) Expletive deleted. *See* Expletive deleted

Judah, Sophie, 1949-

Dropped from heaven. Schocken Books 2007 243p ISBN 978-0-8052-4248-5 LC 2006-26003

July, Miranda

No one belongs here more than you; stories. Scribner 2007 205p ISBN 978-0-7432-9939-8; 0-7432-9939-6 LC 2006-51156

Just after sunset. King, S.

Justice, William E.

(ed) California uncovered. *See* California uncovered

K

Kadare, Ismail

Agamemnon's daughter; a novella and stories; translated from the French of Tedi Papavrami and Jusuf Vrioni by David Bellos. Arcade Publishing 2006 226p ISBN 9781559707886; 1-55970-788-7 LC 2006-18639

Kadushin, Raphael

(ed) Barnstorm. *See* Barnstorm

Kalotay, Daphne

Calamity and other stories. Doubleday 2004 193p ISBN 0-385-51358-5 LC 2004-52701

Kaye, Jessica

(ed) Meeting across the river. *See* Meeting across the river

Keane, John B., 1928-2002

The teapots are out; and other eccentric tales from Ireland. Carroll and Graf Publishers 2004 192p ISBN 0-7867-1298-8

Keeble, John, 1944-

Nocturnal America. University of Nebraska Press 2006 267p (Prairie schooner book prize in fiction) ISBN 978-0-8032-2777-4, 0-8032-2777-9 LC 2006-5908

Kitahara, Aiko, 1938-
The budding tree; six stories of love in Edo; translated by Ian MacDonald. Dalkey Archive Press 2008 170p ISBN 978-1-56478-489-6; 1-56478-489-4 LC 2007-26628
Original Japanese edition, 1993

Klages, Ellen, 1954-
Portable childhoods; stories. Tachyon Publications 2007 210p ISBN 978-1-892391-45-2; 1-892391-45-7

Klassen, Sarah, 1932-
A feast of longing. Coteau Books 2007 279p ISBN 978-1-55050-357-9

Klimasewiski, Marshall N.
Tyrants; stories. W. W. Norton & Company 2008 218p ISBN 978-0-393-33096-0 LC 2007-36233

Knightly, Robert
(ed) Queens noir. *See* Queens noir

Knockemstiff. Pollock, D. R.

Koënings, N. S.
Theft; stories. Back Bay Books/Little, Brown & Company 2008 264p ISBN 978-0-316-00186-1; 0-316-00186-4 LC 2007-33062

Kolchak: the night stalker chronicles; 26 original tales of the surreal, the bizarre, the macabre; edited by Joe Gentile, Garrett Anderson, Lori Gentile; Kolchak created by Jeff Rice. Moonstone 2006 329p il ISBN 1-933076-04-6

Kontis, Alethea
(ed) Elemental. *See* Elemental

Koren, Brittiany A.
(ed) Places to be, people to kill. *See* Places to be, people to kill

Koretsky, J. Lea, 1949-
Snapshot; collected stories. Regent Press 2009 169p ISBN 978-1-58790-158-4; 1-58790-158-7 LC 2008-936079

Krasikov, Sana, 1979-
One more year; stories. Spiegel & Grau 2008 229p ISBN 978-0-385-52439-1; 0-385-52439-0 LC 2007-47992

Kress, Nancy, 1948-
Nano comes to Clifford Falls and other stories; with a forward by Mike Resnck. Golden Gryphon Press 2008 324p ISBN 978-1-930846-50-0; 1-930846-50-9 LC 2007-38575

Krysl, Marilyn, 1942-
Dinner with Osama. University of Notre Dame Press 2008 194p (Richard Sullivan prize in short fiction) ISBN 978-0-268-03318-7; 0-268-03318-8 LC 2007-50580

Kulpa, Kathryn
Pleasant drugs; stories. Mid-List Press 2005 219p LC 2005012760

Kun, Michael
Corrections to my memoirs; collected stories. MacAdam/Cage Pub. 2007 241p ISBN 978-1-59692-195-5; 1-59692-195-1 LC 2006-19867

L

Labors of the heart. Davis, C.

LaBrie, Aimee, 1969-
Wonderful girl. University of North Texas Press 2007 163p (Katherine Anne Porter Prize in Short Fiction series) ISBN 978-1-57441-240-6; 1-57441-240-X LC 2007-27204

LaBute, Neil
Seconds of pleasure; stories. Grove Press 2004 221p ISBN 0-8021-1785-6 LC 2004-49137

The **ladies** of Grace Adieu and other stories. Clarke, S.

Lahiri, Jhumpa
Unaccustomed earth. Alfred A. Knopf 2008 333p ISBN 978-0-307-26573-9; 978-0-676-97934-3 LC 2007-17612

Lain, Douglas
Last week's apocalypse; stories; with an introduction by Eileen Gunn. Night Shade Books 2006 253p ISBN 1-59780-034-1

Lake, Jay
(ed) Other earths. *See* Other earths

Lalumière, Claude
(ed) Witpunk. *See* Witpunk

Lam, Vincent
Bloodletting & miraculous cures. Weinstein Books 2007 353p ISBN 978-1-60286-000-1; 1-60286-000-9
First published 2006 in Canada

Lamb, Harold, 1892-1962
Riders of the Steppes; the complete Cossack adventures v3; edited by Howard Andrew Jones ; introduction by E.E. Knight. University of Nebraska Press 2007 524p map ISBN 978-0-8032-8050-2; 0-8032-8050-5 LC 2006034006
Swords of the steppes; the complete Cossack adventures v4; edited by Howard Andrew Jones ; introduction by Barrie Tait Collins. University of Nebraska Press 2007 615p map ISBN 978-0-8032-8051-9; 0-8032-8051-3 LC 2006035910
Warriors of the steppes; the complete Cossack adventures v2; edited by Howard Andrew Jones ; introduction by David Drake. University of Nebraska Press 2006 629p ISBN 978-0-8032-8049-6; 0-8032-8049-1 LC 2005-35140
Wolf of the steppes; the complete Cossack adventures v1; edited by Howard Andrew Jones; introduction by S. M. Stirling. University of Nebraska Press 2006 602p ISBN 978-0-8032-8048-9; 0-8032-8048-3 LC 2005-35138

L'Amour, Louis, 1908-1988
The Collected short stories of Louis L'Amour; the frontier stories: v3. Bantam Books 2005 436p ISBN 978-0-553-80452-2; 0-553-80452-9
The Collected short stories of Louis L'Amour: the adventure stories: v4. Bantam Books 2006 662p ISBN 978-0-553-80494-2; 0-553-80494-4

Lamsley, Terry, 1941-
Conference with the dead; stories; with an introduction by Ramsey Campbell. Night Shade Books 2005 242p ISBN 1-597800-00-7

Lanagan, Margo, 1960-
Red spikes. Alfred A. Knopf 2007 167p ISBN 978-0-375-84320-4; 0-375-84320-5; 978-0-375-94577-9 (lib bdg); 0-375-94577-6 (lib bdg) LC 2007-04805
First published 2006 in Australia

Land of exile: contemporary Korean fiction; translated and edited by Marshall Pihl, Bruce Fulton, and Ju-Chan Fulton. Expanded ed. M.E. Sharpe, Inc. 2007 343p ISBN 978-0-7656-1810-8 LC 2006-32197

Lane, Joel, 1963-
The lost district and other stories. Night Shade Books 2006 190p ISBN 1-59780-039-2; 978-1-59780-039-6

Langan, John
Mr. Gaunt and other uneasy encounters. Prime Books 2008 239p ISBN 978-0-8095-7249-6

Lange, Richard, 1961-
Dead boys; stories. Little, Brown and Co. 2007 241p ISBN 978-0-316-01736-7; 0-316-01736-1 LC 2006-26482

The **language** of sharks. MacEnulty, P.

Lansdale, Joe R., 1951-
The God of the Razor. Subterranean Press 2007 295p il ISBN 978-1-59606-115-6
Analyzed for short stories only
Mad dog summer and other stories. Golden Gryphon Press 2006 c2004 261p ISBN 1-930846-42-8 LC 2006-3259
Sanctified and chicken-fried; the portable Lansdale. University of Texas Press 2009 250p ISBN 978-0-292-71941-5 LC 2008-49636
The shadows, kith and kin. Subterranean Press 2007 287p ISBN 978-1-59606-081-4; 1-59606-081-6

Lapcharoensap, Rattawut
Sightseeing; stories. Grove Press 2005 250p ISBN 0-8021-1788-0 LC 2004-54131

Larbalestier, Justine, 1967-
(ed) Daughters of earth. *See* Daughters of earth

LaSalle, Peter
    Tell Borges if you see him; tales of contemporary somnambulism. University of Georgia Press 2007 256p ISBN 978-0-8203-2998-7; 0-8203-2998-3 LC 2007-30601
        "Winner of the Flannery O'Connor Award for Short Fiction"

Lasdun, James
    It's beginning to hurt. Farrar, Straus and Giroux 2009 227p ISBN 978-0-374-29902-6; 0-374-29902-1 LC 2008-54251

The **last** chicken in America. Litman, E.

The **last** communist virgin. Wang Ping

Last evenings on Earth. Bolaño, R.

Last exit to Babylon. Zelazny, R.

The **last** leaf of Harlem. West, D.

Last night. Salter, J.

Last notes and other stories. Dobozy, T.

The **last** science fiction writer. Steele, A. M.

The **last** time I saw you. Brown, R.

Last week's apocalypse. Lain, D.

Late in the standoff. Daugherty, T.

Later, at the bar. Barry, R.

Later novels and stories. Maxwell, W.

Law on the Flying U: western stories. Bower, B. M.

Lawson, John Edward, 1974-
    Discouraging at best. Raw Dog Screaming Press 2007 196p ISBN 1-933293-19-5 LC 2006-928777

Layne, Cathy
    (comp) Inside and other short fiction. *See* Inside and other short fiction

Le, Nam
    The boat. Alfred A. Knopf 2008 271p ISBN 978-0-307-26808-2; 0-307-26808-X LC 2007-37820

Le May, Alan, 1899-1964
    Tonopah Range; western stories. Five Star 2006 215p ISBN 1-59414-347-1 LC 2005-30481

Learning to kill. McBain, E.

Lebbon, Tim, 1969-
    (ed) British invasion. *See* British invasion

Lefer, Diane
    California transit. Sarabande Books 2007 237p ISBN 978-1-932511-47-5; 1-932511-47-4 LC 2006-15982

Legend of a suicide. Vann, D.

Lehane, Dennis
    Coronado; stories. William Morrow 2006 232p ISBN 978-0-06-113967-3; 0-06-113967-X LC 2006-44968

Lellenberg, Jon L.
    (ed) Ghosts in Baker Street. *See* Ghosts in Baker Street
    (ed) Sherlock Holmes in America. *See* Sherlock Holmes in America

The **lemon** table. Barnes, J.

Leonard, Elmore, 1925-
    The complete Western stories of Elmore Leonard. William Morrow 2004 528p ISBN 0-06-072425-0 LC 2004-55969

Lethem, Jonathan
    Men and cartoons; stories. Doubleday 2004 160p ISBN 0-385-51216-3 LC 2004-50039

Let's do. Meacham, R.

A **letter** to Harvey Milk. Newman, L.

Leung, Brian, 1967-
    World famous love acts; stories. Sarabande Books 2004 202p ISBN 1-88933-016-7 LC 2003-11923
        "Winner of the 2002 Mary McCarthy Prize in Short Fiction, selected by Chris Offutt"

Levi, Primo, 1919-1987
    A tranquil star; unpublished stories of Primo Levi; translated by Ann Goldstein and Alessandra Bastagli. W.W. Norton 2007 164p ISBN 978-0-393-06468-1 LC 2007-4961

Levithan, David, 1972-
    How they met, and other stories. Alfred A. Knopf 2008 244p ISBN 978-0-375-84886-5; 978-0-375-94886-2 (lib bdg) LC 2007-10586

Levitin, Alexis
   (tr) And other stories. *See* Gospodinov, Georgi, 1968-. And other stories
Levitsky, Alexander
   (ed) Worlds apart. *See* Worlds apart
Levy, Magdalana
   (tr) And other stories. *See* Gospodinov, Georgi, 1968-. And other stories
Lewis, William Henry, 1967-
   I got somebody in Staunton; stories. Amistad 2005 202p ISBN 0-06-053665-9 LC 2004-55128
Li Yiyun
   A thousand years of good prayers; stories. Random House 2005 205p ISBN 1-4000-6312-4 LC 2004-62891
Liebrecht, Savyon
   A good place for the night; stories; translated from the Hebrew by Sondra Silverston. Persea Books 2005 249p ISBN 0-89255-320-0 LC 2005-21802
      "A Karen and Michael Braziller book"
Like you'd understand, anyway. Shepard, J.
Limit point. Brodsky, M.
Lin, Tao, 1983-
   Bed; stories. Melville House 2007 278p ISBN 978-1-933633-26-8 LC 2007-27311
The **line** between. Beagle, P. S.
Link, Kelly
   (ed) The Best of Lady Churchill's rosebud wristlet. *See* The Best of Lady Churchill's rosebud wristlet
   Magic for beginners; illustrated by Shelley Jackson. Small Beer Press 2005 272p il ISBN 978-1-931520-15-7; 1-931520-15-1 LC 2005-5394
   (ed) The Year's best fantasy and horror: eighteenth annual collection. *See* The Year's best fantasy and horror: eighteenth annual collection
   (ed) The Year's best fantasy and horror: nineteenth annual collection. *See* The Year's best fantasy and horror: nineteenth annual collection
   (ed) The Year's best fantasy and horror: seventeenth annual collection. *See* The Year's best fantasy and horror: seventeenth annual collection
   (ed) The Year's best fantasy and horror: twentieth annual collection. *See* The Year's best fantasy and horror: twentieth annual collection
   (ed) The Year's best fantasy and horror: twenty-first annual collection. *See* The Year's best fantasy and horror: twenty-first annual collection
Lippman, Laura
   Hardly knew her; stories. William Morrow 2008 292p ISBN 978-0-06-158499-2; 0-06-158499-1
Litman, Ellen
   The last chicken in America; a novel in stories. W. W. Norton Company 2007 236p ISBN 978-0-393-06511-4 LC 2007-15563
Little, Denise
   (ed) The Magic toybox. *See* The Magic toybox
Little criminals. Reinheimer, K.
Little Edens. Moss, B. K.
Little Star of Bela Lua. Monteiro, L.
A **little** street music. Stern, D.
The **littlest** Hitler. Boudinot, R.
Livability. Raymond, J.
The **lives** of rocks. Bass, R.
The **living** dead; edited by John Joseph Adams. Night Shade Books 2008 487p ISBN 978-1-59780-143-0; 1-59780-143-7
Living shadows. Shirley, J.
Lone Star literature; from the Red River to the Rio Grande; edited by Don Graham. W. W. Norton & Co 2003 733p ISBN 0-393-05043-2 LC 2003-16321
Lone Star sleuths; an anthology of Texas crime fiction; edited and with an introduction by Bill Cunningham, Steven L. Davis, and Rollo K. Newsom. University of Texas Press 2007 265p (Southwestern Writers Collection series) ISBN 978-0-292-71737-4; 0-292-71737-7 LC 2007-5813

Long after fathers. Rees, R.

Long walks, last flights & other strange journeys. Scholes, K.

Looking for war and other stories. Unger, D.

Los Angeles noir; edited by Denise Hamilton. Akashic Books 2007 348p
ISBN 978-1-933354-22-4; 1-933354-22-4 LC 2006-938153

The **lost** district and other stories. Lane, J.

Lost in Uttar Pradesh. Connell, E. S.

Lost stories. Hammett, D.

Lost worlds. Smith, C. A.

Lott, Bret
(ed) The best Christian short stories. *See* The best Christian short
stories

The difference between women and men; stories. Random House 2005
188p ISBN 0-375-50262-9 LC 2004-58442

Love and hydrogen. Shepard, J.

Love and obstacles. Hemon, A.

Love and other stories. Dery, T.

Love stories in this town. Ward, A. E.

Love today. Biller, M.

Lovecraft, H. P. (Howard Phillips), 1890-1937
H.P. Lovecraft; tales; edited by Peter Straub. Library of America 2005
838p ISBN 1-93108-272-3 LC 2004-48979

Lowry, Malcolm, 1909-1957
The voyage that never ends; fictions, poems, drafts, and letters; edited
by Michael Hofmann. New York Review Books 2007 518p ISBN
978-1-59017-235-3; 1-59017-235-3 LC 2007-17329

Lucky dip and other stories. Cody, L.

Lucky Hans and other Merz fairy tales. Schwitters, K.

Luminous fish. Margulis, L.

Lumley, Brian, 1937-
Necroscope: Harry and the pirates and other tales from the lost years.
Tor 2009 189p ISBN 978-0-7653-2338-5; 0-7653-2338-9
LC 2009-12920
"A Tom Doherty Associates book"
Screaming science fiction; horrors from out of space. Subterranean
Press 2006 171p il ISBN 1-59606-042-5
The taint and other novellas; best Mythos tales, volume one.
Subterranean Press 2007 279p ISBN 978-1-59606-125-5

Lunstrum, Kirsten Sundberg, 1979-
Swimming with strangers; stories. Chronicle Books 2008 197p ISBN
978-0-8118-6076-5 LC 2008-13340

Luongo, Margaret, 1967-
If the heart is lean; stories. Louisiana State University Press 2008
156p ISBN 978-0-8071-3376-7 LC 2008-10719

Lupoff, Richard A., 1935-
Terrors. Elder Signs Press 2005 360p ISBN 0-9759229-6-3

Luvaas, William, 1945-
A working man's apocrypha; short stories. University of Oklahoma
Press 2007 208p ISBN 978-0-8061-3837-4 LC 2007-00363

Lynn, David Hayden
Year of fire; stories. Harcourt 2006 262p ISBN 978-0-15-603077-9;
0-15-603077-2 LC 2005-2399
"A Harvest original"

M

Ma Jian, 1953-
Stick out your tongue; translated from the Chinese by Flora Drew.
Farrar, Straus and Giroux 2006 93p ISBN 0-374-26988-2
LC 2006-4282
Original Chinese edition, 1998

MacDonald, Ian
The budding tree. See Kitahara, Aiko, 1938-

MacEnulty, Pat
The language of sharks; stories by Pat MacEnulty. Serpent's Tail 2004
216p ISBN 1-85242-849-X LC 2003-115193

MacLaverty, Bernard
  Matters of life & death and other stories. W.W. Norton & Co. 2006
    231p ISBN 978-0-393-05716-4; 0-393-05716-X LC 2006-18536
MacLeod, Ian
  Breathmoss and other exhalations; [by] Ian R. MacLeod. Golden
    Gryphon Press 2004 309p ISBN 1-930846-26-6 LC 2003-26207
MacLeod, Ken, 1954-
  Giant lizards from another star; edited by Sheila Perry. NESFA Press
    2006 349p ISBN 1-886778-62-0
      Analyzed for short stories only
Macy, Caitlin
  Spoiled; stories. Random House 2009 220p ISBN 978-1-4000-6199-0
    LC 2008-28839
Mad dog summer and other stories. Lansdale, J. R.
Mad professor. Rucker, R. v. B.
Magdaleno, Jana Sequoya
  (ed) Reckonings. *See* Reckonings
Magee, Kelly, 1976-
  Body language. University of North Texas Press 2006 197p ISBN
    978-1-57441-219-2; 1-57441-219-1 LC 2006-22580
The **Magellan** House. Gardiner, J. R.
Magic for beginners. Link, K.
The **Magic** toybox; edited by Denise Little. DAW Books 2006 308p
    ISBN 0-7564-0379-0
Maguire, Emily, 1972-
  (tr) Stories of little women & grown-up girls. *See* Rivera-Valdés,
    Sonia. Stories of little women & grown-up girls
Maḥfūẓ, Najīb, 1911-2006
  The seventh heaven; stories of the supernatural; translated by
    Raymond Stock. American University in Cairo Press 2005 151p
    ISBN 977-424-940-2
The **maker** of gargolyes and other stories. Smith, C. A.
Malae, Peter Nathaniel
  Teach the free man; stories. Swallow Press/Ohio University Press
    2007 258p ISBN 978-0-8040-1098-6; 0-8040-1098-6;
    978-8040-1099-3 (pa); 0-8040-1099-4 (pa) LC 2006-34871
Male of the species. Mindt, A.
Malla, Pasha, 1978-
  The withdrawal method; stories. Soft Skull Press 2009 321p ISBN
    978-1-59376-238-4
Malouf, David, 1934-
  The complete stories. Pantheon Books 2007 508p ISBN
    978-0-375-42497-7; 0-375-42497-0 LC 2006-37694
Mamatas, Nick, 1972-
  (ed) Realms. *See* Realms
The **Mammoth** book of golden age science fiction; edited by Isaac
    Asimov, Charles G. Waugh and Martin H. Greenberg. Carroll &
    Graf 2007 532p ISBN 978-0-7867-1905-1; 0-7867-1905-2
The **Mammoth** book of vintage whodunnits; edited by Maxim
    Jakubowski. Carroll & Graf Publishers 2006 566p ISBN
    978-0-78671-698-2; 0-7867-1698-3
The **man** back there and other stories. Crouse, D.
Man vs. machine; edited by John Helfers and Martin H. Greenberg.
    DAW Books 2007 308p ISBN 978-0-7564-0436-9 LC 2007-298573
The **man** who could fly and other stories. Anaya, R. A.
The **man** with the strange head and other early science fiction stories.
    Breuer, M. J.
Mandelbaum, Paul, 1959-
  Garrett in wedlock; a novel-in-stories. Berkley Books 2004 303p ISBN
    0-425-19637-2 (pa) LC 2004-46319
Mandelman, Avner
  Talking to the enemy; stories; Avner Mandelman. Seven Stories Press
    2005 144p ISBN 1-583-22669-9 LC 2004-23304
Manguel, Alberto
  (ed) The Ecco book of Christmas stories. *See* The Ecco book of
    Christmas stories
Manhattan noir; edited by Lawrence Block. Akashic Books 2006 257p
    ISBN 1-888451-95-5; 978-1-888451-95-5 LC 2005-934818

Manhattan noir 2; the classics; edited by Lawrence Block. Akashic Books 2008 273p (Akashic noir series) ISBN 978-1-9333-5457-6 LC 2008-925934

Manley, Carol
Church booty. Livingston Press at The University of West Alabama 2008 140p ISBN 978-1-60489-008-2; 978-1-60489-009-9 (pa) LC 2007-942224

Mann, James A.
(ed) Works of art. *See* Blish, James, 1921-1975. Works of art

A **mansion** in the sky. Taraqqi, G.

Many bloody returns; edited by Charlaine Harris and Toni L. P. Kelner. Ace Books 2007 355p ISBN 978-0-441-01522-1 LC 2007-11450

Map of dreams. Rickert, M.

Maravelis, Peter
(ed) San Francisco noir. *See* San Francisco noir
(ed) San Francisco noir 2. *See* San Francisco noir 2

Marcus, Ben, 1967-
(ed) The Anchor book of new American short stories. *See* The Anchor book of new American short stories

Margulis, Lynn, 1938-
Luminous fish; tales of science and love. Chelsea Green Pub. 2007 180p ISBN 978-1-933392-33-2; 1-933392-33-9 LC 2006-25902
"A Sciencewriters book"

Marley, Louise, 1952-
Absalom's mother & other stories. Fairwood Press 2007 230p ISBN 978-0-9789078-3-9; 0-9789078-3-3

Martel, Yann, 1963-
The facts behind the Helsinki Roccamatios. Harcourt 2004 208p ISBN 0-15-101090-0

Martin, George R. R.
Dreamsongs: volume I. Bantam Books 2007 c2003 v1 683p il ISBN 978-0-553-80545-1
First published 2003 as part of GRRM: a retrospective by Subterranean Press
Dreamsongs: volume II. Bantam Books 2007 c2003 740p ISBN 978-0-553-80659-8
First published 2003 as part of GRRM: a retrospective by Subterranean Press
Analyzed for short stories only

Martin, Jana
Russian lover & other stories. Yeti 2007 221p ISBN 978-1-891241-52-9 LC 2007-00438

Martin, Valerie
The unfinished novel and other stories. Vintage Contemporaries 2006 212p ISBN 1-4000-9550-6 LC 2005-48613

Marusek, David
Getting to know you. Ballantine Books/Del Rey 2008 c2007 267p ISBN 978-0-345-50428-9; 0-345-50428-3
First published 2007 by Subterranean Press

Mary, Mary, shut the door and other stories. Schutz, B. M.

Masiello, Francine, 1948-
(tr) Dreams and realities. *See* Gorriti, Juana Manuela, 1818-1892. Dreams and realities

Mason, Alane Salierno, 1964-
(ed) Words without borders. *See* Words without borders

Mason, Bobbie Ann
Nancy Culpepper; stories. Random House 2006 224p ISBN 0-375-50718-3 LC 2005-541241

Mason, Jeanne
(ed) Trinidad noir. *See* Trinidad noir

Master of the grass. Gabrielyan, N.

The **mathematics** of magic. De Camp, L. S. and Pratt, F.

Matheson, Richard, 1926-
Collected stories v 1; edited by Stanley Wiater. Edge Books 2003 399p ISBN 1-887368-62-0
Collected stories v2; edited by Stanley Wiater. Edge Books 2005 453p ISBN 1-887368-79-5
Collected stories v3; edited by Stanley Wiater. Edge Books 2005 349p ISBN 1-887368-81-7

McKenzie, Elizabeth
Stop that girl; a novel in stories. Random House 2005 207p ISBN 1-4000-6224-1 LC 2004-50873
McKillip, Patricia A., 1948-
Harrowing the dragon. Ace Books 2005 310p ISBN 0-441-01360-0; 0-441-01443-7 (pa) LC 2005-51311
McLean, Stuart, 1948-
Home from the vinyl cafe; a year of stories. Simon & Schuster 2005 262p ISBN 0-7432-7000-2 LC 2004-65327
McLoughlin, Tim
(ed) Brooklyn noir. *See* Brooklyn noir
(ed) Brooklyn noir 2. *See* Brooklyn noir 2
McNair, Wesley
(ed) Contemporary Maine fiction. *See* Contemporary Maine fiction
McNally, John, 1965-
(ed) Who can save us now? *See* Who can save us now?
McNally, T. M.
The gateway; stories. Southern Methodist University Press 2007 211p ISBN 978-0-87074-516-4 LC 2007-30732
McNett, Molly, 1966-
One dog happy. University of Iowa Press 2008 118p (The John Simmons short fiction award) ISBN 978-1-58729-687-1; 1-58729-687-X LC 2008-10759
McSweeney's enchanted chamber of astonishing stories; edited by Michael Chabon; illustrations by Mike Mignola. Vintage Books 2004 328p ISBN 1-400-07874-1 LC 2004-54617
McSweeney's mammoth treasury of thrilling tales; edited by Michael Chabon. Vintage Books 2003 479p ISBN 1-400-03339-X LC 2002-192265
McVeigh, Daniel, 1948-
(ed) The best American Catholic short stories. *See* The best American Catholic short stories
Meacham, Rebecca, 1970-
Let's do. University of North Texas Press 2004 181p ISBN 1-574-41185-3 (pa) LC 2004-14252
"2004 Winner, Katherine Anne Porter Prize in Short Fiction"
Mean streets; [by] Jim Butcher ... [et al] New American Library 2009 343p ISBN 978-0-451-46249-7 LC 2008-44845
'A ROC book.'
Means, David
The secret goldfish; stories. Fourth Estate 2004 211p ISBN 0-00-716489-0 LC 2004-50617
Meat eaters & plant eaters. Treat, J.
The **mechanics** of falling and other stories. Brady, C.
Medium of murder; edited by Susan Budavari and Suzanne Flaig. Red Coyote Press 2008 205p ISBN 978-0-9766733-4-7; 0-9766733-4-7 LC 2008-920921
Meeting across the river; stories inspired by the haunting Bruce Springsteen song; edited by Jessica Kaye and Richard J. Brewer. Bloomsbury 2005 206p ISBN 1-58234-283-0 LC 2005-41152
Mehan, Uppinder, 1961-
(ed) So long been dreaming. *See* So long been dreaming
Melko, Paul
Ten sigmas & other unlikelihoods. Fairwood Press 2008 254p ISBN 978-0-9789078-6-0; 0-9789078-6-8
Meloy, Maile
Both ways is the only way I want it. Riverhead Books 2009 219p ISBN 978-1-59448-869-6; 1-59448-869-X LC 2008-50342
Men and cartoons. Lethem, J.
Menger-Anderson, Kirsten
Doctor Olaf van Schuler's brain. Algonquin Books of Chapel Hill 2008 290p ISBN 978-1-56512-561-2; 1-56512-561-4 LC 2008-26850
Meno, Joe
Bluebirds used to croon in the choir. Northwestern University Press 2005 180p ISBN 0-8101-5167-7; 0-8101-2424-6 (pa) LC 2005-19766
Demons in the spring. Akashic Books 2008 272p il ISBN 978-1-933354-47-7 LC 2007-939617

Molodowsky, Kadya
    A house with seven windows; short stories; translated from the
        Yiddish by Leah Schoolnik. Syracuse University Press 2006 315p
        ISBN 0-8156-0845-4 LC 2005-33513

Monk, Bathsheba, 1966-
    Now you see it . . .; stories from Cokesville, PA. Farrar, Straus and
        Giroux 2006 228p ISBN 0-374-22330-0 ISSN 978-0-374-22330-4
        LC 2005-22284
        "Sarah Crichton books"

Monson, Ander, 1975-
    Other electricities; stories. Sarabande Books 2005 167p il ISBN
        1-932511-15-6 (pa) LC 2004-14389

Monteiro, Luana
    Little Star of Bela Lua. Delphinium Books 2005 228p ISBN
        1-883285-26-7 LC 2005924879

Monteleone, Thomas F.
    Rough beasts and other mutations. Five Star 2003 432p ISBN
        0-7862-5344-4 LC 2003-49280

Montemarano, Nicholas, 1969-
    If the sky falls; stories. Louisiana State University Press 2005 211p
        (Yellow shoe fiction) ISBN 0-8071-3122-9 LC 2005-10257

Montgomery, Lee
    Whose world is this? University of Iowa Press 2007 93p ISBN
        978-1-58729-614-7; 1-58729-614-4 LC 2007-8810

Moody, Rick
    Right livelihoods; three novellas. Little, Brown 2007 223p ISBN
        978-0-316-16634-8; 0-316-16634-0 LC 2006-26937

Moon, Elizabeth
    Moon flights; with an introduction by Anne McCaffrey. Night Shade
        Books 2007 272p ISBN 978-1-59780-109-6; 978-1-59780-108-9

Moon flights. Moon, E.

Moorcock, Michael, 1939-
    The best of Michael Moorcock; edited by John Davey with Ann &
        Jeff VanderMeer. Tachyon Publications 2009 403p ISBN
        978-1-892391-86-5; 1-892391-86-4
    (ed) New worlds. *See* New worlds

Moore, James A.
    (ed) British invasion. *See* British invasion

Moore, Lorrie
    (ed) The Best American short stories, 2004. *See* The Best American
        short stories, 2004

Moral disorder. Atwood, M.

Mordecai, Pamela
    Pink icing and other stories. Insomniac Press 2006 243p ISBN
        1-897178-32-8

More twisted. Deaver, J.

Morgan, Jill M.
    (ed) Creature cozies. *See* Creature cozies

Morita, Ryuji
    Tokyo fragments. *See* Tokyo fragments

Morrow, James, 1947-
    (ed) The SFWA European hall of fame. *See* The SFWA European hall
        of fame

Morrow, Kathryn L.
    (ed) The SFWA European hall of fame. *See* The SFWA European hall
        of fame

Mortimer of the Maghreb. Shukman, H.

Mosley, Walter
    The right mistake; the further philosophical investigations of Scrates
        Fortlow. Basic Civitas 2008 269p ISBN 978-0-465-00525-3

Moss, Barbara Klein
    Little Edens; stories. Norton 2004 332p il ISBN 0-393-05712-7
        LC 2003-18196

The **most** of it. Ruefle, M.

Mother Aegypt and other stories. Baker, K.

The **mother** garden. Romm, R.

Mother of sorrows. McCann, R.

Mothers & other monsters. McHugh, M. F.

Mothers and sons. Tóibín, C.

Mystery Writers of America presents the blue religion; new stories about cops, criminals, and the chase; edited by Michael Connelly. Little, Brown and Company 2008 374p ISBN 978-0-316-01251-5; 978-0-316-01265-2 (pa) LC 2007-42278

Mystery Writers of America presents the prosecution rests; new stories about courtrooms, criminals, and the law; edited by Linda Fairstein. Little, Brown and Co. 2009 418p ISBN 978-0-316-01252-2; 0-316-01252-1; 978-0-316-01267-6 (pa); 0-316-01267-X (pa) LC 2008-45351

N

Nadelson, Scott, 1973-
The cantor's daughter; stories. Hawthorne Books & Literary Arts 2006 257p ISBN 0-9766311-2-1 LC 2006-1025

Naiyer Masud
Snake catcher; translated from Urdu by Muhammad Umar Memon. Interlink Books 2006 276p ISBN 1-56656-629-0 LC 2005-13183

Nancy Culpepper. Mason, B. A.

Nano comes to Clifford Falls and other stories. Kress, N.

Nayman, Shira, 1960-
Awake in the dark; stories. Scribner 2006 290p ISBN 978-0-7432-9268-9; 0-7432-9268-5 LC 2006-48444

Nebula awards showcase 2002; edited by Kim Stanley Robinson. Roc 2002 304p ISBN 0-451-45878-8

Nebula Awards showcase 2005; the year's best SF and fantasy; selected by the Science Fiction and Fantasy Writers of America; edited by Jack Dann. Roc 2005 327p ISBN 0-451-46015-4
Analyzed for short stories only

Nebula Awards showcase 2006; the year's best SF and fantasy; selected by the Science Fiction and Fantasy Writers of America; edited by Gardner Dozois. Roc 2006 372p ISBN 0-451-46064-2; 978-0-451-46064-6
Analyzed for short stories only

Nebula Awards showcase 2007; the year's best SF and fantasy; selected by the Science Fiction and Fantasy Writers of America; edited by Mike Resnick. Roc 2007 383p ISBN 978-0-451-46134-6
Analyzed for short stories only

Nebula Awards showcase 2008; the year's best SF and fantasy; selected by the Science Fiction and Fantasy Writers of America; edited by Ben Bova. Roc 2008 375p ISBN 978-0-451-46188-9; 0-451-46188-6
Analyzed for short stories only

Nebula Awards showcase 2009; the year's best SF and fantasy; selected by the Science Fiction and Fantasy Writers of America; edited by Ellen Datlow. Roc 2009 436p ISBN 978-0-451-46255-8; 0-451-46255-6
Analyzed for short stories only

Necessary lies. Bakken, K. N.

Necroscope: Harry and the pirates and other tales from the lost years. Lumley, B.

Need. McCauley, W.

Nelson, Antonya
Nothing right; short stories. Bloomsbury 2009 296p ISBN 978-1-59691-574-9; 1-59691-574-9 LC 2008-20318
Some fun; stories and a novella. Scribner 2006 237p ISBN 0-7432-1873-3; 978-0-7432-1873-6 LC 2005-54424

Nelson, Randy F., 1948-
The imaginary lives of mechanical men; stories. University of Georgia Press 2006 210p ISBN 978-0-8203-2845-4; 0-8203-2845-6 LC 2005-37661

Neugroschel, Joachim
(ed) No star too beautiful. *See* No star too beautiful

New and collected stories. Sillitoe, A.

New Dubliners; edited by Oona Frawley. Pegasus Books 2006 152p ISBN 1-933648-09-0

The **New** Granta book of the American short story; edited and introduced by Richard Ford. Granta Books 2007 756p ISBN 978-1-86207-847-5

A **New** omnibus of crime; edited by Tony Hillerman and Rosemary Herbert; contributing editors Sue Grafton and Jeffery Deaver. Oxford University Press 2005 434p ISBN 978-0-19-518214-9; 0-19-518214-6 LC 2005-11606

New Orleans noir; edited by Julie Smith. Akashic Books 2007 281p ISBN 978-1-933354-24-8; 1-933354-24-0 LC 2006-938151

The **new** space opera; edited by Gardner Dozois and Jonathan Strahan. Eos 2007 517p ISBN 978-0-06-084675-6; 0-06-084675-5

The **new** space opera 2; edited by Gardner Dozois and Jonathan Strahan. Eos 2009 544p ISBN 978-0-06-156235-8

New stories from the South; the year's best, 2008; selected from U.S. magazines by ZZ Packer with Kathy Pories; with an introduction by ZZ Packer. Algonquin Books 2008 428p il ISBN 978-1-56512-612-1; 1-56512-612-2

New stories from the South: the year's best, 2005; edited by Shannon Ravenel; with a preface by Jill McCorkle. Algonquin Books of Chapel Hill 2005 311p ISBN 1-56512-469-3

New stories from the South: the year's best, 2006; selected from U.S. magazines by Allan Gurganus with Kathy Pories; with an introduction by Allan Gurganus. Algonquin Books of Chapel Hill 2006 xx, 340p ISBN 1-56512-175-9

New stories from the South: the year's best, 2007; selected from U.S. magazines by Edward P. Jones with Kathy Pories; with an introduction by Edward P. Jones. Algonquin Books of Chapel Hill 2007 372p ISBN 9781565125568

New stories from the Southwest; edited by D. Seth Horton; foreword by Ray Gonzalez. Swallow Press/Ohio University Press 2008 285p ISBN 978-0-8040-1106-8; 0-8040-1106-0; 978-0-8040-1107-5 (pa); 0-8040-1107-9 (pa) LC 2007-43471

The **new** valley. Weil, J.

The **new** weird; Ann & Jeff VanderMeer, editors. Tachyon Publications 2008 414p ISBN 978-1-892391-55-1 (pa); 1-892391-55-4
> Analyzed for short stories only

New worlds; an anthology; edited by Michael Moorcock. Thunder's Mouth Press 2004 386p ISBN 1-56858-317-6
> Analyzed for short stories only

Newman, Lesléa
A letter to Harvey Milk; short stories. University of Wisconsin Press 2004 175p (Library of American fiction) ISBN 0-299-20574-6 (pa) LC 2004-53567

Newsworld. Pierce, T. J.

Nice big American baby. Budnitz, J.

Night and fear. Woolrich, C.

A **night** in the cemetery and other stories of crime & suspense. Chekhov, A. P.

The **night** land and other perilous romances. Hodgson, W. H.

Night train. Erdrich, L.

The **nightingales** of Troy. Fulton, A.

The **nightmare,** and other tales of dark fantasy. Stevens, F.

Nightshadows. Nolan, W. F.

The **Nimrod** flipout. Keret, E.

Nisbet, Robert, 1941-
Downtrain. Parthian Books 2004 176p ISBN 1-902638-37-9 (pa)

No man's land. Parra, E. A.

No one belongs here more than you. July, M.

No star too beautiful; Yiddish stories from 1382 to the present; compiled and translated by Joachim Neugroschel. Norton 2002 710p ISBN 0-393-05190-0 LC 2002-69222

The **Nobbie** stories for children and adults. James, C. L. R.

Nocturnal America. Keeble, J.

Noise; fiction inspired by Sonic Youth; edited bt Peter Wild; introduction by Lee Ranaldo. Harper Perennial 2009 228p ISBN 978-0-06-166929-3

Nolan, William F., 1928-
  Nightshadows; the best new horror fiction by a living legend in dark fantasy. Darkwood Press 2007 303p ISBN 978-0-9789078-4-6; 0-9789078-4-1
  Wild galaxy; selected science fiction stories; introduction by the author. Golden Gryphon 2005 199p ISBN 1-930846-31-2 LC 2004-15223
Nora Jane. Gilchrist, E.
North of nowhere, south of loss. Hospital, J. T.
North of the port. Bukoski, A.
Not a matter of love. Alvarado, B.
Not your average bear & other Maine stories. Stelmok, J.
Nothing like an ocean. Tomlinson, J.
Nothing right. Nelson, A.
Novakovich, Josip
  Infidelities; stories of war and lust. HarperPerennial 2005 241p ISBN 0-06-058399-1; 978-0-06-058399-6 LC 2004-65068
Now you see it . . . Monk, B.
Numbers don't lie. Bisson, T.

O

The **O.** Henry Prize stories, 2005; edited and with an introduction by Laura Furman. Anchor Books 2005 398p ISBN 1-4000-7654-4
The **O.** Henry Prize stories, 2006; edited and with an introduction by Laura Furman; jurors: Kevin Brockmeier, Francine Prose, Colm Toibin. Anchor Books 2006 361p ISBN 1-4000-9539-5; 978-1-4000-9539-1
The **O.** Henry Prize stories 2007; edited and with an introduction by Laura Furman; with essays on the story they admire most by jurors Charles D'Ambrosio, Ursula K. Le Guin, Lily Tuck. Knopf Publishing Group 2007 384p ISBN 978-0-307-27688-9
The **O.** Henry Prize stories 2008; edited and with an introduction by Laura Furman; with essays on the stories they admire most by jurors Chimamanda Ngozi Adiche, David Leavitt, David Means. Anchor Books 2008 xxiv, 372p ISBN 978-0-307-28034-3
Oates, Joyce Carol, 1938-
  (ed) The Best American mystery stories, 2005. *See* The Best American mystery stories, 2005
  Dear husband,. Ecco 2009 326p ISBN 978-0-06-170431-4; 0-06-170431-8
  (ed) The Ecco anthology of contemporary American short fiction. *See* The Ecco anthology of contemporary American short fiction
  The female of the species; tales of mystery and suspense. Harcourt 2005 275p ISBN 978-0-15-101179-7; 0-15-101179-6 LC 2005-05068
    "An Otto Penzler book"
  High lonesome; new & selected stories, 1966-2006. Ecco 2006 664p ISBN 0-06-050119-7; 978-0-06-050119-8 LC 2005-51147
  The museum of Dr. Moses; tales of mystery and suspense. Harcourt 2007 229p ISBN 978-0-15-101531-3; 0-15-101531-7 LC 2006-35431
    "An Otto Penzler book"
  Wild nights!; stories about the last days of Poe, Dickinson, Twain, James, and Hemingway. Ecco 2008 238p ISBN 978-0-06-143479-2; 0-06-143479-5 LC 2008-273051
Obejas, Achy, 1956-
  (ed) Havana noir. *See* Havana noir
Obradoviʹc, Nadežda
  (ed) The Anchor book of modern African stories. *See* The Anchor book of modern African stories
The **ocean** and all its devices. Spencer, W. B.
Ochsner, Gina, 1970-
  People I wanted to be. Mariner Books 2005 204p ISBN 0-618-56372-5 (pa) LC 2004-65132
Ockert, Jason
  Rabbit punches; stories. Low Fidelity Press 2006 182p ISBN 0-9723363-5-4 LC 2005-25303

Ofri, Danielle
  (ed) The Best of the Bellevue Literary Review. *See* The Best of the Bellevue Literary Review
Oh don't you cry for me. Shirley, P.
Ohlin, Alix
  Babylon and other stories. Knopf 2006 275p ISBN 0-375-41525-4 LC 2006-40985
Olafsson, Olaf
  Valentines; stories. Pantheon Books 2007 215p ISBN 978-0-375-42468-7 LC 2006-25508
The **old** child & other stories. Erpenbeck, J.
Old girlfriends. Updike, D.
Olsen, E. J.
  (ed) Detroit noir. *See* Detroit noir
On the Mason-Dixon line; an anthology of contemporary Delaware writers; edited by Billie Travalini and Fleda Brown. University of Delaware Press 2008 279p ISBN 978-0-87413-030-0 LC 2007-52996
On the way to my father's funeral. Baumbach, J.
Once more with footnotes. Pratchett, T.
Once upon a time (she said). Yolen, J.
One dog happy. McNett, M.
The **one** marvelous thing. Ducornet, R.
One more year. Krasikov, S.
One night stands and lost weekends. Block, L.
The **One** right thing. Coville, B.
Oranges in the sun; short stories from the Arabian Gulf; edited and translated by Deborah S. Akers, Abubaker A. Bagader. Lynne Rienner Publishers 2008 239p ISBN 978-0-8941-0893-8; 0-8941-0893-X; 978-0-8941-0869-3; 0-8941-0869-7 LC 2007-26837
Ordinary genius. Averill, T. F.
Orson Scott Card's Intergalctic medicine show; [edited by] Edmund R. Schubert and Orson Scott Card. TOR 2008 432p ISBN 978-0-7653-2000-1; 0-7653-2000-2
  "A Tom Doherty Associates book"
Orton, Marie, 1965-
  (ed) Multicultural literature in contemporary Italy. *See* Multicultural literature in contemporary Italy
O'Shaughnessy, Perri
  Sinister shorts. Delacorte Press 2006 302p ISBN 0-385-33797-3; 978-0-385-33797-7 LC 2005-51981
Other earths; edited by Nick Gevers and Jay Lake. Daw Books 2009 308p ISBN 978-0-7564-0546-5
Other electricities. Monson, A.
The **other** Teddy Roosevelts. Resnick, M.
Other worlds, better lives: a Howard Waldrop reader. Waldrop, H.
Otis, Mary, 1961-
  Yes, yes, cherries; stories. Tin House Books 2007 214p ISBN 978-0-9776989-0-5; 0-9776989-0-4 LC 2006-100131
Our former lives in art. Davis, J. S.
Our lady of the artichokes and other Portuguese-American stories. Vaz, K.
Our story begins. Wolff, T.
Out of space and time. Smith, C. A.
Out of the depths & other stories. Brenner, Y. H.
Overclocked. Doctorow, C.
Oxford anthology of the Brazilian short story; edited by K. David Jackson. Oxford University Press 2006 523p ISBN 978-0-19-516759-7; 0-19-516759-7; 978-0-19-530964-5 (pa); 0-19-530964-2 (pa) LC 2005-28860
Ozick, Cynthia
  Dictation; a quartet. Houghton Mifflin 2008 179p ISBN 978-0-547-05400-1; 0-547-05400-9 LC 2007-52331

P

Pachter, Adam Emerson
  (ed) Fenway fiction. *See* Fenway fiction

The **Pacific** and other stories. Helprin, M.

Packer, ZZ, 1973-
 (ed) New stories from the South. *See* New stories from the South

Page, Michael R., 1967-
 The man with the strange head and other early science fiction stories. See Breuer, Miles John, 1889-1945

Palazzeschi, Aldo, 1885-1974
 A tournament of misfits; tall tales and short; translated by Nicolas J. Perella. University of Toronto Press 2005 xliii, 200p (Lorenzo da Ponte Italian Library) ISBN 0-8020-3850-6; 0-8020-4889-7 (pa) LC 2006-276324

Pale morning dun. Dokey, R.

The **pale** of settlement. Singer, M.

Palwick, Susan
 The fate of mice. Tachyon Publications 2007 218p ISBN 978-1-892391-42-1; 1-892391-42-2

Pandora's closet; edited by Jean Rabe and Martin H. Greenberg. Daw Books, Inc. 2007 308p ISBN 978-0-7564-0437-6 LC 2007-541873

Panek, LeRoy, 1943-
 (ed) Early American detective stories. *See* Early American detective stories

Panning, Anne, 1966-
 Super America; stories. University of Georgia Press 2007 232p ISBN 978-0-8203-2996-3; 0-8203-2996-7 LC 2007006700
 "Winner of the Flannery O'Connor Award for Short Fiction"

Paper cities; an anthology of urban fantasy. Senses Five Press 2008 271p ISBN 978-0-9796246-0-5 LC 2007-928152

Parati, Graziella
 (ed) Multicultural literature in contemporary Italy. *See* Multicultural literature in contemporary Italy

Paretsky, Sara
 (ed) Sisters on the case. *See* Sisters on the case

Paris noir; capital crime fiction; edited by Maxim Jakubowski. Serpent's Tail 2007 336p ISBN 978-1-85242-966-9

The **Paris** review book for planes, trains, elevators, and waiting rooms; by the editors of the Paris review; with an introduction by Richard Powers. Picador 2004 386p ISBN 0-312-42240-7 (pa) LC 2004-44461

Paris tales; stories; translated by Helen Constantine. Oxford University Press 2004 243p il map ISBN 0-19-280574-6 LC 2005295486

Parker, Michael, 1959-
 Don't make me stop now; stories. Algonquin Books of Chapel Hill 2007 276p ISBN 978-1-56512-485-1; 1-56512-485-5 LC 2006-45872

Parks, Tim
 Talking about it. Hesperus Press Limited 2005 356p ISBN 1-84391-704-1

Parra, Eduardo Antonio, 1965-
 No man's land; selected stories; translated by Christopher Winks. City Lights Books 2004 211p ISBN 0-87286-429-4 LC 2003-24976

Parry, Owen, 1952-
 Strike the harp!; American Christmas stories. Morrow 2004 179p ISBN 0-06-057236-1 LC 2004-44951

Passion. Mozetič, B.

Passport to crime; the finest mystery stories from International Crime Writers; edited by Janet Hutchings. Carroll & Graf 2007 420p ISBN 978-0-7867-1916-7; 0-7867-1916-8

Patchett, Ann
 (ed) The Best American short stories, 2006. *See* The Best American short stories, 2006

Patterson, David, 1922-2005
 (tr) Out of the depths & other stories. *See* Brenner, Yosef Haim. Out of the depths & other stories

Patterson, James
 (ed) Thriller. *See* Thriller

Peacock, Irvine
 (il) Lucky Hans and other Merz fairy tales. *See* Schwitters, Kurt, 1887-1948. Lucky Hans and other Merz fairy tales

Pihl, Marshall R.
(tr & ed) Land of exile: contemporary Korean fiction. *See* Land of exile: contemporary Korean fiction

Pink icing and other stories. Mordecai, P.

Pitlor, Heidi
(ed) The Best American short stories, 2007. *See* The Best American short stories, 2007

Pizzolatto, Nic, 1975-
Between here and the yellow sea; stories. MacAdam/Cage 2006 272p ISBN 1-59692-168-4 LC 2006-688

Places to be, people to kill; edited by Martin H. Greenberg and Brittianey A. Koren. Daw Books 2007 309p ISBN 978-0-7564-0417-8

Platinum Pohl. Pohl, F.

Playboy's college fiction; a collection of 21 years of contest winners; edited by Alice K. Turner; foreword by Thom Jones. Playboy Press 2007 332p ISBN 978-1-58642-134-2; 1-58642-134-4 LC 2007-23854

Pleasant drugs. Kulpa, K.

Plots and misadventures. Gallagher, S.

Poems, prose, and letters. Bishop, E.

Poe's children; the new horror: an anthology; [edited by] Peter Straub. Doubleday 2008 534p ISBN 978-0-385-52283-0; 0-385-52283-5 LC 2008-3013

Poe's lighthouse; all new collaborations with Edgar Allan Poe; edited by Christopher Conlon. Cemetery Dance Publications 2006 326p ISBN 1-58767-128-X

Pohl, Frederik, 1919-
Platinum Pohl; the collected best stories. TOR Books 2005 463p ISBN 0-312-87527-4 LC 2005-43965
"A Tom Doherty Associates book"

Politically inspired; edited by Stephen Elliott; assistant editor, Gabriel Kram; associate editors, Elizabeth Brooks [et al.] MacAdam/Cage Pub. 2003 276p ISBN 1-931561-58-3; 1-931561-45-1 (pa) LC 2003-17623

Politics noir; dark tales from the corridors of power; edited by Gary Phillips. Verso 2008 264p ISBN 978-1-84467-161-8; 1-84467-161-5 LC 2008-299172

Pollack, Eileen, 1956-
In the mouth; stories and novellas. Four Way Books 2008 257p ISBN 978-1-884800-82-5; 1-884800-82-3 LC 2007-37691

Pollock, Donald Ray, 1954-
Knockemstiff. Doubleday 2008 206p ISBN 978-0-385-52382-0 LC 2007-39806

Pories, Kathy, 1961-
(ed) New stories from the South. *See* New stories from the South
(ed) New stories from the South: the year's best, 2006. *See* New stories from the South: the year's best, 2006
(ed) New stories from the South: the year's best, 2007. *See* New stories from the South: the year's best, 2007

Portable childhoods. Klages, E.

Porter, Andrew, 1972-
The theory of light and matter. University of Georgia Press 2008 178p (Flannery O'Connor Award for Short Fiction) ISBN 978-0-8203-3209-3; 0-8203-3209-7 LC 2008-23989

Porter, Joseph Ashby, 1942-
All aboard; stories; [by] Joe Ashby Porter. Turtle Point Press 2008 187p ISBN 978-1-933527-17-8; 1-933527-17-X LC 2007-910440

Porter, Katherine Anne, 1890-1980
Collected stories and other writings. Library of America 2008 1093p ISBN 978-1-59853-029-2 LC 2008-927625

Portions from a wine-stained notebook. Bukowski, C.

Potato tree. Sallis, J.

Power & light. Zelazny, R.

Powers, Tim
Strange itineraries. Tachyon Publications 2005 206p ISBN 1-892391-23-6

Q

Qi, Shouhua
　　Red Guard fantasies and other stories. Long River Press 2006 235p
　　　　ISBN 978-1-59265-068-2; 1-59265-068-6 LC 2006-4097
Qissat; short stories by Palestinian women; edited by Jo Glanville.
　　　　Telegram 2007 c2006 188p ISBN 978-1-84659-012-2;
　　　　1-84659-012-4
Quay, James
　　(ed) California uncovered. *See* California uncovered
Queens noir; edited by Robert Knightly. Akashic Books 2008 342p
　　　　ISBN 978-1-933354-40-8 LC 2007-926099
The **quick-change** artist. Holladay, C. C.
Quincannon's game. Pronzini, B.
Quiroga, Horacio, 1878-1937
　　The decapitated chicken and other stories; selected and translated by
　　　　Margaret Sayers Peden; introduction by George D. Schade;
　　　　illustrations by Ed Lindlof; new foreword by Jean Franco.
　　　　University of Wisconsin Press 2004 166p ISBN 0-299-19834-0 (pa)
　　　　LC 2004-41930

R

Rabbit punches. Ockert, J.
Rabe, Jean
　　(ed) Pandora's closet. *See* Pandora's closet
Radio Elvis and other stories. Irsfeld, J. H.
Rahman, Imad, 1970-
　　I dream of microwaves; stories. Farrar, Straus and Giroux 2004 244p
　　　　ISBN 0-374-17401-6 LC 2003-17791
Rand, Ken, 1946-
　　Where angels fear. Fairwood Press 2008 372p ISBN
　　　　978-0-9789078-4-6; 0-9789078-4-1
Randisi, Robert J.
　　(ed) Greatest hits. *See* Greatest hits
　　(ed) Hollywood and crime. *See* Hollywood and crime
Randolph, Ladette
　　This is not the tropics; stories. University of Wisconsin Press 2005
　　　　280p ISBN 0-299-22510-5 LC 2005-05452
Raphael, Lev
　　Secret anniversaries of the heart; new & selected stories. Leapfrog
　　　　Press 2006 242p ISBN 978-0-9728984-7-8; 0-9728984-7-6
　　　　LC 2005-27524
Rash, Ron, 1953-
　　Chemistry and other stories. Picador 2007 230p ISBN
　　　　978-0-312-42508-1; 0-312-42508-2 LC 2007-13086
Raymond, Jonathan
　　Livability; stories; [by] Jon Raymond. Bloomsbury USA 2008 272p
　　　　ISBN 1-59691-655-9; 978-1-59691-655-5 LC 2008-30834
Realm of the dead. Uchida, H.
Realms. Wyrm 2008 256p ISBN 978-0-8095-7248-9
Rear view. Duval, P.
The **reasons** I won't be coming. Perlman, E.
Reckonings; contemporary short fiction by Native American women;
　　　　edited by Hertha D. Sweet Wong, Lauren Stuart Muller, Jana
　　　　Sequoya Magdaleno. Oxford University Press 2008 312p bibl ISBN
　　　　978-0-1951-0924-5; 0-1951-0924-4; 978-0-1951-0925-2 (pa);
　　　　0-1951-0925-2 (pa) LC 2007-24147
Red car. Bingham, S.
The **red** carpet. Sankaran, L.
The **red** convertible. Erdrich, L.
Red Guard fantasies and other stories. Qi, S.
Red spikes. Lanagan, M.
Reed, Eric Melvin
　　(ed) Adventures in the West. *See* Adventures in the West

Reed, Kit, 1932-
Dogs of truth; new and uncollected stories. Tor Books 2005 286p ISBN 978-0-765-31414-7; 0-765-31414-2 LC 2005-40578
"A Tom Doherty Associates book"

Reed, Robert
The cuckoo's boys. Golden Gryphon Press 2005 315p ISBN 1-930846-37-1 LC 2005008247

Rees, Roberta
Long after fathers. Coteau Books 2007 205p ISBN 978-1-55050-358-6

Refresh, refresh. Percy, B.

Reid, Gilbert
So this is love; lollipop and other stories. Thomas Dunne Books/St. Martin's Press 2006 223p ISBN 978-0-312-34985-1; 0-312-34985-8 LC 2006-42500

Reidy, Dave, 1977-
Captive audience; stories. Ig Publishing 2009 197p ISBN 978-0-9815040-4-9 LC 2009-08211

Reinheimer, Kurt
Little criminals; Kurt Reinheimer. Eastern Washington University Press 2004 274p ISBN 0-910055-96-3 (pa) LC 2004-13173

Reinhorn, Holiday
Big cats; stories. Free Press 2005 214p LC 2005-40021

Rescue missions. Busch, F.

Resnick, Mike, 1942-
Dreamwish beasts and snarks; with a foreword by Kristine Kathryn Rusch. Golden Gryphon Press 2009 278p ISBN 978-1-930846-60-9; 1-930846-60-6 LC 2008-55454
(ed) Nebula Awards showcase 2007. *See* Nebula Awards showcase 2007
The other Teddy Roosevelts. Subterranean Press 2008 204p ISBN 978-1-59606-137-8; 1-59606-137-5
(ed) This is my funniest. *See* This is my funniest
(ed) This is my funniest 2. *See* This is my funniest 2

Rewired; the post-cyberpunk anthology; James Patrick Kelly & John Kessel, editors. Tachyon Publications 2007 424p ISBN 978-1-892391-53-7; 1-892391-53-8

Rhodes, Dan, 1972-
Don't tell me the truth about love; stories. Canongate 2005 191p ISBN 1-84195-738-0

Rich, Mark, 1958-
Across the sky. Fairwoods Press 2009 250p ISBN 978-0-9820730-1-8 ISSN 0-9820730-1-1

Richard goes to prison, and other stories. Granville-Barker, H.

Richards, Susan Starr
The hanging in the foaling barn; stories. Sarabande Books 2006 157p il (Woodford Reserve series in Kentucky literature) ISBN 1-93251-133-4; 978-1-93251-133-4 LC 2005-16823

Richter, Stacey, 1965-
Twin study; stories. Counterpoint 2007 261p ISBN 978-1-58243-371-4; 1-58243-371-2 LC 2006-35397

Rickert, M., 1959-
Map of dreams; with a foreword by Christopher Barzak ; and an afterword by Gordon Van Gelder. Golden Gryphon Press 2006 313p ISBN 1-930846-44-4 LC 2006-11153

Riders of the Steppes. Lamb, H.

Right livelihoods. Moody, R.

The **right** mistake. Mosley, W.

Riley, Gwendoline, 1979-
Tuesday nights and Wednesday mornings. Carroll & Graf Publishers 2004 231p ISBN 0-7867-1326-7 LC 2004-45749

Rivas, Manuel, 1957-
Vermeer's milkmaid and other stories; translated from the Galician by Jonathan Dunne. Overlook Press 2008 c2002 120p ISBN 978-1-59020-002-5

Rivera-Valdés, Sonia
Stories of little women & grown-up girls; translated by Emily Maguire. Editorial Campana 2007 223p ISBN 978-0-9725611-6-7; 0-9725611-6-1 LC 2006-38021

The **road** from prosperity. Welch, N.

Roberson, Jennifer
Guinevere's truth and other tales. Five Star 2008 321p ISBN 978-1-59414-150-8; 1-59414-150-9 LC 2008-31534
Roberts, Adam
Swiftly; stories that never were and might not be. Night Shade Books 2004 247p ISBN 1-892389-71-1
Robinson, Kim Stanley
(ed) Nebula awards showcase 2002. *See* Nebula awards showcase 2002
Robinson, Roxana
A perfect stranger; and other stories; Roxana Robinson. Random House 2005 235p ISBN 0-375-50918-6 LC 2004-59537
Robinson, Todd
(ed) Hardcore hardboiled. *See* Hardcore hardboiled
Rock, Peter, 1967-
The unsettling; stories. MacAdam/Cage 2006 329p ISBN 1-59692-171-4 LC 2006-361
Rodgers, Susan Jackson, 1960-
The trouble with you is and other stories. Mid-List Press 2004 (First series--short fiction) ISBN 0-922811-60-1 LC 2004-960
Romani, Gabriella
(ed) Writing to delight. *See* Writing to delight
Romano, Tony, 1957-
If you eat, you never die; chicago tales. Harper Perennial 2009 257p ISBN 978-0-06-085794-3; 0-06-085794-3 LC 2008-32948
Rome noir; edited by Chiara Stangalino & Maxim Jakubowski; translated by Anne Milano Appel, Ann Goldstein, and Kathrine Jason. Akashic Books 2009 268p ISBN 978-1-933354-64-4 LC 2008-925936
Romm, Robin, 1975-
The mother garden; stories. Scribner 2007 191p ISBN 978-1-4165-3902-5; 1-4165-3902-6 LC 2007-61711
Ronk, Martha Clare
Glass grapes; and other stories; [by] Martha Ronk. BOA Editions, LTD. 2008 215p (American reader series, no. 10) ISBN 978-1-934414-13-2 LC 2008-19126
Rose, Alex
The musical illusionist; and other tales. Hotel St. George Press 2007 143p il map ISBN 978-0-9789103-1-0 LC 2007-930631
Rosenbaum, Benjamin, 1969-
The ant king and other stories. Small Beer Press 2008 228p ISBN 978-1-931520-52-2; 978-1-931520-53-9 (pa) LC 2008-13685
Rosie Little's cautionary tales for girls. Wood, D.
Roskies, David G., 1948-
(ed) Scribblers on the roof. *See* Scribblers on the roof
Rottensteiner, Franz
(tr) The black mirror and other stories. *See*. The black mirror and other stories
Rough beasts and other mutations. Monteleone, T. F.
Row, Jess, 1974-
The train to Lo Wu; stories. Dial Press 2005 190p ISBN 0-385-33789-2 LC 2004-56201
The **royal** ghosts. Upadhyay, S.
Rozan, S. J.
(ed) Bronx noir. *See* Bronx noir
Rucker, Rudy von Bitter, 1946-
Mad professor; the uncollected short stories of Rudy Rucker. Thunder's Mouth Press 2007 301p ISBN 978-1-56025-974-9; 1-56025-974-4
Ruefle, Mary, 1952-
The most of it. Wave Books 2008 95p ISBN 978-1-933517-30-8; 978-1-933517-29-2 (pa) LC 2007-41633
Ruffin, Paul
Jesus in the mist; stories. University of South Carolina Press 2007 197p ISBN 978-157003-699-6; 1-57003-699-3 LC 2006-101063
Runaway. Munro, A.
Running mother and other stories. Guo, S.

Russell, Karen, 1981-
St. Lucy's home for girls raised by wolves. Knopf 2006 246p ISBN 0-307-26398-3 LC 2006-45156

Russian lover & other stories. Martin, J.

Rust, Elissa Minor, 1977-
The prisoner pear; stories from the lake. Swallow Press/Ohio University Press 2005 193p ISBN 0-8040-1083-8; 0-8040-1078-1 (pa) LC 2005-18721

Rust and bone. Davidson, C.

Rylands, Jane Turner, 1939-
Across the bridge of sighs; more Venetian stories. Pantheon Books 2005 354p ISBN 0-375-42341-9 LC 2005-47674

S

Saffron and Brimstone. Hand, E.

Sallis, James, 1944-
Potato tree. Host Publications 2007 180p ISBN 978-0924047-39-8; 978-0-924047-40-4 LC 2006-934723
A collection of short stories.

Salmon, Eric
(ed) Richard goes to prison, and other stories. *See* Granville-Barker, Harley, 1877-1946. Richard goes to prison, and other stories

Salmonella men on planet porno and other stories. Tsutsui, Y.

Salon fantastique; edited and with an introduction by Ellen Datlow and Terri Windling. Thunder's Mouth Press 2006 396p ISBN 1-56025-833-0; 978-1-56025-833-9

Salter, James
Last night. Knopf 2005 132p ISBN 1-4000-4312-3 LC 2004-57793

The **Sam** Gunn omnibus. Bova, B.

San Francisco noir; edited by Peter Maravelis. Akashic Books 2005 291p ISBN 978-1-888451-91-7; 1-888451-91-2 LC 2005-925465

San Francisco noir 2; the classics; edited by Peter Maravelis. Akashic Books 2009 330p ISBN 978-1-933354-65-1; 1-933354-65-8 LC 2008-925933

Sanctified and chicken-fried. Lansdale, J. R.

Sankaran, Lavanya
The red carpet; Bangalore stories. Dial press 2005 214p ISBN 0-385-33817-1 LC 2004-60918

Sargent, Pamela
Thumbprints; with an introduction by James Morrow. Golden Gryphon Press 2004 281p il ISBN 1-930846-29-0 LC 2004-5745

Saunders, George
In persuasion nation; stories. Riverhead Books 2006 228p ISBN 1-59448-922-X LC 2005-57715

Savile, Steven
(ed) Elemental. *See* Elemental

Say you're one of them. Akpan, U. C.

Sayles, John, 1950-
Dillinger in Hollywood; new and selected short stories. Nation Books 2004 256p ISBN 1-56025-632-X LC 2004-304724

Schaper, Julie
(ed) Twin cities. *See* Twin cities

Schnapp, Patricia, 1936-
(ed) The best American Catholic short stories. *See* The best American Catholic short stories

Schnee, Samantha
(ed) Words without borders. *See* Words without borders

Schnitzler, Arthur, 1862-1931
Bachelors; stories and novellas; selected and translated from the German by Margret Schaefer. Ivan R. Dee 2006 268p ISBN 978-1-56663-611-7; 1-56663-611-6 LC 2006-12726

Scholes, Ken
Long walks, last flights & other strange journeys. Fairwood Press 2008 265p ISBN 978-0-9820730-0-1; 0-9820730-0-3

Schor, Lynda
The body parts shop. FC2 2005 177p ISBN 1-57366-120-1 LC 2004-27534

Schubert, Edmund R.

  (ed) Orson Scott Card's Intergalctic medicine show. *See* Orson Scott Card's Intergalctic medicine show

Schutt, Christine, 1948-

  A day, a night, another day, summer; stories. TriQuarterly Books/Northwestern University Press 2005 155p ISBN 0-81015-153-7 LC 2004-26517

Schutz, Benjamin M.

  Mary, Mary, shut the door and other stories. Five Star 2005 327p ISBN 1-59414-371-4 LC 2005-19743

Schwartz, Lloyd, 1941-

  (ed) Poems, prose, and letters. *See* Bishop, Elizabeth, 1911-1979. Poems, prose, and letters

Schwarzschild, Edward

  The family Diamond; stories. Algonquin Books of Chapel Hill 2007 212p ISBN 978-1-56512-410-3 LC 2007-7968

Schwitters, Kurt, 1887-1948

  Lucky Hans and other Merz fairy tales; [by] Kurt Schwitters; translated and introduced by Jack Zipes; illustrated by Irvine Peacock. Princeton University Press 2009 235p il ISBN 978-0-691-13967-8 LC 2008-24836

    Translation of selections from: Der gluckliche Hans and Merz

Science fiction: the best of the year 2007 edition; edited by Rich Horton. Prime Books 2007 377p ISBN 978-0-8095-6297-8; 0-8095-6297-9

Scithers, George H., 1929-

  (ed) Cat tales: fantastic feline fiction. *See* Cat tales: fantastic feline fiction

Scott, Joanna

  Everybody loves somebody; stories. Back Bay Books/Little, Brown and Co. 2006 260p ISBN 978-0-316-01345-1; 0-316-01345-5 LC 2006-12310

Scoville, Shelagh, 1928-

  Ulu's dog and other stories. Fithian Press 2003 301p ISBN 1-56474-415-9 LC 2002-156646

Screaming science fiction. Lumley, B.

Scribblers on the roof; contemporary American Jewish fiction; edited by Melvin Jules Bukiet and David G. Roskies. Persea Books 2006 301p ISBN 0-89255-326-X LC 2006-2819

    "A Karen and Michael Braziller book"

Sea dogs. Bensko, J.

Searls, Damion

  What we were doing and where we were going. Dalkey Archive Press 2009 101p ISBN 978-1-56478-547 LC 2008-50050

Sears, Olivia E.

  (ed) Best of contemporary Mexican fiction. *See* Best of contemporary Mexican fiction

Seconds of pleasure. LaBute, N.

Secret anniversaries of the heart. Raphael, L.

The **secret** goldfish. Means, D.

The **secret** lives of people in love. Van Booy, S.

Sedaris, David

  (ed) Children playing before a statue of Hercules. *See* Children playing before a statue of Hercules

Segal, Lore Groszmann

  Shakespeare's kitchen; stories; [by] Lore Segal. The New Press 2007 225p ISBN 978-1-59558-151-8; 1-59558-151-0 LC 2006-30107

Sekirin, Peter

  (tr) A night in the cemetery and other stories of crime & suspense. *See* Chekhov, Anton Pavlovich, 1860-1904. A night in the cemetery and other stories of crime & suspense

Selgin, Peter

  Drowning lessons; stories. University of Georgia Press 2008 235p (Flannery O'Connor Award for Short Fiction) ISBN 978-0-8203-3210-9; 0-8203-3210-0 LC 2008-20377

The **send-away** girl. Sutton, B.

Sensation stories. Collins, W.

Shomer, Enid

Tourist season; stories. Random House 2007 254p ISBN 978-0-345-49442-9; 0-345-49442-3 LC 2006-45690

The **short** fiction of Ambrose Bierce, volume 1. Bierce, A.

The **short** fiction of Ambrose Bierce, volume 2. Bierce, A.

The **short** fiction of Ambrose Bierce, volume 3. Bierce, A.

Short stories of the civil rights movement; an anthology; edited by Margaret Earley Whitt. University of Georgia Press 2006 343p ISBN 9780820327990; 0-8203-2799-9; 9780820328515 (pa); 0-8203-2851-0 (pa) LC 2006-12104

Showdown at Anchor. Dawson, P.

Shrayer, Maxim, 1967-

Jonah and Sarah. See Shrayer-Petrov, David, 1936-, and Shrayer, Maxim, 1967-

Shrayer-Petrov, David, 1936-, and Shrayer, Maxim, 1967-

Jonah and Sarah; Jewish stories of Russia and America; edited by Maxim D. Shrayer. Syracuse Univ. Press 2003 184p (The library of modern Jewish literature) ISBN 0-8156-0764-4 LC 2003-9848

Shroff, Murzban F.

Breathless in Bombay; stories. St. Martin's Griffin 2008 306p ISBN 978-0-312-37270-5; 0-312-37270-1 LC 2007-38265

Shukman, Henry

Mortimer of the Maghreb; stories. Knopf 2006 460p ISBN 1-4000-4325-5 LC 2005-57862

Shuteye for the timebroker. Di Filippo, P.

Sideways in crime; an alternate mystery anthology; edited by Lou Anders. Solaris 2008 363p ISBN 978-1-84416-566-7; 1-84416-566-3

Sightseeing. Lapcharoensap, R.

Signaling for rescue. Herrmann, M.

Sillitoe, Alan

New and collected stories. Carroll & Graf 2005 614p ISBN 0-7867-1476-X

Silverberg, Robert

Phases of the moon; stories of six decades. Subterranean Press 2004 625p ISBN 1-931081-99-9

Something wild is loose 1969-72. Subterranean Press 2008 408p (The collected stories of Robert Silverberg, vol. 3) ISBN 978-1-59606-143-9

To be continued. Subterranean Press 2006 392p (Collected stories of Robert Silverberg, vol. 1) ISBN 1-59606-061-1

To the dark star 1962-1969. Subterranean Press 2007 391p (The collected stories of Robert Silverberg, vol. 2) ISBN 978-1-59606-089-0; 1-59606-089-1

Trips, 1972-73. Subterranean Press 2009 411p (The collected stories of Robert Silverberg, vol. 4) ISBN 978-1-59606-212-2

Silverston, Sondra

The girl on the fridge. See Keret, Etgar, 1967-

Simpson, Helen

In the driver's seat; stories. Alfred A. Knopf 2007 177p ISBN 978-0-307-26522-7; 0-307-26522-6 LC 2006-37215

Sims, Michael, 1958-

(ed) The Penguin book of Gaslight crime. *See* The Penguin book of Gaslight crime

Singer, Isaac Bashevis, 1904-1991

Collected stories: One night in Brazil to The death of Methuselah. Library of America 2004 899p ISBN 1-931082-63-4 LC 2003-66081

Singer, Margot

The pale of settlement; stories. University of Georgia Press 2007 213p ISBN 978-0-8203-3000-6; 0-8203-3000-0 LC 2007-15079

Singleton, George, 1958-

Drowning in Gruel. Harcourt 2006 307p ISBN 978-0-15-603061-8; 0-15-603061-6 LC 2005-17974

"A Harvest original"

Sinister shorts. O'Shaughnessy, P.

Sisters on the case; celebrating twenty years of Sisters in Crime, edited by Sara Paretsky. Obsidian 2007 335p ISBN 978-0-451-22239-8

Skids. With, C.

Sonechka. Ulitskaya, L.

Sorry I worried you. Fincke, G.

Soueif, Ahdaf, 1950-
   I think of you; stories. Anchor Books 2007 182p ISBN
      978-0-307-27721-3

The **spaces** between the lines. Crowther, P.

Spangler, Amy
   (ed) Istanbul noir. *See* Istanbul noir

Spencer, William Browning, 1946-
   The ocean and all its devices; stories. Subterranean Press 2006 195p
      ISBN 1-59606-047-6

Spicehandler, Ezra
   (tr) Out of the depths & other stories. *See* Brenner, Yosef Haim. Out
      of the depths & other stories

Spit baths. Downs, G.

Spoiled. Macy, C.

St. Lucy's home for girls raised by wolves. Russell, K.

Stabenow, Dana
   (ed) At the scene of the crime. *See* At the scene of the crime
   (ed) Powers of detection. *See* Powers of detection
   (ed) Unusual suspects. *See* Unusual suspects

Stable strategies and others. Gunn, E.

Stackpole, Michael A., 1957-
   Perchance to dream, and other stories. Five Star 2005 396p ISBN
      1-594-14149-5 LC 2004-29573

Stafford, Jean, 1915-1979
   The collected stories of Jean Stafford. Farrar, Straus and Giroux 2005
      487p ISBN 0-374-52993-0 LC 2005-47705

Stagestruck vampires and other phantasms. Charnas, S. M.

Stamm, Peter, 1963-
   In strange gardens and other stories; translated by Michael Hofmann.
      Other Press 2006 243p ISBN 1-59051-169-7 LC 2005-29502

Stangalino, Chiara
   (ed) Rome noir. *See* Rome noir

The **Starry** rift; tales of new tomorrows: an original science fiction
      anthology; edited by Jonathan Strahan. Viking 2008 530p ISBN
      978-0-670-06059-7; 0-670-06059-3; 978-0-14-241438-5 (pa);
      0-14-241438-7 (pa) LC 2007-32152

The **stars** above Veracruz. Gifford, B.

Starwater strains. Wolfe, G.

Stashower, Daniel
   (ed) Ghosts in Baker Street. *See* Ghosts in Baker Street
   (ed) Sherlock Holmes in America. *See* Sherlock Holmes in America

Staudohar, Paul D.
   (ed) Murder short & sweet. *See* Murder short & sweet

Stavans, Ilan
   (ed) Collected stories: One night in Brazil to The death of Methuselah.
      See Singer, Isaac Bashevis, 1904-1991. Collected stories: One night
      in Brazil to The death of Methuselah
   The disappearance; a novella and stories. TriQuarterly Books 2006
      130p ISBN 0-8101-2374-6 LC 2006-8898

Steampunk; edited by Ann & Jeff VanderMeer. Tachyon Publications
      2008 373p ISBN 978-1-892391-75-9

Steele, Allen M.
   The last science fiction writer. Subterranean Press 2008 310p ISBN
      978-1-59606-152-1

Steinberg, Susan
   Hydroplane. 2006 204p ISBN 1-57366-129-5 (pa) LC 2005036138

Stelmok, Jerry
   Not your average bear & other Maine stories. Tilbury House 2007
      250p ISBN 978-0-88448-290-1 LC 2007-112

Sterling, Bruce
   Ascendancies; the best of Bruce Sterling. Subterranean Press 2007
      547p ISBN 978-1-59606-113-2
   Visionary in residence; stories. Thunder's Mouth Press 2006 294p
      ISBN 978-1-56025-841-4; 1-56025-841-1

Stern, Daniel, 1928-2007
   A little street music. Texas Review Press 175p ISBN 1-881515-61-3
      LC 2003-25948

Stern, Richard G., 1928-
Almonds to zhoof; [by] Richard Stern. TriQuarterly Books/Northwestern University Press 2005 610p ISBN 0-8101-5149-9 LC 2004-30002

Stevens, Francis, b. 1884
The nightmare, and other tales of dark fantasy; edited and with an introduction by Gary Hoppenstand; illustrations by Thomas L. Floyd. University of Nebraska Press 2004 404p il (Bison frontiers of imagination) ISBN 0-8032-9298-8 LC 2004-9710

Stevens, J. David, 1969-
Mexico is missing and other stories. Ohio State University Press 2006 148p ISBN 0-8142-5153-6; 0-8142-9104-X (pa) LC 2005-28819

Stevenson, Jane, 1959-
Good women; three novellas. Houghton Mifflin 2006 232p ISBN 978-0-618-46217-9; 0-618-46217-1 LC 2005-10752
"A Mariner original"

Stewart, Pamela, 1946-
Elysium & other stories. Anvil Press 2008 198p ISBN 978-1-895636-91-8; 1-895636-91-4 LC 2008-411429

Stick out your tongue. Ma Jian
Stop that girl. McKenzie, E.
Stories of little women & grown-up girls. Rivera-Valdés, S.
The **stories** of Mary Gordon. Gordon, M.

Strahan, Jonathan
(ed) The Best science fiction and fantasy of the year: volume three. *See* The Best science fiction and fantasy of the year: volume three
(ed) The Best science fiction and fantasy of the year: volume two. *See* The Best science fiction and fantasy of the year: volume two
(ed) Eclipse one. *See* Eclipse one
(ed) The new space opera. *See* The new space opera
(ed) The new space opera 2. *See* The new space opera 2
(ed) The Starry rift. *See* The Starry rift

Strange itineraries. Powers, T.

Straub, Peter
(ed) H.P. Lovecraft. *See* Lovecraft, H. P. (Howard Phillips), 1890-1937. H.P. Lovecraft

Straub, Peter, 1943-
(ed) Poe's children. *See* Poe's children

Strike the harp! Parry, O.

Strom, Dao, 1973-
The gentle order of girls and boys; four stories. Counterpoint 2006 341p ISBN 1-58243-343-7 LC 2006-4190

Stross, Charles
Toast. Cosmos Books 2006 247p ISBN 0-8095-5603-0
Wireless. Ace Books 2009 352p ISBN 978-0-441-01719-4 LC 2009-10394

Stumbling and raging; more politically inspired fiction; edited by Stephen Elliott; with associate editors Greg Larson [et al.] MacAdam/Cage Pub. 2005 331p ISBN 1-59692-158-7 LC 2005-24832

Sukrungruang, Ira
(ed) What are you looking at? *See* What are you looking at?

Summer chills; strangers in stranger lands; edited by Stephen Jones. Carroll & Graf Publishers 2007 476p ISBN 978-0-78671-986-0; 0-7867-1986-9

Sundaresan, Indu
In the Convent of Little Flowers; stories. Atria Books 2008 216p ISBN 978-1-4165-8609-8; 1-4165-8609-1 LC 2008-34437

Sunstroke and other stories. Hadley, T.
Super America. Panning, A.

Sutton, Barbara
The send-away girl; stories; by Barbara Sutton. University of Georgia Press 2004 202p (Flannery O'Connor Award for Short Fiction) ISBN 0-8203-2655-0 LC 2004-7421

Swain, Heather
(ed) Before. *See* Before

Swan, Gladys, 1934-
A garden amid fires. BkMk Press 2007 158p ISBN 978-1-886157-58-3; 1-886157-58-8 LC 2006-34004

Swann, Maxine
  Flower children. Riverhead Books 2007 211p ISBN
    978-1-59448-945-7 LC 2006-39269
Swanwick, Michael
  The best of Michael Swanwick. Subterranean Press 2008 469p ISBN
    978-1-59606-178-1; 1-59606-178-2
  The dog said bow-wow. Tachyon Publications 2007 296p ISBN
    978-1-892391-52-0; 1-892391-52-X
Sweet land. Weaver, W.
Swiftly. Roberts, A.
Swimming with strangers. Lunstrum, K. S.
Swords of the steppes. Lamb, H.
Szereto, Mitzi
  (ed) Getting even. *See* Getting even

T

Tabor, Mary L., 1946-
  The woman who never cooked; stories. Mid-List Press 2006 175p
    ISBN 978-0-922811-68-7; 0-922811-68-7 LC 2005-37908
Taha, Muhammad 'Ali, 1942-
  Mohammad Ali Taha's "A rose to Hafeeza's eyes" and other stories;
    translated by Jamal Assadi. Peter Lang 2008 142p ISBN
    978-1-4331-0363-6 LC 2008-23760
The **taint** and other novellas. Lumley, B.
The **taker** and other stories. Fonseca, R.
Tales before Narnia; the roots of modern fantasy and science fiction;
    edited by Douglas A. Anderson. Del Rey/Ballantine Books 2008
    339p ISBN 978-0-345-49890-8; 0-345-49890-9 LC 2007-41373
Tales of pain and wonder. Kiernan, C. R.
Tales of the out & the gone. Baraka, I. A.
Tales of the ten lost tribes. Yellin, T.
Talking about it. Parks, T.
Talking to the enemy. Mandelman, A.
Taraqqı, Gulı
  A mansion in the sky; and other short stories. University of Texas
    Press; Combined Academic 2003 160p ISBN 0-292-70226-4
The **task** of this translator. Hasak-Lowy, T.
Tawada, Yoko, 1960-
  Facing the bridge; translated from the Japanese by Margaret Mitsutani.
    New Directions 2007 186p ISBN 978-0-8112-1690-6;
    0-8112-1690-X LC 2007-1148
Tea & other Ayama Na tales. Bluestein, E.
Teach the free man. Malae, P. N.
The **teapots** are out. Keane, J. B.
Tell Borges if you see him. LaSalle, P.
"**Tell** it to us easy" and other stories; a complete short fiction anthology
    of African American women writers in Opportunity magazine,
    (1923-1948); edited by Judith Musser. McFarland & Company, Inc.
    2008 360p ISBN 978-0-7864-3510-4 LC 2007-50805
Telling tales; edited by Nadine Gordimer. Farrar, Straus and Giroux
    2004 305p ISBN 0-312-42404-3 LC 2004040124
Templeton, Edith, 1916-
  The darts of Cupid and other stories. Pantheon Books 2002 312p
    ISBN 0-375-42159-9 LC 2001-36645
Ten sigmas & other unlikelihoods. Melko, P.
Tenney's Landing. Tudish, C.
The **terminal** project and other voyages of discovery. Chase, M.
Terrestrial intelligence; international fiction now from New Directions;
    edited by Barbara Epler. New Directions 2006 406p ISBN
    978-0-8112-1650-0; 0-8112-1650-0 LC 2006-3820
Terrors. Lupoff, R. A.
Tervalon, Jervey
  (ed) The cocaine chronicles. *See* The cocaine chronicles
Texas heat and other stories. Harrison, W.
Text: Ur; the new book of masks; [edited by Forrest Aguirre] Raw Dog
    Screaming Press 2006 226p ISBN 1-933293-19-5 LC 2007-920993
Thank you for the music. McCafferty, J.

Thanks for listening. Buckler, E.

O **the** clear moment. McClanahan, E.

Theft. Koënings, N. S.

The **theory** of light and matter. Porter, A.

There a petal silently falls. Ch'oe, Y.

There are Jews in my house. Vapnyar, L.

Theroux, Paul

The Elephanta suite. Houghton Mifflin 2007 274p ISBN 978-0-618-94332-6; 0-618-94332-3 LC 2007-13978

Thieves' world; enemies of fortune; edited by Lynn Abbey. TOR Bks 2004 352p ISBN 0-312-87490-1 LC 2004-49575

"A Tom Doherty Associates book"

The **thin** tear in the fabric of space. Trevor, D.

The **thing** around your neck. Adichie, C. N.

Things kept, things left behind. Tomlinson, J.

Things will never be the same: a Howard Waldrop reader. Waldrop, H.

Third and long. Fisher, C.

Third class superhero. Yu, C.

This day in history. Varallo, A.

This is a voice from your past. Gerber, M. J.

This is my funniest; leading science fiction writers present their funniest stories ever; edited by Mike Resnick. Benbella Books 2006 427p ISBN 978-1-932100-95-2; 1-932100-95-4 LC 2006-14201

This is my funniest 2; leading science fiction writers present their funniest stories ever; edited by Mike Resnick. Benbella Books 2007 410p ISBN 978-1-933771-22-9 LC 2007-281439

This is not chick lit; original stories by America's best women writers; edited by Elizabeth Merrick. Random House Trade Paperbacks 2006 321p ISBN 978-0-8129-7567-3; 0-8129-7567-7 LC 2006-45206

This is not the tropics. Randolph, L.

This mortal mountain. Zelazny, R.

Thomas, Donald Serrell, 1934-

The execution of Sherlock Holmes; [by] Donald Thomas. Pegasus 2007 351p ISBN 978-1-93364-822-4; 1-93364-822-8

Sherlock Holmes and the king's evil and other new adventures of the great detective; [by] Donald Thomas. Pegasus Books 2009 324p ISBN 978-1-60598-043-0

Thomas, Edward, 1878-1917

The ship of swallows; a selection of short stories; edited and introduced by Jeremy Hooker; preface by Myfanwy Thomas. Enitharmon Press 2005 108p ISBN 1-904634-16-8

Thomas, Jeffrey

Punktown. Prime Books 2005 223p ISBN 0-894815-74-2; 1-894815-75-0

Thompson, Jean, 1950-

Do not deny me; stories. Simon & Schuster 2009 292p ISBN 978-1-4165-9563-2; 1-4165-9563-5 LC 2008-41316

Throw like a girl; stories. Simon & Schuster Paperbacks 2007 291p ISBN 978-1-4165-4182-0; 1-4165-4182-9 LC 2006-51259

Thoreau's laundry. Harleman, A.

Thormählen, Axel, 1945-

A happy man and other stories, or/oder, Der Glückliche und andere Erzählungen; authorized translation by Marianne Thormahlen; with an introduction by Judith Freeman. Les Figues Press: Distributed by SPD/Small Press Distribution 2008 101p (TrenchArt.Parapet series, v3) ISBN 1-9342-5404-5; 978-1-9342-5404-2 LC 2008-922863

Text in English and German; introduction in English

Thormählen, Marianne, 1949-

(tr) A happy man and other stories, or/oder, Der Glückliche und andere Erzählungen. *See* Thormählen, Axel, 1945-. A happy man and other stories, or/oder, Der Glückliche und andere Erzählungen

Thou shalt not kill; biblical mystery stories; edited by Anne Perry. Carroll & Graf 2005 299p ISBN 0-7867-1575-8

A **thousand** deaths. Effinger, G. A.

A **thousand** years of good prayers. Li Yiyun

Threshold. Zelazny, R.

Threshold shift. Brown, E.

Thriller; edited by James Patterson. Mira 2006 568p ISBN 0-7783-2299-8

Thriller 2; stories you just can't put down; edited by Clive Cussler; [stories by] Kathleen Antrim . . . [et al.] Mira 2009 506p ISBN 978-0-7783-2723-3

Throw like a girl. Thompson, J.

Thumbprints. Sargent, P.

Tierra del Fuego. Coloane, F.

Times like these. Ingalls, R.

To be continued. Silverberg, R.

To the dark star 1962-1969. Silverberg, R.

Toast. Stross, C.

Toer, Pramoedya Ananta, 1925-2006
  All that is gone; translated from the Indonesian by Willem Samuels. Hyperion East 2004 255p ISBN 1-401-36663-5 LC 2003-56675

Tognazzini, Anthony
  I carry a hammer in my pocket for occasions such as these; stories. BOA Editions 2007 142p ISBN 978-1-929918-90-4; 1-929918-90-9 LC 2006-30020

Tóibín, Colm, 1955-
  Mothers and sons; stories. Scribner 2007 271p ISBN 978-1-4165-3465-5; 1-4165-3465-2 LC 2006-47181
    First published 2006 in the United Kingdom

Tokyo fragments; Ryuji Morita [et al.]; translated by Giles Murray. Stone Bridge Press 2005 206p ISBN 4-925080-88-1

Tolstaia, Tat´iana, 1951-
  White walls; collected stories; [by] Tatyana Tolstaya; translated by Antonina W. Bouis [and] Jamey Gambrell. New York Review Books 2007 404p (New York Review Books classics) ISBN 978-1-59017-197-4; 1-59017-197-7 LC 2007-5450

Tomlinson, Jim, 1941-
  Nothing like an ocean; stories. University Press of Kentucky 2009 163p ISBN 978-0-8131-2540-4 LC 2008-49851
  Things kept, things left behind. University of Iowa Press 2006 153p (Iowa short fiction award) ISBN 0-87745-991-6 (pa) LC 2006-41803

Tonopah Range. Le May, A.

Tooth and claw. Boyle, T. C.

Touchy subjects. Donoghue, E.

Tourist season. Shomer, E.

A **tournament** of misfits. Palazzeschi, A.

Tower, Wells, 1973-
  Everything ravaged, everything burned. Farrar, Straus and Giroux 2009 238p ISBN 978-0-374-29219-5; 0-374-29219-1 LC 2008-42757

The **train** to Lo Wu. Row, J.

A **tranquil** star. Levi, P.

Transgressions; edited by Ed McBain. Forge 2005 783p ISBN 0-765-30851-7 LC 2004-61960
    "A Tom Doherty Associates book"

Transparency. Hwang, F.

Travalini, Billie
  (ed) On the Mason-Dixon line. *See* On the Mason-Dixon line

Treat, Jessica, 1958-
  Meat eaters & plant eaters; stories. BOA Editions 2009 159p (American reader series, no. 11) ISBN 978-1-934414-22-4 LC 2009-01762

Tregebov, Rhea, 1953-
  (ed) Arguing with the storm. *See* Arguing with the storm

Tremayne, Peter
  Whispers of the dead; fifteen Sister Fidelma mysteries. St. Martin's Minotaur 2004 370p ISBN 0-312-30382-3 LC 2003-70096

Tremblay, Paul
  (ed) Bandersnatch. *See* Bandersnatch

Trevor, Douglas, 1969-
  The thin tear in the fabric of space. University of Iowa Press 2005 164p (Iowa short fiction award) ISBN 0-87745-950-9 LC 2005-41758

Trevor, William, 1928-
  A bit on the side. Viking 2004 244p ISBN 0-670-91507-6 LC 2004-42035

U

Ulu's dog and other stories. Scoville, S.

Unaccustomed earth. Lahiri, J.

Uncle Peretz takes off. Shabtai, Y.

The **uncollected** Henry James. James, H.

The **unfinished** novel and other stories. Martin, V.

Unger, Douglas

Looking for war and other stories; Douglas Unger. 1st ed. Ontario Review Press 2004 189p ISBN 0-86538-111-9 LC 2003-63451

Unkempt. Eldridge, C.

The **unsettling**. Rock, P.

An **unthymely** death and other garden mysteries. Albert, S. W.

Unusual suspects; stories of mystery & fantasy; edited by Dana Stabenow. Ace Books 2008 306p ISBN 978-0-441-01637-2; 0-441-01637-5 LC 2008-37153

Upadhyay, Samrat

The royal ghosts; stories. Houghton Mifflin 2006 207p ISBN 978-0-618-51749-7; 0-618-51749-9 LC 2005-16737

"A Mariner original"

Updike, David

Old girlfriends. St. Martin's Press 2009 212p ISBN 978-0-312-55001-1; 0-312-55001-4 LC 2009-07634

Updike, John, 1932-2009

My father's tears and other stories. Alfred A. Knopf 2009 292p ISBN 978-0-307-27156-3; 0-307-27156-0 LC 2008-54376

Urban Welsh; new short fiction; edited by Lewis Davies. Parthian 2005 273p ISBN 1-902638-42-5

Use once, then destroy. Williams, C.

The **usual** mistakes. Flanagan, E.

V

Valdés, Javier

People like us; short stories; translated by Stephen Lytle. Atria Books 2006 213p ISBN 0-7432-8646-4 LC 2005-57180

Valentines. Olafsson, O.

Van Booy, Simon

The secret lives of people in love. Turtle Point 2007 155p ISBN 978-1-933527-05-5; 1-933527-05-6 LC 2006-906038

Van Gelder, Gordon

(ed) Fourth planet from the sun. *See* Fourth planet from the sun

VanderMeer, Ann

(ed) Best American fantasy. *See* Best American fantasy

(ed) Fast ships, black sails. *See* Fast ships, black sails

(ed) The new weird. *See* The new weird

(ed) Steampunk. *See* Steampunk

VanderMeer, Jeff

(ed) Best American fantasy. *See* Best American fantasy

(ed) Fast ships, black sails. *See* Fast ships, black sails

(ed) The new weird. *See* The new weird

(ed) Steampunk. *See* Steampunk

Vanilla bright like Eminem. Faber, M.

Vann, David

Legend of a suicide. University of Massachusetts Press 2008 172p ISBN 978-1-55849-672-9; 1-55849-672-6 LC 2008-35381

Vapnyar, Lara, 1971-

Broccoli and other tales of food and love. Pantheon Books 2008 148p ISBN 978-0-375-42487-8; 0-375-42487-3 LC 2007-41537

There are Jews in my house. Pantheon Books 2003 160p ISBN 0-375-42250-1 LC 2003-42975

Varallo, Anthony, 1970-

This day in history. University of Iowa Press 2005 166p (John Simmons short fiction award) ISBN 0-87745-951-7 LC 2005-45703

Vaz, Katherine

Our lady of the artichokes and other Portuguese-American stories. University of Nebraska Press 2008 151p il (Prairie Schooner book prize in fiction) ISBN 978-0-8032-1790-4; 0-8032-1790-0 LC 2008-9969

Las **Vegas** noir; edited by Jarrett Keene & Todd James Pierce. Akashic
    Books 2008 311p map ISBN 978-1-933354-49-1 LC 2007-939596
Venus on the half-shell and others. Farmer, P. J.
Vermeer's milkmaid and other stories. Rivas, M.
The **vicious** circle; mystery and crime stories by members of the
    Algonquin Round Table; edited by Otto Penzler. Pegasus Books
    2007   205p   ISBN   978-1-933648-67-5;   1-933648-67-8;
    978-1-605980-24-9 (pa); 1-605980-24-2 (pa)
Vidal, Gore, 1925-
    Clouds and eclipses; the collected short stories. Carroll & Graf 2006
        166p ISBN 0-78671-810-2
The **view** from Castle Rock. Munro, A.
The **view** from the seventh layer. Brockmeier, K.
Viewpoints critical. Modesitt, L. E., Jr.
A **vintage** from Atlantis. Smith, C. A.
Violations; stories of love by Latin American women; edited and with
    an introduction by Psiche Hughes; foreword by Brian Matthews.
    University of Nebraska Press 2004 186p (Latin American women
    writers) ISBN 0-8032-2418-4; 0-8032-7347-9 (pa) LC 2004-4123
Visigoth. Amdahl, G.
Visionary in residence. Sterling, B.
Visit me in California. Windsor, C.
Voices in a mask. Green, G.
Vollmer, Matthew
    Future missionaries of America; stories by Matthew Vollmer.
        MacAdam/Cage   2008   224p   ISBN   978-1-59692-312-6
        LC 2008-33632
Vonnegut, Kurt, 1922-2007
    Armageddon in retrospect; and other new and unpublished writings on
        war and peace; [illustrations by the author; introduction by Mark
        Vonnegut] G. P. Putnam's Sons 2008 232p il ISBN
        978-0-399-15508-6; 0-399-15508-2
Voodoo heart. Snyder, S.
The **voyage** that never ends. Lowry, M.

W

Waisman, Sergio Gabriel, 1967-
    (tr) Dreams and realities. *See* Gorriti, Juana Manuela, 1818-1892.
        Dreams and realities
Waiting for Elvis. Graham, T.
Waldinger, Albert, 1936-
    (ed) Shining and shadow. *See* Shining and shadow
Waldrop, Howard
    Heart of whitenesse. Subterranean Press 2005 274p ISBN
        1-59606-018-2
    Other worlds, better lives: a Howard Waldrop reader; selected long
        fiction 1989-2003. Old Earth Books 2008 260p ISBN
        978-1-882968-37-4; 1-882968-37-9; 978-2-882968-38-1 (pa);
        1-882968-38-7 (pa)
    Things will never be the same: a Howard Waldrop reader; selected
        short fiction 1980-2005. Old Earth Books 2007 311p ISBN
        978-1-882968-35-0; 1-882968-35-2; 9781882968367 (pa);
        1882968360 (pa)
The **wall** of America. Disch, T. M.
Wallace, Sean, 1976-
    (ed) Bandersnatch. *See* Bandersnatch
    (ed) Realms. *See* Realms
Wang Ping, 1957-
    The last communist virgin; stories. Coffee House Press 2007 204p
        ISBN 978-1-56689-195-0; 1-56689-195-7 LC 2006-38522
War by candlelight. Alarcón, D.
War stories. Haldeman, J. W.
Ward, Amanda Eyre, 1972-
    Love stories in this town. Ballantine Books 2009 205p ISBN
        978-0-8129-8011-0; 0-8129-8011-5 LC 2009-05868
Warriors of the steppes. Lamb, H.
Water. Miller, A. L.

Waters, Don, 1974-
Desert gothic. University of Iowa Press 2007 152p (The Iowa short fiction award) ISBN 978-1-5872-9624-6; 1-5872-9624-1 LC 2007-8812

Watkins, Steve
My chaos theory; stories. Southern Methodist University Press 2006 195p ISBN 978-0-87074-512-6; 0-87074-512-3 LC 2006-44384

Waugh, Charles G. (Charles Gordon), 1943-
(ed) The Mammoth book of golden age science fiction. *See* The Mammoth book of golden age science fiction

We never talk about my brother. Beagle, P. S.

We should never meet. Phan, A.

Weaver, Will
Sweet land; new and selected stories. Borealis Books 2006 179p ISBN 978-0-87351-556-6; 0-87351-556-0 LC 2006-22483

Weber, David, 1952-
Worlds of Weber: Ms. Midshipwoman Harrington and other stories. Subterranean Press 2008 609p ISBN 978-1-59606-177-4

Weil, Grete, 1906-1999
Aftershocks; stories; translated from the German by John S. Barrett. David R. Godine 2008 113p ISBN 978-1-56792-282-0 LC 2008-19741
"A Verba Mundi book"
Original German edition, 1992

Weil, Josh, 1976-
The new valley; novellas. Grove Press 2009 344p ISBN 978-0-8021-1891-2; 0-8021-1891-7

Weird shadows over Innsmouth; edited by Stephen Jones; illustrated by Randy Broecker [et al.] Fedogan & Bremer 2005 297p il ISBN 1-878252-56-9

Welch, Nancy, 1963-
The road from prosperity; stories. Southern Methodist University Press 2005 240p ISBN 0-87074-499-2 LC 2005-41200

We'll always have Paris. Bradbury, R.

Welsh, Irvine
If you liked school, you'll love work . . . W.W. Norton and Company 2007 391p ISBN 978-0-393-33077-9 LC 2007-14665

Wendroff, Zalman, d. 1971
When it comes to living; selected stories by Zalman Vendrof; [by] Zalman Vendrof; translated by Irene Jerison. Fithian Press 2004 239p ISBN 1-56474-435-3 LC 2003-16120

We're all in this together. King, O.

We're in trouble. Coake, C.

Wescott, Glenway, 1901-1987
Goodbye, Wisconsin; with an introduction by Jerry Rosco; illustrated by Steve Chappell. Borderland Books 2008 184p il ISBN 978-0-9768781-7-9 LC 2008-922545

West, Dorothy, 1907-1998
The last leaf of Harlem; selected and newly discovered fiction by the author of The Wedding; edited by Lionel C. Bascom. St. Martin's Press 2008 xxxii, 285p ISBN 978-0-312-26148-1; 0-312-26148-9 LC 2007-32503
Analyzed for Short Stories only

Western animal heroes. Seton, E. T.

What are you afraid of? Hyde, M.

What are you looking at?; the first fat fiction anthology; edited by Donna Jarrell and Ira Sukrungruang. Harcourt 2003 274p ISBN 0-15-602907-3 LC 2003-40633

What begins with bird. Holland, N.

What gets into us. Crone, M.

What we were doing and where we were going. Searls, D.

What you call winter. Jones, N.

What you've been missing. Desaulniers, J.

When I was a horse. Domecq, B.

When it comes to living. Wendroff, Z.

When the nines roll over and other stories. Benioff, D.

Where angels fear. Rand, K.

Where is home and other stories. Burke, T.

Where the money went. Canty, K.

Wingate, Steven

Wifeshopping; stories. Houghton Mifflin 2008 190p ISBN 978-0-547-05365-3 LC 2008-4733

"A Mariner original"

Winn, Tracy, 1953-

Mrs. Somebody Somebody; stories. Southern Methodist University Press 2009 189p ISBN 978-0-87074-554-6 LC 2008-49038

Winton, Tim

The turning; new stories. Scribner 2005 321p ISBN 978-0-7432-7693-1; 0-7432-7693-0 LC 2005-44073

Wireless. Stross, C.

With, Cathleen, 1967-

Skids. Arsenal Pulp Press 2006 151p ISBN 1-55152-215-2

The **withdrawal** method. Malla, P.

Witpunk; edited by Claude Lalumière and Marty Halpern. Four Walls Eight Windows 2003 346p ISBN 1-568-58256-0 LC 2002-192768

Wizards; edited by Jack Dann and Gardner Dozois. Berkley Books 2007 400p ISBN 978-0-425-21518-0 LC 2006-101534

Wolf of the steppes. Lamb, H.

Wolf Woman Bay; and nine more of the finest crime and mystery novellas of the year; edited by Ed Gorman and Martin H. Greenberg. Carroll & Graf 2007 556p ISBN 978-0-7867-1980-8; 0-7867-1980-x

Wolfe, Gene, 1931-

The best of Gene Wolfe; a definitive retrospective of his finest short fiction. Tor 2009 478p ISBN 978-0-7653-2135-0; 0-7653-2135-1 LC 2009-12889

"A Tom Doherty Associates book"

Starwater strains. TOR Bks. 2005 352p ISBN 0-765-31202-6 LC 2004-60115

"A Tom Doherty Associates book"

Wolff, Tobias, 1945-

Our story begins; new and selected stories. Alfred A. Knopf 2008 379p ISBN 978-1-4000-4459-7 LC 2007-44262

Wolven, Scott, 1965-

Controlled burn; stories of prison, crime, and men. Scribner 2005 212p ISBN 0-7432-6011-2 LC 2004-58310

The **woman** who never cooked. Tabor, M. L.

Women and power in Argentine literature. Díaz, G. J.

Women I've known. Johnson, G.

Women of mystery; an anthology; Katherine V. Forrest, editor. Harrington Park Press 2006 257p ISBN 1-56023-543-8 LC 2005-7953

Wonderful girl. LaBrie, A.

Wong, Hertha D.

(ed) Reckonings. *See* Reckonings

Wood, Danielle, 1972-

Rosie Little's cautionary tales for girls. MacAdam/Cage 2006 255p ISBN 978-1-59692-252-5 LC 2007-15661

Woolrich, Cornell, 1903-1968

Night and fear; a centenary collection of stories by Cornell Woolrich; edited with an introduction by Francis M. Nevins. Carroll and Graf 2004 394p ISBN 0-7867-1291-0 LC 2004-270318

Woolson, Constance Fenimore, 1840-1894

Constance Fenimore Woolson: selected stories & travel narratives; edited by Victoria Brehm and Sharon L. Dean. University of Tennessee Press 2004 ISBN 1-57233-353-7 LC 2004-12282

Analyzed for short stories only

Words without borders; the world through the eyes of writers; an anthology; edited by Samantha Schnee, Alane Salierno Mason, and Dedi Felman. Anchor Books 2007 367p ISBN 978-1-4000-7975-9 LC 2006-22501

Analyzed for short stories only

Working, Russell, 1959-

The Irish martyr. University of Notre Dame Press 2006 164p (Richard Sullivan prize in short fiction) ISBN 978-0-268-04408-4; 0-268-04408-2 LC 2005-35137

A **working** man's apocrypha. Luvaas, W.

Works of art. Blish, J.

World famous love acts. Leung, B.

Worlds apart; an anthology of Russian fantasy and science fiction; edited and with commentary by Alexander Levitsky; translated by Alexander Levitsky and Martha T. Kitchen. Overlook Duckworth 2007 655p ISBN 978-1-58567-819-8; 1-58567-819-8; 978-1-58567-820-4 (pa); 1-58567-820-1 (pa)

Analyzed for Short stories only

The **World's** finest mystery and crime stories, fifth annual collection; edited by Ed Gorman and Martin H. Greenberg. Forge 460p ISBN 0-765-31146-1

"A Tom Doherty Associates book"

The **World's** finest mystery and crime stories, fourth annual collection; edited by Ed Gorman and Martin H. Greenberg. Forge 2003 638p ISBN 0-765-30848-7; 0-765-30849-5

"A Tom Doherty Associates book"

Worlds of Weber: Ms. Midshipwoman Harrington and other stories. Weber, D.

Woronov, Mary

Blind love. Serpent's Tail 2004 148p ISBN 1-85242-807-4 LC 2003-101114

Partially analyzed

The **wreck** of the Godspeed. Kelly, J. P.

Wrestling with angels. Clayton, J. J.

Writing to delight; Italian short stories by nineteenth-century women writers; edited by Antonia Arslan and Gabriella Romani. University of Toronto Press 2006 210p il (Toronto Italian studies) ISBN 978-0-8020-3874-6; 0-8020-3874-3; 978-0-8020-3810-4 (pa); 0-8020-3810-7 (pa) LC 2006-462946

Y

Yasuoka, Shōtarō, 1920-

The glass slipper and other stories; translated from the Japanese by Royall Tyler. Dalkey Archive Press 2008 146p ISBN 978-1-56478-504-6; 1-56478-504-1 LC 2007-45756

Translation of 'Garasu no kutsu' and eight other works selected by the Japanese Literature Publishing Project (JLPP).

Yates, Dwight, 1942-

Bring everybody; stories. University of Massachusetts Press 2006 143p ISBN 1-55849-525-8 LC 2005-35189

"Winner of the 2005 Juniper Prize for Fiction"

Year of fire. Lynn, D. H.

Year's best fantasy 6; edited by David G. Hartwell & Kathryn Cramer. Tachyon Publications 2006 354p ISBN 978-1-892391-37-7; 1-892391-37-6

Year's best fantasy 7; edited by David G. Hartwell & Kathryn Cramer. Tachyon Publications 2007 372p ISBN 978-1-892391-50-6; 1-892391-50-3

Year's best fantasy 8; edited by David G. Hartwell, Kathryn Cramer. Tachyon Publications 2008 375p ISBN 978-1-892391-76-6; 1-892391-76-7

The **Year's** best fantasy and horror: eighteenth annual collection; edited by Ellen Datlow, Kelly Link & Gavin J. Grant. St. Martin's Griffin 2005 cxxviii, 608p ISBN 978-0-312-34193-0; 0-312-34193-8; 978-0-312-34194-7 (pa); 0-312-34194-6 (pa)

The **Year's** best fantasy and horror: nineteenth annual collection; edited by Ellen Datlow and Kelly Link & Gavin J. Grant. St. Martin's Griffin 2006 cxxiii, 480p ISBN 978-0-312-35615-6; 0-312-35615-3; 978-0-312-35614-9 (pa); 0-312-35614-5 (pa)

The **Year's** best fantasy and horror: seventeenth annual collection; edited by Ellen Datlow, Kelly Link and Gavin J. Grant. St. Martin's Griffin 2004 564p ISBN 0-312-32927-X; 0-312-32928-8 (pa)

The **Year's** best fantasy and horror: twentieth annual collection; edited by Ellen Datlow and Kelly Link & Gavin J. Grant. St. Martin's Griffin 2007 cxxxi, 472p ISBN 978-0-312-36943-9; 0-312-36943-3; 978-0-312-36942-2 (pa); 0-312-36942-5 (pa)

The **Year's** best fantasy and horror: twenty-first annual collection; edited by Ellen Datlow and Kelly Link & Gavin J. Grant. St. Martin's Griffin 2008 cxiii, 458p ISBN 978-0-312-38047-2; 0-312-38047-x; 978-0-312-38048-9 (pa); 0-312-38048-8 (pa)

The **Year's** best science fiction: twenty-fifth annual collection; edited by Gardner Dozois. St. Martin's Griffin 2008 li, 652p ISBN 978-0-312-37859-2; 0-312-37859-9; 978-0-312-37860-8 (pa); 0-312-37860-2 (pa)

The **Year's** best science fiction: twenty-first annual collection; edited by Gardner Dozois. St. Martin's Griffin 2004 xxxviii, 665p ISBN 978-0-312-32478-0; 0-312-32478-2; 978-0-312-32479-7 (pa); 0-312-32479-0 (pa)

The **Year's** best science fiction: twenty-fourth annual collection; edited by Gardner Dozois. St. Martin's Griffin 2007 xli, 662p ISBN 978-0-312-36334-5; 0-312-36334-6; 978-0-312-36335-2 (pa); 0-312-36335-4 (pa)

The **Year's** best science fiction: twenty-second annual collection; edited by Gardner Dozois. St. Martin's Griffin 2005 xl, 663p ISBN 978-0-312-33659-2; 0-312-33659-4; 978-0-312-33660-8 (pa); 0-312-33660-8 (pa)

The **Year's** best science fiction: twenty-third annual collection; edited by Gardner Dozois. St. Martin's Griffin 2006 xlii, 660p ISBN 0-312-35335-9; 978-0-312-35335-3; 0-312-35334-0 (pa); 978-0-312-35334-6 (pa)

Years in the making. De Camp, L. S.

Yellin, Tamar

Tales of the ten lost tribes. Toby Press 2008 156p ISBN 978-1-59264-213-7

Yes, yes, cherries. Otis, M.

Yesterday's weather. Enright, A.

Yolen, Jane

Once upon a time (she said); edited by Priscilla Olson. NESFA Press 2005 378p ISBN 1-886778-61-2

    Analyzed for short stories only

You are not the one. McIntyre, V.

You must be this happy to enter. Crane, E.

You won't remember this. Blackwell, K.

The **young** Apollo and other stories. Auchincloss, L.

Young Irelanders. Donovan, G.

Your body is changing. Pendarvis, J.

Yu, Charles, 1976-

Third class superhero. Harcourt 2006 173p ISBN 978-0-15-603081-6; 0-15-603081-0 LC 2006-4786

    A Harvest original

Z

Zambian text. Smith, M.

Zebrowski, George, 1945-

Black pockets and other dark thoughts; with a foreword by Howard Waldrop. Golden Gryphon Press 2006 275p ISBN 1-930846-40-1 LC 2005-25437

Zelazny, Roger

Last exit to Babylon; edited by David G. Grubbs, Christopher S. Kovacs, Ann Crimmins. NESFA Press 2009 v4 576p (The collected stories of Roger Zelazny, v4) ISBN 978-1-996778-79-5

Power & light; edited by David G. Grubbs, Christopher S. Kovacs, Ann Crimmins. NESFA Press 2009 576p (The collected stories of Roger Zelazny, v2) ISBN 978-1-886778-77-1; 1-886778-77-9

This mortal mountain; edited by David G. Grubbs, Christopher S. Kovacs, Anne Crimmins. NESFA Press 2009 576p (Collected stories of Roger Zelazny, v3) ISBN 978-1 886778-78-8; 1-886778-78-7

Threshold; edited by David G. Grubbs, Christopher S. Kovacs, Ann Crimmins. NESFA Press 2009 575p (The collected stories of Roger Zelazny, v 1) ISBN 978-1-886778-71-9; 1-886778-71-X

Zhu Wen

I love dollars and other stories of China; translated from the Chinese by Julia Lovell. Columbia University Press 2007 228p (Weatherhead books on Asia) ISBN 978-0-231-13694-5; 0-231-13694-3 LC 2006-8129

Ziyalan, Mustafa, 1959-

(ed) Istanbul noir. *See* Istanbul noir

Zoshchenko, Mikhail, 1895-1958

The galosh and other stories; translated from the Russian with an introduction by Jeremy Hicks. Overlook Press 2006 c2000 208p ISBN 1-58567-631-4

Zumas, Leni, 1972-

Farewell navigator; stories. Open City Books 2008 168p ISBN 978-1-890447-49-6; 1-890447-49-8 LC 2008-5955

PERIODICALS INDEXED

A

AA Files. semi-ann ISSN (0261-6823) Architectural Association, 34-36 Bedford Sq., London WC1B 3ES England

Abitare. 11 times a yr ISSN (0001-3218) Editrice Abitare, Segesta s.p.a., 15 Corso Monforte, 20122 Milan, Italy
Text in Italian and English; summaries in French, German, and Spanish

The Advocate (Vancouver, B.C.). 6 times a yr ISSN (0044-6416) Vancouver Bar Association, 4765 Pilot House Rd., West Vancouver, B.C. V7W 1J2, Canada

African American Review. q ISSN (1062-4783) African American Review, Arts & Sciences Administration, Saint Louis University, Ritter Hall 125, 220 N. Grand Blvd., St. Louis, MO 63103-2007

Agni. semi-ann ISSN (1046-218X) Agni, Boston University Writing Program, 236 Bay State Road, Boston, MA 02215

Amerasia Journal. 3 times a yr ISSN (0044-7471) University of California, Los Angeles, Asian American Studies Center, 3230 Campbell Hall, Los Angeles, CA 90024-1546

American Medical Association Journal. See JAMA

The American Scholar. q ISSN (0003-0937) The American Scholar, Editorial and Circulation Offices, 1606 New Hampshire Ave., NW, Washington, DC 20009

American University Journal of Gender, Social Policy & the Law. 3 times a yr ISSN (1557-3753) Washington College of Law, 4801 Massachusetts Ave. NW, Ste. 632, Washington, DC 20016-8084
Formerly American University Journal of Gender & the Law; name changed with v. 7, no. 1 (1999)

Américas. 6 times a yr ISSN (0379-0940) Americas, P.O. Box 3000, Denville, NJ 07834-3000

ANQ. q ISSN (0895-769X) Heldref Publications, 1319 Eighteenth St., NW, Washington, DC 20036-1802

The Antioch Review. q ISSN (0003-5769) Antioch Review, Subscriptions, P.O. Box 148, Yellow Springs, OH 45387

Arizona Attorney. m (Ag/S combined) ISSN (1040-4090) State Bar of Arizona, 111 W. Monroe St., Ste. 1800, Phoenix, AZ 85003-1742

Arizona Highways. m ISSN (0004-1521) Arizona Highways, 2039 W. Lewis Ave., Phoenix, AZ 85009

Art On Paper. 6 times a yr ISSN (1521-7922) Fanning Publishing Company Inc., 39 E. 78th St., New York, NY 10021
Formerly On Paper; name changed with Sept./Oct. 1998

Artes de Mexico. q ISSN (0300-4953) Artes de Mexico, Administracion de correos no7, Mexico D.F., C.P. 06700

Atlanta Magazine. m ISSN (0004-6701) Emmis Broadcasting Corp., 1330 W. Peachtree St, Ste. 400, Atlanta, GA 30309

Atlantic Monthly (1993). m (bi-m Ja/F and Jl/Ag) ISSN (1072-7825) Atlantic Subscription Processing Center, Box 52661, Boulder, CO 80322

Aztlán. bi-ann ISSN (0005-2604) Chicano Studies Research Center Publications, University of California, Los Angeles, 405 Hilgard Ave., Los Angeles, CA 90024

B

The Banking Law Journal. 10 times a yr ISSN (0005-5506) Warren, Gorham & Lamont, Banking/A.S. Pratt & Sons, 1911 Fort Meyer Dr., Arlington, VA 22209

Beaux Arts Magazine. 11 times a yr ISSN (0757-2271) Publications Nuit et Jour, tour Montparnasse, 33, avenue du Maine, 75755 Paris Cedex 15, France

Best Life. 10 times a yr ISSN (1548-212X) Rodale, Inc., 33 E. Minor St., Emmaus, PA 18098
Ceased publication with Vol. 6, No. 4 (May 2009).

Blind Spot. semi-ann ISSN (1068-1647) Blind Spot Inc., 49 W. 23rd St., New York, NY 10010

Bomb. q ISSN (0743-3204) New Art Publications, Subscriptions Dept., P.O. Box 3000, Denville, NJ 07834

Border Crossings. q ISSN (0831-2559) Arts Manitoba Publications Inc., 500-70 Arthur St., Winnipeg, MB R3B 1G7, Canada

Boston Review. 6 times a yr ISSN (0734-2306) Boston Critic, Inc., 30 Wadsworth Street, Suite 407, Cambridge, Massachusetts, 02139

C

Les Cahiers de la Femme. See Canadian Woman Studies

Cahiers du Musée National d'Art Moderne. q ISSN (0181-1525) Musee National d'Art Moderne, Centre George Pompidou, 75191 Paris Cedex 04, France

California Lawyer. m ISSN (0279-4063) California Lawyer, Circulation, 1115 H St., Sacramento, CA 95814

Callaloo. q ISSN (0161-2492) Johns Hopkins University Press, Journals Publishing Div., 2715 North Charles St., Baltimore, MD 21218-4363

Calyx. semi-ann ISSN (0147-1627) Calyx Inc., PO Box B, Corvallis, OR 97339-0539

Camerawork. semi-ann ISSN (1087-8122) S F Camerawork, 115 Natoma St., San Francisco, CA 94105

Canadian Literature. q ISSN (0008-4360) Canadian Literature, Buchanan E158, 1866 Main Mall, Vancouver, B.C. V6T 1Z1, Canada

Canadian Woman Studies. q ISSN (0713-3235) Inanna Publications and Education, Inc., 212 Founders College, York University, 4700 Keele St., Downsview, ON M3J 1P3, Canada

Centro Journal. semi-ann ISSN (1538-6279) Centro de Estudios Puertorriquen?os, Hunter College, 695 Park Avenue, East Building, Room 1429, New York, NY 10021

Ceramics Monthly. m (except Jl, Ag) ISSN (0009-0328) Ceramics Monthly, Circulation Dept., P.O. Box 6102, Westerville, OH 43086-6102

Chicago Review. q ISSN (0009-3696) Chicago Review, 5801 S. Kenwood, Chicago, IL 60637

The Christian Century. bi-w ISSN (0009-5281) Christian Century Subscription Service, 407 S. Dearborn St., Chicago, IL 60605-1150

Christianity Today. m (semi-m Ap, O) ISSN (0009-5753) Christianity Today Subscription Services, P.O. Box 37059, Boone, IA 50037-0059

Commentary. m ISSN (0010-2601) Commentary, Inc., 165 East 56th Street, New York, N.Y. 10022

Commonweal. bi-w (except Christmas/New Year's; m in Jl, Ag) ISSN (0010-3330) Commonweal Foundation, 475 Riverside Dr., Room 405, New York, NY 10115

Communication Arts. See Communication Arts Magazine

Communication Arts Magazine. 6 times a yr ISSN (0010-3519) Communication Arts Magazine, P.O. Box 51785, Boulder, CO 80328-1785

Configurations. 3 times a yr ISSN (1063-1801) Johns Hopkins University Press, Journals Publishing Division, 2715 N. Charles St., Baltimore, MD 21218-4319

Confrontation. semi-ann ISSN (0010-5716) Long Island University, C.W. Post College of Long Island University, Brookville, NY 11548

Critical Quarterly. q ISSN (0011-1562) Blackwell Publishers, Subscriber Services Coordinator, 238 Main St., Cambridge, MA 02142

D

Daedalus. q ISSN (0011-5266) MIT Press Journals, 5 Cambridge Center, Cambridge, MA 02142

Dalhousie Review. 3 times a yr ISSN (0011-5827) Dalhousie Review, Dalhousie University, Halifax, Nova Scotia, Canada B3H 4R2

Discover. m ISSN (0274-7529) Discover, P.O. Box 420105, Palm Coast, FL 32142-0105

Duke Journal of Comparative & International Law. semi-ann ISSN (1053-6736) Business Manager, Duke University School of Law, Box 90364, Durham, NC 27708-0364

E

Early American Studies. semi-ann ISSN (1543-4273) The McNeil Center for Early American Studies, University of Pennsylvania, 3619 Locust Walk, Philadelphia, PA 19104
　　Preceding Title: Explorations in Early American Culture, 1534-1267

The East. bi-m ISSN (0012-8295) East Publications, Inc., Kasuga Mansion Roppongi #200, 4-27, Roppongi 3, Minato-ku, Tokyo 106-0032

Ebony. m ISSN (0012-9011) Ebony, 820 S. Michigan Ave., Chicago, IL 60605

The Ecologist. 10 times a yr ISSN (0261-3131) Ecosystems, Ltd., Subscriptions Dept., Worthyvale Manor Farm, Camelford, Cornwall PL32 9TT, England

Eighteenth-Century Fiction. q ISSN (0840-6286) University of Toronto Press, Journals Dept., 5201 Dufferin St., Downsview, Ont. M3H 5T8, Canada

English Language Notes. semi-ann ISSN (0013-8282) English Language Notes, Editor, Dept. of English, Campus Box 226, Univ. of Colorado, Boulder, CO 80309

Esquire. m ISSN (0194-9535) Esquire Subscriptions, P.O. Box 7146, Red Oak, IA 51591

Essence. m ISSN (0014-0880) Essence, P.O. Box 53400, Boulder, CO 80322-3400

Etc. q ISSN (0014-164X) International Society for General Semantics, Box 728, Concord, CA 94522

F

Feminist Studies. 3 times a yr ISSN (0046-3663) Women's Studies Program, University of Maryland, College Park, MD 20742

Femspec. semi-ann ISSN (1523-4002) Lexington Books, 4501 Forbes Boulevard, Suite 200, Lanham, Maryland 20706

Fiberarts. 5 times a yr ISSN (0164-324X) Interweave Press, LLC, 201 E Fourth St., Loveland, CO 80537

Film Comment. bi-m ISSN (0015-119X) Film Comment, P.O. Box 3000, Denville, NJ 07834-9925

FMR (Black Edition). 6 times a yr ISSN (0394-0462) Art'e S.p.A. Societa Internazionale di Arte e Cultura, via Cavour 2, 40055 Villanova di Castenaso, Bologna, Italy

Franco Maria Ricci Magazine. See FMR (Black Edition)

Frontiers. 3 times a yr ISSN (0160-9009) University of Nebraska Press, Lincoln, NE 68588-0255

FS. See Feminist Studies

G

Gastronomica (Berkeley, Calif.). q ISSN (1529-3262) University of California Press, Journals Division, 2000 Center St., #303, Berkeley, CA 94704-1223
　　Electronic resource

Gay and Lesbian Quarterly. See GLQ

Georgia Bar Journal. 6 times a yr ISSN (1085-1437) State Bar of Georgia, 800 The Hurt Bldg., 50 Hurt Plz., Atlanta, GA 30303-2934

The Georgia Review. q ISSN (0016-8386) University of Georgia, Athens, GA 30602

Gettysburg Review. q ISSN (0898-4557) Gettysburg Review, Gettysburg College, Gettysburg, PA 17325-1491

Glamour. m ISSN (0017-0747) Glamour, P.O. Box 37690, Boone, IA 50037-0690
　　Incorporating: Mademoiselle

GLQ. q ISSN (1064-2684) Duke University Press, Journals Fulfillment, 905 W. Main St., #18-B, Durham, NC 27701

Good Housekeeping. m ISSN (0017-209X) Good Housekeeping, P.O. Box 7186, Red Oak, IA 51591-0186

Grand Street. semi-ann ISSN (0734-5496) Grand Street Press, 214 Sullivan St., Ste. 63, New York, NY 10012
　　Suspended publication with no. 69 (Summ. 1999); Resumed publication with no. 70 (Spr. 2002); Ceased publication after Issue 73 (June 2004)

Granta. q ISSN (0017-3231) Granta Publications, 12 Addison Avenue, London W11 4QR

H

Hanging Loose. semi-ann ISSN (0440-2316) Hanging Loose Press, 231 Wyckoff Street, Brooklyn, N.Y. 11217

Harper's. m ISSN (0017-789X) Harper's Magazine, P.O. Box 7511, Red Oak, IA 51591-0511

Harvard Review (1992). semi-ann ISSN (1077-2901) Houghton Library of the Harvard College Library, Lamont Library, Harvard University, Cambridge, MA 02138

The Higher. See The Times Higher Education Supplement

The Hudson Review. q ISSN (0018-702X) The Hudson Review, 684 Park Ave., New York, NY 10021

The Humanist. bi-m ISSN (0018-7399) Humanist, 7 Harwood Dr., P.O. Box 1118, Amherst, NY 14226-7188

I

Idaho Magazine. m ISSN (1552-6240) Idaho Magazine, Inc., 4301 W Franklin Rd, Boise, ID 83705

IEEE Computer Graphics and Applications. bi-m ISSN (0272-1716) IEEE Computer Society, 10662 Los Vaqueros Circle, P.O. Box 3014, Los Alamitos, CA 90720

Iowa Review. 3 times a yr ISSN (0021-065X) The Iowa Review, The University of Iowa, 308 English-Philosophy Building, Iowa City, Iowa 52242

J

JAMA. 4 times a month ISSN (0098-7484) American Medical Association, Circulation and Fulfillment Division, 535 N. Dearborn St., Chicago, IL 60610

Journal of Gender, Social Policy & the Law. See American University Journal of Gender, Social Policy & the Law

Journal of Medical Ethics. m ISSN (0306-6800) British Medical Journal, P.O. Box 590A, Kennebunkport, ME 04046
　　Includes supplement: Medical Humanities

Journal of the American Geriatrics Society. m ISSN (0002-8614) Blackwell Science, Inc., 350 Main St., Malden, MA 02148-5018

Journal of the American Medical Association. See JAMA

K

The Kenyon Review. q ISSN (0163-075X) The Kenyon Review, Kenyon College, Gambier, OH 43022

Koreana. q ISSN (1016-0744) Korea Foundation, 526 Namdaemunno 5-ga, Chung-gu, Seoul 100-095, S. Korea

L

Lapham's Quarterly. q ISSN (1935-7494) American Agora Foundation, Inc., 33 Irving Place, Eighth Floor, New York, N.Y. 10003

Legacy. semi-ann ISSN (0748-4321) University of Nebraska Press, 233 North 8th Street, Lincoln, NE 68588-0255

Legal Studies Forum. semi-ann ISSN (0894-5993) American Legal Studies Association, College of Law, West Virginia University, P.O. Box 6130, Morgantown, WV 26506-6130

The Literary Review (Madison, N.J.). q ISSN (0024-4589) Fairleigh Dickinson University, 285 Madison Ave., Madison, NJ 07940

M

The Massachusetts Review. q ISSN (0025-4878) University of Massachusetts, Memorial Hall, Amherst, MA 01002

The Mathematical Intelligencer. q ISSN (0343-6993) Springer-Verlag New York Inc., 233 Spring Street, 7th Floor, New York, NY 10013

Medical Humanities. See Journal of Medical Ethics

Men's Health Best Life. See Best Life

Meridians. semi-ann ISSN (1536-6936) Indiana University Press, 601 N. Morton St., Bloomington, IN 47404

The Michigan Bar Journal. m ISSN (0164-3576) Michigan Bar Journal, 306 Townsend St., Lansing, MI 48933-2083

Michigan Quarterly Review. q ISSN (0026-2420) University of Michigan, 3032 Rackham Bldg., Ann Arbor, MI 48109

Modern Painters. m ISSN (0953-6698) LTB USA Inc., 111 Eighth Avenue, Suite 302, New York, NY 10011

Modernism/Modernity. q ISSN (1071-6068) Johns Hopkins University Press, Journals Publishing Div., 2715 N. Charles St., Baltimore, MD 21218

Monthly Review (New York, N.Y.). 11 times a yr ISSN (0027-0520) Monthly Review, 122 W. 27th St., New York, NY 10001

Ms. q ISSN (0047-8318) Ms. Magazine, P.O. Box 5299, Harlan, IA 51593

Tribal College Journal of American Indian Higher Education. q American Indian Higher Education Consortium, 2509 Montgomery Way, Sacramento, CA 95818

Earlier title: Tribal College, 1052-5505

TriQuarterly. 3 times a yr ISSN (0041-3097) TriQuarterly, Northwestern Univ., 2020 Ridge Ave., Evanston, IL 60208

U

U.S. Catholic. m ISSN (0041-7548) U.S. Catholic, 205 W. Monroe St., Chicago, IL 60606

UMKC Law Review. q ISSN (0047-7575) University of Missouri-Kansas City School of Law, 5100 Rockhill Rd., Kansas City, MO 64110

Formerly The University of Missouri at Kansas City Law Review; name changed with v. 35, no. 1 (winter 1967)

UN Chronicle. q ISSN (0251-7329) United Nations Publications, Room DC2-0853, Dept. 502, United Nations, New York, NY 10017

USA Today (Periodical). m ISSN (0161-7389) The Society for the Advancement of Education, 99 W. Hawthorne Ave., Valley Stream, NY 11580

V

The Virginia Quarterly Review. q ISSN (0042-675X) The University of Virginia, One West Range, Charlottesville, VA 22903

VQR. See The Virginia Quarterly Review

W

Wagadu. ann ISSN (1545-6196) The Research Foundation of The State University of New York, SUNY Cortland, P.O.B. 2000, Cortland, N.Y. 13045

The Walrus. 10 times a yr ISSN (1708-4032) The Walrus Foundation, 19 Duncan St., Suite 101, Toronto, ON M5H 3H1, Canada

Western Humanities Review. 3 times a yr ISSN (0043-3845) Western Humanities Review, University of Utah, English Dept., 255 South Central Campus Dr., Rm. 3500, Salt Lake City, UT 84112-0494

Women's Studies. 8 times a yr ISSN (0049-7878) Taylor & Francis, Inc., 325 Chestnut St., Philadelphia, PA 19106

Women's Studies Quarterly. q ISSN (0732-1562) The Feminist Press at CUNY, The Graduate Center, 365 Fifth Avenue, Suite 5406, New York, NY 10016

Continues: Women's Studies Newsletter with Vol. 9, No. 1 (Spring 1981).

World Literature Today. bi-m ISSN (0196-3570) University of Oklahoma Press, Editorial Office, 110 Monnet Hall, Univ. of Oklahoma, Norman, OK 73069

World Watch. bi-m ISSN (0896-0615) Worldwatch Institute, P.O. Box 879, Oxon Hill, MD 20750-0879

The Writer. m ISSN (0043-9517) The Writer, Inc., 120 Boylston St., Boston, MA 02116-4615

Y

The Yale Review. q ISSN (0044-0124) Blackwell Publishers, Yale Review, Subscriber Services Coordinator, 238 Main St., Cambridge, MA 02142